AFRICA SINCE 1875
A Modern History

The University of Michigan History of the Modern World

Edited by Allan Nevins and Howard M. Ehrmann

AFRICA SINCE 1875

A Modern History

BY ROBIN HALLETT

Ann Arbor: The University of Michigan Press

For Inge, Biddy, Susan, and Stephen

Preface

By far the greater part of this book was written while I was holding the post of research officer at the Institute of Commonwealth Studies of the University of Oxford. Without the benefit of such an appointment it would hardly have been possible to undertake the task of attempting to write a history of the whole of Africa. So my first obligation is to the members of the Committee for Commonwealth Studies for their support from 1965 to 1971. I had the good fortune to have had Oxford as my base while working on this book. In the first place I had the magnificent range of the university's libraries at my disposal—and here I must express a very special obligation to the library of my own institute and to its librarian, R. J. Townsend, for his indefatigable helpfulness in dealing with almost daily requests for material. Residence at Oxford also brought with it the opportunity to participate in three or four postgraduate seminars a week and to meet a wide range of visiting speakers. Indeed, this was an intellectual bonanza and a source of constant stimulus. Again I have a special obligation to my friends in the field of African studies who kept alive a climate of interest in African history in these years: Edwin and Shirley Ardener, Thomas Hodgkin, Antony Kirk-Greene, Kenneth Kirkwood, Colin and Trude Newbury, Christine Nicholls, Peter Sanders, Christopher Saunders, Alison Smith, and Charles Stewart. I also owe a debt of gratitude to Jon James and his cosmopolitan group of students in Ruskin College with whom I discussed African history and the problems and aspirations of the Third World in one of the most warmhearted and exciting classes in which I have ever participated.

Families inevitably get involved in the chores and traumas of authorship. So it seems fitting to dedicate this book to my own family with love and gratitude.

Garsington, Oxford
Rondebosch, Cape Town

Contents

MAPS

Introduction

AFRICA, the second largest of the continents, covers a total area of eleven and a half million square miles. Its landscapes range from the Sahara's arid and desolate expanses to the claustrophobic luxuriance of the forests of the Congo, from the immense plains of the Sudanic belt covered with the varied vegetation of the African "bush" to the rich, well-watered highlands of Kenya and Ethiopia, from the sharply detailed Mediterranean scenery of the coastal Maghrib and of the South African Cape to the dense swamps that obstruct stretches of the Niger and the Nile, from the valleys of broad, majestic rivers to the imposing ranges of the Atlas, the Drakensberg, and the Ruwenzori.

The continent's population, estimated in 1973 to number three hundred and seventy-five million, presents an equally astonishing range of contrasts in physical type, in language, in economy, and in political organization. People of Negroid stock predominate only in the tropical parts of the continent. Northern Africa is dominated by a population of Caucasoid stock which extends from the Berber of the Maghrib to the Somali of the Horn of Africa. Southern Africa also contains an important Caucasoid group in its European minority. Indonesian immigrants to Madagascar have left a clear Mongoloid strain in the present Malagasy population. A few thousand people of Pygmoid stock survive in the equatorial forests, and small groups of Bushmanoids are to be found in parts of Southern Africa. This fivefold "racial" division—Negroid, Caucasoid, Mongoloid, Pygmoid, and Bushmanoid—should be regarded as no more than a fairly crude system of classification. It does not allow for the constant process of interbreeding that has taken place between peoples of different physical type, nor does it provide for the broad range of variants within any one "racial" group. To walk around such cities as Kano, Cape Town, or Zanzibar is to gain a vivid impression of the variety of physical types that Africa affords.

Language provides the most satisfactory criterion in distinguishing one ethnic group, "tribe," or people from another. The number of distinct languages in Africa is variously estimated to be between six and eight hundred. Recent linguistic research has succeeded in classifying this plethora of languages into a number of language-stocks or families. Most of the languages spoken in Northeast and Northwest Africa fall into the group termed by some scholars "Afro-Asiatic." Most West African languages are incorporated in the "Western Sudanic" language-family. The term "Nilo-Saharan" has recently been applied to a group of languages spoken by peoples living in a wide expanse of territory stretching from the central Sahara to the northern parts of East Africa. Almost all the languages spoken in Equatorial and Southern Africa form part of the Bantu language-family. Finally, the term "Khoisan" has been applied to the click-language spoken by peoples of Bushman-oid stock. The majority of these languages are confined to small areas and limited populations, but a few, such as Berber, Hausa, and Swahili, have spread much more widely; and three languages of alien origin, Arabic, English, and French, have become *linguae francae* of continental significance.

Most Africans obtain their livelihood from the land, the majority as farmers, some as pastoralists, and a few as hunters and gatherers. Some communities possess a long tradition of craft industry, and in the course of the last century there has been a slow, still modest but steadily ramifying, development of modern forms of mining and factory industry. African settlement patterns reflect these variations in the economy: at one extreme the camps of Saharan nomads or Bushmen hunters, at the other the skyscrapers, the factories, and office blocks of modern African capitals. But for the majority of Africans, home means some lonely farmstead in the bush, a compact village of thatched huts, or the compounds and alleyways of a provincial town.

In political terms, modern Africa, together with the adjoining islands of the Eastern Atlantic and of the Western Indian Ocean, is divided into more than fifty political units, forty-one of which possessed in 1973 the status of independent sovereign states.[1] These states varied in size from Mauritius (805 square miles) and Gambia (4,000 square miles) to Zaire (Congo) (906,000 square miles) and the Sudan (977,000 square miles). Four independent states—Equatorial Guinea, Gabon, Gambia, and Swaziland—had a population of less than half a million. Three exceeded twenty million: Ethiopia (estimated 23 million), Nigeria (over 50 million), and the Arab Republic of Egypt (32 million). Africa contains today a greater number of independent states than any other continent. However complex the political map of modern Africa may appear, it should be remembered that the continent has been subjected to a massive process of political simplification in the course of the last ninety years, largely as a result of the European conquests of the late nineteenth century. The number of autonomous political units to be found in "precolonial" Africa was to be reckoned in tens of thousands. In purely numerical terms the vast majority of these polities consisted of very small independent communities, sometimes made up of a group of pastoral nomads but more frequently based on a settlement of farmers. Africa also contained a striking variety of states; some were comparable in size to the city-states of ancient Greece or medieval Europe and others—such as Morocco, the Sokoto Caliphate, or Buganda— were substantial kingdoms whose rulers held sway over populations to be numbered in hundreds of thousands, even in some cases in millions. Each of these polities, whatever its size, possessed its own distinct tradition of development. To these records of historical achievement the states of modern Africa have become the heirs.

Given a continent of such exuberant and inexhaustible variety, the historian may well ask himself—and he will certainly have the question put to him by his professional colleagues—whether Africa as a whole represents a proper subject for individual study. The continental historian can begin by framing an apologia for his work in purely historiological terms. Clearly one of the tasks incumbent on the historian is to help himself and his contemporaries to achieve a fuller understanding of the complex processes that have led to the emergence of human society in the form that it presents today. With this end in view there are many different scales on which the historian may choose to operate. He may adopt narrow limits of time and space, reconstructing in great detail the history of a particular locality or social group over a period of a few years. Alternatively, he may take a whole country as his subject and a span of several centuries as his time scale. Or he may choose to survey the whole world and provide a vision of a period of the past on a universalistic scale. All these varied approaches contribute to that constant cross-fertilization of ideas, that continually envigorating debate needed to preserve the healthy development of historical studies. There is an abundant need for the proliferation of well-chosen microhistories, but a historiography made up only of microstudies—of doctoral theses and articles in learned journals—would seem to all but a small band of specialists too atomized, too obviously deficient in an overall intellectual framework. Broad historical themes, which are of such interest to any lively intelligence, imply by their very nature the construction of some sort of diagram capable of serving as a guide to the multifarious phenomena of the past. The microhistorian, who succeeds in presenting his subject in such richly documented detail that he leaves nothing to be done by later scholars in his particular field, may well be compared to the skillful craftsman producing an object designed to last for a long period of time. The macrohistorian, on the other hand, must from the very nature of his approach be aware of his own fallibility, engaged as he is in a constant process of generalization, selection, and compression; he is like the architect of a prefabricated building of some utilitarian value whose construction will soon be in need of repair, enlargement, or even total demolition.

If a valid general case can be made for the writing of macrohistories, then a special case can be advanced for attempting to construct a history of Africa. The division of the known world into continents was first suggested by Greek geographers of the fifth century B.C. Thus "Africa" began as a purely European concept. From classical times onward Europeans and other peoples influenced by European culture have been in the habit of generalizing about a part of the world whose sheer size and variety defy generalization. "Always something new out of Africa," "Africa and her prodigies," "the Dark Continent"—phrases such as these, so evocative, so distorting, form part of the intellectual baggage of Western man. "Africa" has been seen as something "mysterious," "backward," "barbarous," "primitive," "savage," the home of cannibals and witch doctors, of fetish and juju, of bizarre superstitions and exotic rituals.

If "Africa" exists as an entity in the European mind, it has also developed into a distinct concept in the minds of many Africans. The events of the last hundred years have given to many African peoples, hitherto almost completely isolated from the outside world and therefore oblivious of the existence of other peoples not altogether dissimilar from themselves, a certain uniformity of experience, as their countries were conquered by people of European origin and their native cultures exposed to the exhausting impact, at once abrasive and invigorating, of the new culture of nineteenth- and twentieth-century Europe. At the same time members of the African diaspora, who were living in the West Indies, in the Americas, and in Europe and therefore were even more directly affected than most native Africans by the attitudes of racial superiority displayed by many people of European culture, began to develop new concepts of Africa, in response to the crude denigrations implicit in the European image, by stressing "Africa's possession of modes of social thought, action, and belief that are unique, valuable, and fruitful of civilizing virtue." [2] In cultural terms this upsurge of new ideas led to the definition of the concept of the African personality; in political terms, to the emergence of a Pan-Africanist movement and the organization of an institutional structure for African unity. In the post-colonial world of the second half of the twentieth century "Africa" has become both a rallying cry and a verbal counter used more frequently than ever before. In these circumstances the historian may feel some justification in placing so familiar a concept under the microscope of disciplined examination.

There is another justification for studying Africa in its entirety—the impossibility of finding a satisfactory means of dividing the continent into two parts. Such a division has of course been practiced and popularized by those who talk of *Afrique blanche* and *Afrique noire,* of North or Mediterranean Africa and sub-Saharan Africa. This bisection of the continent obviously seems valid if Africa is viewed from its extremities, from Cape Town or from Cairo. It loses its apparent precision when the viewpoint is transferred to the great Sudanic belt that runs from the Atlantic to the Red Sea. The people of Dakar, of Kano, or of Khartoum may be regarded, by virtue of their physical appearance, inhabitants of *Afrique noire,* but they possess many cultural ties with the peoples of Egypt and the Maghrib and no links of any kind with the southern half of the continent. The Sahara has always been much less of a barrier to the peoples living on its fringes than outsiders have tended to assume; and as one moves further east to the valley of the Nile and the highlands of Ethiopia, the concept of a geographical divide disappears almost completely.

Clearly, however, there is a need for some broad subdivisions in studying a continent of such immensity. Yet even here it is not possible to devise a rational set of divisions likely to command universal assent. In the present study the mainland of Africa has been divided into seven regions—Northeast, Northwest, West, Equatorial, Central, East, and South, together with a section on those islands usually regarded as being more closely attached to Africa than to any other continent. This regional division possesses the arbitrary quality characteristic of most frontiers anywhere in the world. The dividing lines between regions should not be overstressed.

If the student of any one region needs constantly to be aware of developments taking place beyond his region's borders, the historian of the continent as a whole must develop the habit of looking outward to a wider world. It is sometimes worth thinking of history in oceanic terms, for the seas and oceans, no less than the great landmasses, have been invested by human enterprise with a certain measure of unity. Many historical ties bind together the peoples living around the Red Sea and the

Mediterranean. And even those whose homelands face the vast expanses of the Atlantic and of the Indian Ocean have acquired a measure of common experience. Today, with man's ever more pronounced mastery of the air, one can go still further and for the first time point to a measure of global unity. With increasing frequency as he moves toward the present, the historian of Africa must direct his gaze to the Middle East, to the lands of Asia, to Europe, to the Americas. Few historical subjects possess so cosmopolitan a character. To study the history of Africa is to equip oneself for an understanding of the history of the universal.

▲▼ THE HERITAGE OF THE PAST

The date at which this study opens—1875—should not be thought of as commemorating any particular event. Given a field as massive and complex as the whole of Africa, it is rarely possible to point to any single event as having truly continental significance. The year 1875 must be thought of rather as possessing a certain symbolic value. Set as a median point in the second half of the nineteenth century, it may be taken as marking the end of the "old order." In 1875 Europeans were in control of less than 10 percent of the total area of the continent, and no really substantial African state had yet been brought completely under their domination. By 1900, so rapid had been the European advance that three quarters of the continent was subject to their hegemony and almost all the major African polities had been totally destroyed, forced to accept European "protection," or reduced to a position where their surrender seemed imminent. By taking 1875 rather than 1900 as the starting point for a study of modern African history it becomes possible to perceive the colonial period in its true character as an interlude—in some areas a very brief interlude—in the broad sweep of largely autonomous African development.

For most students of history the African past still has about it something of the character of an iceberg. The broad outline of the events that have occurred in the course of the past century shows clearly above the surface, but the history of what is sometimes described as "precolonial" or "traditional" Africa seems to lie in unilluminable depths. Old myths die hard: the notion, so vigorously expounded by many Europeans even as late as the 1950's, of Africa as "the continent without a history" still enjoys a measure of support in some intellectual circles in the West. The notion might be regarded as absurd on purely a priori grounds: every human society obviously represents the end product of a long process of historical evolution, even if the sources needed to describe this process are lacking. Since many African societies had not acquired the technique of literacy at the time when they first came into contact with the outside world and so could not produce written records of their own, it was generally assumed that they could have no "history." However, as the recent work of scholars in many different disciplines has shown, the sources relevant to an investigation of the African past are very much more copious than even the most optimistic African historian would have thought possible ten or twenty years ago. As a result of the latest research it is now possible to discern with reasonable clarity the broad outline of African historical development, even if for many periods of the African past there is still—and perhaps always will be—a lack of that detailed documentation with which historiographers working in parts of Europe and of Asia are so familiar.

Three general points that emerge from a consideration of the total sweep of African history may be emphasized here, for they contribute greatly to a proper understanding of the most recent period of African development. The first concerns the antiquity of man in Africa. A hundred years ago Charles Darwin suggested that Africa was "the cradle of mankind." His hypothesis, based on what was known of the distribution of the higher apes, has been brilliantly confirmed by recent archeological research. The skeletal remains of hominids, ancestral to *Homo sapiens,* capable of making very primitive stone tools, and reckoned by the latest dating techniques to have lived about two million years ago, have been discovered in sites in East Africa. From the favored environment of the savannas of Eastern and Southern Africa a slowly increasing hominid population appears to have spread to other parts of Africa, to Europe, to Asia, and finally, probably no more than thirty thousand years ago, to the Americas. The earliest men were—like the modern Bushmen of the Kalahari—seminomadic hunters and gatherers. The emergence of communities able to maintain themselves in settlements sited for long periods in one particular location is a more recent development that dates back about ten thousand years. It was made possible by the gradual discovery of new methods—fishing, vegeculture (the regular collecting of semiwild plants), and agriculture—for obtaining food. Some parts of Africa contain permanent settlements of great antiquity. Many villages in the valley of the Egyptian Nile must have been under permanent occupation for five or six thousand years. Some settlements in North Africa, Ethiopia, and the Sudanic belt have probably been occupied for close on three thousand years. Even in the southern half of the continent where the expansion of an agricultural population is a much more recent phenomenon, some sites can be traced back more than one thousand years. In the contemporary world, Africa is often presented as a continent of "new nations." It needs to be remembered that these nations are made up of peoples whose ancestors have lived in the same area for periods reaching back over many centuries.

The second generalization to be deduced from a study of the African past is concerned with the process of change. Most Europeans, their concepts shaped by their own relatively recent experience of rapid technological progress, have tended to regard African peoples as "backward," their economies as "stagnant," their cultures as "unprogressive" and "incapable of change." Given the natural tendency of any people to generalize from their own experience, it is hardly surprising that Europeans should have accepted the speed at which their own societies have changed as the norm. Every human society is involved in the process of change, but the rate at which this process occurs varies from society to society and from period to period. Even the most "primitive" of contemporary societies—the hunting bands of the Bushmen and of the Pygmies—can point to an immense advance on the societies of paleolithic times. Their technology is obviously far more elaborate, and it is reasonable to assume that their knowledge of the ecology, the product of a long intellectual tradition developed by observation and experimentation, is more sophisticated and their language more refined and precise than that of their distant ancestors. With more elaborate societies based on an agricultural economy the evidence of progressive change is naturally far more apparent.

The gradual increase in the population and its movement into new areas of settlement, the emergence of more complex forms of political organization, the development of a more productive economy utilizing an expanding range of materials and making possible more refined forms of specialization—these basic processes can be as clearly discerned in Africa as in any other continent. Their operation, played out over many different environments, has led to the emergence of Africa's striking variety of cultures. Every human society possesses its own innate dynamism. The historian of Africa needs to acquire an imaginative awareness of the dynamic quality, the resilience, the adaptability inherent in all African societies.

The third general point concerns Africa's association with the cultures of other continents. European historians have been accustomed to stress the measure of Africa's isolation from the main centers of human progress. It is true that many African societies came into direct contact with aliens possessing cultures greatly different from their own only in very recent times. But material innovations, techniques, and even institutions and ideas can be transmitted indirectly and still exert a forceful impact on the recipient society. Viewed in this light, African societies appear as rather less isolated from the developments taking place in other countries than their lack of direct contact with Europeans or Asians would lead one to suppose.

In the course of the last hundred years Europe has exerted so forceful an impact on Africa that it is difficult for both Europeans and Africans to realize that the continent has been far more profoundly influenced by innovations of Asian origin than it has yet been influenced by the ideas and technology of Europe. From Western Asia, about seven thousand years ago, came the new techniques of food production associated with the cultivation of certain cereals and the tending of certain domesticated animals, techniques which were transmitted gradually, and with many local modifications, to almost all African societies. From Western Asia, too, in the course of the first millennium B.C., was introduced the technique of working iron, the most easily accessible of all the metals to be found in Africa, a technique enabling those who acquired it to replace some of their instruments manufactured from stone, wood, or bone with tools or weapons made of the new and more adaptable material. Another part of Asia, the humid lands of Malaysia and Indonesia, provided the tropical regions of Africa with their first staple food crops, the Asian yam and the banana. These crops, brought to the shores of Eastern Africa by Indonesian seafarers of the first millennium A.D., gradually found their way—transmitted, one may surmise, from community to community by the normal processes of human intercourse —across the tropical regions of the continent. Their introduction gave to peoples hitherto dependent on hunting and vegeculture a much greater control over their environment, made possible a steady increase in population, and so set in motion a wide range of other changes. Asia's fourth major contribution to African development was the culture of Islam, a highly elaborate culture whose diffusion involved not only the transmission of new ideas about the place of man in the universe and about the right ordering of society but also the introduction of some material innovations and a number of new techniques, including that of literacy in the Arabic script. Carried first, in the course of the seventh century A.D., by the victorious armies of Arabia into Egypt and the Maghrib and transmitted more slowly over a still wider area by wandering Muslim merchants and holy men, Islam profoundly modified the cultures of almost all the peoples of the northern half of Africa.

By contrast with the long-sustained impact on Africa of material innovations, techniques, and ideas of Asian origin, the influence of Europe appears, especially when viewed from the date at which this study opens, relatively modest. In the latter half of the first millennium B.C. Europeans established their hegemony over the Mediterranean lands of North Africa. But this first period of European colonial rule contributed remarkably little of enduring value to the indigenous cultures of the region, and with the Arab conquests of the seventh century the unity of the Mediterranean world was destroyed. There followed a period of eight hundred years in which the European presence disappeared almost completely from the North African scene, a period in which the material cultures of European societies could offer relatively little in comparison with the far more sophisticated cultures of the Islamic world. Not until the fifteenth century, when seamen from the maritime states of Western Europe began to explore the unknown coasts of the continent's great western bulge, did Africa again begin to feel the forceful impact of its northern neighbor. From the beginning of the sixteenth to the end of the eighteenth century European traders— Portuguese, French, Dutch, and English for the most part—exerted what may well be described as a revolutionary influence on certain parts of the continent, the coastal districts of West, Equatorial, and East Africa, while making a deeper penetration inland in parts of South and Central Africa. These alien intruders brought with them a number of material innovations, including two food crops of American origin, maize and manioc, both of which proved to be of considerable importance in the development of many local African economies. By providing new commercial opportunities for some African communities through their demand for certain forms of African produce and especially for African slave labor, they helped to create conditions favorable for the growth of more elaborate polities, particularly on the Guinea coast. At the same time the African trade served to accelerate the economic development of the Caribbean and of the tropical regions of the Americas. Without the steady increase in the flow of African labor across the Atlantic, it would have been impossible to create the rich and sophisticated cultures of many of the European communities of the New World. The consequences of the slave trade for Africa as a whole are less easy to determine. Clearly, the trade brought impoverishment, desolation, and destruction to some African communities, but for others it provided new opportunities for enrichment and stimulating contacts with a wider world.

The first seventy-five years of the nineteenth century witnessed a steady increase in the scope of European involvement in African affairs. Three areas of the continent became the scene of European military operations, a grueling experience for the local communities involved: Egypt—swiftly conquered and briefly occupied by the French between 1798 and 1801; Algeria—"pacified" by the French army between 1830 and 1860; and South Africa—where Afrikaner farmers and British soldiers were involved in almost continuous fighting with

African communities along a turbulent and steadily expanding frontier. At the same time many Europeans, particularly in Britain, came to view with deep repulsion the commerce in human beings that had contributed not a little to the enrichment of their own societies and urged their governments to take positive action to ensure the abolition of the African slave trade. Naval pressure, exerted chiefly by the British, proved the most effective deterrent and forced many coastal African communities to abandon the export of slaves. The decline of the slave trade coincided with the emergence of new commercial interests as European traders, stimulated by the expanding demands of new European industries, began to seek a wider range of African products, including cotton, groundnuts, palm oil, and rubber.

Yet another powerful current leading Europeans to interest themselves more deeply in Africa was generated by the tide of evangelical sentiment that swept through many Western European communities in the late eighteenth and early nineteenth centuries and led to the formation of new Christian missionary societies. To the African communities in which they settled the agents of European missionary enterprise brought not only new religious concepts but also many material manifestations of their own local culture. Thus the nature of their impact could be compared, though it was still on a very much smaller scale, to those other proselytizers of a faith with universalistic pretensions, the Muslim traders and teachers of the ever-expanding *Dar al-Islam*.

Beside the European soldiers, traders, and missionaries now appearing in Africa in steadily increasing numbers must be set a small but well-publicized group of adventurous travelers. Their exploits were directly inspired by that intellectual tradition of scientific curiosity in the remote places of the earth which had been so greatly expanded and refined in the course of the past four hundred years. The reports sent back by these explorers of peoples and polities hitherto unknown to Europe were read with eager attention and served to diffuse an interest in Africa among a very much wider public.

This rapid ramification of European activities was partly matched by a steady expansion in Asian enterprise in Africa. In the early sixteenth century most of North Africa was brought under the control of the Ottoman Turks. Three hundred years later the Ottoman province of Egypt became a base for the conquest of most of the modern Sudan, and the Turkish governors of Tripoli extended their hegemony deep into the central Sahara. Meanwhile enterprising Arabs from Oman on the Persian Gulf established a position of paramountcy on the East African coast. Early in the nineteenth century Arab traders began to penetrate the interior in search of new commercial opportunities, gradually extending their activities over most of Eastern Africa and the eastern Congo basin.

To outside observers this proliferation of alien activities is the most easily discernible feature of the years between 1800 and 1875. But the historian who seeks to gain a balanced view of the entire continent must always be on his guard against exaggerating the importance of aliens in an African context. The most easily accessible sources are almost all of European origin and therefore contain a built-in bias in favor of recording the exploits of Europeans. In any African community the appearance of the first "white" man, Arab, Turk, or European, could certainly be regarded as an augury of change, but in itself it might call forth no more than an expression of wonderment or derision. Moreover, it needs to be remembered that as late as 1875 there were still many African communities which had not yet gained their first view of a stranger from another continent.

To overstress the force of the impact of aliens is to play down the extent of autonomous development within African societies. Alien influences contributed little or nothing to the emergence of the powerful kingdoms of the interlacustrine area of East Africa or to the rise of military autocracies among the Southern Bantu. The Muslim revolutionaries who launched the series of holy wars that led to the creation of a number of large theocratic states in the Sudanic belt of Africa in the course of the eighteenth and nineteenth centuries were all local men. Much of their inspiration was indeed derived from ideas that could be traced back to the founder of their faith, but few of them were directly influenced by advocates of change coming from countries outside Africa. Some of the more powerful African rulers of the mid-nineteenth century were glad to make use of the services of the occasional European or Asian strangers—missionaries, traders, or adventurers—who visited their countries, valuing the new skills and the wider range of knowledge offered by these unusual intruders. But the material innovations, techniques, and ideas brought by the newcomers were restricted, controlled and censored to accord with the local ruler's own sense of priorities.

Some African communities were completely overwhelmed by the impact of alien forces. In parts of South Africa the Bushmen were hunted down like wild beasts by Afrikaner cattle farmers, and the Hottentots were deprived of their grazing lands and decimated by the unfamiliar diseases introduced by newcomers from Europe or Asia. In central Angola, southern Tanzania, and the southern Sudan some peoples suffered the destruction of their ancestral way of life in the violence associated with the slave trade. But most African communities revealed remarkable qualities of resilience, adapting themselves to new conditions and assimilating those innovations of alien origin most relevant to their needs. The Basuto chief who made use of European missionaries to advise him in his dealings with the European polities surrounding his territory, the Malagasy monarch who employed European instructors to transform his ill-disciplined levies into an efficient standing army, the merchant prince of the Niger Delta who sent his sons to England for a commercial education, the Egyptian Shaikh who set about translating the seminal works of modern European literature for the benefit of his compatriots—men such as these may be regarded as symbolic figures, demonstrating by their actions that intelligent eclecticism needed to sustain any vigorous culture.

▲▼ THE THEMES OF MODERN AFRICAN HISTORY

When European or American historians or Western-educated African intellectuals speak about modern African history, the discussion usually centers on the theme of European imperialism and African nationalism. Recent studies have enlarged the vocabulary of debate and introduced some variations into the original theme. The great historical movement can be discussed in terms of conquest, resistance, collaboration, and liberation, of colonialist suffocation and African renaissance, of imperialist exploitation and the search for freedom from alien pressures. But however expressed, the basic premise remains the same: of all the varied forms of human activity that have taken place in Africa in the course of the last century those associated with the imposition of European rule and its later rejection are to be regarded as the most significant. To say the least, this is a somewhat simplistic view of the past. For the past may be regarded as the sum of the lives of many millions of men and women. A phenomenon so complex can hardly be summarized by concentrating on only one of its aspects. The need is for a pattern rather more complex.

It is salutary for the European historian to realize that other patterns are likely to emerge if he makes the effort to change his viewpoint, puts out of mind all he has been told by the historians of his own culture, and makes the imaginative effort of looking back on the recent past through the eyes of a particular African people. Take, for example, the experience of the Uduk, a small, distinct group of Negroid agriculturalists, living astride the Sudan-Ethiopian border.[3] For the Uduk the most significant period in their recent history is represented by dreadful "time of troubles" in the last decades of the nineteenth century when they were driven from their peaceful villages by well-armed raiders from Ethiopia and the Mahdist Sudan, were chased into the bush like "wild antelopes," and saw many of their friends and relations killed before their eyes or carried off into slavery. This cataclysmic interlude ended with the coming of the "Turks," the officers of the Anglo-Egyptian condominium set up after the collapse of the Mahdist state in 1899. Many great events have taken place since then in the countries of which the Uduk nominally form a part—the Italian invasion of Ethiopia, the campaigns of World War II, the political transformation of the Sudan. But to the farmers of Udukland, living in isolated and largely self-sufficient communities, events such as these are barely comprehensible, producing hardly a ripple on the stream of local life.

Of course there are many other African communities, especially those placed in areas of intensive European activity, whose peoples have been handled far more roughly by the great historical movements of modern times. But the majority of Africans still live in relatively isolated rural communities, and over the greater part of the continent, aliens have been, even in recent years, very thin on the ground. It seems reasonable to assume that for most Africans the stuff of history, the content of their impressions of the past, remains what it has probably always been—natural disasters, feuds and quarrels, and the exploits of remarkable local personalities. Yet even the remotest African community cannot have remained totally unaffected by processes set in motion by developments taking place far beyond its own horizons.

The conventional emphasis on imperialism and nationalism provides too narrow a perspective to represent properly the complex process of change that has operated within Africa in the course of the last century. The need is for an intellectual framework capacious enough to provide a place for the experience of all African peoples, for a set of themes which bring out something of the special character of the last century of African history and yet do not distort the seamless web of historical continuity by suggesting a violent and entirely unreal break between past and present.

The first theme to suggest itself may be defined as the erosion of isolation: clearly the peoples of Africa have come more closely in touch with the peoples and products of other continents than ever before. In the course of the past century aliens of European or Asian origin have made their appearance in parts of Africa where they were previously quite unknown and have congregated—at least until ejected by postcolonial governments—in very much greater numbers in those parts with which they already possessed some contacts in the middle of the nineteenth century. At the same time Africans going abroad as soldiers, students, emigrant workers, or diplomats have become familiar with peoples and places entirely unknown to their forefathers and have returned—unlike those earlier generations of African emigrants, the victims of the slave trade—to tell their contemporaries something of what they have seen.

No less significant than this intercontinental traffic of men and women but affecting a very much greater number of people has been the increased circulation within the continent. In the past, certain areas witnessed the growth of a vigorous local, regional, or, as with the trans-Saharan commerce, even interregional trade. The rewards of commerce or the necessities of war led some Africans to venture far from their homes. But the opportunities for movement have become infinitely greater in the course of the past hundred years as a result of the establishment of new political structures capable of preserving law and order over very much wider areas than the smaller polities of the past, accompanied by the introduction of improved forms of communication and transportation. The produce buyers, government officials, and wandering traders finding their way to remote villages and the sons and daughters of peasant farmers lured by the glittering novelties of the towns or forced to gain a livelihood away from their ancestral homes —all over Africa the movements of people such as these can be observed. Other innovations—the new-style school, the radio, the church or mosque, the political meeting—contribute to the same end, the widening of intellectual horizons, the pouring of the heady wine of novel experiences and new ideas into the old bottles of traditional culture.

The erosion of isolation also implies a gradual transformation of the old patterns of economic self-sufficiency. The nineteenth and twentieth centuries have seen an immense increase in the flow of material objects in and out of Africa. In 1800 Africa's main exports to the outside world, leaving aside the massive trade in slave labor, consisted of relatively modest quantities of gold, gum, ivory, timber, animal skins, and cereals. By the middle of the nineteenth century this list had been expanded to include wool, cotton, palm oil, groundnuts (peanuts), and cloves. By the early twentieth century the range of Africa's agricultural exports had widened still further, with sugar, rubber, coffee, tea, cocoa, sisal, tobacco, and a variety of fruits being sold in increasing quantities on the world market. At the same time the growth of an African mining industry has supplied foreign buyers with diamonds, gold, tin, copper, bauxite, manganese ore, iron ore, phosphates, oil, and natural gas, the list of products steadily lengthening as improvements in mining technology make possible the exploitation of new resources.

In return for its raw materials Africa has received manufactured goods and processed foodstuffs in an increasingly sophisticated variety. Gradually the staples of the early nineteenth-century African trade— textiles and metalware—have been supplemented by beverages and foodstuffs from other continents (tea, beer, rice, sugar, dried fish, and flour), by new forms of building material (cement, glass, and corrugated iron), and by an ever more elaborate range of implements and machinery, starting with firearms and simple tools, expanding to include bicycles, sewing machines and motorcars, and now embracing almost every form of product offered by the most highly industrialized countries in the world. A vigorously developing internal trade has ensured the diffusion of many of these novel objects from the major towns to the villages of the countryside, stirring new currents of desire and suggesting forms of economic activity more gainful than the practices of the past.

The steady acceleration of the processes of change represents a second major theme in the modern history of Africa, one that is obviously closely related to the first. Change manifests itself in half a dozen general ways: the introduction of material innovation, the acceptance of new techniques, the establishment of new lines of communication and new patterns of settlement, the growth of new institutions, and the diffusion of new ideas. But change implies loss as well as gain: objects fall out of use, techniques become obsolete, settlements are abandoned, institutions modified or rejected, and ideas discredited. The rate of change obviously varies not only from period to period but also from community to community and from country to country. In most African countries the people of the capital or of the major cities are more likely to have witnessed changes of a radical nature than those who have spent their lives in the quiet backwater of some provincial town. And the townsmen of the provinces are themselves more conscious of change than those whose homes lie in the lonely farmsteads of the veld or the remote villages of the bush. Again when one contrasts African countries, it becomes clear that some have experienced greater changes than others. In recent decades Egyptians have witnessed a profounder transformation of their society and their environment than Ethiopians; Algerians, than Mauritanians; Ghanaians, than their neighbors in Upper Volta; Kenyans, than Tanzanians; South Africans of every race, than their contemporaries in Angola.

A third major theme running through modern African history is to be found in the practice of violence. About this there should be nothing surprising: conflict between competing groups is a natural phenomenon in every period of history. The annals of indigenous polities contain many records of violence—feuding in stateless societies, destructive raids launched by major polities against their smaller neighbors, and full-scale wars between the larger states. Nor was the establishment of European hegemony so peaceful a process as imperial apologists sometimes imply. The "partition" of Africa involved a long series of military campaigns, some of which were accompanied by heavy fighting. In these circumstances it seems more honest to speak of the European conquest of Africa rather than to indulge in genteel euphemisms. Conquest involved pacification, the denial to hitherto autonomous polities of the right to take up arms not only against the alien invader but also against one another. Thus, the period of colonial rule saw the establishment of a *pax* such as the greater part of Africa had never known before.

The most serious outbreaks of violence in the colonial period arose out of conflicts between the new alien rulers of the continent, between the British and the Afrikaners in South Africa, and later, in World War I and World War II, between the rival blocs of European powers. But the colonial period also witnessed a number of armed revolts by African peoples, of which some may be regarded as representing a last phase in the process of armed resistance to the invader, while others, occurring several decades later, clearly form part of the process of liberation. New patterns of conflict have emerged in the years since independence. There have been bloody disputes, though no major wars, between some neighboring states, while in four of Africa's largest states—the Sudan, the ex-Belgian Congo, Nigeria, and Chad—sharply defined cultural differences have contributed to outbreaks of violence on a massive scale. One may detect, too, a less prominent skein of violence running through the practice of politics in Africa at every period of its recent history. The imprisonment or execution of political opponents has been a device favored by many African rulers, by colonial governors, and by the leaders of modern African states no less than by the monarchs of earlier African kingdoms. And terrorism or planned insurrection remain today, as in the past, the ultimate form of political protest.

Another aspect of this theme of violence requires emphasis. It is possible to detect in Africa, no less than in other continents, a mounting strain of destructiveness in man's attitude toward his environment. The annihilation of so much of Africa's larger fauna, the devastation of thousands of square miles of forest, the ruination of grasslands by overgrazing, the erosion of irreplaceable soil as a result of faulty cultivation —these are processes which have occurred on a scale without precedent in earlier centuries. The historian of the future may well regard processes such as these as exerting an infinitely more profound impact on the quality of men's lives in Africa than the highly publicized political changes that tend to monopolize the attention of contemporary commentators.

One final theme is needed to provide an adequate vision of the past:

it involves the creative achievements of individual men and women. Man by his very nature is a maker: it is impossible to conceive of any normal human community that is completely incapable of constructive activity. "Constructive" and "creative" are terms which must be applied, in the widest possible sense, no less to the development of viable human relationships and to the efficient performance of apparently routine tasks than to the more conventionally life-enhancing pursuits of the artist or the poet. The skill in arbitration of a chief or councillor, the prowess of a hunter, the enterprise and business acumen of a trader, the perseverance and ecological knowledge of a pastoralist or a farmer— qualities such as these represent accomplishments worthy of great respect. Such accomplishments are to be found in every African society.

More obviously apparent to the superficial observer are the achievements of recent decades, and especially those associated with the enterprise of Europeans, those "fabulous artificers" of the modern world. The modern cities of Africa, the highways and the railroads, the dams and the irrigation schemes, the university campuses and the hospitals—what astonishing creations these would have seemed to our fathers and grandfathers. If we admire the relics of the past, Luxor and Meroe, Leptis and Axum, Zimbabwe and Kilwa, Ife and Timbuktu, we ought also to honor those who have produced the great monuments of the present. There are other achievements less tangible but no less impressive—the construction of the administrative framework needed to maintain the structure of an effective state or the organization of a church, a school, a trade union, a political party. And there has come from Africa a steadily broadening stream of intellectual and artistic contributions capable of appealing to men the world over, enriching still further the great and glorious exhibition of universal human culture— the novels, the poems, the sculpture, the painting, the music, the ballet. It seems churlish here to make crude divisions along "racial" lines. So much has been the product of cooperative endeavor. The gold-mining industry of South Africa is as much a monument to the courage and fortitude of African miners as to the financial shrewdness of European capitalists and the technological brilliance of European engineers. The state systems of modern Africa are in large part the product of years of conscientious devotion to duty by civil servants both African and European. The African doctor in his hospital in the bush makes use of medicines and techniques of healing developed by research workers in many different countries. The modern African poet may draw his inspiration from the land of his birth, yet choose to write in a European language and to use the verse forms developed by European masters.

The erosion of isolation, accelerated change, violence, creative achievement—to view the recent African past in terms of themes such as these is to gain a measure of liberation from the glib morality of so much contemporary comment, to realize that African history presents a pattern basically not dissimilar from that of any other continent, and to become increasingly aware of the wonderful richness of the African scene.

▲▼ THE SOURCES OF MODERN AFRICAN HISTORY

The historian's apprehension of the past is entirely dependent on the sources at his disposal. For many aspects of African history before 1875 the amount of written material is extremely modest, and some periods of the African past are unillumined by a single written document. In these circumstances the historian must turn to scholars in other disciplines—archeology, linguistics, ethnology, botany, and zoology— for assistance. By contrast the historian of the recent past finds himself faced with a superabundance of written material, but he too has much to learn from the distinctive approaches developed by his colleagues in the fields of social anthropology, political science, economics, and geography. The general historian in particular cannot afford to neglect any illuminating approach to an understanding of human society.

Accepting the conventional division between primary and secondary sources and leaving the latter the works of reconstruction or analysis produced by scholars remote in time or place from the events they are concerned to study—to later consideration, one may begin by listing the former in order of accessibility. Some primary sources lie within reach of any one who enjoys access to a good library; others can be brought to light only after a laborious and often expensive process of research.

The most easily accessible source is to be found in the books and articles written by contemporaries. Most of these have been produced by aliens: the narratives of explorers, the reminiscences of soldiers, traders, missionaries, or colonial officials, the impressionistic surveys of journalists, and the imaginative reconstructions of novelists. A vivid style, capable of recapturing a scene or re-creating an atmosphere, makes the best of these works extremely attractive to the general reader. But the authors of this type of material are essentially impressionistic in their approach and sometimes possess only a modest acquaintance with the African environment they set out to describe. Indeed, the main interest of such works may often be found to lie not in any illumination they shed on the African scene but in the more oblique insight they afford into the attitudes and preconceptions of a particular European observer.

Far less numerous at present are the works written by Africans. But a sizeable body of easily accessible African literature is now beginning to emerge, consisting of novels, poems, and plays in English, French, or Portuguese together with translations from African languages. To these should be added a number of autobiographies, collected speeches, and political commentaries. All personal accounts serve to enlarge the historian's capacity for sympathetic understanding, but he is likely to find a particular value in those works that enable him to see the world through the eyes of men and women of a culture often greatly different from his own. Unfortunately for the historian, the vast majority of books by African authors presently in print have been written only in the course of the last twenty or thirty years. Earlier works do indeed exist, but their number is limited. This dearth of written material is, of course, a reflection of the preliterate character of many African societies until quite modern times. But a mass of literary work is still to be found in the manuscript collections preserved in most of the Muslim countries of Africa, and the origins of a native African press can be traced back to the latter half of the nineteenth century. There is an urgent need for more translations from the Arabic and for a series of anthologies drawing their material from the earliest African newspapers and thus providing an introduction to the first literary productions of many African peoples.

A second major source of printed material, usually to be found only in specialized libraries, consists of official publications. One of the innovations introduced by the European rulers of Africa was the regular publication of a mass of informative material contained in annual reports, collections of official correspondence and other documents (parliamentary papers and blue books), statistical surveys, handbooks, and encyclopedias. For the first time in his study of the African past the historian finds at his disposal a multitude of exact facts and figures—staff lists, budgets, censuses, development plans, and cartographical surveys. This tradition of copious official publications has been maintained, with varying degrees of efficiency, by the successor states to the old colonial territories and is now increasingly supplemented by the publications of international agencies.

A third source of printed material, one to which brief mention has already been made, is to be found in more ephemeral publications— newspapers, journals, and periodicals. Tattered pages and smeary or closely packed type make many of these publications exhausting to read. Yet here, in the leader columns, one may trace the genesis of new political ideas and catch the first murmurs of modern nationalism. The schedules of shipping lines or the reports of business companies illuminate the growth of local economies. And from pages of advertisements or letters to the editor the perceptive historian will learn much about those subtle shifts in taste and fashion that mark the emergence of new desires, the formulation of new concepts about the pattern of society.

A fourth source, one of immense richness, is provided by the manuscript material contained in archives or other collections. To the great archival depositories of the metropolitan powers—the Public Record Office in London, the *Ministre d'outre-mer* in Paris, the German *Zentralarchiv* in Potsdam, and others—must now be added the new archival centers recently established in most African countries. In addition, many institutions of metropolitan origin—geographical societies, missionary societies, and business firms—have maintained their own private archives. And the papers of many individuals associated with Africa have now been deposited in the manuscript sections of major libraries in Africa, Europe, and America. The extent to which archival material is made available to the individual researcher varies from one depository to another. In some countries the ideologically inspired obscurantism of the local regime may close the archives completely or prohibit inspection of certain important documents. Every official depository and some private ones will naturally impose a closed period. The length of this period varies from country to country. In Britain a "thirty-year rule" has recently been substituted for the long-established "fifty-year rule." In the Sudan, on the other hand, recent historians have had access to official material dating from the last years of British rule in the early 1950's. Confidential material of an even more recent date may suddenly be made available as the result of violent political changes, especially when a new regime finds that it can discredit its predecessor by publishing its secrets.

Manuscript material often serves to illuminate the process of decision making by documenting those aspects of a situation—the clash of personalities, the arguments behind closed doors—usually glossed over or sedulously concealed in published accounts. Archives also contain other information of a kind not available elsewhere. Thus the unpublished reports of some nineteenth-century missionaries contain many interesting comments on the politics and personalities of the African states in which they worked; the police files kept by the colonial authorities often preserve the documentary evidence needed to reconstruct the development of early nationalist movements; and the private letters of colonial administrators reveal their hopes and fears, their ambitions and frustrations, far more vividly than the staid paragraphs of official reports.

The final source, the oral record of the past, presents the researcher with the most obvious practical difficulties. The discovery of reliable informants, the transcription, and, where necessary, the translation of their evidence are laborious occupations, requiring tact, patience, and perseverance. Yet the historian in Africa who sets out in search of oral material is offered many compensations: he enjoys a refreshing period of liberation from his study and his books, finds himself in places— palaces of local chiefs, hamlets deep in the bush, back-street compounds in provincial towns—to which he would not otherwise have entrée, records many memorable personal encounters, and in general accumulates a range of new experiences of a kind well calculated to stimulate and refine a historical imagination.

The importance of the oral record to the student of the recent history of a preliterate or largely illiterate community is obvious enough, but it should be noted that oral information may also serve to supplement or correct the written record. The narrative of the European conquest of Africa has hitherto been derived almost entirely from the annals of the conquerors. To appreciate the historical situation of the conquest in its true complexity, far more needs to be known about the sentiments and reactions of the conquered. The memories of a rapidly dwindling body of old men may often provide the only source. Again a study of the oral record—and especially of the recollections of "ordinary" people—may serve as a much-needed counterbalance to that tendency, so pronounced in many sections of African historiography, to concentrate on the actions and ideas of an elite. This is a field where historians have much to learn from the techniques evolved by social anthropologists and sociologists. Indeed the early works, based on intensive field research, of scholars in these two disciplines already represent historical documents of exceptional significance.

The works of social anthropologists lie astride the conventional watershed between primary and secondary sources. The studies of recent historians, based entirely or almost entirely on written materials, fall clearly into the latter category. African historiography represents an intellectual tradition whose origins can be traced back to the scholars of classical antiquity and the historians and geographers of medieval Islam. Herodotus, Sallust, al-Bakri, ibn Khaldun, Abd ar-Rahman as-Sadi, João de Barros, Job Ludolphus, James Bruce, Heinrich Barth are some of the great names in a tradition of scholarship enriched by the works of men of many different countries and cultures. During the colonial interlude a number of scholars, European administrators and missionaries or Western-educated Africans for the most part, made many valuable contributions to the corpus of historical knowledge. These part-time historians were the precursors of modern African historiography, suffering the hardships—isolation, lack of interest, absence of encouragement—of the pioneer in any field of scholarship. Their successors, the historians of the present generation, have been far more fortunate. The proliferation of new universities, the more generous provision of grants for research, the multiplication of scholarly journals—developments common to most countries in the world—have coincided with the growth of African nationalism into a powerful and highly vocal force, to provide the means and to create the climate of opinion needed to sustain a rapid growth in African historical studies. The 1960's may well be regarded as a golden age of African historiography. Indeed almost all the secondary sources drawn on in the present study have been published in the course of the last decade.

But the continent is vast, the span of historical time is immense, the fields still open for original research are innumerable. The tasks that face the historian of pre-nineteenth-century Africa—especially the need for more archeological and historical linguistic research—may be mentioned here only in passing. But it should be noted, both for the early and for the more recent history of Africa, that the coverage of research has been extremely uneven. Many factors influence the progress of scholarship, with the result that far more tends to be known about some countries, some subjects, and some periods than others. Compare, for example, the historiography of the caliphate of Sokoto with that of the sultanate of Wadai, both Sudanic states to be placed among the most powerful indigenous polities of late nineteenth century Africa. Early in the twentieth century Sokoto was conquered by the British and incorporated in the colony of Nigeria, but its institutions were treated with respect and the descendants of the old imperial elite given the opportunity of playing a prominent part in modern Nigerian politics. In the 1960's a well-endowed university was established at Zaria, one of the main provincial centers of the former caliphate, providing an ideal base for intensive scholarly research. Wadai, on the other hand, came to form part of the French colony of Chad and was roughly treated by its colonial overlords. The Republic of Chad is far too poor a country to afford a university, and the area around Wadai has been the scene in recent years of violent political disturbances. Is it surprising in these contrasting circumstances that much more work should have been done on Sokoto than on Wadai? Similar examples might be cited from every part of the continent. Yet with the steady increase in the number of African historians, working both in Africa and in other parts of the world, the gaps are steadily being filled up, the previously neglected periods examined, and the detailed local studies undertaken. To engage in a field of study constantly enriched by significant discoveries is an invigorating experience for any scholar.

The continental historian finds himself hard-pressed to keep abreast of all the developments taking place in his all too capacious area of interest. Indeed, given the remarkable proliferation of African historical studies in recent years, there must be some interesting projects of which he is totally unaware and many others to which he is unable, through ordinary human limitations, to devote sufficient attention. But his difficulties become all the more formidable when he turns to write about the most recent period of the past. The scholarly analyses and the accurate documentation on which he had been dependent for earlier periods are not yet available, and he finds himself turning to files of press cuttings and articles in journals on contemporary affairs. Any honest historian must possess a highly developed sense of his own ignorance. But it is peculiarly aggravating to realize how little one can know, through the paucity of easily accessible material, of the many aspects of the contemporary world. As for the more publicized events of the most recent past, the historian stands so close to them that he must inevitably find it hard to judge their significance. But the practice of his profession makes him instinctively aware of the interconnection of past and present and he can certainly conceive of no sounder intellectual basis for an understanding of the contemporary world than the disciplined knowledge a study of history provides.

▲▼ THE PROBLEM OF BIAS

In conclusion something needs to be said about the difficult problem of bias. It is fashionable for contemporary historians to assert that they are entirely "objective," that they are concerned to write a truly "scientific" history. For the general historian to make any such claim would be absurd. He may not feel himself consciously affected by any well-defined ideology, but in dealing with a subject of such complexity as the history of a country, a period, or a continent, he is constantly having to make choices—stressing this fact, ignoring that. On this necessary process of selection the inescapable pressures of time and place exert a powerful influence.

The historian cannot entirely divest himself of the preconceptions bred of his own background and culture. Whatever his nationality, he is likely to find it easier to establish a certain rapport with the sentiments of his compatriots than with the views expressed by peoples of other cultures. If he is a devout Muslim, he will probably find it almost impossible to see the world clearly through the eyes of Christians or animists. If he is a congenital rebel, he may become prone to an uncontrollable tendency to mock or denigrate the upholders of established society. If he is a successful member of his own "establishment," he may lack the capacity to feel much sympathy for the revolutionaries, the misfits, and the apparent failures of the world.

Nor can the historian shut out from his mind the promptings of the *Zeitgeist*. In a postcolonial age it is very much easier to feel sympathy for the heroic leaders of gallant "resistance" movements than for their conquerors, the agents of the imperial powers. "Imperialism," indeed, has become something of a dirty word. So, too, has that useful term "collaboration." Africans who decided to cooperate with a colonial regime are seen as toadies and sycophants, as ambitious self-seekers, as "running dogs of imperialism." Fashions have changed rapidly in the field of recent African historiography. European proconsuls have been knocked off their pedestals and nationalist politicians—those "agitators" and "demagogues" of an earlier generation—exalted in their place. With changing perspectives subjects lose their former significance or acquire a previously unexpected importance. Diplomatic crises—the Jameson Raid, Fashoda, Agadir—on which so much has been written by Europeocentric historians seem far less significant when placed in the general context of African history. The conflict between Boer and Briton in South Africa examined in such detail by an earlier generation of European historians now seems far less important than the struggle taking place on the same stage between Africans and Europeans. And to a generation of European agnostics the spread of Islam in Africa represents a phenomenon quite as interesting as the once highly dramatized advance of Christianity.

Obviously the historian cannot divest himself of his own preconceptions, but by identifying them he may be able to guard himself against being led too far astray by their seductive promptings. Moreover, there are two guidelines to assist him as he gropes his way through the mists of the past. They may be defined as the appreciation of complexity and the practice of compassion. All research, in any field of study, represents a movement from the simple to the complex. To examine any historical event in detail is to realize the many currents and pressures to which the actors on the historical stage are subject. All men are the prisoners of time and place, possessing only limited opportunities for successful initiatives, faced usually with a choice not between the good and the bad but between the bad and the worse. Hence the sense of fallibility that haunts all human actions; hence the inability of the historian who remains honest to his material to indulge in facile moral judgments. Out of an awareness of complexity grows compassion, as the historian learns to place himself in the position of the men and women whose lives he is concerned to study. Compassion does not of course imply pity, nor does it involve approval. But the historian who accepts the virtue of compassion may well feel that he is always in the position of the defending counsel, not of the prosecuting attorney, and never of the hanging judge.

Toward the end of *War and Peace* Tolstoy brings one of his leading characters, Pierre Bezukhov, to a "recognition of the possibility of every one thinking, feeling and seeing things each from his own point of view." "This legitimate peculiarity of each individual, which used once to excite and irritate Pierre, now became a basis of the sympathy he felt for, and the interest he took in, other people." [4] To any student of the past—and especially, perhaps, to a historian concerned as in Africa with peoples of many different cultures—Pierre's humane approach to experience may well commend itself as the surest guide to wisdom.

Africa: Major Indigenous Ethnic Groups

27

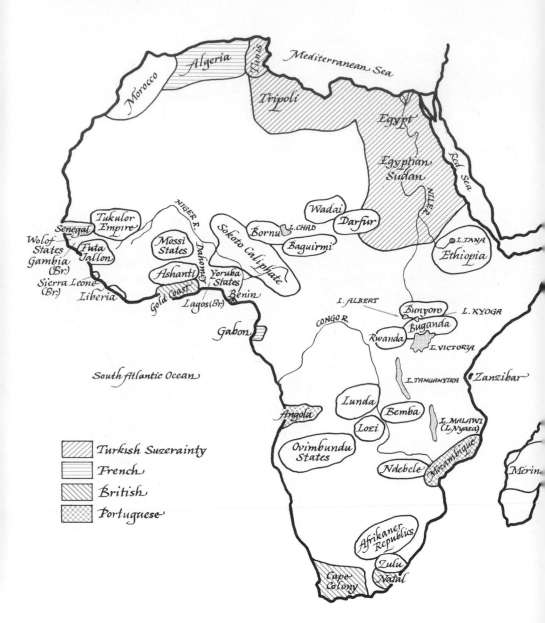

Morocco

Algeria

Tunis

Mediterranean Sea

Tripoli

Egypt

Egyptian Sudan

NIGER R.

Wadai

Darfur

Red Sea

NILE R.

Senegal

Tukulor Empire

Bornu

L. CHAD

Baguirmi

L. TANA

Ethiopia

Wolof States

Gambia (Br.)

Futa Jallon

Mossi States

Dahomey

Sokoto Caliphate

Sierra Leone (Br.)

Ashanti

Yoruba States

Liberia

Gold Coast

Lagos (Br.)

Benin

I. ALBERT

Bunyoro

L. KYOGA

CONGO R.

Buganda

Gabon

Rwanda

L. VICTORIA

South Atlantic Ocean

L. TANGANYIKA

Zanzibar

Lunda

Bemba

Angola

Lozi

L. MALAWI (L. Nyasa)

Ovimbundu States

Ndebele

Mozambique

Merin

Turkish Suzerainty

French

British

Portuguese

Afrikaner Republics

Zulu

Cape Colony

Natal

Africa in 1875: Major Polities

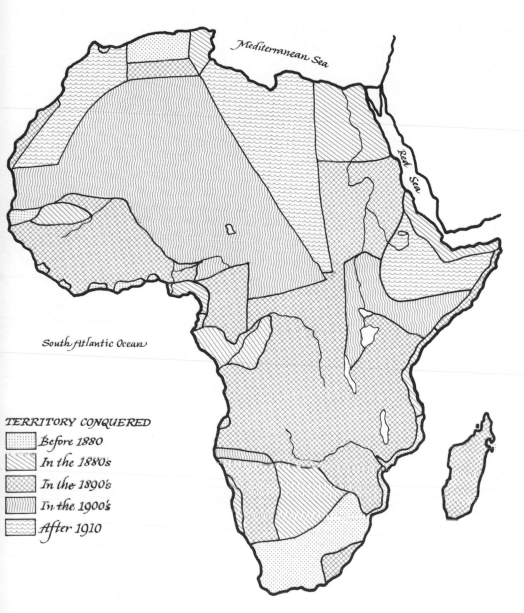

TERRITORY CONQUERED

Before 1880

In the 1880's

In the 1890's

In the 1900's

After 1910

Mediterranean Sea

Red Sea

South Atlantic Ocean

The European Conquest of Africa

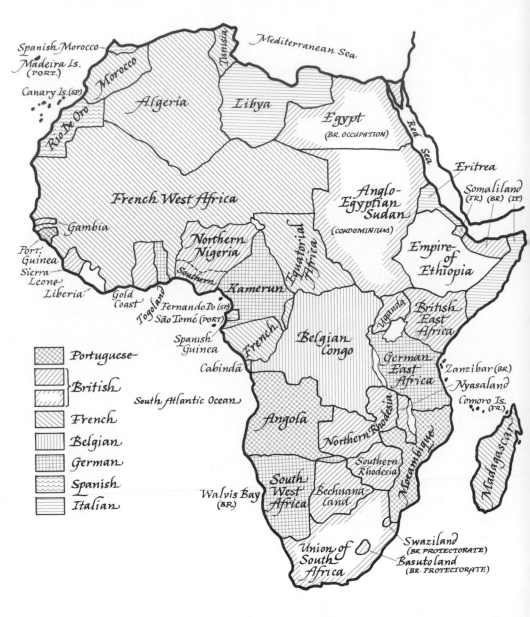

Spanish Morocco
Madeira Is. (PORT.)
Canary Is. (SP.)
Rio De Oro
Morocco
Algeria
Tunisia
Mediterranean Sea
Libya
Egypt (BR. OCCUPATION)
Red Sea
Eritrea
Somaliland (FR.) (BR.) (IT.)
French West Africa
Anglo-Egyptian Sudan (CONDOMINIUM)
Empire of Ethiopia
Gambia
Northern Nigeria
Equatorial Africa
Port. Guinea
Sierra Leone
Liberia
Southern
Gold Coast
Togoland
Kamerun
Fernando Po (SP.)
São Tomé (PORT.)
Spanish Guinea
French
British East Africa
Uganda
Belgian Congo
German East Africa
Zanzibar (BR.)
Nyasaland
Cabinda
South Atlantic Ocean
Comoro Is. (FR.)
Angola
Northern Rhodesia
Madagascar
Southern Rhodesia
Mozambique
South West Africa
Bechuana-land
Walvis Bay (BR.)
Union of South Africa
Swaziland (BR. PROTECTORATE)
Basutoland (BR. PROTECTORATE)

	Portuguese
	British
	French
	Belgian
	German
	Spanish
	Italian

Africa in 1914

30

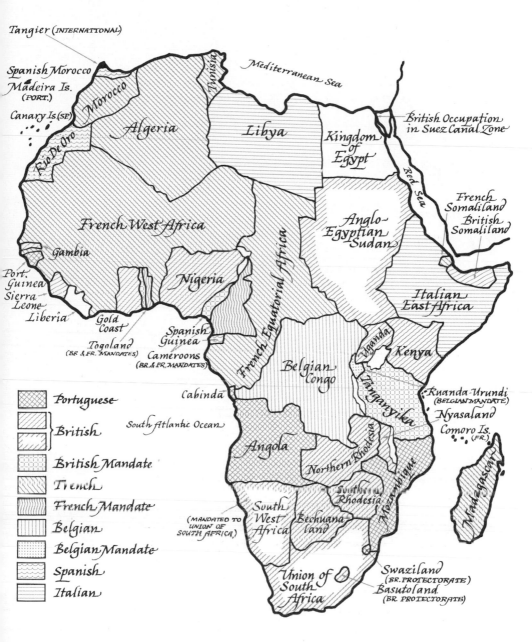

Tangier (INTERNATIONAL)

Spanish Morocco
Madeira Is.
(PORT.)

Canary Is (SP.)

Morocco

Rio De Oro

Algeria

Tunisia

Mediterranean Sea

Libya

Kingdom
of
Egypt

British Occupation
in Suez Canal Zone

Red Sea

French
Somaliland
British
Somaliland

French West Africa

Gambia

Port.
Guinea
Sierra
Leone
Liberia

Gold
Coast

Nigeria

Spanish
Guinea

Togoland
(BR. & FR. MANDATES)

Cameroons
(BR. & FR. MANDATES)

Cabinda

French Equatorial Africa

Anglo-
Egyptian
Sudan

Italian
East Africa

Uganda

Kenya

Belgian
Congo

Tanganyika

Ruanda-Urundi
(BELGIAN MANDATE)

Nyasaland

Comoro Is.
(FR.)

South Atlantic Ocean

Angola

Northern Rhodesia

Mozambique

Madagascar

	Portuguese
	British
	British Mandate
	French
	French Mandate
	Belgian
	Belgian Mandate
	Spanish
	Italian

South
West
Africa

(MANDATED TO
UNION OF
SOUTH AFRICA)

Southern
Rhodesia

Bechuana-
land

Swaziland
(BR. PROTECTORATE)

Basutoland
(BR. PROTECTORATE)

Union of
South
Africa

Africa in 1939

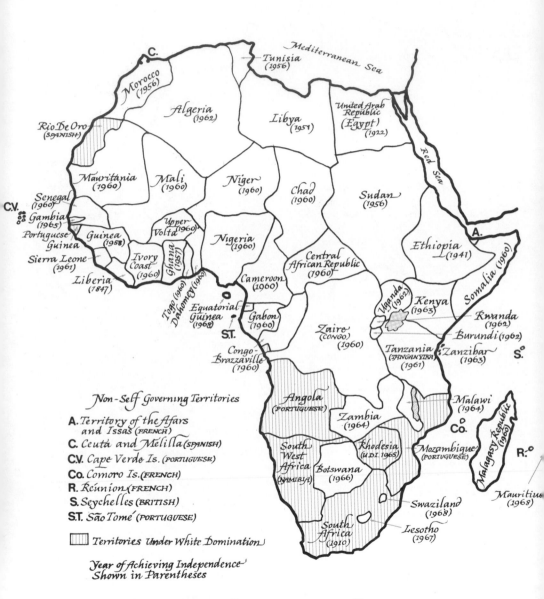

Mediterranean Sea

C.

Morocco
(1956)

Tunisia
(1956)

Algeria
(1962)

Libya
(1951)

United Arab
Republic
(Egypt)
(1922)

Rio De Oro
(SPANISH)

Red Sea

Mauritania
(1960)

Mali
(1960)

Niger
(1960)

Chad
(1960)

Sudan
(1956)

C.V.
Senegal
(1960)
Gambia
(1965)
Portuguese
Guinea

Guinea
(1958)

Upper
Volta (1960)

Nigeria
(1960)

Central
African Republic
(1960)

Ethiopia
(1941)

A.

Sierra Leone
(1961)

Ivory
Coast
(1960)

Ghana (1957)

Somalia (1960)

Liberia
(1847)

Togo (1960)
Dahomey (1960)

Cameroon
(1960)

Uganda
(1962)

Kenya
(1963)

Equatorial
Guinea
(1968)

Gabon
(1960)

Zaire
(CONGO)
(1960)

Rwanda
(1962)
Burundi (1962)

S.T.

Tanzania
(TANGANYIKA)
(1961)

Zanzibar
(1963)

S.°

Congo-
Brazzaville
(1960)

Angola
(PORTUGUESE)

Zambia
(1964)

Malawi
(1964)

Co.

Malagasy Republic (1960)

South
West
Africa
(NAMIBIA)

Rhodesia
(U.D.I. 1965)

Botswana
(1966)

Mozambique
(PORTUGUESE)

R.°

Mauritius
(1968)

Swaziland
(1968)

South
Africa
(1910)

Lesotho
(1967)

Non-Self Governing Territories

A. *Territory of the Afars and Issas* (FRENCH)
C. *Ceuta and Melilla* (SPANISH)
C.V. *Cape Verde Is.* (PORTUGUESE)
Co. *Comoro Is.* (FRENCH)
R. *Réunion* (FRENCH)
S. *Seychelles* (BRITISH)
S.T. *São Tomé* (PORTUGUESE)

◫ *Territories Under White Domination*

*Year of Achieving Independence
Shown in Parentheses*

The Decolonization of Africa

Mediterranean Sea

4.8 Tunisia

Morocco 15.4

Algeria 14.8

Libya 2.0

Egypt 34.1

Spanish Sahara 0.05

Mauritania 1.2

Mali 5.1

Niger 4.1

Chad 3.8

Sudan 16.1

Red Sea

Territory of the Afars and Issas 0.10

mbia 0.4

Senegal 4.0

uguese nea 0.6

Guinea 4.0

ra Leone 2.6

Liberia 1.6

Upper Volta 5.5

Ivory Coast 4.0

Nigeria 56.5

Cameroon 5.4

Central African Republic 1.7

Ethiopia 25.2

Somalia 2.9

Ghana 8.9 Togo 2.0
Dahomey 2.8

Equatorial Guinea 0.3

Gabon 0.5

Congo Brazzaville 1.0

Zaire 22.5

Uganda 10.1

Kenya 11.7

Rwanda 3.8

Burundi 3.6

South Atlantic Ocean

Tanzania 13.6

(Population in Millions)

Continent as a whole
1950: 217
1960: 270
1970: 344

Island Population 1970-71
Cape Verde Is. 0.3
Comoro Is. 0.3
Mauritius 0.8
Réunion 0.5
São Tomé 0.06
Seychelles 0.05

Angola 5.7

Zambia 4.3

4.3 Malawi

South West Africa 0.6

Botswana 0.7

Rhodesia 5.5

Mozambique 8.3

Malagasy Republic 6.8

Swaziland 0.4

Lesotho 0.9

South Africa 22.1

Indian Ocean

Africa: Population 1970-71

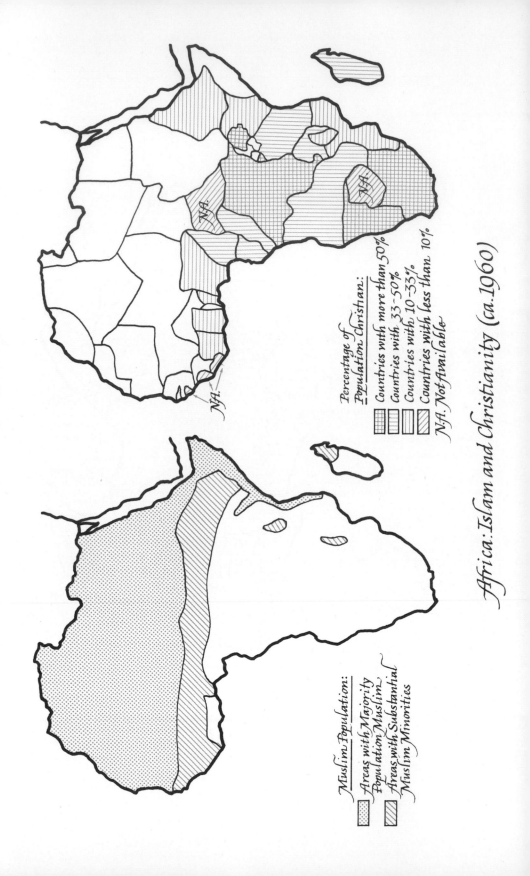

Percentage of
Population Christian:

Countries with more than 50%
Countries with 33–50%
Countries with 10–33%
Countries with less than 10%
N.A. Not Available

Africa: Islam and Christianity (ca. 1960)

Muslim Population:

Areas with Majority
Population Muslim
Areas with Substantial
Muslim Minorities

RAILWAYS ┼┼┼┼┼

☐ *CASH CROPS*

BA *Bananas*	**GN** *Groundnuts*	**T** *Tea*
CA *Cocoa*	**PO** *Palm Oil*	**TI** *Timber*
CF *Coffee*	**R** *Rubber*	**TO** *Tobacco*
CL *Cloves*	**S** *Sugar*	**W** *Wine*
CO *Cotton*	**SI** *Sisal*	**WO** *Wool*

◯ *MINING*

B *Bauxite*	**I** *Iron Ore*
C *Copper*	**NG** *Natural Gas*
CH *Chrome*	**O** *Oil*
D *Diamonds*	**P** *Phosphates*
G *Gold*	**TN** *Tin*

Africa: Railways, Mining, and Cash Crops (1970)

35

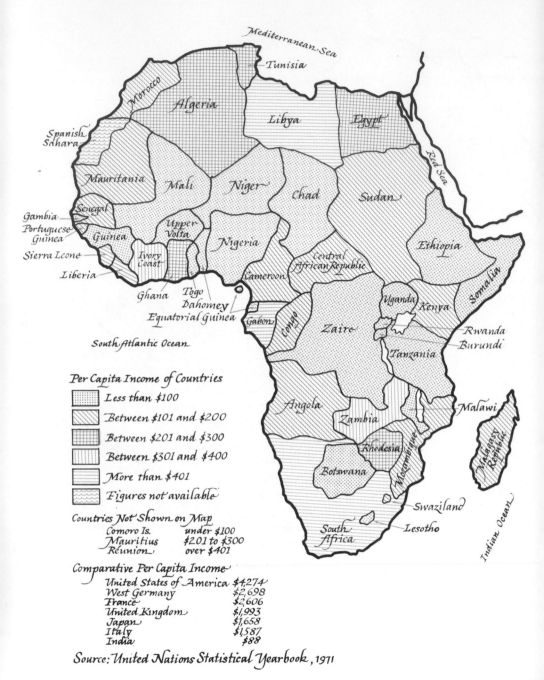

Per Capita Income of Countries

Less than $100

Between $101 and $200

Between $201 and $300

Between $301 and $400

More than $401

Figures not available

Countries Not Shown on Map

Comoro Is.	under $100
Mauritius	$201 to $300
Réunion	over $401

Comparative Per Capita Income

United States of America	$4,274
West Germany	$2,698
France	$2,606
United Kingdom	$1,993
Japan	$1,658
Italy	$1,587
India	$88

Source: United Nations Statistical Yearbook, 1971

Africa: National Income Per Capita (1971)

CHAPTER I

Africa from 1875 to the Present Day: A Chronological Survey

▲▼ AFRICA IN 1875: THE COMPARISON
WITH OTHER CONTINENTS

Compare Africa in the middle of the latter half of the nineteenth century with Europe, Asia, and the Americas and a number of striking contrasts emerge. In the first place Africa clearly contained a far larger number of polities, of autonomous political units, than any other continent. By the 1870's, with the unification of Italy and Germany recently completed, Western Europe presented the pattern of a relatively small number of nation-states. Eastern Europe by contrast was uneasily dominated by three great multinational empires, the Hapsburg, the Russian, and the Ottoman. Asia, too, was a continent of empires, Ottoman, Persian, Russian, Chinese, Japanese, with three European peoples steadily extending their hegemony over extremely heterogeneous collections of minor polities, the British in South Asia, the French in Indochina, and the Dutch in the East Indies. In the Americas a similar process had occurred somewhat earlier, with intrusive groups of Europeans, English, French, Spanish, and Portuguese imposing new forms of political organization over a great variety of subject peoples.

African societies were soon to undergo the same experience of conquest by intrusive Europeans, but in 1875 the process was not yet very far advanced. The most substantial European conquests were to be found in the two extremities of the continent. French Algeria had by now acquired close to 300,000 European inhabitants, while the four European polities in South Africa—Cape Colony, Natal, Orange Free State, and Transvaal—numbered about 325,000 white people. Elsewhere in Africa, however, the European presence was still relatively modest or indeed over vast stretches of the continent totally nonexistent.

Vigorous European commercial and immigrant communities had recently grown up in Egypt and Tunis. Parts of the West African coast were also the scene of a considerable amount of European commercial activity, though no settlers were to be found here and the areas under direct European control—the French colony of Senegal, the British colonies of the Gambia, Sierra Leone, the Gold Coast, and Lagos—were still very small. Farther south, in Angola and Mozambique, the Portuguese preserved a somewhat shaky claim to the status of a colonial power. Far out in the Indian Ocean, but closer to Africa than to any other continent, lay two European island plantocracies, French Réunion and British Mauritius. For the rest the European presence in Africa was largely a matter of isolated individuals, consuls, traders, missionaries, explorers, and adventurers. Europeans were not the only alien intruders in Africa. The Turks were masters of Egypt, Tripoli, Tunis, and the greater part of the area covered by the modern Republic of the Sudan, while the Omani Arabs had built up a position of hegemony on the East African coast and were establishing trading posts as far inland as the Congo. But even when the areas of Asian domination were added to those of European colonization there still remained more than three quarters of the continent where African rulers held sway or where independent groups organized their own affairs undisturbed by the pressure of any alien authority.

African polities presented an extraordinary variety of types of political organization. At one extreme lay ancient kingdoms such as Morocco, Ethiopia, or Benin or more recently established monarchies such as those built up by the Ashanti, the Sokoto Fulani, the Ganda, the Ndebele, and the Zulu, states which at their height might extend over 100,000 square miles of territory. At the other extreme were the innumerable "stateless" societies—bands of hunters, groups of nomadic pastoralists, settlements of agriculturalists—held together by the ties of kinship, each one usually numbering no more than a few score individuals but owing no political allegiance to any external authority. In between these two broad categories of states and stateless societies lay a third type to which, for want of a better word, the term "demi-state" may be applied. The characteristic example of a "demi-state" was the chiefdom dominated by a particular individual but not yet equipped with that administrative infrastructure which is the essential feature of the state and therefore constantly faced with the danger of fragmentation. It is hardly possible to enumerate all the states of late nineteenth-century Africa, for certain areas—Western Nigeria, for example, or the interlacustrine area of Uganda—contained large clusters of small kingdoms, some of which are hard to distinguish from "demi-states." As for the stateless polities, only highly detailed local studies would provide a satisfactory count for limited areas. Over the continent as a whole their numbers must have run into tens of thousands.

The sheer number of political units makes it impossible to construct a satisfactory political map of mid-nineteenth-century Africa. Moreover, many African polities lacked well-defined boundaries. This was not the case with the smallest political units: independent village communities knew the extent of their own territory quite precisely. The rulers of African states on the other hand often had a far less exact notion of their dominions. The nucleus of most kingdoms was made up of a cluster of closely administered provinces, but toward the periphery were usually to be found semi-independent communities whose degree of subordination to the ruler might vary from year to year. This pattern of uncertain marchlands was one that had once been common enough in Europe and it could still be found in 1875 in parts of Asia and the Americas. In general, however, Europe, Asia, and the Americas had come to be divided by a large number of carefully defined frontiers. The Turks had introduced the concept of the linear boundary into North Africa in the seventeenth century, but by 1875 Africa contained very few major territorial divisions that could be defined with cartographical accuracy.

There was then in 1875 a profound contrast in the political pattern of Africa when compared with that of Europe, Asia, and the Americas. A second striking characteristic of the continent, and a corollary of its kaleidoscopic political structure, was cultural diversity. This diversity could best be assessed in the linguistic field. No other continent could rival Africa in the number of its distinct languages; Europe and Asia could provide many examples of individual languages—Latin, Chinese, or Russian, for example—adopted by diverse peoples spread over very large areas. A similar development in the use of Arabic had occurred in Africa. Indeed, over much of the northern part of Africa the Arabic language and the religion of Islam had produced an area of cultural homogeneity comparable in size to other broadly homogeneous areas elsewhere in the world, the sphere of Latin Christendom in Western Europe or of Buddhism and Confucianism in the Far East. But in Africa, south of the Sahara, the measure of cultural diversity—manifested not only in language, but in architecture, in dress, in handicraft, in forms of political and social organization—was very great. This diversity persists, of course, to this day. No countries of comparable size elsewhere in the world can compare in sheer heterogeneity of population with such modern African states as Nigeria, Cameroon, Kenya, or Uganda.

The basic cause of this cultural diversity was to be found in another striking characteristic of late nineteenth-century Africa—the degree of isolation from external influences of most African communities. Of course, communities which by modern standards would be regarded as extremely isolated were to be found in every part of the late nineteenth-century world. But in Europe and in Asia the visits of royal officials, of packmen and hucksters, of the missionaries and ministers of universalistic religious faiths had done much to erode rural isolation and to bring to peasant societies some notion of a wider world. Visits of this kind of course could be recorded in many parts of Africa, but in general political authorities were less powerful, commercial currents less vigorous, religious organizations less well endowed than in Europe and in Asia. Moreover, the sheer size of Africa tended to emasculate and discourage movements, and in general most parts of the continent were by European or Asian standards very thinly populated.

To late nineteenth-century observers Africa seemed the most "barbarous" and "uncivilized" of the continents. "Barbarous" and "uncivilized" were imprecise and emotive epithets which contemporary Europeans applied to many alien cultures whose *mores* they did not attempt to understand. But certainly it would be true to say that no nineteenth-century African society displayed that vigorous high culture manifesting itself in a wide range of creative achievements, which Europeans had in mind when they used the term "civilization." But there had been African civilizations in the past. Ancient Egypt provided the continent's most spectacular example. In classical times Carthage, Alexandria, Meroe, and Axum, though fertilized in varying degrees by the work of aliens, also owed something to local African enterprise, while the remarkable flowering of culture in the Muslim states of medieval North Africa and in Christian Ethiopia bore witness to the skill and vigor with which African communities could adopt and develop alien ideas and techniques. Nineteenth-century Africa offered nothing to compare with these splendid achievements, though many African peoples could demonstrate in the splendor of their ceremonial occasions a marvelous combination of aesthetic qualities. Indeed, even the simplest African societies could point to remarkable examples of creativity in the field of religious speculation, oral literature, and social engineering, but it is clear that nowhere in nineteenth-century Africa could anything be found to match the astonishing inventiveness displayed by some contemporary European communities.

Many late nineteenth-century Europeans came to accept a simple explanation for this striking fact. Clearly, there were easily identifiable physical differences between Europeans on the one hand, and Asians and Africans on the other, differences most obviously apparent in the pigmentation of the skin. Was it not reasonable, then, to assume that there must be some correlation between culture and physical type, that a man's "race"—by which was often meant little more than the color of his skin—somehow determined his intellectual capacity? Simple, forceful, immensely gratifying to the white man's self-esteem by putting him on the top rung of an imagined ladder of evolution, racist explanations acquired an increasingly popular appeal in the last years of the century. In fact the causes of European superiority required a far more complex analysis. Certainly the biological element could not be entirely discounted. Particular mental aptitudes appear to be capable of transmission by inheritance. But one still has to ask how it was possible for these aptitudes—the skills of the doctor, the musician, the artist, or the engineer—to be developed in the first place. When compared with almost all African societies most European communities possessed two great advantages: they were able regularly to accumulate a surplus of wealth; at the same time they were in a position to maintain constant contact with other communities possessing cultures differing slightly from their own. For the development of a high culture wealth is essential. High cultures require the services of a very wide range of specialists, many of whom are not directly involved in productive activities. If, as happened in many African communities, the entire population has to devote almost all its time and energy to the acquisition of food, then its members find themselves constantly deprived of the opportunity to engage in more intellectual pursuits. If a community's food supply is limited, then the number of specialists it can afford to support is limited also. Specialists stimulate one another. In societies containing only a small number of specialists, the atmosphere of intellectual activity is less intense, too few questions are asked, and there is little urge to discover and invent. Indeed, the custodians of tradition, jealous of their own prerogative, are likely to discourage severely too much intellectual activity. It was the good fortune of Europe that the peculiar configuration of the continent made for easy intercourse between its various parts. Especially in its great urban centers, Rome, Paris, London, and a score of other cities, men had been able for many centuries, even before the invention of printing immensely facilitated the circulation of ideas, to keep in touch with the intellectual activity of centers other than their own, enriching their languages by loan words from their neighbors, adopting new techniques sometimes pioneered by distant peoples, extending their own stock of information by absorbing the discoveries of others. Similar processes had of course occurred in certain parts of Africa—but always in a much less vigorous manner.

The contrasts between Africa and other continents must not be overstressed. The similarities also need emphasizing. Human nature is much the same the world over. Differences of physique, of dress, of social structure might lead Europeans to regard Africans as highly "exotic." Of course, men in Africa were concerned with much the same fundamental objectives as men in Europe and Asia—the struggle to maintain life, to provide for dependents, to create a system of harmonious relationships. The vast majority of Africans looked to the land for their livelihood, as did the vast majority of Asians and Europeans—for the late nineteenth century was still an age before the urban explosion when most men lived in rural surroundings. Was the Yoruba farmer any worse off than the Scottish crofter, the Russian muzhik, or the Indian ryot? It is always difficult to compare the living standards of different peoples: all one can say is that many contemporary European travelers were struck by the sense of well-being of many African communities. What then of the "barbarism" of Africa, the hideous rituals, the summary executions, the human sacrifices, the cannibalism, the fear provoked by witch doctors, the unceasing violence in certain areas? Certainly all these horrors did exist though their incidence was often exaggerated by interested Europeans. Regrettably cruelty seems to be an element in almost every society. Africans might well argue that their wars were less destructive of human life than the internecine struggles fought by Europeans, that few men in Africa had to labor under such degrading conditions as those experienced by factory workers in the "dark satanic mills" produced by Europe's industrial revolution, that the fear of the witch doctor might be matched by the fear of the secret police in some brutal European autocracy. Again African politics might seem at first sight quite unlike the politics of Europe on account of sharp contrasts in protocol or obvious differences in scale. But the game of politics is much the same the world over, being concerned with the distribution of wealth and power. The thought processes of the half-naked African monarch holding audience outside his mud-walled palace were not so far removed from those of the frock-coated European minister receiving petitioners in his office with chandeliers as the differences in decor might suggest.

By the 1870's European travelers in certain parts of the continent might find that African monarchs, too, were beginning to take to frock coats or at least to adopt certain cultural innovations of European provenance. The world was shrinking. Everywhere the age-old walls of isolation were beginning to crumble. Africa was soon to be subjected to those processes of political change—involving the creation of large political units—that had occurred centuries earlier in all the other continents. But the European tide which swept over Africa at the end of the nineteenth century was not powerful enough totally to destroy the older cultures that lay in its path. Africa today has far more in common with the other continents than was ever the case a hundred years ago, but like every other continent it remains unique, its peoples each working at their own cultural synthesis, assimilating alien innovations to a rich indigenous core. For the sake of clarity it is essential to construct some sort of chronological framework in studying any period of history. But the chronological approach has its limitations: it is concerned only with the unusual event, the remarkable innovation. Thus this chapter gives only a very partial overview of modern African history. Chapter X, entitled "The Process of Change in Modern African History" and placed by way of summary at the end of this book, attempts to correct this imbalance by identifying certain forces and manifestations of change which cannot be fitted into the narrow straitjacket of a brief chronology.

▲▼ THE 1880'S

For Europeans the 1880's was the decade of the "scramble" for Africa. Between 1875 and 1889, with the tempo of events steadily mounting in the mid-1880's, the major powers of Western Europe established political claims to many parts of Africa in most of which they had shown no previous interest. A brief chronological summary provides perhaps the most compact and vivid means of illustrating this process.

In 1877 the British in South Africa took over the Afrikaner Republic of the Transvaal. Two years later they destroyed the powerful Zulu kingdom which bordered their colony of Natal and annexed an extensive stretch of territory (Fingoland and East Griqualand) on the Eastern Frontier of the Cape. In the same year, 1879, French army officers on the Upper Senegal began an advance toward the Niger, establishing a military post on the river in 1883. In 1881, shortly after the British had been compelled to withdraw from the Transvaal in the face of Afrikaner revolt, the French invaded Tunis and forced the ruler to accept a treaty putting himself under French protection. The year 1882 was marked by what may well be regarded as the most important single event in the history of nineteenth-century imperialism in Africa—the British invasion and occupation of Egypt, the culmination of a process of foreign intervention in Egyptian affairs, initially provoked by the financial collapse of the khedive's government in 1876. The year 1882 also saw the ratification by the French parliament of a treaty concluded two years earlier by the French explorer, Savorgnan de Brazza with an African ruler on the Middle Congo, an event of seminal importance in the foundation of a French empire in Equatorial Africa. In 1884–85 a new imperialist power, Germany, suddenly burst onto the African scene, with the German government establishing protectorates over a number of minor African polities on the coasts of Togo, Cameroon, and South West Africa and later, as a result of Carl Peters's treaty-making expeditions, in the interior of East Africa. Meanwhile another newcomer to Africa, King Leopold of the Belgians, working in an entirely personal capacity, was busy laying claims to an immense stretch of territory in the heart of the continent. Taking astute advantage of the international conference on Africa held at Berlin in the winter of 1884–85 Leopold succeeded in obtaining international recognition for his Congo Free State. The mid-1880's also saw the Italians laying the foundations of their Red Sea colony of Eritrea, while the British occupied the Somali coast opposite Aden. The British also continued to expand in South Africa, absorbing further territory on the Eastern Frontier of the Cape and taking under their control three Tswana chiefdoms, an acquisition needed to ensure a safe route to the little known lands of Central Africa. West Africa, too, was the scene of vigorous British activity, with the establishment of a protectorate over the African trading communities of the "Oil Rivers" and the granting of a charter to a commercial enterprise, the Royal Niger Company, whose agents were thus authorized to conclude treaties with local rulers and to set up a system of administration over a sphere of influence that covered the valleys of the Niger and the Benue. Two other British chartered companies were founded at the end of the decade, the British South African Company, of which Cecil Rhodes was the most prominent member, and the Imperial British East African Company.

How was this astonishing outburst of activity to be explained? The first point that needs to be made bears on the role of individuals. While it is an unavoidable form of historical shorthand to talk about "the British," "the French," or "the Germans," it should be remembered that the policies followed by the European powers in Africa were often in large measure the product of the initiative of single individuals whose actions were not frequently subjected to intense criticism by their compatriots. Had men such as Carl Peters, Savorgnan de Brazza, or George Goldie, the founder of the Royal Niger Company, never set foot on African soil, the course of events would have been significantly different in those fairly extensive areas affected by their actions. The importance of individual initiative was even more astonishingly demonstrated in the case of Leopold of the Belgians who drew on his own private resources to carve out for himself an immense African estate; in so doing he laid the foundations of one of the continent's largest modern states. Individual enterprise introduces an element of unpredictability into the unfolding of events, and this provides the historian with a warning not to set his reconstruction of the past in too rigidly deterministic a mold. But it is still necessary to ask why extraordinary individuals like Peters, de Brazza, or Leopold should have made their appearance when they did and to consider how they should have found it possible to operate in such a remarkable manner. The answers to these questions are to be found not in Africa but in Europe, in the changes that were profoundly affecting every aspect of European life.

Many European societies were richer in the 1880's than they had been ever before. Every European government had always felt itself short of money, and the harsh imperative of financial stringency was a fact of life that no imperialist in the field could ever afford to ignore. But governments, commercial firms, and missionary societies did have infinitely greater resources at their disposal than had been the case twenty or thirty years earlier and could therefore afford to contemplate ventures which in the past would have been beyond their means. Not only were Europeans richer but their technology was becoming increasingly efficient. To mention an example of particular significance for Africa: the contrast between the breech-loading magazine rifle of the 1880's and the muzzle-loading flintlock musket which European armies had used up to the 1840's was considerably greater—bearing in mind the accuracy, range, and rate of fire of the rifle—than that between the musket itself and the bow and arrow.

The undeniable evidence of Europe's technical progress and the steady widening of the technological gap between Europeans and others were immensely flattering to European self-esteem and helped to equip individual Europeans with that carapace of arrogance and assurance, that moral élan, that intense conviction of the rightness of their actions that every expansionist people needs to fuel their dynamism. Moreover, this sense of intense self-assurance received what seemed to be scientific justification as a result of the development of contemporary ideas about race. Black men and brown men were "lesser breeds" over whom it was natural for white men to hold dominion.

These profound changes in European consciousness were taking place at a time when Europeans were becoming more conscious of Africa than ever before. There were many forces serving to bring the two continents closer together. The improvement in maritime communications as a result of the establishment of regular steamship services—a development begun in the 1850's—brought Africa nearer to Europe than ever before. The steady expansion of trade gave an increasing number of Europeans some stake in African affairs. No less important was the increase in the activities of missionary societies: the mission sermon and the Sunday school tract provided many Europeans with their first introduction to Africa. Finally the mounting spate of books on Africa and the proliferation—particularly evident in the 1870's—of geographical societies bore witness to a more intense intellectual interest in a part of the world many Europeans had previously been quite content to ignore.

By the 1880's Europeans in general were more interested in Africa than they had been in the past, and their governments possessed both the technical means and the financial resources needed to impose a measure of political control over African societies should they choose so to do. But why should they make such a choice? Why, indeed, were the major powers of Western Europe induced to embark on a movement that led within a generation to the conquest of almost the entire continent of Africa? Many theories have been put forward to explain the extraordinary phenomenon of late nineteenth-century European imperialism. But imperialism like all great historical movements is in essence a process of great complexity. Theories are valuable in helping to illuminate one aspect or another of this process, but no one theory can do justice to the intricate interweaving of diverse motives that lay behind European actions. The events of the 1880's provide clear evidence of this diversity of motive.

Strategic necessity was the reason behind the British occupation of Egypt. As the possessors of a lucrative Indian empire, the British were particularly sensitive about the security of the main routes leading to the East. They had taken over the Cape and Mauritius during the Napoleonic Wars to protect the approaches to their eastern dominions; the construction of the Suez Canal gave to Egypt an even greater strategic significance than the Cape. In 1882 Egypt seemed to some British statesmen to be in the grip of anarchy. Reluctantly Gladstone's Liberal government decided to intervene to restore order and to save the canal.

An entirely different set of circumstances accounted for the French invasion of Tunis in 1881. For several years Tunis had been the scene of bitter Franco-Italian rivalry, French businessmen were anxious to present and strengthen their interests in the country, and a number of influential French statesmen felt that their own country's prestige would suffer a grievous blow if Tunis were allowed to fall into Italian hands. Trouble on the Tunisian-Algerian border provided a convenient pretext for intervention.

The more positive quest for prestige or, more precisely, for military glory played no little part in encouraging French army officers to embark on a campaign of conquest on the Upper Senegal. Military glory was a peculiarly invigorating tonic for France at a time when the country was still suffering from the humiliation of defeat at the hands of an upstart European rival.

In the German occupations of Togo and of Douala in the Cameroons, on the other hand, considerations of prestige were of much less significance. German traders in West Africa were afraid of being forced out of business by the French extending their control along the coast and imposing protectionist tariffs in areas where Europeans had previously been able to trade quite freely. In the field of national German politics commercial interests in Hamburg were of sufficient importance for Bismarck to take their representations seriously and to initiate action on their behalf.

As for the abortive British annexation of the Transvaal in 1877, commercial considerations were in no way involved. The move was part of an ambitious scheme to unite the four white polities in South Africa. The unprovoked British attack on the Zulu kingdom could be regarded as part of the same scheme, for it was designed to reconcile Afrikaner opinion to British overrule by showing that the British, too, were prepared to use tough methods against African polities.

Only in the case of King Leopold and the Congo Free State can the Marxist historian find a case of crude economic imperialism, for the Belgian king was concerned to acquire as large a domain as possible and to squeeze out of it the last ounce of profit—yet even this was a highly risky enterprise and in the late 1880's Leopold found himself on the verge of bankruptcy.

The factor common to almost all the episodes of late nineteenth-century imperialism in Africa was the intense sense of rivalry between the powers of Europe. There had, of course, always been much rivalry between European states, but rivalry grew more intense as the mounting nationalism of the 1860's and 1870's stoked the fires of aggression and competitiveness. Africa provided a vast and relatively safe field for European nations to give rein to their aggressive and competitive instincts. The leading statesmen of Europe were realistic enough to appreciate that Africa was basically a continent of secondary importance and therefore took pains to ensure that crises provoked by rivalries over an African territory never exploded into full-scale conflicts. Nevertheless the emotions generated by these rivalries were deep and bitter. Thus, the British occupation of Egypt in 1882 aroused the angry resentment of the French whose intimate links with Egypt went back to Bonaparte's expedition of 1798. This intense anti-British sentiment affected French politics and actions in other parts of the continent.

To concentrate on the activities of Europeans in Africa in the 1880's is to gain a very misleading impression of the actual character of these events. Even at the end of the decade there were still a large number of African polities whose peoples were hardly aware of so strange a phenomenon as a man with white skin. African societies possessed their own dynamic; much of African history in the 1880's is taken up naturally enough with those perennial themes—internal power struggles or the expansion of one people at the expense of another. The 1880's provide many examples of local imperialism: the Malinke adventurer, Samory, building up a state of his own in the Upper Niger; another adventurer, the Sudanese Rabih Zubair, following much the same policy in the country between Darfur and Lake Chad; Arab and Swahili traders creating substantial states in the Upper Congo; an Angolan people, the Cokwe, expanding eastward to destroy the ancient Lunda kingdom; and the Hehe, under a resolute chief, building up a conquest state in southern Tanzania. As for the internal disturbances of this period, among the best documented—partly because they were witnessed by European missionaries—were those that affected the East African kingdom of Buganda. But perhaps the most astonishing development of the decade was the revolutionary movement created by the Mahdi, a Muslim religious leader preaching a millenarian doctrine—a movement that shattered Turco-Egyptian rule in the Sudan, caused the death of a famous British hero, General Gordon, and led to the creation of an entirely new Muslim state. If the Mahdist revolt was the most dramatic event of the decade, perhaps the most far-reaching in its long-term consequences was the discovery in 1885 of the richest gold deposits in the world in the middle of the remote Afrikaner Republic of the Transvaal. Hitherto South Africa had been among the poorest regions in the continent; the discovery of gold, coming only eighteen years after South Africa had been found to contain the richest diamond mine in the world, was to set in motion a train of events whose consequences were still to be troubling the world almost a century later.

▲▼ THE 1890'S

By 1890 European rule was firmly established over a large part of Northern Africa with the French controlling Algeria and Tunisia and the British occupying Egypt. Italian, French, and British posts had been established on the Red Sea littoral, while the British and the Germans had made themselves masters of the East African coast. In West Africa the French had recently conquered much of the country between the Senegal and the Upper Niger, while agents of the British Royal Niger Company were pushing vigorously up the Lower Niger and the Benue. Elsewhere in the region the area of European domination was still confined to the coast. In Equatorial Africa the French stake in Gabon and the German stake in Cameroon were still very modest, but Leopold's Congo Free State was pursuing a vigorous policy of expansion along the line of the great rivers of the interior. In South Africa Britons, Afrikaners, and Germans had forced almost all the African communities in the region to accept their overrule, but north of the Limpopo River, Central Africa was only just beginning to come under European attack with the Portuguese advancing inland from their posts in Angola and Mozambique and the British moving up from the south. In Madagascar the French were in command of a number of coastal districts and had maintained since 1885 a loose form of protectorate over the powerful kingdom of Imerina in the center of the island. Nevertheless, for all the encroachments made by Europeans in the past decade nearly all the great indigenous states of Africa were still independent in 1890. By 1900 most of them had succumbed to European attack. If the 1880's could be described as the decade of the scramble, the 1890's was clearly the decade of conquest.

The 1890's began with two recently formed chartered companies establishing the British presence deep in the interior, in Uganda and in Mashonaland (Rhodesia). In the same year the British and the Germans defined their spheres of influence in East Africa, an agreement which left the British free to proclaim a protectorate over the sultanate of Zanzibar. Another important international agreement between Britain and France left both the island of Madagascar and the entire Sahara within the French sphere of influence. In 1891 the French completed the conquest of the Tukulor empire, the powerful Muslim state which had dominated the country between the Upper Niger and the Senegal for the past thirty years. A year later the French shattered another major West African state, Dahomey, while the British conquered the Yoruba kingdom of Ijebu and began, by more peaceful means, to extend their hegemony over the other Yoruba polities. Elsewhere in tropical Africa small European expeditions were probing deep into the interior, forcing local rulers to sign treaties renouncing their sovereignty. In dealing with the more powerful rulers violent methods often had to be used. Msiri, the immensely powerful Nyamwezi warlord of Katanga, was killed by an officer of the Congo Free State in 1891; Lobengula, the Ndebele monarch, saw his kingdom overrun by the forces of the British South Africa Company in 1893; and in 1894 the powerful Arab slave traders on the Upper Congo were defeated in a full-scale war with Free State forces.

While European agents were busy on the ground, European diplomats were actively engaged in defining on the map their countries' respective spheres of influence. In 1891 the British forced the Portuguese to accept a series of frontiers in the Zambezi Valley that did less than justice to ancient Portuguese claims. In the same year the British and the Italians defined their spheres of influence in Northeast Africa. In 1893 and 1894 the Germans created their colony of Kamerun on the map, defining its eastern borders with the French and its western borders with the British. The year 1894 also saw Leopold of the Belgians defining the southern frontier of his Congo Free State by agreement with the British and obtaining direct access to the Nile through the "lease" of the "Lado enclave."

In 1896 the movement of European conquest reached something of a crescendo. Anglo-Egyptian forces launched a full-scale assault on the Mahdist state in the Sudan. In West Africa the French occupied the imamate of Futa Jallon (Guinea) and the Mossi states (Upper Volta), while the British conquered the great kingdoms of Ashanti and Benin and established a protectorate over the hinterland of Sierra Leone. In East, Equatorial, and Central Africa a score of small-scale expeditions gradually extended the sphere of European hegemony, while in Madagascar the French made themselves masters of the powerful kingdom of Imerina. But the year also contained three episodes which showed that the great imperialist powers could not always count on smooth conquests or automatic victories. In Central Africa the British South Africa Company was severely tested by a revolt of the Ndebele and the Shona. In South Africa a bold but ill-conceived British attempt—the famous Jameson's raid—to overthrow the Afrikaner government of the Transvaal ended in fiasco, adding greatly to the already bitter tension between Britons and Afrikaners. Most spectacular of all, Ethiopians under their emperor Menelik inflicted a crushing defeat on the Italian invaders of their homeland at the battle of Adowa.

As the decade wore on, rivalry between the European powers, and particularly between the French and the British, grew more intense. Egypt was the main source of Anglo-French contention. In British eyes the country had become the hub of imperial strategy; but to ensure the security of Egypt it was necessary, so imperially minded British statesmen believed, to dominate the entire valley of the Nile or at least to prevent the Upper Nile from falling into the hands of a potentially hostile European power with the technical capacity to interfere with the water flow of the great river and so to threaten the entire economy of Egypt. Many influential Frenchmen, on the other hand, saw in the continuing British occupation of Egypt an affront to French prestige and sought to undermine the British position by establishing a French presence on the Upper Nile. In 1898 Anglo-Egyptian forces, advancing up the Nile, shattered the Mahdist state and occupied Khartoum. At the same time a small French expedition, striking eastward from the Congo, established itself at Fashoda on the Upper Nile. The resulting crisis—one of the most serious diplomatic incidents in modern African history—brought the two great powers to the verge of war. But the French were in the weaker position and eventually conceded British claims to paramountcy in the basin of the Upper Nile. Meanwhile, an even more violent crisis was developing in South Africa, provoked in large part by the position of the European minority in the booming goldfields of the Afrikaner Republic of the Transvaal. Behind the grievances of the *uitlanders* lay the determination of the British to assert their hegemony over the two Afrikaner republics. The Afrikaners for their part were no less resolved to maintain their independence. Before the decade ended the two sides were at war.

In the course of the 1890's many African peoples became aware of the force of European arms. One African ruler, Menelik of Ethiopia, was astute enough to obtain from the Europeans themselves sufficient modern weapons to enable him to resist the Italian assault and later to embark on a vigorous expansionist policy in the Horn of Africa. Another African ruler, the Malinke Samory, held up the French advance in West Africa for seven years by the brilliance of his guerrilla tactics. In most other parts of the continent African military resistance was broken after a short sharp struggle. But not all African peoples chose to resist the invader by military means. In East Africa the Ganda, many of whom had recently been converted to Christianity, established an extremely profitable modus vivendi with the British. The warlike Masai, too, accepted the British presence in a remarkably peaceful manner. In Central Africa the Lozi ruler, Lewanika, was able to preserve his kingdom relatively undisturbed in sharp contrast to his neighbor, Lobengula. In every part of the continent there were groups or individuals who found it to their interest to work closely with the invaders; in every part, too, there were some communities still so isolated that they were hardly aware of the changes that were taking place beyond their borders. Always Europeans found themselves intruding into an already complex political situation. To some African peoples the newcomers were welcome as liberators or allies: thus the pagan Bambara of the Upper Niger cooperated with the French in destroying the oppressive system of Muslim Tukulor overlordship, while the rulers of Buganda were delighted to be able to count on British assistance in their wars with their traditional enemy, Bunyoro. On the other hand, for those whose power was based on the military domination of their neighbors, Europeans often appeared as unacceptable rivals and conflict became inevitable.

Behind the ever-expanding colonial frontier, in territories where settled administration had taken the place of the military regimes of the years of conquest, European officials were at work, taking up "the white man's burden," deeply conscious of their "civilizing mission," leading the "new-caught sullen peoples . . . slowly toward the light." The age of the reforming proconsul had begun. In Egypt Cromer was so successful in restoring financial stability that he was able to devote an increasing portion of the country's revenue to the construction of dams and irrigation canals designed to transform Egyptian agriculture. In Tunisia the French started to modernize the ramshackle government of the dey. In tropical Africa where the area under direct European control was still relatively small, the older urban centers—St. Louis, Lagos, Dares Salaam, Zanzibar—experienced substantial improvements. New colonial capitals—Brazzaville, Leopoldville, Salisbury, Nairobi, and others —were founded, and colonial administrators at their lonely stations in the bush, with little but their prestige and a handful of native troops or policemen to guard them, embarked on the constantly demanding work of tax collection, road construction, and the settling of innumerable local disputes. A start was made with the vital task of railroad-building; in the 1890's Djibouti, Mombasa, Tanga, Dakar, Lagos, and Matadi were developed as the termini for railroad lines pushing into the interior. Throughout the decade metropolitan taxpayers had to meet most of the expense of maintaining the new colonial structures; but every colonial power hoped to make its new acquisitions not merely self-supporting but also a source of positive profit. By 1900 only Leopold of the Belgians could claim to have achieved much success in this respect. Large areas of the Congo Free State were handed over to European concessionary companies whose agents compelled the local people to bring in rubber and other wild produce.

Improvements were not confined to the territories under European control. Four of the rulers of independent African states—Mulay Hassan of Morocco, Menelik of Ethiopia, and the two military adventurers, Samory and Rabih—were deeply conscious of the need to build up more effective political structures than the regimes of the past and paid particular attention to the provision of modern equipment for their armies. But Samory lost his country to the French; Rabih with his power base in the Lake Chad area was too remote to receive much assistance from the outside world; and Mulay Hassan and Menelik were constantly distracted by the intrigues of covetous Europeans and by the need to suppress local revolts. The Afrikaner rulers of the Transvaal found themselves in a similar position, but with the revenue from the gold mines of the Rand at their disposal, they were in a better situation to build up their resources.

▲▼ THE 1900'S

The decade of conquest was followed in the 1900's by the decade of consolidation, the construction of new colonial infrastructures, the creation of novel links between African communities and the outside world. But there was no hard and fast line between conquest and consolidation. The 1900's witnessed a great deal of fighting. Indeed, the decade opened with the greatest war yet recorded in African history—a conflict in which the British were forced to deploy nearly half a million troops in order to impose their will on the resolute and daring farmer-guerrillas of the two Afrikaner republics of the Orange Free State and the Transvaal. Very much smaller in scale but no less momentous in their consequences for the African communities involved were the campaigns of conquest undertaken by Europeans in the savanna country of the Central Sudan—the French against Rabih in 1900 and against Wadai in 1907–8, the British against the Fulani caliphate of Sokoto between 1900 and 1905. There was fighting too in many other parts of Africa —in the Sahara, in the Somali lands of the Horn, in the Ivory Coast, in northern Uganda, in Kenya, in Angola and Mozambique, in Madagascar. The European invaders usually had at their disposal relatively modest forces, almost invariably made up of locally recruited levies under white officers. Most of the larger African polities, with their brittle centralized structures, collapsed at the first shock of the European assault, their rulers hastening to make peace on terms that would allow them to maintain some semblance of their old power. But the stateless peoples with their highly diffuse system of authority were better equipped to counter the invaders. "Pacification," the mounting of innumerable "punitive" expeditions, was a process which went on in some parts of Africa as late as the 1930's.

Once African resistance had been overcome, the colonial rulers found themselves with little to fear from their new subjects. Indeed, it was astonishing how modest a force was needed in most parts of Africa to maintain European authority. The three major revolts of the decade— in German South West Africa in 1904 (the Herero and Nama rising), in German East Africa in 1905 (the *Maji-Maji* rebellion), and in Zululand in 1906 (the Bambata rebellion)—affected relatively small areas and were the product of peculiar local conditions. Elsewhere Africans appear either to have been stunned by the shock of defeat, by the Maxim gun's brutal indication of the reality of European power, or to have been genuinely appreciative of the benefits of the new order. For the European conquerors imposed a peace such as most parts of the continent had never known before. The strong could no longer raid the weak with impunity; brigandage, endemic in some areas, was suppressed, and bloody feuds gradually gave way to gentler methods of settling disputes. The colonial *pax* made it easier for men and women to devote themselves to productive activities, montagnards moving down from their embattled hilltop villages to cultivate the empty fertile plains, traders to penetrate safely into hitherto insecure areas, and adventurous individuals to leave their homes and make long journeys in search of new forms of employment.

The new colonial infrastructures with their bureaucracies, their police forces, their modest technical services were expensive to maintain. Colonies were supposed to pay for themselves; in fact, in the first years of their existence most African colonies needed regular grants-in-aid from their metropolitan governments. In these circumstances every senior colonial official had to devote much thought to the problem of development, seeking means of increasing taxable forms of wealth. The pressing need of local officials for ready cash tied in with the views of progressive imperialists in the metropolitan countries. Africa was seen as "a vast undeveloped estate," whose peoples could be encouraged to produce a wide range of commodities required by Europe. Let Africa provide the raw materials required by the voracious industries of the metropolitan powers; in return Europe would supply Africa with the manufactured goods for which its peoples clamored. An expanding trade would benefit both the colonies and the metropoles and make it possible for colonial governments to increase local sources of revenue. The basis for such a solution already existed in West Africa with its long established trade in palm oil, groundnuts, and timber. To these was added another export staple, cocoa, a new crop whose development was almost entirely due to the enterprise of peasant farmers in the Gold Coast. Cocoa was not the only new African product to appear on the world market in the 1900's. The Sudan and Uganda followed the example of Egypt and concentrated on the growing of cotton. In all these countries—Egypt, the Sudan, Uganda, and throughout West Africa—the production of cash crops was left almost entirely to African farmers. Elsewhere in the continent another pattern of economical development came to be followed, with European immigrants acquiring land for farms or plantations.

European farming or planter communities had been in existence for many decades in Algeria, South Africa, and the Mascarenes. In the 1890's and 1900's new European immigrant communities came to be established in other parts of the continent: Frenchmen and Italians in Tunisia, Englishmen and white South Africans in Kenya and Southern Rhodesia, Germans in South West Africa and Tanganyika, Frenchmen

in Madagascar. Not all of them looked to agriculture for their livelihood. Rhodesia, for example, attracted a substantial number of miners.
In Equatorial Africa Europeans worked as the employees of the concessionary companies set up in the German, French, and Belgian territories to explore the natural resources of the region. Most European immigrants brought with them both capital and new techniques and were
prepared to experiment with a wide range of crops. They made substantial contributions to colonial economies, but at the same time they severely dislocated the life of many African communities by their demand
for land and labor and caused many political complications by their
claims to a privileged status. Europeans were not the only immigrants
to settle in Africa at the turn of the century. Small groups of Lebanese
and Syrians began to make their way on the West Coast, and larger
numbers of Indians crossed over to East Africa. These Asian newcomers found that the new colonial structures offered increasing opportunities for commercial skills, based on industry, enterprise, and thrift, of a
kind rarely possessed by Europeans in tropical Africa. In many areas
their contribution to the development of local trade was greater than
that of either Europeans or Africans.

In every territory brought under European rule the earliest structures
of alien authority had been extremely modest in character, a hastily
proclaimed protectorate, a status designed to ensure a measure of legality, a handful of white administrators, and some detachments of troops,
usually African mercenaries. Gradually, however, with metropolitan
support and slowly increasing local revenues, every territory found itself
able to afford a more elaborate structure of government. More and
more white officials were brought out. In most parts of Africa army officers, seconded from their normal military duties, had provided the first
generation of colonial administrators. In the 1900's metropolitan governments began devising more professional methods of recruitment.
With the advance in medical knowledge tropical Africa, and especially
the West Coast, began to lose its reputation as "the white man's grave."
In the older West African colonies educated Africans who had filled
many senior posts in the colonial establishments of the 1880's and
1890's found themselves pushed aside by new arrivals from Europe. So
the structure of colonial government became more elaborate. Frontiers
hastily demarcated on the map were surveyed and laid down on the
ground. Territories were divided into provinces and districts. New technical departments were founded—for agriculture, forestry, posts and
telegraphs, health, education, and public works. Agricultural research
stations were started. Work pressed forward on the railroads begun in
the 1890's and on the construction of a number of new lines.

The expansion of the base of a colonial pyramid was accompanied by the reorganization of its apex. Metropolitan foreign offices handed over the task of supervising protectorates to newly established or greatly enlarged colonial offices. In the French sphere two great administrative federations were set up to cover West Africa and Equatorial Africa. In 1908 King Leopold of the Belgians was forced in the face of mounting international protest at the atrocities associated with his regime to renounce his personal control of the Congo and to hand over the territory to the Belgian government. Another transfer of power, even more momentous for the future, was arranged in South Africa. After their defeat in the South African War the two Afrikaner republics were transformed into British colonies. But in 1907 the two Afrikaner polities were granted local autonomy. A new mood of conciliation brought Afrikaners and English-speaking South Africans together and enabled the two groups to work out a scheme acceptable to the British government for the long-sought unification of the four European territories. In 1910 the newly created Union of South Africa became the first colonial territory in Africa to be granted independence by its metropolis.

The achievement of South African independence was in large measure due to the strength of Afrikaner nationalism, a movement that could be traced back to the 1870's. The only other country in Africa to develop at this period a clearly recognizable nationalist movement was Egypt. The first manifestations of Egyptian nationalism in the late 1870's were interpreted by many Europeans as symptoms of "anarchy," and the early nationalist movement was crushed by the British in 1882. By the 1900's, however, a new generation of nationalists had appeared, of whom Mustapha Kamal, founder in 1907 of the National Party, was the representative figure. There were signs too of the stirring of a new spirit in Tunisia, in the Gold Coast, in Lagos (Nigeria), and among certain sections of the African population of South Africa. Those who took the lead in the modest protest movements of the 1900's had one thing in common: they had all received a considerable measure of Western education and had therefore been able to learn for themselves the liberal ideas developed over the past three centuries in Western Europe. In most parts of colonial Africa the most active champions of Western education were the Christian missionaries. The mission schools could indeed be regarded as revolutionary cells within the body of traditional Africa, introducing their students to a wide range of new techniques, new social patterns, new systems of values, and an awareness of an infinitely wider world. By the end of the 1900's those who had passed through the new schools and gained employment as clerks, teachers, evangelists, or, as in the case of a fortunate few, even as lawyers, doctors, businessmen, and journalists were beginning to take on the distinct appearance of a new social group, the "educated Africans" or, in the crude racist jargon of many contemporary Europeans, the "trousered niggers." Forced to accept a subordinate status in the local political and economic structure, some of these "new men" found, however, one sphere in which they could achieve a measure of autonomy—by breaking away from the mission congregations and founding new Christian communities of their own. In their rejection of white domination and their emphasis on the importance of certain traditional values and practices the independent African churches, the earliest of which dates back to the 1880's, were a significant pointer to the shape of things to come.

▲▼ THE 1910'S

The second decade of the twentieth century was overshadowed by the terrible conflict which ravaged Europe for four years, a conflict whose consequences were directly felt in many parts of Africa. Though events connected with World War I dominated the history of the 1910's, the decade also produced other important developments. Some of these represented a continuation of the process of European conquest. In 1911 the Italians, inspired almost exclusively by considerations of prestige, launched an attack on the Turkish province of Tripoli. Within a year the Ottoman government had sued for peace and withdrawn its troops, but the invaders found themselves confronted with far more tenacious opponents in the Bedouin Arabs of the interior. The year 1912 witnessed the formal termination of Moroccan independence with the French and Spanish governments assuming protectorates over their respective spheres of influence. By 1914 the French under General Lyautey, one of the most humane colonial soldiers and administrators of the day, were in control of the cities and plains of the ancient kingdom, but the fiercely independent Berber communities of the Atlas remained to be subdued. For the French and for the Spaniards whose protectorate covered the Rif in the extreme north of Morocco, as well as for the Italians in their newly named colony of Libya, much hard fighting lay ahead. Another event of the immediate prewar period possessing immense significance for the future was the British decision to amalgamate their possessions in the Niger-Benue area of West Africa to form the single colony of Nigeria. The dominant ethnic groups of the area, Fulani-Hausa, Yoruba, and Ibo, differed profoundly in culture and political experience and had previously been little in contact one with another. Now they found themselves brought together under the same political superstructure, but sharp contrasts in the style of British administration in the northern and southern provinces were still preserved and formed one of the most striking characteristics of the most populous colonial territory in the entire continent.

The impact of World War I was felt most severely in the territories under German rule. Within little more than a year the Germans were deprived of most of their African possessions, but in East Africa their forces fought a brilliant rearguard action and refused to surrender until the end of the war in Europe. The war placed a heavy burden on those African peoples called upon to provide soldiers and carriers for European armies. Nor was their service confined to Africa: many thousands of conscripts from the French African colonies fought alongside French troops on the Western Front. Wartime experience was a powerful solvent in breaking down the isolation of many African communities, while the spectacle of white men trying to kill each other served to erode the mystique of unquestioned white superiority. Yet the war also demonstrated the strength of the new colonial regimes. Weakened and distracted though they were, the colonial powers had little difficulty in maintaining their hegemony. Such revolts as occurred during the war years—among the Tuareg of the Central Sahara, in Nyasaland (a strange, symbolic gesture of protest led by an African clergyman, John Chilembwe), and in South Africa (the rebellion of a small group of disgruntled Afrikaners)—were repressed with little difficulty. By far the most serious threat to European power in Africa developed a few months after the termination of hostilities when the British in Egypt found themselves faced with what might well be described as a revolutionary situation. During the war Egypt had served as a base for many hundreds of thousands of British troops, drawn from many parts of the empire and used first to guard the Suez Canal and then to launch an assault on the Ottoman Turks in Palestine. The presence of this large alien force added greatly to the grievances which many Egyptians had begun to express in the years before the war. The foundation of a new political party, the Wafd, was a highly significant event in African history, for the Wafd was a nationalist party with a mass following, the first of its kind in Africa, capable of developing a force that even a great imperial power such as Britain would find impossible to resist.

▲▼ THE 1920'S

During the 1920's the profound changes wrought by World War I in many European attitudes clearly began to affect European relations with Africa. The aggressive self-confidence of prewar days had been severely shaken by the horrifying experiences of war. There was a widespread feeling that the colonial policies of the European powers needed to be informed by a deeper sense of moral purpose. This new mood found its most practical expression in the transformation of the former German colonies into mandates under the supervision of the newly created League of Nations. On the ground the administration of the mandated territories might seem little different from that of conventional colonies, but the various powers which had been granted mandates— France in Cameroun and Togo, Belgium in Ruanda-Urundi, Britain in Tanganyika and parts of the Cameroons and Togoland, South Africa in South West Africa—solemnly bound themselves to observe "a sacred trust of civilization" in governing the mandated territories until they were able to "stand on their own feet." This new emphasis on the duty of the governors to the governed was further emphasized by many of the ablest colonial administrators of the day: colonial peoples must be actively helped to develop their economies and improve and modernize their societies. But the final goal of imperial policy—whether independence for the colonies or assimilation with the metropolis—lay in so remote a future that even the most liberal-minded administrators of the 1920's could hardly regard it as a proposition of any immediate concern. The vast majority of Europeans working in Africa were far too preoccupied with the routine chores of office or the practical problems of earning a livelihood to worry about matters of high policy.

There were, however, certain sections of metropolitan opinion, represented for the most part by left-wing intellectuals and humanitarians, which had for a long time taken a highly critical attitude toward imperialism. The voice of anti-imperialism was now immensely strengthened by the establishment of a Communist government in Russia. The Marxist-Leninist analysis of society, vigorously promulgated by Communist supporters, provided many critics of imperialism with a set of ideas that served to bolster their confidence and sustain their conviction of ultimate victory in their struggle with monolithic and seemingly impregnable regimes. Other intellectual currents contributed to the same end. Particularly significant to the still small group of intellectuals in sub-Saharan Africa was the black nationalism of Marcus Garvey. Designed first to appeal to the members of the African diaspora in the New World, Garvey's simple but dynamic ideas—his glorification of the "black race," his belief in the ultimate liberation of Africa—helped powerfully to counteract the mood of resignation based on a passive acceptance of European superiority to which many Africans had given way. For the Muslim peoples of North Africa, to whom Garvey's ideas could have little or no appeal, the most potent ideological force to set against European imperialism was to be found in a complex of ideas associated with Arab nationalism and the regeneration of Islam. Turning back for inspiration to the great centuries of Muslim achievement but accepting the need to modernize their concepts so as to assimilate the technological and scientific advances made by the West, groups of Muslim thinkers in Egypt and the Middle East had begun even before World War I to work out an intellectual riposte to European dominance. In 1922 Egypt achieved nominal independence, for the British protectorate was brought to an end, though British troops continued to be stationed in the country. From Egypt nationalist ideas could flow southward to the Sudan and westward to the French territories of the Maghrib.

European imperialists might find themselves faced in the course of the 1920's with increasingly forceful intellectual criticism, but on the ground their position seemed stronger than ever. Two peoples noted for their exceptionally resolute opposition to European intrusion, the Berbers of the Atlas and the Rif and the Bedouin Arabs of Cyrenaica, were finally defeated after some of the hardest fighting of the colonial period. Half a million French and Spanish troops were deployed to overwhelm Abd al-Karim and the guerillas of the Rif, while the Italians were forced to employ an army 100,000 strong in order to assert their hegemony over the barren confines of Libya. In the Sudan, after a series of demonstrations culminating in the mutiny of a Sudanese battalion, the British countered the spread of Egyptian influence by sending home most of the Egyptian personnel in the administration, thus depriving the concept of an Anglo-Egyptian condominium of much of its meaning. Elsewhere in Africa minor military activity, often no more than police patrols, was sufficient to complete the process of "pacification" begun thirty years earlier.

With their control over African peoples now firmly established, colonial governments could set about improving the infrastructure needed to hold their territories together. Better communications were of the first importance. Most of the continent's major railroads were constructed before 1914 but important extensions were added in the 1920's and the introduction of motor vehicles made it necessary to provide many areas with a rudimentary network of roads. Improved communications encouraged the flow of commerce and led many Africans to turn to the production of cash crops. By levying duties on imports and exports, the easiest and least painful form of taxation, colonial governments were able to acquire greatly enhanced revenues parts of which could be used to finance the work of their embryonic medical and educational departments. But the most spectacular economic developments of the decade came not from the tropical colonies but from South Africa where the well-established mining industry served both to attract foreign investment and to generate capital that could be used to finance other industries. Thus, South Africa became the first country in the continent to experience the strains and the benefits of industrialization.

South Africa and Egypt, having passed through colonial rule to independence, were the only African countries to exhibit in the 1920's the spectacle of vigorous party politics. In South Africa where political rights were confined almost exclusively to the white community, the electorate was divided between two major parties, both led by Afrikaners and both dedicated to the preservation of white supremacy but the one enjoying the support of the English-speaking group and in favor of maintaining some sort of connection with Britain, the other more concerned to further the special interests of Afrikanerdom. In Egypt the main line of division was between the Wafd and a number of smaller and more conservative groups, some of which were closely associated with the ruling dynasty. Elsewhere in Africa the only signs of open political activity were to be found among the *colons* of Algeria, a territory regarded by the French as forming part of the metropolis; among the *citoyens* of the four *communes* of Senegal who had elected a black deputy to the French parliament as early as 1914; in certain urban areas in British West Africa, notably Lagos, Freetown, and Accra, accorded the right to elect members to the colonial legislative councils established in the early 1920's; and among the European settlers of Kenya and Southern Rhodesia. For the two British colonies of settlement, 1923 proved to be a date of crucial importance. In that year the British government declared that in Kenya African interests must be regarded as paramount, thus imposing a decisive check on the aspirations of those settlers who dreamed of creating a great white dominion in East Africa. At the same time the white settlers of Rhodesia were allowed to choose between union with South Africa and a large measure of internal autonomy. By rejecting absorption by their powerful southern neighbor they secured for themselves a quasi-independent status without precedent elsewhere in the continent. In other colonial territories, whatever the nationality of the colonial power, whether British, French, Belgian, Portuguese, or Italian, the form of government could only be described as autocratic, with major decisions being made by a small group of European officials subject to a limited amount of supervision from the metropolitan governments.

Unruffled though the surface of colonial rule might appear to most contemporary observers, it was possible to detect some symptoms of the momentous changes in store for the continent. The emergence of such varying forms of political organization as the Destour (Tunisia), the White Flag League (the Sudan), the National Congress of British West Africa (Nigeria and the Gold Coast), the Kikuyu Central Association

(Kenya), the Tanganyika African Association and the African National Congress (South Africa) provided clear evidence of a growing political consciousness among certain elements of the subject population. Colonial officials might dismiss these new groups as being entirely unrepresentative of the people as a whole, but the ideas which they put forward —their request for a greater measure of local participation in the work of government, their concern to ameliorate some of the harsher manifestations of colonial rule—were to come to seem increasingly relevant to the needs of their particular territories. In the 1920's African reformers lacked a power-base strong enough to ensure that proper attention would be paid to their views. But the future was on their side. Gradually with the expansion of education, the spread of Christian evangelization, the growth of urban centers, and the development of commercial agriculture and mining, a new, more modern Africa was coming into existence.

▲▼ THE 1930'S

Throughout the 1930's European hegemony in Africa remained intact and indeed in most areas virtually unchallenged. In 1935 Ethiopia, the only African kingdom to retain its independence into the colonial period, was overrun by Italian armies in a war deliberately provoked by the Italian dictator, Mussolini, with the object of distracting the Italian people from their own pressing internal problems. The conquest of Africa was now complete. But already some of the weaknesses of the imperial structure were becoming apparent. The Great Depression of the early 1930's brought with it a sudden fall in the price of most colonial raw materials. Colonial governments, faced with rapidly declining revenues, were forced to halt development projects launched a few years earlier and even to cut down the numbers of their European staff. Not until the last years of the decade did the economic situation improve sufficiently to allow a resumption of the more dynamic policies of the 1920's.

Nevertheless, though the rate of change was slow, especially in comparison with the pace of the two succeeding decades, the general direction was becoming clear. The isolation which had been such a marked characteristic of most African communities was steadily being eroded. Young men were beginning to acquire new ideas about the world as a result of a few years of schooling or of journeys away from home to seek work in distant towns, on plantations, or in mining compounds. Equipped with this wider experience, the new generation could no longer observe their elders with the degree of respect deemed proper in most traditional African societies. Hence the growth of tensions in

local politics, tensions often aggravated by the support given by the colonial authorities to local chiefs and headmen who were thus able to ensure for themselves far greater power than they had ever enjoyed in the
past. In the 1920's the policy of "indirect rule" advocated by many
British administrators with its stress on the preservation of traditional
African institutions seemed humane and progressive. But by the end of
the 1930's some colonial officials were beginning to complain that the
system strengthened the position of the most conservative elements in
local society.

The impact of a new generation was also apparent in the evolution of
those organizations created for the expression of nationalist sentiments.
In Egypt the aging radicals of the Wafd found themselves under attack
from the young zealots of the Muslim Brotherhood. In the Sudan the
creation of the Graduates' Congress in the late 1930's showed that
members of the country's small Western-educated elite were beginning
to think in terms of political action. In Tunisia a group of young men,
exasperated by the cautious policy pursued by the respectable, elderly
leaders of the Destour, broke away to found the Neo-Destour and began
vigorously to canvas for the support of the masses. Among Algerian
Muslims there developed an increasingly animated debate on the future
of the country, with some emerging politicians favoring an assimilationist policy based on cordial collaboration with the French, with others
looking forward to the establishment of an independent Algeria. But
differences of opinion did not go so deep as to nullify the prospects of
united action, and in 1936 all the nationalist groups came together to
form the Algerian Muslim Congress. Morocco, too, was the scene of increasing restlessness of which the first symptoms were the violent protests that greeted French attempts to interfere with the application of
Muslim law among the Berber communities of the Atlas. In 1937 Moroccan nationalists came together to found the country's first modern
political party, the *Comité d'Action Marocaine*. In their political development all the countries of the Maghrib presented a common pattern,
with nationalist sentiment spreading from the urban bourgeoisie to the
urban workers and peasants, while Islam served both as a dynamic and
a cement.

In tropical Africa there was far less evidence of the growth of strong
anticolonial feeling. Unlike the countries of North Africa, most of the
sub-Saharan territories, with their heterogeneous populations, seemed to
lack that powerful stimulant to nationalist sentiment, the sense of a historic personality. Thus, in Kenya Kikuyu activists were vividly aware of
the grievances of their own people but had no interest in the problems
of neighboring ethnic groups, while in Nigeria the politicians of Lagos

rarely showed any concern for the state of affairs in other parts of the colony. The tropical colonies were still to be regarded as geographical expressions rather than as nations in embryo. For their future leaders the 1930's was a period for education and apprenticeship. Some of the most prominent figures of the 1940's and 1950's—Senghor (Senegal), Nkrumah (the Gold Coast), Azikiwe (Nigeria), Kenyatta (Kenya), and Banda (Nyasaland)—were far from home studying in Europe or America. Others were still at school or had not yet turned their minds to politics. Perhaps the most significant political development of the decade in sub-Saharan Africa was the emergence of a new form of Afrikaner nationalism in South Africa, with the formation of the Purified National Party, a breakaway group made up of those who rejected the policy of cooperation between English-speakers and Afrikaners favored by the older generation of Afrikaner politicians and who worked assiduously toward the goal of Afrikaner domination. The stridency and aggressiveness of the new Afrikaner nationalism did not seem out of place in a decade which witnessed the spread of extremist political sentiment in many of the states of Europe.

▲▼ THE 1940'S

The 1940's brought to an end more than half a century of European dominance in the Afro-Asian world. The collapse of France in 1940, the destruction of the Italian empire in Africa in 1941, the Japanese assault on the European colonies in Southeast Asia in 1941–42, the Anglo-American invasion of French North Africa in 1942–43, and finally, the European withdrawal from South Asia and much of the Middle East in the immediate postwar years—this dramatic sequence of events presaged the eventual renunciation by the major colonial powers of their empires in Africa. Though no fighting took place in sub-Saharan Africa, the peoples of the African colonies found themselves deeply affected by the course of World War II. Men from French Africa fought in Europe; from South Africa, in North Africa and Italy; from the British tropical colonies, in Ethiopia and Burma; while Egypt once again served as a base for a massive alien military force. The war brought about many strange encounters between Moroccans and Americans, Nigerians and Indians, Senegalese and Germans. Talk of freedom, a constant strain in Allied war propaganda, fell on receptive ears in many parts of Africa. To the growing number of politically conscious Africans the Atlantic Charter was a highly significant document.

It was no coincidence, then, that the mid-1940's, the last years of the war and the first years of peace, should have seen the foundation of new political organizations capable of appealing for mass support in the cause of local nationalism. Istiqal (Morocco), the *Rassemblement Démocratique Africain* (French West Africa), the United Gold Coast Convention and the Convention Peoples Party, the National Council of Nigeria and the Cameroons, the Kenya African Union, and the Nyasaland National Congress were among the political parties born of these years, while older political organizations such as Neo-Destour (Tunisia) and the Tanganyika African Association resumed their operations with fresh vigor.

Among the European colonial powers, wartime experience served to foster a mood of liberalism and idealism. In the British colonies this found practical expression in a number of significant changes in the structure of government designed to allow Africans greater opportunity to participate in the decision-making processes both at local level and —through the provision of African representation in colonial legislative councils—at the center. Even more striking were the political changes in French Africa where, under the provisions of the new constitution of the Fourth Republic, all the colonies were enabled to send locally elected deputies to sit in the French parliament. To militant nationalists these reforms fell far short of their demands, but they were symptomatic of a willingness to reshape colonial structures and to adopt an evolutionary approach to political problems that augured well for the future. But the latter half of the 1940's also witnessed a series of incidents—abortive insurrections in Algeria and Madagascar, demonstrations, riots, or strikes in Nigeria, the Gold Coast, the Ivory Coast, and Southern Rhodesia—which brought to the surface a violence such as the colonies had not experienced since the ending of the period of conquest and pacification. Britain and France were strong enough to maintain their hegemony in Africa by repressive measures, but to important sections of public opinion in the two metropolitan countries simple repression no longer seemed an adequate solution to political problems. Colonial authorities in Belgium and Portugal, on the other hand, could see no virtue in the liberal policies of the British and the French. In the Belgian and the Portuguese territories European rule remained essentially autocratic in character, with no provision made for African representation on colonial councils. The apparent passivity of the subject populations of the Belgian Congo, Angola, and Mozambique seemed in Belgian and Portuguese eyes to indicate the success of this approach.

South African politics were more complex than those of any other country in the continent. The 1940's saw the development of a somewhat more liberal sentiment among certain sections of the white electorate and the injection of a new militancy into the policies of the old-established African National Congress by a younger generation of African radicals. But the decade ended with the electoral victory of the exclusively Afrikaner National Party. The more militant Nationalists were determined to establish Afrikaner supremacy in relation to the English-speaking section of the white population and at the same time to implement a rigid policy of apartheid or racial segregation. In South Africa there was nothing novel about these ideas, but the Nationalists were prepared to implement them with a dogmatic zeal that contrasted sharply with the more pragmatic and easygoing approach of earlier governments.

The ferment of ideas produced by World War II in many parts of Africa was only one of the factors making for accelerated change. The war also had a profound effect on African economies, producing acute, if only temporary, hardships and at the same time providing new opportunities for development. Shortages of consumer goods, inflation, the compulsory production of raw materials needed for the war effort—to many African peoples such aspects of the wartime economy of their territories were the cause of bitter resentment, resentment that might serve to erode older feelings of loyalty to the colonial power. But the war also brought a welcome rise in the price of most colonial products, a rise that continued even more vigorously in the immediate postwar years, so that colonial governments found themselves with much more buoyant revenues at their disposal than ever before. At the same time the liberal ideas generated by the war in Britain and France produced a new approach to the problems of colonial finance. The old idea that colonies should be self-sufficient was abandoned. Both the British and the French governments now accepted it as their duty to provide direct financial assistance to their colonial territories, thus helping them to develop their resources and expand their social services. Thus colonial governments found themselves in a position to recruit more "technical assistants"—engineers, doctors, agriculturalists, and teachers— than they had ever been able to employ in the past and to embark on ambitious plans for balanced and rational development. One highly significant indication of the new approach was the foundation by the British of new universities for their East and West African territories. No less significant was the steadily swelling stream of African students who found their way to institutions of higher education in Britain and France. These new university graduates, these "been-tos," as the students who had studied abroad were sometimes called, were destined to form the dominant elite of the next two decades.

Inevitably the pace of change varied greatly from territory to territory and from area to area. In those parts of the West Coast where an educational infrastructure was already firmly established and where peasant farmers were growing rich on the production of lucrative cash crops, the manifestations of change were far more apparent than in those much more extensive parts of the continent where local economies were still largely dependent on subsistence agriculture and where the Western-educated group still formed only a tiny minority of the population. The manifestations of change—new buildings going up, more cars on the roads, new skills being transmitted, a wider range of consumer goods finding their way into homes that never had them before—were even more apparent in those parts of the continent which were affected by the development of mining or factory industry, the South African Rand, the copper belt of Katanga and Northern Rhodesia and in those urban centers which possessed a substantial alien immigrant population. In the fast-growing cities of Africa it was possible to trace patterns of social stratification totally without precedent in older African communities.

▲▼ THE 1950'S

In 1950 by far the greater part of Africa was still firmly under European control. By the end of the decade the process of decolonization was almost half completed. The unscrambling of the major European empires in Africa was proceeding as swiftly and to many observers as unexpectedly as the original scramble for African territory was done. In 1951 Libya, the former Italian colony whose constitutional progress had been supervised by the United Nations, achieved independence. The year 1952 was the year of the Egyptian revolution, with the overthrow of the dynasty founded more than a hundred years earlier by Muhammad Ali and the establishment of a notably dynamic government under the eventual leadership of Gamal Abdul Nasser. The next year an Anglo-Egyptian agreement provided the necessary conditions for the granting of independence to the Sudan. In 1954 the French found themselves confronted with a serious revolt in Algeria, a revolt that was to develop into a long-drawn-out war of liberation. Little more than a year later the French government concluded the agreements that led to the independence of Morocco and Tunisia. At the same time French territories in other parts of Africa were granted a large measure of autonomy. The last vestiges of a British military presence in Egypt were removed in 1956 after the fiasco of the Anglo-French attack on the Suez Canal. In 1957 the Gold Coast, changing its name to Ghana, became the first British colony in tropical Africa to achieve independence. In 1958 all the French territories in Africa were given the opportunity to choose by means of a referendum between independence and continued association with the metropolis. At the time only one colony, Guinea, opted for independence. Within a year, however, it was clear that the other French territories were changing their mind over the issue of independence. In Nigeria political progress had been complicated by the need to devise a constitutional structure for an exceptionally large and heterogeneous population, but by 1959 this colony too was on the verge of independence. In East Africa all the British territories were caught up in the process of constitutional change, though in Kenya progress toward independence was retarded by the presence of a vocal white settler community and by the need to defeat a savage revolt launched by Kikuyu extremists. The political development of British Central Africa was dominated by the decision made by the British government in the early 1950's to federate the three territories of Northern and Southern Rhodesia and Nyasaland. By 1959, however, the federation was clearly threatened with collapse in the face of militant African opposition. Belgian authorities in the Congo had deliberately sought to insulate their subjects from disturbing political ideas, but by the end of the decade the bankruptcy of this policy had become apparent as the peoples of the Congo found themselves caught up in the mood of nationalist euphoria sweeping the continent. Only the Portuguese colonies appeared unaffected by these vast changes. As for South Africa, the Nationalist government, with the tacit support of the great majority of the white population, introduced increasingly stringent measures effectively designed to curb the activities of nonwhite political parties.

Throughout the 1950's there was much discussion as to when a colony was "ready" for independence. Readiness, it gradually became apparent, did not depend on economic viability or on educational advancement but on the existence of a mass party capable of disrupting the life of a colony if its demands were not met. Later, once the principle of decolonization had been accepted by the metropolitan power, even the existence of a mass party was not necessary. All that was needed was a group of local politicians willing to take on the burdens of self-government. So it was the mass party that must be regarded as the main instrument for the political changes of the 1950's. The main African political parties could trace their origins back to the 1930's or 1940's, but it was only during the last years of the colonial period that they developed the techniques of appealing for mass support. In the last resort, however, the success of the mass parties was dependent not so much on the skill and determination of their leaders as on the attitude of the colonial power. The Portuguese, the South African, and—at least until the late 1950's—the Belgian governments were not prepared to accord to their African subjects those freedoms of expression and association that were allowed in the British and French colonies. Beyond the differences in political philosophy of the various metropolitan powers lay profoundly different assessments of the relevance of the African territories. Britain and France and in the last resort Belgium could all afford to renounce their African empires without incurring any substantial loss of prestige or suffering any serious economic hardships. But to many Portuguese their very existence as a nation seemed to depend on the maintenance of an African empire, while to the Afrikaners and to many English-speaking South Africans the preservation of white supremacy seemed integral to their way of life.

There is another set of factors which need to be borne in mind when considering what may well be described as the African revolution of the 1950's. Revolutions always proceed by a process of chain reaction. To some extent the English revolutionaries of the seventeenth century, the American and French of the eighteenth, and the Russian of the twentieth were the intellectual ancestors of the African nationalists of the 1950's. Even more relevant in building up the self-confidence of the opponents of colonialism in Africa was the collapse of colonialism in Asia in the 1940's. The political victories gained by nationalists in countries such as Egypt, the Gold Coast, and Guinea encouraged and inspired local nationalists in other parts of the continent. As more and more territories achieved independence, the process of decolonization was correspondingly accelerated. It seemed hardly logical for a metropolitan power to deny to one of its territories what it had already granted to another. Once a country had achieved independence it could become a much more effective base for passing on nationalist and revolutionary ideas to its neighbors. Thus one of the first acts of the government of Ghana was to organize the first Pan-Africanist conference ever held on African soil. For the delegates from countries still under colonial rule the conference proved a dramatically inspiring experience.

The political changes of the 1950's had a profound effect on the social and economic development of the continent. Nationalist politicians made a point of demanding better facilities and accelerated progress for their peoples. Even when the nationalists were in opposition, colonial authorities had to go some way toward meeting their demands in order to allay mounting discontent. Thus both the French in Algeria and the British in Kenya began pouring unprecedented amounts of money into plans for local development at a time when they were still engaged in fighting a formidable guerilla movement. Once the nationalists had gained power, they were able to impart a new dynamism to the work of development, a dynamism to which many expatriate officials responded with considerable enthusiasm. Over the continent as a whole vast sections of the population, and especially the young, were caught up in "the revolution of rising expectations." Two aspects of development contributed directly to this new mood which contrasted so sharply with the passivity or conservatism of many older African societies: the expansion of communications and the extension of education. During the 1950's many African communities were brought for the first time within reach of a motorable road, the most potent of all instruments for breaking down isolation. At the same time, with many African countries embarking on greatly enlarged programs for school building, a far wider range of children were given the opportunity of experiencing a few years of Western-type schooling. Roads and schools were probably the most important elements in the development plans of the 1950's. At least in the early years of the decade the price of raw materials remained buoyant, and there were substantial increases in production. Some countries were fortunate enough to discover hitherto untapped mineral resources—Guinea, for example, bauxite; Sierra Leone, Tanganyika, and South West Africa, diamonds; or the Belgian Congo and Northern Rhodesia, copper—and to witness a rapid expansion in the exploitation of already known resources. Thus at a time when they were being called on to shoulder a wide range of new tasks, most governments in Africa found themselves with larger revenues at their disposal than they had ever possessed before—revenues which were supplemented by increased sums of aid provided not only by the metropolitan countries but also, once they had achieved independence, by other developed countries including the United States and the Soviet Union.

The nationalism of the 1950's also helped to stimulate something of a cultural renaissance. In the high colonial period many aspects of African culture had been denigrated or regarded as curiosities by European commentators, an attitude passed on to many Western-educated Africans who were thus moved to reject parts of their own heritage. But it is one of the characteristics of nationalism to exalt every aspect of a people's distinctive achievements—the deeds of their ancestors, their craftsmanship, their forms of political organization, their religious concepts, and so on. African culture was enriched by the emergence of new art forms and new syntheses, African writers using European languages and adapting European literary techniques for the expression of African themes, African artists using novel materials and experimenting with novel styles, African musicians learning to make use of a wider range of instruments, and so on. Many of these achievements evoked the enthusiastic appreciation of outside observers. The old European concepts of racial superiority began to seem increasingly outmoded and absurd.

At last Africans were beginning to find themselves accepted as equal members of the world community.

▲▼ THE 1960'S

In 1960 Nigeria, Somalia, the Belgian Congo, Madagascar, and a cluster of French colonies in West and Equatorial Africa achieved independence. Sierra Leone and Tanganyika became independent states in 1961; Algeria, Burundi, Rwanda, and Uganda in 1962; Kenya and Zanzibar in 1963; Malawi (Nyasaland) and Zambia (Northern Rhodesia) in 1964; Gambia in 1965; Botswana (Bechuanaland) and Lesotho (Basutoland) in 1966; Equatorial Guinea (formerly the Spanish colonies of Fernando Po and Río Muni), Mauritius, and Swaziland in 1968. In the early 1960's nationalist forces in Angola, Portuguese Guinea, and Mozambique launched a guerrilla war against the Portuguese colonial regime. In 1965 the white settler government of Southern Rhodesia issued a unilateral declaration of independence and succeeded in maintaining its position despite the pressure of economic sanctions imposed first by the British, then by other members of the United Nations. Thus the 1960's witnessed a fundamental transformation of the political map of Africa with the almost total disappearance of the British, French, Belgian, and Spanish empires. (In 1970 a few small European-dominated enclaves still remained, the French in Réunion and in the Territory of the Afars and the Issas on the Somali coast, the Spanish in the presidios of Ceuta and Melilla in northern Morocco and in a strip of territory on the northwestern coast of the Sahara.) The only country apparently unaffected by the political changes of the decade was South Africa, where by the end of the 1960's the white government seemed better equipped than ever before to resist the assault of black nationalism.

For five of the largest states of Africa, Chad, Ethiopia, Nigeria, the Sudan, and Zaire (Congo) the 1960's brought serious outbreaks of violence. The governments of Chad, Ethiopia, and the Sudan found themselves involved in long-drawn guerrilla campaigns against dissident groups whose support was based on the peoples of particular areas, the Muslims in northern Chad and in the Ethiopian province of Eritrea, the non-Muslims in the southern Sudan. In Zaire a highly confusing situation developed in the immediate aftermath of independence, with one province, Katanga, attempting to assert its independence and rebellions breaking out later in other parts of the country. By the late 1960's, however, the government, assisted initially by United Nations forces, had succeeded in establishing its authority in every part of the country.

In Nigeria a complex series of events led to an attempt by the Ibo of the Eastern Region to break out of the federation and establish the independent Republic of Biafra. There followed one of the bloodiest conflicts in modern African history involving two and a half years (1967–70) of fighting before the secessionists were driven to surrender. Two of the smallest African states, Rwanda and Zanzibar, also experienced periods of violent internal turmoil when the dominant ethnic groups, the Tutsi in Rwanda, the Arabs in Zanzibar, were overthrown and exposed to savage massacres. Elsewhere in Africa the newly independent states enjoyed a considerable measure of internal stability. In 1970 almost half the former colonial territories were still being governed by the men who had led their countries to independence and whose power was initially based on the organization of a mass political party. Leaders such as Bourguiba (Tunisia), Senghor (Senegal), Houphouët-Boigny (Ivory Coast), Kenyatta (Kenya), Nyerere (Tanzania), Kaunda (Zambia), and Banda (Malawi) established themselves as father figures of their newly created nations: all of them possessed gifts of statesmanship of a high order. Equally remarkable were the achievements of the heads of the three of the older independent states: Nasser of Egypt, Haile Selassie of Ethiopia, and Tubman of Liberia. Other African countries experienced one or more changes of regime in their first decade of independence. In most cases these changes were brought about by means of military coups. The emergence of the army as a major political force was one of the most striking features of the African scene in the 1960's. A natural corollary to this development was the eclipse of the old-style nationalist politician. But every military regime was dependent on civilian support and cooperation, and some military governments were concerned to hand over power to civilians as soon as possible. In most parts of Africa it was not the army or a political party but the civil service, its structure based on the colonial model, its personnel largely Africanized, that served as the major binding force holding newly independent states together. Thus some of the basic institutions of the colonial period were preserved intact and the transition from colony to independent state proved in practice to be far less revolutionary than many observers had predicted.

The emergence of so large a number of independent states was accompanied by remarkably little interstate friction. With one or two exceptions of which Somalia was the most important, the much-criticized frontiers laid down by the colonial powers at the end of the nineteenth century were accepted as they stood. The creation of the Organization of African Unity in 1963 provided a forum in which all the newly independent states of Africa could discuss common problems. Considerable attention was also given to the task of creating effective institutions for regional cooperation, though here it should be noted that the administrative federations of the colonial period, as formed by the French in West and Equatorial Africa and by the British in Central Africa, were far more effective as practical instruments for cooperation than any of the interterritorial institutions of the postcolonial era.

Every independent African state found itself obliged not only to devise a policy toward its neighbors but also to decide on its attitude toward outside powers. In general relations between former colonies and their former metropolitan overlords remained remarkably cordial, most former British colonies remaining members of the Commonwealth, most former French territories retaining close ties with France and becoming associate members of the European Economic Community. Sentiment as well as self-interest played a part in these alignments—an appreciation of the practical assistance the former metropolis was capable of rendering being supplemented by the attraction of an engaging and familiar culture. Even more significant, however, for the future was the fact that Africa was now opened up as never before to the enterprise of other countries. All the most highly developed nations of the non-Communist world, including Israel, Japan, and Taiwan, offered various forms of technical assistance and financial aid. For virtually the first time in their history the Soviet Union, the Communist states of Eastern Europe, and China began to take a keen interest in African affairs. No African state was anxious to become involved in Great Power rivalries and most defined their foreign policies in terms of nonalignment. Two major issues in the field of foreign affairs were of special interest to many African states: the position of Israel and the situation in the white-dominated states of Southern Africa. Egypt had been deeply involved with Israel ever since the creation of the Jewish state in the late 1940's. After the Egyptian defeat at Israeli hands in the Six Days' War of 1967 sentiments of Muslim solidarity induced many of the Muslim states of Northern Africa to offer practical assistance to the Egyptian government. There was also widespread sympathy, most vigorously expressed in states with an avowedly radical orientation such as Algeria, Guinea, and Tanzania, for the African nationalist forces in their struggle with the white-dominated regimes of Southern Africa. But the military strength and internal solidarity of both Israel and the white communities in Southern Africa were such that the largely verbal assaults of independent African states proved ineffectual in producing any significant changes in the situation either in the Middle East or in Southern Africa. Nevertheless, with the rapidly growing African membership of the United Nations it became clear that African opinion was a factor that could not be entirely disregarded by the policy makers of the great powers.

During the 1960's most African countries faced considerable difficulties in maintaining the pace of development. Fluctuating prices of raw materials in the world market, adverse trade balances, mounting debt charges, vagaries in the flow of foreign aid and investment—factors such as these had a deleterious effect on the implementation of many development plans. Yet the 1960's witnessed a wide range of substantial achievements. The economy of certain countries was transformed by the exploitation of newly discovered mineral resources: oil in Libya, Algeria, Nigeria, and Gabon; iron ore in Mauritania and Liberia. The remarkably rapid growth rate achieved by the Ivory Coast showed that it was possible to base a flourishing economy on the export of a fairly wide range of agricultural products. Factory industry began to emerge as a significant element in the economy of many of the larger African states. Great engineering projects involving the construction of highways, port facilities, irrigation schemes, and hydroelectric works were carried out in many parts of the continent. Among the most spectacular undertakings were the construction of the Aswan Dam in Egypt and the building of the Tan-Zam railway, linking Tanzania and Zambia—the first, undertaken with Russian aid; the second, the work of Chinese engineers. In the field of education many countries achieved a rate of progress, especially in the expansion of secondary schools and institutions for more advanced studies, that would have seemed astonishing only a decade earlier. The output of a very much greater number of university graduates made it possible for most African countries to reduce drastically the number of expatriates in their service. Some countries sought to establish their control over the main foreign-owned companies, banks, and business firms by introducing wide-reaching measures of nationalization. But with so important a sector of their economy still dependent on the prices paid for their raw materials in the world market, most African countries still found their plans for development aggravatingly subject to forces over which they could exert no control.

Rapid development brought with it other problems. As a result of improved medical facilities leading to the control or elimination of once fatal diseases, population began rising at a faster rate than ever before. The average annual growth rate for the entire continent in the years 1960–66 was put at 2.3 percent per annum. Many African countries could still be regarded as underpopulated, but in certain areas, including the Nile Valley in Egypt, the Ibo country of Nigeria, and some of the native reserves or Bantustans of South Africa, pressure of population was an alarming phenomenon. Population growth was particularly marked at the continent's major urban centers, some of which were increasing at the rate of 10 percent per annum. Many African cities lacked the solid industrial core which supported the economies of the older urban centers of Europe and America, with the result that substantial sections of their population were never able to find opportunities for regular employment. In these new urban environments the contrasts of wealth and poverty became brutally apparent. Members of the local elite—politicians, civil servants, and businessmen—enjoyed a standard of living such as few Africans had ever experienced in the past. At the same time many of their compatriots, the inhabitants of the *bidonvilles* or shanty towns, lived in conditions of insecurity and squalor of a kind hardly known by their forebears in their villages in the bush. These contrasts, vivid enough in Casablanca or Lagos or Nairobi, became even more crudely apparent in those countries in the southern part of the continent still dominated by a white oligarchy.

▲▼ AFRICA IN THE 1970'S: OVERVIEW

This chapter began with a brief account of Africa as it appeared in the 1870's in comparison with other continents. Certain broad characteristics were identified: the political fragmentation, the cultural diversity, the isolation of most African societies, the absence in almost every part of the continent of what could unquestionably be described as "high culture." It seems appropriate to end this chapter with another succinct overview. To look at the most striking characteristics of the African scene of the 1970's and to set these against the earlier pattern is to gain some insight into the changes produced by what has surely been the most momentous century in the history of the continent.

In the last hundred years the political face of Africa has undergone a massive transformation. The "demi-states," the stateless polities, have disappeared as independent political units, though most of them still survive as organs of local government. Gone, too, are many of the old states of nineteenth-century Africa, destroyed in the period of European conquest or broken up by the nationalist successors to the European rulers. Today, the whole continent is covered by the superstructures provided by a mosaic of states of varying sizes. Some of these states are among the most modest, both in population and in resources, of all the independent political units of the modern world, but even these "mini-states" represent an advance on the political fragmentation of the past. At the other extreme a handful of African states—notably Egypt, Nigeria, and South Africa—can be counted among the more substantial polities of the late twentieth century.

Africa still remains a continent of striking cultural diversity. But again, as in the field of politics, one can trace a movement toward greater uniformity. The expansion of Islam and Christianity, the establishment of educational structure based on European models, the spread of new *linguae francae*—developments such as these have made it possible for Africans from different parts of the continent to communicate both with one another and with people coming from other parts of the world in an intimate manner that would have been inconceivable a century ago. This movement toward a greater measure of cultural uniformity can also be seen as one aspect of that erosion of the isolation of African societies, a process even more powerfully hastened by changes in their economy. Many African communities still remain largely cut off from many of the forces for change in the modern world, but the immense improvement in the continent's system of communications, the development of cash economies, and the rapid growth of urban areas have served to bring many millions of Africans into a contact with the varying stimuli of modernity much closer than that experienced by their fathers or grandfathers.

Can African countries of the late twentieth century be regarded as providing evidence of the existence of a high culture? In comparison with the situation a century ago one might well give a resounding yes to this question. One of the most notable developments of recent African history—particularly noticeable in the years since colonial territories achieved their independence—has been the emergence of an African intellectual community, a community made up of professional men and politicians, writers and artists, students and scholars. The members of this community may well be regarded as creative synthesizers, taking ideas and techniques from the outside world and adapting them to the needs of their own societies, at the same time giving back to the outside world fresh concepts and novel insights and so contributing to the consciousness of humanity as a whole. The size of this community obviously varies from country to country. Yet today no African country is so isolated and impoverished that it cannot make some contribution to the culture of the continent as a whole.

Against this interpretation of the broad lines of African development must be set two other interpretations that enjoy a more popular currency. One of these interpretations, frequently encountered in conservative circles outside Africa, stresses those events—military coups, tribal revolts, or failures in economic development—which are regarded as providing evidence of African instability, backwardness, or incapacity. There is something aggravatingly naïve, ungenerous, and unbalanced about such an interpretation. In intellectual terms it must be regarded as the product of a threadbare sociology and an impoverished historical imagination. The other popular interpretation of modern African history, current among many radicals and among African nationalists, sees the recent African past almost exclusively in terms of "colonialist (or neocolonialist) exploitation." To question this interpretation is not to deny that some African societies have been violently disrupted by the intrusion of outsiders and that external pressure groups sometimes did seek to manipulate the economy of independent African states for their own ends. Narrow interpretations of history often, indeed, possess a useful function in drawing attention to aspects of the past that historians have previously tended to ignore. Nevertheless "exploitation" remains a loose and emotive term. Applied as a blanket expression to cover the whole of recent African history, it serves to conceal the fact that the impact of outsiders varied very greatly from area to area, that many of the innovations associated with outsiders were in their immediate or long-term effects beneficial to the continent as a whole, and that most African societies did not react passively or supinely to external pressures, but responded vigorously to the new opportunities of a changing situation. History as a whole, the product of the thoughts and actions of innumerable individual men and women, possesses an exuberance which can never be caught within the straitjacket of any monistic theory. To attempt to understand the history of Africa as a whole, one needs a generous imagination and a capacity to appreciate the achievements of all those, whatever their culture or country of origin, who have left their mark on the African scene.

CHAPTER II

Northeast Africa

▲▼ INTRODUCTION

Northeast Africa embraces the four modern states of Egypt (United Arab Republic), the Sudan, Ethiopia, and Somalia. Thus defined, this area of two million square miles lacks that measure of natural unity found in the continent's other regions. On the map certain dominant features stand out—notably the valley and basin of the Nile and the long Red Sea littoral. But there is nothing on the ground comparable to the mountains of the Maghrib or the savanna plains of West and Central Africa to impose the stamp of uniformity on a large part of the region. Over the region as a whole landscapes present sharp and striking contrasts: the green luxuriance of the valley and delta of the Egyptian Nile hemmed in by tawny deserts on either side; the cool, fertile, deeply dissected highlands of Ethiopia rising above the scorching plains of the Red Sea coast; the rough mountains of Darfur overlooking the savanna of Kordofan; and in the south the dreary expanse of marshland that borders the White Nile. Northeast Africa may indeed be thought of as presenting a wider range of environments than any other region of the continent.

No less striking are the contrasts presented by the peoples who today inhabit the region. Compare the Egyptians with their astonishing historical record, their long tradition of urbanization, and their ancient skill in cultivating the "good earth" of their valley home with the Dinka and the Nuer living amid the swamps of the southern Sudan, pastoralists with no settlement larger than their cattle camps and with a history of which nothing is known until they were brought into rude contact with the outside world in the middle of the nineteenth century. Or set the Ethiopian Amhara with their elaborate and decorative culture, the product of two thousand years of checkered growth within the context of organized states, against the austere Somali, the camel herders of the Horn, whose history is largely taken up with the kaleidoscopic movements of small groups of pastoral nomads. These pairs of opposites represent extreme contrasts, but in many parts of the region one can still see, within relatively limited areas, the sharp division between pastoralists and sedentary cultivators. In the northern Sudan Bedouin Arabs are in close touch with the long-settled Nubian population of the Nile Valley. The Baqqara, cattle-owning Arabs, have moved in among the varied groups of negroid cultivators in Kordofan and Darfur. And in southern Ethiopia the sedentary Sidama have been profoundly affected by the impact of the pastoralist Galla.

Beneath these easily visible contrasts some unifying features may be detected. Most of the peoples of the region are of caucasoid stock, differing sharply in physical type from the negroid peoples to their south and west. (Attitudes of "racial" superiority are no less apparent in Northeast Africa, it may be noted in passing, than in other parts of the world where "black" and "white" find themselves in contact.) Most of the languages spoken in Northeast Africa belong to the language family known as Afro-Asiatic. Ancient Egyptian, Berber, Semitic, and Cushitic are the main branches of this family, with Semitic being represented in Northeast Africa by Arabic and Amharic and Cushitic by the languages of the Beja, the Galla, the Somali, and the Sidama.

Over the greater part of the region Islam has become the most powerful force for cultural uniformity. The religion of Muhammad was brought to Egypt by the invading Arab armies of the seventh century A.D., carried by Muslim merchants and by wandering holy men along the trade routes of the interior, and so introduced to a steadily widening arc of peoples. Christianity was brought to some parts of the region several centuries before the advent of Islam. Egypt, indeed, was once an almost entirely Christian country, but after the Arab conquest the number of Egyptian Christians (Copts) steadily declined, and by the end of the nineteenth century they formed a small minority, no more than 6 percent of the total population. In Nubia, also once a Christian country, the practice of the faith disappeared by the end of the sixteenth century. Only in Ethiopia was the position of Christianity vigorously maintained as the religion of state, though the total number of Ethiopian Christians does not exceed 20 percent of the country's present population.

Egypt has always played a dominant part in the history of Northeast Africa, though the Egyptian people themselves have been fated to suffer a long succession of alien masters. The last of the long series of indigenous Pharaonic dynasties was overthrown by the Persians in 525 B.C.

After the Persians, the Macedonian Greeks, the Romans, the Byzantine Greeks, the Arabs, the Turkish and Circassian Mamluks, and the Ottoman Turks—each established their hegemony over the country for periods running into several centuries. In 1798 a French expedition led by General Bonaparte invaded Egypt, occupied the country for three years, and in so doing opened a new era in its long history. For the French expedition introduced to Egypt the ideas and techniques of modern Europe, directed the attention of Europeans to a country in which for centuries they had shown little interest, and inadvertently created the conditions that made possible the career of one of the most extraordinary figures in modern history, the Albanian adventurer Muhammad Ali.

Muhammad Ali arrived in Egypt during the anarchic period that followed the French withdrawal, obtained from the Ottoman sultan, the country's nominal suzerain, the temporary post of governor, and immediately set about providing himself with a base from which he could not be removed. After disposing of all his political rivals, he proceeded by logical degrees to assume complete control over the agricultural land of Egypt, to build up a large standing army, and to introduce many new techniques and institutions of European origin, thus becoming the first major political figure in the Afro-Asian world to undertake the task of modernization on a countrywide scale. In the 1830's this astonishing provincial governor would probably have succeeded in shattering the structure of Ottoman rule in the eastern Mediterranean and in making his country a completely independent state had the powers of Europe not intervened to restrain him. As it was, he was able to acquire for himself a substantial imperial domain through the conquest of the Sudan, which was begun in 1820 with a victorious expedition up the Nile that led to the total destruction of the major Sudanic state of Sennar. By the time of Muhammad Ali's death in 1849 several hundred thousand square miles of territory stretching from Kordofan to the Red Sea coast had come under Egyptian control. Twenty years later the movement of official expansion was revived by the great pasha's grandson, Ismail. In the early 1870's Darfur, Ethiopia, the cities of the Somali coast, and the interlacustrine kingdoms of East Africa came within range of Egyptian aggrandizement. Never in the country's five thousand years as an organized state had Egypt's direct influence penetrated so deeply into the interior of Africa. In 1875 Egypt was still nominally a province of the Ottoman Empire, but it possessed most of the attributes of a major independent state and it could be regarded as the most actively imperialist power in the entire continent.

Modern Ethiopia embraces nearly 400,000 square miles of territory.

The traditional Ethiopian kingdom, the domain of the dynasty whose rulers claimed to be descended from the biblical King Solomon, controlled a very much smaller area, which covered only the northern half of the Ethiopian highlands and was inhabited mainly by people of Tigre or Amhara stock. To the south of the Amhara lived many different peoples of whom the Galla and the Sidama were the most numerous. Early in the second millennium A.D. the Sidama had founded a number of substantial kingdoms of which only Kaffa survived the Galla invasions of the sixteenth century. The Galla were by origin pastoral nomads, but by the nineteenth century many Galla communities had taken to agriculture, and some Galla groups succeeded in founding well-organized states—a remarkable innovation for a people with no tradition of state formation. Other Ethiopian peoples, including the southern and eastern Galla, the Danakil, or Afar of the Red Sea coast, and the small Negroid groups of the western borderlands still lived in small-scale polities. This pattern of political fragmentation was also characteristic of most of the Horn of Africa, as the Somali who occupied the arid plains of the interior and exerted constant pressure on the modest city-states of the coast were divided into a multitude of autonomous clans.

Before 1798 the peoples of Northeast Africa had been for centuries almost oblivious of the existence of Europe. After 1798 European interest in the region steadily increased. By 1875 Egypt contained the third largest European community to be found in Africa, exceeded only by those of Cape Colony and Algeria. Almost all the Europeans resident in Egypt were recent immigrants, drawn for the most part from Italy, Greece, and Malta. A small European community was also to be found in the Sudan. Ethiopia attracted only a handful of Europeans. The massive British expedition of 1868, mounted to rescue the British subjects held captive by Emperor Theodore, did nothing, for all its success, to create an effective British interest in the country. The Red Sea, on the other hand, was becoming increasingly important to the maritime powers of Europe. In the 1820's the British began making regular use of the Red Sea route with its extension, the short overland stretch at Suez, for mails and passengers passing to and from India. The completion of the Suez Canal in 1869 vastly enhanced the importance of this line of communications and made it one of the main commercial arteries of the world. In 1839 the British acquired possession of the South Arabian port of Aden and began to develop an interest in the Somali coast on the opposite side of the gulf. In the 1860's French and Italian agents purchased modest concessions on the Danakil coast further north. In 1875 these concessions were the only pieces of land to which Europeans could lay claim in the whole of Northeast Africa, for the region contained no formal European colonies. But few parts of the continent had been so well explored by European travelers, and no other region could present a country to compare with Egypt in arousing the interest of European statesmen, businessmen, and scholars.

▲▼ THE EGYPT OF KHEDIVE ISMAIL

"This country," wrote Lucy Duff Gordon, one of the few European residents in the Egypt of Khedive Ismail to gain a sympathetic understanding of the life of the mass of Egyptians, "is a palimpsest in which the Bible is written over Herodotus, and the Koran over that. In the towns the Koran is most visible, in the country Herodotus . . . the ceremonies at births and burials are not Muslim but ancient Egyptian." [1] To most alien observers the villages of the valley of the Nile—"slight elevations on the mud banks cut into square shapes . . . with palm-trees and tall pigeon-houses and here and there the dome over a saint's tomb" [2] seemed immune to all the processes of change. Yet since Muhammad Ali's accession to power in the first decade of the nineteenth century, Egyptian rural society had been subjected to three innovations of a profoundly disturbing character—the establishment of an efficient structure of direct administration by the central authority, an alteration in the system of land tenure, and the introduction of a new crop, long-staple cotton, grown almost entirely for the export market.

Both Muhammad Ali (1805–49) and Ismail (1863–79) were passionately concerned to build up a state strong enough to allow them to assert their independence from their suzerain, the Ottoman sultan. To this end they sought every means of increasing the wealth of Egypt, while at the same time squeezing as much revenue as possible out of the unfortunate fellahin (peasantry). In the days of the Mamluks—Turkish or Circassian warriors of slave origin who dominated Egypt in the seventeenth and eighteenth centuries—the Egyptian countryside had been divided into a large number of tax farms. The Mamluks and their retainers held most of these farms, acted as feudal lords in the districts under their control, and handed over to the imperial treasury little more than a third of the produce they collected in taxes from the fellahin. Such a system was entirely unacceptable to a ruler determined to establish a highly autocratic regime. Within the space of a few years Muhammad Ali broke the power of the Mamluks, greatly reduced the prestige of the ulama (the class of religious notables) who had also profited from the tax-farming system, and asserted his right to all cultivable land, thus transforming Egypt into a vast estate of which he was the sole proprietor.

Officials appointed by the ruler replaced the tax farmers of Mamluk days. The new regime brought with it an immediate decline in the lawlessness that had afflicted Egypt in the eighteenth century. No longer could the Bedouin of the desert continue to raid the rich lands of the Nile. Harassed by punitive expeditions or seduced by offers of land, increasing numbers of Bedouin abandoned their nomadic way of life. A threat to which the valley dwellers had been exposed since the days of the pharaohs was finally overcome. For the fellahin this was certainly a substantial advantage. In other respects the new regime had little to commend it. Efficient government as interpreted by Muhammad Ali and Ismail brought with it greater oppression, heavier taxes, more frequent demands for forced labor, and conscription for indefinite periods of military service. "The taxation makes life almost impossible," wrote Lucy Duff Gordon in 1867, ". . . a tax on every crop, on every annual fruit, and again when it is sold in the market; on every man, on charcoal, on salt, on the dancing girls. . . . New taxes and the new levies of soldiers are driving the people to despair and many are running away from the land which will no longer feed them after paying all exactions, to join the Bedouin in the desert, which is just as if your peasantry turned gypsies." [3]

A regime so brutal for most Egyptians brought substantial benefits for those who enjoyed the ruler's favor. Muhammad Ali found it necessary to reward senior officials with grants of land, often made in lieu of a pension. Other notables, including village headmen, received similar grants in return for their assistance in ensuring the payment of taxes by the community in which they lived. In many such village communities land was still held collectively, strips being redistributed every year in accordance with the extent of the Nile flood. A series of ordinances issued by Muhammad Ali and his successors led to the gradual disappearance of the old collective system and produced a rapid increase in the private ownership of land.

These changes transformed the social structure of the countryside. In the eighteenth century a small group of wealthy notables, tax farmers of Mamluk or ulama origin, dominated an undifferentiated mass of fellahin. From the mid-nineteenth century a more complex structure emerged. Its base was formed by an ever-increasing number of landless laborers, peasants forced to abandon or to sell their land in the face of crippling taxation and its top, by a small group of very large landowners, foremost among them the khedive himself and the members of his family. In between came a wide variety of private landowners, of whom some—particularly the influential village headmen—were finding it possible to build up substantial estates of their own.

This process of social stratification was greatly assisted by the introduction of long-staple cotton as a cash crop of major importance. Muhammad Ali had begun experimenting with the production of this species of cotton as early as 1822. In the last years of his reign cotton was providing 25 percent of Egypt's exports. In the early 1860's the collapse of American cotton production as a result of the Civil War provided the Egyptians with an opportunity to break into many new markets, and though there was some recession after the war, the demand for Egyptian cotton still remained high. By the late 1870's exports of cotton and cottonseed were worth more than eight million pounds sterling compared with less than half a million pounds thirty years earlier. With cotton accounting for 75 percent of the country's total exports Egypt now presented a pattern destined to become increasingly familiar in other parts of Africa—that of an economy dominated by a single export crop.

Most Egyptian cotton was grown in the Delta where improvements in the network of irrigation canals made possible a substantial increase in the amount of land under cultivation. For wealthier landowners the development of so lucrative a cash crop was clearly beneficial. But for the peasantry as a whole the new crop appears to have been of questionable advantage. Fluctuations in cotton prices forced many small farmers to borrow money and thus they found themselves caught in the vicious spiral of indebtedness that often led to total bankruptcy. Moreover, the peasantry profited little from those other changes in the Egyptian economy that seemed to outsiders the most spectacular achievements of Ismail's reign—the construction of the railways, the establishment of an efficient system of posts and telegraphs, the "improvement" of the major cities, the introduction of modern education.

In promoting the construction of a system of administration more elaborate than Egypt or, indeed, any other African polity had ever known before, the country's nineteenth-century rulers needed an ever-widening range of collaborators. Under Muhammad Ali all the most important posts in the army and in the civil administration were confined to Turks or Circassians, but native Egyptians were recruited into the lower ranks of the army and members of the ulama class were sent on educational missions to Europe. After the great pasha's death the Turkish aristocracy began to decline in importance; Arabic replaced Turkish as the official language; and many of the young Egyptians who had been trained in Europe or educated at the new schools founded in the 1820's and 1830's achieved high office in government service or were permitted to enter the officer corps of the army with a bar to promotion above the rank of colonel. The career of the most notable of these new men, Ali Mubarak, provides a striking illustration of the changes that were beginning to affect Egyptian society.

Ali Mubarak was born in 1824, the son of a village notable from the Delta. At the age of twelve he entered one of the militarized state schools, passed on to the Egyptian school of engineering, and completed his education in France at the Metz school for army engineers. Mubarak began his career as an engineer officer in the Egyptian army, took part in the Crimean War, and became chief of the fortifications at Alexandria. Later he turned to civilian employment, was engaged in the construction of the Delta Barrage at Cairo, and moved on to a series of high offices which included the posts of minister of education, minister of public works, and director-general of the state railways. In the course of this remarkably varied career, Ali Mubarak found time to write a great many books, among them a series of manuals on engineering and a massive topographical survey of Egypt, an encyclopedic compilation which has provided modern historians with a rich mine of information. For his public services Mubarak was rewarded with valuable gifts of land; in these circumstances it is hardly surprising that he should have remained a loyal servant of the dynasty. He was by temperament "a reformer, not a political revolutionary in the sense of a man alienated from the established authority of the times." Yet the practical schemes that he implemented in many fields of Egyptian life were, as a recent historian has pointed out, "in a sense revolutionary for Egypt." [4] This remarkable technocrat was, indeed, a symbolic figure, a portent of the changes to occur eventually in almost every part of the continent.

The rulers of nineteenth-century Egypt were not solely dependent on local collaborators. They needed the assistance of foreigners capable of introducing the novel techniques recently developed in Europe. Muhammad Ali made a point of recruiting army officers, engineers, and doctors mainly of French or Italian origin. The schemes for Egyptian development conceived by his grandson, Ismail, were on an even more grandiose scale. Consequently, Ismail's reign saw a rapid increase in the number of Europeans in Egyptian service. Some occupied posts of great responsibility—the chief of staff of the Egyptian army was for a time an American officer who had served on the Confederate side in the Civil War. But many Europeans were to be found in quite humble positions, in the public works department, in the post office, even in the police force which contained as many as one hundred Europeans by 1870. Other Europeans were attracted to Egypt by the commercial opportunities to be found in a fast developing country. Prominent among them were a number of financiers, some respectable bankers, other adventurous speculators, and men adept at seducing the khedive and his entourage with ingenious schemes for rapid development based on the liberal application of European credit. In the early years of Ismail's reign

"Egypt," in the acid judgment of Lord Cromer, "must have been an earthly paradise for all who had money to lend at usurious rates of interest, or third-rate goods of which they wished to dispose at first-rate prices." [5]

Foreigners added a new strain, at once dynamic and discordant, to the life of Egypt. Their presence was most brashly manifest in the country's two great cities, Cairo and Alexandria. Alexandria was developing, in the words of a contemporary observer, into "a cosmopolitan city of French houses, Italian villas, Turkish lattice-windowed buildings and native mud-huts, where excellent European shops of all descriptions stand amongst Eastern coffee-houses and bazaars." [6] The impact of the West was even more harshly displayed in Cairo, the greatest city in the world of Islam, where the destruction of ancient mosques and palaces to make room for European hotels could be interpreted as a symbolic event, deeply shocking to every devout Muslim.

By 1875 there were about 80,000 Europeans resident in Egypt. They constituted a highly favored minority. As early as the sixteenth century Europeans resident in Ottoman territory had been granted by the sultan special privileges contained in a series of imperial diplomas, known as "Capitulations." As Ottoman power declined, the European was "gradually transformed from being a humble receiver of 'privileges' into an imperious possessor of 'rights' " [7]—rights which were pushed further in Egypt than in any other part of the Ottoman domains. The European resident in Egypt was virtually exempt from khedival jurisdiction: the Egyptian authorities could not force him to pay taxes, arrest him without the consent of his consul, or reject his right to be tried in a consular court. In these circumstances "the European concession-hunter and loan-monger, the Greek publican and pawnbroker, the Jewish and Syrian money-lender and land-grabber, who could always with ease obtain the protection of some European Power, had battened on the Egyptian Treasury and the poor Egyptian cultivator to an almost incredible extent." [8] These are the words not of an Egyptian nationalist but of a British administrator, Lord Milner. Certainly there were arguments in favor of some sort of special jurisdiction for Europeans living in a Muslim land. But there can be no doubt that the abuses of which Europeans were guilty played a large part in provoking those outbursts of violent anti-European sentiment that were to occur in the years ahead.

Of Ismail it may be said that by his actions and by his ambitions he greatly accelerated the processes of change in almost every sphere of Egyptian life. In so doing the khedive presented an extraordinary mixture of shrewdness and folly. Many of his schemes—the expansion of the railways, the development of education, the establishment of a sugar industry—were well thought out and ably implemented. But the khedive was also prone to extravagance on a quite grotesque scale. Much of the money he acquired from foreign borrowers was spent on "urban embellishments, palaces, wedding feasts, and similar luxuries." [9] The construction of the Suez Canal—to many alien observers the most spectacular achievement of his reign—was made possible only by the employment of the peasantry as forced labor and by the borrowing of large sums from Europe. The later course of Egyptian history suggests that it might well have been better for the Egyptian people if the Suez Canal had never been built.

As for Ismail's ambitious attempt to create a great African empire by sending expeditions to Ethiopia, Somalia, and the lake regions of East Africa, the series of disasters that befell Egyptian armies from 1875 to 1885 showed how grossly the khedive had overestimated his country's power. The price of all these failures in judgment was bankruptcy leading to alien occupation. There was nothing inevitable about the course of events. Had Ismail been a wiser and a more moderate man, he might have retained his throne and Egypt might well have been preserved as an autonomous province of the Ottoman Empire until as late as World War I.

▲▼ EGYPT AND THE POWERS: 1875 TO 1882

In 1863, the year of Ismail's accession, Egypt's public debt stood at £3.3 million. Thirteen years later it had risen, as a result of the khedive's reckless borrowing, to £91 million. In 1875 Ismail found he was no longer able to meet the interest payments due to foreign bondholders. His European creditors had acted in a purely private capacity in lending him money, but they found little difficulty in persuading most of their own governments to put pressure on the khedive to accept a measure of foreign supervision of his financial affairs. European statesmen would hardly have shown such concern in the affairs of so improvident a potentate had his country not occupied a position of quite exceptional importance. In 1875 Egypt was of infinitely greater interest to the powers of Europe than any other part of Africa.

Egypt had been brought dramatically to the attention of Europe by the French expedition of 1798. Before that time the country had been for three hundred years an economic and political backwater, relegated to this position by the Portuguese discovery of the sea route to the Indies. In invading Egypt the French had hoped to extend their influence eastward, thus counteracting the spread of British hegemony in India. Their action made British statesmen forcibly aware of the strategic importance of a country in which they had hitherto shown no interest.

Subsequent developments—the expansion of British power and commerce in Asia and the improvement in communications—vigorously underlined Egypt's significance as a halfway house to the East. This was only one aspect of the country's importance; as a province of the Ottoman Empire, Egypt could be regarded as one of the major pieces in the complex pattern of the "Eastern Question." Should the Ottoman Empire disintegrate, a dangerous vacuum of power would suddenly emerge in the Balkans, in the eastern Mediterranean, and around the Persian Gulf. Russia would be involved, as would Austria and Germany. It was impossible for contemporaries to envisage an international crisis of wider dimensions.

In the years between 1875 and 1878 the possibility of a total Ottoman collapse seemed far from remote. In 1876 the Serbs rose in revolt against their Turkish overlords and were joined in the following year by the Bulgars. The year 1876 also saw a serious political crisis at the heart of the empire with the deposition of two sultans and the temporary grant of a constitution—unprecedented novelty for the autocratic Ottoman regime—by their successor, Abdul-Hamid. In 1877 the situation deteriorated still further when Russia, exasperated by the Turkish refusal to grant concessions to the Christian subjects of the empire, declared war and advanced on Constantinople. A vigorous British countermove—the dispatch of a fleet to the Bosphorus and the movement of a body of troops from India to the Mediterranean—helped deter the Russians from pushing home their military advantage. When a settlement was finally concluded at the Congress of Berlin, the Ottoman Empire was seen to be still intact, though shorn of some of its territory both in the Balkans and in Asia.

While Russia and Austria were pressing down on the northern flanks of the Ottomans, Britain and France were becoming more deeply involved in the affairs of Egypt. In 1876 the khedive set up a Commission of the Public Debt (*Caisse de la Dette*); the commissioners were nominated by those European governments whose nationals had been involved in lending money to Egypt. The commissioners soon found that they lacked the power to introduce the necessary financial reforms. Thus, in 1877 Ismail was persuaded to appoint two Europeans, an Englishman and a Frenchman, as controllers-general of revenue and expenditure. When this measure proved insufficient, diplomatic pressure compelled the khedive to renounce his autocratic powers and appoint a ministry whose decisions he promised to accept. The ministry, headed by a Christian Armenian, Nubar Pasha, contained two European ministers who promptly set about strengthening their position by appointing European civil servants to senior posts in the Egyptian bureaucracy.

As the nature of this system of "Dual Control" became manifest, resentment spread through the leading sections of Egyptian society. Though Ismail had ruled as a complete autocrat until 1878, he had found it convenient to establish early in his reign a consultative assembly, most of whose members were drawn from the ranks of village notables. As the khedive's financial troubles increased, some members of the assembly abandoned their former subservience and began to voice their opinions of the ruler's policy. Much bolder, however, was the line taken by a small group of young intellectuals who gathered around an intriguing and mysterious figure, Jamal al-Din al-Afghani.

Al-Afghani was the stormy petrel of the Muslim world of the last quarter of the nineteenth century, the proponent of a doctrine of revolutionary Pan-Islamism that represented "a blend of religious feeling, national feeling and European radicalism." [10] Born in 1837 probably in Persia, he traveled and taught in India, Afghanistan, and Turkey before reaching Egypt in 1871. His Indian experience gave him a loathing of European imperialism but provided him with some insight into the reasons for European superiority. "Science," he discovered, "makes one man have the strength of ten." [11] But the basic cause of Muslim weakness lay, he believed, not in technological inferiority but in a failure of the spirit. The times called for the regeneration of Islam, for a return to the pristine vitality of the faith, for the re-creation of a sense of Muslim unity, and, so it followed, for the removal or restraint of those Muslim autocrats whose incompetence played into the hands of the European aggressors. These were the ideas on which al-Afghani elaborated in endless conversations to his disciples, urging them "to write, to publish newspapers, to form a public opinion." Thus al-Afghani, though a foreigner, had a part in "bringing about the first stirrings of national consciousness and discontent under Ismail." [12] His ideas were to achieve still wider circulation through the work of the most eminent of his followers, Muhammad Abduh and Sa'ad Zaghlul.

Army officers of *fellah* origin formed a third group of politically conscious Egyptians—a group particularly well equipped to take decisive action. For some years past Egyptian officers had nourished a sense of grievance over a system that reserved all senior military posts for members of the Turco-Circassian aristocracy. In February, 1879, their resentment boiled over into active protest against the Nubar ministry's decision, made on grounds of economy, to put two thousand officers on half-pay. The khedive astutely took advantage of the growing tide of anti-European sentiment, dismissed Nubar and the European ministers, and put himself at the head of the nationalist-constitutionalist movement by summoning Sharif Pasha, the leader of the consultative assembly, to form a ministry. The financial program put forward by the new government could be interpreted as a complete rejection of the reforms pressed on the khedive by his European advisers. In this situation the European powers felt bound, in the words of the British foreign secretary, Lord Salisbury, "to do all that lies in their power to arrest misgovernment before it results in . . . material ruin and almost incurable disorder." [13] The khedive appeared to be "the sole obstacle to reform": therefore the khedive must go. A firman, obtained by European diplomatic pressure from the Ottoman sultan, secured Ismail's immediate abdication.

Ismail was succeeded by his son Tawfiq, a colorless young man vividly conscious of the weakness of his position and quite unable to stand out against his European advisers. So the "Dual Control" was reestablished, yet nothing had been done to abate the serious discontent of the last years of Ismail's reign. Indeed, any rational attempt at financial reform served only to turn influential groups of Egyptians against the government—landowners exasperated by the removal of their exemption from taxation or army officers worried about plans for their retirement.

Army officers, who took as their leader a colonel of *fellah* origin, Ahmad Urabi, proved the most effective spokesmen of national discontent. At first the soldiers appear to have been concerned only with their own professional grievances. By threatening mutiny they forced the khedive to dismiss the ministers of his own choice and appoint men acceptable to themselves. This success led the civilian opponents of the khedive to join forces with the army officers. As early as 1879 more than three hundred leading Egyptians—deputies, army officers, civil servants, religious leaders, and merchants—had come together to form a National Party. In December, 1881, the party issued a lengthy manifesto declaring that its aim was "the intellectual and moral regeneration of the country," proclaiming "its intention to permit no renewal of the despotic reign of injustice," referring to the army as "the armed guardian of the unarmed people" but studiously refraining from attacking the khedive in person or from criticizing the system of "Dual Control." [14] Here indeed was evidence of a new phenomenon, a genuine nationalist movement of a kind rarely known before among a Muslim people, a movement that held out real hope of a new era in Egyptian affairs. For the shattering of this hope the British and French governments were largely responsible.

To Gambetta, the fiery and forceful politician who became prime minister of France in November, 1881, the Egyptian Nationalist Party appeared as "the ludicrous invention of some badly informed or too well-paid journalist," while Colonel Urabi, the leader of the movement, was sarcastically dismissed as "an ambitious intriguer." [15] Gambetta was at this time seriously worried by Muslim revolts in Algeria and in the newly acquired protectorate of Tunisia, linked these insurrections with Urabi's movement, and saw in this alarming combination evidence of a Pan-Islamic conspiracy inspired by the Ottoman sultan. A vigorous Anglo-French gesture in Egypt, going as far as armed intervention should the need arise, would serve, Gambetta reckoned, to put the Muslim dissidents in their place and reestablish European prestige throughout North Africa. Consequently he recommended to the British government the dispatch of a "joint note" to Cairo informing the khedive that the two governments were "resolved to guard by their united efforts against all cause of complication, internal or external, which might menace the order of things established in Egypt."[16] In Britain Gladstone and the members of his Liberal government took a cooler view of the situation. They felt some sympathy for a movement that had taken as its slogan "Egypt for the Egyptians," but they were anxious to remain on good terms with the French and above all to prevent their partner from acting unilaterally in a country of such importance to Britain. In these circumstances it seemed advisable to follow the French lead.

The "joint note" reached Cairo at a time when the deputies were in session and had begun to draw up plans for a constitution. Less than a year had passed, it should be remembered, since the French had invaded and in practice annexed the Ottoman dependency of Tunis. Was it not obvious that the same fate now awaited Egypt? Thus the immediate effect of the "joint note" was to exacerbate anti-European feeling and consequently to weaken still further the position of the khedive, who now found himself with no alternative but to appoint Urabi as minister of war.

"A typical *fellah,* tall, heavy-limbed and somewhat slow in his movements," Urabi seemed, in the words of a sympathetic European observer, "to symbolize that laborious bodily strength which is so characteristic of the peasant of the Upper Nile." [17] Urabi was indeed a symbolic figure who spoke for the mass of Egyptians when, in a tone notable for its calmness and moderation, he described to an English official the grievances of the people: "they were imprisoned, exiled, strangled, thrown into the Nile, starved and robbed according to the will of their masters. . . . the most ignorant Turk was preferred before the best of the Egyptians . . . yet men came of one common stock and had equal rights of personal liberty and security." [18]

Urabi was a genuine nationalist who found himself riding a whirlwind. Egypt was in a state of revolutionary excitement. The movement of protest had spread from the leaders to the masses, arousing in the minds of European residents dreadful fears of "anarchy" and of "Muslim fanaticism." Lord Cromer expressed what became the official British view that if Urabi and his followers had been kept at the head of affairs without any control, a state of the utmost confusion would have been produced in Egypt. But the historian needs to be on his guard when confronted with the magisterial judgments of contemporary observers. In fact, there is no means of knowing what would have happened if Urabi had remained in power. Possibly, after a period of confusion, a stable Egyptian regime would have been established. Speculation is vain: by 1882 Britain and France had acquired such a stake in the country that some sort of intervention was inevitable.

In May, 1882, the British and French governments decided to send naval squadrons to Alexandria as a gesture of support for the khedive. A few weeks later Alexandria was swept by violent riots in which a number of Europeans were killed. At this time the British, anxious to avoid becoming too deeply involved in Egyptian affairs, hoped to be able to persuade the Ottoman government to take action in its capacity as Egypt's suzerain. The French, however, were quite unwilling to accept Turkish intervention, thinking that such a move might adversely affect their position elsewhere in North Africa. But French policy had lost its recent vigor: Gambetta was no longer in power and his successor, Freycinet, reckoned that he could not count on sufficient parliamentary support for decisive action. Meanwhile, an important section of the British cabinet had come to believe that the Suez Canal, Britain's major imperial stake in Egypt, was in real danger. Reluctantly Gladstone accepted this group's proposition that a short sharp blow would bring the Urabists down. On July 11 the British fleet bombarded the Egyptian shore batteries at Alexandria.

Far from achieving the desired results this crude maneuver, clumsily executed by the admiral in charge, played into Urabi's hands. Anti-European riots spread to other parts of the Delta; Urabi issued a proclamation asserting that "irreconcilable war existed between the Egyptians and the English"; and the khedive and his supporters fled in panic to place themselves under British protection. Swiftly an expeditionary force under the command of Sir Garnet Wolseley was dispatched to Egypt. Within four weeks of landing it had overwhelmed the Urabists at the battle of Tel-el-Kebir. "Never," in the words of a British historian, "was there a tidier operation." [19] There were thorns in the laurels of victory: the British government was now saddled with a responsibility it had sought anxiously to avoid. Of all their imperial commitments in Africa none was to cause the British so much trouble over so long a period as Egypt, the country of which they had made themselves the masters in so muddled and reluctant a manner.

▲▼ EGYPT, THE SUDAN, AND THE POWERS: 1882 TO 1904

The British intervention in Egypt did not change the legal status of the country: it remained a province of the Ottoman Empire, from which the British were sincerely anxious to withdraw their troops as soon as possible. The military occupation of a populous Muslim country involved the risk of dreadful and expensive complications, rendered the government unpopular in the eyes of many of its own supporters at home, and imposed a heavy strain on Britain's relations with other European powers and especially with France. Yet how could Britain withdraw from Egypt when the removal of British troops seemed likely to lead to a recrudescence of Egyptian "anarchy"? Should Egypt again be plunged into a revolutionary situation and the British government refrain from action, the French might well act on their own by sending troops to guard the Suez Canal; in so doing they would place in jeopardy the most important lifeline of the British Empire. These were the reflections—the self-invoked chimeras they may seem to a later generation—which tormented British cabinet ministers in the winter of 1882–83.

A seemingly satisfactory way out of this dilemma was provided by the highly experienced diplomat, Lord Dufferin, sent out by the government to report at first hand on the situation. Britain must stay in Egypt only for so long as was needed to reform the khedive's government. Having taught the Egyptians how to govern themselves, the British could safely withdraw their troops, confident that the new Egyptian government would continue to look to Britain for assistance. This process, Dufferin implied, would not take more than a year or two to complete. It was an ingenious argument but a fallacious one. Before long Sir Evelyn Baring, the newly appointed British consul-general in Egypt, was writing to point out the illogicality of Dufferin's policy.

The British maintained the facade of khedival government, but the khedive was clearly only a puppet in their hands. "Recent events have completely shattered the system of government," Baring pointed out. "The whole tendency of the reforms we now have on hand is to weaken it still further." [20] Baring and his subordinates among the ever-increasing number of British advisers were not unhappy to accept the reform of Egypt as a long-term process, but to cabinet ministers in London, conscious of the implications of the Egyptian question both in domestic politics and in Britain's relations with other European states, such "civilizing" zeal might seem imprudent and excessive. Fortunately for Baring news from an unexpected quarter served greatly to strengthen the case against a British withdrawal.

The complex turn of events in Egypt's massive colony, the Sudan, is described in a later section of this chapter. Here it is sufficient to note that in 1881 the Turco-Egyptian authorities in the Sudan found themselves faced with a native revolt led by a religious leader, Muhammad Ahmad al-Mahdi. In 1883 a strong body of reinforcements, commanded by a British general, Hicks Pasha, was sent from Egypt to smash the rebellion only to suffer an annihilating defeat on the plains of Kordofan. The British government had no desire to involve itself in the expense of saving the Sudan for the Egyptians, but it was forced to accept some responsibility for the defense of Egypt. Consequently, it was decided to send a British officer with considerable Sudanese experience, General Charles Gordon, to arrange for the evacuation of Egyptian personnel from Khartoum. Gordon's subsequent fate, his death at the hands of the Mahdists in Khartoum, had little immediate effect on the course of events. But the drama of his last months stirred the British public to its depths and created an emotional British stake in the affairs of the Sudan that was to have some bearing on the events of the next decade.

Meanwhile, in Egypt the British were finding that for all the military power at their disposal they were in no position to act as entirely free agents. The international *Caisse de la Dette* still played a dominant part in the regulation of Egyptian finances; its members included French, German, and Russian representatives. With every month that passed the British were forced to recognize the international complexities provoked by their reluctant occupation. French criticism became steadily more virulent: behind it could be detected injured pride and an uneasy awareness that the British were now in a commanding position in the southern Mediterranean. Germany was prepared to help the British counter French hostility—but at a price. Bismarck "is perpetually telling us," Lord Salisbury remarked in 1886, "of the offer France is making of reconciliation on the basis of an attack upon England in Egypt and of the sacrifices Germany makes by refusing these proposals, sacrifices for which, he adds, England must make some return, and then he demands this and that." [21] The British stake in Egypt had become an important counter in the game of European diplomacy and in the late 1880's the game seemed to be hotting up.

For the remainder of the decade British governments—Liberal to 1886, Conservative from 1886 to 1892—continued to talk of evacuating Egypt. Indeed, in 1887 the British went so far as to reach an agreement with the Ottoman government, providing for the withdrawal of their troops at the end of a three-year period but securing for themselves the right of reentry, should Egypt again show signs of becoming unsettled. The French were enraged by this reentry clause and forced the sultan to abandon the agreement. British influence was clearly on the decline in Constantinople. Meanwhile, a new crisis in Bulgaria provided renewed evidence of Ottoman weakness, and there were signs, ominous in their implications for Britain's stand in the Eastern Question, of a diplomatic rapprochement between Russia and France. Ten years earlier Disraeli had described Constantinople as the "key to India." Were the Russians, he argued, ever to gain control of the Ottoman capital, then, with the military forces at their disposal, they would find it easy to send an army across Syria to attack Egypt and seize the Suez Canal. Now the situation had changed. The fate of Constantinople was more uncertain than ever, but Cairo was firmly in British hands. For the next sixty years Cairo was to remain the hub of British policy in the Middle East.

Thus, by 1890 Egypt had acquired in British eyes an importance even greater than it had possessed in 1882. If the country was now to be firmly held, it must be protected from every possible line of attack. By 1890 the Mahdists could be regarded as a spent force in military terms. But what if a "civilized" power took over the Sudan? The entire economy of Egypt was dependent on the flow of the Nile River. In technical terms it did not lie beyond the bounds of possibility for a European power, once in possession of the Sudan, to construct a dam across the White Nile and thus, by reducing the supply of water, threaten Egypt with ruin. "Whatever Power holds the Upper Nile Valley must," wrote Baring in 1889, "by the mere force of its geographical situation, dominate Egypt." [22] Hindsight may suggest that this was a highly questionable statement: would any rival power really have embarked on the immense task of building a dam in the wastes of the southern Sudan, simply to spite the British? But for British governments in the 1890's the supposition had the compulsive force of dogma.

No less than four European powers could be regarded by the British as potential rivals in the area of the Upper Nile. The Italians were pushing inland from the Red Sea port of Massawa which they had taken over from the Egyptians with British approval in 1885. The Germans were rapidly expanding their influence from the East African coast into the area around Lake Victoria, the source of the White Nile. Agents of the Congo Free State established by Leopold of the Belgians were engaged in a vigorous advance across the heart of the continent, while the restless French were moving eastward across the Sudanic belt and northeastward from their bases in Equatorial Africa. In 1890 the British prime minister, Lord Salisbury, concluded a series of agreements with the governments of Germany, Italy, and France. The Germans were willing to recognize a British sphere of influence in the country lying to the north of Lake Victoria. The Italians were persuaded to renounce all claims to territory lying within the Nile Basin. Thus the British could feel that they had succeeded in fencing off the southern and eastern sides of the threatened territory, but the agreement with the French referred only to land lying between the French North African possessions and Lake Chad and so left open the western approaches to the Nile Valley.

For the next three years the French colonialist lobby was preoccupied with the drive for Lake Chad, but Egypt was not forgotten. The passing of a decade had done nothing to efface the "humiliation" of 1882. For certain powerful elements in France the British occupation of Egypt represented "an almost intolerable affront to French self-esteem," "a stain upon national honour which it was an imperative duty to remove." [23] These deeply irrational sentiments found favor not only with right-wing politicians but also with many of the permanent officials of the French colonial ministry. Permanent officials can usually exert some influence on the shaping of policy: in the mid-1890's officials in the French colonial ministry found themselves in a strong enough position, as a result of the play of personalities on the French political scene, to press their ardently expansionist views to the point of forceful action. From 1893 onward plans were afoot for a French expedition to the Upper Nile. Let the tricolor be raised somewhere in the wastes of the southern Sudan and the French would automatically find themselves in possession of a lever powerful enough to shift the British from their position of dominance in Egypt.

By 1894 the British were aware of the danger of a French thrust for the Nile and planned an elaborate countermove. The lands lying to the west of the Upper Nile were to be "leased" to the Congo Free State in return for Congolese recognition of Britain's ultimate rights in the area. The French refused to sanction the Anglo-Congolese agreement, exerted strong diplomatic pressure on Leopold, and forced him to accept greatly modified terms by which he was allowed no more than the lease of a narrow strip of territory—the Lado enclave—that gave the Congo Free State access to the southern reaches of the White Nile. Direct negotiations between the British and French failed to produce an acceptable solution and in March, 1895, the British foreign secretary, Sir Edward Grey, warned the French government that an expedition "into a territory over which our claims have been known for so long" would be regarded as "an unfriendly act."

An unexpected turn of events in Ethiopia prompted the next major British move in the valley of the Nile. In the course of their advance from the Red Sea coast the Italians had occupied the important Sudanese town of Kassala, from which they agreed to withdraw as soon as the Egyptians were in a position to reestablish their rightful authority in the Sudan. In March, 1896, the Italians suffered a crushing defeat at the hands of the Ethiopians at Adowa. Fearing that this disaster might be followed by the fall of Kassala to the Mahdists, the Italians appealed to the British to make a diversionary move by threatening the Mahdists from the north.

Ever since the fall of Khartoum in 1885 the British in Egypt had followed a strictly defensive policy in their cold war with the Madhists. In due course the Sudan would have to be reconquered, but a full-scale campaign would be an expensive operation which Baring, now Lord Cromer, was anxious to defer until Egyptian finances were in a better shape to stand the strain. Moreover, a sudden Anglo-Egyptian advance from the north might well provoke the French to a countermove from the west. But it was impossible in the 1890's to divorce European policies in Africa from the complexities of Great Power diplomacy in Europe. Italy was at this time in alliance with Germany and Austria; yet Italian membership of the Triplice was largely dependent on British goodwill since Britain alone was in a position to offer Italy the naval support that would be needed in the event of a war with France. For the Italians the defeat at Adowa meant a really serious crisis. If Britain was not prepared to make some show of support in such an emergency, then the Triplice lost much of its meaning and Germany might well find it advisable to try to create a new diplomatic combination. Already there was evidence of a growing rapprochement between Germany and Russia. Should this be transformed into a genuine alliance, British interests in many parts of the world would be seriously threatened. On the other hand, the German government would certainly not object to a British move to help their Italian allies in Northeast Africa, nor would parliamentary opinion in Britain, which might well oppose a full-scale assault on the formidable Mahdist state, be critical of a modest diversion to help a friend in distress. All things considered, the Italian appeal for help provided the British government with an excellent opportunity to strengthen a European alliance peculiarly favorable to British interests and at the same "to plant," in Lord Salisbury's words, "the foot of Egypt rather farther up the Nile." [24] Within a fortnight of

Adowa the Egyptian army received orders from London to advance southward to Dongola. Within a few months military necessity transformed this cautious offensive into the first stage of a full-scale war for the reconquest of the Sudan.

For the British public the new war in the Sudan turned out to be one of the most agreeable campaigns of the Age of Imperialism. It was war on the cheap, for the hard-pressed Egyptian treasury met two-thirds of the cost, and the Egyptian army, reinforced only in the last phase by 8,000 British troops, bore the brunt of the fighting. It was a war that brought a plentiful harvest of honors for the British officers taking part in it, and especially for the commander-in-chief, General Kitchener. Above all it was a war which could be invested with a powerful moral cause: heroic Gordon was to be avenged and the Sudan freed from the barbarous yoke of the fanatical "dervishes." From a military point of view the "river war"—the description popularized by the vivid account written by the young Winston Churchill—was one of those unromantic campaigns in which supply and transportation are of decisive importance. The Mahdists found it impossible to feed a large concourse of men and horses in the narrow desert-fringed valley of the Nile and so were forced to keep the greater part of their fighting strength in the vicinity of their capital, Omdurman. The invaders, on the other hand, could count on two decisive technological advantages—the possession of a fleet of powerful river gunboats and the ability to construct a railway across the desolate wastes of the Nubian Desert.

In retrospect the campaign appeared to have been conducted, as Salisbury told the House of Lords, "with absolute accuracy, like the answer to a scientific calculation." [25] In fact, there were many uneasy moments. Kitchener presented to the world a formidable mask of surly efficiency, but in times of crisis he lacked the nerve of the really great commander. Fortunately for the invaders, the Mahdists were also beset by many difficulties, and so the campaign rolled slowly on over a period of thirty months to its climax, the battle of Karari near Omdurman at which in the course of a morning the splendidly courageous Mahdist cavalry was shattered by the firepower of the Anglo-Egyptians.

Karari, one of the few decisive set battles in the European conquest of Africa, was fought on September 2, 1898. On the very next day, while the Anglo-Egyptians were busy with the occupation of Khartoum, Captain J. B. Marchand, the leader of a French expedition which had been established since July at Fashoda, a point several hundred miles up the Nile from Khartoum, signed a treaty with the local ruler, the Shilluk *reth,* that established a substantial French protectorate on the Upper Nile. Marchand's mission had been planned as early as November, 1895, by the permanent officials of the French colonial ministry using methods which, in the opinion of the latest historian to make an exhaustive study of the evidence, "can only be described as conspiratorial." [26] Marchand's journey from the Ubangi to the Nile was a heroic undertaking, but his mission provoked a major international crisis that brought Britain and France to the verge of war. In Britain the government enjoyed the support of almost every section of public opinion in demanding a French withdrawal. In France opinion was sharply divided. Many solid businessmen would have agreed with the French president, Felix Faure, when he remarked, "We have been like fools in Africa, letting ourselves be dragged on by those irresponsible colonials." [27] Moreover, the French government had to reckon with two brutal facts: the massive superiority of the British navy and the unwillingness of their ally, Russia, to support their stand. In these circumstances the French had no alternative but to give way.

The abandonment of French claims to the Upper Nile cleared the way for a series of agreements that settled the international status of a large part of Northeast Africa for a generation. In January, 1899, the British and Egyptian governments signed an agreement "relative to the future administration of the Sudan." Direct annexation by the British of the newly conquered territory was out of the question. International opinion would have been provoked by the open flouting of Egyptian rights. Even more important, the parsimonious British Parliament would never have agreed to vote the sustantial sums needed to establish a new administration. On the other hand, the Sudan could clearly not be governed by the Egyptians alone, nor was it desirable to create too close a link between the two countries, for this would involve saddling the Sudan with "all the cumbersome paraphernalia of internationalism" [28] which the British found so vexatious in Egypt. The solution devised by Cromer was an ingenious one: the Sudan was to become an Anglo-Egyptian condominium with supreme power vested in a governor-general appointed by the khedive but nominated by the British. The British were in a position to manipulate this agreement to serve their own interests. They obtained complete control of all the policy-making posts in the new administration, while leaving to the Egyptian government the burden of providing the loans and subsidies needed by the Sudan in the first decade of Anglo-Egyptian rule.

In March, 1899, an Anglo-French agreement placed the basin of the Nile and of its western tributary, the Bahr al-Ghazal, firmly within the British sphere of influence. Five years later a more comprehensive agreement was reached between the two governments. Since the Fashoda crisis a more pragmatic group of colonialists had made their influence felt in French official circles. To these men the still independent state of Morocco was a country of infinitely greater significance than Egypt. For decades the British had worked to preserve Moroccan independence and struggled to introduce a measure of internal reform. By the first years of the twentieth century the bankruptcy of this policy had become apparent. Morocco's weaknesses had grown so pronounced that the sultan's government seemed on the verge of total collapse. Given the new mood of realism in London and Paris, it proved possible to hammer out an agreement whereby the French allowed the British a free hand in Egypt, while the British agreed to allow the French freedom of action in Morocco.

The Anglo-French agreement of 1904 removed Egypt from the agenda of international discussion for nearly half a century. Sixty years earlier, in the time of Muhammad Ali, the English traveler A. W. Kinglake had predicted that "the Englishman, straining far over to hold his loved India, will plant a firm foot on the banks of the Nile and sit in the seats of the Faithful." [29] All this had come to pass. The British were masters of the Nile from Lake Victoria to the sea. No foreign power could challenge them. The really formidable enemy lay much nearer at hand—in the cafes and alleyways, the schools and newspaper offices of Cairo and Alexandria. Already by 1904 there was clear evidence of the growth of a new spirit of Egyptian nationalism, though few could have predicted the cataclysmic force it was destined to acquire. This fierce local nationalism was in large part a reaction to the presence of a ruling group more alien in culture than any that Egypt had ever known in its long record of subjection to foreign powers. "Not even the wisest or most humane of princes, if he be an alien in race, in customs and religion, can ever win the hearts of the people." [30] It is significant that this maxim of the historian Gregorovius should have been quoted by Lord Cromer, the British ruler of Egypt for almost a quarter of a century. It might well serve as an epitaph on the first period of British hegemony in the most sophisticated of African states.

▲▼ EGYPT UNDER BRITISH OCCUPATION: 1882 TO 1918

Sir Evelyn Baring, raised to the peerage as Lord Cromer in 1892, was appointed British agent and consul-general in Egypt in September, 1883. This modest title came to conceal a position of immense power, for Baring made himself the de facto ruler of Egypt and dominated the Egyptian scene until ill health forced him to retire in 1907. Earlier in the nineteenth century a number of British diplomats—Stratford Canning in Constantinople, Warrington in Tripoli, Drummond Hay in

Morocco—were able to exert great influence for periods running into decades on the Muslim states to which they were accredited, but their power was far eclipsed by Baring's. Nor were any of the outstanding colonial administrators of the age—Faidherbe in Senegal, Lyautey in Morocco, Wingate in the Sudan, Lugard in Nigeria—permitted to hold positions of supreme responsibility for a span comparable to the twenty-four years granted to Baring in Egypt. "The Lord," as Cromer became known to his subordinates, may indeed be regarded as the model of the "great proconsul" of the Age of Imperialism, his character and career presenting in striking fashion the strength and weakness of the imperialist approach.

Baring was forty-two when he took up his appointment as consul-general. Born into a well-to-do English family possessing valuable connections in the world of politics and of business, he began his career as an officer in the Royal Engineers but left the army in 1872 to serve as private secretary to his cousin, Lord Northbrook, the viceroy of India. In 1877 Baring made his first acquaintance with Egyptian affairs as British commissioner on the *Caisse de la Dette,* returning to India in 1880 to serve as financial member on the viceroy's council. Baring's years in India proved an ideal apprenticeship for the tasks confronting him in Egypt, giving him practical experience of the problems of government and development in a dependent territory and at the same time strengthening his confidence in his own powers.

Toward the end of his life Cromer confessed that he had been moved by the ambition of "leading the Egyptian people from bankruptcy to solvency and then onward to affluence, from Khedival monstrosities to British justice, and from Oriental methods veneered with a spurious European civilization towards the true civilization of the West, based on the principles of the Christian moral code." [31] Such an ambition, blending arrogance with compassion, was peculiarly characteristic of the imperialist humanitarianism of the age. Cromer felt a genuine sympathy for the toiling masses of the "subject races," whether Indian or Egyptian, but his vision was blinkered by that intellectual failing so often to be found among "superior" individuals in any high culture—a total inability to appreciate the worth of cultures other than their own. Cromer fervently believed that there was "only one civilization in the world, and that was the civilization of Europe"; [32] he regarded Islam as a "moribund" culture; and like so many of his contemporaries he indulged in facile generalizations about "national character" of a kind peculiarly flattering to one who saw himself as a member of an "imperial race."

Cromer's mind was indeed, as one of his subordinates perceptively remarked, "not subtle or mentally agile," but the same observer went on to point out that he was "endowed with that curious combination of character which lends authority even to doubtful decisions and makes those who possess it respected in counsel and obeyed as rulers." [33] The British prime minister, Lord Rosebery, put the same point more vividly when he described Cromer as "a good man to go tiger-shooting with." [34] This massive reliability in a post of great responsibility ensured for Cromer an exceptionally long tenure of office, rendering him acceptable to all the British governments of the day, Liberal and Conservative alike.

"Sound finance," so ran one of Cromer's favorite maxims, "is the foundation of the independence of states." [35] Egypt in 1883 was a bankrupt country more than half of whose revenues were pledged to meet interest payments to foreign creditors. Financial stability could come only as the end result of a long period of reform. Yet in a country not legally subject to British sovereignty such reforms had to be introduced through Egyptian intermediaries. Thus, the British consul-general was faced with the delicate task of finding and maintaining a group of Egyptian collaborators who would be prepared to follow his advice. Sentences of exile had removed Urabi and his fellow officers from the Egyptian political scene; seventy years were to pass before the army once again became a force in Egyptian politics. But most of the other leading political figures of the last decade were still active and not unprepared to try working with the British. Thus, the first Egyptian ministry under the British occupation was headed by Sharif Pasha, one of the most popular politicians of the day. Early in 1884 Sharif resigned in protest against the British decision to enforce the evacuation of the Sudan, and Baring called on Nubar Pasha, the Europeanized Armenian who had made his mark under Ismail, to take his place. But Nubar too quarreled with his British mentors and it was not until the 1890's that Cromer found in Mustapha Falmi the compliant collaborator that he needed.

Mustapha Falmi's appointment as prime minister in 1895 came after two years of crisis centered round the person of the young Khedive Abbas, who succeeded his father Tawfiq in 1892. Abbas had received part of his education at the imperial court of Vienna and came to the throne determined to assert the prerogatives attached to his office. The "foolish young man," as Cromer came to call him, could in the last resort be put in his place by the threat of deposition, but the trouble caused the British by this eighteen-year-old prince provides striking evidence of the extreme delicacy of their position. With the young khedive providing the focus for a new generation of nationalists, the British found it advisable to alter the character of their "veiled protectorate."

In 1896 there were 286 British officials occupying senior posts in the Egyptian administration. By 1906 the number had risen to 662 and it was to increase still more in the course of the next decade, as young Englishmen, fresh from university, were brought out to "advise" and "inspect" the work of Egyptian colleagues. The first generation of British officials to serve in Egypt contained many extremely able men with Indian experience behind them, but as the alien bureaucracy expanded, its quality declined and many British administrators became increasingly out of touch with the people they were supposed to assist. To make matters worse Cromer—in the opinion of one of the ablest British officials of the day—"sedulously depressed and kept down every independent Egyptian and filled all the higher pots with cyphers." [36]

Yet for all these failings—failings of a kind inherent in any colonial regime—the British in Egypt could look back by 1914 on a number of substantial achievements. Cromer had succeeded magnificently in restoring financial stability: indeed, by the 1890's he had found it possible both to reduce taxes and to raise the money needed for the reconquest of the Sudan and for new capital works. Of these works the most spectacular was the dam at Aswan, one of the great engineering projects of the age, by means of which much of the cultivatable land of Middle and Upper Egypt was brought under perennial irrigation. Few aliens have made so massive a contribution to the economic development of an African country as the English agricultural scientists and irrigation engineers who worked in Egypt before World War I. Much land that had formerly been capable of producing only one crop a year, now gave two or even three harvests; indeed the total "cropped" area increased by 75 percent between 1882 and 1914. Cotton production more than doubled, and with rising prices the value of the crop increased even more substantially from £E13 million in 1885 to £E35 million in 1910.

At the same time the British labored to purge the Egyptian administrative system of its many inhumane features. The institution of forced labor (the *corvée*) was gradually abolished; the use of the kurbash, the lash of hippopotamus hide, was made illegal; recruitment for the army and the collection of taxes were carried on in a less arbitrary fashion; and a vigorous attempt was made to purge the judiciary and the bureaucracy of corruption. All these reforms were clearly beneficial for the much exploited fellahin.

In other fields the British record was less impressive. Shortage of funds made it impossible to do much to alleviate the appalling burden of disease borne by the peasantry. Indeed, the extension of perennial irrigation increased the incidence of bilharzia, a debilitating disease contracted through working in infected water. In education, too, lack of money hampered development, but more might well have been done had Cromer himself been prepared enthusiastically to embrace a wide-ranging educational program. Like many colonial administrators of the day, the British consul-general's attitude to education was an ambiguous one. He accepted the need to equip a certain number of Egyptians with the professional skills required by a modern government, but he was un-easily aware that the more widely these skills came to be diffused, the more vigorous would grow Egyptian criticism of the British presence. "While it may reasonably be held," Cromer wrote in 1908, "that some-thing has been done in the direction of imparting rectitude, virility and moral equipoise to the Egyptian character, it must be admitted that there is still abundant room for improvement in all these directions." [37] To intelligent Egyptians the tone of such a remark—the simplistic mo-rality, the hectoring schoolmasterish judgment—must have seemed deeply offensive.

There was another field in which the British showed even less interest—industrial development. In his lack of concern for indigenous industry Cromer was in a double sense a prisoner of his age. He ac-cepted dogmatically the tenets of free trade and was therefore opposed to the erection of the tariff barriers needed to protect a newly formed local industry; at the same time he was subject to powerful pressure from foreign businessmen worried lest Egypt should be changed from a passive recipient of their wares into a dangerous competitor. As a measure of prosperity returned to the country, Egypt once again be-came an acceptable field for European investment, with mortgage com-panies, land companies, and banks offering handsome returns. With a single raw material, cotton, providing 80 percent of the country's ex-ports and with so much of the country's commerce and finance domi-nated by aliens, by 1914 Egypt had come to present a classic example of a dependent economy. It was a situation that Muhammad Ali, with his passionate desire to make his pashalik self-sufficient, would surely have regarded with stupefaction.

To write the history of the colonial period of any country only in terms of the policies and actions of the colonial power is to take far too simple a view of historical reality. In Egypt the years of the British oc-cupation witnessed the continuation of processes, social, economic, and cultural, that had begun to be apparent during the reign of Ismail and whose development was often only marginally affected by the British presence. Population continued to increase rapidly, rising from about 7 million in 1882 to close to 13 million in 1917. Partly as a result of this increase social differences became more and more apparent in the coun-tryside. An estimate made in 1907 reckoned that out of 1,700,000 rural families "only just over one-twelfth owned sufficient land to secure an adequate living for themselves, another two-thirds possessed some property but not enough to satisfy their needs, while a quarter had no land at all." [38]

By this fortunate upper twelfth the years before World War I could indeed be regarded as a time of mounting prosperity. Many of the sons of these well-to-do rural landowners passed through the westernized government schools into the ranks of the liberal professions or found jobs in the rapidly expanding bureaucracy. At the beginning of the twentieth century many young Egyptians would have agreed with the remark made by Ali Mubarak in his autobiography, when accounting for his own choice of government service as a career, that "clerks were good-looking in appearance, regarded with respect and close to the rulers." [39] But when the rulers were an alien people, occupying many of the most lucrative posts in the bureaucracy, a sense of frustration was bound to set in. In Egypt, as in so many other countries in modern times, the frustration of able and ambitious professional men was to prove one of the major stimulants of nationalist sentiment.

Ismail had boasted that during his reign Egypt had come to form part of Europe. Europeanization proceeded even faster under his successors. By 1907 the European community, mostly resident in Cairo and Alexandria, had risen to 150,000. For all their special privileges Europeans in Egypt did not represent an entirely self-contained minority. Many of the schools run by European communities were open to Egyptian children whose parents could afford the necessary fees. Formal education provided the swiftest initiation to Western culture. But even those Egyptians whose education had proceeded along traditional lines and whose only language was Arabic could now gain access to contemporary European thought through the steady stream of translations. The works of Marx and of Darwin, of the English Fabians, and the Russian novelists were among those that appeared in Arabic translations in this period.

A vigorous press, whose origins may be traced back to Ismail's reign, came to be established and enjoyed a remarkable measure of freedom to comment on the political scene. Newspapers were an innovation for the Muslim world; the language itself had to be transformed to meet their needs. Literary Arabic had previously been regarded as "a device by which professional literateurs regaled each other by means of subtle and elaborate expressions." Now in the hands of able journalists it was transformed into a "tool for conveying ideas and feelings to the entire literate population." [40]

The changes wrought by contact with the West affected the intellectual culture of Egypt still more deeply. Educated Muslims who had acquired some familiarity with contemporary Western thought saw that it was necessary to try to reconcile their traditional religious beliefs with these powerful new intellectual currents. The most eminent of these Muslim reformers, Muhammad Abduh, began his career by studying in the traditional manner at al-Azhar, Cairo's famous Muslim university, came under the influence of Jamal al-Din al-Afghani in the 1870's, supported the Urabist cause, was exiled and spent some years abroad first in Paris, then in Beirut, returned to Egypt in 1889, and with British support achieved high office in the country's judicial and educational establishments. By the time of his death in 1905 Muhammad Abduh had gained a reputation as the greatest Muslim thinker of his day, but in the last years of his life he also showed himself to be a devoted public servant whose work touched the lives of his coreligionists in many different ways.

Traditional Muslim education was bound in a narrowly dogmatic straitjacket: Muhammad Abduh sought to improve its quality by introducing new teaching methods and by adding new subjects to the curriculum. The bitter opposition of the conservative *sheikhs* of al-Azhar prevented many of his reforms from being realized until long after his death. In his post as Mufti he became the supreme interpreter of the *Shari'a* (the law of Islam) and sought to reconcile the traditional code with the circumstances of the modern world. Thus, in one of his most famous *fatwas* (judicial opinions) he declared it lawful for Muslims to deposit money in the interest-paying post-office savings bank—a decision that contradicted the belief current in traditional Muslim society that it was unlawful for Muslims either to give or to receive interest. Finally as a theologian, Muhammad Abduh sought to reconcile Islam with modern science by emphasizing the essential rationality of the Muslim religion in its pristine form and by stressing the right of personal interpretation of the Koran and the *Shari'a*. A later and more secular-minded generation might find Muhammad Abduh's teaching inadequate, but to those of his contemporaries, both in Egypt and in other parts of the Muslim world, who were struggling to free themselves from a blind resignation to tradition, he was the great intellectual liberator.

Unlike his former master al-Afghani, Muhammad Abduh was a gradualist in politics, not a revolutionary. Believing that social reform should precede political emancipation, he was prepared to accept the British occupation for the stability it brought to Egypt. Other Egyptians, coming of a younger generation that had not experienced the disastrous last years of Ismail's reign, viewed the situation differently. The first significant gesture of political protest came in 1893 when the young Khedive Abbas sought to nominate ministers of his own choice. Failing in this direct assault on British hegemony, the khedive fell back on more circuitous means by giving financial support to journalists prepared to take an anti-British line. Among those who benefited from the khedive's patronage was a young lawyer, Mustapha Kamil, a fiery orator and a prolific journalist many of whose anti-British articles were published in the French press. To the British Mustapha Kamil was a tiresome, impractical extremist—a view that revealed an inability to appreciate the force of disturbing ideas, an intellectual failing typical of most "establishments." In fact, Mustapha Kamil had a great and lasting achievement to his credit: in the course of his short life—he died in 1908 at the age of thirty-four—he succeeded, in the words of a recent Egyptian historian, "in making the thinking Egyptian conscious of himself as a nationalist." [41]

Mustapha Kamil caught the mood of the age. The circumstances of the 1900's made the revival of Egyptian nationalism inevitable. The Egyptian middle class had increased in numbers and grown more prosperous. Yet the alien British seemed more firmly established than ever. Freed through the entente with France of the international complications that had bedeviled the early years of their occupation, the British were beginning to talk as if they intended to stay on in Egypt for generations. Suddenly and dramatically the implications of this situation were highlighted by a relatively trivial incident that was blown up by British clumsiness into a cause célèbre. In June, 1906, a party of British officers were involved in a fracas over pigeon-shooting with the villagers of Dinshawai, and one of the officers died as a result of his injuries. The British authorities, seeing in the incident evidence of an "insubordinate spirit sedulously fostered by unscrupulous agitators," [42] arrested fifty-four villagers, established a special tribunal for the trial, and promptly carried out the harsh sentences, including four executions, on the twenty-one found guilty. The Dinshawai incident marks something of a watershed in Anglo-Egyptian relations, for it aroused a widespread mood of protest of a kind that had not been openly apparent since Urabi's downfall a generation earlier. Henceforward the British would be forced to recognize in local nationalism a factor of mounting importance in the Egyptian situation.

Nevertheless, in the years before World War I Egyptian nationalists were unable to make much headway, while the divisions inherent in their ranks became increasingly apparent. Khedive Abbas certainly wanted to see his country independent, but he aimed also at recovering the autocratic powers possessed by his grandfather, Ismail, and so fell out with the majority of nationalists who favored a liberal constitution.

The National Party, founded by Mustapha Kamil in 1907, took the extreme line of demanding an immediate British withdrawal; some of its members were organized in secret societies and discussed the use of violence. By contrast the far more exclusive *Umma* Party, also founded in 1907, took its inspiration from Muhammad Abduh and advocated a gradualist approach. Neither party succeeded in building up a strong organization, but the local Arabic press provided an effective channel for the transmission of nationalist ideas to the literate public. The schoolboys who shouted for independence on public occasions were true harbingers of a new Egypt.

World War I affected Egypt more directly than any other country in Northern Africa. The last links with the nominal suzerain, the Ottoman sultan, were snapped when Turkey entered the war on the German side in November, 1914, prompting the British to retaliate by declaring a formal protectorate over Egypt, deposing Abbas who happened to be temporarily resident in Constantinople, and according the illustrious title of sultan to his successor. At the same time the British kept a tight hold on the Suez Canal which was guarded by an imperial army, quarter of a million strong. For the majority of Egyptians the presence of this massive alien force brought new burdens. Peasants were conscripted to serve in the army's labor corps, while their families were further impoverished by mounting inflation. But the countryside was afflicted by a more profound malaise, whose most alarming symptom, noted by the British as early as the 1890's, was a marked increase in the number of crimes of violence. Lawlessness must in part have been associated with landlessness: a rising population combined with the constant division of inherited properties meant that more and more of the fellahin were finding themselves without land of their own. At the same time the administrative structure of rural Egypt was in the process of transformation. In Ismail's day the villages of Egypt had been isolated and self-contained communities dominated by their local headmen. Now, under the reforms introduced by the British, village headmen had been brought more closely under the supervision of the central government and stripped of much of their power. But the reforms had not yet produced a new bureaucratic structure strong enough to hold the rural communities together. Thus, for all the advances achieved in the last thirty years, Egypt in 1918 was a country full of discontents, and the discontented were to be found in almost every section of society. A country in such a state might well be thought ripe for revolution.

▲▼ THE MAHDIST REVOLUTION IN THE SUDAN

The affairs of the Sudan have hitherto been considered only from the point of view of outsiders, Turco-Egyptians (the hyphenated form is used since almost all the senior officers in Egyptian service in the Sudan were of Turkish origin), or Europeans. But the development of the Sudan in the last quarter of the nineteenth century—a period when the territory aroused quite exceptional interest in the outside world—cannot be understood unless it is seen from the angle of its own people. Only thus is it possible to explain that extraordinary reaction against alien pressures—the revolutionary movement known as the Mahdia.

The modern Sudan has an area of nearly 1 million square miles with a population at present numbering little more than 13 million. In the composition of this population there is a sharp division between northerners and southerners, the former being Arabic-speaking Muslims, the latter being peoples from a variety of indigenous negroid stocks, each with its own language and distinct culture. This division is the product of changes that can be traced back to the last centuries of the first millennium A.D., when men of Arab origin, some Bedouin camel herders, others wandering merchants or holy men, began to settle among the pastoral Beja of the Red Sea hills and the Nubian agriculturalists of the Nile Valley or made their way to the grazing lands of the savanna plains. The differences in climate forced many of the nomads to abandon their camels and take to cattle, thus acquiring for themselves the generalized name Baqqara, derived from the Arabic *baqar* cow.

The Turco-Egyptian conquest, confined at first to the riverine lands and to the plains of Kordofan, served to accelerate greatly the Muslim penetration of the pagan communities of the south. A flourishing trade in ivory and slaves came to be developed by an enterprising group of merchants, most of whom came from the riverine towns and villages lying between Dongola and Khartoum. Using the two main rivers—the White Nile and its tributary, the Bahr al-Ghazal—to provide an avenue of relatively easy access into the interior, these adventurous frontiersmen fanned out over a wide area, bringing to many hitherto isolated peoples, the Nuer, the Dinka, the Zande, and others, their first direct and usually brutal contact with a wider world. Some of the *jallaba* (the Arabic term applied to these petty traders of Sudanese origin) acquired great riches. Zubair Pasha, the most successful of them all, maintained a princely court and was powerful enough to defeat with his own privately recruited followers the armies of the sultan of Darfur whose ancient polity—for centuries one of the most substantial states of the entire Sudanic belt—was then transformed into an Egyptian province.

The conquest of Darfur in 1874 was the high-water mark of Egyptian expansionism in the Sudan. Thereafter the Turco-Egyptian regime had to suffer the successive shocks of Ismail's bankruptcy, his deposition, and the subsequent occupation of Egypt by the British. However much these events may have lowered morale, the total collapse of Turco-Egyptian rule was by no means inevitable. Local administrators might well have succeeded in weathering the storm had they not found themselves confronted with a revolutionary movement of quite exceptional power. This movement did not take the form of a violent insurrection launched by those on whom alien rule had weighed harshest and longest. It had its origin in the preaching of a Muslim divine whose most ardent supporters were drawn from Sudanese living on the perimeter of the Egyptian domain.

In 1881 a certain Muhammad Ahmad, the son of a boatbuilder from Dongola, let it be known that he was the Mahdi, "the Rightly Guided One" whose coming many Muslim prophecies foretold, "the divine leader sent by God at the end of time to fill the world with justice and equity, even as it had been filled with oppression and wrong." There was certainly a charismatic power about Muhammad Ahmad's personality to lend credence to his extraordinary claim. "His unruffled smile, pleasant manners, generosity and equable temperament, though at times somewhat severe, all tended to enhance the popular idea of him," wrote a European missionary who knew the Mahdi at the height of his power.[43] Even as a boy, he had acquired a remarkable reputation for piety and learning: stories were told of his arduous routine—days devoted to study followed by nights spent in prayer and meditation. In 1870, at the age of twenty-six, he left his former masters and settled at Aba, an island in the White Nile, one hundred and sixty miles south of Khartoum. Here, in the manner of many other Muslim holy men, he gradually began to attract a crowd of disciples. The gospel that he came to preach was simple and dynamic. "Look on the things of this life," he urged his followers, "with a piercing eye. Be sure of the nothingness of it, turn your heart to things above. . . . Prepare always for your own salvation, repent, and ask God's forgiveness for having ever indulged in the trifles and enjoyments of this world." [44] This was the creed of all those Muslim reformers who have urged the faithful to return to the purity of primitive Islam, as exemplified in the life of the Prophet and his companions. As with most Muslim reformers, there were profound political implications in Muhammad Ahmad's teaching. "I am a humble servant," he declared, "a lover of poverty and of the poor, one who hates the pride and haughtiness of those rulers whom I wish to lead into the way of truth." [45]

Muhammad Ahmad's decision to announce himself as the Mahdi is associated in Sudanese tradition with the arrival at Aba of a man from the far west, Abdallahi ibn Muhammad, the son of a soothsayer of the Ta'aisha section of the Baqqara Arabs of southern Darfur. Whatever the precise nature of Abdallahi's influence on his master, it is clear that the two men provided between them that combination of qualities needed to launch any effective political movement, Muhammad Ahmad being the visionary who inspires, Abdallahi the man of action who compels obedience. When in 1881 Muhammad Ahmad publicly announced that he was the Mahdi, he did not urge his followers to launch a jihad against the existing regime. But his claim was clearly a serious threat to the Turco-Egyptian authorities and to their Sudanese collaborators. At this stage resolute action might well have nipped the incipient revolt in the bud, but the two companies of government troops sent by steamer up the Nile to Aba allowed themselves to be beaten off by the Mahdi's followers. After this seemingly miraculous victory of sticks and swords over modern firearms, the Mahdi prudently decided to abandon Aba and retreat westward to a place of refuge in the wild Nuba hills of southern Kordofan, a province he had visited on two recent occasions and where he was assured of a good deal of support.

The men who now thronged to join the Mahdi fell into three main groups. The first was made up of genuine religious idealists, devout Muslims shocked by the sacrilegious conduct of the existing authorities. The second group consisted of *jallaba* from Dongola, Khartoum, and other riverine centers, men whose livelihood had in large part depended on the slave trade. The commerce in slaves flourished exceedingly in the Sudan in the 1850's and 1860's, but early in his reign Khedive Ismail outlawed the trade, and in the 1870's he appointed Europeans to senior posts in the Sudan administration to ensure that the antislave trade regulations were strictly enforced. In 1877 the khedive went so far as to give the post of governor-general to an English army officer, General Charles Gordon. Gordon, a man of demonic energy, was determined to stamp out the slave trade. He promptly set about establishing what he himself described as "a sort of Government of Terror" against the slavers.[46] Gordon resigned his post on Ismail's deposition in 1879. He and his European subordinates were men of great courage and devotion, but they were infidels in a Muslim land and their actions brought much obloquy on the Turco-Egyptian regime. In supporting the Mahdi's cause the *jallaba* were seeking redress for their own bitter sense of grievance. The third group among the Mahdists, the Baqqara, were animated by equally mundane considerations. In the 1870's these independent-minded nomads, formerly the largely autonomous tributaries of the sultans of Darfur, found themselves subjected to the much more stringent administration of the Turco-Egyptians. For the Baqqara, whose horsemen were to provide the shock troops of the revolutionary armies, the message of revolt could be spelt in the simplest of terms: "kill the Turks and cease to pay taxes."

Within a few months of his retreat to southern Kordofan the Mahdi was strong enough to turn to the offensive. In January, 1883, El Obeid, the provincial capital, fell to his followers. Ten months later a hastily recruited Egyptian army, commanded by a British officer, General Hicks, sent from Khartoum to repress the rebellion, was annihilated south of El Obeid. This astonishing victory over superior firepower transformed a local revolt into a countrywide insurrection. Mahdist supporters seized power in the provinces of Darfur and Bahr al-Ghazal, while the Beja, living to the east of the Nile, responded to the Mahdist propaganda of a local merchant, Uthman Diqna, and forced the government to abandon all its posts but Suakin, the main port on the Red Sea coast. To the British, the new overlords of Egypt, there seemed no point in becoming deeply involved in the affairs of the Sudan, though a small force was sent to defend Suakin, a place of potential strategic importance on the route to India. Accordingly in January, 1884, the British government decided to recommend the evacuation of all Egyptian troops and officials from the Sudan. The difficult task of supervising the evacuation was entrusted to General Gordon, an obvious choice in view of his outstanding qualities and unrivaled practical experience of the Sudan.

There followed one of the most dramatic episodes of nineteenth-century African history: Gordon's decision on arriving at Khartoum that evacuation was impossible; his growing obsession to "smash the Mahdi"; the steady advance of the Mahdists leading to the complete investment of Khartoum; the reluctant decision of Gladstone and his colleagues to send out a relief expedition; the agonies of the besieged in Khartoum; the Mahdists' victorious assault and Gordon's death on the steps of the governor's palace; the final irony of the arrival of the streamers of the relief expedition within sight of the town only two days after it had fallen to the besiegers. Five months later the Mahdi himself died in Omdurman, the capital he had established on the west bank of the Nile, opposite Khartoum. At an early stage in the Mahdist movement Muhammed Ahmad had given the title of *khalifa* (successor) to three of his leading supporters. Of the three, Abdallahi was by far the most powerful. On the Mahdi's death Abdallahi rapidly set about consolidating for himself a position of primacy.

The situation with which Abdallahi was faced presented all those difficulties that occur when a revolutionary movement has achieved its immediate objective, has overthrown the existing political regime, and then finds itself confronted with the mundane practicalities of government. Idealism falters, dissension emerges, and the sacred cause is endangered by its own former supporters. At Muhammad Ahmad's death the Mahdist camp was divided into two powerful factions: the Baqqara Arabs from the west, with whom Abdallahi himself was closely associated, and the *Awlad al-balad,* the riverine people, a group which included both the Ashraf, the Mahdi's own relatives, and many of the *jallaba.* There was a sharp contrast in character between the two factions. The riverine people, rendered relatively sophisticated by the trading contacts which gave them some experience with a wider world, despised the Baqqara for their backwardness. To the "simple-minded" Baqqara, on the other hand, the *Awlad al-balad* appeared "cunning, corrupt and quite untrustworthy." [47] During the Mahdi's lifetime most of the important posts in the administration had been given to people of riverine origin, but the Baqqara possessed the commanding advantage of forming by far the largest military force in Omdurman. With Baqqara support Abdallahi was gradually able to oust his political opponents among the *Awlad al-balad* from positions of power, replacing them with Baqqara nominees. In 1889 the Khalifa, as Abdallahi came to be known, increased the Baqqara element in Omdurman still further by summoning the men of his own tribe, the Ta'aisha, to the city, a move dictated in part by the need to keep a close watch on these turbulent nomads. The arrival of this horde of emigrants from the west at a time when the city was suffering from a disastrous famine increased still further the unpopularity of Abdallahi's rule among the riverine people. In 1891 a group, led by members of the Mahdi's family, conspired to overthrow the Khalifa. The revolt, which broke out in the heart of Omdurman, was crushed without difficulty; the power of the riverine people was completely broken; and the arrests and executions that followed presented the melancholy but not unfamiliar spectacle of "the revolution eating its own children."

The Baqqara were fine warriors, some of whose leaders made able provincial governors, but they could not provide the wide range of skills needed to maintain an efficient state. Gradually, under the impulse of the Khalifa's consuming ambition and love of power, the character of the original Mahdist theocracy was transformed to produce a highly autocratic Muslim polity. The Khalifa began to surround himself with regal pomp, built a massive wall around his quarters in Omdurman, and—in sharp contrast to the Mahdi who had always been easily accessible—made increasingly infrequent appearances on public occasions. He expanded his personal bodyguard, partly composed of Negro slaves, into a force 9,000 strong and set about creating an effective system of central administration by following Turco-Egyptian practice. A fair proportion of the clerks employed by Khalifa in his treasury and other government departments in Omdurman were Copts or Muslim Egyptians, formerly in the service of the khedive. The steamers on the Nile and the mint at Khartoum were maintained or developed by the new ruler of the Sudan, but the telegraph service created by the Turco-Egyptians collapsed after the fall of Khartoum and was replaced by an efficient camel post which enabled Khalifa to maintain a regular correspondence with his provincial governors.

To create a new structure of government strong enough to maintain law and order in a ravaged land was not the Khalifa's only task. He and his followers were the champions of a revolution with universalistic aspirations. "Not to flee from the *jihad*" was part of the oath they had sworn on entering the Mahdi's service. The sovereigns of the world must be made to recognize the supremacy of the Rightly Guided One. Accordingly, letters were dispatched to all the rulers known to the Mahdists, including Queen Victoria, the Ottoman Sultan, and the Emperor of Ethiopia, urging them to embrace the Mahdist cause. "The men of the Mahdi," Khalifa declared in his letter to Queen Victoria, "are men of iron: God gave them a nature to love death. He made it sweeter to them than cool water to the thirsty. Hence are they terrible to the unbelievers, as were the noble Companions of the Prophet of God." [48]

This bellicose policy involved the Mahdists in war on every front— against the Anglo-Egyptians on the Egyptian border, against the Ethiopians on the eastern marches of the Sudan, and against local dissidents in Darfur, Bahr al-Ghazal, and Equatoria. Ethiopia was the scene of the Mahdists' greatest success. Their raiding parties reached the high plateau and ravaged Gondar, the ancient capital. In 1889 they scored an even more spectacular victory by killing the Emperor John as he was leading an Ethiopian counterattack. A few months later, however, the Mahdists suffered their first major defeat, when the force ordered by the Khalifa to invade Egypt was wiped out by the Anglo-Egyptians at the battle of Tushki. Only in the south did the Mahdist cause continue to advance after 1889. But to the non-Muslim peoples of the southern Sudan Mahdist activities were completely devoid of ideological content. Mahdist soldiers behaved no differently from the Arab slavers who had devastated the villages and cattle camps of the south twenty years earlier, and Mahdist governors were in no position to erect an effective administrative structure over an anarchic land. Southerners already had ample cause to fear and distrust men from the north; the Mahdist incursions served only to increase their store of bitter memories.

By the mid-1890's the Mahdist state found itself faced with new enemies. In the east the Italians were advancing from their base at Massawa; in the west the Belgians of the Congo Free State were sending well-armed expeditions toward the Upper Nile; most serious threat of all, the Anglo-Egyptian forces on the northern frontier were capable of advancing south at any moment. Had the Khalifa and his counselors adopted a less inflexible attitude toward the outside world, they could have attempted to play their opponents off one against another—a policy followed by their neighbor, Menelik of Ethiopia, with conspicuous success. Pride and ignorance blinded them to the realities of their predicament.

To most contemporary European observers the Anglo-Egyptian victory at Karari heralded the dawn of a new era in the history of the Sudan. The Mahdist period was seen as a dark age: "Civilization was swamped in the flood of fanaticism . . . the flag of tyranny waved over smoking ruins from Darfur to the Red Sea. . . . Mahdism is founded on plunder and violence." [49] Changing perspectives and the lapse of time have enabled recent historians to view the Mahdia in a more objective light. Khalifa Abdallahi is seen less as a "malevolent despot," more as "the prisoner of his circumstances." [50] The Sudan was a vast territory, many of whose peoples had behind them a long tradition of violence. Its material resources had never been extensive and were still further reduced by the disastrous famine of 1889–91. That Khalifa should have failed to improve the standard of living of his people was hardly surprising. That he should have succeeded in developing an increasingly elaborate superstructure of government constitutes a very remarkable achievement. It was an achievement of great significance for the future: the Turco-Egyptian regime had shown that all the lands of the eastern Sudanic belt of Africa could be administered as a single polity; Khalifa's government served to consolidate this tradition and so contributed to the emergence of the Sudan in its modern shape.

▲▼ THE ANGLO-EGYPTIAN CONDOMINIUM OF
THE SUDAN: 1899 TO 1919

The old Turco-Egyptian administrative structure of the Sudan had been destroyed by the Mahdist revolution. With the total collapse of the Mahdist state the new rulers of the country found themselves presented with a tabula rasa on which to erect a superstructure of government of their own devising. The Anglo-Egyptian condominium agreement of 1899 provided a legal constitution for the new authority. Its terms, discussed in an earlier section of this chapter, gave to the British a commanding position in the government of the country. The officers on the spot responded enthusiastically to the opportunity of showing their initiative. "The task before us all," Kitchener, the first governor-general under the condominium, told his provincial governors, "is to acquire the confidence of the people, to develop their resources and to raise them to a higher level." [51] The British saw themselves as liberators, following in the footsteps of the heroic Gordon, "endeavouring," in Cromer's words, "to introduce the first rudimentary elements of civilization into this vast and remote region." [52] By the end of the first decade of their rule they had a very substantial achievement to their credit. "I do not believe that in the whole world," declared former President Theodore Roosevelt, who visited the Sudan on a big game hunting expedition in 1910, "there is to be found any nook of territory which has shown such astonishing progress from hideous misery to well-being and prosperity as the Sudan has shown during the last twelve years while it has been under British rule." [53]

The British were adept at claiming a major share of the credit for the regeneration of the Sudan, but without the practical support of the Egyptians the task could never have been accomplished. Between 1899 and 1908 the hard-pressed Egyptian treasury provided £E8 million in loans and subsidies to meet the cost of the new administration. The British paid for a battalion of British troops to be stationed in the country—the only financial commitment accepted for a territory whose acquisition added greatly to imperial prestige. But the greater part of the garrison needed to maintain law and order was provided by the Egyptian army. Egyptian officials filled the subordinate posts in the administration, together with a small group of Syrian and Lebanese Christians, whose fluency in English and Arabic made them invaluable intermediaries between the British and their Egyptian colleagues.

"Autocracy on military lines for civil purposes" was the accurate description applied by a British official to the form of government developed in the Sudan in the first decades of the condominium.[54] While nominally subordinate to the British agent in Egypt and through him to the Foreign Office in London, the governor-general of the Sudan possessed virtually dictatorial powers. When Kitchener left the Sudan for South Africa in 1899, his place was taken by another soldier, Sir Reginald Wingate. Wingate had come out to Egypt as a young artillery officer in 1883. Appointed director of Egyptian military intelligence in 1889, he had been intimately involved in the campaign against the Mahdists. He remained in the Sudan as governor-general until 1916 when he was appointed British high commissioner in Egypt since his remarkably long tenure of office provided the continuity needed in building up a new system of administration. Wingate's right-hand man was an Austrian, Rudolf von Slatin, whose career stands out as one of the most extraordinary ever recorded in the annals of European intercourse with Africa. Slatin's acquaintance with the Sudan dated back to 1874 when he visited the country as a youth of sixteen. In 1878, shortly after being commissioned in the Austrian army, he was invited by Gordon to join his staff, and soon Slatin took over the difficult post of governor of Darfur. Forced to surrender to the Mahdists, he spent eleven years in captivity in Omdurman, often in close contact with the Khalifa, before he made a dramatic escape. The condominium government was delighted to make use of his exceptional knowledge of the Sudan and created the special post of inspector-general for his benefit. But he retained his Austrian citizenship and resigned on the outbreak of World War I.

In the first years of the condominium almost all Wingate's British subordinates were army officers. But as early as 1901 a handful of English university graduates, carefully selected by interview, were recruited for the administration. From this experimental scheme there developed the Sudan Political Service. Its members, favored by exceptionally generous terms of service (including three months' annual leave in Europe), soon came to regard themselves as a corps d'élite of administrators without rival elsewhere in Africa. Limited in numbers —as late as the 1940's membership did not exceed 150, and in earlier decades it was very much smaller—the service provided a remarkably economical means of governing a vast territory.

Pacification was the first task that confronted the new conquerors of the Sudan. In the course of 1899 the Khalifa Abdallahi and his many loyal supporters were hunted down and killed or captured. But the threat of renewed Mahdist activity still remained, and between 1900 and 1912 troops were used on a number of occasions to repress minor revolts, some provoked by the messianic preaching of Muslim divines. Meanwhile in Darfur Ali Dinar, a member of the old ruling family, had seized power on the collapse of Mahdist rule, revived the ancient sultanate, and built up a slave army to consolidate his position. Thus he achieved the distinction of being the last Muslim ruler in Africa to retain independence. But with the British manning his eastern frontier and the French threatening his western borderlands by their advance from Lake Chad, his chances of survival seemed poor. Desperately, after the outbreak of World War I, he turned to the Turks for assistance, thus playing into British hands and providing a pretext for an Anglo-Egyptian invasion of his country. Ali Dinar's death in battle in November, 1916, may be seen not only as marking the end of Muslim resistance in the Sudan but also as the last act in the European conquest of the entire Sudanic belt of Africa.

During the first decades of the twentieth century hard experience taught the European colonial authorities that the task of pacifying a cluster of miniscule African polities was often more demanding than the rapid campaign, highlighted by one or two pitched battles, needed to shatter the power of major African states. The Sudan provided striking illustrations of this general rule. Darfur and the riverine areas of the north were conquered in the space of a few months; certain districts in the south, on the other hand, were not brought under effective administration until the late 1920's. The southern Sudan had never been fully subject to an ordered government. Distances were vast, communications exceptionally poor, and the British personnel very thin on the ground. (The administration of Bahr al-Ghazal, a province the size of Italy, at first constituted no more than eight British officials.) Bitter experience made the local people distrustful of all strangers, while frequent, long-drawn-out feuds between neighboring villages or clans rendered the general atmosphere of violence and unrest still more intense. Slowly, however, using peaceful cajolery in some places, modest punitive expeditions in others, the "Bog Barons"—as the British district commissioners living in the swamps of the Bahr al-Ghazal were known to their northern colleagues—brought to the southern Sudan a measure of tranquility such as its peoples had never known in the seven or eight decades which covered the span of their ascertainable intercourse with the outside world.

In the Sudan, as in other parts of tropical Africa, the peace established by the European conquerors was seen by many contemporaries as a novel and undisputed blessing. "That a woman could go unescorted to the well, or return after dark from the market laughing and chattering with her sisters, that a man could travel long distances unarmed, that robbery and house-breaking were rare and the offenders usually caught and punished, that policemen were respected, that the soldier drew rations from the government and kept himself in barracks—all these things," one British administrator has recorded, "were still a positive good" in the eyes of the Sudanese a quarter of a century after the establishment of the condominium.[55] The coming of peace provided an obvious stimulus to local economic activity. In Mahdist days Sudanese society had been kept permanently on a war footing, with vast armies consuming the surplus foodstuffs of the main agricultural districts and foreign trade being deliberately restricted. With the frontiers open and the armies dispersed, traders and peasants immediately found it possible to gain a better livelihood.

The British were anxious to encourage this natural process of re-generation. But in their plans for economic development they could not claim, as they were justified in doing elsewhere in tropical Africa, to be complete innovators. "Practically every plan canvassed or implemented by British administrators had already occurred," a recent historian has noted, "to Muhammad Ali Pasha" almost a hundred years earlier.[56] The Sudanese recognized the similarity of the condominium to the old Turco-Egyptian regime by referring to it as *al-Turkiya al-thaniya* ("the second period of Turkish rule"). But the new rulers were able to count on a much greater measure of financial support from Egypt than had ever been possible in the days of Muhammad Ali, and their material achievements were consequently all the more striking.

Muhammad Ali's conquest of the Sudan in 1820 had been largely in-spired by the hope of extracting a plentiful supply of gold and slaves from his new dominion. In antiquity the Sudan had been the greatest producer of gold known to the Mediterranean world, but by the nine-teenth century most of the country's gold deposits were exhausted. Eu-ropean prospectors in the first decade of the condominium were no more successful than the geologists employed by Muhammad Ali in find-ing traces of other minerals in commercial quantities. As for the slave trade, the British promptly set about stamping it out completely—a task not accomplished in some of the remoter districts until the 1920's. Of the Sudan's other products ivory and ostrich feathers were exports of declining value by the beginning of the twentieth century, but there was a considerable demand for gum arabic from Kordofan and opportunities for expansion in the export to Egypt of grain and hides. Cotton had been introduced to certain districts during the Turco-Egyptian period, but its cultivation was dependent on the extension of irrigation. Werner Munzinger, a Swiss adventurer in Ismail's service, wrote in 1871, "The Sudan ought to be one large cotton-field." [57] The British were prompt to realize the possibilities of cotton-growing in the Sudan, encouraged a number of pilot projects, and started to investigate the problems of irri-gating the Gezira, the "island" of land lying between the Blue Nile and the White Nile. Not until after World War I, however, did cotton begin to make a really substantial contribution to the Sudan's economy.

In the meantime it was imperative to provide the country with an ef-ficient system of communications. In the northern Sudan the stress was on railways rather than roads. The military railway built by Kitchener was pushed southward to Khartoum, while a branch line ran east to connect the Nile with the Red Sea coast. In 1906 work started on the construction of a modern harbor complex, named Port Sudan and de-signed to replace ancient Suakin. By 1911 the railway had been extended to Sennar and Kordofan. In the southern Sudan the White Nile provided the obvious line of communications but a channel had first to be cut through the sudd, the barrier of floating vegetation, before the river could be used for regular steamer services. These were expensive undertakings which took up no less than three quarters of the £E8 million spent by the Sudan government on capital projects between 1899 and 1918.

As the range of government activities increased, the need for locally trained personnel became more pressing. British administrators in the Sudan shared Cromer's view, bred of his experience both in Egypt and in India, that too much education of a purely academic nature served only to increase the numbers of "the dissatisfied class who necessarily become patriots and demagogues." [58] The education department received a spectacular boost when subscribers from all over the English-speaking world responded to an appeal launched by Lord Kitchener a few weeks after the battle of Karari and raised £135,000 for the erection of a college to the memory of General Gordon in Khartoum, but the aims set by the first generation of British educationalists to work in the Sudan were pragmatic rather than liberal. They accepted the view of their colleagues in the administration that their job was to turn out efficiently trained clerks, technicians, subordinate administrators, and junior army officers. Ironically enough experience was soon to show that Sudanese civil servants in reasonably well-paid jobs could also become "patriots and demagogues."

By 1920 there were 1,544 Sudanese holding classified posts in government service compared with 535 British and 1,824 Egyptians. By 1918 government revenue which stood at £E242,000 in 1902, had risen to £E2.8 million, while exports had increased from £E395,000 to over £E4 million in the same period. This is an impressive battery of statistics. In the difficult years ahead some British administrators were to look back to the Wingate era as a "halcyon age."

▲▼ THE FOUNDING OF MODERN ETHIOPIA:
1875 TO 1908

In 1850 Ethiopia was a land of warlords. Descendants of the ancient Solomonid dynasty were still invested with the splendid imperial title, "Elect of God, Conquering Lion of the Tribe of Judah, King of the Kings of Ethiopia," but for nearly a century every emperor had been a nonentity, a puppet in the hands of the warrior princes who dominated the politics of the high plateau. By 1900 an amazing transformation had taken place: anarchy had given way to order, and Ethiopia was now the most powerful indigenous polity in all Africa, a kingdom capable of parrying the assaults of foreign invaders and of pursuing a vigorous policy of territorial expansion. Ethiopia could indeed be counted among the imperialist powers participating in the "scramble for Africa." A generation later the country was fated to succumb to an immensely formidable Italian invasion, but the Italian occupation lasted no more than five years (1936–41), far too short a time for the impact of alien rule to produce much effect on the social structure and cultural life of the country. Thus, alone of all the indigenous polities of Africa Ethiopia escaped the profoundly disturbing experience of a generation of colonialism.

A number of factors help to account for the unique character of recent Ethiopian history. In geographical terms the country could be regarded as one of the most isolated in Africa, the peculiar nature of its terrain placing the natural obstacles of high escarpments and deep ravines in the path of an invader. But these obstacles were not sufficient to deter a really well equipped adversary, as the British proved in 1868 and the Italians in 1935. More significant was the fact that Ethiopia occupied a position of no great strategic importance either to Britain or to France, the two great imperialist states of the age. Nor could the country be said to offer any really enticing material prizes to a conqueror. Egypt launched a number of assaults on Ethiopia in the 1870's; Italy followed the same policy in the 1890's. But in both cases these aggressive actions were prompted by little more than a meretricious search for "prestige," a substance too nebulous to provide the driving force needed to maintain a really vigorous policy of expansion. Moreover, both Egypt and Italy were, by the standards of the late nineteenth-century world, second- or third-class powers. The Ethiopians were fortunate in not being called on to face the French army that conquered Algeria. They were fortunate, too, in the timing of later events. Had World War II not broken out so soon after the eventual Italian conquest of their country, the Ethiopians would certainly have found themselves forced to suffer a much longer period of Italian domination.

Whatever happened a generation later, in the 1890's Ethiopians were masters of their own destiny. In part their success in repelling alien invaders must be ascribed to the inspiration of a long tradition that enabled peoples from provinces differing greatly in recent political experience to develop a certain spirit of national unity in the face of external danger. Xenophobia, an attitude noted by many European travelers in Ethiopia and in other African states in the latter half of the nineteenth century, may well be regarded as one aspect of protonationalism. But this proud and defiant spirit needed resourceful commanders to direct it. Again the Ethiopians were fortunate: between 1850 and 1900 the country produced three outstanding political leaders, the emperors Theodore (Tewodros), John (Yohannes), and Menelik.

Theodore was born in 1818, began his career as leader of a band of freebooters, and fought his way to supreme power by defeating all the warlords of his day. In 1855 he had himself crowned emperor and set about the herculean task of building up a strong centralized state. But his centralizing policy offended too many vested interests among the clergy and the nobility, and by 1865 the greater part of his kingdom was in revolt against his authority. As his own power declined, his judgment became distorted by an almost lunatic strain of megalomania. Provoked by a trivial misunderstanding with the British, he took the fatal step of imprisoning a group of British subjects. The British government retaliated by mounting a massive rescue operation in the form of a large military expedition which invaded Ethiopia in 1868. The emperor shot himself, as the British were storming his final stronghold of Magdala. Few reigns have ended so disastrously, yet Theodore's career, viewed in the broad context of Ethiopian history, had a stimulating and creative aspect. After a century of warlordism he had shown that it was not impossible for an outstanding individual to revive the power and prestige of the imperial office. Moreover, the total failure of the last years of Theodore's reign spelt out a lesson his successors, John and Menelik, were careful to take to heart: in a country where local loyalties are still immensely powerful, it is the height of imprudence in a ruler to attempt to impose too rigid a superstructure of government.

John was crowned emperor in 1872. Basing his power on the control of Tigre, Ethiopia's northernmost province, he succeeded, in the years after Theodore's death, in forcing or persuading all his rivals to accept his overlordship. Wisely abandoning Theodore's practice of replacing local rulers by his own nominees, the new emperor allowed the great provincial magnates to retain most of their privileges so long as they paid him tribute in recognition of his suzerainty. This flexible imperial hegemony—basically not unlike a federal system of government—was much better adapted to Ethiopian realities than Theodore's brittle centralization.

In John's reign Ethiopia came under attack from the Egyptians, the Italians, and the Mahdists of the Sudan. It was the first time that the country had been called on to face an invasion since the Somali and Galla onslaughts of the sixteenth century. This external threat greatly assisted the emperor in his work of unification by promoting a growing sense of interdependence between hitherto autonomous provinces. John himself was particularly well placed to lead Ethiopian resistance, as his own home territory of Tigre was the province most exposed to foreign invasion. In the mid-1870's two Egyptian expeditions suffered crushing reverses at the hands of the Ethiopians. Little more than a decade later, after the Egyptian base at Massawa, the main port on the Eritrean coast, had passed into Italian hands, one of John's vassals wiped out an Italian force 500 strong. In the meantime Mahdist forces from the Sudan were ravaging the heart of the country, and one of their armies was devastating Gondar, the onetime capital. In 1889 John prepared a massive counterattack against the Sudanese town of Gallabat. The Ethiopians carried all before them, but in the moment of victory the emperor received a mortal wound from a stray bullet. His death turned success into disaster. The Ethiopians fled the field, abandoning to the Mahdists even the body of their emperor, whose head was cut off and displayed among the trophies of victory at Omdurman.

The sudden death of the valiant Emperor John seemed bound to compound the country's many afflictions. "Civil war, famine, and an epidemic of cholera have, within the last decade, wrought dreadful havoc," wrote a contemporary European traveler. "It is scarcely possible to realize without visiting the country the abject misery and wretchedness which has fallen upon the Ethiopian empire during late years. . . . Bands of robbers haunt all their mountains. . . . Gondar is now almost a desert, having been raided three times by the Dervishes. Tigre is convulsed with the quarrels of rival chiefs, and it would seem, if help in some form or other does not come, that the great plateau of Ethiopia will become practically depopulated." [59] In circumstances such as these who could have predicted that Ethiopia was on the point of experiencing one of the most remarkable periods in the country's long history, or foreseen that John's successor, Menelik of Shoa, would prove the most successful African ruler of his day?

Menelik was born in 1844 into the royal family of Shoa, the southernmost province occupied by Amharic-speaking peoples. His father, King of Shoa, died in 1855 at the time of Theodore's conquest of the kingdom, and the young prince was taken away to be brought up as a page in the imperial household, a post that provided a grueling apprenticeship in the harsh realities of Ethiopian politics. In 1865, when Theodore's power had begun to decline, Menelik managed to escape, made his way back to Shoa, and gradually gained control of his father's kingdom. In the 1870's he put in a bid for the imperial title, but Shoa was not yet strong enough to challenge the might of Tigre and Menelik found himself forced to accept John's overlordship. Shrewdly he set about consolidating his own position by building up a massive store of modern firearms. Many of these guns were presented by official Italian agents eager to weaken Ethiopia by playing the king of Shoa off against the emperor. Others were purchased from French traders animated by a less sinister motive: guns bought in France for seven francs could be sold in Ethiopia for forty. By equipping his army so effectively with modern weapons Menelik gained a commanding advantage over his immediate neighbors. In the course of the 1880's he conquered the Galla principalities that bordered Shoa to the west and south and advanced eastward to occupy the ancient sultanate of Harar.

Thus, at the time of John's death Menelik was by far the strongest local ruler in Ethiopia. In April, 1889, he was crowned emperor. Shortly afterward he concluded with an Italian emissary the important Treaty of Ucciali (Wichale), one article of which defined the boundary between Ethiopia and the Italian possessions on the Red Sea coast. Even more important was another article (XVII) which dealt with diplomatic communications between Ethiopia and the outside world. In the Amharic text of the treaty this article merely implied that Menelik might make use of the Italian authorities to act as diplomatic postmen if he so desired. But in the Italian text of the same clause Menelik appeared to have agreed to avail himself of the services of the Italian government in all his negotiations with foreign powers. The Italians were quick to claim that by this article they had obtained Menelik's agreement to the establishment of an Italian protectorate over Ethiopia—a claim the validity of which Menelik hastened with every justification to deny. Behind the wrangling over legal niceties powerful emotions could be detected, on the Italian side a mounting desire for empire, on the Ethiopian a resolute determination to preserve national independence.

The Italian threat had blown up very suddenly. In 1887, when Francesco Crispi, the most ardent Italian imperialist of his day, became prime minister, the Italians controlled no more than 2,000 square kilometers of territory on the Red Sea coast. Crispi immediately embarked on a vigorous policy of expansion, his first aim being to avenge the disaster recently suffered by a small Italian force in the mountains of Tigre. "We must," he declared, "teach the barbarians that we are strong and powerful." [60] A special expeditionary force was promptly sent to the Red Sea; Massawa was strongly fortified; Italian columns advanced inland to establish posts on the high plateau that overlooks the sweltering coastal plains; the new colony of Eritrea—its name derived from the *Mare Erythraeum* of classical geographers—was officially proclaimed in 1890; and by 1891 Italian-occupied territory measured eighty five thousand square kilometers in extent.

With his own home territory of Shoa lying far to the south, Menelik was not immediately threatened by the Italian advance. But any sign of weakness was bound to compromise his position as emperor among his own subjects. In 1893 he denounced the Treaty of Ucciali but took no hostile action against the Italians until a new Italian advance in the autumn of 1895 made war inevitable. By this time Menelik had at his disposal an army more than 100,000 strong, equipped with artillery, machine guns, and a plentiful supply of modern rifles, many of which had been presented to him by the Italians. But Ethiopian armies suffered from one serious weakness: like the armies of medieval Europe, they lacked the means to feed themselves in a campaign lasting many months. In these circumstances it would have paid the Italians, whose force numbered 10,000 European troops and 7,000 native askaris, to have remained on the defensive until Menelik's host broke up of its own accord. But in December, 1895, an Italian detachment suffered a minor defeat and the impetuous Crispi forced the cautious field commander into action by means of telegrams that combined sarcasm—"this is military phthisis, not a war"—with bombast—"I expect a victory so complete that it will liquidate the Abyssinian question for ever." [61] On March 1, 1896, the two armies clashed unexpectedly a little to the east of the important town of Adowa. The three Italian brigades, advancing through a wild country of rugged hills, became separated one from another. Each of them was overwhelmed in turn by the sheer mass of their well-armed opponents. A morning's hard fighting ended in the greatest defeat suffered by a European power in Africa in the course of the nineteenth century.

The battle of Adowa was one of those rare events the ripples of whose consequences spread wide and deep in space and time. Crispi was the first to feel the impact of the disaster: his political career ended abruptly when a wave of national indignation forced him to make an immediate resignation. "Never again," declared his successor, Di Rudini, "will we embrace a policy of expansion." [62] Not all Italians shared these sentiments. The young Mussolini found that the tally of Italian losses—of soldiers killed and cannon captured—kept hammering on his brain for years afterward. It was an age in which European nations were not accustomed to accept as final any defeat at the hands of the "barbarians." The totality of the Ethiopian victory sowed in some Italian minds the seeds of a war of revenge.

Of the impact of Adowa on British policy something has already been said. As for the consequences of the battle for the victors, Adowa brought to Ethiopia a measure of international prestige, to the emperor enhanced authority, and to his people "a new legend and a pride" which, in the course of the next generation, was to "impede even military modernization." [63]

In the years after the battle Addis Ababa, Menelik's capital, became the scene of intense diplomatic activity, as European missions—French, British, and Russian—hastened to reestablish contact with the victorious emperor. Europeans unfamiliar with Ethiopia regarded Menelik —so Rennell Rodd, the leader of the British mission, recorded in his memoirs—"as little more than an exceptionally enlightened savage." But it did not take long for European visitors to realize that they were dealing with a very remarkable personality, "dignified and at the same time cordially unreserved" in his manners and possessed of "astonishing energy." "Accessible to all his subjects from the highest to the lowest, he had succeeded," Rennell Rodd discovered, "in winning universal regard and affection." Most impressive trait of all, this African monarch was "a man of quick and keen intelligence capable of appreciating political situations with a clearness of apprehension which," Rodd confessed, "I hardly anticipated." [64] Menelik was indeed a master of statecraft, revealing his skill not only in his manipulation of the infinitely complex politics of his own country but also in his handling of intrusive Europeans who were soon forced to abandon their arrogant delusion that the emperor of Ethiopia was a man they could use to their own advantage.

In the decade after Adowa Menelik reaped the fruits of victory. He made no attempt to drive the Italians from Eritrea, for such a task would have been beyond his powers. Instead he turned to expand his domains in other directions by sending expeditions westward to the borders of the Sudan, southward into the country of the Borana Galla, north of Lake Rudolph, and eastward to drive a wedge of Ethiopian territory across Somali lands in the dusty plains of the Ogaden. A series of treaties, concluded with the neighboring imperial powers between 1897 and 1908, confirmed the frontiers of this vastly expanded Ethiopian realm along lines most of which have endured to this day.

One characteristic of the emperor noticed by most European visitors was his interest in modern technology. While he was still king of Shoa, Menelik had begun to make use of the services of European technicians, one of whom, a Swiss engineer named Ilg, served him for many years in a variety of capacities. The establishment of Addis Ababa, founded by Menelik as his capital in the 1880's, provided a focus for the modernizing activities of the emperor. In the first decade of the twentieth century the city presented "a great sprawling mass of thatched mud huts with only a few square buildings intervening," in the midst of which there rose a small hill set with "a collection of hutments and houses" that represented the imperial palace.[65] Nevertheless, this "medieval capital of a feudal king" was beginning to acquire some of the trappings of modernity. Among the innovations introduced through Menelik's initiative were to be found a telephone system, a generating plant for electricity, and a government school, the first of its kind in Ethiopia, where the sons of the nobility received instruction in foreign languages from an Egyptian teacher. By 1910 more than a thousand foreigners were resident in Addis Ababa, with Greeks, Arabs, Indians, and Armenians forming the largest communities. And in 1917 work was finally completed on the railroad, begun by a French company in 1898, that linked the Ethiopian capital with the French Red Sea port of Djibouti.

These developments, though of great significance for the future, affected only a tiny proportion of the population. Moreover, they met with a good deal of popular disapproval. Indeed, in 1908 the emperor felt obliged to issue a proclamation chiding his subjects for their obstructive attitude to certain innovations. "In European countries when people undertake new kinds of work and make cannon, guns, trains, and other things revealed by God, the people concerned are called engineers; they are praised and given more assistants, not insulted on account of their craft. But you," the emperor admonished his subjects, "are going to leave my country without people who can make the plough. . . . From this time forth anyone found insulting another on account of his work will be punished by a year's imprisonment." [66]

Menelik's innovating zeal could make little headway against the natural conservatism of his subjects. Ethiopia, all foreign visitors were quick to note, was a country possessing a rich, ancient, and satisfying culture of its own. A culture made vividly explicit in the great ceremonies of the Ethiopian church: "the priests dancing at Timkat [the Feast of the Epiphany] before the Ark of the Covenant to the muffled throbbing of their silver drums" or "the hierarchy of the Ethiopian church in their many coloured vestments blessing the waters." [67] A way of life that could offer on occasion, as Wilfred Thesiger, son of a British minister at Addis Ababa later recalled, the delirious excitement of some great parade after a successful expedition: the chiefs wearing "their full panoply of war, lion's-mane head-dresses, brilliant velvet cloaks stiff with silver and golden ornaments, long silk robes of many colours and great curved swords, . . . the frenzied tide of men surging past the royal pavilion to the thunder of the war-drums and the blare of war-horns . . . horsemen half concealed in dust and a great press of footmen, screaming out their deeds of valour and brandishing their swords." [68]

Only a handful of Ethiopians—among them Menelik's trusted friend Ras Makonnen, the father of Haile Selassie—were in a position to appreciate, through the stimulus of frequent intercourse with Europeans, something of the vision of their emperor. In early twentieth-century Ethiopia, as in its contemporary, the still independent sultanate of Morocco, there did not exist any social group large enough to maintain a policy of modernization comparable to that pushed through by Muhammad Ali and his successors in Egypt.

Unlike the rulers of Egypt, Menelik was far from omnipotent. He possessed no corps of administrators to enforce his commands. Provincial governors, drawn for the most part from leading local families, were left largely to their own devices, provided that they abstained from acts of overt rebellion. In the newly conquered territories Shoan hegemony was maintained by the establishment of military colonies or garrisons. The local population, distinguished in every aspect of their culture —language, religion, political organization—from their Amhara overlords, were reduced to servile status and divided up among their conquerors with two to five serfs attached to each foot soldier and several hundred to each provincial governor. There was ample room here for the crudest forms of exploitation. Kaffa, once one of the most prosperous little kingdoms in all Africa, suffered particularly. A European traveler who visited the country in 1905, only eight years after the Shoan conquest, reported that "the native culture had almost disappeared." Thirty years later another European traveler found no improvement: much once cultivated land had reverted to forest, one-quarter of the remainder was now in the hands of great Amhara landowners, the slave trade, though officially proscribed, was still carried on, and the original population had suffered a disastrous decline in numbers.[69]

National histories are almost invariably written from the standpoint of the contemporary elite. As an antidote to the Amhara-centered stance of Ethiopian historiography it is salutary to place oneself imaginatively in the position of all those Ethiopian peoples—Galla, Sidama, Somali, and a multitude of smaller ethnic groups—who were subjected to the pressures of Amhara imperialism. One may reflect, too, on the Galla proverb: "where the Amhara trod, the grass grows no more."

▲▼ THE ALIEN PENETRATION OF THE HORN
OF AFRICA: 1875 TO 1920

To the outside world the Horn of Africa presents a face forbidding in the extreme. Between the modest urban centers of the coast—Berbera, Zeila, Mogadishu, and the towns of the Benadir—and neighboring lands around the Arabian Sea, maritime commercial intercourse has been maintained for centuries. But, except in the extreme south, behind the coastal cities there lies "a desert of surpassing desolation"[70] and beyond the desert barren, boulder-strewn mountains through which the camel tracks lead to the water-starved plains of the interior. As late as 1875 these inland plains were almost completely unknown to the outside world. Their only inhabitants were the pastoral Somali, nomads moving with their camel herds from grazing land to grazing land, a virile, liberty-loving, intensely egalitarian people, toughened by their harsh environment. In the course of the past millennium two themes had dominated their history—the introduction and diffusion of Islam and the gradual expansion of the Somali-speaking population over the entire area of the Horn. Never, the Somali could claim in 1875, had they been subjected to an alien conqueror; never, on the other hand, had they succeeded in constructing a unified state of their own. Events following 1875 were to negate both these statements. In sharp contrast to their earlier history alien penetration and conquest and the growth of a movement for national unification provide the major themes in the recent historical experience of the Somali people.

In the latter half of the nineteenth century the Somali presented "a congeries of disunited and often hostile clans which themselves were regularly divided by their internecine feuds." [71] A greater measure of political stability existed in the urban centers of the coast. Most of these towns had been founded centuries earlier by outsiders of Arab or Persian origin, but, as on the Swahili coast further south, these alien urban aristocracies had merged increasingly with the local population. The political influence of the towns extended no more than a few miles inland. Frequently during the nineteenth century the ruling urban groups found it impossible to prevent the Somali clan leaders of the immediate hinterland from intervening in their internal affairs. But they were also under pressure from another direction. By 1875 new forms of foreign influence were becoming increasingly apparent on the Somali coast.

Half a century earlier the Omani sultan of Zanzibar had asserted his hegemony over Mogadishu and the Benadir towns. In 1839 the British occupied the South Arabian port of Aden and began to look to Zeila and Berbera on the other side of the gulf to supply the meat needed to feed their newly established garrison. In 1862 the French government purchased the port of Obock, about a hundred miles north of Zeila, from the local Danakil chief. Seven years later an Italian agent staked out a claim to another Danakil port, Assab, lying to the north of Obock. In the mid-1870's the northern Somali coast felt the impact of Egyptian expansionism when the ambitious Ismail sent troops to occupy Zeila, Berbera, and the inland sultanate of Harar. A decade later the Egyptians were forced by the disastrous course of events in the Sudan to evacuate all their posts on the Red Sea coast south of Suakin. The early 1880's saw a notable increase in French and Italian interests in an area whose commercial opportunities had been considerably enlarged by the opening of the Suez Canal. Obock became the base for a number of French companies anxious to develop trade with Ethiopia, while in 1882 Assab was made into the first official Italian colony. With the French expanding southward from Obock and the Italians northward from Assab, the British thought it advisable to put forward their claims to the Somali ports evacuated by the Egyptians. Between 1884 and 1886 they asserted their hegemony over the territory that came to be known as British Somaliland by means of a series of treaties signed with local chiefs.

By the mid-1880's a handful of Italians had begun to show an interest in the Indian Ocean coast of the Somali country. One of the most active members of this group was a trader named Filonardi who served as Italian consul in Zanzibar. By this time the sultanate was under strong pressure from Britain and Germany. Filonardi was anxious to obtain concessions for his own country but realized that his government was in no position to take decisive action on its own. But the very weakness of the Italians was not without advantages. Early in 1889 the rulers of two northern Somali sultanates with capitals at Obbia and Alula decided, for reasons of calculated self-interest, to place their territories under Italian protection. Some months later the British, reckoning that of all the European powers with an interest in East Africa the Italian would make the most desirable neighbors, helped the Italian government to stake out a claim to the Benadir ports belonging to Zanzibar. In the course of the next few years Italian explorers visited parts of the interior, signing treaties with local chiefs and thus enlarging the Italian sphere still further.

Throughout the 1890's effective European activity was confined to the coast. The French sphere—officially but misleadingly termed *Côte Française des Somalis*—was the scene of the most vigorous enterprise. In 1896 Djibouti replaced Obock as capital. Djibouti's development was remarkably rapid. In 1888 Djibouti was no more than a group of coral islands, inhabited, according to one account, only by "a jackal dying of hunger under a thorn tree." [72] But the site possessed a sheltered road and offered easy access to the interior. Within ten years Djibouti had grown into a town with a population of 10,000 including 200 Europeans and had become one of the main entrepôts of the Red Sea, the starting point for the newly planned railway to Addis Ababa, the center of a flourishing traffic in firearms and an important coaling station for French ships bound for the East. Neither the British nor the Italian spheres offered comparable opportunities for commercial expansion. The British were content to maintain law and order along their stretch of coast by employing a minimum of force: in 1899 their total establishment numbered 10 officials and 130 Indian sepoys. In the Italian sphere the maintenance of Italian authority was left to a private company started by Filonardi. But the task of establishing half a dozen administrative posts soon exhausted the company's modest financial resources. In 1896 Filonardi's company was wound up, but two years later another commercial concern, the Benadir company, was allowed to take Filonardi's place. Italians on the coast could count on the support of a small Italian naval squadron. In the interior their position was much more hazardous. Indeed, in 1896 an Italian expedition attempting to advance inland along the line of the Shibeli River was almost completely wiped out by the local Somali.

European activities on the coast affected only a limited number of Somali tribes. Infinitely more serious for the majority of the Somali was the threat suddenly posed by Ethiopian expansionism. In the 1890's Ethiopian raiding parties struck deep into the Ogaden and pushed as far south as the middle reaches of the Juba River. At the same time Emperor Menelik put forward ambitious claims for Somali territory in the Ogaden, many of which were eventually accepted by Britain, France, and Italy in the treaties negotiated after Adowa to define Ethiopia's borders. In years to come no frontiers in all Africa were to provoke so much argument and conflict as those laid down by rival imperialists for the division of Somali lands.

Compared with the fate of other African peoples during the age of European conquest, the Somali might be said to have escaped comparatively lightly. No foreigners had sought to take away their land; no alien administrators had attempted drastically to transform their traditional way of life. Yet for a people possessing a ferocious pride in their own independence the presence of any alien power with claims to political superiority was a cause for resentment—and resentment grew all the more bitter when the stranger was a man of different religion. The existence of this widespread mood of intense xenophobia, stiffened by pride and strengthened by a vigorous martial tradition, helps to explain why Somaliland became the scene in the first decades of the twentieth century of one of the longest wars fought in Africa during the colonial period.

As so often in Muslim history, the course of events was dominated by an outstanding religious leader, Muhammad Abdille Hassan, known to his followers by the Arabic honorific Sayyid ("Master"), nicknamed the "Mad Mullah" by his opponents. Muhammad Abdille Hassan was born in 1864 into one of the clans of the Ogaden. The first thirty years of his life followed a path rendered familiar through the biographies of many Muslim divines: an early acquired reputation for piety and learning; *wanderjahre* spent in traveling widely in search of knowledge on journeys to Aden, to the Sudan and East Africa, and inevitably to the holy cities of Arabia; finally membership in a new religious fraternity, the Salihiya, and ardent devotion to its reformist ideals. Settling in Berbera in the 1890's Muhammad Abdille Hassan soon attracted attention by his preaching. Eloquently he denounced the laxity of his coreligionists, earnestly he warned them, laying particular stress on the recent foundation of a Catholic mission station outside Berbera, of the dire consequences of infidel subversion and aggression. But the people of the coast rejected his teaching. Members of the local Muslim establishment were outraged by his attacks on their ancient fraternity, the Qadiriyya, while the coastal merchants found little to complain of in a modest system of British administration that had greatly improved local security and so created favorable conditions for a flourishing commerce. Discomforted, Muhammad Abdille Hassan decided to retire to the interior where he could take up his residence among tribes not yet brought under British protection.

Rapidly the Sayyid's oratory, piety, and diplomatic skill in settling disputes gained him a following among the pastoral nomads of the Ogaden. But he also made many enemies, particularly among local tribal leaders. To assert his authority he resorted to the most ruthless methods: doubtful followers ran the risk of summary execution; distant opponents lived under the threat of assassination at the hands of the Sayyid's agents. Nevertheless, in 1899, little more than a year after leaving Berbera, he could count on at least 3,000 supporters and felt himself strong enough to declare formally a jihad against the infidels. The Ethiopians were the first to feel the impact of this new mood of Somali militancy when the Dervishes—as the Sayyid's followers called themselves—attacked their post at Jijiga. Two months later a band of Dervishes made a daring and immensely profitable raid on the camel herds of one of the clans under British protection. Reluctantly the British authorities accepted the necessity of taking firm countermeasures.

The next four years witnessed a steady escalation of the conflict. In their first expeditions against the "Mad Mullah" the British reckoned that a force of Somali levies, commanded by British officers and acting in cooperation with the Ethiopians, would suffice. But war against a master of guerrilla tactics in a land possessing exceptionally difficult problems of transport and supply required far more elaborate preparations. In 1903 the British gathered a substantial expeditionary force made up of detachments drawn from many parts of their empire— battalions of the King's African Rifles from East Africa, British and Boer mounted infantry fresh from the war in South Africa, camel corps detachments from India, and a large staff of British officers. The campaign turned out to be one of the most expensive colonial wars ever fought by the British in Africa—the total cost to the British taxpayer was put at more than £5 million—and it was only partially successful. For the Sayyid eluded capture to the end, and though his forces suffered such losses that he found it advisable to open peace negotiations, he was able to obtain highly favorable terms. In the course of the fighting he had moved into the Italian sphere, settling in an unadministered wedge of territory lying between the two northern Somali sultanates. Here, by the terms of a treaty concluded with the Italians in March, 1905, he was allowed to remain as an autonomous ruler nominally under Italian protection.

The Italians were in far too weak a position to impose any irksome restrictions on their latest protégé. As for the Sayyid, having thus skillfully secured a respite for himself and his followers, he set about preparing his comeback by waging a vigorous war of words, for he was a brilliant propagandist in the Somali style, a master of language whose poems of scathing satire and virulent invective have come to form part of the heritage of Somali literature. Before long his agents had reestablished contact with the clans from whose territories he had been driven. Neither the British nor the Italians were prepared to involve themselves in further large-scale military operations. Accordingly, in 1910 the British took the drastic step of withdrawing from the interior of their protectorate. There followed a dreadful period known to the Somali as "the time of eating filth," in which intertribal violence flared up with an intensity quite unprecedented. Profiting from this situation the Sayyid moved westward to establish his headquarters at Taleh on the eastern borders of the British protectorate. Here, with the aid of stonemasons brought over from the Yemen, he constructed a massive fortress whose sixty-foot stone walls and thirteen bastions make it one of the most astonishing monuments of its kind in all Africa. Of the actual machinery of Dervish government, of the political and economic organization that made possible the construction of a fortress such as Taleh much remains to be discovered. But it is clear that the Sayyid was attempting not only to create a polity in which the laws of Islam would be more rigorously observed but also to build up a supratribal political structure in which unswerving loyalty to the Dervish cause would replace the old attachment to lineage and clan.

In the period after 1910 the Sayyid failed to extend his influence as widely as his opponents had feared. The formation of a Somali camel corps led by British officers provided the protectorate authorities with a cheap and effective means of policing their hinterland. Although the Sayyid made contact with Ethiopian Emperor Iyasu during World War I and even received technical assistance from a German armorer, the Dervishes failed to take decisive advantage of the difficulties facing the British. With the war over, the British decided finally to rid themselves of their old opponent. Planes were used to bomb Taleh and within a few weeks the Sayyid and his fast-diminishing band of supporters were fleeing southward into the Ethiopian Ogaden. The end came in November, 1920, when, after rejecting the tempting peace offers made him by his enemies, the Sayyid Muhammad Abdille Hassan died of influenza.

The Somali people were the chief sufferers in the twenty years' war waged by the Dervishes. Many tens of thousands died in what might well be regarded as a pointless struggle. The extent of the European penetration into the interior of the Horn was far too slight, it might be argued, to constitute a real threat to the way of life of the nomadic Somali. Pointless or not, the war fought by the Dervishes and especially the personality of their leader contained the stuff of legend. "Intensely as the Somalis feared and loathed the man whose followers had looted their stock, robbed them of their all, raped their wives, and murdered their children, they could not but admire and respect one who, being the embodiment of their idea of Freedom and Liberty, never admitted allegiance to any man, Moslem or infidel." [73] So wrote Douglas Jardine, a British administrator with many years' experience in Somaliland. In British eyes the "Mad Mullah" might seem no more than a "romantic, but none the less consummate, scoundrel." [74] To many of his Somali contemporaries he might appear, especially in his last years, as "a monomaniac who believed that he was the only true adherent of Islam left in an otherwise infidel world." [75] But to Somali of a later generation Sayyid Muhammad has been, as Jardine wisely predicted, a national hero, the forerunner of modern Somali nationalism whose "patriotic achievements are lauded today even by the descendants of those who suffered most in the Dervish period." [76]

The Italians were fortunate in escaping direct military involvement in the long-drawn-out struggle between the British and Muhammad Abdille Hassan. Fears that the Dervish movement would spread to the hinterland of the Benadir coast failed to materialize, and though there was some fighting between the Dervishes and the Italian-protected sultans of northern Somalia, the Italians were never called on to initiate large-scale military action. Thus while the British were faced with the devastation of much of their protectorate as a result of the constant wars between the Dervishes and their opponents, the Italians found themselves free to press forward with the pacification of their own very much larger sphere of influence.

In 1905, after more than a decade of chartered company administration on the Benadir coast, the Italian government at last decided to assume direct responsibility for the colony—a move largely prompted by the public attacks made on officials of the Benadir company who were accused of failing to take vigorous enough measures to abolish slavery and repress the slave trade. Some of the most powerful groups of Somali nomads living in the hinterland of the Benadir coast kept Bantu agriculturalists as slaves to provide them with grain for their own consumption and regarded any attack on the institution of slavery as a social revolution to be warded off by all possible means. The matter could be decided only by force of arms. Six years of vigorous campaigning (1908–14) were needed before the Italians could claim control of the greater part of southern Somalia. A practical system of indirect rule, based on the payment of subsidies to local chiefs, formed the basis of the new Italian administration. In economic terms the Italians had little to show for their new conquest. A young agronomist sent to report on the agricultural possibilities of the territory is said to have become so depressed after several years of unrewarding work that he committed suicide. High hopes of economic advancement soon evaporated in the dust and glare of an arid land.

Both the Italians and the British came to refer to their Somali territories as the "Cinderella" of their colonies. Of the three European powers with a stake in the Horn of Africa only the Fench could claim by 1920 to have gained any material profit. Their territory was by far the smallest, they made little attempt to interfere with the lives of its nomadic inhabitants, but they succeeded in creating in Djibouti one of the great new commercial centers of Northeast Africa.

▲▼ EGYPT. 1918 TO 1952

On November 13, 1918, two days after the signing of the Armistice that ended World War 1, a self-appointed delegation of Egyptian notables, led by Sa'ad Zaghlul and claiming to speak for the entire Egyptian people, presented themselves at the residence of the British high commissioner, Sir Reginald Wingate, demanded independence for Egypt, and requested permission to proceed to London to lay their case before the British government. It was the first move in a new era of Egyptian affairs.

Four years earlier no Egyptian politician would have dared contemplate making so direct a request to the alien rulers of his country. But the war had profoundly affected Anglo-Egyptian relations. Military necessity had made British rule harsher and less beneficient. Yet at the same time the British had encouraged other Arab peoples to revolt against their imperial masters, the Ottoman Turks. If the uncouth Bedouin of the desert were permitted to send representatives to the forthcoming peace conference, was it not absurd that sophisticated Egyptians who had contributed loyally to the Allied war effort, should be prevented from stating their case? By 1918, educated Egyptians, reading of President Wilson's Fourteen Points or following the course of events in Russia, could feel that a new spirit, sympathetic to their own deepest aspirations, was abroad in the world. Moreover, in Egypt itself nationalist sentiment, largely confined before 1914 to members of the bourgeoisie, was spreading to other sections of the population. As the main sufferers from wartime conscription and inflation, the peasantry and the urban proletariat had reason to curse the British more heartily than ever before. The combination of the two emotions—hope and resentment—transformed Egyptian nationalism into a truly nationwide movement.

The modest delegation of November, 1918, became the nucleus of the first mass party to be formed in Africa. For the next thirty years the Wafd—the new party took its name from the Arabic word for "delegation"—was to be a major force in Egyptian politics. At first Sa'ad Zaghlul seemed an unlikely person to lead the new movement. Now in his early sixties, he had first made a name for himself as a reforming judge. In the early 1900's he worked closely with Muhammad Abduh and with Lord Cromer. Indeed, Cromer publicly praised him as one of the ablest Egyptians of his generation and appointed him minister of education. Zaghlul proved himself an able and forceful administrator, but in 1913 he found it impossible to continue working so closely with the British and resigned from his ministry. Shortly afterward he was elected to the newly created legislative assembly and in the legislature's one brief session in 1914 established himself as leader of the opposition. Politics suited him, for he was by temperament both a man of action and a man of the people—"in some ways," a British diplomat wrote of him, "the first really representative Egyptian and racy of the soil. Whether he thunders like a minor prophet or chaffs in dialect, he speaks a language every Egyptian understands." [77]

In November, 1918, the British government was understandably too preoccupied with other matters to devote serious attention to the Egyptian problem. A few weeks later Zaghlul and his followers began organizing mass demonstrations in support of their demand for independence, a move promptly countered by the British who arrested the leading nationalists and deported them to Malta. Zaghlul's arrest in March, 1919, sparked off yet more violent protests. "In every center disorderly crowds gathered, terrorizing the executive and demonstrating when and where they pleased: in the country the fellahin gave themselves up to the lust of destruction and murder. It was," wrote one British observer, "the slaking of indiscriminate passion. Anarchy prevailed in some places, self-appointed committees replaced government in others." [78] The British still possessed sufficient troops in the area to enable them to restore law and order fairly swiftly, but they could no longer count on the support of any influential group of Egyptians. Even the civil servants whom they had trained went out on strike against them, while the ministers, drawn mostly from the conservative ranks of the Turco-Circassian aristocracy, tendered their resignations to avoid becoming too far out of touch with popular feeling. Egypt, it was clear, would never be the same again.

A new high commissioner, General Allenby, the victorious commander in the Palestine campaign against the Turks, was given the task of dealing with the situation; Zaghlul was released and allowed to go to Paris to lay Egypt's case before the peace conference; and a high-powered mission led by Lord Milner, one of the most experienced of imperial statesmen, was sent out to make recommendations on future relations between the two countries. There followed two and a half years of inconclusive argument, terminated by a unilateral declaration made by the British government in February, 1922. The declaration formally put an end to the protectorate and proclaimed Egypt to be a sovereign independent state but reserved four vital matters—the security of imperial communications, the defense of Egypt, the protection of foreigners, and the Sudan—for further discussion. No one could have foreseen that discussion on some of these matters would drag on with mounting acrimony for more than thirty years.

So long as British troops remained on Egyptian soil, relations with Britain provided the most obsessive theme in Egyptian public life. But for the first time in centuries Egyptian politics was not completely dominated by the presence of an alien ruling class. The constitution promulgated in 1923 established a parliamentary form of government and so gave many Egyptians a chance to participate in national politics in a manner quite without precedent in the country's long history of autocratic rule. The power struggle between rival groups—especially between the Wafd and the Palace—represents a second major theme in the political history of the thirty years that lead up to the revolution of 1952. Two other themes must also be noted, both of which became of importance only in the 1940's: the gradual involvement of Egypt in the affairs of other Arab lands and the growing demand for social reform. And all these political movements must be set in the context of a steadily accelerating process of change in the country's social and economic life.

In the first half of the twentieth century Egyptian society conformed more closely to that of many European states than to the much less richly diversified society to be found in other African countries. Its structure was clearly pyramidal, with the king—first in the person of Ismail's youngest son, Fuad (1917–36), then of Fuad's son, Faruq (1936–52)—standing undisputedly at the apex. Brought up as descendants of Muhammad Ali to regard autocracy as the proper form of government for Egypt, invested by the constitution with powers considerably more extensive than those normally accorded to constitutional monarchs, possessed of immense wealth derived partly from an overgenerous civil list, partly from the ownership of vast estates, and thus enabled to dispense a wide range of patronage, both Fuad and Faruq proved to be shrewd, highly self-interested political manipulators who made of the "Palace" a force of the first importance in Egyptian political life.

Of the political parties participating in parliamentary activities the Wafd was by far the largest. Under the leadership first of Zaghlul (d. 1927), then of Nahas Pasha, the Wafd retained throughout the 1920's and 1930's the character of a truly national party, its militant tactics and mass support marking it off sharply from the small, "moderate" parties such as the Liberal Constitutionalists, most of whose members were drawn from the wealthier ranks of society. Finally, the Egyptian parliament always contained a powerful caucus of "king's friends," some of whom might describe themselves as independents, while others were former Liberals or dissident members of the Wafd.

In the 1930's, with the Wafd showing signs of losing its old fire, other more radical groups began to appear outside the formal parliamentary arena. Of these by far the most widely supported was the Muslim Brotherhood founded in 1928 as a religious association by Hassan al-Banna, a primary schoolteacher gifted with rare powers of eloquence and inspirational leadership. As a student in Cairo in the 1920's Hassan al-Banna had been deeply shocked by the corrupting influence of the West. "I saw," he wrote later, "that the social life of the beloved Egyptian nation was oscillating between her dear and precious Islamism . . . and this severe Western invasion which is armed and equipped with all the destructive and degenerative influences of money, wealth, prestige, ostentation, material enjoyment, power, and means of propaganda." [79] Totally rejecting the attempts being made by other

Muslim thinkers to reconcile Islam with modern scientific thought, the Muslim Brotherhood dreamed of recreating a purely Islamic polity governed according to the strict rules of the Shari'a. By the late 1940's the Brotherhood was reckoned to have as many as 2 million members, while its strong Pan-Islamic ideals had gained it supporters in other Arab lands. Another movement inspired by the same mood of Muslim revivalism but more narrowly nationalistic in its aims was Young Egypt, founded by a lawyer, Ahmad Husayn, in 1933. Obviously influenced by contemporary Fascist techniques of political action—the core of the movement lay in its paramilitary youth organization, the Greenshirts—Young Egypt preached a martial and intensely xenophobic form of nationalism. Dynamic, idealistic, highly simplistic in their political concepts, the Muslim Brotherhood and Young Egypt were movements well calculated to appeal to the young and to the socially underprivileged. Far more effectively than the aging politicians of the Wafd, the organizers of these extraparliamentary associations brought a measure of political consciousness to a new generation of Egyptians.

Beside all these groups must be placed the British. After 1922 the number of British personnel in the higher ranks of the civil service rapidly declined, but the army still remained, a force never less than 10,000 strong, as an aggravating reminder of the British presence—and the British Residency in Cairo was still a center of power, influence, and intrigue. In the years immediately after 1922 the British were quite prepared to intervene directly and forcefully in Egyptian affairs. When Sir Lee Stack, governor-general of the Sudan, was murdered in the streets of Cairo in 1924, Allenby presented Zaghlul, who had become prime minister for the first time some months previously, with so stiff an ultimatum that the nationalist leader had no alternative but to resign. Three years later when there was a likelihood of Zaghlul returning to power, Lord Lloyd, Allenby's successor, made it clear to the Wafd that Zaghlul would not be acceptable to the British and used the arrival of a British battleship at Alexandria to emphasize his words. But by the late 1920's Lloyd's inflexible imperialism could be seen as presenting far too crude an approach to the situation in Egypt. In 1929 the British Labour government dismissed the anachronistic proconsul and set about trying to reach an agreement over the four matters left unsettled by the 1922 declaration, only to find negotiations breaking down over the Sudan, a subject which aroused much bitter feeling in Egypt on account of the expulsion of Egyptian military personnel after the murder of Sir Lee Stack in 1924.

Six years later Mussolini's invasion of Ethiopia created an entirely new situation in the Eastern Mediterranean. Both sides were now more prepared to compromise, the British to ensure their hold on the Suez Canal, the Egyptians to gain a measure of protection against possible Italian aggression. The Anglo-Egyptian treaty of 1936 substituted a formal military alliance for the unilateral British occupation and allowed the British to station troops in the canal zone. The treaty also led to the abolition of the Capitulations, through whose provisions foreigners had long been able to enjoy a privileged status in Egypt. "For the first time since the age of the Pharaohs, Egyptian nationality ceased to be a badge of inferiority; and Egyptians, instead of courting foreigners, began to be courted by them." [80] With Britain acting as sponsor, Egypt was accepted as a member of the League of Nations. At last the country appeared to have achieved real independence.

But with the coming of World War II Egyptians were once again forced to recognize the aggravating and in many ways deeply humiliating nature of their position. Even more drastically than in World War I their country was transformed into a massive military base for an alien power. And though Egypt remained officially neutral until the last months of the war, much fighting took place on Egyptian soil. Worst of all, the war brought with it a revival of high-handed British intervention in the country's internal affairs. One incident achieved particular notoriety. In February, 1942, at a moment of acute military crisis, the British threatened to depose Faruq if he did not immediately replace ministers suspected of pro-German sympathies with ministers drawn from the Wafd. To the British the affair was a relatively trivial incident, perfectly justified by the brutal necessity of war. But for many Egyptians the British action had a profound political significance: the young king who had yielded so cravenly lost much of his popularity; the Wafd was discredited for profiting so shamelessly from British intervention; and the British were revealed as unregenerate imperialists. "Until now," a young army lieutenant, Gamal Abdul Nasser, wrote at this time, "the officers only talked of how to enjoy themselves; now they are speaking of sacrificing their lives for their honour." [81]

The years between 1945 and 1952 witnessed a steady worsening in Anglo-Egyptian relations as the two sides failed to reach agreement over a new treaty relationship. In 1947 negotiations broke down not over the position of British troops in Egypt—the British were prepared to evacuate their garrison by 1949—but over the status of the Sudan. Nationalist sentiment, more vociferously expressed than ever before, took as its slogan "the unity of the Nile Valley" and demanded the recognition of Egyptian sovereignty over the Sudan—a claim the British, mindful of Sudanese aspirations for self-government, were not prepared to accept. In October, 1951, the Egyptian government, feeling itself under heavy pressure from extremist groups, announced the unilateral abrogation of the 1936 treaty and of the 1899 condominium agreement. Immediately the extremists, with the Muslim Brotherhood in the van, launched a guerrilla war against the British troops stationed in the canal zone. In January, 1952, British countermeasures provoked an appalling outburst of mob violence in the heart of Cairo, when gangs of incendiaries burned down many buildings—bars, cinemas, and restaurants along with Shepherd's Hotel and the British Turf Club—that could be regarded as symbols of the Western presence. Deeply alarmed by the revolutionary implications of mass action against the British, the old-style politicians decided to return to the safer methods of diplomatic negotiation. Before they could reach a settlement, they were swept from power by the July revolution.

Leaving aside the friendships of individuals, there is something peculiarly sad and sterile about Anglo-Egyptian relations in the years after 1922. Contemptuous irritation on the one side, and fanatical xenophobia on the other—generalized attitudes such as these make a singularly unattractive pair of opposites. Apart from the protection afforded by the British against a possible German or Italian occupation, it is difficult to see what the Egyptians gained from their association with the British during these years. On the other hand, the constant and perfectly natural obsession over the British presence distracted attention from the increasingly serious internal problems facing the country. It might also be suggested that bad relations with Britain served to discredit a form of government based in part on a British model. But the failure of Egypt's parliamentary regime had much deeper causes.

The constitution of 1923 introduced a form of political organization for which there was no precedent in Egyptian history. The successful operation of a system of parliamentary government depends in large part on the existence of a set of attitudes and conventions of a kind that could never have developed under the autocratic regimes of the past. When Zaghlul came to power in 1924 and immediately set about muzzling his parliamentary opponents and replacing critical civil servants with his own nominees, his actions horrified British observers brought up to regard the "Westminster model" as the *summum bonum* of political organization, but his actions would not have appeared in the least surprising to a Mamluk pasha of the old school. When Faud or Faruq and their supporters rigged elections and found other means of perverting the constitution, they could argue that autocracy was Egypt's traditional form of government and that any moves designed to rid the country of popularly elected Wafdist politicians notorious for their corruption and their inefficiency were justified. When the Muslim

Brotherhood launched a terrorist campaign against established authority, its members could assert that they were using the only means open
to them to transform a completely discredited regime; moreover, Islamic history provided in the example of such sects as the tenth-century
Ismailis, the founders of Egypt's Fatimid dynasty, respectable precedents for revolutionary extremism. By their actions and their attitudes
all three groups—the Wafd, the Palace, and the Brotherhood—
demonstrated that Egypt's constitutional setup was a sham. Yet not one
of the three was capable of transforming the situation. The Wafd was
weakened by internal divisions and tarnished by the corruption of so
many of its members. Fuad could count on too little public support and
Faruq, immensely popular at the start of his reign, ended up as a "por-
nographically obsessed buffoon," [82] utterly discredited in the eyes of his
people. As for the Muslim Brotherhood, it became the victim of its own
methods; its terrorist activities begun in 1945 provided the government
with the justification for violent countermeasures.

During the years of British hegemony Egypt was in no position to exercise any political influence on neighboring territories, though the
country's intellectual primacy in the Arab world, achieved partly
through the development of a vigorous press and partly through the
work of a number of outstanding men of letters, carried with it a moral
prestige that provided an invaluable foundation for later expansion.
Popular awareness of the problems of other Arab lands dated from the
mid-1930's when the Palestine Arabs launched their revolt against the
British mandate in protest against the increasing immigration of European Jews. But it was the Muslim Brotherhood not the Wafd or the Palace who showed most sympathy for the Arab cause. By the middle of
World War II the British government had come to regard the movement
for Arab unity as a desirable development, likely to bring a measure of
stability to the uncertain politics of the Middle East. Thus encouraged,
the Wafd which was then in power took the lead in summoning a conference to discuss the establishment of an organization of Arab states.
This new body, the Arab League, was formally founded in 1945.

Opposition to Zionist ambitions in Palestine was the one point on
which all the Arab rulers and governments were agreed. In May, 1948,
the British withdrew from Palestine, the Palestinian Jews immediately
proclaimed their new state of Israel, and the leaders of the Arab
League found themselves forced to transform into action their grandiose
declarations of support for the Palestinian Arabs. In the fighting that
followed the Egyptian army suffered an unexpected and deeply humiliating defeat. Among the few Egyptian units which distinguished themselves were those formed by volunteers drawn from the Muslim Broth-

erhood. With its prestige thus enhanced and its own paramilitary organization strengthened by the arms obtained during the war with Israel the Brotherhood seemed well-set to achieve its revolutionary ambition. Boldly the government decided to outlaw the Brotherhood. In January, 1949, hundreds of the Brotherhood were arrested and imprisoned, while the movement's "Supreme Guide," Hassan al-Banna, died at the hands of an assassin, widely rumored to have been a member of the Palace's counterterrorist organization.

Social distress added a deeper dimension to Egypt's political malaise. The war years had brought great hardship to the majority of Egyptians. Food was short and in 1943–44 part of the country was ravaged by a terrible malaria epidemic which is reckoned to have caused 200,000 deaths. In 1945 the misery of the urban masses was increased still further by a drastic rise in unemployment following the closing of many British military establishments. Before the war there had been little talk of social reform, and organized labor was too weak to make its influence felt. But the war made possible the rapid growth of Egyptian industry, accompanied by a proportionate increase in the power of labor unions. Egyptians in touch with the main currents of Western thought, whether liberal-socialist or Marxist, began to talk openly of the need for greater social justice—a need no less clearly felt by those who, with the Muslim Brotherhood, found an ideal model in the egalitarian structure of primitive Muslim society. "Democracy," an Egyptian novelist, Tawfiq al-Hakim, wrote bitterly in 1938, "is a group of hungry, bare-footed men paying a monthly salary of forty pounds to another group [their parliamentary representatives] composed of wealthy men," a group made up of "a few hundred people who monopolize all the good, while leaving millions in the throes of nakedness and hunger." [83] After 1938 the gap between rich and poor visibly widened, thus making the truth of Tawfiq al-Hakim's words all the more glaringly apparent.

To present the development of Egypt in the 1930's and 1940's in terms of a society moving ineluctably through its own contradictions toward political revolution would be to convey far too crude an impression of a period of immensely complex change. For all the country's political tribulations, there were many positive achievements to be recorded: the emergence and rapid development of Egyptian-owned industry; the expansion of education; the erosion of rural isolation; the growing sophistication of the elite. Statistics, with which Egypt is much better supplied than most African countries, convey some aspects of these changes. The production of mechanically woven cotton cloth increased from 9 million square yards in 1917 to 20 million in 1931; from 159 million in 1939 to more than 250 million by 1950. Output of electricity was raised from 288 million kilowatt hours in 1938 to 978 million in 1952. The school population stood at 1,900,000 in 1951 compared with 942,000 in 1932 and 324,000 in 1913. There were 4,000 buses on the roads in 1938, 20,000 in 1952; the circulation of daily papers doubled in the same period; the number of wireless sets greatly increased. As for the intellectual quality of its elite, by the early 1950's Egypt was beginning to produce "a body of first-class natural and social scientists, engineers, and economists in addition to the more traditional supply of lawyers and historians." [84] Western observers, glibly applying the standards of their own more fortunate societies, could easily find much to criticize in many aspects of the Egyptian achievement. Yet when the Egypt of 1950 is compared either with other contemporary African countries or with its own state only fifty years earlier, the contrast is astonishing. Even the villages of the Nile Valley, often regarded as the most tenaciously conservative of all human communities, began to respond to the new currents, as some of their young men, stimulated by the experience of a wider world started to question the hitherto unchallenged domination of that "sinister trio"—poverty, ignorance, and disease.

▲▼ NATIONALISM AND COLONIALISM IN THE
SUDAN: 1919 TO 1953

No Muslim people can ever accept with complete equanimity domination by rulers of a different faith. Whatever the material advantages of the Anglo-Egyptian condominium, Sudanese Muslims were bound to question the assumptions on which the alien regime was based. Close contact with Egypt was a powerful stimulant in arousing a critical attitude toward British hegemony. British officials working in the Sudan often appeared arrogant and aloof: Egyptian teachers, civil servants, and army officers, on the other hand, spoke the same language and in most cases professed the same religion as their Sudanese colleagues and subordinates. After the Egyptian revolution of 1919 the Sudanese were better placed than any other people in sub-Saharan Africa to familiarize themselves with the concepts of revolutionary nationalism. But close association with Egypt also presented awkward problems for Sudanese nationalists. Egyptian politicians of the 1920's stood in the vanguard of the struggle against imperialism, but Egypt itself had recently been an imperial power in the Sudan. Was it really worth rebelling against the British, Sudanese of an older generation asked themselves, if the price to be paid was renewed subjection to Egypt?

Before the emergence of the first modernist political groupings in the 1920's, political sentiment in the Sudan found expression in the activities of the various Muslim fraternities (*tariqa*). Of these fraternities the one formed by the Mahdists (known also as the Ansar ["companions"], the term applied by Muhammad Ahmad al-Mahdi to his original followers) was by far the most powerful. But in the first years of the condominium the Mahdists were regarded by the Anglo-Egyptian authorities as a serious security risk and found themselves subjected to many irksome restrictions. The eclipse of the Mahdists added greatly to the prestige and influence of the Khatmiyya, the most prominent of the rival fraternities. Members of the Khatmiyya were indeed exceptionally well placed to profit from the new situation. In the past they had been on friendly terms with the Turco-Egyptian authorities. To escape Mahdist persecution the head of the order, Sayyid Ali al-Mirghani, and many of his followers had sought refuge in Egypt and returned to the Sudan after the establishment of the condominium. The British were delighted to receive the wholehearted support of so distinguished and influential a Muslim leader as Sayyid Ali, and they expressed their appreciation by conferring on him in 1916 the honor of a British knighthood.

A few months after the outbreak of World War I the British found themselves faced with a new and extremely disquieting development: their new enemies, the Ottoman Turks, were engaging in virulent Pan-Islamic propaganda on a large scale. To strengthen their hold on the Sudan the British felt in need of support from another powerful group of Sudanese Muslims. Ironically enough no group was better placed or more inclined to offer the British the backing which they needed than their one-time enemies, the "fanatical" Mahdists. The Mahdists had sound historical reasons for loathing the Turks, and their leaders were glad of any opportunity to free themselves from the restrictions to which they had been subject for the last fifteen years. In regional terms their support nicely complemented that of the Khatmiyya, for while the older fraternity—the Khatmiyya had been founded early in the nineteenth century—drew most of its adherents from the riverine provinces, the Mahdists dominated Kordofan and Darfur. In 1919—a year in which the explosion of Egyptian nationalism made Sudanese loyalty all the more precious to the British—Sayyid Abd ar-Rahman al-Mahdi, leader of the Ansar and a posthumous son of the Mahdi, accompanied a delegation of Sudanese notables to London and presented King George V with his father's "sword of victory" as "a sure token of my fealty and submission to your Exalted Throne." [85] The coalition between the British and the Mahdists—for such in a political sense it may well be termed—was to endure for the duration of British hegemony in the Sudan.

Abd ar-Rahman al-Mahdi was a shrewd politician. With British goodwill he was able to secure a number of lucrative business contracts. His rapidly growing personal fortune provided the financial resources needed to sustain and promote his movement. The goal which he and his followers set themselves was expressed in the slogan "Sudan for the Sudanese"; the approach was to be—in the words of a contemporary Mahdist statement—"through loyalty and cooperation with the British Imperial Idea." [86] These tactics were also favored by members of the Khatmiyya. By this time, however, a new element had appeared on the Sudanese scene—a small, slowly expanding group of younger men, clerks, schoolteachers, and junior army officers for the most part, educated at the schools recently established by the British. Reading Egyptian newspapers, talking to Egyptian acquaintances, the members of this newly emerging elite became increasingly familiar with the concepts of modern Arab nationalism and increasingly critical of the cautious, collaborationist tactics of their country's religious leaders. To these "Young Sudanese" Egypt seemed the natural ally in the struggle against imperialism. Once the British had been driven from the valley of the Nile, it would be easy, so they argued, for Sudanese and Egyptians to work out a harmonious relationship between their respective countries.

In 1921 a crop of semisecret leagues and societies sprang up in the main towns of the Sudan providing the country with its first direct experience of modern nationalism. Three years later the nationalist movement clearly came out into the open when Ali Abd al-Latif, former army officer of Dinka origin, founded a militant organization, the White Flag League. With Egyptian encouragement nationalist agitation steadily mounted in the summer and autumn of 1924, and Khartoum was the scene of the most frequent demonstrations. In November Sir Lee Stack, Wingate's successor as governor-general, was assassinated in Cairo. Immediately the Egyptian government was presented with a British ultimatum, demanding the withdrawal of all Egyptian troops from the Sudan. As soon as the news reached Khartoum, a Sudanese battalion stationed in the city mutinied, its soldiers barricading themselves in the military hospital where they became engaged in a pitched battle with a battalion of British troops. To the disgust of the Sudanese, Egyptian detachments stationed nearby failed to come to their aid. The mutineers fought on to the last man; the Egyptians, their reputation gravely tarnished in Sudanese eyes, meekly allowed themselves to be placed on trains and sent back to their own country.

The events of 1924 were deeply disturbing to British administrators in the Sudan. The most ardent nationalists had been drawn not, as might have been expected a few years earlier, from the ranks of the

Mahdists but from their own protégés, the former students of Gordon College. If British hegemony was to be preserved—and on this point there was, in the mid-1920's, clearly no room for argument—then a firm new policy must be devised. The British promply set about eliminating the subversive influence of Egyptian nationalists by depriving many Egyptian teachers and officials of their posts and at the same time transforming Sudanese battalions of the Egyptian army into the Sudan Defense Force. British and Egyptian flags continued to fly side by side over government buildings, but the condominium was clearly a sham; the Sudan was in reality a British colony.

The withdrawal of so many Egyptian officials made it easier for the British to reshape their policy of provincial administration. Hitherto a hierarchy of officials—British governors and district commissioners, Egyptian or Sudanese *mamurs* or *submamurs*—had imposed a form of direct administration on the provinces into which the country had been divided. Between 1919 and 1924 Sudanese, mostly graduates of Gordon College, began to take over many of the posts previously held by Egyptians, but this vigorous policy of sudanization soon aroused doubts in the minds of British administrators. "It is our business," one provincial governor pointed out in 1920, "to strengthen the solid elements in the country, sheikhs, merchants, etc., before the irresponsible body of half-educated officials, students and town riff-raff takes control of the public mind." [87] After 1924 this view came to dominate official policy. The talk was now of "indirect rule," of "native administration," of "devolution."

"Indirect rule" had been developed into a theory of colonial administration by Lord Lugard, the most influential colonial administrator of his day, during his governorship of Northern Nigeria. But the emirates of the caliphate of Sokoto possessed an administrative structure almost unique in Africa and certainly without parallel in the Sudan where local communities had been violently disrupted during the revolutionary years of the Mahdia. In practice, therefore, the establishment of "native authorities" worked only for the benefit of a small group of local notables who soon developed into "a privileged salaried hierarchy." Within such a system, as one senior British administrator wrote in the 1940's, there could be "no seeds of progress," "no scope for educated or ambitious citizens." [88] But this was not the way things appeared to British administrators in the 1920's. Having developed a strong paternalistic style of government and established a cordial rapport with the nomads and the peasants of the rural areas, these deeply conscientious, somewhat narrow-minded officials saw it as their duty to protect and strengthen the position of the country's "natural rulers" against what one governor-general, Sir John Maffey, described as "the septic germs which will inevitably be passed on from the Khartoum of the future." [89]

This deliberate attempt to cordon off the provinces, to "parcel out the country," in Maffey's words, "into nicely balanced compartments" was carried furthest in the Southern Sudan. British administrators, working in areas where memories of slave raiding were still vivid, saw the peoples of the south as the victims of northern exploitation; in their eyes every Muslim trader from the north was to be regarded as an "undesirable immigrant battening on the villages, selling rubbishy goods at vast profit and introducing venereal disease." [90] These views were held even more strongly by the Christian missionaries of various denominations whom the government barred from working in the Muslim north but allowed to proselytize in the "pagan" south. In 1930 the authorities in Khartoum produced a precise definition of their "southern policy." To achieve the aim of building up "a series of self-contained racial or tribal units . . . based upon indigenous customs, traditional usage and belief," active steps were to be taken to purge the three southern provinces (Bahr al-Ghazal, Upper Nile, and Equatoria) of all forms of northern influence.[91] Northern officials were to be posted elsewhere and southerners educated to take their place; northern traders were to be discouraged from carrying on business; and English was to be developed to take the place of Arabic as a *lingua franca*. To such extremes was this policy carried in some areas that Greek shopkeepers were forbidden by local district commissioners to sell Arab dress.

It is easy, given the advantage of hindsight, to recognize the absurdity of a policy that attempted to set the country in an artificial mold. But colonial administrators in the 1920's could still feel that they were living in an age in which time was on their side. Behind them lay a record of unquestioned achievement, all power was firmly in their hands, and the country was enjoying a peace such as it had never known before— indeed no more than a single battalion of British troops was needed to provide the sanction of force for the government of a territory nearly a million square miles in extent. As for the most vociferous opponents of colonial rule, the urban nationalists could be dismissed as a bunch of wild young men utterly ignorant of the problems of government. In the Sudan, as in other parts of Africa, British administrators of this period could be described as "quietly ambling along, very just, very humane, very patient," [92] the dispensers of "a vague, purposeless benevolence." [93]

Yet these years of administrative "reaction" and educational "stagnation," as they have been described by later historians, present a number of substantial achievements. The railway network was extended; a school of medicine, the first of its kind in northern tropical Africa, was founded; and work started on the Gezira scheme, the most successful large-scale agricultural project ever implemented by a colonial government in tropical Africa. The construction of a dam at Sennar on the White Nile, completed in 1925, made possible the irrigation of a steadily increasing acreage on which long-staple cotton was grown as the main crop. The tenants of the scheme, carefully selected and superintended, provided with expert technical advice, and rewarded with a substantial share of the profits, soon developed into one of the most prosperous agricultural communities in all Africa.

The prosperity of the late 1920's was cut short by the great depression. Government revenue which had risen from £E 4.3 million in 1924 to £E 7 million in 1929 fell steadily to £E 3.6 million in 1933. For the first time many Sudanese were made vividly aware of the ties that bound their economy, now largely dependent on the production of cotton, to the world market. Economies introduced by a deeply worried government—cuts in salaries and the dismissal of staff—caused bitter resentment among educated Sudanese and in 1931 led to the first overt demonstration of discontent since the revolt of 1924, a well-organized strike by Gordon College students. Meanwhile, a new generation of British administrators and education officers were beginning to look critically at the principles which directed government action. "Education alone," wrote one British reformer, "can cure the crudities of many kinds that not only make the people unhappy, but hinder the government, and dirty its name—indifferent agriculture, fanatical Mahdism, disease-carrying dirt, female circumcision, and all the cruelty and barbarity of a backward people. . . . The Sudan native can neither administer nor be peacefully administered unless he progresses." [94] In the context of its time and place this was a revolutionary doctrine, but it commanded increasing assent. In this new and more liberal atmosphere educated Sudanese found themselves back in the position of official favor from which they had been thrust in 1924. There was talk now of promoting Sudanese to more senior posts in the administration; Bakht er Ruda, a teacher training college destined (through the willingness of its staff to experiment with new ideas) to become one of the most influential institutions of its kind in Africa, was founded in 1933; and Gordon College, described in the 1920's by one of the Arab members of its staff, as "a military, not a human institution," [95] was transformed into a liberal secondary school.

With the conclusion of the Anglo-Egyptian treaty of 1936 Egyptian soldiers and officials were allowed to return to the Sudan. They brought with them the breath, so invigorating in the stuffy atmosphere of colonial society, of new political ideas. Two years later a group of Sudanese intellectuals, led by Ismail al-Azhari, a mathematics teacher at Gordon College, founded the Graduates' Congress. With membership confined to Sudanese who had "graduated" from intermediate or secondary schools, the new association devoted most of its energies to educational reform by sponsoring the establishment of private intermediate schools to meet the growing demand for postelementary education in the towns. But al-Azhari and his supporters were deeply aware of the political implications of their activities. In calling their association a "congress" they deliberately implied some comparison with the great Indian movement of political protest; they regarded their members as forming "the only educated element" [96] in the country; and they developed a form of organization that could rapidly be transformed into an "embryonic Sudanese parliament." [97]

In April, 1942, the Graduates' Congress took its first overt political action when it produced a memorandum demanding that the British and Egyptian governments should formally recognize the right of the Sudanese to self-determination as soon as the war was over. The condominium government could certainly not accept the claim of a self-appointed body to be representative of the Sudanese people. The memorandum was returned with a stiff rebuke to its authors. But British officials in Khartoum were aware that the time had come for some measure of political reform. Hitherto the Sudan had been ruled autocratically with a governor-general's council composed of officials but no form of Sudanese representation at the center. In 1944 a new consultative body was established: an advisory council for the Northern Sudan with eighteen elected and ten nominated Sudanese members.

By this time the traditional rivalry between the Ansar and the Khatmiyya had made its appearance in the ranks of the Graduates' Congress. Arguments over the tactics to be followed after the rebuff of 1942 made the rift still wider. In 1943 Ismail al-Azhari formed his own political party, *Ashiqqa* ("blood brothers"), gained the patronage of Sayyid Ali al-Mirghani, the leader of the Khatmiyya, put forward a policy of union with Egypt, and made himself, by his militant and uncompromising attitude, the hero of the students and of the urban population. His opponents retaliated by forming a rival party, *Umma* ("nation") with the support of Sayyid Abd ar-Rahman al-Mahdi, summed up their political ideas in the old Mahdist slogan "Sudan for the Sudanese," and continued the old Mahdist policy of collaboration with the British.

The immediate postwar years represent a period of exceptionally rapid change for parts of the Sudan. With cotton commanding high prices on the world market, the economy boomed. Government revenue, which had barely exceeded £E 5 million in the late 1930's, rose to £E 8 million in 1946 and £E 19 million in 1949. In these years Khartoum was transformed from an "old African-colonial cantonment" dominated by British officials into a new city "modern and cosmopolitan-Mediterranean in appearance." [98] The metamorphosis of the capital was symbolic of the flood of new ideas powerfully affecting the lives of people in the main urban areas. In 1944 a group of Sudanese students in Cairo formed the Sudan's first Communist party. Railway workers at Atbara laid the foundations of one of the most vigorous trades union movements in tropical Africa. And Gordon College was made the nucleus for a new university.

Political excitement mounted steadily as the religious fraternities conveyed the ideas of the intelligentsia to the mass of the population. But the country lacked an effective arena for political debate. The advisory council possessed no legislative powers, its members were drawn from the more conservative sections of Sudanese society, and it contained no provision for representatives from the three southern provinces. Clearly the time had come for a measure of constitutional reform which would bring the Sudanese nearer to their goal of self-determination. But the position was complicated by the need of the two codomini to agree on the next stage of advance. By this time most Egyptian politicians had come to regard "the unity of the Nile Valley" as an irrevocable principle of Egyptian policy. *Ashiqqa* party members accepted the Egyptian claim, but the *Umma* interpreted it as a bid for mastery over the destinies of the Sudan and organized violent demonstrations of protest. In 1947 the Egyptian government, finding that it was impossible to reach agreement with the British, brought the issue of the Sudan before the Security Council of the United Nations—but to no avail.

The accelerated pace of political development forced the British authorities in Khartoum to revise their "southern policy." As late as 1945 there had been some discussion of the possibility of linking the southern provinces with Uganda. Little more than a year later it was evident that the time for cordoning off or separating the south from the north was past. In an official policy statement issued in December, 1946, the peoples of the south were described as "inextricably bound" by "geography and economics" to the northern Sudan; by "educational and economic development" they were to be "equipped to stand up for themselves . . . as socially and economically the equals of their partners of the Northern Sudan in the Sudan of the future." [99] If the government's old "southern policy" could be described as "negative and sterile," [100] its new approach might be termed generous but chimerical. In the south income per head was reckoned to be about half that of the average figure for the north; in education the disparity was even more glaring. Yet, if it was an illusion to assume that the newfound panacea of development could redress the balance, it is difficult to see what other policy the government could have followed.

In 1948 the Sudan's advisory council was replaced by a legislative assembly with seventy-five directly or indirectly elected members, including thirteen from the south. At the same time the governor-general's council was transformed into an executive council half of whose members were Sudanese. The *Ashiqqa* and other pro-Egyptian groups boycotted the elections while the Egyptian government continued to insist on its rights over the Sudan. This inflexible policy reached its logical conclusion in October, 1951, when the Egyptian parliament formally abrogated the condominium agreement of 1899 and proclaimed Faruq "King of Egypt and the Sudan." Meanwhile in the Sudan members of the *Umma,* the dominant group in the legislative assembly, were pressing the British for a rapid advance toward self-government. In the late 1940's the British had reckoned that the Sudan was not likely to achieve independence before 1966. The pressure of Sudanese nationalists was already making this date appear unrealistic when the situation was transformed by the Egyptian revolution of July, 1952. The new Egyptian government, led by General Neguib, was prepared to accept the Sudanese right to self-determination. An Anglo-Egyptian agreement concluded in February, 1953, prepared the way for a rapid transfer of power.

The British withdrawal from the Sudan marked the beginning of the decolonization of tropical Africa. As they departed the administrators of the Sudan Political Service could feel that they were leaving behind them a record of fine achievement. "What a magnificent job the British did!" wrote John Gunther, the noted American journalist, when he visited the Sudan in 1953. "For fifty years their administration gave the Sudan education, justice, public order, and almost complete political tranquillity, even during periods of most effervescent crisis . . . all this in a territory that could easily have exploded into chaos at any moment, if administration had ever been arbitrary, selfish or unwise." [101] A fortunate combination of circumstances made this achievement possible. In the years between 1820 and 1880 the Turco-Egyptian authorities had provided a large part of the Sudan with an administrative structure of a kind not to be found elsewhere in tropical Africa. Thus, the British came not as complete innovators but as the inheritors of an older, though still comparatively recent, tradition of bureaucratic government. Moreover, their close association with Egypt made them familiar with the practice of leaving a wide range of responsible posts in the hands of non-British personnel. By 1953 "localization"—the appointment of local people to senior posts in the civil service—had proceeded very much further in the Sudan than in any other colonial territory in Africa. In framing local policy British administrators in the Sudan enjoyed great freedom of action. They were subjected to a minimum of supervision from Whitehall and did not have to contend with the type of pressure exerted in other African territories by white settlers and businessmen. Yet, profiting from their long annual leaves in Europe, they never became intellectually isolated and so were quick to respond to new ideas and situations. Thus, there developed in the last stage of the condominium a relationship between the British and the Sudanese nicely characterized by one outside observer, himself one of the staunchest British critics of colonial rule, as "unusually genial and tolerant." [102]

▲▼ ETHIOPIA: 1908 TO 1945

In 1908 the great emperor Menelik was left almost totally paralyzed by a stroke. He lingered on, a broken man, until 1913, his last years providing a melancholy epilogue to a remarkable reign. From 1908 until the proclamation in 1930 of Menelik's distant kinsman, Tafari, as Emperor Haile Selassie, the politics of Ethiopia were dominated by a ferocious struggle for power among a number of contestants. To the historian of medieval Europe many of the details of this struggle must have a familiar ring: set in the context of the twentieth-century world how strange, by contrast, these labyrinthine intrigues appear. Personality and territorial basis are more important than ideology; family connections, marriage alliances, and the ties of clientship take the place of party groupings; and the strength of each of the contestants is usually best measured by the number of rifles in the hands of his followers. Yet it is worth trying to trace briefly the complex course of Ethiopian politics in the 1910's and 1920's—not only as an essential prelude to the contemporary Ethiopian scene. The interest is more general: here one is given an illuminating indication of the stuff of politics in other African monarchies of an earlier and therefore less-documented age.

Of the leading figures of these two decades four held or were destined to hold an imperial title: Menelik's consort, Empress Taitu who died in 1918, his daughter Zauditu, his grandson Iyasu, and his kinsman, Tafari. Empress Taitu was a formidable old lady whose eight marriages vividly illustrate the vicissitudes experienced by many members of the Ethiopian aristocracy. Her first husband, one of Emperor Theodore's military commanders, died of poison. Her third rebelled at her instigation against Emperor John: the revolt failed and Taitu was forced to attach herself to a common soldier. Later she moved to Shoa—new

ground for one whose family connections were all with the northern nobility. Here she married a noncommissioned officer, followed this marriage by two progressively more advantageous unions, and ended up as
Menelik's third wife in 1883. The empress took a vigorous part in the
counsels of state and was even known to have ridden into battle at the
head of a regiment of cavalry. She bore Menelik no children, but one of
her nephews, Ras Gugsa, was married to her stepdaughter Zauditu. If
she could not obtain power for herself, then she was prepared to support Zauditu's claim. Had the old empress been able to have her way,
the seat of power might well have been transferred from Addis Ababa
to the northern town of Gondar, Ethiopia's capital in the seventeenth
and eighteenth centuries.

Iyasu, Menelik's grandson, was a youth of sixteen in 1913. His
mother, like Zauditu, had been an offspring of one of Menelik's earlier
marriages, and his father, Ras Mikael, was a Galla who had been forced
by Emperor John to renounce Islam and embrace Christianity. By 1913
Mikael was the most powerful man in Ethiopia, with numerous supporters in Tigre and in his own province of Wallo and an army fifty thousand strong, well-equipped with rifles smuggled in from French Somaliland. As for Tafari, the future Haile Selassie, his claim to the imperial
succession was more remote than those of his immediate rivals. He was
a member of the royal family of Shoa, and his father, Ras Makonnen, had
been Menelik's most trusted adviser. But Makonnen had died in 1906
and though the young Tafari had been brought up in the imperial court
and had gained the affection of the old emperor, he was only twenty-
one when Menelik died and could count on few influential supporters.
He inherited, however, a valuable base in Harar of which his father had
been governor since the occupation of the sultanate by Shoan troops in
1887.

In 1907 Menelik, feeling that his powers were failing, appointed a
council of ministers drawn from members of the Shoan nobility. Two
years later he nominated Iyasu as his heir, a decision which Empress
Taitu schemed to have reversed. The empress was unsuccessful and
Iyasu succeeded his grandfather in 1913. The young emperor is one of
the strangest and most controversial figures in Ethiopian history. In
many accounts he appears as an utterly dissolute youth, coward, sadist,
and pervert. Viewed more dispassionately he can be seen as a leader of
some originality. All previous imperial regimes had been based on the
dominant position of the Christian Amhara, whether of Shoa or of the
northern provinces. Iyasu attempted to introduce a revolutionary change
by appealing to the partly islamized Galla and to other Muslim peoples
of the empire. By 1916 his behavior suggested that he was contemplat-

ing the utterly unprecedented step for an Ethiopian emperor of conversion to Islam. He was surrounded by Muslim confidants, had formed matrimonial alliances with many Muslim chiefs, was in close touch with the Somali resistance leader, Muhammad Abdille Hassan (the "Mad Mullah") and was on cordial terms with the Turkish and German representatives in his country.

In the conflict then raging not only in Europe but also in the Middle East and East Africa, Ethiopia was officially neutral. But to the representatives of Britain, France, and Italy Iyasu's extraordinary activities suggested the horrifying possibility of a jihad led by an apostate emperor supported by German and Turkish agents and capable of inflaming the entire Muslim population of Northeast Africa. Members of the Shoan "establishment"—and indeed all Christian Amhara—had infinitely greater cause for alarm. A Muslim emperor of Ethiopia—such a prospect threatened nothing less than the reversal of more than one thousand years of history, the undermining of the country's long-established social structure, and the dislocation of its religious life. In September, 1916, a group of Shoan noblemen, supported by church leaders, staged a coup d'état, declared Iyasu deposed, proclaimed Zauditu empress, and appointed Tafari regent and heir apparent. The coup was a bold one, for the conspirators had few troops at their disposal, while Mikael, the deposed emperor's formidable father, possessed the largest army in Ethiopia and Iyasu himself could count on many supporters among his Muslim subjects. But Mikael made the mistake of advancing on Addis Ababa without waiting for his son's reinforcements, and then allowed himself to be delayed by a ruse, thus giving the Shoan nobility more time to gather their forces. There followed a hard-fought battle ending in Mikael's defeat and capture. Iyasu remained at large until 1921 when he was caught and handed over to the most trustworthy of the northern *rases* ("provincial governors") to be kept in gilded captivity for more than a decade.

Neither the new empress nor the new regent possessed sufficient power to assert their hegemony over the troubled land. They were indeed intensely suspicious of one another, but Tafari was the stronger of the two. Zauditu's husband, Ras Gugsa, was a member of the northern nobility. Tafari secured his removal from the center of power by requiring Zauditu to divorce him. To avoid further matrimonial complications the empress was made to swear to remain celibate. But Tafari's own position was weakened by his lack of supporters among the Shoan nobility. During a brief spell as governor of Harar he had shown himself a liberal administrator whose serious attempt to increase the wealth of his province contrasted sharply with the extortionate rapacity practiced by provincial governors of the old school. To keep a check on this dangerous young man the nobles appointed Habta Giorgis, one of Menelik's generals, as minister of war. The old warrior was a fervent patriot and a passionate conservative who boasted that he had never set eyes on the train that now ran regularly from Djibouti to Addis Ababa and described airplanes as "childish toys, an affront to the Almighty or a devilish device by the foreigner to spy out the land." [103] Zauditu, Tafari, and Habta Giorgis formed a governing triumvirate in which the empress supported the war minister in his opposition to change.

Tafari could count on the advantage of youth, knew the importance of patience, and possessed to the full that combination of qualities—subtlety in intrigue, ruthlessness in applying force—needed to survive the fierce strain of Ethiopian politics. He revealed his ability by the swift and well-planned action with which, on Habta Giorgis's death in 1926, he took over the war minister's estates, together with all his soldiers and the government posts in his patronage. The next year Tafari dealt with the most recalcitrant of the provincial governors. The *ras* rejected the regent's first summons to present himself at the capital, then changed his mind and arrived with his private army of ten thousand men. When Tafari invited him to a feast at the imperial palace, the suspicious *ras* insisted on bringing with him a bodyguard six hundred strong. But while the feast was in progress, Tafari's agents set about bribing the governor's soldiers to desert and disperse. Within a few days the now defenseless *ras* found himself condemned to a monastery to atone for his sins. "Do not underestimate the power of Tafari," he is said to have remarked. "He creeps like a mouse but has jaws like a lion." [104]

In 1928 Tafari forced the empress to accord him the title of *negus* ("king") and to allow him complete control of public affairs. But he still had formidable enemies to contend with. Early in 1930 Ras Gugsa, Zauditu's former husband, raised the standard of revolt in the northern province of which he was governor, denounced Tafari as a secret Roman Catholic who was seeking to subvert the established church, and advanced on the capital with a substantial army. By this time, however, Tafari was able to count on the firm support of the ecclesiastical hierarchy. He possessed considerable armed forces of his own and had recently acquired a small air force consisting of four biplanes flown by French pilots. The use of this novel weapon—the planes dropped first leaflets, then small bombs—did much to lower the morale of the rebels. But a battle in the old style had still to be fought. It ended in total disaster for the rebels with Gugsa numbered among the slain. Two days after her former husband's death Empress Zauditu expired—allegedly of a broken heart. Six months later with a splendiferous ceremony attended by a wide range of foreign notables and covered by a battery of newspapermen Tafari celebrated his coronation as Emperor Haile Selassie I.

The emperor was now in a position to push forward his plans for modernization. His father, Makonnen, had made a number of visits to Europe in Menelik's reign, and he himself had been on an extensive European tour in 1924. Thus, his knowledge of the outside world was far wider than that of the vast majority of his subjects. But his greatest asset lay in the quality of his intellect. "Elegant, reflective, a lover of neatness, order, tenure," as one foreign observer described him, the young emperor clearly possessed "an immensely able mind" and an astonishingly detailed grasp of the work of government.[105] He knew that his country was backward and that this backwardness constituted a threat to its independence. "We need European progress," he told one European visitor, "only because we are surrounded by it." [106] At the same time he was able to equate the well-being of his country with his own personal and dynastic ambitions. By strengthening his own position as head of the central government, he would be able steadily to erode the power of his still formidable rivals, the great povincial *rases*.

Modernizing autocrats in "backward" states inevitably tend to concentrate their energies on a small range of interconnected objectives. Thus, the program pursued by Haile Selassie in Ethiopia in the early 1930's presents obvious parallels to that of Muhammad Ali and Ismail in Egypt, of Mulay Hassan in Morocco or even of Radama I, the early nineteenth-century ruler of the Malagasy kingdom of Merina. The establishment of an efficient standing army, partly trained by European instructors, came high on the list of the emperor's priorities. So, too, did the formation of a central bureaucracy, with the assistance of a small group of European advisers. Great stress was laid on education, new schools were founded, and students sent to Europe for higher studies. Concessions were granted to foreign companies willing to help develop the country's natural resources. And the capital was adorned with buildings and monuments designed to enhance the prestige of the dynasty.

The task of building an efficient centralized government was as formidable in twentieth-century Ethiopia as it had proved in late nineteenth-century Morocco. The greater provincial *rases*—with their vast estates, their substantial private armies, and their princely style of living —remained a constant threat to the imperial authority. In 1932 one of the most powerful of the *rases*, Hailu of Gojjam, contrived the escape of the former emperor Iyasu as the first move in a major conspiracy to unseat Haile Selassie. The attempt was nipped in the bud, Hailu was stripped of his possessions and sentenced to life imprisonment, and Iyasu was confined in a more secure jail in Harar province where he died in 1935 shortly after the Italian invasion. Iyasu's death—like that of so many members of the Ethiopian nobility—was clouded with the uncertainty of conflicting accounts.

For a generation Ethiopia had been an anomaly in Africa—the only indigenous state to have escaped European conquest. The maintenance of Ethiopian independence could not be ascribed solely to the shock of Adowa. In 1906, only ten years after the battle, Britain, France, and Italy, the three European nations most closely interested in the country, anticipating a period of anarchy after Menelik's death, signed a treaty formally recognizing Ethiopian independence but defining their own spheres of interest. The British, with their preoccupation over the Nile waters, staked out a claim to the country round Lake Tana, source of the Blue Nile; the French, to the strip of land needed for the railway between Djibouti and Addis Ababa; and the Italians, to a vast wedge of territory bounded by a line running west of Addis Ababa and designed to link their two colonies of Eritrea and Somalia. Should intervention ever become necessary, the three powers pledged themselves to act in harmony.

Of the three powers Italy showed the most vigorous interest in Ethiopia, but Italian governments found themselves beset by many internal difficulties and burdened with a long-drawn-out war in Libya. Consequently, Italy was in no position to pursue an active policy in Northeast Africa until the late 1920's. By this time Tafari had secured for his country membership of the League of Nations, a shrewd move that helped to break down Ethiopia's diplomatic isolation in a world still dominated by the great powers of Europe. Its value was shown in 1926 when Tafari protested to the League about a recent Anglo-Italian agreement. The British were anxious to build a barrage at Lake Tana, the Italians, a railway across Ethiopia linking Eritrea with Somalia. Under the terms of the agreement the two governments were to cooperate in putting pressure on Ethiopia to obtain the necessary concessions. "Throughout their history," Tafari declared in his note to the League, "the peoples of Abyssinia [Abyssinia is derived from the Arabic equivalent, Habash] have seldom met with foreigners who did not desire to possess themselves of Abyssinian territory." [107] With their plans so awkwardly exposed to international scrutiny, the British and Italian governments hastened to declare their innocence of any aggressive intent. Nothing more was heard of the projected concessions.

Italians with an interest in Ethiopia were by no means unanimous on the policy their government should follow. There was much to be said for cordial collaboration with Tafari: a stable Ethiopia would provide an agreeable field for Italian economic activity. It was in this spirit that an Italo-Ethiopian treaty of peace and amity was signed in 1928. But some influential officials in the colonial ministry in Rome and in the colonial administration of Eritrea preferred to play the more dangerous game of supporting Tafari's rivals among the nobility of northern Ethiopia. When nothing was done to stop their intrigues, the brief entente between the two countries collapsed. At the same time Mussolini, the dictator of Italy, began to show an increasing interest in a country to which, in the first ten years of his rule, he had devoted little attention.

The reasons for Mussolini's new-sprung interest in Ethiopia had nothing to do with Africa. By 1933 the Fascist leader was finding himself faced with the bankruptcy of all his policies, internal and external alike. In Europe his attempt to achieve a resounding diplomatic success through the formation of a four-power pact embracing Italy, Germany, France, and Britain had ended in fiasco. Meanwhile, his own country was suffering severely from the consequences of the great economic depression, and it was becoming increasingly obvious that Fascism could offer no effective solution to the problems of mounting unemployment and declining trade. In circumstances such as these some diversion was essential, especially for a party so wedded to the cult of action. With the conquest of Libya now complete, Ethiopia offered the only field open for a display of Italy's dynamic qualities. But in the summer of 1934 the Nazis launched their abortive coup in Austria—an incident in which Mussolini saw a warning of graver crises soon to come. Prompt action was now essential if Ethiopia was to be conquered before the storm broke over Europe.

In December, 1934, Ethiopian and Italian forces clashed briefly at Walwal, a group of wells in the Ogaden province recently occupied by the Italians but lying well within Ethiopian territory. The consequent dispute provided the prologue to the Ethiopian crisis, the first in that dismal series of major international incidents marking the rapid drift of Europe toward World War II. In Menelik's time it had been Ethiopian policy to deal with the European powers that threatened the country's independence by playing one against the other. In 1935 Haile Selassie followed the less tortuous policy of placing all his faith in the League of Nations. By referring the dispute with Italy over Walwal to the League and by stating the Ethiopian case with dignity and moderation Haile Selassie was able to gain "almost world-wide moral support." [108]

Effective action by the League depended on the willingness of France and Britain, its two most powerful members, to use forceful measures to deter a possible Italian attack on Ethiopia. But by 1935 both the British and the French governments were becoming increasingly preoccupied with the direct threat to their security presented by the growing power of Nazi Germany. In these circumstances Italy was to be regarded as a potential ally, while Ethiopia occupied a position of no strategic importance. Moreover, in the eyes of many influential Englishmen and Frenchmen the Ethiopians were "barbarians" who might well benefit from a dose of European "civilization."

Steadily in the spring and summer of 1935 the Italians built up their military forces in Eritrea and Somalia. Meanwhile, Mussolini and his propagandists worked on Italian public opinion with such skill that almost all sections, including some long-standing opponents of the Fascist regime, were caught up in the mood of martial exhilaration and eagerly looked forward to a "totalitarian" solution of the Ethiopian problem. Only the serious threat of vigorous military countermeasures on the part of Britain and France would have deterred Mussolini by this time—and this was a threat neither the British government nor the French government was prepared to make. The measures adopted finally after the entirely unprovoked Italian invasion of Ethiopia in October proved completely ineffective. The almost unanimous condemnation of Italy as an aggressor by the Assembly of the League of Nations and the imposition of limited sanctions assured Mussolini of an even greater measure of public support in his own country. The League's action was interpreted by many Italians as a crowning example of the hypocracy and meanness of those "sated imperialists," the British and the French, in denying to a young "proletarian" nation the opportunity to fulfill its legitimate colonial ambitions.

The Italian-Ethiopian war was, according to Mussolini, "a war waged and won in the very spirit of Fascism"; the armed conflict "which, according to the most optimistic calculations, was expected to last not less than six years, was over in seven months." [109] The last of the colonial campaigns of conquest was by far the swiftest. The Italians had taken the lessons of Adowa to heart. Their European troops, well armed and motorized, numbered 120,000, supported by 350 planes and reinforced by 100,000 native irregulars from Eritrea and Somalia. The Ethiopians, by contrast, had learned nothing. "Overweening bravery and superlative arrogance," as Haile Selassie himself once remarked, were their worst faults.[110] "A descendant of the Negus Yohannes makes war," one of the leading *rases* declared, "but cannot carry on guerilla warfare like a brigand chief." [111] So the Ethiopian commanders continued to deploy their men in vast masses and to fight a campaign of pitched battles. No tactics could have been more fatal when employed against an enemy possessing not only superior firepower on the ground but also complete mastery of that new element in African warfare, the air. "Italian air supremacy," wrote a British correspondent whose sympathies were clearly on the losing side, "made of the Ethiopians a rabble which could not think for itself. It demolished, in fearful explosions and vibrations of the solid earth, the aristocracy which was the cadre of their military organization." [112]

Ethiopia was the last African state to suffer the experience of European conquest. But in Ethiopia the means by which European hegemony was established were a good deal more violent than those employed in most other parts of Africa. In Tunis, in Morocco, and in many of the major polities of sub-Saharan Africa local rulers had been forced to sign treaties placing their countries under European protection; at the same time they had been able to preserve for themselves some semblance of their old authority. In Ethiopia, once an overwhelming Italian victory became inevitable, the emperor prudently decided to retreat into exile, leaving the Italians free to construct a political superstructure of their own devising but at the same time preserving intact, in the eyes of most of his subjects, his own legitimate claims to authority.

No sooner was the war officially over than the Italians set about redrawing the map of Northeast Africa to allow for the creation of a great new European dominion, *Africa Orientale Italiana*. Ethiopia ceased to exist as an administrative entity, being divided into the four provinces of Amhara, Shoa, Galla-Sidamo, and Harar, while the Ogaden was added to the province of Somalia. Never before, in all history, had so large a political unit ever been seen in this part of Africa. Men and money were poured into the recently conquered territory. By 1939 the Italian government had spent more than £100 million on Ethiopian development, brought sixty thousand Italians to work on construction projects, and built more than two thousand miles of first-class roads. "In her approach to the task of developing the resources of the country," wrote Lord Hailey, one of the foremost British authorities on colonial administration, "Italy has shown a comprehensive energy and a liberality in the provision of finance to which there is no parallel, nor indeed anything approaching a parallel, in the history of Colonial Africa." [113]

This remarkable achievement, of which the Ethiopians themselves have not been unappreciative, could not disguise the fact that the Italians were operating as conquerors in a hostile land. And so Ethiopia became a stage for that range of reactions—collaboration, resistance, reprisal—which so many other African countries had witnessed in the first years of colonial rule, and which many Europeans were shortly to become familiar with as the vicissitudes of World War II affected their own homelands. With some success the Italians sought Ethiopian supporters for their new order among the dissident *rases* of the north and the discontented non-Amhara peoples of other provinces. Ethiopians who collaborated with the Italians did so in pursuit of personal ends, seeking advantages for their own local dynasties and provinces. Thus, it was hardly surprising that the Italians' most notable supporter should have been the old warlord, Hailu of Gojjam, detained by Haile Selassie after the revolt of 1932. Other Ethiopians refused to admit military defeat, formed "patriot" groups, took to the hills, and began to wage a guerrilla war against the Italian forces. In February, 1937, the Italian viceroy, Marshal Graziani, was wounded in a bomb attack in Addis Ababa. Several thousand Ethiopians died in the violent reprisals that followed the incident, among them many of the small group of young men who had received a Western education.

Italian East Africa collapsed as swiftly as it had been formed. Within a year of Italy's entry into World War II Haile Selassie was back in his capital after British Commonwealth forces, moving into northern Eritrea from the Sudan and into Somalia from Kenya, had inflicted a series of crushing defeats on the vastly more numerous Italian armies. Seven years after the ending of World War II Ethiopia received the fruits of the Allied victory. For a decade the Italian colony of Eritrea had been subject to British military administration, while its fate was discussed by the great powers. Finally the matter was referred to the United Nations where it was agreed that Eritrea should become "an autonomous unit federated with Ethiopia." The agreement was implemented in 1952. For the first time in centuries an Ethiopian government found itself in firm control of the country's natural outlets on the Red Sea coast.

▲▼ COLONIAL RULE IN THE HORN OF AFRICA:
1920 TO 1960

In 1920 the European occupation of the Somali lands of the Horn of Africa was far from complete. Italian Somalia had an area of nearly 200,000 square miles (almost three times the size of the British protectorate), but the Italians were in direct control of no more than a third of the entire territory. The death of the "Mad Mullah," Muhammad Abdille Hassan, in 1920 freed the British of an enemy who had ravaged the interior of their protectorate for twenty years and forced them to spend vast sums on military operations in a territory of marginal imperial interest. After this experience they had no intention of becoming involved in further expenditure on a large scale and were content to maintain an extremely modest administrative superstructure staffed by a handful of British officials assisted by Arab and Indian clerks. As for the French, in their small territory of 8,400 square miles, all their interests were concentrated on the flourishing port of Djibouti to the almost total neglect of outlying areas.

The establishment of a Fascist government in Rome in 1922 brought a new vigor to Italian colonialism. De Vecchi, the first Fascist governor of Somalia, denounced "the policy of weakness" followed by his predecessors and with the full support of the metropolitan government set about consolidating Italian rule over the entire territory. The northern sultanates, which had enjoyed almost complete autonomy under the earlier regime, presented the Italians with their most formidable task. Between 1925 and 1927 12,000 troops were employed on military operations in northern Somalia before the region was completely pacified and the sultanates abolished. Meanwhile, southern Somalia received a valuable accession of territory when, after years of haggling, the British agreed to transfer to Italy the British East African province of Jubaland, as part of the reward promised to the Italians for their support of the Allied cause in World War I.

Somalia alone was too unrewarding a country to satisfy colonialists inspired by grandiose ambitions. As early as 1924 De Vecchi described his colony as presenting "the sure and infallible way of access for the inevitable penetration of the great Ethiopian plateau." [114] In the late 1920's the Italians made contact with Somali groups living over the border in the Ethiopian Ogaden and from 1931 Italian patrols began probing Ethiopian territory. The Ethiopians retaliated by employing the tactics of countersubversion, giving arms and money to Somali leaders known to be hostile to the Italians. The affair at Walwal in December, 1934, was in essence no more than a major incident in the cold war being waged by the two rival imperialist powers for the control of the Ogaden. Considerations that had nothing to do with Africa led Mussolini to transform the incident into a pretext for his attack on Ethiopia.

Early Italian pioneers in Somalia had dreamed of the possibility of transforming part of the colony, particularly the relatively fertile lands in the valleys of the Juba and the Shibeli, into centers of Italian colonization and settlement. These dreams were never realized. But in the course of the 1920's some progress was made in the development of a new plantation in southern Somalia. The impulse came from an Italian aristocrat, the Duke of the Abruzzi. In 1920 the duke founded the *Societa Agricola Italo-Somala,* raised a substantial amount of capital, and succeeded, with considerable help from the colonial government, in establishing a number of plantations on which were grown a wide range of tropical crops including cotton and sugar. Inspired by this example a government agricultural scheme pioneered the development of banana plantations. Between 1927 and 1934 banana production increased from 50 tons to 14,000 tons and by the mid-1930's bananas were established as Somalia's main export crop. The real cost of this development was borne by the Italian consumer who was forced by the Italian State Monopoly to pay twice as much for the short red Somali bananas as other Europeans were paying for bananas from Central America.

In other fields the achievement of the Italian authorities was more modest, but it must be contrasted with the almost total stagnation in the British Protectorate. In Somalia in 1934 no more than 1,265 Somali children were attending government subsidized schools, but in the British Protectorate there was no public educational system at all. This stagnation was in part a product of British weakness. A proposal to levy a tax on livestock to pay for the construction of a number of elementary schools aroused intense resentment and led to a riot in which a district commissioner was killed. Terrified at the possibility of being faced with another large-scale rebellion, the British authorities abandoned the scheme completely.

The lack of interest shown by the Somali in innovations of European origin was in part a reflection of their complete satisfaction with their own culture. Somali nomads possess a grueling educational system of their own; boys sent off at the age of seven to tend their father's or elder brother's livestock soon develop, as I. M. Lewis has pointed out, "those attributes of resourcefulness, fortitude and fierce independence that are so strongly engrained in the Somali character." [115] Some sections of Somali society did, however, succeed in initiating significant economic changes of their own accord. Since the beginning of the century nomads living in the better-watered districts of the British Protectorate had begun the cultivation of sorghum, using ox-drawn plows of Ethiopian origin and were thus able to develop a flourishing trade in grain with their purely nomadic neighbors. Another significant innovation was the invention by a certain Isman Yusuf Kenedid of "a highly sophisticated and accurate alphabet and script" known as Osmaniya,[116] which provided a much more effective medium for writing the Somali language than the Arabic script then in use. Yet another manifestation of change was to be found in the main urban centers of both the British and the Italian territories where in the late 1930's small groups of Somali, civil servants and merchants for the most part, came together to discuss questions of public interest, thus earning for themselves a place in Somali history as the progenitors of modern nationalism.

In 1935 the dreams of local Italian expansionists were realized when Somalia served as one of the bases for the assault on Ethiopia. The next year Somalia, enlarged by the addition of the Ogaden, became a province of the new dominion of Italian East Africa. Shortly after the outbreak of war between Britain and Italy in 1940, Italian troops occupied the British Protectorate. And so for the first time in history almost all the Somali people found themselves under a common administration. The new superstructure was preserved after the Italian defeat in 1941, for the British Military Administration which took over responsibility for the government of Somalia and of the liberated British Somaliland, also looked after the Ethiopian province of the Ogaden. This unified system of administration was clearly in the best interest of the Somali people. Accordingly in 1946 Ernest Bevin, the British foreign secretary, suggested that the temporary military administration be transformed into a permanent trusteeship. Rational though the proposal might appear to an impartial observer, it soon encountered insuperable diplomatic objections. No other great power was prepared to countenance a scheme that would involve the Ethiopians in a loss of territory they were unwilling to accept. Moreover, the British were legally bound by agreements made with Ethiopia in 1942 and 1944 to return the Ogaden as soon as the Ethiopians were in a position to take over the administration of the territory. In 1949 the British withdrew from the Ogaden but retained control of the Haud, a stretch of territory regularly frequented by pastoralists from the British Protectorate but lying to the south of the Protectorate's border with Ethiopia. In the years after 1948 the Ethiopians were able to assert their presence in the Ogaden far more effectively than they had ever done in the past. But for the Somali the smart of disappointed ambitions was aggravated by the rasp of new grievances. Of such emotions conflict and bloodshed are born.

In compensation the people of Somalia could feel that the war years had brought a distinct advance in their political fortunes. They had welcomed the British as liberators and soon found that their confidence was not misplaced. For the British were indeed prepared to follow a liberal pro-Somali policy. The restrictions imposed by the Fascist authorities on political associations were abolished, thus making possible the emergence of the first legal political parties yet seen in Somalia. The Somali Youth League, founded in 1943 as a club in Mogadishu, was the first and most important of these new associations. By 1947 the League had established branches not only in other parts of Somalia but also in the British Protectorate, in the Ogaden, and even among the Somali community in Kenya. In a manifesto issued at this time the League defined its object as being "to unite all Somalis generally . . . to educate the youth in modern civilization . . . and to take an interest in and assist in eliminating by constitutional and legal means any existing or future situations which might be prejudicial to the interests of the Somali people." [117] In Somali terms this was a profoundly revolutionary document: it specifically repudiated as "harmful old prejudices" those clan and tribal distinctions that had formed the main lines of division in traditional politics. At the same time it showed an openness to new ideas that contrasted sharply with the deeply entrenched suspicion of European innovations shown by most Somali in prewar years.

In 1949 the General Assembly of the United Nations decided that before achieving independence Somalia should be placed under Italian trusteeship for a period of ten years. This proved a wise decision, for the Italians soon succeeded in allaying initial Somali fears and showed themselves exemplary trustees. A vigorous educational and training program—31,000 children attending primary school in 1957 compared with less than 2,000 before the war; steady progress in the somalization of the higher reaches of the administration; the establishment of democratic institutions at local and national level; new schemes to develop the economy—banana production, for example, was increased to 50,000 tons—all these must be counted among Italian achievements in the last and most creative phase of Italian colonialism. They were made at considerable cost to the Italian taxpayer, for Somalia remained a desperately poor country where development could only be rendered possible by a liberal transfusion of foreign aid.

Development in the British Protectorate proceeded at a much more leisurely pace, for the British authorities had no target date for independence to stir them on. Nevertheless, by the early 1950's it was possible to detect innovations, particularly in the field of education, that would have been inconceivable in prewar days. During the war the Somali of Berbera and other towns had made contact with East African troops who were "capable clerks, telegraphists, hospital dressers and mechanics," an experience which produced, at least in the townspeople, something of "a change of heart" and led them to ask for an educational service provided by the government.[118] The first elementary schools were started in 1943; by 1959 over 7,000 Somalis, including some girls, were attending government or government-supported schools and over one hundred Somali were studying abroad.

Not until 1954 did the British Protectorate become the scene of vigorous political activity of a nationalist kind. In that year the British handed the grazing areas of the Haud over to the Ethiopians, a decision which aroused a storm of protest, led to the emergence of new political groupings, and persuaded many northern Somali that they should press for union with Somalia. Constitutional change barely kept pace with these vigorous new currents of public opinion. The colony's first legislative council was not established until 1957; two years later the council received its first elected, as opposed to nominated, members. Once it had been announced that Somalia was to become independent on July 1, 1960, the colonial authorities found themselves faced with a flood tide of public opinion demanding independence for the Protectorate in time to allow an immediate union with Somalia. Whatever the practical difficulties, such a demand could not be resisted. The British Protectorate achieved independence on June 26, 1960. Little more than a week later the union with Somalia was consummated when the legislatures of the two territories met in joint session at Mogadishu to form the National Assembly of the Somali Republic.

▲▼ NASSER'S EGYPT

On the evening of July 22, 1952, a small group of middle-ranking Egyptian army officers led their troops to occupy the key strategic centers in Cairo. A few days later, with Alexandria also in their hands, they forced King Faruq to abdicate and so completed a military coup that was soon to acquire the significance of a major revolution in Egyptian affairs. Since 1952 the world in general, and Africa in particular, has become very much more familiar with the spectacle of army officers seizing power from politicians in the avowed cause of national regeneration. The military coup in Egypt was the first of its kind in the modern history of Africa. It gave birth to a regime that has endured for nearly two decades and can now lay claim to a considerable range of achievements. And in the manner of other major revolutions it presented a model that other countries have sought to copy.

The conspirators of 1952 were all members of a group known as the Free Officers who had come together in the late 1940's to discuss means of achieving radical reforms in a country burdened with many afflictions— the rampant corruption of many politicians, the scandalous disasters of the war in Palestine, the humiliating presence of British troops still on Egyptian soil. The Free Officers chose a fifty-year-old general, Neguib, a man with a jovial manner and a gallant record in Palestine, to act as their nominal leader. But the organizing genius behind the coup was a thirty-four-year-old colonel, Gamal Abdul Nasser, the son of a minor postal official from Upper Egypt. Nasser could be described as a passionate but undoctrinaire nationalist with a profound sense of Egyptian history. His associates encompassed a wide range of ideologies: some were closely connected with the Muslim Brotherhood, others had been strongly influenced by Marxist thought. But they were bound together by the ties of comradeship and by a common detestation of the existing regime.

"The Egyptian government," Nasser had written as a schoolboy of seventeen, "is based on corruption and favors. Who can change it?" [119] With the seizure of power by the Free Officers the opportunity for change had come. But though the junta had certain broad objectives— the expulsion of the British, the elimination of corruption, the acceleration of social reform and economic development—clear in their minds, its members possessed no carefully formulated blueprint for revolution and so had to proceed in a largely empirical manner. Moreover, with the exception of General Neguib, they suffered from the disadvantage of being completely unknown to the mass of the Egyptian public. At this early stage the officers saw themselves only as a "vanguard." Realizing their own inexperience, they were quite prepared to accept the advice of established politicians. And they looked forward to the creation of a new government truly representative of the people. Romantically they had imagined, as Nasser wrote later, "the whole nation . . . would fall in behind in serried ranks ready for the sacred advance towards the great objective." To their dismay they found nothing but "chaos," "dissension," and "indolence." "Every man we questioned had nothing to recommend except to kill someone else. Every idea we listened to was nothing but an attack on some other idea." [120] Failing to find sincere collaborators among the politicians of the old regime, the officers decided to establish an authoritarian government with supreme power concentrated in the hands of a revolutionary council of which they themselves were the members.

To give the new regime legitimacy an interim constitution was promulgated, and a new party, the Liberation Rally, was organized to the accompaniment of a formidable barrage of propaganda. But the junta found itself still faced with a wide range of opponents. The well-to-do politicians of the old regime proved the easiest to deal with. In October, 1952, a number of politicians accused of gross corruption were put on trial and given severe prison sentences. Three months later all the old political parties were officially banned with the exception of the Muslim Brotherhood which claimed to be a nonpolitical association. The Brotherhood with its massive membership and long experience of terrorist activity was in fact a far more serious threat to the revolutionary council than the discredited politicians of the Wafd. The leaders of the Brotherhood accepted many of the objectives announced by the Free Officers, but they were naturally anxious to secure power for themselves in order to implement their own more rigidly Islamic ideas. In January, 1954, Muslim Brothers clashed openly with supporters of the Liberation Rally, thus providing the revolutionary council with a pretext for ordering the suppression of the Brotherhood and the arrest of many of its members, but the risk of subversive action remained.

More serious still for the members of the revolutionary junta was the danger of a rift within their own ranks. By early 1954 relations between Nasser and Neguib were becoming increasingly strained. Though Nasser occupied a key position on the revolutionary council, he was still a little-known figure to the mass of Egyptians, whereas Neguib had acquired immense popularity as head of state. By temperament Neguib was a conservative. Irritated by the pretensions of his junior colleagues, he began to envisage a return to civilian rule. To Nasser and his associates Neguib's ideas threatened to jeopardize the entire revolution: under a civilian regime there would be nothing to prevent the old-guard politicians from resuming their former malpractices. By a series of adroit maneuvers Nasser succeeded in restricting Neguib's presidential powers and in purging the army of his supporters. In October, 1954, Nasser narrowly escaped assassination at the hands of a member of the Muslim Brotherhood. By showing that Neguib possessed certain contacts with the Brotherhood, Nasser was able to secure his dismissal. With the fall of Neguib in November, 1954, Nasser achieved a position of uncontested primacy that he retained until his death in 1970.

In his years of supreme power in Egypt Nasser earned himself a place among the great political figures of the twentieth century. At the same time his regime was frequently criticized for its authoritarian character. In fairness to Nasser and his supporters three points need to be borne in mind. In the first place, Nasser's rule, though tough, was not excessively inhumane. The original coup was almost completely bloodless. And though many hundreds of political opponents were sent to detention camps, there were very few executions and many former detainees were allowed to return to positions of some responsibility. Moreover, Egypt is a country in which the tradition of autocratic rule is deeply entrenched. For a period reaching back over thousands of years the inhabitants of the Nile Valley have been accustomed to subordinate themselves meekly to a higher authority. Finally, it must be noted that Nasser was always aware of the weakness of personal dictatorship. He and his associates tried to create a political party—first the Liberation Rally, later the National Union and the Arab Socialist Union—that would transmit their own dynamic sense of purpose to every sphere of political life. They also tried to create political institutions in which all sections of the country could participate. The National Assembly, first convened in 1964, is the most truly representative parliament in Egypt's history, for half its seats were reserved by law for "farmers or workers." On paper the Assembly's powers are considerable, but the political crisis through which Egypt has lived since the Arab-Isreali war of 1967 has discouraged the government from taking any further steps to democratize its regime. All that can be said categorically is that Egypt enjoyed under Nasser's rule a measure of political stability that contrasts favorably with the recent experience of many other Afro-Asian states. And this stability was maintained in the years immediately following Nasser's sudden death in September, 1970. His successor as president, Anwar al-Sadat, was regarded as a middle-of-the-road man, his election being seen as the result of a compromise between the regime's leftist and rightist factions. In 1971 al-Sadat strengthened his position by successfully countering a serious threat posed by his most formidable radical opponent, Ali Sabry. At the same time the new president made some attempt to liberalize his regime, but internal Egyptian politics were still overcast by the baleful possibility of open war with Israel.

To the outside world Nasser's most spectacular achievements were in the field of foreign affairs. In 1952 Egypt could still be regarded as a client-state of the British. Ten years later the country had achieved a position of considerable prominence among the nations of the Afro-Asian world. "Imperialism," Nasser wrote in his *Egypt's Liberation: The Philosophy of the Revolution,* "is the great force that is imposing a murderous, invisible siege on the whole region." [121] The first stage in freeing Egypt from this "siege" was to get rid of the British whose troops still occupied the canal zone in force. In 1947 negotiations with Britain had broken down over the question of the Sudan. Shrewdly the revolutionary junta decided to abandon their predecessors' insistence on the "unity of the Nile Valley" and proposed that the Sudanese be allowed to decide their future status for themselves—a proposal it was not politic for the British to reject. With the Sudan problem finally solved in 1953, discussion turned to the future of the massive military base—the largest of its kind in the world—constructed by the British in the canal zone. In 1954 the British agreed to withdraw all their troops, but the base remained as British property, maintained by British civilian technicians. The Egyptian government was not prepared to commit itself to any Western-inspired defense pact that might involve the country in the cold war, but it conceded to Britain the right to bring troops back to the canal base should Turkey or any other member of the Arab League be attacked by the Soviet Union.

With the withdrawal of British troops from the canal, Egypt found itself free, for the first time since the Ottoman conquest of 1517, to pursue a truly independent foreign policy. Yet the sense of living in a part of the world under siege from foreign aggressors still persisted. When Arab nationalists in Egypt looked westward to the Arab lands of the Maghrib, they could see the French colonialists implacably at grips with the local nationalist parties, some of whose leaders had sought refuge in Cairo even before the revolution. Equally depressing was the spectacle of the "feudalistic" rulers of some Middle Eastern states signing defense pacts with the West and thus threatening to involve the entire region in the horrors of a nuclear war. Most dangerous of all, on Egypt's very borders lay the state of Israel, a state which would never have come into existence without "imperialist" support and which was now displaying alarming symptoms of expansionist ambitions. In such a situation there was much to be said, so it seemed to Nasser and his associates, for pursuing a dynamic policy aimed at undermining the forces of "imperialism." Hence the practical support given to the small group of Algerians who opened their country's war of liberation in November, 1954. Hence the cordial welcome accorded nationalist leaders from other Afro-Asian countries and the vitriolic propaganda directed against colonial regimes. Hence the bitter attacks on the Baghdad Pact devised by the Western powers as an extension of NATO (North Atlantic Treaty Organization) into the Middle East. Hence, too, the vigorous proclamation of a policy of "neutralism" or "nonalignment," an approach to the greatest international issue of the day—the cold war between the Soviet Union and the West—which placed the still relatively unknown President Nasser on the same footing as Nehru of India or Tito of Yugoslavia.

In his *Philosophy of the Revolution* Nasser wrote of a role waiting for a hero to fill it. On his return from the Bandung Conference in April, 1955, he found that he himself had become for many Arabs the hero of whom he had once dreamed, a genuinely popular leader whose portrait was to be seen in shops and cafes from Aden to Tripoli and whose ideas had suddenly developed into a widely accepted ideology. "The appeal of Nasserism," wrote a perceptive observer in 1956, "lies in the fact that it has transferred, if only partially, to the Arab world itself the centre of decisions concerning the future of that world, from the Western European capitals where those decisions have been taken for more than a century. It has also restored to the Arabs a feeling of confidence in themselves and thus has largely counterbalanced the psychological shock of the loss of Palestine." [122] For all the aggressive tone of Egyptian propaganda Nasser's policy was notably cautious in its approach toward Israel. But the Egyptians were unable to prevent a steady deterioration in the situation on their borders with Israel where modest raids launched by Palestinian refugees provoked massive Israeli reprisals. Reluctantly Nasser accepted the necessity of building up the Egyptian army. Finding that the West would not supply the arms he needed, he turned to the Communist bloc for assistance.

By 1956 Nasser's independent policy was causing intense irritation in London, Paris, and Washington. In July the British and United States governments decided to turn down Egypt's request for a loan to help build the High Dam at Aswan, a project which occupied a key position in the regime's plans for economic development. To this rebuff Nasser retaliated in the most provocative manner possible by nationalizing the Suez Canal. This bold action aroused immense enthusiasm in Egypt but seemed to certain Western statesmen to confirm their suspicion that Nasser was a dangerously irresponsible demagogue. Acting on this misleading assumption, the British and French governments joined Israel in an invasion of Egyptian territory. But the three aggressors were not strong enough to ride the tide of outraged world opinion, nor could they afford to ignore the stern disapproval of their closest ally. With the withdrawal of the invaders Nasser's triumph was complete. No African leader in modern times has ever enjoyed so spectacular a diplomatic victory over European intruders. There could be no hesitation now about taking over the fifteen thousand British and French firms and other establishments to be found in Egypt, together with the massive British base in the canal zone. By January, 1957, Egypt was free at last of the excessive influence of Western European powers.

In February, 1958, the Syrian government approached Nasser with a request of a kind that he himself as the apostle of Arab unity could not possibly turn down: Egypt and Syria were to form a political union under the name of the United Arab Republic. Five months later Nasser's archenemy, Nuri as-Said of Iraq, was overthrown in a bloody revolution in Baghdad. Nasserism now seemed triumphant throughout the Middle East. But 1958 turned out to be the apogee of Nasser's fortunes on the international stage. The next decade brought with it a series of frustrations and defeats. In 1961 a coup in Syria led to the collapse of the union with Egypt. In 1962 Nasser committed a third of the Egyptian army to a long and inconclusive war in the Yemen in support of the Republican insurgents. On the African stage Egypt's active sponsorship of the cause of radical Pan-Africanism failed to achieve any positive results. Finally in 1967 came a third war with Israel, which ended more disastrously than the two earlier conflicts with Israeli troops in control of all Egyptian territory east of the Suez Canal. Yet, even this shattering reverse could not shake Nasser's popularity among his own people, though the regime as a whole was weakened by serious dissension in the army and became the target for public criticism more freely expressed than ever before. Nevertheless, Nasserism still remained an immensely potent force in the Arab world. The military coups that occurred in the neighboring states of Libya and the Sudan in 1969 brought into power young men who had been profoundly influenced by Nasser's ideas. In 1971, the year after Nasser's death, Egypt, Libya, and Syria came together to form the Federation of Arab Republics. (The new association brought with it a change in nomenclature: from being the "United Arab Republic" Egypt now officially became the "Arab Republic of Egypt.") In 1972 Egypt and Libya established an even closer form of union, but the attitude of the Sudan to the new movement for Arab unity appeared equivocal.

The long-drawn-out conflict with Israel forced the Egyptian government to look for allies in the outside world. There was in fact no room for choice: only the Soviet Union could offer the large-scale military assistance needed by the Egyptians. During the nineteenth century the area covered by the Ottoman Empire, of which Egypt formed an autonomous province, was always of major concern to Russian statesmen. But for more than three decades after the 1917 revolution Soviet policy makers showed little interest in the successor states based on the former Arab subjects of the Ottomans. An Egyptian Communist party was founded in the early 1920's, but most of its members were of foreign origin and its appeal to native Egyptians was very limited. Not until after World War II did Communist ideas begin to circulate widely among Egyptian intellectuals. Communist reaction to the 1952 revolution was far from cordial. One of the first acts of the Free Officers had been to use troops to break a violent strike by factory workers in Alexandria—an action for which they were inevitably condemned as "Fascist reactionaries." There followed for Egyptian Communists a dark period of persecution and imprisonment which ended when increasingly cordial Soviet-Egyptian relations brought to local Communists a measure of toleration and even of some official favor.

In the late 1950's and throughout the 1960's the Soviet Union provided Egypt with an ideal ally. There were no bitter historical memories of Russian domination in Arab lands to cloud the relationship. Soviet spokesmen showed themselves consistently willing to support the Arab cause against Israel. The Soviet Union and its allies in Eastern Europe supplied armaments, financial aid, and technical assistance without asking for much in return. Resistance to "imperialism" served as a common aim on which the two powers were united. "We do not want foreign influence in our part of the world," President Nasser frequently pointed out. "For its part, the Soviet Union is most anxious to oppose imperialism and to liquidate the imperialist concentrations to the south of its borders." [123] To those who warned him of the dangers of Communist penetration Nasser replied, "All our people are politicians and very smart. . . . I am certain that no Communist will, whatever happens, influence Arab nationalism. On the contrary, the ideas of Arab nationalism will finally and forever prevail." [124] After Egypt's disastrous defeat at the hands of Israel in 1967, Soviet military aid was greatly increased. By 1971 more than fifteen thousand Russian servicemen were reported to be stationed in Egypt, with the primary purpose of helping the Egyptians to construct an effective system of defense designed to ward off Israeli air attacks. At the same time the Soviet government was clearly anxious to prevent the renewal of armed conflict in the Middle East. This cautious approach to a highly inflammable situation appears to have been one of the reasons for the serious strain in Soviet-Egyptian relations which became apparent in mid-1972 when President Sadat requested the Russians to withdraw all their military personnel from his country. Yet with Israel still enjoying a position of military preponderance based in part on equipment received from the United States, the Egyptian government could not escape looking to the outside world and especially to the Communist bloc for assistance.

To many foreign observers Nasser's dynamic foreign policy seemed a luxury too extravagant for the leader of a poor country to afford. Yet this policy gave Nasser the standing of a world statesman, vastly enhanced his prestige among his own people, and thus provided his regime with a greater measure of stability. Moreover, in the eyes of many Egyptians the need to free their part of the world from "imperialist" influences abundantly justified a revolutionary approach to international affairs. Finally, it could be argued that by "making a nuisance of itself" in an area of major strategic importance to all the great powers, the Egyptian government was able to secure a greater volume of aid than would ever have come its way had it pursued a quieter policy. Few countries in the Third World, indeed, received so generous an amount of assistance as the United Arab Republic, or were able to count on the support of so wide a range of donors. Financial assistance came as copiously from the West as from the East. Leaving aside military credits, in the years between 1957 and 1964 the United Arab Republic received £E 483 million in grants and loans from Communist countries and £E 782 million from the non-Communist world. Of this latter sum more than two-thirds was provided by the United States of America, mainly in the form of food shipments under Public Law 480. "One of every two Egyptians," an American historian of Egypt pointed out in the mid-1960's, "is fed by the grain surplus of the United States" [125] More recently, substantial subsidies from the oil-rich Arab states have helped to offset the losses incurred by the closing of the Suez Canal as a result of the third Arab-Israeli war.

Whatever the distractions involved in the pursuit of a vigorous foreign policy, the rulers of Egypt cannot be accused of neglecting the ur-

gent tasks of internal development. In the course of the past two decades Egypt has undergone a transformation far more profound than
that experienced by most other African countries. In 1952 the Egyptian
economy was overwhelmingly agricultural. Industry, finance, and trade
were controlled by private capitalists, many of whom were foreigners.
Taxes were low, and glaring inequalities of wealth were to be seen in
town and country. With population steadily increasing—from 13 million in 1918 to 19 million in 1947—the lot of most of the fellahin was
growing worse, not better. To provide themselves with an adequate livelihood a peasant family needed at least two *feddans* ("acres") of land.
Yet in 1952 72 percent of all peasant proprietors possessed less than
one *feddan* of land, and there was a large class of landless laborers.

One of the first acts of the military junta was to push through an
agrarian reform law that fixed land rents at lower levels and broke up
the largest estates. But during their first few years in power the Free Officers were too preoccupied with political problems to devote much attention to further economic reforms. Local businessmen were encouraged to invest in industry, and favorable terms were offered even to
foreign capitalists. By the mid-1950's, however, some Egyptian economists were beginning to argue that private enterprise was failing to provide the dynamics needed for rapid economic growth and that a measure of centralized planning was essential. The nationalization of a large
number of foreign firms in the aftermath of the Suez war provided the
government with a more substantial stake in many sectors of the
economy, and the process of nationalization was carried still further in
the course of the next few years as many Egyptian-owned companies
were taken over by the state. Political reasons were mixed inextricably
with economic arguments. Indeed, one might compare "the dismantling
of the Egyptian bourgeoisie," many of whose members had grown bitterly hostile to Nasser's regime, with the elimination of the Mamluks by
Muhammad Ali in the early years of his reign, though the methods used
by the Egyptian government in dealing with its political opponents were
far less brutal than those employed by the great pasha or indeed by the
revolutionary regimes of modern Europe. To be judged fairly the actions of Nasser's government need to be seen in the context of the
country's long history: in Egypt powerful rulers, from the pharaohs to
Muhammad Ali, have always sought to consolidate their position by assuming control of the greater part of the economy. But it would be
wrong to describe the post-1952 regime as truly totalitarian or to equate
its system of government with those of Communist states. Private enterprise still prevails in some important sectors of the economy; the concept of a class struggle has been rejected; and the regime has shown a

humane concern to improve the immediate lot of the Egyptian worker and peasant that contrasts sharply with the brutal priorities adopted by most Communist regimes.

The changes wrought by these new policies are most easily visible in the upper strata of Egyptian society. The country's new elite, made up of army officers and scientists, engineers, and factory managers, contrasts sharply with the land-owning pashas and beys of the *ancien régime*. "Any one who mixed with the witty, cosmopolitan, self-confident members of the pre revolutionary Egyptian cultural elite is likely," an English observer has remarked, "to find their successors philistine, serious and dull. But they have a much better understanding of their country's needs." [126]

After the technocrats, the urban population—and especially the factory workers—have benefited most markedly from the changes of the last fifteen years. The development of industry was one of the first goals set by the regime, and its achievements in this field have been substantial. In 1952 Egyptian industry was confined largely to a number of processing operations. Today Egyptian factories are turning out an ever-expanding range of increasingly elaborate manufactured articles, some still partly dependent on imported components, that include refrigerators, television sets, bicycles, and automobiles. Most of these articles are intended for the Egyptian home market, but a modest export trade has recently been developed with neighboring Arab states.

The proportion of Egyptians engaged in industry is still relatively small. An estimate made in 1960 showed that 607,000 workers were occupied in manufacturing and handicrafts compared with 4,200,000 occupied in agriculture. All observers agree that most of the Egyptian fellahin are "as poor, hungry and diseased as anywhere on earth." [127] Clearly the major task of any avowedly socialist regime must be to seek to improve the lot of the peasantry. The breakup of the large estates—a second agrarian reform law passed in 1961 took over all holdings exceeding 100 *feddans*—was a first step in this direction. Politically it was an act of great significance, for it shattered the power of the old land-owning aristocracy. Only one peasant family in twelve, however, is likely to benefit from the redistribution of the land thus acquired. Of more immediate concern to a very large number of tenant farmers was the fixing of rents by the law of 1952, a measure which had the effect of increasing, at least for a time, the money income of a hitherto depressed class. A strenuous effort had also been made to provide villages with social services of a kind they had never enjoyed before. But to tackle the immense task of regenerating the Egyptian countryside, some observers believe that even more radical changes are necessary. They see a model in the government cooperatives to which all the peasants who received land on the breakup of the large estates were required to belong. In economic terms the cooperatives have proved successful, and an attempt is now being made to persuade other villages to organize themselves on the same lines.

Meanwhile, population continues to increase more rapidly than ever before: by 1968 there were over 30 million Egyptians. In these circumstances, with industry absorbing only a limited number, it becomes imperative to extend as rapidly as possible the amount of land under cultivation. In 1950 total cultivatable land amounted to about 6 million *feddans,* a figure that had not changed in the course of forty years. The construction of the High Dam at Aswan—possibly the greatest engineering project ever undertaken in Africa—creates many new opportunities for irrigation and may, in time, serve to increase the cultivatable area by 25 percent. Moreover, the dam will contribute to other sectors of the economy by providing electricity at a very cheap rate. Other schemes of land reclamation have been undertaken in the oases and depressions lying to the west of the Nile. Even more ambitious plans involve the distillation of seawater by solar energy. Recent mineralogical surveys have shown that the previously unutilized deserts contain considerable resources, including oil. The prospects thus invoked are truly revolutionary; advances in modern technology will enable the Egyptians to "break out of the narrow valley in which they have been cooped up for the last six or seven millennia, ever since the desiccation of the Libyan and Eastern Deserts." [128] In no African country is the pressure of population so intense as in Egypt. Yet few African farmers possess skills comparable to those acquired over the centuries by the fellahin of the Nile Valley. Given the steady introduction of new techniques—involving among other developments the replacement of grain and rice by more profitable crops such as fruit and vegetables— the transformation of the Egyptian countryside appears as a task that is certainly within the realm of possibility.

Many of the developments that have taken place in Egypt since 1952 may be regarded as the continuation of processes already well established before the present regime came to power. The expansion of modern education—a movement that can be traced back to the days of Muhammad Ali—has continued. Between 1952 and 1965 the total school population doubled from 1.9 to 4 million. Particularly striking—at least in statistical terms—has been the expansion of higher education. With more than 100,000 university students Egypt has a ratio of students to total population higher than that of many much richer countries. The past twenty years have also witnessed a wide range of achievements in many forms of cultural activity—the novel, drama, cinema, and television. These developments have been vigorously encouraged by the state; yet the disadvantages of an authoritarian regime remain. As a European historian of modern Egypt has recently observed, "one sometimes feels that, despite the relatively great attainments in education and culture, there is in Egypt (though less than in the rest of the Arab world) with all due respect a bureaucratic intelligentsia with a political consciousness, but not an intellectual elite with a civilizational potential." [129]

Few regimes in modern Africa have aroused such intense controversy as that established by the brash young army officers who seized power in Egypt in 1952. With popular discontent feeding on mounting economic difficulties and the bitter frustrations provoked by the "setback" of 1967, the closing years of President Nasser's rule cast something of a shadow on his regime's earlier achievements. Of the reality of some of these achievements there can be no doubt. For the first time since the fall of the last pharaonic dynasty Egypt has been ruled by men of indigenous stock. For the first time, too, in the country's long history a genuine attempt has been made to improve the lot of all classes of Egyptians. Never before has the country's influence extended over so wide an area of Africa and the Middle East. And even if many of the regime's political initiatives have ended in failure, its vigorous domestic policies have made of Nasser's Egypt "a pace-setter for social and economic change in the Arab world and even beyond in Africa." [130] In population the second largest of African states, in trained manpower by far the best endowed, it has been both natural and fitting that modern Egypt should over the course of the past two decades have played so notable a part in recent world affairs.

▲▼ THE INDEPENDENT REPUBLIC OF THE SUDAN

"The new Sudan," wrote an English journalist, Basil Davidson, summing up his impressions of the country in 1958, "combines an Arab dignity with an African tolerance, an Islamic stillness with a pagan verve, a population almost entirely illiterate with an almost casual confidence in a literate future, an economy still in the pre-income-tax era with a whacking big ambition for development; and lastly (but not least) a good administrative framework. It is not exactly bliss to be alive in the Sudan today, but it is certainly exciting." [131] Five years earlier the American John Gunther made much the same point when he described the Sudan as "politically the most exciting country in all Africa, with the possible exception of Nigeria. . . . It is crowded with zest to get ahead; it boils and sparkles with euphoria." [132] In the course of the past fifteen years the independent Sudan has certainly lived up to its early reputation; with three changes of regime in Khartoum and a long-drawn-out guerrilla war in the south the republic's recent political history has been among the most eventful of any country in the world.

The Anglo-Egyptian agreement of February, 1953, paved the way for the Sudan to become one of the first colonial territories in Africa to achieve independence. By its terms the two codomini formally accepted the Sudanese right to self-determination and agreed on arrangements for a transitional period lasting not more than three years in which to wind up their administration. Elections for a new Sudanese parliament were held at the end of 1953 and took the form of a contest between two major parties—the Mahdist-backed *Umma* party which drew most of its support from rural areas and the urban-based National Unionist Party which had grown out of the smaller *Ashiqqa* party founded by Ismail al-Azhari in 1943. NUP members had boycotted the legislative assembly founded in 1948, leaving that body to be dominated by *Umma*. British officials and *Umma* politicians had worked amicably together for five years, but to the dismay of both groups the 1953 elections resulted in a resounding victory for the NUP.

A victory for the NUP could be interpreted as a victory for the Egyptians since the party was—as its name implied—in favor of some form of union between Egypt and the Sudan. To *Umma* members, with their long tradition of hostility to Egypt, such a prospect was utterly abhorrent; they gave violent expression of their views by staging a massive demonstration of protest when the Egyptian president, General Neguib, arrived in Khartoum in March, 1954, for the ceremonial opening of the new parliament. Neguib possessed close family ties with the Sudan and had become a popular hero for many urban Sudanese, but he fell from power in November, 1954. At the same time Nasser began to attack the Egyptian Communists and the Muslim Brotherhood, both groups with influential supporters in the Sudan. In these altered circumstances even Sudanese radicals found themselves growing disenchanted with the idea of union.

Other considerations—besides the very real threat of civil war posed by *Umma* demonstrations— helped al-Azhari and his ministers to make a complete volte-face by abandoning the idea of union. In the course of 1954 most British administrative police and army officers were required to resign their posts. The government's declared policy of "Sudanization" would become meaningless if these vacancies were filled by Egyptians. With all parties now enthusiastically in favor of complete independence, there was clearly no need to put the question of union with Egypt to the popular vote. In December, 1955, members of the Sudanese parliament unanimously approved a unilateral declaration of independence. The end of the condominium was formally recognized on New Year's Day, 1956. But the achievement of independence was clouded by ominous happenings in the south. In August, 1955, southern soldiers in the Equatoria battalion of the Sudan Defence Corps mutinied, killed their northern officers and many other northerners and plunged some districts of the three southern provinces of Bahr al-Ghazal, Upper Nile and Equatoria into a state of anarchy. Their action marked the opening of a new phase of misery and violence in the history of one of the most turbulent areas in all Africa.

The new republic's first experience of parliamentary government lasted for less than three years. In February, 1956, al-Azhari was forced to accept a coalition government which included members of the *Umma*. Four months later members of the Khatmiyya sect broke away from the NUP to form their own party, the People's Democratic Party. A few weeks later PDP and *Umma* members came together, voted al-Azhari out of office and gave the premiership to a leading *Umma* politician, Abdullah Khalil. The PDP–*Umma* coalition survived the general election of March 1958 and came out with a working majority of 89 out of 173 seats. But there could be no real harmony of interest between two parties which drew their support from rival religious sects, and every major question of policy tended to cause dissension in the ranks of the unnatural alliance. At the same time the cynical and opportunist behavior of most politicians brought the entire parliamentary system into discredit. "We used to watch the files accumulate on the Minister's desk," one senior civil servant recalled afterward, "while he gossiped with numerous place-seekers for whose protégés we were then instructed to find jobs." [133] In November PDP politicians were rumored to be flirting with their old associates in the NUP as part of a plan to seize power with the aid of President Nasser. Suddenly, on November 17, the army under the command of General Ibrahim Abboud, staged a bloodless coup to rescue the country from "degeneration, chaos and instability."

The military regime lasted for almost six years. Its members showed considerable ability in tackling the country's economic problems, some of which were clearly the product of inefficiency and short-sightedness on the part of the discredited politicians. By 1963 Abboud could point to a wide range of achievements in the field of development. He could claim, too, to be engaged in a sincere attempt to transform the autocratic structure of his regime by making arrangements for a measure of representation at the center "as a prelude to a parliamentary system by universal election . . . free from all the errors of the past." [134] But beneath the country's apparent stability could be traced a swelling tide of popular discontent.

Abboud himself was widely liked for his genial and humane manner, but the arrogant behavior of other army officers caused bitter resentment, especially among the population of the main towns. All political parties were suppressed immediately after the coup, but their leaders were left at liberty until July, 1961, when twelve prominent politicians were interned for openly criticizing the regime. More violent forms of protest were employed by railway workers on strike and by Mahdist demonstrators in Khartoum. Meanwhile, in the south heavy-handed action on the part of the military had driven many local dissidents to participate in a full-scale revolt. Suddenly, in October, 1964, the military government found itself faced with a revolution in the streets of Khartoum. On October 22, police attempted to break up a political meeting in the university, a student was killed, and crowds gathered in their thousands for the funeral procession. Before long policemen and soldiers found themselves confronted with a frightening display of mob violence which they were quite unable to control. Doctors, lawyers, civil servants, and trade unionists joined in the movement of protest, their leaders forming a Committee of Public Safety capable of taking over the reins of government from General Abboud and his army officers.

The Sudan's "October Revolution" was a triumph for the urban radicals, some of whom had never possessed any political affiliations while others were active members of the small but well-organized Communist Party. But the radicals were not strong enough to reap the fruits of their victory over the military regime. With the restoration of parliamentary government, the old political parties made a vigorous comeback. Elections in June, 1965, resulted in a victory for the *Umma,* but the party had lost its great patron, Abd al-Rahman al-Mahdi who died in 1959, and was soon rent by a feud between two powerful factions. One was led by Abd al-Rahman's grandson, Sadiq, young, Oxford-educated, and an enthusiastic modernizer; the other, by Sadiq's uncle, the Imam al-Hadi, religious leader of the Mahdists and a staunch conservative. When the two factions formed themselves into separate parties, opportunities for political maneuvering were greatly enhanced. Meanwhile, the NUP, whose old leader, Ismail al-Azhari, had been rewarded by being appointed president, merged with the PDP to become the Democratic Unionist Party. The DUP emerged as the single largest party when new elections were held in April, 1968, but it needed the support of the Imam's wing of *Umma* to attain a majority in the Assembly.

Ever since the October Revolution, northern political leaders had attempted to bring peace to the south by measures far more conciliatory than those employed by General Abboud. The new approach won the support of southern moderates but failed to satisfy the extremists. So the guerrilla war in the south dragged on, a severe strain for a country whose economy was now far from buoyant. Thus the Sudan's second spell of parliamentary government seemed to repeat all the failures of the first. Once again the army stepped in to redress the situation. But there was a profound difference between the military coups of November, 1958, and May, 1969. General Abboud was an aging soldier of conservative outlook; Major-General Jaafar al-Nimairi was only thirty-nine when he seized power in 1969, the oldest of a group of middle-ranking army officers of "progressive" views. The new regime regarded itself as the true heir of the October Revolution; accordingly one of its first acts was to invite those civilians, including members of the Communist Party, who had taken a leading part in the events of October, 1964, to participate in the government. Nimairi's policy could also be regarded as an attempt to apply a Nasserist solution to the problems of the Sudan. Inevitably this new radicalism angered the traditionalists, and in March, 1970, the government found itself engaged in a series of bloody clashes with the Mahdists, leading to the death of the Imam al-Hadi and many of his followers. In July, 1971, Nimairi's regime faced an even more serious threat, when a group of radical army officers, supported by leading members of the Sudanese Communist Party launched a coup and succeeded in gaining power for a day only to be overthrown by Nimairi's vigorous countercoup. The executions that followed deprived the Communists of their most able leaders.

Four themes in this brief narrative require further comment: the causes of the Sudan's political instability; the problem of the south; the shaping of the country's foreign policy; and the development of its economy. The Sudan is at once the largest in area and one of the most heterogeneous in population of all the countries of Africa. Physical size and ethnic diversity produce problems of a kind that the rulers of compact, homogeneous states such as Egypt or Tunisia are never called on to face. Separatism in the Sudan finds its most violent expression in the south but is not confined to this area. In the 1968 elections the Nuba of Kordofan and the Beja of Kassala province, both peoples ethnically distinct from the Arabic-speaking majority of the north, launched their own "tribal" parties. Tribal sentiment or local patriotism has certainly contributed to a second divisive force in Sudanese politics—religious sectarianism. The rivalry between the Mahdists and the Khatmiyya dates back to the nineteenth century, but it has found new expression in the struggle between the *Umma* and the NUP or the PDP. Yet many younger Sudanese feel that religion—and especially sectarianism—

should not be allowed to intrude into politics. This secular approach is most evident in those strongholds of Sudanese radicalism—the Gezira and "the three towns" (Khartoum, Khartoum North, and Omdurman). The tenants of the Gezira and many of the townsmen have profited more than any other sections of the population from the economic and social developments of recent years. Their relative prosperity contrasts sharply with the unchanged lot of the people of most rural areas, thus stressing still further the division between town and country.

The northern Sudanese have been described as "socially the most democratic people in the world." [135] Their contempt for the pompous and the arrogant finds expression in a satirical sense of humor and a sardonic vein of political journalism. Given a people of such a temperament, given the play of a wide range of political forces, it is difficult to imagine the Sudan ever being dominated for long by any one political regime. The country has the advantage of possessing one of the best civil services in Africa. So long as the administration maintains its efficiency, political vicissitudes need not be taken too seriously. The history of nineteenth-century France has shown that a country can be subjected to many violent changes of regime, yet still develop a brilliant culture of its own.

Whatever the local tensions in Khartoum, the leaders of the independent Sudan have never been able to forget that their country is saddled with the daunting problem of the south. The three southern provinces of Equatoria, Bahr al-Ghazal and Upper Nile, whose inhabitants differ so markedly in culture, physical appearance, and way of life from the people of the north, cover an area of 250,000 square miles with a population numbering about 3 million. The size of the area involved and the nature of the ethnic differences have presented politicians in Khartoum with an extremely formidable task. It is indeed not unreasonable to compare the situation to that which faced the English in Ireland or the French in Algeria. Northerners point out that Muslim traders have done business in the south for more than a century, that Arabic has been widely accepted as a *lingua franca,* and that many southerners have been converted to Islam. In these circumstances they feel justified in regarding the southern provinces as forming an integral part of their republic. But viewed through southern eyes, the position looks quite different: northerners appear as aliens, the descendants of slave-raiders, the heirs of a colonialist tradition of government.

With southern opposition ruling out the possibility of total integration, three alternative solutions came to be canvassed in the 1960's: autonomy, federation, and secession. Some southerners were prepared to collaborate with successive governments in Khartoum and showed themselves willing to accept recent northern proposals for autonomy. Others, while still participating in national Sudanese politics, pressed for federation. A third group, intent on secession, set up a government-in-exile. Finally, many of the soldiers who participated in the 1955 mutiny became the nucleus of a terrorist organization, *Anya Nya,* and waged a not unsuccessful guerrilla war against government troops operating in the south. To render the situation even more intractable the differences between southern politicians were further complicated by tribal divisions and personal jealousies. For fifteen years the south lived in a state of fluctuating insecurity, with many districts experiencing the dismal cycle of terrorist attacks, punitive expeditions, ravaged villages and refugees in their thousands fleeing into the bush or over the frontiers. In February, 1972, however, to the surprise of many observers, representatives of the government in Khartoum and of some of the most militant southern parties came together in Addis Ababa and succeeded in working out a peace settlement. The settlement provided for constitutional changes in the Sudan designed to allow the three southern provinces a far greater measure of autonomy than earlier Sudanese governments had ever been prepared to accord. By agreeing to incorporate the guerrilla fighters of the *Anya Nya* into the Sudanese army the Khartoum government provided southerners with a practical guarantee that the terms of the settlement would be carried out. At last southerners could turn their energies to the immensely formidable task of developing their isolated and impoverished region.

The movement of refugees had not been only in one direction. In the course of the 1960's small groups of dissidents from Ethiopian Eritrea, from Chad, and from the ex-Belgian Congo sought refuge in the Sudan and succor from the Sudanese government. But the support given by the authorities in Khartoum to rebel groups from Chad or Eritrea provoked violent countermeasures by the governments in Fort Lamy and Addis Ababa. The continuation of the armed struggle in the south left the government in Khartoum in no position to pursue a "revolutionary" foreign policy. The Sudan's neighbors could easily counter any attempt at Sudanese intervention in their internal affairs by offering practical assistance to southern militants. Only on one occasion since independence has the Sudan made a notable contribution to the affairs of a wider world. In the frantic weeks after the disastrous Six Days' War of June, 1967, the Sudanese government "took the lead in rallying Arab states to the cause of unity," [136] succeeded in persuading Saudi Arabia and the U.A.R. to settle their long-standing differences over the Yemen and made Khartoum the venue for an Arab summit conference. But the

Sudan occupies too peripheral a position to maintain a leading role in Arab politics. Nor, with its image spoiled in many African eyes by the running sore of the south, can the country claim to have lived up to the potentialities of its geographical position and formed a viable "bridge" linking the continent's Arab Muslim North with its Negroid Christian South. A vigorous foreign policy is a luxury only politically stable countries can afford. "While Sudanese politics remain in an unsettled state, the Sudan's impact on Africa and the outside world is likely to remain insignificant." [137]

In a very real sense the Sudan may be regarded as one of the most underdeveloped countries in Africa. Population density—less than fifteen people to the square mile—is among the lowest in the world, and only 6 percent of the country's cultivable land is at present utilized. The success of the Gezira scheme provided economic planners with striking evidence of the country's potentialities for agricultural development based on the expansion of irrigation. Accordingly, great stress has been laid in recent development plans on the implementation of similar schemes in other parts of the Sudan. But the concentration on cotton production which these schemes imply is a policy not without drawbacks. In recent years cotton has provided between 40 and 60 percent of the total value of all Sudanese exports. But, as a plant, cotton is vulnerable to a wide range of diseases, and as a commodity, its price subject to massive fluctuations on the world market. In 1961 the Sudan's cotton exports produced £S28.7 million, in 1963 £S43.7 million, and in 1965 £S31.0 million. The country's other exports, of which gum arabic is the most important, are more stable in their return but far less lucrative. Surprisingly, in view of its massive size, the Sudan has not yet been found to contain mineral deposits of any value. Thus the country can hardly look forward to more than a modest increase in export earnings through improved cotton production and a limited range of minor developments.

Throughout the 1960's there was an alarming tendency for the Sudan's imports greatly to exceed exports and government expenditure to run far ahead of revenue. Technical assistance and financial aid from a wide range of countries and international agencies enabled the government to press forward with its development plans. Loans offered by Egypt, Saudi Arabia, Czechoslovakia, and Bulgaria in 1968 helped in part to compensate for the aid withdrawn by the United States of America when Sudan broke off diplomatic relations after the Six Days' War and by West Germany after Sudanese recognition of East Germany. But even with a generous provision of outside aid and an increasing number of foreign trading partners the Sudan's economic prospects remain among the cloudiest in Africa, economic uncertainty adding yet another element of strain to the country's febrile political situation.

▲▼ HAILE SELASSIE'S ETHIOPIA

In contrast to the dramatic press of events that has marked the history of most African states in the years since the ending of World War II, in contrast, too, to its own turbulent history in the early decades of this century, the record of Ethiopia in the past twenty-five years seems at first sight almost monotonously barren of incident. In 1973 Haile Selassie was still ruling with apparently undiminished authority and vigor, thus establishing a record for length of tenure of high office quite unparalleled not only in any African state but also in any other country in the world. For the aging emperor of the early 1970's was the same man as the young Ras Tafari, appointed regent of Ethiopia as far back as 1916. Great monarchs have a baleful influence on contemporary historiographers: so pervasive is their influence that it is hard not to write the history of their reigns in terms approaching biography. Looking beyond the monarch to the complex society over which he ruled, one needs to try to identify significant changes that occurred during a period seemingly almost untroubled by violent political incidents.

For almost its entire history Ethiopia has been a country noted for its isolation. The most remarkable aspect of the last two decades has been the extent to which Ethiopians have sought to make contact with the outside world, thus opening their country to the impact of alien forces. This movement has taken many forms. There has been the development of Western-style education, the dispatch of students overseas, the foundation of a university and of other specialized institutions for higher studies, all largely staffed by foreigners. There has been a willingness to accept financial and technical assistance and, more recently, capital investment from a wide range of countries, among whom the United States has been particularly prominent. Communications with the outside world have been immensely improved by the development of one of the most efficient airlines in Africa. Most remarkable of all, Ethiopia has pursued an outward-looking foreign policy that has led to the formation of an unusual variety of diplomatic contacts. Few heads of states have traveled so widely in recent years as the Emperor Haile Selassie. In support of the United Nations Ethiopian troops were sent to fight in Korea and to serve in the Congo. Finally, Ethiopia has played a leading part in the movement for African unity, with Addis Ababa providing the headquarters for the Economic Commission for Africa and for the Organization of African Unity. Taken as a whole, these developments have enabled a small but steadily increasing number of young Ethiopians to acquire a range of new techniques and to familiarize themselves with a variety of new ideas in a manner unprecedented in the country's long history.

Basically the Ethiopian experience may seem not dissimilar in this respect from that of most other African countries. But there is an important difference in the method by which these stimulating contacts have come to be established. In African countries experiencing a long period of colonial rule most innovations were imposed by aliens. In Ethiopia the process of innovation has been strictly controlled by the indigenous authority of the emperor. Thus considered, Ethiopia's recent development may be seen as a continuation of old-established trends. The creation of institutions of higher education has served to provide the emperor with the trained officials needed to staff the apparatus of central government, the strengthening of which has been the concern of every powerful ruler in Ethiopian history. A great deal of foreign aid, particularly that received from the United States of America, has been used to build up one of the largest and best equipped armies in Africa. The employment of foreign technicians and advisers represents the continuation of a practice followed by Theodore, Menelik, and other powerful rulers in the nineteenth century. Throughout their history the emperors of Ethiopia have always been conscious of the need to assert, through ceremonies and legend, the dazzling regality of their office: Haile Selassie could have devised no more effective way of enhancing his own prestige than the vigorous foreign policy which he himself has both directed and implemented with its multitude of state occasions and its frequent gatherings of the rulers of modern Africa presided over by the emperor in person.

Thus, by the 1960's, Haile Selassie could feel that he had achieved all the objectives that his predecessors in the imperial office had set before them. As Dame Margery Perham has recently written, "improved communications, an efficient standing army, a settled revenue, a modernized yet still subservient bureaucracy, and an immensely increased range of patronage, have all appeared to give to the throne a greater height and range of power than at any time in its long history. All the ceremonies and trappings of power, all the publicity of an official press, are used to advertize the height of the Emperor's royalty and to create a *Roi Soleil* in Ethiopia, the source of all benefits and progress." [138] And yet, through the irony of history, as the great emperor's reign draws to a close, the country begins to find itself confronted with problems that are bound to create a daunting situation for Haile Selassie's successors.

Ethiopia's problems stem in part from its ethnic composition: in its mixture of peoples and cultures the country is one of the most hetero-geneous in Africa. Over the past seventy years the empire has been held together by Amhara expansion and Shoan hegemony. A vigorous policy of amharization, aided by frequent intermarriage between Amhara and the people of other communities, especially the Galla of the high pla-teau, has done something to lessen the alien quality of Amhara rule. But the Amhara are staunch Christians and their domination has inevi-tably provoked bitter resentment among the Muslim peoples most re-cently brought under the control of the central government—and espe-cially among the Somali of the Ogaden and the Tigray-speaking peoples of northern Eritrea. Historical memories of long centuries of conflict between Muslims and Christians on the borders of the high plateau make present grievances all the harder to eradicate, and the dissident groups can look beyond Ethiopia's borders for support from their core-ligionists. The aspirations of the Ethiopian Somali are best considered in the wider context of Somali nationalism. As for the Muslims of Eri-trea, an immediate deterioration in their relations with the central gov-ernment occurred in 1962 when Eritrea's federal status was revoked and the territory reduced to a mere province. The Muslim separatist movement, whose origins can be traced back to the period of British ad-ministration after World War II, turned to violence. Today the Eritrean Liberation Front is engaged in guerrilla warfare with Ethiopian troops in the wild country along the border with the Sudan and appears to be receiving a measure of practical support from the governments of other Muslim states.

Clearly any weakening of the central government could lead to a wid-ening of the movement of provincial dissidence. But most observers now agree that the power of the old provincial nobility has suffered a disastrous decline. No longer can they gather round them their own pri-vate armies or hope to challenge the military power at the disposal of the central government. Nevertheless, members of the old nobility still retain great prestige and derive substantial fortunes from their landed estates. In terms of political influence the Ethiopian aristocracy remains one of the most powerful classes of its kind in the world.

But even in the midst of Ethiopian high society new and perplexing strains have arisen. The first indication of serious discontent came with the bloody but abortive coup of December, 1960. The coup, which oc-curred at a time when the emperor was on a state visit to Brazil, was organized by a small group of highly placed members of the Amhara elite. Their avowed motive was a desire to accelerate the rate of eco-nomic development in Ethiopia so as to bring the country into line with the measure of progress achieved by other African states. The movement which was never directed overtly against Haile Selassie lacked popular support and so was repressed with relative ease. Yet in retrospect the coup has begun to assume the quality of a symbolic event. For the rebels were expressing ideas that have gained still wider acceptance in the course of the last decade.

Basically the situation is the familiar one of new wine in old bottles. With its monarchy, its nobility, and its church, Ethiopia possesses the most impressive range of traditional institutions to be found anywhere in Africa. Self-interest, combined with a deep attachment to an old-established mode of living make those who control these institutions—the courtiers, the nobles, and the priests—unwilling to make way for a seemingly brash and disrespectful younger generation. Moreover, the conservatives know that they can count on the support of the mass of Ethiopia's peasant population most of whom are still entirely unaffected by the forces that make for rapid change. Yet the young men who have traveled abroad or spoken to foreign visitors are becoming increasingly conscious of the fact that Ethiopia, for all the glory of its great historical tradition and in spite of all the changes that have occurred in the past generation, is to be counted among the most backward states in the world in terms of social and economic development. To take but one example of many, no country in Africa possesses so rudimentary a medical service. In 1962 there was one doctor to every 96,000 inhabitants in Ethiopia: comparable figures for Nigeria showed one doctor to every 27,000, for Morocco, one to every 9,000. Statistics for educational development, for income per capita, or for government spending per capita of population showed Ethiopia far behind most independent African states. Only in one aspect of the modern sector—the size of the standing army and the quality of its equipment—can Ethiopia show its superiority. Its army of 35,000 men is one of the largest in Africa. Whatever the precise course of events after the emperor's death, the army seems bound to play a role of major importance.

▲▼ INDEPENDENT SOMALIA AND SOMALI IRREDENTISM

Compared with other newly independent states, the Somali Republic possesses a measure of ethnic and cultural homogeneity that is almost unique in Africa. The possession of a common culture—manifested in language, religion, traditions, and social and political institutions—gives to the Somali people a sense of nationhood that the leaders of other African states, bedeviled by acute ethnic divisions, have cause to envy. But it would be misleading to assume that the Somali are completely immune to political differences of a kind that may loosely be described as "tribal." Contemporary Somali politics have in fact been profoundly influenced by group divisions that can be traced back over several hundred years.

Every Somali can feel himself a member of the Somali nation by finding his place on a national genealogy that starts with the supposed common ancestor of all the Somali people. But every Somali also finds himself involved in a widening range of loyalties, to his immediate kin, to his lineage, to his clan, and to his clan-family. The Somali are divided among six large clan-families. Two of these clan-families, known collectively as Sab, are confined to the semiagricultural people of southern Somalia, the remaining four, the Samale, being made up of the more widely dispersed nomadic pastoralists. The largest of these Samale clan-families, the Darod, numbers about a million people and is spread across the entire length of the Horn. Other clan-families have a membership of several hundred thousand but occupy more compact areas. In the past, clan-families and even clans were social units too widely dispersed and too deeply riven by internal divisions to have much significance in local politics, but with the development of political parties on a national scale clan-family affiliations have become a matter of great significance.

Political divisions do not, however, follow simply along the lines of clan-families. Somali politics have been characterized by the emergence of a large number of small parties, more than sixty of which competed in the general election of 1969. Many of these parties confine their appeal to members of a particular lineage. Some parties, especially in the south, possess an obvious territorial base. Only a handful can be regarded as truly national. Of these, by far the most important has been the Somali Youth League, an alliance of many different elements, with members of the Darod, the largest of the clan-families, predominating.

Somali society is noted for its egalitarianism. Clanship provides an effective link between the nomadic herdsman and his Western-educated relative working as a civil servant in an office in Mogadishu. A certain hierarchical element has recently been introduced into Somali life through the establishment of a modern administrative structure, but this development has not led to the emergence of a remote and arrogant elite with authoritarian tendencies. Nevertheless, the obligations of clanship and the efficient running of a modern bureaucracy obviously go poorly together. The successful coup led by army officers in October, 1969, was intended as a protest against the nepotism and corruption of the "old gang" of politicians. The new civilian administration, set up by the army and made up of "the cream of the country's youngish technocrats," [139] may well succeed in reforming some abuses; it can hardly hope to free itself from the basic pressures of Somali political life.

In the years between 1960 and 1969 Somali politics presented a kaleidoscopic pattern of frequent ministerial changes, set in a basically democratic framework. In these years the young republic faced three basic tasks: the integration of the former British protectorate with the former Italian trusteeship territory; the unification of all Somali peoples; and the social and economic development of a country that could be represented in statistical terms as one of the poorest in the world. Of these three tasks the first may be said to be nearing completion. When the two parts of the republic achieved independence in 1960, no communication links of any kind existed between the two capitals of Mogadishu and Hargeisa, British-trained civil servants had to make use of translators when writing to their Italian-trained colleagues, and differences in rates of pay, in legal codes, and in administrative procedure provoked constant friction. The first years of the union were marked by a good deal of bitter feeling in the north. Indeed, in December, 1961, a group of young Sandhurst-trained officers stationed at Hargeisa launched a revolt against the government at Mogadishu, but the vast majority of northerners were not prepared to destroy the unity of the new republic and the mutineers were disarmed by their own soldiers.

The claims of Somali irredentism soon proved a potent force in fostering a spirit of national unity. Every Somali was conscious of the plight of his brothers beyond the borders, more than 1 million in Ethiopia, 200,000 in northern Kenya and 40,000 in French Somaliland. "There is no future for us," the Somali Youth League had declared in 1948, "except as part of a Greater Somalia. . . . Union with other Somalilands is our greatest demand which must take priority over all other considerations." [140] Unification remains the declared objective of the Somali government, but experience has shown that such a goal can hardly be achieved without the shedding of much blood.

The years immediately after independence were marked by a steady worsening of the republic's relations with its neighbors. By 1964 Somalia had reached a state of undeclared war with Ethiopia and with Kenya. In the Ogaden Ethiopian troops clashed with well-armed Somali nomads, supported on occasion by detachments of the Somali army. As for Kenya, the Somali government hoped that Britain, as the colonial power, would allow the cession of the Somali-populated areas before the country achieved independence. When Kenyan African politicians showed themselves resolutely opposed to any loss of territory, Somali partisans began to wage a guerrilla war against the Kenyan army in the arid Northern Frontier District.

In French Somaliland, Somali claims clashed with Ethiopian interests
—Djibouti was one of Ethiopia's main outlets to the sea—and with the
local nationalism of the Danakil or Afar who formed a substantial proportion of the territory's population. In 1968 the French government
offered the people of the territory a choice between limited autonomy
under French control and complete independence without further
French aid. Voting in the referendum followed ethnic lines, the Somali
favoring independence, the Afar continued association with France. The
result showed a majority for the Afar, to the disgust of the Somali who
claimed that many of their supporters had been unfairly prevented from
voting, but to the relief of those observers who feared that a Somali victory would have provoked a serious crisis with Ethiopia. Renamed
"Territory of the Afars and the Issas" (Issa being the clan-family of the
local Somali), the 8,000 square mile enclave is the last French colonial
possession on the mainland of Africa.

By 1967 the Somali Republic's aggressive tactics had clearly failed.
Bravely the government of the day decided to change to a policy of conciliation. The propaganda war was called off, guerrilla activities across
the borders discouraged, an accord reached through Zambian mediation
with Kenya, and more harmonious relations established with Ethiopia.
But Somalia's frontiers, with long stretches still not properly demarcated, remained among the most sensitive in Africa and Somali irredentism retained its explosive force.

Somalia is one of the poorest countries in Africa. Bananas and livestock continue to provide its principal exports. During the past decade
the republic has received aid from many different sources and in a variety of forms. New harbors have been constructed by the Russians at
Berbera in the north, and by the Americans at Kismayu in the south.
The Italians have provided schools and bridges, the West Germans a
textile factory, while the Chinese Communists have organized a state
farm and equipped a national theater. In addition the Soviet Union has
helped Somalia to modernize and expand its army and air force. These
developments can affect only marginally the livelihood of most Somali.
Magnificently adapted to their harsh but stimulating environment, the
nomads of the Horn of Africa seem destined to maintain their ancestral
way of life for many generations to come.

CHAPTER III

Northwest Africa

▲▼ INTRODUCTION

Northwest Africa is defined here as a region that embraces both the Maghrib—the Arabic term meaning "west" that covers the four modern states of Morocco, Algeria, Tunisia, and Libya—and the Sahara, whose vast expanse is today divided among no less than ten distinct political units. Thus defined Northwest Africa has a total area of about 3 million square miles.

Despite its size the geographical structure of the region is not difficult to grasp. The desolate Sahara takes up nine-tenths of the total area, leaving to the lands of the Maghrib a relatively narrow strip, never much more than 200 miles—a day's drive—in breadth and disappearing completely in some places, as in parts of Libya, where the desert reaches to the sea. The Maghrib is dominated by its mountains, the mighty chain of the Atlas with its outlying ranges and massifs. But in western Morocco, in parts of northern Algeria, and over much of Tunisia, the Maghrib contains some of the most fertile plains of the Mediterranean world. These contrasts of mountain and plain, fertility and desolation are also to be encountered in the Sahara where rocky massifs—Tibesti, Ahaggar, Air—tower spectacularly above the stony wastes, and lonely oases form green islands amid huge and shifting dunes of sand.

An overall impression of the population of Northwest Africa also suggests simplifications of a kind not possible in the adjoining regions of Northeast and of West Africa. Even today despite its vast extent the region does not contain more than 30 million inhabitants. Thus in its entirety the population of the Maghrib and of the Sahara is not greater than that of modern Egypt and it is considerably smaller than that of modern Nigeria.

Three factors—Berber ancestry, the religion of Islam, and the Arabic language—have profoundly affected the lives of the vast majority of the people of Northwest Africa and so contributed to the region's relative homogeneity. In the course of the past three thousand years parts of the region have been profoundly influenced by the activities of seven distinct groups of alien immigrants—Phoenicians, Romans, Vandals, Greeks, Arabs, Turks, and Western Europeans. With the first four groups and with the Turks the numbers involved appear not to have exceeded a few score thousand. The Western European immigrants of the nineteenth and twentieth centuries, numbering almost 2 million at one time, kept themselves so sharply aloof from the native population that not much intermarriage took place. The Arabs came in two great waves, with the invading armies of expanding Islam in the seventh century, and as Bedouin migrants three centuries later; but however profound their cultural influence, they remained in numerical terms a relatively modest minority. Thus the vast majority of the population of Northwest Africa must be regarded as the descendants of that ancient indigenous stock known to the Romans as *barbari,* the Berbers of modern ethnography.

The Berber language must once have been spoken throughout the region. It is still used by one Moroccan in three and by about a quarter of the population of Algeria. In Tunisia and in Libya, on the other hand, it has died out almost completely, while in the Sahara the Tuareg remain the only major group of Berber-speakers. But though the Berber language would seem to be gradually disappearing in favor of Arabic, there continues to exist in rural areas of the Maghrib a body of beliefs and customs reaching back to a very remote past and forming part of a general Berber culture.

Islam and the Arabic language, the other major factors shaping the lives of the people of Northwest Africa, were introduced by the invading Arab armies of the seventh century A.D. Today the only non-Muslims in Northwest Africa are to be found among the old-established Jewish communities and the more recently settled communities of Europeans, both of which have been greatly reduced by emigration in the course of the last decade. Thus well over 90 percent of the population of the region is Muslim in religion. As for the Arabic language it has been accepted for centuries as the language of the cities and the plains and is spreading steadily to the remote communities of the mountains.

But one must not exaggerate the extent of the region's uniformity. Even before the impact of modern technology, the people of Northwest Africa pursued their livelihoods in many different ways, some as merchants, religious teachers, or craftsmen in the cities or in the oases of the Sahara, others as peasant farmers in the mountains or in the plains, yet others as nomadic pastoralists herding cattle, sheep, goats, or camels. Sharp contrasts exist, too, in the character of individual countries. Tunisia, with its fertile plains and easily accessible coast, has been far more open to alien influences than Morocco where an exceptionally rugged terrain has made it easy for the local people to repel intruders. "The Tunisian," according to a Maghribi proverb, "is a woman, the Algerian is a man, but the Moroccan is a lion."

Today Northwest Africa is divided among a number of independent states. In 1875 the overall political pattern of the region was more complex. Libya was a province of the Ottoman Empire directly under the control of Turkish officials. Tunisia too nominally formed part of the Ottoman domains, but its beys, members of a dynasty founded early in the eighteenth century, enjoyed most of the attributes of sovereignty, while paying a modest annual tribute to Constantinople. Algeria had also been under Ottoman suzerainty, but in 1830 the country was invaded by the French, the Turkish regime overthrown, and the entire territory gradually conquered and transformed into a French colony. Morocco still possessed its ancient status as an independent kingdom, with a record of statehood reaching back through dynastic changes over a thousand years. No ruler of Morocco could, however, claim to have succeeded in asserting his authority over all the communities within his domains. The village republics of the Berber *montagnards* of the Atlas and the Rif were for the most part completely autonomous units. So too were most Saharan communities, as represented by the complicated tribal groupings of the Bedouin Arabs, the Moors, the Tuareg, and the Tebu, the four distinct people each of whom dominated a different sector of the great desert.

Between 1880 and 1930 this political pattern was transformed as every part of the region found itself exposed to European invasion. Three European nations, France, Spain, and Italy, participated in this movement, with the French playing by far the most active part. The consequences of this invasion form the dominant theme for this period of the region's history and provide for the peoples of the Maghrib and of the Sahara a new bond of common experience.

▲▼ ALGERIA: COLONS AND INDIGÈNES

The Maghrib has known many empires in the course of its long recorded history. But until the nineteenth century every imperial power —the Algerine Turks alone excepted—had been based on the region's extremities. Northern Tunisia was the center from which the Phoenicians, the Romans, and the Arabs gradually extended their hegemony westward, while the two great Berber dynasties of the Middle Ages, the

Almoravids and the Almohads, first conquered Morocco before advancing in other directions. In striking contrast to these earlier processes, the French conquest of Algeria, begun in 1830 and formally completed by 1860, made the Central Maghrib the dominant section of the entire region, a base from which the French advanced eastward into Tunisia, southward into and across the vast Sahara, and finally westward into Morocco. Algeria played a crucial role in this movement of French expansion that led to the creation of the most extensive—and the most ephemeral—imperial structure ever imposed on the Maghrib. But Algeria was also a country continually beset with a fearful problem of its own, a "racial" problem involving the relationship between Europeans and Muslims, *colons* and *indigènes*. In the late 1870's the territory contained about 300,000 Europeans out of a total population of 3 million; by 1911 the number of Europeans had increased to 752,000, the total population to 5.6 million. In no other part of the Islamic world were Muslims confronted with so large or so formidable a community of aliens settled in their midst. Nowhere else in Northern Africa did the clash of cultures produce so harsh and discordant a note.

Up to 1870, French Algeria had been dominated by the army, with a governor-general, invariably a military man, possessing virtually autocratic powers and with a large part of the country administered by army officers. To the *colons,* the European settlers, the *régime du sabre* was a doubly distasteful system, denying them many of the rights they would have enjoyed in metropolitan France and paying insufficient attention to their own interests. Particularly obnoxious to the *colons* was Napoleon III's famous declaration that Algeria was "not a colony but an Arab kingdom" and that both Arabs and Frenchmen were equal in his eyes. For this reason the emperor's fall in 1870 was greeted with rapture by the ardent republicans of Algiers who immediately set about constructing a system that would guarantee forever their status as a dominant minority.

Politically, the last decades of the nineteenth century were a golden age for the *colons* of Algeria. Under the constitution of the Third Republic they were able to send representatives—six deputies and three senators—to the parliament in Paris, thus ensuring the presence of a vocal Algerian lobby at the center of affairs, a lobby which found ample opportunity to assert itself in the kaleidoscopic instability of republican politics. Meanwhile in Algiers the powers of the governor-general were rigorously curtailed. A large part of the country was transferred from military to civilian rule and, for a time, government departments were placed under the control of the appropriate ministry in Paris. When this system of *rattachements* proved unsatisfactory, the colonists succeeded in attaining a measure of local self-government through the establishment of the *delegations financières,* a body which after 1900 was able to control a large part of the Algerian budget.

Between 1870 and 1891, the civil territory of Algeria was expanded from 6,000 to 60,000 square miles. In the formerly military territory native affairs had been the responsibility of the officers of the *bureaux arabes,* the best of whom showed a real, if paternalistic, sympathy for their subjects; the *indigènes* of the civil territory found themselves under the control of officials, many of whom were of local origin and in full accord with the views of the *colons.* To the *colons,* obsessed with the difficulties of earning a livelihood in a particularly harsh environment, the native population seemed, in the words of a later historian, "the evil genius of the land, apart and impenetrable, partly a menace and wholly a nuisance." [1] In 1871 the French had been faced with a great revolt in Kabylia, an uprising which was suppressed with great brutality after months of hard fighting. In the late 1870's and early 1880's fresh outbreaks in other parts of the country reminded the settlers that they were living amid a hostile population. "The Arab," wrote a French settler after the defeat of the Kabyle revolt, "must accept the fate of the conquered. He must either become assimilated to our civilization or disappear. European civilization can have no sympathy for the life of savages." [2]

The process of *refoulement,* of pushing natives out of their lands to make room for European colonists, had begun at an early stage in the conquest. It was continued even more vigorously after 1870, with every unsuccessful native revolt providing the opportunity for confiscations on a massive scale. At the same time, new legislations encouraged the division into individual holdings of land previously held collectively by tribal groups and made it easy for European colonists to buy land at very cheap prices. Despite their loss of land the native population still had to bear a heavy burden of taxation. In the early years of the twentieth century 70 percent of the proceeds of direct taxation came from the *indigènes;* yet no more than 3 percent of the country's total expenditure was devoted to social services for the Muslim population. Finally, as if to emphasize their position as a defeated people, Muslim Algerians were subjected to a harsh disciplinary code, the *indigénat,* which required all Muslims to carry passes and imposed prison sentences for a wide variety of offenses, including begging, delay in paying taxes, or making a journey without having obtained permission from the authorities.

These harsh administrative measures shattered the structure of traditional Algerian society. "The Algerian nobility," in the words of

Jacques Berque, "still knew how to sweep majestically through the waiting rooms of the *bureau des affaires indigènes*. But its function was no longer that of the true feudal lord, adjudicator, representative, and apex of the tribe. With few exceptions it consisted solely of official dignitaries and debt-ridden opportunists." [3] Almost the entire native population was faced with the dismal process of apparently irreversible pauperization. From the mid-1870's the Muslim population began to increase steadily, doubling itself from 2½ to 5 million in the course of half a century. So unprecedented an increase taking place at a time when the native economy remained completely stagnant, meant a serious decline in the standard of living for the majority of Muslims. Pastoralists were deprived of their grazing grounds, peasants forced back into lands of poorer fertility. In 1911 no more than 80,000 Algerian Muslims were able to find employment in industry and commerce. For the vast majority migration overseas was not yet possible, but in the decade before World War I a few enterprising men, mainly from Kabylia, made their way to France in search of a livelihood.

Many Frenchmen in metropolitan France were aware of the abuses of the Algerian situation. In the French parliament the native question in Algeria was the subject of a number of memorable debates, instigated by a small group of liberal-minded reformers who made scathing oratorial assaults on the colonial regime. "There is no longer any justice for the natives of Algeria," a leading reformer, Senator Pauliat, declared in 1891, "they are oppressed by the Algerian colonists who are the real masters and the tyrants of the colony." [4] But colonial reformers faced a double problem—to devise a practical ideal and to ensure that the measures needed were successfully implemented. Inevitably, given the tenor of French thought, the ideal of most reformers was one of progressive assimilation, a development which implied the removal of all those humiliating restrictions to which Algerian Muslims had for so long been exposed. In the years immediately before and after World War I the reformers were able to make some progress. But to the vast majority of Algerians, *colons* and *indigènes* alike, assimilation was utterly unacceptable. The *colons,* conscious always of their position as a minority outnumbered ten to one, could never contemplate a development which was bound to diminish their power, while the vast majority of Muslims were not prepared to renounce their own culture for that of their masters.

Perceptive observers could see the dangers in the situation. "Security? We shall have it," remarked a great Algerian administrator, Charles Jomart, "when we cease to exploit the native under the pretext of emancipating and assimilating him." [5] This was said in 1893. It was no less true forty years later, after half a century of internal peace, when superficial impressions suggested that the colonial regime was destined to last forever. And yet, as Berque has pointed out, "the whole set up lived under an indefinable threat. . . . A sense of precariousness, the dread of an imminent settling of accounts which might lead to bloodshed, whetted men's appetites, sharpening their desire for gain and pleasure. The very prosperity enjoyed by a few made them more apprehensive of what was in store." [6]

▲▼ FRENCH HEGEMONY IN TUNISIA

"It is pitiable," wrote the United States consul in Tunis in 1878," to see a country like this with a docile people, an excellent climate, rich soil and abundant resources reduced to the most abject poverty and misery by the misgovernment of a few men whose only thought is to find the means of gratifying their inordinate love of luxury and bad passions." [7] Basically the tribulations of the Regency of Tunis bore a close resemblance to those of Egypt, for in both countries the members of the small governing class had allowed themselves to be seduced by the alluring novelties that could now be offered by Europe. For the rulers the cost was loss of power; for their countries, subjection to a new group of alien masters.

As rulers the nineteenth-century beys of the Hussainid dynasty were lesser men than Muhammad Ali and his descendants, with the result that effective power came to lie in the hands of the small group of Mamluk ministers appointed to the great offices of state. These Mamluks arrived in the regency as aliens. Of Greek or Circassian descent, most of them had been captured as slaves in their youth, converted to Islam and placed at an early age in the household of the bey. Bound to the land of their adoption by few ties of sentiment, brought up in an atmosphere of constant intrigue, occupying posts from which they could be dismissed at a moment's notice, the members of this highly exclusive elite inevitably devoted most of their energies to the advancement of their own private interests. The most prominent of these Mamluk ministers, Mustapha Khaznadar, was shrewd enough to succeed in holding the highest offices of state from 1837 to 1873. "Sidi Mustapha," wrote a well-informed European observer in 1871, "has never had and will never have any other political system than that of pillaging and ruining the country he governs." [8] As for Mustapha's master, the bey Muhammad as-Saduk (1859–82), he was a noted devotee of the pleasures of the harem, and consequently delighted to leave the cares of state to his industrious minister.

The events of the 1860's bore witness to the disastrous nature of

Mustapha's rule. Ambitious schemes of modernization were started that could be paid for only by accepting high-interest loans from European financiers. To meet the debt charges, taxes were sharply increased. The peasantry, oppressed beyond endurance, promptly revolted, only to suffer savage repression. Finally, as the situation continued to deteriorate, the government of the regency found itself forced to hand over complete control of its finances to an international financial commission. By 1875 a marked improvement could be noted. The rascally Mustapha had at last been removed from office. His successor, Kheredin, was able, public-spirited, and animated by a spirit of Tunisian patriotism rarely found in a Mamluk minister. Working harmoniously with the members of the international commission, Kheredin embarked on a program of practical administrative reform aimed at eliminating the corruption of his predecessor's regime. He also sought ways of involving the Tunisian bourgeoisie more closely in the work of government. But the bey, for all his effeteness, still had the power to dismiss ministers at will. In 1877 he replaced Kheredin by one of the most corrupt of his favorites. Within a few months all Kheredin's reforms had been undone.

The country's wretched situation was made still worse by the intrigues of foreigners. From the 1850's on, a motley crew of European adventurers, British, French, and Italian for the most part, made their presence felt in the regency, "like flies," in the expressive Arab simile, "swarming around a wounded ass." Their grandiose schemes for mining concessions or for the construction of railroads contributed little to the development of the country but were skillfully devised to extract the maximum amount of money from the coffers of the bey. European consuls in Tunis spent much of their time furthering the commercial enterprises of their compatriots, but they were also concerned with broader political considerations.

Four powers had an interest in the affairs of Tunis. In Constantinople the regency was still regarded as forming part of the Ottoman Empire. The frequently troubled frontier with Algeria made Tunis a country of major concern to the French. Nationalist politicians in an Italy newly unified were well aware that their own compatriots formed by far the largest element in the regency's European population. As for the British, they were accustomed to regard any country that lay alongside the lifelines of their empire as possessing strategic importance.

Until the 1870's, British policy in Tunis as in other parts of North Africa sought to preserve the status quo by supporting Ottoman claims to hegemony. These claims the French encouraged the bey's government to throw off, for it was reckoned in Paris that an independent Tunis could be drawn more easily into the French sphere of influence. In the late 1870's the British, thinking that recent events showed the Ottoman Empire to be on the verge of collapse, made a drastic reappraisal of their Mediterranean policy. In 1878 they acquired possession of Cyprus, thus strengthening their position in the eastern Mediterranean but providing the French with what was then regarded as legitimate cause for seeking compensation. By this time Italy was beginning to assume the role of a considerable power. Should Tunis fall to the Italians, a potentially hostile European nation would be in control of both sides of the Mediterranean at its narrowest point. In these altered circumstances the British foreign secretary, Lord Salisbury, let it be known to the French that his government would not object to a French move to take over the regency. Bismarck urged the French even more vigorously "to pick the ripe Tunisian pear." French ministers rightly saw in the German chancellor's suggestion a ruse designed to distract them from their preoccupation with the lost provinces of Alsace and Lorraine. They knew too that their compatriots had no desire to become involved in overseas adventures. And so, despite an exceptionally favorable international climate, French statesmen hung back.

Meanwhile in Tunis, an intensely bitter rivalry was developing between the French and Italian consuls, Roustan and Maccio, both energetic champions of their country's interests. Considerations of prestige now complicated the situation. "A new show of feebleness," wrote the French ambassador in Berlin, "and we shall end up by reducing ourselves to the rank of Spain." [9] Financial interests with a stake in the regency were no less ardent in demanding action. This small clique— Roustan, the diplomats, and the businessmen—proved persuasive advocates. Once the French government had been convinced of the need for action, there was no difficulty in finding a pretext for intervention. Algeria's eastern frontier had frequently been troubled by the Kroumir, a turbulent group of *montagnards,* living nominally within the bey's domains but never subject to his authority. In the spring of 1881, French troops were involved in yet another incident with the Kroumir. Orders were promptly given for a French expeditionary force to march on Tunis. On May 12, the bey agreed to sign the treaty of Bardo under whose terms control of the regency's finances and of its foreign relations was placed in French hands, while a French military occupation was to be maintained until such time as the local administration should prove itself capable of maintaining law and order.

The devious nature of French policy did not escape contemporary critics. "The real object," wrote the London *Daily Telegraph,* "is to drill the unfortunate Regency into a happy hunting ground for French speculators." [10] And in France the government was assailed both from the extreme right and from the extreme left. In the regency the first phase of the invasion passed with little fighting. But in July, 1881, the people of the south rose in protest against the French occupation. Several months' campaigning were needed to break Tunisian resistance, and some groups near the border with Tripoli continued to wage a guerrilla war against the invaders until 1888.

Tunisia—the name the French began to apply to their new possession—had been conquered without much difficulty. The more taxing task of establishing an effective system of administration remained to be accomplished. There was no desire in official quarters to create another Algeria by annexing the regency outright and transforming it into a colony for European settlement. An alternative formula could be found in Southeast Asia where in 1863 the French had declared a protectorate over the kingdom of Cambodia and placed a French resident by the side of the local ruler. In Tunis Consul Roustan became the first resident-general, but the term "protectorate" was not formally applied until 1883. By this time Roustan had been replaced by Paul Cambon, a highly efficient civil servant who had made a name for himself as a departmental prefect and was later to become even more widely known as French ambassador in London in the years before World War I.

To Cambon Tunisia seemed a country in a state of complete collapse. "Misery, waste and ruin exist throughout," he wrote shortly after his arrival. [11] To transform the country he needed greater powers than those allowed him by the treaty of Bardo. To this end he set about negotiating a new convention which was signed at La Marsa in 1883. "In order to make it easier for the French Government to accomplish its protectorate, His Highness, the Bey of Tunis," ran the crucial first article, "promises to proceed with the administrative, judicial and financial reforms that the French government will judge necessary."

The bey was allowed to retain the trappings of his royal office, but with such a legal instrument at their disposal French residents-general were in a position to intervene in almost every sphere of Tunisian life. Tunisian offices were not abolished, but by the side of every important Tunisian official there came to be placed a French official acting in a supervisory capacity. Thus the old system of administration was overlaid by a new administrative structure, manned solely by Frenchmen and reaching from the resident-general and his deputy, the secretary-general, in the capital to the civil controllers and their assistants in the provinces appointed to keep a check on the behavior of local *caids*. At the same time new departments of state were created to administer the newly established social and technical services (education, public works, agriculture, etc.), with Frenchmen occupying all the senior posts. Officials familiar with the techniques of the modern world were, of course, essential, if the protecting power was to fulfill its self-imposed task by introducing all the reforms that seemed necessary. Given the lack of qualified Tunisians, the officials needed could only be drawn from France, from Algeria, or from French-settler families in Tunisia. But as the number of French officials increased, it became obvious that the concept of a protectorate was little more than a fiction, a sop to liberal consciences.

By the 1890's it was clear that the protectorate of Tunisia represented what Paul Leroy-Beaulieu, the leading French colonial theorist of the day, termed *une colonie d'exploitation* in which "the superior race directs, raises, and guides the inferior race, provides the capital, develops the natural resources, and by means of an intelligent staff of administrators, engineers, men with capital, businessmen, teachers, foremen, and workers transforms a country that has long been sunk in poverty, on account of the lack of initiative and the absence of accumulated material resources among its people, into a rich and prosperous territory." [12] As French administration became increasingly more direct, as the number of alien immigrants steadily mounted—there were 130,000 Europeans in Tunisia in 1910 compared with 18,000 in 1880—the protectorate might well have seemed to be developing into another Algeria. But the fiction of a protectorate allowed a consciousness of the country's historic personality to survive. By the first decade of the twentieth century a handful of educated Tunisians had begun to speak the language of a new nationalism.

▲▼ THE EROSION OF MOROCCAN INDEPENDENCE:
1875 TO 1912

To late nineteenth-century Europeans the Sharifian Empire of Morocco, one of the most historic states in Africa, presented a spectacle of anarchy and decay. The romantically inclined were entranced by features that could be described as "medieval" or "picturesque"—the walled cities, the ceremonial of the imperial court, the prancing horsemen, the lonely *kasbahs*. "Somber Morocco," wrote that arch-romantic traveler, the Frenchman Pierre Loti, in 1889, "long may you remain immured, impenetrable to novelty. Turn your back on Europe; abide motionless in time past. Long may your ancient charms persist." [13] Prosaic observers could only see, as one of them wrote in the 1890's, "that everything is crumbling. The towns on the coast exhibit a gloss of Europe and the nineteenth century; those of the interior are to a large extent semi-ruins amid all-abounding filth." [14] In European eyes Morocco was on the verge of complete collapse; only a liberal transfusion of reforms, based on European models, could transform the ancient kingdom.

Events were to confirm the validity of this diagnosis. Nevertheless, the contemporary European view provided no more than a superficial impression of a highly complex situation, and most European observers possessed scant understanding of the realities of the Moroccan predicament. Moroccans could look back on a history rich in cultural achievements and distinguished by periods in which their country had clearly been one of the major powers of the Mediterranean world. Dynastic traditions associated with an organized Moroccan state reached back as far as the eighth century and were therefore no less ancient than those of the longest-established European monarchies. Moreover, this dynastic tradition had been maintained in spite of the fact that Morocco's peculiar geographical configuration made it an exceedingly difficult country to control. Indeed there were mountain villages in the lonely valleys of the Rif or the Atlas only a few score miles from the imperial cities of Fez and Marrakesh where even the most powerful sultan had never succeeded in asserting his authority. In recent centuries, a large part of the country had come to be termed *bilad as-siba* ("land of dissidence") and this rebel territory increased rapidly in area whenever the *makhzen* ("the imperial government") showed any sign of weakness. Nevertheless even if the sultan's authority was constantly slighted, his prestige remained very great. The traditions of the dynasty embodied a large part of the historical experiences of the Moroccan people, a situation unique in the world of Islam. "Morocco," as an eminent French historian pointed out in 1953, "has been for almost five hundred years the only Islamic country which was aware of itself as constituting a nation." [15]

To hold the country together, to preserve the *bilad al-makhzen* and diminish the *bilad as-siba* was the primary task of every Moroccan sultan and one that required exceptional qualities of energy, courage, and diplomatic skill. If at the same time the sultan sought to introduce fundamental reforms, he was likely to run up against the opposition of those conservative groups which would, in other circumstances, have proved his most powerful supporters. Finally, from the middle of the nineteenth century on, every Moroccan sultan had to cope with a constantly worsening international situation. Faced with growing pressure from the powers of Western Europe, it became impossible to maintain the policy of haughty isolation favored by early nineteenth-century sultans. Along Morocco's long and troubled eastern borders the relatively weak Turkish regime based in Algiers had been replaced after 1830 by a powerful French presence. For centuries the Spaniards had possessed in their *presidios* of Ceuta and Melilla small enclaves in Moroccan territory, while across the narrow straits lay the major British base of Gibraltar. Thus for reasons of security or prestige the governments of France, Britain, and Spain all had cause to interest themselves in Moroccan affairs. They were joined in the last decades of the nineteenth century by Germany, for Bismarck was quick to perceive the significance of Morocco as a pawn on the diplomatic chessboard of Europe. All these interested powers had a stake in the external trade of Morocco and were concerned to preserve and to extend the privileges accorded to their own nationals and to those Moroccans who had placed themselves under consular protection.

The reign of Mulay Hassan (1873–94) clearly indicated the difficulties, amounting at this period to sheer impossibility, involved in the task of equipping Morocco with a modernized infrastructure. Mulay Hassan was vividly aware of his country's problems and anxious to introduce moderate reforms. He was, moreover, a ruler of inexhaustible energy: "The imperial tents are never stored," men said in his reign, referring to the sultan's constant peregrinations through his dominions. Realistically, Mulay Hassan grasped the paramount importance of replacing his ill-disciplined tribal levies with an efficient standing army equipped with modern weapons. Such a force would enable him to extend the territory of the *bilad al-makhzen* and thus ensure a greater volume of tribute, part of which could be used to meet the cost of constructing roads, harbors and other useful projects. As respect for the authority of the *makhzen* increased, the sultan hoped to be able to prevent the recurrence of unfortunate incidents involving foreigners that had in recent years provided European governments with a pretext for exacting diplomatic pressure on his country.

To improve the quality of his army Mulay Hassan accepted the services of foreign military instructors, arranged for young Moroccans to attend training courses at many of the military academies of Western Europe, bought modern equipment from a wide range of European and American firms, invited a group of Italians to set up a munitions factory at Fez, and gave a contract for coastal artillery to the German firm of Krupp. These expensive innovations could be paid for only by squeezing more taxes out of the people of the *bilad al-makhzen* and by launching regular tribute-collecting expeditions—known to Moroccans by the expressive term *harka* ("burning")—against the communities of the *bilad as-siba*. Particular attention needed to be paid to the extreme southwest of the country, a remote province that Mulay Hassan's predecessors could afford to ignore, for groups of European adventurers had established bases on the Saharan coast and were attempting to siphon off the lucrative trans-Saharan trade—for their own profit and the *makhzen*'s loss.

In terms of the immediate present the sultan's policy proved successful. Mulay Hassan preserved his country's independence. Moreover, unlike most of his predecessors, he never found himself faced with a serious internal revolt. But the methods he was forced to employ laid up serious trouble for the future. *Harkas* destroyed the prosperity of the districts through which they passed; at the same time, the people of the *bilad al-makhzen* grew increasingly resentful of the cost, expressed in mounting taxes, of these expensive expeditions. Here indeed was a vicious circle from which even a ruler of Mulay Hassan's ability could not escape.

To make matters worse, economic forces over which the sultan had no control were steadily working against him. In the 1860's Morocco had enjoyed a decade of relative prosperity, with wool and corn, the country's major exports, securing good prices in a steadily expanding European market. But the price of Moroccan exports began falling in the 1870's in the face of steadily mounting competition from the pastures of Australia and the prairies of North America. Meanwhile, Morocco was attracting the attention of more and more European businessmen as a market. In the years between 1864 and 1894, the number of Europeans resident in Morocco, the majority of them engaged in trade, rose from 1,350 to 9,000. Mounting imports created an unfavorable trade balance and led to a steady movement of currency out of the country. Prudently, Mulay Hassan avoided becoming entangled in the disastrous policy followed by his contemporaries in Egypt and in Tunis of raising foreign loans, but the financial reserves of his government and country were being steadily drained away and there was little he could do to prevent this happening; the growing influence, the constant jealousy, and the frequent intrigues of the representatives of the European powers blocked all his attempts at constructive fiscal reform.

For the European countries doing business with Morocco the total volume of their commerce might seem extremely modest. (In the early 1890's, for instance, about 50 percent of Morocco's external trade was done with Great Britain; yet trade with Morocco represented no more than 0.2 percent of total British overseas commerce.) But for the Moroccans a vigorous maritime trade was an innovation that produced a radical transformation in the structure of their economy. It was almost as if the country had been given a new face. After 1850 the ports developed a dynamism that contrasted sharply with the economic stagnation of the rest of the country. Their population increased rapidly: Tangier, with 45,000 inhabitants in 1900, had experienced a fivefold increase since 1850; over the same period Casablanca had been transformed from a village to a town of 11,000. Steamship lines founded in the 1870's and 1880's, provided regular contact with Liverpool, Marseilles, and Hamburg and so drew the Moroccan ports into the orbit of a wider economy. Small groups of Moroccans, some of Jewish origin, others Muslim merchants from Fez or Rabat, were quick to take advantage of the new commercial opportunities. Settling in the ports, placing themselves whenever possible under the "protection" of a European consul —a legal device that enabled the protégé to escape many of the taxes imposed by the *makhzen*—and rapidly acquainting themselves with the techniques of modern commerce, these enterprising men developed into a prosperous bourgeoisie. Their familiarity with European ways and their keen interest in personal profit prepared them for the role of collaborators with a European protecting power.

When Mulay Hassan died in 1894, his son and heir, Abd al-Aziz, was still a minor and so for six years the country was governed by Bu Ahmad, the powerful court chamberlain. Abd al-Aziz who took over the practical duties of sultan on Bu Ahmad's death in 1900 was described by a European friend as "intelligent, thoughtful and desirous of doing well," [16] but he was a weak young man who allowed himself to be seduced by a crowd of European hangers-on into wasting his resources on the toys of European technology, ranging from elaborate firework displays to barrel-organs and cameras mounted in gold. Before long, picture postcards of the sultan dressed in fancy European uniforms were on sale in Tangier to the horror and disgust of his devout Muslim subjects. "Foreigners are the original cause of all our troubles," declared the ulama of Fez. "Our ancestors lived in peace and quiet at a time when foreigners had no means of interfering in our affairs and when it was impossible for them to corrupt us. What use have these foreigners been to us? What new sciences have they taught us and what advantages have we gained from them?" [17]

Inevitably there were revolts. An adventurer nicknamed Bu Hamara, "father of the she-ass," made himself out to be a brother of the sultan, gained control of most of northeastern Morocco and, with the aid of arms sent to him by the French settlers of Oran, held his own from 1902 to 1911. At the same time, Morocco's international standing was severely shaken by a drastic change in British policy. For sixty years the British, ever anxious to preserve the security of the Straits of Gibraltar and to develop open markets for their traders, had constituted themselves the most vigorous defenders of Moroccan independence and the foremost advocates of the necessity for internal reforms. But by

1903 it had become exasperatingly clear to the British that external advice could never bring about satisfactory changes. Of the countries of North Africa, Egypt was by now much more important to the British than Morocco. On the other hand, French interest in Egypt had declined since the settlement of the Fashoda crisis of 1898, but a powerful lobby, recently formed by Eugène Etienne, the deputy for Oran, was urging the need to "tunisify" Morocco. There was room here for profitable horse trading. Under the terms of the Anglo-French treaty of 1904 the French recognized British paramountcy in Egypt; in return the British agreed to recognize that it "appertains to France to preserve order in Morocco and to provide assistance for all administrative, financial, and military reforms that it may require." Some months earlier the French and Spanish governments, reckoning that the sultan's authority was likely to break down completely, had drawn up plans for a partition of the country. These arrangements suited British interests, for they reserved to Spain, in British eyes a relatively harmless power, control of the northern coast of Morocco opposite the British base at Gibraltar. Accordingly they were endorsed in a secret clause of the Anglo-French treaty.

In these negotiations one major European power had been ignored. Since the 1870's German interest in Morocco had steadily increased. By 1904 the Germans were doing almost as much trade with the country as the French. In these circumstances the Germans had some reason to feel themselves affronted. As they brooded on their grievances, French policy began to take on in their eyes a brutally Machiavellian guise. Clearly Delcassé, the forceful French foreign minister, was making a deliberate attempt to exclude Germany from a field of perfectly legitimate interest. National prestige was at stake. A vigorous countergesture must be made. In April, 1905, Kaiser Wihelm II landed at Tangier. "Germany," he was reported as saying, "regards Morocco as an independent state. Germany will not tolerate an attempt by any power to establish its supremacy over Morocco." The Kaiser's words were interpreted as a calculated rebuff to the French. A long-drawn-out diplomatic crisis followed. For the first time in thirty years, French and German statesmen dropped veiled hints of war. "The long Bismarckian peace" was "shattered." It was, as one eminent historian has pointed out, "a turning point in the history of Europe." [18] But for Morocco the crisis brought no relief, nor did it provide the Germans with the compensation they had sought. An international conference in the Spanish town of Algericas early in 1906 confirmed that in the reform of Morocco France should play the leading role.

Rapidly the situation deteriorated. In 1907, incidents in which a number of Europeans were killed provided the French with a pretext for occupying a number of Moroccan towns including Casablanca. In 1908, Abd al-Aziz was overthrown in a revolt led by his brother, Mulay Hafiz. The change of sultan did little to arrest the mounting disorder. In 1911, Mulay Hafiz found himself beseiged in his capital, Fez, by hostile tribesmen and appealed to the French for assistance. The dispatch of a French column to Fez made it clear that the days of Moroccan independence were numbered. Feeling themselves entitled to "compensation," the Germans sent a gunboat to the south Moroccan port of Agadir. The second Moroccan crisis stirred public opinion in Germany, France, and Britain far more vigorously than the crisis of 1905. After months of tough bargaining in an atmosphere embittered by ominous hints of war an agreement was hammered out. The French gave the Germans a substantial slice of their equatorial colony of the Congo; in return the Germans agreed to drop their objection to a French protectorate over Morocco. In March, 1912, four months after the Franco-German accord, a treaty was signed at Fez whereby Sultan Mulay Hafiz placed his country under French protection. In the European view this seemed the logical culmination of events, the opening of a new and happier phase in Moroccan history. But to the Muslim population of the ancient kingdom, the treaty of Fez appeared as a shameful "act of sale." The sultan of Morocco was also the *imam,* the religious leader of his people; yet he had made over part of *dar al-Islam* ("the domain of Islam") into the hands of the unbelievers.

▲▼ THE CONQUEST OF MOROCCO: 1912 TO 1934

One of the clauses of the treaty of Fez provided for the division of the protectorate of Morocco into two zones, one French, the other—no more than 8,500 square miles in extent—Spanish. This paper protectorate had now to be transformed into an effective administrative superstructure. The task was formidable. The French and Spanish authorities were dealing with a people noted for their passionate devotion to Islam and their staunch love of independence—qualities usually referred to in European parlance as "fanaticism" and "xenophobia." They were attempting to assert control over a country that had never, in its thousand years of history as a Muslim state, been successfully conquered by an invader of alien faith. And they were confronted with a situation in which law and order appeared to have broken down completely. In the spring of 1912, Berber tribesmen moved down from their mountains to harrass the cities of the plain. In Fez soldiers of the imperial army mutinied shortly after the signing of the protectorate treaty and murdered their European officers. Most serious of all, far to the south, a religious leader from the western Sahara, known as al-Hiba, proclaimed a jihad against the infidels, attracted to his cause the warriors of the desert and of the mountains, and advanced on the southern capital of Marrakesh where in August he was proclaimed sultan.

Massive military force promptly and vigorously deployed was essential to cope with such a situation. Between them, the French and Spanish authorities soon had more than 100,000 troops in Morocco. But force alone would not suffice to introduce those reforms which provided the sole justification for the establishment of the protectorate. This more delicate task needed the touch of the skillful administrator and the insight of the shrewd and sensitive diplomat. It was a piece of rare good fortune both for Morocco and for France that General (later Marshal) Hubert Lyautey, the first resident-general in the French zone, should prove himself not only an outstanding soldier but also an administrator of genius, in achievement the greatest, in personality the most engaging of all the Europeans who have left their mark on the history of Northwest Africa.

Lyautey was fifty-eight when he came to Morocco as resident-general. Born of an aristocratic family from Lorraine, he had spent all his life in the army and acquired a remarkable range of experience, making a name for himself in France as one of the brightest young officers of his generation, serving under another great military administrator, Galliéni, in Indochina and in Madagascar and holding high command in Algeria in a post which brought him directly into contact with Moroccan affairs. Lyautey represented that rare and admirable combination, the man of action who is also an intellectual; moreover, he was blessed with an immense charm of manner. To his subordinates he was the ideal *patron,* gay, sympathetic, "friend-creative" in the phrase of one of his English acquaintances,[19] and he had no difficulty in gathering round him a group of young army officers whom he inspired with his own ideals. To Lyautey the task of the colonial administrator was creative, life-enhancing. "Wherever I have gone," he wrote in 1915, "it has been to construct. . . . In Morocco, among these ancient lands of lethargy what a rich joy there has been in giving them desire, in quickening the blood in their veins." [20] With his practical experience of road-building, of developing medical services, of founding new towns and markets Lyautey possessed a remarkable grasp of the problems involved in economic development. But this constant concern for fruitful innovations was accompanied in the mind of this many-sided man by a deep and humane respect for tradition. "The longer I live in this country," Lyautey once said of Morocco, "the more I am convinced of the greatness of this nation." [21] Thus Lyautey came to develop an intensely personal sense of mission, loving Morocco, in the words of a modern historian, "with a passion that saw its future not as a colony but as a noble friend unified and exalted by his hand." [22]

Lyautey's primary task was to gain control of the *bilad as-makhzen,* the land of fertile plains and populous cities which he termed *Maroc utile.* "Show force in order not to use it" was one of his favorite maxims; by observing it he aimed to avoid unnecessary bloodshed. He also subscribed vigorously to the old imperialist adage "divide and rule" and made use of all the techniques of local diplomacy to gain supporters for the French cause from among his Moroccan opponents. This policy was worked out on a grand scale in the south where Lyautey won over the great Berber *caids,* the members of the al-Glawi family, and other "lords of the Atlas," by confirming them in the possession of their recently acquired domains. The pretender, al-Hiba, was defeated by a French force and compelled to abandon Marrakesh. With the Berber *caids* acting as marcher lords on their behalf the French had no cause to fear a renewed assault from the men of the desert. By the summer of 1914, the greater part of *Maroc utile* was in French hands, but soon after the outbreak of war in Europe, Lyautey received orders from Paris to send more than half his 70,000 troops back to France and to retreat to the Atlantic coast. Realizing that any sign of weakness would provoke an immediate revolt, Lyautey disregarded the latter part of these instructions, skillfully succeeded in retaining all the recently conquered territory, and was able in 1917 to resume the offensive. As the French columns moved into the valleys of the Atlas, the traditional *bilad as-siba,* fighting increased in intensity. "No tribe," a French army officer wrote later, "submitted without fighting and some did not submit until they had exhausted their last means of resistance." [23] Finally, to pacify the Berber tribes of the Atlas it became necessary to impose a permanent system of military occupation.

Lyautey conquered Morocco in the name of the sultan. He himself subscribed vigorously to the ideal of a protectorate. "Govern with the mandarins, not against them. Do not offend a single tradition, do not change a single habit. Identify the governing class with our interests." [24] These were the imperatives by which French policy should be directed. In practice it was impossible to observe them. One of Lyautey's first acts had been to force Mulay Hafiz to abdicate in favor of his more pliant brother, Yusuf. As the structure of French administration developed along lines similar to those established a generation earlier in Tunisia, it became clear that a system of government by control was turning into a form of direct administration. "Practically everyone within the French Administration," the resident-general wrote ruefully in 1920, "succumbs to the tendency to regard the natives as belonging to an inferior race, of being of no account." [25]

Lyautey himself was well aware of the dangers inherent in this attitude. He could see that a new generation of Moroccans educated in the schools established by the French authorities was beginning to emerge; he realized that some at least of these young men were bound to be attracted by the nationalist fervor sweeping through the countries of the Muslim East, and he regarded it as essential to win over this new elite by appointing its members to posts of some responsibility in the administration. In the context of the times this was a remarkably enlightened attitude for a colonial administrator. But Lyautey was not prepared to go so far as to allow young Moroccans to study in France for fear that they should become exposed to subversive influences. He saw France as fulfilling in Morocco the noble role of a "tutor" or of a "benevolent elder brother." In so doing he laid himself open to the reproaches likely to be leveled by the more vigorous of its subjects against any paternalistic regime, no matter how benevolent its intentions.

But there was a deeper contradiction, a graver weakness in Lyautey's policy. To ensure French control he was glad to accept the collaboration of a small class of feudal magnates, the great *caids* of the Atlas; to promote economic development he was eager to encourage French businessmen to invest in the country; and he was prepared to allow a limited amount of European agricultural settlement. As in other parts of the Maghrib, the French *colons,* whether businessmen or farmers, soon developed into an immensely powerful pressure group determined to maintain a system that ensured to them the maximum amount of advantages. Thus, by the time of Lyautey's resignation in 1925, Morocco had come to be saddled with a regime whose three main supporting groups, administrators, *colons,* and Berber *caids,* were deeply concerned to preserve a situation so profitable to themselves. Men such as these were to prove narrow-minded and inflexible in their reactions to the aspirations newly conceived by an increasing number of Moroccans. Inevitably, therefore, Lyautey's achievement seems less commendable to a postcolonial generation than it did to European observers of the 1920's when it could reasonably be argued that within the space of a decade Lyautey and his assistants had wrought an extraordinary transformation, making possible the "regeneration" of one of the most ancient states in Africa.

The French achievement looked all the more remarkable when it was contrasted with the situation in the Spanish protectorate. The Spanish zone was dominated by the mountains of the Rif. In the old days the Rif had always formed part of the *bilad as-siba,* and its Berber inhabitants possessed the reputation of being among the most turbulent and independent of all the peoples of the Maghrib. From the start, Spanish troops were faced with bitter opposition as they advanced from their bases on the coast. By 1921 they were in control of no more than a third of the territory nominally under their protection when they found themselves confronted with a revolt that soon developed into a major war.

The revolt was led by two brothers, both named Muhammad ibn Abd al-Karim, sprung from one of the Berber tribes living in the heart of the Rif. Both men had been able to observe European ways at close quarters. The elder, the Abdelkrim of contemporary European accounts, worked in the Spanish presidio of Melilla first as a Muslim judge (*cadi*), then as a newspaper editor, while the younger spent several years in Spain training to become a mining engineer. Their aim was to unite the deeply divided tribes of the Rif and to create a modern nation-state, to be known as "the Confederal Republic of the Tribes of the Rif." Though their revolt had many traditional overtones, it represented a movement far more modern in character, and therefore far more formidable to the colonial power, than the petty wars of resistance waged by Berber *montagnards* in other parts of the Maghrib.

The brothers were devout Muslims. They were anxious to ensure that their compatriots observed the ritual obligations of the faith, and they sought to replace customary Berber law by the Muslim code (the Shari'a). But they rejected the idea of a jihad against the Christians. "The time for holy wars is past," the elder is recorded as saying. "We are no longer in the Middle Ages. . . . We wish simply to be independent and to be governed by God alone." [26] "The Rifian government," one of the new state's leading supporters declared in a letter to the Spanish authorities, "established upon modern ideas and on the principles of civilization, considers itself independent politically and economically—privileged to enjoy our freedom as we have enjoyed it for centuries, and to live as other people live." [27] This was a remarkable statement to come from what many observers regarded as one of the most backward, turbulent, and disunited parts of the Maghrib.

The war began with a Rifian victory at Anual over a large Spanish force advancing westwards from Melilla. Not since the Italian defeat at Adowa twenty-five years earlier had a European army in Africa suffered a catastrophe on such a scale. Making good use of the vast supply of war material abandoned by the Spaniards, the triumphant tribesmen carried their struggle into the western Rif and inflicted further defeats on the Spanish army. Abd al-Karim and his followers might well have succeeded in establishing their state on secure foundations, had Spain been their only enemy. But many Rifian tribes lived astride the ill-defined frontier between the two protectorates and could not be prevented from engaging in operations against the French. In the spring of 1925, a massive Rifian assault on French frontier posts met with some spectacular local successes but provoked the French into energetic countermeasures. Marshal Pétain, regarded as the greatest French soldier of the day, was sent out to take over military command from Lyautey. Troops were poured into the country. Meanwhile, the Spanish forces were being reorganized by the dictator, General Primo de Rivera. By the autumn of 1925, Spain and France had more than a half-million troops at their disposal in northern Morocco, by far the largest European-controlled force ever to have been deployed against an African opponent. Even the Rifians, for all their courage, tenacity, and resourcefulness, could not hope to hold out against such overwhelming odds. In May, 1926, the brothers Abd al-Karim and other members of their family surrendered to the French and were exiled to Réunion. In 1947 the French authorities gave permission for Abd al-Karim to come to France. When the ship in which he was traveling touched at Port Said, Abd al-Karim managed to escape and was given asylum in Egypt where he lived until his death in 1963.

In the aftermath of the Rif war, the Spanish authorities were at last able to establish their control over every part of their protectorate. Meanwhile in the French zone of Morocco, extensive areas, particularly in the High Atlas and in the Saharan borderlands, still remained to be conquered. In 1931 the French embarked on the final phase of "pacification." It was a major military operation, requiring the use of squadrons of bomber planes and massive concentrations of artillery, with most of the hard fighting being done not by French troops but by Moroccan levies. By 1935 the last trace of a *bilad as-siba* had been erased from the political map of Morocco. For all the advances in military technology, the conquest of Morocco had taken almost as long as the subjugation of Algeria eighty years earlier. No sooner was the fighting finished than the conquerors found themselves confronted with a modern nationalist movement. The young politicians of Fez and Rabat were soon to present French authority with a threat far more serious than any they had had to face from the stubborn warriors of the mountains and the desert.

▲▼ EUROPEAN COLONIZATION AND THE DEVELOPMENT OF THE MAGHRIB

In 1930 the French authorities in Algeria staged an extravagant series of celebrations to commemorate the centenary of the French conquest of Algiers. The colonial regime was at the height of its power. Imperially minded Frenchmen could regard themselves as the worthy heirs of ancient Rome, engaged as their classical forbears had been in the demanding task of civilizing barbarians on the southern shores of the Mediterranean. So firmly had France's new North African empire been established that it was impossible to foresee its disintegration. Forty years later, the perspectives are very different. The relatively brief interlude of European rule in the Maghrib is over: some assessment of its achievement needs to be made.

The most obvious manifestation of European rule in North Africa was the presence of a large alien community. In 1830 there were no more than 200 Europeans resident in Morocco, slightly larger numbers in Algiers and in Tripoli, and about 8,000, mainly of Maltese or Italian origin, in Tunis. By the early 1950's, in the last years of the colonial regime, the total European population of the region numbered almost 2 million, with just over 1 million in Algeria, 600,000 in Morocco (350,000 in the French zone, the remainder in the Spanish zone, Tangier, Ceuta, and Melilla), nearly a quarter-million in Tunisia, and 38,-000 in Libya. In addition, the French and Spanish authorities maintained large garrisons, partly made up of troops from the metropolis, in their North African territories. In northern Morocco Spanish forces numbered as many as 200,000 men, while in the late 1950's the French found themselves forced to deploy an army half a million strong in Algeria. "Barracks," an English observer has pointed out, "form a notable feature of the North African cultural landscape." [28]

The great age of European settlement in Algeria occurred in the generation before World War I when the country's European population rose from 279,000 in 1872 to 752,000 in 1911. Tunisia, too, received a flood of European immigrants in the same period, the European population rising from 18,000 in 1880 to 128,000 in 1906. In the French zone of Morocco, the European population was put at 10,000 in 1911; it reached 191,000 in 1936 and continued to rise rapidly in the years immediately after World War II. The vast majority of European immigrants to North Africa came from the lands lying within the basin of the western Mediterranean, from the Spanish provinces of Valencia, Catalonia, and the Balearics, from French Corsica and Provence, from Malta, Sicily, Sardinia, and southern Italy. The European population of northern Morocco was almost entirely Spanish in origin, and much of the European population of the department of Oran in Algeria was of Spanish descent. Maltese and Italian were particularly numerous in the department of Constantine in eastern Algeria and in Tunisia. Indeed, in Tunisia Italians outnumbered Frenchmen until as late as the 1920's. In the French protectorate of Morocco, Frenchmen drawn either from Algeria or from the metropolis accounted for more than four-fifths of the European population.

Ethnic diversity then was a feature of the European population of French territories in North Africa, and especially of Algeria. But whatever their origin, all Europeans shared certain common interests. Mixed marriages occurred fairly frequently. And the process of frenchification was greatly accelerated by the educational system and by universal military service. Thus there emerged, particularly in Algeria, a new type of European, the *pieds noirs,* men who prided themselves on their virility, labeled their compatriots in metropolitan France with the pejorative nickname *patos* (Spanish: "ducks"), and usually regarded them as fools.[29] This was a development remarkably similar to that which was occurring at the same time in the colonial or ex-colonial territories of Anglo-Saxon culture. The *colons* thought of themselves as pioneers, and so, in the first stages of colonization, many of them had been. But by the middle of the twentieth century more than 80 percent of the European population was concentrated in the towns of the Maghrib, and especially in the great urban conglomerations of Algiers, Casablanca, and Tunis. In this urban environment there grew up both a European bourgeoisie of government officials, businessmen, and shopkeepers, and a European proletariat of bus drivers, factory hands and dock workers. But whatever the differences in wealth and status that divided the European community, they lost much of their significance in face of the infinitely greater contrasts in culture and way of life that separated the European townsmen from the Muslim peasant. Moreover, in every part of the Maghrib, even in Algiers itself where the European population numbered 300,000 in the 1950's, the *colons* found themselves in the position of a minority.

In the heyday of colonial rule this minority could regard itself as a beneficent, creative force. Jules Cambon, governor-general of Algeria in the 1890's, applied to his compatriots in North Africa the praise bestowed by Edmund Burke on the English settlers in North America: "Our ancestors have turned a savage wilderness into a glorious empire: and have made the most extensive and the only honorable conquests, not by destroying, but by promoting the wealth, the number, the happiness of the human race." [30] In confirmation of this proud assertion the French could point to a wide range of achievements. In the colonial view the Maghrib had been ruined by centuries of anarchy and misgovernment. The disappearance of the last *bilad as-siba* ushered in a period of unprecedented peace, in which the colonial authorities could devote themselves to the task of equipping their territories with the infrastructure of a modern economy.

By 1930 much had already been done. An efficient system of communications had been established, with arterial roads or railroads being laid along the lines of dusty mule tracks, and modern harbors built to replace the dangerous roadsteads of the past. Particularly striking were the advances in the field of agriculture. In Algeria the malarial swamps of the Mitidja valley were transformed into a rich landscape of citrus orchards and vineyards. In parts of southern Tunisia, ruined over a period of centuries by the depredations of Bedouin nomads, olive trees flourished once again as vigorously as they had done in Roman times. Geologists and mining engineers were revealing aspects of the region's mineral wealth—in phosphates, iron ore, zinc, and lead—hitherto barely, if ever, exploited. And the Maghrib's first modern industries had been established.

And yet—to quote the judgment of one of the most perceptive observers of the North African scene, the sociologist, Jacques Berque— "the colonial achievement in the Maghrib was not intended for, and only indirectly affected, the welfare of the country itself. Exploitation may have been frequently judicious and sometimes even benevolent, but it was always focused on unilateral advantage." [31] The criticism was not a new one. As early as 1896, the British consul in Tunis pointed out that the government of the protectorate "worked not for the benefit of the mass of the population but for that of the army of functionaries, a few French financial adventures, and of the few thousands of Frenchmen settled in it. For them taxes are levied; for them bridges are built; for them roads, useless to the Arab, are made; for them, in fact, the revenues of the Regency are drained." [32]

Thus there developed both an economy and a social structure that had about them something of the nature of an excrescence. To superficial observers the great estates of the French *colons* seemed to represent magnificent examples of European enterprise. Yet, as Berque has pointed out, "there is something terribly weak about a system that shows such disregard for the whole rural humanity of North Africa, and mobilizes so many collective means to create in the end at best only a freak landscape and to enrich only a minority." [33]

Few communities were to suffer so catastrophic a fall from power as the *colons* of North Africa. Looking back over their own experiences, these vigorous, hot-blooded men could feel that they had fought, sweated, and suffered to transform a backward land only to find themselves caught in an impossible position by the floodtide of Maghribi nationalism. The moral weakness of their position lay in a fault of the heart. "The French simply do not *like* the Tunisians," John Gunther noted in the early 1950's, "and cannot resist treating them with indiffer-

ence or contempt." [34] The same point could be made with equal justification in Algeria and in Morocco. Yet, throughout the colonial period,
individual Frenchmen found ways of bridging the gulf that separated
them from their Muslim neighbors. There were always to be found
some Europeans of whom Muslims would say approvingly "He's one of
us." Included in this category were a number of settlers "of the good
old type, reliable in business, Arabic-speaking, jovial, well thought of far
and wide," consulted by the local peasantry on agricultural matters,
even asked on occasion to act as arbiter in lawsuits.[35] And there existed
too a small but distinguished band of French scholars and scientists who
devoted themselves enthusiastically to the study of the Maghrib in all its
aspects, and whose researches made it possible for Maghribi Muslims to
become more deeply aware of the nature of their environment and the
wealth of their historical heritage. Their achievements confirm the truth
of Napoleon's aphorism: "The true conquests, the only conquests that
cost no regret are those achieved over ignorance." [36]

▲▼ MAGHRIBI-FRENCH RELATIONS IN THE
COLONIAL ERA

Few African peoples have been so roughly subjected to the experience
of alien rule as the inhabitants of the Maghrib. In the Sudan, in the Somali lands, and over much of tropical Africa, the colonial presence was
relatively modest in character. In many African colonies the cadre of
European administrators, soldiers, and technicians numbered no more
than a few hundred individuals. With so small a group of alien rulers it
was possible for most of the local people to pass long periods without
even setting eyes on a European. In French North Africa, on the other
hand, as in the white-dominated countries of the south, the fact of alien
domination was a daily reality for a large proportion of the population.
European quarters in the towns, barracks and police posts, European-
run farms and factories—institutions such as these provided painful reminders of the changed political status of countries with a noble historical tradition behind them.

The peoples of the Maghrib reacted to the colonial regime in a
variety of ways ranging from impassioned resistance to enthusiastic collaboration. Collaboration came most easily to the region's largest indigenous minority, the Jews, whose numbers reached close to half a million for the Maghrib as a whole by the 1950's. Some members of the
Jewish community, marked by their sophistication, wealth, and enterprise, were the descendants of refugees from Spain in the sixteenth century or of immigrants from Italy in the eighteenth, but the majority were
simple people, basically of Berber stock, the conversion of whose ances-

tors dated back to a period before the advent of Islam. Concentrated in the main urban centers, the Jewish population was well placed to take advantage of the opportunities offered by the new order. An enthusiasm for education, leading to the foundation of a large number of private Jewish schools, paid off handsomely by providing Jewish youths with the qualifications needed for jobs in the administration, in commerce, and in the professions. In Algeria assimilation was expedited by the government's decision, made at a time of acute crisis in 1870, to grant French citizenship to the entire Jewish population. In the 1890's and again in the 1940's, Algerian Jews suffered from the tantrums of European anti-Semitism, but their lot was infinitely more comfortable than that of the Muslim population, and the maintenance of French supremacy was clearly to their advantage.

Individual Muslims also found it possible to find a secure niche in the new establishment. In this respect the Berber *caids* of southern Morocco, especially the members of the al-Glawi family, proved particularly successful, achieving a position of opulent autonomy comparable to that allowed to the maharajahs of the princely states of British India. The massive *kasbahs* built by these "lords of the Atlas" during the French protectorate bear witness to their skill in extending their power and enlarging their revenues. It suited French policy to treat these feudal magnates as equals. It was no less convenient to win over by means of subsidies and special privileges the most conservative elements in the Muslim population and, in particular, the leaders of the *confrèries*, the Muslim *tariqas* or brotherhoods.

It would be wrong to think that Muslim collaboration was obtained only by political subterfuge. Many Muslim soldiers who saw service in the French army, particularly during World War I, developed a sincere devotion for the *patrie* they had helped to defend. At the same time, most members of the small group of *évolués*, Muslims who had received a higher education in French schools in North Africa or taken university courses in France, were forcefully impressed by the contrast between the best of French culture, so assured, so stimulating, and so humane, and the poverty and intellectual stagnation of their coreligionists. Many *évolués* were won over, at least for a time, to the cause of assimilation. And inevitably there were individuals who sought to preserve their own interests or to satisfy their private ambitions by filling the posts of petty authority left open to them in the colonial hierarchy. To their fellow-countrymen the most obsequious of the collaborators came to be known as the *Beni Oui-Oui,* "the tribe of yes-men."

Only a small minority of Maghribi Muslims could enjoy the uneasy advantages of collaboration. A handful of the more prominent members of the community sought refuge through a self-imposed exile in the Muslim countries of the Middle East. But during the high-noon of the the colonial era there was for the mass of the population no alternative to submission. Islam, despite the aspersions cast on it by Europeans, retained its strength as a spiritual bastion, a religion which could give a man strength to endure the sufferings and the humiliations of the present. And despite life's hardships inevitably there remained many private occasions—"long days of rest, festivities, wanderings and meditations" [37]—that served to give something of a savor to the experience of living. But one has only to read some of the popular poetry circulating in rural Algeria in the years between 1870 and 1920 to gain some insight into the greyness of this period.

> *I weep for my country which has been conquered*
> *by force, in which oppression and immorality*
> *now reign supreme.*
> . . . .
> *If anyone enjoys a bit of luck or finds himself*
> *a little better off, immediately his heart*
> *grows hard.*
> *In our time all people are wicked, thinking only*
> *of themselves.*
> . . . .
> *No one knows my despair save He who knows all,*
> *All I reveal of myself is my physical appearance,*
> *My heart lives in a perpetual state of anguish.*[38]

In the first years of the twentieth century many Algerian peasants must have felt themselves trapped in a hopeless situation, but already new perspectives were beginning to reveal themselves to the urban bourgeoisie. Intellectually the Maghrib was one of the least isolated of the regions of Africa. Members of the ulama class, teachers and jurists trained in traditional Muslim studies, were able to maintain some contact with their coreligionists in the Muslim lands of the Eastern Mediterranean and so to learn of the new ideas being put forward in the Ottoman Empire and in Egypt. Meanwhile the *évolués* were made aware through their education of the powerful liberal tradition in French thought. In the first decade of the twentieth century, groups of French-educated Muslims formed their own associations in Tunis and Algiers, and began publishing journals in French or Arabic. These "Young Tunisians" and "Young Algerians," as they were called by contemporaries, numbered only a few hundred individuals; their political ideas differed little from those of the colonial reformers in France; their tactics, involving the presentation of petitions and the drafting of memoranda, revealed their moderation. But administrators considered it advisable to keep a close watch on these "loquacious natives" (*indigènes loquaces*), while French *colons* talked of "ambitious young men, who want to supplant us by turning all the native population against the French population." [39]

▲▼ NATIONALISM IN TUNISIA AND MOROCCO

Under French protection both Tunisia and Morocco retained a semblance of their historic personalities. Thus their experience of colonial rule differed markedly from that of other African territories where substantial states, such as Ashanti, Buganda, or the Caliphate of Sokoto, found themselves incorporated in entirely novel political structures. Clearly it was much easier for a citizen of Fez or of Tunis, living among the monuments of a noble past, to think of himself as a Moroccan or a Tunisian than it was for a man from Ashanti or Buganda to accept the notion of Ghanaian or Ugandan nationalism. Thus the nationalist movement in the two French protectorates of the Maghrib was never weakened by the tribal divisions that affected the modern political development of other African territories containing elaborate polities with long historical traditions. Both Moroccans and Tunisians possessed a certain national consciousness at the time when they were first brought under colonial rule.

In both countries certain sections of the population, the nomads of southern Tunisia and the *montagnards* of the Atlas and of the Rif, fortified by a long tradition of opposition to external authority, were able to put up a stiff resistance to the European invaders. But these last-ditch resisters were concerned only with local issues. Even Abd al-Karim and his followers fought for an independent Rif, not for the freedom of all Morocco. To arouse and make explicit a sense of national consciousness, to speak in terms of the country as a whole, was a task which in its initial stages could be undertaken only by urban intellectuals.

For the Maghrib as a whole the intellectual stimulants emanating from beyond the region's borders acquired a more potent force in the 1920's when it became easier to achieve direct contact with outsiders. Maghribi students who began going to Paris in increasing numbers found themselves meeting Frenchmen of a type refreshingly different from the general run of *colons* and *administrateurs,* men of the left, socialists or communists, colonial reformers or anticolonialists who saw themselves as the heirs and upholders of the liberal and humane traditions of 1789. Other young men who preferred to follow a more traditional course, studying in the Muslim universities of Fez or of Tunis and reading in Arabic rather than in French, were in a position to receive the new ideas put forward by Muslim reformers in Syria and

Egypt. Particularly influential for the Maghrib was the teaching of the Amir Shakib Arslan, member of a noble Lebanese family and disciple of Jamal al-Din al-Afghani and Muhammad Abduh. Arslan settled in Geneva in 1918 and lived there till his death in 1946. He was visited by many of the leading Maghribi politicians of the day and was able to achieve a wider circulation for his ideas through the publication of a journal, *La Nation arabe*.

Obsessed, as were so many thinking Muslims of his generation, with the apparent "degeneration" of their coreligionists, Arslan saw the basic cause of the decline of Islam in a failure of will. He elaborated this idea in a series of articles written in the early 1930's and later published in the book, *Our Decline and its Causes*.[40] "It is not bombs, aeroplanes, fire-throwers or torpedoes that endow a nation with mettle and resolution. On the contrary," he asserted, "it is honor, mettle, courage and the will-to-be that brings the bombs, torpedoes and aeroplanes into existence," and he went on to cite the example of the Japanese to prove his point. The material poverty of Muslims was due, he believed, to their indifference to the study of modern science. And this indifference was in turn a product of the "lazy fatalism," the excessive other-worldliness of conservative Islam. In reality, Islam was "a religion that inspired men to a life of intense activity and constant striving." This could be proved by reference to the great centuries of Muslim achievement: it could be documented by numerous quotations from the Koran. Will, resolution, and willingness to make sacrifices—these were the qualities that Muslims must cultivate if they were to recover their lost greatness. Many young Maghribi nationalists found ideas such as these immensely attractive: they felt perturbed about the consequences of assimilation and its implicit abandonment of cherished traditions, they shared Arslan's hatred and contempt for the sycophantic collaborators and his exasperation at the impotence of the *vieux turbans* (the ultra-conservative Muslims), and they desperately needed a cause to which they could devote themselves with passionate enthusiasm.

The fund of ideas, some originating in the reformist Muslim East, others in the rationalist West, from which they drew their inspiration was not the only element the nationalist movements of Morocco and Tunisia—and also of Algeria—had in common. There was also a certain similarity in the pattern of development followed by the early nationalist movements. In Tunisia and Morocco the first modern nationalists were to be found among the prosperous urban bourgeoisie, a bourgeoisie whose members tended, as Charles Gallagher has pointed out, to be "conservative, property-conscious, family-oriented, and deeply religious" and so to present a type very different from the "middle-class, venturesome entrepreneur active in the great movements of post-Reformation Europe." [41] About 1930 members of a younger generation began to make their ideas felt. Under this new impulse nationalist sentiments spread first to the members of the petty bourgeoisie, then to the urban proletariat, and finally to the peasantry of the countryside, the tone of the nationalists becoming ever more vigorous, strident, and assured as the size of their following increased. This was a development common to many nationalist movements. But Moroccan and to a lesser extent Tunisian nationalism presented one unusual feature—the role in the nationalist movement played by the traditional ruler.

The French needed a puppet as sultan of Morocco or bey of Tunis. In Morocco the Sultan Yusuf who reigned from 1912 to 1927 suited their purpose admirably, and in choosing Yusuf's eighteen-year-old son, Sidi Muhammad, as his successor the French thought they had found a young man as peaceable and pliant as his father. But widening experience made of the new sultan a staunch nationalist and he emerged in the 1950's as a true leader of his country. In Tunisia a curious law of succession whereby the oldest member of the Husainid family was regarded as the natural successor to the office of bey provided the country with exceptionally elderly heads of state. But at least one of the beys, Moncef, proved himself a vigorous supporter of the nationalist cause. Both Moncef and Sidi Muhammad paid for their audacity with their thrones. Moncef was deposed in 1943 after a reign of less than a year and died in exile in 1947. Sidi Muhammad was more fortunate. Forcibly removed from his throne and country in 1953, he made a triumphal return in 1955.

The Moroccan and Tunisian nationalists found the French settlers and civil servants, who between them controlled so many of the seats of power, tough, even ruthless opponents. In Morocco opposition to the nationalists was rendered all the more formidable by the support the French obtained from the great caids and from the leaders of the religious fraternities. Among the most dramatic incidents of recent Maghribi history were the two occasions when al-Glawi, the immensely powerful pasha of Marrakesh, vigorously supported by members of the French administration, assembled a force of several thousand horsemen in plots designed first, in 1951, to put pressure on the sultan to force him to abandon the nationalist cause, and later, in 1953, to secure his removal. Tunisia by contrast was more fortunate. In the last phases of the nationalist struggle the country's political leaders could count on the support of every section of the Muslim population.

Tunisian nationalism enjoyed other advantages. In a country that is relatively compact—Tunisia has an area rather smaller than Oklahoma

—and, by African standards, highly urbanized, political organization was easier to develop. In these circumstances Neo-Destour, the country's dominant party, constructed one of the most efficient political machines to be found in Africa. As early as 1937, only three years after its foundation, the party had more than 400 local branches and 28,000 active members. Such an achievement was the product of able and energetic leadership. In the 1930's a dominant figure had already emerged in the person of Habib Bourguiba, a young French-educated lawyer with a French wife, a man so steeped in French culture that many Europeans have remarked that he he could easily pass for a Parisian, yet destined to establish himself as one of the outstanding figures in the contemporary Muslim world, and to occupy the leading position in the political life of his own country for a span that has not yet reached its term.

The Moroccan political scene was more complex. Istiqal ("Independence Party") was the most vigorous force in the nationalist movement since its foundation in 1944. But it had to share the political limelight with the sultan, Sidi Muhammad, who by virtue of his office could not function simply as a party leader, and it was subjected to greater internal stresses and so never developed the monolithic character of Neo-Destour in Tunisia.

As for the actual course of events, political developments in the two countries, being subject to much the same external pressures, ran on broadly parallel lines. Tunisia, a country which throughout its history has always been remarkably open to the outside world, inevitably seemed more advanced than Morocco. As early as 1906, small groups of educated Tunisians were beginning to voice their criticism of the protectorate. These "Young Tunisians" founded Tunisia's first political party, the Destour ("Constitution Party") in 1920. Their aim was to bring about the establishment of a parliamentary regime which would, in the words of their first program, "bring Tunisia to maturity and free her from slavery," [42] but no attempt was made to obtain a mass following. In these circumstances the French had little difficulty in rejecting their proposals. Frustration bred lethargy. A new generation was needed to revive the dormant cause of Tunisian nationalism. But to young men like Habib Bourguiba, who made his first appearance on the political scene about 1930, the old Destour seemed "to distrust all contact with the people." Exasperated with the attitude of their elders, Bourguiba and his followers broke away in 1934 to form the Neo-Destour.

In Morocco a number of very young men, some still in their late teens, came together in 1926 under the leadership of Allal al-Fasi in Fez and of Ahmad Balafrej in Rabat to discuss the future of their country. The two groups represented different strands in the nationalist movement, the Fasis being students at the Muslim university inspired by the ideals of Muslim reformism, the Rabatis French-educated *évolués* influenced by their contacts with French thought. Many of these young men possessed the social advantage of coming from some of the most distinguished families in the country but they found it hard to make much impact on public opinion until French policy provided them with an admirable pretext for agitation.

By 1930 the pacification of Morocco was almost complete. In the past there had always been a sharp political division between the dissident Berbers of the mountains and the Arabs or Arabic-speaking peoples of the cities and the plains. In the interests of French hegemony it seemed desirable to the French administrators of the time to maintain this old division in a new guise. With this end in view they issued a decree, known as the Berber *dahir*, establishing a special system of jurisdiction that confirmed traditional customs but limited the application of the Shari'a (Muslim law) in Berber areas. Coming at a time when Catholic missionaries in Morocco were openly discussing the chances of converting the Berbers, the *dahir* was regarded as an affront to Islam and aroused a storm of protest that spread from Morocco to almost every part of the Muslim world. In this period of agitation the young nationalists found themselves being listened to with respect by their elders, a novel experience in a deeply conservative and traditional society. Fortified by their success in forcing the French authorities to withdraw the *dahir*, the nationalists sought new ways of extending their activities. But it was not until 1937 that they formed the country's first modern political party, the *Comité d'Action Marocaine.*

The success of the left-wing Popular Front in the French elections of 1936 roused the hopes of Moroccan and Tunisian nationalists and incited them to engage in increasingly vigorous political activity. But though the nationalists talked of independence, they accepted the need for a program involving a gradual French withdrawal. To the French, however, the time was not propitious for far-reaching reforms. In France public opinion was unsympathetic or preoccupied with the country's own internal problems; in North Africa settlers and administrators were resolutely hostile to concessions; and the French military, vividly aware of the threat posed to French security by the growing power of Nazi Germany and Fascist Italy, were unwilling to accept any weakening of the French presence in the Western Mediterranean. As for the nationalist leaders, once they had decided to appeal to the masses, they found themselves in the position of the sorcerer's apprentice who unleashes a force he is unable to control. Protests and mass demonstrations led to violent scenes, to repression, and to the arrest of the nationalist leaders. By 1939 with the nationalist parties banned, Allal al-Fasi exiled to Gabon and Bourguiba imprisoned in France, the colonial authorities could feel that they were fully in command of the situation.

The illusion of French omnipotence was shattered by their defeat in 1940 and by the Anglo-American invasion of North Africa in 1942. Early in 1943 Sidi Muhammad of Morocco had a meeting with Franklin D. Roosevelt. In the course of their conversation the American president left the young sultan in no doubt of his own anti-colonialist sentiments. Roused by Roosevelt's words into conceiving a new future for his country, Sidi Muhammad is said to have emerged from the interview a changed man. From henceforth he was to take an increasingly vigorous part in the nationalist struggle. As for the nationalist politicians, they too became aware of new opportunities. Early in 1944 the Istiqal party was founded in Morocco; the party's first manifesto contained a stirring and unequivocal demand for independence. In Tunisia, too, the last years of the war saw a revival of political activity, the return of Bourguiba and the establishment of new organizations well suited to support the nationalist cause, including a vigorous body of trade unionists, the *Union Générale Tunisienne du Travail.*

For both countries the immediate postwar years represented a period of *détente,* when the protectorate authorities introduced a number of modest reforms, providing Muslims with greater opportunities for employment in government service and for membership of the protectorates' consultative councils. But while the French thought of the future of the protectorates in terms of cosovereignty, hoping to devise a system that would allow the *colons* to retain a commanding position in local affairs, the nationalists were committed to outright independence. In these circumstances conflict was inevitable; but it was not until 1954 that really serious outbreaks of violence occurred. In Tunisia, where the French had turned from negotiation to repression in 1952, groups of guerrillas, known as the *fellagha,* began operating in the countryside. Even more serious was the situation in Morocco after the deposition of Sidi Muhammad in 1953. With their sultan in exile in Madagascar and their leaders in prison, the rank and file of Istiqal began to take action, launching terrorist attacks in the towns on police informers and the supporters of the puppet sultan, Muhammad ben Arafa, and later organizing a guerrilla force, the Moroccan Liberation Army, on the borders with Algeria.

This disastrous deterioration of the situation in the two protectorates occurred at a time when France was beset with other difficulties. In

1954 the humiliating end of the war in Indochina was followed by the outbreak of a serious insurrection in Algeria. At the same time, French delegates were finding themselves increasingly isolated in the United Nations where Tunisian and Moroccan nationalists could count on many friends prepared to speak on their behalf. Eventually, following the initiative of Pierre Mendès-France, the French government, acting with a speed and boldness that nothing in its previous North African policy had led contemporaries to anticipate, concluded a series of agreements first with the Tunisian nationalists, then with the Moroccans. In March, 1956, the two protectorates recovered their position as independent states. Shortly afterward the Spanish government teminated its protectorate over northern Morocco. Finally the important city of Tangier which in accordance with the terms of an agreement made in 1923 had enjoyed a special status as an "international zone" was returned to the administration of the sultan.

▲▼ THE STRUGGLE FOR INDEPENDENCE
IN ALGERIA

The difficulties facing Muslim nationalists in Algeria were very much greater than those confronting their corcligionists in Tunisia and Morocco. Not only did Algeria contain a deeply entrenched settler population numbering close to a million, but the country was regarded, even by liberal-minded Frenchmen, as a projection of France overseas, a province whose political amputation from the metropolis was unthinkable. In the 1920's and 1930's Muslim *évolués* were prepared to accept this situation. They looked to the future for a more effective policy of assimilation, for a gradual expansion of the meager political opportunities granted to Muslims, and for the extension of the privileges of French citizenship to a wider section of the Muslim population. French commentators laid much stress on a famous article entitled *La France, c'est moi,* written in 1936 by Ferhat Abbas, the most prominent political figure among the *évolués* and one of the leaders of the recently formed Federation of Algerian Elected Members which was supported by many Muslim representatives on municipal councils. "If I had discovered the Algerian nation," wrote Ferhat Abbas, "I would be a nationalist. I cannot die for the 'Algerian fatherland,' because this fatherland does not exist. . . . We must," he concluded, "definitely link our future with that of the work of Frenchmen in this country." [43]

The sincerely collaborationist approach of Ferhat Abbas and the *évolués* never commended itself to the mass of Algerian Muslims, and it was vehemently rejected by the two other Muslim parties that emerged in Algeria at this time, one based on the liberal-minded ulama, the other on radical Muslim workers. The Association of Reformist Ulama in Algeria, a body whose members were strongly influenced by the ideas of the Egyptian, Muhammad Abduh, was founded in 1931. The association's leader, Ben Badis, attacked the views of Ferhat Abbas, asserting that "a Muslim Algerian nation," with its own history, its religious and linguistic unity, its own culture and traditions, did indeed exist. "This Muslim Algeria," Ben Badis declared, "is not France, cannot be France, and does not want to be France." He went on to suggest that Algeria might evolve peacefully to independence along lines similar to those followed by the white dominions of the British Empire.[44]

An independent Algeria was also the goal of the *Étoile Nord-Africaine* ("North African Star"), a party founded in 1926 among Algerian workers in Paris and led by Messali Hadj. But there was a world of difference between the ulama and the radical workers. The ulama were members of the bourgeoisie and tended to be more interested in the reform of Muslim culture than in vigorous political action. The members of the ENA, on the other hand, had been strongly influenced by their contacts with the French Communists and talked in revolutionary terms. In the early 1930's Messali Hadj came under the influence of Shakib Arslan. Thereafter the concepts of militant Islam played an increasingly important part in his political doctrine. In 1936 he returned to Algeria and founded the Party of the Algerian People. The support gained by this new party among Muslim workers in the larger towns was in sharp contrast to the failure of the European-dominated Algerian Communist Party to attract large numbers of Muslim members. In the Algerian context Islam could provide the mass of Muslims with a revolutionary doctrine far more congenial than Marxism.

Algerian nationalists were, then, deeply divided both over tactics and over ultimate objectives. Nevertheless on two occasions Ferhat Abbas succeeded in bringing the various nationalist groups together—in 1936 to form the Algerian Muslim Congress, and again in 1944. In 1936 the program put forward by the congress contained no mention of independence, but demanded a wide range of reforms involving the abolition of the special laws to which Muslims were subject and leading to a greater measure of integration between France and Algeria. The Popular Front government accepted the need for reform and put forward a plan which would have enabled all the members of the Muslim Algerian elite to claim French citizenship without being required to renounce, as had previously been the case, their legal status as Muslims. This reform, known from its sponsors as the Blum-Violette project, was never even discussed by the French parliament. So violent was the reaction of *colon* opinion—the Federation of Algerian Mayors threatened to resign *en bloc* and so to paralyze the administration of the country if the proposals were laid before parliament—that the project was quietly buried. The episode was of crucial importance for the future of Franco-Algerian relations. A golden opportunity of gaining the support of moderate Muslim opinion had been abandoned; such an opportunity was never to occur again.

In March, 1944, the French Committee of National Liberation established by General de Gaulle in Algiers issued an ordinance that went even further than the Blum-Violette project in granting immediate political rights to the Muslim elite. But by this time the political atmosphere of the country had changed completely. Early in 1943, shortly after the Anglo-American invasion of North Africa, Ferhat Abbas composed a "manifesto of the Algerian People." This widely distributed tract contained a scathing indictment of French colonialism, demanded the application of the right to self-determination for the whole country, and asked for the promulgation of a special Algerian constitution guaranteeing the equality of all Algerians. Using this challenging document as his platform, Ferhat Abbas set about forming a new party, the Association of Friends of the Manifesto, designed to unite the various strands of nationalist opinion.

As the war drew to an end in Europe, political excitement grew ever more intense in Algeria. Suddenly, on May 8, the very day on which the armistice was signed in Europe, Algerian politics turned to violence. A riot occurred in Sétif, a town in the department of Constantine, leading to the death of a number of Europeans. As news of the incident spread, bands of Muslims began roaming the countryside killing other Europeans. It was the most serious rising Algeria had known since 1871 and showed signs of developing into a country-wide rebellion. Confronted with such a situation and uneasily conscious of the limited number of troops at their disposal, the French authorities in Algeria retaliated with extreme harshness. In the repression that followed several thousand Muslims lost their lives. European dead numbered ninety-seven.

There followed nearly a decade of superficial quiet. In retrospect this may seem a period of lost opportunities for the French. Political reforms were introduced: under the constitution of the Fourth Republic Algerian Muslim deputies were given a seat for the first time in the metropolitan parliament, and in Algeria itself there was greater provision for Muslim representation on local councils. But these reforms never went far enough to satisfy Muslim opinion, and when the French administration began to make a point of rigging local elections to ensure the return of its own supporters, it became clear that little could be expected through normal political channels. Meanwhile the European population continued to increase in wealth, the Muslim to increase in numbers.

Inevitably the basic inequality between Algeria's "two nations" became ever more glaringly pronounced. But the rise in numbers of the Muslim population had consequences that lie far beyond the ability of statistics to illuminate. "When a population doubles," the French anthropologist, Germaine Tillion, one of the most penetrating observers of the Algerian scene, has written, "it finds the number of its conflicts, its difficulties, its problems quadrupled, but the collective passions multiply still more quickly, inevitably rousing the people, according to circumstances, to a pitch encouraging dynamism and the spirit of enterprise—but also hostility and even outright hysteria." [45]

It is easy to accuse the French authorities of complacency. Yet in fact the government of the Fourth Republic was hamstrung by its own weakness. With the Communists in permanent opposition it was impossible to secure the majority needed to ensure the passage of radical reforms through the French parliament. And even if such reforms had been accepted in Paris, it would have been extremely difficult to achieve their implementation by a settler-dominated administration in Algeria. The maintenance of the status quo might satisfy most Frenchmen; by the early 1950's it was becoming increasingly irksome to most Algerian Muslims. Violence provided the only way out of the impasse, yet to almost all Algerian Muslim politicians even violence seemed unlikely to succeed, for France was still an immensely powerful nation and French sentiment was adamant on the need to maintain *l'Algérie française*. To launch a rebellion was an act of supreme foolhardiness.

The decision to attempt such a revolt was taken by a group of nine Algerians, the founders of a revolutionary committee that became the nucleus of the National Liberation Front (FLN). Though unknown to most of their compatriots, these men had been among the most militant members of Messali Hadj's Party of the Algerian People, but had broken away when internal feuds, provoked in part by the leader's domineering personality, showed signs of reducing the party to a state of complete ineffectiveness. In April, 1954, the revolutionaries made contact with the Egyptian government and obtained from Colonel Nasser invaluable assistance in the form of arms, money, and other supplies. On November 1, 1954, their followers launched a series of small-scale attacks on French posts in various parts of Algeria. Though few people could have realized it at the time, these were the first shots fired in the Algerian war of independence.

The war thus modestly begun developed into one of the most astonishing conflicts in modern times, intensely dramatic in some of its major episodes, horrifyingly brutal in many of its minor incidents. In retrospect it can be seen as the greatest colonial war Africa had known since the original French conquest of Algeria more than a century earlier, a struggle that dragged on for more than seven years and was the cause of death and destruction on a terrible scale. Insurgent losses in battle are put at more than 141,000 killed, while the French and their Muslim auxiliaries suffered 15,000 casualties. About 20,000 Muslims and 3,000 Europeans lost their lives as a result of terrorist activities. Some 2 million Algerian Muslims were forced to leave their homes, and many thousands died of hunger or disease in these cruel upheavals.

Had the French been able to treat the insurrection simply in terms of a military struggle as they had done when dealing with Abd al-Krim in the 1920's, there can be no doubt that they would have emerged victorious. Supported by a half-million troops and guided by the experience gained from years of antiguerrilla activities in Indochina, the French were able to force the National Liberation Army onto the defensive. But almost from the start the conflict became not merely a burning political issue in France itself but also a matter of widespread international concern. The leaders of the FLN established one wing of their movement, the External Delegation, first in Cairo and then in Tunis and were thus able to remain constantly in touch with their supporters in the outside world, particularly the Arab states, the Communist countries of Eastern Europe, and Communist China. Without such contacts it would have been impossible to obtain all the arms and equipment needed to maintain the fight in Algeria. At the same time, the rebel leaders showed notable adroitness in presenting their case openly at international gatherings and privately through diplomatic contacts in the major capitals of the world. With international opinion becoming ever more favorable to the rebel cause the French found themselves reduced to a position of diplomatic isolation. In 1958 the External Delegation was transformed into an Algerian Government-in-Exile which received prompt diplomatic recognition from a number of Afro-Asian states.

In the last analysis, however, the key to peace in Algeria lay not in Algiers, Cairo, or New York but in Paris. In 1958, after four years of war, it was clear that nothing had occurred to make the *colons* renounce their passionate determination to keep Algeria French. Indeed their position had been strengthened, for many French army officers had come to share their views. (It was widely believed by both army officers and *colons* that a surrender to the FLN was surrender to Communism: a naïve analysis of a complex situation.) Conscious of their power and exasperated by the weakness of the politicians in Paris, army officers and *colons* came together in Algiers in May, 1958, to stage the revolt that brought General de Gaulle to power.

The task which de Gaulle accomplished in freeing his country of the incubus of Algeria stands out as one of the greatest feats of statesmanship in modern times. Twice the new president was faced with a direct threat to his own authority—in January, 1960, when the European *Ultras* seized power for some days in Algiers, and again in April, 1961, when many senior army officers mutinied and seemed poised to launch an attack on the seat of government in Paris. In dealing with these insurrections de Gaulle was assured of the support of the vast majority of his countrymen, for most Frenchmen, sickened by the tales of atrocities committed by both sides, were thoroughly weary of the long war and had grown indifferent to the fate of French Algeria. By purging the army of disaffected officers de Gaulle was able to establish a tight control over the military in Algeria. At the same time he set in motion the long-drawn negotiations with the leaders of the FLN that culminated in the Evian Agreement of March 1962. In the months that intervened before the proclamation of the Algerian Republic in July, French Algeria collapsed, totally and ignominiously, the terrorist outrages of the embittered *Ultras* of the Secret Army Organization (OAS) being followed by the mass exodus of Europeans.

Most long wars are likely to involve an acceleration of the processes of change. For the Muslims of Algeria their struggle for independence was certainly no exception to this rule. It was a struggle that involved far more than the ejection of an alien master. In the course of the war hundreds of thousands of Muslims were forced to leave their ancestral homes: the new contacts made in the ranks of the National Liberation Army or in the resettlement camps established by the French brought a rough awareness of a wider world and of the meaning of an Algerian nation. "Tribal partition, authority of the elders, family organization, the special position of women—all these had already suffered encroachments but nothing," wrote Germaine Tillion in 1961, "comparable to today's collapse." She went on to provide a vivid illustration of this process by referring to "a number of stern, traditionalist Moslem families in which the daughter of the house has switched from the veil to blue jeans and from the harem to the *maquis,* while her old father wavers between consternation and patriotic pride." [46]

In retrospect, the Algerian war of indepence seems bound to appear as one of the most revolutionary episodes in the long history of the Maghrib. In retrospect, too, the war seems invested with a dreadful inevitability, the culmination of a process which began with the French conquest of Algiers in 1830. "This land," a group of Algerians told

Governor Bugeaud in 1841, "is the country of the Arabs. You are here only as passing guests. Even if you stay here as the Turks did for 300 years, you are bound to leave in the end." [47]

▲▼ LIBYA: ARABS, TURKS, AND ITALIANS

In 1875 the country now known as Libya formed one of the largest, poorest, and remotest parts of the Ottoman Empire. In the 1880's this vast territory—Libya's present area is 679,000 square miles—was divided for administrative purposes into the *Vilayat* of Tripoli (embracing most of Tripolitania and the Fezzan) and the *Sanjuq* of Benghazi (covering Cyrenaica), the local governors at Tripoli and Benghazi being directly subject to the control of the government at Contantinople. The Turks were an imperial people, but the prudence of their methods and the moderation of their aims gave to their regime a character very different from that of the colonial governments established by European powers in other parts of North Africa. No doubt Turkish prudence could be ascribed partly to weakness: the Turks, beset with many other difficulties, could only afford to maintain a small force, not exceeding 8,000 men, in this relatively unimportant part of their empire. But prudence was also derived from a realistic assessment of self-interest. The imperial authorities expected little more of their Libyan provinces than the payment of a regular but not exorbitant amount of tribute. Provincial governors who fulfilled this obligation without troubling their superiors with demands for additional troops to put down native insurrections could count on being left in peace.

By the standards of contemporary Algeria or Tunisia the administrative superstructure imposed by the Turks was exceedingly modest but it met the needs of the time well enough. Turkish officials, supported by small detachments of troops, were based on the coastal towns and the main urban centers of the interior such as Murzuk, the capital of the Fezzan and Ghadames, one of the richest oases of the northern Sahara. Little attempt was made to establish a system of direct administration over the numerous tribes of Bedouin Arabs. Instead, Turkish officials aimed at developing harmonious relations with the local tribal chiefs, blending cajolery with the threat of force to induce them to extract from their followers the taxes required by the Turkish administration.

In bringing a reasonable measure of law and order to a naturally turbulent land the Turks were greatly assisted by the expansion of a remarkable Muslim order, the *Sanusiyya,* a brotherhood founded in the 1830's by a devout Algerian Muslim, Sayyid Muhammad ibn Ali as-Sanusi. After spending many years in the Hejaz, the Grand Sanusi, as

Sayyid Muhammad was known to his followers, decided in the 1850's to move the center of his new order to the remote oasis of Jaghbub in southern Cyrenaica. Under the Grand Sanusi's inspiration Jaghbub became one of the most vigorous intellectual centers in the contemporary Muslim world, a place where, as one visitor remarked, one could meet "literary men of distinction whose writings eclipse those of the poets of Iraq and Andalusia." [48] But missionary enterprise rather than scholarship was the main concern of the new order, for the Grand Sanusi was intent on converting the heathen and bringing the ill-instructed to a deeper knowledge of the faith. The order's missionaries were the Grand Sanusi's disciples, many of whom had travelled from the distant Maghrib to study under his direction. Responding to invitations from other communities, the Grand Sanusi and his successors sent out the shaikhs of the order to form local lodges (zawiya). Rapidly and by entirely peaceful means the order spread, following the line of the trade routes of Libya and the central Sahara. In 1895 the headquarters of the order were moved from Jaghbub to Kufra, an even more remote oasis, well-sited to superintend the order's growing responsibilities in the central Sahara. Cyrenaica contained the greatest concentration of Sanusi zawiya, but there were by now numerous lodges in the Fezzan, Tripolitania, western Egypt, and Arabia, and even a few in the Sudanic belt between Kano and Darfur.

The Bedouin of Cyrenaica were organized in a multitude of independent political units, constantly at war one with another. For these anarchic warriors of the desert the spread of the Sanusiyya was a development of profound political significance. They soon began to appreciate the services offered by the shaikhs who superintended the local Sanusi lodges. These holy men were well fitted to act as arbiters in local disputes and as mediators between the tribes and the Turkish authorities. In this way the order, without losing its primary character as a religious movement, began to assume political responsibilities and to take on the form of a "theocratic empire."

In 1902 the French advance northeastward from Lake Chad brought the Sanusi for the first time into violent conflict with a European power. They were unable to prevent the French from asserting their hegemony over Kanem, Tibesti, and Wadai, destroying as they did so every Sanusi zawiya in the area. But French expansion affected only the outer provinces of the order. Far more serious was the threat to the Sanusi heartland in Cyrenaica produced by the Italian invasion of Libya in 1911.

"Italy went to Tripoli," wrote the Italian historian, Benedetto Croce, "because she could not resign herself to the idea of the French, the English, and the Spaniards establishing themselves before her eyes along the

African coast, if the Italian flag was not to be planted in any part of it, and if Italy did not share with them in the Europeanization of Africa." [49] Italian imperialists supplemented the dictates of prestige with other arguments, talking about strategic considerations, indulging in grandiose predictions of the opportunities Libya would offer to Italian emigrants or grumbling about the obstructions being placed in the path of Italian economic enterprise by the Turkish authorities.

The Italians had learned nothing from the experience of the French in their assaults on other parts of the Ottoman Empire. In Egypt in 1798 and in Algiers in 1830 the French imagined they would be accepted as liberators coming to free the local Arabic-speaking peoples from Turkish tyranny. Inspired by the same illusion, the Italians were soon chagrined to find the Arabs making common cause with their "oppressors." The combined Turco-Arab resistance to Italian aggression provided yet another indication of the dynamic quality of Islam, for it was religion alone that bound the two peoples together.

In the face of complete Italian mastery of the sea, the Turks could not hope to defend the main coastal towns successfully. Prudently they fell back on a line of military camps established in the hinterland and resorted, in collaboration with their Bedouin allies, to the tactics of guerrilla warfare. In this guise the war might have dragged on for years had not other pressures—in particular the Italian invasion of the Aegean and the growing crisis in the Balkans—forced the Turkish government to negotiate a peace in October, 1912. The Turkish withdrawal marked the end of the first phase of a war that was to involve the Italians in twenty years of fighting, for the Bedouin tribes of the Libyan desert proved as resolute in their resistance to European encroachments as the Berber *montagnards* of Algeria and Morocco.

The second stage of the war, lasting from 1912 to 1917, brought to both sides unexpected reverses. In the winter of 1913–14 the Italians, stirred to vigorous action by the French advances in the central Sahara, pushed rapidly south to occupy the main oases of the Fezzan. But with their lines of communications exposed to constant Bedouin raids, they were soon forced to withdraw in disarray to the coast. In May, 1915, Italy joined Britain and France in the war against the Central Powers and the Ottoman Empire. Before long Turkish and German officers, bringing with them arms and other supplies, were landed by submarine on the Libyan coast, but the Bedouin soon found themselves having to pay an unwelcome price for this assistance. The Sanusi regarded the Italians as their main enemy; with the British in Egypt they had maintained reasonably cordial relations. But in the winter of 1915–16 they agreed, in response to an urgent Turkish request, to mount an attack on the British troops in western Egypt. The British parried this assault with little difficulty and retaliated by inflicting on the Bedouin a defeat far more chastening than any they had ever suffered at the hands of the Italians.

In the course of 1917, British, Italian, and Sanusi negotiators hammered out an agreement which allowed the Sanusi of Cyrenaica much the same rights as they had enjoyed under the Turkish administration. But by conferring the title *amir* on the new head of the *Sanusiyya,* Sayyid Muhammad Idris (later to become King Idris I of Libya), the Italians recognized how greatly the political responsibilities of the order had increased under the impact of war. With an army and a regular revenue at his disposal the leader of a movement, until recently purely religious in character, had now acquired the attributes of a secular sovereign.

Meanwhile, in those parts of Tripolitania lying outside the limited area controlled by the Italians a somewhat similar development was taking place, involving the emergence of an indigenous political structure of a kind larger than any the province had ever known before. In 1918 a group of local notables, assisted by a pan-Islamic agent from Egypt, announced the foundation of a Tripolitanian Republic. But Tripolitania did not present the same measure of ethnic or religious homogeneity as Cyrenaica. The province contained a substantial Berber-speaking minority, while the *Sanusiyya* possessed only a limited number of supporters. In these circumstances the history of the republic was one of bitter internal dissensions leading to mounting anarchy.

In the troubled years after 1918 Italy was in no state to embark on the reconquest of Libya. But the task was one that no Italian government could afford to renounce entirely. With internal political stability restored after the Fascist coup of 1922, an energetic Libyan policy became one of the main preoccupations of Italy's new rulers. The war against the Libyan Arabs was promptly resumed. The Italians, profiting from the advances in military technology that had taken place during World War I, were now in a position to use mechanized transport and aircraft on a lavish scale, and their troops were led by able and enterprising commanders. Even so, the conquest of Tripolitania, Cyrenaica, and the Fezzan required ten years of continuous fighting, for the Italians found themselves faced, particularly in Cyrenaica, with immensely stubborn resistance. In their conflict with the Bedouin of Cyrenaica the Italians were fighting "a people, not an enemy"—and "a people," as Evans-Pritchard has remarked in his study of Sanusi resistance, "can only be defeated by total imprisonment or extermination." [50] The Italians resorted to both methods. The Bedouin population is thought to have been "reduced by half to two-thirds by death and migration between 1912 and 1932." [51] In the closing phase of the war the Italians rounded up the Bedouin and placed them in large concentration camps to prevent them from continuing to assist the guerrillas. In 1930 the heroic leader of Cyrenaican resistance, Umar al-Mukhtar, an elderly Sanusi shaikh of Bedouin origin, was captured and hanged before a large crowd of his compatriots.

Eight years after the ending of the Italo-Sanusi war, Cyrenaica once again became a battlefield, the scene of some of the most momentous fighting of World War II. In 1943 Tripoli fell to the British Eighth Army, and the period of Italian rule in North Africa was ended. In the coastal towns it had lasted for no more than thirty years, in many other parts of the country for less than two decades.

In this brief period the Italians proved themselves enterprising colonists. Italian architects and town planners transformed Tripoli into one of the most pleasant cities of the Mediterranean and gave a distinctly Italianate character to many of the smaller towns. In the countryside the colonial authorities faced a more formidable task, for Libya was essentially a desert land—"a crate of sand" in the phrase popularized by Italian anticolonialists—offering few opportunities for agricultural development. Nevertheless the Fascist government was determined to carry through a program of "demographic colonization" designed to relieve population pressure in Italy itself and to provide Libya with half a million Italian colonists of peasant stock by the 1960's. In the late 1930's Italo Balbo, the immensely energetic governor of Libya, organized a scheme—probably the most elaborate of its kind ever known in the history of European colonization in Africa—that allowed 30,000 Italians to move within the space of a few months into well-planned agricultural settlements. Economically the scheme was far from being a failure. The Italian farms represented, in the words of a postwar United Nations report, "a remarkable feat of pioneering and land reclamation." But for the local people in Libya as in Algeria, European settlement involved *refoulement*, the loss of agricultural or pasture lands essential to their own economy, and for the Italian people as a whole, the colonization of Libya demanded a vast outpouring of money and of energy that could, so it seems in retrospect, have been far more profitably employed in the development of the many extremely backward areas of the Italian mainland.

In the years after 1943 British military administrators in Tripolitania and Cyrenaica and French officers in the Fezzan provided the country with a basic superstructure of government. Libya seemed to possess no natural unity; its three parts were geographically remote one from another and their populations differed greatly in character and sentiment. But in the immediate postwar years the great powers failed to agree on a system of trusteeship for the country and the matter was referred to the United Nations. In November, 1949, the General Assembly resolved that Libya should become an independent state within two years. Assisted by an able United Nations commissioner the Libyans set about devising a constitution for their country. Sayyid Muhammad Idris, the head of the Sanusi order, was the country's outstanding political personality. Though he had not taken a direct part in the war against the Italians—from 1922 to 1943 he lived in exile in Egypt—he was accepted by the Cyrenaicans as their leader. The Tripolitanians too were prepared to recognize Sayyid Idris as the constitutional monarch of a united kingdom, a federal constitution being devised to link the country's three parts together. In December, 1951, Libya became the first colonial territory in Northwest Africa to achieve independence.

▲▼ THE SAHARA TRANSFORMED

On a world population map no land area of comparable size, the polar regions excepted, presents so vast a blank as the Sahara. To outsiders the great desert seems a land mysterious, desolate and forbidding. Yet the Sahara is far from being completely uninhabited. Today it contains a population numbering about 2 million, the vast majority of its inhabitants being the descendants of groups long resident within its borders.

Before the coming of the French at the end of the nineteenth century, four distinct peoples played dominant roles in the history of the desert. The great massif of Tibesti was the preserve of the negroid Tebu, a people whose language is now classified as Nilo-Saharan. Berber-speaking Tuareg were the lords of the central Sahara from the mountains of Ahaggar to the great bend of the Niger River. The northern reaches of the desert were controlled from the eleventh century on by Bedouin who could trace their ancestry back to Arabia, while the western Sahara was the domain of the Moors, a people of mixed Arab and Berber stock. These four peoples were all nomadic pastoralists, possessing a political organization that appeared at first sight fragmented to the point of anarchy; in fact there existed many subtle ties of vassalage or clientship serving to bind seemingly autonomous tribal units loosely together. Amid the domains of the pastoralists lay the Sahara's urban centers, the oases with their cosmopolitan sedentary population. Many of these oasis-dwellers were black slaves of Sudanic origin.

Ties of culture, of commerce, and occasionally of politics linked the Saharan peoples with their neighbors to the north and to the south. For nearly a thousand years the Sahara had formed part of *dar al-Islam* (the land of Islam) and some Saharan groups were noted for their piety and learning. For centuries the desert had been traversed by trade routes connecting the Mediterranean lands with the wealthy Sudanic states of West Africa. In 1875 the trans-Saharan caravan trade still represented one of the most vigorous currents of long-distance commerce in the interior of Africa. Politically most of the communities of the desert could be regarded as autonomous units, but on a number of occasions in the past great states, formed either in the Maghrib or in the Sudanic belt of West Africa, had sought to establish their hegemony over neighboring Saharan peoples. In the early sixteenth century the Songhai emperors controlled a vast stretch of the southern Sahara, but the Songhai were shattered by a Moroccan army in the 1590's and Moroccan garrisons were established at Timbuktu and other towns on the Niger. A century later the sultans of Morocco again sent their military forces into the western Sahara on operations that reached as far south as the Senegal. At the same time many of the oases of the northern Sahara accepted Moroccan suzerainty. In the nineteenth century, Moroccan rulers still regarded most of the western Sahara as lying within their sphere of interest, but they lacked the power to maintain their claims in the face of French expansion.

Between 1850 and 1935 the French made themselves masters of by far the larger part of the great desert, establishing as they did so the most extensive imperial superstructure the desert had ever known. Direct French contacts with the Sahara date back no further than the 1850's when troops based in Algeria moved south to occupy the northern oases of Laghouat, Wargla, and Tuggurt. At this time there seemed little prospect of a rapid expansion of French hegemony, for the terrain of the desert was exceptionally forbidding and the Saharan peoples were regarded as fanatically hostile to alien intruders. But the French were well aware of the existence of a regular trans-Saharan commerce and were eager to find means of attracting this apparently lucrative traffic to the markets of Algeria. In the 1870's an ambitious scheme for the construction of a trans-Saharan railroad received considerable support in official circles, only to be abandoned in 1881 after a military surveying party led by Colonel Flatters was wiped out by the Tuareg of Ahaggar. For more than a decade fear of Tuareg hostility prevented the French from resuming their advance in the northern Sahara.

In 1890 the French obtained from their rivals, the British, diplomatic recognition of their claim that the greater part of the Sahara lay within their own sphere of influence. Meanwhile French forces based in Senegal were advancing eastward in a movement that gave them by 1900 complete control of the borderlands of the southern Sahara. At the turn of the century the French resumed their advance into the desert, moving northward from the Senegal to achieve the conquest of southern Mauritania, occupying the important northern oasis of In Salah in 1900, inflicting a crushing defeat on the Ahaggar Tuareg in 1902, and sending detachments from the Niger area to occupy Agades and Bilma, the major oases of the south central Sahara, in 1906.

The small group of army officers who led the French advance rapidly learned to adapt themselves to the peculiar nature of war and politics in a desert environment. Their success was due in large measure to their own initiative, for they were operating in an area where the metropolitan authorities could do little to assist or advise them. In these circumstances the support of native collaborators was essential. The French found the allies they needed in the Chaamba, a Bedouin Arab people of the northern Sahara. Before the French occupation of their territory, the Chaamba had been largely dependent on raiding neighboring tribes for their livelihood. By recruiting them into a newly formed Saharan Camel Corps, the French provided the Chaamba with a respectable outlet for their martial propensities. Armed with modern rifles, mounted on swift camels, and led by French officers, these one-time robbers became the policemen of the desert, finding in their new vocation ample opportunity to settle old scores with their traditional enemies, the Tuareg and the Moors.

In dealing with these two formidable peoples the French proved themselves masters of the tactics of "divide and rule," taking advantage of the continual feuds that set tribe against tribe and faction against faction. Nevertheless, there were occasions when the French found themselves confronted with a considerable measure of concerted resistance. A series of short sharp encounters fought in the first decade of the twentieth century forced the Tuareg to acknowledge French hegemony. But by 1916 the tide seemed to have turned against the European intruders, when the Italians were driven from their posts in southern Libya, and the Tuareg, urged on by Sanusi emissaries, rose against the French in a revolt which spread throughout the central Sahara and which was not finally mastered until 1919.

Even more serious was the opposition the French encountered from some of the Moors of the western Sahara. In the years between 1900 and 1910, Moorish resistance was led by the Shaikh Ma al-Amin, a widely revered religious leader whose home territory, the Seguiet al-Hamra, lay in the extreme northwestern corner of the desert. Ma al-Amin's base was strategically sited for resisting French encroachments, enabling him to establish direct contact with the sultan of Morocco, to purchase arms from the German and Spanish traders who visited his stretch of the Saharan coast, and to encourage the Moorish tribes living further south in their resistance to the French. Ma al-Amin died in 1910, but one of his sons, al-Hiba, carried on the policy of vigorous resistance. Something has already been said of al-Hiba's invasion of southern Morocco after the establishment of the French protectorate in 1912, of his proclamation as sultan in Marrakesh, and of his eventual repulse by the French—an episode in Moroccan history strongly reminiscent of that eleventh century onslaught by the warriors of the desert from which arose the great Almoravid dynasty. For all their dash and courage the Moors were outfought by the French and their native allies, but the establishment of French hegemony proved a long-drawn-out process. Not until 1934 was the conquest of northern Mauritania completed. In the final phase of pacification the French were assisted by Spanish troops, for Spain had claimed a protectorate over a large part of the western Sahara as early as the 1880's and received diplomatic recognition of her rights over a more modest stretch of territory in a series of Franco-Spanish treaties negotiated between 1900 and 1912. Without the advance of French arms in adjoining areas the Spanish authorities would hardly have been able to establish any form of control over the 100,000 square miles of territory that came to be known as the Spanish Sahara.

The European pacification of the Sahara represented one strand in a complex process of change that transformed the lives of many Saharan peoples. By 1914 the trans-Saharan trade, maintained so vigorously for more than a thousand years, had disappeared, though a local trade in Saharan products, dates in the north and salt in the south, continues to provide the owners of camels with some employment to this day. But there was no point in doing business across a span of 1,500 miles of desert, when Mediterranean goods could be transported so much more cheaply by steamship to West Africa, and the produce of the Sudan carried in much greater quantities on the new railroads built by the French to link the Niger with the Senegal and by the British to connect Kano with Lagos.

The years before World War I saw not only the decline of the camel caravan but also the introduction of the first motor vehicles to the Sahara. "Of all the innovations introduced by the French into the Sahara," an eminent French geographer has written, "none, not even the peace nor the multiplication of wells, has had such a profound effect on conditions of life as the motorcar: to discover a fact of comparable importance one must go back to the domestication of the camel." [52] For the slaves and serfs of the oases the coming of the long-distance lorry or bus provided an opportunity for escape to the enticing cities of the

Maghrib. But the gradual diminution of the servile population seriously affected the economy of the oases, as herds declined for want of herdsmen and irrigation channels became blocked for lack of labor to maintain them.

For the nomadic tribes, and especially for the previously favored groups of warriors and nobles, the collapse of the trans-Saharan trade, the check on raiding, and the emigration of many of their serfs involved "a loss of prestige, a reduction of employment and a fall in income." [53] In place of the old aristocracy a new bourgeoisie has arisen made up of shopkeepers, traders, civil servants, and soldiers, all of whom enjoy the advantage of a regular salary.

The social structure of the desert has been still further transformed by the extraordinary development of its economy in the course of the last fifteen years. The discoveries made by mineralogists and oil prospectors have brought wealth on a scale inconceivable a generation ago to one of the poorer regions of Africa. The first major oil strike was made in the Algerian Sahara in 1955. Four years later immensely rich oil deposits were discovered at a number of sites in the Libyan desert. By 1967 Saharan wells were producing 124,000,000 tons of oil, two thirds of which came from the still rapidly expanding Libyan oil fields. The Algerian Sahara was also found to contain one of the world's richest deposits of natural gas. As early as the 1930's Mauritania was known to possess valuable deposits of copper and high-grade iron ore; but it was not until the late 1950's that a start could be made to establish, through the work of an international consortium, a Mauritanian mining industry. The latest, but surely not the last, of the mineral discoveries made in the Sahara is a rich deposit of uranium in the Air massif that now forms part of the Republic of Niger.

These developments must be counted among the great pioneering achievements of modern industry. They have led to the establishment of many new settlements populated by the cosmopolitan personnel of the oil or mining companies. The intrusion of these aliens, with their enticing material culture, may well come to be regarded as an event of revolutionary significance in the history of the Saharan peoples. By their demands on the local population for labor and by their mere example the newcomers serve to undermine still further the old economy and the old way of life. "Simply to obtain workmen for the oil fields, it is planned to transform these lordly people who command our respect by the dignity of their attitudes and the wisdom of their utterances into a rabble seeking jobs and doles." [54] So the decline of the great camel nomads appears to a veteran French Saharan hand. But to the young men of the desert picking up the new skills of the motor mechanic in place of the ancient skills of the herdsmen, and acquiring in the process the vision of an infinitely wider world, the future probably presents itself in far less desolate terms.

▲▼ THE INDEPENDENT STATES OF
NORTHWEST AFRICA

With the withdrawal of the French from Algeria in 1962, the Maghrib as a whole achieved a measure of political independence such as it had not known since the early sixteenth century, in the years before the coming of the Turks, when the Hafsids ruled in Tunis and the Merinids in Fez. Morocco, Algeria, Tunisia, and Libya, the newly independent states of the Maghrib, could each lay claim to a long tradition of historical identity and so did not present that quality of "newness" so noticeable in the recently created sovereignties of tropical Africa. But they faced the same basic tasks as other "new nations" in Asia and Africa —reconstructing the political and administrative superstructure established by colonial authorities, devising a foreign policy to accord with the aspirations of a truly independent state, and pressing forward with the manifold activities involved in the process of social and economic development.

In 1951 it seemed ironic that Libya, at that time by far the poorest and most backward territory in the Maghrib, should be the first to achieve independence. Some contemporaries gloomily predicted that the deep divisions existing between the country's three provinces, Tripolitania, Cyrenaica, and the Fezzan, would lead to a rapid disintegration of the hastily devised federal structure. In fact, the years since independence have witnessed a steady growth in Libyan national consciousness, a process that made possible in 1963 the replacement of the federal constitution by a unitary system of government. The king, Idris I, an elderly man of scholarly temperament, provided an effective focus for national unity and made himself the source of ultimate authority, but he preferred to lead a secluded life in his palace near Tobruk and left most of the affairs of state to a coterie of wealthy families whose members soon found that the practice of politics offered many opportunities for personal enrichment. Under this plutocratic regime Libya enjoyed a "record of rather tremulous stability," [55] which ended suddenly in September, 1969, when a group of army officers, led by Colonel Mu'Amar al-Qadhafi, staged a swift and almost bloodless coup, abolished the monarchy, and proclaimed a republic. The young officers—most of them were in their mid-twenties—were Arab radicals, deeply inspired by the career of President Nasser. They saw themselves as the agents of a profound revolution in Libyan affairs. Within a few weeks of seizing power they had removed from office all the politicians, senior civil servants, and army officers associated with the old regime, launched a vigorous attack on such manifestations of European influence as the teaching of English in primary schools, demanded the removal of the British and American bases at El Adem and Wheelus Field, and created a new diplomatic axis through the development of extremely cordial relations with the governments of the United Arab Republic and the Sudan. By 1972, Libya's international position had been transformed by the flamboyant foreign policy of its new rulers, who exploited to the full the opportunities for freedom of action made possible by their country's immense wealth. From a position of relative obscurity Libya emerged as one of the most dynamic of Arab states, the most vigorous advocate of Arab unity, the architect of a political union with Egypt, and the dispenser of lavish quantities of aid to other African countries, including Tunisia, Mauritania, Niger, and Uganda.

The political stability maintained by Tunisia in the years since 1956 contrasts sharply with the stormy politics of other newly independent states. The country's modest size and the homogeneity of its population certainly facilitate the tasks of government, but so stable a polity would never have been achieved without the organizing ability shown by prominent members of the Neo-Destour (renamed the Destourian Socialist Party in 1964) under the immensely popular leadership of the president, Habib Bourguiba. Bourguiba—regarded by many Tunisians as the "father, prophet, and savior of his country"—has spoken of the state and nation as being founded on a "dialogue" with the people. Few leaders in modern times have indeed been so open in explaining their policies or so frank in expressing their thoughts as the Tunisian president. Though other parties are not banned, Tunisia is in practice a one-party state. Yet the opportunities provided for participation in political activity and for discussion of the country's problems gave to the present regime a genuinely popular character. Nevertheless, by the early 1970's there were signs of a serious malaise in Tunisian politics, with deep divisions appearing within the ranks of the ruling party and a liberal wing voicing its criticisms of the president's excessively paternalistic leadership. One familiar symptom of social and political tension was presented by the violent demonstrations launched by university and high school students which convulsed the Tunisian capital in February, 1972.

The politics of postcolonial Morocco reflect the country's complex social structure. Three major groups may be distinguished—the monarchy and its supporters, Istiqal, the leading party in the struggle for independence, and the National Union of Popular Forces, formed in 1958 by a breakaway group of radical members of Istiqal. Minor groups include the Democratic Party of Independence, founded in rivalry to Istiqal as early as 1946, and the Popular Movement, a rural, predominantly Berber party founded in 1957. In the years since independence the Moroccan monarchy has succeeded in maintaining its dominant position. By virtue of the religious nature of his office the king is regarded with deep reverence by the majority of his subjects. His political power is based on control of the armed forces and the rights of patronage that place a large number of official appointments at his disposal. To these constitutional advantages Muhammad V, first king of newly independent Morocco, could add the immense personal prestige acquired through taking so active a part in the struggle against the French. Between 1956 and 1960, the king acted as an arbiter, striving to achieve a measure of consensus between conflicting parties. Istiqal ministers played a prominent part in the governments of these years but they were never able to establish an all-Istiqal cabinet to the exclusion of ministers from other parties. Meanwhile the king was shrewdly using the patronage at his disposal to increase the number of his supporters. By 1960 he felt strong enough to take over the post of prime minister for himself.

Muhammad V died suddenly in 1961. His son, Hassan II, gave evidence of the same political dexterity as his father. In 1965, after a period of some confusion in which the minor political parties attempted to maintain a government in the face of strong opposition from Istiqal and the radicals of the National Union, the king dissolved parliament and made himself prime minister. Hassan II drew his support from the more conservative elements in Morocco's population, the Berbers of the countryside, the urban bourgeoisie and the religious leaders; but the "palace set" with which he surrounded himself was made up largely of high-ranking army officers and wealthy aristocrats. The most vigorous criticism of the regime has come from the students and the urban proletariat. Monarchical rule has been authoritarian but not dictatorial. With Istiqal describing itself as a "loyal opposition," political debate continued and the king showed himself vividly aware of his country's problems, but by the end of the 1960's there was increasing talk of exorbitant corruption in the royal entourage. In the early 1970's two dramatic attempts were made to overthrow the regime. In July, 1971, a group of senior army officers incited officer cadets to attack the royal palace near Rabat while the king was celebrating a lavish birthday party. Thirteen months later pilots of the Moroccan air force opened fire on the royal plane with the king on board. From both conspiracies the king escaped unscathed, though on both occasions a number of high-ranking Moroccans lost their lives. The conspirators in both cases appear to have been animated by a desire to purge the court of its grosser excesses. The Moroccan monarchy is one of the oldest political institutions in Africa. By the early 1970's many observers were beginning to wonder how long it could survive.

No country in Africa achieved independence in an atmosphere of such violence as Algeria. In the last weeks of nominal French rule in the summer of 1962, Algeria presented a spectacle of near-anarchy and incipient civil war: European residents abandoning their properties and fleeing by the thousands; freedom fighters paying off old scores by killing Muslim collaborators; and the civilian and military leaders of the nationalist cause quarreling bitterly among themselves. From this period of utter confusion one man emerged with supreme power in his hands. Ahmad Ben Bella was one of the few surviving members of the small group of militants who launched Algeria's war of liberation in 1954. In 1956 he was kidnapped by the French while on a flight from Morocco to Tunis and spent the remainder of the war in French custody. On his release he did not become a member of the Algerian Provisional Government, but astutely gained for himself the backing of the country's best-equipped military force, the detachments of the National Liberation Army built up by Colonel Boumédienne in Tunisia but prevented by the French policy of cordoning off Algeria's eastern frontier from taking a direct part in the armed struggle. With the support of Boumédienne and his soldiers Ben Bella gained control of Algiers, set up a political committee, made sure that his own nominees were returned in the elections for a national assembly held on the eve of formal independence and thus ensured his constitutional appointment as premier. In the course of Algeria's first year as a sovereign state, many of the men who had played a leading part in the liberation struggle disappeared from the political scene; some fell foul of Ben Bella, were arrested and placed in detention, others sought safety in exile.

Ben Bella was dedicated to the achievement of a socialist revolution. He sought to achieve this end by transforming Algeria into a one-party state, with the FLN as the sole party, creating for himself the office of an executive president invested with supreme power. But the personal nature of his rule became increasingly irksome to the old-guard militants who had grown accustomed to the wartime practice of collective leadership, and his grandiloquent revolutionary aspirations exasperated the technocrats who were grappling with the immense practical difficulties of reconstructing a shattered economy. In June, 1965, Ben Bella was unexpectedly toppled from power in a coup led by his most powerful supporter, Colonel Boumédienne. With ironical timing his downfall occurred on the eve of a highly publicized Afro-Asian conference which he had invited to meet in Algiers.

Boumédienne brought with him a new style, less flamboyant, less personal, more pragmatic, laying greater stress on Algeria as an Islamic state but no less conscious of the country's "revolutionary" aspirations. The new president provided Algeria with a period of much needed stability.

In political terms the greater part of the Sahara is divided between states whose center of power lies either in the Maghrib (Algeria and Libya) or in the Sudanic belt of West and Equatorial Africa (Mali, Niger, Chad). But there exists today one truly Saharan state— Mauritania. Under colonial rule the country formed a part of the administrative federation of French West Africa and seemed to lack a distinct political personality of its own. French colonial officials referred to the territory as *la vide* ("the emptiness") and finding it lacking in suitable urban centers, chose to administer it from the Senegalese town of St. Louis.

Of Mauritania's 1 million inhabitants, 200,000 are Negroid agriculturalists, mainly of Tukulor or Fula stock, living on the northern bank of the Senegal, and forming a clearly defined minority in comparison to the light-skinned Moors who make up the remainder of the country's population. The Moors are nomadic camel-herders, but they have been profoundly influenced by Islam, possess a long tradition of literacy, and have acquired through their position on one of the main Saharan trade routes considerable experience of a wider world. The years immediately after World War II saw the emergence of the country's first modern political parties. One of these parties, *Parti du Regroupement Mauritanien,* led by Mokhtar Ould Daddah, developed into a moderate and broadly based national front and formed a government to whom the French could transfer power in 1960. The same party, which changed its name to the Party of the Mauritanian People in 1963, provided the country with a remarkably stable administration in the first decade of independence.

The four independent states of the Maghrib find themselves occupying an international position of some complexity. In geographical terms they are all Mediterranean countries and so possess considerable strategic significance both for the NATO powers and for the USSR. Culturally they form part of the world of Islam, watch with particular interest the political changes taking place in the Arab states to their east, and have shown themselves keenly responsive to the latest developments in the Arab-Israeli conflict. But close cultural links also exist with the countries of Western Europe, where most members of the present ruling groups received at least part of their education. The relations between Algeria, Tunisia, and Morocco and their former colonial overlord have been far more cordial than the bitterness engendered during the period of nationalist struggle led contemporaries to expect. France remains the major source of aid for all three countries, but valuable assistance has also been received from many other countries, including the United States and the Soviet Union. Finally, all the states of the Maghrib have been involved in the movement for African unity.

To outsiders the Maghrib appears to possess a certain natural unity. Yet only twice in the region's long history—under the Almohads in the twelfth century and more recently under the French—have its various parts been subjected to a measure of political unification, and the stress laid on national consciousness in all the newly independent states has strengthened traditional differences. Moreover, Algeria's revolutionary panache jars on the sensibilities of many Moroccans and Tunisians, and Morocco's quasi-imperialistic pretensions have led to bitter disputes with Mauritania and Algeria.

At the time of Morocco's emancipation from French rule in 1956, the Istiqal leader, Allal al-Fasi, demanded the "reconstitution of Greater Morocco," citing the exploits of Moroccan armies in the sixteenth and seventeenth centuries to show that Moroccan suzerainty had once been extended over the western Sahara as far south as the Niger and the Senegal. With these grandiose claims in mind the Moroccan government refused to recognize Mauritania as an independent state. A number of political leaders in northern Mauritania were prepared to accept the Moroccan claim, but the Mauritanian government refused to discuss the matter and made use of the threat of Moroccan expansionism to stimulate the growth of a feeling of Mauritanian unity. Both Morocco and Mauritania laid claim to the Spanish Sahara, a territory recently found to contain immensely rich phosphate deposits, but their dispute played into Spanish hands. By the early 1970's, there was clear evidence of increasing restlessness among the inhabitants of the colony, and the Spanish government found it necessary to maintain an army of 15,000 troops to enforce its authority over a territory whose total population numbered no more than 50,000. Even the Spanish position in the presidios of Ceuta and Melilla, both of which had been in Iberian hands since the fifteenth century and were therefore by far the oldest European possessions in the continent, no longer seemed entirely secure.

Morocco's dispute with Algeria was also concerned with frontiers in the northwestern Sahara. Toward the end of the nineteenth century certain communities, long accustomed to recognize the suzerainty of the sultan of Morocco, were brought under the control of the French administration in Algeria and came in time to form part of the territory of the Algerian republic. In the autumn of 1963, fighting broke out between Moroccan and Algerian troops in the area under dispute. The Organization of African Unity succeeded in negotiating a cease-fire but it was not until 1970 that Morocco and Algeria finally settled the dispute by agreeing to establish two joint commissions, one to demarcate their Saharan frontiers, the other to study means of exploiting the rich iron ore deposits that lay beneath the disputed area. The agreement was symptomatic of the emergence in the late 1960's of more cordial sentiments between the states of the Maghrib.

Relations between France and her three former North African dependencies were disturbed by a number of dramatic and violent incidents. In the years immediately after independence the French had been allowed to retain the use of the important Tunisian naval base of Bizerte. In 1961 the French base was attacked by Tunisian volunteers who were beaten off with heavy casualties. Two years later the base was handed over to the Tunisian government but memory of the bloodshed at Bizerte soured relations between the two countries for the duration of the 1960's. Relations between France and Morocco were affected in much the same way by the mysterious Ben Barka affair. In 1966, Ben Barka, the leader of one of Morocco's opposition parties, was abducted from the house in Paris where he was living as an exile and was never seen again. Among those implicated in the ensuing police investigation was the Moroccan General Oufkir, one of the king's most trusted ministers. Oufkir was tried *in absentia* by a Paris court and sentenced to life imprisonment. The affair caused a considerable breach in the hitherto cordial relations between the two countries. For the duration of General de Gaulle's presidency official relations between France and Algeria were astonishingly warm, but there were many minor disputes between the two countries, and in 1971 the Algerian decision to nationalize French oil companies, in apparent contravention of an earlier agreement, caused great bitterness in Paris. Nevertheless, in spite of so much friction, sharply contrasting with the harmonious relationship it maintained with the francophone states of *Afrique noire,* France continued to be a generous source of aid to the countries of the Maghrib. But the general trend was clear. Tunisia, Morocco, and above all Algeria were determined to reduce their links with their former colonial power and to adopt a more independent stance. One symptom of change was to be found in the altered pattern of trade: in 1962 80 percent of Algeria's trade was carried on with France; ten years later the French share had dropped to 45 percent. In the mid-1960's the Soviet Union established close relations with Algeria and began to develop a flourishing trade with Morocco. The United States also began to play a more vigorous part in the development of the Maghrib, so too did France's partners in the EEC. By the early 1970's, the state system in the Western Mediterranean was beginning to recall a pattern that had not been seen since the early eighteenth century when Morocco, Algiers, and Tunis could all be regarded as vigorous and independent powers.

In the 1960's Algeria stood out as one of the few countries in Africa intent on pursuing a "revolutionary" foreign policy. "Unlike other nations," the country's foreign minister declared in 1968, "we have not lost all illusions. We are still spurred on by faith, by conviction, by a flame, by a fire." [56] Algeria's ardor found an outlet in vigorous support for the Arab cause in the struggle against Israel and for the freedom-fighters in Southern Africa. At the time of the Six Days' War between the Arab states and Israel, Algeria showed itself one of the most militant members of the anti-Israeli coalition. The Algerian leaders, with their own hard-earned experience of the effectiveness of violent methods in a revolutionary struggle, naturally felt considerable sympathy for the Palestinian guerillas. Other Maghribi leaders adopted a more moderate line. King Hassan of Morocco has stressed the need to settle disputes by peaceful means and President Bourguiba of Tunisia, mindful of the fact that his own political opponents have found refuge on occasion in Algeria and in the U.A.R., showed scant sympathy for the "revolutionary" approach to international problems.

Involvement in the affairs of distant peoples may indeed be regarded as something of a luxury for the governments of states whose own peoples are more concerned to see some improvement in their immediate livelihood. With the recently created exception of Libya, all the countries of the Maghrib are poor. The difficulties they face in increasing their wealth derive in part from the physical nature of their environment—the irregularity of the rainfall and the poor quality of many soils—in part from the historical forces set in motion in the course of the past century.

Morocco, Algeria, and Tunisia are all beginning to feel the pressure of a rapidly increasing population. Between 1946 and 1966 the population of Morocco rose from 9.4 million to 13.5 million, of Algeria from 8.2 million to 12 million, and of Tunisia from 3.3 million to 4.5 million. One consequence of this rapid population growth has been the emergence of an appallingly high rate of unemployment and of underemployment. In 1968, no less than 2 million Algerians were reckoned to be unemployed and as many underemployed. Rural unemployment is a serious problem in some districts, but it is in the towns, especially in the *bidonvilles* of Casablanca and the *medina* of Algiers, that poverty takes on its most savage aspect. These are the places of which Franz Fanon wrote: "It is a world without spaciousness; men live there on top of each other, and their huts are built one on the top of the other. The native town is a hungry town, starved of bread, of meat, of shoes, of coal, of light. The native town . . . is a town on its knees, a town wallowing in the mire." [57]

Fanon wrote at a time when it was still possible to point a sharp contrast between the *medina* and the prosperous suburbs inhabited by the *colons*. By the end of the 1960's the contrast was less apposite, for the vast majority of Europeans had left. Between 1956 and 1964 the European population of the Maghrib fell from nearly 2 million to 300,000. The exodus of Europeans achieved its most massive proportions in Algeria, with a fall from over a million to 70,000. At the same time all the countries of the Maghrib witnessed the departure of a very large number of Jews, of whom about 200,000 found new homes in Israel, while 90,000, mainly from Algeria, were resettled in France. Emigration on such a scale deprived the countries of the Maghrib of a vast fund of administrative ability, commercial acumen, and entrepreneurial energy. The departure of the Europeans removed a major source of political tension but it produced a severe dislocation in the structure both of the economy and of the social and administrative services. The technical assistance provided by France and other countries can do no more than partially plug a gap that must in time be filled by trained Maghribi civil servants, teachers, factory managers, agricultural advisers, and other technicians.

The years since independence have some notable achievements in the field of development. Something has already been said of the spectacular discoveries of oil, natural gas, and iron ore in the Sahara. New industries—including a fast growing tourist industry—have been established in Tunisia and Morocco. And every country can point to impressive advances in education at all levels. Agriculture, the most important section of the economy, remains, as in most Afro-Asian countries, the least dynamic. Indeed Algeria presented the depressing spectacle of agricultural regression. Local workers proved unable to maintain both the quantity and the quality of the products of the great estates abandoned by French proprietors. Some Algerian wine failed to satisfy French palates and had to be sold to the Russians for use as industrial alcohol. But the agricultural potentialities of all the countries of the Maghrib are very considerable. Indeed it has been estimated that the thorough application of the latest techniques, with particular stress laid on the expansion of irrigation, could lead to a sixfold increase in the region's agricultural production.

CHAPTER IV

West Africa

▲▼ INTRODUCTION

West Africa is defined here as a long quadrilateral of territory, extending about 2,000 miles from the Atlantic to Lake Chad and about 700 miles from the Gulf of Guinea to the Sahara. Modern West Africa is divided into fourteen distinct political units. Eight of these were formerly under French domination: Senegal, Mali, Guinea, Ivory Coast, Upper Volta, Togo, Dahomey, and Niger. (Mauritania, which also formed part of the administrative federation of French West Africa, is a truly Saharan state and has been considered in this study as a part of Northwest Africa.) The two most populous countries of modern West Africa, Nigeria and Ghana (the Gold Coast), once formed part of the British Empire, together with the smaller territories of Sierra Leone and Gambia. Liberia, dominated by its ruling class of Afro-American immigrants, has been an independent republic since 1849. In 1973 Portuguese Guinea was the only remaining colonial territory in West Africa. The off-shore islands of the Cape Verde archipelago and of Fernando Po (now part of the Republic of Equatorial Guinea) are considered in Chapter IX.

The geography of West Africa can be simplified into two distinctive subregions stretching from west to east, the northern belt of the savanna and the southern belt of the rain forest. To the former, geographers and historians have found it convenient to apply the term "Sudan"; to the latter, "Guinea." (*Bilad as-Sudan,* "land of the blacks," was the expression applied by medieval Arab geographers to all the countries lying to the south of the Sahara; Guinea is derived from the Berber word for "black" and was the term applied by the earliest Portuguese explorers to the coastal lands of West Africa.) Historians find it convenient to divide the Sudan into three parts: Western, extending from the Atlantic to the western borders of modern Nigeria; Central, incorporating most of northern Nigeria, Niger, and Chad; and Eastern, the territory now forming part of the modern Sudan Republic.

The contrast between the northern and southern belts of West Africa is sharp and striking, but it is derived not from any sharp variations in relief but from marked differences in rainfall, climate, and vegetation. Freetown, the capital of Sierre Leone, has an average rainfall of 138 inches, Bamako, capital of Mali, 44 inches, and Niamey, capital of Niger, 21 inches. Niamey, which may be taken as typical of the northern savanna, is virtually rainless from October to March. In the coastal districts of West Africa, on the other hand, some rain may be expected every month, though rainfall is heaviest between May and October. The traveler who flies from Dakar to Freetown or from Kano to Lagos in the "dry season," is made vividly aware of these geographical contrasts. Around Dakar or Kano the landscapes seem arid, the air filled with the dust blown by the *harmattan*, a north wind from the Sahara. Many rivers dry up completely, thus greatly facilitating the opportunities for travel, and the climate is often refreshingly cool. By contrast most of the coastal lands of West Africa are green and humid throughout the year. During the rainy season the contrast between the two parts of the region is less apparent. During the summer months most parts of the Sudanic belt receive enough rain to transform the dun landscape of the dry season into a verdant and delectable countryside, capable of supporting a flourishing agriculture.

A certain monotony in the relief deprives West Africa of the spectacular scenery possessed by other regions of the continent. In compensation the peoples of West Africa present a remarkable and exhilarating variety of cultures. In physical terms most indigenous West Africans are of Negroid stock, but in the northern Sudanic belt a certain admixture of Caucasoid groups has taken place over the centuries, as people of Saharan origin have come to settle in the more fertile lands to their south, while in many districts from Senegambia to Darfur the light-skinned pastoral Fulani stand out sharply from their Negroid agriculturalist neighbors.

Linguistics provides a rather more precise tool than physical anthropology for distinguishing one ethnic group from another. One section of West Africans—among whom the Hausa of northern Nigeria are the most prominent group—speak languages classified as forming the Chadic branch of the Afro-Asiatic family—a family of which Berber and Arabic are also branches. Two West African languages, Songhai, spoken by a largely riverine people living on the great bend of the Niger, and Kanuri, the main language of Bornu in northeastern Nigeria, are now classified as forming part of a Nilo-Saharan family of languages. All other West African languages are incorporated in a language family which some scholars term Western Sudanic. This family contains six branches: West Atlantic, embracing most of the languages spoken in Senegambia, together with Fufulde, the language of the widely dispersed Fulani; Mande, a group of languages whose principal speakers are the Sarakole or Soninke, the Malinke or Mandingo, and the Bambara; Voltaic, a large number of languages spoken by peoples, of whom the Mossi and the Senufo are the most prominent, living within the area of the Niger bend; Kwa, an even more widely extended group of languages stretching from the southern Ivory Coast to eastern Nigeria and including most of the languages spoken in Ghana, Togo, and Dahomey; Benue-Congo, a complex group of languages spoken by a cluster of smaller ethnic groups living in the "middle belt" of Nigeria and in western Cameroon; and Adamawa, a group of languages confined, at least in so far as West Africa is concerned, to the Nigerian province of that name.

Language provides, of course, only one of the criteria that can be used for classifying the peoples of West Africa. Political organization offers another sharply marked manifestation of differences. No African region presented in 1875 so diverse a range of polities as West Africa. In Ashanti, the caliphate of Sokoto, and the Tukulor empire created by al-Hajj Umar Tall, the region contained three of the largest and most dynamic indigenous polities to be found in the entire continent. The kingdoms of Benin and Bornu possessed a longer record of historical continuity than any other polities in sub-Saharan Africa. The Wolof, the Yoruba, and the Mossi were among the most prominent of West African ethnic groups; all of them had created a cluster of medium-sized states. Some of the region's major commercial centers, such as Timbuktu, Kong, Bonny, and Calabar, were autonomous or virtually autonomous polities. Many areas, such as the Gambia and much of modern Sierra Leone, possessed a striking variety of smaller states and chiefdoms. But there were also many belts of territory, in the plateau area of northern Nigeria, for example, or in parts of northern Ghana or the Ivory Coast, where people lived, as they had done for centuries, in completely autonomous village communities.

For more than a thousand years West Africa had been exposed to the profound impact exerted by alien immigrants coming from areas whose peoples had evolved a more sophisticated culture. Toward the end of the first millennium A.D. a series of regular caravan routes was developed across the Sahara to link the Sudanic belt of West Africa with the Mediterranean world of Egypt and the Maghrib. The North African merchants who traveled these routes brought with them many manifestations of the culture of Islam—new religious, political, and social concepts, new techniques (including that of literacy), and the experience derived from a knowledge of a very much wider world. In the first half of the second millennium A.D. Islam was established in some of the major polities of the Sudanic belt. Many of the rulers of the dynasties which had accepted Islam proved somewhat lax in their observance of the faith, but small groups of Muslim merchants and holy men acted as a constant leaven, preserving the vitality of local Islam and gradually extending its influence, largely as a result of their trading enterprises, to areas lying farther to the south. The second quarter of the eighteenth century saw the outbreak of the first of a series of jihads which continued into the nineteenth century and led to the establishment of a number of new states, including the caliphate of Sokoto, the imamate of Futa Jallon, and the Tukulor empire, in which the principles of Islam were observed with much greater strictness than in the older Muslim polities.

In the fifteenth century direct contact had been established between West Africa and Western Europe as a result of the success of the Portuguese in pioneering the sea routes around the western bulge of the Sahara. As news of the commercial opportunities offered by the newly discovered land of Guinea gradually spread, other Europeans—especially the English, the French, and the Dutch—began to do regular business in West African waters. The development of plantation economies in the tropical lands of the Americas led to a steadily increasing demand for African labor, and many thousands of Africans were shipped across the Atlantic. The organization of the slave trade could be regarded as a cooperative venture between Europeans and Africans. European posts were confined almost entirely to the coast and African middlemen grew rich and powerful on the profits the trade afforded. Before the coming of the Europeans, the coastal areas of West Africa must have been among the least developed and the most thinly populated in the entire region. The creation of a string of new entrepôts, comparable to the commercial centers fed by the trans-Saharan traffic in the Sudanic belt, exerted a profound influence on the political and cultural development of the peoples of Guinea. When the export of slaves was suppressed by European action in the course of the nineteenth century, Guinea was able to offer new products—particularly groundnuts and palm oil—of value to the fast growing economy of Europe. By this time, however, European interest in West Africa was no longer purely commercial. The movement to abolish the slave trade had served to arouse a powerful current of humanitarian sentiment, especially in England. At the end of the eighteenth century a settlement for freed slaves was established on the Sierra Leone peninsula and became in 1808 the first British crown colony in tropical Africa. In the first decades of the nineteenth century Protestant missionaries began to preach their revolutionary gospel at a number of mission stations founded at various centers between the Gambia and Calabar. The activities of missionaries, of naval officers serving in the anti-slave-trade patrols, and of administrators provided a practical manifestation of the new attitude developed by many Europeans toward the people of West Africa. By 1875 the French, with their main settlements at St. Louis, Gorée, and Dakar, the British with their control of the Sierra Leone peninsula, the Gold Coast, and Lagos Island, held in their hands the growing points of new political structures whose expansion and evolution were to affect a massive transformation in the lives of many West Africans.

▲▼ SENEGAMBIA: AFRICAN POLITIES, MUSLIM REVOLUTIONARIES, AND EUROPEAN CONQUERORS

The term "Senegambia" covers the western extremity of West Africa, the basin of the Senegal and Gambia rivers, from which two of the modern states of the region derive their names. Immediately to the south lies the Portuguese "province" of Guinea, 14,000 square miles in extent, and the last colonial enclave in West Africa, a territory which may most conveniently be considered an extension of Senegambia.

No part of sub-Saharan Africa possesses so long a record of association with Europeans. In the middle of the fifteenth century the Portuguese made their first contacts with the people of Senegambia, to be followed a hundred years later by the French and the English. By the nineteenth century Portuguese activities were largely confined to the creeks and estuaries of the district known to the French as "the Rivers of the South" where the fortified posts of Bissau and Cacheu represented the only substantial Portuguese settlements. French activities were concentrated on the Senegal River and on the Cape Verde Peninsula. St. Louis, the capital of the colony, was founded in the mid-seventeenth century at the mouth of the Senegal. It had grown by 1875 into a town of 16,000, many of whose inhabitants had been strongly influenced by French culture. In the late seventeenth century the French began moving up the river, establishing a number of small posts as entrepôts for the trade in slaves and gum. Gorée, a rocky island lying off the Cape Verde Peninsula, had been in French hands since the seventeenth century, but it was not until the 1850's that the French laid the foundations of Dakar on the adjacent mainland. At the same time French traders, eager to develop the trade in groundnuts (peanuts), the area's major export after the abolition of the overseas slave trade, began to establish trading posts in the Casamance, the district to the south of the Gambia.

The Gambia, whose broad estuary presents the most easily navigable highway into the interior of any of the rivers of West Africa, had been associated with the British ever since the seventeenth century. Immediately after the Napoleonic Wars the British established the post of Bathurst at the mouth of the river, intending it primarily as a base for activities against illegal slavers. By the middle of the nineteenth century British traders, many of them Creoles from Sierra Leone, had developed a flourishing trade in groundnuts with the riverine peoples.

Senegambia had never provided the base for any of the major indigenous polities of West Africa, but the area contained a number of small states of some antiquity. The eleventh-century Arab geographer, al-Bakri, described a Negro kingdom, Takrur, lying in the valley of the Middle Senegal. Takrur is probably to be identified with Futa Toro whose people are known as the Tukulor. To the southwest of Futa Toro lay a group of six states established by the closely related Wolof and Serer peoples. Along the Gambia a dozen smaller states had come to be formed by ruling groups mostly descended from emigrants from the Malinke (Mandingo) heartland on the Upper Niger. To the south of the Gambia on off-shore islands or among the swamps of the coast lived a variety of smaller ethnic groups, such as the Jola, the Mandjak, and the Balante, groups whose polities took the form of independent village communities over which the superstructure of a state had never been erected. Two other ethnic groups played a prominent part in the life of the area: the Sarakole or Soninke and the Fulani (known also as Fula, Peul or Fulbe). The Sarakole heartland lay to the northeast in territory that had once formed part of the ancient empire of Ghana. The Sarakole were vigorous traders, many of whom had migrated southwards in search of new commercial opportunities. The movements of the Fulani had extended over an even wider area. The Fulani are a pastoral people, sharply distinguished from their Negroid neighbours by their lighter skin. It is possible that they derive their origin from a group of Berber pastoralists. In the course of the first millennium A.D. such a group may have moved south from the Sahara across the Senegal and come into contact with the Negroid agriculturalist Tukulor whose language the pastoralists adopted. The pressures of a cattle-raising economy forced many Fulani groups to break away in search of new pastures. By the mid-nineteenth century groups of Fulani pastoralists were to be found in many parts of West Africa, on the Gambia, in the highland of Futa Jallon, on the Upper Niger, and in many of the districts lying between the Niger and Lake Chad.

Islam was introduced to Senegambia in the eleventh century when the ruler of Takrur, probably prompted by Maghribi traders from across the Sahara, accepted the new religion and began to apply the Shari'a. Despite this early start, the progress of Islam was slow and unspectacular. The new culture had little appeal for other ruling groups in the area, and even the kings of Takrur allowed the true faith to be overridden by animist practices. Nevertheless, over the centuries small Muslim communities came to be formed in many parts of Senegambia, as Muslim traders and holy men (known locally as *marabouts*) moved into the area. Most of these Senegambian Muslims were of Sarakole or Tukulor origin, others were Moors from Mauritania, while some individuals came from distant Morocco. Richard Jobson, an Englishman who visited the Gambia in the early seventeenth century, reported that "the Mary-buckes [*marabouts*] are separated from the common people both in their habitations and course of lives" and was particularly struck by the large number of Arabic manuscripts in the possession of local Muslim communities.[1] Another Englishman, Winwood Reade, who traveled in Senegambia in the 1860's, described in crude but vivid terms the contrast between the pagan and Muslim communities living side by side in the Casamance. "The first are drunkards, gamblers, swine: as diseased in body as debased in mind. The latter are practical Christians . . . sober; truthful; constant in their devotions; strictly honest; they treat kindly those who are below them; they do good only to their neighbors." [2]

In the Wolof and Malinke states of Senegambia the *marabouts* formed a distinct clerical class, esteemed by local rulers for the services they could offer. As the "commercial travelers" [3] of Senegambia, making journeys as far afield as Timbuktu, they acquired a mass of information about a wider world and so were well equipped to become shrewd diplomatic advisers. Their literacy also stood them in good stead. In animist eyes many *marabouts* were regarded as the dispensers of powerful magic and some Muslims developed a useful trade by selling amulets containing sentences from the Koran. But temporal power lay firmly in the hands of the ruling dynasties and their powerful feudatories, the commanders of bands of pagan warriors, many of whom—like the Mamluks of North Africa—were of slave origin. Devout Muslims had frequent cause to deplore the sacrilegious conduct of these hard-drinking captains and sometimes found themselves the victims of their depredations. Thus, though Muslim and pagan communities often lived peacefully side by side, the possibility of conflict along cultural and ideological lines was always present.

By 1875 Senegambia had indeed been troubled for over a century by wars of religion. The first major religious conflict between Muslims and pagans broke out in the second quarter of the eighteenth century amid the plateaus of Futa Jallon, where Fulani pastoralists, attracted by the area's excellent grazing lands, had come to nomadize among the scattered small-scale polities of the pagan Jallonka. The pastoralists were accompanied by Muslim clerics through whose influence the inevitable conflicts between Fulani and Jallonka were transformed into a jihad. After fifty years of fighting the Muslims succeeded in establishing a loosely structured theocratic state, whose ruler was given the title of *al-mami,* derived from the Arabic *al-Imam.*

The revolution in Futa Jallon inspired a similar movement in Futa Toro where in the last quarter of the eighteenth century the Torodbe, the Tukulor clerical class, overthrew the old-established pagan dynasty and formed a confederation of seven largely autonomous provinces under the presidency of an *almami,* elected for a brief span of office by an electoral body made up of the main Torodbe families. By 1850 Futa Toro had become one of the most thoroughly Islamized polities in West Africa. "The Koran is the only law in the political and civil order there," wrote two contemporary French observers. "All social life is regulated according to the principles, more or less well understood, of their sacred books." [4] The rulers of Futa Toro controlled an area too confined to serve as an effective base for political expansion. But Tukulor emigrants moved into the countries to the south and west, carrying with them the disturbing ideology of a strict adherence to the principles of Islam.

The most remarkable of these Tukulor emigrants was a certain Umar Tall, who was born in Futa Toro about 1795. In the 1820's Umar Tall accomplished the arduous feat of the pilgrimage to Mecca, thus earning himself the title of al-Hajj. On his return journey he stayed for some years at the court of Muhammad Bello, the ruler of the recently founded caliphate of Sokoto, and thus learned much about the practical problems of administering a theocratic state created as a result of a revolutionary war. Before leaving his homeland he had become a member of the Tijaniyya, a newly founded religious fraternity whose members believed themselves to be greatly superior to all other Muslims. During his residence in Mecca Umar was appointed leader of the order in the Western Sudan. In the late 1840's, after more than twenty years of traveling, he settled down and founded a Tijani colony at Dinguiray, on the eastern borders of Futa Jallon. The combination of vast learning, wide knowledge of the world, and an assurance of divine inspiration made an exceptionally impressive personality, and disciples from Futa Toro and Futa Jallon flocked to his *zawiya.* In 1852 al-Hajj Umar announced a formal declaration of jihad, and for the next twelve years this astonishing elderly scholar was engaged in the formidable tasks of waging a revolutionary war on many different fronts and building up a vast new

Tukulor empire between the Niger and the Senegal. French opposition prevented al-Hajj Umar from gaining control of his own homeland in Futa Toro and the struggle between the French and his successor, Ahmadu, took place outside the borders of Senegambia. But the constant movement of clerics and traders meant that the Muslim communities of Senegambia were kept closely in touch with the currents of opinion affecting their coreligionists living further to the east. By the 1850's the petty states on the Gambia had been caught up in a series of violent conflicts that dragged on for forty years and came to be known as the Soninke-*Marabout* wars, Soninke being the term confusingly applied to the largely pagan Malinke ruling classes.

Even before 1850 a profound alteration in the local economy was producing signs of revolutionary change on the Gambia. In the days of the slave trade it was possible for local rulers to establish an effective monopoly over external trade. But when groundnuts replaced slaves as the area's principal export, local peasant-farmers found it easy to sell direct to European traders. As the rulers' hold over their kingdoms relaxed, local notables took power into their own hands, began erecting walls around their towns, and even made occasional bids for complete independence. With the gradual breakdown of the old order Muslim communities seized the chance to emancipate themselves from the restrictions imposed by their pagan overlords. In 1862 a leading *marabout,* Ma Ba, gained control of the Malinke state of Badibu on the north bank of the Gambia. Muslim rebels in neighboring states appealed for his assistance and he found himself engaged in a series of wars, losing his own life while fighting against the Serer kingdom of Sine in 1867.

The European presence in Senegambia served to complicate still further an already confused situation. The British on the Gambia were restrained by their home government from becoming too deeply involved in local conflicts. "It will be one of the governor's most important duties," wrote a colonial office official in 1877, "to afford to the trade of the river facilities and encouragement, so far as he may be able to do so without exercising undue interference with the native tribes . . . or imposing heavy charges on the Colonial revenue." [5] Some years earlier the British had withdrawn their small garrison from MacCarthy's Island, their only post up stream, and they were seriously prepared to discuss handing over the Gambia to the French in return for territorial concessions in other parts of West Africa.

By 1875 the French on the Senegal could claim to have pursued a far more vigorous line of policy than the hesitant British. The founder of this dynamic tradition was Louis Faidherbe, governor of Senegal from

1854 to 1861 and again from 1861 to 1863. Faidherbe saw the colony as the growing point for a great West African empire "worthy of comparison with Canada or India." [6] The first stage in such a policy was to gain control of the line of the river and of the country to the south by creating a number of strategic posts from which French agents could exercise their influence over neighboring politics, taking advantage of the constant local conflicts and making sure that their allies were always victorious. By 1875 the French had established a system of direct administration over 10,000 square kilometers of territory in the vicinity of St. Louis and of an area no more than 1,000 square kilometers in extent in the neighborhood of Dakar. The rulers of Futa Toro had accepted French protection but the local Wolof states could be regarded as no more than doubtful allies of the French. The story of Lat-Dior, *damel* ("king") of Cayor, illustrates the way in which a Senegambian ruler could find himself painfully caught up in the two movements of Muslim revolution and European conquest.

Cayor, one of the most substantial Wolof states, occupied most of the territory lying between the two French bases of St. Louis and Gorée-Dakar. To the French authorities, Cayor was a constant trouble-spot, where the ruling class—the *tiedo* or pagan nobility—seemed no better than a gang of brigands, its members gaining their livelihood by pillaging the peasantry and harassing peaceful traders. In 1861 the French invaded Cayor and with some difficulty succeeded in securing the appointment of a *damel* of their own choice. Within a few months the French nominee had been overthrown in a revolt led by Lat-Dior, one of the younger members of the royal family. For two years Lat-Dior reigned as *damel,* but he showed himself a dangerous neighbor to the French, was driven from his country by a French expedition in 1863, and sought refuge with Ma Ba, the revolutionary Muslim leader of the little state of Badibu. At this time Lat-Dior was a pagan but under Ma Ba's influence he was converted to Islam. Ma Ba now attempted to extend his own influence over the Wolof states to the north, but was countered by a French force which invaded his country and destroyed his capital. "More than thirty fine villages," wrote Faidherbe in his account of the operation, "their granaries bursting with the annual harvest, were put to the flames." [7] Two years later Ma Ba was killed. Some time after his death Lat-Dior was allowed to return to Cayor, over which the French had attempted to enforce a more direct system of administration. In 1871 he was again recognized as *damel.*

All previous rulers of Cayor had been dependent on the support of the *tiedo,* the pagan warrior-nobility who were usually powerful enough to act as king-makers. But by his conversion to Islam Lat-Dior had broken with the ancient tradition of the dynasty and so he was forced to find new bases of support. He surrounded himself with reforming *marabouts* and set about the conversion of the Wolof peasantry. The time was clearly one in which the old order was breaking down. Faidherbe described the period as one of "great religious excitement," though he chose to ascribe the mood of the people to the effects of famine and a serious cholera epidemic.[8] Lat-Dior was clearly moved by a shrewd sense of self-interest. When, in the early 1870's, another Muslim revolutionary, Ahmadu-Seku, began building up his power in Futa Toro and threatening Cayor with his raids, Lat-Dior joined forces with the French and took part in the expedition which led to the *marabout*'s downfall and death. But there could be no enduring alliance with the French, especially when they began to prepare plans for a railway across Cayor, joining Dakar and St. Louis. To the French the construction of the railway represented an essential stage in the consolidation and economic development of their colony of Senegal. To Lat-Dior it was a clear threat to his independence; he dreamt of it, so he told his followers, in the image of a sinister black dog passing backward and forward across his land. The outcome was predictable. In 1882 Lat-Dior was deposed. After four years of guerilla warfare he was killed fighting against the French. Meanwhile French attempts to establish a puppet ruler proved ineffective. Accordingly the ancient office of *damel* was abolished and the kingdom divided up into a number of chiefdoms, supervised by French officials.

In 1876 negotiations for an exchange of territory between Britain and France in West Africa broke down. Had they succeeded, the political geography of colonial West Africa might well have been "strikingly different," [9] with the French in complete control of Senegambia and the British masters of the territory between the Gold Coast and Lagos. The protest launched by British African subjects in Bathurst against being handed over to French administration contributed significantly to the failure of the negotiations. But the British made little attempt to assert their hegemony up river until French forces began operating on the banks of the Gambia in the late 1880's. Finally, in 1889, as part of a general convention on West African frontiers, the French accepted the British claim to a narrow strip of territory on both banks of the river stretching for 200 miles inland, thus erecting the strangest-shaped territory in colonial Africa. Three years earlier the French had signed a treaty with the Portuguese defining the frontier between the territories of the two colonial powers in Guinea and the Casamance.

In the 1890's, while the French were engaged in the final stages of the pacification of Senegal, the British reluctantly undertook the task of bringing law and order to the war-torn states along the Gambia. By 1900 the task of pacification had been virtually completed in the British and French spheres of Senegambia. Portuguese Guinea, on the other hand, remained one of the last parts of West Africa to be fully subjected to alien domination. During the 1910's a series of campaigns were undertaken to ensure the pacification of the interior, and as late as 1936 the Portuguese authorities found it necessary to launch a full-scale expedition against "rebellious" Bijagos islanders. Twenty-five years later Portuguese Guinea again became the scene of a long-drawn-out guerrilla war.

▲▼ THE FRENCH MILITARY AND THE MAJOR STATES OF THE WESTERN SUDAN

The Western Sudan is defined here as that section of the Sudanic belt of West Africa stretching from Senegal to the western borders of Nigeria. In the course of the past thousand years this extensive territory—the distance from Dakar to Niamey is about the same as that from Amsterdam to Moscow—had seen the rise and fall of three of the most substantial indigenous polities Africa had ever known. Toward the end of the first millennium A.D. the Soninke rulers of Ghana—a state possessing no ascertainable connection with the modern republic of the same name —had established their hegemony over 100,000 square miles of territory lying between the Niger and the Senegal and including the steppe country of southern Mauritania. In the thirteenth century, after the total collapse of Ghana, a second great Sudanic kingdom, Mali, gained control of most of the territory that now forms part of its modern successor, the state of the same name. Two centuries later a third imperial power created by the Songhai, a riverine people with their capital at Gao on the Middle Niger, dominated the entire bend of the great river and forced the rulers of many outlying polities to pay them tribute. The Songhai empire was shattered by an invading Moroccan army in the last decade of the sixteenth century and broke up, as the Mali empire had already done, into a large number of petty independent chiefdoms.

In the early nineteenth century the most powerful polities in the Western Sudan were the two Bambara kingdoms of Segu and Kaarta and the cluster of Mossi states lying within the Niger bend. The states of Bambara and the Mossi were dominated by ruling groups whose members had never accepted Islam. But ancient urban centers such as Timbuktu and Jenne survived as important foci of Muslim activity, and Muslim traders of Malinke origin, known in many areas as *dyula,* had created substantial new settlements in the southern belt of the Western Sudan. In the 1880's Kong, the most important of these new towns, was described by the first European traveler to visit it, as possessing five mosques, an industrial quarter devoted to weaving and dyeing, a well-stocked market, and a population estimated at 15,000.

In the second decade of the nineteenth century a Fulani *marabout,* Seku Ahmadu, inspired by the astonishing achievements of his coreligionists in the Hausa states to the east, launched a successful revolt against the pagan Fulani rulers of the little state of Macina, and went on to establish his hegemony over most of the country lying between Segu and Timbuktu. The theocratic polity of Macina has been described as "the most genuine Islamic state West Africa has ever known," [10] but the religious devotion of its ulama offered no protection against the aggressive revolutionary fervor of al-Hajj Umar Tall. In 1862 the great conqueror and prophet entered Hamdallahi, the capital of Macina. Two years later Umar was killed attempting to put down a Macina resistance movement.

The task which faced Ahmadu, al-Hajj Umar's eldest son and successor, was one of quite exceptional difficulty. He could not hope to claim the immense personal prestige enjoyed by his father; he possessed a large number of brothers, some of whom were extremely jealous of his promotion; and he was expected to hold together a rambling, ill-constructed state largely based on his father's conquests of the two Bambara kingdoms of Segu and Kaarta. To the Bambara the Tukulor regime represented a particularly brutal form of alien domination. When al-Hajj Umar occupied Nioro, the capital of Kaarta, he destroyed the hallowed symbols of the ancient religion and ordered the inhabitants to shave their heads, build mosques, and limit themselves to four wives. Many of his lieutenants, the majority of whom were of Tukulor or Fulani origin, behaved with even greater brutality. Little wonder that the Tukulor rulers found themselves faced with the constant threat of revolt.

In coping with these manifold problems Ahmadu proved himself one of the most competent African rulers of his age. He imprisoned some of his brothers and appointed others to act as provincial governors. He concentrated the greater part of his empire's resources at his capital of Segu and devised an efficient system for keeping a check on the governors of outlying provinces. But he was unable to prevent some of the remoter provinces from achieving virtually complete autonomy, nor could he effectively pacify certain areas of determined Bambara resistance. These local preoccupations were constantly in his mind when he found himself confronted with an even greater threat to his authority— the aggressive activities of French army officers on the Upper Senegal.

The French were not the only aggressors in the area. Across the

Niger in an area that now forms part of eastern Guinea and southern Mali, a remarkable adventurer named Samory Toure was engaged in the 1860's and 1870's in building up a powerful new Sudanese state. Samory's family was of Malinke origin and could trace its line back to an ancestor who had taken part in the great dispersal of Muslim Malinke throughout much of the country lying between the Niger and the forest. Samory's forefathers had settled in Konyam, a remote district not far from the northern border of modern Liberia, where they had taken to cattle-rearing, intermarried with the local animist population, and gradually forgotten their old religion.

As a young man Samory had taken the only opening available to an enterprising individual anxious to escape from the suffocating atmosphere of a strictly gerontocratical society and become an intinerant trader, a *dyula,* thus following a profession in which many other Malinke had made their fortune in the past. Traveling over the country between Sierra Leone and the Upper Niger, dealing in gold, cattle, kola, slaves, and firearms, he acquired an intimate knowledge of local affairs over a wide area. But he abandoned this profitable career when his mother was captured in a slave-raid and he decided to attach himself to the chief, his mother's captor, to work for her ransom.

At this time the Malinke country was divided up into innumerable petty chieftaincies, some of which had succeeded in building up more substantial polities through the conquest of their neighbors. To his knowledge of local commerce Samory was now able to add practical experience of warfare. He soon acquired a name for himself as a warrior. Having secured his mother's release and regained his own independence of action, he found no difficulty in setting up his own power base, attracting adventurous young men to his side and turning war-captives into devoted soldiers. Clearly he possessed a genius for administration. As his state expanded, he devised effective means for holding it together. By 1887 his empire was said to cover over 100,000 square miles of territory and to be divided up into 162 districts, each containing up to twenty villages. By this time he had built up a substantial standing army made up mainly of foot-soldiers, known as *sofas,* armed with guns mostly bought from the British in Sierra Leone.

During his years as a private trader Samory had been converted to Islam. But he was never a scholar nor a religious leader of outstanding piety in the manner of Seku Ahmadu of Macina or of al-Hajj Umar. Indeed he seems to have been a supreme pragmatist who saw in Islam an ideological cement that would serve to create a uniform culture among peoples hitherto divided by many cultural differences. For this reason he ordered the destruction of the manifestations of the old religion, replacing sacred groves by mosques and pagan priests by Muslim imams. Samory was indeed a unifier, an innovator, a progressive, the protagonist of a *"dyula* revolution," [11] bitterly hated by members of the old local ruling classes whose privileges he undermined, deeply admired by the young and adventurous who found in his new political structure the opportunity of a career open to talents. Thus, as in Senegambia, so in many parts of the Western Sudan, the latter half of the nineteenth century was a period of revolutionary upheaval. Into this confusing situation was thrust the new, powerful, and alien force represented by the French military.

The French on the Senegal had long been attracted by the reputed riches of the Western Sudan. Though contemporary travelers such as Caillié and Barth had provided sober accounts of the reality, a number of influential Frenchmen were prepared to talk of the Western Sudan as a vast unexploited market with a population which some guesses put as high as 100 million occupying districts of "unbelievable fertility." As early as 1847 the French minister in charge of colonies could declare that it was "absolutely vital" for France "to prevent any European nation from challenging our pre-eminence in the Upper Senegal or from sharing the commercial advantages we are seeking to develop there." [12] During his two spells as governor of Senegal, Faidherbe was able to formulate this concept of French penetration of the interior even more vigorously. But the government of Napoleon III, saddled with costly imperialist ventures in Indochina and in Mexico, was in no position to afford a vigorous policy of West African expansion. Even before the catastrophe of 1870 metropolitan subsidies to the Senegalese budget had been severely cut. In 1876, the newly appointed governor of Senegal, Colonel Brière de l'Isle, was formally instructed that the needs of national reconstruction at home made it impossible for the country to engage in expensive overseas commitments. Yet within three years the French had embarked on the first of a series of campaigns that brought them into violent contact with all the major polities of the Western Sudan and led, by the end of the century, to the creation of the most extensive imperial structure ever known in the history of West Africa.

A combination of circumstances help to explain this remarkable change in policy. Brière himself was a military governor of the same stamp as Faidherbe, resolute, energetic, and ambitious. Moreover, as a recent historian has pointed out, he was "astute enough" to perceive the difficulties that faced the metropolitan government in attempting "to control a determined local subordinate" and be "bold enough to exploit them." [13] Both Brière and Faidherbe were the heirs of a tradition of resolute action by French army officers on an African stage that could be traced back to the years of intensive campaigning in Algeria and perhaps even to that extraordinary episode, Bonaparte's conquest of Egypt. French officers with experience of Algerian warfare became skilled in tactics involving the daring deployment of small mobile columns, of a kind that could never have been practiced on European battlefields. They learned, too, to regard with the deepest apprehension any manifestation of Muslim "fanaticism" and to retaliate with prompt and brutal countermeasures. And they acquired a scathing contempt for the politicians at home and a sense of supreme self-confidence in their own capacity to understand the local situation and to provide the right solutions to local problems.

But military operations are always expensive. Brière and his successors would have shared the same fate as Faidherbe had not a series of shifts in the center of French political life brought about a climate of opinion in influential circles propitious to a forward policy in West Africa. In the mid-1870's certain sections of the French public began to see in overseas expansion not a wasteful line of policy that would serve to distract Frenchmen from their proper preoccupation with national security and the fate of the lost provinces but a means of reasserting national prestige. "France," declared a leading parliamentarian, Maurice Rouvier, in 1879, "lying closer to Africa than most other nations . . . cannot afford not to participate in a movement which is drawing Europe towards those regions of Africa whose riches are just beginning to be revealed. Are we not bidden by our concern for the greatness and the interests of our fatherland to place ourselves at the head of this movement?" [14] A well-defined series of projects provided an exciting focus for these expansionist aspirations. The 1870's was an age of transcontinental railroad construction. It was not surprising that railroad enthusiasts in France should dream of spanning the Sahara or providing a link between St. Louis and the Niger to enable French traders to tap more effectively the markets of the Western Sudan. Governor Brière profited directly from the railroad schemes of the late 1870's. It was obvious that the Sudan railroad could not be built until security had been established in the troubled districts between the Senegal and the Niger —and security, in the last resort, implied military conquest. Thus Brière was able to use the money voted for a preliminary survey of the Sudan railroad to raise a new battalion of colonial troops and to provide for the construction of a chain of forts along the line of route.

Other circumstances helped to further French expansion into the Western Sudan. There was much talk of the need to forestall a British move into the same area. In fact the British in Sierra Leone possessed only a modest interest in the Upper Niger, and the British government was not concerned to oppose French advances in West Africa until a very much later date. Thus the French were confronted with a minimal likelihood of serious international complications. Other considerations helped to disarm criticism: an advance in the Sudan did not require the deployment of a large number of metropolitan troops nor—unlike the contemporary French stake in Tunis and in Egypt—could it be associated with the private interests of a furtive group of businessmen. Even so ardent an anti-imperialist as Clemenceau did not attempt to attack what the colonial propagandists of the day described as the "heroic exploits" of a handful of Frenchmen operating in the midst of a "barbarous" and "fanatical" population. Finally, it was fortunate for the expansionists that in 1879 one of their most ardent supporters, Admiral Jauréguibery, a former governor of Senegal, should have been appointed minister of marine and colonies.

In 1880 Jauréguibery created a special military command on the Upper Senegal and gave the post to a highly aggressive artillery officer, Borgnis-Desbordes. "We are not in the Sudan to talk but to act," Desbordes told his subordinates on taking up his new command. "We must go to the Niger and we will." [15] Acting on his own initiative Desbordes set about destroying the Tukulor strongholds that lay in his path and even led a flying column on a raid across the Niger. "The peaceful conquest of the Niger," he warned his superiors, "is an illusion." [16] Desbordes' activities provided the Tukulor with a clear indication of the aggressive nature of French intentions. But Ahmadu was in no position to concentrate all his energies on warding off the French threat. Far more pressing was the need to deal with dissident provincial governors and rebellious Bambara subjects. To establish a position of military supremacy within his own domains Ahmadu needed a steady supply of modern firearms—and these could hardly be obtained except by trade with the French. Moreover the French controlled the routes leading to Futa Toro, the homeland of the Tukulor and the main source of recruits for the administrative cadre of Ahmadu's empire. In these circumstances Ahmadu realized that it was clearly in his own best interest to pursue a cautious policy toward the French, hoping that in time this might lead to the development of a more cordial relationship. This was not the reaction of a "fanatical" Muslim zealot but of a shrewd statesman anxious to maintain the integrity of his own patrimony.

In February, 1883, after three years of campaigning, Desbordes achieved his immediate objective; he advanced with a strong French force to the Niger and constructed a permanent fort at Bamako, today the capital of the Republic of Mali, then a small independent Bambara market-town which had never been conquered by the Tukulor. The retention of Bamako posed the French with many difficulties. No effective progress had yet been made with the railroad, and only two forts had been constructed between Kayes on the Upper Senegal and Bamako on the Niger. To the north lay Ahmadu's domains, to the south and east territory controlled by Samory with whose troops the French had already been in contact, while to the west, in country lying between the Senegal and the Gambia, a new religious leader, Mahmadu Lamine, had just begun a career of conquest and even attacked the old-established French post at Bakel. An aggressive policy might well have helped to consolidate and even extend the French sphere, but the French parliament was no longer willing to vote the extra money needed for expensive military campaigns. Desbordes himself left Senegal and his immediate successors showed no trace of his capacity for profitable insubordination.

In 1886 Colonel J. S. Galliéni was given command of the Niger-Senegal area. Galliéni had already made a name for himself by his conduct of a diplomatic mission to Ahmadu in 1880 and was to go on to win further laurels in Indochina and Madagascar, earning a place for himself among the great proconsuls of French colonial history, the inspirer of a generation of colonial administrators whose most distinguished representative was Lyautey of Morocco. Galliéni, an austere intellectual very different in temperament from the run of French army officers, thought long and deeply about the problems of colonial administration, without ever being troubled by doubts as to the justification of his country's self-appointed "civilizing mission." Pacification he saw as the first stage in a creative process that would lead through reorganization to a greater measure of prosperity for the conquered. The "patch of oil" spreading slowly outward was Galliéni's favorite metaphor to describe the steady process of pacification. There must be no rash advances; territory once conquered must be effectively occupied. In this process the collection of detailed information was imperative. "An officer who has succeeded in producing a reasonably exact ethnographic map of the territory under his command," Galliéni wrote, "is well on the way to having assured its complete pacification." [17]

One of Galliéni's first acts was to ensure the defeat of Mahmadu Lamine whose newly created state posed a real threat to French lines of communication. Toward Ahmadu and Samory his approach was more oblique. "We must look on all these chiefs," he told his successor, Archinaud, "as people to be removed and made to disappear before very long." [18] But this objective was to be achieved by guile and infiltration, not by head-on conflict. Diplomatic missions sent to the two great Sudanese leaders succeeded in establishing a formal *modus vivendi,* important in diplomatic terms, for the two sovereigns nominally agreed to accept French protection and so placed their territories clearly within the French sphere of influence. But even while Galliéni was professing peace, he was assisting Ahmadu's and Samory's local enemies with gifts of arms. His approach could indeed be described as profoundly revolutionary, for he regarded the existing ruling classes, the territorial elite, with the deepest mistrust and sought to gain the support of "the people, the working mass of the population whose interests are closely linked to ours and who learn to realize this quickly enough, if only we take the trouble to show them." [19]

When Galliéni left the Sudan in 1888, he was able to hand over to his successor a bloc of territory firmly in French hands and linked to the Upper Senegal by the construction of ninety kilometers of railroad. Moreover, though there had been no substantial new conquests, French officers, sent out on missions of exploration, had made contact with many previously unvisited African polities lying to the south and east. The most spectacular of these missions, undertaken in 1888–89 by Captain L. G. Binger, involved the exploration of territory lying between the Upper Niger and the headwaters of the Volta and represented the first French contact with an area that today forms part of the Republics of Upper Volta and the Ivory Coast.

Archinaud, Galliéni's successor, was of the same stamp as Desbordes, an intensely ambitious army officer eager to perform those feats of arms that would serve to ensure his accelerated promotion. He was fortunate in taking over command at a time when changes in the French political scene helped to produce an atmosphere more favorable to a dynamic forward policy than that which had prevailed in the mid-1880's. Abandoning Galliéni's policy of waiting for the Tukulor empire to collapse after Ahmadu's death, Archinaud obtained permission in 1890 to launch a frontal attack on Segu, Ahmadu's capital. By 1891, with Nioro, the second town of the empire in French hands, the Tukulor state was shattered. Ahmadu, accompanied by many of his followers, fled eastwards, dying in 1898 while on his way to Sokoto.

No sooner had Archinaud completed the destruction of the Tukulor empire than he turned, in flagrant disregard of his official instructions, to attack Samory. Samory was better placed than Ahmadu to resist the French assault. His territories were remote from the main French bases, yet he had been able to maintain commercial contacts with Freetown, where his agents found no difficulty in purchasing modern firearms. By 1891 he had at his disposal the best-equipped native army in sub-Saharan Africa. Eight thousand of his *sofas* were armed with modern breech-loading repeating rifles and several hundred specially trained blacksmiths provided him with a modest armaments industry. "Samory's troops," wrote one French officer, "fight exactly like Europeans, with less discipline perhaps but with much greater determination." [20] Given the superiority of French arms, especially in respect of artillery, Samory realized that he had little chance of defeating the invaders in pitched battle. Instead he turned to guerrilla tactics, ambushing French detachments and harassing their supply lines. While one part of his army was thus engaged in holding up the French advance, another part was given the easier task of conquering new territories to the east. Thus Samory, even when forced to abandon his homeland on the Upper Niger, continued to possess a firm territorial base on which to re-create the basic structure of his state.

It took the French seven years' hard campaigning to break Samory's power. Not until 1898 did they succeed in running him to earth, capturing him in a surprise attack, and sending him to end his days in exile. Samory proved himself one of those towering personalities whose exploits become the stuff of legend. But he remains a deeply controversial figure. French officers who fought against him were greatly impressed by his abilities: one of them summed him up as "an outstanding leader of men, possessing audacity, energy, the ability to follow up an advantage and plan an advance, and above all an irrepressible tenacity which could not be destroyed." [21] Naturally enough to a later generation of African nationalists Samory became one of the great heroes of African resistance. But to many of the peoples living in the area which he dominated, his name still remains a by-word for cruelty and oppression. To maintain his state he was forced to engage in the slave trade on a large scale, for slaves represented the only exportable commodity left to him, the only product he could offer in exchange for the horses and firearms needed to maintain his resistance. Moreover, it became his policy to devastate all the country that he was forced to evacuate, leaving to his enemies "not an old man nor a single grain of millet." [22] Samory had always ruled as a despot and his fear of treachery and intrigue must have grown more acute as his plight became more desperate. One of his many savage acts was to destroy the famous town of Kong, razing the mosques to the ground and executing forty of the ulama, after some of the inhabitants had collaborated with the French. Like his contemporary, the Mahdist Khalifa Abdullahi, Samory must be seen as a prisoner and ultimately a victim of his times. More pragmatic in his politics than the Khalifa, he was always prepared to negotiate with the French and even, on several occasions, to seek British support. But he refused to accept a French resident at his court, realizing clearly enough the implications of such an agreement. He stands out in his last years as a heroic, brutal, tragic figure.

Ahmadu and Samory were the most formidable opponents faced by the French in the Western Sudan, but there were many other local leaders who fought against the inevitable. In January, 1894, a French force which had occupied Timbuktu was wiped out by the local Tuareg—an episode whose detailed narrative would provide a vivid illustration of that blend of gallantry, rashness, and insubordination so characteristic of the activities of many French army officers operating in the Sudan. By 1896 the French were masters of the Mossi states of the Upper Volta. The next year they were in a position to launch expeditions eastward from the Niger toward Lake Chad.

Ever since the end of the 1880's, Lake Chad had tended to replace Timbuktu as the goal, the lodestar of French expansionists. This shallow, mosquito-ridden expanse of water in the middle of the Central Sudan was seen as the pivot of a great French African empire, the meeting-point for the three French thrusts for the interior—from Algeria, from Senegal, and from the Congo. "This great interior lake," wrote a French foreign office official in 1890, "may well hold some surprises in store for the future of civilization in Africa. It might become the focal point of the continent's major trade routes. . . . There is here a reservoir for the future which our policy cannot afford to neglect." [23] The Anglo-French agreement of 1890 provided the French with a diplomatic foothold on the shores of the lake. All the country lying south of the Mediterranean and extending to a line drawn between Say on the Niger and Barruwa on Lake Chad was recognized as falling within the French sphere of influence, a division of territory that left within the British sphere "all that fairly belongs to the kingdom of Sokoto." Lord Salisbury, the British prime minister, possessed a far shrewder sense of reality than the colonial enthusiasts in Paris. The French, he remarked drily, had certainly "laid claim to a very considerable stretch of country," but land must be judged "not merely by its extent but also by its value." The land acquired by the French was "what agriculturalists would call 'very light land.' " [24]

The conquest of the small Hausa states lying to the north of the caliphate of Sokoto presented no great difficulty, but it led to one of the most extraordinary episodes in the history of French imperialism. A military column under the command of Captain Voulet behaved with such brutality, pillaging and destroying villages on its march from the Niger toward Lake Chad, that a senior officer, Colonel Klobb, was sent out to take over command. Voulet refused to hand over, shot Klobb dead, talked crazily of going off to found a new African empire for himself, only to be killed a few days later by one of his own *tirailleurs*.[25] Early in 1900, the soldiers of Voulet's column, under new command, joined forces with two other French expeditions, one that had set out from Algeria across the Sahara, while the other had advanced northward from the Congo. The combined force defeated and killed Rabih Zubair, the military adventurer from the Eastern Sudan whose exploits—more fully recounted in the next chapter—included the conquest of the Central Sudanic kingdoms of Baguirmi and Bornu.

The territory conquered by the *officiers soudanais* of the French army between 1880 and 1900 was later to become the modern republics of Mali, Upper Volta, and Niger. Meanwhile other Frenchmen had been pushing northward from the coast of Guinea to assert their country's claims over the territories that came to be known as Guinea, the Ivory Coast, and Dahomey. In this southern belt of West Africa the situation was complicated by international rivalries, as other imperialists, British, German, and Liberian, sought to gain control of the hinterland of their coastal possessions. Here, as in every part of Africa, the people of the local indigenous communities were not to be regarded as passive spectators of the act of alien intrusion but rather as active participants in a political game that had suddenly acquired new players and new rules.

▲▼ UPPER GUINEA: THE FOUNDATIONS OF THE MODERN STATES OF GUINEA, SIERRA LEONE, LIBERIA, AND THE IVORY COAST

No part of nineteenth-century West Africa displayed so bewildering a variety of minor polities and distinct ethnic groups as Upper Guinea, the area covered by the modern states of Guinea, Sierra Leone, Liberia, and the Ivory Coast. This high degree of political fragmentation was partly accounted for by the nature of the terrain. Though heights rarely exceed four thousand feet, Upper Guinea contains in the massif of Futa Jallon and in the Guinea highlands the greatest expanse of mountainous country in West Africa. Dense forest, much of which has since been destroyed, covered the greater part of southern Sierra Leone, Liberia, and the southern Ivory Coast, while the coasts of Guinea and Sierra Leone, cut by many barely navigable rivers and bordered by numerous offshore islands, presented a proliferation of natural barriers between local communities.

The modern history of much of Upper Guinea has been dominated by the same broad movements as that of Senegambia. An autochthonous population made up of the speakers of West Atlantic languages—

represented today by such groups as the Baga of Guinea and the Temne and Limba of Sierra Leone—has over the last five centuries experienced the intrusion of Mande-speakers from the east, of Fulani from the north, and of Europeans and Africans influenced by European culture from the west. The expansion of Mande-speakers from the area of the Upper Niger led to the emergence of such distinct groups as the Susu of Guinea, the Mende of Sierra Leone, and the Vai of Liberia, people whose political development took the form of a proliferation of petty chiefdoms. In 1875 the largest indigenous polity in the area was the imamate of Futa Jallon created by the Fulani in the eighteenth century. Though subject to constant internal dissensions the influence of the imamate was powerful enough to affect many neighboring polities. Chiefdoms on the Guinea Coast paid tribute to the *almamys* of Futa Jallon, and Fulani adventurers often rose to positions of prominence in non-Fulani states. Fulani influence did not extend as far south as the territories that now form part of the Ivory Coast. But many of the Kwa-speaking peoples of the southern half of the modern republic were exposed to the pressure of Mande-speakers from the north, with *dyula* traders spreading along the trade routes of the interior as the pioneers of Mande expansion.

Europeans had been active on the coast of Upper Guinea since the sixteenth century. Individual Europeans established trading posts on the coast and sometimes married African women, becoming the founders of locally influential Eurafrican families. But the area lacked a major center of European influence until the last decade of the eighteenth century when a group of British philanthropists founded Freetown in Sierra Leone as a settlement for freed slaves. In 1808 the British government made Sierra Leone into a crown colony. Though confined to the Sierra Leone peninsula, the colony's population rapidly increased as slaves, drawn mainly from ethnic groups living within the area of modern Nigeria, were "recaptured" by British warships from Portuguese and Brazilian slavers in the Bights of Biafra and Benin and brought to Freetown to be liberated. Finding themselves completely cut off from their own societies some of the ex-slaves responded eagerly to the opportunities offered by their new environment and adopted the religion, language, technical skills, dress, and other cultural traits of the colony's elite of English administrators and missionaries. Thus there emerged a new type of African, the Creole, a man of two worlds, looking to Europe for intellectual inspiration but able to achieve a closer rapport with African societies than the vast majority of Europeans. In the latter half of the nineteenth century the Creoles of Sierra Leone clearly represented one of the most dynamic and enterprising groups in tropical Africa. Some achieved local fame as Protestant missionaries, as government officials, or as professional men, others acquired considerable wealth through their enterprise in business and commerce. Sierra Leone alone could not offer sufficient opportunities for these forerunners of a new order. Many sought employment in other parts of British West Africa; others became pioneers of empire, establishing trading posts in parts of Upper Guinea beyond the frontiers of the colony and becoming the most vigorous advocates of an extension of the sphere of British jurisdiction.

The American-financed settlement of Liberia, founded in the early 1820's, possessed some of the same characteristics as Sierra Leone in that its early settlers were of slave origin. But the "Afro-Americans" of Liberia all came from across the Atlantic. Culturally they were much further removed from local African societies than most of the Creoles of Sierra Leone. In 1847 lack of official support from the United States government forced the Liberians to declare their territory an independent republic. The country's first president, J. J. Roberts, talked bravely of a "manifest destiny" to bring "civilization" to the hinterland. Outside observers doubted the new republic's capacity to survive. "The Liberians have no money," wrote the not unsympathetic English traveler, Winwood Reade, in 1873, "immigration is slack, they do not intermarry with the natives and population is decreasing. Nothing can save them from perdition except the throwing open of the land . . . the free admission of European traders and Negro settlers of Sierra Leone." [26]

The French were destined to acquire by far the largest part of Upper Guinea, but in 1879 they possessed no more than a few modest posts on the stretch of coast north of Sierra Leone known to officials in Senegal as "the Rivers of the South." The country immediately to the north of Freetown, traversed by the Mellacourie and Scarcies rivers, was an area of particularly intense rivalry between French and British traders until a frontier was defined by diplomatic negotiation in 1882. But the French position still remained very weak. "Our *commandants de cercles,*" wrote a French administrator, "shut up in their residencies, more like prisoners than the representatives of a great power, had to perform prodigious feats to maintain French influence in the midst of continual local wars." [27]

On the Ivory Coast the French position was even less impressive. Indeed, in 1871 the French abandoned their posts, established in 1843, at Grand Bassam and Assinie. Only the enterprise of an energetic trader from La Rochelle, Arthur Verdier, preserved a French stake in the territory that was later to become the richest colony in French West Africa. Between 1878 and 1885 Verdier held the post of official French resident at Grand Bassam, but he himself remained in France, delegating his duties to his agents on the spot.

In the Western Sudan the French presence was entirely military in character; in Upper Guinea, by contrast, the French were represented by civilian administrators and traders possessing no great incentive to expand into the interior. But the military advance into the valley of the Upper Niger made it possible for the French to approach the coastal districts from the north. Thus, in 1889 Binger ended his great journey of exploration in the Upper Volta by traveling southward from Kong, where he was met by one of Verdier's agents, Treich-Laplène, who had made a daring journey northward from Grand Bassam. The treaties of protection negotiated by Binger and Treich-Laplène with the local rulers between Kong and Grand Bassam provided the legal basis for French claims which were accepted by the British in an agreement defining the western frontier of the Gold Coast signed in 1893. The same procedure—persuading local rulers to sign treaties of protection—was used to extend French hegemony in the area of modern Guinea.

Early in the 1880's, the French began to develop an interest in Futa Jallon. This highland Muslim territory presented the combined attractions of a pleasant climate, a relatively sophisticated population, and reputed mineral riches, but alarm at the possible consequences of British "intrigues" provided the French with an even sharper incentive for vigorous action. Futa Jallon had indeed long been an area of some interest to British officials in Freetown anxious to develop trade with their hinterland. In 1881 the senior British official in the Gambia led a mission to Futa Jallon. He returned with a treaty of friendship, but wrote so dismal a report on the country's commercial possibilities that officials in the colonial office decided it was a waste of money trying to foster trade in such unpromising circumstances. Nevertheless, the mere fact of British activity alarmed the French and led to the immediate dispatch of a mission to Futa Jallon and the conclusion of a highly dubious treaty of protection. More than a decade passed before the French were strong enough to transform this paper protectorate into formal occupation. At first the French posts on the "Rivers of the South"—the term French Guinea did not come into use until 1893—were controlled from Senegal, but in 1890 they were made into a separate colony, the first governor, Dr. Ballay, being an extremely able naval surgeon who had made a name for himself working with de Brazza in the Congo. Six years later French troops were sent into Futa Jallon. By shrewdly taking sides in the imamate's continual internal divisions, the French had little difficulty in making themselves complete masters of the country.

By 1890 officials in London had at last begun to share the concern at

French activities long felt by the leading residents, British and Creole alike, of Freetown. On New Year's Day, 1890, Colonial Secretary Lord Knutsford wrote to the governor urging that "efforts should be made . . . to prevent the French from further surrounding and hemming in the Colony." [28] Accordingly two officials were appointed to act as "traveling commissioners" and given the task of negotiating treaties of friendship with the chiefs of the interior. At the same time, a modest force of Frontier Police was formed to put an end to the continual wars between rival chiefdoms. In 1896, after an Anglo-French agreement on Sierra Leone's eastern frontier, a formal protectorate was proclaimed over all the territory lying between the borders of the colony and the new frontier.

The British established their protectorate with relative ease, but when they attempted to enforce their authority, they found themselves faced with serious trouble. Local chiefs resented the way in which British district commissioners interfered in the internal affairs of their chiefdoms. Undisciplined detachments of the Frontier Police were guilty of many acts of wanton brutality. Worst grievance of all, the governor in Freetown decided to impose a form of direct taxation—a tax of five shillings on each hut—to meet the cost of administration. "Our own true fear," explained a group of Temne chiefs, "is that paying for our huts naturally means no right to our country." [29] Early in 1898 protest turned to violence. A Temne chief, Bai Bureh, proved himself a redoubtable guerrilla leader, who held the colony's troops at bay for the greater part of a year. Further south a savage revolt broke out, leading to the massacre of several hundred Creole traders and missionaries, many long settled in Mende country but still regarded as aliens. The "Hut Tax War" of 1898 brought out in sharp relief many of the tensions involved in the clash of cultures that occurred whenever Europeans asserted their hegemony over hitherto relatively isolated African peoples.

Not dissimilar in its causes to the "Hut Tax War" was the long-drawn-out crisis faced by the French in the forest areas of the Ivory Coast. Here, too, a multitude of undemanding protectorate treaties with minor chiefs provided a "legal" basis for European hegemony. In 1900 the French imposed a land tax and stepped up demands for forced labor to construct a railroad from the coast. So fierce was the resistance of the Baule and other peoples that the French were left in control of no more than a small coastal strip. In 1908 a tough new governor, Angoulvant, decided to launch a full-scale military operation to break the resistance of the forest people. The Baule lived in independent villages, a form of political organization far less brittle than that of more imposing polities.

Every village could be turned into a fortress, forcing the invader to bring in artillery to smash the strong wooden stockades. Nowhere in West Africa, except in the campaign against Samory, was a colonial power faced with so exhausting a war, for it was not until 1916 that the Baule were finally subdued.

To many Europeans and Americans the Republic of Liberia seemed to possess the character of a truly African state. But to the indigenous inhabitants of the area the republic's Afro-American elite represented an intruding group no less alien in culture than the European conquerors of other parts of West Africa. The Liberians participated vigorously in the scramble for African territory. Many of their claims were brushed aside by the British and the French, but they were still able to obtain 43,000 square miles of territory, an area one and a half times the size of neighboring Sierra Leone, the greater part of which could never in the early days be submitted to an effective system of administration. "Even today," according to a study of the country made in the late 1960's, "there are still vast tribal areas where the writ of the Liberian government is still very weak." [30] Given the difficult nature of much of the terrain and the limited resources at the Liberian government's disposal, it is hardly surprising that the construction of an effective political superstructure should have proceeded so slowly. Nor was it remarkable that the small polities of the hinterland should have long resisted the assaults of an invading group whose most significant difference from other imperialists lay not so much in the color of their skin as in their freedom from the restrictions which metropolitan governments and a critical public opinion in Britain and in France were often able to impose on their agents in the field.

▲▼ FROM THE GOLD COAST TO DAHOMEY: AFRICAN POLITIES AND EUROPEAN INVADERS

In 1875 the three most substantial polities in the rectangle of territory, nearly 200,000 square miles in extent, that comprises the modern states of Ghana, Togo, and Dahomey, were the two African kingdoms of Ashanti and Dahomey and the recently established British colony of the Gold Coast. In addition, the area contained a very large number of smaller polities, some fairly substantial minor chiefdoms such as those established by the warlike Bariba of northern Dahomey, others independent village communities, many of them, as in the mountainous country of northern Togo, distinguished from their neighbors by differences of language.

Ashanti has been variously described as an empire, a union, and a confederacy, a confusion of terms which reflects the polity's complex structure. The kingdom was founded in the latter half of the seventeenth century, when a cluster of small Akan-speaking village-states, lying in the forest country of central Ghana, formed a union, headed by the chiefs of Kumasi, to protect themselves against the attacks of their larger neighbors. Guided and inspired by a succession of remarkable leaders, the Ashanti union soon developed the most powerful military force in the area. Other Akan states accepted Ashanti paramountcy, and wars of conquest forced a number of non-Akan polities, including Gonja and Dagomba, both of which lay within the savanna belt to the north, to pay regular tribute to the *asantehene* (the ruler of Ashanti). By the beginning of the nineteenth century at least twenty states were tributary to Kumasi.

The task of holding together this far-flung empire was the major preoccupation of every *asantehene*. These great provincial magnates, descendants of the chiefs of the states that had formed the original union, possessed virtually autonomous powers within their own territories. To ensure their own position of paramountcy, the *asantehenes* needed to develop the resources of their own territory and to maintain a tight hold on the outer ring of tributary provinces. From the late eighteenth century on the rulers of Ashanti began to build up a rudimentary bureaucracy made up of officeholders entirely dependent on royal favor. Able men, whatever their origin, had a chance of rising high in the royal service. Even foreigners were not excluded. Muslim shaikhs, possessors of the valuable new technique of literacy, were employed to build up an Arabic chancery, and, in the 1870's, a French trader was appointed to a local governorship and a Danish adventurer employed to raise Hausa troops for the Ashanti army and later chosen to lead a diplomatic mission to a neighboring state.

In the early nineteenth century the Ashanti came into conflict with the British trading posts on the Gold Coast. The Ashanti had no desire to drive the British into the sea. They needed the firearms and appreciated the wide range of luxury goods provided by European traders in exchange for gold and slaves. But they were anxious to assert their hegemony over the small Fante states that adjoined the European trading settlements. To protect themselves against Ashanti aggression the Fante sought British assistance. Fante rulers also appreciated British arbitration in settling local disputes. In 1844 a number of Fante rulers put their signatures to a document formally acknowledging British "power and jurisdiction." At this time there were still several Dutch and Danish trading posts on the Gold Coast. By purchasing the Danish forts in 1850 and the Dutch in 1872, the British strengthened their hold on the coastal areas, but in so doing they caused bitter resentment in Kumasi, where the former Dutch fort of Elmina was regarded as being legally subject to Ashanti sovereignty. In 1873 an Ashanti army invaded British-protected territory, provoking the British to undertake a spectacular counteroffensive. A force made up largely of British troops under the command of Sir Garnet Wolseley marched on Kumasi, burnt the town and blew up the royal palace. A few months later the protected territories on the Gold Coast were transformed into a British Crown Colony.

For the Ashanti the last decades of the nineteenth century brought many tribulations. Much more needs to be known about Ashanti economic history before any confident generalizations can be made about this period. But it is reasonable to assume that the final suppression of the overseas export of slaves must have caused the late nineteenth-century Ashanti rulers considerable financial hardship and made it more difficult for them to obtain the firearms and gunpowder on which their military power was partly dependent. The shock of defeat in 1874 brought an immediate increase in internal tensions. Some of the remoter provinces took advantage of the weakness of the *asantehene* to reassert their independence. Even more serious was the revolt of some of the original states of the Ashanti union, whose chiefs had long resented the amount of power accumulated by the rulers of Kumasi.

British administrators on the coast showed scant sympathy for the difficulties of the *asantehene*. To them the once-great kingdom appeared as "a petty despotism, from which no good government is to be expected . . . and whose history is a chronicle of deceit, cruelty and breach of treaty regulations." Their vision of Ashanti was profoundly influenced by the fact that the *asantehene* still sanctioned "the horrifying practice of sacrificing human victims." [31] In 1895 a colonial office official summed up the view held by most Europeans—missionaries, traders, and administrators—and by many western-educated Africans on the Gold Coast when he asserted that "the continued existence of a savage and barbarous power like Ashanti" represented "a constant menace to the Gold Coast Colony," "a formidable hindrance to the development and advance of civilization," "an obstacle to trade" and "a disgrace to humanity." [32]

Whatever the opinions of the men on the spot and of the experts in the colonial office, British cabinet ministers had no desire to see their country saddled with the expensive and difficult task of asserting a protectorate over so rambling and ill-defined a kingdom. Thus in the twenty years after 1874 the general line of British policy toward Ashanti was essentially negative in character. At the same time, British officials on the Gold Coast were often involved in internal disputes within Ashanti territory and often showed themselves willing to support the political opponents of the *asantehene*. Two developments brought about the final decision to occupy Ashanti: the growing danger of French and German intervention in the hinterland of the Gold Coast and the appointment to the colonial office of an exceptionally vigorous minister, Joseph Chamberlain. In 1896 a British force invaded Ashanti, deposed the *asantehene* Prempeh I, and installed a British resident at Kumasi. Surprisingly, in view of the Ashanti people's long military tradition, no attempt was made to resist this shattering blow. The British followed up their initial success by dismembering the empire, signing separate treaties with the chiefs of the various tributary and confederated states, some of whom appear to have genuinely welcomed the opportunity of throwing off the hegemony of Kumasi.

But the British went too far. In 1900 Governor Hodgson, intent on asserting British paramountcy, visited Kumasi and demanded the surrender of the Golden Stool, the most sacred object in the *asantehene*'s regalia, for it was held to be the dwelling-place of the soul of the Ashanti nation. Exasperated by this insult and bitterly resentful of many minor afflictions suffered at the hands of their conquerors, the people of Kumasi and surrounding districts broke into a revolt that took the British several months of hard fighting to suppress. "The real origin of the rising," wrote Hodgson's successor, Nathan, "is the profound dislike on the part of the chiefs and leading people of Ashanti to British rule." This dislike seemed to him "not unnatural"; "we take away from them all they care about, and have given them in place conditions of life which have no attractions to them." What did "protection against external aggression" mean to a people who for two hundred years had shown themselves perfectly capable of waging successful war against their neighbors, or internal peace to men whose "recognized source of power and wealth lay in feats of war"? Nathan concluded by referring to the Ashantis' "complicated system of administration, hallowed by antiquity and by historic precedents, which our ignorance and policy have alike tended to break down" and to "a deep-rooted superstition which we are unable to understand and from which our presence in the country has detached a portion of the people." [33] In circumstances such as these— circumstances reproduced in many other parts of Africa at this time— was it surprising that the first phase of alien rule should be so bitterly resented?

The kingdom of Dahomey covered an area not exceeding 20,000 square miles, no more than one sixth the size of the territory dominated by the Ashanti at the height of their power. Over this relatively compact area, corresponding to the southern half of the modern republic, the kings of Dahomey had developed one of the most highly centralized systems of government to be found in tropical Africa. Throughout the eighteenth century Dahomey was a vassal state of its eastern neighbor, the great Yoruba kingdom of Oyo. But with the collapse of Oyo in the first decades of the nineteenth century, Dahomey asserted its independence and went on, in the reign of the great king Gezo (1818–58), to acquire the reputation of a formidable military power. To Europeans Dahomey symbolized the "dark ferocity" of "savage Africa." Its rulers grew rich on the "diabolical practices" of the slave trade and regularly engaged in the hideous public ritual of human sacrifice. In the 1840's and 1850's the enterprise of Brazilian merchants, many of whom were in fact of mulatto stock, made Dahomey the last great market of the Atlantic slave trade. But in 1851 the British established a protectorate over the neighboring state of Lagos, and, with the closure of the last slave markets in the New World, the Atlantic trade came to an end in the 1860's.

Thus Gezo and his successor, Gelele (1858–89), found themselves deprived of their major source of wealth. Whatever the internal strains this major economic calamity may have provoked, the two monarchs showed the outside world that they could face their problems with vigor and determination. As the European demand for palm oil increased, Gezo began to establish royal oil-palm plantations worked by the slaves who could no longer be sent overseas. At the same time, new administrative measures were devised to ensure a strict control over the production of individual farmers. "Dahomeans," in the opinion of some recent historians, "were the most heavily taxed West Africans in the nineteenth century." [34] An aggressive foreign policy was an essential element in these overall plans for economic consolidation. In the eighteenth century Dahomean armies had devastated the smaller polities lying to the west and north in their search for slaves; from the 1830's on, they turned eastward to ravage their Yoruba neighbors. In the mid-nineteenth century the Dahomeans launched three formidable assaults on Abeokuta, the capital of the Egba state founded by one section of the Yoruba after the collapse of Oyo. Had the Dahomeans conquered the Egba, they would have gained control of a rich palm-oil-producing area, but all three of their attacks were beaten off with heavy losses.

"Weakened by frequent failure, this breed of black Spartans," wrote Richard Burton, the famous traveler who led a consular mission to Dahomey in 1863, "is rapidly falling into decay." [35] Nevertheless, the kingdom continued to hold its own for another thirty years. Stringent restrictions were imposed on Europeans doing business at the country's main port, Whydah (Ouidah), but it was impossible to prevent the white men from gaining control of neighboring territories. In 1861 the British transformed Lagos into a crown colony and gradually took over a number of neighboring communities. French traders, fearing that the British would soon acquire the entire stretch of coast from Lagos to Accra and so be in a position to impose heavy duties on the import of foreign goods, pressed their government to annex the little state of Porto Novo, lying on the lagoon half way between Lagos and Whydah. Porto Novo was brought under French protection in 1863, but the protectorate was renounced two years later in the face of local difficulties. In 1883, Tofa, the ruler of Porto Novo, alarmed by the threatening attitude of Dahomey, placed his territory again under French protection. A few years earlier the French had obtained from Dahomey a treaty which was interpreted as providing for the cession of the coastal village of Cotonou. Thus, by the mid-1880's, with Porto Novo and Cotonou under their control, the French had at last acquired a satisfactory base for their commercial activities on this stretch of coast, but they had no desire to become involved in a conflict with Dahomey.

In 1889, the elderly Gelele was succeeded by his son Behanzin, a strong man determined to preserve the rights of his kingdom. He questioned the French claim to Cotonou, and pointed out to the French resident at Porto Novo that Tofa had grossly insulted him, that he could easily have taken revenge by sacking the town but that he had refrained from doing so out of consideration for the French. At the same time, he succeeded in reviving the slave trade, obtaining modern firearms from German merchants in exchange for slaves, most of whom were shipped to the Congo or the Cameroons. Behanzin chose an unpropitious moment to defy the French, for in Paris the mood of aggressive expansionism was at its height. In 1892 the French finally made the decision to invade Dahomey, occupied the capital Abomey, deposed Behanzin, and divided the kingdom into two protectorates.

The British and the French were not the only European powers with an interest in the stretch of coast between Lagos and Accra. Portuguese and Brazilian merchants still retained some commercial contacts in the area. Indeed, in 1885 the Portuguese made an abortive attempt to claim a protectorate over Whydah. But neither the Portuguese nor the Brazilian governments were in a position to support their nationals with vigorous political action. German traders and missionaries—relative newcomers on the Guinea coast—were in a more fortunate position. Firms from Bremen and Hamburg began trading on the Guinea coast in the 1830's. (One German firm, O'swald, developed a profitable line of business by shipping cowrie-shells from Zanzibar to Lagos and Dahomey where they were still used as currency.) German trade increased particularly rapidly in the 1870's: Hamburg's exports to the Guinea coast rose by

560 percent between 1871 and 1883. In 1884 Bismarck decided to make a gesture in support of German commercial interest in West Africa. The chancellor was no enthusiast for colonial expansion. Constantly engaged in an elaborate juggling act to preserve both his own personal ascendency over German internal politics and his country's newly acquired position of dominance in Europe, he saw in colonial affairs no more than a number of minor issues that might be manipulated to his own advantage. Support for German trade would gratify the important Hanseatic towns; a few minor colonial conflicts with Britain might serve to improve German relations with France. To this end, a leading German Africanist, Gustav Nachtigal, best known for his travels in the Sahara and the Sudan, was sent out to visit German trading posts on the coast of West Africa, with instructions authorizing him "to extend German protection to territories where German traders seemed threatened by foreign encroachment." [36] Among the places visited by Nachtigal was Lome, today the capital of the Republic of Togo, where the local ruler signed a curious document. "King Mlapa of Togo," ran the first article, "desirous to protect the legitimate trade in this country principally by German merchants . . . begs the protection of H.M. the German Emperor, so that he may become able to maintain the independency of his territory." [37]

German fears of "foreign encroachments" were not misplaced. The British authorities on the Gold Coast were anxious to extend their protectorate eastward in an attempt to stamp out the "smuggling" around the unguarded ends of their territory. The local British agent had indeed drawn up a "provisional agreement" for the cession of the Togo seaboard only a fortnight before Nachtigal made his totally unexpected appearance. Thus the natural reaction of the men on the spot was to regard the German treaty as "disastrous to British prestige." [38] Officials at the colonial office regarded the matter much more coolly. "I suppose," one official wrote ironically, "we have a divine right to levy toll on all trade with the interior." "Before we annex more territory," he went on to reflect, "we ought to do something more for the trade we already tax so heavily by opening up roads and improving harbour facilities." [39] Five months later, the colonial secretary, Lord Derby, delighted with the outcome of the West African Conference at Berlin, made it plain to the governor of the Gold Coast that the British government now had "no disposition to dispute the German acquisitions." [40]

The anger of the men on the spot at being beaten to the post by a rival, the sober appraisal of wider realities by metropolitan officials, the final agreement reached by placing the matter under dispute alongside many other disputed claims in a manner calculated to produce the bar-

gaining that leads to compromise: this sequence of reaction was followed many times in the course of the next fifteen years, as Frenchmen,
Germans, and Britons pushed northward into the unexplored interior.
European rivalry reached its most hectic pitch on the Middle Niger
where the French, advancing northward from Dahomey and eastward
from their conquests in the Western Sudan, sought to establish a post on
the navigable stretch of the great river below the Bussa rapids, and thus
break into a domain over which the British Royal Niger Company was
ruthlessly asserting its monopoly. By March 1898, British and French
officers, backed by detachments of African troops, were glaring angrily
at each other in the barren lands of Borgu. To sober European contemporaries, including the British prime minister, Lord Salisbury, and
many of his cabinet colleagues, disputes such as these might well seem
"trivial brawls over expendable places." [41] For the African peoples concerned, the matter could not be so lightly dismissed. For the quarrels
and compromises of outsiders dictated the shape of the new political
structures that were later to be transformed into the independent successor states of the European colonies. To diplomats in Europe, most
minor African communities could not be more than names on a map,
but in deciding whether a particular community should come under
British, French, or German hegemony, European statesmen were in fact
determining an important element in the cultural heritage of generations
yet unborn.

▲▼ NIGERIA: THE BRITISH OCCUPATION
AND AFRICAN REACTIONS

In historical terms "Nigeria" is a neologism. First coined in the 1890's,
it was applied to those parts of the Niger area over which the British
were engaged in extending their hegemony. Before the 1890's there was
no one term that could be used to embrace all the territories that today
form part of the modern republic. Northern Nigeria is best regarded as
forming part of the Central Sudan, while southern Nigeria represents the
eastern extension of the subregion of Guinea. When the Atlantic slave
trade was at its height, the term "Slave Coast" was applied to the littoral
of Guinea lying between the Gold Coast and the Cameroons. Later, with
the development of the trade in palm oil, the term "Oil Rivers" was used
to describe the labyrinth of waterways most of which form part of the
Niger's broad delta.

Modern Nigeria has an area of 356,000 square miles. In 1875, this
substantial territory was divided up among a very large number of independent polities formed by peoples of strikingly different cultures. The
largest polity in the area—and indeed the most substantial indigenous

state in sub-Saharan Africa—was the caliphate of Sokoto, formed as a result of the victorious jihad launched in the first decade of the nineteenth century by Fulani groups living in the cluster of Hausa kingdoms—Gobir, Zamfara, Kano, and others—that occupied most of northwestern Nigeria. The caliphate could be described as a confederation of provinces, each of which was ruled by a dynasty founded by the local leaders of the jihad. Some provinces were based on the old Hausa kingdoms, others, such as Bauchi and Adamawa, were entirely new political structures in which the framework of Muslim Fulani rule had been laid over the miniscule polities of a variety of distinct ethnic groups. The caliphate must not be thought of as covering a solid bloc of territory. There were many areas, of which the Jos plateau is the most easily definable, where the local people preserved their independence often in the face of regular raids by Fulani slavers. Nor should the caliphate be thought of as even roughly conterminous with the Northern Nigeria of modern times. The province of Adamawa extended far eastwards over a large part of modern Cameroon, while in the northwest the Kanuri kingdom of Bornu, whose history, linked with that of the earlier kingdom of Kanem, could be traced back over a thousand years, occupied about 25,000 miles of territory and proved strong enough to beat off all Fulani assaults. Some of the peoples living south of the Benue—the Idoma, the Igala, and the Tiv—had not yet been seriously affected by Fulani expansion.

The Yorbua were the dominant ethnic group of western Nigeria. The political pattern of Yorubaland, always one of great complexity, was rendered still more confused by the collapse of Oyo, the greatest of Yoruba kingdoms, in the 1830's. Oyo, gravely weakened by internal dissensions, was finally destroyed by the attacks launched by the Fulani from their base at Ilorin. Thousands of Oyo refugees flooded southward, disturbing the old political balance, creating a number of new states, and inaugurating a long period of inter-Yoruba strife. By 1875 the Yoruba presented a great variety of independent polities, many no larger than a single town, some—notably Ijebu, Ibadan, and the Egba kingdom of Abeokuta—states possessing considerable resources. To the east of Yoruba country lay Benin, one of the most ancient of all the kingdoms of West Africa, already a highly organized state when first visited by the Portuguese at the end of the fifteenth century. The hegemony of Benin had once been undisputed over a wide area, but by 1875 it was being challenged by the Fulani to the north, by the growing power of Ibadan to the west, and by the gradual extension of European influence on the Niger.

Eastern Nigeria was largely dominated by the Ibo people. Most Ibo polities took the form of independent village groups, for the Ibo had never formed a state comparable to the kingdoms west of the Niger. Further east, along the modern Nigeria–Cameroon frontier, lay an area of great ethnic and linguistic complexity, where the languages spoken in neighboring villages often proved mutually incomprehensible. On the coast, the Niger delta was dominated by the Ijaw, and the area around the Cross River by the Ibibio, but the Ijaw population had been considerably modified by the large number of Ibos brought in by the slave trade and settled in the main Ijaw centers. The major Ijaw polities —Bonny, Opobo, Brass, and New Calabar—together with the Efik (Ibibio) polity of Old Calabar, presented some of the most unusual political structures to be found in tropical Africa. Deriving their wealth first from the export of slaves, then of palm oil, and possessing a record of intercourse with Europeans that reached back to the sixteenth century, their ruling groups had developed a distinctive eclectic culture of their own.

European intercourse with the people of southern Nigeria could be traced back to the contacts made by the Portuguese in the last decades of the fifteenth century. Three hundred years later the Nigerian coast contained some of the most active slave markets in all Africa. But despite the volume of their trade Europeans never established any forts or factories on this stretch of the "Slave Coast," preferring to do their business from "hulks" moored alongside the main trading centers. So great was European ignorance of the interior that the waterways they frequented were never seen as forming part of the mouth of a mighty river. Indeed, until the 1790's, most European geographers regarded the Niger as a westward-flowing river whose waters reached the sea by way of the Gambia and the Senegal. A great movement of exploration, sponsored first by private, then by official British agencies between 1788 and 1830, served to correct these erroneous notions and provided a mass of information on the polities of the Nigerian area, as British explorers visited Bornu, Sokoto, and some of the Yoruba states. The Niger, its lower course accurately charted, now presented itself as a magnificent highway into the interior. But the ravages of disease brought disaster to the first commercial expeditions up the river until the 1850's when it was found that regular doses of quinine offered reasonably effective protection against malaria—a discovery that served immensely to facilitate the European penetration of the interior.

By this time the British had found it necessary to establish a definite political presence on the Nigerian coast as part of their campaign to stamp out the export trade in slaves. In 1827 a temporary base was constructed on the Spanish island of Fernando Po. In the 1830's British naval officers began to exert direct pressure on the rulers of the coastal polities to make them abandon the trade on which so much of their economy was dependent. In 1849, a British trader, John Beecroft, was appointed first British consul for the Bights of Biafra and Benin. Two years later the British intervened in the affairs of the coastal state of Lagos, the main port of Yorubaland and one of the centers of the clandestine trade in slaves. In 1861 Lagos was formally annexed as a British crown colony.

No further acquisitions of territory took place in the course of the next twenty years, but this period witnessed a steady expansion of European activities in the southern Nigerian area, largely as a result of the work of British or British African traders and missionaries. In the late 1830's a number of Sierra Leoneans, liberated slaves of Yoruba birth, returned to their homeland, settling mainly at Badagry and Abeokuta. A few years later they were joined by a handful of European missionaries sent out by Protestant churches of different denominations. In the course of the next two decades, Christian missionaries—European, American, and African—carried their profoundly revolutionary message to many of the towns of Yorubaland and to the principal commercial centers of the "Oil Rivers" and the Lower Niger. At the same time there was a steady increase in the European trade with the Nigerian coast. In Lagos, where a number of British, French, and German firms came to settle in the 1850's, the value of imported goods rose from £121,000 in 1864 to £515,000 in 1870. A similar increase was taking place in the trade of the "Oil Rivers" where in 1871 the permanent staff of the twenty foreign trading companies numbered 2,500 Europeans and British Africans. There were five European firms on the Niger in 1871, fourteen in 1879, and the value of exports rose from £54,000 to £310,000 in the same period. Hindsight makes it easy to appreciate the significance of this gradual expansion. For European contemporaries, mindful of the heavy cost in human lives extorted by that fever-stricken coast, the meaning of these developments was less apparent. "Probably, with the exception of the Arctic regions, in no portion of the globe," wrote a British official in 1871 with special reference to the Niger, "has the British Government and British enterprise devoted so much persistent energy, and expended so much life and treasure hitherto to [so] little advantage." [42] Little more than thirty years after these words were written the British were masters of Nigeria, the most populous and in many ways the richest territory in tropical Africa.

The occupation of Nigeria was an extremely complex process which brought the British into conflict with many different indigenous communities. Here there is only space to consider four episodes, selected to illustrate the variety of African reactions to the British intrusion: the revolution in Bonny and the rise and fall of Jaja of Opobo, the establishment of British hegemony over the warring Yoruba states, the activities of the Royal Niger Company, and the British conquest of the caliphate of Sokoto. These episodes must first be set in a chronological framework—a narrative of the British occupation too brief to allow more than the barest mention of other important events in this highly dramatic period.

In 1875 the British possessed a firm political base in the island-colony of Lagos together with a strip of the adjoining coast. Further east, in the "Oil Rivers," British consuls had developed a tradition of intervening in the affairs of the coastal polities and could call on the warships of the West African squadron to add force to their behests. But the home government had no intention of becoming more deeply involved in expensive operations against the "savages" of a pestilential coast. Nevertheless, in the 1870's, when African traders, enraged at the intrusion of European rivals into their commercial preserves on the Lower Niger, began to attack British trading posts, gunboats were sent up the river to bombard the towns of the offenders. At the same time, a newcomer among the British merchants on the Niger, an ex-army officer named Goldie, succeeded in amalgamating the fiercely competitive British firms into the United African Company.

The early 1880's was marked by a new threat to British interests—the establishment of two vigorous French companies on the Niger. Goldie managed to buy up his French rivals, but the danger of political action by the French still remained. To ensure his country's position, the local British consul was instructed in 1884 to negotiate a series of treaties with the rulers of the coastal polities, a process which culminated in the proclamation of the "Oil Rivers Protectorate." The British position was made all the more secure by the decision reached at the international conference meeting at Berlin in 1884–85 to recognize British paramountcy on the Lower Niger. Meanwhile, agents of Goldie's United African Company were busy persuading local rulers to sign treaties ceding their entire territories to the company. Two hundred and thirty-seven such treaties could be produced in 1886 when the company was granted a royal charter authorizing it to set up a formal system of administration over its sphere of influence in the valleys of the Niger and the Benue.

"So long as we keep Europeans out," wrote one of the officials of the "Oil Rivers Protectorate," "we need not be in a hurry to go in." [43] Gradually, however, the pressure of local circumstances—the demands of British merchants, the initiative of British officials, the breakdown of indigenous polities—transformed the "paper protectorate" into a *de facto* colonial regime. This alien intrusion was vigorously resisted by the two ablest coastal rulers, Jaja of Opobo and Nana of the Itsekiri.

Jaja was deported in 1887, Nana driven from his country in 1894. Behind Nana's domains lay the ancient kingdom of Benin whose rulers attempted to protect themselves by avoiding all contact with the British. In 1896 a peaceful British embassy to Benin was attacked and massacred, an incident that inevitably provoked the British into mounting a powerful "punitive" expedition. The invaders entered a city adorned with extraordinary works of art—the famous Benin bronzes—but besmirched with the hideous evidence of human sacrifice—corpses crucified to "sacrifice trees," "altars covered with streams of dried human blood." [44] These dreadful sights contributed a new set of images to the European concept of Africa. They served to confirm contemporary notions of "Negro degradation" and to justify the "morality" of a "civilizing mission."

The years between 1890 and 1897 also saw the assertion of British hegemony over the warring states of the Yoruba. The British authorities in Lagos had long been interested in the affairs of Yorubaland. They had watched Ibadan, the most powerful of the successor states of the old Oyo empire, attempt to assert its paramountcy over its neighbors. And they had suffered from the conflicts between Ibadan and the Egba and Ijebu states that lay to its south. For Ibadan looked to Lagos for war materiel, yet the trade routes between the two greatest Yoruba cities lay through Egba or Ijebu territory and were naturally closed in time of war. The closing of the roads had a disastrous effect on the economy of the British colony. "Canoes were drawn up," a contemporary wrote of Lagos during one such period of interrupted trade in the late 1880's, "markets were extremely poor, shopkeepers sat gazing at their goods, there being no buyers, and the streets seemed to have put on a mournful appearance." [45] Little wonder that in these circumstances those ardent imperialists, the leading members of the Christian Yoruba community of Lagos, should have urged the British authorities to intervene directly in the affairs of their homeland. But in Yorubaland as on the "Oil Rivers," fears of French intervention, rendered more acute by French operations in Dahomey, rather than the pleas of missionaries or the exasperation of the merchants appear to have been the really decisive factor in stirring the British government to vigorous action. In 1892 a series of incidents, discussed in more detail later in this section, led the British to launch a strong military force against Ijebu. The governor, Carter, followed up this successful coup by an imposing tour of Yorubaland, signing treaties with the principal rulers, and establishing British residents and small garrisons of troops in the principal towns of the interior. In few parts of Africa was the coming of alien rule so cordially welcomed, for the Yoruba were exhausted by their internal dissensions and many communities had suffered gravely from the closing of trade routes and from the banditry and slave-raiding or kidnapping that flourished during the country's endemic state of insecurity. The financial statistics of the colony of Lagos soon provided striking evidence of the economic advantages of the *pax Britannica:* between 1892 and 1893 revenue jumped from £68,000 to £115,000 and by 1898 it had passed the £200,000 mark.

Meanwhile the Royal Niger Company was busily engaged in asserting its commercial monopoly over the Middle and Lower Niger and the Benue. In 1885 the company obtained by treaty from the sultan of Sokoto "entire rights" to the country on either side of the two rivers. Five years later the French agreed that "all that fairly belongs to the kingdom of Sokoto" lay within the company's sphere. These two agreements provided the legal basis for British claims to the territory that later became Northern Nigeria. In 1897 the company came into direct conflict with Nupe and Ilorin, the two southernmost provinces or emirates of the Sokoto caliphate. In a short, sharp campaign the company's well-equipped constabulary won two decisive victories over the massed Fulani cavalry of the emirates. But the company lacked the resources to impose a vigorous system of administration over the conquered provinces, nor was it strong enough to mount effective countermeasures to a French thrust from northern Dahomey across Borgu to the Niger. By this time, however, the colonial office, now under the vigorous direction of Joseph Chamberlain, was prepared to take active measures to support British interests on the Niger. In the summer of 1897 Chamberlain obtained the money needed to set up a small colonial army, the West African Frontier Force. By September he was talking of the need to "expropriate" the Niger Company "lock, stock and barrel." [46] By April, 1898, the British were able to counter the French move into the disputed area of Borgu with a convincing show of force. Three months later the diplomats in London and Paris reached agreement over a frontier on the long-disputed Middle Niger.

On January 1, 1900, after revoking the charter of the Royal Niger Company, the British government assumed responsibility for the "Protectorate of Northern Nigeria." The new protectorate embraced more than a quarter of a million square miles of territory, only a fraction of which was under direct British control, while many districts had never even been visited by a European. The first British high commissioner, Sir Frederick Lugard, was well-qualified to undertake the arduous task of imposing British authority over this vast area. Born in India in 1858, the son of an Anglican clergyman, Lugard spent the first ten years of his career as an army officer in India, until an unhappy love affair led him, "an almost hopeless and penniless adventurer," [47] to seek solace and distraction in Africa. Between 1888, when he arrived in Africa, and 1900 his life was one of extraordinarily varied action—fighting Arab slavers in Nyasaland, taking service with the Imperial British East Africa Company and playing a leading part in establishing the British presence in Uganda, undertaking a dramatic mission to Borgu on behalf of the Royal Niger Company, leading another expedition to Bechuanaland, and finally taking over command of the West African Frontier Force on the Niger. A vivid and prolific writer, Lugard produced a spate of articles recounting his exploits. His marriage in 1902 to Flora Shaw, colonial correspondent of *The Times* and one of the most influential women of her day, provided new opportunities for indulging in what seemed to some contemporaries an inordinate taste for self-advertisement. "Lugard writes," one of his critics remarked, "as though he were the Special Commissioner of Heaven invested with authority." [48] Lugard was indeed one of the most ardent imperialists of his generation, utterly convinced of "the genius," as he described it, of the British "race to colonize, to trade and to govern," [49] supremely confident of his own ability to assist his country to achieve its destiny. His industry was phenomenal, his courage undoubted, but he was by temperament an autocrat and he possessed a strictly limited range of sympathies. In his view the peoples of southern Nigeria were "lower negroid types" in contrast to the "superior and civilized races" of the north.[50] Most "educated natives" he regarded with distaste, and he found it difficult to feel much real interest in the work of those of his compatriots who were businessmen and missionaries.

As a soldier Lugard believed in the efficacy of military conquest. In a series of swift campaigns between 1900 and 1903 he succeeded in breaking the power of the Sokoto caliphate. In northeastern Nigeria no fighting was required. In the 1890's, Rabih, a remarkable military adventurer from the Eastern Sudan whose dramatic career is described in the next chapter, conquered the ancient kingdom of Bornu, only to be defeated and killed by the French in 1900. As for the pacification of more remote areas, of lonely communities sited in the rugged terrain of the Jos plateau or the Adamawa highlands, this involved, as in so many other parts of Africa, a long-drawn-out process in which local administrators blended persuasion with the threat of force as they sought to bring hitherto independent polities under the jurisdiction of the new regime. Thus, by the end of the first decade of the twentieth century Nigeria was firmly in British hands. Seen from the angle of the paramount power, the expansion of British hegemony may seem a relatively simple process. To appreciate the situation in its true complexity, and to understand the varied reactions of local peoples, one must turn to examine a number of case studies.

In the middle of the nineteenth century, Bonny, with its capital sited on an island at one of the easternmost arms of the Niger, was the wealthiest and most powerful of the delta polities. The state possessed a tradition of monarchical rule reaching back at least as far as the sixteenth century, and its ruling dynasty, the Pepples, were surrounded with something of that divine aura characteristic of so many African monarchies. Bonny's original population consisted of Ijaw-speakers, but by the nineteenth century it had been strongly modified by the influx of Ibo slaves. Indeed, by 1850 men and women of slave origin appear to have been in a majority. Servile status did not, however, condemn a man to a position of permanent inferiority. In Bonny, as in some of the other trading polities of the delta, society was divided into a number of "houses," each "house" containing as many freemen and slaves as were needed to man one of the great war-canoes on which Bonny's power was based. "Houses" also served as trading corporations, their dual role offering able and ambitious men abundant opportunity to reveal their prowess in war and their enterprise in business. In the first half of the nineteenth century some of the most powerful "houses" passed under the control of men of slave origin, but so great was the prestige surrounding the royal house that no ex-slave could aspire to the highest office in the land.

For Bonny, as for other coastal polities, the first half of the nineteenth century was, then, a time of growing social tension, as the "new men" of slave origin sought to extend their influence. But the situation was rendered all the more confusing by the intrusion of a new political force manifested in the warships of the West African squadron of the British navy. Bonny had been profitably engaged in selling slaves to Europeans since the seventeenth century, but its traders were able to make the transition to "legitimate commerce" with relative ease, for they enjoyed easy access to a hinterland rich in oil-palms and were soon able to develop a flourishing commerce in palm oil. This transition was expedited by the pressure exercised by the British navy to force the rulers of Bonny to extirpate the last traces of the slave trade. British intervention naturally caused bitter resentment, and the presence of a substantial community of British merchants, living in hulks moored in the Bonny River, brought with it the risk of further complications. In the early 1850's, the chief European and African merchants set up a "court of equity" which provided a satisfactory mechanism for solving minor disputes. But in 1853, the king of Bonny, William Pepple, began to impose restrictions on his subjects' trade with the hinterland. The king's action was a move in the struggle between the monarchy and the leading "houses," but it also had a serious effect on the polity's overseas trade and thus angered the European merchants as much as the house-chiefs. By appealing to the British consul the two groups were able to secure William Pepple's deposition.

The king was allowed to return to Bonny in 1861, but during his exile his opponents had looted the royal treasure and taken over the royal trading preserves, thus depriving the monarchy of its economic base. William Pepple's son, George, who succeeded his father in 1866, had been educated in England and converted to Christianity. His foreign manners impressed foreign visitors—one of them was amazed to find in this African monarch a shrewd critic of the comic operas of Gilbert and Sullivan—but inevitably alienated him from the mass of his subjects and forced him to rely on the support of the British consul. In 1867 Consul Livingstone reported that the king "wished me to bring a Man-of-War and compel his chiefs to do what I thought fit." [51] Thus almost two decades before the establishment of a formal protectorate, the British had achieved a position of paramountcy in the most powerful state of the Niger Delta.

In 1869 the long-simmering rivalry between the traditionalists, the supporters of the Bonny monarchy, and their opponents boiled over into civil war. The "new men" were led by Jaja, an Ibo brought to Bonny as a slave in the 1830's, who had worked his way up through sheer ability to the headship of one of the leading "houses." Realizing that he could never gain complete control of Bonny, Jaja retreated eastward, taking with him fourteen of the eighteen Bonny "houses," to found a new settlement significantly named Opobo after the greatest ruler in Bonny's history. Opobo was skillfully sited, allowing Jaja to control the richest palm oil markets of the interior. Within a few years Bonny was in eclipse, and Jaja of Opobo had become the most powerful ruler in the entire area later to be known as Eastern Nigeria.

In 1884, Jaja, in company with the other rulers of the "Oil Rivers," signed a treaty designed to provide the legal basis for a British protectorate. Shrewdly the king asked for the term "protectorate" to be defined. "The Queen," Consul Hewitt explained in reply, "does not want to take your country or your markets, but at the same time is anxious that no other nation should take them." [52] At the same time Jaja insisted on deleting a clause in the treaty that mentioned "free trade." Jaja's refusal to open up the markets of the interior was based on a reasonable assessment of the bases of his own power. In the same way, his unwillingness to allow Christian missionaries to operate in his territory derived from a vivid appreciation of the disturbances likely to be produced by their revolutionary doctrines. By thus seeking to preserve his own independence Jaja fell foul of both the traders and the missionaries, the two most vocal European pressure groups on the coast. The traders' view of Jaja became still more hostile when he was presumptuous enough to draw up plans for shipping palm oil direct to Britain, thereby threatening to undermine their entire business.

The British consuls naturally supported their compatriots, the traders. Acting Consul Johnston, later to achieve wider fame for his work in Nyasaland, put the matter vigorously but crudely when he described Jaja as "one of the most grasping, unscrupulous and overbearing of mushroom kings who ever attempted to throttle the growing commerce of white men with the richer interior." [53] In September, 1887, Johnston resorted to what can only be described as a singularly shabby trick to lure Jaja aboard a British gunboat and thus secure his arrest and deposition. Jaja died in Tenerife in 1891.

Very different from the clash of rival businessmen in the trading polities of the "Oil Rivers" was the pattern of events that led to the establishment of British hegemony in Yorubaland. The reaction of the Yoruba to alien intrusion contrasted sharply with that of many other African peoples: many Yoruba positively welcomed British intervention in their affairs. Two sets of circumstances help to explain their reaction: their country had been ravaged by war for more than sixty years; at the same time, the expansion of Christian missionary enterprise, due in large part to the work of Sierra Leonians of Yoruba origin, had given the people of many Yoruba towns some familiarity with the ways of white men. So much can be said by way of generalization. But the Yoruba must be seen as a complex people, divided among a large number of independent polities. Every local situation had its own special characteristics and every Yoruba ruler had his own ideas about the role he wanted outsiders to play in his community. The people of Kishi, for example, a little state in northeastern Yorubaland on the borders of Borgu, had good reason to welcome British intervention. When Lugard visited Kishi in 1894, the king told him that his people lived in "daily dread" of Borgu attack, that the Borgu people were constantly raiding Kishi, carrying off the townsfolk as slaves. "The British had introduced law and order into all Yoruba," Lugard reported the ruler as telling him. "They prayed God my coming was the beginning of peace; all they desired was peace." [54]

In sharp contrast to the case of Kishi may be set that of Ijebu, a state whose rulers resolutely resisted alien intrusion. Ijebu, lying between Lagos and Ibadan, was one of the largest Yoruba states. It had escaped the worst consequences of the Yoruba wars and had never been exposed to attack by other peoples. Thus there was no great political incentive to seek a British alliance. Relations with the British in Lagos were further complicated by the lie of the trade routes, for the Ijebu were in a position to control the route to their northern neighbor, Ibadan, and thus to deprive Lagos traders of one of their most valuable markets. Yet another source of conflict lay in the fact that Ijebu was one of the few major Yoruba polities to refuse admission to Christian missionaries, even though some of the missionaries were Ijebu people who had settled in Lagos or returned from Sierra Leone. The Ijebu attitude was logical enough. Members of the Ijebu ruling class were vividly aware of what had happened in Lagos in the 1850's when the local ruler, Kosoko, had been deposed by the British largely as a result of missionary prompting. Clearly all missionaries, European and African alike, were to be regarded as "spiritual intruders" seeking to subvert the kingdom's traditional institutions. As with Jaja, the uncompromising stand of the Ijebu earned them the bitter hatred of missionaries, traders, and colonial officials. Viewed from Lagos, the Ijebu took on the guise, in Governor Carter's words, of "heathens of the most uncompromising description." [55]

Missionary pressure was a factor of some importance in the British decision to launch a punitive expedition against Ijebu in 1892. The Ijebu, for their part, first attempted to resist the invaders by spiritual means. "Charms of imprecation for which they were famous were uttered over the creek that the vessels might founder and the expedition might end in failure." The Ijebu then attempted to hold up the British force at a well-chosen position, only to be terrorized by the sight of rockets "with horrid noises and streaming fiery tails bursting into the forest." [56] Within a few days the campaign was over."The taking of Ijebu Ode," wrote the Christian Yoruba historian, Samuel Johnson, "sent a shock of surprise and alarm throughout the whole land. The people felt instinctively that a new era was about to dawn on them. . . . To the vast majority of the common people it was like the opening of a prison door. . . . Even among the Ijebus themselves very few of any outside the high officials of the capital who had hitherto maintained the iron system of inexorable exclusiveness and rigour suffered much from the change; the Ijebus were exclusively traders and they benefitted by the increased trade." [57] With the collapse of the old order many Ijebu turned enthusiastically to Christianity. Indeed, within a few years the Ijebu came to be regarded as the missionaries' most ardent supporters. Islam, said to have been introduced into Ijebu by a Hausa slave in the 1860's, also made many converts. By 1921, 23 percent of the people of Ijebu were classified as Christian, 29 percent as Muslim. In Abeokuta, on the other hand, to which Christianity had been introduced as early as the 1840's, 71 percent still followed the traditional religion in 1921, and only 8 percent were counted as Christians.[58]

To turn from Ijebu to the activities of the Royal Niger Company and the reactions of its opponents is to enter yet another world. "The spirit and energy of the Royal Niger Company have, without the expenditure of Imperial funds, or the sacrifice of the life of a single British soldier, placed under the protection of the Crown, the whole of the Lower, a great portion of the Central Niger, and its affluent, the Benue." [59] So wrote Lord Salisbury in 1892. Thus within the space of fifteen years Goldie, the founder of the company, had succeeded in achieving that ambition, conceived at the time of his first visit to West Africa in 1877, of "adding the region of the Niger to the British Empire." It is tempting to linger over the details of Goldie's strange career and arresting, even hypnotic personality. Here was a man who, on inheriting a fortune in his early twenties, had chucked an army career and rushed off to Egypt where, on his own testimony, he spent three years living with an Arab girl in the desert until she died of consumption; a man described by one of his friends, the poet Dorothy Wellesley, as "an incongruous mixture of reason and passion . . . rapid and violent in his movements, his nervous force extraordinary." [60] But the historian must resist the seductions of biography, when a much more important matter needs to be considered—the impact of the Royal Niger Company on the Nigerian peoples with whom it came into contact.

The company was basically a commercial enterprise, which pursued commercial objectives with great ruthlessness. "In the vast territories of the Niger Company," wrote Sir Claude Macdonald, consul-general of the Niger Coast Protectorate in 1895, "there is not one single outside trader, black, white, green, or yellow. The markets are all theirs. They open and shut any given market at will, which means subsistence or starvation to the native inhabitants of the place. They can offer any price they like to the Producers, and the latter must either take it or starve. And why, in heaven's name, why? Because they must pay 6 or 7 percent to shareholders." [61] Goldie's response to these criticisms was to provide a moral gloss to the company's monopolistic policies by describing the African traders excluded from the company's territories as "disreputable coloured men . . . (generally inferior clerks dismissed for peculation), who lived by surreptitious dealing in slaves . . . stirring up the natives to discontent and bloodshed, under a mask of false piety." [62] This was clearly a jibe at the new class of Western-educated Africans who were playing so large a part in bringing Christianity to the Niger area. To men such as these Goldie's attitude was symbolic of the new mood of racial arrogance that became increasingly apparent among the British in West Africa in the last decade of the nineteenth century.

There was little that most African communities could do to resist the company's invasion of their territory. But in 1895 one group, the people of the Niger Delta polity of Brass, exasperated beyond endurance by the restrictions imposed on them by the company, launched a savage attack on the company's coastal depot at Akassa. Retaliation was swift and brutal. A British naval bombardment destroyed a large part of the Brass settlements. But a judicial inquiry followed this bloody incident, allowing the Brassmen an opportunity of explaining their grievances. Trade up the Niger played a vital part in their economy, for their own soil was too poor to provide them with all the food they needed. Yet now when they tried to reach their old markets to purchase yams and palm oil, their canoes were stopped or fired on by the company's officials and many of their people maltreated or even killed. "A person who has been accustomed to eat bread," the Brass chiefs explained, resorting to figurative language to emphasize their case, "and knows its sweetness from his youth to manhood happens to offend (*sic*) by another man to eat dust instead of bread. At the very time he hears the word dust, he will go mad." [63]

On paper the company developed an imposing system of administration, with a chain of command running from the senior local administrator, the agent-general, to district agents at the smaller stations along the rivers. Moreover it possessed in its constabulary the most effective fighting force in the whole area. But the constabulary was used not for conventional police duties but for punitive expeditions against towns and villages whose people refused to obey the company's trading regulations. The impact of the company's harsh regime on African communities was indeed, in the opinion of the company's most recent historian, "almost totally negative." "Little or nothing was done to alter society, to change beliefs, or even to develop the economy." [64] Yet for all the company's shortcomings its work represents an important link in the chain of events that led to the creation of the greatest of all the states of modern tropical Africa.

Few episodes in the European conquest of Africa were so vividly narrated as the British occupation of the great caliphate of Sokoto. The conqueror, Sir Frederick Lugard, was his own historiographer and produced an interpretation of events that is still widely accepted. "The Fulani race," wrote Lugard, "are aliens to the country whose population they have oppressed. Their power has become effete and their rule has degenerated in most places into tyranny. They recognize themselves that their day is past. Already in 1900, the process of disintegration had begun. In every direction the peoples subject to them were in rebellion or had thrown off their yoke." [65] The approach is a familiar one: the French had invaded Egypt in 1798 and Algeria in 1830 to liberate the Arabs from the brutal Turks; the British likewise could pose as the liberators come to free the Hausa and other Central Sudanese people from the oppression of the alien and degenerate Fulani. The reality was, of course, considerably more complicated.

The Fulani could hardly be regarded as alien conquerors, for they had been settled in parts of the Central Sudan for many generations before the revolutionary wars that brought them to power in the first decade of the nineteenth century. The caliphate certainly possessed a ruling class of largely Fulani extraction, but the ties of marriage or concubinage provided an intimate link between the rulers and many of their non-Fulani subjects, and Islam served to strengthen the bond between the *sarakuna* (the nobility) and the *talakawa* (the peasantry). Further, the Fulani had never succeeded in overcoming the resistance of all the peoples of the Central Sudan. Indeed, many of the "rebellions" to which Lugard referred represented the continuation of local wars of resistance whose origins could be traced back to the first years of the jihad. There was nothing new about the violence with which Europeans found themselves confronted in many of the areas nominally controlled by the caliphate. Local chronicles provide evidence of intensive slave-raiding in certain areas at least as early as the fifteenth century. Nor is there any reason for supposing that the caliphate was on the verge of total disintegration. In the last decade of the nineteenth century the "sultans of Sokoto"—the form of title applied by the British to the paramount rulers of the caliphate—appear to have had little difficulty in ensuring the payment of tribute by distant provinces.

The swift and sudden collapse of Fulani resistance was a reflection of the relative technological backwardness of the caliphate. The Fulani rulers lacked that stimulating experience of a wider world acquired by such men as al-Hajj Umar or Samory. They were not entirely ignorant of modern firearms but they preferred to put their trust in the cavalry formations that had brought them victory in so many local conflicts. Given the great area covered by the caliphate, its rulers found it impossible to develop an effective plan for concerted resistance. Consequently each province fought and lost its own battles.

For the devout Muslim—and many of the Fulani nobility were exceedingly devout—defeat at the hands of the infidel was a terrible but not an overwhelming experience. Shortly after the fall of Kano but before the capture of Sokoto, the emir of Kano wrote to the *waziri* (vizier or chief minister) of Sokoto, "I have found no more useful plan for all

Muslims . . . than that we leave this country all of us . . . as the dogs [i.e. the Christians] have surrounded us and threaten to overcome us." [66] To flee a country that had fallen under infidel domination could be interpreted as *hijra,* a religious act sanctioned by the Prophet himself. Accordingly, after the defeat of his army outside the walls of Sokoto in March, 1903, Sultan Attahiru decided to flee eastward, probably regarding Mecca as his ultimate objective. "The people appear to rise en masse at the Sultan's call," wrote a worried British official, "men, women and children leaving their towns and villages deserted to follow him, thus showing a fanaticism which I, for one, never thought they possessed." [67] For the valiant sultan and many of his followers flight ended in death at the hands of British forces in the battle of Burmi.

For those who could not take the path of *hijra* and were therefore forced to accept alien rule and even to collaborate with the infidel conquerors, an alternative line of action was regarded as permissible— *taqiyya* or dissembling in order to preserve the faith. "This is legal in every land where Islam is not strong," wrote a learned shaikh of Sokoto, to whom the *waziri* turned for advice after the British conquest. "We show regard to them with the tongue and have intercourse with them in affairs of the world but never to love them in our hearts or adopt their religion." [68] This attitude soon brought satisfactory results. The British were uneasy conquerors, haunted by the fear of Mahdist insurrections, of "fanatical" Muslim jihads. They were scrupulous in avoiding any gesture likely to offend Muslim susceptibilities. In time many members of the Fulani aristocracy reconciled themselves to the British presence. "The British," wrote a prominent Sokoto Fulani, later to become the premier of Northern Nigeria, "were the instruments of destiny and were fulfilling the will of God. . . . They made no drastic changes. . . . Everything went on more or less as it had done, for what could the Resident, an assistant and a few soldiers in Sokoto do to change so vast an area as Sokoto Emirate?" [69]

A different view of the British occupation is to be found in the autobiography of an old Hausa woman, Baba of Karo. "The Europeans . . . found a lot of tyranny and oppression here, people being beaten and killed and sold into slavery . . . We Habe [i.e. Hausa] wanted them to come, it was the Fulani who did not like it. When the Europeans came the Habe saw that if you worked for them then they paid you for it. They didn't say, like the Fulani, 'Commoner, give me this! Commoner, bring me that.' Yes, the Habe wanted them, they saw no harm in them." [70] Historians cannot make valid generalizations from the testimonies of a handful of individuals, but statements such as these serve to indicate the variety of reactions provoked by the sudden British intrusion.

▲▼ THE STRUCTURE OF EUROPEAN HEGEMONY IN WEST AFRICA: BRITISH AND FRENCH SYSTEMS OF RULE

By 1905 the greater part of West Africa was firmly under European control. By 1960 most West African territories had regained their independence. Thus in most parts of the region the period of European rule lasted for little longer than a single lifetime. In the years between the two World Wars the European regime appeared to have acquired an unshakeable permanence; yet it was soon to prove no less ephemeral than any of the other empires West Africa had seen in the course of the past thousand years.

The structure of the European regimes—the hierarchy of officials ranging from the governor or governor-general at the apex of the pyramid to the district officer or *administrateur* at his station in the bush— is not difficult to describe. Nor is it hard to find striking contrasts in the administrative policies of Britain and France, the two major imperial powers in the region. But such relatively facile generalizations tend to conceal the wide range of variables that lie beneath the deceptively simple surface. Precolonial West Africa was made up of an extraordinary variety of independent polities. Inevitably the structure of the alien regime was affected by the character of the indigenous institutions over which it was laid. Thus the British district officer working in one of the Muslim emirates of the former caliphate of Sokoto found himself confronted with problems very different from those faced by his colleagues stationed among the "pagan" communities of the Benue valley. Relations between overlords and subjects were further affected by the circumstances of the initial act of occupation or conquest. Some major West African polities—the Tukulor empire, Samory's state, and the kingdom of Dahomey provide the most prominent examples—lying in the path of the French advance had been completely shattered by the years of hard fighting that preceded the final establishment of French rule. In the British sphere, on the other hand, military campaigns were shorter and sharper, and the damage inflicted on such polities as Benin, Ashanti, or the Sokoto caliphate not completely irreparable. Nor had all African rulers been forced to taste the bitter fruit of military defeat, for there were some who had deliberately chosen to place their states under European protection, only to find that treaty-forms implying a semi-autonomous protectorate status provided no security against the steady increase of alien intervention in their internal affairs.

To the variables of place must be added those of time. The character of colonial rule changed subtly from decade to decade. In part these changes were provoked by the impact on West Africa of major events and processes in the outside world, the two World Wars, the Great Depression, the gradual shift in European ideas about imperialism. But change in the character of colonial rule was also a product of the pressure of local circumstances. The subjects of a colonial power must never be thought of as a passive mass of humanity, totally incapable of autonomous action. The notion of passivity seems particularly absurd when applied to West Africa, many of whose societies struck outside observers as exhibiting a peculiarly dynamic quality. Moreover, West Africans as a whole were fortunate in escaping the harsher manifestations of colonial rule produced in areas of extensive European settlement. In such circumstances many West Africans, responding to the stimulus of the new techniques and the new ideas introduced by the Europeans in their midst, were able to formulate new ambitions, thus generating a current of emotion strong enough to help shatter the foundations on which their overlords' power was based.

A third and less easily definable variable lies in the field of human personality. Many Africans learned that the quality of colonial rule depended in large measure on the character of the man on the spot, the European—district officer, schoolmaster, or P.W.D. foreman—with whom they came into direct contact. It is impossible to make any overall generalizations about the quality of European officials serving in West Africa. In the first place, the character of the administration was constantly changing. In Northern Nigeria, for example, many of the first generation of administrators were army officers fresh from the Boer War. About 1908, the administration began to attract Oxbridge graduates, Northern Nigeria being invested, through Lugard's works, with a glamor that made it the most prestigious of British West African possessions. After the end of World War I, another generation of ex-army officers entered the Northern Nigerian administration where their influence served, in the opinion of one of their juniors, a member of the new wave of Oxbridge recruits who came out in the late 1920's, "to intensify the drift towards literalism and clerkliness" at the expense of more dynamic qualities.[71] A similar generation gap with its resulting tensions could be traced no less clearly in the French service. The young Frenchmen holding passionate left-wing views who arrived in Dakar during the period of the Popular Front in the late 1930's were a world apart from the *rois de la brousse* ("kings of the bush"), the hard-bitten administrators of the old school.

Comments on the differences between the generations take no ac-

count of the range of individual character to be found within the service, and since individual administrators possessed, especially in the
early days, a great deal of power within their particular district, province, or colony, any detailed historical study must rest on a mass of biographical material. Some European administrators, by virtue of their energy or eccentricity, won a place in the folklore of their districts: such a
one was Henri Fleury, *commandant de cercle* at Zinder in the early
1920's, whom the local Hausa nicknamed "thief-purger." [72] Others,
with a sharp eye on the opportunities for promotion, speedily abandoned the splendors and miseries of life as a bush district officer for the
sedentary occupation of a file-pushing bureaucrat in the secretariat.
Others found themselves being shuttled from one province or even—in
French West Africa—from one colony to another, with little opportunity to make much impression on the people under their charge. But
there were a few men, especially in the higher ranks of the service, who
were able to exercise a profound influence on the development of their
temporary domain. Of these creative administrators, Governor Guggisberg of the Gold Coast, may serve as an example.

Guggisberg, a Canadian of Swiss descent, started his career as an army
officer in the Royal Engineers. Between 1900 and 1914 he was employed as a surveyor in West Africa, an occupation which brought him
into close and sympathetic contact with a wide variety of Africans.
During World War I he commanded a brigade on the Western Front, an
experience which determined him "to dedicate the rest of his life to the
service of his fellow-men." [73] A fortunate combination of circumstances secured him the governorship of the Gold Coast, a post which
he held from 1919 to 1927. Guggisberg believed that it was the duty of
government "to lay the foundations of development in every
direction." [74] Accordingly, within six weeks of his arrival at Accra he
had drawn up a ten year development program based on ideas of planning and financing development that were far in advance of his time.
Before he retired, many of his plans, ranging from the construction of
an artificial harbor at Takoradi and the foundation of a secondary
school at Achimota to the beginning of a vigorous policy of africanization, had become reality. To his "fantastic capacity for work," his
"orderly and systematic approach to his problems," and his "drive
and determination"—characteristics common to many able colonial
administrators—Guggisberg added a rarer and more original quality,
defined by his biographer Ronald Wraith as "an obsessional belief in
the potentialities of the people whom he governed, coupled with a flair
for putting himself across and appearing to them as the embodiment of
their own aspirations." [75] On his arrival on the Gold Coast Guggisberg

was hailed in the local press as "the New Messiah"; when he left, people wore cloth on which was printed his portrait above the inscription "Guggisberg forever Governor in the hearts of the Gold Coast people." [76] Few proconsuls have earned so endearing an epitaph.

"The Colonial Service," wrote a critical Australian observer in the 1940's, "includes Governors of outstanding personality and ability; but it also contains too many who are outstandingly unfit for their high function. The doings of some of them could, if told in a book, not be believed." [77] This was said about the British; the same comment could, no doubt, be made about the French. But it will not be possible to test these dark allegations by documentary evidence until all the personal files of the colonial era have been opened—an intriguing expansion of historical source material not likely to occur for many years.

Whatever the local variations of place, time, and individual personality, every imperial establishment faced the same basic problems: a viable administrative framework must be devised for the newly acquired domains, men recruited to staff the new organization, money raised to meet its costs, and finally a system of local administration worked out effective enough to allow the necessary contacts between the rulers and the ruled. These were the tasks which faced the British and the French in West Africa, and, on a very much smaller scale, the Germans in their colony of Togo, until its conquest by Anglo-French forces in the first weeks of World War I, the Portuguese in Guinea, and the Afro-Americans in Liberia.

The largest indigenous polity established before the colonial era, the caliphate of Sokoto, covered an area of about 150,000 square miles. Most other West African kingdoms were very much smaller, and many independent polities were limited to single towns and villages. Two of the British territories—the Gambia (4,000 square miles) and Sierra Leone (28,000 square miles)—were among the smallest colonies in Africa, but the Gold Coast (to which was added a part of German Togo) had an area of 91,000 square miles and Nigeria of 373,000 square miles. The administrative federation of French West Africa included extensive stretches of the Sahara in Mauritania, the Soudan (later Mali), and Niger; with a total area of 1,816,000 square miles, it formed by far the largest administrative unit in all Africa.

It took the French twenty years to work out a satisfactory structure for their territories in West Africa. Up to 1891, French possessions on the coast of Guinea were nominally under the control of the governor of Senegal. In the early 1890's, Guinea, the Ivory Coast, and Dahomey were made into autonomous colonies, while the ambitious army officers who held command in Soudan usually acted as a law unto themselves.

But as the lines of French expansion converged in the interior, the need for some overall system of cooperation became increasingly pressing. Accordingly, in 1895 the post of governor-general for French West Africa was created, but the first incumbent also served as governor of Senegal and possessed only modest supervisory powers over the other West African territories. Not until 1904 was the government-general placed on a firm footing, with its own capital at Dakar, and its own revenue derived from the control of customs duties. There was no legislature in French West Africa, all legislation emanating from France usually in the form of a presidential decree drawn up in the colonial ministry. The governor-general alone had the right to communicate directly with the metropolitan authorities and so found himself well-placed to supervise the activities of his subordinates, the lieutenant-governors of the different colonies. At the same time, the government-general acquired direct control over the technical services concerned with agriculture, health, posts and telegraphs, and public works and so was able to exercise a profound influence on the development of the federation as a whole. As for the pattern of territorial organization, this was a matter involving the constant redrawing of inter-colonial boundaries in the first two decades of the twentieth century, as "pacification" gradually gave way to settled administration and civilian *administrateurs* took over from army officers. Particularly unstable was the administrative structure that covered the territory which now forms the Republic of Upper Volta. In the years immediately after the French conquest most of Upper Volta was administered as part of Soudan and Ivory Coast, but it was formed into a distinct colony in 1920, only to be dismembered in 1932 and reestablished in 1947.

The British were faced with the same problem of erecting new political structures to cover the territories brought under their control. In the Gambia, Sierra Leone, and the Gold Coast the administrative task was relatively simple: the new "protectorate"—in the case of the Gold Coast, Ashanti, and the Northern Territories—could be tacked on to the old "colony." The Nigerian area, on the other hand, presented an administrative problem far more complex. In the 1890's the territory contained the colony of Lagos, with its recently acquired Yorubaland protectorate, the "Oil Rivers," later renamed the Niger Coast Protectorate, which covered most of the areas later known as Midwest and Eastern Nigeria, and the riverine strip along the Niger and the Benue administered by the Royal Niger Company. In 1900 the Royal Niger Company handed over its responsibilities to the colonial authorities of the newly created Protectorate of Northern Nigeria. At the same time, the Niger Coast Protectorate, which had previously been under foreign office supervision, was renamed the Protectorate of Southern Nigeria and handed over to the colonial office. In 1906 Southern Nigeria was linked with Lagos under a single governor. Eight years later the two Nigerias, Northern and Southern, were amalgamated under the governor-generalship of Sir Frederick Lugard.

The decision to create a unified Nigeria—a polity possessing a larger and more heterogeneous population than any other territory in Africa —was clearly one of the most momentous taken by a colonial power in the first half of the twentieth century. Some West African colonies could be regarded as an expansion or even as a re-creation of older indigenous polities. French Soudan, for example, renewed the unity once established in the area of the Upper Niger by the rulers of medieval Mali, while the British Gold Coast embraced little more than the territory once dominated by Ashanti. But Nigeria was something entirely new. There was no historical precedent for a superstructure that linked such diverse peoples as the Yoruba, the Ibo, the Hausa-Fulani, and the Kanuri. Naturally, given the circumstances of the time, the decision to unify Nigeria did not result from the pressure of local political groups; it derived from considerations of administrative convenience as interpreted by a colonial power. In the eyes of Governor Lugard, the two Nigerias presented the "anomaly of a territory, undivided by any natural boundaries, of which one portion [Southern Nigeria] was wealthy and able to spend large sums on developments not of paramount urgency, while the remaining portion [Northern Nigeria] . . . could not balance its budget, and the British taxpayer was called upon to pay the larger part of its bare necessities of administration." [78] (Between 1900 and 1912 the British government had, in fact, contributed more than £3 million to the cost of the Northern Nigerian administration, reluctant liberality in an age when colonies were generally required to be self-supporting.) Disputes between the two Nigerian governments over plans for railroad construction emphasized still further the need for a greater measure of coordination. Finally, it must be remembered that Lugard, an administrator of highly autocratic temperament, had gained all his Nigerian experience in the North. He regarded most of the peoples of the South as being of "a low and degraded type" and considered that the system of administration developed by the British in Southern Nigeria, a system which allowed many of the Yoruba states a great measure of autonomy, "left the authority of the Colonial Government very ill-defined." [79] It was natural that such a man should attempt to impose on the South the system of native administration he had developed in the North. The act of amalgamation provoked bitter controversy at the time, arousing the resentment of many Western-educated Nigerians and

of some British administrators. It saddled the country with an issue—
the relationship between North and South—that has dominated its politics to this day.

Of the variations in the character of the personnel engaged in the
work of colonial administration in British and French West Africa
something has already been said. But there are two other points, one
concerning numbers, the other the degree of africanization, that need to
be made about the colonial services in West Africa. In the late 1930's
there were about 3,600 French officials working in French West Africa,
about 1,500 British officials in Nigeria, and another 1,100 in the three
remaining British West African territories. These are very modest figures, especially when it is remembered that the term "official" covers
officers in technical services and that a substantial proportion of every
colony's European staff was likely to be out of the colony on leave at
any one time. To provide the sanction of force for their authority the
British were almost entirely dependent on locally recruited troops and
policemen. Thus in Nigeria in the late 1920's there were only 233 European officers and noncommissioned officers among the 4,000 men of the
Nigerian regiment of the Royal West African Frontier Force, and 75
European officers in a police force also numbering 4,000. In French
territory the colonial military presence was far more noticeable. A British traveler of the 1930's commented on what seemed to him "the excessive militarization of the country." "In any conglomeration of any size
was a barracks . . . the bugle has completely ousted the tom-tom as a
background to local colour." [80] In the years between the two World
Wars, the French made all their West African subjects liable to conscription, though only a small proportion of conscripts proved fit
enough for army service. Many of the troops raised in West Africa
were stationed in France and in other parts of the French empire. A
British estimate made during World War II reckoned that there were
40,000 troops in French West Africa, of whom 15,000 were of local
origin.[81]

Until the 1890's the British were glad to appoint suitably qualified
black men, whether Creoles from Sierra Leone or West Indians, to senior posts in the various West African establishments. In Lagos, for example, in 1875 "the heads of the Police, of the Posts and Telegraphs and
of the Customs departments were all Africans, as was the Registrar of
the High Court." [82] By 1910 such a state of affairs would no longer
have been possible. A number of factors account for the rapid europeanization of senior posts in the civil service and the consequent
blocking of African opportunities. Advances in medical science—
particularly the discovery that malaria and yellow fever were trans-

mitted by mosquito—made possible the introduction of new measures designed to safeguard the health of Europeans, measures that served slowly to dispel the notion of West Africa as "the White Man's Grave." At the same time, the growth of racial feeling in Britain led to the acceptance of views that would have been sharply questioned thirty years earlier. In 1886 the head of the African department of the colonial office expressed the opinion that "the educated native is the curse of the West Coast." [83] Before long this notion had become one of the clichés of the British community in West Africa, and it continued to influence the "official mind" of British West Africa until as late as World War II. An experienced British observer, writing in 1938, remarked that "the preference for the uneducated over the educated native . . . is so much more conspicuous in British than in French territories." [84]

By the 1920's the British had developed a unified colonial service which included both administrative and technical branches. Appointment was by interview, not by written examination, and the possession of a university degree came to be regarded as an essential qualification. These conditions made it extremely hard for local men to obtain appointments in the senior grades of the civil services of the British West African territories. Indeed, Africans found themselves deliberately excluded from applying for admission to the administrative service by a ruling, in force until 1942, that required candidates to be "of pure European descent." [85] Individual governors, acting on their own initiative, could do something, as Guggisberg showed on the Gold Coast, to advance local men, but the necessity of africanization was not generally accepted until the mid-1940's.

The structure of the French colonial service differed in a number of ways from the British. Candidates aspiring to join the higher grades of the service were required to take a competitive examination. If successful, they trained for three years at the *École Nationale de la France d'Outremer* in Paris. All French citizens could compete for entrance, but the only West Africans to enjoy the status of "citizens" were the inhabitants of the four *communes* of Senegal. The French were never animated by the intense color-consciousness of the British. A number of black West Indians—among them Felix Eboué, governor-general of French Equatorial Africa in 1944—found employment in the colonial service between the wars. But the artificial distinction between *citoyens* and *sujets* served as a barrier to ambitious francophone Africans as effective as the racial prejudices encountered by their contemporaries in British West Africa. Indeed the opportunities for professional advancement were even fewer in French territories than in British, for African education was less highly developed and the colonial authorities made a practice of appointing Europeans to subordinate posts.

Recruitment to the administration was a subject for discussion only among the *évolués,* the intelligentsia of West Africa in the 1920's and 1930's. For the mass of West Africans the incidence of taxation provided the most effective means of gauging the burden represented by alien rule. Here again there was a sharp contrast between British and French territories. British territories had developed a flourishing export trade in agricultural and mineral products. In 1924, Nigeria and the Gold Coast could afford imports worth £23 million, while the total imports of the whole of French West Africa did not exceed £9 million. In these circumstances British colonial governments found that customs duties provided an easy and painless means of raising the greater part of the revenue that they required. (In 1928 a single item—the duty on imported gin—provided nearly a third of the Gold Coast's total revenue.)

Most British administrators were relieved to be able to raise revenue by indirect means. As early as the 1860's the British had been forced, in the face of popular resistance, to abandon their attempt to impose a poll tax on Africans under their protection on the Gold Coast. The Sierra Leone "Hut Tax War" of 1898 provided an even more stringent warning of the resentment that could be aroused by the hasty introduction of a system of direct taxation. Consequently it was not until as late as the 1940's that the colonial authorities in the Gold Coast and Sierra Leone, finding themselves faced with the absolute necessity of raising more revenue to pay for expending development, at last managed to introduce effective systems of direct taxation. In Nigeria the situation was somewhat different. Under Fulani rule the northern emirates had already acquired considerable experience in extracting tax revenues from the local peasantry, part of the revenue being dispatched as tribute to Sokoto. Thus the British found little difficulty in ensuring that a proportion of the taxes raised by local authorities was paid to the new suzerain, the colonial government. But when, in the years after the amalgamation of Nigeria in 1914, British administrators attempted to graft the local government practices developed in the Fulani emirates onto the vastly different polities of the Yoruba and the Ibo, they ran into immediate difficulties. The serious disturbances that broke out in Yoruba Abeokuta in 1918 and in Ibo Aba in 1929 had complex causes, but the imposition of novel forms of direct taxation was an issue of major importance in both cases. The system of "indirect rule" developed by the British in Nigeria allowed native authorities to retain for their own benefit a substantial proportion of the tax which they collected, and British administrators were concerned to develop a flexible system of taxation that took into consideration the varying resources of different districts. By the late 1930's, when direct taxation had been accepted throughout the country, "the Nigerian system" struck a liberal South African observer as "such an advance on the unscientific hut and poll taxes prevailing elsewhere." [86]

West Africans living in border areas must have become sharply conscious of the contrasts between British and French taxation systems. Since their colonies had developed a less lucrative external trade, the French authorities found it necessary to rely far more heavily on direct taxation than the British. (The contrast between French West Africa as a whole and the British Gold Coast was particularly striking: in 1937, 27 percent of French West Africa's revenue came from direct taxation, while the Gold Coast derived less than 1 percent of its revenue from direct taxes.) The French authorities demanded of their subjects both a capitation tax, to which even children over the age of ten were liable in some territories, and a *prestation* payable in the form of a definite amount of labor but redeemable in cash. Without such a labor-tax the French administration would have lacked the means to construct many essential public works. But the imposition undoubtedly caused great hardship when, as frequently happened in Upper Volta and the northern Ivory Coast, people were required to work far from their homes, in some cases even in plantations belonging to Europeans. Nor was this the only burden to which France's new African subjects found themselves liable. From 1919, French Africans could be conscripted for military service or for service in special labor battalions. "Although we have abolished slavery," wrote Governor Delafosse, one of the pioneer administrators of Soudan, "the heads of families regard the tax and blood which we exact as much more severe than that which the local princes formerly demanded, because they are now reduced to giving us their own children and they find it difficult to accept this obligation which appears unnatural. . . . They complain . . . that we disintegrate their family and social organization. Many of them are coming to regret the tyranny of an al-Hajj Umar or a Samory which was undoubtedly more capricious but the caprices of which had less general importance and were marked by greater intervals of calm than our own." [87] This was written shortly after World War I when French West Africa had supplied the French army with 181,000 recruits; but French rule was criticized for its harshness no less severely in the 1930's or 1940's, when many young men took the only path of escape open to them and slipped over the border into British territory to evade the often crushing burden of labor service and conscription.

The contrast between British and French rule in West Africa was equally evident in the differing attitudes of the two regimes to indigenous institutions. Between the British resident calling on a Northern Nigerian emir in his spacious palace to discuss local business and a French *commandant* summoning a *chef de canton* to his office to hear his orders lay two very different philosophies of administration. Every energetic colonial administrator, French or British, could regard himself as a modernizer, as "the unknown electrician"—in the vivid metaphor of one French official—"in the powerhouse of a new mode of life . . . releasing the powers of Europe and Africa and transforming them into socially valuable forces." [88] But the French, faced with the task of constructing novel forms of local administration, took their models from their own country or from Algeria. (The *indigénat,* the disciplinary code which permitted a *commandant* to inflict summary punishments for a wide range of minor offences, had first been evolved in Algeria.) British officials, on the other hand, became increasingly concerned, especially in the inter-war years, to work through indigenous political structures. "In my view," wrote Lugard, whose prolific writings made him the most widely read theoretician of British colonial administration, "the tradition of British rule has ever been to arrest disintegration, to retain and build up again what is best in the social and political organization of the conquered dynasties, and to develop on the lines of its own individuality each separate race of which our Great Empire consists." [89]

To the historian anxious to re-create the complex human variety of a particular time and place, the semi-theoretical discussion of colonial administration makes frustrating reading. One needs to get beyond the facile contrast between the "direct" administration of the French and the "indirect rule" of the British to see how colonial overrule really affected the political evolution of particular West African peoples. Fortunately, in recent years a number of scholars, basing their research on oral records and on newly available archival material, have produced detailed local studies of the colonial period. A brief summary of three such studies may provide a more penetrating impression than that conveyed by the conventional textbooks on colonial administration of certain political aspects of the colonial situation before the rise of modern nationalist parties. The first of these studies concerns the Northern Nigerian emirate of Zaria; [90] the second, the impact of British administration on the Tiv, a politically highly fragmented people living in the

Benue valley of Northern Nigeria; [91] the third, the attitude of the French to chieftainship in their colony of Guinea. [92]

The emirate of Zaria formed one of the major provinces of the caliphate of Sokoto. At the time of the British invasion, the emir, Kwassau, was on bad terms with his suzerain at Sokoto and so found it convenient to accept a British garrison peacefully, only to be deposed in 1903 by his new overlords for plotting with their enemies. The British were careful to follow traditional practice in appointing Kwassau's successor. The new emir, Aliyu, was nominated by the sultan of Sokoto on the advice of the electoral council of Zaria and confirmed in office by the British to whom he swore a solemn oath of fealty. One of the first acts of the British had been to put a stop to slave raiding and the crueller forms of punishment. The British then put pressure on the new emir to rationalize and improve his system of administration. In the past, the great fief-holders of the emirate had resided in the capital and made use of intermediaries, known as *jekada,* to act as their agents and tax collectors. The British abolished the office of *jekada* and forced the fief-holders to leave the capital and reside in the districts submitted to their charge. Later, the number of district heads, as the fief-holders came to be known, was reduced, thus easing still further the burden borne by the peasantry of maintaining a horde of office-holders. At the same time, justice was made more easily available by the creation of new *alkali's* courts at district levels, while the judiciary, its numbers greatly expanded, enjoyed a measure of independence such as it had never known under the old regime.

The British brought with them many new techniques designed to improve many aspects of local life. As these techniques came to be accepted, new departments of local government were created in Zaria and an increasingly numerous local bureaucracy came to be formed. By 1950, every district possessed its own agricultural, veterinary, and forest officers, together with a number of teachers, "a warder, scribes, District Treasury officials, police, an *Alkali* and judicial assessors." [93] All senior appointments lay in the hands of the emir. Since the emir was concerned to maintain his own authority to the utmost, he naturally arranged for these posts to be given to his own kinsmen and supporters. When heads of departments controlled appointments to offices under their charge, they too worked on the same basis, paying more attention to family connections than to educational qualifications. The British could force the dismissal of those found guilty of gross corruption but, being anxious not to reduce the prestige of the emir unduly, they made it a rule that a local official should always be present, whenever a private individual wanted to lodge a complaint—a routine that effectively served to muzzle criticism from the grass roots. In these circumstances the emirate of Zaria could be described as "an autocracy ineffectively supervised by the British." [94] But in the course of half a century of British overrule the emirate had been transformed from the "unstable, unqualified absolutism" of the last years of independent Fulani rule into "an effective limited absolutism which showed signs of considerable stability." [95]

In contrast to the hierarchical structure of society and the highly developed political institutions found among the Hausa and Fulani of Zaria emirate, the Tiv of the Benue valley presented the British with the difficult task of working out an effective system of administration for a highly egalitarian people whose largest form of traditional polity was represented by a group of compounds described by early administrators as a "township" and governed by a council of elders made up of compound-heads. The Tiv, whose numbers were estimated at 350,000, were one of the last Nigerian peoples to be brought under British administration. The first British administrators in the area were quick to realize that nothing would be gained by military expeditions and set about extending British rule by making friendly contact with the communities living in the neighborhood of their headquarters. They saw no advantage in attempting to impose the alien notion of taxation until the Tiv had received practical evidence of the advantages of British rule. Whatever local district officers might feel about the peculiar nature of Tiv society, to their superiors, the senior administrators who controlled the government of Northern Nigeria and who had gained almost all their experience in the emirates of the Sokoto caliphate, the Tiv presented a tiresome anomaly. By the second decade of the twentieth century the notion that every African society possessed its own traditional "chief" had become part of the dogma of "indirect rule." District officers in Tiv country were accordingly ordered to find chiefs, who could be given the same responsibilities as district heads in the Hausa emirates. In the early 1920's a historically minded lieutenant-governor, H. R. Palmer, noted that the Jukun, northern neighbors of the Tiv, had once formed a substantial empire with an elaborate culture some aspects of which could—in Palmer's opinion—be associated with ancient Egypt. The Jukun empire collapsed in the seventeenth century but Palmer was determined to revive something of the glories of this once-imperial people by placing half the population of Tivland under the administration of the Jukun chief, the Aku of Wukari. This extraordinary exercise in administrative antiquarianism ended in total failure. Nor was the attempt to transform certain compound-heads into district chiefs any more successful. The newly promoted men began to abuse their authority, behaving in a way so untypical of normal Tiv society that their neighbors accused them of turning into witches and of indulging in anthropophagous rites to increase their power. By the late 1920's popular resentment burst out into a series of violent "witch-hunts" which completely shattered the structure of local administration.

The British then set about devising a new scheme more in keeping with traditional Tiv institutions. A three-tier system of councils was established at kindred, clan, and tribal levels. Kindred councils were required to elect spokesmen, but the new office, originally intended to rotate from one compound-head to another, often came to remain in the same hands, and the new spokesmen indulged in the same abuses as the old district chiefs, thus provoking in the late 1930's a renewed outburst of antiwitchcraft agitation. There followed a long-drawn-out investigation into local institutions by a British district officer who concluded, erroneously so it appears in the light of later anthropological research, that the Tiv possessed certain custodians of authority whom he described as "patriarchs." These "patriarchs" were identified and invested with authority. At the same time, a careful watch was maintained to prevent the recurrence of outbreaks of antiwitchcraft agitation. A few years later the Tiv took a more positive role in shaping their political future. Aware of the great prestige enjoyed by Muslim emirs in other parts of Northern Nigeria, they pressed the British administration to allow them to create a paramount chief of their own. Accordingly, in 1947 the office of Tor Tiv was established, an ex-sergeant-major being installed as the first incumbent. Two years later an executive council was appointed to assist the new paramount in his responsibilities.

There was a sharp contrast between the British acceptance of a diversity of forms of local political organization and the French drive toward a measure of administrative uniformity. A study of French administration in the colony of Guinea provides a vivid illustration of French methods. In precolonial days Guinea contained a wide range of forms of political organization. In the center lay the imamate of Futa Jallon with its powerful Fulani aristocracy. The coastal areas to the west were divided up among a large number of minor chiefdoms. The Malinke country to the east was also divided up, at least until its incorporation in Samory's empire, among many petty principalities, while the communities living in the forest country along the Liberian border presented the spectacle, superficially interpreted as anarchic, of a multitude of independent villages.

For some years after its occupation by French troops the imamate of Futa Jallon enjoyed the status of a protectorate. But French administrators soon made their authority felt, deporting local notables suspected of hostility to the new regime, dividing up the territories formerly controlled by the greater provincial chiefs and, in 1910, abolishing the office of the paramount, the *almami*. With its territory carved up among a number of administrative *cantons,* Futa Jallon ceased to exist even as the hollow shell of an ancient state.

Every colonial regime needs native intermediaries. The French had destroyed the *grands chefs,* the rulers of the major African polities in their territories, but they could not afford to dispense with the services of lesser notables, the more important of whom were designated *chefs de canton,* their subordinates *chefs de village.* But as Governor-General van Vollenhoven pointed out in a famous circular issued in 1917, these chiefs possessed "no power in their own rights." "Only the *commandant de cercle* commands . . . the native chief is only an instrument, an auxiliary." [96] In most parts of Guinea the French found it possible to make use of notables sprung from families which had enjoyed chiefly status in precolonial times. Only among the egalitarian village communities of the forest area along the Liberian frontier was chieftainship an entirely novel institution. In these areas, the position of the man, often an ex-soldier or one-time government clerk, appointed by the local administrator to act as village or *canton* chief, usually proved a peculiarly difficult one. Reviled by his neighbors for his novel authority, yet constantly in trouble with his French superiors for failing to carry out their orders, he found himself threatened on the one side by "the prison of the *commandant,*" on the other by "the poison of the 'witchdoctor'." [97]

In other areas of Guinea local chiefs found it possible to use their position for their own advantage. Their duties were onerous—collecting taxes, providing men for labor or military service, arresting malefactors, keeping a check on their community's food reserves, and so on, and their salary was meager. But so long as they performed their duties effectively—inefficiency could be punished by dismissal or even imprisonment—French officials were usually prepared to turn a blind eye to their exactions and misdeeds. It was easy enough for a *canton* chief to find ways of enriching himself at the expense of the local peasantry. During World War II the pressure exerted by the chiefs became even more burdensome. For the French colonial authorities, eager, after the collapse of the Vichy regime, to demonstrate their enthusiastic devotion to the Allied cause by increasing the production of raw materials, required individual territories to meet totally unrealistic quotas, and the chiefs were naturally given the task of ensuring that the peasantry met these exorbitant demands. After the war many of the chiefs developed new and highly extravagant tastes. In the past they had required local people to render labor service by working in their fields or by helping to build their houses. Now they began to demand cash contributions to meet the cost of American cars or pilgrimages by air to Mecca. By this time, however, a new force had appeared in the countryside— the agents of the first political parties. Soon the chiefs found themselves powerless in the face of collective resistance to their depredations. In 1957, the last year of the colonial regime in Guinea, with nationalist politicians and French administrators both equally convinced of the need to put an end to an outdated system, the office of chief was abolished.

The contrasting systems of native administration in the British and French West African territories formed the subject of constant debate during the last decades of the colonial era. Most Western-educated British West Africans were bitterly critical of the concept of "indirect rule" which seemed to them to leave power in the hands of the most autocratic and "reactionary" elements in the community. And certainly it was true that the most ardent British advocates of "indirect rule" had no use for the "educated native." More "lugardist" than Lugard, they were romantically intent on preserving the picturesque culture of "traditional" Africa from the "corrosion" of the modern world. But there were other administrators, no less sympathetic to traditional culture, who came to share the doubts of educated Africans. "The masses of the people," wrote R. S. Rattray, an administrator famous for his studies of Ashanti, "are likely to become estranged owing to the undoubted tendency of Indirect Rule, as now applied, to build up centralized African autocracies, disregarding the bases of former African constitutions and states which were essentially decentralized and democratic." [98] In the light of hindsight one can see clearly enough that most senior British officials, in their preoccupation with local government, were giving far too little thought to the strengthening of that overall administrative structure needed to maintain the unity of a modern nation-state. But men may never fairly be blamed for lacking prophetic vision. In the 1930's the emergence of independent African states was a development almost impossible for most European administrators to conceive. In spite of these criticisms there was much that could then and can still be said in favor of the policy of "indirect rule." The system served to shield many African communities from the more abrasive effects of the colonial impact. It provided a considerable number of Africans with an opportunity to follow useful and satisfying careers, or, as paternalistic administrators preferred to put it, "to develop a spirit of responsibility and initiative." And it made for the gradual transformation of older institutions by exposing them to the stimulus of new ideas and new techniques.

In the years between the two wars, French theorists writing about colonial administration preferred to speak of *association* rather than *assimilation* in describing the relationship between the metropolis and the colonies. To outside observers, however, the French system appeared to be based on the basically assimilationist assumption that it was "to the African's own interest to pass as rapidly as possible from the use of his own institutions and his own language to a regime of French civilization and French language." [99] Englishmen and Frenchmen both shared an arrogant and quite unshakable conviction in the superiority of their own culture. But there was something hermetic about the early twentieth-century Englishman's concept of his own culture: he could not see it as a commodity suitable for export. On the other hand, to French administrators there seemed nothing illogical about attempting to turn Africans into "black Frenchmen." French rule was often harsh, it permitted many abuses, but it possessed a certain intellectual generosity that struck many Africans as immensely attractive. A British observer, writing in 1936, noted that "the French attitude towards the educated native arouses the bitter envy of his contemporary in neighboring British colonies." [100] Sixteen years later, the American, John Gunther, noted that "the Africans whom the French do succeed in turning into Frenchmen are on the whole more loyal to France than British-educated Africans of the same class are to Britain." [101] Yet one must not overestimate the good fortune of the French West African *évolué*. Many educated Senegalese found it preferable to take employment in France rather than endure the humiliations of colonial society. The *évolué* could also be seen in African eyes as a "renegade," scathingly described by the Senegalese poet, David Diop, as his "poor brother in immaculate evening dress . . . pleading in the parlours of condescension." [102]

Whatever the cost to the sensibilities of two or three generations of Africans, the alien rulers of West Africa succeeded, in a remarkably short period, in constructing a framework of more stable and extensive polities than the region had ever known in the past. In the years after World War II the foreign overlords found themselves compelled by a variety of forces rapidly to liberalize their regimes. But the political developments of the postwar years can be understood only when seen against the background of the complex changes that affected many aspects of the economic and social life of the region in the decades of undisputed alien hegemony.

▲▼ WEST AFRICAN ECONOMIES IN THE COLONIAL ERA

In the course of the second millennium A.D. the peoples of West Africa had developed a pattern of economic activity more complex than that to be found in any other region of sub-Saharan Africa. As in every other part of the continent, the vast majority of the population earned their living from the land. But few West African communities were constricted by the straitjacket of a purely subsistence economy. A vigorous local trade flourished in almost every district, finding its outlet in a multitude of markets of varying size. A vivid impression of the variety of goods available at one of the larger markets of the forest zone is provided by a list compiled by an American missionary who lived in Yoruba country in the 1850's: "various kinds of meat, fowls, sheep, goats, dogs, rats, tortoises, eggs, fish, snails, yams, Indian corn, Guinea corn, sweet potatoes, sugar cane, ground peas, onions, pepper, various vegetables, palm nuts, oil, tree butter, seeds, fruit, fire-wood, cotton in the seed, spun cotton, domestic cloth, imported cloth, as calico, as shirting, velvets, etc., gunpowder, guns, flints, knives, swords, paper, raw silk, Turkey-red thread, beads, needles, ready-made clothing, as trowsers, breeches, caps, shirts without sleeves, baskets, brooms." [103] A list such as this gives some indication of the wide range of foodstuffs produced in one of the more highly developed areas of West Africa. It also reveals the variety of manufactured objects, some of local origin, the majority imported, available in areas lying about a hundred miles from the coast.

A host of traders were involved in the internal distribution of imported goods and local produce. A few West African merchants, based on the main entrepôts of the coast or of the Sudanic zone, possessed substantial capital resources, but the vast majority of men and women trading at local markets obtained from their petty transactions no more than a modest supplement to a family income basically derived from agriculture. Naturally the range and type of goods offered for sale varied from area to area. There were striking variations too in forms of transport. Sixty-ton canoes carried rice, millet, and honey, together with minute quantities of gold dust from Jenne and other markets on the Upper Niger to Timbuktu, one of the entrepôts to which the trans-Saharan camel caravans brought salt from mines deep in the desert, together with the varied and enticing merchandise produced by the Mediterranean world. Caravans, made up of a multitude of small traders, some with donkeys, others carrying their wares on their heads, plied regularly between the main Sudanic towns and the kola-producing areas in northern Ashanti and the forest country to the west. Yet other traders collected the goods sought by Europeans and brought them by canoe or head-porterage to the flourishing commercial centers on the coast.

Often, before the establishment of the colonial *pax,* the current of local commerce found itself dammed. Predatory nomads closed some of the Saharan routes for months, even years at a time. Local wars interrupted the activities of traders at the region's major outlets, the entrepôts of the northern savanna and of the Guinea coast. And a few areas were virtually denuded of population by the depredations of slave-raiders. Nevertheless, the impression vividly conveyed by the narratives of contemporary European travelers is often one of exuberant activity—of thronged markets and well-trodden paths. Moreover, it is clear from available statistics that during the third quarter of the nineteenth century, when groundnuts and palm oil had firmly replaced slaves as the region's major export, commercial activity was steadily increasing. Between the 1850's and the 1880's "the value of West Africa's import and export trade roughly doubled." [104]

The establishment of colonial rule introduced a new element into the economies of West Africa. To the activities of local people, farmers, traders and craftsmen, and of alien merchants was added the driving force of new governments, at once more stable and far better endowed in material terms than even the most powerful of the old indigenous polities. To an age such as the present, obsessed with the problems of economic development and accustomed to think pejoratively of all colonial regimes, "driving force" may well seem a term inapplicable to the governments that ruled West Africa in the first half of the twentieth century. Yet even the most conservative of colonial governments was forced to think seriously about the problems of development, if only to meet the cost of maintaining an administrative structure far more elaborate than any the region had ever known before. Moreover, European expansion in West Africa occurred at a time when Europeans were becoming increasingly conscious of their ability to master almost any natural environment, to extract wealth from the "undeveloped estates" of the world. No doubt the majority of imperially minded politicians in Britain and France were more concerned with the advantages West African colonies might offer as producers of raw materials and consumers of manufactured goods. No doubt the majority of European officials, often working under conditions of great hardship, lonely, sometimes frightened, often in indifferent health, found it impossible to lift their eyes beyond the exhausting routine of administration. Nevertheless, throughout the period of colonial rule there existed a creative minority of Europeans, intellectual heirs of the humanitarians of the anti-slavery movement, upholders of the "civilizing mission" in the best sense of that much-abused term, men and women who would have accepted Victor Hugo's dictum that "to improve material life is to improve moral life."

The extent to which colonial officials could devote their energies to the tasks of development varied from decade to decade. In the late 1890's, the British in Lagos were able to embark on a series of schemes for urban improvement on a scale that would have been unthinkable ten years earlier. A glance at the colony's revenue statistics shows how this new development became possible: before 1892 revenue rarely exceeded £60,000; between 1893—the year of the establishment of the British protectorate over Yorubaland—and 1902 it rose from £115,000 to £364,000. Again it was very much easier to think constructively about development in the buoyant early 1950's, when the rising prices of most West African products was putting more money than ever before into the hands of colonial governments, than in the gloomy years of the Great Depression when governments found themselves with no alternative but to reduce expenditure and even dismiss staff. (In the Gold Coast revenue fell from £5.2 million in 1927 to £2.3 million in 1931; it rose from £3.7 million in 1938 to £50 million in 1953.) Nevertheless, whatever the fluctuations of the world economy, development in some form remained a constant preoccupation of the region's new rulers. And the more imaginative would have agreed wholeheartedly with Governor Macgregor when he said of Lagos in 1903, "the future development of this country must be by its own people, through its own people and for its own people." [105]

To many colonial officials, as to a later generation of African nationalists and their European sympathizers, metropolitan governments seemed exceedingly mean in their attitude toward colonial finance. Until the 1930's, British politicians and treasury officials acted on the principle that colonial territories should be self-supporting. Assistance in the form of direct grants-in-aid was provided only in the event of dire necessity. The Gold Coast government, for example, was given £619,000 between 1898 and 1901 to meet the initial cost of administering the newly acquired Northern Territories and to cover emergency expenditure on the military forces needed to suppress the Ashanti rebellion. In 1929 the British government set up the Colonial Development Fund, but by 1936 the West African territories had received less than £1 million from this source. Not until after World War II were the British prepared to make substantial grants to assist West African development.

The French were more willing to make direct grants to their colonies, the poorest of which could, indeed, not have survived without regular subsidies, but the complex system of official accounting makes it impossible to deduce from the published figures the exact amount of French grants-in-aid. However it is clear that until the late 1940's the French, no less than the British, preferred to render assistance by the painless and indirect method of underwriting loans raised by colonial governments at commercial rates of interest. By 1936 British West African governments raised £44 million by this means, the Federation of French West Africa about £15 million. This total of £59 million for the region as a whole seems very small when set against the £224 million raised by South African governments in publicly listed loans between 1870 and 1936. Nevertheless, seen in historical perspective, this novel process of borrowing from abroad represented an infusion of wealth into the region of a kind and on a scale such as West Africa had never known before. Without this borrowed money the colonial governments would never have been able to undertake many of the public works that provided the essential foundations for future development.

By the standards of late nineteenth-century Europe, West Africa was a land without roads. In the dry season a man on foot could travel easily enough along the bridle tracks of the savanna or the narrow paths of the forest. But the rains turned tracks into quagmires and rendered many streams and rivers temporarily impassable. Except on the few navigable rivers, head-porterage and pack animals provided the only means of transportation. In the savanna both the British and the French introduced horse-drawn wheeled vehicles, but the innovation proved abortive. Until the widespread diffusion of motor transport in the 1920's colonial governments could do little more than widen existing paths and construct a few bridges. Of French West Africa it was said that "roads hardly existed outside certain urban areas in 1914." By 1937, however, 50,000 kilometers of motorable roads had been constructed.[106] Thus, in the first decades of the century the governments of every territory—the Gambia with its navigable river alone excepted— were forced to undertake the formidable task of railroad construction as an essential preliminary to "opening up the country." West Africa's first railroad was built by the French between 1882 and 1885 to connect St. Louis with Dakar. The more ambitious plan, begun at the same time, to link the Senegal with the Niger by rail took forty years to complete. More spectacular was the British achievement in linking Lagos with Kano by a railroad begun in 1896 and completed with the construction of a rail bridge across the Niger at Jebba in 1916. The turn of the century also saw the construction of a number of shorter railroads in French, German, and British territories, each constructed with the aim of linking the cash-crop producing areas of the hinterland with the coast. Many of these lines were extended in the 1920's.

"Our railways will revolutionize the conditions of the Protectorate," wrote Governor Bell of Northern Nigeria in 1911. "Not only is the construction of the Baro–Kano railway having a great effect on markets and districts within a wide radius, but it is also having a remarkable educative influence on the primitive inhabitants of districts which had never before come into touch with Europeans and their methods"—a point he was able to illustrate from the report of one of his residents who described how "a few sections of low-grade Pagans arrived on the work stark naked . . . and returned to their homes with clothes on their bodies and money in their hands." [107] Northern Nigeria's commercial statistics soon confirmed the governor's prediction that the railways would "render the territory self-supporting." In 1911, the protectorate's exports were worth £836,000. The completion of the railroad made possible for the first time the export of groundnuts from the Kano area. By 1925 Northern Nigeria was sending overseas more than 100,000 tons of groundnuts worth more than £2 million.

The construction of improved port facilities was a necessary sequel to the building of the railroads. The wharves and warehouses of Dakar, Conakry, and Abidjan, of Takoradi, Lagos, and Port Harcourt must be counted among the monuments of the colonial era. Abidjan, sited on the landward side of a coastal lagoon, was not accessible to ocean-going vessels until the completion of the Vridi Canal in 1950. So great was the improvement offered by the new harbor compared with the old ports of Grand Bassam and Port Bouet, where ships had to transfer their cargoes to lighters, that traffic immediately increased by 50 percent. Without this great feat of engineering the dramatic expansion in the economy of the Ivory Coast would not have been possible.

The "communications revolution" in West Africa, the greatest technical achievement of the colonial powers, served to confirm a development that could be traced back to the arrival of the first European traders on the coast of Guinea in the late fifteenth century. At that time the Sudanic belt of West Africa with its powerful states and its vigorous commercial links with the Mediterranean world was clearly the most favorable area in the region for the absorption and diffusion of cultural innovations. The growth of the Atlantic trade brought a gradual increase of wealth to many coastal communities. By the end of the colonial era it was clear that the major centers of creative activity were to be found not in the distant interior but on or near the coast. The trans-Saharan links with the Mediterranean world gradually withered away. Famous cities—Jenne, Timbuktu, Sokoto, and others—declined into sleepy backwaters.

Some of the capitals chosen by the colonial administrations had been no more than fishing villages in 1875; brash new towns, they became the pace-setters of a new age.

The colonial governments made other contributions to the development of West African economies. They alone were in a position to introduce an effective system of currency. At the time of the European conquest West African societies possessed a variety of locally accepted currencies: brass rods, iron bars, gold dust, bottles of gin, and, commonest of all, cowrie shells, were among the commodities used as media of exchange. But these currencies were either in short supply or so bulky that their use served to inhibit the development of trade. To many early administrators "the circulation of coinage" represented "one of the most important signs of progress in a new country," [108] and much attention was paid to the manifold problems involved, the diffusion of the new coins, the gradual elimination of other currencies, the introduction of the strange novelty of paper money, the establishment of banks and currency boards.

All the West African colonial governments developed specialized departments for agriculture, veterinary services, and forestry. Given the limited staffs at their disposal—there were less than 300 Europeans employed in these departments in the British West African territories in the late 1930's—the total impact of this aspect of the colonial governments' work on the economy of the region as a whole could hardly be more than marginal. Moreover, government agricultural and veterinary officers were forced to start from a basis of almost total ignorance of the peculiar nature of the West African environment. They were, however, able to profit from the development of a tradition of practical research into the problems of tropical agriculture to which European botanists and agronomists had contributed throughout the nineteenth century. Special stress was laid on the diffusion of "useful plants" and the botanical gardens founded and maintained by the colonial governments provided centers for experiments with new species introduced from other parts of the tropical world and for the detailed investigation of the complex problems associated with pests, plant diseases, and soil fertility. The gradual accumulation of a mass of exact information relating to the agricultural economy of West Africa must be counted among the most valuable achievements of the colonial era.

It is difficult to generalize about the changes introduced by colonial officials into the economy of West African peoples. The Germans during their relatively brief spell as rulers of Togo embarked on a comprehensive policy for agricultural improvement that greatly impressed contemporary observers. (The invitation extended by the German government before World War I to American Negro agricultural students to come over to Togo and teach local farmers improved methods of cotton cultivation was a particularly imaginative gesture.) The French were prepared to use coercive measures to ensure that local farmers adopted new crops. By contrast "the common British alternative of persuading local farmers here and there to experiment" seemed, to one shrewd British observer, "desperately slow and by no means sure." [109] In fact, the responsiveness of local communities was dependent on a number of variables. The oil-palm research center established by the British near Benin appears to have "made very little, if any, impact on the peasant-controlled oil-palm economy," its officers failing to persuade farmers to go to the trouble of replacing their semi-wild palms by higher-yielding species introduced from overseas.[110] Cocoa farmers, on the other hand, proved far more willing to accept advice given them on ways of improving the quality of their crop and of combatting pests and diseases.

European traders made a substantial contribution to the development of precolonial African communities by opening up new markets for their products. The European conquest of West Africa immensely extended the range of opportunities open to the alien trader. In 1875 the banks of the Senegal, the Gambia, and the Niger were the only parts of the interior where European trading establishments were to be found. By 1910 it was possible for European traders to travel freely in almost every part of the region, untroubled by the restrictions formerly imposed by local chiefs. One consequence of these enlarged opportunities was a rapid increase in the number of Europeans engaged in commerce. Thus in Northern Nigeria the "nonofficial" European community rose from 65 in 1905 to 493 in 1919. But Europeans were not the only aliens to profit from the new commercial situation. In the last years of the nineteenth century a number of Syrians and Lebanese, emigrants from their poverty-stricken homeland to Brazil and the United States, found themselves rerouted to Dakar where they were allowed to settle. In 1897 there were twenty-eight Syrians in French West Africa, but as news of their success in business reached their families at home, friends and relations came out to join them. By 1909 the Syrian community exceeded 1,000. Forty years later the Syrian population of West Africa numbered 15,000.

The primary function of these alien traders was to provide an effective channel between African producers and consumers and European manufacturers. In historical terms the Syrian peddlers who made their way up country from Freetown in the 1890's, the European agents of trading firms maintaining stores and buying stations in districts where white men had never been seen before were fulfilling the same purpose as the *dyula* traders and the Maghribi merchants of earlier centuries. Pioneers of new commercial frontiers, they added new strands to the fragile links between West African peasant communities and the outside world. Alien traders possessed certain advantages over their indigenous competitors—wider contacts, more substantial sources of capital, more sophisticated commercial techniques, but their enterprises remained hazardous, for the price of African products was subject to constant fluctuations in the world market. Moreover, much of their business was dependent on credit, with goods or money being advanced to the African middlemen who dealt directly with local producers and consumers, a practice that inevitably brought with it the risk of default.

In these circumstances it was natural that European merchants doing business in West Africa should seek to find a measure of protection through cooperation, mergers, and partnerships. By the 1930's the relatively large number of small European traders to be found in West Africa in the first decades of the century had been replaced by a few great commercial concerns, described as "oligopolies" by some economists and regarded by their critics as capable of exerting a baneful influence on the economy of the region as a whole. A brief account of the genesis of the largest of these firms, the United Africa Company, serves to illustrate this new development. Shortly before World War I, the British firm of Lever Brothers, the largest soap manufacturer in the United Kingdom, bought up a number of small trading companies in West Africa, as part of a policy designed to bring the manufacturer more closely in touch with the producer of his raw material (palm oil) and thus achieve a valuable economy by cutting out the profits hitherto obtained by middlemen. The rise in raw material prices during and immediately after World War I led Lever to carry this policy still further by buying up the famous Niger (formerly Royal Niger) Company in 1920. In the previous year a number of old-established British West African firms, some with a history going back to the eighteenth century, merged to form the African and Eastern Trading Corporation. In 1929 this corporation merged with the Niger Company to form the United Africa Company, itself a subsidiary of the massive concern of Unilever. The new company had at its disposal in the persons of the employees of the old firms that had been taken over an impressive repository of commercial experience; at the same time it could draw on infinitely greater sources of capital than any other European firm in the region. Thus equipped, the new company was able constantly to diversify its activities beyond its primary function as an import-export agency. By the late 1930's, the U.A.C.'s interests had expanded to include "shipping, river and motor transport, oil palm and rubber plantations, mining royalties, cold storage depots, automobile and agricultural machinery agencies, bakeries, cotton ginning, tank installations and timber concessions." [111]

During the 1930's the European "oligopolies" came under attack from African nationalists for a variety of reasons. They were accused of forming "price-rings" designed to keep down produce prices, of employing Europeans in jobs for which Africans should have been trained, and of handing their profits over to European shareholders rather than plowing them back into the country from which they were derived. For their part the directors of the great trading firms could reply that "few commercial companies had to conduct their affairs in a more delicate and difficult *milieu*," [112] that they had in fact poured a lot of money into the region (£66 million of private capital had been invested in British West Africa by 1936 and £14 million in French West Africa), and that it was clearly in their own interests, given the fact that the European working in the tropics was the "most expensive of God's creatures," requiring special housing, medical facilities, and overseas leave, to train and promote Africans as rapidly as possible. The historian cannot hope to reach a satisfactory conclusion on this matter until the firms themselves have opened all their archives to impartial researchers.

Two other smaller groups of Europeans, the miners and the planters, were directly concerned with the economic development of West Africa. European miners, frequently backed by capital raised on the London money-market, brought with them technical equipment more elaborate than that possessed by old-established African miners and so were able to reach deposits of tin and of gold that would otherwise have remained inaccessible. On the Gold Coast European gold-mining began in the late 1870's, but production remained on a modest scale until the turn of the century when the sudden fall in South African exports of gold as a result of the Anglo-Boer War brought a minor "rush" to the Gold Coast. As a result, exports rose from 6,000 oz. in 1901 to 400,000 oz. in 1914. In the years before World War I another "rush" brought European prospectors to the tin fields of Northern Nigeria, where fifty companies or private individuals invested £4 million by 1913. In 1915 West Africa's first and only colliery was opened at Enugu in Eastern Nigeria, being managed and run as a state enterprise by the colonial government. Most of the coal produced was used by the Nigerian railways. In 1919 another important source of wealth, accessible to both Africans and Europeans, was revealed when a government geologist came across alluvial diamonds in the Gold Coast. In the French territories mining enterprise developed very much more slowly, French investors showing themselves much more cautious than their British contemporaries in providing capital for enterprises outside Europe. As early as

1912 easily workable deposits of bauxite were discovered on the Isles de Los off the coast of French Guinea, but a serious attempt to exploit the site was not made until after World War II, when the French government embarked on a massive survey of French West Africa's mineral deposits.

The role of European planters was less important in West Africa than in most other tropical lands. As early as the last decades of the eighteenth century Europeans had attempted to establish plantations of commercial crops in the neighborhood of their West African settlements, but local disturbances and the high mortality rate among Europeans led to the collapse of all these experiments. During the colonial era powerful economic arguments were advanced in favor of plantations, and a number of European estates were formed in French West Africa, mostly in the Ivory Coast, where European planters played a leading part in the introduction of coffee as an agricultural crop and in the development of an export trade in bananas. But the total amount of land alienated was very small, 422 square miles, a mere 0.06 percent of the total cultivatable area of French West Africa. In the British territories, colonial administrators, apprehensive of the disturbances European planters might cause with their demands for native labor, resolutely refused to allow the establishment of commercial plantations on a substantial scale, an act of political wisdom that brought down on them the bitter criticism of disappointed commercial interests in Britain.

During the colonial era most writers on West Africa overstressed the contribution made by outsiders to the economic development of the region. Achievements associated with alien enterprise should certainly not be underestimated, but it seems reasonable to suggest that the greatest contribution to the economic development of West Africa came from West African peoples themselves. Obviously the great works of construction—the roads, the railroads, and the harbors—could never have been undertaken without the assistance of African labor. In this field the initiative usually came from Europeans. In two other fields of economic activity, however, the diffusion of cash crops and the expansion of internal trade, West Africans, spontaneously taking advantage of new opportunities, were able to make a massive contribution to the transformation of their economy.

The most spectacular example of African enterprise is provided by the history of the cocoa industry in the Gold Coast, Nigeria, and the Ivory Coast. Cocoa, a plant indigenous to the New World, was carried across the Atlantic by the Spaniards and the Portuguese who established plantations in their island colonies of Fernando Po and São Tomé. In 1879, Tetteh Quashie, a blacksmith from the Gold Coast, obtained a few cocoa seeds from Fernando Po, planted them on his farm in Akwa-pim, and became the first West African successfully to grow the new crop. Ten years later, Governor Griffiths of the Gold Coast, an administrator with long experience of the West Indies, set up botanical gardens at Aburi, imported cocoa seeds, and arranged for young plants to be distributed to local farmers. About the same time, a number of enterprising Yoruba businessmen from Lagos established the first cocoa plantations in Western Nigeria. Cocoa was introduced to the Ivory Coast in the same decade, but the first plantations failed through being sited on unfavorable soil. In 1912, Governor Angoulvant resumed the attempt in another area where the local people were compelled to plant the new crop. Once cocoa had become firmly established in an area, local farmers were quick to realize its money-making potentialities. In all three territories production rose very rapidly. On the Gold Coast a mere 80 lbs., worth no more than £4, was exported in 1891; by the 1920's production had passed the 200,000 ton mark, and sales brought in between £4.7 million (1921) and £11.7 million (1928), three-quarters of the total value of the country's exports. Nigeria began exporting cocoa in 1907 and earned between £1 and £2 million a year from the crop in the 1920's, while the Ivory Coast's exports rose from 1,000 tons in 1920 to 52,000 tons in 1938.

The stimulus afforded by colonial governments played some part in the diffusion of the new crop, but the successful establishment of this highly lucrative addition to the local economy must be seen as a great pioneering achievement carried out by African businessmen and peasant farmers. "This man," wrote Governor Clifford of the Gold Coast cocoa-farmer, "has carved from the virgin forest an enormous clearing, which he has covered with flourishing cocoa farms. Armed with nothing better than an imported axe and machete and a native-made hoe, he has cut down the forest giant, cleared the tropical undergrowth and kept it cleared. With no means of transport, no railways and few roads, he has conveyed his produce to the sea, rolling it down in casks for miles and carrying it on his own sturdy cranium." [113]

In the Sudanic belt groundnuts (peanuts), another plant of American origin, played much the same role in the local economy as cocoa and palm oil in the forest areas. Groundnuts were first exported from Senegambia in the 1840's. With the construction of railroads, first in Senegal and later in Northern Nigeria, production for export increased very rapidly. Rural landscapes in Senegal were transformed by the expansion of the new crop. "Villages and towns sprang up as the rails [of the St. Louis-Dakar and Dakar-Niger railroads] advanced, and areas that formerly had been almost wasteland became fertile with groundnuts." [114]

A new Muslim fraternity, the Muridiyya, played a large part in the expansion of the new cash-crop economy in Senegal. "Work," Ahmad Bamba (d. 1927), the founder of the fraternity, urged his followers, "is part of religion." Accordingly *marabouts* of the new order gathered their students round them and went out into the hitherto uncultivated bush to found farming settlements organized on cooperative lines. In Northern Nigeria the stimulus to expand groundnut production came not from European businessmen and officials, who were more interested in encouraging the growing of cotton, but from Hausa merchants who toured the villages of Kano emirate telling headmen and farmers of the good price and the attractive imported goods they could obtain by selling groundnuts, a crop hitherto grown on a modest scale for local consumption. Agricultural innovations adopted by local farmers were not confined to crops intended mainly for the export trade. The growth of towns and the expansion of internal trade led to a rising demand for a wide range of basic food crops. As a result a number of food crops of alien origin came to be grown in areas where they had been quite unknown in precolonial times. Thus in Western Nigeria cassava (manioc), whose introduction was associated with the return of freed slaves from Sierra Leone in the 1840's and 1850's, spread farther inland, even replacing yams in some districts as the staple foodstuff, while citrus fruits and tomatoes provided a novel and nutritive supplement to the diet of many Yoruba communities.

The expansion of agriculture and the improvement in communications created many new opportunities for enterprising traders. Shortage of capital and lack of managerial skill prevented West Africans from moving into the commanding heights of the colonial economy. But it is worth noting that between the 1890's and the 1920's, when the fall in price of most export crops led to many bankruptcies in the business world of the West Coast, a number of African businessmen succeeded in carrying on a flourishing import-export trade. *The Red Book of West Africa,* an entertaining and informative commercial directory published in 1920, gives details of some of these men. S. Thomas and Co., for example, an African-directed firm of general merchants with its head office in Lagos, possessed twenty branches up country and employed eight Europeans and fifty African clerks. Another successful African-owned firm was directed by S. H. Pearce, born in Lagos in 1866, educated at the C.M.S. Grammar School and apprenticed to a British firm in whose service he acquired "a great knowledge of general merchandise and commercial law." Setting up in business on his own, he eventually succeeded in making a fortune out of the ivory trade in Calabar. By the age of fifty he was one of the pillars of Lagos society, a leading member of many boards, societies, and committees, and the owner of a massive mansion, "Elephant House," widely famed for the elegance of its ballroom.[115]

The growth of the European "oligopolies" and of some smaller Lebanese firms presented men such as Thomas and Pearce with competition they were unable to resist. But the European trading companies were themselves dependent on the collaboration of many smaller African traders. In the 1930's European firms on the Gold Coast were making use of the services of 1,500 brokers and 37,000 subbrokers to bring in the export crops to their buying stations. Moreover, there were certain fields, such as local transport or the trade in indigenous foodstuffs, which European firms did not attempt to enter. Here it was possible for an exceptionally enterprising man to achieve remarkable results. A cattle dealer living in Accra in the 1950's, who had begun life as an immigrant farm laborer, was importing cattle from as far afield as Timbuktu, Lake Chad, and Duala in the Cameroons and had developed "secondary interests" that included "grain dealing and the operation of a transport enterprise serving places as far afield as Khartoum." "Although he cannot sign his name," an admiring British economist recorded, "he recently gave a deposit of £50,000 on a government contract." [116] A detailed study of many West African communities in the first half of the twentieth century would certainly reveal many more modest success stories, the record of enterprising men and women who responded vigorously to the opportunities presented by a new age.

▲▼ SOCIAL AND INTELLECTUAL CHANGES IN
WEST AFRICA DURING THE COLONIAL PERIOD

Even as late as the 1950's, the last years of the colonial era, the traveler in many rural parts of West Africa might well assume that little or nothing had changed in the life of the people in the course of the last half-century. Men still pursued the traditional agricultural routine of shifting cultivation, using implements no more elaborate than a locally made iron hoe and a machete. Women walked long distances to obtain water from muddy streams or the pools left in dry-season river beds. In areas untouched by the Christian mission or the Muslim *mallam* ("teacher"), dress was sometimes confined to a leather girdle and an apron of freshly picked leaves. Appallingly high rates of infant mortality were common. Features such as these were—and indeed still are— to be found in the many thousands of West African villages that lie lost in the bush, to be reached by hours, sometimes even days, of walking from the nearest motor road. (The study of a large scale map, detailed enough to show every major path and hamlet, provides a salutary lesson in the isolation of many African communities.) In West Africa, as indeed in every other part of the world, one must look to the towns for the most striking manifestations of change.

In many parts of West Africa urbanization does not represent a purely modern phenomenon. Some of the cities of the Sudanic belt—Kano, Katsina, Gao, Timbuktu, Jenne, and others—have a recorded history reaching back at least seven hundred years. In the densely populated Yoruba country, large towns must for a long time have been one of the most striking features of the landscape. The capitals of Benin (Benin City), of Ashanti (Kumasi) and Dahomey (Abomey) have a history as long as that of the states themselves. And there are many other small urban centers whose dating awaits the research of the archaeologist. But, as in every other part of the continent, the period of European rule brought a rapid increase in the pace of urbanization. In some areas the European rulers found it necessary to found entirely new towns as administrative or commercial centers. Two of the regional capitals of Nigeria, Kaduna in the north and Enugu in the east, fall into this category; so, too, does the Eastern Nigeria harbor-town and railway terminal, Port Harcourt, named after the British colonial secretary of the day. Elsewhere Europeans transformed native villages, such as Abidjan or Conakry, into colonial capitals, or grafted new suburbs onto older indigenous centers. Thus at Kano, the largest town in Northern Nigeria, there grew up outside the walls of the old city a "government residential area," designed primarily for Europeans, and two African suburbs, Sabon Gari ("new town"), populated mainly by clerks and traders from Southern Nigeria, and Tudun Wada, occupied by immigrants from other parts of the north—a pattern of residential segregation followed in many other West African cities.

The growth in size and population of the major urban centers of West Africa was directly related to the expansion of commerce and the increase in government revenue. Before World War I, Lagos, with a population of 75,000, was the largest political and commercial center in West Africa. Accra at this period had a population of 20,000, Dakar of 25,000, Bamako of 6,500. By 1931, Lagos contained 126,000 inhabitants, Dakar 53,000, while the new town of Enugu rose from 10,000 in 1921 to 15,000 in 1939. The most spectacular figures of growth came in the last two decades of the colonial period. By the mid-1950's, the population both of Lagos and of Dakar had reached 300,000; Bamako shot up from 22,000 in 1939 to 68,000 in 1955; and Accra rose from 135,000 in 1948 to 325,000 in 1960.

This process of urban growth was accompanied, so it seemed to many observers, with changes in urban character. Thus the compiler of a commercial handbook described Accra in 1920, its main streets lined with "great stores built of reinforced concrete cement" and busy with "innumerable motor vehicles speeding hither and thither in the feverish race for the new wealth that is flooding the colony with cocoa aroma," as a town entirely different from the "quiet, little, old-fashioned place much given to dozing and dreaming" which he had known before 1914.[117] A similar change occurred a generation later in the colonial capitals of French West Africa: "those who knew the sleepy towns which were Abidjan, Bamako, Conakry or Dakar in 1939 would hardly recognize," wrote a student of francophone Africa in the 1960's, "the bustling cities which bear the same names today." [118] This almost tangible increase in vitality was not confined to the major urban centers. There was also a marked growth in the number of smaller agglomerations. In the Gold Coast, for example, there were only 29 centers with a population exceeding 3,000 in 1921 (28 in the Colony, 1 in Ashanti, none in the Northern Territories); by 1960 the country contained 98 towns with a population exceeding 5,000, 37 of which had more than 10,000 inhabitants.

Towns lying in the main cash-crop producing areas of West Africa acquired a population at once more cosmopolitan and more specialized in its occupations than any to be found in the old market centers. "Middlemen and brokers, dealers in cloth, lorry-drivers, garage proprietors, hotel-keepers, *marabouts,* jobbers of all descriptions, officials, bank clerks, domestic servants, labourers and dockers"—so runs a list, compiled in the late 1940's, of occupations in the small port of Kaolack in the groundnut producing area of Senegal.[119] Similar lists could have been drawn up, with minor additions and variations, for many small towns in the cocoa belt of the Gold Coast or Western Nigeria, in the groundnut farming districts around Kano, or in the oil-palm districts of Eastern Nigeria.

For the young men and women who poured into the new towns, seeking work, seeking excitement, seeking escape from the restraints of parental authority or the officiousness of some local despot, whether native chief or alien official, the urban environment served as a powerful stimulant, creating new desires, eroding old beliefs, filling the mind with a wide range of novel experiences. The street lined with shops, the cinema, the bar, the brothel, the building site, the factory—in all these places the immigrant to the town could come into contact with material objects, techniques, ideas, and institutions of which he had previously possessed no concept. But of all the institutions capable of producing a profoundly disturbing impact on those coming into contact with them, three stand out, especially in the early years of the colonial period, as being of paramount importance—the mosque, the church, and the school.

It is one of the ironies of the period of European hegemony in West Africa that the religion of Islam should have spread more widely in the course of these fifty or sixty years than in the entire span of time, some nine or ten centuries, that had passed between the introduction of the new faith to West Africa and the establishment of colonial rule. Yet this development was not really surprising. Islam had received a massive impetus as a result of the revolutionary jihads of the eighteenth and nineteenth centuries. By 1875 it was firmly established in certain key areas, in the valleys of the Senegal and of the Middle Niger, in Futa Jallon, and in much of the savanna country between the Niger and Lake Chad. Islam's main line of advance had always been along the line of the trade-routes, an advance not deflected by the so-called barrier of the forest. By the middle of the nineteenth century there were influential Muslim communities established as Kumasi, Ibadan, and many other smaller towns lying well to the south of the savanna.

A striking indication of the intellectual vitality and wide-ranging contacts to be found in many West African Muslim communities in the late nineteenth and early twentieth centuries is provided by the career of one of the greatest West African Muslim poets of the age, al-Hajj Umar al-Salghawi (c. 1850–1934). Umar, who came of Hausa stock and was a great-grandson of one of the associates of Uthman dan Fodio, received his early education in Kano where his father was a trader, before moving to Salaga, a town in the Northern Territories of the Gold Coast to which many Hausa merchants came to purchase kola-nuts. Umar achieved a high reputation as an Arabic scholar, making a special study of one of the poets of pre-Islamic Arabia, some of whose verses he translated into Hausa. But he was also a poet in his own right. "His major contribution to the Islamic literary tradition," a Western scholar has written, "might be described as making poetry the vehicle of social commentary, social criticism, and reflections on the history of his time," his poems taking as their themes such subjects as the civil war in Salaga in the early 1890's, the decline of morals and religion, and the Christian conquest of the Western Sudan.[120] Like most Muslim scholars, al-Hajj Umar gathered many students around him, some of whom went on to become writers of distinction.

The colonial *pax* provided Muslim traders with the opportunity to move into areas whose pagan inhabitants had in the past staunchly resisted the assaults of Muslim raiders. A handful of Muslim traders settled on the outskirts of a pagan village might succeed in attracting a few converts. But most men who had been brought up to worship the old gods were not likely to grasp the attractions of the new universalistic faith until they found themselves placed in an entirely new environment. For the old religions, derogatively lumped together as "paganism" both by Muslims and by Christians, were local and intensely ethnocentric in character. The pagan villager who moved away from his own home territory was cut off from the shrines of his ancestors and often found himself among men who regarded his beliefs with deep contempt. Pagan Mossi, for example, leaving their homes in Upper Volta to seek work further south, usually traveled in lorries many of whose passengers were Muslims. It was galling to find that the Muslims "all prayed together during the frequent stops on the roads and shared food and water with each other but never with the pagan 'kaffirs'." It was even more aggravating to be set to work under a Muslim supervisor who naturally favored his coreligionists. Succumbing to these powerful social pressures many Mossi became Muslims and on their return home urged their relatives to do the same.[121]

The spread and consolidation of Islam was positively encouraged by the colonial authorities, once they had overcome their initial dread of Muslim "fanaticism" and realized that certain groups, properly handled, could provide a valuable bulwark to their regime. "In a purely voluntary manner," wrote a French Islamist, "we have shown favor to the leaders of Muslim brotherhoods and organized the round of visits made by the grands marabouts, asking of them nothing in return but that they tell the people to keep quiet; we have showered them with the highest honors; at their request we have built schools, medersas ("Muslim colleges"), even mosques, and we have brought over teachers from Egypt and Algeria." [122] The British, for their part, showed their respect for Islam by their support of the great emirs of Northern Nigeria and their reluctance to allow Christian missionaries to operate in predominantly Muslim areas. "We want no violent changes, no transmogrification of the dignified and courteous Moslem into a trousered burlesque with a veneer of European Civilization," declared Governor Bell of Northern Nigeria in 1911,[123] expressing a point of view held by many later British administrators working in Muslim areas.

For most first-generation West African Muslims the new religion represented, no doubt, little more than a novel veneer over deeply held ancestral beliefs. But there were powerful currents working in favor of Muslim orthodoxy. New schools helped to improve the quality of Muslim education. Printed works on religious subjects circulated much more widely than the laboriously prepared manuscripts of the nineteenth century. And the steady stream of West African pilgrims to Mecca—their number rapidly increasing with the advent of cheap air travel in the

1950's—enabled the Muslim community to maintain closer contacts than ever before with their coreligionists in other parts of the world of Islam. By 1960 West Africa contained more than twenty million Muslims. Far more clearly than in 1900, many parts of the region could be regarded as *Dar al-Islam*.

The impact of Christianity on West Africa was a historical phenomenon even more remarkable than the expansion of Islam. In 1875, the number of West African Christians, gathered around mission stations —none more than seventy years old, the majority of much more recent foundation—could hardly have exceeded 50,000. By the 1960's West Africa was reckoned to possess a Christian population numbering 10 million. The initiative in this massive work of conversion came from Europe and America. But with an appallingly heavy mortality among early white missionaries—fifty-four out of the eighty-nine Anglican missionaries who came out to Sierra Leone between 1804 and 1825 died prematurely—most missionary societies found it advisable to train a native pastorate at a very early stage. Thus almost from the start, the work of evangelization in West Africa must be seen as an Afro-European enterprise.

Afro-European cooperation in the early mission churches gave way to spontaneous African initiative in the "independent" churches that began to appear in the 1880's. The earliest of these churches were founded by breakaway groups from the older missionary congregations. Resentment at the domineering manner and racist attitudes of individual white missionaries was a frequent cause of the bitterness that led to separation. But the "independents" were also inspired by a positive belief that the evangelization of Africa was a task that must be carried out by Africans, for African Christians could understand far better than any alien evangelist the complexities of the societies from which they were sprung. Refusing to follow the harshly censorious view of polygamy taken by most white missionaries, the independent churches made a point of accepting polygamists as converts. At the same time, they began to adopt forms of worship more in keeping with the aesthetic tastes of many African congregations, colorful vestments taking the place of austere cassocks, drums and calabashes providing an accompaniment for the vigorous singing of native hymns far more appropriate than the dreary harmonium used in most mission churches.

By the second decade of the twentieth century the development of purely African Christianity was carried further by the emergence of a number of "prophets" who became the founders of new churches. One of the first and most successful of these striking innovators was a Liberian of Kru origin, William Wade Harris, a teacher in the Methodist Episcopal

Church. In 1910 he announced that the Archangel Gabriel had appeared to him in a vision and instructed him to go forth and preach the gospel to the heathen. Three years later, clad in a long white robe, wearing a white turban, and carrying a roughly hewn cross, he began his work of evangelization in the southern Ivory Coast among a people whose morale had been shattered by their experiences during the savage campaigns of "pacification" waged against them by the French. His success was phenomenal. In village after village people "cut down their sacred groves, destroyed the symbols of the old religion, built churches and elected leaders to conduct Christian worship. About 120,000 were converted in one year, giving Harris the distinction of having inspired the greatest Christian mass movement in West Africa." [124]

A survey of religious observances in the Yoruba city of Ibadan carried out in the early 1950's revealed the extraordinarily complex pattern that had emerged in an area where both Christianity and Islam were steadily gaining more and more adherents. The 1952 census showed that no more than 13 percent of the inhabitants of Ibadan were still adherents of the old "pagan" religion, while 30 percent were Christians and 57 percent Muslims. Traditional Yoruba religion was founded on a pantheon numbering about four hundred deities. As late as the 1890's, a visitor to Ibadan could speak of seeing "a great number of small idol-houses"; by 1950 the city contained no more than fifty modest pagan shrines. Two hundred mosques had been constructed to meet the needs of Muslim worshippers, while the Christian community, divided among nine foreign missionary societies and fourteen separatist sects, maintained fifty-eight churches. Many of the mission churches and the sects ran their own schools, but those run by the missionaries were both more numerous and better-equipped, an advantage which helps to explain why the mission churches, with more than 8,000 adult members, enjoyed four times more support than the sects. [125]

But a pattern of religious affiliations typical of Yorubaland as a whole is impossible to detect. In the district of Oyo, for example, lying immediately to the north of Ibadan, 43 percent of the population were shown by the 1952 census to be still pagan; in the relatively remote district of Ekiti, on the other hand, only 23 percent of the population were pagans, as many as 69 percent were Christians, and Muslims numbered no more than 8 percent. Striking contrasts also emerge between the two former regions of Southern Nigeria. In 1921 there were about half a million Christians in Eastern Nigeria, a quarter of a million in Western Nigeria. Today the numerical difference is even more sharply marked with about 4 million Christians in Eastern Nigeria, 1 million in Western Nigeria. Contrasts such as these, repeated in other parts of West Africa, provide a warning to the generalizer. A really satisfactory history of religious change in the region as a whole can be constructed only from a multitude of detailed local studies.

From the start, the movement of Christian evangelization was associated with a wide-ranging program of innovation. Every mission station, with its church and its school, its hospital and its orphanage, its workshops, farms, or vegetable gardens represented an entirely novel community, an island of alien culture in an African sea or—to use the type of metaphors beloved by missionary writers—a cell of "civilization" in a "barbarous" land, a "beacon" of "true" religion in the "darkness" of "heathendom." The more closely African converts attached themselves to the persons of European missionaries, the more profound the impact of the stream of new ideas generated by these avowedly revolutionary alien innovators. In some mission stations the wives of European missionaries made a point of taking into their homes African girls of marriageable age to provide them with practical training in housecraft and Christian living. "In my opinion," an African clergyman has written, "this service went further than formal education in introducing the Christian way of homelife among the people." [126] And many other West Africans have testified to the deep influence on their early lives of certain European missionaries.

That the missionaries should have been associated with a culture so rich in technological achievement was of course a powerful argument in favor of their doctrine. No doubt many of the Africans who attached themselves to the local mission station were interested only in acquiring the new techniques introduced by the white man. But there were others, deeply involved in the work of the church, who could see a close connection between the religion of Christ and European technological progress. "If even the white man finds that his wisdom, his knowledge, his wealth, his steamships, his cannons, his railways and his bicycles cannot help him to stand before God," declared an African evangelist in a sermon preached about 1912, "how much less can we deluded, ignorant, lazy, wicked Africans save ourselves from superstition and the fear of spirits? Seek first the kingdom of God and His righteousness, so will these blessings come to you. What help to my father were his many amulets, what help has he had from his fetish?" [127]

The early missionaries set themselves a well-nigh impossible task. They sought to reproduce on African soil the contemporary culture of their own homelands. Their success was greatest with those who had been violently torn from their own local society. The liberated slaves of Sierra Leone, atomized individuals, bereft of all the ties of kinship, deprived of the solace and security offered by an ancestral religion, provided exceptionally favorable material for the early church in West Africa. It was not surprising that Sierra Leone should have provided the most ardent African evangelists of the mid-nineteenth century, nor that many of the Sierra Leonean converts should have become so strikingly anglicized in their culture. When Christianity was carried to other parts of West Africa, the new religion tended to appeal first not to the upper strata of local communities but to outsiders, to the socially deprived. The nucleus of the Roman Catholic community in Eastern Nigeria, for example, was made up of slaves actually purchased by the missionaries from local dealers and settled in Christian villages. As soon as the new religion began to spread to other sections of the community, strains became apparent. "To become a Christian," a Nigerian historian has pointed out, "meant a complete dissociation of oneself from the family compound, and consequently loss of social family privileges and undesirable estrangement." [128] By many missionaries such cruel dislocations were interpreted as "the price to be paid for progress."

Late nineteenth-century West Africa certainly presented many sights deeply offensive to the Christian mind. "Those who have never with their own eyes beheld the spectacle of a man, with a rope around his neck, being led through the country like a dog," wrote a British traveling commissioner in Sierra Leone in the 1890's, "cannot imagine what the sight makes a Britisher feel." [129] "Slavery, polygamy, drunkenness, bloody quarrels, brutality and cruelty," wrote a German missionary on the Gold Coast, "revealed the pagan life of the people." And he followed established missionary practice in launching a savage attack on the "fetish priests" who "by the use of poison and magic incantations exploited the people and made them the slaves of fear." [130] Complacently, with the easy advantage of hindsight, one can appreciate now that most nineteenth-century missionaries were doubly blinkered— blinkered by their profound ignorance of African thought and culture, blinkered too by the often fanatical dogmatism of their faith. To work for the abolition of the more inhumane features of African life they needed to be men and women of quite exceptional strength of purpose. But their total condemnation of certain African practices often produced consequences of a kind that proved brutally disruptive of the stability of local societies. A study made by an anthropologist among the Ibibio of Eastern Nigeria provides a striking illustration of this ironic process. [131]

In traditional Ibibio courts of law, witnesses were required to swear an elaborate oath, by which they were understood to invoke the "oath-spirit," a powerful supernatural being capable of inflicting instant punishment on those who dared to tell an untruth. In the late 1940's the missionaries succeeded in persuading the administration to allow Ibibio Christians to swear on the Bible. But these converts had been taught that their new God was merciful, always ready to forgive those who made confession of their sins. Freed of the fear of the "oath-spirit," many Ibibio Christians felt no compunction about telling lies in court. Paradoxically their behavior led to an increase in magical practices, as persons who felt they had been cheated of justice in the courts turned to more sinister methods to obtain redress.

Inevitably the development of indigenous Christianity has brought with it a constant process of adjusting new ideas to traditional practices. Thus many West African Christians prefer to celebrate their marriages in the customary manner rather than with a church service. Concubinage, a veiled polygamy, is widely found among the members of churches whose leaders censure open polygamy. Christians participate in traditional ceremonies of a kind that would have been censured by many nineteenth-century missionaries. At the same time, many contemporary European evangelists have come to develop a more sympathetic approach to traditional religion. Although it is widely asserted that the old gods are dying, more than half the population of West Africa is still classified as "animist" or "pagan," and traditional practices and beliefs still exert a profound influence on many nominal Muslims and Christians. In West Africa, more vigorously than in any other part of the continent, three cultural streams—traditional, Muslim, and Western Christian—have converged, producing for the region as a whole the impression of a cultural life of exuberant heterogeneity.

The novel institution of the formal school provided the means by which many West Africans first became familiar with the universalistic faiths of Christianity or Islam. But it would be utterly misleading to assume that "education" itself was an alien import. All societies, whatever their character, must devise some method for passing on traditional skills and knowledge from one generation to another. Thus among the Mende of Sierra Leone—to cite one specific example—a secret society, the Poro, was responsible for carrying out an elaborate program for training the young. By the Poro, Mende boys were taught many practical skills—farming techniques, basketry, bridge-building, and the making and setting of animal traps. The holding of mock courts and trials gave the boys some insight into native law and custom. At the same time, they became skilled in the social art of drumming, learned many Poro songs, practiced acrobatics together, and came to develop among themselves "a strong sense of comradeship." [132]

Mende practice exemplifies what an African educationalist from Mali has called the "multivalent nature" of traditional African education, its capacity to "embrace all sides of the personality of the child and the adolescent." [133] By contrast the educational system developed in Muslim and in European schools may well seem significantly narrower, for the main task of the teachers both in Muslim and in Christian mission schools was to impart to their pupils the technique of literacy, thus enabling them to read for themselves the sacred writings on which these two "religions of the book" are based. In the primary stages of Muslim education attention concentrated—to the exclusion of all other subjects —on the Koran, boys being taught enough Arabic to enable them to memorize the text. Those competent enough to advance to higher studies attached themselves to distinguished scholars under whose direction they embarked on the study of Muslim law books and commentaries on the Koran. Muslim education, with its modestly endowed institutions, was far less spectacular in its manifestations than the new type of schooling introduced by Europeans. But throughout the colonial period it continued to act as a powerful stimulant in many West African societies, breaking down ethnic particularities, encouraging the diffusion of a uniform culture, and serving to strengthen the position of Muslim scholars whose prestige, backed by independent sources of income obtained from teaching, enabled them to serve both as the advisers and as the critics of secular authorities.

Muslim education has a history reaching back more than five hundred years in some parts of West Africa. By contrast European or Western education represented an entirely novel phenomenon in the cultural life of the region. But this alien method of training the young, with its increasingly complex institutional structure and its ever widening range of innovations, developed into one of the most powerful forces for change in modern West African history. The expansion of the European type of education was brought about by three agencies; the colonial governments, the missionary societies, and, at a later stage, by various indigenous organizations, ranging from local authorities to groups of private individuals. But the extent of the contributions made by each of these agencies varied from territory to territory, and there were sharp contrasts in the educational policies followed by the two main colonial powers in the region. The French, accustomed to a highly centralized system of education in their own country, were more clearly aware than the British of the potential political function of education. As early as 1857, Governor Faidherbe of Senegal could describe the purpose of the recently founded school for the sons of chiefs at St. Louis as being to build up "a native elite to assist us in our work of civilization." [134] Consequently mission schools were allowed relatively little freedom and made only a modest contribution to the development of education in French West Africa. The British, on the other hand, were prepared in most of their West African territories—with the notable exception of parts of Northern Nigeria—to allow missionary societies to open as many schools as they wanted, the colonial authorities finding it more satisfactory to subsidize the best of the mission schools by grants-in-aid rather than to open a large number of government-maintained schools.

Statistics from the Gold Coast serve to illustrate the rate of educational expansion and the proportionate contributions made by the different agencies. In 1890 there were 5 government and 49 "assisted" mission schools in the colony, with an enrollment of 5,000 pupils. By 1920, when figures for "nonassisted" schools, whether run by missionary societies or by other groups, appear for the first time, the colony contained 20 government, 188 "assisted," and 309 "nonassisted" schools, the total school population numbering 43,000. By 1940, there were 91,000 children attending Gold Coast schools. A decade of dramatic expansion followed; by 1950 there were 279,000 pupils in close to 3,000 schools, only 45 of which were directly maintained by the government. The vast majority of these children were, of course, attending primary school. Figures for secondary school enrollment show 207 students in 3 schools in 1920, 2,635 students in 17 schools in 1940, and over 6,000 students in 57 schools in 1950.

The Gold Coast was fortunate in being the richest and therefore the most educationally advanced territory in West Africa. In 1950, 43.6 percent of the colony's school-age children were attending school compared with 21.4 percent in Nigeria. In French West Africa educational development was more modest: in 1947, 12.4 percent of school-age children were attending school in Senegal, 10 percent in Dahomey, 5 percent in Soudan (Mali), and 3.7 percent in the Ivory Coast. Figures such as these, which incidentally take no account of children attending Koranic schools, disguise the sharp variations in educational provision to be found within every West African country. Nigeria provided the most striking example of such variations. In 1912, close to 36,000 children were attending school in Southern Nigeria, less than 1,000 in Northern Nigeria. By 1947 there were more than half a million children at school in the South, compared with 71,000 in the North. Differences in secondary education were particularly marked: in 1947 Northern Nigeria contained only 251 secondary school students, while the two southern regions had more than 10,000 students in secondary schools. These variations were in large part a reflection of differences in demand. Throughout West Africa the demand for Western education was strongest in urban areas, in the coastal zone, and in societies receptive to Christian evangelization, weakest in remote rural districts, in the hinterland, and in societies strongly influenced by Islam.

From the start, the European schools, whether staffed by government teachers or by missionaries, introduced a wide range of innovations—the technique of literacy, knowledge of a European language, more efficient methods of computation, some familiarity with a wider world and with other cultures. The gradual diffusion of a knowledge of French or of English provided large areas with acceptable *linguae francae,* making it possible for West Africans, in the words of Leopold Senghor, to "communicate to our brothers and to the world the unheard-of message which only we could write." [135] Other skills learned at school had some bearing on the economic development of the region: a knowledge of simple arithmetic, for example, could rapidly be put to commercial advantage. ("We do not want religious instruction," the chiefs of Bonny told Bishop Crowther in 1874, "for that the children have enough at home . . . we want them to be taught how to gauge palm oil and the other mercantile business as soon as possible.") [136] Most attractive of all to many young West Africans were the social implications of western education, for a school graduation certificate showing proficiency in the three R's often provided an "open sesame" to employment as a clerk, schoolteacher, or junior civil servant, a position carrying a salary more substantial and more regular, and invested with a status more exalted than anything the mass of the "uneducated" could ever hope to achieve.

The curricula of the colonial period have often been criticized for being too "academic" or "literary" in character, too strongly influenced by European models, too little concerned with African realities. Such simplistic judgments convey a misleading impression of the educational situation in colonial West Africa. In the French territories the government laid great stress on the importance of vocational training, especially at the highest levels of the educational structure. Among the institutions established with a distinctly vocational purpose was the medical school at Dakar. Founded in 1918, the school was regarded by a British observer in the 1930's as "the most successful effort in Africa to provide a colonial medical and health service with adequate African assistance." [137] In the British territories the importance of technical education was a commonplace frequently stressed in government reports. In the Gold Coast, for example, "the whole period of the twenties was marked," so a student of colonial educational policies has recently pointed out, "by a systematic attempt to alter the basis of primary and secondary education in the direction of technical and agricultural studies." [138] That such attempts should have met with so poor a response was a reflection of the economic climate of the colonial period. There were relatively few openings for trained African craftsmen, and the rewards, whether in money or in status, offered the skilled carpenter or mechanic were far less attractive than those gained by the successful clerk or schoolteacher.

In British West Africa the educational system was subject to strong popular pressure not only to maintain its academic character but also to model itself on a metropolitan pattern. "Only the best is good enough for Africa" was a popular slogan in British West Africa during the late colonial period. Any attempt to deviate from British models—to substitute, for example, a local examination board for the old metropolitan examiners—was liable to be interpreted as an attempt to fob Africans off with the second-rate. The unconsciously assimilationist trend in British colonial education is to be seen, ironically enough, as being in large part due to African pressures. French educational policy, on the other hand, was far more explicitly assimilationist in its objectives. "We must," as one governor-general put it, "educate the masses to bring them closer to us." [139] Language teaching provided the clearest reflection of this difference in emphasis. In the primary schools of British West Africa, teaching in the first forms was usually in the vernacular; in the French schools, by contrast, the French language was used from the start. Equipped with a greater mastery of a European language, francophone Africans often appeared to be more truly assimilated to the culture of their metropolis than their anglophone contemporaries. To a postcolonial generation, the virtues of educational assimilation, whether on the British or the French model, appear highly questionable. Assimilationist educational policies "resulted," in the critical view of a modern African educationalist, "in a real alienation among Africans. . . . It was only a step, often made eagerly, from attraction to foreign culture to scorn of national culture." [140]

Many West African boys and girls dropped out of the colonial education system after little more than a year or two of schooling. To rise to the top, to win a place in the region's most prestigious institutions—École Normale William Ponty at Dakar (the most famous school in French West Africa), Fourah Bay College (Sierra Leone), Achimota College (Gold Coast), King's College, Lagos, or Katsina College (Northern Nigeria)—"probably involved," it has been suggested, "more effort than the attainment of a Harvard degree by an immigrant American slum-dweller during the depression." [141] Gradually, however, as the educational system expanded, a new social category, "the Western-educated elite," began to appear in many West African societies. Its members were drawn from a wide variety of backgrounds: some were the sons of chiefs and notables, others the descendants of slaves. A few had completed their education overseas and achieved the highest educational qualifications; the majority could claim no more than seven or eight years of primary schooling. But set against the vast mass of their contemporaries, all the Western-educated stood out by virtue of their new skills, their knowledge of the "white man's world," their possession of material innovations—a European suit, a bicycle, a well-furnished house—which most ordinary peasant farmers could never hope to acquire. "In my part of the world," Chief Awolowo has written of the Yorubaland of his boyhood in the 1910's, "the elite of society were the pastors, catechists, teachers, clerks and interpreters. They were respected, admired and adored." [142] "These petty officials," another West African, Abdou Moumouni of Niger, has written, "were as submissive as they were zealous, generally conducting themselves with as much base servility and obsequiousness towards 'whites' as they displayed arrogance, scorn and cupidity towards their fellow Africans." [143] Whatever subjective judgments contemporaries passed on the members of this new social group, it is clear that in political terms the emergence of the "educated native"—the somewhat derogatory term used by colonial administrators of the time—was a phenomenon of the utmost significance.

The educated elite became subject to two sets of frustrations. The first was clearly a product of the colonial situation. Able Africans in subordinate positions found themselves denied opportunities of promotion by governments whose policy was to reserve all the best jobs for Europeans. The other frustration had its cause in the nature of contemporary West African economies which were not rich enough to offer to every aspirant the rewards which he considered to be his due as a result of his years of schooling. The problem of the unemployed school graduate is an old one in West Africa. As early as the 1850's it is mentioned in reports from the Gold Coast. Not every boy was lucky enough, on leaving school, to become a clerk or a teacher. As the educational system expanded, as more boys came to the towns after completing their schooling to look for jobs, so the volume of disappointed ambitions steadily increased. In time these two sets of frustrations were to combine into an explosive political force—the relatively prosperous clerks and teachers becoming the leaders, the disgruntled young men the shock troops of a nationalist movement.

▲▼ THE ORIGINS OF WEST AFRICAN NATIONALISM

"Nigeria," declared Chief Awolowo, one of the country's rising politicians, in 1947, "is not a nation. It is a geographical expression." [144] The remark has a familiar ring: Metternich had applied the same phrase to Italy in the 1840's, Ferhat Abbas to Algeria in the 1930's, while one of Nigeria's most able British governors, Sir Hugh Clifford, had made exactly the same point in 1920 when he described the country as "this collection of self-contained and mutually independent Native States, separated from one another, as many of them are, by differences of history and traditions, and by ethnological, racial, tribal, political and religious barriers." A polity so composed could never, Clifford believed, "be welded into a single homogeneous nation." [145] Remarks such as these might well have been applied to almost every other colonial territory in sub-Saharan Africa. Egypt, Ethiopia, Morocco, Tunisia— these were countries with a centuries-old tradition of historical identity, with an easily ascertainable record of creative achievement behind them. It was not excessively difficult to imagine these Northern African territories emerging from the experience of alien rule as stable national units. By contrast the colonial territories of West Africa appeared as entirely novel political formations whose very names were in some cases purely alien designations. For two generations after 1875 those members of the Western-educated West African elite who thought critically about the present and speculatively about the future might be described as nationalists without a nation. A truly Nigerian or Ghanaian (Gold Coast) nationalism did not emerge until the 1940's, while in French West Africa "independence" remained "a nasty word banned in polite political society" until as late as the mid-1950's.[146] Yet every colonial society is likely to contain elements who are disturbed by local grievances, moved by a sense of ancestral pride and stimulated by the contemplation of other political patterns. Grievance, pride, and external stimulus combined in the minds of a growing number of West Africans to create the vision of a new political order.

The forerunners of modern West African nationalism were to be found in those communities where Africans were in a position to come into close contact with the novel culture of Europe. Here in St. Louis and Freetown, Cape Coast and Accra, Lagos and Calabar there had emerged small groups of African professional men—government servants, lawyers, journalists, schoolteachers, clergymen—well equipped to comment constructively on the development of their society. Profoundly conscious from their own experience of the benefits to be derived from association with Europe, these men rarely if ever gave vent to narrowly chauvinistic views. Even so rumbustious an advocate of traditional African virtues as the Reverend Samuel Attoh-Ahuna, a Methodist clergyman from the Gold Coast, could speak of the need for Africans to revert to the "simplicity" of their forebears "sobered and matured with all that is excellent in Western civilization and religion." [147]

But however grateful educated West Africans might feel to their European beneficiaries, there were certain aspects of colonial rule that roused bitter resentment. Particularly obnoxious was the growing mood of racial arrogance, combined with a dogmatic denigration of African ability, to which the behavior of many Europeans bore witness. It must have been a deeply wounding experience for an educated Creole from Sierra Leone to find himself described as "insufferably vain," "besotted by ignorance," and possessed of an "overpowering odour." [148] These phrases occur in a book published in 1881 by an English army officer with long experience of West Africa: they might be regarded as typical of the stock of clichés used by many Europeans to define and describe their image of the "educated native."

As colonial administrations and missionary societies developed the practice of appointing white men to posts previously occupied by educated West Africans, men who found their career prospects blighted were provided with an easily definable grievance. "When the white man came to us a hundred years ago," a Freetown newspaper editor wrote in 1912, "it was as an angel . . . everywhere he bestowed joy . . . . assisting untiringly the development of the black man. . . . The Angel of peace has changed into a veritable Assyrian. . . . Force is the enthroned deity, and nothing seems to give pleasure like the scampering of bewildered blacks over hill and dale before masters who whack and kick." [149]

In an age of triumphant imperialism it was impossible for local opponents of the colonial regime to exert enough pressure to ensure a radical change in government policy. But in the old-established colonial centers it was usually possible to launch a vigorous protest against specific acts of the colonial government when these aroused the resentment of the great mass of the local population. Thus when in 1908 the British administration imposed a water-rate on the people of Lagos to pay for the cost of supplying the town with fresh drinking water, sections of the local population, believing that the scheme was devised purely for the benefit of Europeans, staged a series of demonstrations against the measure. Mass meetings were held, gangs of youths roamed the streets smashing the windows of Europeans offices, and two leading African doctors "organized the People's Union for the purpose of defending native rights in general and of opposing expropriation, changes in land tenure, and the water rate in particular." [150]

Protest movements are essentially negative and defensive in character. An effective nationalism needs a positive ideology. In a situation of alien hegemony nationalists inevitably look to the future, to the "dawn of freedom," to "self-government" or "independence." But some nation-

alist thinkers must also look back to the past, affirming the peculiar virtues and values of their own society as revealed in its institutions and
its historical traditions and thus constructing the intellectual foundations
for their claim to the right to manage their own affairs. Just as Muslim
intellectuals in North Africa and the Middle East looked back to the
great age of Islam to fortify themselves in their struggle with intrusive
Europeans, so in West Africa vigorous minds began to play on the past,
the little known and often derided past, of their own communities. For
the generation of West African poets whose works began to appear
after World War II, the past could be evoked in haunting images:

> *Africa of proud warriors on ancestral savannahs,*
> *Africa of which my grandmother sings*
> *On the banks of distant rivers.* (David Diop, *Africa*) [151]

*   *   *

> *I must hide him in my inmost veins*
> *The Ancestor. . . .*
> *He is my faithful blood that demands fidelity*
> *Protecting my naked pride against*
> *Myself and the scorn of luckier races.* (L. S. Senghor, *Totem*) [152]

*   *   *

> *Let us listen to the voices of our*
> *Forbears. . . .*
> *In the smoky cabin, souls that wish us well are murmuring.*
> (L. S. Senghor, *Nuit de Sine*) [153]

The emergence of a group of West African historians preceded the
appearance of the first notable West African poets by close to half a century. In 1889, C. C. Reindorf, a mulatto clergyman of mixed Ga and
Danish ancestry, published his *History of the Gold Coast and Asante,*
while Samuel Johnson, a Yoruba clergyman of Oyo origin, completed
his massive *History of the Yorubas* a decade later. Both men, though
openly appreciative of many European innovations, were "concerned,"
as Robert July has pointed out, "with reviving the past of their people
precisely in order to build permanently into the popular mentality a
sense of pride in age-old accomplishments as the basis of a new African
nationalism." [154] Yet other educated West Africans were led, partly as a
result of their legal training, to examine in detail their communities' traditional institutions. Thus in 1889 a group of influential citizens at
Cape Coast came together to form the Fanti National Political Society;
declaring themselves "dissatisfied with the demoralizing effects of certain European influences," they "determined to stop further encroachments into their nationality and planned to compile a record of native

sayings, customs, laws and institutions." [155] Prominent among them was John Mansah Sabrah who was one of the first Western-educated men on the Gold Coast to wear national dress—the splendid toga of rich kente cloth—in preference to the formal black European frock-coat in public, and who compiled three substantial volumes on Fanti laws and institutions.

It was not enough to exalt the past or to protest against isolated acts of injustice in the present. An effective West African nationalism needed a structure of ideas capacious and modernistic enough to allow local nationalists to argue their case effectively in terms which European opinion would understand. As in the Maghrib, so in West Africa some of the intellectual tools needed could be taken from Europe itself. The Gold Coast lawyer who spoke of "no taxation without representation," the Senegalese politician who quoted the "Declaration of the Rights of Man" were turning against their colonial masters' concepts deeply cherished by many Englishmen or Frenchmen and so could be assured of a measure of sympathy among liberal elements in London or Paris. Even more potent than the doctrines of European liberalism were the Marxist ideas with which a few West Africans became familiar in the 1920's. The colonial authorities kept a close watch on subversive literature, but it was impossible to control the movements of West Africans who found their way overseas. Thus French West Africans who came to Paris, whether as demobilized soldiers after World War I or as students of a later generation, often found it possible to make contact with European Communists or Asian revolutionaries. One of the most active West African nationalists in Paris in the 1920's was a Senegalese veteran, Lamine Senghor. He was a founder-member of the *Ligue contre l'impérialisme et l'oppression coloniale* whose inaugural meeting was attended by Nehru and Mme Sun Yat Sen, and later established the *Comité de la défense de la race nègre*. During the regime of the Popular Front in the late 1930's, a number of French Communists obtained official employment in West Africa and exerted a considerable influence on many of the Africans with whom they came into contact. "The Communists won the trust of Africans by behaving in ways that Africans had never seen Europeans behave. They were personal friends and comrades, rather than superiors; they taught political ideas and doctrines which strongly attracted Africans who had had little access to any acceptable alternative political education." [156]

Europe was not the only source of new ideas. From the African diaspora in the New World there came another powerful intellectual current peculiarly well-fitted to strengthen the self-confidence of African nationalists. Of the many individual Afro-Americans who spanned the Atlantic in their thought, two acquired a special significance for West Africa, Edward Blyden and Marcus Garvey. Blyden, born in the Danish West Indies in 1832, came to Liberia in 1850 and spent most of his life in Liberian service, but he traveled widely in West Africa, the Middle East, Europe, and North America, wrote prolifically, and could be regarded from the 1880's to his death in 1912, as the most articulate and widely known black African of his generation. A man of outstanding intellectual ability, Blyden was ideally qualified to shatter the widespread notion of "Negro inferiority." The aim of all his writing was to re-establish African dignity or rather—for he accepted the simplistic theories of his day whereby mankind was divided into a number of distinct races—the dignity of the black race. Races, Blyden argued, could not be regarded as superior or inferior one to another; on the contrary, each race made its own unique contribution to universal civilization. The Negro race had been present, so Blyden proved to his own satisfaction, in ancient Egypt, the world's first great civilization, and so could claim credit for its share in passing on to posterity "the germs of all the arts and sciences." [157] In modern times "the African race," Blyden admitted, "has filled a very humble and subordinate part in the work of human civilization." Nevertheless, "Africa may yet prove to be the spiritual conservatory of the world. . . . When the civilized nations, in consequence of their wonderful material development, shall have had their spiritual perceptions darkened and their spiritual susceptibilities blunted through the agency of a captivating and absorbing materialism, it may be that they may have to resort to Africa to recover some of the simple elements of faith." [158]

A series of related themes came together in Blyden's thought to form a comprehensive philosophy of Africanism. He defined the particular characteristics of the "African personality"—the intense spirit of community, the deep sense of religion. He urged his fellow Africans to preserve the fundamentals of their own society and culture against the insidious influence of European innovations; "be yourselves," he told a Freetown audience in 1893, "honor and love your Race." [159] Though himself a Christian minister, he developed a deep appreciation for the achievements of Islam which he came to regard as "the form of Christianity best adapted to the Negro race." [160] And he called for the establishment of a truly African university in West Africa.

The core of Blyden's teaching was taken up by Marcus Garvey. Both men pursued the same goal—the reestablishment of the dignity of the black race, but they differed greatly in character, method of working, and experience. Blyden, the brilliant conversationalist and lecturer, the contributor to scholarly journals, moved with assurance in the international world of learning. Moreover, most of his working life was spent in Africa, holding a variety of official appointments in Liberia and Sierra Leone. Garvey never once set foot on African soil. Born in Jamaica in 1887, he achieved his greatest success in the United States between 1916 and 1927, and died in obscurity in London in 1940. To his critics Garvey appeared as a flamboyant and egocentric demagogue all of whose schemes ended in total disaster. Certainly it could be said that Garvey's most spectacular creation, the Universal Negro Improvement Association, to be regarded until the 1960's as "the largest Negro mass organization in modern times," [161] collapsed largely as a result of Garvey's own failings as a leader. But Garvey's words were more important than his deeds. His oratory and his writings struck a new note, vibrant and deeply enthralling to many young blacks on both sides of the Atlantic. "Be as proud of your race today as your fathers were in days of yore. We have a beautiful history and we shall create another in the future that will astonish the world. . . . Wake up, Ethiopia! Wake up, Africa! Let us work towards the one glorious end of a free, redeemed and mighty nation. . . . The masses of Negroes in America, the West Indies, South and Central America are in sympathetic accord with the aspirations of the native Africans. We desire to help them to build up Africa as a Negro Empire where every black man, whether he was born in Africa or the Western world, will have the opportunity to develop on his own lines." [162] *Philosophy and Opinions of Marcus Garvey,* from which these quotations are taken, must be seen as one of the seminal books of the age, more influential, as Kwame Nkrumah has testified, on the thinking of many West African nationalists than the works of European radicals from Mazzini to Lenin.

Against this background of converging forces one can set the history of West African nationalism in the first decades of the twentieth century by tracing the careers of the three outstanding nationalist politicians of the period, Blaise Diagne of Senegal, J. E. Casely-Hayford of the Gold Coast, and Herbert Macaulay of Nigeria. A brief biographical sketch of each of these remarkable men serves to illustrate both the achievements and the limitations of the early nationalist movement in three of the region's most vocal communities.

Blaise Diagne was born in Gorée in 1872. Despite his humble parentage—his father was a Serer cook—he was able to obtain a reasonable education and so to qualify for a post in the French colonial customs service. As a customs official Diagne acquired a remarkably wide knowledge of the world through service in many different parts of the French empire. He gained the reputation of being a truculently outspoken defender of the interests of black people, but he also made a number of influential French friends, and in 1909 he married a French woman. Five years later he took a bold decision; he abandoned his official career and entered Senegalese politics. The peculiar constitutional status of his home town made this step possible: under the constitution of the Third Republic all the inhabitants of Gorée and of the three other Senegalese *communes,* St. Louis, Dakar, and Rufisque, whatever their ethic origins, were accounted French citizens. As such they were allowed to elect their own municipal councils and to send one deputy to represent their interests in the Chamber of Deputies in Paris. Until 1914, the politics of the four *communes* seemed to offer little scope for African initiative, given the dominant position enjoyed by two rival interest groups, the agents of the Bordeaux merchants who controlled most of the colony's trade, and the Creoles or *métis* ("mulattoes") who had achieved wealth and status in a variety of professional occupations. This situation was transformed by the sudden entrance of Blaise Diagne.

To the astonishment of most European observers, Blaise Diagne narrowly won the election of 1914, thus proving himself a far abler politician than his European or Creole opponents who ruined their own chances by their bitter internal rivalries. Diagne's 1914 election campaign presented an entirely novel phenomenon in black Africa. Here was a completely unknown African customs officer conducting a campaign, so a contemporary Dakar newspaper recorded, "as it would have been done in France," organizing committees, acquiring a newspaper, putting up posters long in advance and changing them often.[163] Diagne's supporters came from many different elements of local African society, ranging from the intensely conservative Lebu fishermen of Dakar to the radical clerks and schoolteachers who had recently formed an association known as the "Young Senegalese." By playing on their well-justified fears of French moves to curtail their rights as citizens, Diagne succeeded in knitting these diverse groups together. His achievement was a remarkable one, a portent of later political developments which he himself, dying in 1934, did not live to see.

Superficially Diagne's long career as a French parliamentarian—"our blackest deputy" in the affectionate phrase of some of his colleagues—was remarkably successful. Toward the end of World War I he was given the special post of high commissioner of African troops with the task of encouraging recruitment in French West Africa. After the war he held office in most of the governments of the 1920's. Succumbing to the metropolitan embrace, he gradually shed his former radicalism. "We Frenchmen of Africa," he declared in 1922, "wish to remain French, for France has given us every liberty and accepted us without reservation along with her European children." [164] The ennunciation of such suavely assimilationist sentiments transformed Diagne into one of the most persuasive and eloquent defenders of French colonialism in his generation. He ended his career, in the words of a recent biographer, "a living picture of the assimilated man who sought his roots and rationale in Africa but who preferred to work and play in Europe." [165]

The career of J. E. Casely-Hayford followed a pattern not dissimilar to Diagne's, the youthful radical ending up as a staunch upholder of the colonial regime. Casely-Hayford was born in 1866 into a prominent Gold Coast family, prosperous enough to send him to Cambridge and London to study law. On his return as a promising young barrister to his home in Cape Coast, Casely-Hayford threw himself into the work of a proto-nationalist organization, the Aborigines' Rights Protection Society. The ARPS was founded in 1897 by many of the chiefs and wealthy professional men of the Gold Coast to protest against the colonial government's attempt to interfere with the traditional system of land tenure by introducing a lands bill "to regulate the administration of public land." In the view of members of the ARPS there was no such thing as "public land," all land, even untouched forest, being held either by private individuals or by chiefs on behalf of their people. The government, on the other hand, was acutely conscious of the fact that much land, especially in the gold-mining areas, was being alienated to foreign concession-hunters to the benefit not of the people as a whole but of local chiefs who pocketed the proceeds of any sale and of local lawyers whose business swelled with the growing volume of litigation. The situation was ironic, an alien administration attempting to protect the native community as a whole against the narrow self-interest of the local elite, but it proved no exception to the rule that disputes over land are likely in any society to develop into highly emotional issues. Before long the colonial government found itself faced with a volume of protest so strong that it was forced to retreat.

By the turn of the century Casely-Hayford, who had made a name for himself by drawing up the legal brief for the ARPS, could be described as "fast becoming the most articulate and influential advocate of African national consciousness." [166] In 1911 he published *Ethiopia Unbound,* a rambling, largely autobiographical work, thinly veiled as fiction and containing many arresting statements about the present state and future destiny of his people. He presented Europeans as coming out to Africa "with the gin bottle in one hand and the Bible in the other," "dismembering [the African's] tribe, alienating his land, appropriating his goods and sapping the foundations of his authority and institutions." Against this spectacle of European greed and hypocrisy he set the image of African virtue, following Blyden in asserting that Africa was "the cradle of the world's systems and philosophies and the nursing mother of its religions." [167] These were ideas capable, as the later history of the Gold Coast was to reveal, of stirring the hearts of men still unborn.

In 1920 Casely-Hayford became involved in the most ambitious form of political activity of his career when he played a leading part in founding the National Congress of British West Africa. At its inaugural conference in Accra in 1920, the congress—which drew its membership from educated groups in every British West Africa territory—put forward an ambitious program, demanding a wide range of reforms and innovations, all designed to allow Africans a greater measure of control over their own affairs. Every territory's legislative council was to be transformed by the provision that half the members should be elected African representatives; racial discrimination was to be abolished in the civil service; restrictions were to be imposed on immigration of Syrians and Lebanese whose commercial activities had forced many Africans out of business; and a university was to be established for British West Africa. The delegates were sound prophets; most of their objectives were to be achieved in the course of the next thirty years. To contemporary British administrators, however, they appeared to be nothing more —as Governor Clifford caustically remarked—than "a self-selected and self-appointed congregation of African gentleman . . . whose eyes are fixed, not upon African native history . . . nor upon their own tribal obligations and the duties to their Natural Rulers which immemorial custom should impose upon them, but upon political theories evolved by Europeans to fit a wholly different set of circumstances." [168]

In his political concepts Casely-Hayford displayed, as July has noted, "a curious blend of law-abiding constitutionalism and racial belligerence." [169] Certainly he was no revolutionary, and it was not inappropriate that he should end his career as a highly respected member of a mildly reformed Gold Coast Legislative Council. "Our fundamental policy," he declared in 1929, "is to maintain strictly inviolate the connection of the British West African dependencies with the British Empire." [170] Born in an age when members of the Gold Coast intelligentsia were far more closely in touch with their contemporaries in Freetown and Lagos than with the people of Ashanti and the Northern Territories, it was natural for Casely-Hayford to think in terms of the emergence of a great West African dominion rather than of the creation of a series of more narrowly based nation-states. In this respect Casely-Hayford's predictions were to be belied by events, though his vision of a more closely united West Africa placed him in the main stream of pan-Africanist sentiment. Casely-Hayford's thought could not compare in range or originality with Blyden's, but living in an age—he died in 1930—when European colonial regimes were at the height of their power, he stands out as the most vigorous and stimulating West African thinker of his day.

The most prominent figure in Nigerian politics in the years before World War II was Herbert Macaulay, an engagingly flamboyant personality whose inexhaustible capacity for launching verbal assaults on the British administration earned him the popular title of "father of Nigerian nationalism." A grandson of Bishop Crowther, Macaulay was born in Lagos in 1864, studied civil engineering in England, and set himself up in private practice as a surveyor. By the end of the century Lagos, in common with Freetown and Cape Coast, had developed a flourishing, largely African-owned local press. Macaulay soon found first in journalism and later in political activity an ideal medium through which to display his ebullient intelligence. Throwing himself into all the political disputes and protest movements of his day, many of which were concerned with the position of the traditional dynasty of Lagos, the House of Docemo, Macaulay rapidly established his position as the gadfly of the local "establishment," and the most outspoken Nigerian critic of British rule.

In 1923, the Nigerian Legislative Council, hitherto a largely official body, was enlarged to allow for the inclusion of four African representatives, three from Lagos and one from Calabar, elected on the basis of a strictly limited franchise. Macaulay himself was debarred from standing for election, as he had been convicted, once for fraud, the second time for criminal libel, and had served prison sentences on both occasions, but he was in a position to organize and lead the Nigerian National Democratic Party (NNDP) whose members successfully contested the three Lagos seats in every election from 1923 to 1938. The party's title was a misnomer: Macaulay was obsessed with Lagos politics and made no serious attempt in the prewar period to gain supporters in other parts of the country. Nor, for all Macaulay's tirades on the British, could the party be described as truly radical. Grandiosely, the party's aims were defined as being "to carry the banner of 'Right, Truth, Liberty and Justice' to the empyrean heights of Democracy"; but at the same time the party pledged itself "to maintain an attitude of unswerving loyalty to the Throne and Person of His Majesty the King Emperor, by being strictly constitutional in the adoption of its methods and general procedure." [171] In the Lagos elections of 1938, the NNDP's candidates were defeated by the supporters of a new political group, the Nigerian Youth Movement, whose appearance on the political stage was symptomatic of a profound change that was occurring in many parts of West Africa at this time.

The older generation was passing away. It had been represented by Diagne, Casely-Hayford, and Macaulay, all of whom were associated with the aristocracy of the Coast. The new men, products of the gradually expanding system of Western education, were drawn from farther afield. Their attitudes soon revealed them to be less respectful of European authority, less wedded to European norms than the highly assimilated nationalists of the first decades of the century. In the 1930's, the political expression of these "youngmen" (a term strictly applicable only to a distinct social group in some of the Akan chiefdoms of the Gold Coast but useful in a wider connotation) could best be observed in the new associations they were creating, particularly in the larger urban centers. These associations took many different forms, ranging from friendly societies (*amicales*), social clubs, and tribal unions to literary groups, trade unions, and professional associations. (The Society of Native Therapeutists, the Youths' Literary Improvement Circle, the Merry Rose Sporting Club, the Lagos Night Soil Removers' Union, the Urhobo Renascent Convention; names such as these, of associations to be found in Southern Nigeria in the early 1940's, convey something of the rich flavor of the local scene.) Many of the activities of these associations could in no sense be regarded as political, but whatever their purpose, these voluntary bodies brought like-minded people together, gave to "an important minority," as Thomas Hodgkin has pointed out, "valuable experience in modern forms of administration—the keeping of minutes and accounts, the handling of records and correspondence, the techniques of propaganda and diplomacy," and finally served "to provide the cells around which a nation-wide political organization could be constructed." [172]

The development of "tribal unions" in Southern Nigeria provides a particularly clear illustration of the way in which these apparently highly localized institutions could exert an influence on the politics of a wider area. Formed originally as a means of bringing together men and women from the same town, village, or ethnic group who found themselves living far from home in some strange town, many of these associations acquired a markedly progressive character, as their members "began to export to their rural homelands the enlightenment, modernity and civilization they encountered in urban centers." [173] In 1944, 101 "tribal unions" came together in Lagos and affiliated themselves to the newly founded National Council of Nigeria and the Cameroons (NCNC), thus giving to this novel political organization a far more truly national character than any earlier Nigerian party had ever possessed by providing through their own system of membership a direct channel of communication between Lagos and many communities in other parts of the country.

The veteran Herbert Macaulay was elected president of the NCNC, but the party's outstanding personality was its secretary-general, Nnamdi Azikiwe, regarded throughout the 1940's as the outstanding nationalist leader of his time without a rival anywhere in tropical Africa. "Zik"—even his nickname conveyed onomatopoetically something of the brashness, the militancy, the modernity of the man—was a novel phenomenon on the African political stage. He was not a member of the West Coast aristocracy but the son of a modest Ibo clerk in government service, and the first of the Ibos to achieve prominence beyond the bounds of Eastern Nigeria. He had gone not to Europe but to the United States for his education, and his nine years (1925–34) spent mainly in Negro colleges profoundly influenced the evolution of his political ideas. His racial consciousness was sharpened by first-hand experience of the tribulations of American Negroes. He was won over by the "black nationalism" of Marcus Garvey, and he learned to appreciate the value of journalism—the more hard-hitting and sensational the better—as a weapon to use against his political opponents. In 1934 he returned to West Africa, and edited a paper on the Gold Coast until he found himself served with a charge of sedition; he then moved to Lagos where he founded a paper of his own, the *West African Pilot,* and played an active part in the Nigerian Youth Movement. Rapidly he gained for himself a position as the idol of a large section of Nigerian youth, "the Saviour of Africa," "a Super Genius more than a super man" in the words of one of his supporters.[174] He was indeed a man of astonishing versatility —a successful journalist and businessman (the papers that he founded were profitable commercial concerns), a patron of sport, the holder of a string of academic distinctions, above all a man who showed that he cared about the problems of junior clerks, could set before them the vision of a more enticing future, and exhilarate them with his verbal assaults on the "colonial dictatorship." "Explosive," "magnetic," "a wonderfully effective demagogue," as John Gunther described him,[175] "Zik" could indeed be regarded as the prophet of a new age in which the swelling force of African nationalism would swiftly transform the political face of West Africa.

▲▼ THE DECOLONIZATION OF BRITISH WEST AFRICA

In comparison with many other parts of the Afro-Asian world, British West Africa was relatively little affected by the turmoil of World War

II. Nevertheless, for the steadily increasing groups of politically conscious young men in Lagos, Freetown, and Accra the war brought some stimulating and disturbing experiences: the extraordinary sight of Englishmen, servicemen in transit through West Africa, doing menial jobs; the ironic spectacle of British administrators denouncing racialism and imperialism—as practiced by their rival "tribesmen," the Germans; the irksome sacrifices demanded by the war effort in the form of a shortage of consumer goods; and the stirring, hopeful affirmations of the Atlantic Charter. For the forty or fifty thousand West African soldiers who saw service with the allied armies in Ethiopia and Burma there was an even wider range of novel sensations. Once demobilized, these ex-servicemen showed that "their contacts with other peoples" had led them, in the words of an official report, to develop "a political and national consciousness." Their familiarity with better living conditions during their army service and their disillusionment with the hardship of life on their return home made for "a general communicable state of unrest." [176]

West African intellectuals and ex-servicemen were not the only people to see the colonial situation in a new light. Many people in Britain, stirred by the mood of war-time idealism, were anxious to give the colonies a better deal. Yet no one in Britain could have predicted how swiftly the process of decolonization would take place. "Somewhere in West Africa within a century, within half a century—and what is that in the life of a people—a new African state will be born," wrote a group of Englishmen, notably sympathetic to African aspirations, in an official report on higher education in West Africa published in 1945.[177] No more than twelve years later the Gold Coast had achieved independence, and by 1965, with the transformation of the miniscule colony of Gambia into a sovereign state, the process of decolonization was complete.

In retrospect the British disengagement from West Africa appears to have taken place in a remarkably smooth and ordered manner and in an atmosphere of great cordiality. In fact, as the course of events in Nigeria and the Gold Coast clearly indicated, the process of decolonization was accompanied with many unexpected twists of fortune. "We lived," wrote a British governor of the Gold Coast, "in an atmosphere of perpetual crisis." [178] Such an atmosphere might well be regarded as normal in a time of rapid political change: before the process had been completed decolonization invariably seemed like a leap in the dark. Fortunately for the British, the features which complicated their withdrawal from other colonial territories—considerations of strategic importance and the presence of British settlers—did not affect West Africa. And the British enjoyed an inestimable advantage over other colonial powers in having at their disposal a great deal of practical experience relating to the process of decolonization.

A century earlier in Canada, later in the other white dominions, and finally and very recently in South Asia, the British had worked out an effective formula for the transfer of power from expatriate officials to local politicians. First, the legislative council with its majority of official members was transformed into something approaching a national parliament through the addition of an increasing number of locally elected members. Then local politicians were taken into the governor's executive council and given a gradually enlarged range of responsibility. Parliamentary elections involving a steadily widened electorate enabled the colonial government to be sure that it was handing over power to local leaders who enjoyed a wide measure of popular backing. As for the functioning of the newly established system of democratic government, Westminster itself, as "the mother of Parliaments" provided the model. There were many sceptics who argued that the institutions evolved over many centuries to suit a particular European society could not possibly be transferred effectively to other peoples of alien culture, who doubted whether Africans possessed the experience, or even the capacity, needed to manage the complicated machinery of a modern state, or who wondered how colonies made up of a wide variety of mutually hostile "tribes" could ever be effectively transformed into modern nations. Decision-makers, both in Britain and in West Africa, could not afford to be mesmerized into inaction by such reflections. By 1948, West African nationalism had developed in the Gold Coast and in Nigeria into a force that could only be held in check by a massive show of counterforce—a line of action the British, with no vital interests at stake, were not prepared to consider. In these circumstances there was no alternative but to apply the formula of the "Westminster model." British parliamentary procedure was functioning reasonably effectively in India—perhaps it might also work in Africa. In any case, given the nationalists' assumption that only the best is good enough for Africa, it would have been impossible for the British to have attempted to introduce some other system of government that they themselves regarded as falling short of the "best," nor indeed could they have manufactured some new system completely alien to their own traditions. These guiding lines of metropolitan thinking must be borne in mind when following the course of action on the West African stage.

In no West African territory was the transfer of power beset with so many difficulties as in Nigeria. This was hardly surprising. The country possessed a population—put at 35 million in the 1953 census—at once far larger and considerably more heterogeneous than that of any other European colony in Africa. Over an extraordinarily varied conglomeration of older polities—the ancient kingdoms of Benin and Bornu, the caliphate of Sokoto, the warring Yoruba states, Ibo village groups, and a multitude of smaller units—the British had erected the superstructure of colonial administration. In the past forty years much had been done to modernize native systems of government at local levels. But the British had been exceedingly reluctant to allow Nigerians to participate in the work of government at the regional or national level. Relatively few local men—barely exceeding one hundred in 1945—had succeeded in entering the higher ranks of the civil service, and the country's legislative council drew its four elected members from Lagos and Calabar, leaving the other parts of the country to be represented only by European officials whose presence in the legislature ensured the government of a permanent majority.

In 1945, Governor Richards (later Lord Milverton) took the first step toward equipping Nigeria with a more representative set of institutions. Stressing the need for unity in diversity, he introduced a constitution which enlarged the legislative council to allow for an unofficial majority and set up three regional houses of assembly. But the governor made the mistake of not consulting Nigerian opinion over the new constitution and immediately found himself faced with a spate of bitter criticism from the nationalists. Most of the unofficial members of the new assemblies were either nominated or appointed through a system of indirect election by the native authorities, thus creating the impression that the British were concerned only to allow conservative interests a say in regional and national affairs. Later critics were to blame the constitution for giving to the country's three regions, originally intended only to serve as administrative divisions, a degree of political significance that was seriously to affect Nigeria's future development. Of these regions, the North, an area ten times larger than that of the East, eight times that of the West, and possessing 54 percent of the country's total population, was by far the largest.

Disputes between the regions were to assume an ever more prominent place in Nigeria's political evolution, but in the last years of Richards's governorship the British administration provided the main target for nationalist attack. The NCNC, led by Azikiwe, established itself the spokesman of the discontented and in so doing created for the first time in Nigeria's history a genuinely popular movement capable of drawing support from many parts of the country. Particularly striking was the success of the NCNC's nation-wide fund-raising tour of April, 1946. "Accompanied by brass bands, flute bands, cowhorn bands, dancers and soldiers, in schoolrooms, halls, compounds, cinemas, and churches," Azikiwe and his fellow politicians "touched the lives," wrote a contemporary observer, "of hundreds of isolated communities in a way never known before." [179]

By the late 1940's, the British authorities in Nigeria might well have found themselves faced with an extremely dangerous situation. A group of young militants, members of the Zikist Movement, preached the need for "positive action" of a revolutionary kind. But the nationalist cause was already plagued by the "tribalism" that was destined to become the most characteristic feature of Nigerian politics. To its critics, the NCNC, for all its pan-Nigerian pretensions, appeared to be dominated by its Ibo supporters, and the presence of large numbers of hard-working but clannish Ibo immigrants in the main towns of the North and West lent substance to the fears felt by other groups of mounting Ibo influence. In 1949, two new political parties made their appearance, the almost exclusively Yoruba Action Group and the Northern Peoples Congress (NPC), most of whose leading supporters came from the Hausa, Fulani, and Kanuri aristocracy of the most strongly islamized provinces of Northern Nigeria. At the same time, the British put themselves in a position to counter the arguments of all but the most extreme nationalists by initiating a program of more liberal reforms.

The new policy was initiated by a new governor, Sir John Macpherson. The Richards Constitution had been intended to last for nine years. But Macpherson considered that "progress" in the last two years had been "so rapid and so sound" that the timetable needed revising. "I suggest that we might consider together what changes should be made." [180] For a colonial governor still possessing virtually autocratic powers to make such a statement in an address to a largely nominated legislative council was clear evidence of a profound change in the spirit of British policy, a change which must in large part be ascribed to the liberal ideas generated by the Labour government in Britain. Evidence of the new spirit could be detected at many levels. In the past the British had shown special respect to Nigeria's traditional rulers. Now they began to seek to win the good will of educated Africans. "District officers began to invite more and more Nigerians to tea or cocktails; mixed clubs became increasingly popular; . . . all along the line cracks began to appear in the great barriers that had separated the European from the African." [181]

There were many strands to Macpherson's policy: a clear recognition of the need to Nigerianize the senior civil service; reforms designed to make the structure of local government more democratic; and plans for a rapid expansion of education. But the most original aspect of the new

British approach was to be found in the scheme devised to allow Nigerians at every level to participate in putting forward suggestions for their country's constitution, through a series of discussions held at first in the village, then in the district, followed by provincial, regional, and national conferences. Thus began one of the most intense processes of political self-education that the people of any country have ever experienced. Young men used their savings to print pamphlets putting forward their political ideas; newspapers printed the speeches of politicians verbatim; and clerks and junior civil servants discussed the niceties of constitution-making with as much expertise as their contemporaries in other countries would devote to baseball or football.

The process of Nigerian constitution-making lasted for more than a decade. There were many difficult questions to be settled: along what lines was power to be divided between the regions and the center; what provision should be made to allow Nigerians to take an increasing share in the executive work of the government; how was revenue to be allocated between the central and regional governments; was Lagos, at once a Yoruba city and capital of Nigeria, to form part of the western region or be made a special federal territory; what rights were to be allowed the many minority groups in each region; what date should be fixed for the final achievement of independence. With the three major political parties building up solid political bases for themselves in their respective regions, the NPC in the North, the Action Group in the West, and the NCNC in the East, a federal constitution in which a great deal of power was allowed to the regions appeared to provide the only feasible answer to Nigeria's political problems. But this solution was not reached smoothly or easily. Interparty rivalry was intense to the point of bitterness, and there were moments of acute crisis. Thus in 1953, NPC leaders rejected an Action Group's motion calling for independence in 1956, were ridiculed by southern politicians as "imperialist stooges," and seriously considered plans for Northern secession.

Given the vast cultural differences between North and South, political tension could hardly have been avoided. But the situation was exacerbated by the fears felt by the Northerners that "unscrupulous" Southern politicians would use their greater familiarity with the techniques of modern politics to dominate their region, and by their resentment at the openly contemptuous attitude often displayed by Southerners to many aspects of Northern culture. No less understandable was the exasperation of many Southerners who were convinced that the process of Nigerian political development was being held back by ultra-conservative forces in the North.

The Nigerian situation as it developed during the 1950's, cannot, however, be presented only in the simple terms of a conflict between North and South. Serious strains could be detected within each region. In the North, the aristocratic NPC was challenged, though with little success, by the radical Northern Elements Progressive Union. At the same time, fear of Hausa–Fulani domination induced some politicians drawn from the predominantly non-Muslim peoples of Nigeria's "middle belt" (composed of the southern provinces of the Northern Region) to come together and form the United Middle Belt Congress (UMBC). Similarly, fear of Yoruba domination led a number of non-Yoruba groups in the Western Region to press for the creation of a mid-West state whose boundaries would roughly coincide with the area controlled by the old kingdom of Benin. While these anti-Yoruba Westerners looked to the NCNC for support, anti-Ibo Easterners, drawn mainly from the Ijaw and Ibibio peoples of the coastal provinces, turned to the Action Group to help them in their struggle with the ruling NCNC. This criss-cross pattern of inter-regional alliances was carried still further by the links formed between the Action Group and UMBC and between NCNC and NEPU. Thus both Southern parties had sufficient support in regions other than their own to present themselves as truly national in character.

Ironically it was the most regionally-minded of the major parties, the NPC which secured the greatest success in the federal elections of 1959, winning 143 of the 312 seats, a result made possible by its control of the greater part of Nigeria's most populous region. Nevertheless, had the NCNC and the Action Group decided to form an alliance, the two parties between them would have secured a convincing majority in the federal parliament. But Action Group–NCNC relations had been embittered by years of struggle in the Western Region. Accordingly, the NCNC decided to accept the NPC's offer to form a coalition, leaving the Action Group with its apparently secure base in the Western region to form the opposition in the federal parliament. A solution of sorts had been achieved, allowing the British to make the final act in the transfer of power in October, 1960. Thus Africa's most populous state achieved its independence.

In the late 1950's Nigerians developed the habit of describing their country as "Africa's giant," but it was the very much smaller Gold Coast (its population, 4.1 million in the 1948 census) which stole most of the limelight in the 1950's. In comparison with the often tedious complications of Nigerian constitutional development, Gold Coast politics posssessed a simple dramatic quality. When, by the mid-1950's, it was apparent that the country was to become the first colonial territory in Black Africa to achieve independence, international interest was immensely heightened. Rarely indeed in the whole course of African history has a single event been attended with so great a measure of publicity as the Gold Coast's achievement of independence in March, 1957.

A decade earlier, in the mid-1940's, the Gold Coast was regarded by its British administrators as a model colony, and its inhabitants—in the words of Governor Burns—as "extremely sensible people" who knew "their limitations" and were "very keen to take advice." [182] Sir Alan Burns, governor of the Gold Coast from 1941 to 1946, was a liberal reformer. In 1944 he introduced a new constitution, regarded at the time by African public opinion as "a bold and imaginative advance," [183] for it increased the African membership of the legislative council, creating a majority of elected African members. With its well-developed educational system, its flourishing economy—exports rose from £12 million in 1944 to £27 million in 1947, and its apparent lack of tension between major ethnic or racial groups, the Gold Coast seemed well set for a period of smooth, harmonious development. Even the colony's one major political party, founded in 1947, the United Gold Coast Convention, had a highly respectable character. Its aim "to ensure that by all legitimate and constitutional means the direction and control of government should pass into the hands of the people and their chiefs in the shortest possible time" might appear, in the contemporary West African context, mildly revolutionary, but the party's leadership, headed by Dr. J. B. Danquah and largely made up of well-to-do lawyers from the coastal towns, was far removed from the "rabble-rousing" nationalists with their backing among the masses with whom worried British officials had recently had to deal in such countries as Egypt and India.

Yet even if the Gold Coast did not have the appearance of a country on the verge of a revolution, certain ominous strains could be detected. In the eastern cocoa-growing districts many farmers were bitterly indignant at the drastic measures introduced by the government to compel them to cut down trees attacked by the disease known as "swollen shoot." In the towns, people were suffering from a classic inflationary situation—too much money, partly produced by high cocoa prices, chasing too few imported consumer goods—a situation particularly exasperating for ex-servicemen who saw their hard-earned gratuities being rapidly frittered away by rising prices and for African businessmen who found that under the system of import control introduced during the war import licenses were more readily granted to old-established European or Syrian firms. To these recent grievances must be added a more deep-rooted cause for discontent. In the Akan chiefdoms, including Ashanti, there had been, even in precolonial days, frequent incidents produced by tension between the chiefs and their counsellors or "elders" on the one side and the mass of commoners or "youngmen" on the other. Two developments in the 1930's and 1940's served to increase such tension—the British policy of supporting chiefs and even of allowing them to obtain powers in excess of those sanctioned by native custom, and the rapid expansion of primary education among commoners. "Youngmen," leaving their villages to seek work in the towns, freed themselves from many of the constraints of their local society. By joining the new associations springing up in the towns—tribal unions, trade unions, or debating societies—they had a chance of meeting other "youngmen" who shared their grievances and aspirations. The "intelligentsia," to use the term locally applied to the lawyer politicians of the UGCC (United Gold Coast Convention), lacked both the flair and the inclination to appeal to these "angry youngmen" of the back street. An apparently trivial decision transformed the situation. Some months after its foundation, the UGCC appointed as its first full-time secretary, an ex-teacher in his late thirties, who had been out of the country for the past twelve years. His name was Kwame Nkrumah.

Nkrumah, the son of a goldsmith from the southwestern corner of the Gold Coast, had trained as a teacher at Achimota, but had abandoned teaching in 1935 and taken the bold step of going to the United States to continue his education. After ten years in American universities, he moved to England in 1945 to study law. During his twelve years of absence from the Gold Coast, he was deeply involved in the politics of the African diaspora, being elected president of the African Students Organization of America and Canada, and later playing a prominent part in the Pan-African Congress held at Manchester in October, 1945. All this time he was searching, in his own words, "for a formula by which the whole colonial question and the problem of imperialism could be solved." [184] The writings of Marx, Lenin, Mazzini and, above all, Marcus Garvey helped to inspire and shape his mental development, while observation of the American political scene provided some insight into the techniques of political organization. Self-consciously the revolutionary, he gradually introduced a new style into Gold Coast politics, a compound of passion, simplicity of utterance, single-minded pursuit of certain ends, and a brilliant handling of public relations that contrasted sharply with the long-winded constitutionalism of the intelligentsia. A shrewd observer saw in him "a born actor, with all the magnetism, emotional sensitivity and *panache* of the good player." [185] Later experience was to bring out the obverse of these qualities—intolerance of criticism, indifference to many important aspects of a country's activities, and an overweening egocentricity.

In February, 1948, the image of the model colony was suddenly shattered. In Accra a mob started looting European and Syrian shops after police had fired on and dispersed a threatening demonstration organized by the ex-serviceman's union. Riots also occurred in Kumasi and other towns. The British authorities handled an ugly situation with shrewd magnanimity. A commission was appointed to investigate the cause of the disturbances. Its report, a remarkably frank and perceptive document, analyzed Africans' "distrust and suspicion" of Europeans and came to the conclusion that "every African of ability" must be given "the opportunity to help govern the country" and so "to experience political power." [186] An all-African committee was then appointed to submit proposals for constitutional reform. Most of the committee's proposals were accepted by the British and became the basis for the constitution of 1951. Particularly important was the provision that the executive council, hitherto the preserve of European officials, should include a majority of African members, appointed by the governor from the elected members of the legislature, and holding ministerial office.

While the constitutional committee was engaged in its deliberations, Nkrumah decided to break with the UGCC and found his own party, the Convention People's Party. The new party was based on the radical youth groups whose support Nkrumah had been successfully canvassing while still secretary of the UGCC. The "verandah boys"— "those who slept in the verandahs of the rich because they had no home of their own" [187]—provided the CPP with its cadre of tough, hard-working militants. They were joined by other groups, including the ex-servicemen and the formidable market mammies, together with many trade unionists and members of the farmers' associations. Rapidly the CPP developed into a mass party, seeking as it did so to substitute, as Thomas Hodgkin has pointed out, "a new sense of solidarity based upon the party for the solidarity based upon older, more restrictive groupings," "to dispel the inertia and irresponsibility" produced by the system of colonial rule, and "to put in its place a belief in the 'historic role' of Africans in general and of a given African community in particular." [188] The party's methods of propaganda were brilliant, gay, irreverent, dynamic, neatly blending ancient and modern—the forceful slogans: "Freedom," "Self-Government Now," "Seek ye first the political kingdom"; the songs often based on familiar hymns ("Fight the good fight with all thy might, Kwame Nkrumah is thy right"); the rallies, the dances, the flags, the propaganda vans painted in party colors, the cult of the leader as hero, as "Man of Destiny," "Star of Africa," "Deliverer of Ghana," or even engagingly as "Great Leader of Street Boys."

In January, 1950, Nkrumah, urged on by his more radical followers, announced that the proposals being put forward by the constitutional committee did not go far enough and launched a campaign of "positive action," involving widespread strikes and riots. The government retaliated by arresting Nkrumah and other CPP leaders, but they did not proscribe the CPP as a party nor did they abandon their plans for a general election in 1951. The election results vindicated the CPP's policy: of the popularly elected seats the party won thirty-four, the UGCC two. Bowing graciously to the inevitable, Governor Arden-Clarke released Nkrumah from prison and invited him to become "leader of government business."

The CPP's victory in the 1951 elections marked the climax of the nationalist struggle. Between Nkrumah and Governor Arden-Clarke there developed, in the governor's own words, "A close, friendly and not unfruitful partnership." [189] Thus the British were able to hand over power gradually and in an atmosphere of goodwill. But as independence drew nearer, the CPP leaders found themselves faced with a mounting tide of opposition. The bitter hostility of many of the intelligentsia and of the chiefs in the coastal areas was only to be expected: their party, the UGCC, had been crushed and humiliated by the CPP. It was almost inevitable too that there should be a steady group of CPP dissidents who for personal, moral, or doctrinal reasons decided to break with the party. These opponents of the CPP were joined by groups whose attitude, the product of many local grievances, was pejoratively described by CPP militants as "tribalistic." They include the Ewe of Togoland, anxious for unity with their kinsmen in French Togo, and the Dagomba and Mamprussi of the Northern Territories who saw themselves in "danger of being subjected to over-hasty, over-radical politicians" from the South. [190] The most serious threat of all came from Ashanti where cocoa farmers were indignant at the low price being paid to them by the official marketing board, and where many people, deeply mindful of the past glories of their "nation," were growing increasingly critical of the CPP's "dictatorial tendencies." Each of these local groups formed political parties—the Northern Peoples's Party, the Togoland Congress, and, in Ashanti, the National Liberation Movement—and began to press for the introduction of a federal constitution.

In the general election held in 1954 for an enlarged legislative assembly the CPP won 79 out of 104 seats. But so vigorous did the opposition parties become in the course of 1955—their members' exuberance often leading to savage street-brawls with CPP militants—that the British government decided to test the CPP's popularity in yet another general election before reaching a final decision about the granting of independence. The election of 1956 proved a bitter disappointment to the CPP's opponents, for Nkrumah's party won 71 of the 104 seats. But by gaining 43 percent of the total vote the opposition parties succeeded in proving the extent of their support. Thus the Gold Coast achieved independence as a country deeply divided, yet endowed with certain unquestionable assets—a buoyant economy, a well-developed educational system, and a highly efficient administrative structure. The country's new name symbolized the hopes felt by its people. By harking back to one of the greatest of the early kingdoms of West Africa, "Ghana" could well be regarded the clarion call of an African renaissance.

In sharp contrast to the rumbustious tone of Ghanaian or Nigerian politics in the last years of the colonial period, the decolonization of Sierra Leone was a relatively smooth and quiet process, reflecting what one Sierra Leonean writer has described as the country's "nonmilitant, acquiescent and almost apologetic nationalism." [191] Socially, the two most influential groups in Sierra Leone's population were the traditional chiefs of the protectorate and the Creole bourgeoisie of the colony (Freetown and its peninsula). The Creoles, immensely proud of their achievements in education and the professions, regarded the "tribesmen" of the protectorate with a mixture of fear and contempt. But once the British had decided to enlarge the legislative council to allow a reasonable measure of representation to the people of the protectorate, the days of Creole predominance were over. In the election of 1951, the first to be held on a country-wide basis, Dr. Milton Margai's Sierra Leone People's Party (SLPP) gained the largest number of seats. Margai was a Mende and the first man from the protectorate to qualify as a medical doctor; born in 1895, he was a good deal older than most contemporary African politicians and had spent his entire career in government service. His party, founded to advance the interests of the people of the protectorate, could count on the full support of the traditional chiefs. Given this backing and Margai's own cautious and undemonstrative manner, it was natural that the SLPP should pursue a conservative line based on cordial collaboration with the British administration. Younger men, among them Milton Margai's brother, Albert, anxious to pursue a more radical line, broke away from the party, formed rival groups, but usually ended by returning to the fold of the SLPP. Only in 1960, the year before independence, with the foundation of Siaka Stevens' All People's Congress (APC) did Sierra Leone acquire an effective opposition party with a radical base. Stevens himself was secretary of the Mineworkers Union and could count on the support of the younger radicals and the trade unionists.

The last weeks of the colonial period gave an unpleasant foretaste of the violence which was to characterize so much of Sierra Leone's politics in the first decade of independence. Ferocious clashes between rival groups of SLPP and APC supporters led the government to declare a state of emergency and to hold Siaka Stevens in temporary detention. Milton Margai died in 1964 and was succeeded by his brother, Albert. Under its new leader the SLPP rapidly declined in popularity, as the ministers in power gave evidence of increasing arrogance, extravagance, and incompetence. Taking Nkrumah's CPP as his model, Albert Margai talked of establishing a one-party state, but he was unable to prevent the APC from participating in the election of 1967. In the confusion that attended the announcement of the election results, with both parties claiming a victory and accusing each other of corruption and violence, the army stepped in. There followed a year of military rule, marked by faction fights within the army itself, but ending in the restoration of the civilian regime and the appointment of Siaka Stevens as prime minister. By 1970 Sierra Leone had regained something of the stability it had known under Milton Margai.

During the 1950's, The Gambia remained a political backwater. By far the smallest British colonial territory on the mainland of Africa (area, 4,000 square miles; present population about 320,000), the country was gradually propelled toward independence more by the prompting of its British administrators than by the demands of local politicians. Country-wide elections for the legislature were not held until 1960—previous elections had been confined to the capital, Bathurst. They led to the emergence of a pattern of political parties not unlike that seen in Sierra Leone in the early 1950's. For The Gambia presented the same unequal division between colony (Bathurst and neighborhood) and protectorate; and, as in Sierra Leone, the party representing the protectorate, the People's Progressive Party (PPP), led by Daudu Jawara, gained a convincing electoral victory. Independence came in 1965; eight years later the PPP was still in power.

Before independence there was talk of a federation between The Gambia and Senegal. But protracted discussions led to nothing more positive than a loose "treaty of association" between the two governments. And once The Gambia had found that it was capable of surviving as an independent state, nothing was done to press forward the plans for a closer association with its relatively powerful francophone neighbor. Indeed, in economic terms The Gambia gained something from its curious position, for many of its people took advantage of differences in prices to carry on a flourishing smuggling trade with neighboring Senegalese traders. But The Gambia's gain meant a serious loss to the Senegalese government. Gambians could hardly forget that their country is, in the vivid local metaphor, "a finger resting in Senegal's jaws." The time might come when a government in Dakar, less moderate than President Senghor's, might seek to bite off the offending member and so put an end to one of the strangest political entities created by the European partition of Africa.

▲▼ THE DECOLONIZATION OF FRENCH WEST AFRICA

By the end of 1960, the nine French territories in West Africa— Dahomey, Guinea, the Ivory Coast, Mauritania, Niger, Senegal, Soudan (Mali), Togo, and Upper Volta—had all achieved the status of sovereign independent states. Thus, in chronological terms, the transfer of power by the French had run roughly parallel to the gradual withdrawal of the British. Moreover, in both French and British territories the process of decolonization had been remarkably peaceful. But there was a sharp contrast in the methods used by the two metropolitan powers. The French concept of empire, harking back to a Roman model, made no allowance for the emergence of independent states. The French record of decolonization in other parts of the world—Syria, Indochina, North Africa—could be interpreted not as a gracious withdrawal but as a reluctant retreat in an atmosphere of violence and bitterness. And the French political scene, when contrasted with the British, was marked by greater instability and more intense party rivalry. The evolution of British West Africa in the 1940's and 1950's can be traced with only passing reference to political events in the metropolis. But the shifting politics of French West Africa cannot be understood without a fairly detailed knowledge of internal French politics. Another difficulty faces the student of French West Africa in the last decade of the colonial period. Unlike the British colonies, each of which can reasonably be studied in isolation, the French West African territories were linked closely together in an administrative federation. Some of the political parties which emerged after 1945 were formed on an inter-territorial basis, though each of them also possessed strong links with particular territories. Thus it is necessary to study French West African politics at three levels—territorial, inter-territorial, and metropolitan. Here there is only space to consider briefly first the development of metropolitan and inter-territorial politics, then the particular course of political change in four of the nine territories.

French West Africans were more deeply affected by World War II than their contemporaries in the neighboring British territories. Black troops were an important element in the French army and many African soldiers witnessed at first hand the catastrophic events of 1940. Africans were made aware, too, of the deep rift in the ranks of their masters between the supporters of the Vichy regime who controlled West Africa from 1940 to 1942 and the Free French under General de

Gaulle. Indeed, the only fighting to occur in West Africa took place between Frenchmen when a Free French force, with British naval support,
launched an unsuccessful attack on Dakar in September, 1940. In 1944,
after all the French colonies had rallied to the Free French cause, de
Gaulle summoned senior administrators to a conference at Brazzaville,
the capital of French Equatorial Africa, to discuss the future of the
French empire. A new spirit was clearly abroad, for many Frenchmen
were moved by a deep sense of gratitude to those African territories,
especially in Equatorial Africa, which had supported the Free French
from the first. Consequently there was much talk of reform, of the need
to make the system of colonial rule more equitable, to improve social
services, to plan vigorously for economic development. But there was to
be no fundamental political reappraisal. "The aims of the civilizing
work accomplished by France in the colonies," the preamble to the conference's "final resolutions" resoundingly declared, "exclude any thought
of autonomy . . . the idea of establishing, even in the distant future,
'self-government' in the colonies must be discarded." [192]

Nevertheless, even with autonomy ruled out, the new mood of liberalism made for significant political changes. Before the war only the *citoyens* of Senegal's four *communes* possessed political rights, being allowed to elect one member for the French parliament. In 1945, each of
the French African territories was invited to elect two African representatives to the Constituent Assembly. Provision for the continuing
representation of the African territories in the metropolitan parliament
was then formally incorporated in the constitution of the Fourth Republic. (Of the sixty-seven members of the French West African delegation
to Paris—twenty senators, twenty deputies, and twenty-seven counsellors of the French Union—forty-five were black or *métis,* of mixed descent.) At the same time the terms "union" and "overseas territories"
were substituted for "empire" and "colonies." Other important innovations included the abolition of the inferior status of *sujet,* thus transforming all French Africans into *citoyens,* and the establishment of territorial assemblies to serve as local legislatures. These constitutional
changes set in motion a vigorous outburst of political activity in many
parts of French Africa, with a multitude of parties being formed to
compete for the various metropolitan and territorial seats now open for
African election. At the same time, African deputies in Paris were
drawn into the main stream of French political life, attaching themselves to those parties, usually the socialists or the Communists, most
likely to serve their interests.

"Faithful to her traditional mission France intends," so the preamble
to the constitution proclaimed, "to lead the people she has taken into

her charge towards freedom to administer themselves and to regulate their own affairs democratically." [193] To many Africans these brave words had a hollow ring, as the liberal euphoria of the immediate postwar years began to evaporate. The worst abuses of the old system— forced labor and the *indigénat*—were abolished, but in other respects colonial administrators seemed as autocratic as ever. Little was done to Africanize the administration; educational development proceeded very slowly; and the territorial assemblies possessed extremely limited powers and paid too much attention to the interests of local French residents. Worried by the evidence of a move to the right in French politics, a number of prominent African politicians came together at Bamako in October 1946 to form an inter-territorial party, the *Rassemblement Démocratique Africain*. For tactical reasons the RDA worked closely with the French Communists. But when the Communists left the postwar coalition government in 1947 and decided to adopt a policy of undeviating hostility to the constantly shifting governments formed by other French parties, the leaders of the RDA found themselves in an increasingly frustrating position, attacked by the colonial authorities as much for their Communist affiliations as for their nationalist aspirations. In 1950, after two years of outright persecution, especially in the Ivory Coast, the RDA broke with the Communists. Colonial administrators still continued to intervene in territorial politics in support of the more conservative parties led by local notables anxious to preserve their privileged position, but they were stuggling against the tide. By the mid-1950's, the pressure of outside events—the withdrawal from Indochina, the surrender to the nationalists in Tunisia and Morocco, the rapid advance toward independence of Nigeria and the Gold Coast— made some change in French West African policy inevitable.

The "outline law" (*loi cadre*) introduced by Guy Mollet's Socialist government in 1956 went some way toward satisfying the demands of the nationalists for a substantial measure of internal self-government. Suffrage, hitherto restricted, was made universal; African representation was greatly increased in the territorial assemblies; and a post equivalent to that of prime minister was established in each territorial executive council and offered to the leader of the party to win the greatest number of seats in the territorial elections of 1957. But the structure of the federal government at Dakar remained unchanged, with executive power over a wide range of subjects still firmly in the hands of the French high commissioner. So, despite the reforms introduced by the *loi cadre,* independence on the Ghana model still seemed out of the question. Many African politicians were prepared to accept that their territories were too small and poor to stand on their own feet. At the same time, it was evident that the hold maintained by the French over the federal government precluded the possibility of a bid for independence by the federation as a whole. The situation was further complicated by a sharp division of opinion among French West African politicians on the future of the federation. Houphouët-Boigny, leader of the Ivory Coast, president of the inter-territorial RDA, and a member of the French government, had no desire to see preserved a federal structure to which his own territory, the richest in French West Africa, made by far the largest financial contribution without receiving much in return. Senghor of Senegal, on the other hand, expressed the views of many other West African politicians when he accused the French of following the old imperialist tactics of "divide and rule," of deliberately encouraging the "balkanization" of French West Africa by granting a measure of autonomy to individual territories. At this stage neither federalists nor antifederalists were prepared to contemplate a complete break with France, preferring to see themselves as members of a Franco-African Community, a super-federation in which French protection and French economic aid would still be assured.

In May, 1958, the political situation was suddenly transformed by the collapse of the Fourth Republic and the assumption of supreme power by General de Gaulle. The constitution of the Fifth Republic, in whose drafting Houphouët-Boigny played a prominent part, created the institutions needed for a French Community, but made no provision for the continuation of intermediate federations. In September, 1958, the constitution was put to the test of a referendum. In a promise that was also a threat, President de Gaulle made it clear that any territory which chose to vote "no" and thus signify its rejection of the constitution, would be granted immediate independence. To most French West African politicians the idea of a complete break with France was unthinkable. Though often exasperated by the shifts of French policy, they were deeply wedded to French culture and felt themselves bound to France by many intimate associations acquired in their student days and during the years spent as members of the French parliament. Moreover, they were vividly aware how greatly the economies of their respective territories were dependent on French aid. So it was only Guinea, under the leadership of Sékou Touré, the most radical of all French African politicians, that voted to reject the constitution.

Guinea's resounding "no" served ultimately to shatter the plan for a well-ordered Franco-African Community. The territory was granted immediate independence, but on terms apparently deliberately devised to warn other territories against choosing the same path; all French officials were withdrawn, and the flow of French aid was cut short. Nevertheless, Guinea survived and by surviving demonstrated to other French territories that total independence was not beyond their powers. Guinea's independence also disrupted the plans of those politicians who wished to preserve the federal structure of French West Africa. In 1959 Senegal and Soudan worked out plans for a smaller federation to be known as Mali after the great Malinke empire of the fourteenth century. Upper Volta, Niger, and Dahomey considered joining Senegal and Soudan, but were dissuaded by the resolute hostility of the Ivory Coast to any form of political federation and had to be content with a loose association, the *Conseil de l'Entente,* formed under the leadership of the Ivory Coast.

Early in 1960 the Federation of Mali lodged a formal request for independence. After long negotiations the request was granted, thus establishing a precedent which the other French African territories hastened to follow. The Federation of Mali lasted for only two months after independence. For reasons that will become apparent when the internal politics of Senegal and Soudan have been considered, the partnership proved unworkable. The name, Mali, was taken over by independent Soudan. Thus, by the end of September 1960, French West Africa had been finally broken up into its nine constituent parts. But most territories had achieved independence reluctantly and were anxious to maintain a close relationship with France. The French, for their part, were no less anxious to preserve as much influence as possible in their former African colonies. Consequently an elaborate series of "cooperation agreements" were drawn up between the metropolis and its ex-colonies. Mali alone gradually extracted itself from the French embrace, moving toward a position of independence similar to that of Guinea. The other former French territories were glad of the financial and technical assistance provided by the French and of the protection afforded by the continuing presence of French troops within their borders. Radical critics would say that independence on these terms was a sham; sympathizers that cordial cooperation with the French enabled the former colonies to enjoy the best of both worlds.

To appreciate to the full the politics of decolonization in French West Africa, it is essential to examine the particular experience of individual territories. The French territories differed in all the ways that serve to distinguish one country from another: area—Togo, the smallest, measured 22,000 square miles, Soudan (Mali), the largest, 465,000 square miles; population—the range lay between Mauritania with three quarters of a million people and Upper Volta with four and a half million; culture—Senegal, Mauritania, Mali, and Niger were strongly Islamized, the Ivory Coast, Togo, and Dahomey combined older African religions with a recent infusion of Christianity; and historical traditions —memories of great Sudanic empires in Soudan, of substantial kingdoms in Dahomey and among the Mossi of Upper Volta, of a multitude of miniscule polities in Togo and the Ivory Coast. Given these and other differences it was natural that each territory should develop its own unique form of political expression. Here there is space to consider the late colonial politics of only four French territories but those chosen —Senegal, Soudan, Guinea, and the Ivory Coast—present a remarkable variety of political experience.

Senegal was the only territory in French West Africa to have experienced open political activity in the years before World War II. But the right to participate in elections was limited to a favored minority, the *citoyens* of the four *communes*. And though Senegal had been represented by a deputy of African origin in Paris ever since Blaise Diagne's spectacular election victory in 1914, the politics of the four *communes* had degenerated in the 1930's into faction fights between rival personalities. In 1936 Lamine Gueye, a lawyer from Dakar and the first African to own a villa and a car, formed Senegal's first major political party as a branch of the French Socialist party (SFIO). In 1945 Gueye was elected as one of Senegal's two deputies to the constituent assembly in Paris. His co-deputy, Léopold-Sédar Senghor, was a schoolteacher of Serer origin, who had lived in France since 1932, made a considerable name for himself as a poet in French literary circles, and served in the French army in 1940. Both men stood out for their intellectual brilliance, their sophisticated assimilation of French culture. But there was a subtle distinction between them: Gueye was a *citoyen* and therefore a member of Senegal's privileged minority; Senghor was the son of a *sujet*.

The reforms of 1946 abolished the legal distinction between *sujets* and *citoyens,* but the *citoyens* of Dakar and St. Louis retained their sense of social superiority, and those who were members of the SFIO succeeded in gaining control of most of the new political posts created by the postwar reforms. Gradually Senghor established himself as the spokesman of the former *sujets,* expressing their resentment at the arrogance and nepotism of the former *citoyens* and taking issue with the leaders of the SFIO for following too slavishly the political line laid down by the French Socialists. In 1948 Senghor and his political associates broke away from the SFIO to form the *Bloc Démocratique Sénégalais* (BDS). The poet of *négritude,* the theoretician of "African Socialism" now proved himself a practical politician of consummate ability. A series of extended tours of the bush made him deeply familiar with the problems of the neglected peasantry and brought him into touch with many influential local personalities—the traditional chiefs, the leaders of Muslim fraternities, wealthy groundnut traders, prominent trade unionists, and war veterans. In this way he was able to construct the nexus of political alliances needed to provide the BDS with a mass backing. In 1951 Senghor's party achieved its first major electoral victory over the SFIO and went on to establish an impregnable position in Senegalese politics.

In 1958 Lamine Gueye's Socialists merged with the BDS, the combined parties taking on the name, *Union Progressiste Sénégalaise* (UPS). By this time Senghor's most bitter critics were to be found among the radical intelligentsia of the towns. For a time Senghor succeeded in persuading many of them to work within the UPS, but they broke away in protest against the UPS's decision to accept the 1958 constitution and founded their own political parties. To these "young Turks" of the left, with their passionate Marxist views, Senegal on the eve of independence seemed a country still largely dominated by the French, and they called for a more vigorous approach to africanization. But their appeal was to a limited circle and their hopes of practical support from the radical political leaders of Soudan were shattered with the collapse of the Federation of Mali. In 1960 Senghor could be regarded as one of the most firmly established leaders in French Africa.

Superficially the peoples of Senegal and Soudan appeared to have much in common: members of the same ethnic groups—Fulani, Sarakole, Malinke, and others—were to be found, though in varying proportions, in both territories; Islam was firmly established as the dominant religion; and for the vast majority of peasant farmers between the Atlantic coast and the Niger groundnuts provided the main source of cash-income. But there were also substantial differences between Senegalese and Soudanese. In the past, the territory of Soudan had provided the base for three of the most substantial polities in West African history, the great states created by the Malinke in the thirteenth and fourteenth centuries, by the Songhai in the sixteenth, and by the Tukulor under al-Hajj Umar in the latter half of the nineteenth century. Senegal's indigenous polities, the Wolof states and Futa Toro, had been by contrast much more modest constructions. On the other hand, the Senegalese had been far more powerfully influenced by French culture than the Soudanese, their country was richer and more urbanized, and their educational system more highly developed.

In the years immediately after World War II Soudanese politics was dominated by the struggle between two newly formed political parties, the *Parti Soudanais Progressiste* (PSP) and the *Union Soudanaise*. The parties originated as rival groups from the small educated elite of the territorial capital, Bamako, but as they extended their activities to other parts of the territory, they attracted different sections of the Soudanese population and so began to acquire radically different shades of political coloring. The PSP gained the support of many of the *chefs de canton* and found its securest bases in remote rural areas where many of the peasantry were still animists. Many PSP supporters were noted for their long record of amicable collaboration with the French authorities, a record which could be traced back to the 1890's when Bambara and Fulani groups living in the Upper Niger area had welcomed the French as liberators and rejoiced at the destruction of the Tukulor regime founded by al-Hajj Umar. The *Union Soudanaise,* on the other hand, appealed strongly to the Muslim intelligentsia of the urban centers, many of whose members came from families with a long record of resistance to French domination.

As the party of the chiefs, the PSP enjoyed the favor and support of many French administrators and so was able to achieve substantial majorities in all the elections held between 1946 and 1952. But for the *Union Soudanaise* the years spent in opposition served as a blessing in disguise, providing party militants both with the incentive and the opportunity to construct a highly efficient political machine powered by a forceful and well-defined ideology, "a blend of history, Islam and Socialism." [194] History allowed the people of the Soudan to feel a strong sense of national greatness. ("To the peoples of the richer forest states," a foreign observer recorded in the early 1960's, "Malians proudly say, 'Our wealth is our civilization.' ") [195] Islam, as propagated by the great religious leaders of the nineteenth century, provided a structure of ideas, at once puritanical and dynamic, to which most Soudanese could respond. Socialism in a Marxist-Leninist form was introduced to Soudanese intellectuals in the late 1940's by French Communists closely associated with the RDA, of which the *Union Soudanaise* was itself a branch. The new doctrine offered an attractive and coherent line of action to a modernizing and militantly anti-colonialist party. In building up their organization members of the *Union Soudanaise* laid constant stress on the need for collective leadership, for continual self-criticism, and for a regular flow of comment and information between the central political bureau and the local town and village branches.

After the *loi cadre* of 1956, French administrators ceased intervening in local politics: the PSP, denounced as the party of the collaborators, rapidly crumbled; and the *Union Soudanaise,* after winning a substantial majority in the elections to the territorial assembly in 1957, emerged under the leadership of Mobido Keita as a truly national party. Mobido Keita and his associates showed remarkable skill in restraining the tensions inevitably inherent in the relations between different ethnic, social, and occupational groups. In 1959 they even succeeded in persuading their old rivals in the PSP to dissolve their party and join the *Union Soudanaise,* thus ensuring that Soudan should achieve independence as a genuine one-party state. With their people solidly behind them, the Soudanese leaders committed themselves to erecting a still wider grouping by joining with Senegal in the Federation of Mali. But their audacious radicalism led to constant disputes with the more conservative Senegalese. The break with Senegal, though attended with many practical difficulties, was greeted with a sense of relief. "Now we are ourselves," Mobido Keita declared, "The secession from Senegal . . . will provide the opportunity for the Soudanese Republic to reach its political, economic, social and cultural goals by truly Socialist methods and with essential concern for the welfare of our poorest elements." [196]

The political transformation of Guinea in the course of the 1950's from one of the quietest of French colonies to the most revolutionary and controversial independent state in tropical Africa was a development even stranger and less predictable than the emergence of a strongly Socialist Mali. Compared with Senegal in the years immediately after World War II, Guinea could be regarded as a very backward territory. Senegal's exports were worth five times those of Guinea, while there were only 546 students attending upper primary and secondary schools in Guinea, compared with 3,000 in Senegal. For eight years after 1945 Guinean politics took the form of bitter rivalries between regional associations based on the main ethnic groups, the Fulani of Futa Jallon, the Malinke of Upper Guinea, and the various smaller groups of the coastlands, with local chiefs and French administrators constantly intervening in these political disputes. In 1947 the *Parti Démocratique de Guinée* (PDG) was founded as a branch of the interterritorial RDA, but the new party seemed unlikely to make a mark, for its membership was soon divided along ethnic lines into squabbling factions, and its most active supporters were persecuted by the French administration for their affiliation with the Communists.

Fortunately for the PDG's future, a young trade unionist of marked energy and ability, Sékou Touré, became secretary-general of the party in 1952. Born in 1922, Sékou Touré came of a younger generation than almost all the other leading politicians of French West Africa. He differed from them, too, in never having received a full secondary education. But his work as a trade unionist had brought him into close contact with the French Communist officials of the *Confédération Générale du Travail* (CGT). By the sophisticated *évolués* of Conakry, Sékou Touré might be contemptuously dismissed as an "illiterate demagogue"; in reality he had acquired from his European associates an education in

Marxist ideology and in political organization ideally suited to his temperament and his needs. "Trade unionism," Sékou Touré believed, "is a faith, a calling, an engagement to transform fundamentally any given social and economic regime, always in the search for the best and the beautiful and the just." [197] This was a profoundly revolutionary doctrine which might well—like so many idealistic aspirations—have fizzled out, had not circumstances strongly favored the growth of trade unions in Guinea. The early 1950's was a period of spectacular economic development as a result of the opening of iron ore mines and the exploitation of bauxite deposits. (The total quantity of Guinea's exports was 23,000 tons in 1946, over 1 million tons in 1954.) The rapid expansion of the industrial labor force provided Sékou Touré with the dynamic base needed for an effective political party. In 1953, Sékou Touré, in his capacity as secretary-general of the local section of the CGT, led a two-month-long strike in Conakry which forced the government to grant a 20 percent wage increase to the poorest paid workers. This spectacular victory made Sékou Touré a popular hero throughout French West Africa.

From the start of his political career Sékou Touré had stressed the need "to unite in democratic organs . . . men and women of all races, of all religions, around a common program for a common action." [198] A superb orator, tirelessly touring the country, he preached in speech after speech the gospel of fraternity and equality. "At sunset when you pray to God," he urged his hearers, "say over and over that each man is a brother and that all men are equal." [199] As a radical, he appealed to all those who were growing increasingly critical of the privileges enjoyed by traditional chiefs. As a Muslim, he was able to secure the support of some of the country's most influential religious leaders. As a clansman of the great warrior Samory, he was able to associate himself personally with the heroic tradition of resistance to French rule. But victory did not come without a struggle. Not until 1957, when the PDG won fifty-four out of sixty seats in the elections for the territorial assembly, was the party in a position to occupy the formal seats of power. As with the Union Soudanaise in Soudan, a prolonged period of opposition gave the PDG time and incentive to build up an effective system of political organization in the countryside and to develop among party stalwarts the revolutionary élan born of a not too violent struggle in which "history" was clearly on the side of the "militants."

Guinea's resounding vote of "no" in the 1958 referendum was the logical culmination of the PDG's policy. "We have to tell you bluntly, Mr. President," Sékou Touré told de Gaulle, when the French president visited Conakry in August, 1958, "what the demands of the people are.

. . . We have one prime and essential need: our dignity. . . . But there is no dignity without freedom. . . . We prefer freedom in poverty to opulence in slavery." [200] In voting for independence, the PDG leaders never envisaged a total break with France. But de Gaulle decided that Guinean independence should be interpreted in the most literal terms: French administrators and technicians were ordered to leave immediately, and French financial aid was cut off. If de Gaulle's intemperate reaction was intended to demonstrate to other African leaders that an ex-French colony could not survive on its own, it failed completely in its purpose. Guinea achieved a sudden international renown. Other nations, especially from the Communist bloc, came to its assistance. By demonstrating the practicability of independence even under the most adverse conditions, Sékou Touré provided African nationalists in many other parts of the continent with a lesson they took deeply to heart.

In sharp contrast to the mounting radicalism of Guinea and Soudan, the political evolution of the Ivory Coast took the form of a movement from revolutionary extremism to a cautious conservatism based on exceptionally cordial relations with the metropolis. Culturally the Ivory Coast was the most heterogeneous of French West African territories: its population, numbering little more than 3 million, was divided among sixty ethnic groups. With an economy based on constantly expanding exports of coffee, cocoa, timber, and bananas, the Ivory Coast established itself in the 1950's as the richest territory in French West Africa: in 1961 average per capita income in the Ivory Coast was estimated to be $223, compared with $198 in Senegal, $70 in Guinea, $68 in Mali, and $49 in Upper Volta. The wealth of the Ivory Coast was reflected in the emergence of an African bourgeoisie, a social group far less evident in other parts of French West Africa.

As early as the 1930's, a number of Africans in the Ivory Coast were making substantial incomes from their newly established coffee and cocoa plantations. They were not the only planters in the country, for the French authorities, unlike the British in the neighboring Gold Coast, had encouraged Europeans to acquire land. The European plantocracy was small in numbers—probably never exceeding 300 estate owners—but it acquired great influence, especially during the war years when the pro-Vichy colonial authorities allowed Europeans a higher price for their crops than African farmers, awarded them more generous subsidies, and arranged for them to have exclusive access to supplies of forced labor. After the fall of the Vichyites in 1943, African planters formed their own union, the *Syndicat Agricole Africain,* to press for the removal of the bitterly resented forms of discriminations in favor of Europeans. The union was led by Félix Houphouët, a prosperous plantation owner who was also a *chef de canton* and a doctor trained at the medical school in Dakar. In 1945 Houphouët was elected to the French constituent assembly; at the same time he set about constructing a party on a territory-wide basis, the *Parti Démocratique de la Côte d'Ivoire* (PDCI), linking the many urban associations which had sprung up after the war with his own well-endowed planters' union. In Paris Houphouët soon gave proof of his effectiveness as a politician, being actively involved in the passing of a law abolishing the hated system of forced labor. To the mass of his fellow countrymen who had suffered more from the *corvée* than most other French Africans this was a heroic achievement. An enthusiastic local poet, expressing the idolatry with which many Ivorians regarded their champion and their liberator, wrote:

> *You are the king of the factories,*
> *You are the king of the fields,*
> *You are the people,*
> *You are the master. . . .*[201]

And Houphouët himself bore witness to his own intense self-confidence by adding to his name the Baule word *boigny*, "irresistible force."

Hard days lay ahead. In 1946 Houphouët-Boigny played a leading part in the foundation of the inter-territorial RDA and gladly accepted the new party's close association with the French Communists. But in 1947 the Communists left the French government and turned to violent opposition. To the colonial authorities on the Ivory Coast, the spectacle of a well-organized nationalist party closely in league with the Communists was deeply alarming, while the European planters, tormented by exaggerated fears of possible massacre, were loud in their demands for strong measures. There followed in 1949 and 1950 a series of the most violent "incidents"—involving the death of at least fifty Africans—in the late colonial history of French West Africa, as the French administration attempted to crush the power of the PDCI. Chiefs and civil servants known to support the party were summarily dismissed; hundreds of party militants were thrown into prison; and every effort was made to encourage and support the party's African opponents. Deeply alarmed by the turn of events, Houphouët-Boigny decided to break with the Communists and follow the path of conciliation and cooperation with the colonial authorities. The new policy paid off handsomely. French officials, too, were becoming increasingly worried about the situation. There were many opportunities for local conflict in Ivorian society—between different ethnic groups, between chiefs and commoners, between *originaires* (locally-born people) and "strangers" (traders and migrant laborers from other parts of West Africa). The PDCI had temporarily succeeded in uniting all these groups; the French policy of openly favoring the PDCI's opponents had aroused such bitter animosities that some districts seemed on the verge of civil war. Yet the French had failed to discover a viable alternative to the PDCI. Cooperation between the colonial authorities and the dominant political party was essential if the country was to be prevented from falling into a state of anarchy. With his personal influence steadily growing in Paris—in 1956 he became a member of the French cabinet—Houphouët-Boigny was able to exploit to the full his indispensability to the French authorities, securing the removal of unpopular French officials, and making sure of the provision of a steady flow of financial aid for development.

Houphouët-Boigny was in no hurry to achieve independence for his country. As a supreme pragmatist he must have found ideas such as those put forward by Sékou Touré absurdly romantic. "National independence" seemed to him "meaningless in the face of economic underdevelopment." "Freedom," he declared, "will never thrive in the midst of misery." [202] Such a line of thinking was hardly calculated to appeal to the students returning from French universities and to local trade unionists who, by the late 1950's, came to represent Houphouët-Boigny's most scathing local critics, but his own prestige was so immense that he had little difficulty in warding off these attacks. Moreover, his personal authority was greater than that of any other leader in French West Africa. The PDCI provided an efficient machine for bringing in the votes at elections: in 1957 and again in 1960, the party won all the seats in the territorial assembly. But the party's organization had never been effectively rebuilt after the troubles of 1950 and many of the old rancours still persisted. Indeed, in 1957 some party officials "found it unsafe to venture outside the towns because of widespread hostility to them in the rural areas." [203] The higher echelons of the party were completely dominated by Houphouët-Boigny and his hand-picked group of loyal supporters. "The people," one of the members of this inner circle explained to a foreign observer, "are amorphous, they cannot study problems such as questions of economic development. We need a system in which the alternatives are debated by an elite." [204]

There was another striking difference between Houphouët-Boigny's ideas and those of most other French West African politicians. Though Houphouët-Boigny had played a leading part in the inter-territorial RDA of which his own party was a section, he had come to reject completely all plans for retaining a federal structure in French West Africa. Again his approach was entirely pragmatic. As the richest territory in French West Africa, the Ivory Coast was required to make the largest contribution to the federal government at Dakar. Why should the Ivory

Coast continue to tolerate such a drain on its resources, when it needed every franc for its own development? On the other hand, Houphouët-Boigny was whole-heartedly in favor of de Gaulle's plans for a Franco-African Community, believing that the new association would result in an increased flow of aid to the Ivory Coast. For this reason he was deeply angered by Guinea's vote of "no" in the 1958 referendum, and he was also opposed to the projected Federation of Mali. But he was prepared to construct a much looser association between the Ivory Coast, Upper Volta, Niger, and Dahomey, an association which came to be known as the *Conseil de l'Entente*. Finally, when the Mali federation pressed for independence in 1960, Houphouët-Boigny saw that the plans for a Franco-African Community had proved abortive and had no hesitation in demanding independence for his own country.

▲▼ THE INDEPENDENT STATES OF WEST AFRICA

By 1970 most West African countries had experienced a decade of independence. The gloomiest prophets had been confounded: no former colony had shown itself totally incapable of assuming the heavy responsibilities of sovereignty. With the major exception of the Nigerian civil war there had been no violent outbreaks of disorder in the former French and British territories. Nor had events confirmed the views of those observers who thought they could detect a political pattern common to all West African countries. In the early 1960's there was much talk both in West Africa and in the outside world of the inevitability of single-party rule in newly independent states whose leaders were grappling with the problems of national integration and could not therefore tolerate the existence of a potentially disruptive opposition. By the mid-1960's a series of military coups—in Dahomey, Togo, Upper Volta, Nigeria, Ghana, Sierra Leone, and Mali—showed that the politicians who led their countries to independence were far from invulnerable. Yet military rule was never regarded, even by most soldiers, as a desirable system in itself; military regimes were seen as essentially transitional in character, providing an opportunity for the construction of a new political system purged of the abuses that had done so much to discredit the old structure which the soldiers had demolished. By 1969 civilian governments were back in power in Ghana and Sierra Leone, and civilians, whether former politicians or civil servants, were closely associated with the work of government in all the other countries that had experienced military coups. To disprove the assumption that military coups were the inevitable sequel to one-party rule, five West African states—Senegal, Guinea, Ivory Coast, Niger, and Gambia—were still ruled by the leaders who had brought them to independence.

Given this striking diversity—a diversity that contrasts sharply with the relative uniformity of the colonial period—any historian, looking at postcolonial West Africa, must be on his guard against facile generalizations. All West African countries may indeed be seen as facing the same basic problems of national integration and social and economic development. But environments differ sharply from country to country. With recent historical experience varying so greatly from territory to territory, each of the countries of West Africa may be seen as gradually evolving its own personality. In these circumstances there is no alternative but to consider, albeit briefly, the political developments of the region's six most prominent states—Nigeria, Ghana, Senegal, Guinea, Mali, and the Ivory Coast.

That Nigeria should have experienced in its first decade of independence a greater measure of tribulations than any other country in West Africa was hardly surprising. The sheer size and heterogeneity of the country's population presented obvious problems to the men who took over the reigns of government from the British, and the deep and often bitter divisions that had emerged between rival political parties in the decade before independence gave a clear warning of troubles ahead. Yet to superficial observers at the time of independence in 1960 the prospect for a stable Nigerian democracy did not seem unfavorable. The constitution had been hammered out after years of discussion between Nigerian politicians and was provided with an elaborate range of safeguards designed to prevent illiberal practices. In each of the three regions one of the country's major parties was in control; the Northern People's Congress in the North, the Action Group in the West, and in the East the National Council of Nigerian Citizens—"citizens" had been substituted for "Cameroons" in the party's name, after the West Cameroons had voted in 1961 to leave the Nigerian Federation and join French Cameroon. The federal government was controlled by a coalition between the NPC and the NCNC with the Action Group forming a parliamentary opposition.

Some indication of the complexity of Nigerian politics could be seen in the position of the federal prime minister, Alhaji Sir Abubukar Tafawa Balewa, who was only vice-president of the NPC and therefore in a sense subordinate to the leader of the party, the premier of the Northern Region, Alhaji Sir Ahmadu Bello, Sardauna of Sokoto. By contrast, the leader of the Action Group, Chief Obafemi Awolowo, chose to become leader of the opposition in the federal parliament, leaving to his deputy, Chief Samuel Akintola, the premiership of Western Nigeria. No less paradoxical was the fact that so consummate a politician as Dr. Nnamadi Azikiwe, leader of the NCNC and former premier of the

Eastern Region, should have chosen to take the largely apolitical post of governor-general and later president under the republican constitution of 1961.

The first sign of a serious rift in this apparently satisfactory balance was produced in 1962 by a split in the Action Group. Awolowo and his supporters, faced with the frustrations of opposing the coalition government in the federal house, were developing increasingly radical ideas; at the same time Akintola and the Action Group ministers in Ibadan, the capital of the Western Region, were enriching themselves from the wide range of emoluments available to Nigerian politicians in power. A complicated train of events led to the imprisonment of Awolowo, sentenced for plotting against the federal government after a trial of doubtful impartiality, and the creation by Akintola of a new party, the Nigerian National Democratic Party. With federal assistance Akintola established himself even more firmly than before as regional premier in Ibadan. Shortly afterward, the Western Region was reduced in size as the result of the creation of a Midwest Region with its capital at Benin, and its regional government under the control of the NCNC. These changes in the political balance of the West were soon to be linked to a crisis of nation-wide dimensions as tension steadily increased between the North and the South.

In the early 1950's many Northerners had been fearful of "Southern domination." A decade later the situation was reversed: with the NPC clearly the dominant partner in the federal government in Lagos, Southerners began to feel the pressure of "Northern domination." Southern attitudes to the North were made up of a mixture of fear, ignorance, and contempt. In Awolowo's phrase the North was "a dead weight on the country as a whole," "a gradual but sure brake on the fast-moving South." [205] Yet with more than half the seats in the federal parliament allocated to the Northern Region, the NPC seemed assured of a permanent majority. Many Southerners hoped that the results of a new census held in 1962 would show that the population of the North had been overestimated at the previous census of 1953, but when, after a second count, the census figures were finally published in 1964, the North was given a population of 30 million, the South of 26 million. As a population count the Nigerian census was attended with so much chicanery as to be totally useless. As a political issue it led to such bitter feeling between the NPC and the NCNC that the coalition disintegrated just at a time when all political parties were preparing for the federal general election due to be held at the end of 1964.

To fight the election, the two main Southern parties, the NCNC and the Action Group, together with the small opposition parties in the

North, formed the United Grand Progressive Alliance (UGPA). To counter this apparently formidable force the NPC joined with Akintola's NNDP and small opposition groups in the East to establish the National Nigerian Alliance (NNA). In essence the election might be regarded as a contest between North and South, but the split in Yoruba ranks between Awolowo's Action Group and Akintola's NNDP meant that the NPC could now count on far more powerful support in the South than the UGPA could ever hope to obtain in the North. The election campaign was conducted in an atmosphere "reeking" in President Azikiwe's words, "of mutual antagonisms, bitter recriminations and tribal discrimination." [206] Finding that many of their candidates in Northern constituencies were being prevented from securing nomination, the UPGA leaders decided to boycott the election. In so doing they assured their opponents of victory in the North and West; with 197 of the 310 seats in their possession the NNA thus gained a comfortable majority in the federal parliament. Reluctantly, after a week of acute crisis, President Azikiwe asked Tafawa Balewa to re-form the government. Unable to resist the lure of office, many of the NCNC ministers in the last government again accepted ministerial appointments.

Ten months later regional elections were held in the West. The NNDP's popularity had steadily declined and it was widely assumed that the party would suffer a crushing defeat at the hands of the UPGA. But Akintola and his supporters had grown so adept in the techniques of rigging elections that they were able to return a massive majority, "winning" seventy-one of the eighty-eight seats. It was a hollow victory. During the elections both sides had used gangs of thugs to support their cause. After the results had been announced violence increased alarmingly. UPGA demonstrators were shot down by the police, NNDP supporters murdered by their opponents; "anarchy" and "civil war" were not inappropriate terms to apply to the situation in the West in the last months of 1965.

Political violence was only one symptom of the deep malaise gripping Nigeria. More irksome to ordinary Nigerians was the wide-spread corruption of which almost all Nigerian politicians seemed guilty. The large cars, the lavish expense accounts, the grandiose official residences provided the man in the street with clear evidence of the rewards which his rulers were gaining from their periods in office. Politicians at regional and federal levels had become expert at building up highly profitable systems of patronage, dispensing—at a suitable price—jobs, scholarships, contracts, and commercial loans to their clients. A commission of inquiry held in the Western Region in 1963 after the fall of the Action Group revealed that the party had diverted to its own coffers millions of pounds of public money. Had similar commissions been established in other parts of the federation they might well have produced even more startling figures.

By early 1966 Nigeria might well be regarded as a country ripe for revolution. Yet the events which occurred on the night of January 14–15 were more surprising and more shocking than any close observer of the Nigerian scene could ever have predicted. Groups of middle-ranking army officers, Ibo in origin but avowedly unaffected by "tribal considerations," operating simultaneously in Lagos and in the Northern and Western regional capitals, Kaduna and Ibadan, murdered four of Nigeria's leading politicians—the federal prime minister, Tafawa Balewa; the premiers of the North and of the West, the Sardauna of Sokoto and Chief Akintola; and the vastly corrupt federal finance minister, Chief Festus Okotie-Eboh—together with almost all of the most senior Northern and Western army officers. But the young officers failed to set up a government of their own choice and had to see power pass into the hands of the commander of the Nigerian army, another Ibo but one not involved in the coup, General Aguiyi-Ironsi, and to the military governors appointed in each of the regions. On the other hand, as a purely destructive operation, the coup proved brilliantly effective. Amid scenes of popular rejoicing in the South, the "old gang" of corrupt politicians were driven from office. It seemed a Nigerian 1789, the birth of a new era, a second chance to fulfil the high hopes of 1960.

It was not surprising in the Nigerian context that Ironsi, as an Ibo, should turn for advice to other Ibos, particularly to these who occupied senior civil service posts in Lagos. The new military government found itself in an exceptionally difficult position. Almost all Nigerian politicians had been discredited; Ironsi himself was a nonpolitical soldier; many of his advisers harbored "ingrained technocratic sentiments" and regarded "the vocation of politics" with contempt.[207] Yet the country's problems were essentially political in nature and needed to be tackled with tact and imagination. The solution proposed by the military government was in accordance with the ideas advanced by the NCNC in the early 1950's. Excessive "regionalism" had been, it was argued, a major cause of the downfall of the old regime; Nigeria needed a strong central government to preserve its unity. With substantial Ibo communities settled in every region it was much easier for Ibos than for any other ethnic group to think in terms of national unity. Northerners viewed the situation quite differently. Their two leading politicians, Tafawa Balewa and the Sardauna, had been murdered by Ibo officers. By most Northerners "strong central government" was equated with a sinister plot to achieve Ibo domination. Suddenly, in May, after the military government had issued a decree formally abolishing the federation and transforming the old regions into "groups of provinces," Northerners hit back in a series of murderous attacks on Ibos living in the main centers of the North. This savage pogrom appears to have been "both organized and spontaneous" [208] with former NPC politicians urging on the urban mobs.

In June many Northerners began seriously to consider the possibility of secession. But at the end of July another violent episode gave a new twist to the political situation. Northern troops stationed in Lagos and Abeokuta mutinied, murdered many of their Ibo officers, and arrested and shot Ironsi. A young Northern officer, Colonel Yakubu Gowon, now became "supreme commander." Gowon represented a new type of Northerner, for he was a Christian from the Middle Belt, and his sudden rise to power could be seen as symptomatic of the emergence of a powerful new force in Nigerian politics, that of the Northern Middle Belters. In the days of NPC domination in the North, many Middle Belters had seen themselves as an oppressed minority. Unable to achieve their goal of a separate Middle Belt region, the Tiv, the largest ethnic group in the area, had turned so violently against the NPC supporters in their midst that the regional government had brought troops into the Tiv districts in 1960 and again in 1964 to restore order. Now, in 1966, the Middle Belters found themselves in an unexpectedly powerful position, for their numbers far exceeded all other ethnic groups among the soldiers of the Nigerian army.

With order re-established after the countercoup of July, Nigerians could turn to the major political problem that confronted their country, that of discovering a new political formula acceptable to all sides. Meetings of "leaders of thought" were held in the regions and a Constitutional Review Conference met in Lagos. Its most prominent members were politicians with a record of sustained oppositon to the old federal regime—Awolowo, recently released from prison, Aminu Kano, leader of the radical Northern Elements' Progressive Union and J. S. Tarka, leader of the United Middle Belt Congress. The discussions revealed that a remarkable shift had taken place in the views of the various regional representatives. Easterners abandoned the idea of a strong central government and talked in terms of a loose confederation of regions. Northerners, on the other hand, ceased threatening secession and suggested that each region should be broken up into a number of separate states. Catastrophically, these discussions were interrupted by one of the most horrifying outbreaks of violence that Africa has ever known. Allegedly provoked by reports of attacks on Hausa communities in the Eastern Region, Northern mobs, assisted by mutinous soldiers, launched a renewed attack on the Ibos in their midst. At least as many as 10,000 Ibos are reckoned to have been killed in these September massacres, and about 1 million panic-stricken Ibo refugees streamed back from the North and West to an already densely-populated Eastern Region.

The Ibos could now claim with some justification that a federation which offered them no guarantee of safety beyond their regional borders was a meaningless political structure. Rapidly the gulf between the East and the rest of Nigeria widened, with Colonel Ojukwu, military governor of the Eastern Region, assuming the role of popular leader within his own region. On May 30, 1967, Ojukwu, in response to immense popular pressure, proclaimed the transformation of the Eastern Region into the independent Republic of Biafra. On the same day Gowon made an equally momentous announcement: the regions were abolished and Nigeria was to be divided into twelve states. With the Northern Region divided up into six states the image of a monolithic North, capable of dominating the rest of Nigeria, was finally shattered. But the new constitutional structure was still unacceptable to the Ibos, for the former Eastern Region was divided into three states, two of which—Rivers and South-East—would probably be dominated by the Ijaw, the Ibibio, and other non-Ibo peoples, leaving to the Ibos the small East-Central State. With the federal government branding Ojukwu's proclamation as "an act of rebellion," war became inevitable.

The Nigerian Civil War lasted from July, 1967, to January, 1970. Measured by the number of troops deployed by the two sides, the war represented by far the most substantial conflict ever recorded in the history of West Africa. No accurate figures for casualties exist, but deaths, particularly among the famine-stricken civilian population of Biafra, may well have been numbered in the hundreds of thousands. So stubborn was Biafran resistance, particularly in the Ibo heartland, that the outcome of the war often seemed in doubt, but the federal army had the advantage not only of larger numbers but also—as supplies of British and Russian arms steadily mounted—of infinitely greater fire-power. African and Commonwealth statesmen made many attempts to bring the two sides together, but the determined insistence of Colonel Ojukwu and his supporters on Biafra's right to sovereignty proved an insuperable barrier to a negotiated settlement. So the war was fought to the bitter end, culminating in a defeat for Biafra as complete as that suffered by the Southern States of America in a not altogether dissimilar conflict more than one hundred years earlier.

Both the American and the Nigerian civil wars were fought to preserve the unity of a great federation. Certainly in 1970 Nigerian unity

seemed more firmly established than at any time since the British withdrawal. But the country was still faced with a formidable range of political problems. Military government was a form of rule irksome to many
Nigerians. Yet the military could not hand over power to a civilian regime until the country had been provided with a constitution acceptable
to all the main groups. Such a constitution would need not only to define the powers to be allowed to the states established in 1967, but also
to lay down the exact number of such states. For by 1970 the twelve-
state structure hastily introduced in 1967 was under severe criticism,
with many Nigerians pressing for the creation of new states to satisfy
the demands for autonomy of often quite small ethnic groups. Here, indeed, was a danger of "tribalism" running riot.

Two other imponderables cast a shadow over the future—the position of the army and the destiny of the Ibo people. Federal Nigeria had
begun the civil war with an army less than 10,000 strong; by 1970 the
federal army numbered more than 100,000 men and the government
had no plans for rapid demobilization. Even after a return to civilian
rule, an army of such a size was bound to exert a profound influence
on Nigerian life at many different levels. Even more problematical appeared the future position of the Ibo people. Their homeland, the East-
Central State, was the most densely populated area in the whole of Nigeria. In the past, population pressure had forced many Ibos to migrate
to other parts of the federation in search of employment. By 1970,
many of the posts in government and commerce once occupied by Ibos
had passed as a result of the events of the previous four years to local
people not only in the North and West but also in the non-Ibo parts of
the former Eastern Region. The Ibos enjoyed a well-earned reputation
for energy and enterprise. Their neighbors in the Mid-West and Rivers
states seemed likely to grow rapidly richer as a result of the discovery
of large quantities of oil in the Niger Delta area. The East Central
State, with an economy based mainly on agricultural produce, could
nourish no such hopes of easy economic development. Should Nigeria's
Ibos find themselves impoverished, frustrated and embittered by the
country's new political structure, fresh tensions of an extremely grave
nature seemed bound to arise. Indeed, it is difficult to imagine an independent country with a population as large and as heterogeneous as Nigeria's ever experiencing those long stretches of political stability which
smaller nations, especially in Europe, accept as the norm.

The first decade of Ghanaian independence was dominated by the
figure of a single man. For Kwame Nkrumah, prime minister and later
president of Ghana, and leader of the Convention People's Party, came
to develop a system of rule whose peculiarly personal character was

without exact parallel elsewhere in postcolonial Africa. If political systems be judged by their durability, then Nkrumah's must be accounted a failure, for it lasted no more than nine years. Yet in his heyday the Ghanaian leader enjoyed a measure of international esteem accorded to few other political leaders of modern times. To peoples in many parts of the world Kwame Nkrumah seemed a heroic and symbolic figure, the reviver of African dignity, the scourge of the "imperialists," the first black African to achieve the status of a world statesman. In his own country, on the other hand, though he certainly enjoyed immense popularity among certain sections of the population, Nkrumah's standing had always been more questionable. By many of the older leaders of Ghanaian society, the chiefs and the intelligentsia, he was cordially disliked as a social and political upstart. In certain parts of the country, especially in Ashanti and in the Northern Territories, his party, the CPP, had encountered bitter opposition as early as 1955. And the first months of independence were clouded by violent disturbances among the Ewe of Togoland and the Ga of Accra.

These potential threats were countered by harsh measures including the "preventive detention" of many of the CPP's political opponents. In 1960 Nkrumah increased his formal powers when, after an election designed to convey the impression of public support, he assumed the position of an executive president under the country's new republican constitution. At the same time, the power of the governing CPP was greatly increased and the influence of its more militant members brought to bear on many sections of Ghanaian life through the operation of "patriotic organizations" based on models mainly of Communist origin. These new bodies—the Young Pioneers, the revised Trade Union Congress, the United Farmers' Council and others—were intended to "mobilize" the activities of those groups in the population most likely to support the interests of the CPP. Rapidly in the first years of independence the CPP came to be identified "not only with 'the general will of the nation,' but with the total power of the state." [209]

The activities of the opposition provided Nkrumah with a means of justifying the increasingly authoritarian nature of his regime. Frustrated by the failure of constitutional forms of opposition, some anti-CPP politicians began to consider lines of action that the government could reasonably describe as "subversive." The first in a series of "plots" against the regime was uncovered in 1958. Later a number of attempts were made to assassinate the president. These violent incidents served as pretexts for harsh and oppressive measures but they do not in themselves provide a sufficient explanation for the emergence of a highly authoritarian regime among a people possessing a deeply ingrained tradition of political discussion. The CPP state in Ghana must be seen as the creation of a man obsessed with his own highly emotional view of the world, incapable of understanding the aspirations of those whose ideas differed from his own, prepared to accept with equanimity "the need," to quote his own words, "for extreme measures of a totalitarian kind," [210] and supported by a group of followers who soon found the tenure of high office so entrancing that they were prepared to do all in their power to bolster up their own positions of authority.

With his power apparently firmly based on the support of a loyal party, Nkrumah came to devote an increasing amount of his time to external affairs, transferring his revolutionary aspirations to the international stage, preaching the gospel of pan-Africanism, and launching constant verbal tirades against the "sinister forces" of "neo-colonialism." These ideas formed a major part of that curious intellectual phenomenon, too ill-structured to be defined as an ideology, to which he gave his name. "Nkrumahism," in the words of a CPP leader-writer of the time, "is the quest for African unity and independence, a way of life that ensures security, abundance and prosperity for all through brotherly love." To a sympathetic American observer Nkrumahism seemed to possess some of the qualities of "a modern religious crusade"; by critical Ghanaians, on the other hand, the new doctrine was wittily dismissed as "the highest form of opportunism." [211]

These external and intellectual pursuits of "a romantic African Marxist" determined, as one well-informed English critic remarked, "to play the part of a revolutionary" [212] offered a dangerous distraction for a man who was also leader of a political party and ruler of a volatile people and a fast developing country. Moreover, by 1960 it was clear that the CPP was losing its early radicalism. Party militants, deprived of the stimulus offered by a formidable opposition, and eagerly profiting from the new sources of wealth put at their disposal by the offices to which they had been appointed, became increasingly divorced from the common people. In 1961 Nkrumah attempted to restore something of the old spirit by purging the party of its right wing, thus depriving himself of the support of some of his oldest and ablest collaborators. Yet the loyalty of the extreme left wing, to whom the president turned for support, was soon called in question when leading left-wingers were arrested after a bomb-attack on the president in August, 1962. In the course of the next three years, other important sections of the community, including the judiciary, the police, and the army, were humiliated by Nkrumah's erratic displeasure. An efficient civil service still maintained the machinery of government, but several of the country's ablest officials resigned in exasperation and took employment with international agencies.

Meanwhile Nkrumah continued to push forward his plans for Ghanaian development. Some of the large-scale projects of the Nkrumah era—notably the Volta Dam and the new harbor at Tema—could be regarded as highly impressive achievements. But many of the later schemes, proposed to the president by self-seeking businessmen from both the Communist and the non-Communist world, proved disastrously ill-conceived. Thus a massive system of silos for storing cocoa was constructed before it had even been ascertained that cocoa could be safely stored for long periods in the tropics. Equally irksome to the Ghanaian public was the construction of a number of grandiose state buildings erected to satisfy the whims of the president. Nkrumah's economic policy in the early 1960's bears a striking resemblance to that of the extravagant Khedive Ismail of Egypt almost exactly a century earlier. In both cases large scale capital projects could be paid for only by borrowing at increasingly high rates of interest from overseas creditors. Between 1963 and 1965 Ghana's total external debt rose from 38 million to 378 million new *cedis*. At the same time, a fall in the price of cocoa on the world market added to the government's economic difficulties. Mounting inflation was a direct consequence of the president's economic policy. Even the price of local foodstuffs rose sharply, thus posing, in the words of an official report, "a very real threat to the morale of our people." [213] In the past the market mammies of Accra had been among the most enthusiastic supporters of the man who once called every Ghanaian woman his bride. That they should now turn against the president was evidence of a serious loss of support among the common people.

Nevertheless Nkrumah might still have weathered this storm, had he followed the example of his fellow radical, President Sékou Touré of Guinea, and taken the trouble to maintain an efficient party machine. But by 1965 the CPP was a party in decline and Nkrumah himself a lonely and frightened man who rarely dared to show his face in public, preferring to live surrounded by a personal bodyguard and by a court of foreign "advisers." The end came suddenly in February, 1966, when the president was out of the country on a visit to Peking. A swift and almost bloodless army coup, greeted with tumultuous rejoicing by Ghanaians in all sections of society, shattered within a few hours the structure of Nkrumahist rule.

To provide an interim government the officers formed themselves into the National Liberation Council. Civilian support came from the civil service and from anti-CPP politicians, many of whom had spent years in prison or in exile. The tasks which the NLC set itself were necessarily austere: to expose, through a series of commissions of inquiry, the misdeeds of the CPP; to correct, through strict measures, the costly mistakes of an economic policy that had brought the country to the edge of ruin; and finally to ensure a return to civilian rule after the drawing up of a new constitution. By 1969 all these tasks had been successfully completed. General elections, held in the same year, resulted in a decisive victory (105 out of 140 seats) for the newly formed Progress Party led by Dr. Kofi Busia. Busia could be regarded as a representative of the intelligentsia and of the more conservative forces in Ghanaian society. A vigorous opponent of the CPP from the early 1950's, he had gone into exile in 1959 and became a university professor in Europe. His quiet, academic, low-key style of leadership offered the sharpest possible contrast to the flamboyance of his predecessor. By permitting political opponents freedom to express their views inside and outside parliament, the new Ghanaian government gave evidence of a degree of liberal thinking that seemed strange and refreshing in the contemporary context. Unfortunately, Dr. Busia's government failed to live up to the expectations of its well-wishers, proving itself particularly inept in its handling of a difficult economic situation. In January, 1972, it was overthrown in a bloodless military coup. The new government, the National Redemption Council under the chairmanship of Colonel Ignatius Acheampong, showed considerable toughness in its handling of the country's problems, introducing a note of radicalism that had not been heard since Nkrumah's downfall. Nkrumah himself died in exile in May, 1972.

The political history of independent Senegal seems smooth and uneventful when compared with that of modern Nigeria or Ghana. Clearly the relatively small size of the country's population— with 3½ million inhabitants Senegal contained half as many people as Ghana—made the task of government somewhat easier. But Senegal also enjoyed the signal advantage of a greater measure of cultural homogeneity among its main ethnic groups than any other country in West Africa. Its four major groups, Wolof, Serer, Fulani, and Tukulor, comprising 75 percent of the total population, had developed broadly similar social and political institutions, while the Wolof language had become the *lingua franca* of the country and Islam the religion of the vast majority of the people. Other factors capable of breaking down the barriers between ethnic groups—notably the French policy of assimilation and the rapid growth of towns were of much greater significance in Senegal than in other parts of francophone West Africa.

Yet Sengalese society also contained potential sources of tension. The country's non-African population, made up mainly of French and Lebanese and numbering about 50,000, represented the largest distinctly alien community to be found in any part of West Africa. Senegalese Muslims offered spiritual allegiance to a number of rival religious leaders. Sharp contrasts in the manner and standard of living existed between such groups as the industrial workers of Dakar and the improverished Tukulor peasantry of the *Valleé du Fleure*. And there had been a distinct growth of regional consciousness in the isolated Casamance lying between Gambia and Portuguese Guinea. To hold such divisive forces in check Senegal needed firm and prudent government. The regime built up by President Senghor admirably satisfied the country's immediate postindependence needs.

In the years before independence Senghor had shown his skill as a politician: a Catholic, he gained the support of the leading *marabouts;* an intellectual of great sophistication, he showed himself able to establish close contact with the peasantry; an ex-*sujet,* he won over many of the former *citoyens* of the four *communes.* Thus Senghor's political technique could be regarded as the exact opposite of Nkrumah's. While the Ghanaian leader moved towards a position of almost total isolation, losing the support of one section of the community after another, Senghor sought to incorporate all the sections of Senegalese society in one political party, the *Union Progressiste Sénégalaise* (UPS). In 1966 the president succeeded in persuading members of the left-wing *Parti du Regroupment Africain,* who had opposed his regime since 1958, to merge their party with his own. Two years later, Senghor suddenly found himself faced with a really serious threat to his regime when students from Dakar University joined with local trade unionists in violent demonstrations against the government. The situation bore a striking resemblance to contemporary events in Paris; indeed the Dakar movement was profoundly influenced by the French students' campaign against de Gaulle. Senghor's government was saved not by its political supporters—the UPS proved useless in an emergency—but by the army.

The crisis of 1968 revealed the limitations of Senghor's achievement. Politically he had been brilliantly successful in securing a wide measure of consensus. But his government had failed to produce a substantial improvement in the material conditions of Senegalese life. The country's economy was still largely dependent on groundnuts, yet with groundnut prices steadily falling—largely as a result of the removal of the subsidy previously provided by the French government—many peasant farmers were faced with a decline in their cash income. At the same time, more than half the country's annual revenue was spent on the salaries of an excessively large bureaucracy. (Like Austria after World War I, Senegal found itself saddled with a capital, Dakar, designed for a very much larger political structure and containing a substantial population of civil servants.) Senegalese businessmen were faced with a situation in which the "commanding heights of the economy" were controlled by Frenchmen and French advisers were still prominent in ministerial offices. Here, then, were many grievances for radical critics of the regime to seize on. By 1972, however, the aging but adroit president had made a substantial comeback. By delegating some of his powers to an able prime minister, Abdou Diouf, the president created the preconditions for a rather more vigorous conduct of internal affairs, at the same time leaving himself free to pursue a more active foreign policy than at any other time in his career. Even more important, in the opinion of some commentators, than this shift in the structure of power at the center was the fact that after three years of near-drought, 1971 was a year of ample rainfall, with a consequent doubling of the groundnut harvest over the previous years' yield and more cash in the pockets of the country's peasant farmers.

Few West African countries faced the challenge of independence with so meager a range of assets as the Republic of Mali. Landlocked, and with an economy based on limited agricultural resources, the country offered few opportunities for rapid development. The collapse of the short-lived federation with Senegal added still further to the new state's difficulties. So intense was the animosity provoked on both sides by the break-up of the federation that for three years (from 1960 to 1963) the railroad between Dakar and Bamako, Mali's only rail link with the sea, was closed at the Mali-Senegal frontier and Malians were forced to send their export crops long distances by road to points on the railroad between Ouagadougou and Abidjan. In compensation Mali had the advantage of a ruling party, the *Union Soudanaise* which enjoyed a very wide measure of public support. President Mobido Keita and his closest associates knew how to inspire a spirit of national pride and were confident that with austerity, dedication, and a strict application of Socialist principles a better life could be created for the mass of the people.

Socialist planning involved a rapid expansion in the size of the bureaucracy as state control was extended to cover almost every section of the economic life of the country. In 1962, the government, in a gesture designed to emphasize the total nature of Mali's independence, broke away from the monetary union to which all other ex-French colonies, except Guinea, belonged and created an independent Mali franc. Already Mali was beginning to face a serious balance of payments problem, and when it was found that the new currency was not easily convertible, the country's foreign trade was seriously affected. In 1962 there were demonstrations in Bamako when traders protested violently against official restrictions. (Two leading members of the *Parti Souda-nais Progressiste,* the *Union Soudanaise's* rival of the 1950's were implicated in the disturbances, put on trial and sentenced to life imprisonment, dying in prison a few years later in mysterious circumstances.) As the economic situation steadily worsened, local traders turned to smuggling and black-marketeering, thus exposing themselves to the risk of heavy punishments. Civil servants, the most influential section of the community, were exasperated by the gradual disappearance of imported consumer goods from the shops. Many peasants, seeing the value of money steadily declining, abandoned the cultivation of cash-crops and returned to subsistence farming. Export statistics revealed the stagnant nature of the country's economy: in 1960 Mali's exports were worth $14 million, in 1966 $13 million. In the same period, imports, swollen by purchases of capital equipment required to meet the needs of an ambitious development plan, were running close to $40 million a year.

Confronted with this gloomy situation, the government followed the advice of its more moderate members and sought a financial agreement with France. After lengthy negotiations concluded in 1967, the Malians devalued their franc by 50 percent in return for a French offer to provide the financial backing needed to render Mali's currency freely convertible. The radical members of the *Union Soudanaise* interpreted this agreement as a betrayal of the revolution. Mobido Keita was anxious to hold a balance between the two wings of his party, but he was also deeply worried by the implications of Kwame Nkrumah's fall in the Ghanaian army coup of February, 1966, and thought it advisable to strengthen his position by allowing the radicals more scope than ever before. "Active revolution" now became the government's watchword; "centralization" replaced "dialogue" as the formula used to define the party's relationship with the masses; a new body, the *Comité National de Défense de la Révolution,* took over from the party's old-established *bureau politique,* and the young men of the *milice populaire* were allowed to emulate the exploits of the Chinese "Red Guards," accusing older party members and civil servants of corruption and securing their dismissal. ("What kind of traitor are you?" listeners to Bamako radio were regularly invited to ask themselves.) In these circumstances the government's political base steadily narrowed. There was no sign of any improvement in the country's dismal economic situation; many people were deeply offended by the antics of young party militants; and officers in the regular army could see in the growing power of the militia a direct threat to their livelihood. Exasperated by this situation a group of young officers decided to act. In a bloodless coup launched in November, 1968, they overthrew Mobido Keita's government.

By the end of 1972 the *Comité Militaire,* set up by the army officers, had succeeded in maintaining itself in power for four years. But it had failed to implement its promise to hold democratic elections: it had made no significant contribution to solving the country's economic problems; it had narrowed its political base by replacing the civilian ministers appointed immediately after the coup by army officers; and it was faced with increasingly determined opposition from two powerful urban pressure groups, the students and the trade unionists. In such a situation, Mali's military regime looked somewhat unstable.

In 1958, the year of Guinea's independence, Sékou Touré, leader of the *Parti Démocratique de Guinée,* showed himself to be the most aggressively radical nationalist politician in Black Africa. That he should still have been in power fifteen years later was a tribute not so much to his ideological fervor as to his immense energy and remarkable dexterity as a political manipulator. Guinea achieved independence in an atmosphere of revolutionary enthusiasm unparalleled elsewhere in West Africa. The sudden withdrawal of French officials created many practical difficulties; in compensation, the country's new rulers found themselves in a position to plan its future development without constantly having to defer to the advice of ex-colonial French civil servants. To the militants of the PDG, the leaders of other francophone states, with the exception of Mobido Keita of Mali, appeared as pusillanimous collaborators, accepting all too meekly a "neo-colonialist" situation.

By 1963 the high hopes of 1958 had faded. As in Mali, the brave attempt to achieve total independence in the economic sphere—a nonconvertible Guinean franc was created in 1960—and to establish a large measure of state control over almost all aspects of the economy created much hardship and provoked much bitterness. Many intellectuals were repelled by the dictatorial nature of the regime and highly critical of the increasing corruption evident among party cadres. As in Mali, traders resorted to smuggling on a large scale only to find themselves becoming the victims of more and more severe restrictions. A very large number of ordinary Guineans—put in some reports as high as half a million—voted against the government "with their feet" by moving across the frontiers to settle in Senegal or the Ivory Coast.

Sékou Touré interpreted the worsening political and economic situation in terms of the class struggle. "A bureaucratic bourgeoisie has installed itself within the Party," he declared, "it has spawned about itself a 'clientele' of merchants, *transporteurs* and rural land proprietors—an embryonic national bourgeoisie." Such a bourgeoisie was "slothful," "hypocritical and treacherous," "ready to sell the Nation to any imperialist power that presents itself." Even the most militant party member was liable to succumb to the process of "embourgeoisement"; "subversion," Sékou Touré asserted, "inhabits every heart." [214] To protect the revolution against its enemies the president turned to the youth of the country, creating a range of new institutions including a people's militia staffed by an "uncorrupted" generation of militants. These innovations could be interpreted as the creation of a man whose early experience had taught him that he "could transform a political and even a social situation by the enthusiastic mobilization of large masses of people." [215] But they could never offer the president complete protection against his enemies. In 1969 Sékou Touré narrowly escaped assasination. In 1970 government forces beat off a sea-borne attack on Conakry in which Guinean exiles appeared to have been supported by the Portuguese authorities in Bissau.

The most prolific African ideologue of his day—by 1969 his published works, based mainly on his speeches, ran to seventeen substantial volumes—Sékou Touré was clearly assured a prominent place in the history of his times. Like Kwame Nkrumah and Mobido Keita, he had been animated by a belief in "the primacy of the political." The sad economic state of his country after twelve years of independence bore witness to the limitations of this doctrine. Endowed with a wider range of mineral resources than any other country in West Africa, Guinea appeared to present excellent prospects for rapid development. Yet export figures—$52 million in 1960, $43 million in 1964, $58 million in 1966—revealed an almost stagnant economy. Indeed without the continuing investments made by Western European and American firms in the bauxite industry, the major source of foreign exchange, Guinea would have been faced with economic ruin. To some foreign observers in the late 1960's, Sékou Touré took on the guise of a tragic figure, despairingly attempting to force his people to accept the sacrifices needed to create a new society. To others he appeared "a monumentally inept head of state," ruling "by whim and impulse" and "using his country as a laboratory to try out experiments of social and economic development." [216] Only when the people of Guinea find themselves free to express their opinions of their president will it be possible for the historian to reach a more assured assessment of one of the most controversial figures in modern Africa.

The contrasts in political style between Guinea and Mali on the one hand and the Ivory Coast on the other, already clearly discernible in the last years of the colonial period, became glaringly apparent in the first decade of independence. Few countries anywhere in the Third World could match the Ivory Coast's average growth rate of 8 percent per annum; no country in Black Africa presented so striking "an economic miracle" with exports steadily rising in value from $151 million in 1960 to $310 million in 1966. This achievement had been brought about by methods that African radicals could only describe as "neo-colonialist." Every effort had been made by President Houphouët-Boigny's government to attract foreign investment. No attempt had been made to expel or replace French administrators and technicians. Indeed the country's French community, numbering about 15,000 in 1960, had more than doubled by 1970. With a detachment of French troops stationed for a time in Abidjan, French intelligence experts manning the security service, French officials holding high office in all the ministries, and with the government consistently maintaining cordial relations with Paris, the Ivory Coast might well have seemed to have changed little in ethos since the last years of the colonial era.

The regime, like that of colonial governments at the high noon of their authority, was autocratic, with all decisions being taken by the president and his small group of advisers. But Houphouët-Boigny enjoyed a prestige far greater than that of any colonial governor; by 1970 he had dominated the politics of his country for twenty-five years, he was "the father of his people," the chief above all chiefs, the modernizing politician who had acquired an almost monarchical status in his own country, the symbol of Ivorian unity and independence. Yet his position was not uncontested: in 1963 two major plots against the president were uncovered, leading to the arrest of several of the country's most prominent politicians. Inevitably, too, Houphouët-Boigny's regime was the target for constant criticism from student radicals. In dealing with his opponents, Houphouët-Boigny, like Senghor, showed himself to possess the flexibility of the consummate politician. Dangerous opponents could be chastened by a spell in prison; young radicals won over by the offer of a good job in the bureaucracy; public discontent in the late 1960's allayed by a series of *dialogue à l'africaine* in which the president held informal meetings with a wide variety of social groups and invited and answered frank criticism of the current situation.

In the 1960's few countries in Africa enjoyed as great a measure of political stability as the Ivory Coast. Yet the country still contained serious sources of tension. Tribal feeling was strong, indeed, one local group, the Agni of the "kingdom" of Sanvi even went so far as to attempt a Biafran type of secession. "Strangers," non-Ivorian Africans, were far from being truly integrated in local communities. And even though a fair measure of the prosperity of recent years had reached most members of the community, social differences had inevitably become more acute, the opulence of the main beneficiaries of the regime—party officials, civil servants, planters, and European businessmen—contrasting sharply with the penury of the unemployed. Should the country continue to prosper, thus allowing the government constantly to extend the range of its patronage and its bounties, these tensions could probably be constrained. With economists predicting that the country would soon achieve the stage of "take-off," of self-sustained growth, the Ivory Coast appeared in 1970 to be one of the most fortunate countries in the Third World.

▲▼ PORTUGUESE GUINEA AND LIBERIA

Two of the smaller West African territories were not directly involved in the process of decolonization that transformed the status of all the other parts of the region in the years after World War II. In the case of Portuguese Guinea the metropolitan government in Lisbon totally refused to accept the concept of independence, regarding all its colonies as "overseas provinces" of Portugal. Liberia, on the other hand, had no need for formal decolonization, having existed as an independent state since the proclamation of the republic in 1847. Nevertheless, until the 1950's both Portuguese Guinea and Liberia presented a pattern of historical development not dissimilar to that found in other parts of the region, with groups of alien intruders, the Portuguese and the Americo-Liberians, establishing their hegemony over a multitude of small indigenous polities. Only in very recent years have the sharp contrasts between these two territories and other West African countries become apparent.

Portuguese Guinea (Guiné-Bissau) has an area of no more than 14,000 square miles, yet the Portuguese found it a difficult country to conquer. Military operations continued in some districts until as late as the mid-1930's. Under the highly authoritarian system of Portuguese colonial government (a system more extensively discussed in the context of Angola and Mozambique in Chapter VI) there was no room for the emergence of open political associations among the colonial peoples. But the colony could not be completely insulated from the changes taking place elsewhere in West Africa, and the authorities were not able to prevent a small group of Africans from coming together secretly in Bissau, the capital of Portuguese Guinea, in 1956 to found a party whose name, the African Independence Party of Guinea and the Cape Verde Islands (PAIGC), defined its basic aims. The new party's leader, Amilcar Cabral, was a young *assimilado* who had studied in Portugal to become an agricultural engineer and had then spent some years in government service in Guiné-Bissau. Cabral and his followers began their political campaign by seeking support among the urban workers, but in

August, 1959, they suffered a disastrous reverse when fifty African dock-workers, on strike in Bissau for higher wages, were shot down by the Portuguese police. In the face of such brutal repression it was clear that nothing could be gained by the organization of peaceful demonstrations in the towns. Accordingly the PAIGC decided to prepare for "a struggle by all possible means including war" by concentrating their activities on mobilizing "the peasant masses" as "the main force in the struggle for national liberation." [217]

Cabral was peculiarly well-qualified to organize the peasantry. During his years in government service he had been given the task of conducting an agricultural census, a task which took him to every part of the colony and made him deeply familiar with the problems of the peasantry. With former French Guinea now an independent state, the PAIGC was assured of a friendly base in a neighboring territory. Arms and equipment were supplied by most of the countries of the Communist world. In 1963, after four years of intensive preparation, building up a cadre of supporters and persuading the peasantry that armed revolt could be successful even against the well-armed Portuguese, the PAIGC launched a full-scale guerrilla war. By 1968 the party claimed to be in control of two-thirds of the country, leaving the Portuguese confined to the main towns, to a few isolated military strongholds, and to the area in the west where the colonial authorities could still count on the support of the Fulani chiefs.

To the PAIGC the war was also a revolution. "Always bear in mind," Cabral instructed party militants, "that the people are not fighting for ideas. They are fighting to win material benefits, to live better and in peace, to see their lives go forward." [218] In the liberated areas the PAIGC set about improving the local economy, seeking ways of offering the peasants higher prices for their produce than those paid by the monopolistic Portuguese company which dominated the trade of the colony; tackling problems of rural health by establishing dispensaries; and founding primary schools in many villages never touched by the modest educational efforts of the colonial government. At the same time, several hundred Guineans were sent overseas, mainly to the Soviet Union and Eastern Europe, to be trained as doctors, nurses, electricians, and motor mechanics. By 1970 the war appeared to have reached a stalemate. The Portuguese, with 30,000 troops at their disposal, maintained an apparently invincible hold on the towns and were attempting to win over the countryside by ambitious plans for development and social reform. On the other hand the PAIGC had behind it an astonishing achievement. As Basil Davidson has pointed out, "an almost completely nonliterate people, lacking all the minor aids to punctuality and orderly procedure, such as watches and clocks, which we take for granted, has managed to transform itself into an integrated and efficient military and political organization." [219] As in Algeria, peace seems likely only through a negotiated settlement.

For the Vai, the Kru, the Kpelle, and other indigenous groups of the Liberian hinterland the establishment of Americo-Liberian hegemony brought with it a range of experiences little different from those inflicted on the Balante, the Mandjak, the Pepel, and other peoples of Guiné-Bissau by the slow process of Portuguese conquest. The Americo-Liberians were the descendants of African slaves, but they behaved little differently from other colonial rulers. In their contempt for "tribal" culture, their expropriation of "tribal" lands, their destruction of "tribal" authorities, the Americo-Liberians often gave evidence of a more ruthless attitude toward their subjects than that displayed by their European contemporaries in West Africa. And they found themselves faced with the range of reactions—collaboration, resignation, revolt— familiar in every colonial situation. (In 1915 the Kru, exasperated by the exactions of Americo-Liberian officials, took to armed resistance: to re-establish its authority the government in Monrovia was forced to call on the United States for naval and military assistance.) But the position of the Americo-Liberians differed from that of other colonial rulers in one important respect. Until the sudden discovery and exploitation of the country's magnificent deposits of iron ore in the 1950's, the Liberian government was always desperately poor. In the early 1920's official revenue came to less than a quarter of that of the neighboring British colony of Sierra Leone, and much of the money collected by the government had to be paid out to meet the interest on foreign loans. Given such poverty, given, too, the unsympathetic attitude of outside powers ready to seize on every Liberian failing, merely to survive as an independent state was an achievement. This sense of struggle against a hostile world helped to nourish among the Americo-Liberains a lively spirit of nationalism, while the experience of running their own country gave to the elite "a *savoir faire*" which struck a sympathetic American observer in the 1920's as being "unique through the continent of Africa." [220]

In numbers the Americo-Liberians have never exceeded more than 2 percent of the total population of Liberia. (In 1962 they numbered 23,000 in a population slightly exceeding 1 million.) From the earliest days of the settlement the Americo-Liberian community was beset by factional divisions and with differences in wealth it soon came to develop a well-defined class structure. But political stability was essential for the survival of the community. This stability was eventually achieved through the construction of what may well be regarded as Africa's first one-party state. Since the 1870's Liberia has been dominated by the True Whig Party. A constitution modeled on that of the United States and involving regular elections disguised the fact that Liberia was in reality a highly autocratic state controlled by a few prominent families. Within the charmed circle of the ruling few, political manipulation provided the only means of access to wealth, prestige, and power. By leaving the major tasks of economic development to foreigners, the Liberian oligarchy prevented the growth of a class of local entrepreneurs who might in time have challenged their domination. At the same time, the cruder forms of social distinction, as practised in European-dominated territories maintaining a strict color bar, were avoided. Some intermarriage took place between Americo-Liberians and people of "tribal" origin; some "tribesmen" were assimilated into Americo-Liberian society. But with the army and the police firmly under presidential control and with the distribution of jobs decided by the innermost caucus of the True Whig Party, critics of the regime, whether "tribesmen" or Americo-Liberians, could easily be broken or brought to heel.

This autocratic regime, with its police-state atmosphere, prevails to this day. But the last twenty-five years have produced substantial changes in the Liberian scene, changes closely associated with the policies of William V. S. Tubman, president of Liberia from 1944 until his death in 1971. Tubman used the terms "unification" and "open door" to describe his new and dynamic approach to the problems of Liberian development. The Open Door Policy involved the opening of the Liberian hinterland to foreign economic enterprise. Before World War II only one large foreign firm—the American-owned Firestone Plantations Company—operated in Liberia. Firestone's achievement in developing rubber plantations was remarkable: from the 1920's to the 1950's plantation-produced rubber was the mainstay of the Liberian economy. But there were obvious disadvantages in being so heavily dependent on a single commodity and on a single foreign company. Since 1945 Liberia has attracted no less than forty foreign concessionaires together with a large number of smaller firms. The most spectacular development has been the astonishing growth in iron-ore mining. Before 1945 no iron ore was mined in Liberia; by 1967 Liberia was the third largest exporter of iron ore in the world. Many consequences flowed from the Open Door Policy. The country's economy was diversified and it was no longer tied exclusively to a single alien source of capital. Government revenue shot up from a mere $1 million in 1945 to $55 million in 1968. The country, virtually roadless and harborless thirty years ago, acquired the foundations of a good system of communications. And the extreme isolation of the "tribal" peoples was steadily broken down.

With his Unification Policy, Tubman attempted to bridge the political gap between Americo-Liberians and "tribal" peoples. No previous Liberian president ever paid such attention to the hinterland. By regular tours of inspection, by frequent public meetings at which local people could address their complaints and requests to the president in person, by occasionally wearing native dress, by encouraging the preservation of "tribal" arts and crafts, Tubman worked out a policy that permitted "the tribal people to identify with the Liberian nation through the personality of the President." [221] But Tubman's genuine popularity could not disguise the strains produced by the changes of recent years. As in so many other African countries, education has been the agent of revolution. Until the 1950's the country's modest number of schools was monopolized by the Americo-Liberians. The expansion of education, greatly assisted by generous American aid and by the use of Peace Corps volunteers, has brought many young people of the hinterland into touch with modern ideas and created the inevitable demand for better opportunities of employment. Were the economic structure of the country developing in such a way as to produce ways of meeting this demand, political strains might be avoided. But in the 1960's the Liberian economy presented an extreme case of "growth without development." Too much was dependent on foreigners: were the foreign firms suddenly to withdraw, "the modern sector of the economy would virtually cease to function." [222] For this situation critical foreign observers blamed the ruling group of Americo-Liberians. In their preoccupation with the politics of patronage and with the niceties of social etiquette, in their disdain for the practical work of commerce and industry, in their fundamental lack of interest in the hard tasks of development, and their thinly-veiled sense of superiority over the mass of the population, the Liberian elite presents most of the characteristics of an outdated aristocracy. Given a situation in which the country's political structure continues to be dominated by its traditional oligarchy and its economy to be controlled by foreigners but in which the mass of younger people are becoming increasingly exposed to new ideas, "it is difficult," in the opinion of one well-informed observer, "to see how the country can be forever insulated against a violent nationalist reaction . . . by both the tribal element and the lower ranks of the Americo-Liberian community." [223] Nevertheless, the smooth and strictly constitutional manner in which Vice-President William R. Tolbert succeeded to the presidency after Tubman's unexpected death in 1971 provided a remarkable indication of the degree of political stability which the country still enjoyed.

▲▼ THE FOREIGN RELATIONS OF WEST AFRICAN STATES

As in all newly independent states, political leaders in West Africa were faced with the task of formulating their country's foreign policy, of working out a system of relationships with their former metropolis, with neighboring West African states, and with countries in other parts of the world, and of deciding what part to play in the emerging movement for African unity. The line of foreign policy taken by any one country depended in part on its internal political situation. No less important was the character and ideas of the individual who occupied the office of head of state. Thus Kwame Nkrumah of Ghana, an avowedly radical leader with a temporarily secure power base, pursued a more "dynamic" or at least a more vocal policy than his contemporaries in the Ivory Coast and in Nigeria. But however anxious any West African leader might have been to pursue a truly independent foreign policy, he was forced to recognize that in world terms his country came low, in most cases very low, in the power rating, and that the necessity of depending on a measure of foreign aid imposed certain unavoidable restraints. Few contemporary Third World leaders have gone so far in taunting the Great Powers as Sékou Touré of Guinea. Between 1961 and 1966 Sékou Touré found cause to expel a Soviet ambassador, arrest an American ambassador, and abruptly break off relations with France —but for all his Marxist rhetoric the Guinean president has refrained from attempting to nationalize the French and American firms which run the bauxite industry, the country's main source of foreign exchange.

In the first decade of independence, relations between the anglophone states and Britain, though not uncordial, fell far short of the intimacy that marked the relationship of France with most of the ex-French colonies. All the former British territories remained in the Commonwealth and continued to receive fluctuating amounts of technical assistance and financial aid from Britain. But there were no formal pacts between Britain and the anglophone states, with the exception of a short-lived Anglo-Nigerian defense agreement, abandoned in 1962 as a result of wide-spread Nigerian protests. During the Nigerian Civil War Britain made a substantial contribution to the victory of the federal forces by maintaining a steady flow of arms, but any goodwill this policy might have earned was largely dissipated by the vigorous support accorded the Biafran cause by a large section of British public opinion and by the harsh criticisms leveled against the federal government for its conduct of the war.

Many factors accounted for the peculiar intimacy of France's relations with most of her ex-colonies in West Africa. The magnetic personality of President de Gaulle served as a revered model for many African leaders. Most influential politicians and civil servants in francophone Africa felt a sense of deep personal attachment to France and to French culture. Not that the French were regarded uncritically: to so ardent a francophile as Léopold Senghor they often appeared "irritating," "deceiving," "imperialistic," "striving to impose their ideas and sentiments on facts"—and yet, Senghor concluded, "when you resist them, when you face them with a solid dossier of facts, they end by giving in to truth—through reason and humanity." [224] Many practical considerations served to strengthen the ties of sentiment. For some years after independence detachments of French troops continued to be stationed at Dakar and Abidjan, providing a comforting support for the governments of Senghor and Houphouët-Boigny. French technical assistance supplied many of the specialists needed to meet the requirements of ambitious development plans. Above all, French financial aid was still generously lavished on those countries which had signed cooperation agreements with France at the time of independence, and it was supplemented by the assistance provided by other members of the European Economic Community. Thus the francophone states of West Africa, Guinea and Mali excepted, found themselves in receipt of a greater amount of aid than any other ex-colonial territory in Africa. Senegal, for example, received in aid, both bilateral and multilateral, in the years 1964–67 an annual average of $13.90 per capita of population; comparable figures for Ghana and Nigeria in the same period are $7.70 and $2.10, respectively. The price to be paid for this assistance was the continuation of a massively visible French presence—French banks, French businesses, French civil servants, French teachers—which seemed of its very nature to deny the reality of independence.

The colonial powers were often accused by their nationalist critics of "balkanizing" Africa. In fact, independent West African governments were themselves largely responsible for breaking down the larger political and economic structures created during the colonial period. In the anglophone countries, services which had been organized on a collective basis, such as the West African Currency Board, were reorganized to allow for the creation of distinctive national institutions. The change was even more apparent in francophone countries as a result of the collapse of the administrative federation of colonial days. But by the early 1960's political opinion throughout the region was insistent on the need for cooperation between neighboring territories as part of a general movement toward African unity. Such cooperation involved three different forms of interrelationship—between individual francophone states, between anglophone and francophone states, and between West African states and the rest of Africa.

The foundations of an effective system of cooperation between francophone states were laid by Houphouët-Boigny of the Ivory Coast in 1959 when he persuaded the leaders of Upper Volta, Niger, and Dahomey to join him in establishing "a cooperative association," the *Conseil de l'Entente,* described as being designed "to give a practical form to economic solidarity." [225] The *Conseil* might be regarded as a West African equivalent to the East African Common Services Organization, for it was responsible for the management of the four states' harbors and railways. At the same time a "solidarity fund" was set up as a device to provide the means for the Ivory Coast to offer financial assistance to its poorer neighbors. The *Entente* served as the nucleus for wider groupings embracing all ex-French colonies in tropical Africa, with the exception of Guinea and Mali, but including Madagascar. Two organizations were set up in 1961, the *Union Afrique et Malgache* (UAM) and the *Organisation Africaine et Malgache de Coopération Économique* (OAMCE). The UAM was dissolved two years later in response to criticisms that its existence was rendered unnecessary by the creation of the Organization of African Unity, but it was resurrected under a new name, *Organisation Commune Africaine et Malgache* (OCAM), in 1965 when it became apparent that the OAU was not likely to develop into a strong continental organization. The main political aims of OCAM can be understood only in the wider context of continental politics. But the organization also possessed the advantage of enabling its members to present a common front in negotiations with France and other members of the EEC, and it encouraged the creation of a number of subsidiary agencies concerned with cooperation in specific fields such as telecommunications. From these groupings of the moderate francophone states Guinea and Mali stayed away, but the two radical states hesitantly agreed to join the Senegal River Committee set up as a result of Senegalese initiative.

In the days of colonial rule there had been remarkably little contact between the French and British territories, except as a result of labor migration. Hardly any African politicians or civil servants knew more than one European language and most members of the elite were ignorant of even the basic facts concerning the territories of a metropolis other than their own. After independence international gatherings did something to bring representatives from different parts of West Africa together, but the cultural divide between anglophones and francophones remained—and still remains—very wide. The most spectacular political attempt to bridge this gap was the union between Ghana and Guinea, established in November, 1958, a few weeks after Guinea's dramatic emergence as an independent state, and enlarged in 1961 by the adherence of Mali. Avowedly formed as "the nucleus of the United States of Africa" [226] and grandiosely entitled the Union of African States, the new association provided an institutional expression of the community of views between West Africa's three radical states but it never developed into an effective political organization. Nevertheless, the Ghana-Guinea-Mali Union clearly represented a rival bloc to the moderate francophone states grouped around the Ivory Coast. From 1960 on, Ghana's francophone neighbors had good reason for resenting the line of action followed by President Nkrumah. Not only did the Ghanaian leader offer sanctuary to groups outlawed in their country of origin but he also provided them with the means to carry on subversive activities in their homelands. Nkrumah was openly denounced for his interference in the internal affairs of other African states at the first OCAM meeting in 1965, and his downfall a year later was greeted with rapture by the governments of the *Entente* countries. By 1968, with Mobido Keita of Mali no longer in power and Sékou Touré of Guinea in a position of diplomatic isolation, the radical cause was at a low ebb. But even with ideology removed as an irritant, there were still many ways in which West African governments could fall apart. Relations between Nigeria and the Ivory Coast, for example, were seriously affected by President Houphouët-Boigny's support of the Biafran cause during the civil war, while the Ghanaian government of Dr. Busia upset all its neighbors by its hasty decision to expel all non-Ghanaians not in possession of resident permits. It was a sad commentary on the professions of goodwill made at the time of independence that by 1970 the barriers on inter-territorial movement should have become more formidable than at any time during the colonial period.

As the first countries in Black Africa to achieve independence, the West African states were caught up from the start in the movement for African unity. Here the role of Kwame Nkrumah was outstanding. As early as 1946, while still a student in England, Nkrumah had organized the West African National Secretariat and spoken of the need to establish a West African Federation as the first step towards a United States of Africa. Twelve years later, his position firmly established as prime minister of an independent Ghana, Nkrumah organized two international conferences at Accra. The first, the Conference of Independent Africa States, was attended by Egypt, Ethiopia, Liberia, Libya, Morocco, Sudan, and Tunisia; the second, the All-African Peoples' Conference, was organized on a nongovernmental basis and attracted many

African politicians from countries still under colonial rule. The effect of these conferences might be compared to a loud-speaker. Individually African states were too small and too weak for much attention to be paid to their leaders' pronouncements. Collectively they could produce a new voice in world affairs. Critical observers of the African scene might regard with some scepticism communiqués—such as that issued after the first Accra conference—asserting "a fundamental unity of outlook in foreign policy" which would allow "a distinctive African Personality to further the cause of peace"; representatives of the Great Powers disregard the call "to discontinue the production and testing of nuclear weapons"; European governments pay no attention to the demand that "a definite date be set for the attainment of independence by each of the colonial territories." [227] But for men and women throughout Africa, brought up in the "colonial situation," accustomed to a world in which white men made all the pronouncements, it was immensely exhilarating to hear a powerful, public pronouncement of many of their own opinions and aspirations. With Nkrumah achieving the status of a popular hero in countries far removed from Ghana, the pan-Africanism of which he was the leading exponent offered a powerful ideological reinforcement to the force of local nationalisms.

Nevertheless, no sooner had other West African countries gained their independence than it became apparent that their leaders were sharply divided in their attitude toward African unity. While Nkrumah spoke in terms of the immediate creation of a grandiose continental superstructure, politicians in Nigeria and the moderate francophone states adopted a cool, cautious, pragmatic approach, preferring to build not in the Nkrumahist fashion from the top downwards but from the bottom upwards, through the multiplication of practical forms of cooperation. Events in other parts of Africa soon served to widen the gap between moderates and radicals. The radicals strongly supported the FLN in its struggle with the French in Algeria; the moderate francophone states, with 15,000 of their nationals still serving in the French army, were far less critical of French policy. Even more bitter was the controversy provoked by the Congo crisis in which the two West African groups supported rival Congolese politicians. By 1961 the division had spread to other independent African states, with separate meetings being held— the moderates at Brazzaville and Monrovia, the radicals at Casablanca, where Ghana, Guinea, and Mali were joined by the United Arab Republic and Morocco. But the sentiment for African unity was still strong enough to allow all parties to come together at Addis Ababa in 1963 and formally establish the Organization for African Unity. The OAU fell far short of the "union" envisioned by Kwame Nkrumah in which all states would surrender their sovereignty to a supranational body. With its elaborate machinery for consultation between independent states and for the development of practical forms of cooperation, the OAU might be regarded as an African variation of the United Nations. Increasingly after 1963 the OAU devoted its attention to the situation in Southern Africa. To the francophone states this was an area of no great interest, while Nigeria and Ghana were too deeply preoccupied with their own internal problems to become closely involved in a part of the world where they lacked any practical means to make their influence felt. In the late 1960's West African voices sounded somewhat muted in the councils of African statesmen.

At the time of their achievement of independence in the late 1950's and early 1960's, West African states attracted the attention of many countries which had previously had little cause or opportunity to interest themselves in this part of Africa. Americans and Russians, Czechs and Germans, Israelis and Egyptians, Chinese and Japanese began to explore this new area of the world suddenly opened to outsiders by the removal of the fences maintained by the colonial powers. They came, seeking to win new friends, new trading partners, new supporters for their own national causes, transforming by their presence many West African capitals into excitingly cosmopolitan places. West African governments were glad to accept the gifts brought by the newcomers—scholarships, grants for capital projects, the loan of technicians—and eager to find new ways of expanding their own export trade, but they were careful to avoid becoming entangled in international controversies. Everywhere the talk was of "nonalignment" of "neutralism." Nevertheless, it was clear that the radical states were prepared to accept closer relationships with the countries of the Communist world than their moderate neighbors would have done. Trade figures provide a convenient means of measuring changes in alignment. Guinea presented the most striking reorientation. In 1958, more than 70 percent of the country's trade was carried on with France; three years later the French stake had fallen to less than 20 percent, and the Soviet Union had become Guinea's major trading partner. In Senegal, on the other hand, diversification and a move away from the former metropolis occurred much more gradually: in 1968, 55 percent of the country's trade was carried on with France, compared with 70 percent in 1961. The proportionate decline in British trade with Nigeria was far more clearly marked. In the early 1950's two-thirds of Nigeria's trade had been carried on with Britain; by the late 1960's the British stake had fallen to one-third. In the late 1950's, nineteen countries were listed in U.N. trade returns as trading with Nigeria; ten years later the number had increased to forty-two—Finland, Hungary, Israel, Pakistan, Spain, and Yugoslavia being among the newcomers on the Nigerian commercial scene.

The countries of West Africa possess one vital negative advantage in their dealings with the outside world. Their region is of no great strategic importance to the Great Powers. This fact greatly facilitated the process of decolonization in the 1950's. It may well serve to protect the peoples of West Africa from whatever shocks the international scene may produce in the last decades of the twentieth century.

▲▼ RECENT CHANGES IN WEST AFRICAN LIFE

Outside observers often overestimate the significance of political changes. For the vast majority of West Africans the gentle ending of the colonial period brought no sudden break in the pattern of their lives. New men of local origin, politicians and administrators, took over the posts hitherto occupied by Europeans, but the superstructures girding West Africa together retained their basically hierarchical character. Far more significant to most West Africans were the changes affecting certain aspects of their daily lives, changes symbolized by such diverse objects as the artesian well, the Land Rover or "mammy wagon," the groundnut decorticator, the gas-driven flour mill, and the transistor radio.

A variety of forces account for the accelerated pace of change in modern West Africa. Much must be ascribed to a self-generating process with roots deep in the past. Already before World War II many West Africans, the heirs of long traditions of enterprise in various fields, had shown their capacity to respond to the new opportunities associated with the establishment of European overrule. The expansion of cocoa-farming in Ghana and the Ivory Coast, the rapid increase in groundnut production in Senegal and Northern Nigeria, the multiplication of schools in areas touched by the activities of Christian missionaries, the steady expansion of the main administrative and commercial centers—developments such as these provided clear evidence of the forcefulness of the local response to new conditions. A fresh stimulus to the initiative of many West Africans came with the growth of local nationalism. Nationalist parties, though primarily concerned with "seeking the political kingdom," were quick to appreciate the need to incorporate social and economic objectives in their programs. Thus the 1951 election manifesto of the Convention People's Party on the Gold Coast spoke of introducing a "five-year economic plan," designed to provide for a rapid expansion of the country's communication system, "progressive mechanization of agriculture" and energetic industrialization, together with "a planned campaign to abolish illiteracy." [228] In the atmosphere of free debate that characterized the 1950's even the most conservative West African political parties were forced to concern themselves with development programs, to offer their supporters, in the succinct formula popularized by the Nigerian Action Group, "Life more Abundant."

To colonial governments there was nothing particularly novel about the concept of development. Most colonial governors had been concerned to improve the basic infrastructure of their territories and some, notably Guggisberg on the Gold Coast in the 1920's, had thought in terms of a carefully planned use of resources. During World War II circumstances forced West African governments to interest themselves more directly than ever before in the commerce and production of their respective territories. In British West Africa official marketing boards took over from the great commercial firms the task of purchasing cash-crops and selling them on the world market. In theory, the new boards were intended to protect the peasant producer against sudden variations in price on the world market; in practice, they provided an effective administrative machinery enabling the government to accumulate fresh resources. For at a time of rapidly rising prices it was thought advisable to pay the producer considerably less than the market price and to spend some of the sums thus acquired on worthwhile development projects. Later, local politicians, moving into positions of power, found easy ways of milking the marketing boards for their own personal advantage. But large-scale corruption, the bane of West African politics, was hardly envisaged in the optimistic atmosphere of the postwar years when both British and French colonial authorities were sincerely anxious to make amends for past neglects by doing all in their power to encourage local development.

The remarkable harmony that prevailed between West African politicians and European officials in the last years of the colonial period could in large part be ascribed to the fact that both sides accepted the basic need for rapid development. Material factors contributed greatly to the agreeable intellectual climate of these years. With the prices of most West African export commodities steadily rising on the world market, the early 1950's proved to be the most prosperous period the region had ever known. In Ghana the value of imports rose from £15 million in 1945 to £114 million in 1954. In Nigeria—to quote figures that convey some impression of the expansion of building activity, a sure indication of prosperity—imports and local manufacture of cement rose from 107,000 tons in 1947 to 573,000 in 1958. Most other West African countries could also provide striking indices of growth in the

1950's. In the 1960's the momentum was maintained more effectively in some countries than in others. Between 1959 and 1967, exports from Niger showed an annual increase in value of 14.7 percent, from the Ivory Coast of 12 percent, from Nigeria of 6.7 percent, from Senegal of 2.6 percent, but in Ghana there was a decline of 1.4 percent and in Dahomey of 2.1 percent. But even allowing for temporary set-backs, it is clear that in the years since World War II more money from export earnings flowed into West Africa than ever before.

The profit of an expanding trade was supplemented by a flow, vastly increased when measured by pre-1945 standards, of foreign money in the form of governmental grants and loans and of private investment. Particularly notable was the assistance provided by the French government, both before and after independence. The Special Investment Fund for Social and Economic Development (FIDES) set up by the French in 1947 channeled more money into the French West African colonies in the space of ten years than the territories had received from all sources, both public and private, in the period from 1903 to 1946. After independence the French continued to give most of their ex-colonies extraordinarily generous financial assistance. The British, too, provided substantial financial aid for their West African territories, though the volume of British aid tended to decline after independence. In the 1960's West African countries also received assistance from many other sources. The bare statistics of trade and aid need to be translated into goods and people, into sewing machines and corrugated iron roofing and bulldozers and patent medicines, into civil engineers and science teachers, soil chemists and pediatricians. More forcefully than ever before, the people of West Africa were exposed in the years after 1945 to a wide range of stimuli of alien origin.

Of all the changes that have taken place in West Africa in recent years possibly the most fundamental are those associated with the growth of population. The absence of accurate population statistics for most parts of the region before 1950 makes it difficult to speak with any assurance about the rate of population growth in the past. Current estimates indicate that the population of most West African countries was expanding in the 1960's at rather more than 2 percent per annum. On this reckoning the population of the region as a whole is likely to rise from 86 million in 1960 to 147 million in 1980.[229]

Throughout the colonial period the pattern of the distribution of population was little different—save only in respect of the growth of a few large towns—from what it must have been in the mid-nineteenth century. With one notable major exception, the densest populations were all to be found in areas that had previously formed the territory of major indigenous states—Dahomey, Ashanti, Benin, the Yoruba and Wolof kingdoms, and the Sokoto caliphate. Yet the security provided by the larger polities was clearly not the only factor responsible for the emergence of high population densities for the most crowded area in the whole region lay in that part of Nigeria occupied by the independent village groups of the Ibo. Here, certain rural districts contained as many as 800 people to the square mile; here, more strongly perhaps than in any other part of Africa outside the Nile Valley, the pressure of population could be felt in an extreme form. By contrast, many districts, particularly in the savanna belt stretching from Senegal to Northern Nigeria, contained less than twenty-five people to the square mile.

Though the colonial period witnessed no massive shifts in the distributions of West African populations, the establishment of the colonial *pax* and the development of new forms of economic enterprise led to a considerable amount of temporary migration, as young men from the more impoverished or overcrowded areas mored elsewhere, often for only a few months at a time, in search of a livelihood. Two currents of migration were particularly striking—from Upper Volta to the rich forest lands further south, and from Iboland to other parts of Nigeria. But there were many other minor currents—civil servants from Dahomey, for example, taking employment in other parts of French West Africa, or Yoruba and Hausa traders from Nigeria settling in Kumasi, Abidjan, or Accra. In the years after independence, a series of political crises dammed or diverted, possibly only temporarily, some of the currents of movement that had flowed so strongly during the colonial period. In Niger a trivial frontier dispute with Dahomey provided the government with a pretext for expelling 769 civil servants of Dahomeyan origin. Far more serious was the mass exodus of Ibos from Northern and Western Nigeria after the massacres of September, 1966, a movement which may have involved no less than one million people. As many as a half-million people, drawn from many parts of West Africa, were reckoned to have been affected by the decision made by the government of Ghana in November, 1969, to expel all aliens not in possession of residence permits. And in the Ivory Coast the position of "strangers," estimated to number about one quarter of the entire population, often seemed precarious in view of the openly expressed hostility of native-born Ivorians.

Developments such as these bore witness to a strain, novel in its intensity, of xenophobia in many West African societies. In part this resentment of "strangers" was associated with an increasingly fierce competition not only for the richest rewards in wealth and power that each society had to offer but often for mere employment in a job with a regular wage. Thus xenophobia could be regarded, at least in part, as a product of those cosmopolitan urban communities which had grown up during the colonial period. Expulsions, followed by restrictions on interterritorial or even, in the special case of Nigeria, of interstate movements might render the cities of West Africa rather less diverse in their population than they had been in the past. But nothing seemed likely to sap the major cities' capacity for continuous expansion. The capitals of West Africa, with new offices, factories, schools, and hospitals constantly being built within their bounds, became more alluring than ever before. Thus they continued to attract a steady stream of newcomers, of diverse origin. (The composition of the African population of Dakar in 1954—to quote but one example of diversity—showed that 54 percent of the inhabitants were drawn from the neighboring Wolof, Serer, and Lebu people, that most of the remainder of the population—Tukulor, Bambara, Fulani, and Jola—came from more distant parts of Senegal, and that there were also small minorities of Moors from Mauritania, Susu from Guinea, and people of mixed ancestry from the Cape Verde Islands.) Statistics covering the late 1950's and early 1960's reveal that in every West African country, except Guinea and The Gambia, the population of urban centers with more than 20,000 people increased at rates exceeding 10 percent per annum. In 1950 the population of Lagos, the largest city in West Africa, was put at 230,000; by 1963 it had risen to nearly 700,000.

The new urban graces of the capitals of West Africa—the imposing public buildings, the multistoried office blocks, the well-laid-out city centers—were accompanied all too often with an expansion of urban squalor. Increasingly, West African governments were faced with the problems associated with rapid urbanization the world over—overcrowding, sewage disposal, broken families, destitution, and delinquency among the lowest paid workers and among the unemployed. Yet with Africans rather than Asians and Europeans, as in East and South Africa, dominating so much of local commerce, the cities of West Africa, for all their alien innovations, displayed a vigorously indigenous character. With their color and clamor and gaiety—the piles of vividly patterned cloths on pavement stalls, the "high-life" music blaring from transistors, the good-humored bargaining of the market place—the citizens of West Africa offered a refreshing contrast to the disciplined, atomized, time-haunted inhabitants of the great conurbations of Europe and America.

Parallel to this movement from "bush" villages to the cities there ran another kind of movement as the sons and daughters of peasant fathers acquired, through schooling, the qualifications needed to enter the charmed circle of the Western-educated elite. A few figures serve to illustrate the phenomenal expansion of West African education in the 1950's and 1960's. In 1948, Niger, the poorest country in West Africa, had no more than 3,000 children in school. By 1958, the number had risen to 13,000; a decade later, school enrollments were approaching 80,000. In 1958, 546 students were attending secondary schools; by 1968 more than 4,000. For a country with a population of more than 3 million, even the latest figures could be used to indicate extreme educational backwardness. Yet seen in the context of local society, the present production of several hundred secondary school graduates every year represents a development of profound political, social, and economic significance. In Nigeria a massive campaign to extend primary education, especially in the two southern regions, in the 1950's was followed in the early 1960's by an equally vigorous effort to expand secondary schooling. As a result, the number of secondary school students rose from 24,000 in 1960 to 150,000 in 1966. No less remarkable was the expansion of higher education. In 1948, Nigeria's first university was opened at Ibadan; twenty years later the country had five universities with a total enrollment of 10,000 students.

Contemporary observers could find much to criticize in West Africa's rapidly developing educational structure. Standards in many schools were often low, due in large part to a shortage of trained teachers. Many children dropped out of the system, some without even completing primary education. The spread of educational facilities was extremely uneven both within the region as a whole and within individual countries. (In 1963, 77 percent of all school-age children were attending primary school in Ghana, compared with 44 percent in the Ivory Coast and 9 percent in Upper Volta, while in Nigeria 51 percent attended school in Eastern Nigeria compared with only 7 percent in Northern Nigeria.) Education at all levels still seemed to be caught in the mold established during the colonial period, with too much emphasis on the acquisition of literary skills, too little on technical training. Yet viewed in historical perspective, the development of West African education in the twenty years after World War II represented an extraordinary achievement, involving the transfer of a wide range of novel techniques and new ideas, made always through the difficult medium of alien languages, French or English, to many millions of West Africans.

The expansion of higher education was closely linked to the need to provide trained men and women capable of doing the work hitherto monopolized by Europeans. In the first years after independence political leaders concentrated on securing the "localization" of decision-making posts in the administration and the technical services. The speed with which "localization" took place varied from country to country. In

Ghana there were only 30 expatriate officials left in pensionable posts in 1962 compared with almost 600 at the time of independence. In francophone countries, on the other hand, with the exception of Guinea and Mali, many French administrators continued to hold positions of authority for some years after independence. In 1960 more than 3,000 French administrators were employed in the newly independent African states (including Madagascar and Equatorial Africa as well as francophone West Africa); by 1966 the number had fallen to 1,267. All the countries of West Africa found it necessary to look overseas for the personnel needed to undertake essential work in their developing economic and social structures. Technical assistance took different forms in different countries. Guinea, finding itself suddenly deprived of French support, turned in the first months after independence to the Communist bloc for assistance. By 1960, as many as 1,500 Soviet and Eastern European technicians were reported to be at work in the country. Mali, too, received considerable technical assistance from the Communist bloc: Chinese technicians, for example, were involved in half the country's industrial projects. But French aid was not completely discontinued: in 1965, 300 French teachers were working in the country's secondary schools. Other francophone countries were naturally far more heavily dependent on French personnel. In 1965, about 5,000 French technical assistants, half of them teachers, were working in West Africa. Anglophone West Africa received a more cosmopolitan range of technical assistants, drawn not only from Britain but also from other Commonwealth countries and the United States.

The unemployed school graduate, usually a boy in his late teens with no more in the way of qualifications than a smattering of English or French and a modest ability to read and write, had posed problems which worried administrators even in the early decades of the colonial regime. By the 1950's the rapid expansion of primary education had made the problem even more acute, as young men flocked to the towns in search of jobs more exciting and more remunerative than the seemingly dreary round carried on by their fathers and grandfathers. Statistics from Western Nigeria in 1961 showed that of the 261,000 young people leaving school that year, only 50,000 could hope to receive any further education, leaving over 200,000 looking for work. By the end of the 1960's most West African governments—radical and conservative alike—had experimented with some form of "civic service" designed to provide further training and employment for those who would otherwise have spent their time loitering around the streets. But "workers' brigades" proved expensive to organize and were able to absorb only a few thousand young people at a time.

To many West African politicians in the 1950's industrialization appeared as the panacea which would not only create vastly expanded opportunities for employment but also free individual territories from their dependence on foreign-produced goods. Until as late as 1950 West Africa was almost totally devoid of modern forms of factory industry. Since 1950 the larger and wealthier countries of West Africa have witnessed the emergence of a significant amount of modern industry. In Nigeria more than 500 factories were established between 1953 and 1966, and industry's contribution to the Gross Domestic Product rose from 5 percent to 12 percent. Textile mills, cement works, assembly plants for cars, bicycles, and radios, food canneries, and processing factories connected with major exports such as timber, groundnuts, and palm oil were the main forms of industrial activity. At their most successful, the new industries, almost invariably set up in partnership with foreign firms, made a useful contribution to the economy by substituting home-produced for imported goods. But the new factories offered employment to only a very small proportion of the working population. In 1954, no more than 16,000 Nigerians were employed in manufacturing industry; by 1962, the number had increased to 53,000 but still represented no more than 10 percent of the total wage-earning population.

By far the most substantial development in the West African economy since World War II was to be found in the expansion of the production of certain well-established cash-crops, and in the exploitation of some hitherto untapped mineral deposits. By the mid-1960's, farmers in Northern Nigeria were producing three times the prewar tonnage of groundnuts. In the Ivory Coast cocoa production increased three-fold in thirty years. Even more striking was the growth in coffee production. Before the war the Ivory Coast exported a few thousand tons annually; by the mid 1960's Ivorian exports of coffee reached 250,000 tons. No West African country had been a major producer of minerals before the war. By the 1960's bauxite had become the main export of Guinea, iron ore of Liberia, and oil of Nigeria, while Niger seemed likely to acquire substantial wealth from the deposits of uranium discovered by French geologists in the Air Mountains.

The improvement of communications was a major concern of all West African governments. The 1950's and 1960's was an age of intensive road-building, of the tarring of major trunk roads, and the construction of an increasingly elaborate network of feeder-roads reaching out to remote villages in the bush. In 1951 no more than 16,500 motor vehicles were in use in Nigeria. Sixteen years later the figure had increased to 103,000. Bold statistics such as these must be translated into human terms—more opportunities for local enterprise in the roles of taxi-driver, transport operator, mechanic or garage proprietor, an end, for good or ill, of the immemorial isolation of many rural communities.

With this vigorous process of modernization there has come a new pride in the past, in the distinctive manifestations of West African culture, together with an exhilarating outburst of new forms of creativity. In the course of the past decade West African scholars have made significant contributions to knowledge, particularly in the field of history. West African novelists, dramatists, and poets have produced works which form part of the literature of the mid-twentieth-century world and in so doing have helped outsiders to gain a deeper understanding of the nature of their society. West African artists and sculptors have presented their own distinctive visions. And West African musicians have excited foreign audiences with their vigorous rendering of traditional themes. Achievements such as these can, of course, be recorded in other parts of Black Africa—but not to the same extent. Few regions of the world convey so striking an impression of cultural richness and variety as West Africa or seem so well-equipped to produce a balanced synthesis between traditional and modern.

CHAPTER V

Equatorial Africa

▲▼ INTRODUCTION

Equatorial Africa is defined here as a region embracing the modern states of Cameroon, Central African Republic, Chad, Congo (Brazzaville), Zaire (Congo), and Gabon. In a strictly geographical sense only a small part of the region can be regarded as equatorial. The savanna plains of the southern Congo form part of a broadly uniform bloc of territory that includes much of Angola, Zambia, and Rhodesia —three countries defined here as forming part of Central Africa. Similarly the savanna plains of northern Cameroon, southern Chad, and the Central African Republic make up the central part of the great Sudanic belt that stretches across Africa from the Atlantic to the Red Sea. Finally northern Chad is a purely Saharan territory. A region of such diversity takes its shape not from any natural divisions but from those arbitrary lines drawn by European frontier-makers in the late nineteenth century.

However illogical these frontiers, the historian of colonial and postcolonial Africa obviously cannot afford to ignore them. For the student of Equatorial Africa in precolonial times, modern frontiers, though in a strict sense anachronistic, are useful in helping to define the limits of his field of study. For the region presents considerable ethnic and cultural complexity, despite the fact that its population is relatively modest in numbers. (With an area of almost 2 million square miles the region contained in 1960 no more than 25 million inhabitants, less than half the population of Nigeria.) All the ethnic groups in the southern half of the region speak Bantu languages, but in the northern half the linguistic pattern is more complex with languages of Afro-Asiatic, Western Sudanic, and Nilo-Saharan stock to be found among the peoples of the northern savanna plains. The vast majority of the peoples of Equatorial Africa are Negroid in physical appearance; but the region also contains about 100,000 pygmies, while some groups—notably the Shuwa Arabs of Chad, and the Fulani of northern Cameroon—stand out by reason of their partly Caucasoid features.

It would be virtually impossible to represent on a map the political geography of the region in the last half of the nineteenth century, for the majority of the peoples of Equatorial Africa lived not in substantial states but in independent village communities. This highly fragmented pattern, seemingly anarchic to outside observers, was to be found among the Kirdi (pagans) occupying the mountains of northern Cameroon, among the warlike Fang of Gabon, among the Sara, the Banda, the Baya, and other groups of southern Chad and the Central African Republic, and among the peoples whose villages lined the course of the Middle and Upper Congo and its tributaries. In contrast to these minuscule polities were a few substantial states formed during the sixteenth and seventeenth centuries: Wadai on the borders of the Sahara, Baguirmi south of Lake Chad, Bamum in the high grasslands of Cameroon, and the Lunda kingdoms of the Mwata Yamvo and the Kazembe. And there were a number of peoples—among them the Bamiléké of southern Cameroon, the Teke of the Lower Congo, the Zande living astride the Nile–Congo watershed, the Kuba and the Luba of the southern Congo basin—who had created polities, whether in the form of loosely structured kingdoms or, as with the Zande, an expanding cluster of chiefdoms, that provided links between larger numbers of peoples than the more isolated communities of stateless peoples.

In contrast to West Africa, with its long record of intercourse with peoples of the Maghrib and its briefer yet intense association with Europeans, most of Equatorial Africa had, by the beginning of the nineteenth century, been little affected by direct contact with the outside world. The coastal peoples of Cameroon and Gabon had carried on some trade with Europeans, but this trade could not match in volume that of their western neighbors, the Efik, the Ijaw, or the Ibo, nor was the impact of Europe nearly so disruptive north of the Congo as it had proved among the peoples of Kongo and Angola living to the south of the great river. Similarly, the northern peoples living between Lake Chad and Darfur had been drawn very much more slowly into the current of trans-Saharan trade than their western neighbors, the Kanuri and the Hausa. Indeed the route between Wadai and Benghazi, by way of the lonely oasis of Kufra, appears never to have been used until the second decade of the nineteenth century. Yet for all its relative isolation, Equatorial Africa must not be thought of as culturally impoverished. The wide range of craft industries developed by the people of Bamum or by the Kuba, the skill in wood-carving of the Bamiléké or in metalwork of the Mangbetu are vivid reminders of the development of an elaborate culture which must be seen as the end product of a vigorous cross-fertilization of techniques and ideas, a process reaching back into a past at present unilluminated by exact historical knowledge.

▲▼ PRE-EUROPEAN CONQUERORS IN EQUATORIAL AFRICA

The history of Equatorial Africa in the last decade of the nineteenth century was dominated by the activities of small groups of intrusive Europeans who succeeded within a remarkably short period in asserting their hegemony over the entire region. But Europeans were not the region's only intruders. From the mid-nineteenth century onward, peoples living on the periphery of Equatorial Africa were subjected to the impact of a variety of newcomers—Fulani in the northwest, Sudanese in the northeast, Swahili-Arabs in the east, Nyamwezi from Tanganyika in the southeast, and Cokwe in the southwest. Each of these intrusive groups was powerful enough to shatter the indigenous polities that lay in its path and to impose many aspects of its culture on the Equatorial peoples subjected to its domination. These pre-European conquerors were defeated in their turn by the Europeans who followed in their wake and their achievements obscured or eclipsed, but they made a massive contribution to the historical development of many parts of Equatorial Africa, and some of their descendants continue to play a prominent part in the political and economic life of the region.

Today there are about 400,000 Fulani living in the northern part of the Republic of Cameroon. The presence of Fulani groups in the area has been traced back to the end of the eighteenth century when bands of pastoralists, continuing a movement of slow migration that had carried their ancestors eastward from the Senegal across the Sudanic belt of West Africa, began to frequent the rich grazing lands of the Middle and Upper Benue. Early in the nineteenth century this easternmost group of Fulani was caught up in the movement of revolutionary excitement produced by Usuman dan Fodio's jihad against the rulers of the Hausa states. At this time the Fulani of the Benue valley were divided into a large number of autonomous clans, some of which were tributary to local pagan chiefs, but they were given a measure of unity by an outstanding local leader, Mobido Adama. Mobido Adama accepted the suzerainty of the caliph at Sokoto but enjoyed complete autonomy in his remote territory. He made his capital at Yola on the Benue, gave his name to a province, Adamawa (later divided by the frontier laid down by the British and the Germans to demarcate their territories in Nigeria and Kamerun), and founded a dynasty which rules in Yola to this day. Mobido Adama's vassal chiefs, who bore the title *lamido,* extended Fulani rule eastward and southward, conquering the pagans (Kirdi) of the plains but never subduing the resolute *montagnards* in their well-sited villages in the boulder-strewn Cameroon mountains. By 1875 the Fulani had reached as far south as the Sanaga River and one of their easternmost chiefdoms had as its capital a town, Ngaoundere, with a population of 20,000.

Further to the north the two substantial Muslim states of Wadai and Baguirmi served much the same function as the emirates of the Sokoto caliphate in producing a number of able but restless individuals who sought an outlet for their energy and scope for their ambition by carving out principalities for themselves in the pagan territories that lay beyond *Dar al-Islam* ("the land of Islam"). The process may be illustrated by the career of a certain Uthman, a member of the royal family of Baguirmi, who embarked on the pilgrimage to escape being blinded by his brother, the sultan. On his return from Mecca Uthman settled for a time in Dar Runga, south of Wadai, where he married the daughter of the local sultan and was given the task of subduing the pagans living to the south of the river Aouk in one of the northern districts of the modern Central African Republic. Uthman's domain, known as Dar Kuti, was rich in ivory and soon began to attract adventurous men from Dar Runga, Wadai, Baguirmi, and Bornu, together with Hausa returning from the pilgrimage and *jallaba,* Sudanese traders from the Nile valley. By 1870, the year of his death, Uthman could claim to have absorbed several hundred square miles of territory into "the land of Islam."

Far more spectacular than this modest success was the achievement of Rabih Zubair, the man whom some of his European contemporaries described as "a black Napoleon." Rabih, a Sudanese of humble origin from Sennar, took his second name from Zubair Pasha, the greatest of the merchant princes of the Turco Egyptian Sudan, in whose service he rose to prominence as an exceptionally energetic and courageous fighting man. In the late 1870's, after Zubair himself had been detained in Cairo, Rabih attached himself to the pasha's son, Sulaiman, and was involved in the gruelling campaign which followed Sulaiman's revolt against the government in Khartoum. Sulaiman was hunted down in the country south of Darfur by Gessi, an Italian officer in Egyptian service; he surrendered and was promptly executed. But Rabih, refusing to surrender, broke away, and taking with him a thousand of Sulaiman's best troops, many of them ex-slaves of Shilluk or Dinka origin, struck westward into the country south of Wadai.

Rabih's force, though modest in size, was yet immensely formidable, for it was made of tough, well-disciplined *bazingers* familiar with the use of modern firearms. Within a few years Rabih was master of the eastern half of the modern Central African Republic. Many independent village communities were wiped out, some of their people were incorporated in Rabih's steadily expanding band of followers, the men as soldiers, the women as wives or concubines; others were sold as slaves to *jellaba* merchants in exchange for vitally needed supplies of gunpowder and firearms. The rulers of the more substantial local principalities, including Dar Kuti and some of the Zande chiefdoms on the river Bomu to the south, were allowed to retain their position, so long as they paid tribute to the conqueror. Only Wadai was strong enough to resist him and in the late 1880's Rabih's army suffered a severe defeat at the hands of the Wadaians.

To the conquistador whose very existence depended on obtaining a regular supply of arms and ammunition the hostility of Wadai was a particularly serious matter. For Wadai lay at the southern end of one of the main trans-Saharan caravan routes, along which a regular supply of arms, smuggled into Benghazi by Greek fishermen, was known to flow. These arms the sultan of Wadai needed for his own army, and he took stringent precautions to prevent them from reaching his adversary. Meanwhile, constant raiding had left much of the country south of Wadai a desert. In these circumstances, Rabih had little option but to move westward and so came into direct conflict with the ancient sultanates of Baguirmi and Bornu. Twenty years earlier Rabih had taken part in the campaign in which his master, Zubair Pasha, conquered the sultanate of Darfur. He must have been well aware of the many lines of weakness which the pomp and splendor of an old-established Sudanic court often concealed. In 1893 Rabih conquered Baguirmi. Little more than a year later, after several hard-fought battles, he was master of Bornu. Controlling a territory which reached from the borders of Kano in the West to the borders of Darfur in the east, Rabih was the master of the most substantial empire ever recorded in the history of the Central Sudan.

Rabih's empire was also destined to be the most short-lived in Sudanic history. But, in the few years that remained to him, Rabih gave abundant proof of his quality as an administrator. Having destroyed Kuka, the old capital of Bornu, he created a new capital for himself at Dikwa, south of Lake Chad, a place strategically sited to allow easy access to the eastern and western halves of the empire. Dikwa was equally well placed to develop into an important commercial center to which came merchants from Tripoli, from Hausaland, from the Nile valley, and from many nearer lands. Over the conquered territories Rabih imposed an administrative superstructure not unlike that later to be established by the British and the French, leaving local chiefs in place but using his own officers to supervise their activities and to ensure the regular payment of taxes. Basically, Rabih's power rested on force—his army had by now increased to 5,000 gunmen and a large number of irregulars. But he could count on the cordial collaboration of certain important groups. Most of the Shuwa Arabs of Bornu, for example, had hastened to abandon their overlord, the Kanuri sultan, and join forces with the invader. Moreover, Rabih had come to provide himself with a distinctive ideology for he claimed to be a follower of the Sudanese Mahdia and could thus base his hostility to the established authorities of his day on the grounds of Muslim doctrine rather than of self-aggrandizing *realpolitik*. Inevitably Rabih was denounced by his opponents as a brutal despot, and there is no doubt that he was responsible for many cruel deeds. But brought up as he was in an atmosphere of continual violence, he showed an astonishing capacity to master one daunting situation after another, to infuse a new element of discipline and efficiency into the older polities of the Central Sudan, thus laying the foundations of an empire which might well have developed into one of the most substantial states in the history of Black Africa, had it not been so suddenly confronted with new groups of conquerors—French, German, and British—whose expeditions began to converge on Lake Chad in the last years of the nineteenth century.

More than a thousand miles to the southeast of the area dominated by Rabih and his Sudanese, another group of Muslim intruders were making their impact on a cluster of Bantu-speaking peoples living in independent village-communities in the country known as Manyema, west of Lake Tanganyika. Arab and Swahili traders from the East Coast first appeared in Manyema in the late 1840's. Like the Khartoumers operating in the Southern Sudan, they were moved to push ever deeper into the heart of Africa by the demands of the ivory trade. By 1860 there was an Arab settlement at Nyangwe on the Lualaba (the name locally given to the Upper Congo), and in the late 1870's, enterprising Arabs, partly influenced by the ease with which their one-time guest, the European explorer, Stanley, was able to journey down the river, moved northward as far as Stanley Falls. The impact of the Swahili-Arabs on the peoples of the Eastern Congo was not unlike that of the Khartoumers on the stateless polities of the Southern Sudan. There was an immediate increase in violence for the newcomers needed slaves as personal attendants, as porters, and as merchandise whose sale would help swell the profits of the ivory trade. Ghastly incidents could occur when groups of well-armed, lawless and avaricious men were let loose among a population ill-equipped to resist them. (The massacre witnessed by Livingstone at Nyangwe when Arab gunmen opened fire on a market crowded with women and children provided Europe with a vivid example of Arab brutality.) But there were among the newcomers shrewd, moderate, and business-like men who saw the need to end the mounting anarchy by creating new political structures. The most famous of these merchant princes was Tippu Tib, a dark-skinned Arab from Zanzibar who made his headquarters at Kasongo on the Lualaba. Kasongo and other large Arab settlements astonished European visitors. At Kasongo "even the common soldiers slept on silk and satin mattresses, in carved beds with silk mosquito curtains," and the town was surrounded by large plantations, the land cleared of virgin forest yielding "splendid crops of sugar-cane, rice, maize" and a variety of fruits, including oranges, guavas, pineapples and pomegranates.[1] As agricultural innovators, bringing in not only a wide range of new crops but also new breeds of cattle, the Arabs made a major contribution to the economic development of the area under their control. They were responsible too for the diffusion of Swahili as a *lingua franca* over a wide area. And the trading states which they established represented the largest polities yet known in this part of Africa.

Arab and Swahili traders were not the only newcomers from the east to be found in the Congo basin. Three hundred miles south of Manyema lay the substantial Lunda kingdom of Kazembe. Early in the nineteenth century, Nyamwezi traders whose homeland lay to the east of Lake Tanganyika, began to purchase the copper for which Kazembe was famous. Of the Nyamwezi one European traveler remarked that they were "like Scotchmen," to be found "almost everywhere throughout central Africa," having "a knack of pushing themselves into prominence."[2] The most successful of these Nyamwezi adventurers was Msiri, the son of one of the earliest traders to reach Kazembe. In the 1850's, Msiri created a political base for himself on the western borders of the Lunda kingdom and set about conquering neighboring chiefdoms —including one whose ruler, Katanga, gave his name to the entire area —which had previously been vassals of Kazembe. Msiri's force was made up of young Nyamwezi, known to the Lunda as Yeke, "elephant hunters." To keep these soldiers-of-fortune happy and to prevent them from returning to their homeland, Msiri needed a constant supply of women, cattle, and other booty, of a kind to be obtained only by incessant raids on independent chiefdoms or by the establishment of a regular system of tribute from those who accepted his overlordship. Through a policy of constant expansion Msiri created a new state that embraced the greater part of modern Katanga and far eclipsed the ancient kingdom of Kazembe. He called his new dominion Garenganze, a name derived from a district in western Nyamwezi.

By the 1880's, Msiri's capital, Bunkeya, had grown into one of the largest commercial centers in Central and Equatorial Africa, attracting traders from countries as distant as Angola and Zanzibar, from Uganda, the Zambezi, and the Congo basin. But for all its cosmopolitan character Bunkeya was singularly lacking in urban graces. Unlike his contemporaries, Samory, Rabih, or the Arab traders on the Upper Congo, with all of whom his career had obvious similarities, Msiri had never been influenced by the refining culture of Islam. Force was his only sanction, terror his favorite weapon. Thus he preferred to execute a thief rather than inflict the traditional punishment of cutting off a hand. "I stab them in the heart," he is reported as saying, "because the hand never stole anything yet, it is the heart who is the thief." [3] This crude psychology served to justify and explain his actions. And his subjects were presented with a constant *memento mori* in the human skulls that decorated the palisades of his *boma*. A kingdom so constructed was too heavily dependent on the will of a single man. Even before a European expedition rendered the *coup de grâce* to Msiri in 1891, Garenganze appeared on the verge of collapse, with local chiefs starting to rebel against the aging tyrant of Bunkeya.

The export of ivory played a vital part in the economy of all the new states of Equatorial Africa, for it represented one of the few products which could be exchanged for the firearms of European origin that were essential for the maintenance of the new political structures. Ivory, too, was of crucial importance in the rise of the Cokwe, a relatively small group of people who succeeded in the last half of the nineteenth century in dominating most of the southwestern section of the Congo basin, including the great Lunda kingdom of Mwata Yamvo. In the eighteenth century the Cokwe were overshadowed by their neighbors, the Ovimbundu and the Imbangala, who acted as middlemen in the trade that brought a constant flow of slaves from the Congo basin to the Portuguese in Angola. The collapse of the overseas slave trade in the 1840's and the sudden expansion in the demand for ivory gave the Cokwe an opportunity to establish themselves as successful traders. They already possessed a reputation as elephant-hunters, and observers had noticed that they were particularly interested in obtaining European firearms, though little attracted by other European trade-goods. By 1855, the Cokwe had exterminated all the elephants in their own well-forested homeland of Quiboco, and small groups of hunters began to move eastward in search of fresh herds. From the Lunda chiefs they received a ready welcome, for the Lunda were suffering from the decline in the slave trade and were glad to strike a bargain with the migrant Cokwe who gave them one tusk of every elephant they killed. The hunters used much of their new-found wealth to purchase slave-women from neighboring peoples. In areas where their skill as hunters was in less demand, particularly among the Lulua and Luba living east of the Kasai River, the Cokwe turned directly to trade and established themselves as middlemen on routes not frequented by the Imbangala and the Ovimbundu. As a result, many Congolese communities which had previously lain beyond the network of long-distance trade, were caught up in the atmosphere of violence that accompanied the trade in slaves and ivory in every part of Africa.

With their own numbers greatly increased by the constant absorption of slave women, the Cokwe began to suffer from acute population pressure in their homeland of Quiboco. At the same time, they were able to benefit from a rising European demand for a previously ignored tropical product, the wild rubber that grew abundantly in most of the forests of Equatorial Africa. To profit from the rubber trade and to ease population pressure, entire Cokwe villages began moving eastward, following the line of the gallery forests which had been left uninhabited by the Lunda. Thus the arrival of a large group of Cokwe immigrants caused no immediate upheaval in a Lunda district, especially as the newcomers were careful to preserve good relations with the host community. But within a few years the Cokwe usually came to dominate the local economy, and to undermine local Lunda society by attracting Lunda women to attach themselves voluntarily to their prosperous communities, where they rapidly came to adopt Cokwe culture. Thus by the 1880's, the Cokwe settled in Lunda county had the advantage of substantial numbers, of considerable wealth, of skill in the use of firearms, and of a fund of political, diplomatic and administrative experience acquired through their management of large trading caravans. Moreover, by this time some Cokwe groups had taken to living as free-booters, pillaging villages, robbing caravans and using effective guerilla tactics when confronted with more substantial forces. With such assets it was inevitable that the Cokwe should find many local chiefs seeking their support.

By the 1880's, the Lunda kingdom of Mwata Yamvo, for long the greatest state in the southern Congo basin, was afflicted by a disastrous economic crisis. The long-distance trade in slaves, on which the kingdom's early prosperity had depended, had disappeared, the country's supply of rubber and ivory had rapidly been exhausted, and the kingdom's geographical position in the center of the continent ruled out the possibility of its merchants taking on the profitable role of middlemen. Constant disputes occurred at the court of the Lunda paramount, the Mwata Yamvo, and at the lesser capitals of provincial governors. As the kingdom fell apart, Lunda power-seekers turned to Cokwe chiefs and their bands of followers for assistance. By 1890 the once prosperous Lunda kingdom east of the Kasai had been reduced to a desert. Like the Galla in eighteenth-century Ethiopia, with whose turbulent political activities the actions of Cokwe mercenary leaders bear a striking resemblance, the Cokwe lacked the capacity to create a powerful unified state. By the mid-1890's there were clear signs of a Lunda revival. European intervention confused the later outcome of events. But even without European assistance it seems likely that the Lunda would have recovered much of the land the Cokwe had devastated.

As in West Africa, so in Equatorial Africa, large areas appear to have experienced a period of unprecedented violence in the 1870's and 1880's. But the causes which made for bitter conflicts among the Yoruba states or plunged the Upper Niger into years of warfare as a result of the state-building ambitions of Samory or al-Hajj Umar have little in common with forces which lay behind the actions of Rabih, the Congo Arabs, Msiri's Yeke and the Cokwe. One factor alone is common to both regions—the increasing use of firearms. In other aspects there is a sharp contrast between the two regions. West African wars arose from local causes. The major conflicts in Equatorial Africa, on the other hand, were started by outsiders, of Asian or African origin, many of whose activities were set in motion by the demand developing both in Europe and in Asia for African ivory. Ironically, indeed, the trade in ivory, an apparently innocuous produce used to manufacture billiard balls and bangles, appears to have been conductive of quite as much violence as the earlier trade in slaves. Inter-African violence clearly facilitated the European conquest in both West and Equatorial Africa. It made it easy for intruding groups of Europeans to find Africans who welcomed their arrival and eagerly offered their assistance. It also enabled the Europeans to adorn their actions with a palpable moral gloss, presenting themselves as liberators come to free oppressed African communities from the scourge of the slave trade. Nor was this chivalrous sentiment a sham: to Europeans living in the 1870's, and still blissfully unaware of the appalling miseries their descendants were to inflict on one another in two world wars, Equatorial Africa presented a ghastly spectacle of cruelty, superstition, and vice. Here indeed was Livingstone's "open sore of the world" which Europe was called on to heal. But in 1875 the European presence in Equatorial Africa was modest to the extreme, being confined to a few trading posts and mission stations on the Atlantic Coast. Nowhere in the world, outside the polar regions, was European geographical knowledge so limited. Even the course of the Congo was still unknown. It would have been totally impossible for any observer to have predicted in 1875 that within a mere twenty-five years the whole of Equatorial Africa would have been divided up among the nations of Europe, and that the largest and richest part of the region would have become the property of the sovereign of one of the smallest states in Europe.

▲▼ THE CONGO FREE STATE

The creation of the Congo Free State presents one of the most extraordinary examples of state-formation in modern history. For the state owed its origin to the driving force of a single individual—the constitutional monarch of one of the smallest countries in Europe, Leopold II, king of the Belgians. Leopold was an extraordinary head of state. Strictly correct in the performance of his constitutional duties, he displayed in his private actions the temperament of a tycoon—immensely energetic, highly intelligent, a brilliant man of business, dreaming big, yet capable of translating his dreams into reality, but with a strong strain of coarseness, of crude, ugly, self-seeking materialism vitiating much that he achieved.

Leopold ascended the Belgian throne in 1865 at the age of thirty. Already he had traveled widely, acquired a mass of information about the non-European world, and formulated the ideas that were to shape his later actions. "Belgium does not exploit the world," he wrote in 1863. "It's a taste we have got to make her learn." [4] By acquiring overseas possessions even a small country could become great. But colonies must be organized so as to produce the maximum profit for the metropolis. Forced labor was "the only way to civilize and moralize . . . idle and corrupted [native] populations." [5] Restlessly he searched the world for an opening, considered plans for Belgian colonization in China, the Philippines, North Borneo, the Pacific islands, Argentina, and finally decided in 1875 "to make discreet enquiries as to whether there is not something to be done in Africa." [6]

In the early 1870's Equatorial Africa was still a vast and provocative blank on European maps. But European interest in the region was steadily mounting as explorers, starting either from Gabon on the Atlantic Coast or from Zanzibar, attempted to penetrate deep into the interior. Taking advantage of this favorable climate of opinion, Leopold invited the leading Africanists of the day, including both travelers and humanitarians, to a geographical conference held in Brussels in 1876. The conference led to the foundation of a new international body with Leopold himself as chairman. The *Association internationale pour reprimer la traite et ouvrir l'Afrique centrale,* usually known in England as the International African Association, appeared, as its full title suggested, to be concerned only with humanitarian and scientific objectives; in reality it had been devised by Leopold himself, as his most recent biographer has pointed out, "to serve as a smoke-screen to confuse stronger nations," while the king, operating in a purely personal capacity, laid the foundations of a colony in Equatorial Africa.[7]

Two years later Leopold secured the services of Henry Morton Stanley, the most famous African explorer of his day and a man ideally equipped to help the king achieve his aims. Stanley had just returned to Europe after his three year journey "through the dark continent," a journey that had taken him from Zanzibar through Uganda to the Upper Congo. There he had taken to the river and paddled down to its mouth, engaging in the course of his odyssey in a series of "desperate conflicts" with various riverine peoples whom he chose to describe as "the insensate forces of savage-land." [8] Thus he was able to provide the outside world with its first detailed account of Equatorial Africa's complex system of waterways and to show how greatly these rivers facilitated communication in a region previously regarded as impenetrable. Exasperated to find that the British were not greatly interested in the commercial possibilities of his discoveries, he was glad to accept Leopold's offer of employment. The king was anxious to advance his own schemes further than the formal purposes of the International African Association would allow. To this end he organized a commercial syndicate, the *Comité d'Études du Haut Congo,* to finance a mission to be led by Stanley to explore the commercial opportunities of the Congo and to meet the expense of the commercial stations the explorer was instructed to set up. These stations, Stanley was secretly informed, were to be developed into "little republics," populated by free and freed Negroes but under the control of white men and linked together to form a "republican confederation of Negro freedmen." [9] Here, again presented in a piously humanitarian guise, was the blueprint for a new political structure.

Stanley served Leopold well. In five years he founded a chain of stations from the mouth of the Congo to Stanley Pool and beyond, building a road around the cataracts that blocked the lower course of the river. At the same time, he concluded several hundred treaties with local chiefs. Meanwhile Leopold made sure of his own undisputed control over these operations by winding up the *Comité d'Études* and replacing it with a new body, the *Association Internationale du Congo,* a body which seemed to Leopold's contemporaries more or less identical with the International African Association. In reality there was nothing international, humanitarian, or scientific about the new association. It was created solely as a blind; Leopold was its only member and its activities were financed by the king's private fortune, much of which was said to have been acquired by successful speculation on the stock exchange.

Leopold was now faced with the difficult task of securing international recognition for the AIC. The situation was one of great complexity. Four European powers—Portugal, France, Britain, and Germany —were keenly interested in the future of the Congo. The Portuguese had once—in the sixteenth and seventeenth centuries—dominated much of the country to the south of the Lower Congo. Though they no longer maintained any administrative posts in the area, they still considered themselves to possess a moral claim to the stretch of coast on both sides of the river. Further north the French had established a colony on the coast of Gabon, and French agents were actively exploring the interior in search of an overland route to the Congo. Already a sense of rivalry was developing, and in 1880 the most successful of French explorers, Savorgnan de Brazza, reached Stanley Pool from the north and concluded a treaty with the local Teke chief. This treaty was enthusiastically ratified by the French parliament two years later. The British had no territorial ambitions in the area but British merchants were increasingly active on the coast of Equatorial Africa and feared that the extension of French influence might eventually serve, through the erection of prohibitive tariffs, to exclude them from a profitable market. The Portuguese, too, were growing seriously alarmed at French expansion. Common fears brought the two sides together and led early in 1884 to the conclusion of an Anglo-Portuguese treaty whereby the British, in return for certain trading concessions, recognized the Portuguese claim to the coast on either side of the Congo estuary.

Fortunately for Leopold, who could see his newly acquired possessions being deprived of direct access to the sea, the treaty was never ratified. It aroused a storm of protest in Britain, especially among humanitarians who accused the Portuguese of still dealing in slaves, and its territorial provisions were rejected both by the French and by the Germans. The policy followed by Germany in the Congo in 1884 can be fully understood only when seen as part of that immensely complex web of political and diplomatic relationships woven by Bismarck to maintain a dominant position for himself in the political life of his own country and for his country in the councils of Europe. Temporarily estranged from Britain, Bismarck was glad to cooperate with France in inviting all the powers of Europe, together with the United States, to a conference at Berlin to discuss the future of the Congo basin.

An international conference provided Leopold with the ideal milieu in which to advance his claims. Before the conference met, the AIC had been recognized as possessing the status of a sovereign state by the United States and France. In the course of the conference recognition came from the other powers of Europe, and the AIC was able to secure a preliminary territorial settlement with France and Portugal. The conference ended in February 1885 with the promulgation of a "general act," some of whose articles had an important bearing on later developments. The first article laid down that "the trade of all nations shall enjoy complete freedom in all the regions forming the basin of the Congo"; the sixth article bound the powers "exercising sovereign rights" in these regions "to watch over the preservation of the native tribes, and to care for the improvement of their moral and national well-being"; further articles made it clear that "the navigation of the Congo" and its tributaries was "free for the merchant ships of all nations" and that the territories covered by "the free trade system" should be neutral in time of war. Two other articles of the Berlin Act were of general import. The first required any power taking "possession of a tract of land on the coasts of the African Continent" or assuming a protectorate to notify the "Signatory Powers" of its action. Under the terms of the second article, the "Signatory Powers" recognized "the obligation to insure the establishment of authority in the regions occupied by them." [10] The Berlin Conference did not, as is sometimes supposed, bring about the "scramble for Africa"; it served merely to lay down the rules for a game already begun.

Given the special provisions relating to the Congo, it was hardly possible to devise a more effective political arrangement than that which allowed an "international association" with allegedly humanitarian aims under the presidency of the constitutional ruler of a small European country whose own neutrality had been internationally guaranteed to establish its control over the greater part of the Congo basin. Within a few weeks of the ending of the Berlin Conference the AIC was transformed into the Congo Free State, and Leopold, still acting in a purely private capacity but with the hesitant consent of the Belgian parliament, assumed the title of the new state's "sovereign."

Leopold never once set foot in his new domain, yet he exerted over the Congo a measure of autocratic power such as no other contemporary African ruler, indigenous or alien, could claim to possess. Seeing himself as the "proprietor" of the Congo, the king could have asserted far more truly than Louis XIV, *"L'état, c'est moi."* The Congo was ruled from Brussels where Leopold assiduously supervised the work of the officials of the "central government" and kept as tight a check as possible on his agents in the field. In the Congo itself a hierarchy of officials—a governor-general, fourteen district commissioners, and an increasing number of junior officers commanding individual *postes*— built up the rapidly expanding structure of alien rule. Belgian army officers and N.C.O.'s formed the largest element in the new administration. But it was necessary, especially in the early stages, to supplement the Free State's cadre of officials by recruiting the nationals of many other countries. The 430 whites resident in the Congo in 1889—not all of whom were Free State officials—included 175 Belgians, 58 Portuguese, and smaller numbers of Dutchmen, Englishmen, Danes, Swedes, Frenchmen, and Americans, Mortality rates were high: no less than 179 of the 600 Belgian officers to serve in the Congo between 1877 and 1908 died of disease or were killed in action, and many more were invalided home. The Free State's army, the *Force Publique,* was 6,000 strong in 1895; eleven years later it contained 16,000 African troops led by 360 European officers. In the early days, many of the soldiers came from other parts of Africa, including Liberia, Sierra Leone, and Zanzibar. Gradually more and more Congolese, many of them former slaves of Arab masters, were recruited for seven years' military service.

Administrators and army officers were not the only agents of European authority. In the late 1870's the Congo began to attract the attention of Protestant missionary bodies in Europe and America. By 1890 American and English Baptists had established many mission stations on the Lower and Middle Congo, American Presbyterians were expanding from their base at Luelo on the Kasai, and English Plymouth Brethren were firmly settled in Katanga at the court of the redoubtable Msiri. The work of Protestant missions in the Congo was inspired and financed by private philanthropists in Europe and America. The establishment of Roman Catholic missions, by contrast, owed much to the initiative of Leopold himself, for the king was anxious to see his own compatriots play a leading part in the evangelization of the Congo. By 1900 six Roman Catholic missionary orders had started work, some in areas already opened by the Protestants, others in remoter districts, such as the country between the Uele and the Aruwimi rivers in the extreme northeast of the Free State's territory. Mission stations rapidly developed into substantial communities in which the white missionary could not avoid operating in an administrative capacity. "Many a little Protestant Pope is forced," wrote an English missionary working in Katanga, "to be prophet, priest, and king rolled into one—really a very big duck in his own private pond." [11]

There were heroic and dedicated men among the administrators and missionaries of the Congo Free State. But the country also attracted many adventurers and ne'er-do-wells, men "whose talk was the talk of sordid buccaneers . . . reckless without hardihood, greedy without audacity, and cruel without courage." So Joseph Conrad, whose great novel, *Heart of Darkness,* was based on personal experience of the Congo in the 1890's, wrote of one such group, the members of a prospecting expedition, adding savagely, "to tear treasure out of the bowels of the land was their desire, with no more moral purpose at the back of it than there is in burglars breaking into a safe." [12]

In 1885 Stanley remarked that the driving force of the Congo Free State was an "enormous voracity." [13] Other imperial powers took over territory in Africa to protect already established economic interests, to safeguard areas deemed to be of strategic significance, or even to bolster national prestige. Leopold's expansionist policy was based on a less complex rationale: "its sole principles," as the Belgian historian, Jean Stengers, has recently written, "were those of greed." [14] As an acquirer of land Leopold was brilliantly successful. When the frontiers of his territory were finally demarcated, they embraced more than 900,000 square miles. But he had planned to take over an even vaster domain which would include much of the territory of the upper Nile. Indeed, in the late 1890's he went further and opened negotiations with Italy, after that country's colonial ambitions had been shattered by the defeat of Adowa, in the hope of obtaining the lease of Eritrea and thus ensuring that his empire should stretch across the entire continent.

Empire-building on such a scale in the heart of Africa involved four daunting tasks: the territory, largely unknown, had to be explored; its frontiers defined by agreement with rival European powers; the resistance of local African polities overcome; and, most difficult of all, the new domain made not only to pay for the cost of its administration but also to fulfil the basic purpose of a colony as Leopold understood it by yielding a substantial profit. All these tasks Leopold and his agents accomplished in their fashion.

Within ten years of the formal establishment of the Free State most of its territory had been explored in the most concentrated burst of activity ever to be recorded in Europe's long record of acquiring geographical information about Africa. Most of the work was done by administrators and missionaries serving in the Congo, but the most impressive—and by far the most widely publicized—feat of this period, involving the crossing of the dense Ituri rain-forest, was accomplished by H. M. Stanley as leader of the Emin Pasha Relief Expedition. Emin Pasha, a German doctor of somewhat eccentric character, was governor of Equatoria, the only province of the Turco-Egyptian Sudan not to be overrun by the Mahdist revolution. The relief expedition was financed by a generous grant from the Egyptian government and by the donations of English supporters; nevertheless, Leopold, with his eyes on the Upper Nile, hoped to turn it to his own advantage by persuading Emin to enter the service of the Free State, retain his governorship of Equatoria, but transfer his allegiance from Cairo to Brussels. Emin was not the man to fall in with such a scheme, and in any case his power was undermined when his Sudanese troops began to mutiny and he found himself forced to return with Stanley to Zanzibar. Equatoria now became a no-man's-land invested with a far-fetched strategic significance by those European statesmen who believed that control of the Upper Nile could have some effect on the destinies of Egypt.

Something has already been said in Chapter II of the intense diplomatic activity over this remote and commercially valueless part of Africa. In 1894 the British government, it will be recalled, in its anxiety to prevent the French from securing a foothold on the Upper Nile agreed to "lease" the lands lying west of the Nile as far north as Fashoda to the Congo Free State in return for Congolese recognition of Britain's ultimate rights in the area. Angry protests from the French forced Leopold to abandon this treaty and to be content with a narrow strip of territory, the Lado enclave, which allowed the Free State access to the river at a point north of the modern Sudan-Uganda frontier. Dissatisfied with this modest concession, Leopold made an about-face, turned to the French, agreed to support the French plans which resulted in the Marchand expedition to the Upper Nile, and set about preparing a large-scale expedition of his own to march on Equatoria. Leopold's expedition ended disastrously with the mutiny of its Congolese soldiers, but a number of smaller detachments from the Free State reached the Nile valley, came into direct conflict with Mahdist forces, and continued to operate in Equatoria and Bahr al-Ghazal for several years after the establishment of the Anglo-Egyptian condominium. Finally, in 1905 the British forced Leopold to accept the Nile-Congo watershed as the boundary between the Free State and the Sudan and restricted the lease of the Lado enclave to the king's lifetime, thus shattering Leopold's long-cherished hopes for an empire on the Nile.

Far more significant for the future of the new state than these frustrated efforts at expansion toward the Nile valley was the successful occupation of the extreme southeast, the area covered by Msiri's conquest-state of Garenganze, better known to Europe as Katanga. Maps published in the 1880's showed Katanga as forming part of the Free State, but Leopold, ignorant of the vast mineral resources of an almost entirely unexplored territory, was in no hurry to uphold his claims by effective occupation. Meanwhile, since 1886 a succession of British missionaries, members of the Plymouth Brethren, had established themselves at Msiri's court. The old tyrant gladly accepted the presence of these "white slaves" at his capital, finding them transparently devoid of political ambitions and appreciating their skill as medicinemen and their usefulness as secretaries, but he could not prevent the first missionary, F. S. Arnot, from returning to England and presenting so attractive an account of Garenganze that English interest in this previously neglected part of Africa steadily began to increase. Already a British imperialist with an appetite for territory no less voracious than Leopold's was beginning to look from a South African base northward across the Zambezi. In 1889 Cecil Rhodes obtained a charter for his British South Africa Company and set about laying the foundations for British hegemony in Central Africa. As part of Rhodes' grand strategy, a British agent, Alfred Sharpe, visited Bunkeya and attempted to persuade Msiri to put his signature to a treaty. But Msiri, warned by his missionary friends that such a treaty meant "giving away his country," [15] stoutly rejected Sharpe's demands and forced him to beat a hasty retreat. This success gained Msiri a year's respite, but it offered no protection against the advance of the Free State expeditions already set in motion by Leopold. In December 1891, Msiri, refusing to the last to raise the Free State flag over his capital, was shot dead in the course of an angry argument with a Belgian officer. The Free State's control of Katanga was formally recognized in the Anglo-Congolese treaty of 1894, by which the curiously shaped frontier between the modern states of Zambia and Zaire was laid down.

Msiri's kingdom fell apart with his death, leaving a cluster of warring feudatories incapable of uniting to oppose the European intruders. Indeed, nowhere in the entire Congo basin did any local African group succeed in presenting a really formidable resistance to the Free State forces. Only when the Europeans came into contact with a body of rival imperialists, the Arab and Swahili traders of the Upper Congo, were they faced with really serious fighting. In the mid-1880's, the Arabs were vigorously engaged in expanding their search for ivory and slaves northward along the line of the Congo when they came into contact with the post established by the Free State at Stanley Falls. Lacking the strength at this time to resist the Arab advance, the Free State authorities resorted in 1887 to the device of appointing Tippu Tib, the most prominent of the Arab merchant-princes of the Upper Congo, to act as governor of the whole territory on condition that he made every effort to stop Arab slave-raiding. Tippu Tib was influential enough to restrain his compatriots from coming into direct conflict with the Europeans, but he was bitterly reviled by Congolese Arabs for collaborating with infidels, and after his return to Zanzibar in 1891 he was too far removed from the Congo to exercise much influence over the course of events. Finally, in 1892, after a series of incidents involving the killing of Europeans, the local Free State commander, Dhlamis, acting on his own initiative, launched an all-out war on the Arabs. Within eighteen months Arab power had been completely broken. In Europe the campaign was presented as a campaign against the slave trade—a crusade to which Leopold had shrewdly dedicated himself by taking a leading part in the Conference for the Abolition of the Slave Trade held in Brussels in 1890. For Belgian public opinion, Dhlamis' victories struck a patriotic chord, investing the Congolese adventure with a new-found glamor. "Africa," declared a Belgian minister, "gives us an ideal outside ourselves to pursue, and a nation, like an individual, cannot do without an ideal." [16]

As a cynical old materialist, Leopold was prepared to make use of any form of idealism that might serve his own ends. His basic aim was crude and simple: to develop the Congo Free State in such a way as to ensure that it yielded, like any other commercial undertaking, a satisfactory return in terms of hard cash profits. The whole adventure was a gamble, and in the late 1880's it looked as if it well might fail. Under the terms of the Berlin Act, the Free State authorities were precluded from collecting import duties, the main source of revenue for most European colonies in Africa. Thus in its first years the Free State was faced with a constant deficit which the king could meet only by drawing heavily on his own private resources. By 1889 Leopold was so short of money that he was reduced to mortgaging the livery of his palace servants. He was saved the next year when the Belgian government, influenced by the favorable publicity accorded the royal venture by the Brussels Anti-Slave Trade Conference, agreed to grant the Free State a loan of 25 million francs. At the same time Leopold benefitted from those clauses in the Brussels Act which allowed colonial governments in the free-trade area to impose limited import duties. But even with these concessions the Free State still remained close to bankruptcy. In 1887 receipts covered no more than a third of all expenses; by 1893, largely as a result of an increase in ivory exports, revenue had improved substantially but still met no more than one third of the cost of government. Solvency came only when the government found a way of exploiting the most easily procurable of all the Congo's products—the rubber that grew wild in most forest areas.

As early as 1885 the Free State had laid claim to all "vacant lands" within its territory. The implications of this claim became apparent in the early 1890's when about half the total area of the State, including all those districts most likely to produce wild rubber, were declared to form the State's *domaine privé*. To this was added another extensive tract of territory around Lake Leopold II which was reserved for the king's exclusive profit and known as the *domaine de la couronne*. Other large tracts of territory, such as Katanga, which appeared to offer less immediately exploitable commercial opportunities were granted to private concessionary companies, in most of which the state possessed a share. Rubber could be obtained only by compelling local Africans to go out into the forest to collect the wild produce. State and company officials were encouraged by the commissions they received on the amount of rubber produced in the areas under their charge to concentrate all their energies on this crude system of exploitation. Inevitably such a system gave rise to many abuses. An official on the Ubangi described how he would arrive at a village by canoe with a detachment of Congolese soldiers; the villagers would promptly bolt into the forest, leaving their homes to be looted by the soldiers; the soldiers would then pursue the villagers, capture some of the women and hold them hostage until the local chief had brought in the prescribed amount of rubber; the captured women would then be "sold back to their owners for a couple of goats apiece"; "and so he continued from village to village until the requisite amount of rubber had been collected." [17] Thirty years later, a Dutchman who had worked in the Congo in the first decade of the twentieth century described the usual method of obtaining rubber. "You dumped a handful of rubbishy goods—beads and bracelets and so forth —on the local chief, and demanded a certain quantity of rubber by a certain date. If it was not forthcoming the chief was put down and given fifty of the best on the backside with a rhino-hide whip." [18]

In narrow financial terms this savage policy of exploitation proved exceedingly profitable. The Free State's deficits were replaced by surpluses from 1900 onward. These surpluses were not plowed back into the country to assist its development but were used to finance a series of grandiose public works in Belgium itself. Leopold was always a thorough-going imperialist. "It is the White Man," he declared, "who has made and will make the Congo into a civilized country. To maintain that everything the White Man is likely to produce in the country ought to be spent only in Africa and for the benefit of the Blacks is a real heresy, an injustice and a mistake." For all their work of "civilization" the whites were entitled to their "legitimate compensation." [19] Even in Belgium, Leopold found few supporters for his economic policy, and some of his earliest collaborators were so critical of the monopolistic practices introduced by the king that they preferred to leave his service. In general, however, the vast majority of Belgians felt no great interest in the Congo, until the pointed criticisms of foreign critics forced them to look more closely at the actions of their sovereign.

Early in the 1890's English and American missionaries working in the Congo began to send home stories of the brutal behaviour of some state officials. (Particularly atrocious were the incidents which occurred when Congolese troops were let loose on native communities accused of failing to meet the demand for rubber.) The Congo Free State was open to attack on legal grounds for failing to honor those articles in the Berlin Act which required all sovereign powers in the Congo to guarantee free trade and to consider the welfare of the native inhabitants. Worried by the mounting reports of atrocities, the British government instructed its consul in the Congo to investigate the situation. In 1904, the consul, Roger Casement, produced a vividly documented report that was also a damning indictment of the Free State's system of government. The indictment was driven home by the Congo Reform Association, one of those powerful *ad hoc* bodies, of a kind to be found more frequently in England than in any other European country, devised to give organized expression to outraged humanitarian sentiment, and looking back to the great antislave trade movement of the late eighteenth century as model and inspiration. The Clarkson of the Congo Reform Association was a young journalist, E. D. Morel, who had started his career as a clerk in the service of the shipping firm of Elder Dempster and become one of the best informed observers of West African affairs to be found anywhere in Europe. As a result of vigorous lobbying by the Association, the British government began to press Leopold to introduce effective reforms. Leopold countered his foreign critics by appointing an impartial commission of enquiry to investigate the situation in the Congo. The commission's report confirmed many of Casement's findings and made a profound impression on public opinion in Belgium where the earlier attacks by foreign critics had been dismissed as the products of greed or malevolence. Gradually more and more influential Belgians came to accept the suggestion first put forward by the British government that Belgium itself should take over responsibility for the Congo. But the final decision to annex the Congo was taken by the Belgian parliament in April 1908 only after many months of debate. "Never before," observed a contemporary English newspaper, "was greatness forced by circumstances upon a more reluctant people." [20]

▲▼ THE FOUNDATION OF FRENCH EQUATORIAL AFRICA

French Equatorial Africa covered an area equal in size to that of the Congo Free State and embraced an even wider range of geographical environments, extending from the rain-forests of the Congo in the south to the wastes of the Sahara in the north. This massive bloc of territory was one of the most thinly populated parts of the continent; in 1930 it was reckoned to contain no more than 3.2 million inhabitants compared with 10 million in the Belgian Congo, 14.6 million in French West Africa, and 19 million in Nigeria. This extremely low population density —put at 3.7 per square mile in 1935—helps to explain two of the most striking features of the territory's modern history: the relative ease and swiftness of the initial European penetration and the failure of the colonial regime to develop an infrastructure comparable to those built up in the first half of the twentieth century in other parts of tropical Africa.

Europeans had carried on a considerable trade along the Atlantic coast of Equatorial Africa from the sixteenth century onwards. By 1790, as many as seventy French firms were doing business on the coast of Gabon and French missionaries had worked for some years in the kingdom of Loango. In 1839, the French made their first territorial acquisition when a local chief agreed to cede them a plot of land on the estuary of the Gabon River. Ten years later, Libreville, also on the Gabon estuary, was founded as a settlement for freed slaves, a francophone Freetown.

At this time Europeans were totally ignorant of the nature of the country that lay behind the coast but the many rivers flowing into the Atlantic presented intriguing possibilities to explorers. Many attempts were made to strike inland, but not until the late 1870's did the French expedition led by a young naval officer, Savorgnan de Brazza, succeed in following the Ogowe, the largest river in Gabon, to its headwaters, turning back only after reaching the Alima, one of the tributaries of the Congo. This first feat of exploration marked the opening of one of the most remarkable careers in the annals of late nineteenth-century European imperialism.

Savorgnan de Brazza was an Italian by birth, born in Rome in 1852, the scion of an ancient and aristocratic family. Through the influence of a family friend, the French admiral, Montaignac, de Brazza, though a foreigner, gained admittance to the French naval college. Later, after some years naval service, he became a naturalized Frenchman. In 1872 he was posted to the South Atlantic squadron of the French navy and was soon gripped with the urge to explore the mysterious hinterland of Gabon. With his patron Montaignac serving as minister of marine in the French government, de Brazza, though still in his early twenties, was well placed to obtain official support for his first expedition of exploration. Thus launched, de Brazza abandoned the navy for the exciting career of an explorer and empire-builder, achieving before he was fifty a reputation as one of the great proconsuls of his age.

From the start de Brazza stood out as a highly unusual, even eccentric individual among the hard-bitten traders of the coast. "Full of high thought and proud reserve," he seemed to one of his English contemporaries, the famous Trader Horn. "He'd have done better at poetry, perhaps," Horn reflected. "But a man for all that. Aye, he stepped as if earth was his heritage." [21] In his exploits as an explorer de Brazza showed himself a man of deep humanity. "Keep in close touch with the blacks," he advised his fellow-explorers. "Struggle to understand their mentality. Go on your own without arms or an escort. Never forget that you are the uninvited intruder." [22] De Brazza was also an ardent French patriot. This blend of sentiments was not unusual; humanitarianism and a desire to see a rapid extension of European rule often went together in late-nineteenth-century Africa. In de Brazza's mind humanity and patriotism were reconciled in the beguiling concept of France's "civilizing mission."

De Brazza's first expedition up the Ogowe overlapped with Stanley's epic journey down the Congo. On his return to Europe in 1878, de Brazza was alarmed to learn that Stanley was planning to return to the Congo in the service of Leopold of the Belgians. To the Frenchman, Stanley, with his brutal methods of forcing his way through unknown country, appeared as an uncouth but highly dangerous rival. Accordingly de Brazza hastened to gain support for a second expedition both from official sources and from the French committee of the International African Association and set out with what he himself defined as the specific object of "safeguarding by means of treaties our political future in the countries" of the Ogowe-Congo area.[23] In 1880, after traveling overland from Gabon, he reached the Congo at Stanley Pool and concluded a treaty of protection with the Teke chief, Makoko. De Brazza was acting largely on his own initiative. There was, in fact, no compelling reason why the French government, preoccupied with many other far more important matters, should be anxious to ratify a treaty concluded with an obscure African chief whose territory lay many hundreds of miles from the nearest French post. Accordingly on his return to France in 1882, de Brazza and his supporters launched a vigorous press campaign, designed to advertise the riches of the Congo in the most glowing terms and to warn their compatriots that a failure to ratify the treaty with Makoko would be a serious dereliction of patriotic duty. The time was peculiarly propitious for such an appeal: a few weeks earlier the British had occupied Egypt, a move regarded by many influential Frenchmen as a humiliating defeat for their national interests. A countermove in Equatorial Africa would apply some balm to a wounded *amour-propre*. In a mood of patriotic enthusiasm untroubled by rational calculations, the French parliament voted unanimously in November 1882 in favor of ratifying the treaty with Makoko. The whole incident might seem trivial but coming as it did two years before the German intervention in the Cameroons and the summoning of the Berlin conference, it must be seen as marking the opening of the European "scramble" for Equatorial Africa.

In 1883 de Brazza returned to Gabon for a third spell of exploration, taking with him a staff of 48 Europeans and 130 Senegalese sailors. Within three years he and his companions had established French claims to most of the territory contained in the modern states of Gabon and Congo-Brazzaville. But even while grappling with the task of providing a rudimentary administrative structure for an area considerably larger than France, de Brazza had begun to look to more distant horizons. "We must hurry up," he told a mass meeting held on his return to France in 1886, "Our rivals [the British and the Germans] are setting out from the coast for the interior. We must surprise them by our march on Chad." [24]

For many French imperialists of the late 1880's Lake Chad—in reality a mosquito-infested swamp on the borders of the Sahara—acquired a mystical significance. Here was the point where the three French thrusts—from Algeria, from Senegal, and from the Congo—would converge to link the isolated French colonies together to form a massive African empire. From Chad a new French thrust could be developed eastward toward the valley of the Nile. But Chad itself was deemed far from worthless. "This great interior lake," wrote a senior official in the French foreign ministry in 1890, "may well hold some surprises in store for the future of civilization in Africa. It might become the focal point of the continent's major trade routes. There is here a reservoir for the future which our policy cannot afford to neglect." [25] Expansionist sentiments such as these might well strike a sceptical posterity as being based on a phoney concept of geopolitics, but they were held not only by romantic enthusiasts like de Brazza but also by senior civil servants occupying positions in important ministries and therefore well placed to translate territorial ambitions into policy and action. Nor did French expansionists follow the example of their rival Leopold and keep their ideas to themselves. In 1890 an influential group of Frenchmen came together to found the *Comité de l'Afrique Française* with the express object of arousing public interest in African expansion and of raising the money needed to finance new missions into the interior.

Within ten years of the *Comité*'s foundation, the French had established their claim to all the country lying between the Ubangi—defined as the frontier with the Congo Free State—and the Central Sahara. In French eyes it was an era of heroic achievement, culminating in 1900 in the battle of Kousseri when three French expeditions starting from Senegal, Algeria, and the Congo came together south of Lake Chad and defeated the great conqueror, Rabih. Both Rabih and the French commander, Lamy, whose name was commemorated in the capital of Chad, died on the field of battle. Another decade was needed to complete the conquest of the substantial kingdom of Wadai and the smaller but still powerful sultanate of Dar Kuti, whose ruler, Muhammad as-Sanusi, held his own as a highly successful slave-raider until he was killed by the French in 1911.

It might be said crudely that in acquiring so vast an accession of their empire, the French had bitten off more than they could chew. It was easy enough to devise a formal administrative structure, to follow the pattern of French West Africa and divide French Equatorial Africa into four territories—Gabon, Moyen-Congo, Oubangui-Chari, and Tchad—linked together in an administrative federation with its capital at Brazzaville. Infinitely more difficult was the task of securing effective administration on the ground. The colony was poor, so officials were badly paid despite their exceptionally rigorous conditions of service. As a result there was a constant shortage of personnel. In 1908 administrative posts covered only 26 percent of the territory. "The remainder of the country remained much as it was before the French annexation." [26] Eighteen years later, despite some improvement brought about in the

years immediately before World War I, the governor-general had to report that "our skeleton personnel does not allow us to occupy the territory sufficiently and to fulfill all of our duties towards the native
population." [27]

De Brazza, who served as Equatorial Africa's first governor from
1886 to 1898, wanted to see the colony developed in the interests of its
African inhabitants. Constantly he preached the importance of patience,
of personal example, of getting to know the natives. But to practical
men of the world his methods had one disastrous defect—they produced
a colony which not only offered scant opportunity for commercial profit
but was also a constant drain on the resources of the metropolis. In
1891 local revenue amounted to 1.1 million francs; six years later it
was no more than 1.4 million francs while subsidies from the French
government had increased from 2.4 million to 5.2 million francs. At the
same time, the revenues of the Congo Free State were rising rapidly as
a result of Leopold's methods of exploitation. It was hardly surprising
that a group of influential businessmen and politicians, some of whom
possessed close links with Belgian interests, should demand that the
Free State's system of concessions be introduced into the poverty-
stricken French territory. They were powerful enough to secure de
Brazza's dismissal in 1898, a shabby end to the career of one of the
most humane imperialists of his generation. Shortly afterward de Brazza's secretary visited the colonial ministry in Paris; in every office he
saw a map of the French Congo divided up into squares like a chessboard. The entire colony was given to concessionary companies, forty-
two in all. "The calf of gold," he wrote to his old chief, "is rampant
still." [28]

The concessionary companies acquired vast domains many hundreds
of square miles in extent over which— in return for the payment of a
modest rent and 15 percent of their profits to the government—they
were allowed to claim a complete commercial monopoly. Development
economists of the day might see in the system the only means of attracting foreign capital and trained personnel to an impoverished colony.
Moreover, at a time when the most active merchants on the coast of
Gabon were not Frenchmen but Englishmen and Germans, the concessionary system had the advantage in French eyes of concentrating a
major share of the colony's commerce in the hands of their own compatriots. The foreign firms were powerful enough to launch a vigorous
protest and to obtain financial compensation for the losses incurred as a
result of the new system. The native inhabitants of the French Congo
were less fortunate.

The imposition of local monopolies meant that Africans could never obtain a fair price for their produce. Ivory, for example, was bought in the early 1920's for one-twentieth of the price being paid on the world market. Within their own domains the agents of the various companies enjoyed virtually sovereign powers, and some of them were guilty of acts of wanton brutality in their efforts to obtain African labor. Nor was brutality confined to commercial agents. Administrative officers in certain districts were required to find a constant supply of porters to carry northward the tons of equipment needed by the French forces operating in the Chad area. To meet these requirements some officers resorted to methods which bore comparison to the slave-raiding they claimed to have suppressed. In 1905 some of the scandals of the regime came to the attention of the French public. There was an immediate outcry, and de Brazza was called from retirement to lead a commission of inquiry. Deeply grieved by the ruin of the colony he had founded, de Brazza died on his way back from the Congo and his report was never published. But liberal opinion in France had learned enough of what was being done in the Congo to launch a vigorous attack on the government and to secure some modification of the concessionary regime.

But the concession companies were not abolished, and their malpractices continued. Twenty years later the famous French writer, André Gide, visited Equatorial Africa and reported a number of horrifying cases of brutality. Gide traced the source of the evil to the "occult powers" of the big companies in Paris.[29] Journalists sent to check on his allegations found that the local administration was far from innocent. Appalling rates of mortality were found among the workers conscripted to build the Congo-Océan Railroad connecting Brazzaville with Pointe Noire. Seventeen thousand Africans were reported to have died in the construction—without modern machinery—of one hundred miles of track through difficult forest country. Slowly, as a result of these disclosures, a serious attempt began to be made to remedy the worst abuses.

French Equatorial Africa might well be presented in the first forty years of its existence as a classic example of "colonial exploitation." Abstract expressions of this nature need always to be translated by the historian into human terms. Of African reactions to the colonial regime something will be said in a later section of this chapter. Here, it should be recalled that for Europeans too the price of maintaining such a regime was a heavy one. An English woman, the wife of a French colonial official, living in the French Congo in the early 1920's, described one concessionary company founded by five brothers. "They have made a small fortune but at a heavy price. After thirty years of extreme personal activity, two are dead, one is ill, the fourth will never return to

France, and the fifth only keeps things going by dint of strong character, robust health and unrivalled energy." [30] The same writer, Gabrielle Vassal, also conveyed a vivid impression of the colonial society of Brazzaville: the businessmen, British, Greek, Portuguese, and French, willing "to risk life, health, capital, earnings and an unlimited number of years of exile without misgiving," their enterprise hampered, their advice scorned by a complacent bureaucracy; the middle-aged military men "often the worst for wear physically and mentally," "seeing everything from a point of view exclusively military"; the doctors, usually remarkable for their great devotion to their work, "kind, patient, unsparing," charitable in the extreme "to the lowest type of native," "relentless" and "brutally sincere" in their judgments of their European superiors; finally, the average official, "a man who fears and often shirks his responsibilities," spinning out time with innumerable pointless "palavers." "Nature is hostile, not with a living but a dead hostility. Humanity is lifeless, birds are songless, heat is without sunlight." In such an atmosphere "the faith and enthusiasm which inspire an exceptional few in this part of Africa seem incredible." [31]

▲▼ CAMEROON: GERMAN COLONY, BRITISH AND FRENCH MANDATE

The modern Republic of Cameroon is nearly 200,000 square miles in extent, shaped roughly like a triangle with its northern apex touching Lake Chad, its southern base set in the dense rain-forests of the Congo basin. By the early 1960's, the country's population was put at just over 4 million, divided up into a very large number of ethnic groups. (In West Cameroon alone as many as eighty "tribal units" could be counted in a total population of about 1 million.) Certain broad distinctions help to clarify this highly confusing ethnographic situation. As in Nigeria, there is a sharp contrast both geographically and in terms of ethnicity between north and south. Northern Cameroon, with its savanna plains broken along the western borders by the mountain ranges of Mandara and Alantika, is clearly a part of the great Sudanic belt, a land of confrontation between Muslims and "pagans," largely dominated since the early nineteenth century by the intrusive Fulani. Southern Cameroon, on the other hand, extending westward from the Atlantic coast to the Congo basin, possesses many natural links with the equatorial countries to the south. Thus the Beti-Pahouin cluster of peoples, the largest group of Southern Cameroon, numbering today about three-quarters of a million people, are closely related in cultural terms to the Fang, the dominant people of Gabon. Between the dense forests of the South and the dusty savannas of the North lies a broad belt of grassy plateaus rising to the Bamenda highlands in the west. This is the most densely populated area in Equatorial Africa, the home of peoples—Bamiléké, Bamum and others—distinguished for their elaborate political systems and for their remarkable artistic achievements. Over this conglomeration of peoples and polities was imposed in the years between 1884 and 1914 the structure of German hegemony.

German contacts with the country that was destined to become the colony of Kamerun date back no further than 1868, the year in which the Hamburg firm of Woermann opened a trading establishment at Douala on the estuary of the Cameroons River. The Douala people had a long record of commercial intercourse with Europeans and particularly with the English who had been the dominant group of aliens in the area since early in the nineteenth century. English traders carried on business from hulks moored in the Cameroons River. A few miles farther west, at the foot of Mount Cameroon, lay the English mission-station of Victoria, founded by Baptists in 1858 after they had been expelled from the Spanish island of Fernando Po, and presenting in political terms what may best be described as a miniature theocracy. In Douala British initiative had led to the establishment of a "court of equity" to settle disputes between Europeans and African traders. And the British consul appointed to the Bights of Biafra and Benin regularly visited the area in his gunboat. Throughout the 1870's the Cameroons clearly lay within the sphere of Britain's "informal empire." Indeed, in 1879 a number of Douala chiefs, appreciating the usefulness of British support as a prop to their own shaky authority, formally sought British protection. "We wish to have your laws in our towns," they wrote in a petition addressed to Queen Victoria, adding appealingly, "Plenty wars here in our country. Plenty murder and plenty idol-worshippers." [32] Their request was turned down by a parsimonious British government. But in the early 1880's, mainly as a result of fears not of German but of French encroachments, official opinion in London began slowly to swing in favor of a British protectorate over the Cameroons. In November 1883, the British cabinet finally gave its consent to the establishment of a protectorate along the Niger Delta–Cameroons stretch of coast. But officials in Whitehall needed six months in which to work out the complicated legal and financial problems caused by this decision. Consequently, it was not until May, 1884, that Hewitt, the British consul on the coast, received formal instructions to conclude the necessary treaties. In June he was busy working on the chiefs of the Niger Delta. When he reached Douala in mid-July he found to his astonishment that the German flag had been raised there a few days earlier.

The initiative in establishing a German protectorate in the Cameroons came from the small group of German businessmen with an interest in the country. German traders were no less alarmed than their English contemporaries at the French practice of imposing heavy duties on non-French goods imported into their colonies. Clearly French expansion threatened to undermine the legitimate commercial activities of other European nationals. But the British too came in for criticism. German traders in Douala had accumulated a good many grievances against the British-dominated "court of equity." Accordingly in July, 1883, the Hamburg Chamber of Commerce presented Chancellor Bismarck with a memorandum urging the acquisition, before it was too late, of a strip of territory in the Cameroons. Bismarck was well known at this time to be resolutely opposed to all forms of colonial expansion. But the Hamburg merchants had a powerful spokesmen in Adolf Woermann, head of the firm of the same name, and a personal friend of the chancellor. Events, too, served to confirm their warning; the Anglo-Portuguese treaty of February 1884 was interpreted as a direct threat to German interests. By May Bismarck had come to accept some measure of official responsibility for German commercial interests in West Africa as an unavoidable necessity. In July, Commissioner Nachtigal, whose treaty-making activities in Togo have been described in the previous chapter, arrived at Douala. A few days before his arrival the local German traders, acting on instructions received from Adolf Woermann, succeeded in concluding a treaty with "the independent Kings and Chiefs of the Country called 'Cameroons.' " Under the terms of the treaty the signatories agreed to convey "our rights of Sovereignty, the Legislation and Management of this our Country" to the German firms under certain conditions, one of which required that "during the first time of establishing an administration here, our country's fashions will be respected." [33]

Since the protectorate had been created at the request of the traders, Bismarck expected them to meet the cost of administration. But the traders were unwilling to meet this unwelcome addition to their expenses and events soon forced the government in Berlin to involve itself more deeply in the affairs of a territory in which the solitary representative of the imperial presence in the first months after annexation was Nachtigal's assistant, Dr. Buchner, living in a room rented from Woermann's. Buchner found himself faced with the hostility both of the English and of many of the local people. The English, determined to confine the German territory to as narrow a strip as possible, were delighted to make use of the services of an adventurous Polish officer of the Russian army, Stefan Rogozinitski, who had come to West Africa on a scientific expedition. "Rogue-Gin-and Whisky," as he was nick-named by the missionaries at Victoria, hated the Germans and set about concluding treaties on behalf of the British with the village-chiefs of Mount Cameroon, carrying out his instructions with such vigor that he ran out of treaty-forms and was reduced to making use of wrapping-pa-per. Even more alarming to the Germans was a violent demonstration launched against their authority by one of the towns of Douala. To re-store order Buchner called for a German warship; a naval bombardment and the landing of a detachment of marines followed. Reluctantly Bis-marck accepted the necessity of asking the Reichstag for money to es-tablish an embryonic colonial regime. A year after annexation Kamerun received its first German governor.

By the end of 1886 the Germans had reached agreement both with the British and with the French on the new colony's boundaries. In re-turn for concessions elsewhere on the Nigerian coast the British aban-doned Victoria and their claims, secured by Rogozinitski's treaties, to Mount Cameroon, and agreed to a frontier striking northeastward from the Cross River to the Benue. The Campo River was taken as the boundary between Kamerun and French Gabon. (In 1900 northern Gabon was ceded by France to Spain and became the Spanish colony of Río Muni.)

For the first ten years of Kamerun's existence little attempt was made to extend German rule deep into the interior. A number of explorers brought back reports of Adamawa and Bamenda and some merchants were eager to reach the hinterland markets hitherto controlled by the native traders of Douala. But money was short and neither the imperial government nor its local representatives were anxious to incur new re-sponsibilities. Kamerun seemed to lack the expansionist drive so clearly visible in other European colonies in West and Equatorial Africa in the early 1890's. The most vigorous demand for rapid expansion came from the members of the *Deutsche Kolonialgesellschaft,* an influential and extremely well-organized metropolitan pressure group founded in 1887. The play of international rivalries was more important than any show of local initiative in securing a substantial accession of new territory. An agreement with Britain in 1893 carried Kamerun's western border from the Benue to Lake Chad. The next year the colony's eastern bor-der was defined by agreement with the French. By far the greater part of this northern wedge of territory had not yet been visited by any Ger-man explorer.

Jesko von Puttkammer, governor of Kamerun from 1895 to 1907, was the real architect of German hegemony. At the start of his governorship the colony's total budget was a mere 600,000 marks. Its only armed force, the *Polizeitruppe,* most of whose members were ex-slaves purchased from the still independent king of Dahomey, had been weakened by a serious mutiny in 1893. And German authority was still virtually nonexistent in the hinterland. By 1907 the colonial budget had risen to more than 6 million marks, half of which came from an imperial grant-in-aid. In addition to the police the colony now possessed its own army, the *Schutztruppe,* which numbered 1,550 men under 185 white officers in 1914. And German rule had been firmly established as a result of a large number of small military expeditions carried out in almost every district. To Puttkammer this work of conquest and consolidation was the essential preliminary to the basic task, as the governor conceived it, of economic exploitation in the interest of the metropolis. With this end in view, two concession companies, organized on the same lines as those already functioning in the Free State and French Congo, were allowed to assert a monopoly over the rubber, ivory, and other wild produce of two vast areas, one in the south, the other in the northwest. Neither company proved as profitable as their promoters had anticipated. Far more significant for the future was the development of extensive plantations producing cocoa, rubber, palm oil, and bananas, on the fertile volcanic soil of Mount Cameroon. In economic terms the plantation policy could be regarded as a success. The colony's exports, which never exceeded 5 million marks in value in the 1890's, rose to 15 million in 1907 and to 23 million marks in 1912. Inevitably it was the native population which was called on to bear the main burden of these developments. Particularly gruelling was the constant demand for labor not only for the plantations but also for the tasks of porterage between the coast and the interior. Almost 100,000 men—four-fifths of them as porters—were needed at any one time to meet the demands of planters, traders, and administrators. Conditions of work were usually arduous, methods of recruitment often oppressive, and mortality rates high.

From the start the new German colonialism was subjected to vigorous parliamentary criticism, particularly from the Social Democrats and the Catholic Centrists. Since every colonial budget had to be submitted to the Reichstag, anti-imperialists found ample opportunity to air their views. Some Social Democrats preferred to lambast their country's colonial policy on doctrinaire grounds, accusing it of producing nothing but "murder, robbery, syphilis, and the curse of liquor." [34] But many Socialist attacks were more specific, often being based on detailed information supplied by missionaries and traders working in Kamerun. "Their public airing of abuses has resulted," an American historian of

Kamerun noted in 1938, "in Germany's having an undeserved reputation for poor colonial administration." [35] Less well known than German shortcomings, widely advertised by the victorious Allies after 1918, is the fact that as a result of informed criticism a vigorous effort was made to improve the quality of German colonial administration in the seven years before World War I. Puttkammer, who showed scant respect for African interests, was dismissed as a result of a scandal in 1907. (He has an enduring memorial in the baronial *schloss* at Buea which he built for his mistress, a cabaret dancer from Berlin.) Puttkammer's successor, Dr. Theodor Seitz, was notable for his vigorous protection of native rights, a policy in which he could count on the support of Germany's first colonial minister, Bernhard Dernburg, a man of equally humane views.

In 1911 Kamerun received a massive accession of territory. As a result of the Agadir crisis the French agreed to hand over the westernmost districts of their Equatorial African colonies in return for German recognition of French rights in Morocco. This was the first in a series of frontier changes which were to have a serious effect on the lives of many of the peoples of Cameroon in the course of the next half-century. In 1914, a few weeks after the outbreak of World War I, the colony was invaded by French and British troops. Within two years the German forces had surrendered or been interned in Río Muni. Kamerun was divided into two unequal parts, four-fifths of the territory going to the French, the remainder, including the rich plantation area around Victoria, to the British. This *de facto* division was confirmed after the war, when the conquered territories were accorded the new status of mandates under the League of Nations.

Under the terms of the mandate agreement Britain and France were made "responsible for the peace, order and good government of the territory, and for the promotion to the utmost of the material and moral well-being and the social progress of its inhabitants." [36] In spite of these high-sounding principles it is doubtful whether the lot of most Cameroonians was greatly improved by the change of masters. The war itself led to much material destruction, while the expulsion of the Germans involved the breakdown of an administrative machine of considerable efficiency. The new rulers introduced their own distinctive styles of administration. The British were generally regarded as being much milder than the Germans; the French, with their use of forced labor, their *indigénat,* and their tough methods of dealing with native chiefs, quite as harsh. In these circumstances a certain nostalgia for German rule developed among some Western-educated Africans, particularly in the French mandate.

In the years immediately before World War I the Germans had taken up the task of developing Kamerun with great vigor. Between 1908 and 1914 the government in Berlin provided the colony with 20 million marks (£1 million) in grants-in-aid and 50 million marks (£2½ million) in loans. Particularly notable was the intensive scientific exploration of the country's natural resources, largely financed by the economic committee of the *Kolonialgesellschaft*. Of the two mandatory powers in the interwar years the British contributed little to their share of the ex-Germany colony. The northern part of the British Cameroons was attached for administrative purposes to the adjoining provinces of Northern Nigeria, the southern part formed a distinct but geographically isolated province of Southern Nigeria. A visitor to the Southern Cameroons in the late 1930's found the British presence "apologetic and unproductive" and noted sadly that the splendid botanical gardens established by the Germans at Victoria were "slowly being re-absorbed into the bush." [37] The British raised no objection to the re-purchase of the expropriated plantations by their former German owners. By 1938 there were almost 300 Germans living in the Southern Cameroons compared with less than 100 British, and four-fifths of the territory's exports were being sent to Germany.

Many Englishmen argued that as the fate of the mandates was uncertain, it was not worth spending much money in them. The French took a very different view of the situation. Cameroun was one of the richest of the territories under French rule in Africa and its new masters were determined to hold on to it. Most of the ex-German property remained in French hands; by 1938 there were less than a hundred Germans in a total European population of 2,000. Not unmindful of the fact that their actions were subject to scrutiny by the League of Nations' Mandates Commission in Geneva, the French threw themselves vigorously into the work of development. Considerable attention was paid to the improvement of native agriculture. The colony was equipped with one of the best road systems to be found in tropical Africa in the 1930's. And, by 1937, it could be shown that 25 percent of the local budget was being devoted to the social services, compared with a mere 11 percent in the adjoining territories of French Equatorial Africa. For younger members of the small but expanding group of Western-educated Cameroonians memories of the German past were gradually submerged by cultural innovations introduced by their French or British masters. But one heritage of the German past remained, the myth of a "Kamerun nation," a myth powerful enough to make possible the eventual "re-unification" of the divided country.

▲▼ BELGIAN RULE IN THE CONGO

The Belgian Congo was in many ways the most unusual European colony in Africa. Exceptional in its size—its area of over 900,000 square miles was surpassed only by that of the Anglo-Egyptian Sudan—it was exceptional also in the peculiar nature of the ties that bound it to its metropolis. As founder of the Congo Free State, Leopold of the Belgians had always intended to bequeath his vast African estate to his country, but he had been forced by international criticism of his regime to accelerate the transfer. The legacy was received in a mood that combined reluctance with a strong sense of duty. This sense of duty, this determination to eliminate the scandals by which the Belgian name had been sullied provided a substitute for that spirit of imperial destiny which did so much to animate other European powers but which never really inspired the people of Belgium. Nevertheless, in the manner of all imperialists the Belgians sought to impose on their new African domain their own characteristic qualities—a strong sense of justice, a belief in the virtues of industry, thrift, self-help—the approach to life of "a people without imagination, a people who do not dream, a people whose thoughts are fixed on reality and do not get beyond it, but who make reality yield up useful fruits." [38] And so, less explicitly perhaps but no less firmly than their British, French, and Portuguese contemporaries, the Belgians came to develop their own distinct colonial doctrine. Belgian colonial officials struck one perceptive English observer as formulating for themselves a role similar to that of the philosopher-king in *Plato's Republic:* their task, as members of "a benevolent, wise and highly trained elite," was to manipulate the "plastic mass" of their African subjects, to instil in them certain "unquestioned and unquestionable moral values," to provide them with certain amenities, but to prevent them from ever coming into contact with such disturbing concepts as liberty and self-determination.[39] Such a doctrine was to achieve substantial results. In many respects the Belgians could claim that they had done more for their African subjects than other colonial powers. But the doctrine also possessed fundamental defects—defects whose consequences became tragically apparent in the last years of Belgian rule.

The most obvious characteristic of Belgian hegemony lay in the simple fact of numbers. There were more Europeans at work in the Congo at the height of the colonial era than in any other territory in tropical Africa. In 1936 there were approximately 19,000 Europeans in the Belgian Congo, a figure to be set against the 9,000 Europeans to be found in British West Africa and the 7,000 in French Equatorial Africa and French Cameroun. It is true that the Belgian Congo attracted a number of white settlers, but their influx was severely restricted—the Belgian authorities were determined to prevent the emergence of a class of poor whites—and their political influence kept within stricter bounds than that of any other permanent white community in Africa. The vast majority of Europeans in the Congo were employed by the administration, the missions, and the great commercial companies. State, Church, and Business—that "unholy trinity" in the eyes of Congolese nationalists—interlocked far more closely than in other colonial territories, creating a seemingly monolithic system of alien rule whose representatives interfered in the lives of the African population far more frequently than did the colonial officials of other more loosely governed territories.

The problems involved in administering the Congo were formidable in the extreme. The territory was vast, communications were poor and most of the African inhabitants lived in small-scale polities, while the few substantial states found within the Congo basin—the Lunda kingdom of the Mwata Yamvo, for example, or the Yeke paramountcy created by Msiri in Katanga—had been severely battered or even completely broken in the Congo's "time of trouble," during the last decades of the nineteenth century. The Belgians were not unwilling to recognize traditional authorities, but inevitably they had to proceed from a position of ignorance. Years of research were needed to unravel the complexities of Congolese society, and it was to the credit of the Belgian authorities that they were prepared to subsidize such research more generously than their colonial contemporaries in other parts of Africa. But the Belgian system had many fundamental weaknesses. By 1917 the territory had been divided up into more than 6,000 *chefferies*. Yet many of these new political units had little meaning for the local communities they were intended to serve. In some *chefferies*, so administrative officers were warned in 1918, "the quarrelsome and the ambitious have seen their intrigues crowned with success and have obtained by official investiture a dignity and advantages to which they could not legally pretend"; in others, "genuine chiefs have substituted for themselves men of straw, intended to suffer the remonstrances of administrators, whilst they themselves continued clandestinely the administration of their communities." [40] Another glaring weakness of the Belgian administration lay in the quality of the subordinate European officials, the *agents territoriaux*, who were brought by their work into much closer contact with the "natives" than were their superiors, the *administrateurs territo-*

riaux. The *agents* were the N.C.O.'s of the colonial administration, fulfilling a role not undertaken by Europeans in most British colonies: usually very young and poorly trained, many of them seem to have developed into caricatures of the white man in the tropics, lying on their verandahs, so one Belgian critic recalled, shouting *katuka* ("go away") to the Africans who brought them their problems and disputes. [41]

The best minds in the Belgian administration were well aware of the faults of their system of administration. In the early 1920's substantial reforms were introduced through the initiative of a vigorous colonial minister, Louis Franck. The training of colonial officials was greatly improved by the establishment of a colonial university at Antwerp. The training given right up to the end of the colonial era struck an English critic as being essentially authoritarian in character and as making "too few demands on the critical intelligence," but "it did produce a professional sense of a high order." [42] One aspect of Belgian administrative routine greatly impressed observers from other colonial territories: officials were required to spend twenty days in every month touring their districts. At the same time, steps were taken to check the administrative fragmentation of the Congo by grouping the small *chefferies* into a new administrative division, the *secteur*. There was even talk of attempting to recreate the old African paramountcies in the form of *protectorats*. These reforms were interpreted as a move toward a system of "indirect rule," but this movement was fatally distorted when the colonial government introduced a decree in 1933 making it compulsory for all male Africans still living in their traditional communities to perform sixty days paid or unpaid labor a year. From the start the colonial regime had made use of African labor for the construction of roads but the new decree laid particular stress on the compulsory cultivation of useful crops. The decree was introduced with the best of intentions. The colony was suffering from the effects of the slump; the economy needed to be diversified; peasant agriculture must be vigorously encouraged. But the means employed were far too crude, and their crudity became all the more apparent during the war-years when the administration was concerned to increase Congolese production to its maximum and stepped up the number of days of compulsory work to one hundred and twenty. Administrators thus found themselves having to give more and more time to the implementation of these requirements, while chiefs became even more obviously than before the agents of the administration. On paper, two days a week of compulsory labor might not seem excessive, especially when the peasant farmer was paid for the crops he was required to grow; in practice, the system led to manifold abuses—

bullying by local officials, excessive punishment for trivial offences, the constant threat of alien intervention into the daily course of life. Not surprisingly many young men began to leave the villages for the towns. As one young urban Congolese remarked, "In the villages there are no longer any young people and no longer any pleasures. Here [in the towns] at least one can be happy some days." [43] "At each full moon," in the haunting and evocative phrase of Governor-General Ryckmans, "the circle of dancers grows smaller." [44]

The excessive stress on production continued during the postwar years. There were some substantial achievements in the last years of Belgian rule: notably an ambitious scheme for the resettlement of peasant farmers and an improvement in rural medical services. But the essential weaknesses of the Belgian approach were not remedied. "Our old conception of indirect rule—timid and attenuated as it had been from the beginning—had not ceased to grow weaker," Governor-General Petillon confessed in 1952. "Under the pressure of economic circumstances . . . we have wanted to take everything in hand and direct the Congolese masses, willy-nilly, to a happiness comfortable to our ideas." [45] There can be no doubt that the Belgian administration contained a number of exceptionally able men, dedicated, energetic, paternalistic in the best sense of the word, but they were inevitably the exception. The poor quality of many of the subordinate *agents* was a point much commented on in the last years of the regime. Men such as these were singularly ill-fitted for the role of "philosopher-kings."

The second group of Europeans with whom Africans came into regular contact was made up of the missionaries. No other territory in tropical Africa could rival the Congo as a field for missionary endeavor. In the mid-1920's there were 2,000 missionaries working in the country, a far larger number than was to be found anywhere else in tropical Africa. (Nigeria at this time contained 600 European missionaries and French Equatorial Africa 400.) By the 1950's no less than 6,000 missionaries were at work in the Congo. A few bald statistics give some impression of the ever-widening range of their impact: in 1925 the Congo contained 400,000 Christians, in 1936 1½ million, in 1954 3½ million. In purely statistical terms, the Belgian Congo could be regarded, after South Africa and Ethiopia, as the most Christian country in Africa. This vigorous proliferation of missionary activity owed a great deal to the support which the colonial government was prepared to accord to "national" missionaries—support which went far beyond the normal colonial practice of subsidizing the more efficient mission-schools to include grants of land for mission stations and financial assistance in the construction of new missionary establishments. Since Belgium itself was an almost entirely Catholic country, "national" missions proved almost without exception to be those run by Roman Catholics. Thus the Protestant missionaries of other nationalities, British, American, Scandinavian, who had done much of the pioneering work in the 1880's and 1890's found themselves overtaken by their Catholic rivals. The Catholic missions could be regarded as the spiritual arm of the state. "Through their teaching and preaching, their rituals and ceremonial, their pastoral and social work, their network of satellite associations, their range of vernacular periodicals and journals, they exercise or seek to exercise," an English observer remarked in the 1950's, "a large measure of control over African minds." [46]

In contrast to the situation in other colonial territories where many of the most important schools were run by the colonial government itself, education in the Congo was virtually a monopoly of the missionary societies. The philosophy behind educational work in the Congo was clearly defined: "The Belgians," in the words of Colonial Minister Franck, "wish to produce better Africans: they have no wish to make copies of Europeans who will be no more than 'humans of a third category.' " [47] Hence the stress on the importance of teaching in the vernacular—a total rejection of the French concept that "the vernacular was a prison-house holding back African intellectual development." [48] Hence, too, the great emphasis on the importance of technical and agricultural training, so that the Congolese would be equipped to take a useful place in their country's expanding economic structure. In the field of primary and technical education the Belgians could be described as being "by general agreement outstandingly successful." [49] But the obverse of their system lay in an intense reluctance to expose their subjects to the disturbing intellectual currents of a truly liberal education. Congolese students were prevented from coming to European universities because, as the colonial minister remarked in 1954, "natives who have been shown Europe and given a very advanced education do not always return to their homelands in a spirit favourable to civilization and to the Mother Country in particular." [50] Therefore little attention was paid to the development of secondary education, at least until the late 1950's, with the result that the country was completely lacking in those higher educational institutions, such as Achimota College or the *École William Ponty* in West Africa, which played so vital a role in producing national elites. "The colonizer must never lose sight of the fact," wrote an eminent Belgian official, a man highly esteemed for his humane and reforming spirit, "that the Negroes have the spirits of children, who are moulded by the methods of the educator: they watch, listen, feel—and imitate." [51] This was written in 1947. At the roots of Belgian educational policy lay a suffocating spirit of paternalism.

The great commercial companies formed the third leg to the tripod of European power in the Congo. The practice of attracting European capital to the Congo by the grant of generous concessions had been an essential element in the system devised by Leopold for the Congo Free State. In most of the concessionary companies thus formed the state itself obtained a share and was represented on the board of directors. Most of the companies founded in Leopold's day had been concerned to organize the collection of wild produce, especially rubber; under the new regime rubber, the source of so many abuses, declined rapidly in importance to be replaced by mining and plantation agriculture as the major elements in the modern economy of the country. But the principle of state participation in nominally private business was still maintained. "Nowhere else in the world (except in Communist areas)," wrote John Gunther in the early 1950's, "are the government and economy of the country so wedded and welded as in the Congo. The Congo probably represents the highest development of state capitalism ever attained by a country." [52] Five great holding companies or trusts were reckoned to control about 70 percent of the entire business of the colony. Of these five companies by far the largest was the famous *Société Générale de Belgique,* "the kind of colossus that might be envisaged," Gunther suggested, "if the House of Morgan, Anaconda Copper, the Mutual Life Insurance Company of New York, the Pennsylvania Railroad, and various companies producing agricultural products were lumped together, with the United States government as a heavy partner." [53] There are few aspects of the colonial period so ill-documented as the history of the great commercial companies and the record of their influence on colonial and metropolitan governments. (To the academic historian the representatives of large commercial undertakings often seem to suffer from a pathological fear of objective research into their histories: Do they really, one wonders, have so many skeletons locked in the vaults of their head offices?) At any rate, it is clear that the links between the administration and business concerns were very close. Government officials were instructed to help the companies in obtaining the labor and the food supplies they required. Officials were retired after twenty-three years' service, and many of them looked to the companies for further, well-remuncrated employment. Finally, the organization of the whole commercial sector, with its high degree of concentration of ownership, made it all the easier to bring pressure on the government. Senior directors of the *Société Générale* were men to whom even governor-generals would lend an attentive ear. This was a situation very different from that prevailing in British colonies where "commercials" were usually regarded by members of the administration as a distinctly inferior caste.

The contrast between the British and the Belgian approach to the problems of development in tropical Africa was vividly illustrated by the experience of the great commercial concern of Lever Brothers. In 1911, the company obtained from the Belgian government the right to lease up to three-quarters of a million acres of land for the establishment of oil-palm plantations. After World War I the company sought similar concessions in Nigeria. "The African native," declared Lord Leverhulme, "will be happier, produce the best, and live under the larger conditions of prosperity when his labour is directed by his white brother who has had all these million years' start of him." [54] Leverhulme's arguments cut no ice with British administrators anxious not to complicate their problems by interfering with native land rights, so his application was turned down. But his view of African development was one that seemed natural to most Belgians in the Congo.

There were powerful arguments to be put forward in favor of plantation agriculture. Production could be more efficiently organized, new techniques more rapidly introduced, and native laborers provided with a wider range of social services than they could ever hope to enjoy in their homes in the bush. Yet the establishment of plantations—and indeed of most other forms of European economic enterprise, especially mining—had a profoundly disruptive effect on many rural communities. For the plantations and the mines required labor, a commodity in particularly short supply in thinly populated areas such as Katanga. So pressing were the demands of labor-recruiters in some areas that the demographic balance of whole districts was upset. "It is not difficult to imagine," wrote one Belgian observer, "the sombre *ennui,* the profound demoralization into which a village is plunged where 54 percent of the able-bodied men are normally absent. . . . Everything weighs on the women: the cultivation of food crops, the care of children and of cattle, the upkeep of dwellings." [55] This might be regarded as an extreme case, but the situation in the country as a whole was sufficiently serious for the colonial government to decree in the 1920's that no more than 5 percent of the adult males of any village should be absent from their homes as migrant laborers at any one time.

In the 1920's many Belgian companies came to realize the serious economic disadvantages of a system of migrant labor and embarked on a policy of labor stabilization. Particularly impressive in this field were the achievements of the great copper mining company, the *Union Minière du Haut Katanga.* The company's *cité des travailleurs* became one of the show-pieces of colonial Africa. Workers were encouraged to bring their wives with them and provided with first-class welfare facilities—good housing, excellent health services, a wide range of schools. To many European observers companies like *Union Minière* were undertaking an essential service, transforming the "raw African" from the bush into an efficient and contented member of an industrial society. A different point of view has been put with great vividness and insight by Guy Hunter. Writing of plantation villages in West Africa— but his remarks apply equally to the Congo—he commented on "the thoroughly aseptic and slightly dead feeling" produced by the "beautifully clean row of houses." "Near one estate visited was a real village . . . chickens running about, a Hotel and Bar, a carpenter, a market, three gramaphones playing, children everywhere in the dusty paths, shady shanties of thatch selling everything under the sun, a photographer, a chief's council meeting going on . . . some banana trees, an antique but functioning motor-car and a lot of pretty girls. Here, in fact, was life with a great number of hazards and a great deal of satisfaction." [56]

"The object of paternalist policy," wrote Guy Malengreau, a liberal critic of his country's colonial record, "is to make the African a being assisted, insured and pensioned, instead of making him a free man. . . . Man is turned into a sort of vegetable . . . but at all times men have found freedom in misery preferable to comfortable slavery." [57] Yet it would be unfair to press these criticisms too hard. John Gunther who visited the Congo in the early 1950's formed the impression that Congolese Africans were "by and large much happier than those in the surrounding territories. The Belgian system denies them much; but it also gives them much. They are certainly far and away better off than their fellows in the Union and the Rhodesias. Men smile; children are fat; women look contented. And they have not succumbed to the pervasive, creeping drabness that afflicts so much of southern Africa. They wear costumes gleaming with intricate color; they prettify themselves with unashamedly barbaric devices; they preen and prance and giggle, showing off." [58]

▲▼ AFRICAN REACTIONS TO THE COLONIAL IMPACT ON EQUATORIAL AFRICA

It seems reasonable enough to affirm that the African inhabitants of the Belgian Congo felt the weight of the colonial regime bearing down on them more heavily than their contemporaries in other parts of tropical Africa where the colonial powers had fewer administrators or missionaries at their disposal and interfered less officiously in the life of the people. But it is not easy to present a balanced assessment of African reactions, for the nature of the colonial impact varied from district to district and from decade to decade. All that one can do in a short space is to take a number of well-documented examples and present them in such a way as to provide a spectrum of the range of African responses.

Toward the end of the colonial period a young English anthropologist, C. M. Turnbull, gained the confidence of a certain Matungi, an elderly traditional chief from the eastern Congo. It is worth quoting at some length from Matungi's narrative of his experience in dealing with white men, for it provides a rare opportunity of gaining some insight into the reactions of the upholders of traditional values who saw their world gradually falling apart. Matungi's first contact with white men occurred when the Belgians sent their soldiers, African mercenaries from another part of the country, to compel his people to provide labor for building a road. "The soldiers stood with their guns in case we tried to escape . . . the white men often carried whips and they beat us like animals." Later the white men "came around and told us we had to plant cotton and other things we did not want to plant. They said they would pay us and I explained that if we planted cotton we would have to grow less food. They said we could buy food with the money we got for the cotton and I told them this was like the play of children, because we could easily grow our own food without money, and have enough left over to give them." For this plain speaking Matungi was denounced as a troublemaker, dismissed from his chieftainship and replaced by a local collaborator, a Christian named Masoudi.

Because the new chief was a Christian, "he could not lead the people as the representative of their ancestors" nor conduct the initiation ceremonies that played a vital part in the social life of the community. But the white men regarded initiation as "thoroughly evil and a wasteful thing." When Matungi made it clear that his people could never accept Masoudi as their true chief, the white men had him beaten by a Zande soldier. "To have been beaten by one of those savages from the north," Matungi exclaimed, "is a shame I shall never forget. Even our enemies we treat like men, not like children. For a long time this made me burn inside with a fire, eating at my stomach, eating at my strength and my sense. . . . I have tried hard to understand the white man and his ways, but I can only see harm. What happiness have they brought us? They have given us a road we did not need, a road that brings more and more foreigners and enemies into our midst, causing trouble, making our women unclean, forcing us to a way of life that is not ours, planting crops we do not want, doing slave's work. At least the BaNgwana [a neighboring people and the traditional enemies of Matungi's community] left us our beliefs, but the white man even wants to steal these from us. . . . I have tried to maintain my dignity. I have tried to remain a man in the eyes of my father. Whatever I may have done with my body, I have never betrayed my beliefs with my mind. But for my children it is different. They do not know good and bad as I know it; the white man fills their heads with different ideas and they doubt." [59]

Throughout colonial Africa there were many elderly men who reacted to the colonial situation in the same way. Stubborn, proud, and bitter, they came to form a conservative "underground" implacably opposed to the new regime. The nature of this group varied from society to society. In the French Congo, for example, an official report of 1920 noted that the *zozi,* the judges of the ethnic groups of the area, were "the only natives who are feared and respected by their compatriots." "They live in remote villages with no external indication of their status to attract the attention of Europeans. Yet it is through them that the traditions and customs of the country are maintained." [60] "This concealment of authentic social reality behind official appearances had two effects," George Balandier has pointed out. "In the long run it led to semi-secrecy losing its dynamism and, because of its ambiguity, it brought into the open antagonisms within customary society that had previously been held in check. In these circumstances, customary society is much more likely to deteriorate than to adapt." [61]

The profound transformation experienced by certain societies during the colonial period is well illustrated by the case of the Fang, the dominant ethnic group of Gabon. Throughout the nineteenth century the Fang who were organized in a series of small, mobile clans, were expanding from the interior to the coast, conquering and absorbing many of the peoples who lay in their path. French administrators spoke highly of "their vivacity of spirit, their robustness, their passion for work." [62] In the 1920's the French began to recruit large numbers of Fang for work first in newly created timber-camps, then on the construction of the Congo-Océan Railroad. To the Fang this period of recruitment for the railroad was known as "the Terror." To escape recruiting agents many men took to the bush or made their way across the frontier into Spanish Guinea. The depopulation of many Fang villages was carried further by the ravages of epidemics of influenza and smallpox, and the onset of famine, the shortage of food being ascribed to the fact that there were not enough young men left to clear the land for cultivation. Depopulation and the breakdown of older communities created a deep sense of crisis. In the 1930's the French began to encourage the cultivation of coffee and cocoa, a development which served greatly to stabilize and eventually to enrich the population of certain districts.

To many Fang it appeared, as Weinstein has pointed out, that "the old methods of dealing with disorder, of insuring conformity to the group's rules were weakened and new capricious forces were introduced." [63] Traditional Fang society had been profoundly egalitarian in character. Now differences in wealth were becoming increasingly apparent. Men who accumulated great wealth were regarded as witches, as persons possessing magical powers that enabled them to acquire the goods of ordinary people. Many of the old cults designed to maintain the social order disappeared increasing this sense of insecurity. The Fang believed that their ancestors could help to protect them against evil forces; the cult of the ancestors centered round a basket containing bones of long-dead members of the community, but European missionaries found the cult improper and wantonly destroyed the sacred baskets. To protect themselves the Fang gradually began to devise or make use of new institutions. New antiwitchcraft societies were founded; a pan-Fang movement developed in the 1940's which brought together Fang living in Gabon, Cameroun, and Spanish Guinea and laid special stress on the preservation of traditional customs. At about the same time, a syncretistic religion known as *Bwiti,* made its appearance. An amalgam of traditional and Christian doctrines, it gave its adherents a sense of protection against the evils of the world. Later, in the 1950's, when the Fang had come to participate vigorously in the new political order, the administration started to regroup Fang villages, to produce larger communities which could be provided with schools and hospitals.

Not all Gabonese communities reacted to the colonial impact as vigorously as the Fang. The leaders of one group whose birthrate suffered a sharp decrease, were reported as saying, "We are lost; we don't want children, for our values do not fit the world; we are becoming cut off from our ancestors." [64] But the example of the Fang showed that it was possible for a people to suffer a profound and long-drawn-out crisis and yet emerge with their innate dynamism still unimpaired.

The peoples of the Lower Congo, a melange of different groups to whom the term Kongo is applied, suffered the colonial impact even more severely than the Fang. Kongo men were recruited as porters to carry loads from the Congo estuary round the cataracts to Stanley Pool in the first years of the Free State. Later they were employed on railway construction. There followed a devastating epidemic of sleeping sickness. And to all these afflictions was added the disruptive impact of European administrators, missionaries and businessmen. Against this background of social disruption must be set the rise of a new religion, Kimbanguism. The prophet of the new faith, Simon Kimbangu, was born in 1889 and educated at a Baptist mission school. As a young man he had a series of visions culminating in one in which he believed himself to have been "touched by the grace of God" and given the power to heal the sick. Early in 1921 Kimbangu began his ministry. His reputation as a healer spread with amazing rapidity and his home village was soon crowded with pilgrims. In his sermons Kimbangu exhorted his followers to "abolish and abjure all *nkisi* [the figurines regarded by the Kongo as possessing the power to combat witchcraft], practice monogamy, and worship the one true God." [65] Kimbangu preached a form of Christianity to which the missionaries could not take exception, and there is no evidence to suggest that he openly proclaimed any anti-European doctrines. But to his followers the sight of one of their own people speaking with such an air of authority was profoundly disturbing: here at last was a popular champion, a black David to be set against the white Goliath. Nervously aware of the movement, the Belgian administration stepped in, arrested Kimbangu, sentenced him to life imprisonment —he died in Elisabethville in 1951—and in so doing created a martyr whose renown, kept alive by small secretive groups of followers, put him on a level, in the eyes of his compatriots, with the other great religious leaders of the world. "God promised us to pour out his Holy Spirit upon our country. We besought him, and he sent us a Saviour of the Black Peoples, Simon Kimbangu. He is the Leader and Saviour of the Black People in the same way as the Saviours of other races, Moses, Jesus Christ, Mahomet and Buddha." [66] So ran one of the main themes of Kimbanguist literature. And a catechism used by some Kimbanguist congregations spoke of their leader as being "the cup with the oil of blessing," "the mighty sword of government," "the banner of Dominion" given by God for the black races. [67]

The followers of Simon Kimbangu were not allowed to practice their faith openly until the late 1950's. In the intervening years other prophets and sects arose among the Kongo people. Their significance as a response to the colonial situation has been summed up by George Balandier. "These Congolese movements brought about a revival of initiative and, at the same time, an attempt to reorganize society. They helped to counteract the processes responsible for the breakdown of communities and the weakening of cohesion: antagonism between pagans and Christians, and between Christians themselves; growing individualism among the ever-increasing modernist elements; new sources of conflict between the sexes, intensified competition as a result of the establishment of a money economy; disintegration of clans, lineages and villages. More or less consciously, the new movements sought to restore the broken ties and rebuild the community." [68]

If the majority of people in Equatorial Africa endured the first stages of the colonial impact while still residing in their ancestral homes, there were from the start a considerable number of individuals who cut themselves off from their own communities and attached themselves to the new organizations established by the colonial powers—the army camps, the mission stations, the administrative headquarters, the plantations, the offices of commercial companies—each of which in their different ways offered "avenues to modernity." Particularly significant was the role of the military forces maintained by all the colonial powers. "Even before the missions, the army," Crawford Young has written with special reference to the *Force Publique* in the Belgian Congo, "was able through its iron discipline and the complete removal of the recruit from his traditional moorings to create a group of people sharply distinct from the rest of the population." [69] Ex-soldiers, unwilling to return to their home villages, formed a major element in the population of the new towns established by the administration. The mission stations fulfilled a not dissimilar function to the army camps. They provided a base outside the traditional structures of society where men could acquire relatively rapidly the new techniques introduced by the white man. The first generation converts became the domestic servants of the Europeans or worked as catechists for the missions. Their sons, equipped with a better education, entered the administration as clerks or became the priests and teachers of the expanding missions. In the Belgian Congo, ordination to the Catholic priesthood provided the only way in which an ambitious young man could obtain higher education until the reforms of the 1950's. The third generation, the grandsons of the original converts, provided most of the university graduates of the period of independence. In most parts of Equatorial Africa the emergence of a commercial bourgeoisie of native origin was hampered by the activities of alien traders, Sudanese or West African in French Equatorial Africa, Portuguese or Greeks in the Belgian Congo. Gradually, however, a class of native businessmen began to emerge, particularly in towns such as Léopoldville or Elisabethville, though not on the same scale as in West Africa.

As in every part of Africa, the new towns served as magnets for the young, the discontented, the adventurous. Almost without exception the major towns of Equatorial Africa were European creations. These *agglomerations urbaines* with their housing estates and their government quarters differed sharply, as Thomas Hodgkin has pointed out, from the older towns of West Africa, which could be described, like London or

Paris, as "syntheses of villages" and displayed "more of an organic character." [70] In the Belgian Congo the process of urbanization was particularly rapid. In 1936, 7 percent of the population was classified as urban, in 1957, 23 percent; a remarkably high figure for tropical Africa. In these years Léopoldville rose from a modest 26,000 to 370,000. The growth of Douala and Brazzaville was more restrained. In the 1930's their populations were not much smaller than that of Léopoldville. By the end of the colonial era neither town was more than a third the size of the Belgian colonial capital. The young men and women who came to the towns were not, as their colonial masters sometimes imagined, suddenly detribalized. Caught up almost from the start in tribal associations, friendly societies or *amicales,* they were able to retain many links with their home areas. Indeed ethnic affiliations came to be a major factor in the growth of urban politics. In Elisabethville, conflict between Luba immigrants from the Kasai and "authentic Katangans"; in Brazzaville, clashes between groups coming from different parts of the French Congo, the Mbochi from the north, the Lari from the south; in Libreville, tension between the local Mpongwe and the immigrant Fang; in Fort Lamy, a sharp rift between Muslims from northern Chad and the Christian Sara from the south—situations such as these were to have a profound influence on the development of political parties in the 1950's. But newcomers to the towns were also able to make contact with peoples from other ethnic groups more frequently perhaps than in the more homogeneous cities of West Africa. They saw too the white man's world at close quarters. Constraints in the form of a color-bar were certainly less evident in the French and Belgian colonies than in the Anglo-Saxon territories to the south, but there was plenty of evidence of discrimination—in jobs, in wages, in material amenities. In Equatorial Africa as in other regions of the continent, the towns were the crucible in which an explosively vigorous new culture was coming to be formed.

▲▼ THE DECOLONIZATION OF FRENCH EQUATORIAL
AFRICA AND CAMEROON

It is a mistake to assume that the spirit of nationalism which swept through Africa in the 1950's produced in all African countries the same intensity of excitement. The four French territories that made up the federation of *Afrique Equatoriale Française*—Gabon, Moyen-Congo, Oubangui-Chari, and Tchad—achieved independence not as a result of the struggles of their own politicians but because they formed part of a remarkably unified imperial structure and so benefited from the changes brought about by events in other parts of the world. That the peoples of the A.E.F. should have played a relatively passive role in the decolonization of their territories was not really surprising. None of the four territories had yet developed that peculiar combination of conditions needed to sustain a vigorous nationalist movement. In all four territories population density was extremely thin—no more than two people to the square mile throughout A.E.F. as a whole compared with six to the square mile in the Belgian Congo, seven in Cameroun and thirty-nine in Nigeria. Gabon, with its resources of timber, manganese, and oil, came in the late 1950's to hold out the promise of becoming the Ivory Coast of Equatorial Africa. The other three territories, with their meager agricultural resources—timber in Moyen-Congo, cotton Tchad and Oubangi-Chari—and their inadequate systems of communications were among the most backward countries in Africa. Their backwardness was reflected in the poverty of their educational structures. By 1960, the entire federation contained no more than five university graduates. Effective nationalist movements could hardly be said to exist in French Equatorial Africa.

In such a situation the political changes brought about in the A.E.F. during the 1940's and 1950's were the result of decisions made in Paris and imposed on the territories of Equatorial Africa from above. "Political reforms of French origin, especially elections themselves, produced," as John Ballard has pointed out, "the impetus for the formation of political groups." [71] In most other parts of Africa the parties preceded the reforms. One consequence of this unusual situation was that it allowed local Europeans, whether administrators or businessmen, exceptionally favorable opportunities to manipulate the growth of parties for their own advantage. This process could be seen particularly clearly in Chad in the late 1940's and early 1950's. At the time of the first elections to the newly-established territorial assembly, the French governor, Jacques Rogué, "a fantastically energetic administrator who ruled Europeans and Africans alike with a firm hand," [72] set up what has been described as "the most effective regime of paternalism and repression in French Africa." [73] He did this by founding a party, the *Union Démocratique Tchadienne* (UDT) which drew its support from local chiefs, officials, and notables. Those who dared to question the governor's policy were liable to find themselves posted to a remote district. The governor's most formidable opponent was a radical young colonial official from the West Indies, Gabriel Lisette. Lisette, a protégé of the governor-general in Brazzaville, won one of the seats on the National Assembly in Paris and organized his supporters into the *Parti Progressiste du Tchad* (PPT). But the PPT which drew most of its support from the young educated elite was no match for the UDT in the rural areas. For nearly ten years, then, until the introduction of the reforms that made up the *loi cadre* in 1956, this administration-supported party dominated the political scene. But the widening of the electorate enabled the PPT to make a dramatic comeback, and in 1957 Gabriel Lisette was able to form a government, though he himself was replaced two years later by a native-born Chadian, François Tombalbaye.

European intervention in local elections to an extent that would seem astonishing to a contemporary observer from a British West African colony was, then, one of the features of the Equatorial African political scene in the last years of colonial rule. Another prominent feature—the growth of ethnic rivalries and their bearing on political development— was of a more familiar nature. The process may be illustrated by the course of events in Moyen-Congo. In the years between 1946 and 1956, the country was divided between two parties, one drawing its support from the south, the other from the Mbochi and other northern groups. But an important section of the population, the Lari, a branch of the Kongo people who lived in the neighborhood of Brazzaville, refused to participate in local politics. In the late 1920's the Lari had come strongly under the influence of a proto-nationalist movement led by a remarkable Congolese, André Matswa, who had lived for some years in Paris. After Matswa's arrest and imprisonment his followers demonstrated their rejection of the colonial regime by a long-drawn-out campaign of passive resistance. Matswa died in 1942 but lived on in the minds of his followers as the central figure of a messianic cult. In Brazzaville elections of the late 1940's many of the Lari either refused to participate or wrote in Matswa's name on the ballot paper. In 1956 a young Catholic priest of Lari origin, the Abbé Fulbert Youlou, put himself forward as the spiritual heir of Matswa and succeeded in involving his fellow-tribesmen in his own newly-formed political party. By this time the older southern party was in a state of dissolution, and Youlou now emerged as a leader of the south. His rise was bitterly contested by the northern party which held power by a majority of one from 1956 to 1958. In November 1958, one of the government's supporters announced his decision to join Youlou's party thus allowing the Abbé to claim that he now possessed a majority. There followed a violent scene in the territorial assembly in the course of which the Abbé "slipped out of his cassock and in the middle of the meeting armed himself with a gun." [74] Three months later Brazzaville became the scene of violent rioting between the Lari and the Mbochi in which one hundred Africans lost their lives.

Violence on an even larger scale was also a feature of Cameroun's advance toward independence. The territory possessed certain obvious advantages over its neighbors in A.E.F. It was richer and more densely populated. Education was far more advanced: in 1958 there were more than a thousand Camerounians studying in France compared with a mere sixty-five students from A.E.F. Finally, by the virtue of the country's special status as a trust territory, Camerounians enjoyed certain political advantages. During the 1950's it became evident to local politicians that petitions submitted to the Trusteeship Council of the United Nations were an effective means of putting pressure on the French administration to introduce reforms. The pace-setter in the Camerounian drive for independence was the *Union des Populations du Cameroun* (UPC), a party founded by left-wing trade unionists in 1948 and closely linked with the radical *Rassemblement Démocratique Africain* (RDA) of French West Africa. In the course of the early 1950's the UPC built a "highly sophisticated organizational structure" [75] with a network of local branches, a wide range of front organizations, and a number of party newspapers. Although it fully controlled only a relatively small area in the southwest of the country and so was never able to win more than a few seats in territorial elections, the party carried on its work of propaganda in many other parts of the country and in so doing served powerfully to stimulate other political groups into expanding their range of action and developing more efficient forms of organization. In 1955 the UPC turned from radicalism to revolution, probably as a result of the influence of one of its leaders, Dr. Felix Moumié, a dedicated Marxist and a believer in direct action. Finding itself subjected to increasing restrictions, the UPC responded by a series of violent demonstrations, including the storming of the radio station at Douala and an attack on the police station in Yaoundé. The administration retaliated by banning the party and arresting many of its activists though the leaders succeeded in fleeing the country.

The UPC's revolt came at a time when French colonial policy, powerfully affected by developments in Tunisia and Morocco, was already beginning to move in a more liberal direction. In 1956 new elections were held for an enlarged territorial assembly with greater power. The UPC was still banned and its leaders attempted to disrupt the election by a campaign of sabotage and violence, but their activities affected only a relatively small part of the country. The new assembly contained four major parties, each of which drew its support from a particular area, the largest, with a third of the seats, being the northern-based *Union Camerounaise* led by Ahmadou Ahidjo. In 1958 Ahidjo formed his own government, based on an alliance of northern and southern groups. Meanwhile the UPC remained the major focus of opposition. One group of UPC activists established themselves first in

Cairo and later in Conakry and kept up an unremitting propaganda barrage, demanding immediate independence and the holding of new elections. Another group, led by Reuben Um Noybé, carried on the struggle within the country, launching a new campaign of violence in September 1957 with attacks on plantations, mission stations, and administrative posts in the Sanaga-Maritime province. Um Nyobé was killed a year later. For his people, the Bassa, he had become a legend in his lifetime, and even his political opponents honored him after his death as the founder of Camerounian nationalism. Meanwhile Ahidjo was using a skillful combination of tactics—tough counterinsurgency measures combined with promises of an amnesty for surrendered rebels—to break the revolt. In 1959, however, violence broke out yet again and on an even more alarming scale in the Bamiléké country. The Bamiléké, like the Ibo of Nigeria, occupied one of the most densely populated areas in Africa. Land shortages forced many young men to move to the towns in search of work. When they returned home, they were often involved in conflict with their traditional chiefs. The UPC with its revolutionary doctrines became a natural spokesman for Bamiléké discontents. For the Camerounian government the Bamiléké revolt was a threat quite as serious as the Mau Mau revolt had been for the British authorities in Kenya. It lasted for three years, involved the death of 10 to 20,000 civilians and 1,000 soldiers, and was accompanied by a great deal of damage to property, including the destruction of nearly one hundred schools.

There was another unusual aspect to the movement for Camerounian independence—the question of reunification with the British Cameroons. The territory under British trusteeship had been divided into two parts, with the northern part being incorporated into Northern Nigeria, while the southern part was eventually given the status of a separate region. There was a difference of opinion in the Southern Cameroons about the future outcome of the territory. Some local politicians felt that their territory had been largely neglected by the Nigerian government, that their people were in danger of being swamped by Ibo immigrants, and that the best policy for the future lay in reunification. Their opponents, on the other hand, stressed the difficulties involved in attempting to merge an anglophone with a francophone territory and pointed apprehensively to the violence that was taking place in Bamiléké country just over the frontier of the British territory. In 1961 the populations of the two parts of the British Cameroons were asked to decide by means of a plebiscite organized by the United Nations between incorporation in Nigeria or in Cameroun. Seventy percent of the southern voters favored Cameroun, 60 percent of the northern voters looked to Nigeria, and so the two parts went their separate ways, with the former Southern Cameroons becoming the state of West Cameroon in the newly created Federal Republic of Cameroon, while the Northern Cameroons became a province of Northern Nigeria.

▲▼ DECOLONIZATION IN THE BELGIAN CONGO

In 1947 an American visitor to Léopoldville asked a group of Congolese *évolués* "how they envisaged the future of their country, if they wanted independence, what their political aspirations were." "To her disappointment, the *évolués* did not seem visibly interested in independence, nor emancipation. They had a certain number of grievances which were centered around . . . human relations." [76] It was hardly surprising that these Western-educated Congolese should have produced a response so very different from that of their contemporaries in Lagos, Accra, or Dakar. The Belgian authorites took great pains to keep "their" Africans cut off from the outside world. Apart from a few Catholic priests, no Congolese student was allowed to attend a Belgian university until 1952. At the same time, stringent precautions were taken to prevent "unhealthy" political influences from entering the country. "Stanley Pool," Basil Davidson noted in the early 1950's, "is watched day and night to prevent 'subversives' from crossing into the Congo out of the 'nightmare liberty' of French territory. . . . Everywhere there is an atmosphere of acute suspicion." [77] Another particularly striking contrast with West Africa was to be seen in the position of the press. In Lagos, Freetown, and Accra there had been a vigorous, independent, and uncensored African-owned press since the latter half of the nineteenth century. In the Belgian Congo the first independent African newspaper was not founded until 1957. Thus those channels of communication that served to propagate new ideas and so to stimulate new forms of thought and action were kept closed until the last years of colonial rule. Add to this the facts that there was no provision for African representation in any legislative assembly or metropolitan parliament, that freedom of association was not legally granted until August 1959—with the result that open political parties could operate only in the last months of colonial rule—and that no more than a handful of Africans had been admitted to the higher grades of the administration —and the contrasts with British and French West Africa and even with British East and Central Africa become strikingly apparent.

The colonial policy of any imperial power is always in part a reflection of certain profound experiences in the historical development of the metropolis. Belgium was a relatively new nation-state; it lacked the wide range of imperial experience acquired over the centuries by Britain and by France. The British had been grappling with the problems of decolonization since the late eighteenth century and had evolved a constitutional formula that had been successfully applied to countries as diverse as Canada, South Africa, and India. The French, with their generous concept of assimilation, had found a means of holding out to their African subjects a larger hope for the future. The Belgians, by contrast, were far less conscious of the need to develop a flexible and evolutionary policy. They were not unaware of the change in the international climate after World War II, but they felt that it would be sufficient to speed up the process of social reform and economic progress. Politics was a dirty subject to be kept firmly out of sight. In the early 1950's the Belgian administration struck one perceptive English observer as being "scared of letting go even a little of its authority." He noticed, too, that "although the Belgians admit literate Africans to the title of *évolué,* they laugh at the literate wretch behind his back and are still a thousand miles from that pleasant intellectual companionship which is now possible in West Africa." [78] Slowly during the 1950's Belgian policy began to change, but it was still characterized by immense caution. "Controlled gradualism," "building from the ground up," "the creation of a black bourgeoise," the need for European participation—these were the phrases and themes that dominated official Belgian discussion of the problem of decolonization while the initiative still remained in the hands of the metropolis.

There were, however, some critical and dissenting voices, notably that of A. J. Van Bilsen, professor of colonial legislation at Antwerp University. In 1955 Van Bilsen published a *Thirty-Year Plan for the Political Emancipation of Belgian Africa.* Van Bilsen was deeply worried by the *immobilisme* of Belgian policy, but he realized the need not to shock his compatriots by putting forward too revolutionary a project, and he therefore proposed a period as long as thirty years in which to complete the process of emancipation. Yet even with this cautious proposal Van Bilsen appeared a dangerous agitator in the eyes of his compatriots, while the minister of the Congo spoke scathingly of the "irresponsible strategists . . . who know nothing or understand nothing of Africa." [79] Nevertheless, for the first time the magic word "independence" had been uttered in a Congolese context. Within a few months Van Bilsen's plan came to the notice of a small group of *évolués* in Léopoldville. In August 1956 they published a manifesto in a Catholic periodical, *Conscience Africaine,* welcoming Van Bilsen's plan and expressing their desire to see the Congo merge as "a great nation in the center of the African continent." [80] The debate on independence had begun.

Before long a new voice, that of ABAKO, the *Alliance des Ba-Kongo,* made itself heard. ABAKO was founded in 1951 as a cultural organization. Its intellectual leaders were concerned to preserve the traditions of the Kongo people, looked back with pride on the ancient Kongo kingdom, and sought to encourage a closer feeling of unity among the Kongo groups living within Belgian, French, and Portuguese territory. In 1956 ABAKO took its first overtly political step, when it produced a countermanifesto, attacking the moderate tone of the spokesmen of the *Conscience Africaine.* "Our patience is already exhausted," ABAKO declared, "emancipation should be granted us this very day." [81] Here suddenly was a totally different tone, strident, uncompromising, impatient, reminiscent in some ways of the CPP in the Gold Coast. But ABAKO could make no claim to be a national party, it spoke only for the people of a single ethnic group, and it thought of the future constitutional status of the country in terms of decentralization and the creation of a federal structure. This was a theme that was to assume increasing importance in the discussion of the country's future. Meanwhile a serious crack had appeared in the once almost monolithic structure of Belgian colonial rule. In 1954 a Socialist-Liberal coalition came to power in Brussels. With anticlericalism forming part of its platform, the new government began to attack the monopoly which the Catholic missions had hitherto exercised over Congolese education. The *question scolaire,* the dispute over mission schools, created intensely bitter feeling between the administration and the missionary bodies. Catholic missionaries began to talk of refusing to collaborate with the administration, Catholic bishops issued a declaration "assuring that all the inhabitants of a country have the right to take part in public affairs," [82] while on the other side of the political fence the colonial minister justified his policy by referring to the "irresistable pressure" of the demand among Africans for lay schools—a statement which made it clear that the old paternalistic assumptions were beginning to wear thin. There were other ways, too, in which the contradictions in Belgian policy became increasingly apparent. In 1955 King Baudouin visited the Congo and spoke on his return of the need for blacks and whites to understand one another better. There was much talk in royal and ministerial circles of the creation of a new Belgo-Congolese community. Yet most Belgians working in the Congo were unprepared to abandon their old condescending approach to their African charges, and an increasing number of Africans were growing aware of the element of racial discrimination involved in their everyday relations with the Europeans in their midst.

But though the existence of currents of opinion which had not been present even five years earlier could now clearly be perceived, the metropolitan government itself did very little in these crucial years of the mid-1950's to introduce positive measures of reform. The most significant development was the establishment in 1957 of urban communes, each with its own burgomaster and a council elected by universal suffrage, in Léopoldville and two other large towns. In Léopoldville the communal elections resulted in a striking victory for ABAKO, which now emerged, under the leadership of Joseph Kasavubu, as a distinct political party. In Elisabethville, the main town of Katanga, the outcome was more confusing. There was little political organization but most of the elected seats went to Luba immigrants from Kasai. Their success aroused the resentment of the "authentic Katangans," a term which embraced Lunda, Yeke, and even some Luba from the northern part of the province. To protect their interests against immigrant pressures, the "authentic Katangans" created an effective piece of political machinery, the *Confédération des Associations Tribales du Katanga* (CONAKAT), under the leadership of Moise Tshombe, a Lunda businessman closely related to the royal family of the Mwata Yamvo, the ancient Lunda paramount.

Both CONAKAT and ABAKO were concerned to preserve local ethnic interests. But during the course of 1958 a number of Congolese became aware of the need to think in less exclusive terms. Two external events served to accelerate their political education. In the summer of 1958 several hundred Congolese from all parts of the country were invited to attend the great exhibition being staged in Brussels. Direct contact with the outside world combined with ample opportunity to discuss Congolese problems among themselves proved a highly stimulating experience for these young men who were becoming increasingly concerned with political matters. Even more significant to many Congolese was the dramatic visit paid by General de Gaulle to Brazzaville in August. Two days after de Gaulle's speech offering the French Congolese the opportunity of immediate independence, a group of Léopoldville *évolués* presented the Belgian minister for the Congo with a petition denouncing the "anachronistic political regime" of the Congo and demanding the fixing of a date for "complete independence." [83] A few weeks later the petitioners founded their own political party, the *Mouvement National Congolais* (MNC). The president of the new party was a thirty-three-year-old ex-postal clerk of Tetela origin from Orientale Province, Patrice Lumumba. Lumumba, who had just served a year in prison on a charge of embezzlement, possessed a remarkable range of qualities. As a member of numerous professional organizations, he had already proved his energy and skill as an organizer. Though his formal education had never taken him beyond primary school, he possessed a remarkably acute mind, capable of achieving a penetrating insight into the contemporary situation and animated by a restless curiosity. Before long he was to reveal the political genius of the charismatic leader.

In December 1958, Lumumba was one of the handful of Congolese delegates who attended the All-African Peoples' Conference at Accra. On his return from this intoxicating experience he addressed a mass rally in Léopoldville. "Independence," Lumumba told his enthusiastic audience, "is not a gift but a fundamental right of the Congolese." [84] "We follow you. We will support you. Down with the Belgians! Long live the Congo!" [85] the crowd replied—and in their clamor could be heard for the first time the distinctive tones, at once menacing and exhilarating, of mass nationalism. A week later Léopoldville became the scene of an exceptionally violent outbreak of rioting. Lumumba's inflammatory speech could be regarded as a contributory cause of the riots. But the disturbances had their roots in something deeper than political excitement: there was a great deal of unemployment in the city and bitter resentment of the favored conditions enjoyed by Europeans, some of whom became the target for mob violence.

A week after the riots, the Belgian government put forward its plans for constitutional reform, the development of more representative institutions at local level, leading eventually to the creation of a Congolese parliament. The king, in a broadcast, spoke of leading the peoples of the Congo to independence "without fatal delays but without inconsiderate precipitation." [86] In the months that followed, the weakness of the Belgian position became increasingly apparent. The "men on the spot," the local administrators and even the governor-general, were confronted with a situation for which their training provided no guidance. Meanwhile the metropolitan government—a coalition of Liberals and the conservative *Parti Social-Chrétien* formed in December 1958—was riven by deep disagreements between those who wanted a bold approach and their conservative critics, disagreements that led in September to the resignation of the colonial minister, Van Hemelrijick when he found that his cabinet colleagues would not support his plans for speeding up the process of decolonization.

Confusion of purpose on the Belgian side was matched by an even greater confusion on the part of the Congolese. In the course of 1959 a crop of new parties sprang up. Some, like Antoine Gizenga's *Parti Solidaire Africain* with its power-base in the Kwango-Kwilu area of southern Léopoldville Province drew their support from fairly wide areas; others were confined to single ethnic groups. During the same period, the first signs of internal fission occurred when Albert Kalondji led a group of Luba dissidents out of the MNC and formed his own party, the MNC–Kalondji in opposition to the MNC–Lumumba. The proliferation of parties was clear evidence of the growth of ethnic consciousness. Congolese "tribalism" could already be seen at its ugliest in the Luluabourg area of Kasai Province. In cultural terms the two opposing groups, Lulua and Luba, had a great deal in common, but the Luba were recent immigrants in the area—to the Lulua they appeared as strangers who took over an increasing amount of the farmland and established a monopoly of clerical posts in the towns. Few issues serve to inflame political passions so violently as competition over jobs and land. So it was in Kasai, with the Belgian administration openly appearing to favor the Lulua. By October 1959, gangs of Lulua were at work burning huts, committing an increasing number of murders, and provoking a growing exodus of Luba peasants to the relative safety of the towns. The breakdown of law and order was hardly less apparent in the Kongo-populated districts of Léopoldville Province. "On the political level," wrote a senior administrator, "contact with the people has become impossible. Everything which comes from the administration is rejected without discussion." And he went on to remark that the ABAKO leader, Kasavubu, virtually unknown before the January riots, had become the "object of a blind and fanatical submission of the mass." [87] By the autumn of 1959 the Congo was demonstrating the classical symptoms of a revolutionary situation.

With the administrative machine beginning to break down, with capital being withdrawn from the Congo in increasing quantities, with Socialist deputies in Brussels asserting their adamant opposition to the use of Belgian troops to restore order, and with Congolese politicians maintaining constant pressure, the Belgian government decided to give way. In December the colonial minister announced that a political conference would be held in Brussels in January and promised that the Congo would achieve independence in 1960. Local elections had been held in the Congo during December, and to the delight of the administration a party of moderates, the *Parti National du Progrès* (PNP) had won the largest number of seats. But when the Round Table Conference met in Brussels, the Belgian government found itself driven from a cautious retreat into a headlong rout. For the Congolese delegates succeeded in overcoming their factional divisions, formed a "common front," and pummeled the Belgian government into granting total independence by June 30, with "all the keys of the house"—some of which, in such matters as defence and foreign policy, the Belgians had hoped to retain for a little time—firmly committed to Congolese hands. The conference then moved on to drawing up a hasty constitution, of a quasi-federal type, with a strong central government but also with a certain amount of responsibility entrusted to the six provincial authorities.

In the history of parliamentary institutions it is doubtful whether there has ever been quite so extraordinary an election as that held in the Congo in May 1960. Voting took place in an atmosphere of mounting confusion, intense excitement, deep anxiety, and spreading violence. There was no time to educate voters, to provide them with some grasp of the meaning of these novel procedures. In some areas the coming of independence was interpreted in apocalyptic terms. In parts of Orientale Province graves were tidied up in expectation of a general rising of the dead. Party militants presented their supporters with a highly simplistic view of the future. "Independence means total equality between blacks and whites," declared a MNC—Lumumba broadsheet, and it went on to illustrate what equality meant. "If you must travel by foot to go somewhere and happen to meet a European who drives a car, he must stop and pick you up if you think there is room for you." [88] But if the young militants saw the future in the rosiest possible terms, many other Congolese were deeply worried at the approaching collapse of the accepted order, particularly if they lived in areas of mounting tribal conflict.

Confusion was worse confounded when the election results were announced. The 137 seats of the National Assembly were divided among more than twenty-five different parties. The MNC–Lumumba emerged as by far the largest party, with thirty-three seats compared to the thirteen of the PSA, twelve of ABAKO, and seven of CONAKAT. The success of the MNC was in large part due to the personality of its leader. As Réné Lemarchand has put it, "Lumumba possessed a special knack for setting people in motion, for arousing an emotional response from his audience, for whipping up enthusiasm for his ideals. His own excitement, as well as his ideals, were infectious." [89] But the election results showed that though the MNC always claimed to be a national party, it possessed a firm power-base only in Lumumba's own Orientale Province where it won twenty-one of the twenty-five available seats; it gained no seats in Katanga and only one in Léopoldville. With the exception of the moderate PNP all the other parties were confined to their own provinces, and in many cases to a limited number of districts. In these circumstances a government could be formed only by a coalition of different groups. Such a coalition was formed only a week before the final hand-over of power. Lumumba became the Congo's first prime minister, Kasavubu its first president. King Baudouin attended the independence celebrations and delivered a euology of his country's achievements in the Congo. Lumumba replied with a fiery and emotional speech which stressed the wounds and the insults suffered by his compatriots under Belgian rule. The two orations provided an embarrassing, yet in some ways singularly appropriate climax to eighty years of Belgian rule.[90]

▲▼ THE INDEPENDENT STATES OF EQUATORIAL AFRICA

Within a fortnight of achieving independence the ex-Belgian Congo was in a state of chaos: the *Force Publique,* which combined the functions of an army and a police force, had mutinied against its white officers; Europeans were fleeing the country in their thousands; and Katanga, the country's richest province, had seceded and declared its independence. Rapidly there developed a situation of extraordinary complexity. For four years the country—like China in the 1920's or Nigeria in the late 1960's—seemed on the verge of total disintegration. But the later 1960's saw a remarkable transformation of the Congolese scene, with the return of a substantial measure of political stability.

Perhaps the most effective way of charting a path through the labyrinth of Congolese history in the years 1960–65 is to begin by identifying the various groups, both Congolese and alien, who played major roles in the exceptionally dramatic events of this period. On the Congolese side five main groups may be distinguished. The first was that of the Léopoldville politicians, Kasavubu, Adoula, and others, who made a base for themselves in the Congolese capital. The second group could be described as the Lumumbists, radical politicians who regarded themselves as Lumumba's heirs after his murder. While the Léopoldville politicians retained their grip on the province of that name, together with Equateur Province and a large part of Kasai, the Lumumbists gained control of Orientale and Kivu provinces for a time, made their capital at Stanleyville (later renamed Kisangani), and had some supporters in northern Katanga and northeastern Kasai. The third and smallest group was made up of Luba politicians from southern Kasai who made strenuous efforts to set up an independent state of their own. The fourth group was formed by members of CONAKAT, the party led by Moise Tshombe, which controlled the greater part of Katanga. The fifth group was represented by the *Force Publique,* later renamed the *Armée Nationale Congolaise* (ANC) one of whose senior officers, Joseph Mobutu, was eventually to emerge as the country's most powerful leader.

Few independent states have been so subject to foreign intervention as the Congo Republic in the first years of its existence. Its former rulers, the Belgians, were still keenly interested in its affairs and possessed many material stakes in the country. A second alien presence was made up of United Nations personnel, both diplomats and civil servants together with a substantial military force formed from contingents sent by a number of different states, including recently independent Ghana and Nigeria. The third alien group, small in numbers but capable of exerting considerable influence on the course of events, consisted of a cosmopolitan band of white mercenaries whose services were used by all the Congolese groups, except the Lumumbists. The Belgians, the United Nations personnel, and the mercenaries operated more or less openly on the Congolese stage. Less easy to determine was the role of the United States and the Soviet Union, both of whom were drawn into the crisis at an early stage and played no small part in the unfolding course of events.

Every long-drawn-out international crisis is made up of a myriad local crises. To catch the full flavor of the Congo in these troubled years one needs a series of local studies which would illuminate the careers of men who played little part on the national stage but were in a position to dominate their own localities. Take, for example, the powerful Luba paramount, Kasongo Nyembo, in northwestern Katanga. In return for his support of CONAKAT this great traditional chief was provided with modern arms by the Katanga regime and so was enabled to build up his own military force. For three years Kasongo Nyembo played the part of a war lord on the frontiers of Katanga until he was overthrown and imprisoned in Léopoldville in December, 1963. In a brief narrative, however, it is impossible to do more than provide an outline of the course of the main events.

The mutiny of the *Force Publique* must be regarded as the seminal event in the history of the newly independent state. It was an astonishing occurrence: as Crawford Young has pointed out, "the successful mutiny of an entire army against its entire officer corps is a phenomenon virtually unique in history." [91] The mutiny was in large measure a product of Belgian stupidity. No serious attempt had been made in the last years of Belgian rule to africanize the officer corps, and on July 5 the force commander, General Jannsens, bluntly told a meeting of African N.C.O.'s, writing the words on a blackboard to emphasize his point, "Before Independence = After Independence." In the highly charged atmosphere of Léopoldville such a remark was tantamount to setting a match to a powder keg. The mutinous soldiers turned not only against their own officers but against other Europeans. The Western world was shocked by terrible stories of atrocity and violence, though in fact fewer than two dozen Europeans lost their lives. Naturally concerned to protect its own nationals, the Belgian government flew in troops. Tension between the Belgian and Congolese governments increased sharply when the Belgian navy bombarded the port of Matadi. On the same day, July 11, the provincial government of Katanga issued a declaration of independence.

The roots of Katangese secession could be traced far back into the colonial past, though the character of Katangese separatism was very different from that of other contemporary separatist movements such as those of the Ganda, the Lozi, or the Ibo. In 1959 there were 33,000 Europeans resident in Katanga, 3,000 of whom could accurately be described as settlers. The white settler element in Katanga had for long represented a vocal political lobby. In the last decade of the Free State the administration of Katanga had been entrusted to a private corporation, the *Comité Spécial du Katanga,* which in the manner of chartered companies in British territories, appointed its own officials and organized its own military force. Katanga's first rail-links with the outside world ran south to the Rhodesias and South Africa; inevitably the first white settlers in Katanga felt that they had more in common with the European communities to the south than with the remote colonial administration in Léopoldville. As early as 1931 white settlers had protested against the vigorous centralizing policy of the Léopoldville administration by talking of independence for Katanga, a line of thought which was later modified to a demand for some sort of federal solution. Until the late 1950's native Katangans had given no thought to the future of the province. With a population made up of many different ethnic groups the province contained no element of ethnic unity. The most prominent of its late nineteenth-century rulers, the renowned Msiri, was an adventurer of alien origin whose rule had been hated and whose kingdom had broken up on his death. The activities of the immigrant Luba from Kasai provided the immediate stimulus for the growth of separatism among the "authentic Katangese." Thus there emerged two rival groups, the CONAKAT of Moise Tshombe and the BALUBAKAT of the immigrants. It was natural for CONAKAT and the European settlers to move closer together and to seek support from commercial interests in Belgium and other capitalist countries. It was equally natural for the BALUBAKAT to gravitate toward the MNC–Lumumba and to gain the backing of those local Europeans who were opposed to the influence of the big companies and the missions. Thus an ideological element was introduced into the struggle, making it still more bitter.

The central government could not accept the secession of the country's richest province, but with the *Force Publique* in a state of almost total disorder, it found itself deprived of the means to assert its authority. In these circumstances Lumumba decided to appeal to the United Nations for assistance. On July 13 the Security Council agreed to organize a U.N. force in the Congo to preserve law and order while the

Belgians withdrew their troops. Lumumba hoped to be able to use U.N. forces to end the secession of Katanga. Disappointed by the refusal of Secretary-General Dag Hammarskjöld, to allow the U.N. forces to be used to settle what could be interpreted as an internal dispute, the Congolese prime minister turned to the Soviet Union for assistance. In so doing he naturally alienated the western powers; at the same time his increasing extremism aroused the resentment of many of his ministerial colleagues. On September 5 Lumumba was dismissed by President Kasavubu. A week later the army, under Colonel Mobutu, intervened to "neutralize" all politicians and to establish a caretaker government made up of university graduates.

In November Lumumba's supporters set up a rival government in Stanleyville. Lumumba, who had been protected by U.N. forces since his deposition, escaped from Léopoldville but was captured by Congolese troops. In January the ex-prime minister was flown to Katanga where he was murdered in mysterious circumstances. Lumumba dead was an even more potent force than Lumumba alive. News of his death caused an explosion of anger throughout Africa, to which the Security Council responded with a resolution recommending a return to government by politicians in the Congo, at the same time providing the United Nations with greater powers to deal with intervention by outsiders in support of Katanga. After protracted negotiations the Léopoldville and Stanleyville politicians came together to form a new government under Cyrille Adoula, an independent politician possessing no close links with any ethnic group or party. In September, 1961, United Nation troops in Katanga came into conflict with the local *gendarmerie*. For months the situation remained violent and confused. But in the course of 1962 Tshombe agreed to renounce secession, though there was another round of fighting before the central government's authority was firmly re-established and Tshombe departed into exile.

Meanwhile the coalition between the Léopoldville and Stanleyville politicians had broken up. By 1964 the country was again faced with the threat of civil war, as Lumumbist leaders took up arms in Kwilu, Orientale, and Kivu. When it became clear that Adoula was no longer capable of dealing with the situation, Kasavubu, who still retained his position as president, invited Tshombe to form a government. Realizing that the Congolese National Army was too weak to deal with the rebellion, Tshombe turned to the Americans for military aid and at the same time recruited a force of 400 white mercenaries, many of whom had been in his service in Katanga. The Lumumbists, for their part, turned to the radical African states for assistance. By 1965 the rebellion had been crushed, but Tshombe's prestige was rapidly waning. His power was based on an alliance of provincial bosses—the number of provinces had been increased from six to twenty-one, thus greatly enlarging opportunities for patronage—and of traditional chiefs. During his period in power government expenditure rose by 50 percent, thus creating a large budget deficit. In the end Tshombe overplayed his hand and made a bid for the presidency which was still occupied by the wily Kasavubu. Kasavubu retaliated by using his power to dismiss Tshombe, a move with consequences curiously parallel to his earlier dismissal of Lumumba. A political deadlock ensued which ended when the army, under General Mobutu, intervened and staged a bloodless coup in November 1965.

By 1970 Mobutu had confounded the sceptics and retained power without a really serious challenge for five years. As a soldier his record was an unusual one. Born in 1930, he had been pushed into joining the army after being expelled from school. Employed as a clerk, he rose to the rank of sergeant-major before securing his release in 1955. He then turned to journalism for a living, worked closely with Patrice Lumumba, and became a prominent member of the MNC. He rejoined the army a day or two after the mutiny and was immediately appointed chief of staff. The army provided Mobutu with his power base, but he excluded army officers from the main posts in his government and looked for support and advice to the radical young graduates now coming out of the University of Lovanium. Benefiting from the almost universal revulsion against local political bosses, Mobutu was able to introduce a greater measure of centralization, reducing the number of provinces from twenty-one to eight. In policy Mobutu might well be regarded as Lumumba's political heir. He had nothing of the dead leader's charisma, but he was as ardent and sincere a nationalist. The success of his measures was remarkable. In the late 1960's the Congo began slowly to recover from its terrible ordeal during the first years of independence. The communications system was repaired. Mineral production—never seriously affected by the troubles—continued to increase. A start was made on the great hydroelectric works at Inga on the lower Congo, a scheme designed to produce electricity at an exceptionally cheap rate. The state took over the *Union Minière* but foreign investment was encouraged and the near-monopoly of the country's major concerns maintained by the Belgians in colonial days was broken as a result of competition from the businessmen of other Western powers. Particularly remarkable was the development of education. In 1958, there were only 30,000 students in secondary school and less than 1,000 receiving higher education; after ten years of independence, secondary school enrollment had risen to 270,000, while 10,000 students were attending universities or other institutions of higher education. Agriculture represented the weakest sector of the country's economy. During the time of troubles production fell by 50 percent, and improvement occurred slowly. All in all, however, it was true to say that the Congo had made a recovery that would have seemed almost impossible to those who knew the country in the grim days of the early 1960's. In 1971 President Mobutu decreed that his country's name should be changed to the Republic of Zaire. The change in nomenclature—Zaire is one of the native terms for the Congo River—was seen as a symbolic gesture intended to stress the country's "authenticity" and to cut it off from its colonialist past.

In their first decade of independence the five states of French Equatorial Africa—Cameroon, Gabon, Congo-Brazzaville, the Central African Republic (formerly Oubangui-Chari), and Chad—were faced with the familiar task of attempting to weld highly disparate populations into the semblance of a nation-state. None of them achieved the international prominence of Congo-Kinshasa (now Zaire) or of some of the other francophone states such as Guinea or the Ivory Coast, but their history—based on a considerable divergence of experience—was not uneventful.

Cameroon in the first decade of independence enjoyed a degree of political stability remarkable for any newly independent state, all the more remarkable when the ethnic diversity of the country and the local violence of the Bamiléké revolt that marked the first years of independence are taken into consideration. Clearly much of the country's success must be attributed to the political skill of its first president, Ahmadou Ahidjo. Still in his mid-thirties when he became president, Ahidjo was a Muslim Fulani, who had served for ten years as a radio operator in the post office. His family background helped to equip him with an instinctive grasp of the intricacies of northern politics, while his later experience brought him into close touch with politicians from the south. In power Ahidjo came to display an impressive combination of qualities: "a total rejection of the flamboyant," a refusal to be swayed by purely ideological considerations, "a hard-headed determination to exercise unrestricted power over his country's government and ruthlessness in dealing with his opponents." [92] Cautious, astute, pragmatic, Ahidjo clearly possessed those political skills so often ascribed to the great Fulani rulers of the nineteenth century.

By contrast the political history of both Chad and Congo-Brazzaville was very much more troubled. In Chad the government of President Tombalbaye found itself faced with a widespread Muslim revolt in the late 1960's. (The situation neatly reversed that prevailing in the neighboring Sudan. There a government which derived its power from the Muslim Arabic-speakers of the north was faced with the revolt of a Christian and pagan south.) In Fort Lamy the government was in the hands of southerners—Tombalbaye himself was a Sara and drew much of his support from people of his own ethnic group—while the rebels operated in the desert country of the north. In Congo-Brazzaville the situation was more complex. There the government of the Abbé Fulbert Youlou was overthrown by a popular revolution in the streets of the capital in 1963. Youlou was denounced for his corruption, his megalomania, and his espousal of reactionary causes—he had established particularly cordial relations with Moise Tshombe. His successors took a sharp swing to the left. Close relations were established with Communist bloc countries, Cuban advisers were brought in to train the youth wing, and when, in 1968, the military took over power in a sudden coup, the army officers justified themselves by explaining their intention to recover the purity of the revolution. Yet, as one foreign correspondent reported in 1970, "socialism has made strikingly little difference either to the vast mass of the people living on subsistence agriculture in the country and largely unaware of the political views of their leaders in the towns; or to the country's economy which remains largely under the control of French interests." [93]

The persistence of the French stake in the former colonies of Equatorial Africa was indeed one of the striking features of the 1960's. French military assistance provided one of the props of regimes in Cameroon, Chad, and Gabon. In Cameroon, French troops and military advisers had stiffened the local armed forces in their struggle with the UPC guerillas. In Chad, more than 3,000 French troops, including a regiment of the Foreign Legion, were sent in to assist the government in curbing the Muslim revolt. In Gabon, the French intervened directly to restore the government of President Mba after it had been overthrown by an army coup in February 1964. French aid and technical assistance continued on a generous scale to all the territories of Equatorial Africa, all of which, with the exception of Congo-Brazzaville, responded by maintaining cordial diplomatic relations with the former metropolis. It was easy to present such a situation as a manifestation of the crudest form of neo-colonialism, with the French preserving their interests by propping up autocratic and unpopular regimes. But the example of Congo-Brazzaville showed that even a country which made a determined attempt to follow a new line of policy was presented by virtue of its poverty with a very narrow range of alternatives.

Under the colonial regime the territories of French Equatorial Africa were among the poorest in Africa. Their poverty had its roots in factors over which even the most beneficient government could have little control. In few other parts of tropical Africa was population density so thin. Distances over the area as a whole were vast, making communications all the more difficult to establish and expensive to maintain. And all five territories seemed devoid of those lucrative mineral deposits which served in other parts of Africa as the most efficient booster of economic development. For Gabon alone the years since independence have brought the prospect of a better life; the country has been found to contain rich deposits of manganese, uranium, and oil and exports have steadily expanded. But for the other ex-French territories the years since independence have brought no dramatic advances in the economic field. With their economies dependent on a limited range of agricultural products whose prices constantly fluctuate on the world market, they present a peculiarly intractable set of problems both to their governments and to outside agencies seeking to ameliorate the poverty of their peoples.

CHAPTER VI

Central Africa

▲▼ INTRODUCTION

Five modern polities—Angola, Zambia, Rhodesia, Malawi, and Mozambique—make up Central Africa, a region with an area of about 1¼ million square miles stretching in a broad belt from the Atlantic to the Indian Ocean. Geographically Central Africa forms part of the great continental plateau fringed on either side by a relatively narrow strip of coastal lowlands, with much of the eastern and central sections of the region lying within the basin of the Zambezi. Scenically Central Africa contains some of the continent's most spectacular landscapes, the Victoria Falls, the mountain-fringed Lake Malawi, the impressive highlands of southern Angola, but much of the region is covered by monotonous bush, the sober vegetation of the savanna.

By the mid-1960's Central Africa possessed a population numbering about 23 million, slightly smaller than that of East Africa or Equatorial Africa. By this time the region had acquired an immigrant population of about three-quarters of a million, mostly of European origin. Though divided into many distinct ethnic groups, the entire African population, a few small Bushman communities excepted, is made up of speakers of Bantu languages. The slow spread of Bantu-speakers throughout the region, a highly complex movement with many crosscurrents, can now, as a result of recent archaeological research, be traced back over a period of about 2,000 years.

At the beginning of the nineteenth century most of the African peoples of Central Africa lived in states or demi-states, grouped together to form a number of distinct ethnic clusters. Two hundred years earlier northern Angola had been dominated by the kingdom of Kongo. In the course of the seventeenth and eighteenth centuries the kingdom broke up into a number of independent chiefdoms, with the royal dynasty still maintaining a shadowy paramountcy from the ancient capital, San Salvador. Central Angola was the domain of the Mbundu, some of whose states had been shattered by the gradual expansion of Portuguese power inland from Luanda, while others maintained a successful resistance to the white invaders. Further east lay the Imbangala kingdom of Kassanje, formed by a group of Lunda origin. The Benguela plateau was covered with another cluster of states, more than twenty in number, formed by the Ovimbundu. Both the Imbangala and the Ovimbundu were exceptionally vigorous traders who regularly visited the countries lying several hundred miles farther east in search of slaves and ivory. The most substantial kingdom of southern Angola was founded early in the nineteenth century by the Kwanhama, a section of the Ambo people, most of whom live today in the northern part of South West Africa.

Most of the kingdoms and chiefdoms lying within the area of modern Zambia were founded by migrant groups breaking away from the Lunda and Luba states of the southern Congo. The two largest Zambian polities were the states formed by the Lozi and by the Bemba. The Lozi constructed a highly elaborate kingdom in the fertile flood-plain of the Zambezi, while the Bemba built up a confederation of chiefdoms under a single paramount based in the relatively arid northeastern plateau.

In 1800 the greater part of Rhodesia and much of Mozambique was populated by Shona-speaking peoples. Three hundred and fifty years earlier a Shona clan, the Rozwi, had created a great kingdom known to Europeans as Monomotapa, extending from the Kalahari to the Indian Ocean and from the Limpopo to the Zambezi. The rulers of Monomotapa were able to preserve their hold over this vast area only for a few decades. Toward the end of the fifteenth century Monomotapa began to break up into a number of Rozwi-dominated successor states all of which survived into the early nineteenth century.

The political geography of early nineteenth-century Central Africa reproduced a pattern to be found in every other part of the continent. Beyond the borders of the major polities lived peoples organized in stateless societies, many of whom had been forced to take refuge in mountainous or swampy areas to escape the attacks of their more powerful neighbors. Stateless peoples often had to accept the fate of incorporation into the larger kingdoms that surrounded them, but occasionally they were favorably placed to develop a dynamic of their own. Thus the Yao, whose independent villages lay between Lake Malawi and the Indian Ocean, came into contact with Swahili-speaking coastal traders and began to set out on trading journeys of their own, seeking slaves and ivory among the Nyanja-speaking peoples living at the southern end of the lake. Early in the nineteenth century, successful Yao traders, some of whom had been strongly influenced by Muslim culture, were using their wealth to build up petty chiefdoms for themselves.

In the 1830's many of the peoples of Central Africa suddenly found themselves confronted by the most formidable invaders the region had ever known—highly disciplined warrior-bands trained in the new military techniques developed by the Zulu under the leadership of Shaka. Three of these groups of invaders were, like the Zulu, of Nguni origin, their leaders being military commanders who had fallen foul of the despotic Shaka. The first group, led by Soshangane, entered southern Mozambique and carved out a kingdom known as Gaza. A second group, the Ngoni of Zwangendaba, devastated the Rozwi states and moved northward along the length of modern Malawi and on into country that now forms the southern part of Tanzania. By the 1850's the Ngoni had broken up into a number of distinct groups some of which settled within the bounds of modern Malawi, others in eastern Zambia. The third group of Ngoni invaders, the Ndebele of Mzilikazi, were driven from the Transvaal by the Boer trekkers and settled in western Shona country. Here Mzilikazi and his successor, Lobengula, were able to construct and maintain a powerful and highly unified military state. Many Shona were assimilated into the Ndebele system, while others were forced to accept a tributary relationship, but in the area that came to be known to Europeans as Mashonaland a number of independent Shona polities survived until the 1890's. The fourth group of South African invaders, the Kololo under Sebitwane, differed from the other three in being not of Nguni but of Sotho origin. The Kololo conquered the Lozi kingdom in the late 1840's but suffering gravely from the malaria of the Zambezi Valley, they found themselves unable to resist a ferocious Lozi counterattack in 1864 which ended in the restoration of the ancient Lozi monarchy and in the extermination of most of the Kololo.

In the last quarter of the nineteenth century Central Africa came under the attack of two new groups of conquerors—the Portuguese and the British—one with a long tradition of contact with the region, the other powerfully moved by newly conceived interests. These two groups were to dominate the history of the region well into the second half of the twentieth century.

▲▼ THE PORTUGUESE CONQUEST OF ANGOLA
 AND MOZAMBIQUE

Portuguese contacts with Central Africa date back to the sixteenth century. In 1505 the Portuguese established a fortified trading post at Sofala on the coast of Mozambique; in 1576 they founded Luanda, a city which developed in the seventeenth and eighteenth centuries into the most substantial European urban center to be found in tropical Africa. From the coast of Mozambique the Portuguese pushed up the Zambezi River into the interior, carrying on a vigorous trade with the Rozwi states of the Rhodesian plateau. In Angola the Lower Kwanza Valley was the main area of Portuguese activity, but Portuguese influence reached northward to the kingdom of Kongo and southward to the Ovimbundu states of the Benguela plateau. Angola's economy was based almost entirely on the export of slaves until the late 1830's when the trade was finally abolished. In the 1850's the Luanda authorities sought to augment the colony's declining revenues by conquering new territory in the area of the old Kongo kingdom and imposing heavy taxes on the conquered peoples. The policy failed; the colony could not afford to meet the cost of maintaining the military posts needed to hold down the newly occupied territory; by 1870 only a very small extent of Angola, the immediate hinterland of Luanda and Benguela, was firmly in Portuguese hands. In Mozambique the Portuguese position was equally shaky, with local officials controlling no more than a few ports and a couple of trading posts on the Zambezi. Away from the coast and the river, part of the colony was dominated by the *prazeros,* landowners of mixed Portuguese, Goanese, and African descent who possessed considerable wealth and were as little respectful of the authority of the Portuguese government as any independent African chief.

There were two fundamental reasons for the weakness of the Portuguese colonies. With the collapse of the slave trade Angola and Mozambique found themselves lacking a sound economic base of a kind which could provide the revenue needed to maintain an efficient system of administration. At the same time, the metropolitan government was itself so poor that it could do little to support the struggling colonists. There was, indeed, little to be said on purely economic grounds for attempting to preserve so extravagant a stake in Africa. But Portuguese imperialism derived its rationale from other considerations. Many members of the Portuguese governing classes were haunted by memories of the "great century" of Portuguese expansion and felt themselves called to be worthy of so illustrious a past. Even more persuasive, in an age of mounting rationalism, was the argument that only through its colonies could a country as small as Portugal achieve any standing in the council of nations. Portuguese imperialists did not find their views passing uncontested by their compatriots. As in other European countries, the opponents of imperialism in Portugal pointed to the oppressive aspects of colonial rule, emphasized the hypocrisy inherent in much of the talk about a "civilizing mission," and argued that the money spent on Africa could be better used at home. But, in the late nineteenth century, a country which already possessed so strong a colonial tradition could hardly escape being swept along by the immensely powerful ideological tide of the new imperialism. Between 1875 and 1900 the Portuguese were able to establish their claim to more than three-quarters of a million square miles of territory in Central Africa.

In 1875 an influential group of Portuguese politicians and officers, colonial officials, and academics came together to found the Geographical Society of Lisbon. Special attention was devoted to Angola and Mozambique, and the society's African committee publicized Portugal's historic role in Central Africa and organized scientific expeditions for the exploration of the interior. "The society's work did far more," a recent historian has pointed out, "than legislation and speeches to dramatize the presence of Africa, and helped restore natural pride in the traditional abilities of Portuguese explorers." [1] Between 1877 and 1885 a large part of the interior of Central Africa was traversed by Portuguese travelers—of whom Serpa Pinto was the best known—in a series of expeditions which helped to provide the foundation for later Portuguese claims.

From the late 1850's the Portuguese had been made painfully aware of the low esteem in which they were held by their most dangerous rivals, the British. British views on the Portuguese colonies were largely based on the highly critical accounts of Portuguese rule produced by David Livingstone and other missionary travelers. The Portuguese were described as "pedlars in human flesh," as "the curse of the Negro race," as "deserving the worst name in Christendom." Their "indolence and apathy" was scornfully compared with British "zeal, energy and humanitarianism." "Let the Portuguese have only the territory where the whites can't live" was a comment frequently heard in the 1880's and 1890's.[2] The practical difficulties faced by the Portuguese in getting other powers to recognize their claims were brought out into the open as a result of the crisis provoked by the Anglo-Portuguese Treaty of 1884. The British government, alarmed at the increase of French activity in Equatorial Africa, agreed to recognize Portuguese claims to sovereignty on the coast on either side of the mouth of the Congo in return for certain commercial privileges. The treaty aroused a storm of protest both in Britain itself and in France and Germany and had to be abandoned. In the negotiations at Berlin in the winter of 1884–85 the Portuguese were able to secure a small enclave, Cabinda, north of the Congo, to have recognized their claim to the coast south of the great river, and to reach agreement with the newly created Congo Free State on the northeastern boundaries of Angola. This could be regarded as a substantial acquisition but it fell far short of Portuguese ambitions. Why should a newcomer like Leopold of the Belgians be granted so much when the oldest European colonizing power in Africa obtained so little? It was time to resurrect the dream, first conceived in the sixteenth century, of a great Portuguese transcontinental empire. In 1886–87 Portugal persuaded France and Germany to recognize the country's "rights of sovereignty and civilization in the territories which separate the Portuguese possessions of Angola and Mozambique." The Lisbon government then went on to publish a map in which these territories were colored rose-pink to denote Portuguese rights.

Empires are built with money and guns and blood and sweat, not with paper treaties, historical memories, and political rhetoric. There had been a British presence in the Lake Malawi area since the mid-1870's as the result of the work of a group of resolute Scottish missionaries. In the late 1880's, the South African industrialist, C. J. Rhodes, probably the richest single individual in the entire continent, began to interest himself in the lands north of the Limpopo. Rhodes, working through his newly chartered British South Africa Company, supplied the money that the British government was unwilling to spend on speculative imperial enterprises. In 1889 the British proclaimed a protectorate over the Shire Highlands in southern Malawi. When it appeared that the British position was being threatened by a Portuguese force in the area, a stiff ultimatum was sent to Lisbon demanding a Portuguese withdrawal. The ultimatum provoked a frenzy of anti-British feeling, but the Portuguese government was in far too weak a position to hold out against the greatest naval power in the world. Eighteen months of tortuous negotiations followed before the frontier between the Portuguese territories and British Central Africa were laid down. After the conclusion of further treaties with the Congo Free State and with Germany, the Portuguese sphere of influence was defined with reasonable precision. By the mid-1890's the Portuguese had acquired as much territory as they could ever hope to develop.

In 1890 the Portuguese controlled no more than one tenth of the total area of Angola. Of Mozambique it could be said that "the province belongs without question to the blacks who live in it." [3] Thirty years of almost continuous fighting were needed before the Portuguese were fully in control of their sphere of Central Africa. The American historian, James Duffy, has given a succinct and ironical summary of "the classic native war" of these years: "The punitive expeditions were organized quickly; the Africans fought bravely but foolishly; every Portuguese soldier was a hero; and, finally, thousands of Africans were killed while Portuguese losses were minimal." [4] Not all the colonial wars of this period ended so easily. In certain areas, particularly in Angola, there was much hard fighting and occasional Portuguese reverses. For the Portuguese these petty campaigns did more than serve to establish their hegemony over a large number of African polities. Victorious wars in Africa served to dispel the colonial pessimism of the late nineteenth century and became the stuff of a new colonial mystique. "To the Portuguese," Douglas Wheeler has pointed out, "proof of their possession and a hint of control indicated a glorious transformation of the nation." [5] The new mood was the creation of new men and particularly of the famous "generation of 1895," the group of young army officers who accompanied the journalist-politician, Antonio Enes, when he served as governor of Mozambique in the mid-1890's. For no other European power did African colonies possess so deep a significance. "Only through these colonies," declared a leading Portuguese imperialist, João de Andrade Corvo, in the late 1870's, "will Portugal be able to take the place she deserves in the concert of nations; only on their preservation and prosperity does her future greatness depend." [6] This theme was constantly to be repeated by Corvo's successors.

▲▼ BRITISH CONQUESTS IN CENTRAL AFRICA

Compared with the Portuguese, the British were upstarts in Central Africa, newcomers whose contacts with the interior dated back no further than the great journeys of exploration undertaken by David Livingstone in the 1850's. Few individuals in the course of European history have done so much to direct the attention of their compatriots to a part of the world which had hitherto lain completely beyond their ken. Livingstone saw Central Africa in moral terms as a land afflicted by the horrors of the slave trade and of intertribal warfare and darkened by the terrible errors of heathendom, "He helped," as Alan Cairns has pointed out, "to create an image of the African as an improvable member of the human species and he emphasized in his writings and his contact that European influences"—succinctly defined in terms of Christianity, Commerce and Civilization—"on tribal peoples should be ameliorating in their broad effects." [7] Livingstone directly inspired much of the missionary activity of the 1860's and 1870's that brought Protestant evangelists to Barotseland, Matabeleland, and the country round Lake Malawi. In practical terms the early missionaries achieved very little. In politically fragmented societies, such as those in the Lake Malawi area, mission stations became places of refuge and the missionaries themselves acquired the status of local chiefs. In the larger polities the missionaries were welcomed as technical assistants or diplomatic advisers, but few Africans were prepared to accept the strange ideas put forward by these curious innovators. As one missionary remarked of the Lozi, "they did not want to know how to pray, they knew that already," and he quoted them as saying, "we do not need these teachers unless they know and teach us to make powder [for guns] and such like things." [8]

Missionaries were not the only white men to make their appearance in the interior of Central Africa in the 1860's and 1870's. A slowly swelling stream of hunters, traders, prospectors, and adventurers flowed northward from South Africa into what was described as "the far interior." Numbers were still very small. In the mid-1870's only twenty trading wagons were reported to be entering Matabeleland every year, while in the late 1880's no more than seventy-two Europeans—missionaries, traders, planters, and hunters—were counted in the Lake Malawi area. Gradually, however, this "no man's land," this "happy hunting ground" of Central Africa as it must have appeared to its first white pioneers, began to assume a more overtly economic and political significance in British eyes. In the late 1860's travelers brought back reports that gold was to be found in Mashonaland, and though the earliest prospecting companies, set up in the 1870's, failed to make any really spectacular strikes, influential South Africans were still prepared to believe in the 1880's that Mashonaland held "some of the richest deposits of alluvial gold in the world." [9] Moreover, the country between the Limpopo and the Zambezi was regarded as enormously fertile. The European communities in South Africa, both English-speaking and Afrikaner, had always possessed a strong expansionist urge. For English-speaking South Africans the safest route to the "far interior" lay through the territory of the Tswana, west of the potentially hostile Afrikaner Republic of the Transvaal. In 1885, the year in which German annexations in South West Africa introduced another European competitor into southern Africa, the British government established a protectorate over the Tswana chiefdom. Thus a British political presence was brought to the borders of Matabeleland. The Afrikaners of the Transvaal were no less interested in the country immediately to their north. In 1887 an envoy from the Transvaal visited Lobengula, the Ndebele ruler, and concluded a treaty of alliance. The Portuguese, too, were developing a keener interest in the lands of the Zambezi. Thus Matabeleland and Mashonaland were caught in the nexus of European rivalries.

Rivalry did not last for long. In 1888 the British signed a treaty with Lobengula whereby the Ndebele monarch agreed never to cede any of his territory to a foreign power without first obtaining British consent. It was at this stage that the man destined to mold events more forcefully than any other European in the history of Central Africa began to take an active interest in Ndebele affairs. Cecil John Rhodes was one of the most formidable men in Africa. Biographers have summed up his character with a string of paradoxical epithets: quarrelsome but conciliatory, vindictive but generous, moody but frank, dictatorial and yet shy, humorless and cynical and at the same time sentimental and romantic.[10] Rhodes's personality might be intriguingly complex: his ideas were compulsively simple. He had made a fortune first in diamonds and then in gold so as to provide himself with the financial base essential for the realization of his great ambition—the extension of the British empire. "If there is a God," he once remarked, "I think that what he would like me to do is to paint as much of Africa British-red as possible." [11]

The first stage in Rhodes's plan to paint Central Africa red was to secure control over mining rights in Matabeleland and Mashonaland. In September 1888 he sent his agent, Rudd, to Bulawayo, the Ndebele capital. Lobengula's court was thronged with Europeans seeking concessions: Rudd outbid them all, offering the monarch £100 a month, a thousand modern rifles, and a steamboat on the Zambezi in return for "complete and exclusive charge over all metals and minerals" within his dominions. Verbally Lobengula was assured that no more than ten European miners would enter his country, and that Rhodes would do all in his power to keep other Europeans out. With the Rudd Concession in his pocket Rhodes moved to London to seek official support for his scheme to establish a chartered company which could administer any territory he might acquire in Central Africa. Overcoming the prejudices which he aroused as a raw colonial, a monopolist, and a friend of the Cape Afrikaners, Rhodes demonstrated to the British government how splendidly his own ambitions fitted in with imperial strategy. A large slice of valuable territory, threatened by Portuguese, Afrikaner, and German expansion, would be taken over for Britain at no expense to the British taxpayer. At the same time, the British presence in Southern Africa would be immensely strengthened. Since 1885 the turbulent Afrikaner Republic of the Transvaal, its economy transformed by newly discovered gold, had been showing signs of a dangerous independence of action. Once most of the country north of the Limpopo was in British hands, the Transvaal would be almost completely hemmed in by British territory and eventually forced to accept that confederation which British statesmen had sought so long to achieve, a scheme which would bring together all four European polities in South Africa under the leadership of the Cape. Lord Salisbury, the prime minister of the day, drawing comfort from glib assumptions about the future, gave Rhodes his charter—and with it freedom of action, in the form of administrative responsiblity for a loosely defined extent of territory lying north of Bechuanaland and the Transvaal and west of the Portuguese possessions. It was a fateful decision. The British South Africa Company had a board of directors adorned by royal dukes, but it was far more South African than British in character. The humanitarian lobby in the metropolis was able to have certain safeguards for African interests written into the terms of the charter, but there were, in the first years, no imperial officials on the spot to see that these safeguards were observed. In 1889 Britain acquired responsibility without power for a large part of Central Africa. The consequences of this decision became starkly apparent three-quarters of a century later when a post-imperial Britain incurred the odium of the greater part of the Afro-Asian world on account of its inability to bend a quarter-million white settlers to its will. The long-drawn-out crisis provoked by the Rhodesian declaration of independence in 1965 had its roots in the granting of a charter to Rhodes's company in 1889.

On his visit to London to arrange about the charter Rhodes made the acquaintance of a young consular official, Harry Johnston, who had just been appointed to Mozambique with instructions to report on the extent of Portuguese rule in the vicinity of the Zambezi. Johnston, who had already spent some years in the consular service in West Africa, was destined to become, with Rhodes, one of the architects of British rule in Central Africa and to emerge as one of the most engaging and versatile of the "great proconsuls" of the age of imperialism. Artist, novelist, naturalist, linguist, and explorer, he has been well described by Margery Perham as "Elizabethan in his range of gifts and in the combination of the aesthetic with the adventurous and of an almost *fin de siècle* refinement with the harshness he brought to bear upon the often bloody business of taming a still wild Africa." [12] Johnston was as passionate an imperialist as Rhodes. In a remarkable article published anonymously in *The Times* in August 1888 he had provided an astonishingly prescient forecast of the still-uncompleted partition of Africa, in which he had envisaged "a continuous band of British dominion" stretching from South Africa to the Egyptian Sudan.[13] "From the Cape to Cairo" was an extravagant and in practical terms totally fatuous concept but it was well calculated to appeal to Rhodes's perfervid imagination. Before long Rhodes was publicizing Johnston's ideas as his own invention. But the man who had made a fortune for himself in his twenties was also a master of the art of getting things done in a hurry. Learning of the crippling financial restrictions imposed by the parsimonious British Treasury on Johnston's projected trip to Zambezia, Rhodes promptly wrote out the young consul a check for £2,000, thus providing him with the means to pursue a more dynamic policy than the British government had intended.

On his arrival in the Lake Malawi area, Johnston set about concluding treaties with all the leading chiefs living in a broad sweep of territory stretching northward from the Shire Highlands along the western shores of Lake Malawi to the southern end of Lake Tanganyika, while Alfred Sharpe, an English solicitor turned hunter, was engaged as honorary vice-consul and given the task of blocking the advance of Congolese agents by negotiating treaties with the chiefs of the Bemba country. These treaties were similar to the one signed by Lobengula a year earlier. The signatories did not renounce their sovereignty but agreed not to dispose of their territories to any other power. When the Portuguese made a serious attempt to gain control of the Shire Highlands, Buchanan, the acting consul appointed by Johnston, promptly declared the territory a British protectorate. In January 1890 a British ultimatum forced the Portuguese to renounce their claims to the area. Six months later an Anglo-German agreement laid down the frontier between Lakes Malawi and Tanganyika. The northeastern borders of British Central Africa had been secured.

While Johnston was laying the foundations of the colony which was eventually to be known as Nyasaland, Rhodes was preparing the conquest of the territory later to bear his own name. In Bulawayo, Lobengula, alarmed at reports of Rhodes's activities, was talking of repudiating the Rudd Concession. Rhodes was not averse to planning a conquistatorial attack on the Ndebele capital but dropped the idea when Lobengula agreed to allow the company's men to prospect for gold in Mashonaland. The Ndebele were deliberately deceived: instead of the handful of miners coming to "dig a big hole" which the discussions over the concession had led Lobengula to expect, a "pioneer column" of 600 hand-picked white men, 400 of them armed police, moved provocatively along the edge of Ndebele territory and ran up the Union Jack at the fort they named in honor of Lord Salisbury, before scattering to take possession of the gold claims and the 3,000-acre farms they had been promised. In the eyes of most contemporary Europeans the pioneers were romantic figures, agents of progress in a land of savagery; for the Shona and the Ndebele, the company's men represented first a new factor in the complex pattern of local politics, then a new race of conquerors.

To the northwest of Matabeleland lay Barotseland. The Lozi king, Lewanika, had been anxious for several years to secure British protection. In the course of 1890 he was visited by Lochner, one of the British South Africa Company's agents, and signed a concession treaty which served to confirm the British claim to approximately 200,000 square miles of territory. Beset with many more pressing concerns, the company could give no further attention to Barotseland. Not until 1897 was a permanent British agent posted to Lewanika's kingdom. By this time the company had survived three major crises in its original area of occupation.

The first crisis arose out of relations with the Portuguese on the eastern borders of Mashonaland. To Rhodes the Protuguese were "a bad race" and "a curse to any place they have occupied." [14] Gladly he would have taken over the greater part of Mozambique, thus providing his own colony with an outlet to the sea and completing the encirclement of the Transvaal. The British government was not prepared to follow so acquisitive a policy in dealing with an ancient ally. The company's men bundled the Portuguese out of Manicaland on the eastern borders of Mashonaland but the frontier finally laid down left Rhodes's major ambition unsatisfied.

The company's second crisis was of a far more serious nature. To the west of Mashonaland lay the still unconquered kingdom of the Ndebele. With remarkable skill Lobengula had restrained his arrogant and hotheaded warriors from any action that might serve to provoke European retaliation. But the company's occupation of Shona territory regularly raided by Ndebele *impis* inevitably led to disturbing incidents. By 1893 the white settlers in Mashonaland had come to accept war as inevitable. Rhodes himself was not a deliberate warmonger, but he was acutely aware that insecurity could prove disastrous for his company's reputation and that the price of its shares had already slumped in the London stock exchange. There was also, of course, a strong acquisitive streak in the attitude both of Rhodes and of the settlers. Matabeleland looked an extremely tempting prize: the Ndebele were rich in cattle, their pasturelands appeared to be agreeably lush, and their country might well contain a reef of gold far richer than anything yet discovered in Mashonaland. The war which Lobengula had tried so valiantly to avoid confirmed the worst of his fears. Within a few weeks the Ndebele *impis* had been shattered and Bulawayo was in British hands. In January 1894 the old king died, a hunted fugitive. The Ndebele kingdom ceased to exist. While impoverished Ndebele warriors sold their ostrich-feather headresses in the streets of Bulawayo, Jameson, the company's administrator, began to allocate 6,000-acre farms to the white troopers who had taken part in the campaign. The conquest seemed complete.

Nevertheless, within two and a half years of the Ndebele war, the company found itself faced with the third and most dangerous of its crises—a violent revolt which began in Matabeleland in March 1896 and spread a few months later to Mashonaland. In two or three years of company rule both the Ndebele and the Shona had accumulated a mounting tally of grievances—confiscation of cattle, expropriation of land, compulsory labor, harsh taxation, brutal treatment at the hands of white officials or settlers and their African subordinates. Jameson's notorious "raid" provided the immediate opportunity for an African revolt. Jameson, as administrator of Mashonaland, had conquered the Ndebele in 1893; now he and many of his men were humiliatingly locked up in a Transvaal prison, after their abortive attempt to overthrow Kruger's republic, leaving Matabeleland denuded of troops. The combined Ndebele-Shona rebellion shook the company's regime to its foundation. "The settlers lost something like 10 percent of their total number, a staggeringly high figure," L. H. Gann has pointed out, when compared with white settler casualties in Algeria or in Kenya two generations later. But there was a profound contrast in the ideological atmosphere of the 1890's and the 1950's. The settlers "felt that history was on their side, that Europe stood behind them, and that they formed the vanguard of civilization in Darkest Africa. . . . The settlers' estimate of themselves was shared by public opinion in Britain and America, so that the whites in Rhodesia never experienced that clammy sense of moral and political isolation which weighed down their successors." [15] With the aid of volunteers from South Africa the revolts were suppressed. In Matabeleland many of the Ndebele retreated to the natural stronghold of the Matopos. Anxious to avoid the expense of a long-drawn-out siege, Cecil Rhodes himself brought the rising to an end by his daring and dramatic gesture in visiting the rebel camp and concluding a negotiated settlement. But in Mashonaland fighting went on well into 1897, with rebel strongholds taken by storm, and rebel bands hunted down and forced to surrender.

Few revolts are ever entirely futile. The Shona and the Ndebele gained something from their courageous acts of defiance. "The company was compelled following the rebellions and under the pressure of public opinion to adopt a less harsh approach and to soften the regime to which the natives were submitted. Today," wrote a shrewd Belgian observer in 1913, "there are no more 'atrocities' with which to reproach the Government or the settlers." But the African population was still "at the mercy of their European conquerors." "Fear of rebellion" might restrain the whites from engaging in "unbounded exploitation," but the settlers were preoccupied with their own well-being. There was no trace of "a genuine social policy inspired by the interests of the blacks." [16]

Southern Rhodesia was emphatically a conquered country. So too was Nyasaland. But in the process of conquest there were sharp contrasts between the two territories. Southern Rhodesia experienced two violent outbursts of warfare, in 1893 and 1896–97; Nyasaland was the scene of a series of minor colonial campaigns from 1891 to 1895. There had, indeed, been fighting between Europeans and Africans in the Lake Malawi area even before the proclamation of a British protectorate. In 1887, European agents of the African Lakes Company—a concern financed by philanthropic Scottish businessmen to assist their missionary compatriots in the Malawi area—clashed with Swahili-Arab traders at the north end of Lake Malawi. In political and economic terms, the position of the Arab traders in their newly created principalities was similar to that of the Yao chiefs established at the southern end of the lake. To the local people both Yao and Arabs were intruders, who derived much of their power from the trade in slaves and ivory. The majority of the Arab and Yao rulers bitterly resented the European incursion which threatened to destroy their own power-structure. But initially they must have felt confident of being able to resist the newcomers for in the first years the British presence was absurdly weak. Harry Johnston who returned to the Malawi area in 1891 with the new title of "commissioner and consul-general for the territories under British influence north of the Zambezi," had at his disposal a force of 150 armed men, 70 Sikhs and 80 Zanzibaris. This force had to be paid for out of an annual grant of £10,000 provided not by the British government, which did little more than meet the commissioner's own salary, but by the British South Africa Company. Thus Johnston was expected, as Roland Oliver has remarked, "to govern a territory the size of England and France together on an income which to many of his contemporaries would have seemed barely sufficient for the upkeep of an English country house." [17]

Johnston achieved a remarkable measure of success. In the course of five years of exceptionally strenuous work he laid the foundations of a modern administrative system for Nyasaland, broke the power of the Yao and Arab slavers, and managed to persuade the British government to provide the protectorate with a reasonably generous grant-in-aid. "I have spared neither the risk of my own life, the abandonment of comfort, nor the right to rest at times like other people," Johnston wrote to Rhodes in 1893. "Sundays and weekdays, mornings and evenings I am to be found either slaving at my desk, or tearing about the country on horseback, or trudging twenty miles a day on foot or sweltering in boats or being horribly sea-sick in Lake Nyasa steamers. I have to carry on in my office, myself, a most onerous correspondence in Swahili, which I have to write in the Arabic character, in Portuguese, in French, and in

English. I have had to acquire a certain mastery over Hindustani to deal with the Indian troops. I have learnt three native languages besides Swahili in order to talk straight to the people. I have undertaken grave responsibilities, and I have devoted myself to the most wearisome and niggling tasks. One day I am working out a survey which has to be of scrupulous accuracy, and another day I am doing what a few years ago I never thought I should be called upon to do—undertaking the whole responsibility of directing military operations. I have even had myself taught to fire Maxim guns and seven-pounder cannon, I, who detest loud noises and have a horror of explosives." [18] This passage might well serve as a memorial to the first generation of imperialists—to their energy, their versatility, their self-confidence, their courage. Moreover, Johnston, like the best of his contemporaries, was man with a vision. "We must devote ourselves to reclaiming Africa from the unintelligent rule of Nature by educating the Black Man and introducing the Yellow Man"— a term which referred not to the Chinese but to the "docile, kindly, thrifty, industrious, clever-fingered, sharp-witted Indian"—"and establishing ourselves in the more healthy districts so that we may direct these operations *in situ*." [19] Though far from unmindful of the contribution which European capital could make to African development, Johnston grew increasingly critical of the crudely materialistic approach of his one-time collaborator Cecil Rhodes, and he deliberately sought to reduce South African influence in his protectorate, regarding South Africans as being "without any conception of justice where natives are concerned." [20]

Johnston's original commission covered not only Nyasaland but also the whole territory of modern Zambia. With such limited forces at his disposal he himself could do no more than establish a few modest administrative posts in the area of Lakes Mweru and Tanganyika. Accordingly, when the British South Africa Company ceased subsidizing the Nyasaland Protectorate in 1895, the British government agreed to allow the company to assume complete responsibility for the administration of what came to be known for a time as North-Eastern and North-Western Rhodesia. North-Western Rhodesia presented the company with relatively little difficulty for Lewanika, the Lozi monarch, and by far the most powerful African ruler in the area, was prepared peacefully to accept European overrule. But in North-Eastern Rhodesia the company faced three potentially formidable opponents, the Bemba confederation, the Lunda kingdom of Kazembe and the Ngoni state founded by Mpeseni. Both the Bemba and the Lunda rulers had come to depend on Arab and Swahili traders for much of the surplus wealth on which their power was based, exchanging slaves and ivory for firearms and luxury goods from the coast. Johnston's attack on the Arab traders in the Lake Malawi area affected both the Bemba and the Lunda economy, and the run of military successes achieved by the British provided a grave warning to potential resisters. Other factors contributed to a relatively peaceful takeover. The Bemba were too divided among themselves to form a united front against the invaders. The most powerful Bemba chief, Mwamba, died in 1898, and a remarkable Catholic missionary, Father Dupont of the White Fathers, gained temporary control of his chiefdom and assisted the company's agents to establish themselves in Bemba country. The Lunda ruler, Kazembe, was overawed by the size of the expedition sent against him in 1899 and fled into Belgian territory. Only Mpeseni's Ngoni, a people with a military tradition comparable to the Ndebele's, risked a head-on conflict with the company's forces and were soon defeated.

The Yao, the Bemba, the Lunda, and the Ngoni had been the terror of the many agricultural communities formed by groups of different ethnic origin to be found in every part of Central Africa. Most of the people of these minor polities had little hesitation in accepting European hegemony. The company's officials, supported by small detachments of native police, toured the country addressing gatherings of notables. "We come from the Great White Queen. We are fresh from conquering the Ngoni. We have three things to say. First, in this country there shall be no more war. Secondly, in this country there shall be no more witchcraft. Thirdly, in this country there shall be no more slavery. In regard to all other things, men shall do as they have done, and as their fathers have done before them." With these words Assistant Collector Stephenson addressed the "chiefs of the Lala nation." "There was," as L. H. Gann, who quotes Stephenson's speech, remarks, "no reference to any treaties past, present or future, but the Lala were impressed by the white man's guns." [21]

▲▼ AFRICAN REACTIONS TO THE EUROPEAN CONQUEST OF CENTRAL AFRICA

Viewed from a distance, the European conquest of Central Africa may well take on the appearance of a smooth, inevitable process, an irresistible tide engulfing every independent African community lying in its path. The reality was of course far more complex. Change one's point of vantage, try to see the situation through African eyes, and one is immediately confronted with a wide range of local crises, in which though the final outcome, the establishment of European overrule, was always the same, the actual course of events varied greatly from community to community. So many factors had a bearing on each encounter—the precise nature of a community's political and economic structure, its relations with neighboring polities, the character of the initial European impact, and so on. Rather than continue along the line of generalization, it seems better to concentrate briefly on three exceptionally well-documented aspects of African reaction to European intrusion—the policies followed by Lobengula and by Lewanika, the Ndebele and Lozi rulers, and the part played by the Shona in the great revolt of 1896–97. From these three episodes it is possible to gain a vivid impression of the human dimension of a conquest situation.

Lobengula's kingdom was the most powerful African polity to be found in Central Africa in the last quarter of the nineteenth century. The area of Ndebele settlement was comparatively modest, extending for no more than a thirty- or forty-mile radius from the capital, Bulawayo, and the Ndebele population probably did not exceed 100,000, but the state was so organized as to allow its power to be felt over a very much larger territory. The Ndebele kingdom derived its entire rationale from war. Beginning as a breakaway group of a few hundred Zulu warriors under the leadership of Mzilikazi, the Ndebele polity had gradually snowballed as the horde moved northward across the Transvaal to settle in the rich pasturelands of the western Shona. "We were always out raiding," a Ndebele warrior recalled later, "and subduing the neighboring tribes and collecting tribute from their chiefs. If they submitted and acknowledged our king's sovereignty and if they gave cattle freely we left them alone but if they refused we fought them and burnt their kraals and took their young people into slavery." [22]

Europeans, it has been suggested, came to hate the Ndebele as much for their arrogance as for their brutality. Nevertheless, it was certainly not impossible for European intruders to establish, if only for a time, reasonably harmonious relations with African military polities. In East Africa the two most formidable people of the interior, the Ganda and the Masai, collaborated profitably with the British. But the pattern of state relationships in Central Africa precluded such an arrangement between the Ndebele and the intruders. The Ndebele's most powerful neighbors, the Lozi and the Ngwato (the latter a Tswana group whose chief, Khama, was converted to Christianity) both found it possible to reach a satisfactory *modus vivendi* with the British, while the Shona polities to the east had too great a fear of the Ndebele to wish to make a common cause with them in resisting the first European incursion. Thus the Ndebele found themselves diplomatically friendless. Had it been possible for them to retreat into what one European observer described as "a Chinese isolation from the rest of the world," no doubt they would have done so. But there could be no retreat. "Did you ever see a chameleon catch a fly?" Lobengula asked one of the European missionaries at his court, and he went on to describe the chameleon's tactics—the movement into position, the stealthy advance, the sudden fatal dart of the tongue. "England," the Ndebele monarch declared, "is the chameleon and I am that fly." [23] Clearly Lobengula realized the tragic nature of his situation, but he fought gamely and shrewdly to ward off the inevitable.

Superficially Lobengula could be described as a despot. His presence was majestic, his manner sometimes affable, sometimes savage, his mind well-equipped to make a statesmanlike assessment of any situation. There could be no doubt that his great authority was the main force holding the Ndebele together, but like any other monarch he could never be indifferent to the views of his subjects. Indeed, internal pressures made his position "most difficult and precarious." This was the view expressed by J. S. Moffat, who visited Bulawayo in 1888 to negotiate a treaty of alliance and who acquired a remarkably sympathetic understanding of Lobengula's predicament. "He has to consult all the great *indunas* on all public questions . . . he has to stave off by all possible means the threatened rebellion of the Matjaha [the young unmarried warriors who believed themselves to be invincible] . . . he has to deal with a steadily increasing influx of European concession hunters . . . whom he can now scarcely protect from the bloodthirsty Matjaha . . . and lastly he has a perpetual dread of an inroad of Boers. . . . He knows all about Majuba and the retrocession of the Transvaal . . . he knows how England, after the fairest promises, handed over 750,000 unwilling natives to the Boers whom they dread and detest. . . . He is sharp enough and farsighted enough to understand that the English alliance might be his best card if only he could trust the English, but there's the rub. England has a bad name in South Africa for breaking faith with natives." [24]

Lobengula succeeded in restraining his arrogant and blood-thirsty young warriors from giving vent to their exasperation by striking down all the white men in their midst. He found means of playing off Rhodes and his associates for the space of five years. But he could do nothing to prevent the final calamitous overthrow of his kingdom. Ndebele society had no room for those mediators—enterprising African traders or Christian converts—who might have served as a peace party and provided the king with the internal support he needed in any attempt to reach a compromise settlement with the British. The inflexibility of the Ndebele system of government, especially manifest in the continuing dependence of the ruling group on an economy based on raiding their neighbors' cattle, made its eventual downfall virtually inevitable. "If he attacks us," the British South Africa Company's secretary wrote of Lobengula some months before the pioneer column set out for Mashonaland, "he is doomed, if he does not, his fangs will be drawn, the pressure of civilization on all his borders will press more and more heavily upon him, and the desired result, the disappearance forever of the Matabele as a power, if delayed, is yet the more certain." [25]

In 1884, when Lobengula, the Ndebele monarch was at the height of his power, Lewanika of the Lozi was a king in exile, recently overthrown by a *coup d'état* in his capital. Lewanika regained his throne a year later, but the experience of his sudden fall must have accentuated an already acute sense of insecurity. Of Lewanika's two immediate predecessors one had been assassinated, the other forced into exile after a reign of a few years. Moreover, in contrast to the victorious sweep of Ndebele history, his people, the Lozi, had experienced a highly troubled half-century with the Kololo invasion and conquest of the 1840's followed by the successful but sanguinary Lozi counterrevolution of the 1860's. A sense of insecurity was not confined to the king; it affected all the leading members of Lozi society. "The chiefs," wrote François Coillard, the French missionary who worked in Barotseland in the 1880's, "are always exposed to secret assassination, are naturally suspicious and afraid of each other." "You will soon discover," Coillard reported some Lozi as saying, "that we have yellow hearts (i.e., are jealous of each other) and that our country is a country of blood. The nation is weary; it sighs for peace: it languishes." [26]

In 1886 Lewanika frankly confessed his difficulties to Coillard: "He did not trust his people and was also afraid of other nations such as the Portuguese and the Boers." In these circumstances his great desire was "to place his country under Queen Victoria's protection as Khama had done." [27] Khama's people, the Ngwato, whose country lay to the south of Barotseland had even more cause than the Lozi to dread Afrikaner expansion. And both the Ngwato and the Lozi had another common enemy, the formidable Ndebele whose raids troubled their borders. Clearly, given the Lozi monarch's highly insecure position, British protection was well worth seeking. In 1888, Lewanika wrote to Khama asking him to explain exactly what "protection" meant. "They say there are soldiers living in your place, and some headmen sent by the Queen to take care of you and protect you against the Matabele. Are you happy and quite satisfied?" [28] But while Lewanika was engaged in seeking the Great White Queen's protection, many of his leading subjects were bitterly critical of his policy. Some chiefs, with pretensions to becoming over-mighty subjects, resented any move by the king that might serve to strengthen his personal power. Others were deeply disturbed by innovations associated with the white man and feared that the whites would come in great numbers and "eat up the land." In 1890 Lewanika secured the protection he sought when Lochner, an agent of Rhodes's chartered British South Africa Company, visited Barotseland and negotiated a concession treaty in which the company pledged to protect Lewanika and his people "from all outside interference and attacks."

Lewanika wanted something more than mere protection. Through his relatively modest contacts with the handful of European traders and missionaries whom he had allowed to reside in his kingdom, the Lozi king had come to conceive a new vision for his people. "He longs for light and knowledge," one European visitor wrote of him, "and wonders why more missionaries do not come to teach him and his people." But Lewanika was not interested in the message of the gospel; "he wants teachers to instruct his people how to read and write, but especially to train them as carpenters, cabinetmakers, blacksmiths and for other trades that they may make furniture and build houses for him. . . . He has great ideas of the ability of the Marotsi [Lozi] to learn the various arts and become wise like Europeans." [29] To Lewanika one of the most attractive clauses in the treaty with the chartered company was that in which the company agreed "to aid in the education and civilization of the native subjects of the King, by the establishment, maintenance and endowment of schools and industrial institutions." In fact the company did nothing to live up to this promise. Indeed, in the years after 1897 when the first British resident was posted to Barotseland, Lewanika was forced to recognize, as Gerald Caplan has pointed out, that his "victory in winning 'British protection' " was entirely pyrrhic: "He succeeded in remaining king only by forfeiting a large proportion of the traditional authority of the kingship," while "his plan to build a modern nation on the Upper Zambezi was an even more abject failure." [30] "We are sometimes made to feel that we are a conquered nation," Lewanika exclaimed bitterly in 1907 in vain protest against a further diminution of his sovereignty. He believed that he had "made an agreement which was said to be just like an alliance between our nation and the Imperial Government." But when he pointed this out to the British South Africa Company, the reply of the company's agents, so the aging Lozi paramount complained to the British high commissioner in Cape Town, was terse and brutal—"Do you want to be conquered?" [31] Lewanika died in 1916. To the end he maintained his dignity and his status. To have preserved even the outward trappings of Lozi monarchy was a considerable achievement.

To the first settlers in Mashonaland the Shona people appeared to "be composed of disintegrated groups of natives, having no common organization and owing allegiance to no single authority, cowed by a series of raids from Matabeleland into a condition of abject pusillanimity and incapable of planning any combined or premeditated action." [32] So wrote the resident magistrate at Salisbury, reporting in shocked surprise the outbreak of the Shona rebellion. Europeans had many illusions about the Shona. They thought of them as a people without a history, not realizing that the Shona were the heirs of the rich cultured traditions associated with Monomotapa and the Rozwi chiefdoms. They regarded them as people completely dominated by the Ndebele, yet there were a number of Shona chiefdoms which lay beyond the range of Ndebele raiding parties, while other Shona groups made skilful use of the country's natural defences to ward off Ndebele attacks. As for the cordial manner in which they received the Europeans of the pioneer column, it would seem that the Shona regarded the white men not as protectors against the Ndebele but as members of an unusually large trading caravan with whom it would obviously be possible to conduct profitable business. Only gradually did the Shona come to realize that these strange intruders intended to become permanent residents in their country. Even then the European presence might well have been peacefully accepted had the British South Africa Company's adminstrators not been guilty of so many brutal actions. In one part of Mashonaland, for example, native constables were sent through the countryside, a missionary reported, "collecting the natives by armed force, compelling them to labour here and there wherever their services happen to be required, whether they are willing or not, their wives being seized as hostages in case they attempt to escape." [33]

However bitter their resentment of European rule, if ever the Shona thought of the possibilities of revolt, they must have been acutely aware of the difficulties they would have to face. Unlike the Ndebele, they were a politically fragmented people. Nevertheless, there did exist in Mashonaland certain religious institutions which could serve to bring together people of many politically independent communities and eventually inspire them to common action. Many of the Shona revered a high god, Mwari, whose shrines, sited in caves, were attended by elaborate hierarchies of priests and messengers. In areas where Mwari was of less importance, the people turned to spirit mediums for religious sustenance, the mediums being men and women who were believed to be possessed by the spirits of dead kings. The Mwari cult extended into Matabeleland and was treated with respect by the conquering Ndebele. Thus it was ideally suited to provide an organizational link between the two otherwise antagonistic people.

The revolt of 1896 was planned by a group of Ndebele *indunas* who aimed at restoring their shattered monarchy. But at an early stage the conspirators gained the support of many of the local priests of the Mwari cult. The most important of these priests, Mkwati, was a man of slave origin, but so great was his prestige that even the supercilious Ndebele aristocrats accepted him as an equal. Mkwati and his associates made the round of all the kraals in his area, telling the people that Mwari expected them to kill all the whites. Before long Mkwati was able to extend his field of operations to Mashonaland by summoning the Shona priests of Mwari to hear his instructions. The priests returned to the kraals of the chiefs of western Mashonaland, often accompanied by small groups of Ndebele warriors who could tell of the success achieved by the rebels in Matabeleland. From western Mashonaland news of the rising spread to other parts of Shona country, where the cause was taken up by some of the leading spirit mediums. When the Ndebele *indunas* decided to seek a negotiated settlement, Mkwati abandoned his original base and turned to strengthening Shona resistance. Certainly the religious enthusiasm which characterized the revolt contained "an element of the super-rational," but, as Terence Ranger has pointed out, "the services of the religious leadership to the 1896–97 risings . . . were eminently utilitarian. The resistances were a defiance of a power which enjoyed great technological superiority and began with a superiority of morale based upon it and upon confidence in its ability to shape the world. The religious leaders were able to oppose to this a morale which for the moment was as confident, if not more so, based upon *their* supposed ability to shape the world; and they were able to oppose to modern weapons the one great advantage that the Africans possessed, that of numbers. . . . Moreover, the so-called superstitious injunctions of the religious leaders . . . ensured the minimum of discipline essential in movements such as these. The great injunction—not to loot European goods but to deliver them to the servants of God—prevented the risings from breaking up into a series of fragmented raids for property, and gave the religious leaders, through their control of the modern weapons seized from the whites, a stronger hold still upon the military side of the rebellion." [34] Mkwati's strange career ended in 1897 when he was hacked to death by a group of Shona who rejected his summons to revolt. Clearly he deserves a place among the major figures of Central Africa at the end of the nineteenth century, along with Rhodes and Lobengula, Lewanika and Johnston, and many others whom there has been no space to mention.

▲▼ PORTUGUESE RULE IN CENTRAL AFRICA: 1900 TO 1950

It is not yet possible to present a satisfactory account of the development of Portuguese rule in Angola and Mozambique in the first half of the twentieth century. The Portuguese authorities have discouraged those detailed studies based on field work and archival research of a kind undertaken by African, European, and American scholars in other parts of the continent with such illuminating results. Contemporary studies of Portuguese Africa are distorted by a tone of polemic which makes it impossible for an outside observer to reach a reasonably balanced assessment of the impact of Portuguese rule. All that a general historian can do in such a situation is to point to certain broad and easily discernible lines of development.

Portugal was by far the poorest of the European colonial powers of the early twentieth century. As late as 1962, the average per capita income in Portugal was no more than £95, compared with £150 in South Africa, £224 in Italy, £368 in Belgium, and £420 in France. Even in the second half of the twentieth century, Portugal with its largely agricultural economy, its high rate of illiteracy, and its dependence on foreign investment still possessed many of the characteristics of an underdeveloped country. The poverty of the metropolis inevitably affected the colonies. It is hardly fair to complain of Portuguese shortcomings in comparison with other colonial powers in the field of development, for there were many tasks the Portuguese simply could not afford to undertake.

Any consideration of Portuguese policy must also bear in mind the country's troubled political history. For Portugal the twentieth century has been less troubled than the nineteenth, but it has contained one period of profound instability. In 1910 the monarchy gave way to a republic. The republican regime lasted for sixteen years during which no less than forty-five governments held office before being brought to an end by a military coup. Thus, in the eyes of many Portuguese, liberalism as practiced during the republican era came to be associated with anarchy in sharp contrast to the remarkable stability achieved by the *Estado Nova,* the authoritarian regime gradually built up by Dr. Salazar and his associates from the late 1920's. "It is the duty of the New State," declared one of the regime's supporters in 1938, "to re-establish the force of Power. With it will be revived all the power-concepts of the Past." "Empire and Liberty," the same writer pointed out, "were incompatible concepts. Empire means Authority and there is no Authority where Power is divided and diluted." [35]

There had been many expressions of imperialist sentiment under the monarchy and the republic, but Portuguese imperialism was transformed into a well-defined ideology by the Salazar regime at a time when other colonial powers were beginning to realize that their imperial responsibilities were a liability rather than an asset. Britain and France could survive as substantial powers without their empires. For Portugal the situation seemed quite different. "Africa," as one newspaper editor wrote in 1935, "is for us a moral justification and a *raison d'être* as a power. Without it we would be a small nation: with it we are a great country." [36] This deep sense of commitment to empire, this feeling that the country's very being depended on its continued existence as an imperial power, was buttressed by an appeal to the past, to faith, and to duty. Portuguese history was seen as an epic in which the men of the present should learn to play their part. "The Portuguese, like no other people, made their enterprises of exploration and conquest a transcendent campaign, a sharing of spiritual values." [37] So wrote one of the prophets of the new imperialism. From this "sharing of spiritual values," this diffusion of Portuguese culture, a new, a pan-Lusitanian community had come into existence. The concept of the "civilizing mission" was so defined as to fit in with this "transcendent" approach to empire. "Our whole policy has been and continues to be," explained a spokesman of the regime in 1939, "to improve the cultural, economic and social level of the Negro, to give him opportunities, to drag him from his ignorance and backwardness, to try to make of him a rational and honorable individual, worthy of the Lusitanian community." [38] Ideologies often have the same effect as strong liquor: they give a man courage and confidence but distort his perception of reality. Many critical outside observers have pointed to the seedy manifestations of colonial oppression behind the grandiose facade of Portuguese imperialism. But it would be entirely misleading to play down the importance of ideology. Without the inner backing provided by their elaborate structure of ideas, the Portuguese could hardly have survived as a colonial power.

In the first half of the twentieth century Angola and Mozambique witnessed three major developments: the emergence of a multi-racial society as a result of steady immigration from Portugal; the consolidation of Portuguese rule, and the beginnings of modern economic development. In 1900 Angola possessed a European population numbering just over 9,000; by 1940 there were 44,000 Europeans in Angola, by 1951, 88,000. The rapid increase in the 1940's was the product of official encouragement of immigration. But most of the new immigrants were poor whites with little to offer in the way of skills or capital. "Creaking old boats dump them on the beaches," an American journalist noted in the early 1950's. "Often they cannot find suitable work, but they are too proud to return to Portugal, inevitably they drift into native villages, take up with African women, live at a bare subsistence level and 'go native.' Africa absorbs the European, instead of vice versa." [39] In Mozambique, with its less salubrious climate, the current of immigration flowed less strongly: the colony's European population numbered 18,-000 in 1928, 52,000 in 1951. With its long tradition of contact with Goa the colony also attracted a few thousand Indian immigrants.

In both territories at least half the European population was concentrated in the main towns—Luanda in Angola, Lourenço Marques and Beira in Mozambique—whose growth represented the most spectacular manifestation of the Portuguese presence in Africa. In the 1890's Lourenço Marques was nothing but "a fever-stricken fortress," Beira "a few hovels sinking in the marsh." [40] Profiting from their function as ports, railway terminals, and tourist resorts, both places developed into well-planned and even elegant urban centers, while Luanda, its ancient graces preserved and embellished, acquired a population of 200,000 and came to be placed, after Lisbon and Oporto, as the third city in the Portuguese empire. In Angola substantial new towns—Nova Lisboa, Lobito, and Sá da Bandiera—were founded as administrative and commercial centers, while in Mozambique old settlements, such as Tete and Inhambane, experienced a renaissance.

In 1900 much of the interior of the two colonies was still unconquered. By 1950 the Portuguese had succeeded in building up "a formidable administrative service larger in proportion to the size of the territory and the number of its inhabitants than that of any other colonial power in Africa." [41] Portuguese administrators, ironically described in the early years of the century as "spending their time collecting taxes and African mistresses," [42] became more professional, more specialized, and rather less venal. Traditional chiefs and headmen were accepted as intermediaries between the administration and the mass of the African population; if they failed to perform their duties faithfully they were replaced by other Africans, often ex-soldiers or petty officials who had given ample proof of their loyalty to the colonial power. As in every other colonial territory, the nature of the Portuguese impact varied from district to district. In parts of northern Mozambique, for example, some groups rarely saw a Portuguese official until the arrival of the army to repress the revolt of the 1960's. Elsewhere official interference became a regular feature of local life.

Two aspects of the Portuguese system of government attracted the special attention of foreign observers—the policy of assimilation and the widespread use of forced labor. In the 1850's David Livingstone had spoken approvingly of "the liberality with which persons of colour were treated by the Portuguese." "Nowhere else in Africa," he declared, "is there so much good will between Europeans and natives as here." [43] Many other travelers made the same point. A century later, John Gunther, arriving in Lourenço Marques from Johannesburg, found himself feeling "an acute sense of social amelioration and relief on leaving behind the stubborn bigotry and intolerance of the Union." [44] The absence of a legal color-bar, the acceptance of mixed marriages, the existence of a distinct group, the *mestiços* of Afro-European ancestry enjoying the same privileges as Europeans, the provision which allowed Africans possessing the requisite qualifications—literacy in Portuguese, a reasonable income, "good conduct"—to become *assimilados* and so enjoy the full rights of citizenship; all these features of the Portuguese colonial system presented a refreshing contrast to the avid racialism of other colonial regimes in southern Africa. But the contrast should not be overstressed. The number of *assimilados* was very small: 4,500 in Mozambique and 30,000 in Angola in 1950. In the same year there were about 60,000 *mestiços* in the two colonies: their position might be compared to that of the "Coloured" group in South Africa, but they formed a very much smaller proportion of the total population. That so small a proportion of the African population should have achieved assimilated status was hardly surprising. Assimilation was dependent on education and educational facilities were extremely limited. As late as 1963 there were only 26,000 children attending primary schools in Mozambique of whom no more than one fifth were African. As for the assumed lack of racial prejudice, many observers over the last fifty years noted the appearance of a new strain of racial discrimination, a direct result of the gradual increase in the immigrant European population. As early as 1912 a high Portuguese official in Angola pointed to a "Germanic mentality" of racial superiority among Portuguese settlers.[45] As in other colonies of white settlement, new immigrants usually displayed a more intense streak of racial prejudice than old-fashioned European residents. But in spite of the rapid increase in immigration, the Portuguese colonies never gave birth to so rigid a racialist philosophy as that developed in other settler communities in southern Africa.

Of all the forms of discrimination practiced in Angola and Mozambique—most of which have their parallels in other colonial territories—none was so painful for the mass of the African population as the widespread use of forced labor. The practice of compelling the subject population to work was to be found to a limited extent in most European colonies, and indeed in many older African polities, but the peculiarity of the Portuguese system lay in the fact that forced labor became, in Basil Davidson's words, the "flywheel of the whole economy." [46] The system had its roots deep in the past. From the seventeenth century, Portuguese residents in Angola and Mozambique, like their contemporaries, the Dutch colonists at the Cape and the French planters of the Mascarenes, had grown accustomed to regard Africans as fit only to be slaves. In 1878, slavery was finally abolished in the Portuguese colonies, but the government in Lisbon, for all its undoubted liberal aspirations at the time, lacked the power to ensure that the letter of the law was strictly applied. The term "contract laborer" was substituted for that of "slave," but the reality of servitude remained. Recruiting agents bribed up-country chiefs to supply them with laborers, many of whom were marched down to the coast and shipped to the plantation-islands of São Tomé and Principe from which, for all the talk of a five-year contract, few men ever returned. In 1899 a new labor code was drawn up by a committee dominated by Antonio Enes, the leading imperialist of his day. "All natives of the Portuguese overseas provinces," the first article declared, "are subject to the obligation, moral and legal, of attempting to obtain through work the means that they lack to subsist and to better their social condition. They have full liberty to choose the method of fulfilling this obligation, but if they do not fulfill it public authority may force a fulfillment." [47] This devious piece of legislation provided the justification for many brutal practices.

The worst excesses of the system were curbed in the first decade of the twentieth century as a result of a campaign waged by English humanitarians and Portuguese liberals. Proper provision was made for returning workers from São Tomé at the end of their contracts. But in Angola forced labor continued to be used for work on the roads or in the plantations. An American journalist writing in 1948 provided a succinct account of the methods employed. "When an Angolan plantation owner requires labor, he notifies the government of his needs. The demand is passed down to the village chiefs, who are ordered to supply fixed quotas of laborers from their communities. If the required numbers are not forthcoming, police are sent to round them up." [48] To escape the demands made on them many Portuguese Africans moved into neighboring British or Belgian territory creating what one Portuguese official described as "an extremely grave state of depopulation" in parts of Angola. [49]

The Portuguese territories were reckoned to be among the poorest in Africa. The low density of population was at once a reflection and a major cause of their poverty: censuses taken in the 1960's showed that there were only 4.3 persons to the square kilometer in Angola and 9 in Mozambique compared with 11.3 in Rhodesia and 15 in South Africa.

Both colonies were capable of growing a considerable range of tropical crops, including coffee, cotton, sugar, and maize, but production remained on a modest scale. Six thousand tons of Angolan coffee were exported in 1910; twenty-five years later coffee exports had risen to no more than 10,000 tons. Mozambique appeared to have nothing to offer in the way of mineral resources, but Angola produced a modest quantity of diamonds. Nevertheless, neither colony could be described as entirely starved of capital investment. By 1935, £67 million had been invested in the Portuguese African colonies, compared with £102 million in the Rhodesias, and no more than £70 million in all the French territories in Africa. Much of this money had gone to construct the railroads needed to connect the mining area of Katanga, the Northern Rhodesian copper belt, and the major urban centers of Southern Rhodesia with ports in Portuguese territory. The Benguela Railroad, for example, was started in the 1900's and finally reached Katanga in 1931; built at a cost of £13 million, most of the capital was provided by British investors. The construction of the railroads and the improvement of the ports provided essential foundations for the unexpected leap forward in the economy of the two colonies that was to occur in the 1950's.

▼▲ BRITISH RULE IN CENTRAL AFRICA

There is a certain monotony in the description of colonial situations in early twentieth century Africa. Everywhere in the continent the European intruders faced certain common problems as they set about erecting the superstructure of their alien hegemony over a mass of hitherto independent polities. Yet there were also significant differences in the approach of the European colonizers. Thus the British never accepted the Roman concept of empire developed by the Portuguese, never saw their African territories as possessing some sort of organic unity with the metropolis. Nor were the British haunted by these memories of a great imperial past which obsessed the impoverished Portuguese. There were then, as the gradual development of colonial rule was to show, many points of contrast between the British and the Portuguese approach. But there were also notable differences between British rule in Central Africa and the policy followed by British administrators in other parts of the continent. For Central Africa witnessed the confluence of two distinct streams in the British imperial tradition. To some men of British stock, especially those with South African connections, Central Africa seemed fore-ordained to become an area of white settlement, a region naturally destined to develop into the last of the great Anglo-Saxon dominions. Others, more vividly aware of the presence and the needs of the indigenous population, saw the future in terms of trusteeship and interpreted the imperial mission in more altruistic terms. Already, before the end of the nineteenth century, two towering figures had come, in the eyes of their compatriots, to symbolize these two partly contradictory approaches: Cecil Rhodes was the most dynamic advocate of white settlement, while David Livingstone lived on as the apostle of trusteeship. Already, too, the Zambezi had come to be seen as a natural divide between the two distinctive spheres of British domination. To the south, wrote Harry Johnston in 1897, "where climatic considerations encourage true colonization, there undoubtedly the weakest must go to the wall and the black man must pay for the unprogressive turn his ancestors took some thousands of years ago." South of the Zambezi, Johnson considered, "the direct rule of Downing Street may cease." But to the north where "we merely impose our rule to secure a fair field and no favor for all races, and inferentially for our own trade, there the local government must depend directly on London." [50]

By the late 1960's the Zambezi did indeed appear to be firmly established as a frontier between Black Africa and the white-dominated south. But this line of political division across Central Africa was not naturally ordained. There was a time during the 1950's when the white thrust from the south seemed likely to lead to white domination north of the Zambezi; and throughout the colonial era the presence of a substantial body of white settlers created a political situation very much more confusing than that existing in other regions where Africans were never confronted with permanent white residents. In 1901 there were 11,000 Europeans in Southern Rhodesia. By 1931 the white population had risen to 50,000, of whom roughly a third were Rhodesian-born, another third had been born in South Africa, while a quarter of the population had come originally from Great Britain. The British character of the colony was firmly established, but about one fifth of the population spoke Afrikaans as their home language. The Britishness of Southern Rhodesia was consolidated by the flood of immigrants who entered the country immediately after World War II. Between 1941 and 1951, 73,000 newcomers settled in Southern Rhodesia, though about 20,000 left after a few years' residence. By 1951, the white population of Southern Rhodesia had risen to 136,000, 70 percent of whom resided in the country's main towns. Northern Rhodesia contained less than 4,000 whites in 1921. By 1946 the European population was 22,000, rising rapidly in the course of the next five years to 37,000. By 1951 more than three quarters of Northern Rhodesia's whites were resident in the copper belt. In Nyasaland, by contrast, there were no more than 4,000 Europeans in 1951, the white population having little more than doubled in the course of the past thirty years. In 1921 Nyasaland contained 400 European planters; ten years later the planter population had decreased by a quarter.

The number of Europeans in each territory had a direct bearing on local constitutional and administrative development. Southern Rhodesia followed a unique path. From the conquest of the country in the 1890's until 1923 the territory was administered by a commercial company, the British South Africa Company. The company developed an administrative cadre whose members were drawn mainly from the Cape, headed by an officer with gubernatorial powers bearing the title of "administrator." The Southern Rhodesian civil service presented certain striking contrasts when compared with the colonial service in other British territories. Europeans were employed in many subordinate posts which elsewhere in British Africa would have been filled by Africans, while most new recruits to the service came to be local Europeans, not expatriates. In the administration of Africans, most of whose polities had been completely shattered as a result of the Ndebele war of 1893 and the rebellion of 1896, the British South Africa Company followed the direct methods developed earlier in South Africa with chiefs deprived of most of their judicial powers and regarded as nothing more than government agents. But after the rebellion of 1896–97 the company was no longer allowed a completely free hand. The British government appointed a resident commissioner to serve as a "watchdog" by reporting on the company's legislation and administration to the British high commissioner at the Cape. The resident commissioner was particularly required to watch out for any legislation that discriminated against Africans. Thus, in 1903 the company was effectively prevented from raising the poll tax paid by Africans from £1 to £2.

Alongside the company with its natural preoccupation with profits —though, in fact, it was never able to pay a dividend to its shareholders during the whole period of its administration—and a metropolitan government with a strong humanitarian tradition must be set a third and increasingly important element in the country's emerging constitutional pattern, that formed by the growing number of white settlers with their practical interests in every aspect of their new country's development. Rhodesia's first legislative council was established in 1898: with a membership of five company nominees and four elected representatives, it was seen by Cecil Rhodes as "the first step in the direction of self-government." Rhodes possessed an intimate rapport with "his" Rhodesians. None of the other directors of the chartered company could emulate his charisma; to the pioneers of the veld these remote commerical magnates offered a standing target for criticism and invectice. Gradually the company began to retreat by offering greater political rights to the settlers, who gained a majority on the legislative council in 1907. Thirteen years later, a majority of the council passed a resolution in favor of "responsible government." Finally, in 1923, Rhodesian voters were asked to decide in a referendum between union with South Africa—a course favored by many of the company's officials and by local mine owners—and a responsible government under the British crown. Out of almost 15,000 voters just under 9,000 voted for responsible government: fear of coming under Afrikaner domination, practical economic arguments against the high tariffs imposed by the South African government, dislike of the punitive measures lately used by Smuts' government against white trade unionists on the Rand, and the natural distaste of an independent minded community to submit itself to the control of another government—such were the reasons advanced for opting to take on their own shoulders the responsibilities of government. Constitutionally, Southern Rhodesia was transformed into a self-governing colony with a governor appointed by the British government which also retained its right to disallow any legislation judged to discriminate against Africans. But effective political power was now clearly in the hands of the settlers.

The territory that now forms the modern state of Zambia was under the control of the British South Africa Company for almost thirty years. In 1911 the two original administrative divisions—North-Eastern and North-Western Rhodesia—were brought together to form a single unit, Northern Rhodesia. The company planned to carry the process of amalgamation to its logical conclusion by placing Northern and Southern Rhodesia under a single administration, but settler opinion in both territories was strongly opposed to this scheme; whites from north of the Zambezi feeling that their interests would be neglected by a government in Salisbury, while Europeans in Southern Rhodesia had no desire to saddle themselves with a "black north." With the breakdown of this scheme the company was glad to divest itself of administrative responsibilities and hand over Northern Rhodesia to the British government in 1924 to be administered as a protectorate of the crown. As for the local settlers who had lacked any form of representation under company rule, they were provided by the new colonial regime with a limited number of seats on the newly created legislative council. For the next twenty years settler politics in Northern Rhodesia revolved around the question of their relationship with the dominant white groups in the area—the London-appointed civil servants whose control of the executive the settlers wished to see reduced, and their compatriots south of the Zambezi whose semi-independent polity sometimes seemed to have much to offer the very much smaller group of whites north of the river.

The pattern was a familiar one in the nineteenth- and early twentieth-century politics of the white communities of Southern Africa: the "native question" seemed a matter of minor significance to the European farmers and miners of Northern Rhodesia in the years of confident white supremacy before World War II.

As for Nyasaland, the territory was regarded by many Europeans in the 1920's and 1930's as a model colony, a country untroubled by politics. The *bwanas,* the "great white chiefs" of the colonial administration, "ruled it," according to one of their European contemporaries "with a fairness, tolerance, and incorruptibility that was the envy of other dependencies"; "but," the same observer noted ironically, "long after 'outposts of empire' and 'the white man's burden' had become music-hall jokes . . . these Bourbons of modern times still believed their colonial world to be immutable," thinking that it "would continue to provide gentlemanly employment for generations of their kinsmen to come." [51]

The contrasts between the three territories so evident in the white population structure and in the differences in constitutional status, were even more deeply emphasized by their divergent patterns of economic development. The "white man's country" of Southern Rhodesia was the scene of a process of economic transformation more drastic than that occurring in any other part of tropical Africa before World War II. In the 1890's European enthusiasts had forecast that Mashonaland and Matabeleland would become a second Rand. Southern Rhodesia never lived up to these ultra-optimistic predictions, but gold mining, much of it carried on in small workings, did provide the country's main source of wealth until the 1940's. In 1938, Southern Rhodesian gold earned £5.8 million, about half the total value of the entire agricultural and mining production. European prospectors also found valuable deposits of coal, asbestos, and chrome. Coal was of immense value both for the railways and the mines, while asbestos overtook gold in the 1950's as the country's most valuable mineral product. Not until after World War II did tobacco become Southern Rhodesia's most important export: in 1938 the value of the crop was no more than £1.1 million.

In the first decades of the twentieth century, white farmers in Rhodesia directed their attention to the needs of the European population in the mines and in the towns. These needs might well have been supplied, at least in part, by African peasant producers, for the Shona had developed a highly effective agriculture, producing a remarkable variety of crops—"mealies, poko corn, kafir corn, millet, ground-nuts, beans (five sorts), egg fruit, cabbages, tomatoes, peas, pumpkins of sorts, watermelons, cucumbers, sweet potatoes, chillies, tobacco, bananas, and lemons, and all these," according to the account of an early European settler, "grown to perfection." [52] By ensuring that most of the land within easy reach of the railroads went to Europeans, the local administration gave white farmers a signal advantage—an advantage consolidated by the subsidies and other forms of official support which the farmers, with their great political influence, found it easy to secure. Thus most African farmers in Southern Rhodesia were locked in the straitjacket of a subsistence economy, discouraged from producing cash crops and from participating in the new market created by the influx of Europeans.

The most spectacular evidence of Southern Rhodesia's economic development was provided by the rapid construction of railroads. Between 1893 and 1898 the chartered company undertook the building of a line from Vryburg in the Cape though Bechuanaland to Bulawayo. At the same time, Beira in Mozambique was linked to Umtali, and by 1902 both the Beira and the Cape lines had reached Salisbury. A few years later branch lines were constructed to meet the needs of the mining industry. To the prosaic European mind all this was part of the normal process of development in a backward area. To Rhodesian Africans, on the other hand, a steam train first appeared as "a monster which spits fire and smoke and swallows people and spits them out alive." According to the testimony of one Rhodesian African, the Ndebele and the Shona, confronted for the first time with the white man and all his marvels, were "simply overwhelmed, overawed, puzzled, perplexed, mystified, and dazzled." [53] In terms of immediate material benefit the new order held out little to the country's African population. On the other hand, Rhodesian Africans, through their experience of work in the European areas, had greater opportunity to familiarize themselves with new techniques than their contemporaries in other parts of tropical Africa.

In the first decade of the twentieth century Southern Rhodesia developed an economy that appeared vigorously progressive when compared with its backward neighbor north of the Zambezi. Poor soil, large areas of tsetse-infested bush, and remoteness from potential markets presented almost insuperable obstacles to the development of Northern Rhodesian agriculture, though a few white settlers were able to earn a living by growing maize for sale in Katanga. In the early 1900's, deposits of copper, lead, and zinc were discovered and by the end of the decade a railroad had been built between the Victoria Falls and Katanga, but the prospects for future expansion were extremely poor. The oxidized ores found in the Northern Rhodesian copper belt had a much lower copper content than those being mined in neighboring Katanga and by 1918 the country's mineral exports were worth no more than £166,000. Two developments, one technological, the other commercial, brought a gradual transformation of Northern Rhodesia's prospects as a copper producer. Shortly before World War I scientists discovered how to extract copper from sulphide ores which had previously been regarded as valueless. After the war there was a rapid increase in demand for copper to meet the needs of the expanding automobile and electrical industries. In the search for new sources of supply attention turned to Northern Rhodesia where some of the early mines had been abandoned as unprofitable. Geological research soon revealed that the copper belt contained enormous quantities of sulphide ores, but, in contrast to the gold deposits of Southern Rhodesia which could be worked by small firms with modest resources, the Northern Rhodesian copper mines required capital on a scale that could be provided only by large companies. After prolonged negotiations two massive combines acquired control of the entire copper belt—the Rhodesian Anglo-American Corporation, which was closely linked to South African mining interests, and the Rhodesian Selection Trust, most of whose capital was raised in the United States. The results of these activities were vividly demonstrated in the spectacular rise in copper production. In 1931, 9,000 tons were produced worth £346,000; 1932 witnessed a sudden breakthrough with production rising to 68,000 tons worth just over £2 million; by 1940, Northern Rhodesia was producing more than 250,000 tons of copper at a value of £12½ million. Initially a large proportion of the profits went to the companies themselves, but slowly the government began to benefit from this extraordinary bonanza, its revenue rising from £371,000 in 1925 to £863,000 in 1936.

In 1936 Northern Rhodesia's exports—of which copper made up about 90 percent—were worth just over £6 million. By contrast Nyasaland's exports, which had slightly exceeded Northern Rhodesia's a decade earlier, brought in no more than £800,000. Nyasaland suffered from a lack of mineral resources; consequently European interests had concentrated on the development of cash crops. For a brief period in the 1890's, coffee, introduced to the country twenty years earlier by Scottish missionaries, was Nyasaland's main export, but in the 1900's European planters found it impossible to cope with Brazilian competition and turned to tobacco which rapidly developed into the country's main export, producing as much as 85 percent of all export earnings in 1932. Tobacco was supplemented by cotton and by tea, a crop which became increasingly important in the 1930's. In the early 1920's by far the greater part of the country's exports was produced on the estates of European planters, but many planters found it difficult to make ends meet and left the country. By the 1930's most of the tobacco and cotton exported by Nyasaland was grown by African farmers. In statistical terms Nyasaland was clearly the poorest of the three British Central African territories. Its transport system left much to be desired: an effective rail link with the port of Beira was not established until 1935, and communications with other parts of Central Africa were very poor. But Nyasaland was the only one of the three territories to produce a substantial class of peasant farmers with a cash income derived from their participation in the market economy.

Behind the varying patterns of economic development in the three territories lay something of supreme importance to both Europeans and Africans—the ownership of land. Here again the contrasts between the three territories had become very marked by the 1930's. In Nyasaland a good deal of land had been acquired by European planters in the 1880's and 1890's, most of it purchased at very cheap rates from local chiefs. By the 1920's as much as 15 percent of the total acreage of the protectorate had been alienated to Europeans. But colonial officials were well aware of the tensions provoked by European ownership and took steps to check European expansion and to reassure African opinion. In 1936 all non-alienated land was declared "native trust land." Gradually much of the alienated land was recovered, and by 1946 no more than 5 percent was still in European hands. But 200,000 Africans—10 percent of the total population—were still resident on European estates. These tenants had many grievances: "Why," they asked, "should we pay rent as well as tax when on Native Trust Land only tax is paid?"; "What is the justice," they shrewdly enquired, "of maintaining forever the sale fifty years ago for a few rolls of calico of vast areas now worth many thousands of pounds?" [54] Questions such as these served as a powerful stimulant to a spirit of militant anticolonialism. Moreover, the nagging fear persisted that one day Europeans might well attempt to secure more land. To appreciate the consequences of such a development Nyasalanders had only to reflect on what they had seen of Southern Rhodesia and South Africa.

In Southern Rhodesia the chartered British South Africa Company had rewarded the first pioneers with grants of 3,000-acre farms. (In many parts of Rhodesia a farm of this size could support no more than 150 head of cattle.) In the course of the 1890's, first in conquered Matabeleland, then in Mashonaland, the company set about demarcating reserves for Africans. At this time the African population was thought to number no more than half a million and there seemed enough land for blacks and whites alike. By 1915, native reserves covered an area of 24 million acres, while Europeans owned 21 million acres, leaving some 50 million acres still unallotted. Ten years later the settler government appointed a commission to make recommendations about the future of these undemarcated lands, recommendations which were largely embodied in the Land Apportionment Act of 1931. Segregation was the keynote of this "Magna Carta" of white Rhodesia. In the past Africans had been free to acquire land in most parts not specifically under European occupation. Under the act, Africans wishing to acquire land found themselves restricted to the 7 million acres defined as Native Purchase Areas. At the same time, Africans living as tenants on European farms were required to move and seek new land in the native areas, a provision which the government eventually found impossible to enforce. Rhodesian whites could claim to have treated Africans very much more generously than their fellow Europeans in South Africa had done. In the early 1930's it was reckoned that thirty-five acres had been set aside for every Rhodesian African compared with less than six acres for every African in the Union. There was a subtle difference, too, between Rhodesian and South African whites in their attitude toward segregation. "Few Rhodesians," Richard Gray has pointed out, "passionately believed, as did the Afrikaners of the Union, that segregation was the one hope for national survival. Most of them rejected the thorough-going doctrinaire approach." [55] Nevertheless, for all the flexibility of which white Rhodesians showed themselves capable, the fact remains that the distribution of land was fundamentally inequitable. Africans tended to be left with the lands of poorer soil remote from the railways, and they were specifically prevented from acquiring property in the expanding towns, all of which were defined as European areas. As the African population began to develop a steadily accelerating rate of increase, rising from three-quarters of a million to one million between 1911 and 1931, then doubling in the course of the next twenty years, pressure on land became more and more insistent, providing a natural focus for African discontent.

The land policies followed by the new administrations in British Central Africa had, then, a profound long-term effect on the African population. Hardly less important was the policy followed by the new governments with regard to African labor. From the start the British invaders of Central Africa required an ever increasing supply of African workers to make possible the development of mines, farms, or plantations and to undertake the construction of roads and railroads. In time the attractions of the white man's marvelous toys—his bicycles and sewing machines and phonographs—would serve to lure young men from their isolated villages, where cash was nonexistent, to places where wages were paid in money. But in the early decades of British rule harsher methods had to be employed to obtain the labor needed. It was not possible for the agents of the chartered company to use the direct forms of compulsion favored by the Portuguese. Had they done so, they would have brought down on their heads the cry of "forced labor" from vocal and influential groups of humanitarians in the distant metropolis. Instead, a less direct but no less effective form of coercion was employed: Africans were required to pay taxes in cash which most of them could obtain only by working for the whites. The impact of this policy on one African people, the Lozi of Barotseland, has been vividly described by a recent historian. "The hut tax hit them directly and powerfully. . . . They suddenly found themselves obliged to pay money they often did not have and for reasons they did not comprehend. Informants talked vividly of arrests, handcuffs, miserable prison food, ticks on the blankets, men often enchained, sometimes being forced to carry buckets of excreta on their heads. . . . To the mass of the Lozi the *bomas* [administrative headquarters] increasingly became symbols of fear and oppression at the hands of the white men." But there could be no doubt about the success of this approach. "Lozi began streaming south in tens of thousands, many on their own, many others recruited by the (Southern) Rhodesian Native Labour Bureau which the Administration had authorized to seek labourers in Barotseland 'for the purpose of benefiting the industries of (Southern) Rhodesia.' " [56] Eventually the new industries might benefit those who worked them. But in the first decades of colonial rule the advantages of the new order must have seemed highly questionable to many Africans.

▲▼ AFRICAN REACTIONS TO COLONIAL RULE IN BRITISH CENTRAL AFRICA BEFORE 1945

"We have governed the native and over-governed him. We have taken from him the power of self-determination and have hedged him in with a network of rules and permits, a monotonous, highly regulated and very drab existence. We save him from war and enslavement but do very little else for him. We have taken the interest and excitement out of life." [57] So, in 1919, wrote a perceptive British colonial judge serving in Northern Rhodesia. Twenty years later a social anthropologist, studying the Ngoni of Nyasaland, made much the same point. "Gone are the age-grades and regiments with their close comradeship and friendly rivalries. . . . The *Inqwala* [a first-fruits ceremony and a time of dancing and feasting] is finished, and the cultivating season has no longer any recognized interval for songs and rejoicing. The young people in the Ngoni Highlands do not dance *ingoma* in village after village after the harvest, as they still do in Northern Ngoniland and the present day dances are childish and lacking in spirit compared with the vigorous rhythm of the *ingoma.*" The same writer quoted the words of a Ngoni chief who lamented the decline in his people's agricultural practices. "Formerly there was no other work than taking care of their own affairs. They were thinking about war, and hoeing, and building their houses, and drinking beer and judging cases. When the Europeans came, they came with other work, adding to the work of the people, such as the tax and work to receive cloth. When they were busy with such things they forgot the cultivation of their ancestors." [58]

No doubt comments and laments such as these could be heard in many other parts of Africa at this time. But there were significant differences between Central Africa and other British colonial territories. In both East and West Africa the British had generally attempted to preserve indigenous institutions. The system of indirect rule was applied to Northern Rhodesia and Nyasaland in the 1930's but with no great success. The failure to resurrect the old polities was hardly surprising. Many of them had been completely shattered in the period of conquest. Those that survived lacked an economic base broad enough to support a flourishing local government structure. In the old days chiefs had grown rich through their monopoly over trade and their command of the labor services of their subjects. The meager stipend provided by government was no substitute for these vanishing perquisites, and many chiefs found themselves poorer than some of their commoners returning with cash and European goods acquired during their period of wage-labor in the urban centers of southern Africa. There were few African farmers in British Central Africa able to derive an income from cash crops comparable to that acquired by their contemporaries in parts of East and West Africa. Consequently the local taxes needed to support an effective system of indirect rule were not available. In 1946–47 there was not one "native authority" in Nyasaland with a revenue exceeding £10,000 and most had to make do with a mere £2000 or £3000; in Northern and Western Nigeria, by contrast, there were at this time a number of "native authorities" with revenues well in excess of £100,000. The one apparent exception to this rule of the decline of the indigenous polities was provided by Barotseland where the Lozi paramount and his advisers maintained the position of a privileged aristocracy and where the local treasury had a revenue of £35,000 in 1946. But Barotseland was, as its British administrators frequently remarked, a "living museum." "Beneath the impressive facade of a state in alliance with the British Crown lay the stark reality of a totally underdeveloped, almost poverty-stricken labour reserve." [59]

There was no aspect of colonial rule that affected the mass of the people of Central Africa so directly as the demand of their masters for taxes and labor. Labor migration was to be found in other parts of colonial Africa—Algerian workers going to France, Mossi from the Upper Volta making their way to the farms and plantations of the Gold Coast and the Ivory Coast, men from Bechuanaland, Basutoland and the reserves of South Africa finding temporary employment in the industrial areas of the Union—but nowhere did the volume of migration reach such massive proportions as in parts of British Central Africa. In the 1930's there were certain districts in Northern Rhodesia and Nyasaland where more than half the adult male population was away from home at any one time. The consequences of labor migration on such a scale were vividly described in a report published by the Nyasaland government in 1936. "As our investigation proceeded," wrote the members of the committee who produced the report, "we became more and more aware that this uncontrolled and growing emigration brought misery and poverty to hundreds and thousands of families and that the waste of life, happiness, health and wealth was colossal." If emigration was allowed to continue on its present scale, thought the investigators, "home life will cease to exist; all belief in the sanctity of marriage will disappear. Large tracts of land will be rendered unfit for habitation, and in consequence the economic life of the whole community will suffer seriously. . . . Resident chiefly in other lands, the Nyasaland-born Natives will have acquired a complete mistrust in and loathing for administration by white people which has made a wilderness and called it peace." [60]

Few contemporary opponents of imperialism could have produced so scathing an indictment of one aspect of colonial rule as the local Europeans—officials, settlers, and a missionary—who produced this report. But the consequences of labor migration were not entirely negative. The migrants were thrown brutally and roughly into strange and frightening urban environments. Those who survived and returned came back with minds enlarged by a wide range of new experiences. For Africans from Nyasaland and Northern Rhodesia migration also had a profound political significance. To work for a time in Southern Rhodesia or South Africa was to come face to face with the reality of white settler domination. Whatever grievances they might have about colonial rule in their own territories, it was clearly infinitely preferable to rule by white settlers. "We know Southern Rhodesia," clerks from Northern Rhodesia told a visiting commission in 1938, "and it is not good. They do not speak to you properly, just get hold of you and push you about and it is not pleasant." [61] But there was also a positive side to this reaction; the development, particularly strongly marked among educated Nyasa migrants, of a supra-tribal spirit of national unity which found expression in a passionate desire to preserve the distinctive character of their country.

There was another way, gentler than the exhausting experiences associated with labor migration, in which Central Africans could begin their initiation into the white man's world—a way provided by the new schools, the majority of which were run by Christian missions. There was no uniformity about the missionary approach to African development. Afrikaner missionaries of the Dutch Reformed Church—the Protestant denomination most actively engaged in mission work in British Central Africa—were naturally profoundly influenced by their South African background; dedicated in a paternalistic way to "improving" their charges, most of them found it impossible to accept notions of racial equality and so came to be regarded by a later generation of African nationalists as obstinate upholders of the colonial regime. Very different was the radical line adopted by many of the Scottish missionaries in Nyasaland. " 'Africa for the Africans' has to be our policy from the start," a group of Blantyre missionaries declared as early as 1895, "and we believe that God has given this country into our hands that we may train its people to develop its marvelous resources for themselves." [62] The Scottish missionaries made a remarkable contribution to educational development in Nyasaland. By the 1930's the country could claim one of the highest percentages of literacy of any territory in Africa and Nyasa men had acquired a reputation for energy and intelligence that enabled them to fill most of the best jobs open to Africans in other parts of Central Africa. But there was one serious limitation in the educational development of British Central Africa in the years before World War II. The three territories did not contain a single secondary school for Africans and those desiring higher education had to seek it in South Africa or overseas.

In their reactions to British rule the peoples of Central Africa displayed that spectrum of attitudes, ranging from whole-hearted collaboration through fatalistic acceptance to bitter hatred and resentment, so familiar to the student of conquest situations. For their white rulers, on the other hand, the first four decades of the twentieth century represented a remarkably peaceful period. Only one incident, the Nyasaland native rising of 1915, disturbed the colonial peace, and even this could be dismissed by contemporary observers as a very minor affair, for it affected only a limited area of the Shire Highlands, led to the deaths of no more than three Europeans and a small number of Africans, was suppressed within a few days, and provoked no major shift in British policy in the protectorate. But the personality of the leader of the rising, the Reverend John Chilembwe, gave to this relatively trivial affray a profoundly symbolic quality, investing it with the aura of legend. It is fortunate that the rising should have been studied in such detail and interpreted with such sympathy by two modern scholars, George Shepperson and Thomas Price, whose biography of Chilembwe, *Independent African,* is one of the classics of recent African historiography. Few incidents in the colonial period of African history are so illuminating as this strange, tragic revolt.

John Chilembwe, a Yao by birth, began his career as a cook-boy in the service of John Booth, an independent missionary of radical views who was inspired by a passionate belief in the need to develop Africa for the Africans. In 1897 Booth took Chilembwe to America where the young Yao convert was enrolled for a course of study at a Negro Baptist college in Virginia. Returning to Nyasaland, Chilembwe set up, with some American Negro support, his own mission, the Providence Interior Mission, at Mbombwe in the Shire Highlands. Chilembwe was not by nature a violent revolutionary. He retained close links with his Baptist supporters in the United States and set about trying to improve the lot of the converts, laying great stress on building an imposing church, encouraging the development of schools and cooperatives, and attempting to advance the position of women. His wife, he wrote in 1912, "is seeking to prevent early marriage among our girls, telling them that marriage has meant too little among our parents for generations, and telling them that it is not thus that happy homes are made and a strong race reared." [63] Chilembwe could not avoid coming into contact with the local whites, for his mission station lay next to one of the largest European estates in the country. At this time it was common form for Europeans to take a strong exception to "natives who got above their station." A native, one African informant recalled, "was often times beaten by a white man if he did not take his hat off his head some thousand yards away, even a mile away of a white man." [64] Treatment such as this was only one item in a long tally of African grievances.

From his own church members Chilembwe must have heard many stories of the brutal exploitation of African workers at the hands of their white masters. Gradually his regard and respect for Europeans came to be replaced by mounting resentment. But it required a sudden shock to provide the catalyst that could transmute frustrated resentment into active acceptance of the need for violent action. This shock Chilembwe experienced as a result of the outbreak of World War I, which was followed, in the autumn of 1914, by heavy fighting between British and German forces in northern Nyasaland. Deeply grieved that African blood should be shed in a conflict between two European powers he wrote a memorable letter to a local newspaper. He spoke of the loyalty

which the people of Nyasaland had always shown toward their government. "We understand that this is a war of free nations against a devilish system of imperial domination." Yet the people of Nyasaland
were "imposed upon more than any other nationality under the sun."
"Will there," he asked, "be any good prospects for the natives after the
end of the war? "Let the rich men, bankers, titled men, storekeepers,
farmers and landlords go to war and get shot. Instead the poor Africans
who have nothing to win in this present world . . . are invited to die
for a cause which is not theirs." [65] When this letter was suppressed by
the government censor, Chilembwe decided that only by the desperate
gesture of an armed revolt could he make his protest effective. In reaching this conclusion he appears to have been powerfully influenced by
the memory of the forlorn, heroic gesture of the American, John
Brown, a martyr in the antislavery cause. "You are to go and strike the
blow and then die," he told his small band of followers. "You must not
think that with that blow you are going to defeat white men and then
become Kings of your own country." All they could hope for was that
"the white man will then think, after we are dead, that the treatment
they are treating our people is almost bad, and they might change." [66]
The principal European victim of the revolt was the manager of the
nearby estate. His head was cut off and displayed in Chilembwe's
church, a grisly episode which served to confirm many local Europeans'
glib assumptions of African savagery. A fortnight later Chilembwe was
shot by African police while attempting to escape into Mozambique.

Chilembwe dead was destined to become the folk-hero of Nyasaland:
his soul, like that of his model, John Brown, "went marching on." But
to many of his African contemporaries his forlorn revolt must have
demonstrated the futility of violence. Fortunately violence was not the
only means open to Central Africans under British rule of expressing
sentiments of protest and dissent. British Central Africa contained a
number of institutions newly created by Africans and designed to serve
as the channel for expressing their grievances and their aspirations.
Among the Ndebele, Lobengula's eldest son, Nyamanda, led a movement whose objects were the restoration of the Ndebele monarchy and
the recovery of some of the alienated lands. With the aid of African
lawyers from South Africa, the Ndebele drew up a petition for presentation to King George V in 1919. Four years later Africans from the
Union also played a prominent part in founding the Rhodesian Bantu
Voters Association (RVBA). Southern Rhodesia had followed the example of the Cape in establishing a "color-blind" franchise, but the settler government imposed such stringent qualifications in regard to income, property, and education that no more than sixty-two Africans

achieved the vote before World War II. In the face of settler opposition neither the Ndebele home rule movement nor the RBVA were able to achieve any positive results. More effective as local pressure groups, if only because they operated in a more sympathetic environment, were the native associations of Nyasaland, the earliest of which was founded in 1912. Confining their membership to "persons of good knowledge and character," the native associations were designed to keep government informed of public opinion and to present local grievances in a coherent and respectful manner. Their members might be regarded as providing a self-appointed loyal opposition to the colonial regime.

Far more radical in character than the highly elitist native associations were some of the independent African churches, founded by dissidents breaking away from European missionary establishments. Of these new currents of religious sentiment by far the most alarming in the eyes of the colonial administration were those associated with the Watch Tower Movement. The millenarian doctrines of the Watch Tower Bible and Tract Society, later better known by the name of Jehovah's Witnesses, were introduced into Nyasaland from South Africa in 1908. Eliot Kamwana, the apostle of the movement, openly prophesied the end of British rule. "These people," he told his followers, pointing toward the local British government office, "you will see no more. . . . We shall make our own ships, make our own powder, make or import our own guns." [67] Inflammatory speeches of this nature soon led to his arrest and deportation. But the seed had been sown. Watch Tower churches were founded in many parts of Nyasaland, and the new doctrine was carried by Nyasa migrants to Northern and Southern Rhodesia. No doubt most of the Watch Tower preachers were incapable of formulating precise demands and of organizing a really effective mass movement. "They left their Party Programme to the Almighty," L. H. Gann has ironically remarked, "and when Jehovah failed to intervene much of their enthusiasm evaporated." [68] Nevertheless, the wide support enjoyed by the movement at certain periods was a clear symptom of a deep malaise in some African communities.

By the late 1920's a new social group was beginning to emerge in British Central Africa—that of the urban industrial workers. In 1930, the copper belt had an African population of 30,000; by 1936, there were 46,000 African residents in Salisbury and 30,000 in Bulawayo. In the view of officials both north and south of the Zambezi the African was still essentially a "tribesman" who might reside in an urban area for a few years but could eventually be expected to return to his tribal homeland. Inevitably, however, an increasing number of Africans began to take up permanent residence in the towns. Urban life brought with it closer association with Europeans than most Africans had ever experienced in the countryside and with it a vivid awareness of the harsh discipline of the color-bar. In the copper belt, native miners were supervised by European miners. "The European only points out to them," one African informant explained, "the places where they should drill holes. After doing this the European sits down and the natives drill the holes." [69] In 1935 the average wage for European workers at one of the largest mines in the copper belt was £506 a year, for African underground workers, £18.18 a year. And these disparities were made all the more irksome by the jeering brutality that many white miners displayed in their attitude toward Africans. In the copper belt, African resentment exploded in two violent strikes in 1935 and in 1940. In Southern Rhodesia, the Industrial and Commercial Union (ICU) opened branches in various towns in the late 1920's. The Union, founded by a remarkable Nyasalander, Clemens Kadalie, had already proved itself the most spectacular mass movement yet seen in black South African politics. In Rhodesia it was far less successful and rapidly declined after the arrest of its leaders in the early 1930's. But it could be regarded as the "forerunner of the urban mass party" and some of the statements made by ICU speakers at well-attended public meetings had a challenging and prophetic ring: "All the workers of the world are united and we must also unite our forces together and so achieve something and have freedom in Africa." [70]

▲▼ WHITE SETTLERS AND AFRICAN NATIONALISTS IN BRITISH CENTRAL AFRICA

In April 1948, Bulawayo, the second city of Southern Rhodesia, was paralyzed by a general strike of African workers. "From the location," wrote a local journalist, "there streamed hundreds of natives armed with knobberies, sticks, hatchets, lead piping, bicycle chains, etc., and they proceeded through the streets yelling, shrieking and beating up any natives who appeared to be going to work." [71] There was also some expression of hostility to Europeans. For most white Rhodesians it was the first time in their lives that they had ever heard such bitter words in the mouths of Africans. As one sensitive observer noted, the world they had known seemed suddenly to have "entered a new era." [72] It was indeed the first serious manifestation of African discontent since the rising in Matabeleland and Mashonaland more than half a century earlier. The Bulawayo riots might be seen as the prelude to fifteen years of mounting political excitement in every part of British Central Africa.

The dramatic political events of the postwar years took place against a background of accelerating change, change which made African communities more conscious than ever before of the powerful alien forces at work in their midst, change that forced many Europeans to become no less aware of the aspirations of the hitherto disregarded mass of Africans among whom they lived. One of the most striking manifestations of change was to be seen in the rapid increase in the European population. In 1946 there were 106,000 whites in British Central Africa—82,000 in Southern Rhodesia, 22,000 in Northern Rhodesia, and 2,400 in Nyasaland. By 1960 the total had risen to 308,000; 223,000 in Southern Rhodesia, 76,000 in Northern Rhodesia and 9,000 in Nyasaland. Less spectacular but of even greater significance in the long run was the steady increase in the African population, which rose from 5½ million in 1946 to 8 million fourteen years later. Caught up in the postwar boom, the three territories came to produce more wealth than ever before. In Southern Rhodesia the gross value of the output of European farms never exceeded £4 million in prewar years; in 1956 it passed the £40 million mark. In Northern Rhodesia copper production doubled in quantity between 1946 and 1956. Copper prices were subject to violent fluctuations: in 1956 Northern Rhodesian copper production was worth £121 million; the next year, in spite of a 10 percent increase in the tonnage produced, the total value was only £88 million. But even this lower figure represented a dramatic increase over the annual average of £10 million earned by Rhodesian copper in the war years. Another striking manifestation of economic growth was to be found in the development of secondary industry, especially in Southern Rhodesia, which could claim by the mid-1950's to be the most highly industrialized country in tropical Africa. As a result of these developments more and more Africans were drawn into the modern sector of the economy. In 1951 just under 600,000 Africans were employed in European concerns in the three territories, by 1956 this figure had risen to 1 million. Equally striking was the rapid expansion of African education. So dramatic was the sudden demand for schooling in parts of Southern Rhodesia that one historian had described it as a "second Shona uprising." [73] In 1936, 104,000 African children were attending school in Southern Rhodesia. By 1950 the number had risen to 224,000. Ten years later more than 75 percent of the children between the ages of five and fourteen were attending primary school, a ratio equaled at the time in only four other African territories.

This massive African awakening was reflected in the political field by the emergence of new institutions created to provide more effective channels for the expression of African grievances and aspirations. In Nyasaland a group of African clerks and teachers who had played an active part in the work of the native associations came together in 1944 to form the Nyasaland African Congress, a body which like its exact contemporary, the National Council for Nigeria and the Cameroons took the form of a federation of local associations rather than of a political party with individual members. A poem written by a local nationalist at this time gives some hint of the new spirit:

> Men of Nyasa, Unite! Unite!
> You have nothing to lose but your chains,
> Join up, Join up and Fight the Good Fight
> And Freedom shall be least of your gains.[74]

The Congress was a less revolutionary body than these words might suggest, confining its initial activities to such strictly constitutional forms of protest as the presentation of long memoranda to the government, requesting improvements in the educational structure and the establishment of direct African representation on the legislative council. In Northern Rhodesia a somewhat similar development took place with the formation of a Federation of African Societies of Northern Rhodesia in 1946, a body which transformed itself in 1948 into the Northern Rhodesian African National Congress. Southern Rhodesia already possessed an African National Congress, a body founded in 1934 which acquired a new lease on life after 1945. The two Rhodesias also witnessed an increase in organized African activity in the industrial field. In 1945 railway workers in Salisbury staged a highly successful strike which gained both a wage increase and official recognition of their union organization. "The railway strike has proved that Africans have been born," a Southern Rhodesian African politician declared. "The old African of tribalism and selfishness has died away. Africans realize as never before that united they stand and divided they fall." [75]

African aspirations provoked varying responses among the different European groups in Central Africa. Colonial officials were aware of the need to devise new institutions to give Africans in Northern Rhodesia and Nyasaland a greater sense of participation in the process of government. During the war provincial councils were established, followed in 1946 by the creation of African Representative Councils for both territories. But these new institutions allowed their members no more than an advisory role in the work of government and there was no guarantee that African advice would be accepted. Officials often showed a complete inability to understand the point of many African complaints. Thus, when members of a Northern Rhodesian provincial council objected to the use of the derogatory term "boy," a senior official remarked tersely, "Africans worry too much about these things." [76] Other Europeans in Northern Rhodesia were even less inclined to sympathize with African grievances. The white artisans and clerical workers of the copper belt occupied a highly insecure position, their future clearly threatened by the gradual process of African advancement. To the hard-living white mining community the colonial officials represented bureaucracy at its most aggravating—arrogant, pampered, and far too sentimental in its approach to Africans. The Northern Rhodesian settlers took as their leader a shrewd and rumbustious trade union official, Roy Welensky, the son of a Lithuanian Jewish father and an Afrikaner mother, a one-time prize fighter and engine driver. "We detest the colonial office government," Welensky exclaimed in 1948,[77] as he set about devising means of freeing his territory from the control of Whitehall.

There was no uniformity of view among the white settlers of Southern Rhodesia as to the policy to be followed in dealing with their African majority. Some Rhodesians, strongly influenced by their South African background, favored total segregation with Africans confined to a position of permanent inferiority. A small group of liberals looked forward to the emergence of a fully integrated community. The vast majority of Rhodesians were glad to follow the lead of Godfrey Huggins (later Lord Malvern), an English-born doctor who dominated Southern Rhodesian politics from the 1930's to the 1950's. Huggins believed that the European community served as "a leaven of civilization"; remove this leaven and "the black man would inevitably revert to a barbarism worse than ever before." [78] Before the war Huggins spoke of "gradual, differential development," of the need to construct two separate social pyramids. In his own areas the African "must be allowed to rise to any position of which he was capable of climbing, but supreme power must always remain in white hands." [79] Huggins was no doctrinaire: in 1941 he was prepared to admit the possibility of "the two parallel lines in our parallel development policy coming together in some very distant future," and he showed by practical action taken to provide permanent residential accommodation for Africans in urban areas that he was no longer prepared to accept the narrowly segregationalist view—widely held in South Africa—that the African must always be regarded as a temporary sojourner in the white man's towns.[80]

African grievances and aspirations, European hopes and fears were brought dramatically together in the great debate over federation that dominated the history of British Central Africa from the late 1940's to the early 1960's. The idea of some sort of closer union between the three territories was not a new one. Indeed, it could be dated back to the first years of chartered company rule in the 1890's. In the 1920's the Southern Rhodesian settlers had turned against the idea of amalgamation with Northern Rhodesia, not wishing to saddle themselves with a poverty-stricken territory possessing only a few thousand European residents. But the emergence of the copper belt set amalgamation in an entirely new perspective. Northern Rhodesia, with its rapidly expanding revenues and its growing white population, began to appear a much more desirable partner. At the same time, settlers in Northern Rhodesia came to see that the only way of throwing off the galling yoke of the colonial office was through a merger with the virtually independent colony south of the Zambezi. In 1938 the British government set up a royal commission under Lord Bledisloe to examine the question of closer union. The commission took evidence from Africans as well as Europeans and was made vividly aware of the strength of African opposition to any plan to amalgamate the three territories. In its report the commission recommended the immediate amalgamation of Northern Rhodesia and Nyasaland—a step which might well have been implemented but for the outbreak of World War II; it also favored the creation of an inter-territorial advisory council, but it regarded as impractical the settlers' demands for total amalgamation.

The Central African Council set up by the British government in 1944 to coordinate a wide range of technical services fell far short of what the settlers wanted. Four years later Huggins and Welensky took the initiative by convening a conference of settler politicians at the Victoria Falls to draw up proposals for closer union. Aware of the need to consider African sentiments and to gain the support of the British government, the settlers dropped the idea of amalgamation and replaced it by the new concept of federation; under a federal constitution, they pointed out, each of the three territories would be able to retain control of African administration and so preserve its distinctive character. No colonial office officials or African representatives were invited to attend the conference, and the settlers' proposals were rejected both in Whitehall and by the vast majority of African spokesmen. Hastings Banda, a Nyasa doctor long resident in Britain, presented a memorandum to the colonial office in which he asserted that the whites of Southern Rhodesia "look upon Africans as inferior beings with no right to a dignified and refined existence." [81] In Northern Rhodesia rumors began to circulate that the Europeans were after African land: "Without land," African peasants were reported as saying, "we shall be like wild pigs driven from place to place." [82]

Despite this initial rebuff, the tide of events began to flow strongly in the settlers' favor. In 1948 the Nationalist Party had swept unexpectedly to power in South Africa. Militant Afrikanerdom, with its long tradition of anti-British sentiment and its dogmatic belief in racial inequality, now began to appear as a serious threat to British interests in southern Africa. Equally objectionable to many Englishmen was the fierce black nationalism emerging in West Africa. In such a situation the creation of a great new Central African dominion dedicated to partnership between the races took on the guise of a worthy and idealistic enterprise to certain sections of liberal English opinion. Clearly, too, powerful economic arguments—the advantage of a wider market, the opportunity for large-scale planning—could be advanced in favor of federation. Particularly important at this stage was the enthusiasm with which a group of senior officials in the colonial office responded to the concept of federation. As a result of their influence, a committee of theoretically impartial British and Central African civil servants was appointed in March 1951 to examine in more detail the possibilities of closer association. The committee produced an elaborate set of proposals for a federal constitution: "Implicitly the officials thought that legal draughtsmanship and cleverly designed constitutional formulas could effectively limit the exercise of power by white settlers." [83] Had the Labour government remained in office it is possible that, on second thoughts, the colonial office might have dropped the idea of federation, for many Labour M.P.'s were acutely conscious of the mounting tide of African opposition. But in October 1951 the Conservatives came to power and immediately proclaimed their unequivocal support for the new venture. By 1953 agreement had been reached and a federal government was finally inaugurated.

During these years of discussion African opposition continued unabated. Faced with the threat of white domination, African political leaders began to think in terms of eventual independence. "The best government for the black people," Harry Nkumbula, president of the Northern Rhodesian Africa National Congress declared in 1952, "is a government fully manned and run by black people." [84] The experience of the first years of federation served only to confirm their worst fears. The federal capital was established at Salisbury; Southern Rhodesian officials came to dominate the federal public service; revenue raised in Northern Rhodesia was used to finance projects south of the Zambezi; even the federation's most spectacular project, the Kariba hydroelectric scheme, benefited Southern Rhodesia far more than the other two territories. As for partnership, how could Africans regard it as anything more than a sham when white politicians consistently talked of Europeans remaining the senior partners for the foreseeable future, when little or nothing was done to remove the color-bar and other forms of racial discrimination, when the safeguards written into the constitution to preserve African interests were gradually eroded, apparently with the tacit consent of the British government? This was the view of the situation held by African political leaders in Nyasaland and Northern Rhodesia. But to Africans in Southern Rhodesia partnership was not entirely a sham. The mid-1950's brought some welcome concessions: more money spent on African education, African representation in the federal parliament, unprecedented opportunities for intercourse with liberal-minded Europeans in the newly founded interracial associations. For some members of the African elite this was "the golden age of participation." [85]

The mid-1950's saw the emergence of a new generation of African nationalists—young men anxious to follow Nkrumahist tactics, to transform elitist organizations into mass parties, and to substitute "positive action" for petition and participation. In Nyasaland two graduates in their late twenties, H. B. M. Chipembere and Kanyama Chiume, came to the fore, greatly improved the organization of the old Congress party, and lost no opportunity of attacking both the federal and the protectorate governments when they had secured a platform for themselves through election to the Nyasaland legislative council. At the same time the Congress leaders maintained close contact with the most distinguished of Nyasalanders, Dr. Hastings Kamuzu Banda. Banda had been away from his homeland for more than forty years. Born in 1902, he had made his way as a boy in his teens to South Africa and eventually saved enough money to pay for a passage to the United States. After ten years of study at American universities, he graduated as a doctor of medicine in 1937, moved to England, and earned his living as a general practitioner. But he never lost touch with his homeland, acted as a spokesman for Nyasaland Africans in the early debates over federation, and left England to settle in the Gold Coast in 1953 as a gesture of disapproval over the establishment of the federal constitution. In 1957 the Young Turks of the Nyasaland Congress urged Banda to return to his homeland. Deliberately they sought to build him up as a "political messiah." [86] Their plan succeeded brilliantly—too well indeed, as later events were to prove, for their own comfort. In July 1958 Banda returned to Nyasaland. Within a few weeks he was appointed president-general of the Congress, on terms which allowed him to exercise complete control over all party offices. Banda was by nature a deeply conservative politician; he was anxious to secure his ends by negotiation. But he left the audiences who flocked to hear him in no doubt of his hatred of federation. Rapidly popular excitement was translated into expressions of hostility toward Europeans. "I have the whole of Blantyre and Zomba on fire," Banda wrote in October. "Very soon I hope to have the whole of Nyasaland on fire." [87] In January 1959 he was able to demonstrate the close ties between local nationalism and the revolutionary movement now sweeping the entire continent by attending the All-African Peoples' Conference at Accra. "To Hell with Federation," he declared on his return. "Let us fill their prisons with our thousands, singing Hallelujah." [88] But the British government, still firmly committed to the cause of federation, refused to be stampeded by such emotional outbursts. In March 1959, faced with a threat of widespread rioting, the protectorate government declared a state of emergency and arrested Dr. Banda and thirteen hundred Congress supporters.

In the development of African political activities during the first years of federation there were obvious parallels between Northern Rhodesia and Nyasaland. The victory of the federationists left members of the Northern Rhodesian African National Congress exhausted and dispirited, but popular resentment found expression in what has been described as a "perpetual cold war in the bush," [89] with hard-core Congress supporters stirring up discontent over specific local grievances, and district commissioners retaliating by deposing chiefs suspected of nationalist sympathies. For urban Africans the continuation of the color-bar—most movie theaters, hotels, restaurants, and even some churches were still closed to black men—remained a standing affront, provoking a series of boycotts and demonstrations which helped to keep the nationalist cause before the public. About 1956 a group of young militants began to make their influence felt, prominent among them a fiery Bemba schoolteacher, Simon Kapwepwe, recently returned from four years of study in India. Before long it became evident that the nationalist cause needed new leadership: Harry Nkumbula, the Congress president and the territory's most prominent African politician since the late 1940's, was criticized as being too moderate in his tactics, too ready to fraternize with European politicians, too obviously attracted by the hedonistic lure of "bright lights and fast living." In 1958 the militants broke away and formed their own party, the Zambian African National Congress. (Zambia, a shortening of Zambezia, was a term coined by Kapwepwe, as a nationalist substitute for Northern Rhodesia.) The militants elected as their leader another ex-schoolteacher, Kenneth Kaunda, a close friend of Kapwepwe and long a loyal supporter of Nkumbula. Born in 1923, Kaunda was the son of a Nyasa clergyman who had worked for many years on a mission station in Bemba country. Unlike most contemporary nationalist leaders, Kaunda had never had the experience of an overseas education; he had risen to prominence through his energy and ability as a political organizer at the grass roots level, touring villages on a bicycle, playing a guitar to attract an audience and singing political songs of his own composition. A devout Christian, at once gay and ascetic in manner, Kaunda was to emerge as one of the outstanding Africans of his generation.

In 1959 the British government provided Northern Rhodesia with a highly complicated new constitution, which increased African representation but still left the settlers as the dominant group in the legislative council. Nkumbula was prepared to accept the constitution, but the militants of the Zambian Congress decided to boycott the forthcoming elections. Kaunda himself was determined to employ non-violent tactics, but by March 1959 the colonial government, deeply alarmed by the course of events in neighboring Nyasaland, had come to believe that the Zambian Congress was a dangerously disruptive organization, comparable, in Governor Benson's highly colored analogy, to the famous "Murder Incorporated" run by Chicago gangsters. Ten days after the arrest of Banda and his supporters in Nyasaland, the Northern Rhodesian government rounded up all the leading Zambian Congress officials and exiled them to remote rural *bomas*.

In Southern Rhodesia African opinion had never been greatly concerned about the issue of federation. Of far more immediate significance were the grievances aroused by a piece of legislation passed by the Southern Rhodesian legislature in 1951, the Natives Land Husbandry Act. To the government the act represented a sincere attempt to bring about a much-needed agrarian revolution in the increasingly densely populated native reserves; a revolution roughly comparable to the enclosure movement in eighteenth century Britain, involving as it did the division of land previously held under communal tenure into individual freehold plots. Many urban Africans still retained a stake in the reserves and saw in their right to communal land a form of insurance policy on which they could fall back when faced with urban unemployment or retirement. These rights were now threatened by the new act. At the same time many rural Africans strongly objected to a series of measures introduced from above and designed to transform the entire pattern of their lives. Here then was an issue ideally suited to bring together town and countryside in a movement of protest.

In 1955 a group of educated young men came together in Salisbury to found the City Youth League. Profoundly influenced by the success of West African nationalism and increasingly critical of the behavior of the participant elite, those "stooges," as Dr. Banda once described them, who "for tea and whisky in white men's houses have betrayed their country," [90] this new generation of radicals introduced a new note of militancy into African politics in Southern Rhodesia. Two years later Youth League members revived the old-established Southern Rhodesian

African National Congress and accepted Joshua Nkomo, the country's most respected trade unionist as their president. Soon Congress activists—landless young men from urban locations—were returning to their home areas to preach the more vigorous doctrine to a peasant audience. "The long smouldering rural resentments were at last brought into modern politics." [91]

To check the mounting tide of rural discontent the Southern Rhodesian government decided to employ draconian measures. In February 1959 a state of emergency was declared, Congress was proscribed and its leaders arrested, while the government rushed through a series of bills giving it the power to detain people without trial for unlimited periods. Thus, by the end of March, the nationalist movement in all three territories had suffered what seemed a crushing reverse. Confidently, Roy Welensky, who had succeeded Godfrey Huggins as federal prime minister in 1955, predicted that 1960 would see the granting of full independence to the Federation. But in fact by forcing the colonial governments to put them in prison, the nationalist leaders in Nyasaland and Northern Rhodesia had won a decisive victory. "The British will always pat stooges at [sic] their backs," Kaunda told his supporters in a letter written in the first weeks of detention, "but at the bottom of their hearts it is the rough guys they have both respect and consideration for. They will put them in jail, they will rusticate them but all these are tests to see if they are ready to rule because to govern is no small job and needs to be handed over to people who can stand the ups and downs of life." [92] There is a good deal of shrewd psychological insight in this remark, even if the situation was not viewed by British cabinet ministers in quite such generous terms. For the British now found themselves faced with a familiar dilemma: they had temporarily removed the nationalist leaders from the political arena but they were not prepared to employ the coercive measures needed to crush a widespread nationalist movement. Thus they did nothing to prevent the formation of two new political organizations—the Malawi Congress Party in Nyasaland, the United National Independent Party in Northern Rhodesia—designed to replace the proscribed parties and to serve as caretakers for the nationalist cause while Banda, Kaunda, and their associates remained in prison. In 1960 the British released the detainees and gradually began to devise the constitutional machinery needed to set both territories on the path to independence. In Nyasaland the process was relatively straightforward. In Northern Rhodesia the white settlers fought hard to maintain their privileged position, leading the Colonial Office to devise a constitution of extraordinary complexity in an attempt to blunt the shock of majority rule. But the outcome was the same in both territo-

ries. Nyasaland achieved independence in July 1964, Northern Rhodesia four months later. The names adopted by the new states—Malawi
(derived from an old term applied to many of the peoples of the Lake
Nyasa area) and Zambia—symbolized their essentially African character. The Federation, which in the mid-1950's had seemed to its supporters so durable a structure, was finally dissolved on the last day of 1963
and "partnership" disappeared from the vocabulary of Central African
politics.

Very different was the course of events south of the Zambezi. Here
African nationalists found themselves in conflict not merely with a minority group of a quarter million whites but with a nationalist sentiment as powerful as their own. Moreover, unlike their compatriots in
the northern territories, the Europeans of Southern Rhodesia retained
under their own control the coercive forces of a modern state. Many
white Rhodesians were recent emigrants from Britain, but whatever political views they may have held in the land of their birth, most of them
found no difficulty in assuming the characteristic attitudes and adopting
the distinctive mores of the society of their adoption. "Rhodesia," L. H.
Gann and Peter Duignan have pointed out, "is the only African settler
country outside South Africa to have produced an accent of its own, a
phonetic amalgam compounded of Afrikaans, Scottish, and Cockney
elements." [93] A distinctive accent was but one manifestation of the
emergence of a clearly defined subculture which could provide the
foundations for an intensely nationalistic spirit. In this relatively small
white community there were many factors that served to produce a high
degree of social cohesion—not least among them the "common feeling
of having to stand together against the blacks." [94] Nevertheless, there
had never been complete concensus in the field of white politics. From
1923 onward, the white electorate had been divided between a government and an opposition party. The parties changed their names from
time to time, but their essential character seemed permanently settled.
From the start the government party drew its support from the local
establishment—business and professional men and large farmers together with the more highly skilled artisans, while the opposition rallied
Afrikaner farmers and the lower paid white workers. Given such a
composition it was not surprising that the "one permanent characteristic" of the opposition should be, as Colin Leys has pointed out, its "appeal to the racial fear of the European population." [95] Until 1958 the
position of the establishment seemed unchallengeable, but the growth of
African nationalism produced a steadily accelerating swing to the right.
In 1958 Garfield Todd, who had succeeded Huggins as premier of
Southern Rhodesia, was forced to resign; his pronouncements on gov-

ernment policy appeared dangerously liberal to his cabinet colleagues. After a general election held a few months later the government party (the United Federal Party) found its position seriously shaken. In the 1954 election it had won twenty-six out of the thirty seats; now it held only seventeen to the opposition's thirteen. Four years later, under a new constitution which increased the number of seats to sixty-five, fifteen of which were reserved for Africans, the ruling United Federal Party was defeated by a newly formed opposition party, the Rhodesian Front. In the history of Southern Rhodesia the election of 1962 has a significance comparable to that of 1948 election in South Africa. Since 1958, the United Federal Party, under the leadership of Sir Edgar Whitehead, had followed a policy designed to combine "social justice with national discipline." [96] Whitehead had been responsible for banning the African National Congress in 1959 and its successor, the Zimbabwe African People's Union (ZAPU) in 1962. On the other hand, his government had introduced many measures designed to remove the cruder forms of discrimination, while the new constitution provided Africans with their first real opportunity to participate in national politics. But to many Europeans, deeply alarmed by the course of events in the Congo and other parts of Africa, Whitehead's policy seemed dangerously "soft" in its insistence on the need to reform, while African nationalist leaders, intent on achieving majority rule, regarded it as hypocritical and instructed their followers to boycott the election. Had Nkomo and other ZAPU members taken a more moderate and flexible line, they might well have helped the UFP to ward off the attack from the right and eventually have secured a foothold in the government. As it was, the African nationalists found themselves condemned to a position of total impotence. In 1963 many of the more educated members of ZAPU, aggravated by the ineffectiveness of Nkomo's leadership, broke away to form the Zimbabwe African National Union (ZANU), but they underestimated the strength of Nkomo's hold on the masses. Denied any opportunity of constructive political activity, supporters of the rival parties turned to attacking each other, and for months the township locations were the scene of savage gang warfare between ZAPU and ZANU activists until the government stepped in and finally banned the two parties.

With the collapse of the Federation, it was natural that the Rhodesian Front government should start putting pressure on the British to grant the colony independence. When Winston Field, the first leader of the Front, failed to gain this objective he was replaced by Ian Smith. Smith was described as "a dedicated man, sincere in his dedication, but fixed, narrow and simple in his beliefs and ideals": narrowness and inflexibility might be regarded as a source of weakness in an international context but, as James Barber has pointed out, these characteristics were "strengths within the confined world of white Rhodesia." [97] Under Smith's highly successful brand of leadership the Rhodesian Front strengthened its hold on the European community. In the election of 1965 the Front made a clean sweep of all fifty European seats. Emotions ran high: white Rhodesians were encouraged by their government to see themselves as standing heroically in the vanguard of a struggle between "civilization" and "barbarism." In circumstances such as these, there could really be no hope of a successful outcome to the negotiations with the British government. For the British would grant legal sovereignty only to a government which was clearly representative of the people of Rhodesia as a whole. All the steps taken by the Rhodesian Front to demonstrate that its government was indeed truly representative—the holding of a referendum, the convening of an *indaba* or grand meeting of African chiefs—appeared to the British as false and deceitful measures. But the Rhodesian Front had committed itself to securing independence. Whatever hesitations individual members of the government might have felt about daring to defy the remote metropolitan overlord, within the party itself there had developed a head of steam so powerful that it would have swept away any leader thought guilty of pusillanimity. So events moved toward their inexorable conclusion. On November 11, 1965, the Rhodesian government presented the world with an "unilateral declaration of independence." Power had triumphed—at least for the time being—over legality.

▲▼ WHITE SETTLERS AND AFRICAN NATIONALISTS IN ANGOLA AND MOZAMBIQUE

Throughout the 1950's Angola and Mozambique seemed to lie outside the main stream of African development. Only very rarely were the two Portuguese territories mentioned in the international press. Their economics appeared to be little affected by the postwar boom that enriched so many African colonies. And their subject populations seemed totally unaware of the new ideas so eagerly imbibed by Africans elsewhere in the continent. These superficial impressions were in fact misleading. Certainly the pace of change was slower in the Portuguese territories than in other parts of Africa, as it was indeed in Portugal itself when that country, with its archaic economy, was compared with other European nations. But by the 1960's it had become abundantly clear that the overall pattern of recent history in Angola and Mozambique was not in its essentials so very different from that of other African territories.

In the course of the 1940's and 1950's the African population of the

Portuguese colonies became more conscious than ever before of the presence of Europeans in their midst. In 1940 there were 44,000 Europeans in Angola and 27,000 in Mozambique. By the mid-1960's Angola contained about 250,000 whites and Mozambique 130,000. Many of the new immigrants came as agricultural settlers on government-sponsored schemes. (There was talk in the late 1960's of settling as many as one million Portuguese peasants and their families in the irrigated area to be created as part of the ambitious Zambezi Valley Development Scheme.) In Angola many settlers started small-scale coffee plantations, and the colony's coffee production rose from 18,000 tons in 1942 to more than 200,000 tons in the 1960's. About three-quarters of Angola's coffee crop was produced on European-owned land. The coffee boom brought wealth to many Europeans, but for the Kongo people in the coffee-growing areas of northern Angola the new development had less welcome consequences—an increase in the incidence of forced labor and a loss of fertile farmland to European planters. No less detrimental to African interests was the influx of poor white migrants to the towns for the newcomers took over many semi-skilled jobs such as taxi-driving which would otherwise have been filled by Africans, while their deep-rooted sense of insecurity made them acutely resentful of any plans for African advancement.

The Portuguese imposed more restrictions on the intellectual development of their native populations than any other power. From the 1920's on the colonial press was subject to a strict censorship. The security police were quick to deal with any signs of political unrest. Educational facilities were among the most backward in colonial Africa: one estimate made in 1959 showed that while the Northern Rhodesian government was spending approximately four dollars per capita on education, the figure for expenditure by the Portuguese government in Angola was about six cents.[98] Nevertheless, there were a number of ways in which Portuguese Africans could make contact with new currents of thought. A small, highly privileged group received their higher education in Portugal. A larger number of Africans attended the schools run by Protestant missionaries. (In official Portuguese eyes these Anglo-Saxon heretics with their talk of self-determination and their reluctance "to educate the native for the Portuguese concept of integration," represented a distinctly subversive element in the colonial community.) Finally many Portuguese Africans made their way as migrants into neighboring territories—from Angola to the Belgian Congo and Northern Rhodesia, from Mozambique to Tanganyika, Southern Rhodesia, and South Africa—and so learned something of the revolutionary new ideas that were beginning to sweep the continent.

Agostinho Neto and Holden Roberto were the two most prominent figures to emerge in the Angolan nationalist movement of the 1950's and 1960's. A brief account of their early careers illustrates clearly the impact of external influences in the growth of African nationalism in the Portuguese territories. Neto was born in 1922, the son of a highly respected Methodist pastor of Mbundu origin. (The Mbundu are the dominant ethnic group in Central Angola and the Luanda hinterland.) One of the very few Africans to complete a secondary education in Angola, Neto spent some years after leaving school as secretary to an American missionary bishop before being awarded a scholarship to study medicine in Portugal. In Lisbon he came into close contact with radical student organizations and was introduced to the intellectual world of European Marxism. His studies were interrupted twice by spells in prison. Not until 1959, after a twelve-year absence from his homeland, was he able to return to Angola, as a qualified doctor, with a growing reputation as a poet. In Luanda he came to be associated with a revolutionary movement, the MPLA (Popular Movement for the Liberation of Angola), which gained most of its support from the young *assimilado* intellectuals. In 1960 Neto was arrested by the Portuguese security police and taken to prison in Portugal. But he escaped in 1962 and became leader of the MPLA in exile.

Holden Roberto was an almost exact contemporary of Neto, but his career lay along very different paths. Born in 1923 on a Baptist mission station at São Salvador, the capital of the ancient Kongo kingdom, he spent most of his early life in Léopoldville and worked for eight years as a clerk in the Belgian administration. In the early 1950's he became involved in the political movement developing among the Kongo people on both sides of the Congo-Angola border. In 1958 he was sent as an emissary of the most prominent Kongolese organization, the UPNA (Union of Peoples of the North of Angola) to the All-African Peoples' Conference at Accra. Here he met most of the leading African nationalists of the day, changed the name of his party to UPA (Union of the Peoples of Angola) in response to criticism that excessive stress on the interests of the Kongo people was an anachronistic form of tribalism, and became a close friend of Frantz Fanon, the philosopher of the Algerian revolution and an impassioned advocate of the necessity of violence in a revolutionary struggle. In the course of 1959 Roberto served for a time on the Guinean delegation to the United Nations and took the opportunity of establishing a wide range of American contacts during his stay in New York. In mid-1960 he returned to Léopoldville, now the capital of the independent Congo Republic, and set about planning to translate Fanon's ideas into action.

The large size of the two Portuguese territories combined with strict censorship and rigorous surveillance by the security police made it impossible for any nationalist leader in Angola and Mozambique to create a truly effective mass movement, as Banda and Kaunda were doing in other parts of Central Africa. Instead, Neto and Roberto emerged as the champions of particular localities, Neto of the Mbundu of the Luanda area, Roberto of certain sections of the Kongo people. But there were many other isolated groups of protesters. In the cotton-growing district of Malange in eastern Angola an African chauffeur, Antonio Mariano, emerged as the leader of a movement known as "Maria" and traveled the district preaching a "sort of nationalist evangelism complete with incense, 'Maria water' and praise for Lumumba." [99] In the southern Angolan town of Sá da Bandiera a mulatto pharmacist, Eduardo Pereira, was the leader of a group which submitted an unsigned memorandum to the Portuguese authorities demanding political reforms; in time the security police learned the names of the members of the group, arrested them, and rusticated them to a remote area on the borders of Katanga. Similar forms of proto-nationalist activity could be detected in Mozambique: the revolutionary poems written by urban intellectuals, the associations formed by ex-secondary school students, the cooperatives founded by peasants on their own initiative to improve their economic lot. All these movements pointed to a growing restlessness, an increasingly vocal spirit of dissatisfaction with Portuguese rule.

But the explosion when it came was sudden, savage, and largely unexpected. Early in 1961 Angola became the scene of one of the bloodiest incidents in the history of African nationalism. Violence broke out first in Malange where the local peasantry, already excited by the preaching of the prophet Mariano, deeply resented being forced to cultivate cotton and to sell their produce at the low prices fixed by a monopolistic concessionary company. Like the participants in another famous revolt, also partly provoked by compulsory cotton-growing, the *Maji-Maji* rebellion in Tanganyika, Mariano's supporters believed that they were invulnerable to bullets. But the movement failed to spread; the Portuguese brought in planes to strafe rebel villages; Mariano was betrayed to the Portuguese and died in prison; and many of his followers fled in disarray to Congolese territory. The second outburst occurred in the capital itself, when several hundred Africans, probably organized by the MPLA, mounted an attack on Luanda's main prison for political offenders. Angered by the deaths of seven Portuguese policemen, white vigilantes retaliated by shooting several hundred Africans. A few weeks later on March 15, 1961 a third and even more serious outbreak of violence occurred in northern Angola, a widespread revolt that could be taken as marking the opening of a long-drawn-out war of liberation.

The revolt appears to have been largely organized by Holden Roberto's UPA from its base in Léopoldville. Throughout 1960 a group of young UPA militants were at work building up an underground organization. Some of them were even able to address revolutionary rallies of several thousand people a few days before the rising, rallies at which instructions were given for the destruction of bridges, airfields, and plantations. At the same time, a group of deserters from the Portuguese army was organized to form the nucleus of a future military force. Within the first few days of the revolt more than 250 Portuguese civilians lost their lives and another 500 were killed in the course of the next three months: in the grisly arithmetic of revolt this was certainly one of the worst massacres in African history. The Portuguese reaction was even more terrible and ruthless: missionary observers reckoned that as many as 20,000 Africans were killed in the first six months of the revolt.

By the autumn of 1961 the Portuguese could claim to have broken the back of the nationalists' assault. Portuguese settlers had not panicked, as the Belgians had recently done in the Congo, but fought back grimly in defense of their plantations. While the army reoccupied the posts overrun by the rebels, the airforce attacked rebel villages. Much of the reoccupied territory appeared a wasteland for the inhabitants had fled for refuge into the bush or crossed the Congolese frontier. Throughout 1961 the Portuguese found themselves faced with another form of attack: through diplomatic channels and in the meetings of the United Nations their colonial record was subjected to a barrage of criticism. This assault was met with considerable skill and determination. In January 1962 a resolution affirming Angola's right to self-determination was passed by a majority of ninety-nine to two (Spain and South Africa) in the General Assembly of the United Nations. When a somewhat similar resolution was introduced into the Assembly in December of the same year, the United States was one of five NATO countries that voted against it. In the months between the two resolutions the United States had been made uneasily aware that Portugal might refuse to renew the contract for American bases in the Azores, if the United States government continued its attacks on Portuguese colonial policy. But though the Portuguese held fast to essentials, they did begin to introduce reforms designed to render their system of rule more humane. The hated system of forced labor was abolished; off.cial rural markets were established to ensure that African producers obtained fair prices from Portuguese middleman; and more money than ever before was spent on education and medical services.

But the rebellion still went on. In 1962 the UPA set up a revolutionary government-in-exile and obtained Algerian assistance in training its military cadres. But nationalist activity in northern Angola was confined to spasmodic guerrilla activity, and the nationalist cause as a whole was constantly troubled by an intense spirit of factionalism. There was a deep divide between the MPLA which had taken no part in the rising of March 15 and the UPA. There were serious divisions within each of these two major parties, leading to the creation of dissident splinter groups. And there were a large number of Angolans living in exile who preferred to establish their own parties as an expression of tribal and subtribal aspirations and to follow a line of their own which led some of them to adopt a veiled form of collaboration with the Portuguese.

For four years the revolutionary cause seemed to languish. Then, in 1966, the MPLA succeeded in opening a new front in eastern Angola. The MPLA, most of whose supporters came from the Luanda area, had never been in a position to develop, as the UPA had shown signs of doing, into a mass party. But the party was led by a group of able men, whose resolve was stiffened by their clear-cut ideology. As Marxists, they looked to the Communist bloc for aid and were not disappointed. In 1963 the MPLA was forced, largely as a result of UPA hostility, to move its headquarters from Kinshasa (Léopoldville) to Brazzaville. From its new base it attempted unsuccessfully to stir up a revolt in the Portuguese enclave of Cabinda. In 1966 the MPLA moved yet again, from Congo-Brazzaville to Zambia, in order to mount an attack on the "soft underbelly" of Angola, the remote and thinly populated southeastern provinces of Moxico and Cuando-Cubango. The MPLA was not the only nationalist party to operate in these *terras do fin do mundo* ("world's end") as they seemed to the authorities in Luanda. In 1966 UNITA (National Union for the Total Independence of Angola), a party formed by Ovimbundu who had broken away from the UPA began guerrilla operations in a bid to capture the Ovimbundu heartland in southern Angola.

By the mid-1960's the Portuguese found themselves committed to yet another colonial war. In September 1964 FRELIMO (the Front for the Liberation of Mozambique) began operations in the country immediately south of the Mozambique-Tanzania frontier. The Front represented a coalition of a number of smaller groups formed by Mozambican exiles living in East and Central Africa. Its leader, Eduardo Mondlane, had lived for some years in the United States, worked for the United Nations, and held a teaching post at Syracuse University. By the late 1960's much of northern Mozambique was caught up in the tribulations of a war of liberation, with thousands of refugees fleeing north across the Rovuma into Tanzania, with FRELIMO establishing a rudimentary system of administration in liberated areas, and with the Portuguese committing more and more troops in their struggle to contain the guerrillas. In 1969 FRELIMO suffered a terrible blow when Mondlane was assassinated in mysterious circumstances: his death deprived the movement of its only leader to have acquired a certain international stature, a humane and sophisticated man inspired by a vision of Mozambican nationhood.

Mondlane's assassination—caused by the explosion of a bomb concealed in a parcel—may well have been the work of one of his political rivals. At any rate it is clear that the Mozambican liberation movement was as much riven and distracted by factionalism as the Angolan. In the politics of the refugees and exiles bitter internal feuds grew out of the soil of frustration. But there were deeper reasons for African factionalism in the Portuguese territories. In Angola and Mozambique, politically minded Africans had never been able to enjoy institutions of a type that did so much to facilitate the growth of powerful nationalist movements in the British and French colonies: an uncensored press, schools and universities where students drawn from many ethnic groups could acquire the intimate experience of living together, political parties with the freedom to thrash out their problems in the open. The very idea of an Angolan or Mozambican nation was barely conceivable to the vast majority of Portugal's African subjects, or even to members of the small educated elite who had been taught to consider themselves primarily as Portuguese. In these circumstances most Africans naturally thought first of the ethnic group or subgroup to which they belonged. In the politics of the refugee camps these tribal divisions were often reinforced or overlaid by ideological differences, between Catholics and Protestants or between Marxists and non-Marxists. In Algeria, the only other country in Africa to wage a large-scale guerrilla war against a colonial power, the population was far more homogeneous, with Islam serving as a powerful ideological cement. One might wonder if the Angolan and Mozambican freedom fighters would ever succeed in overcoming their internal divisions and so be able to wage a really effective war of liberation.

Just as Paris was more important than Algiers in deciding the final outcome of the Algerian struggle, so events in Lisbon are likely to have a profounder influence on the fate of Angola and Mozambique than the fighting in the lonely bush of Moxico or Cabo Delgado. To many European observers it seemed extraordinary that a country as small and poor as Portugal should accept the burden of an immensely expensive colonial war. By the late 1960's almost half of Portugal's annual budget was being spent on defense. Clearly some Portuguese—particularly students and certain members of the Catholic church—were bitterly opposed to the war. But to the Portuguese establishment—the politicians bred in the Salazarist tradition, the senior army officers, the big businessmen, who between them formed the power-base of Portuguese autocracy— the idea of retreat was inconceivable. To abandon Angola and Mozambique would mean nothing less than the renunciation of Portugal's historic destiny. More than that, it would involve throwing away two increasingly valuable assets. In spite of the war—indeed, partly as a result of the war—the economics of Angola and Mozambique were booming as never before. For Angola the 1960's was a golden decade, with the value of the territory's foreign trade doubling between 1960 and 1967. In 1966 rich oil deposits were discovered in the Cabinda enclave and there was talk of many other mineral resources awaiting the enterprising prospector. Portuguese businessmen and financiers had good reason to wish to keep a tight hold on the two colonies. Tropical products, such as cotton and sugar, could be purchased at prices well below those prevailing elsewhere while colonial markets were manipulated to meet the needs of Portuguese producers. The cost of the war could thus in large part be met from the growing wealth of the colonies. Moreover, the war itself was not a particularly bloody affair. The Portuguese deployed a large number of troops—about 70,000 in Angola and 50,000 in Mozambique—but suffered only modest casualties. According to official sources only 1,000 soldiers were killed by the Angolan guerrillas in nearly ten years of fighting. Finally, the Portuguese could reckon that they were not alone. Increasingly close and cordial ties were established with South Africa, whose forces cooperated with the Portuguese military in antiguerrilla operations. Moreover, by encouraging foreign investment in their colonies the Portuguese significantly increased the number of their sympathizers to be found in influential circles in the Western world.

Thus the nationalists found themselves faced with a colonial enemy whose position seemed in some ways more firmly entrenched than ever. The freedom fighters had failed to win a single decisive victory on the field of battle. But their movement could claim one spectacular success: it had forced the Portuguese to abandon the cruder forms of colonial exploitation and pay increasing attention to the policies of welfare. Particularly significant was the very substantial improvement in educational facilities. In Angola there were 106,000 pupils in primary schools and 12,000 in secondary schools in 1960–61. By 1966–67 enrollment in primary schools had risen to 268,000, in secondary schools to 32,000. "The official doctrine" was described in 1970 as being "to 'lusitanify' with the greatest rapidity as many young Angolans as possible to put them out of reach of the sirens of nationalism." [100] The whole course of modern African history suggests that this policy of "lusitanification" is doomed in the last resort to failure.

▲▼ CENTRAL AFRICA SINCE 1965

In the late 1960's Central Africa was potentially the most explosive region of the entire continent, the area of confrontation between two barely reconciliable power blocs, the independent states of Black Africa to the north, the countries dominated by white minority regimes to the south. Yet compared with the major war-zones of the 1960's, Vietnam or Nigeria/Biafra, the scale of violence in Central Africa remained relatively modest. The activities of black guerrillas in Angola, Mozambique, and Rhodesia represented an aggravating threat rather than a mortal danger to the authorities against which they were directed. But no foreign power became decisively involved in the struggle of the freedom fighters, while the governments in Luanda, Lourenço Marques, and Salisbury were able to look to South Africa, the most powerful state on the whole continent for support. Thus by 1970 the region could be said to have experienced a certain basic stability of a kind that would have surprised many well-informed observers five years earlier.

When the government of Rhodesia made its "unilateral declaration of independence" in November 1965, it was widely predicted that the "rebel regime" would collapse within a few months. In fact, the Rhodesian Front government proved to be one of the most stable in Africa. It succeeded in maintaining the support of the vast majority of the white electorate. Indeed, the verbal attacks directed against Rhodesia by a large section of world opinion served to stimulate a more intense spirit of white Rhodesian nationalism and so indirectly reinforced the governing party's hold on the country. As for the punitive measures in the form of economic sanctions adopted first by the British and later by many other governments in response to a United Nations resolution, these clearly failed seriously to damage the Rhodesian economy. With Portuguese and South African assistance, Rhodesians were able to maintain many trade links with the outside world. If some sections of the white community, notably the tobacco farmers, suffered from the closing of old established markets, others with an interest in developing local industries found the new conditions offered considerable opportunities for enterprise. Only the two banned Rhodesian African parties, ZAPU and ZANU, were prepared to use violent methods in an attempt to bring down the white regime by sending guerrilla bands across the Zambezi from their bases in Zambia. In countering this attack the Rhodesian government obtained substantial military support from South Africa.

The victory of the Rhodesian Front in the 1962 election had marked the beginning of a swing to the right in Rhodesian politics, the renunciation of ideas of partnership between the races, the abandonment of a policy of integration. This swing became more evident after independence was declared. Under the republican constitution accepted by a referendum held in 1969, the common voters roll, which Rhodesia had inherited from the Cape, was abolished and separate rolls established for Europeans and Africans. The Land Tenure Act of 1969 introduced a rigid distinction between European and African land, and the government took steps to remove some African communities long settled in land designated as European. In seeking African support the government turned to the most conservative elements in the African community, the traditional chiefs, many of whom were, in fact, government agents without any special prestige in their localities. Nevertheless, by 1970 the white government had not reached the point of attempting to impose so rigorous a system of separation as that enforced in South Africa. The university retained its character as a multi-racial institution. The sixty-six members of the lower house of the Rhodesian parliament contained sixteen Africans, and the new constitution provided for a gradual increase in African representation until eventually there should be parity between the races. (An increase in African representation was made dependent on a rise in the amount of income tax paid by Africans, an ingenious device so designed as to rule out any sudden expansion in the number of African representatives.)

All attempts made by the British and Rhodesian governments to reconcile their differences ended in failure. In a series of protracted negotiations the British made a number of concessions, but they remained determined to find some sort of formula which would allow for "unimpeded progress towards majority rule." No such formula could ever be acceptable to a government so clearly determined to maintain white supremacy. In November 1971 the British and Rhodesian governments agreed on the terms of a settlement which provided for a very gradual political advance by the African majority and so was interpreted by Conservative cabinet ministers in Britain as being in accord with the general principles laid down by their predecessors in the Labour government. But the British insisted that the settlement must be seen to be acceptable to the people of Rhodesia as a whole and forced the Rhodesian government to accept the presence of a British commission under the chairmanship of Lord Pearce whose members were given the task of assessing Rhodesian opinion. The commissioners soon found that the settlement was totally unacceptable to the vast majority of the African population. After the publication of the Pearce report the British government had no alternative but to abandon the proposed settlement.

In terms of international law Rhodesia still remained a British colony. By failing to assert its authority over the government in Salisbury Britain suffered a considerable loss of prestige and incurred the odium of the more radical political leaders in the Commonwealth. Viewed in historical perspective, however, the British failure was hardly surprising. Rhodesia was a South African rather than a purely British creation; under the chartered British South Africa Company the colony acquired its own locally controlled army, police, and civil service. Whitehall had never been able to maintain any really effective form of control over Rhodesian affairs. In the last resort it did not perhaps really matter whether white Rhodesia secured international recognition or not. Of far greater import was the regime's relations with its large African population. This population was increasing at the rate of 3.6 percent per annum. The demands for jobs, land, and educational opportunities were bound to grow more intense. White domination could be maintained only at the cost of increasing African frustration and bitterness.

No Black African state was faced in the first years of independence with so many pressing external difficulties as Zambia. The unilateral declaration of independence made Rhodesia "enemy territory," and Zambians found themselves occupying a highly vulnerable position, a landlocked salient, with hostile or potentially hostile territories on three sides and with a communications system created during the colonial era and designed to link the country to ports and industrial centers in white-dominated territories. In 1964 Zambia obtained 40 percent of its imports from Rhodesia, and 20 percent from South Africa. Almost all the power used in the copper belt was derived from the hydroelectric works at Kariba which the Rhodesians were in a position to control. And all Zambian copper had to be sent out on railways that ran through Portuguese or Rhodesian territory. Vigorously, in the years after 1965, the Zambian government set about freeing the country from the strong hold that the white-dominated territories could exert over its economy. Trade with Rhodesia was steadily reduced, a process that involved considerable sacrifices for the Zambian consumer. Local coal deposits were exploited to replace coal previously obtained from Rhodesia. An oil pipeline and an all-weather highway were constructed between the copper belt and the Tanzanian port of Dar es-Salaam. Finally, in 1969, work started on a major rail link, the Tan-Zam Railroad, a spectacular project, comparable in political and strategic significance to some of the great railroads built in the early years of the colonial era and rendered the more dramatic by the involvement of Communist China. For the governments of Zambia and Tanzania, finding that Western governments were not prepared to help in the construction of the railroad, had been glad to accept an offer from Peking. The project was the largest contribution to African development yet undertaken by Communist China. To cold-war warriors in the West and simplistic geopoliticians in Southern Africa the spectacle of Chinese engineers at work in East and Central Africa was highly alarming, the thin end of the wedge of Communist Chinese penetration into the African land-mass. In fact there was no evidence to suggest that the Chinese were attempting to behave in a subversive manner. But it was clear that African states could learn a good deal from the Chinese experience of modernization and from the industry, frugality, and self-discipline of the Chinese people. As for the threat of subversion, the leaders of independent Zambia and Tanzania were far too deeply committed to preserving and strengthening the independent character of their own countries to allow any foreign government undue influence within their borders.

If Zambia could be seen as a salient of Black Africa, needing for its own security to strengthen its links with the friendly states to its north, it could also be regarded as an advance post of revolutionary black nationalism, a constant threat to the white laager of the south. With the advent of Zambian independence many of the Southern African nationalist organizations in exile transferred their headquarters from Dar es-Salaam to Lusaka and began to use Zambian territory as a base for guerrilla activities. Their actions posed the Zambian government with a cruel dilemma. Though deeply sympathetic to the aspirations of the freedom fighters, President Kaunda and his ministers were constantly aware that guerrilla activities led to reprisals by the infinitely more powerful white-dominated states of a kind that could inflict cruel wounds on Zambia itself. The clearest expression of the Zambian government's own policy toward Southern Africa was to be found in the Lusaka manifesto, a document signed by the heads of fourteen African states meeting at the Zambian capital in April 1969. The signatories pointed out that their "stand of hostility towards the colonialism and racial discrimination in Southern Africa" was derived from their "commitment to human equality and human dignity." The manifesto struck liberal observers in the Western world as "remarkable for its reasoned approach, its recognition of the problems involved, and its assurances that one racialism should not succeed another when the power structure of Southern Africa was eventually altered." [101]

No less worrying for the new rulers of Zambia than these immensely onerous external difficulties were internal tensions of a kind to be found in most newly independent African states. UNIP, the governing party, never achieved in the years before independence so overwhelming a degree of popular support as the Tanganyika African Nation Union in Tanzania or the Congress Party in Malawi. Nkumbula and his supporters in the African National Congress retained a firm base in the Southern province, while there were strong separatist traditions in Barotseland, and Lozi resentment of the government at Lusaka steadily mounted in the years after independence. The contrast between the stagnant countryside and the booming copper belt created another deep dividing line in Zambian society and politics. Local rivalries were reflected in deep personal antagonisms within the ruling party, so that it often seemed as if nothing but the personality, political skill, and widespread popularity of President Kaunda could succeed in holding the country together. In 1971 the tensions within UNIP came out into the open, when Simon Kapwepwe, the president's right-hand man, broke away and formed a party of his own. Kapwepwe's United Progressive Party was banned after a few months of not particularly effective campaigning and many of its members were placed in detention. In the course of 1972 there was much talk of transforming Zambia into a one-party state.

Nevertheless, in spite of all these tribulations, the first years of independence were marked by a number of substantial achievements. In 1964 Zambia was a country whose economy seemed almost entirely dominated by foreign companies, most of which possessed close ties with Southern Africa. By 1970 the government was firmly in control of the commanding heights of the country's economy, having acquired a major share of all the large companies, including the two great mining combines. In the last years of the colonial era Northern Rhodesia had lagged seriously behind other British territories in the field of secondary and higher education. On achieving power the UNIP government immediately introduced a crash program designed to increase the number of secondary school students from 7,500 in 1964 to 70,000 by 1970. At the same time the country's first university was established at Lusaka. With the wealth derived from its mineral resources Zambia was able to meet the cost of most of its new development projects without depending on foreign aid. But though copper made Zambia one of the richest states in Black Africa, excessive dependence on a single commodity whose price was liable to fluctuate violently on the world market introduced a dangerous element of instability into the country's economy. President Kaunda was a sincere and eloquent exponent of the need for economic development to benefit the "common man," but for the rural population independence brought little or nothing in the way of tangible gains. Hence with an accelerating drift to the towns, the population of Lusaka rose by 75 percent, from 195,000 to 343,000 between 1963 and 1969, and the ranks of the urban unemployed swelled steadily.

In comparison with Zambia, Malawi was a smaller, poorer, and more easily governable country, whose development in the years immediately after independence was dominated to a quite remarkable extent by the personality of its leading politician, Dr. Hastings Kamuzu Banda. Once established as supreme ruler of his country, Banda showed himself to be an autocrat, a paternalist, and a realist who seemed positively to enjoy acting in an idiosyncratic manner that deeply exasperated many of his African contemporaries. Within two months of Malawi's independence the prime minister was involved in a bitter quarrel with his younger ministerial colleagues, the radical intellectuals of the nationalist party who had done so much to encourage him to return home and had deliberately set about building up his prestige. Profoundly aware of the perilous nature of his country's position, its poverty, and its dependence on its white-dominated neighbors, Rhodesia, Mozambique and South Africa, Banda found the conventional anticolonialism expressed by other members of his cabinet absurdly impractical. The first stage of the crisis was resolved with the dismissal of three ministers followed by the resignation of three others. A few months later the most prominent of the ex-ministers, Harry Chipembere, attempted to lead an armed revolt against the prime minister, but his followers were dispersed by the security forces and he fled the country to join his colleagues in exile. Two years later, another ex-minister, Yatuta Chisiza, was killed near Blantyre while leading an armed band of infiltrators who planned to assassinate Dr. Banda. With the collapse of the ex-ministers there was no group left strong enough to check the prime minister's assumption of supreme power. While continuing to make use of the services of a comparatively large number of European officials President Banda, as he became with the introduction of a republican constitution in 1966, began to assume the "outward trappings of a traditional chief: a fly-whisk in his hand, his entourage preceded by a modern version of the praise-singer—a Land Rover fitted with loudspeakers—and welcoming groups of ululating women symbolically sweeping the ground with brushwood in front of his path." [102]

Far more controversial in the eyes of most of his fellow-nationalists in other parts of the continent than these dictatorial tendencies was the policy which President Banda followed toward the white-supremist states of Southern Africa. To the ruler of Malawi the security of his regime and the economic development of his country were the lodestars of his policy. With all his country's trade passing through Portuguese territory, it became imperative to establish cordial relations with the colonial authorities in Mozambique. South Africa, the richest country in the continent, could offer Malawi valuable assistance in the economic field: gifts of this nature a poor country could not afford to disregard. On the other hand, Tanzania and Zambia offered hospitality and succor to Banda's political opponents: in such circumstances they must be treated with coolness, even hostility. As for the militants in the Organization of African Unity with their talk of "liberating" Southern Africa, their ideas were both impractical and dangerous, especially for a country occupying so exposed a position as Malawi. Yet Banda would claim that he was no less fundamentally opposed to racial discrimination than the most militant African radical. The disagreement was not over the end, but over the tactics. The president of Malawi spoke of establishing links rather than mounting boycotts, of dialogue rather than ostracism, of "killing apartheid with kindness" rather than with wars of liberation. This shrewd, pragmatic, unheroic policy achieved the results President Banda had set his eyes on. In the late 1960's Malawi showed itself to be one of the most stable black states in the continent. And there was a substantial improvement in the country's economic situation, with exports increasing from £12 million in 1964 to £24 million in 1970, and with real income per head rising at the rate of 2 percent per annum.

The foreign policy of President Banda fitted in with the "outward-looking" policy developed by Prime Minister Voster of South Africa in the mid-1960's. South Africa had two pressing reasons for taking a greater interest in the affairs of Central Africa: security and markets. Clearly for a country that felt itself under attack from sinister outside forces there was much to be said for the creation of a buffer zone to the north and for the establishment of close ties with the other white communities—in Rhodesia and the Portuguese territories—which also faced the same enemy. But South Africa was also anxious to acquire new markets for the products of its rapidly expanding secondary industries. So there began to emerge the concept of a "co-prosperity sphere" under South African leadership ambracing most of the southern half of Africa. In the nineteenth century the history of much of Central Africa had been dominated by the local imperialisms of African groups—the Ndebele, the Ngoni, and the Kololo—of South African origin. It seemed likely that much of Central African history in the last third of the twentieth century would be dominated by another form of South African imperialism.

CHAPTER VII

East Africa

INTRODUCTION

East Africa is usually taken to comprise the three modern states of Kenya, Tanzania (Tanganyika and Zanzibar), and Uganda. To these should be added Rwanda and Burundi, formerly Ruanda-Urundi, whose peoples have been for most of their history far more closely linked with neighboring areas of East Africa than with Equatorial Africa, though for a period of forty-six years, 1916–62, they were under Belgian rule and therefore attached more closely to the Congo. Thus defined East Africa covers an area of about three-quarters of a million square miles and contained a population approaching 40 million in 1970.

Though less than half the size of West Africa, East Africa may well be said to rival or even to surpass the larger region in the variety of its landscapes. The coast, tropical, languorous, with coconut palms and coral reefs and glaring white sands; the highlands, displaying in some parts a truly Alpine vegetation; the lower plains, with their thorn-scrub, their tsetse-infested bush, their meager and impoverished soil; the great lakes of the northwest, bordered in parts by areas of high rainfall, a land of papyrus swamps and banana groves—here in a relatively modest compass is a remarkable range of environments.

Equally remarkable has been the number of distinct streams of people who have contributed in the course of the past two or three thousand years to the population of East Africa. Like most of South and Central Africa, the region once possessed a substantial population of Bushmanoid stock, and a language classified as Khoisan and closely related to the "click" languages spoken by modern Bushmen groups in South Africa is still spoken by the Sandawe of central Tanzania. About 3,000 years ago peoples speaking Cushitic languages moved southward from Ethiopia to the highlands of Kenya. The Iraqw of northern Tanzania, who speak a language classified as Cushitic, are the most easily identifiable of these early settlers. Three other streams of immigrants, each speaking languages now classified as Nilotic, moved into East Africa from the north in the course of more recent centuries: the "highland" Nilotes represented by the Kalenjin of western Kenya and the Tatoga of northern Tanzania; the "plains" Nilotes of whom the Masai are the most numerous modern representatives; and the "river-lake" Nilotes, a group which includes the Luo, now occupying the northeastern shores of Lake Victoria.

Far more numerous, however, than these immigrants from the north were the Bantu-speaking peoples who began to spread over all but the northernmost parts of East Africa in the course of the first millennium A.D. The Kikuyu, the Kamba, the Luhiya of Kenya, the Ganda, and other interlacustrine peoples of Uganda, the Sukuma, the Nyamwezi, the Chagga, and all the peoples of southern Tanzania speak Bantu languages, though some of these peoples have almost certainly absorbed groups of Khoisan-, Cushitic- or Nilotic-speakers. Bantu groups settled on the coast also absorbed many of the immigrant traders, particularly those of Arab origin, whose record of intercourse with the East African littoral can be traced back over many centuries. From this fusion of Bantu- and Arabic-speakers there emerged the distinct Swahili culture, a truly Afro-Asian synthesis which flourished in the chain of city-states of which Mombasa, Kilwa and Zanzibar were the most important.

By the middle of the nineteenth century East Africa presented a political pattern of bewildering complexity. Most East African peoples lived either, as in the case of the Kikuyu or the Luo, in stateless polities, or in demi-states as represented by the petty chiefdoms of the Chagga and the Nyamwezi. Statelessness could not be regarded as any indication of lack of enterprise. The Masai were, strictly speaking, a stateless people, but they dominated an area 80,000 square miles in extent stretching from Lake Rudolph to central Tanzania, and the warrior bands of these formidable pastoralists were known to have raided as far afield as Lake Victoria to the west and the Indian Ocean to the east. Another notably martial people were the Ngoni who invaded the region from the south in the middle of the nineteenth century. The Ngoni already possessed a state organization based on the Zulu pattern. Many of the peoples with whom they came into contact in southern Tanzania began in self-defense to copy their political practices and to adopt their military tactics.

The densest cluster of states in East Africa was to be found in the fertile and well-watered lands north and west of Lake Victoria. By contemporary African standards Buganda, Bunyoro, Ankole, Rwanda, and Burundi were all substantial polities, well able to dominate the smaller groups on their borders. Most of these states had a history reaching back to the sixteenth century. Among the city-states of the coast the process of state formation could be traced back even further. In the course of the nineteenth century the coast came to be dominated by the Omani Arabs from their base on Zanzibar Island, and Arab-Swahili influence began spreading deep into the interior along routes already pioneered by local traders drawn from the Kamba, the Nyamwezi, and the Yao. The nature of the Arab-Swahili impact varied greatly from area to area. West of Lake Tanganyika the coastmen transformed themselves into the rulers of substantial states; east of the lake a great measure of influence lay in local hands. Some chiefs, making effective use of the firearms they obtained from the Arabs, were able to dominate far larger areas than their predecessors had ever done. Particularly successful was the Nyamwezi chief Mirambo who established a loose hegemony over the country south of Lake Victoria until his death in 1884. Thus in 1875 East Africa—and especially the southern half of the region— presented a scene of considerable political fluidity. This scene was soon to be transformed by the appearance of yet another group of intruders, the Europeans.

▲▼ THE EUROPEAN CONQUEST OF EAST AFRICA

For many East African communities the most significant events of the last quarter of the nineteenth century were the product either of natural forces—a famine or an epidemic—or of local political changes in which outsiders might scarcely be involved. But for the region as a whole there can be no doubt that the gradual establishment of European hegemony and the accompanying expansion of European influence represented the most profound cause of change in these years. Given the importance of the European penetration, it seems best to present a brief chronological narrative of the stages by which it occurred before turning to examine the complex interaction of alien and local forces in the northern and southern parts of the region.

Up to the middle of the nineteenth century no part of the continent had been so little affected by European influence as East Africa. Coastal areas had been brought within the sphere of Portuguese hegemony during the sixteenth and seventeenth centuries, but by 1700 the Portuguese had been expelled by the Omani Arabs from all their coastal strongholds north of Cape Delgado. Throughout the eighteenth century Europeans were rarely seen in East African waters; the interior was totally unknown to them; and the coastal markets offered little to attract traders carrying on a far more profitable commerce in other parts of the Indian Ocean. During the first half of the nineteenth century, however, three developments served greatly to encourage European interest in this neglected region: the emergence of Zanzibar as an entrepôt in which traders from Europe and from Asia could carry on business in perfect safety; the growing European demand for tropical produce, especially ivory and cloves; and the mounting concern among British humanitarians over the consequences of the Arab slave trade.

British opponents of the slave trade had concentrated their attention on the destruction of the Atlantic trade, but from as early as the 1810's some attempt had been made to check the growing commerce in slaves in the Indian Ocean. By the 1860's the rulers of Zanzibar had been forced to accept a number of restrictions, and a British naval squadron of seven or eight ships was permanently stationed in the Western Indian Ocean with the task of catching slave-dhows sailing between the East African coast and Arabia. Nevertheless, slaves were still bought and sold in Zanzibar and as many as 20,000 Africans were shipped to Arabia every year.

Had the slave trade not existed, it is very doubtful whether the British would have become deeply interested in East African affairs in the middle of the nineteenth century. As it was, many English people were not only aware of the trade but deeply shocked by the horrifying accounts brought back by travelers and naval officers. ("The slaves are in a most awful state when we get at them, just stewing together, packed like herrings, and one mass of smallpox," wrote one young naval officer serving in the anti-slave-trade squadron, "many of them dead, and they and the living cooped up as tight as they can fit in." [1] At last, in 1873, the British succeeded in persuading Sultan Bargash of Zanzibar to sign a treaty under whose terms he agreed to prohibit the transport of slaves by sea and to close all slave markets in his dominions. In the course of the previous half-century the sultans of Zanzibar had frequently had cause to look to the British for assistance. By accepting a measure so deeply resented by members of the Omani aristocracy on the coast, Bargash found himself forced to rely even more closely than before on British support. By the late 1870's the British representative, John Kirk, whose experience in Zanzibar dated back to the 1860's, though he was not appointed consul until 1873, acquired so great a measure of influence that he could be regarded as a "sort of unofficial prime minister." [2]

Concern over the slave trade led, then, to the establishment of a moderately powerful British presence, personified by the consul at Zanzibar and the naval officers of the anti-slave-trade squadron on the East African coast. But there were other reasons for the growth of European interest in East Africa. The "commercial empire" built up by Seyyid

Said, the first sultan of Zanzibar, attracted a small but gradually increasing number of European traders—English, French, and Germans —together with a few Americans, and a very much larger number of Indians, most of whom came from territories recently brought under British rule. To protect the interests of their nationals British, French, German, and American consuls were appointed to Zanzibar in the 1840's. In the third quarter of the nineteenth century Zanzibar's trade with the outside world increased rapidly. The tonnage of foreign ships calling at Zanzibar rose from 19,000 tons in 1859 to 89,000 in 1879, while the island's total foreign trade grew from half a million pounds to more than 2 million pounds in the same period, with cloves, ivory, and, by the late 1870's, rubber providing East Africa's main exports.

Two other motives brought Europeans to East Africa in the third quarter of the nineteenth century—scientific curiosity and evangelical enthusiasm. In a great spurt of activity much of the interior of East Africa, hitherto completely unknown to Europe, was revealed by the "discoveries" of Burton, Speke, and Grant in the late 1850's and early 1860's. From then on hardly a year passed without some contribution being made to the European knowledge of East Africa by the brave and adventurous men who crisscrossed the interior on missions of exploration.

Of even greater significance for the future of East Africa were the activities of European missionaries. In the 1840's three Swiss Protestant missionaries in the service of the British-supported Church Missionary Society established near Mombasa the first Christian community seen in the region since the expulsion of the Portuguese. Twenty years later, two other missionary societies, the Catholic Holy Ghost Fathers and the Protestant Universities Mission for Central Africa, created mission stations in Zanzibar and sought their converts among the growing number of freed slaves. Before long both Catholics and Protestants were able to advance on to the mainland, the Holy Ghost Fathers establishing a station at Bagamoyo, a costal town opposite Zanzibar, while the UMCA struck inland to found two widely separated stations about one hundred miles from the coast. In the 1840's, Krapf, the first CMS missionary in the East African field, had dreamed of a chain of mission stations gradually extending across the continent from east to west. The actual course of events proved in some ways more spectacular than the most optimistic of the early pioneers could ever have imagined. In 1875 there was published in the English press a letter from the explorer Stanley describing the cordial interest shown by the powerful ruler of Buganda in the principles of the Christian religion. Within a few days of the publication of the letter the CMS received a check for £5,000 from an anonymous donor with a proviso that the money be used for financing a mission to Buganda. The challenge was accepted, and by 1878 there were five CMS missionaries established in the most powerful kingdom of the East African interior, lying several months' journey from the coast. Two years later, a group of Catholic missionaries, White Fathers of the order recently formed for the evangelization of Africa by the fiery Cardinal Lavigerie, were founding their own centers in Buganda and in the country to the south of Lake Victoria. In 1856 there had only been a single European missionary active in East Africa. By the early 1880's the region contained more than one hundred Europeans engaged in the revolutionary work of evangelization.

Humanitarian sentiment, commercial interest, scientific curiosity, and missionary enterprise drew Europeans to East Africa, but none of these forces were in themselves powerful enough to lead any European government to wish to establish its hegemony over any part of the region. In the 1870's the only outside power with imperial ambitions affecting East Africa was Egypt. Khedive Ismail dreamed of annexing the country between Lakes Albert and Victoria and even went so far as to send an expedition to seize an East African port. British pressure forced the Egyptians to withdraw from the coast, and Ismail soon found that he lacked the resources to maintain his claim to hegemony over the lands of the Upper Nile. As the dominant naval power in the Indian Ocean, Britain was clearly in a position to assert its paramountcy over Zanzibar and the neighboring coast. But, in 1881, when Sultan Bargash of Zanzibar asked the British to take over powers of regency after his death, he met with a very cool response. "We should avoid implicating ourselves," wrote the viceroy of India, "in matters over which we could exercise no real influence without an expenditure of money and a display of strength out of all proportion to the advantages to be gained." [3] Only three years later Foreign Secretary Granville was talking of possible French or German annexations in East Africa as being "ruinous" to British influence in the region.[4] Events in other parts of Africa—the crisis over Egypt, the mounting Anglo-French rivalry in West Africa, the unexpected appearance of Germany as a colonial power—were responsible for this sudden change in attitude, inducing British statesmen to view East Africa in an entirely new perspective. The region had been drawn into the vortex of Great Power rivalry.

At this juncture a totally unforeseeable event transformed the situation on the East African coast. In November 1884, a group of young Germans who had traveled out from Europe in disguise arrived in Zanzibar, set off into the interior, and returned six weeks later with a number of treaties. The leader of the group, Carl Peters, "adventurer, thruster, dreamer, orator, liar and imperialist" as one English writer has described him,[5] had been engaged only a few months earlier in founding the *Gesellschaft für Deutsche Kolonisation,* a society whose avowed object was to provide Germany with overseas territories similar to those possessed by "every other civilized nation of Europe." [6] The society was financed by the sale of shares but received no official backing from the government. Nevertheless, as soon as Peters returned to Berlin, he found little difficulty in obtaining Bismarck's support for his treaties. In February 1885, the kaiser signed a *Schutzbrief* placing under German protection the territories whose rulers had allegedly "ceded" and "offered" their domains to Peters, and providing the German Colonization Society with what the British would have termed a "charter," authorizing the society to take over responsibility for the administration of the new protectorate.

The districts claimed by the Germans lay well inland from the coast, covering much of east-central Tanzania and lying for the most part beyond the jurisdiction of the sultan of Zanzibar. Had the British been so minded they could have consolidated the sultan's authority on the coast and so "strangled the new German colony at birth." [7] But in spite of Granville's forebodings only six months earlier, the British soon found a number of sound reasons for acquiescing in the German coup: the expense of vigorous countermeasures, the need to ensure German support over Egypt, the distraction of other crises in the Sudan and in Afghanistan, the opposition expressed by many members of the Liberal government to any expansionist moves, the realization that in the last resort East Africa was not an area of major strategic significance. Accordingly Consul Kirk was instructed to advise the sultan to accept the German move. The arrival in Zanzibar of a German naval squadron, guns cleared for action, made it evident that resistance was useless. Just over a year later, after an international delimitation commission had surveyed the sultan's mainland territories and asserted that they extended no more than ten miles inland, an Anglo-German agreement was signed, defining the German "sphere of influence" as stretching from the Rovuma in the south to the present Kenya-Tanzanian border in the north and extending inland as far west as Lake Victoria.

Soon after acquiring the *Schutzbrief* the German Colonisation Society set up a German East Africa Company. But it was not until May 1887 that a small group of Germans in the company's service arrived at Dar es-Salaam, the one port ceded by the sultan, to establish a formal occupation. A year later the Germans obtained permission to administer on the sultan's behalf all the Zanzibari possessions lying within their sphere of influence. Within a few months of their arrival the intruders were drawing on themselves by their tactlessness a mounting tide of bitterness and hatred from the Muslim population of the coast. By the end of 1888 they found themselves faced with a major resistance movement led by an Arab named Abushiri. The seriousness of this "revolt" served completely to discredit the company's system of administration. Only direct action financed by the home government could restore German prestige. An "imperial commissioner," Hermann von Wissmann, already distinguished as an African traveler, was sent out to Dar es-Salaam with a motley army of African mercenaries recruited from Egypt, the Somali coast, and Mozambique. In November 1890, with Abushiri dead and "order" firmly established on the coast, the German government formally took over the colony from the discredited company. A few months later the sultan of Zanzibar was forced to sell at a modest price his few remaining rights on the coast. German sovereignty was now complete.

The Anglo-German agreement of 1886 left most of the area covered by modern Kenya lying within the British sphere of influence. There was no desire at this time in official quarters to become involved in the expense of administration, but a group of businessmen, retired consular officials, and philanthropists led by a Scottish shipping magnate, Sir William Mackinnon, the founder of the British India Steam Navigation Company, formed themselves into the British East African Association and determined to take more resolute action. In 1887 the association reached an agreement with the sultan of Zanzibar and obtained political rights to the stretch of coast north and south of Mombasa in return for an annual payment to the sultan of the amount previously received in customs duties. The next year the association was granted a royal charter and became the Imperial British East Africa Company. The British government still had no desire to saddle the country with an expensive new African domain, but Prime Minister Salisbury was beginning to look anxiously toward Uganda and the headwaters of the Nile. By the end of the 1880's it had become clear that the British occupation of Egypt was likely to be of long duration. The security of Egypt depended, so many influential Englishmen believed, on the denial of the entire Nile Valley to any European power possessing the technical capacity to interfere with the flow of the Nile waters. Under the terms of the Anglo-German agreement of 1886, the international position of Uganda had been left undetermined. Should the Germans, now beginning to press forward from their coastal bases, lay effective claim to the country, a vital piece in the elaborate structure of British imperial security would pass into the hands of a potential enemy. The device of a chartered company provided the means for establishing a British presence on the ground without involving the embarrassment of asking a reluctant parliament for money. But high-level diplomacy was needed to confirm the British claim. In the first half of 1890 a new Anglo-German agreement was hammered out. The terms were extremely favorable to the British. In return for the cession of the relatively unimportant North Sea island of Heligoland, the British obtained a frontier settlement which defined the northern limits of German East Africa in such a way as to leave Uganda clearly within the British sphere. At the same time they also secured German approbation of their plan to establish a protectorate over the islands of Zanzibar and Pemba. A British East African empire was beginning to take shape on the map.

The new chartered company soon proved ill-equipped to sustain the heavy responsibilities thrust upon it. Its directors lacked the drive, the business acumen, the political shrewdness of a Rhodes or a Goldie. The East African interior offered no opportunities for profitable trade comparable to the rich palm-oil markets of the Niger. Predictably, then, the company was a commercial failure. But the company was also required to fulfil a political role. With no more than £500,000 in capital it soon found itself grievously overextended. At first the company's operations had been confined to the hinterland of Mombasa, but in 1890 it was agreed to dispatch a substantial expedition, led by Captain Lugard, a young Indian army officer who had recently made a name for himself fighting Arab slavers in Nyasaland and was later to achieve even greater fame in Nigeria, to establish the company's presence in Uganda. Lugard based himself in Buganda, the most powerful kingdom in the interior, and persuaded the ruler to sign a treaty recognizing the company's suzerainty, but before long he found himself drawn into a tense, dangerous, and confused political situation (discussed in more detail in a later section of this chapter), and the support of his expedition was soon costing the company far more than it could afford. The certainty of parliamentary disapproval made it impossible for the government to help the company with a subsidy. Yet, by 1892, it was clear that lacking practical official support the company would very soon be forced to withdraw from Uganda.

Should the company withdraw, then the French, so one influential group of British officials believed, would certainly move in. Nor was this the only consequence to be dreaded. In the course of the past decade European missionaries, British Protestants and French Catholics, had been making great headway in Buganda. By the late 1880's Christian converts represented a powerful force in Ganda politics, but they were bitterly opposed by the smaller number of Ganda Muslims and by the many supporters of the traditional religion. A sudden British withdrawal might well lead, so British missionaries in Buganda encouraged the outside world to believe, to a massacre of all Ganda Christians. To Prime Minister Gladstone and most of the members of the Liberal government that took office in 1892 these arguments made little appeal. They were anxious to withdraw from Egypt and could see no point in attempting to protect the headwaters of the Nile. But Gladstone's foreign secretary, Lord Rosebery, "a *realpolitiker* in a party which specialized in matters of faith and morals," [8] possessed the advantage of occupying for domestic reasons so influential a position in the cabinet that his resignation was unthinkable. Even Rosebery, however, could hardly have acted decisively to retain Uganda, had his hand not been strengthened by a "brief, spontaneous, countrywide, strangely componded but truly national movement of British public opinion"—a movement that provided a fascinating insight into the popular springs of imperialism in late Victorian Britain. "Some ideas," D. A. Low has expressed it, "deep seated in the national character had been profoundly stirred." They included "a Christian horror of slavery; fears of the passing of free trade; memories of Gordon and Khartoum, and confidence that the keys to progress had been found and could easily be transferred to Africa." [9]

The campaign achieved its object. Reluctantly Rosebery's colleagues agreed to the dispatch of an "imperial commissionar" to Uganda to report on the situation. The man chosen for this difficult mission, Sir Gerald Portal, a young diplomat with considerable African experience, shared Rosebery's ideas. He arrived in Buganda in March 1893, replaced the company's flag by the Union Jack, set up a skeleton administration, and produced a report strongly advocating the maintenance of what he defined as "some kind of British preponderance." His arguments for retaining Uganda were almost entirely strategic. The country was the "natural key to the whole of the Nile Valley"; as long as the British remained in Egypt, such a key must never be allowed to fall into foreign hands.[10] In the course of 1893 Rosebery's hand was greatly strengthened when he replaced the aging Gladstone as prime minister. In April 1894 he went even further than Portal had suggested and had Uganda declared a British protectorate. A few weeks later an Anglo-Congolese treaty defined the new protectorate's eastern frontier. The partition of East Africa was now complete. The conquest was still to be accomplished.

By 1890 the Germans, with the Tanzanian coast firmly under their control, were in a position to extend their hegemony deep into the interior. An expedition under von Wissmann set off up the Zambezi and along Lake Nyasa to reach the remote southwest. At the same time, the famous Emin Pasha, who entered German service after playing such a notable part in the history of the Southern Sudan, took a force westward to occupy Tabora and the country south and west of Lake Victoria. The conquest of the north, and especially of the Chagga chiefdoms on the slopes of Kilimanjaro, was left to Carl Peters who behaved with such brutality that he was eventually recalled to Germany to face an official enquiry. (Peters came to be regarded in many circles as an epitome of European imperialism at its most savage. "I will show the Wagogo what the Germans are," he wrote on one occasion, after claiming to have been insulted by a Gogo chief. "Plunder the village, set fire to the houses and smash everything to pieces that will not burn.") [11] The extension of German rule naturally involved many small-scale "punitive" expeditions. But only in one area did the invaders find themselves faced with really serious resistance. In 1891 the Hehe of the Southern Highlands inflicted a crushing defeat on a German column sent against them. Three years later the Hehe capital was stormed and taken, but the Hehe chief, Mkwawa, waged guerrilla warfare against the Germans until his death in 1898. Under the terms of an agreement reached with the Congo Free State in 1884, the two important kingdoms of Rwanda and Burundi were left within the German sphere. The kingdoms contained some of the most densely populated districts in all Africa, but they remained almost totally unknown to Europeans until the 1890's. Little force was required to persuade the two rulers to accept a modest form of German hegemony. By 1905 German rule appeared firmly established when a serious revolt, the *Maji-Maji* rebellion, broke out in the south of the country. After the repression of this revolt, the German colonial authorities enjoyed less than a decade of peace before their territory again became a battlefield on a larger scale than ever before in the course of World War I.

In Uganda the British were fortunate in being able to count on the support of most members of the Ganda elite, the ruling class of a kingdom which was by far the most populous of the interlacustrine polities. From Buganda the British extended their system of overrule peacefully to the small Soga chiefdoms in the west and to the kingdoms of Toro and Ankole in the east. But to the north the powerful kingdom of Bunyoro confronted them with a formidable adversary. Between Bunyoro and Buganda there was a long tradition of conflict into which the British inevitably found themselves drawn. In 1894 Bunyoro was invaded by British and Ganda forces and the ruler, Kabarega, driven from his kingdom. The Ganda were rewarded for their part in the victory by a large slice of Nyoro territory, an award that created an issue—the fate of the "lost provinces"—destined to trouble Uganda for the next seventy years. In 1897 the British suddenly found their position seriously threatened by two unexpected developments. Mwanga, *kabaka* of Buganda, exasperated by the steady erosion of his authority at the expense of the local Christian elite, rebelled against the protectorate regime. A few months later three companies of Sudanese mercenaries, representing a substantial proportion of the local British military force, mutinied and began harassing the surrounding countryside. In Buganda the situation was saved for the British by the support of the leading Ganda officials, while Indian troops were called in to deal with the mutineers. Not until the first decade of the twentieth century did the British start establishing their authority in the northern half of the country. As in the neighboring Southern Sudan, the new rulers found themselves confronted with a large number of miniscule polities many of whose people needed to be visibly impressed by European military force before making their submission. The process of pacification took place slowly over a period of more than twenty years.

The Uganda protectorate established by the British in 1894 included also most of the western part of modern Kenya. The remainder of the country lying between the Rift Valley and the coast became the East African Protectorate (E.A.P.) in 1895, when the British government assumed responsibility for its administration after revoking the charter of the almost bankrupt Imperial British East Africa Company. In the years between 1888 and 1895 the company had established posts in the main towns of the coast and at various stages on the route to the interior. To the British government this latest acquisition of African territory was of no interest except in so far as its control was necessary in order to maintain access to Uganda and the headwaters of the Nile. As early as 1891 Lord Salisbury had looked favorably on the project of a railroad from the coast to Uganda, but construction of the line could not start until 1896. Without the seeming imperative of strategic necessity, the need for swift access to Uganda and the Upper Nile, the British government would never have imposed the burden of a £5½ million bill for construction costs on the British taxpayer. And, ironically, by 1901 when the line was completed, the strategic necessity had disappeared with the resolving of the Fashoda crisis and the British conquest of the Sudan.

The building of the Uganda Railroad was an impressive advertisement of the drive and resourcefulness of a great imperial power. "The road," wrote *The Times* in an editorial commemorating the completion of the line, "had frequently to be cut through dense forests or hewn out of the rock, bridges had to be built over streams subject to the sudden rise and fall of tropical rains, in the lowlands malarial fever of a virulent type had to be reckoned with, and the attacks to which working parties were often exposed in the jungle from wild beasts, disturbed for the first time in their hereditary lairs, added a new and serious danger, certainly unprecedented on such a scale, to the task of railway construction." It was no "small thing," concluded the leader-writer, "that the *pax Britannica* has secured order and security over a vast region of nearly 4,000,000 souls which until the advent of British rule was given over to a cruel and sterilising tyranny." [12] In fact, when these words were written in 1901, British rule in the future Kenya was confined to little more than the line of rail. Some people, notably the warlike Masai (whose reactions are considered in the next section) accepted the British intrusion without open protest. But many others had to be intimidated by a show of force. Thus between 1900 and 1908 there were expeditions against the Nandi, the Embu, the Gusii, the Kipsigis, and other peoples, all of whom were organized in stateless polities. Though small in scale, these expeditions often had a shattering effect on the people against whom they were directed. "Operations did not cease," wrote a critical British official of the 1908 Gusii expedition, "until thirty-eight natives had been killed or wounded, many villages burnt and livestock to the value of £2,400 seized, in respect of each one of the six murders actual or attempted of which members of the tribe had been guilty." [13] "There was a strange tendency in the E.A.P.," a later historian has remarked, "encouraged, no doubt, by the frequently dangerous isolation of British officials, to resort to arms without considering possible alternatives; to inflict 'punishment' out of all proportion to any 'offence' which had been committed and to treat as rebellion actions by Africans which, in truth, were only the expression of a natural instinct to preserve their own freedom and be rid of obstinate and unwelcome intruders." [14]

In 1902 the eastern part of the Uganda Protectorate was placed under the administration of the E.A.P. Five years later the protectorate's northern frontier was defined by means of an agreement with Ethiopia. In 1920—the year in which the territory acquired the name "Kenya"—the Somali-populated district known as Jubaland was handed over to the Italians in compensation for their services to the Allied cause in World War I. Much expense and bloodshed would have been saved for the African heirs of the British colonial regime in Kenya, if all the territory's Somali population had been transferred to Italian Somalia at this time. As it was, the colony was saddled with a vast economically useless Northern Frontier District, whose turbulent inhabitants— Somali, Turkana, Boran, and others—could be brought only with much difficulty to accept British hegemony.

The construction of the Uganda Railroad was an event of seminal

importance in the history of British East Africa, for it created the circumstances that made possible—or even, as some contemporaries
would have argued, inevitable—the introduction of two new ethnic
groups—Indian merchants, clerks, and laborers, and European settlers
—into a territory already possessing a remarkably heterogeneous population. The building of the railroad, wrote Sir Harry Johnston in 1899,
"means the driving of a wedge of India two miles broad right across
East Africa from Mombasa to Victoria Nyanza. Fifteen thousand coolies, some hundreds of Indian clerks, draughtsmen, mechanics, survey-
ors and policemen are carrying the Indian penal code, the Indian postal
system, Indian coinage, Indian clothing right across these wastes, deserts, forests and swamps." [15] In fact, of the 32,000 indentured laborers
recruited to build the railway, no more than 7,000 elected to stay in
East Africa. But the Indian population of the region already included a
substantial group of merchants based in Zanzibar and in the main
coastal towns. These enterprising men, their numbers swollen by new
arrivals from India, were quick to take advantage of the new commercial opportunities opened to them by the railroad and by the establishment of new administrative posts. "With considerable fortitude and per-
severence," a recent historian has pointed out, these petty Indian
merchants "pioneered the establishment of *dukas,* of local trading
centres and Indian bazaars in different districts; and by introducing the
local populations to a variety of imported goods and later the rupee
currency, they provided an incentive to greater local production as well
as the transition from a barter to a money-based economy." [16]

Indian enterprise was destined to make a massive contribution to the
economic development of a region which had little of immediate value
to offer its conquerors. Both the British and the Germans could only
support their new colonial structures by means of grants-in-aid. In
1902–03 the East African Protectorate received £314,000 from the
British taxpayer, while interest on the loans advanced to meet the cost
of building the railroad amounted to £319,000. In the 1890's there had
been talk of organizing Indian agricultural settlements in East Africa
—Sir John Kirk spoke of the region as "India's America"—as an effective way of boosting the new colony's economy and thus enabling the
local colonial regime to obtain sufficient local taxes to free it of its dependence on metropolitan support. At the same time, some Englishmen
familiar with East Africa were beginning to suggest that the cool, beautiful, and fertile Kenya highlands might well be transformed by European settlement into a "white man's country." This idea was taken up
"with almost fanatical zeal," as one recent historian has remarked,[17] by
Sir Charles Eliot, a youngish diplomat with no previous experience of

Africa, who was appointed to take charge of the East African Protectorate in 1900. Eliot was a brilliant scholar—his publications included a Finnish grammar, a study of Ottoman history, and a standard work on British molluscs—and a firm believer in the rightness of his country's "civilizing mission." To him and to many of his contemporaries most of the African peoples of the highlands presented nothing but "blank, amorphous barbarism." [18] Moreover, much of the most fertile land was apparently lying waste and idle. The African population of the highlands had never been very dense, and it had suffered from dreadful mortality produced by the epidemics of the late 1890's. A vigorous policy of encouraging white settlement seemed by far the most effective way of transforming one of the most enticing "undeveloped estates" of the African continent. By 1914 there were about 1,000 European farmers and planters in the East African Protectorate, their holdings averaging between four and five thousand acres.

▲▼ AFRICAN REACTIONS TO THE ESTABLISHMENT OF EUROPEAN HEGEMONY IN EAST AFRICA

It is a great deal easier to describe the gradual expansion of European hegemony in East Africa than it is to present the varied reactions of individual East African peoples to this formidable alien intrusion. The broad spectrum of reactions, from enthusiastic collaboration to embittered resistance, is familiar enough, but it is not easy to make watertight generalizations. Much of the East African experience tends, indeed, to invalidate assumptions based on the historical examples provided by other regions. Thus, it is often suggested that pastoral nomads are particularly likely to put up a fierce resistance to any alien intruder attempting to interfere with their traditional way of life, and the examples of the Tuareg, the Somali, the Libyan Bedouin, or the Moors may be cited to confirm this generalization. Yet in East Africa the Masai, a pastoral people with a formidable reputation as warriors, accepted British hegemony with remarkable passivity. Again, much African experience might suggest that well-organized kingdoms usually put up at least a show of resistance to the European intrusion; such a generalization would seem to be justified by the experience of the Sokoto caliphate or the Tukulor empire, of Dahomey or Benin, of the Ndebele kingdom or Ethiopia. Yet in East Africa the most powerful polity of the interior, the kingdom of Buganda, embarked at an early stage in its relations with the British on a remarkably harmonious policy of collaboration. Most African rulers were unwilling, so the late nineteenth-century history of much of the continent suggests, to resort to guerrilla warfare after suffering a crushing defeat at European hands; but the example of

Mkwawa of the Hehe shows that this too is not of universal validity. Finally, it is clearly true that when the European hegemony had been firmly established for more than a decade, most African peoples were not prepared to risk their necks by launching a violent revolt against their powerful new masters. Yet the example of the *Maji-Maji* rebellion in southern Tanzania shows that this too is not an incontrovertible statement. Here then are four cases, the experiences of the Masai, the Hehe, the *Maji-Maji* rebels, and the Ganda, each of which is worth examining in more detail.

In the last half of the nineteenth century, the Masai could be regarded, in D. A. Low's phrase, as "the hinge of Kenya." "Lords of the plains and open plateaus between Mount Kilimanjaro and Lake Nakuru," they had also become through their raiding expeditions "the most ubiquitous of the peoples between Lake Victoria and the sea." [19] "Their superior technique," a British official noted admiringly in the 1920's, "enabled them to cover distances that seemed miraculous. Perfectly trained and organized they were always certain of victory and were regarded as invincible. They even boasted of never attacking without giving notice." [20] Yet the hegemony of these arrogant warriors, these exceedingly "noble savages" as they seemed to many European observers, was based on shaky foundations. Their economy was entirely pastoral, and cattle were to prove a highly vulnerable commodity when East Africa was swept by a terrible epidemic of rinderpest in the 1890's. (The same epidemic was later to cause disaster to another pastoral people, the Herero of South West Africa.) Another serious source of weakness lay in their political disunity, for the group, whose population probably never exceeded 100,000, was divided into a number of completely autonomous sections. The 1880's saw much fierce fighting between these sections, and the atmosphere of violence grew more intense as a result of the cattle shortage caused by the rinderpest epidemic of the 1890's, for every Masai band was accustomed to remedy its losses by raiding the herds of its neighbors. To the afflictions of rinderpest and local war was added another catastrophe, a virulent outbreak of smallpox. In this terrible time of troubles some observers reckoned that three-quarters of the entire Masai population was wiped out.

Nevertheless, the Masai still retained their formidable reputation as warriors. One of the main trade routes from the coast passed through Masai country, and there had been many cases of traders' caravans being attacked by Masai war-bands. At the same time, the pastoralists had gradually become used to the appearance of aliens in their midst. Thus the arrival of the first British officials in the service of the Imperial British East Africa Company aroused no alarm. The British, for their part, were well aware of the weakness of their own position and treated the Masai with caution and respect. In 1896 a violent incident, known as the Kedong massacre, served unexpectedly to strengthen the bonds of trust between British and Masai. A large caravan of Swahili traders and Kikuyu porters was involved in a fracas with a group of Masai; a local white trader was drawn into the quarrel, began shooting at the Masai, and was speared to death only after he had inflicted a large number of casualties. Instead of launching a punitive expedition to avenge their compatriot's death, British officials held an inquiry and found that the Masai were not to blame as the trouble had been started by the Swahili traders attempting to steal Masai girls. At this time the most influential man among the local Masai was the *laibon* Lemana, a ritual expert who also possessed substantial political powers. "When I had explained to Lemana," wrote John Ainsworth, the British official in charge of the inquiry, "that we were satisfied that our own people were to blame for starting the trouble, he came forward with obvious feeling, thanked us and exclaimed that he had heard of the white man's justice but now he knew it was a fact and . . . it was not his wish and never would be to have trouble with the white man." [21] Lemana stuck to this principle for the remainder of his life. "Tell my people," he said on his death-bed in 1911, "to obey the Government as they have done during my life." [22]

Behind this genuine appreciation of British justice lay a shrewd political calculation. The Masai had witnessed on many occasions the power of European firearms. Clearly it was hopeless to attempt to resist such powerful intruders. So the Masai cooperated with the invaders, even joining them in their expeditions against other peoples, some of whom had, of course, been their own hereditary enemies. So complete was their willing subjection to British authority that they raised no fundamental objections when the British decided to delimit their grazing grounds and even to move them, in 1911, from an area which had been solemnly recognized as Masai territory under the terms of a treaty signed in 1904 but which was now coveted by British settlers. So docile a reaction would never have been anticipated by those who had seen the Masai at the peak of their military glory in the 1870's.

The British were not uniformly successful in dealing peacefully with a people possessing a reputation for military prowess. Against the Nandi of Western Kenya it was necessary to lead no less than five punitive expeditions before their power was finally broken in 1905. But in their East African campaigns the British never suffered a defeat comparable to that inflicted on the Germans by the Hehe who lived in the southern highlands of Tanzania. The Hehe emerged as a united people in the 1860's and 1870's when a local ruler, Munyigumba, asserted his hegemony over fifteen petty chiefdoms. By adopting the military tactics of the neighboring Ngoni (tactics originally derived from the Zulu) the Hehe soon acquired a formidable reputation as warriors. Under Munyigumba's son, Mkwawa, their raiding parties were striking eastward to the coast and northward to harry caravans using the important trade route between Bagamoyo and Tabora. In their dealings with the Masai the British were faced with a declining power: the Germans, by contrast, found themselves confronted in the Hehe with a people still experiencing the first flush of successful expansion. Thus German-Hehe relations soon presented the not unfamiliar pattern of a clash of rival imperialisms. In 1891 a German expedition sent against the Hehe was ambushed and overwhelmed, 10 Europeans, including the commander, and 200 native troops being killed. But the Hehe also sustained heavy losses and Mkwawa decided to rely mainly on defensive tactics to counter the German threat. Accordingly he set about fortifying his capital, Kalanga, with a massive stone wall. The Hehe believed this fortress to be impregnable: "there is nothing able to knock down this wall which is higher than any other," local tradition records them as saying.[23] But their confidence was misplaced, their tactics ill-chosen. In 1894 the Germans stormed Kalanga with relative ease, destroyed its fortifications, and built a new post for themselves at nearby Iringa. Mkwawa then turned to guerrilla warfare. So great was the esteem and the fear in which the warrior-chief was held that he was able, though a fugitive, to resist the Germans for another four years. The end came when Mkwawa shot himself to avoid capture by a German patrol.

In defeating Mkwawa the Germans could claim to have liberated the Hehe from a ruthless and savage despot. Even to his own people the great chief was known as "the slaughterer" and "the wild beast." "Give him to the vultures," the order for an execution, was a command frequently heard at Kalanga. But Hehe resistance made a profound impression on the officials of the German administration. They learned to respect "the intelligence, loyalty and discipline" of a people whom they could regard as the *Herrenvolk* of East Africa. Later, British administrators saw in the Hehe a "magnificent opportunity for building up an ideal chieftainship by tact and sympathy." The special treatment accorded Mkwawa's successors by the two colonial administrations, German and British, "has been one of the most important factors," so a student of Hehe history has recently pointed out, "in creating a sense of unity among the Hehe, something that was only just beginning to emerge at the time of Mkwawa's death."[24] Clearly the symbolic value of a gallant defeat possesses a certain creative force that may have a profound influence on the pattern of future developments.

Every ruling group is concerned to preserve its own power and authority. Though the decisions reached by the leaders of different East African peoples might vary widely, they all possessed this common denominator. The concern of those who participated in the *Maji-Maji* revolt of 1905 was very different. The rebellion broke out in a part of southern Tanzania that had been under German rule for more than a decade. It could not be interpreted as an act of "primary resistance" but as a movement of protest or even of liberation. At the same time it was essentially a popular movement, "a revolt of the people," that came to involve a large number of previously disunited small-scale polities. Finally it developed a highly complex pattern with powerful religious overtones.

The revolt began in July 1905 among peoples living near the coast in the valley of the Rufiji and spread rapdily inland to embrace most of the peoples of the Rufiji basin, including the Ngoni and the Bena. Within a few weeks the Germans had broken the main thrust of the revolt, but order was not finally restored until 1907. Famine then vastly exacerbated the suffering caused by war, war and famine combining to cause the death of 75,000 Africans.

Three distinct strands or stages have been detected in this remarkable mass movement: "*Maji-Maji*," the most recent historian of the movement has written, "originated in peasant grievances, was then sanctified and extended by prophetic religion and finally crumbled as crisis compelled reliance on fundamental loyalties to kin and tribe." [25] The grievances were caused by the German decision to compel African peasants in the coastal area to raise cotton on communal plots, a form of forced and virtually unremunerated labor that caused considerable hardship. In their distress the local people turned to the priests of Kolelo, a great spirit widely revered in the Rufiji area, and received from them a water-medicine (*maji*) powerful enough, it was firmly believed, to protect the recipient from the bullets of the white man. In an atmosphere of mounting excitement, with bands of angry peasants attacking isolated Europeans and their African collaborators, representatives of the Kolelo cult began carrying the medicine to peoples quite unaffected by the agitation over cotton-growing. The mood was messianic: men were exhorted to defy the government in the name of a new god: "He will change the world and it will be new," they were told, "his rule will be one of marvels." [26] Not all who heard believed: some chiefs held their people loyal to the Germans, others attempted to resist but were swept aside. Among some communities the movement gained added momentum by appearing in a form already familiar in the area, that of an all-out attack on sorcery. Thus the *maji* symbolized an immensely attractive complex of ideas which was received avidly by peoples of many different ethnic groups. But the new ideology was not in itself sufficient to create the unified political organization required by any successful revolutionary movement. In the face of vigorous German countermeasures, each group was forced to fight on its own, while the mounting toll of dead soon showed that the *maji* lacked the properties claimed of it. Clearly the revolt could be regarded as a catastrophic failure. Yet, even in the short term, it was far from being totally ineffectual. Fear of a great native uprising continued to haunt the Germans long after the final act of suppression had taken place. This fear played no small part in the calculations which led the German authorities to adopt a notably more liberal native policy in the last years of their rule in East Africa. As for the long term consequences of *Maji-Maji,* the revolt has come to be regarded as the national epic of the people of Tanzania. The phenomenon is a familair one: gallant failures in a just cause often tap deeper wells of national pride than the most dazzling successes.

The story of Buganda's reaction to the establishment of European hegemony is strikingly different from that of the minor polities of southern Tanzania. Few people in tropical Africa had developed so complex a political superstructure as the Ganda, whose kingdom stretched crescent-shaped along the northern shores of Lake Victoria. Nor had many African peoples had the chance of acquiring so intimate a familiarity with European ways even before the establishment of colonial rule, despite the fact that from the European point of view Buganda was one of the most remote, least accessible of African kingdoms. By the second half of the nineteenth century, the Ganda could look back on three centuries of continuous expansion and increasing power. The history of their kingdom could be interpreted in terms of a steady process of centralization, a growing concentration of power in the hands of the ruler, known to his people as the *kabaka. Kabaka* Mutesa, the first Ganda monarch to be visited by Europeans, maintained a splendid court, appointed most of the chief officers of state, and had powers of life and death over his immediate entourage, but he faced many practical difficulties in consolidating his power. In a sense it might be said that the kingdom lacked a really secure ideological base. The gods worshipped by the people were all local deities whose priests tended to support local interests and so to resist the centralizing ambitions of the *kabaka.* In the 1860's Mutesa began to take a serious interest in Islam, to which he had recently been introduced by Arab traders, studied the Koran, wore Arab dress, and encouraged the building of mosques. But when some of the Ganda converts to Islam began to put the law of the Prophet above the law of the *kabaka,* Mutesa realized that the new religion could never provide him with a satisfactory ideological support, and he turned savagely against its adherents. By this time he had become aware, through conversation with European travelers, that Europeans, who were clearly the masters of a technology far more elaborate than anything known to the Arabs, also possessed a distinct religion of their own. There was much to be gained by inviting Christian missionaries to reside in his country: they could impart new skills, serve as useful diplomatic agents, and initiate him and his people into the mysteries of their faith. The success achieved by the early missionaries was astonishing. Within a few years of their arrival in the late 1870's they were winning converts among young men of the best families. On these youthful courtiers growing up in a society filled with danger—at court a trivial breach of etiquette might be punished with instant execution—and in which the old gods had been discredited, the new religion made a profound impression. Many of them became devoted followers of Christ and were soon called to put their new faith to the test. For just as Mutesa had come to perceive in Islam a serious threat to his own authority, so his successor, Mwanga, who became *kabaka* in 1884, was not slow in grasping the dangers implicit in Christianity. Indeed, Christianity could well be regarded as the more dangerous of the two faiths for it appeared to have some connection with the sinister moves Europeans were reported to be making on the coast. Shortly after learning from Arab informants of the treaties concluded by the Germans in the East African interior, Mwanga received news that a missionary bishop, the Anglican James Harrington, was on his way to Buganda. Before Harrington could reach the capital, Mwanga had him murdered. Nine months later the *kabaka* sentenced thirty of his pages to be burnt alive after the young men had refused to be the ruler's partners in sodomy and stood resolutely by their new-found faith. Their deaths came to be regarded as one of the most notable martyrdoms in modern Christian history. Their courage proved infectious; more and more men began turning to the missionaries for instruction.

By the late 1880's an unusual and complicated situation had developed in the Ganda capital. For all his doubts about Christianity Mwanga had not attempted seriously to molest the missionaries. But the missionaries and their converts were divided into two rival groups, Protestant and Catholic, with the followers of Islam, an equally revolutionary monotheistic faith, representing a third and no less vocal body of opinion. Referring to the last years of Mutesa's reign, a modern historian has spoken of "colloquies at court, reminiscent of sixteenth century Europe in their manner, bitterness and barrenness of result." [27] By the late 1880's the adherents of the rival faiths were beginning to take on the form of distinct political parties. There was another complicating factor in the situation. Firearms had recently been introduced to Buganda, and it was the young men about court who had become most proficient in their use. Mwanga might have serious doubts about the new ideologies which so intrigued his courtiers, but he was always anxious to consolidate his own power in the perpetual struggle with the great chiefs of the kingdom. Accordingly he set about organizing his young men into new military formations, whose concentrated firepower soon proved their effectiveness. In September, 1888, the *kabaka* became alarmed at the extent of power acquired by his new regimental commanders and plotted to get rid of them. The plot miscarried, precipitating as it did so a countercoup which forced the *kabaka* into temporary exile and left control of the kingdom in the hands of a coalition made up of Muslim, Protestant, and Catholic leaders. Within a month the coalition had broken up, and for the next five years Buganda was torn by a factionalism that came close to developing into a civil war. One thing at least seemed clear: the *kabaka* could never again hope to achieve a position of undisputed supremacy, the real rulers of the country now being found in an oligarchy drawn from the leaders of the new religious parties.

In these circumstances the arrival of the British in 1890 was something of a godsend, for the intruders were well-suited to act as arbiters. Not surprisingly, the Protestants gained most from the British presence, while the Catholics tended to rest their hopes on the establishment of a German protectorate. *Kabaka* Mwanga attached himself to the Catholics but was defeated in a battle with the British and their Protestant allies. In 1894 a settlement was reached under whose terms the great offices of state and the territorial chieftainships were divided almost equally between Catholics and Protestants with a few posts being given to the less powerful Muslim group. The *kabaka* was left with little more than the ceremonial perquisites of his office. Disillusioned by this settlement, resenting the power acquired by the Ganda oligarchs quite as much as he deplored the new hegemony established by the British, Mwanga attempted a revolt only to find that most of his own subjects were prepared to stand by their new foreign overlords. Mwanga ended his life an exile in the Seychelles. His successor was a minor, a fact that made it even easier for the oligarchs, headed by three regents, to consolidate their position. The oligarchs had proved their value to the British not only by their loyalty at the time of the *kabaka*'s revolt but also by their willingness to assist the British in their campaigns against Bunyoro and other neighboring polities. In 1900 they received their reward in the form of a written and carefully negotiated agreement, a remarkable document for any colonial power to offer a nominally subject people. In return for their loyal cooperation, the *kabaka,* chiefs, and people of Buganda were assured that their traditional institutions would remain intact. The *kabaka* was granted the title of "His Highness." The *lukiko,* originally an assembly of all those who had come to pay court to the *kabaka,* was given formal status as a local parliament. The boundaries of Buganda were laid down in such a way as to include a substantial slice of territory recently acquired by force from Bunyoro. And a land settlement provided all the leading chiefs with freehold estates of a kind they could never have possessed in the past when grants of land were made on a temporary basis. Here then was a settlement which satisfied both the Ganda and the British for the next half century.

▲▼ COLONIAL RULE IN EAST AFRICA

The pattern of colonial rule established in East Africa in the first half of the twentieth century varied considerably from territory to territory. Britain was not the only power to exercise dominion in the region. Tanganyika, Rwanda, and Burundi experienced a generation of German hegemony which was followed in the two smaller territories by forty years of Belgian rule. In Kenya, the presence of a vocal body of white settlers gave a distinctive character to the colony's development. Tanganyika, Rwanda, and Burundi suffered the dislocating experience of a change of masters during World War I, then acquired the special status of League of Nations mandates, and later became trust territories under the United Nations. Finally, the development of Uganda and Zanzibar was profoundly influenced by the special position of the kingdom of Buganda in the one and the Arab sultanate in the other. Given these differences it is difficult to work out any valid generalizations for the region as a whole; instead it seems better to describe briefly the special characteristics of each of the various territories.

The position of Zanzibar was unique in tropical Africa. The sultanate, which covered the two off-shore islands of Zanzibar and Pemba, had been founded by a dynasty of Omani origin. The privileged position of the Arab aristocracy, together with the ceremonial manifestations of the sultan's authority, were preserved by the British. But the protectorate regime introduced by the islands' new overlords in 1890 rapidly changed its character, on lines not unlike those evolving in the contemporary French protectorate in Tunisia. At first there was talk of exerting no more than a "friendly influence" on the sultan's government. But when Gerald Portal, one of Evelyn Baring's bright young men, trained in the high-handed methods of the Cairo residency, was appointed consul-general in 1892, the true nature of British hegemony became apparent.

To Portal the sultanate was an "embodiment of all the worst and most barbaric characteristics of primitive Arab despotism." [28] Accordingly he did not hesitate to exert his authority by taking control of the sultan's treasury and using the revenue to pay the salaries of newly appointed British officials. Four years later the Zanzibar Arabs were given an even clearer and more brutal demonstration of British power. On the death of a British-nominated sultan a contender to the throne attempted to assert his claims by barricading himself and his followers in the palace on the waterfront. The British retaliated with a naval bombardment of the palace which caused 500 casualties. It was a very effective "lesson." The next year the British administration, urged on by the antislavery lobby in London, forced the sultan's government to pass a decree abolishing, though in a gradual manner, the status of slavery.

The Arab aristocracy of Zanzibar derived most of its wealth from clove plantations, the labor for which was provided by slaves brought from the mainland. The emancipation of the slaves proved less disastrous to Arab interests than many observers had predicted. Most ex-slaves stayed on as squatters on the estates of their masters, rendering labor-service in return for their tenancy of small plots of land. More serious as a source of Arab economic decline was the heavy burden of debt acquired by many plantation owners as a result of their efforts to keep up an opulent standard of living. Their indebtedness was greatly aggravated as a result of the catastrophic fall in clove prices caused by the Great Depression of the 1930's. A report of the mid-1930's reckoned that half the clove-trees in the protectorate had been mortgaged by their owners.

The census held in 1948 showed that 17 percent of the total population (44,000 out of 264,000) considered themselves Arab and 6 percent (15,000) Asian. In proportion to the total population, the Arabs could be regarded as as large a minority as the Afrikaners and the English of South Africa. Zanzibar never developed as rigid a system of social stratification as South Africa. Unlike the poor whites of the Union, impoverished Arabs, reduced to the position of small peasant farmers, felt no compunction about intermarrying with the indigenous African population, and there were a considerable number of Zanzibari Africans who came, as they prospered, to consider themselves Arabs. This blurring at the edges of ethnic groups helped to create what seemed to many outsiders an extremely attractive atmosphere of racial harmony. Yet to some extent this harmony was an illusion. Ambitious members of the African community soon found that Zanzibar could offer very few opportunities for upward mobility. Most of the protectorate's commerce was in the hands of Asians, while almost all the available jobs in the public service went to Asians or Arabs. As for the educational system, it could be described as a "mechanism through which already over-privileged racial groups increased their social and economic advantages": [29] by 1948 no more than 3 percent of the students in the senior grades of the protectorate's secondary schools were local Africans. Given the extremely limited character of the Zanzibar economy and the virtual impossibility of finding new sources of wealth, the British could have done something to ameliorate existing inequalities only by a ruthless transfer of wealth from one community to another. This the British were not prepared to do. In Zanzibar British colonial rule developed into "an extremely conservative political force." "Its effect, if not its intention," an American observer has pointed out, "was to freeze social class relations in the pattern in which they had existed when the protectorate began." [30]

The two African kingdoms of Rwanda and Burundi resembled Zanzibar in their social structure. Just as the Zanzibari Arabs formed a dominant caste sharply distinguished by their physical features from the mass of the population, so in the two inland kingdoms a distinct ethnic group, the Tutsi, pastoralists remarkable for their great stature and refined features, stood out sharply from the short, stocky peasantry known as the Hutu. The movement of Tutsi pastoralists into the fertile mountainous country lying to the north and northeast of Lake Tanganyika dated back perhaps as far as the fifteenth century. Gradually, over a long period of time, the two kingdoms of Rwanda and Burundi had emerged, growing from modest nuclear cores to conquer and absorb the numerous smaller polities of the area. But the two kingdoms differed sharply in their political structure. Burundi has been described as being "at best a loose aggregate of semiautonomous chiefdoms, at worst a cluster of warring principalities," with the *mwami* (the title borne in both countries by the ruler) little more than *primus inter pares* in relation to the princes of the blood. Rwanda, by contrast, presented a high degree of centralization, with local chiefs entirely dependent on royal favor for their tenure of office, while the *mwami* "came as close to the image of an absolute monarch" as any ruler in Africa.[31] These differences in the two countries' political pattern were closely related to their social structure. In Burundi, local princes engaged in a constant competition for power could not afford to ignore the support offered by their Hutu neighbors; in Rwanda, on the other hand, the absolute nature of royal power, combined with the fact that all subordinate chiefs were of Tutsi origin, created a much more rigidly hierarchical system. These differences between the two kingdoms came to be accentuated by the policies followed by the European overlords of the area in the first half of the twentieth century.

The Germans pursued diametrically opposite policies in the two kingdoms. In Rwanda, once assured of the collaboration of the *mwami,* they did everything in their power to strengthen and extend the influence of the crown. In Burundi, on the other hand, the Germans encouraged the process of fragmentation by supporting the claims of the local chiefs and by reducing still further the prestige of the *mwami.* The Belgians, who took over the area in 1916 and were later given a mandate for the conquered territory, built on the modest foundations laid by the Germans. Under Belgian administration Ruanda-Urundi, as the territory was known, was governed as a separate province of the Congo. The Belgians left the indigenous political structure intact and claimed to be applying to the two kingdoms the principles of indirect rule. But the Belgian interpretation of indirect rule was not quite the same as that of the British. Under the Belgian system, local chiefs were subjected to a much greater measure of supervision and allowed far less responsibility than their opposite numbers in neighboring Tanganyika. Nevertheless, especially in Rwanda where Western-type education was largely monopolized by the Tutsi, Belgian rule tended to stress still further the privileged position of the minority group. The bitterness engendered by this policy was eventually to lead to one of the bloodiest revolutions ever experienced by an African country.

The administration of Tanganyika presented problems very different from those faced by the colonial rulers of Ruanda-Urundi and Zanzibar. The territory was by far the most extensive in East Africa, with a population divided up among an exceptionally large number of ethnic groups, all organized in small-scale polities. In tackling the problem of asserting their hegemony over so diffuse a population the Germans followed the example of the Zanzibari governors on the coast and appointed native officials with the title of *akida* to supervise groups of villages. At first these officials were all coastmen, many of them Arabs, but by 1910, Africans, educated at government schools, were coming forward to provide the German administration with a well-trained local civil service. In the interior the Germans often had no alternative but to make use of local chiefs, while seeking to turn local rivalries to their own advantage. In its first two decades German rule in East Africa was often criticized for its harshness and brutality, but a notable change took place after the suppression of the *Maji-Maji* rebellion. The last seven years of undisturbed German rule are regarded as "an era of reform." The new reforms were initiated by two able and enlightened men, Germany's first colonial minister, Bernhard Dernburg, and the colony's first civilian governor, Freiherr von Rechenberg. Greater stress was laid on the need to develop peasant agriculture rather than to promote the interests of European settlers; active support was given to the missions in their educational work; and the indiscriminate use of the whip was severely censured.

During World War 1 Tanganyika probably suffered greater material destruction and loss of life than any other territory in Africa. For four years the country was a battleground as the Allied forces vainly attempted to compel the Germans to surrender: only after the armistice had been signed in Europe, did the brilliantly elusive German commander, Lettow-Vorbeck, lay down his arms. And not until 1925, with the appointment of an exceptionally able British governor, Sir Donald Cameron, did the colonial administration recover the dynamism that had marked the last years of German rule. Cameron was an unusual man to find in the higher ranks of the British colonial service: born in the West Indies of poor Irish parents, he was entirely self-educated but had secured a post in Nigeria and rapidly come to the fore. Cameron was determined to act in accordance with the principles of trusteeship laid down by the League of Nations. Constantly he stressed "the duty of the Mandatory Power to train the people so that they can stand by themselves." [32] The system of indirect rule, as he had known it in Nigeria, seemed to the governor to offer the best means of encouraging a sense of self-reliance. Accordingly he instructed his administrative officers to search out the traditional rulers, many of whom had been cast aside by the German administrators, and saw that they were provided with the organizational structure in the form of native treasuries and courts needed to fulfil their functions effectively. Initially these reforms were widely welcomed, but in Tanganyika, as in parts of British West Africa, it gradually became apparent that under the new system traditional rulers were able to bolster up their power and influence much more effectively than they had ever done in the old days. Not only did chiefs enjoy the benefit of fixed salaries; they were also given preferential treatment in schemes for agricultural improvement. In one district, for example, the chief was presented with 1,500 coffee trees, while local headmen received only 75. Here in the expanded privileges of traditional rulers was a significant source of social tension.

The peculiar difficulties involved in implementing a system of indirect rule are well illustrated by the story of British relations with Buganda. The agreement of 1900 gave the kingdom a special status not unlike that of an Indian native state under the British raj, and its great men continued to regard themselves as the allies rather than the subjects of the British. Allies they had certainly been in the 1890's and 1900's when they had so vigorously assisted the British in asserting their hegemony over the rest of the protectorate. But the consolidation of British power made the need for Ganda support much less vital. In 1926, Sir Apolo Kagwa, *katikiro* (chief minister) of Buganda, resigned after a clash over a relatively trivial matter with the British provincial commissioner. His departure marked the end of an era, for Kagwa had been one of the architects of the 1900 agreement and had always proved himself a resolute defender of his kingdom's autonomy. From the mid-1920's the British began to intervene much more directly in Bugandan affairs. In so doing they were following what had become common practice in other parts of the protectorate, where the local British commissioner could be described as the "controller and chief executive" of his district, "operating through a hierarchy of chiefs and subordinate chiefs in charge of traditional units." [33] Having unquestionably established its hegemony, the protectorate government showed itself in the 1920's "more concerned with economy, efficiency and welfare than with the maintenance of traditional institutions." [34]

Local administrative policy could, however, always be transformed by a strong and resolute governor, and in 1935 Uganda received such a man in the person of Sir Philip Mitchell. Mitchell had worked under Cameron in Tanganyika, and he accepted Cameron's belief that native authorities should really be allowed to enjoy a measure of autonomy. Accordingly, he interpreted the task of British administrative officers in Buganda to lie in the role not of controllers but of advisers, a new policy that led to a marked relaxation of British supervision of local affairs. But it was the chiefs rather than the people who profited most from this apparently liberal approach. In 1945 and again in 1949, Buganda was the scene of widespread riots directed not against the British administration but against the *kabaka's* government and the chiefs. The British took strong action to restore law and order, and British officials returned to the policy of exercising tighter control over the affairs of Buganda. But the basic policy of ruling through the chiefs was not discredited. British officials might tinker with the system, but as with their counterparts in Nigeria, it was impossible for them, even as late as 1945, to visualize the future of Uganda in a pattern other than that of a congeries of native states.

Few contiguous colonial territories in Africa presented such sharp contrasts as Uganda and Kenya. The difference between the two territories went far deeper than the obvious fact that Kenya had become a land of white settlement while Uganda retained its distinctive African character. Uganda was also a territory most of whose peoples had come in the course of the past few centuries to be organized in states or demi-states, whereas Kenya was for the most part a land of stateless polities, of confusing clusters of peoples whose societies were so structured as to make it virtually impossible for an outsider to distinguish any obvious traditional leaders. Faced with the necessity of establishing a rudimentary administrative superstructure, the British resorted to the device of nominating those Africans best known to them—traders, interpreters, ex-soldiers—to act as chiefs or leaders. This policy was soon found to have many disadvantages. By 1912 administrative officers were describing these "so-called chiefs" as "a partly detribalized riff-raff who enjoyed no confidence among their own people." [35] By the mid-1920's, however, the British had begun to work out a more effective system of administration through the establishment of local district councils. These bodies brought together people from previously independent polities and so helped to create a wider sense of loyalty and unity. Many of the councillors were drawn from the age-grade of the elders, the traditional decision-makers of most Kenyan societies, but younger, Western-educated men also had a chance of making their views known through a modified system of elections. District councils were allowed to dispose of some of the money they collected in tax and so gained some practical experience of the problems of financing local development.

Far more significant to most contemporary observers than the shifts taking place in the political structure of local African communities were the political activities of the colony's European settlers. In numerical terms the European settler community was very small—in 1923 there were 1,183 European landowners, in 1929 just over 2,000—but it included many vigorous, independent, and determined men with a clear vision of what the future should hold: Kenya was to become a "white man's country," another South Africa, the last frontier for the pioneering genius of the British race. Many of the Kenya settlers were members of the English aristocracy—one of Nairobi's leading hotels was jocularly known as "the House of Lords"—and so were well versed in the techniques of manipulating "the old-boy network" when dealing with the government at home or its representatives in the colony. Hardly less important than these English connections were the South African associations possessed by many of the settlers: the South African pattern of government presented indeed a highly acceptable model for this white oligarchy.

By 1920 the settlers had shown themselves extremely adept at gaining the support of many British administrators. They had secured the right to elect eleven members to the colony's legislative council and had succeeded in working out with cooperative governors a system of "government by consent" which enabled them to exert considerable informal influence on the direction of affairs. In the early 1920's, however, the European settlers found their position challenged not by the African majority but by the colony's other alien minority, the Indian community. Indian leaders in Kenya saw the future of the country in terms not of a white but of a brown dominion. Naturally they felt a bitter resentment at the way in which the colonial government had given in to the demands of the white settlers by imposing many restrictions on Indian activities, preventing Indians from acquiring land in the white Highlands, and limiting Indian representation in the legislative council to a single nominated member. British politicians and civil servants with Indian connections, uneasily aware of the mounting tide of nationalism in India itself, were not unsympathetic to the aspirations of Kenyan Indians. In 1923, in response to the pressure exerted by this British Indian lobby, the colonial office came up with a scheme for politiccal reform in Kenya: elections to the legislative council were to be conducted on the basis of a new common-roll franchise. Stringent income and property qualifications would limit the number of Indian voters to no more than 10 percent of the total electorate, but the white settlers argued that with a common roll there would be a steady increase in Indian voting strength, until the whole colony would find itself engulfed in an irresistible brown flood. This nightmarish prospect aroused the white settlers to such a pitch of fury that many of them were prepared to run the risk of armed rebellion should the British government decide to carry its plans through. The settlers gained their point. The British government withdrew the plan for a common roll, but politicians in Whitehall were not prepared to go all the way with the settlers and accept their demands for eventual self-government. Instead, by way of compromise, the colonial secretary of the day, the Duke of Devonshire, issued a statement pointing out that Kenya was "primarily an African country," that "the interests of the African inhabitants must be paramount," and that the British government was "exercising a trust on their behalf." Some years later, under a prosettler colonial secretary, L. S. Amery, there was talk of associating the white settlers more closely with the whole process of trusteeship, but the Labour government of 1930 made it clear that ultimate responsibility for the future of Kenya lay with the British government alone.

By the 1930's, then, Kenyan settlers could see little prospect of ever being able to achieve their ideal of an independent, white-dominated state. In compensation they could console themselves by the degree of power and influence they had secured in the running of the colony. As a result of the inquiries undertaken by the Land Commission of 1932–34, the settlers were granted permanent and exclusive use of 16,700 square miles of territory in the fertile highlands. Separation and privilege now become the hallmarks of Kenyan society: "medical services, education and even sports were organized on strict racial lines with the Europeans always getting the best services, the Indians the second best and the Africans," so a recent African historian has pointed out, "having to do with whatever was left over." [36] As for the settlers' political power, it was considerably enhanced by the appointment in 1937 of two leading settlers to ministerial office in the colony's executive council. The establishment during World War II of numerous boards and committees with the task of directing the colony's wartime economy provided the settlers with new opportunities for gaining office and exerting influence. In retrospect it can be seen that by 1945 the political power of Kenya's settler community was at its height.

▲▼ THE ECONOMIC TRANSFORMATION OF EAST AFRICA

In 1875 most East African communities still found themselves locked in the straitjacket of a subsistence economy and therefore totally unaware of those animating experiences common to so many peoples of North and West Africa—the experiences that come from trade, the social intercourse of the market place, the journeys away from home, the acquisition of a few simple yet life-enhancing luxuries, the opportunity to develop new skills. Not that a subsistence economy necessarily involved grinding poverty. Everything depended on the local environment. Unfortunately, large parts of East Africa were extremely ill-endowed by nature: the soil was poor, rainfall scanty and irregular, and the surrounding bush infested with insect parasites, especially the dreaded tsetse fly. But there were a few areas, of which Buganda provides the most notable example, where it was possible to produce a surplus of basic foodstuffs without excessive labor, unharassed by the constant threat of famine. The economy of Buganda was based on the banana, so easy was the plant to cultivate, that it could be said with only slight exaggeration that one old Ganda woman could produce enough bananas to feed ten men. Supported by the regular yield of their banana groves, the Ganda were able to lead a far more settled life than those many other East African peoples who found it necessary to shift the ground of their meager plots of maize or millet every few years. With food production left largely to the women, Ganda men were able to devote themselves to other pursuits, craftmanship, administration, and war. War, not trade, provided the means of increasing the kingdom's wealth; "the real basis of their economy," as Christopher Wrigley has put it, "was not production but predation." [37] There was really very little that the Ganda could barter with their neighbors. What they wanted—women, either as concubines or laborers, and livestock—could be obtained only by force. To this end the Ganda developed their state into a highly efficient military machine.

By 1875, however, the Ganda and many other peoples of the East African interior were beginning to become aware of new economic opportunities, as traders from the coast made their way into their territories, bringing with them a tempting display of novelties, including firearms. The emergence of long-distance trade routes in East Africa was, by comparison with most of North and West Africa, a very recent phenomenon, dating back little further than the last years of the eighteenth century. The initiative in developing trade between the coast and the interior was taken not, as is often imagined, by the Arabs and the Swahili of the coast but by certain African peoples, notably the Kamba, the Nyamwezi, and the Yao. But by the middle of the nineteenth century, the men of the coast, encouraged by the political support of the Omani rulers of Zanzibar, and greatly assisted by the financial backing of Indian money-lenders, were leading their own caravans into the interior, establishing trading posts at Tabora in Central Tanzania and at Ujiji on Lake Tanganyika, and making their impact felt on many local communities. But East African commerce in the nineteenth century was seriously constricted in two ways. In the first place, the carriage of goods had to be made by head-porterage, the most expensive of all forms of transportation, for the tsetse-fly ruled out pack animals and canoes could not be used on the rivers that flowed down to the coast. Thus, even if the interior had produced valuable agricultural products, the cost of freightage would have rendered their exploitation totally unprofitable. In fact, the interior could offer only three commodities in which the outside world was interested—slaves, ivory, and, for a short period, wild rubber. But ivory and rubber were rapidly wasting assets, and the trade in slaves was outlawed in the 1870's. Here then was a situation very different from that prevailing in West Africa where African producers living near the coast or within reach of navigable rivers had been supplying European merchants with steadily mounting quantities of palm oil, groundnuts, and other tropical produce for many decades.

The basic theme of East African economic history during the colonial period is to be found in the removal of these constrictions, the development of a more efficient system of communications, and the introduction of new forms of agricultural produce, easily saleable on the world market. Economic transformation is never easy to bring about, and in East Africa the difficulties were more formidable than in many other parts of the continent. At first the region seemed entirely devoid of mineral resources, and discoveries made late in the colonial period —diamonds and gold in Tanganyika, copper and tin in Uganda, soda ash and a little gold in Kenya—were on a very modest scale when compared with the vast mineral wealth found in South Africa, Northern Rhodesia, and parts of the Congo. The region, then, offered little or nothing to attract a flow of private capital. In the first years of their existence all the colonial territories, except Zanzibar, were dependent on grants-in-aid from their metropolitan governments. But their poverty was not without its stimulating effects—it forced European officials both at home and in the East African field to give a great deal of thought to the problem of how best to develop their newly and somewhat reluctantly acquired estates.

At the outset of the colonial period communications meant not so much roads but railroads. The first major railroad to be completed in East Africa—the line from Mombasa to Kisumu on Lake Victoria— was built by the British for strategic reasons. But even before the line was completed, its revolutionary impact on the area through which it passed was becoming apparent. At a place called by the Masai *Enkare Nairobi,* "cold stream,"—"a blank, swampy stretch of soppy landscape, the resort of thousands of wild animals," as a contemporary described it,[38] the railroad engineers erected their workshops. Soon, as at every other stopping point on the railroad, an Indian bazaar had sprung up, and enterprising Indian traders were making contact with the local Kikuyu and Masai, bartering cotton cloth, beads, or wire for grain, ivory, or hides. The same process was to occur on all the railroads of East Africa. The Mombasa-Kisumu line, though described as the "Uganda railway," did not, in fact, reach Uganda territory until the 1920's, arriving at Kampala in 1931. By this time a number of branch lines had been constructed to serve the needs of the European farming community in the Kenya Highlands. In German East Africa, the Tanga-Moshi line was begun in 1893 and completed in 1911, while the long central line from Dar es-Salaam to Kigoma on Lake Tanganyika was built in nine years, the last stretch being finished only a few months before the outbreak of World War I.

Concurrently with the railroad engine came the bicycle, a particularly useful innovation in a region where it was hardly ever possible to use pack animals. (In Uganda no import of bicycles is recorded in the customs returns before 1908; between 1908 and 1914 bicycle imports rose in value from £4,000 to £27,000.) The 1920's brought the truck and with it the need for colonial governments to devote more and more of their modest resources to the construction and upkeep of roads. In

Uganda expenditure on public works shot up from £41,000 in 1919 to £315,000 in 1928, fell as a result of the Depression to £161,000 in 1932, but rose to £557,000 in 1938. By this time the colony contained over one hundred townships and twenty-seven trading centers, each of which could be regarded as a relatively isolated "pocket of development" making its impact felt on the surrounding countryside. An efficient road system linked these embryonic urban centers together, thus creating, in Cyril Ehrlich's words, "the complex network of interrelated markets which distinguishes a healthy economy." [39]

The railroads, the roads, the colonial administrations that made their construction possible, all had to be paid for—and after an initial period of metropolitan assistance, the money had to come from the local people. The stress on money represented another innovation for most East African peoples. Colonial officials found that when they tried collecting taxes in kind, they were liable to be presented with barely saleable objects. (In the early years of the Uganda Protectorate officials were prepared to receive one live young elephant as a tax return from one thousand huts.) The introduction of cash crops which could be sold on the world market was an absolute necessity. But two questions remained to be resolved: what crops should be introduced, and who should be encouraged to grow them—local African peasant farmers or alien planters using African labor? The questions were interrelated—certain crops were more suitable for one type of agriculture than others—but it is simpler to consider them separately.

Sisal, cotton, and coffee were the three most important cash crops produced in East Africa during the colonial period. Of these, sisal represented a complete innovation. The plant, a fiber-producing aloe, was brought from Florida to German East Africa in the 1890's. Sisal had the advantage of not requiring either good soil or regular rainfall, so it could be grown in the semiarid country that formed the immediate hinterland to the East African coast, but it was suitable only for plantation production. In the years before World War I, both English and German settlers developed sisal plantations, but after 1918 most of the German estates in Tanganyika passed into the hands of Greeks or Indians.

Under East African conditions cotton, unlike sisal, could not support the high overheads of European management, but it was a crop well-suited to peasant cultivation. Its fortunes varied sharply, however, in the three East African territories. In Tanganyika it became a valuable supplement to coffee and sisal as an export crop. In Kenya, on the other hand, despite vigorous efforts made by the government from 1907 onward to interest Africans in Nyanza Province in this new source of income, it failed to catch on. The peoples of the province apparently found it "more congenial to work for hire [on European farms] than to exert themselves in the production of an unfamiliar and inedible crop." [40] At exactly the same period, in neighboring districts of Uganda, African production of cotton was proving remarkably successful. The British authorities had decided to encourage the growing of cotton because of the high price of the crop on the world market. To this end, large quantities of different strains of seed were imported from Egypt and distributed to selected local chiefs who in turn passed the seed on to the farmers in their area. By 1915, Uganda's export of cotton, which brought in no more than £200 in 1905, was worth £369,000.

If the price of cotton was riding high in the world market during the first decade of the twentieth century, that of coffee was caught up in a long depression. In 1910, however, coffee prices began rising sharply. It was already known that many parts of the region provided suitable conditions for coffee cultivation—indeed *robusta* coffee appears to have been indigenous to southern Uganda. Rising prices showed how much coffee production could contribute to an expanding economy. Again, however, there was a sharp difference between the three territories. In Uganda and Tanganyika, coffee was developed as a peasant crop in the 1920's. In Kenya, on the other hand, wealthy Englishmen, possessing the capital needed for the establishment of substantial plantations, began investing in coffee before World War I. The emergence of this new plantocracy provides "the key," Christopher Wrigley has suggested, "to a great part of Kenya's subsequent history," for the typical planter combined "the economic role of a substantial capitalist and employer of labour with the social outlook of a farming settler." [41] The planters' preoccupation with the need to obtain regular supplies of African labor led them to put pressure on the government actively to discourage the production of lucrative cash-crops by peasant farmers in native reserves. Not until the mid-1950's, when the Mau Mau rebellion forced the Kenya government to reconsider its agricultural policies were the restrictions on African production abandoned.

Given the climate of European opinion in the first decades of the twentieth century together with the obvious economic backwardness of many East African communities, it was hardly surprising that many colonial enthusiasts should have stressed the major part that European settlers could play in the economic development of East Africa. In practice, every settler was faced with a grueling uphill task, and many enterprises ended in bankruptcy and heartbreak. The English aristocrats who dreamed of reproducing the farming practices of the English shires in the splendid landscapes of the Kenya Highlands found their wheat fields ravaged by "rust," their herds of cattle decimated by east coast fever, and their imported sheep dying "with depressing regularity." [42] But they carried on, experimented with new strains and breeds, and so made a massive addition to the country's stock of agricultural knowledge. Moreover, they brought with them a great deal of capital and were able to pass on many new techniques to their African workers. Against these undeniable benefits must be set the strains and tensions produced in many Kenyan African communities by the alienation of land and by the racial arrogance of some of the settlers. In Tanganyika, the European settler community was much smaller and very much more widely dispersed than in Kenya, but in spite of modest numbers it was able to exert considerable pressure first on the German, then on the British administration. Uganda, by contrast, followed the West African model, with the country's major export crops being produced by peasant farmers. But the supremacy of peasant agriculture was not a foregone conclusion. Between 1916 and 1923, many senior protectorate officials argued in favor of encouraging European plantions. But the few European coffee plantations already established failed to live up to expectations, and by 1923 there was clearly no likelihood of being able to interest other Europeans to come and settle in the country. Thus there developed significant variations in the pattern of economic activity in the three major East African territories. These variations were to have a profound influence on the way in which the inhabitants of the three territories reacted to the impact of alien rule.

▲▼ "IMPROVEMENT," "DIFFERENTIATION," AND THE RISE OF NATIONALISM IN EAST AFRICA

"The Age of Improvement and Differentiation" is the title which John Iliffe, one of the contributors to a recent history of Tanzania, has applied to his study of the colonial period of the country's history. The phrase is a stimulating one, for it indicates the dynamic quality of the African response to the colonial situation. Tanzanians, in common with most other Africans, had been made brutally aware of their own weakness by the overwhelming might of the colonial power. Abandoning the tactics of resistance, they turned, Iliffe suggests, to "improvement" which is defined as an "attempt to change people and societies in such a way as to make them both better in themselves and more able to face their rulers on equal terms." "The process was a gradual one which emphasized education, economic development and the modernization of local government. . . . Its heroes were village schoolteachers and shopkeepers, clerks and cotton-growers." [43] With improvement went increasing differentiation. Some groups were better placed than others by virtue of their proximity to good schools or their possession of particularly fertile land to enjoy the advantages of improvement. Within particular societies the process of differentiation was carried further by the fact that certain individuals or families responded more eagerly than others to the new opportunities around them. Sharp contrasts of a kind never seen in the culturally homogeneous societies of the past began to make their appearance. "Improvement" and "differentiation" are concepts of continental, even of universal validity: developments such as these were taking place all over Africa. Alternatively, one may regard the changes occurring during the colonial period as products of that convergence of forces defined as the peaceful pursuit of well-being and the stimulus of intercourse. Contact with European missionaries, traders, and administrators made Africans aware of new opportunities for earning a livelihood or introduced them to new concepts of the good life. In embarking on new forms of activity, in concerning themselves with the techniques of "improvement," individuals may well not have been prompted by any consciously political motive. But the process of improvement inevitably brought about new social situations and these in turn led to the emergence of tensions of a kind well calculated to weaken the authority of the colonial power. "Improvement" may be seen as the seed-bed of modern nationalism.

In the first decades of colonial rule most East African communities experienced only spasmodic contacts with the white man. But by the mid-1920's, the activities of government officials, missionaries, and settlers were beginning to impinge much more directly on the lives of many Africans. As in most other parts of tropical Africa, the missionaries proved themselves the most vigorous alien stimulators of change and their success, measured in the statistics of conversion, was often remarkable. But excessive missionary pressure could serve to produce a countervailing "cultural nationalism" among their converts. This development was vividly illustrated by the conflict over "female circumcision" which came to the surface among the Kikuyu in the late 1920's. According to Kikuyu custom, the operation of clitorodectomy or female circumcision formed an essential part of the initiation rites to which all girls were subjected. In Kikuyu eyes "not to be circumcised was to be debarred from developing the personality and attributes of womanhood." [44] On the other hand, medical evidence had come to show that in a minority of cases the operation could have harmful after-effects. By the mid-1920's, some Kikuyu had agreed to abandon the custom, but certain missionaries were anxious to hasten its abolition by making it the subject of an all-out assault. In so doing they laid themselves open to the charge of attempting to interfere with the whole ceremony of initiation which to most Kikuyu formed an essential part of their traditional life. Members of a newly formed proto-nationalist organization, the Kikuyu Central Association, took the lead in resisting the missionary assault. Their propaganda helped to give to the Kikuyu as a whole, a people divided in the past into many autonomous groups, an awareness of cultural homogeneity such as they had never known before. The crisis over female circumcision had another important consequence: it provided the Kikuyu with a pretext for creating modern institutions of their own. Rather than submit to the demands of the missionaries, many Kikuyu chose to leave the mission churches or resign from teaching posts in mission schools. In so doing they did not turn their backs either on Christianity or on Western education; instead, they set about creating churches and schools of their own. One of the societies formed for this purpose, the Kikuyu Independent Schools Association, defined its object as being "to further the interests of the Kikuyu and its members and to safeguard the homogeneity of such interests relating to their spiritual, economic, social and intellectual upliftment." [45] Whatever limitations the Kikuyu independent schools might have to suffer from lack of funds or shortage of trained teachers, the urge for improvement was clearly apparent.

The tension in Kikuyu country could be presented as a conflict not only between Europeans and Africans but also between Kikuyu and Kikuyu, for a considerable number of Kikuyu Christians decided to stand by their missionary patrons. An intra-tribal conflict of quite a different kind may be illustrated by developments among the Chagga of northern Tanzania. The Chagga, who occupy the fertile slopes of Mount Kilimanjaro, had been among the first East African people to take to the growing of cash crops. In 1925, a group of Chagga coffee-growers established one of the first modern organizations yet seen in a rural area of Tanganyika, the Kilimanjaro Native Planters' Association (KNPA). Within two years the association had 10,000 members. Its primary aim was to provide an efficient means of marketing the coffee produced by local growers but the leaders of the association were led on to interest themselves in many other matters and so became involved in disputes with local chiefs, local European settlers, and even with the government itself. In the eyes of certain Chagga chiefs the association represented an unwelcome new focus of power in an area where they expected to enjoy absolute authority. European settlers seeking to enlarge their holdings soon came under KNPA attack, while government measures seemingly designed to support settler interests, such as the registration of Chagga land-holdings, were stoutly resisted. The average Chagga farmer, so a perceptive administrator noted in 1931, was afraid of the consequences of a possible coalition of interests between European officials and settlers and wanted "to keep his affairs as far as possible out of the hands of the Government." [46] The KNPA collapsed during the 1930's depression, and was replaced by a government-sponsored body, the Kilimanjaro Native Cooperative Union. The new union was largely under the control of the chiefs, but when it attempted to assert its monopoly over the sale of coffee there were violent riots, some of which took the form of demonstrations directed against the chiefs themselves.

A more direct cause of conflict between East African peasants and European administrators was to be found in the government's well-intentioned but often ill-considered attempts to force through schemes for agricultural improvement. A striking example of such a conflict is provided by the controversy that arose in 1938 between the Kenya government and the Kamba over the destocking of cattle. The Kamba, who occupy the drier country to the south and east of the Kikuyu, had evolved a mixed economy in which cattle played an important part. In precolonial times Kamba country was surrounded by a no-man's-land into which the Kamba could drive their cattle for grazing if the rains failed in their own homeland. But with the expansion of European settlement a large part of these empty lands was taken up by white farmers and fenced off as cattle ranches. At the same time, veterinary officers were achieving great success in eliminating the diseases that had decimated Kamba herds in the past. By the 1930's the vicious consequences produced by these changes had become alarmingly apparent. Denied the opportunity of moving into other areas at a time when their own herds were increasing rapidly in numbers, the Kamba found themselves with no alternative but to overgraze their own homelands which soon came to display the brutal scars of soil erosion. After years of prevarication the government attempted to tackle the situation by introducing compulsory destocking. The Kamba provided many recruits for the King's African Rifles and for the colonial police; consequently they were regarded by the British as the most loyal of Kenyan peoples. But their loyalty did not prevent them from feeling a bitter resentment at the way in which destocking was being carried out or from devising highly effective countermeasures. A group of educated Kamba came together, formed the Ukamba Members Association, and embarked on a campaign designed to present their grievances to a wide public through letters to the local press and petitions to the governments in Nairobi and London. Possibly even more effective was the dramatic gesture of 2,000 Kamba men, women, and children who marched on Nairobi and set up a "protest camp" on the race course of the capital. There they stayed for more than three weeks until the government showed signs of a change of mind. Compulsory cattle auctions were given up, and government officials began working out a more effective scheme for marketing. As for the Kamba, the crisis had clearly demonstrated the value and power of organization, developed a new group of political leaders, and led to the establishment of contacts with members of the Kikuyu Central Association.

Tension and protest were not confined to rural areas. As early as 1922 Nairobi had been the scene of a bloody incident in which at least twenty-five Africans were shot dead by the police while demonstrating against the arrest of a popular leader, Harry Thuku. Thuku, a clerk in government service, was one of the founders of the Young Kikuyu Association, a body described in an official report as being "composed largely of office boys and domestic servants." [47] African workers in Nairobi had many grievances, the most immediate of which was caused by a European attempt made at a time of economic depression to cut their wages by a third. By extending his campaign to the Kikuyu countryside, Thuku effectively linked rural and urban discontent. But the strong measures used by the government—Thuku was kept in detention for nine years—temporarily blunted the edge of urban protest. As for the growth of labor organization, there is little evidence of any significant development until 1939 when both Dar es-Salaam and Mombasa were the scene of dockworkers' strikes. "We do not like to be kicked and pushed and abused during the working-time," the "coolies" of Dar es-Salaam declared in a letter of complaint addressed to the local district officer. [48] The Dar es-Salaam strike was a failure: the workers could find no answer to the employers' threat to recruit a new labor force. But four years later the dockers of Dar es-Salaam staged another strike and succeeded in gaining considerable wage increases. Moreover, their example proved infectious. In 1944, domestic servants in the Tanganyikan capital formed a Union of Europeans' Boys and began to press the government for improved working conditions.

Taking East Africa as a whole, it could be said that in the years between the wars protest was the exception rather than the rule. Many East African communities were still barely affected by the pressures emanating from the aliens in their midst and so had little sense of grievance. Moreover, such protests as occurred were all essentially local in character, being confined to individual ethnic groups. All this was gradually to change in the course of the 1940's as colonial governments began to embark on ambitious plans for economic development and in so doing brought many Africans face to face with European officials for the first time in their lives. At the same time, a substantial number of East Africans were made vividly aware of a wider world through their service in the armed forces. The early 1950's saw the emergence of a mass nationalism well designed to put pressure not on the periphery of the colonial administration but on its central councils.

▲▼ THE DECOLONIZATION OF EAST AFRICA

In the late 1940's, hardly any observer of the East African scene would have dared predict that the region would be independent of alien rule within a mere fifteen years. Even as late as the latter half of the 1950's, British officials were confidently talking in terms of another quarter-century of colonial administration. Yet, in fact, by the end of 1963 every country in the region had achieved its independence. No less surprising to contemporary observers than the speed of decolonization was the fact that Tanganyika of all the East African countries should have been the first to gain independence. For Tanganyika could clearly be shown to be the most backward economically, the least advanced in the field of education, and therefore seemingly the worst equipped of all East African territories to meet the burdens of independence. But Tanganyika had one sovereign advantage over its neighbors—the virtual absence of tribalism. The country's population was made up of a very large number of ethnic groups none of which were large enough— unlike the Ganda or the Kikuyu—to offer a serious threat to its neighbors by seizing power at the center and monopolizing jobs and development grants for its own advantage. Moreover, partly as a result of the activities of coastal traders from the nineteenth century onward, partly as a consequence of the language policy followed first by the German, then by the British colonial education department, Swahili had come to be widely spoken throughout the country, thus providing Tanganyika with an indigenous *lingua franca,* an advantage possessed by no other tropical African country of comparable size. It was thus rather less difficult to build up a sense of national unity in Tanganyika than in any other East African country. Tanganyikan nationalists had another asset at their disposal: as a trust territory their country was subject to a measure of surpervision by the United Nations, a situation which made it impossible for the British authorities entirely to disregard the pressures exerted by international opinion.

Against these advantages must be set the fact that Tanganyika contained influential minorities of Europeans and Asians. The numbers involved were not large—23,000 Europeans, among whom only a few hundred could properly be regarded as settlers, and 87,000 Asians— but the two minority groups were regarded by the British authorities as making so important a contribution to the development of the country that it seemed right to allow them a major voice in its affairs. The privileged position accorded to Europeans and Asians was most clearly apparent in the composition of the colony's legislative council. The first African representative was appointed to the council in 1945, and African membership was slowly increased in the course of the next decade, but the government, in pursuit of a policy described as "multi-racial," insisted on parity of representation for the country's three races, European, Asian, and African. No matter how great the numerical superiority of Africans in the country as a whole, in the legislative council African representatives would always, under the parity system, find themselves in a minority when set against the two groups of aliens.

It is a mistake to pay too much attention to the details of colonial constitutional change. Far more significant in the long run were the developments, barely perceptible at the time to most observers at the center, which were beginning to affect Africans in many walks of life, gradually drawing them together into one of the most remarkable mass movements of its time. In 1945, a body known as the Tanganyikan African Association (TAA) held its third territorial conference and discussed, among other things, a motion to the effect that "efforts be made to enroll all Africans, women and men, in the African Association" and passed a resolution calling for the establishment of local branches in every town and district.[49] The TAA had been formed in Dar es-Salaam sixteen years earlier by a group largely composed of African civil servants. In view of its limited membership the association's stated object, "to safeguard the interests of Africans not only in this territory but in the whole of Africa," [50] seemed absurdly grandiloquent. But the association stuck to its guns in the face of much discouragement, extended its influence through the formation of up-country branches, and showed itself to be the only African institution in the country capable of bringing together people of many different ethnic groups.

In the late 1940's and early 1950's the most vigorous assertion of Tanganyikan nationalism came not from the center but from the provinces, particularly from Sukuma country south of Lake Victoria, where African cotton-growers joined together to form a cooperative union in a bid to break the monopoly over the sale of cotton established by Indian businessmen. The work involved in organizing the union helped to politicize the farmers of the area and paved the way for a great extension of TAA activity. In other parts of the country the efforts made by the colonial administration to introduce improved methods of agricultural production often aroused bitter resentment. Thus a group of farmers in the Dar es-Salaam area complained of the behavior of agricultural instructors: "Instead of teaching us how to produce more crops, they tell us to clear our coconut *shambas* [plantations] at once and in case of failing to do so, heavy fines and imprisonment are imposed." [51] One issue proved of particular significance. In 1951 the British forcibly expelled 3,000 Meru farmers from their land in northern Tanganyika to make room for European settlers. The Meru land case seemed to call in question the whole issue of trusteeship: "It aroused political fears and suspicions," noted a U.N. visiting mission, "wherever African political leaders have a following." [52]

In 1954, the TAA transformed itself into the Tanganyika African National Union (TANU), members electing as their president a young Catholic schoolteacher and one of the country's few graduates, Julius Nyerere. The new party immediately embarked on a policy of vigorous expansion, concentrating its attention on those areas where peasant discontents provided fertile soil for nationalist propaganda. At the same time, Nyerere visited the United Nations to press the case for his country's independence with eloquence and assurance. The colonial government viewed the rise of TANU with misgiving and devised two different forms of countermeasure. The first involved simple repression, banning TANU activities in disaffected areas. The second represented a form of tactics more common in French than in British colonies, the creation of a government-sponsored political party, the United Tanganyika Party (UTP), designed to uphold the cause of multi-racialism. Both methods failed. When elections were held early in 1959 for thirty members of the legislative council, ten for each race, TANU won an overwhelming victory, for the elections were held on the basis of a common roll, and those European and Asian candidates who had obtained TANU backing were assured of success over their UTP opponents. With TANU now clearly the major force in the legislative council, with the party's membership increasing at a phenomenal rate throughout the country, and with Nyerere winning golden opinions for his moderate and nonracial approach to the country's minority groups, the way was clear for a speedy transfer of power in an atmosphere of remarkable harmony and goodwill. In December, 1961, Tanganyika became the first country in East Africa to achieve independence.

In contrast to the relatively smooth political evolution of Tanganyika, Kenya's path to independence lay through a period of violent troubles. The incidence of violence was hardly surprising: bitter interracial conflict was the experience of almost every African country which contained a community of white settlers numerous enough to entertain the illusion of being able to maintain a position of privilege forever but lacking the resources to devise a system of repression as effective as that constructed by the white minority in South Africa. Far more unusual was the fact that the violence served to create a climate of opinion that made possible a remarkably rapid and peaceful transfer of power from white officials and settlers to black politicians.

As in other African territories, individuals from many different ethnic groups played a part in Kenya's struggle for independence, but the nationalist movement of Kenya differed from that of other tropical African countries by virtue of the fact that one ethnic group, the Kikuyu, came to occupy a position of quite exceptional prominence. In 1962, the date of the country's first accurate census, the Kikuyu numbered 1.6 million and made up about 20 percent of Kenya's African population. Thus the Kikuyu far outnumbered such groups as the Masai (154,000) or the Nandi (170,000)—both of whom had played a notable part in the late nineteenth-century history of the country—but they were not greatly in excess of the Luo and their neighbors, the Luhiya (both 1.1 million). On the other hand, the Kikuyu possessed the great political advantage of dominating the capital, Nairobi, and they had acquired a more active political consciousness and come to nurture a more bitter sense of grievance as a result of their contacts with European settlers and missionaries. By 1939 the Kikuyu could look back on twenty years of political agitation. Their most vigorous political organization, the Kikuyu Central Association, was proscribed on the outbreak of war, but in 1944 political activity was resumed with the formation of the Kenya African Union. The founders of the KAU were drawn from many different parts of the country, but the new party came increasingly to be dominated by its Kikuyu members. In 1947 Jomo Kenyatta was elected president of the KAU. Kenyatta had just returned home after spending fifteen years in England—the pattern of his career thus bearing a striking resemblance to that of his contemporaries, Hastings Banda and Kwame Nkrumah. In the late 1920's he had served for a time as general secretary of the Kikuyu Central Association, and during his years abroad he had kept closely in touch with Kenyan affairs. He was the author of a remarkable anthropological study of the customs of his people, *Facing Mount Kenya,* a book which could be described as a "text in cultural nationalism." [53] And he had played a prominent part in the Pan-African Congress held in Manchester in 1945. These varied and unusual accomplishments gave to Kenyatta a quite special standing in the eyes of his fellow-Kikuyu.

The late 1940's were marked by increasing discontent in the Kikuyu areas. The pressure of population was growing more acute in the reserves but Kikuyu farmers found themselves prevented from putting their shrinking resources to the best possible use as a result of the government's policy of discouraging Africans from growing the more lucrative cash crops. In the meantime, European farmers in the adjoining white Highlands were visibly enjoying the profits of the postwar boom. The approach adopted by Kenyatta and other KAU leaders were reformist rather than revolutionary: their attention was concentrated not so much on the "political kingdom" as on the issue of the "lost lands" of their people. The Kenya government, however, was quite unwilling to reopen discussion on a subject which it considered to have been satisfactorily settled by the land commission of the 1930's. But official policy was far from being entirely satatic. Sir Philip Mitchell, who governed Kenya from 1944 to 1952, had a clear idea of the way in which the colony should develop. In his opinion, the natives of East Africa were exceedingly backward, "uncivilized, superstitious, economically weak to the point of utter helplessness and quite unable to construct a civilized future for themselves." [54] But with British assistance Africans were clearly capable of advancement. Gradually then there would emerge in Kenya a multi-racial society of "civilized men" in which Africans would play an increasingly prominent part. To politically conscious Africans Mitchell's ideas must have seemed exasperatingly paternalistic, but they were exceedingly liberal when set beside the views of most white settlers.

Faced with a highly frustrating situation, more and more Kikuyu began to turn to thoughts of violence. There were two stages in this development, the first of which was concerned with the spread of "oathing." Oathing cemented political commitment. "If I become an enemy of my land and my people, let this meat and blood kill me straight away. . . . If I am ever tempted to abandon my people, let this oath kill me": [55] words such as these, accompanied by a solemn and mysterious ritual, had a profound effect on the oath-taker, binding him in an almost mystic union with his fellows. Leaders of the KAU were closely involved in the practice of oathing but appear to have been thinking of future action in terms of peaceful demonstrations and passive resistance rather than of violent forms of subversion. The second stage in the movement toward outright violence was marked by the emergence of a group of radical militants in Nairobi who were prepared to use far more brutal methods than the constitutionally-minded members of KAU. It did not take the militants long to discover that they could count on a great deal of support from the slum-dwellers of Nairobi and from many Kikuyu living in rural areas. By 1952, the government found itself confronted with a situation that had many revolutionary characteristics. Rallies organized by the KAU were attracting huge audiences and served to generate powerful currents of mass emotion. At the same time, cases of minor violence such as arson and cattle-maiming were on the increase. Finally, in October 1952, the assassination of one of the government's leading Kikuyu supporters provided the immediate pretext for the proclamation of a state of emergency.

The Kikuyu militants knew that they could not hope to overthrow the colonial regime, but they counted on being able to create a situation which would force the metropolitan government to pay increasing attention to Kenya and eventually to find means of allaying their grievances. This, in fact, is what they achieved, though at great cost in bloodshed and suffering. The proclamation of an emergency produced a steady escalation of violence, as the militants retreated to the dense forests on the slopes of Mount Kenya to escape arrest by the security forces and began to develop the tactics of guerrilla warfare. The government, for its part, believed that it was faced with a conspiracy, to which the mysterious name "Mau Mau" was attached, organized by Kenyatta and the KAU. The militants were undoubtedly guilty of a number of hideous atrocities, and these enabled the government to describe the movement as utterly barbaric and atavistic. Against this well-publicized view of Mau Mau should be set the statement of one of the leading guerrilla fighters, Dedan Kimathi: "I do not lead rebels but I lead Africans who want their self-government and land. I lead them because God never created any nation to be ruled by another nation forever." [56]

By 1956 the colonial government had re-established law and order in the Kikuyu reserves and embarked on a vigorous policy of agrarian reform under which African farmers were at last encouraged to grow export crops, while their land, previously scattered over many holdings, was consolidated into single viable units. At the same time, the British government decided to increase the pace of political reform. Multiracialism served as the guiding concept for the constitutional changes of the 1950's, but the African stake in the central government was steadily increased with the appointment of the first African to the executive council in 1954 and the election, as opposed to the nomination, of African members—eight in 1957, fourteen in 1958—to the legislative council. With the KAU dissolved, Kenyatta and most other leading Kikuyu politicians under detention, and many of their supporters disenfranchised, it was temporarily impossible for the Kikuyu to continue as the spearhead of Kenyan nationalism. This role was taken over in the late 1950's by the Luo under two dynamic leaders, Tom Mboya, a young trade unionist in Nairobi, and Oginga Odinga, a rural militant from Central Nyanza. Meanwhile, the European settler community was falling apart into two political groups, one of which was prepared to go a long way to cooperate with Africans, even to the point of accepting the opening of the white Highlands to African settlement. The broad lines of the country's future were finally settled when the constitutional

conference of 1960 provided for an elected African majority in the legislative council. But there were still substantial political difficulties to be
overcome before the advent of independence. The nationalist movement
failed to preserve its unity, dividing into two rival parties, the Kenya
African National Union (KANU) and the Kenya African Democratic
Union (KADU). KANU, the product of a Luo-Kikuyu alliance, gained
a majority in the 1961 election, but the party's representatives refused
to accept ministerial office so long as their acknowledged leader, Jomo
Kenyatta, remained under detention. Accordingly a government was
formed by a coalition between KADU and European and Asian members. KADU, which drew its support from the country's smaller ethnic
groups, then set about devising a constitution of a federal type designed
to protect the interests of its own members against the threat of KANU
domination. But in 1962 the two African parties came together to form
a coalition government with Kenyatta, now released, as one of its members. A year later KANU won an even more substantial electoral victory than it had done in 1961 and went on to form the government that
led the country to independence at the end of 1963. The dire prophecies of those who anticipated that Kenya would prove itself another
Congo proved to be singularly wide of the mark.

The political development of Uganda in the last years of colonial rule
presented a striking contrast to that of Kenya and Tanganyika.
Throughout the 1950's the country never produced a national movement comparable either to TANU or to KAU. Certainly Uganda was
the scene of a great deal of political activity, but most of the matters
under debate were essentially local, even parochial issues. Those Ugandans who attempted to build up national parties seemed to be doing no
more than playing at politics in the manner of "week-end
politicians." [57] It was hardly surprising that they should feel little of the
compelling urgency of a Nkrumah, a Kenyatta, or a Nyerere to liberate
their peoples. There were no white settlers in Uganda to serve as a
convenient opposition against whose encroachments the forces of African nationalism needed to be rallied. Nor was there really any doubt
from the mid-1950's on that the British government was prepared to
concede independence as soon as the people of Uganda had acquired a
viable government of their own. But how was such a government to be
constructed? Uganda was a deeply divided country. Throughout the period of British hegemony, the Ganda, the colony's largest ethnic group,
had enjoyed a privileged status and so been able to preserve a large
measure of autonomy for the ancient kingdom of Buganda. But would
Buganda find it possible to maintain its position of privilege forever? In
1953 a new British governor, Sir Andrew Cohen, forceful, liberal and

far-sighted, made the unequivocal assertion that "the future of Uganda must lie in a unitary form of central government covering the whole country." "The Protectorate," he pointed out, "is too small to grow into a series of separate units of government, even if these are federated together." [58] To many Ganda, and especially to their ruler, the *kabaka,* such sentiments were anathema. Rapidly relations between governor and *kabaka* deteriorated, creating so tense a situation that the governor felt himself faced with no alternative but to order the *kabaka*'s deposition. It soon became apparent, however, that the British could never hope to reach any sort of agreement with the Ganda as long as their ruler was out of the country. In 1955, after two years of exile, the *kabaka* made a triumphant return and concluded a new agreement with the British which actually increased his kingdom's autonomy. So the fundamental problem facing Uganda seemed even further from solution in 1955 than it had done two years earlier: How could Uganda ever hope to achieve independence if the richest, most advanced, and most densely populated part of the country was set on maintaining its special privileges and even considered "going it alone" as an independent state? Gradually it appeared that developments taking place in the composition of the country's legislative council might provide an answer to this question.

Changes in the composition of Uganda's legislative council followed much the same pattern as in Kenya and Tanganyika. The first nominated African members took their seats in 1945; African membership was gradually increased in the early 1950's; the first direct elections were held in 1956, and the first general election in 1961. These constitutional changes, opening up as they did many new opportunities for achieving power, helped greatly to stimulate the development of national politics. The 1961 election took the form of a contest between two parties with national aspirations, the Democratic Party and the Uganda Peoples Congress. The Democratic Party was a product of that deep division that had affected Ganda politics as early as the 1880's, with the emergence of two rival groups, one made up of Protestant converts, the other of Catholics. The Democratic Party—it might well have called itself the *Christian* Democratic Party—was almost entirely Catholic in membership. It drew its strength from the sense of grievance felt by Catholics throughout the country that most of the best jobs had gone to Protestants. Its leader, Benedicto Kiwanuka, was a Ganda lawyer, and many of the party's supporters came from Buganda. The UPC, on the other hand, was an almost entirely non-Ganda party, whose strongest sentiment was the resentment felt by many Ugandans at Buganda's highly privileged position. The leader of the UPC, Milton Obote, came from Lango in northern Uganda. There was a third, silent party in the 1961 elections—a party made up of many of the most influential men in Buganda. These neo-traditionalists, as they have been called, were concerned only to preserve the interests of their kingdom. They refused to participate in a national election and were able to put effective pressure on the majority of Ganda voters to follow their example. But the boycott played into the hands of the Democratic Party, whose candidates were able in the greatly reduced poll to win all the seats in Buganda and so gain an overall majority.

In the course of 1961, the Ganda neo-traditionalists came to realize that they had done themselves considerable injury by boycotting the election. Accordingly they changed their tactics and struck up an alliance with the UPC. Both groups profited from this convenient arrangement. In the course of further constitutional discussions with the British the Ganda leaders were able, with UPC support, to obtain a quasi-federal status for their kingdom. The UPC, for its part, could now look forward to ousting the Democratic Party and forming a government in coalition with the new party, the *Kabaka Yekka* ("*Kabaka* Only") organized by the Ganda "establishment" in late 1961. Things worked out exactly as Obote and the *kabaka* had planned. The *Kabaka Yekka* trounced their Democratic Party rivals in the election to the *lukiko,* the Ganda parliament, held in February 1962. The general election held a month later resulted in a resounding victory for the UPC-*Kabaka Yekka* coalition. Six months later Uganda achieved independence. Obote had proved himself a remarkably astute and versatile political leader. The *kabaka,* who was elected president of Uganda on the first anniversary of independence, seemed to have preserved brilliantly his kingdom's traditional heritage. In reality, however, as later events were soon to show, Uganda's political problems were far from being satisfactorily solved.

The sultanate of Zanzibar regained its independence, after seventy-three years as a British protectorate, in December 1963. In political terms Zanzibar could well be compared to Kenya, for it had long been dominated by a settler community of alien origin. But whereas in Kenya the settlers found themselves ousted from political power before the coming of independence, in Zanzibar the alien oligarchy was able to retain its position of dominance until the end of British rule. That the Arab minority should have succeeded in holding so firmly onto their privileges after three general elections, two in 1961, one in 1963, based on universal suffrage, is an achievement that requires some explanation. From the late 1950's on, politics in Zanzibar had run on racial lines, with the Zanzibar Nationalist Party representing the Arabs, the Afro-Shirazi Party the mass of African voters. The ASP included both Africans of mainland origin and Shirazi, the term the indigenous inhabitants of Zanzibar and Pemba applied to themselves. Some Shirazi, particularly the Hadimu of Zanzibar whose ancestral lands had been expropriated by Arab plantation-owners, shared the bitter anti-Arab sentiments felt by the "mainlanders," but the Shirazi of Pemba had long been accustomed to live peacefully with their Arab neighbors and resented the note of racial intolerance introduced by the ASP into its electioneering. Accordingly, in 1959 an important group of Pemba Shirazi broke away to form the Zanzibar and Pemba Peoples Party (ZPPP). Meanwhile the ZNP was demonstrating its effectiveness as a nationalist party by pressing for independence far more vigorously than the ASP. At the same time, the Arab landowners who formed the most important element in the party showed themselves as adept as any rural magnate in Victorian Britain in getting their workers and tenants to vote the way they wanted. In the final election before independence, held in June 1963, the ZNP won twelve seats to the ASP's thirteen, and the ZPPP's six, but by forming a coalition with the ZPPP the ZNP was able to dominate the government which led the country to independence.

Arab success was based on shaky foundations. Since the late 1950's many parts of Zanzibar had been wracked by interracial tension, and at least fifty Arabs had lost their lives in the riots that followed the June 1961 elections. The result of the 1963 election, in which the ASP gained 54 percent of the votes, served only to intensify African feelings of resentment and frustration at their failure to achieve power by constitutional means. Meanwhile, the ZNP was seriously weakened when, in mid-1963, some of the party's ablest members, exasperated by the conservatism of their colleagues, broke away, founded a new party, the Umma, and began pressing for a revolutionary socialist approach to the territory's problems. It would have paid the leaders of the ZNP to have attempted to broaden the base of their support by inviting the ASP to join the government; instead, they sought to strengthen their position by purging the police, the sultanate's only armed force, of dissident elements. In so doing they played straight into the hands of their enemies. For when, on January 12, 1964, barely a month after the independence ceremonies, a small group of revolutionaries attacked the police armory in Zanzibar, the police were too ill-organized to put up an effective resistance, while the most experienced of their assailants were ex-policemen bitter at their recent dismissal. The band was led by a young Ugandan, John Okello. Okello received no outside support of any kind; indeed the only weapons his followers could muster were a few bows and arrows. But within a few hours of taking over the armory with its supplies of firearms they were in control of the island. Few *ancien régimes* have collapsed so swiftly or in so unexpected a manner as the Arab sultanate of Zanzibar.

There are obvious analogies between Zanzibar and Rwanda in the political developments of the two territories in the late 1950's and early 1960's. Both the Arabs of Zanzibar and the Tutsi of Rwanda were local elites culturally distinct from the mass of the population and occupying a position which had been greatly strengthened by the support received from their colonial overlords. But the analogy must not be pushed too far, for there was a sharp difference in the actual course of events. In Zanzibar the British gave the Arab aristocracy a measure of support to the end, with the result that violent political change was postponed until after the ending of colonial rule. In Rwanda, by contrast, the Belgian administration, whose members had actively bolstered up the position of the Tutsi in the first decades of the mandate, began to swing around in the 1950's in favor of the oppressed Hutu majority and came positively to encourage the emergent Hutu political movement. One important element in the Rwandan political scene not found in Zanzibar was provided by the missionaries. Before World War II, Catholic priests in Rwanda urged their converts to regard the Tutsi hierarchy as part of the divinely ordained order of things. After 1945 a new generation of missionaries began to lay increasing stress on democratic practices and took pains to provide opportunities for aspiring Hutu to gain higher education of a kind that had been denied to them before the war. Thus out of the mass of the Hutu peasantry a distinct intelligentsia began to emerge. In 1957 a group of young Hutu intellectuals, all former seminarians, published a manifesto denouncing the "political monopoly" of the Tutsi. By 1958 both Tutsi and Hutu groups were organizing their own political parties. In 1959 the first violent incidents occurred, as bands of incendiarists roamed the countryside setting fire to Tutsi huts. The Tutsi attempted to suppress this peasant *jacquerie* by hunting out and killing prominent Hutu leaders. Had the Belgian authorities not intervened to restrain these acts of revenge, the Tutsi might well have succeeded in consolidating their own position by eliminating their opponents. As it was, Tutsi repression served greatly to inflame Hutu resentment without effectively stifling the growing movement of revolt.

In 1960 the Belgian authorities organized country-wide local elections which led to the replacement of many Tutsi chiefs by popularly elected Hutu burgomasters. Many of the new burgomasters then used their ill-defined powers to remove the Tutsi in their areas from all positions of responsibility. Finally, in February 1961, at a mass meeting attended by 3,000 burgomasters and local councillors, the monarchy was formally abolished and a republic established by popular acclamation. Clearly a revolution had taken place, but to many outside observers the movement seemed entirely negative in character, its outcome no more than "the transition from one type of oppressive regime to another." [59] Rwanda achieved formal independence in July 1962, but for the Tutsi further afflictions were still in store.

▲▼ THE INDEPENDENT STATES OF EAST AFRICA

Taking the region as a whole, East Africa's record in the immediate post-colonial period was one of considerable political stability. At the same time, two of the region's smaller territories, Zanzibar and Rwanda, were the scene of some of the most violent incidents in recent African history. The Zanzibar revolution of January 1964 has already been briefly described, but something needs to be said of its aftermath. Having seized power with astonishing ease, Okello and his associates were confronted with the task of forming a government. They decided to form a "revolutionary council" made up of prominent members not only of the Afro-Shirazi Party but also of the Umma, the recently founded, partly Arab party which was emphatically Marxist in its policy statements. Soon afterward Okello disappeared from the scene and Abedi Karume, the veteran leader of the ASP, who was to die at the hands of a mysterious assassin eight years later, emerged as the dominant personality in the island. Three months after the revolution the revolutionary council agreed to the establishment of a union with neighboring Tanganyika to be known as the United Republic of Tanzania. In spite of the ties of friendship between TANU and ASP leaders, relations between the two partners frequently showed signs of strain, and throughout the 1960's Zanzibar maintained virtually total autonomy.

In the decade before independence Zanzibari politics had been marked by mounting bitterness. In the immediate aftermath of the revolution the intensity of interracial feeling burst out in the form of murderous attacks on Arab landowners. Within a few weeks at least 10,000 Arabs—more than one-fifth of the total Arab population—had been massacred or forcibly expelled. As a ruling class the Zanzibari Arabs ceased to exist: those who remained could be described in the late 1960's as a "pariah group" living on "prostitution, beggary and charity." [60] The Asian community also suffered severely. Few Asians were killed, but many shops were looted and some businesses ruined. For many Africans, on the other hand, the revolution brought much that was beneficial. Arab-owned estates were broken up and the land redistributed to peasant farmers; posts in government service, previously monopolized by Arabs or Asians, were opened up to Africans;

and the wages of the lowest-paid workers were increased sometimes as much as three times while the salaries of the professional classes were reduced. For technical assistance and financial aid in implementing its new development plans the revolutionary council turned to Communist countries, particularly to East Germany and China. Problems of development were tackled more vigorously than they had been under the easy-going regime of the British. Though some of its actions, well-publicized in the outside world, were undoubtedly brutal and unjust, the revolutionary council could well claim to have rendered great services to the mass of the Zanzibari population.

When Rwanda became an independent state in July 1962, the revolution which had been vigorously encouraged by the Belgian authorities seemed virtually complete. The ancient Tutsi monarchy had been destroyed and all power was now in the hands of the previously subservient Hutu. But, like members of the French aristocracy after 1789, many Tutsi refused to accept this situation. From their places of exile, whether in foreign capitals or in the refugee camps set up in the countries bordering Rwanda, they began to plan counterrevolution. Between July 1962 and July 1966 there were at least nine major incursions by Tutsi commandos, known locally as *inyenzi*, "cockroaches," into Rwanda territory. Far from undermining the Hutu government, these attacks served to consolidate its power. For the Tutsi still living in Rwanda the *inyenzi* raids had disastrous consequences: more than 10,000 Tutsi men, women, and children were hacked to death in a series of atrocious massacres, a terrible reprisal wrought by the Hutu populace on their former masters. Following the killings, most of the remaining Tutsi left the country to settle in Zaire, Uganda, Tanzania, and Burundi. Seldom in history has a once-dominant group suffered so terrible a reversal of fortune as the Tutsi of Rwanda. But the radical, egalitarian strain which was such a prominent feature of the Zanzibar revolution, was hardly evident in Rwanda. Many Hutu politicians began to demand for themselves privileges previously associated with the feudal regime of the Tutsi and their claims were accepted passively by a peasantry reared in a tradition of subservience. Thus the revolution in Rwanda can be described, in Marx's phrase, as "a partial, merely political revolution which leaves the pillars of the building standing." [61]

Few observers of the East African scene in the 1950's could have predicted that Tanganyika, the poorest and most backward of the British East African territories, would prove itself as an independent state one of the most original countries in the entire continent. Tanzania, as the country became after the union with Zanzibar in 1964, possessed one signal advantage over most other African states of the same size:

tribalism—that disruptive force produced by rivalries between different ethnic groups—never presented a really serious political problem. In these circumstances TANU, the party which had led the country to independence, was able to preserve its position unchallenged. By the mid-1960's, Tanzania presented one of the clearest models of a one-party state to be found anywhere in the world. But the unquestioned primacy of TANU would never have been achieved without the leadership of the president, Julius Nyerere. Nyerere's style of leadership was relaxed, unostentatious, and strongly inspirational: to his people he was *Mwalimu,* the teacher, a philosopher-king, whose ideas as expressed in his speeches reached an audience far wider than that of his own people. By the late 1960's Nyerere had established himself as one of the foremost radical thinkers of the Third World. Nyerere's radicalism owed nothing to Marxist doctrines; it was essentially a home-grown philosophy derived from a deep awareness of the problems and potentialities of the great mass of the Tanzanian people. The president's ideals were at once liberal and puritanical. Tanzania was officially declared a one-party state, but at the same time, with the promulgation of the 1965 constitution, the electorate was given the opportunity of choosing between different candidates for election to the national assembly. In consequence this body remained one of the most vigorous representative institutions to be found in postcolonial Africa. Nyerere's puritanism was clearly apparent in the Arusha Declaration, the document issued by TANU in 1967 as a major statement of policy. Egalitarianism and self-reliance were the key-notes of the declaration: Tanzania was to be transformed into "a classless society free from exploitation." But the country could never enjoy "real" independence so long as it was dependent on outside sources for aid in developing its resources. One of the practical consequences of the new policy was a stringent set of regulations limiting the amount of property held by any private individual— designed to prevent the emergence of a local class of capitalists and to strip the *Wabenzi*—the satirical term applied to members of the local elite who rode around in Mercedes Benz automobiles—of their excessive privileges. Another consequence of the declaration was the introduction of a series of decrees nationalizing foreign-owned banks and other businesses.

To outside observers Nyerere presented himself as that rare, uncomfortable, even aggravating phenomenon—the moralist in politics. The deep sense of morality which informed the Tanzanian president's approach to politics was particularly evident in his shaping of the country's foreign policy. Tanzania was unflinchingly opposed to any form of racism and particularly to the pattern of white supremacy maintained by the Portuguese, Rhodesian, and South African governments. Hence the breaking-off of diplomatic relations with Britain at the time of Rhodesia's unilateral declaration of independence. Hence the practical support given to liberation movements and particularly to those operating across the border in Mozambique. These were not empty gestures: the loss of offers of aid and the diversion of scarce resources involved the Tanzanian government in considerable sacrifices. Yet gestures such as these could be turned into political assets, for they helped to give the country a sense of dignity and pride. Though Tanzania remained one of the poorest countries in the world, it had acquired in the course of the 1960's a remarkably distinctive personality.

Uganda achieved independence in 1962 under a government which represented an uneasy coalition between Prime Minister Milton Obote's Uganda Peoples Congress and the *Kabaka Yekka,* a party formed to represent the interests of the Ganda people and their ruler, the *kabaka.* Within two years Obote had increased the strength of his own party sufficiently through defections from the opposition Democratic Party and from the *Kabaka Yekka* to be able to put an end to the alliance with the Ganda party. He then proceeded to show his strength by tackling the highly controversial issue of the "lost counties," a piece of Bunyoro territory which had been handed over by the British to Buganda at the beginning of the century. A referendum showed that the people of the "lost counties" were overwhelmingly in favor of a return to Bunyoro. The Ganda attempted to retrieve their steadily weakening position by intriguing with non-Ganda members of the UPC who were growing discontented with Obote's leadership. In February 1966, the prime minster met this threat by ordering the arrest of five cabinet ministers suspected of plotting against him. A few weeks later he summarily abrogated the constitution and invested himself with the title and the powers of an executive president. Increasingly alarmed at the seriousness of the threat to Buganda's special status, the *lukiko* (the parliament of Buganda) presented the central government with an ultimatum demanding that all its officials be withdrawn from Buganda within the space of a few days. Interpreting this gesture as an act of rebellion, Obote sent in the army. After a few hours' hard fighting the royal palace in Kampala was in the central government's hands and the *kabaka* fled the country. The next year Obote introduced a revolutionary new constitution which strengthened his own position as president and abolished the institution of kingship not only in Buganda but also in Bunyoro, Ankole, and Toro. To consolidate his position still further Obote needed to be sure of a greater measure of popular support. This he attempted to obtain by making a clear "move to the left," through the introduction of a "com-

mon man's charter," a policy statement designed to inject a new dynamism into the activities of his party, the UPC. But he failed to establish
a tight enough grip on the army. Early in 1971 he was removed from
power by a military coup. For a decade Obote had dominated the
Ugandan political scene: in so divided and potentially turbulent a country this was a highly remarkable achievement. His successor, General
Idi Amin, made sure of his own position by savagely purging the army
of all soldiers whose tribal affinities were close to those of the deposed
president. In August 1972, the general gained international notoriety by
announcing plans to expel the country's entire Asian population.

At the time of Kenya's achievement of independence in 1965, there
was much talk of the country having to run the risk of becoming "another Congo." Preindependence Kenyan politics had provided ample evidence of the tension between different groups, and even—as some of
the ghastly episodes of the Mau Mau rebellion revealed—of a frightening strain of violence. But in its first years as an independent state
Kenya belied the worst fears of outside observers. President Kenyatta
and the leading members of his party, KANU, provided the country
with a ruling group of great ability. Within a year of independence, the
opposition party, KADU had gone into voluntary dissolution, its members deciding either to retire from politics or to join the ranks of the
government. But it proved impossible to maintain for long the structure
of a one-party state. In 1966, Oginga Odinga, after Kenyatta the most
powerful politician in KANU, broke with his old associates and formed
a new political party, the Kenya People's Union. Odinga was a Luo and
therefore opposed to the ascendency acquired by the Kikuyu in most of
the fields of government. He also disagreed with KANU's policy on
ideological grounds, favoring a far more radical approach to the country's problems. Certainly, in the late 1960's Kenya gave many grounds
for radical discontent. In sharp contrast to the situation in Tanzania, the
Kenyan government's policy had encouraged the growth of a class of
local capitalists whose newly acquired wealth contrasted sharply with
the poverty of the growing number of the urban unemployed. But Kenyatta showed his political genius by his skill in reconciling so many apparently irreconcilable groups—Mau Mau freedom fighters and colonial
loyalists, European farmers and Asian businessmen, stalwart KANU
supporters and rebels who had broken away from the party and then
returned—all found some place in Kenyatta's political system. Though
the government found it necessary to detain some of its KPU opponents
including Odinga, the election held late in 1969 showed that Kenya
still possessed a remarkable amount of political freedom.

There was one issue of concern to all the three major states of East

Africa—closer union. As early as the 1920's, British officials had pointed to the economic advantages to be gained from the establishment of some form of federation between the three East African territories. Kenya settlers, too, had responded enthusiastically to the idea, lured on by the mirage of creating a great white dominion in East Africa. Settler support for the scheme aroused the suspicion of the small group of politically conscious Africans and their European friends and advisers. Consequently, after a great deal of discussion in the period 1927 to 1931, the project had been dropped. But the practical advantages of some sort of interterritorial association came to be recognized during the war, and in 1948 the British government set up the East African High Commission, later known as the East African Common Services Organization.

In the early 1950's there was still a large measure of African opposition to projects for closer union, but by the end of the decade a complete *volte-face* had occurred. Most East African nationalist leaders were vigorous advocates of the idea of African unity and had created for themselves in PAFMECSA (Pan-African Freedom Movement of East, Central and South Africa) an organization where matters of common interest could be discussed. As in other parts of Africa, the achievement of independence was marked by the collapse of some of the practical forms of cooperation, such as a common currency and common postal services, effectively maintained during the colonial period. But the Common Services Organization continued to exist, and an East African Economic Community was established in 1967.

The first years of independence brought no really major changes in the economy of East Africa. All the territories remained dependent on a small range of cash crops—coffee, cotton, tea, sisal, or cloves—and so found themselves peculiarly vulnerable to changes in the prices paid on the world market. But the new governments were able to record some achievements. There was a considerable expansion of secondary industry, particularly in the Nairobi area. Tourism emerged as a valuable means of acquiring foreign exchange. In Kenya a considerable amount of land passed peacefully from European to African hands. Interesting experiments were made, particularly in Tanzania, in the field of rural community development. Substantial advances were achieved in the provision of secondary and higher education. At the same time, population was increasing rapidly in most parts of the region, with annual rates of growth in some countries estimated to exceed 3 percent. Given this rapid growth in population, the basic task of development, the struggle against poverty, ignorance, and disease, remained as formidable as ever.

CHAPTER VIII

South Africa

▲▼ INTRODUCTION

South Africa—defined here as a region embracing the modern republic of the same name, together with South West Africa and the three newly independent states of Botswana, Lesotho and Swaziland, has an area of just over 1 million square miles. Relief and rainfall determine the relatively simple pattern of the region's geography. The southern extension of the great plateau that dominates East and Central Africa takes up the greater part of the South African interior, giving to much of the country an altitude of more than 3,000 feet, rising to 6,000 on the high veld of the Transvaal and to mountains almost as high as the Moroccan Atlas in the Drakensberg of Lesotho. Variations in rainfall provide a factor of even greater significance in the historical development of the region. With the exception of the southwestern Cape with its unique ecology, the best-watered and most fertile areas of the region lie in the east, with an average annual rainfall of more than thirty inches on the Indian Ocean coast of Natal. Moving westward across the interior, the rainfall declines steadily to produce the semidesert landscapes of the Kalahari and the Karroo and the total desert of the "skeleton coast" of South West Africa.

Today the population of South Africa presents a more striking degree of heterogeneity than that of any other region in the continent. In 1960, out of a total population of 16 million approximately 70 percent were Africans speaking Bantu languages, rather less than 20 percent were Europeans, 9 percent were "Coloured," (people of mixed origin) and 3 percent Asians. In historical terms, the emergence of so varied a population was a phenomenon of relatively recent occurrence. In 1500 South Africa probably had a smaller population than any other region of comparable size in the continent. Small groups of Bushman (San) hunters and food-gatherers and Hottentot (Khoi-Khoi) pastoralists made up the sparse population for most of the southern and western parts of the region, while in the north and east slowly expanding communities of Bantu-speaking peoples were gradually colonizing the areas later known as Transvaal and Natal. These Bantu-speakers could be divided into four main linguistic groups: Venda in the Limpopo valley of the far north, South Western in modern South West Africa, Sotho living between the Kalahari and the Drakensberg, and Nguni in modern Natal. Pioneers in an almost empty land, some of these negroid migrants from the north met and merged with many of the Bushmen and Hottentots with whom they came into contact.

In 1652 a new element was added to the population of South Africa with the establishment of the first European settlement, a modest victualling station founded by the Dutch East India Company at the Cape. No European settlement anywhere in Africa was to carry within itself the seed of greater changes than this simple Dutch post on the shores of Table Bay which was gradually to develop into the gracious city of Cape Town. By the end of the eighteenth century the Dutch colony contained more than 20,000 Europeans, together with a substantial population of mixed African, Asian, and European descent, the offspring of the unions contracted by Dutch colonists with slave women, and a considerable number of slaves mostly of Hottentot, Malay, or Malagasy origin. For the company officials at Cape Town there was no great incentive to acquire new territories in the hinterland. But one section of the European community, the Trek Boers or "migrant farmers," whose cattle served to victual the ships that thronged Cape Town's harbor, responding to the dynamics of a pastoral economy, began to move farther and farther inland, the younger sons of the large Boer families constantly hiving off to find new pasturelands for their gradually increasing herds. As they spread northward and eastward the Trek Boers came into contact with groups of Bushmen hunters and Hottentot pastoralists. Some groups, especially those of Bushmen, they exterminated, others they forced to retreat beyond their range, yet others they subjugated and absorbed into their slave-owning society. By the beginning of the nineteenth century when the Dutch colony was taken over by the British, most of the country now regarded as forming the western half of Cape Province was firmly in European hands.

Meanwhile, an equally momentous development was beginning to take place farther east in the well-watered lands of Natal. Here the Nguni section of the Southern Bantu were experiencing an apparently unprecedented increase in the population of both men and cattle. Population pressure led to ever more violent conflict between the small, loosely organized Nguni groups, forcing men to experiment with new forms of political organization in their desperate search for security in a time of mounting trouble. The most successful of these truly revolutionary innovators was Shaka, the chief of a small clan, the Zulu. Building on this modest power base, introducing highly effective new military tactics (notably the substitution of the stabbing for the throwing spear), and working out a new system of military organization whereby the young men of his own and allied chiefdoms were brought together in specially created barrack villages and trained to become highly disciplined warriors, Shaka was able to build up the most substantial polity yet seen among the indigenous communities of South Africa. For many African communities the *mfecane* ("time of troubles") of the early nineteenth century was a period of catastrophic loss and destruction. But those who succeeded in riding the storm—some, such as Mzilikazi and his Ndebele, off-shoots of the Zulu system, others, notably Moshesh, the paramount of the Southern Sotho, defenders of a more traditional order —were able to create and preserve more extensive and elaborate polities than the region had ever known before.

By the middle of the 1830's when the turbulence of the *mfecane* was beginning to subside, many of the African communities of Natal and the high veld were suddenly confronted with a new threat, as substantial groups of white men, well equipped with wagons, horses, and firearms, began to make their appearance in areas where no white men had ever been seen before. This dramatic expansion of Dutch cattle-farmers beyond the borders of the Cape—a complex movement succinctly described by an earlier generation of Europocentric historians as "The Great Trek"—was in part a product of those irresistable forces that had led to the earlier expansion of the Trek Boers over the entire Western Cape. But it was also the angry reaction of a people who had developed a highly distinct culture and philosophy of life against the uncomfortable new ideas being introduced by the new masters of the Cape. The Boers, tough and resourceful frontiersmen carving out their careers in a harsh and threatening environment, had acquired an unshakable conviction in their superiority over all people whose culture and physical appearance differed sharply from their own. They were contemptuous of the alluring blandishments of contemporary European civilization and found in a narrow interpretation of their sacred book a secure ideological basis for their beliefs. To many of the new English residents in Cape Colony and to those members of the Dutch communities who preferred the amenities of Cape Town and its surrounding to the rigors of frontier life, the Boers appeared stubborn, uncouth, semi-illiterate, and often guilty of a brutality of attitude and action in their dealings with people of other "races" deeply shocking to those brought up in the liberal and humanitarian traditions of early nineteenth-century England.

By the middle of the nineteenth century the "migrant farmers" had succeeded in establishing two modest independent polities of their own —the Orange Free State and, across the Vaal River, the grandiosely named South African Republic. At the same time the administration of the Cape had been extended farther eastward to include territories occupied by the Xosa and other Nguni groups, and a second British colony, Natal, had driven a deep wedge of white power through the central Nguni area. In the early 1870's another expansion of European-dominated territory took place when the British government annexed Griqualand West, a buffer zone lying between the Cape Colony and the Orange Free State where a number of enterprising leaders of "Coloured" origin had carved out domains for themselves and where diamonds had recently been found in great profusion.

"Gentlemen," the colonial secretary of the Cape told the members of the local house of assembly in 1867 as he showed them one of the earliest gem-stones found in Griqualand, "this is the rock on which the future success of South Africa will be built." [1] Later developments were soon to justify this bold, prophetic utterance. Hitherto the character of the economy of the Cape—by far the most favored of the four European colonies in the region—could be described as "that of a sparsely populated country largely engaged in pastoral farming and self-subsistence agriculture, too poor to advance rapidly by domestic capital formation and lacking any exploitable resources to attract foreign capital." [2] The discovery of diamonds provided the Cape and eventually other parts of South Africa with a stimulant comparable to that experienced by other African countries in more recent years through the discovery of oil. Exports shot up, government revenue rose dramatically, money became available for large-scale projects such as railroads, and the diamond fields witnessed the emergence of a new social phenomenon without precedent elsewhere in the Africa of the 1870's—the appearance of an African urban proletariat, as "tribesmen" from far and wide abandoned their long-established forms of gaining a livelihood and sought their fortunes in the sprawling shanty town of Kimberley.

By 1875, then, the lineaments of modern South Africa were becoming faintly discernible. But there were still large areas of the region where African rulers maintained an independent sway and where African communities lived the same sort of life as their forefathers had done over many generations. All this was to change drastically in the course of the years that lay ahead. By 1900 the superstructure of European administration had been spread over the entire region. At the same time, the two major European groups, the English and the Afrikaners, had become locked in one of the most ferocious conflicts yet witnessed on the African continent. These two themes—of African-European and English-Afrikaner relationships—ran parallel, yet the lines sometimes converge and intertwine. For clarity's sake, however, they must be considered separately.

▲▼ THE SUBJUGATION OF INDEPENDENT AFRICAN POLITIES: 1875 TO 1900

By 1900, the process, begun in the second half of the seventeenth century, whereby African communities found themselves forced to accept European domination was virtually complete. But the nature of European domination varied from area to area and the experience of individual African communities varied accordingly. Some groups, notably the Southern Sotho, the Tswana, and the Swazi, escaped relatively lightly, others were confronted with the terrible experience of seeing their old-established institutions destroyed and their lands taken from them. Some appeared to accept their fate with resignation and made the most of whatever opportunities the new situation offered. Others sought to defend their homelands by military means, only to see their warriors mown down by the superior weapons of the invaders. Yet others submitted to the initial occupation of their territories but rose in armed rebellion when the price to be paid to the new overlords became apparent. The range of reactions is familiar; yet the South African situation as a whole presented a striking difference to that prevailing in most of tropical Africa during the period of European conquest. Conquest is a highly unpleasant experience for any people to undergo. The greater the number of alien intruders, the more unpleasant the experience for the native population. It was the lot of many African communities in South Africa to be confronted with a larger number of aliens than any other African people with the exception of the Muslim population of Algeria.

The Southern Sotho, the people of modern Lesotho, represented a cluster of many previously autonomous groups brought together under the loose paramountcy of the great chief Moshesh in the middle decades of the nineteenth century. In the late 1850's Moshesh's Basuto (as the Southern Sotho were called at the time) came into violent conflict with their western neighbors, the Boer farmers of the Orange Free State. After holding their own in the first Boer-Basuto war of 1858, Moshesh's followers suffered a disastrous defeat in 1866–67 and were forced to abandon their richest farmlands to their enemies. Faced with the total disintegration of his kingdom, Moshesh sought and obtained British protection. In 1871, one year after Moshesh's death, the British government, ever anxious to divest itself of awkward liabilities, handed over Basutoland to the local administration at the Cape. For seven years the Cape Colonial Government maintained a cautious system of overrule, but, in 1878, a decision was made to intervene more directly in Basuto life by requiring all Basuto along with other Africans living in the Cape to surrender their firearms. It was not unreasonable for a colonial government constantly on the *qui vive* against the threat of a great native uprising to disarm its potentially unruly subjects. But when the Basuto, deeply chagrined by the demands made on them, turned to armed resistance, the authorities in the Cape found themselves faced with a struggle they lacked the means to win. The "Gun War," as it was called, dragged on for two years before being ended by a compromise worked out by the British high commissioner at the Cape. Three years later, in 1884, the British government reluctantly agreed to take on the administration of Basutoland. For the Basuto the new regime offered two practical advantages; it preserved their land from the encroachments of white farmers, and it allowed a considerable degree of autonomy to their rulers, Moshesh's successors to the paramountcy and other leading chiefs, whose influence the British were glad to strengthen. But the Basuto homeland was a poor mountainous area, and increasingly its people found themselves compelled to seek their livelihood in the white-dominated lands beyond their borders.

Today the Tswana people are divided between the independent state of Botswana and the Republic of South Africa. In the 1870's they were organized in a large number of petty chiefdoms, situated between the Transvaal high veld and the Kalahari. With Boer farmers encroaching on their grazing lands from the east and British missionaries, traders, and adventurers moving into the country from the south, the Tswana found themselves increasingly exposed to alien interference. Moreover, the country occupied an area of considerable strategic importance, for through it ran the "road to the north" that represented the only line of advance open for British South Africa into the far interior. Early in the 1880's Boer farmers from the Transvaal formed the two independent republics of Stellaland and Goshen in Tswana territory. In 1884 the Transvaal government decided to take over Goshen; in the same year the German government proclaimed a protectorate on the coast of South West Africa. Deeply alarmed at the possibility of a link being established between the fiercely independent Transvaal and a major European power, the British government decided to take prompt action. A large force of troops was sent to occupy the territory south of the Molopo River which became known as British Bechuanaland and which contained the greater part of the two Boer republics. Shortly afterward, the rulers of three major Tswana chiefdoms—formed by the Kwena, Ngwato, and Ngwaketse peoples—living north of the Molopo River agreed to place themselves under British protection. British Bechuanaland was transferred to the Cape in 1894, but the Bechuanaland Protectorate remained, like Basutoland, the responsibility of the metropolitan power. Under this favored status the peoples of the protectorate escaped many of the pressures to which their kinsmen living on the other side of the frontier were increasingly subjected.

In the 1870's the Swazi kingdom was bordered by the South African Republic to the west and the Zulu kingdom to the north. Of the two, the Swazi feared the Zulu more than the Transvaalers; indeed they were frequently glad to obtain assistance from the Transvaal to help them to resist the raids of their formidable African neighbors. By the mid-1880's, however, after the total collapse of Zulu power, the Swazi found themselves increasingly subject to European pressure, as stock-farmers from the Transvaal and concession-hunters from every part of South Africa moved into the kingdom and persuaded the Swazi ruler to sign away almost all the natural resources of his kingdom. In 1894, after protracted negotiations between Britain and the Transvaal, Swaziland was declared to be a "political dependency" of the Afrikaner republic. Less than a decade later, however, in the settlement made after the South African War, Swaziland was detached from the Transvaal and given the same form of administration as Basutoland, though two-thirds of Swaziland had been alienated to white farmers.

The Nguni peoples—Mfengu, Tembu, Mpondo, and others—living in the two hundred-mile stretch of territory between the great Kei River and the western borders of Natal were still nominally independent in 1875. But their political structure was deeply fragmented, their communities were exhausted by almost a century of struggle with advancing European frontiersmen, and their leading men were clearly strongly subject to the influence of the white missionaries, traders, farmers, and officials who had come in recent years to settle in their midst. Most of these white frontiersmen urged on the colonial or imperial authorities a policy of vigorous expansion, arguing that the extension of European overrule would serve to procure for native peoples "the blessings of Christianity and Civilization." Between 1879 and 1894 the expansionists achieved their objective as one Nguni chiefdom after the other was gradually brought under the direct control of the Cape authorities. A somewhat similar process of piecemeal expansion was taking place in the northern and eastern Transvaal, as Boer farmers began moving into land claimed by Northern Sotho and Venda chiefs. Basing their defensive systems on hill-top fortresses, some of these northern groups—

particularly the Pedi—were able to put up a formidable resistance. But they could devise no really effective answer to the destructive "scorched earth" tactics of Boer commanders nor could they resist the skill with which Boer agents, like their counterparts in the Eastern Cape, learned to play faction against faction and shrewdly manipulated to their own advantage the tangled web of local politics.

The gradual erosion of African independence involved many individual tragedies. But for tragedy on a grand, spectacular scale few episodes in late nineteenth-century African history rival the collapse of the Zulu kingdom and nation. In 1875 the Zulu kingdom represented the most substantial native polity in Southern Africa. It possessed in Cetewayo, a nephew of the great Shaka and son of the pacific Mpende whom he succeeded in 1872, an extremely able and intelligent ruler, who set about doing all in his power to strengthen the bonds holding his people together. The Zulu kingdom was confronted with two formidable neighbors, the British colony of Natal to the south, the South African Republic to the west. Cetewayo was careful to maintain extremely cordial relations with Natal while preparing to resist the encroachments of Boer commandos from the Transvaal. A turn of events of a kind that no Zulu diplomat could ever have predicted upset this cautious and sensible policy. In 1877, the British government, as a result of a series of decisions discussed more fully in the next section, annexed the Transvaal. Two years later, in a move undertaken largely to lessen the anti-British sentiment developing among the Afrikaners of the Transvaal by showing that the British were prepared to take tough action against a potentially aggressive state, the British high commissioner, Sir Bartle Frere, ordered the invasion of Zululand. At the battle of Isandhlwana the Zulu *impis* wiped out a British regiment in the most spectacular defeat ever suffered by a European force in South Africa. But there could be no doubt of the final outcome. The Zulu spearmen for all their bravery were incapable of holding up the inexorable advance of the British war machine. In July 1879, six months after the opening of the campaign, Ulundi, the Zulu capital, went up in flames. The British were concerned to destroy the Zulu kingdom, not to annex Zulu territory. Accordingly, Sir Garnet Wolseley, that imperial factotum, recently appointed governor of Natal, devised a scheme of "Machiavellian quality," banishing Cetewayo and dividing the country up into thirteen independent chiefdoms. "Divide and refrain from ruling" was, as Leonard Thompson has pointed out, "a shrewd technique in an area where imperial interests were merely negative." [3] But it was not a policy that could be maintained for very long. As anarchy spread through Zululand, Boer farmers consolidated their power in the northwest of the country, proclaiming a "New Republic" which was incorporated into the Transvaal in 1887. In the same year the British formally annexed the rest of Zululand. In the short space of eight years "the social and psychological bonds of Zulu national life collapsed." [4]

Englishmen and Afrikaners were not the only Europeans to press heavily on the indigenous peoples of South Africa. In 1884 the Germans established a claim to the coastal districts of South West Africa, advanced rapidly into the interior, and succeeded by 1890 in obtaining recognition from the British of their claim to a territory 371,000 square miles in extent. South West Africa is for the most part a land of barren mountains, deserts, and grassy steppes. In the late nineteenth century its population hardly exceeded a half-million. One large ethnic group, the Ovambo, living in the extreme north of the territory, were relatively little affected by the German incursion. For the other major peoples of South West Africa, the Herero and the Nama, the arrival of an increasing number of European settlers was attended with consequences that came close to being utterly disastrous. The Herero were a Bantu people who had moved from the north into the country south of the Ovambo. The Nama were of Hottentot (Khoi-Khoi) origin, a people made up of many different groups, some of which had moved northward across the Orange River (later to become the southern frontier of South West Africa) to escape the pressures exerted by the white colonists of the Cape. Both Herero and Nama were pastoralists. Inevitably, as the two peoples came to compete for grazing-lands in the area round Windhoek, there was savage fighting between them: much of the history of South West Africa in the mid-nineteenth century is taken up with the record of Nama-Herero wars. But the area was becoming increasingly exposed to alien influences as European missionaries and traders began to move inland from the coast or northward from the Cape.

In the first years of their occupation the German overlords found in the Nama their most formidable opponents. The Herero, on the other hand, placidly accepted German "protection." "You will have bitter eternal remorse for this handing of your land and the sovereignty over to the hands of White people," Hendrik Witbooi, the most resolute Nama chief, wrote in 1888 to the Herero paramount. "This giving of yourself into the hands of the Whites will become to you a burden as if you were carrying the sun on your back." [5] Within less than twenty years this dire prophecy was to be dreadfully fulfilled.

In 1897 the Herero suffered a shattering calamity when almost all their cattle died in an epidemic of rinderpest. Such a loss was not only an "economic disaster"; "it undermined," a recent historian has sensitively pointed out, "the cultural self-assurance and stability of the tribes on the widest possible scale. A feeling of general crisis began to spread." [6] This sense of crisis intensified as German settlers began gradually to encroach on Herero land. The total German population, of whom actual settlers represented only a small proportion, was no more than 4,700 in 1903. But to the Herero chiefs it was now abundantly clear that the German presence, already manifested in many irksome ways, was bound to become increasingly oppressive. In January 1904 the entire Herero people rose in revolt. In October they were joined by the Nama who waged a savage guerrilla war against the Germans until 1907. There could, of course, be no doubt of the final outcome. But the war proved to be one of the most terrible and costly conflicts in the history of South Africa. The Germans who brought in 14,000 troops, lost 2,000 men and were forced to spend $120 million to re-establish their authority. For the Herero and the Nama the consequences of defeat were utterly appalling. One-third of all the Nama and three-quarters of all the Herero died as a result of the war. Both peoples lost all their cattle, their land was expropriated, their traditional political structure shattered, many of their chiefs executed, many of the survivers deported to other parts of the country. "The psychological effects," the German historian, Helmut Bley, has written, "were even more terrible. The Herero substantially abandoned their traditional customs and standards. Deprived of their tribal links . . . they became cowed and disorientated. It was only gradually that they began to search for a new form of life in a situation that denied them even the minimum social or economic self-determination." [7]

"Colonisation," wrote Governor Leutwein of South West Africa, "is always inhumane. It must ultimately amount to an encroachment on the rights of the original inhabitants in favor of the intruders. If that is unacceptable then one must oppose all colonisation. . . . What is impossible is on the one hand to take land from the natives on the basis of questionable treaties and risk the life and health of one's countrymen to this end, and on the other to enthuse about humanitarian principles in the *Reichstag*." [8] This was an apt and penetrating comment. Yet it would be a mistake to see the movement of colonization as wholly destructive. All intruders are agents of change, bringing with them material innovations, new techniques, new ideas. In South Africa there were many intruders. By 1900 the region contained well over one million Europeans, a figure which must be set against the few hundred or the few thousand white men to be found in the regions of tropical Africa at this time. Inevitably the impact of such an incursion was profoundly revolutionary. But before discussing the transformation in the life-patterns of many of the African inhabitants of South Africa, the bitter struggle between the European overlords for the supremacy of the region must be considered at some length.

▲▼ BRITISH PARAMOUNTCY AND AFRIKANER NATIONALISM: 1875 TO 1899

Few sets of relationships in late nineteenth-century Africa were so complex as those existing between the various European polities in South Africa and between these polities and the European power with a major stake in the region, Great Britain. The British had taken over the Dutch colony at the Cape during the long war with Revolutionary and Napoleonic France. At the time the British had no desire for territorial aggrandizement in this remote part of the African continent, but as the masters of India and the greatest naval power in the Indian Ocean, they could not afford to see the Cape, a base of major importance on the long sea route to the Indies, fall into the hands of a potentially hostile power. Having acquired the Cape for these basically negative reasons, successive British governments found themselves subjected to many local pressures compelling them to adopt a policy of reluctant expansion. British administrators or settlers at the Cape, caught up in incessant frontier wars with local African polities, saw in the extension of the *pax Britannica* the only feasible way of establishing the necessary foundations of order and security. Missionaries, too, ever able through their metropolitan sponsors to bring some pressure to bear on British cabinet ministers, came to share the same view. Yet the military force needed to maintain the superstructure of British rule imposed a heavy expense on the metropolitan government, and the expense became even greater and more irksome when British troops were involved in long-drawn-out frontier wars. Clearly there was much to be said for devolving as much of the burden and the responsibility of government as possible onto the local European community at the Cape.

The whole situation in South Africa was rendered all the more confusing in British eyes by the establishment of the two Afrikaner republics whose independence the British government agreed to recognize early in the 1850's. The two republics possessed a very much smaller white population than the two British colonies. In 1873, there were 27,000 whites in the Orange Free State and 40,000 in the Transvaal, compared with 18,000 in Natal and 236,000 in the Cape. Thus the total population of the British territories was almost four times as large as that of the Afrikaner republics. Moreover, the colonial governments at Cape Town and Durban had far greater financial resources to draw on; between 1871 and 1875 the annual average revenue of the Cape was £668,000, of Natal and the Orange Free State each £127,000, and of the Transvaal £55,000. But the men who formed the elite of the Afrikaner republics, farmers brought up in the heroic tradition of the Great Trek, were tough, resourceful, extremely independent in their views, and naturally expansionist in their ambitions. The total independence of the republics no British government could easily accept: such a situation could breed an alliance between the republics and one of Britain's European rivals, thus setting in motion a chain of consequences that might fatally undermine the cornerstone of British hegemony in the East. Yet the British had no desire for a head-on conflict with the Afrikaners. Fortunately, in the 1860's and 1870's, the way seemed open for compromise. Following the pattern successfully worked out in Canada in 1867, the four European polities could, it was felt in Whitehall, be encouraged to come together to form "a self-governing, white-controlled, federal Dominion under the British Crown," [9] a political structure strong enough to meet from its own resources the expense of maintaining law and order within its domains. This statesmanlike objective might be achieved by direct British action—an approach attempted, with dramatic consequences, in the late 1870's and again in the 1890's. Alternatively the Cape could be encouraged to draw the other smaller polities into its orbit.

The Cape Colony was granted responsible government by the British in 1872. Compared with other contemporary African polities, the Cape, with its relatively elaborate administrative structure, looked fairly imposing. The discovery of diamonds in 1867 gave a powerful boost to the colony's economy. The total value of the Cape's trade (imports and exports combined) trebled in the course of a decade, while government revenue rose from an annual average of £537,000 in 1866–69 to £1,648,000 in 1875–79. But even these resources were too modest to finance the really vigorous policy of expansion needed to embrace the other European polities of South Africa. Moreover, the grandiose scheme of federation was not one that commended itself greatly to Cape politicians. Many of them were more concerned with local interests and local rivalries. Settlers in the Eastern Cape, for example, had long regarded the government at Cape Town with some suspicion. And if Grahams Town and Port Elizabeth were suspicious of Cape Town, then Cape Town was often uneasy about the pressures and the suggestions emanating from the distant imperial metropolis. Moreover, the colony's white population was divided between two cultural groups, English and Dutch-Afrikaner. Though there had been some measure of fusion through intermarriage, some assimilation of English culture by settlers of Dutch descent, there existed many opportunities for disagreement between the two groups.

Even more fundamental was the rift between the English settlers of
the Cape and Natal and the Afrikaner frontiersmen of the two republics. The Northern Afrikaners, living in their remote and isolated farms,
were totally unaffected by the anglicizing currents that helped to change
the culture of their kinsmen at the Cape. The trekkers regarded themselves as men who had—in the words of one of their statements—"torn
themselves loose . . . from the British Government . . . and had left
our motherland where we were libelled, plagued and humiliated." [10]
This profound anti-British sentiment was never far from the surface of
the consciousness of many Northern Afrikaners. But it was muted in
the 1850's and 1860's when the British government appeared willing to
accept the independence of the republics. In these years the two small
trekker states were wracked by internal differences: "disorder and lawlessness, which led to licentiousness, chaos and anarchy" are the terms
used by a leading Afrikaner historian in describing the internal situation of the Free State in the 1860's, and in the more backward Transvaal conditions were far worse.[11] In such circumstances Afrikaners
might feel a sense of cultural homogeneity, but they had not yet evolved
that intense national consciousness which was later to have such a profound influence on the destinies of South Africa. In the years between
1865 and 1877 signs of a "spiritual metamorphosis" [12]—to use the
phrase of F. A. van Jaarsveld, the historian of Afrikaner nationalism—
began to be apparent among the Afrikaner communities of the Orange
Free State and the Cape. In the Free State the long struggle with the
Basuto and the able and inspiring leadership of President J. H. Brand
gave birth to a spirit of national unity, a sentiment strengthened by the
bitter sense of grievance felt by the Free Staters after the British annexation of the diamond fields to which the republic could make a good
legal claim. In the Cape the position of the Afrikaners was less clear
cut. The Great Trek had divided the Afrikaner population of South Africa into two broad groups—"emigrants" and "colonists." After more
than a generation of separation the disputes between the government of
the Cape and the Orange Free State drew the Afrikaner elements of the
two countries closer together. As Cape Afrikaners became more keenly
aware of their republican kinsmen, a wider sense of "South African"
patriotism began to develop. At the same time, a group of young Cape
Afrikaner intellectuals led by a Dutch Reformed Church minister, S. J.
du Toit, began to lay the ideological foundations of Afrikaner nationalism, stressing the sense of a distinct identity—"neither an Englishman,
nor a Hollander, but an Afrikaner" [13]—by insisting on the value of the
Afrikaans language and encouraging an interest in Afrikaner history.
The titles of du Toit's newspaper, *The Patriot,* of one of his books, *The*

History of Our Country in the Language of Our People, and of the "Society of True Afrikaners" which he founded to advance his aims provided a succinct and eloquent testimony to the nature of his views.

The ideal of South African unity came then to be recognized both by the British government and by far-sighted Afrikaners. But both sides were determined to secure unity on their own terms, and the British, by far the stronger of the two, were clearly in a position to force the pace. In 1875 Lord Carnarvon, the colonial secretary in Disraeli's government and an ardent imperialist, attempted unsuccessfully to convene a conference to discuss the possibilities of confederation. Both the Cape and the Afrikaner republics viewed the prospect coolly or with hostility. At the same time, the Transvaal took active measures to provide itself with a permanent link with the outside world by attempting to raise a loan for a railroad to the Portuguese territory of Delagoa Bay in southern Mozambique. Deeply alarmed by the implications of this move and aware of the grave weaknesses of the republic—the government was facing bankruptcy, while its commandos had suffered a severe defeat at the hands of the Pedi—Carnarvon decided to take strong action and sent a senior colonial administrator, Theophilus Shepstone, to the Transvaal as special commissioner. In April 1877, Shepstone succeeded in persuading a group of leading Transvaal Afrikaners to accept annexation as a British colony.

With the Transvaal firmly in British hands the prospects of achieving federation seemed excellent. But it soon became apparent that to the mass of the Transvaalers the "timorous despotism," as one historian has called it,[14] of the new British regime was intensely distasteful. Opposition to the British annexation provided a cause to which the Transvaal Afrikaners, a people previously noted for their almost anarchic lack of unity, could render enthusiastic support. Mass meetings, the organization of people's committees, and the able leadership of Paul Kruger and P. J. Joubert served to create a novel sense of Transvaal nationalism. In December 1880, the Transvaal Afrikaners, exasperated at the refusal of the British to revoke the hated system, broke out into revolt. Two months later Transvaal commandos wiped out a small British force at Majuba Hill. In August, 1881, the British and the Transvaalers signed the Convention of Pretoria; under its terms the Transvaal acquired "complete self-government subject to the Suzerainty of Her Majesty." The war had done more than put an end to the British attempt to unite South Africa on terms acceptable to the imperial government. The dramatic series of events between the annexation and Majuba Hill served powerfully to stimulate the spirit of Afrikaner nationalism. Afrikaners in the Cape and in the Orange Free State felt an intense bond of sympathy with their long-neglected kinsmen beyond the Vaal. As for the Transvaalers, their spectacular victory over the British provided a powerful boost to their intense feelings of pride and self-reliance.

"South Africa," in the words of an eminent South African historian, "has advanced politically by disasters and economically by windfalls." [15] In 1886 South Africa in general and the Transvaal in particular enjoyed the first fruits of the greatest economic windfall ever experienced by an African country in the nineteenth century—the discovery that among the low hills of the Witwatersrand lay the richest gold-bearing deposits in the whole world. This astonishing discovery completely transformed the political pattern of South Africa. Before 1886, the Cape had clearly been the region's most powerful political unit, the Transvaal the least stable, the most backward of the region's four European polities. After 1886, the Transvaal gradually moved toward a position of political and economic dominance. Ultimately this development was to confer great benefits on the Afrikaner people. But it was one of the ironies of the South African situation that the construction of the economic base for Afrikaner power was the work not of Afrikaners but of "outsiders," of British and other European capitalists and artisans and of African laborers. And it was one of the region's greatest tragedies that the discovery of gold and the consequent settlement of a large foreign element in the Transvaal should have set in motion a series of crises leading directly to the terrible disaster of the South African War.

Two sharply contrasting figures—Cecil Rhodes and Paul Kruger—dominate much that has been written about the history of white South Africa in the last two decades of the nineteenth century. It is not wise of a historian to put excessive stress on the importance of any individual, however remarkable, but in the case of these two men a brief biographical excursus seems excusable. Not only did Rhodes and Kruger both acquire a great deal of power which they used to further ambitious policies of their own devising; both of them could also be regarded as symbolic figures, epitomizing in their personalities something of the characteristics of the very different societies they came to lead. Both of them, too, were clearly "big" men, seen as such by their contemporaries, hero-worshipped by some, execrated by others. And both of them had intensely dramatic careers which ended in both cases under the pall of tragedy.

Rhodes was born in 1853, the son of an English country clergyman. Sent out to South Africa while still in his teens for the sake of his health, he made his way to the diamond fields of Kimberley and rapidly built up a remarkable fortune. Money provided the young English emigrant with freedom and power. Power he used to translate his political vision into reality. Rhodes once confessed to a predilection for "the big, the simple, the barbaric" and his political schemes undoubtedly possessed a certain crude grandeur. Utterly convinced of the pre-eminent virtues of the cultural group from which he was sprung, Rhodes believed that the spread of "civilization" could best be served by the rapid northward expansion of British hegemony. But though he was a passionate British imperialist, he was also a good South African, who dreamed of the emergence of a great white dominion stretching from the Cape to the Zambezi. His own financial empire gave him something of the status of an independent power, so that he could never be accused of acting as the tool of the metropolitan government. At the same time, his obvious devotion to the cause of a united South Africa made it possible for many Cape Dutch politicians, who might otherwise have distrusted him for his Englishness, to accept his leadership when he became prime minister of the Cape in 1890.

As a young boy, Paul Kruger had taken part in the Great Trek. Thus he had been involved from the start in all the tribulations—the wars with "kaffirs," the savage internal feuds—which beset the Boer communities that came to settle north of the Vaal. In the late 1870's he came to the fore as leader of the resistance to the British occupation of the Transvaal. Thus he was a natural choice for the presidency of the revived republic and was re-elected to the same post on three subsequent occasions. His long tenure of office combined with a lifetime's experience of local politics invested him with a prestige comparable to that achieved in much more recent times by the leaders of certain independent African states. Certainly, unlike most modern leaders, Kruger could never be described as a modernizer. Indeed, to many contemporary observers the old man with his "uncouth, surly manner" [16] and his fundamentalist ideas about religion seemed an almost absurd anachronism. To one sophisticated Englishmen indeed the president appeared little better than "a snuffy mendacious savage." [17] In reality Kruger must be seen as an extremely shrewd politician, who stood manfully against a mounting tide of trouble in defense of the best interests of his *volk*.

At Majuba Hill in 1881 the Afrikaners of the Transvaal had fought for and won their independence. This independence Kruger was determined to establish on impregnable foundations. Yet from the mid-1880's he and his compatriots found themselves faced with the apparently irresistible expansion of British imperialism. In 1885 the British took over control of Bechuanaland, thus depriving the republic of the possibility of making contact with the Germans in South West Africa. Five years later, Rhodes launched his conquistatorial expedition into the territory of the Ndebele and the Shona and succeeded in hemming in the republic from the north. And in 1895, after the Transvaalers had established their hegemony over Swaziland, the British government countered their move by annexing Tongaland, the territory lying between Swaziland and the sea. Only one outlet was left to the land-locked republic if it wished to escape total dependence on the British-controlled ports of the Cape Colony and Natal, an outlet that involved the construction of a railroad to Delagoa Bay in Portuguese Mozambique. With the aid of foreign capital this eastern line was completed in 1894. Commercial independence was accompanied by a greater measure of freedom in foreign affairs, as the Transvaal came to establish cordial diplomatic relations with Germany and other European powers. This development caused acute alarm in London and Cape Town. "To have [the Germans] meddling at Pretoria and Johannesburg," wrote the colonial secretary, Lord Ripon, in 1894, "would be fatal to our position and our influence in South Africa." [18]

Kruger's astute manipulation of European powers is reminiscent of the skill with which another contemporary ruler of a land-locked state, Menelik of Ethiopia, handled the Europeans who encroached upon his territory. But Kruger was faced with yet another grave problem of a kind Menelik was fortunate to escape; the establishment of an influential alien minority within the borders of his state. (The khedive of Egypt and the bey of Tunis had been forced, it will be recalled, to face the same problem as a result of the influx of Europeans in the 1860's and 1870's.) The discovery of gold on the Witwatersrand attracted a steadily mounting stream of fortune-seekers to settle in the heart of Afrikaner territory. By 1896, only ten years after its foundation, Johnnesburg possessed a population of 100,000, half of whom were white. Of the city's 50,000 Europeans, only 6,000 were Afrikaners; 16,000 of the *Uitlanders* ("aliens") came from Britian and a similar number from Cape Colony and Natal, while substantial minorities of Russian Jews, Germans, Australasians, Netherlanders, and Americans served to emphasize the city's cosmopolitan character. How extraordinary were the contrasts afforded by the European population of the Transvaal in the 1890's: on the one hand, a society of Afrikaner pastoralists, living in widely dispersed farms and content with a culture more reminiscent of the seventeenth than the nineteenth century; on the other, the brash urban community of the Rand, with its freedom from the restraints of an older order and its intense interest in practical forms of modernization. To have coped with so massive an influx of aliens peacefully would have been a difficult enough task for any people. To Kruger and his fellow-Transvaalers the situation was rendered all the more tense by the fact that many of the leading *uitlanders* appeared to be hand in glove with the hated British imperialists. Was not the prime minister of the Cape himself one of the wealthiest industrialists on the Rand?

The *uitlanders,* for their part, had many grievances. Afrikaner administration in the Transvaal was corrupt and inefficient; yet Kruger and his officials proved themselves extremely adept at devising fiscal measures designed to ensure that a proportion of the mining industry's profits remained in the country. Moreover, the Transvaal government, while taking the *uitlanders'* money, refused to grant to the aliens the political rights which they all too arrogantly assumed to be their due. In this uneasy situation some of the *uitlanders* began to use the vocabulary of revolution. To Rhodes the overthrow of Kruger's government as a result of a swift and bloodless coup was an insidiously attractive idea. Kruger's government was growing steadily richer and more intransigent. How could such a state ever be incorporated in a great South African dominion united under the British flag? Only, Rhodes argued, by replacing the present republican administration by a new regime largely dependent on *uitlander* support. To achieve such a goal Rhodes was prepared to take great risks: encourage the *uitlanders* to revolt, send in the British high commissioner to mediate, and the game was won. He was encouraged to proceed with his plans by the support he received from the ardently imperialist Joseph Chamberlain who became colonial secretary in June 1895. Six months later, Rhodes' trusted lieutenant, L. S. Jameson, invaded the Transvaal with a force of 500 men in an attempt to bolster up the long planned *uitlander* revolt.

Jameson's "raid" was an act of disastrous folly. The raiders were easily rounded up by the Transvaal authorities and so were the *uitlander* rebels in Johannesburg. Rhodes, accepting responsibility for the "raid," resigned immediately. Chamberlain succeeded in covering up his complicity. But irreparable harm had been done to Anglo-Afrikaner relations in South Africa. Clearly, in Afrikaner eyes, the British were no longer to be trusted. The Transvaal government began importing large quantities of firearms from Europe, imposed more stringent restrictions on *uitlander* activity and concluded an alliance with the Orange Free State. In the Cape the alliance which Rhodes had formed with the Afrikaners collapsed, and political divisions ran bitterly along ethnic lines. Angered and humiliated by the course of events, many British South Africans began to see the situation in conspiratorial terms. To uphold British supremacy and to counter the insidious forces of "pan-Afrikanerism," groups of Britons came together in the Transvaal and in the Cape and Natal to found the South African League, a body which soon developed into a powerful lobby advocating strong British action.

What South Africa needed, a senior British official concluded in 1899, was "rest, not surgery." [19] Unfortunately, this was not a view which commended itself either to Joseph Chamberlain or to his appointee, Sir Alfred Milner, British high commissioner in South Africa from 1897. Milner was an intensely public-spirited bureaucrat dedicated to "working for the integrity and consolidation of the British Empire." He was also, by his own definition, a "British Race Patriot." [20] He had been one of Cromer's bright young men in Egypt. Few apprenticeships could have been less appropriate for one called on to deal with the complexities of South African politics. With the arrogant simplicity of a supremely lucid but entirely unimaginative mind, Milner set about "solving" the South African problem. Giving his support to the "jingoes" of the South African League and disregarding the many shrewd and moderate-minded men to be found both in the republics and in the colonies, Milner pressed the government of the Transvaal to accept the demands being put forward by the militant *uitlanders*. It was a policy deliberately intended, as Milner himself confessed, to precipitate a crisis. If British supremacy was to endure in South Africa, then the power of the Transvaal must be broken, even at the cost of a full-scale war. Chamberlain accepted Milner's diagnosis and persuaded his fellow ministers to accept it too. As for the Transvaalers, surrender was inconceivable. When it became apparent that the British were intent on strengthening their forces in South Africa as a prelude to presenting an ultimatum, the governments of the two South African republics decided to strike first. In October 1899, their forces invaded the two British colonies of the Cape and Natal. Wars are never "inevitable." The "jingoes" in the British camp would have done well to have heeded the prophetic words written in 1895 by a great English-speaking South African, Olive Schreiner: "the hour of external success may be the hour of irrevocable failure." [21]

▲▼ THE POLITICS OF WHITE SUPREMACY: CONFLICT AND CONCILIATION, 1899 TO 1910

The South African War stands out as one of the largest and most savage conflicts in the history of Africa. It lasted for two and a half years and involved more than half a million fighting men. But though fought on African soil, it remained throughout a "white man's war." Both sides studiously refrained from making use of "native" combatants. The British, who had used Indian troops in many other African campaigns, in this war looked only to the white dominions of their empire for military assistance. But for all its racial exclusiveness, the war, in its strategy and character, presented a striking similarity to those other campaigns between "aliens" and "indigenes" of which the modern history of the Third World affords so many examples. The Afrikaners were fighting to defend what they had come to regard as their fatherland. The morale of their people was high. The farmers of the veld, born to the rifle and the saddle, possessing an intimate knowledge of the terrain, and often with some previous experience of warfare acquired through their campaigns against African chiefdoms, turned out to be first-class fighting men. The best of their generals combined the essential military virtues of dash and doggedness. And they possessed in the German artillery and rifles that the Transvaal government had prudently stock-piled in the years immediately before the outbreak of war, weapons technically superior to those used by the British. Given these advantages, given the fact that the armed forces of the two republics also enjoyed a significant numerical superiority in the first weeks of the war, then the run of initial Boer successes does not seem surprising. But as reinforcements poured into the Cape, the advantage gradually swung to the British. With 450,000 men at their disposal against the 80,000 fighting men mustered by the two republics, the British generals, Roberts and Kitchener, rapidly succeeded in moving up the main railroads to occupy all the major towns of the Transvaal and the Orange Free State. The war then took a form destined to become oppressively familiar to the student of later campaigns in the Moroccan Rif, in Libya (the Italo-Sanusi wars), and in Algeria—and, of course, in Vietnam: on the one side, elusive guerrilla forces made up of men fighting for their freedom; on the other, a large and cumbersome army mostly composed of regulars and often unimaginatively led. Exasperated by the difficulties involved in breaking the will of so resilient an enemy, the British commanders resorted to increasingly brutal measures. Boer farms were burned or blown up, captured guerrillas were sometimes executed as "rebels," and the families of the Boer commandos were herded into "concentration camps" where about 20,000 men, women, and children—about 10 percent of the total white population of the two republics—died of disease. These tactics had dire consequences for the future. By resorting to such methods the British army did much, as G. H. Le May has pointed out, "to assist in creating an Afrikaner nationalism more cohesive, more vengeful and more ambitious than the 'Afrikanerdom' which Britain had set out to break." [22]

At an early stage in the war the British had demanded the "unconditional surrender" of their opponents, but with antiwar sentiment spreading at home—a process strongly reminiscent of the reactions of French public opinion to Algeria in the late 1950's or of American to Vietnam a decade later—and with the cost of the struggle reaching the figure, astronomical for those days, of one and a half million pounds a week, it became clear that in the absence of a decisive military victory the war had to be ended by negotiation. As for the Boer commandos still in the field, their prospects were growing steadily darker. Many of the Free Staters felt that the struggle was not yet lost, but the Transvaalers were gravely weakened by hunger and becoming increasingly alarmed at the possibility of a general African uprising. "We must not sacrifice the nation," declared the young General Smuts, addressing himself to the "bitter-enders," who refused to accept surrender, "on the altar of independence." [23]

The terms secured by the Afrikaners in the Treaty of Vereeniging (May, 1902) were far from ungenerous. "Military administration" in the Orange River Colony, as the Free State was now termed, and in the Transvaal was to be succeeded as soon as possible by "civil government." "As soon as circumstances permit," the most important clause in the treaty declared, "representative institutions leading up to self-government will be introduced." Equally reassuring for the Afrikaners was the single clause that mentioned "natives": "the question of granting the franchise to natives will not be decided until after the introduction of self-government." The significance of this point did not pass unnoticed in Britain. "The native will never have the franchise," wrote an official in the colonial office. "No responsible government will give it to him." [24] The insertion of such a clause was hardly surprising. The war had not been fought in the cause of African liberation nor—as some contemporary commentators were inclined to believe—had it been inspired by a crude desire to protect the profits of the capitalists of the Rand. The aim throughout had been to preserve British supremacy in South Africa.

The British had won their war. But the basic problem of establishing British supremacy on secure foundations remained to be solved. More than half the European population of South Africa was of Afrikaner stock. How, then, could one be sure that an independent South Africa would ever be a loyal dominion of the British Empire? Milner, with that short-sighted self-confidence so characteristic of the technocratic mind, believed that it was possible to engineer a satisfactory solution to the problem. The Transvaal was clearly the key to the future of South Africa. Accordingly, the Afrikaners of the Transvaal must be swamped by a massive British immigration both to the towns and to the rural areas of the high veld. At the same time the Afrikaners must gradually be "denationalized." Their nationalism was in large part a product of their isolation. Break down that isolation, bring them in closer touch with immigrants from Britain, transform their society by introducing an efficient, modern system of education, educate them in the English manner and in the English language—these were clearly the lines to be followed. As for the "native," certainly he must be "well treated and justly governed," but his role was to serve as "black labor," condemned by implication to a position of permanent inferiority.

"Milnerism" ended in bankruptcy, as Milner himself was forced to recognize when he left the country in 1905. South Africa failed to attract the expected flood of British immigrants and so the basic demographic pattern remained unchanged. As for Afrikaner nationalism, it was not weakened but toughened and stimulated by its ordeal. The war produced a fine crop of legends, heroes, and martyrs; it strengthened the bonds of comradeship; it aroused in many an Afrikaner heart intense pride in the achievements of the *volk* whose members had fought so valiantly for their freedom against the armed might of the greatest empire in the world. Within three years of the end of the war the Afrikaners of the Transvaal formed a new political party, *Het Volk* ("The People") and were pressing vigorously for the grant of responsible government. Such a demand could have been resisted only by an imperial government determined to exercise all the powers at its disposal to maintain its supremacy. But by 1906 there was a Liberal government in power in Britain for the first time in eleven years. Many of the Liberals had been known for their pro-Boer stand during the war; all of them felt a strong obligation to hold out the hand of friendship to the Afrikaner people. "We think that British Authority in South Africa has got to stand on two legs," the young Winston Churchill, colonial under-secretary in the Liberal government, informed the House of Commons. "Hon. Gentlemen opposite have laboured for ten years to make it stand on one." [25]

By this time a new generation of leaders had emerged in the Afrikaner areas. They were men of very different stamp from the patriarchal figures of Kruger's day. Still in their thirties or early forties, they had established themselves as lawyers usually educated abroad—or progressive farmers before the war and made names for themselves as successful guerrilla leaders during the conflict. Three men in particular stood out and were to dominate South African politics for the next decades—Louis Botha, Jan Christiaan Smuts, and James Hertzog. Botha was a farmer from the Transvaal, a man of great bonhomie, described as possessing "a homely insight into the minds of his own people." Smuts, on the other hand, was a highly intellectual lawyer from the Cape, a man whom some men regarded as displaying "an icy coolness," "a rather hard brilliancy." [26] Yet between these two dissimilar men there developed a deep friendship and a remarkable political partnership. "Conciliation" was the word they used to describe their policy—

"conciliation" designed to heal the rifts in the Afrikaner camp, to bring the four provinces of South Africa closer together, to unite English-speakers and Afrikaners, and finally to establish a harmonious relationship between a united South Africa and its imperial suzerain. Herztog, on the other hand, a lawyer from the Free State, trained not in England as Smuts had been but in Holland, regarded the policy of "conciliation" with some reserve and came to establish himself as a vigorous defender of Afrikaner culture.

In 1907 the Liberal government pushed through the first stage of its new policy by according self-government to the Transvaal and the Orange River Colony. Already by this time many responsible people, both British administrators and South African politicians, were working out plans for a system of closer union between the four colonies. A number of practical considerations lent a measure of urgency to their plans. There were serious disagreements between the inland and the maritime colonies over the policy to be followed in regard to customs duties and railroad tariffs. (Somewhat similar complications over railroads and customs duties were of major significance, it may be recalled, in the plans for the unification of Nigeria.) In Natal, a serious native rising in Zululand, the Bambata rebellion, had provided the isolationist English settlers with a salutary warning of the dangers of trying to go it alone. In the Transvaal, Afrikaner politicians, uneasily conscious of the power of the great mining magnates, saw in closer union the most effective means of preserving their own freedom of action.

And so at last, with negotiations between the various groups achieving a degree of harmony that seems incredible when contrasted with the earlier vicissitudes of South African polities, the British government was able to reach its long sought objective and hand over power to a truly South African government competent to manage all its own affairs. Yet in so doing the British government was unable to secure any effective guarantee that the rights of the vast majority of South African peoples would be considered. The Cape still retained its "color-blind" franchise which gave the vote to a limited number of Africans and "Coloureds," but the three other provinces refused to modify their rigid political color-bar, and it was stated in the constitution that every member of parliament should be "of European descent." There were a few uneasy consciences both in England and in South Africa about the implications of these decisions. W. P. Schreiner, for example, a former prime minister of the Cape, described the constitution as "illiberal and shortsighted in its conception of the people of South Africa." [27] "Any final assessment of the achievement of an imperial power," another South African, Leonard Thompson, has written, "must depend largely upon the sort of society it left behind when it withdrew. In withdrawing from South Africa, Great Britain left behind a castle-like society, dominated by its white minority. The price of unity and conciliation was the institutionalization of white supremacy." [28]

▲▼ THE TRANSFORMATION OF THE SOUTH
AFRICAN ECONOMY

In the course of the past century no country in the entire continent has experienced so massive a transformation of its economy as the Republic of South Africa. Today South Africa can claim to be one of the world's most highly industrialized nations. A century ago, before the discovery of diamonds, the vast majority of South Africans earned their living from the land. Many of the Europeans, both English colonists and Afrikaners, were stockmen, the wool from whose merino sheep represented the region's major overseas export. Some African peoples, too, particularly those living in the semiarid areas of Botswana and South West Africa, were entirely dependent on pastoralism for their livelihood. But the majority of Africans, and some European farmers too, derived their livelihood from a mixed economy, herding cattle, producing crops of millet or of maize, and supplementing their diet by hunting the game which was still abundant in many areas. Hunting could also still be carried on as a full-time profession, and the sale of ivory and wild animal skins provided a useful supplement to the meager wealth of many remote communities. Cape Town, the largest town in the region, had a population of less than 30,000 in the mid-1860's; only three other urban centers—Port Elizabeth, Grahamstown, and Durban—exceeded the modest number of 5,000 inhabitants. Commerce and manufacture provided employment for no more than 4 percent of Cape Colony's half-million people. In the other communities of South Africa the percentage was even lower.

The discovery first of diamonds, then of gold, and the consequent development of a large-scale mining industry provided the root-causes for the transformation of South Africa's economy. In the course of a century £700,000,000 worth of diamonds have been produced by the mines at Kimberley, while in eighty years the total amount of gold yielded by the Witwatersrand has reached the figure—amazing when contrasted with the total of other export products in other parts of Africa—of £6,000,000,000. The emergence of a large-scale mining industry was a massive enterprise whose success was dependent on the courage, intelligence, and resourcefulness of a wide range of individuals—engineers, applied scientists, financial experts, and a large company of miners, both European and African. The search for gold and precious stones has been a powerful stimulant in the history of many societies; few episodes in the history of Africa provide so vivid an example of the "peaceful pursuit of well-being" serving as a force for change as the development of the diamond- and gold-mining industries of South Africa. The two industries stimulated a variety of changes that transformed the life-patterns of a very large number of South Africans.

In the first place, the new mining centers acted as magnets whose active force drew men from the remotest parts of the earth. Americans and Australians joined with Russian Jews and Englishmen in seeking their fortune in the new boom-towns of Kimberley and Johannesburg, greatly enriching by their talents and experience the cultural life of the European communities in which they settled. Even more significant, however—for the numbers involved were larger and the cultural consequences more profound—was the movement of Africans to the mines. The majority came only as migrant laborers, returning to their homes at the end of their contract period, but some settled in the new urban areas, where their children, completely cut off from the old "tribal" society, were to develop a rich new Afro-European culture of their own. By 1960, Johannesburg with over 1 million inhabitants, more than half of them Africans, had grown to be the third largest city in Africa (exceeded only by Cairo and Alexandria). With its soaring office blocks, often elegantly designed, and its broad ring of opulent white suburbs it exhibited a visual concentration of wealth astonishing even to a visitor from one of the more prosperous parts of Europe.

It was fortunate for the overall development of the country that the two mining centers should lie deep in the interior. First Kimberley and later Johannesburg served as an obvious focus for the development of communications. In 1870, South Africa contained less than seventy miles of railroad. In the course of the 1870's, 780 miles of track were constructed, with lines reaching out from the four main ports, Cape Town, Port Elizabeth, East London, and Durban, into the interior. Another 1,000 miles were added in the course of the next decade, and by 1919 South Africa had approximately 10,000 miles of track (almost double the total mileage of present-day West African railroads). By this time the railroads were providing employment for 72,000 workers, half of them white. A generation before the coming of the motor car, the railroads were supplemented by another form of transport, massive wagons drawn by eight to ten pairs of oxen and capable in dry weather of carrying loads weighing 8,000 pounds ten to twelve miles a day. Many South Africans, white, black, and "Coloured," left their farms and chose the adventurous life of a transport driver.

Thus gradually, with the coming of the railroads and the expansion of road traffic, the isolation of the European communities of the *platte-land* ("flat land," an Afrikaner expression applied to the European-occupied rural areas) was broken down. New markets began to present themselves both in the mushrooming mining towns and even, as contacts with the ports became easier, in a wider world. The first plantations of sugar cane had been established in Natal in the 1850s. Faced with the problem of finding suitable plantation workers, the farmers of Natal turned, as their contemporaries in Mauritius were doing, to India: from 1860 to 1911 a stream of indentured laborers, together with a large number of free immigrants, reached Natal from India. Many a "frugal and irrepressible coolie," to quote the phrase of an English Natalian,[29] turned to market-gardening, hawking, or shopkeeping when his term of service was over. Many European planters undertook the pioneering of almost virgin land. Farther west, in the southern Cape, enterprising farmers took to breeding ostriches, whose feathers fetched an excellent price in the European market. In 1913, exports of ostrich feathers from South Africa were worth almost £3 million. But the product was too closely attached to a particular style of *haute couture;* the postwar change in female fashion struck a death-blow to the industry. But all was not lost: ostrich farmers had introduced lucerne (alfalfa) grown in irrigated plots to feed their birds; lucerne hay provided an excellent winter fodder for livestock; so farmers were able to give their ostrich pens over to dairy cattle.

Whatever the success achieved by certain aspects of South African agriculture, the industry as a whole was called on to face many hardships. Not a decade passed without at least one severe drought. In the 1890's the vineyards of the Cape were attacked by the phylloxera or vine-aphids, the maize farms in districts near the Kalahari by locusts, while rinderpest, whose ravages in South West Africa have already been mentioned, was no less destructive in parts of South Africa, carrying off between 30 and 90 percent of the cattle of certain districts in the Cape. Even more destructive in the long run was the process of soil erosion set in motion by over-grazing or excessive "veld-burning." "Since the white man has been in South Africa," an official report pointed out in 1922, "enormous tracts of country have been entirely, or partially denuded of their original vegetation, with the result that rivers, vleis and water-holes described by old travelers have dried or disappeared."[30]

The pressures of a harsh environment affected all those, both black and white, with a stake in the land. But there were other difficulties which provided white farmers alone with special cause for complaint. "Every farmer I met with," wrote Anthony Trollope, "swore to me that the country was a wretched country simply because labour could not be had." [31] This was written in the 1870's but the complaint of a shortage of labor continued to be heard decade after decade. White farmers had another grievance, the constant fluctuation in prices to which their products were exposed. But the white farming community was in a position to secure for itself the removal of many of its disabilities. Commanding immense voting strength, it was well placed to put pressure on the state authorities to secure practical advantages for itself.

The earliest white farms established in South Africa had been based on slave labor. "Of all skilled occupations, farming," as a critical South African historian has pointed out, "most surely requires an apprenticeship of calloused hands and a sweated brow." [32] Yet to the vast majority of whites, manual labor on the farm was "kaffir's work." Brought up to expect that black labor should be both cheap and docile, white farmers were determined to maintain their highly favored position. The Natives Land Act of 1913 provided them with a highly effective instrument for this end. The act made it illegal for Africans to purchase lands outside the limited areas designated as reserves, thus putting an end to the practice, particularly prevalent in the Cape, whereby Africans were able to acquire farms in predominantly white areas. The act also contained another set of clauses which prohibited Africans from concluding new agreements with white farmers to rent land. These clauses were aimed at eliminating the practices of "farming-on-the-half" whereby an African tenant handed over half his produce to the owner of the land and of "kaffir farming" whereby Africans were allowed to "squat" on white farms in return for some form of payment. Some white farmers had been only too glad to obtain an easy source of income by making over land in these ways, but to a more influential section of white society the emergence of a class of moderately prosperous African tenant farmers presented a really serious threat to the supply of cheap labor. "Few laws passed in South Africa can have been felt with such immediate harshness," in the opinion of a recent economic historian, "by so large a population." [33] Hundreds of black South Africans were uprooted from white-owned farms, forced to sell their stock, and to seek a new livelihood either in the towns or the reserves or as full-time laborers. "The next three decades were to see the almost total elimination of that class of rural African" described by one contemporary observer as being "fairly comfortable" and "living in many instances just like Dutchmen." [34]

The Land Act served to prevent many Africans from choosing the alternative of working for themselves rather than for a white employer. The numerous Pass Laws, discussed in more detail in the next section, served to restrict the natural mobility of labor, while many African farmworkers were bound to their employer by the ties of indebtedness. All these different forms of restriction helped to ensure that white farmers obtained the labor force needed. In the 1950's, still other methods were used to meet the farmers' requirement. Prisons were established in rural areas so that farmers could make use of convict labor, and petty offenders were encouraged to "volunteer" to pass their short prison sentences working on farms.

White farmers needed more than a supply of cheap labor if they were to make a decent living. Their incomes were affected by the violent fluctuations of primary products on the world market and by competition from imported foodstuffs. From the 1920's on, the farmers found successive governments highly sympathetic to their problems. Generous subsidies helped them when world prices were low; tariff protection shielded them from the threat of foreign competition. One group which benefited greatly from government assistance—the maize farmers of the Transvaal and Orange Free State—became a powerful lobby able to exert considerable pressure on the government after 1948. Between 1948 and 1951, the price of maize was raised from 21s 3d a bag to 30s. Before long, maize was being overproduced, and the surplus was being sold on the external market at a loss. In 1967, £33 million was spent on subsidies to white farmers, almost twice the amount provided from public funds for African education.

Clearly, political considerations exercised as powerful an influence on the development of agriculture in South Africa as they did in Muhammad Ali's Egypt or in French Algeria or, for that matter, in Stalin's Russia. But however questionable some of the country's agricultural policies may have been, it was still possible to point to a record of substantial achievement. From 1910 on, there was a steady and sometimes a spectacular increase in all forms of agricultural production. Maize and wheat, for example, doubled in output between the two world wars, and a rapid increase in the two crops was resumed after 1945. Sugar, fruit, and dairy produce achieved an even higher rate of growth. Another impressive achievement of South African agriculture was the establishment of agricultural colleges well-equipped to serve as the bases for practical research. Increasing attention was paid to the problem of conservation, but in the 1960's the country was still estimated to be losing 400 million tons of scarce topsoil every year. Here was a development with ominous implications for the future; to some observers, indeed, it seemed that in its attempts to preserve the most vital of its natural resources "the country was still fighting a losing battle." [35]

All that has been said so far about South African agriculture relates only to the areas of white land-ownership. In those districts where Africans were allowed to own land, the reserves or "homelands" which comprised no more than one-seventh of the Republic's total area, the situation was very different. "From one community after another," Monica Wilson has written, "there is evidence of a fall of productivity after a period of early prosperity. The tale is one of increasing pressure of population on deteriorating land, and the fall was not only in productivity per head, but in the total crop produced." [36] Some government-sponsored measures designed to improve agriculture on the reserves— notably the construction of dams and wells—have been welcomed by the local people; others, such as the culling of stock and the introduction of fencing, both measures needed to protect the soil from overgrazing, have been bitterly resented and have even led to violent clashes between peasants and officials. Most families living in the reserves began to find it impossible to provide enough food from their own plots to meet all their requirements. To make ends meet, able-bodied men were forced to seek work in the towns as temporary or migrant laborers. By the mid-twentieth century, the lot of the black peasantry of South Africa could be seen as very different from that of the prosperous small farmers to be found in many parts of East and West Africa where the development of lucrative export crops—cocoa or groundnuts, coffee or cotton—brought a substantial increase in the value of rural incomes.

In some tropical African countries the profits of agriculture, creamed off by the marketing boards, have helped to meet the cost of other forms of development. In South Africa, by contrast, agricultural development would hardly have been possible without the support that could be drawn from profits in the mining industry. The rapid growth of mining stimulated the economy in yet another way—by making possible the development of a steadily increasing range of manufacturing industries. Even before the discovery of diamonds and gold, a start had been made in the process of industrialization. In 1860, Cape Town possessed seventy manufacturing concerns, including brickfields, flour mills, soap factories, and iron foundries. In this respect the Cape was well ahead of any other community in Southern Africa, but a substantial increase in the manufacturing sector would never have taken place without the massive influx of capital and the steady widening of the market that accompanied the boom in gold and diamonds. Initially, however, the mining industry absorbed most of the capital and skilled labor available. Not until World War I when imported goods suddenly became at once more expensive, as a result of high insurance rates, and in shorter supply, did South Africa experience the necessary stimulus needed for the diversion of enterprise into new industries. Between 1911 and 1921 the value of factory production trebled. During the 1920's, South Africans began advocating lines of development little different from those to be proposed in other parts of the continent forty years later. South African trade was entirely dependent on primary products; these products were subject to violent fluctuations in the world market; gold, the basis of the economy, threatened to become a wasting asset. Clearly it was necessary to diversify the economy, to industrialize, to erect tariff walls to protect young industries. In 1928 the government established an iron and steel corporation which served as the nucleus for an expanding group of engineering industries. Soon afterward South Africa was hit by the Great Depression. But gold once again proved the country's salvation. Between 1932 and 1939, the price of the precious metal rose from just over £4 an ounce to almost £8. In five years (1932–37) there was a 70 percent increase in the Gross National Product, from £217 million to £370 million. In these years, one economic historian has argued, South Africa became the first country on the African continent to achieve the "take-off" into sustained economic growth.[37]

By the end of the 1960's South Africa was firmly established as the most highly industrialized country in the continent. The contribution of agriculture to the Gross Domestic Product fell from 15.9 percent in 1954–55 to 8.8 percent in 1969–70, while that of secondary industry increased from 23.8 percent to 27.9 percent in the same period. Mining, which contributed just over 11 percent to the GDP in both years, profited from a variety of new developments. Gold was still the most valuable single product, but whereas in the 1930's it had accounted for more than 80 percent of the total value of the mining output, by the 1950's its contribution had fallen to just over 60 percent. By the late 1950's, South Africa had emerged as a major producer of uranium; indeed, in 1959, the value of what official statistics coyly described as "prescribed atomic minerals" was three times that of diamonds. By this time, too, South Africa had become an important producer of copper, zinc, lead, and asbestos. Most significant of all, the country possessed in its rich deposits of coal and iron ore the essential foundations for heavy industry. In 1926, South Africa produced 52,000 tons of iron ore and 14 million tons of coal. By 1959, iron ore production exceeded 3 million tons, coal production 40 million tons.

An ever-increasing labor force was needed to maintain this steadily ramifying industrial structure. Little in the way of coercion was needed: Egoli (the African name for Johannesburg), the fantastic city of gold, became a magnet for young men from almost every part of Southern Africa. "They come on foot, on horseback, on bicycles, by dugout canoes, by lake and river steamers, in lorries, by train and even by air.

They come from all parts of the compass—from the peaceful hills of the Transkei, from the lion country of the Bechuanaland bush, down the broad reaches of the Zambesi, from the tropical shores of Lake Nyasa and the mountain fastnesses of Basutoland. They come, too, in their thousands from the hills and valleys of Portuguese East Africa, from the rocky uplands of Sekukuniland, the tangled swamp country of the Okavango delta and the green fields of Swaziland." [38] A romantic invocation, perhaps—the source is a survey published by the Transvaal Chamber of Mines in 1951—but one that does convey something of the extraordinary nature of this great movement of African laborers. Yet the pull of Egoli was extraordinary only in its range, not in its basic nature. All over Africa, all over the world, industrial towns had for many decades been attracting workers from the countryside. But in the way this movement occurred there was one profoundly significant difference between South Africa and other countries. Elsewhere in the world when the peasant moved to the town, he settled down, brought his family with him, and gradually became a townsman. In South Africa most Africans who came to the town to work were not permitted to make this complete transition. It suited the needs of their white overlords better that they should remain as migrant laborers.

In the early years of industrialization and urbanization it was natural enough that African peasants coming to Kimberley or to Egoli should think only in terms of a few month's work, of returning to their families when they had earned enough money to pay the tax collector or to buy a few simple luxuries. But as the towns increased in size and their amenities became more apparent, and as conditions in many reserves became increasingly difficult, many Africans became anxious to make their homes in the new urban setting, only to find themselves restricted by the regulations devised by their European masters. "The towns of the Colony," declared an official publication from Natal in 1904, "are the special places of abode for the white man who is the governing race." [39] This was a view to which the vast majority of white South Africans would give their assent. Africans were seen only as "temporary sojourners" in urban areas. For their own sakes it was as well that this should be so; life in towns, Europeans argued, was bad for Africans, it "demoralized" and "detribalized" them, it prevented them from "developing along their own lines." Moreover, a large urban African population had dangerous political implications; urban locations were to be seen, in the words of an Afrikaner politician of the 1920's, as "the incubators of unrighteousness." [40] The movement to the towns must be restricted. Africans must not be allowed to bring their families with them. As soon as their period of contract was finished, they should be required to return to their natural "homeland" in the reserve. The Pass Laws (discussed in more detail in the next section) provided Europeans with the legal sanctions needed to restrict a movement on which their own prosperity was based but which was interpreted as a threat to their very identity as a "superior race."

Thus the system of migrant labor came to be established as one of the pillars of white supremacy. Yet it came under increasing fire from economists, social workers, and industrialists. "An evil canker at the heart of our whole society" was the phrase used by an eminent South African economist in 1964; and he went on to describe the system of migrant labor as being "wasteful of labour, destructive of ambition, a wrecker of homes and a symptom of our fundamental failure to create a decent and progressive economic society." [41] No less "destructive of ambition" was the system of job reservation, another pillar in the structure of white supremacy, whereby Africans were proscribed by law from entering a wide range of skilled occupations reserved exclusively for Europeans. As the economy expanded, many European employers found themselves faced with a sometimes almost crippling shortage of white skilled labor. Inevitably a widespread practice developed of using Africans to do jobs legally reserved for whites. But the fundamental injustice of the system remained. Africans could never aspire to rise above a certain modest level, nor when they took over a job from a white man could they expect to be paid at the same rate.

Taken as a whole, the development of the South African economy appeared curiously ambivalent in character. On the one hand, there could be no doubt about the astonishing nature of the South African achievement—a point succinctly illustrated by a few statistics. In 1911, the value of the output of agriculture, mining, and private manufacturing stood at £29 million, £35 million, and £9 million respectively. By 1961, agricultural output had risen to £387 million, mining to £426 million, and private manufacturing to £561 million. In the same period of fifty years, exports (excluding gold) rose from £10 million to £463 million and state revenue from £14 million to £365 million. This vast increase in production had made South Africa one of the most prosperous countries in the world for its dominant white minority. An estimate made in 1954 put the average annual family income of whites at £1616, of "Coloureds" and Asians at £308, and of Africans at £145. Within the African population there was a great disparity between those families living in the reserves whose income was put at £87 and those in cities with an average income of £213. Undoubtedly, some urban Africans today enjoy a greater measure of prosperity than their forefathers, but it is impossible to avoid the conclusion that a very large number of black South Africans are either worse off or no better off than were their parents and grandparents. This is particularly true of the reserves. "The food of most Nguni families," Monica Wilson has written, "is probably less nutritious and less plentiful than it used to be, though fewer die from famine during drought. There is no sense of steadily increasing wealth as there is in some African communities elsewhere, with lucrative cash crops and ample land." [42] In the mining industry real wages for Africans were no higher in the mid-1960's, after thirty years of economic growth, than they had been in 1911. In agriculture real wages for Africans were reported to have declined in the course of the last fifty years. In some industries the disparity between black workers and white had grown, not shrunk. In gold mining, for example, white miners were earning eight times as much as black miners in 1924, nine times as much in 1957. The inevitable expansion of automation had ominous implications for many Africans, for it seemed likely that the demand for unskilled labor would decline, and the urban unemployed could be removed by transporting them back to the reserves. The need to create new employment opportunities by developing industries within the reserves or on their borders was generally recognized in the 1960's, but the decade had little to show in the way of practical achievements. Behind the bright glitter of white South African prosperity lay the dark and ominous shadow of black South African misery and frustration.

▲▼ THE EMERGENCE OF A PLURAL SOCIETY

In 1875 South Africa was made up of a large number of societies, for the most part still distinct one from another, politically, socially, and economically. Already, however, the bonds of interdependence had been laid. Indeed, the process could be traced back over many centuries to the earliest contacts between Bushmen and Bantu peoples. Europeans, too, had found themselves closely involved from the earliest years of their settlement in the life of their African neighbors, the Hottentot of the Cape, trading with them, enslaving them, establishing intimate relations with many of their women. By 1875 the ties linking together people of different ethnic groups had grown still more extensive and complex. White farmers, now spread over many parts of the country, were largely dependent on the services of their African laborers. On the farms, Francis Wilson has pointed out, "the relationship between master and servant had all the distance of a caste society, combined with the closeness that is inevitable when human beings are thrown together in an isolated enterprise." [43] Black and white families often lived within the precincts of the same courtyard; black and white children played happily together; and, inevitably, white men sometimes fell in love with black women, though such unions could never lead to formal marriage. Close relations between black and white developed, too, at the trading posts and in the mission stations, many of which still lay beyond the formal colonial boundaries. By the end of the nineteenth century there were almost 500 mission stations to be found south of the Limpopo. As in other parts of Africa, the mission stations with their church, their school, their store and workshops, their cluster of homesteads, presented a new type of community whose members might be drawn from a variety of local groups. Here, far more than on the farms, there could take place a true meeting of minds, an intellectual symbiosis bred of a proper appreciation of the values of different cultures. Here, as Monica Wilson has written of Lovedale, one of the oldest and most famous mission schools and stations in Cape Colony, "an environment in which respect and friendship could grow was provided . . . an atmosphere in which people of different races could work and grow together in trust." [44]

The expansion of European hegemony, the development of mining and other industries, and the steadily accelerating process of urbanization brought an increasing number of people of different ethnic groups into close contact with one another. European officials largely replaced chiefs as the symbols and bearers of authority, and a rapidly expanding administrative structure provided opportunities for African employment in many subordinate roles. In 1899 there were just over 100,000 Africans and 12,000 whites working in the mines of the Rand. By 1967, the mining industry was employing 62,000 Europeans and more than half a million Africans, two-thirds of whom came from countries lying beyond the borders of the Republic. Even more substantial was the increase in the numbers employed in manufacturing industries: 123,000 workers, of whom 13,000 were Europeans, in 1918; just over 1 million, a quarter of them Europeans, in 1967. In 1904, 25 percent of South Africa's total population were classified as urban, by the mid-1960's the figure had risen to close to 50 percent. (In 1960 the Republic contained eleven cities with a population exceeding 100,000.) In urban locations, factories, and mining compounds Africans of many different ethnic groups came into contact one with another. And though stringent efforts might be made to segregate black from white, contacts across the color-bar in shops, in mining galleries, on the factory floor, on building sites, even if of a seemingly casual nature, were of necessity more numerous and more frequent than they had ever been in the past.

Against this pattern of increasing contact, though of contact often interrupted by political action on the part of the dominant minority group, and of inescapable interdependence must be set the distinctive characteristics of the major groups that serve to make up South Africa's plural society. None of these groups could be regarded as static, none was exempt from the process of change. Each major group—European, African, "Coloured," and Asian—needed to be seen in historical perspective. The student of society must constantly remind himself that there are no fixed "types," except in the mind of those ideologists who think of "culture" as an immutable norm and allow their perception of reality to be obscured by the use of emotive and imprecise terms such as "civilization" and "barbarism."

In 1875 South Africa possessed a European population numbering rather less than 300,000. By 1904, the European population exceeded 1 million; it passed the 2 million mark in the mid-1930's; and it numbered just over $3\frac{1}{2}$ million in the mid-1960's. In the "goldrush" years of the 1880's and again in the 1900's South Africa attracted a substantial number of European immigrants. By the mid-twentieth century, however, the net gain from immigration amounted to no more than a few thousand every year. The most significant aspect of twentieth-century immigration to South Africa was the introduction of new cultural strands in white society. Jewish intellectuals and businessmen, many descended from immigrants who left their homes in the western provinces of Czarist Russia at the end of the nineteenth century, Greek shopkeepers, Italian restaurant owners—individuals such as these have made a distinctive contribution to South African culture, giving a more cosmopolitan atmosphere to life in the larger cities.

In 1960 almost 60 percent of the European population spoke Afrikaans as their home language. The vast majority of Afrikaners could trace their descent back to the Dutch and Huguenot settlers of the seventeenth century. But already by the mid-eighteenth century there were clear cultural distinctions emerging between the Dutch of the Western Cape and the "boers"—the word originally meant no more than "farmer"—of the expanding frontier. The Cape Dutch were more prosperous: the manor houses of successful plantation owners with their distinctive gables and their elegantly furnished rooms contrasted sharply with the modest earth-floored cottages of the frontier. Moreover the Cape Dutch were never completely out of touch with European ideas. They were conscious of subtle social gradations, the product of wealth or professional status, and not feeling themselves threatened by a native population vastly superior in numbers, they were able to maintain a relaxed relationship with the peoples of different color and culture— Hottentot, Cape Malay, or the many people of mixed race—who occupied the subordinate positions in their society. Boer society, on the other hand, as it developed in the two independent republics, came to produce an entirely different set of characteristics. The life of a nine-teenth-century farmer on the veld might at best provide a certain rude plenty, but it was always tough and austere. Inevitably, too, it was al-most completely isolated from the intellectual currents of a wider world, a situation which made it possible for the "ritual experts" of Boer so-ciety, the *predikants* of the Dutch Reformed Church, to establish a posi-tion of unchallenged intellectual authority. In social structure Boer societies were remarkably homogeneous and egalitarian: "true burgher-like freedom, equality and fraternity" were the ideals commemorated in the Transvaal's first constitution. But equality was conceded only to members of the Boer community. Beyond the charmed circle of the laa-ger lay the black hordes, "rapacious, bloodthirsty barbarians." Other small groups of dominant Europeans in nineteenth-century Africa could count on a measure of support from a powerful metropolis. The Boers had no such backing. They had reason to feel insecure. And their sense of insecurity was rendered all the more intense by the intrusion of the imperialist British, with their arrogant, condescending ways. In such circumstances it was natural for a fiercely independent people to de-velop a harsh streak of aggressiveness and an intense spirit of group solidarity.

In the first two decades of the twentieth century ineluctable economic forces combined with the shattering experience of defeat in the South African War to make life even more irksome for many Boer families. In the old days there had been plenty of land for every white man, but as population increased, more and more families found it impossible to earn a decent livelihood on the land. In the mid-nineteenth century the typical Boer farm was 6,000 acres in extent, but under the Roman-Dutch law of inheritance a father was required to give equal shares of his land to all his children. The large size of most Boer families acceler-ated the process whereby many farms were subdivided into completely uneconomic units. Landless men (*bywoners*) were allowed squatting rights by the more prosperous farmers, until the latter began to intro-duce more efficient farming methods. (Wire fencing in early twentieth-century South Africa had much the same social consequences as enclo-sures in eighteenth-century England.) Natural disasters, drought, or rinderpest, combined with the destruction of war to bring almost total impoverishment to many rural Afrikaners. Travelers spoke of seeing "groups of families huddled together on land that could not support them in comfort, condemned to eat the meanest food, so abjectly poor that money was almost as rare as the meat on their plates." [45] White South Africans, largely indifferent to the plight of the "poor blacks" in their midst, found themselves deeply moved by the plight of the "poor whites."

In other societies landless agriculturalists have found a place for themselves in rural society by selling their labor. But to the "poor whites" of South Africa manual labor was "kaffir's work" and therefore only fit for natives. So there was no alternative but to drift toward the towns in a movement which some Afrikaner leaders later described as "the Second Great Trek." It required courage and toughness to survive in the slums of Johannesburg. The "poor white" from the *platteland* brought with him little or nothing in the way of useful skills. He found himself surrounded by other white men of English stock who jibed at his rural ways and spoke a language he did not understand. He felt himself the victim of the mysterious and sinister forces of "Anglo-Jewish" capitalism, personified in such crude satirical images as "Hoggenheimer" and "Goldbug," and he found himself faced with his old enemies of the veld in a new guise, the mass of unskilled black labor remorselessly threatening by unfair competition to engulf the struggling Afrikaner laborer. But "poor whites" possessed one decisive advantage over their black competitors: they could vote and were therefore well placed to attract the attention of those in power. In 1924 South Africa's first Nationalist government, defining its policy under the slogan "civilized labor," set to work to create jobs for white men at rates far higher than those a free market would have allowed. It was not, however, until the mid-1930's, when South African manufacturing industry entered its spectacular phase of expansion, that the number of "poor whites" began to decline rapidly.

By the 1940's the typical Afrikaner was a townsman, not a countryman. (In 1904, 53 percent of the total white population was classified as urban; by 1946, 75 percent; by 1960, 84 percent.) The cultural developments that accompanied this profound social change were basically not much different from those which were occurring among men of different pigmentation in other parts of Africa. Voluntary associations proliferated: being designed to help the people of a single ethnic group, they could be described as basically tribal in character. The intense sense of rivalry with English-speaking South Africans, the feeling of insecurity, of inferiority, and of injustice provided the incentive for Afrikaners to come together to work for the good of Afrikanerdom. Of all the societies formed between the wars a secret organization without exact parallel elsewhere in Africa, the *Afrikaner Broederbond,* was undoubtedly the most important. A broad-based organization—by 1964 it had almost 7,000 members—it provided the machinery needed to coordinate Afrikaner activities in many different spheres. Indeed, to some competent observers the Nationalist party itself appeared to be no more than "the political arm of the *Broederbond*." [46]

The parallels between the growth of Afrikaner national consciousness and similar movements elsewhere in the continent must not be over-stressed. Some aspects of the South African situation were almost unique. No religious institutions elsewhere in Africa occupied quite the same position in the local community as the three Dutch Reformed Churches to which 90 percent of the Afrikaner population belonged. The Calvinist version of Christianity put forward by ministers of the Dutch Reformed Churches was well suited, when adapted to local conditions, to provide Afrikaner congregations with both an ideological boost and an ideological cement. Afrikaners were encouraged to see themselves as God's elect, as a "chosen people," as a nation entrusted with the divine mission of preserving their beloved homeland for the cause of "Christianity and Civilization."

The cement of religion was reinforced by the cement of language. Afrikaans or Cape Dutch as it was known in the nineteenth century developed as a simplified form of spoken Dutch. In the nineteenth century, the English rulers of the Cape introduced a number of regulations to ensure the predominance of their own language. A knowledge of English was made compulsory for the civil service, and English became the sole language of the law courts, of parliament, and of government schools. In the 1870's and 1880's, a vigorous counterattack by the Dutch-speaking inhabitants of the Cape secured a measure of recognition for High Dutch on official occasions. In the first decade of the twentieth century Milner's policy of anglicization provoked an even more vigorous defense of High Dutch and of Afrikaans. Afrikaans language associations were set up in the main towns, and Afrikaans scholars began to draw up rules on spelling and grammar. The Act of Union recognized English and Dutch, the latter replaced by Afrikaans in 1925, as the country's two official languages. But Afrikaners found that in many sections of the country's life the English language still enjoyed a position of predominance. In the civil service, for example, over 80 percent of the officials were English-speaking in 1912, many of them possessing no more than a smattering of Dutch or Afrikaans. Against this threat of English cultural domination the recently founded Afrikaans cultural organizations began to struggle. Meanwhile, Afrikaans was revealing itself to be a language well suited for poetry, "direct, supple, idiomatic, rhythmic, alternately rugged and sonorous—and above all exciting in its freshness and constant growth." [47] Through the work of a group of poets the Afrikaner people began to acquire a literature of their own.

Thus fortified, backed by a wide range of cultural, social, and political organizations, sustained by a well-defined ideology and assured of the survival of a language that once seemed threatened with extinction, the Afrikaner people were able to press forward into many fields of South African life hitherto dominated by their English rivals. A prosperous class of Afrikaner businessmen began to emerge in the 1950's. By 1960, 70 percent of all mine workers and 37 percent of all technical and professional workers were Afrikaner, while government action ensured from 1948 on that the commanding heights of the public service were securely in Afrikaner hands. To the student of other parts of Africa the process of afrikanerization had a familiar ring. Elsewhere in postcolonial Africa certain ethnic groups attempted to establish a dominant position over a wide range of activities; none showed themselves to be so well-organized or proved themsleves so successful as the descendants of the Boer pastoralists of the *platteland*.

In terms of historical development and social structure there was a great difference between the English-speaking and the Afrikaner communities. Despite the well-marked cultural distinctions between Cape Dutch and Transvaalers, Afrikaner society as a whole possessed a certain obvious homogeneity. Its members could trace their descent back to a relatively small group of early settlers. All the van der Merwes, for example—said to number between 25,000 to 50,000—are reckoned to be the descendants of an ancestor of that name who settled in the Western Cape in 1682. By comparison with the clans and kinship ties of Afrikanerdom, English-speaking South Africans presented a much more heterogeneous social mixture. Emigrants from Britain have been coming to South Africa for more than one hundred and fifty years, though at certain periods the flow has shrunk to a trickle, and many English South Africans have returned to their homeland. The English-speaking community, numbering just under 40 percent of the entire white population, has also come to assimilate some groups, such as the descendents of Russian Jews, of an entirely un-English origin. Only in Natal—a province remarkable for its intensely "British" character—and in certain parts of the Cape has an English farming community been established. The vast majority of English-speaking South Africans chose to settle in towns: by 1936, 90 percent of the English-speaking population could be classified as urban.

The contributions made by English-speaking South Africans to the development of their country both in the material and in the cultural field have been succinctly summarized by Leo Marquard. "English-speaking South Africans were responsible for mining and industrial development, for railway construction, for the establishment of towns and cities, for commerce and banking, for shipping and for harbour construction—in fact, for changing South Africa from a backward agricultural community into a semi-industrialized modern state. . . . In primary and secondary education, in the establishment and endowment of universities, in the building of libraries, in the development of the theater and encouragement of the arts, in the spread of learning, in social welfare, and, last but not least, in the establishment of parliamentary traditions and of the rule of law, English-speaking South Africans played a major part." [48] In the decades before the Act of Union, English-speaking South Africans were prominent in the politics of the Cape and of Natal. Since 1910, however, no English-speaker has made an absolutely outstanding contribution to South African political life. English-speaking South Africans have been accused of being more interested in making money or of "not feeling passionately enough about anything political for long enough to take effective action." [49] But there has also been an insuperable deterrent to prevent English-speakers from rising to the top: the numerical superiority of the Afrikaners has ensured that in all the major parties the most important posts have gone almost automatically to men of Afrikaner stock.

The divide between Afrikaners and English-speakers must not be overstressed. There has been a considerable amount of intermarriage between the two groups, especially in the Cape. There has been a steady increase in bilingualism: 42 percent of the white population were bilingual in 1918, 73 percent in 1951. With the increasing urbanization of the Afrikaner, the vast majority of people in both groups find themselves living in broadly similar environments. And most white South Africans feel themselves exposed to the frightening threat of African nationalism and "World Communism." But cultural differences between the two groups are still profound and tribal tensions are very close to the surface. Yet the differences and the tensions that divide white from white are far less than those that lie between white and black.

In 1911 there were just over 4 million Africans living within the boundaries of the Union. By 1936, the African population had increased to 6.5 million, by 1970 to 13 million. To this last figure should be added another 2 million Africans living in South West Africa and in the three small independent states of Botswana, Lesotho, and Swaziland. Thus Africans make up about three-quarters of the population of the region as a whole and 68 percent of the population of the Republic. Between 1911 and 1921 the African population was increasing at the rate of 1.57 percent annually; forty years later (1951–60), the growth rate had risen to 2.48 percent, while the European rate of increase had fallen from 1.76 percent to 1.6 percent in the same period. Clearly the numerical disparity between the two groups was bound to become increasingly evident in the last decades of the twentieth century—a development with highly significant implications.

Before the establishment of European hegemony over African-occupied areas, a process that could be dated back to the late eighteenth century in parts of the Eastern Cape, the Bantu-speaking population was dispersed among a large number of political units. This galaxy of independent chiefdoms could be divided up into a number of distinct clusters whose people shared a common language and certain common customs. Only in the three small territories ruled directly by the British high commissioner and in certain reserves did something of the structure of the nineteenth-century chiefdoms survive into the mid-twentieth century. Cultural differences, most obviously manifested in differences of language, persist to the present day. Many Africans in South Africa are still moved by what Leo Kuper has defined as "subjective attitudes of tribal patriotism," with memories of ancient wars serving to produce disdain for or suspicion of other groups.[50] These attitudes the Nationalist government of the 1950's and 1960's sought to encourage, its spokesmen presenting South Africa as a "multi-national" state. Idealists in the Nationalist ranks, arguing from their own experience as Afrikaners, saw in the "patriotism" of the different African "nations"—Zulu, Xosa, Tswana, and others—a sentiment of such deep significance that it must at all costs be preserved if the people concerned were not to lose their "identity." To critics of government policy, on the other hand, this encouragement of African "tribalism" seemed little more than a sophisticated variation of the familiar "divide and rule" tactics followed by any group occupying a position of uneasy domination.

More significant than the ethnic divisions between African peoples were the differences produced by varying degrees of exposure to European culture and society. At one extreme were those individuals born into families which had been for several generations completely assimilated through education and occupation to the European way of life; at the other, a large group—expressively described as the "reds" in Xosa society because they used red ochre on their blankets—whose members stuck tenaciously to the old ways. Individual life-styles were largely dependent on the environment into which a man was born, for there were profound differences between life in a reserve, on a white farm, or in an urban location. Each of these three environments needs to be considered in turn.

By the first decade of the twentieth century, European settlers had laid claim to the greater part of South African land. The extent of the reserves, the only areas in which Africans were allowed to own land, was defined by the Natives Land Act of 1913. In 1936 more land adjoining the reserves was "released" for African purchase. By 1966, the reserves covered a total area of 56,000 square miles, about 13 percent of the entire country. On the map they spread like a greatly eroded horseshoe from the Ciskei in the Eastern Cape through the Transkei and Zululand and around the northern and eastern borders of the Transvaal. Only the Transkei covered a compact and reasonably substantial area (15,000 square miles); elsewhere the pattern was one of great fragmentation. In the 1960's the government set about removing "black spots," as African-owned land in predominantly white areas was described, providing those required to leave their old homes with land, often of inferior quality, in areas adjoining the main reserves. Into this pattern the three states of Botswana, Lesotho, and Swaziland fitted with little sense of anomaly. Though their peoples might breathe a freer air than the Africans of the Republic, they were bound no less closely by the ties of economic necessity to the powerful neighbor whose territory surrounded them, leaving them isolated, land-locked, and extremely vulnerable.

In 1951, 55 percent of the African population was resident in the reserves, by 1966 the figure had fallen to 37 percent. Nevertheless, the total population of the reserves increased substantially—with consequences whose baleful effect on the livelihood of the people has already been noted. By the 1950's many of the reserves had degenerated into rural slums. The increase in population density was not without effect on the political structure of local society. In the old days, should a chief prove unpopular, his followers could disperse and find new land elsewhere for themselves. With overpopulation this "sanction against tyranny" [51] could no longer be applied. Moreover, chiefs could now count on the support of their white overlords. The old Southern Bantu adage—"a chief is a chief by virtue of his people"—lost much of its meaning. On the reserves most chiefs came to be regarded as the government's "policemen."

Within the reserves the missionaries and their converts, the "school" people, acted as agents of change. The processes were basically similar to those taking place in other parts of Africa. There developed, for example, a new attitude toward disease. In the past, disease was usually attributed to the malevolence of a particular individual. Medical training and attendance at hospitals introduced Africans to the idea of natural causation. But, as Monica Wilson has pointed out, "the shift from a personal to an impersonal view of causation proceeds very slowly, and the same people speak of 'infection' when a neighbour has typhus, but think in terms of witchcraft when they themselves are very ill with pneumonia." [52]

Another parallel between developments among the rural population of South Africa and the peasantry and urban poor of other parts of the continent is seen in the emergence of independent churches. The first independent African church in South Africa was founded in 1884 by Nehemiah Tile, an ordained Methodist minister, who broke away from his missionary body to establish a "national" church among his own people, the Tembu. The rigid segregation practised by many white Christians with its implicit denial of the Gospel's message served powerfully to stimulate the growth of other independent churches. In the 1890's, contact was made with the American Methodist Episcopalian Church, the pioneer independent church among black Americans, and a number of South Africans visited the United States, some to study at black American universities. By 1938 there were over 500 separatist churches in South Africa. Twenty years later—so rapid had been the process of fragmentation—the number had increased to 2,400, with a total membership of 1½ million, 20 percent of the African Christians in the Republic.

Even more powerful as a force for change than the new ideas brought by the missionaries was the steady movement of people toward the new towns. In 1904, no more than 13 percent of the total African population was classified as urban; by 1936 the proportion had risen relatively slowly to 17 percent; thereafter the rate of growth steadily accelerated, and by 1960 almost a third of the entire African population was living in towns. The movement of Africans from rural reserves to urban locations was in its underlying causes no different to that of Afrikaner "poor whites" from their *platteland* farms to the city slums, but the government regarded the two currents of internal migration very differently. The towns were seen as "white areas" to which the "native" came as an alien. From the early nineteenth century on the "masterless native" was seen as a source of potential danger to white hegemony, and an elaborate system of "influx control," based on a series of regulations known collectively as the Pass Laws, was introduced to restrict African movements. It may well be doubted whether any government at any time in history had succeeded in doing more than the white-dominated South African regime to restrict the freedom of movement of so large a proportion of its people. By the 1950's Africans found that they required official permission to stay in a particular location, to work or to look for work in a particular town or district, or to leave a white man's farm. No aspect of white hegemony aroused such intensely bitter resentment as this totalitarian system of restrictions. The inevitable corollary of this system was the creation of an ever more elaborate structure of coercive administration, brutally symbolized for many Africans by the raids of white policemen on black locations. "The number of technical offences of which the African may be guilty" has now reached the point that "any police officer can at any time arrest any African and be sure of obtaining a conviction." [53] In the year 1965–66, to cite but a single set of figures, an average of 1,375 Africans a day were prosecuted for contraventions of the Pass Laws or labor service contracts.

In spite of these regulations the African urban population has steadily increased. This population is far from homogeneous in character. Some men come to the towns for a few months' contract labor, live perhaps in the quasi-regimented isolation of a compound or bachelors' barracks, never accustom themselves to the variegated pattern of urban living, and soon return to their reserves or their countries of origin beyond South Africa's borders. Others, drawn to the towns by their atmosphere of adventure and excitement, learn to swim like fish in the rough urban waters, evading the police, and often turning to crime for a living. Few cities anywhere in the world can have a crime rate to compare with Johannesburg's, "the bloodiest place on earth," in the phrase of one newspaper correspondent. In Soweto, one of the city's African suburbs, armed gangs roam the streets "robbing, raping, killing any one in their path." [54] In this single suburb some 1,000 murders are committed every year.

"It is astonishing," one European observer has remarked, "that Africans are able to maintain such high standards of conduct and behaviour in the midst of such poverty and administrative chaos as they do." [55] Gradually over the decades, a truly urban African society has grown up—in some ways the most deeply rooted urban society to be found anywhere in black Africa. "I am supposed to be a Pondo," Nat Nakasa, a Johannesburg journalist wrote in 1966, "but I don't even know the language of that tribe. . . . I am just not a tribesman, whether I like it or not. I am, inescapably, a part of the city slums, the factory machines and our beloved shebeens." [56] This new urban society devised its own Afro-European culture, one aspect of which has been vividly described —and its deeper meaning underlined—by another Johannesburg writer, Ezekiel Mphahlele. "In every South African town, big and small, there are jazz bands and troupes. . . . It is an escape as well as an assertion. If there is no escape, someone will crack up somewhere, someone will be trampled down and the human mind doesn't give in so easily. You may be arrested for not having a pass or for protesting against certain laws, but no one can arrest you for singing or performing on an instrument. It's one of the last strongholds of human dignity and self-respect." [57]

To the Africans living in the reserves and in the towns must be added a third group, those resident on white farms. In the 1960's 1½ million Africans were employed as labor on white farms, compared with a half-million in the mines, another half-million in manufacturing industry, 400,000 in government service (including the railroads) and just under 200,000 in building trades. The vast majority of Africans in the farming areas were employed as full-time laborers but there are still a number of African tenants who pay in cash or in labor services for their right to make use of land. Such tenancy arrangements have been condemned since 1913, but they persist, though subject to increasing official pressure. Government action might force African tenants to give up their land; it could not prevent an increasing number of white farmers from leaving their farms to the sole occupancy of their African workers. Although some white farmers took great pains to provide decent amenities for their workers, the quality of life for the majority of farm workers left much to be desired. Wages remained very low and while many members of the officially pampered white farming community grew steadily more prosperous, most of their employees enjoyed a standard of living little better in the 1960's than it had been a century earlier. It would seem, too, that African farm workers were no less impoverished in their social life. On the reserves traditional ties still served to bind communities together. In the towns men and women were brought harshly but often stimulatingly into contact with a wider world. On the white farms, by contrast, there was often a greater measure of security, contacts with white people were usually less abrasive, but isolation and poverty and tedium led many young men to try and seek a living elsewhere and so to escape their semiservile status.

Two other groups complete the complex pattern of South Africa's plural society—the "Coloureds" (a term, incidentally, which many members of this group now find offensive but for which no satisfactory substitute has yet been devised) and the Asians or Indians. By 1970 the "Coloureds" numbered 2 million and made up 10 percent of the Republic's total population. In ethnic origin the "Coloureds" may claim —and it is a claim of which in a shrinking and increasingly cosmopolitan world a man may well be proud—to be perhaps the most heterogeneous group of people in the whole world. In the veins of the "Coloured" population flows the blood of Bushman and Hottentot, Malagasy and Malay, West African and Southern Bantu, Englishman and Afrikaner. In physical features it is virtually impossible to distinguish some "Coloured" people from Europeans, others from Asians, others from Africans. Nowhere else on the continent have the races mixed so freely. Ninety percent of the "Coloured" population is to be found in

Cape Province, but in the nineteenth century a number of "Coloured" men followed or even preceded the advancing Europeans, and small "Coloured" communities are to be found in every urban center in Southern Africa. One distinct subgroup, the Cape Malays, have stuck tenaciously to the Islamic faith of their forefathers, but they represent no more than 5 percent of the total "Coloured" population. In other respects the "Coloureds" have become almost completely assimilated into European culture. Afrikaans is today the home language of 90 percent of the "Coloured" community, but only about a third are members of the Dutch Reformed Church. There is a long tradition of missionary activity among the "Coloured" population, leading to the creation of large Anglican, Methodist, Congregationalist, and Roman Catholic congregations. In 1960, 36 percent of the male "Coloured" working population found employment in agriculture and 32 percent in manufacturing and building, while more than half of the "Coloured" women at work were engaged in domestic service.

Politically, socially, and economically the "Coloured" community occupied a position intermediate between Europeans and Africans. In the Cape a limited "color-blind" franchise introduced in 1853 gave the more prosperous members of the "Coloured" community an opportunity to participate in local politics, though they were debarred by the Act of Union from ever aspiring to become members of parliament. Economically, they enjoyed, on the average, a considerably higher standard of living than the African population. A small group of "Coloured" professional men achieved considerable wealth. At the other extreme, many agricultural laborers lived in great poverty, the drabness of their lives relieved by little more than the practice, developed in the wine-growing districts of the Western Cape, whereby farmers provided free tots of wine or brandy. Socially many "Coloureds" aspired to enter white society, and the offspring of some "Coloured" families were able to "pass" as white. (It is well known—though the current political climate makes it improper to mention the fact—that many European families number "Coloured" people among their ancestors.) To visitors from other parts of South Africa the atmosphere of Cape Town seemed —and still seems—unique. In this splendidly sited city "the toleration of colour and social admixture" made it possible for men of different races to mingle freely—as one Natal writer noted in 1911—"in the streets, on the tramcars, in the railway stations, public offices and places of entertainment" in sharp contrast to other South African towns where a black man or a brown man might expect to find himself pushed off the pavement by an arrogant white man.[58] This process of natural mixing the Nationalist government of the 1950's and 1960's set about trying to demolish by a series of legislative enactments to be described in a later section of this chapter.

By the mid-1960's South Africa's Asians numbered just over a half-million and made up 3 percent of the Republic's total population. Indian immigration began in the 1860's when contract laborers were brought over to work on the sugar plantations of Natal. ("For the sake of a sugar crop which was too uneconomical to compete in the world market," one South African historian has ruefully pointed out, "South Africa acquired a permanent Indian population.") [59] The movement of Indians into South Africa came to an end in 1911 when the Indian government prohibited the recruitment of contract laborers and the South African government refused to accept any more free immigrants. In white South African eyes, the Indians were regarded as an unassimilable element in the country's population. The Orange Free State went so far as to forbid them to reside within its borders, but in Natal there were soon as many Asians as Europeans and a substantial Asian minority settled in the industrial areas of the Transvaal. By the 1960's less than 10 percent of the male Asian working population was still engaged in agriculture, 33 percent found employment in manufacturing industry and 20 percent in commerce. As with the "Coloured" community, so with the Asians great extremes in the standard of living were to be found. A few Asian businessmen in Durban became immensely rich, but the majority of Asians earned less than half the annual income of the average European. As with the "Coloureds," the Asians, too, occupied an uncomfortable intermediate position—scorned by Europeans, distrusted by Africans, but protected, at least in the first half of the twentieth century, from the harsher manifestations of white racialism by the influence the government of India was able to bring to bear on their behalf.

"The history of South Africa," a great liberal South African has written, "is the story of strife between the various groups comprising the political union." [60] That this should be so is hardly surprising. It is one of the sad truths of history that when people of different cultures live next to one another, a measure of conflict is almost inevitable. One may recall the struggle between Christian and Muslim peoples in Ethiopia, between Arabic-speakers and non-Muslims in the Sudan, between Fulani, Yoruba, and Ibo in Nigeria, between Ganda and other groups in Uganda—or, for that matter, between English, Scots, Welsh, and Irish in certain periods of British history or between German and Slav in much of Eastern Europe. The remarkable feature of recent South African history has been the skill with which one of the "tribes" of this divided land, the Afrikaners, has succeeded in establishing its hegemony over all the others.

▲▼ SOUTH AFRICAN POLITICS, 1910 TO 1948:
WHITE RIVALRIES AND THE "NATIVE QUESTION"

For more than a century, from 1798 to 1910, the English had been the dominant force in the politics of South Africa. The British governors or high commissioners at the Cape, the English-speaking prime ministers of the self-governing colony—these had been the men in a position to shape the destinies of the region as a whole. In these years both independent Afrikaners and Africans found themselves forced to occupy basically defensive positions, to fight a continual series of rearguard actions. After 1910 the situation changed dramatically as men of Afrikaner stock moved into all the dominant political positions in the country. It would be a mistake, however, to accept the concepts put forward by Afrikaner mythologists about the unity of the Afrikaner *volk* and the purity of the Afrikaner "race" and to assume that the Afrikaners were a truly united people prepared unquestioningly to accept a single line of policy. It is doubtful whether any people, except in brief moments of great stress, ever achieve so total a sense of unity. Certainly, in the years between 1910 and 1948 it is possible to detect three distinct strands in Afrikaner political thought.

The first strand was personified by Botha and Smuts, the two Boer generals who laid constant stress on the need for conciliation between English-speakers and Afrikaners. Both men had been deeply moved by the magnanimity of the Liberal prime minister, Campbell-Bannerman, in according self-government to the Transvaal in 1907. "The contagion of magnanimity," Smuts wrote in his old age, "spread from the leaders to their people." [61] Not only were Botha and Smuts prepared to work harmoniously with English-speaking South Africans; they also expressed in the clearest terms their loyalty to the British Empire–Commonwealth by bringing their country to the aid of Britain in the two world wars. That Smuts, the offspring of an intensely isolationist people, should have become one of the apostles of international cooperation is one of the strangest paradoxes in South African political biography. Smuts played a great part on the international stage, contributed to the foundation of the League of Nations and the United Nations Organization and hastened the transformation of the British Empire, in which the mother country's primacy over the white dominions was still clearly manifest, into the British Commonwealth, "a society," as he defined it, "of free and equal sister states." [62] Smuts' stress on the need for cooperation between the nations might be seen as the logical corollary to his stress on conciliation between the two dominant ethnic groups in South Africa.

The second strand in Afrikaner thinking was expressed by General Hertzog. Hertzog saw the Afrikaner people and their culture as being faced with the possibility of complete disintegration as a result of the steady growth of the English-dominated industrial sector of the economy and the gradual expansion of the process of anglicization. To counter this deeply alarming threat to the very being of his people, he put forward the concept of Afrikaners and English-speakers forming the "two streams" of South African life, equal but separate. To Hertzog "conciliation and loyalty" were "idle words." Distrusting the collaborationist approach of Botha and Smuts to British imperialism, he spoke up boldly in favor of a "South African Nationalism" from which would emerge "a true unity of hearts." [63] Hertzog was no narrow chauvinist. Once the British had accepted, in the terms of the Statute of Westminster in 1931, that South Africa, along with the other white dominions, enjoyed the status of a sovereign independent state, he declared himself content and pressed for no further change in the "special relationship" with Britain. Indeed, in the 1930's he was able to work amicably with Smuts until the crisis provoked by the outbreak of World War II.

The third strand in Afrikaner thought was represented by those passionate nationalists who saw themselves as the heirs of Kruger and of Krugerism. South Africa as a totally independent republic united under Afrikaner hegemony was the ideal they set before themselves. Some of them had been "bitter-enders" in the South African War and dreamed of avenging the defeats and insults suffered at the hands of the "khakis." Others joined in or sympathized with the abortive rebellion launched in the autumn of 1914 as a protest against their country's involvement in "England's war." Their successors, men of the next generation, devoted much of their energies to new organizations such as the *Broederbond* designed to provide Afrikaner nationalism with the machinery needed for effective action. They jibed at Smuts as "the handyman of the Empire" and even went so far as to label him "England's Quisling" during World War II. Hertzog they came to regard as far too conciliatory to the English-speaking South Africans, a group whom they regarded with distrust and even hatred. In the 1930's one section of these ardent nationalists was deeply attracted by the National Socialism of Adolf Hitler and founded a para-military organization, the *Ossewabrandwag,* to publicize their views. Not all Afrikaner nationalists supported this extreme line, but all nationalists were in agreement on the need to achieve the unity of the Afrikaner *volk*.

English-speaking South Africans were also divided in their approach to what seemed to most of them the major issue of the day—the relations between the two dominant white groups. Some English-speakers chose to follow Botha and Smuts from the start. Others organized exclusively English-speaking parties—the Unionists in the 1910's, the Dominion Party in the 1930's—and laid great stress on the need to retain close ties with Britain. A third group, drawn largely from the industrial workers on the Rand, formed the South African Labour Party and concentrated their energies on protecting the high wages of European artisans against the threat presented by cheap black labor to "civilized" living standards.

For more than thirty years after 1910 South African politics was dominated not by the major theme in the country's history, the relations between black and white, but by the struggle between and within the two white groups. This struggle, fought out in a series of regularly conducted elections, must be briefly described, before turning to consider the attitude of the main white parties to what was referred to at the time as the "native question" and to examine the reactions of the most vocal African groups to their European overlords. In 1910 Botha became first prime minister of South Africa and went on to organize his followers into the South African Party. In 1913 Hertzog, after working uneasily with Botha as a member of his government, broke away and later founded the National Party. The general election of 1920 showed that the National Party had become the strongest single party in the country, but the South African Party—under Smuts' leadership since Botha's death in 1919—managed to retain power by forming a coalition with the English-speaking Unionists. Two years later the government came into head-on collision with the white miners of the Rand. Both English-speaking urban workers and Afrikaner nationalists found themselves faced with the same enemies—the "sinister forces" of "Anglo-Jewish capitalism" and the even more alarming black masses. Consequently, the National Party was able to form an electoral alliance with the Labour Party, win the election of 1923, and form a coalition or "pact" government which retained power until 1933.

In 1933, with the country facing the many social and economic difficulties caused by the Great Depression, Hertzog and Smuts agreed to form a coalition, even going so far as to "fuse" their respective parties thus creating the United South African National Party. Fusion was more than some Afrikaner nationalists could stand, and one group, led by D. F. Malan of the Cape, broke away to form the Purified National Party. In 1939 Afrikanerdom was further divided when Hertzog, defeated in his opposition to Smuts' proposal that the country should participate in "England's war," was forced to leave the government. World

War II was a period of bitter tension in Afrikaner society. Some Afrikaners hoped for a German victory, others fought valiantly on the British side: each group denounced the other as traitors. There was still much ill feeling between Hertzogites and Malanites, and when Hertzog retired from public life, his follower, Havenga, organized a separate Afrikaner Party to press for the old leader's "two stream" approach to national politics. But the neo-nationalists under Malan, backed by the *Broederbond* and other Afrikaner organizations, was rapidly becoming the spokesmen of the mass of Afrikaners. In the 1938 election Malan's National Party won 27 seats to the United Party's 111; in 1943, 43 to 89, in 1948 70 to 65. By forming a coalition with the Afrikaner Party which won 9 seats in 1948, the Nationalist were assured of an overall majority. Their victory was in large part due to an electoral system designed to favor rural constituencies. In terms of votes cast, the National and Afrikaner Parties won 462,000 to the United and Labor Parties' 620,000. "My old comrades have turned against me," Smuts said to a friend when he heard the result. "How could they turn against you?" the friend replied, "they are all dead." "This devastating truth," Smuts' most authoritative biographer has pointed out, meant that "Smuts and his ideas and his loyalties had lost their appeal to Afrikaner youth." It was "the end of an epoch." [64]

There were certain premises about the "native question" on which almost all white South Africans were agreed in the years before 1948. The first premise was the necessity to maintain white supremacy. The second pointed to the equation between white supremacy and "civilization"—an emotive and somewhat fuzzy concept which embraced every aspect of European culture from street cleaning to religious ideas. The third stressed the need to maintain some form of separation between people of different color. "There must be no intermixture of blood between the two colours," Smuts declared in 1917. "Instead of mixing up black and white in the old haphazard way, we are now trying to lay down a policy of keeping them apart as much as possible in our institutions." [65] Four years before this declaration was made, the government of which Smuts was a member introduced the Natives Land Act, by which Africans were prevented from holding land except in specially designated reserves. In 1923 Smuts was responsible for another addition to the statute book, the Native (Urban Areas) Act, which helped to erect a new set of barriers between the races. The act required municipalities to create African locations and to see that they were properly maintained—in this respect it could be regarded as a progressive measure, for the old, unsupervised locations represented the worst type of urban slum. But the act also allowed the municipalities to assert certain forms of "influx control" designed to prevent locations from becoming overcrowded. Later amendments to the act provided more effective means of controlling the movement of Africans. Thus women, who had previously been allowed unrestricted movement into the locations, were required, by an amendment passed in 1930, to produce a certificate showing that they had accommodation available before settling in a location.

In 1936 the Union parliament passed an important series of acts for which Hertzog had long been pressing. Hitherto, Africans living in the Cape and possessing the necessary qualifications had been allowed to vote on the same roll as whites and "Coloureds" in parliamentary elections. The legislation of 1936 removed the Cape Africans to a separate roll but allowed them to elect three white members to represent their interests. At the same time, provision was made for the representation of Africans in other parts of the country by the creation of four seats in the senate, to be held, of course, only by whites, for their elected representatives. Two other measures were designed to put the finishing touches to Hertzog's "solution" of the "native question": the establishment of an advisory body, the Natives' Representative Council, with some elected African members, and the provision, through the Native Land and Trust Act of 1936, of a certain amount of additional land for the reserves. To members of the white electorate concerned with a proper ordering of relations between the races these acts appeared as generous and far-sighted measures; to the small band of white liberals who had begun to conceive of their country as developing toward a truly nonracial society they represented a serious set-back, a renunciation of the famous dictum ascribed to Cecil Rhodes, "Equal rights for all civilized men."

In every conquest society the dominant group tends to think of the subject population as a passive mass, an agglomeration of anonymous people, so characterless that their individual features can never be perceived, a section of the community whose political aspirations are dismissed as "agitation," and whose leaders are reviled as "trouble-makers." Moreover, the historian of a conquest society finds himself inevitably influenced and weighed down by the mass of documentation produced by the conquerors. If he is to remain true to his calling to explore a society in all its complexity, he must free himself from these blinkers and make an imaginative effort to understand how a conquest society looks to those who make up the subject population. In the case of South Africa the most effective way to aquire some insight into African reactions to white supremacy is to trace the growth of African political movements.

▲▼ AFRICAN NATIONALISM IN SOUTH AFRICA

1912 may be regarded as a seminal date in the history of modern African nationalism in South Africa. In that year a group of four young African lawyers, all of whom had managed to complete their education in England, organized a conference at Blomfontein to which came representatives from every part of the Union. It was an impressive gathering which brought together members of both the traditional and the modern elites, chiefs and clergymen, lawyers and tribal elders, to form a new political association, the South African Native National Congress, later to be known as the African National Congress. The aim of the ANC was to press by strictly constitutional means for the redress of African grievances and in particular for the removal of the color-bar in education, industry, administration, and in parliament. At a time when African ethnic differences were still sharply defined the conference was remarkable in gathering so wide a range of people from every part of the country. Behind such an event could be traced the slow emergence of a modern political consciousness, a process reaching back to the last decades of the nineteenth century.

The color-blind franchise in the Cape, that was such a distinctive feature of the 1853 constitution, gave the vote to any man, white, black, or "Coloured," occupying property worth £25 or earning £50 a year. In the 1890's the Cape parliament showed how easy it was to diminish African political rights by constitutional means when it raised the property qualifications and added a literacy test. Nevertheless, a small group of Africans did possess the vote and could bring a certain pressure to bear on their white representatives. In Natal the franchise was also theoretically color-blind but so restrictive were the qualifications that in 1909 only six Africans possessed the vote. In the Transvaal and the Orange Free State Africans were rigorously excluded from the political arena. Of the other two nonwhite groups the "Coloured" formed a political association of their own, the African Political Organization, in 1902 to protect against discrimination in the Transvaal. Eight years earlier discrimination had provoked the Indian community of Natal, led by a young lawyer named Gandhi (later to become one of the great anticolonialists of the twentieth century) to form the Natal Indian Congress. In 1906 Gandhi led a successful campaign against the imposition of passes on the Indians of the Transvaal. The tactics which he devised— the practice of nonviolent resistance, the pitting of "soul force" against "brute force," were to have a profound influence on a later generation of African nationalists.

Between Indians and Africans there were at this time no political contacts. But the bolstering of white supremacy in the Act of Union served to bring nonwhite spokesmen and white liberals together in an appeal, inevitably unavailing, to the British government. Thus by 1912 there was already a well-established tradition of political activity among the Western-educated African elite. In the Cape an African political press dated back to the 1880's. More than a hundred Africans had been abroad, to Britain or the United States, to complete their education. And the growing number of separatist churches provided many Africans with practical experience of running their own organizations. In 1912 South Africa clearly possessed a much larger community of Africans familiar with many of the concepts of the modern world that was to be found in almost any other European-dominated territory in the continent.

The 1920's saw two significant developments in the nationalist movement, its extension to the urban proletariat and the establishment of contacts with other bodies both within South Africa and in the outside world. In 1920 a group of African trade unionists under the leadership of Clements Kadalie, a clerk from Nyasaland, came together to form the Industrial and Commercial Workers Union. Kadalie proved himself an organizer of rare ability, and by 1928 the union had about 30,000 members drawn from every part of the country. In 1919 the ANC sent a deputation to the Peace Conference at Versailles, and one of its members attended the Pan-African Congress organized in Paris by W. E. B. Dubois. Eight years later the Congress president was present at the Brussels conference of the Communist-inspired League against Imperialism. Within South Africa the nationalist movement began to receive active support from the newly formed South African Communist Party. But deputations, strikes, and protests were of no avail against a government resolutely determined to preserve total white supremacy. Frustration inevitably served to emphasize the divisions already inherent in the nationalist ranks. Particularly bitter were the quarrels between the Communists on the one side and Kadalie and some of the Congress leaders on the other. By the early 1930's the nationalist movement was in a state of total disarray.

As a force making for change in history, nationalism needs to be regarded not only as an immensely powerful idea capable of stirring men to action, but also as a manifestation of that pursuit of well-being, whether peaceful or violent, which is clearly one of the major impulses for change in human affairs. This purely practical aspect of nationalism was particularly evident among certain sections of the nonwhite population of South Africa. Any African who left the familiar bounds of the traditional society found himself caught up in the toils of the restrictive regulations devised by the local whites to maintain their own supremacy. Even more irksome to any man of spirit than the regulations themselves was the manner, patronizing, curt, or humiliating adopted by many white men toward their African employees. Two brief extracts from the work of the modern Zulu poet, B. W. Vilakazi (1906–47) may serve to illuminate African reactions.

> *Just because I smile and smile*
> *And happiness is my coat . . .*
> *You think that I'm a gatepost*
> *Numb to the stab of pain.*
>
> *Just because of the laugh on my lips*
> *And my eyes lowered in respect . . .*
> *You think I'm like a stone*
> *And don't know what it is to die.*
>
> (*Because*) [66]

> *This our fatherland today and yesterday*
> *Is pillaged by the foreign conquerors*
> *Grown rich out of the spoil of nation on nation*
> *Yet I and this whole line of ours*
> *Who are black are left with nothing of nothing . . .*
>
> *Thunder on, engines of the gold mines . . .*
> *Roar on, only stop jarring on my ears,*
> *I have served the white employers well*
> *And now my soul weighs heavily on me . . .*
> *Come, release my sleep, to rise far off*
> *Far in the ancient birthplace of my race.*
>
> (*On the Gold Mines*) [67]

Pride, anger, bitter resentment at insults suffered, the natural search for human dignity—these are emotions likely to be found in any subjugated society, especially in one whose traditions of independence lay relatively close to the surface, for in the South Africa of the 1930's there were many men whose fathers could have recalled a time before the coming of the white conquerors. In circumstances such as these, nationalist sentiment must be regarded as an emotion which even the most repressive government could never hope to eradicate.

The early 1930's had seen the African nationalist movement at the nadir of its fortunes. A decade later the situation had changed. Internal developments and external stimuli made the movement more vigorous than ever before. With the rapid expansion of industry came an equally rapid rise in the African urban population. At the same time, the strain of the war years particularly manifest in inflation and an extreme shortage of housing forced many urban Africans to live in conditions of acute hardship. Yet there was also much discussion, encouraged by the Atlantic Charter, of a new freedom and a better life after the war. To these factors making for change must be added the conflict between the generations, a conflict particularly apparent in the ranks of the ANC where to the new recruits the "old guard" seemed depressed, played out, defeatist. The new men—among them Nelson Mandela, Oliver Tambo, and others, destined to play a leading part in the nationalist movement of the 1950's and 1960's—formed a Youth League and began to press for a more vigorously African approach, an approach that would stress the virtues of African traditional society and culture and encourage Africans to take a pride in the heroes of the past. The intellectuals of the Youth League represented only one strand in the movement of nonwhite nationalism. There were others, moderate professional men anxious to try and make a success of the Natives' Representative Council set up by Hertzog in 1936; mine workers concerned to improve their abysmally low wages; and a radical group of young Indians concerned to achieve proper equality for their kinsmen in Natal. In the years between 1944 and 1947 all these groups were to run up against the blank wall of white hostility and white power.

In 1945, 70,000 mine workers went on strike after the Chamber of Mines had persistently disregarded all their requests for improved wages: the police were called in and drove the miners back to work with some loss of life. The requests put forward by the moderates of the Natives' Representative Council for a modest increase in membership were turned down and the members adjourned in disgust. The Indians in Natal were confronted with new legislation removing their right to purchase land freely, and some of their leaders were imprisoned when they launched a campaign of nonviolent resistance. A national campaign against the Pass Laws ended in total failure: Hofmeyr, the acting prime minister, refused even to see the leaders of the campaign. Hofmeyr was regarded as the most liberal cabinet minister in the history of the Union. Yet both he and his leader Smuts were trapped by the nature of the white electorate. "The Natives want *rights* and not improvement," Smuts wrote in 1947. Yet all Smuts could hope to offer them was a small measure of improvements as being "less open to white prejudice and opposition." "I dare not do anything," he wrote in 1948, "which will outpace public opinion too much on the eve of an election." [68]

▲▼ AFRIKANER NATIONALISTS IN POWER:
BAASSKAP AND APARTHEID

With the National Party's victory in the election of 1948 a new term made its appearance in South African politics. But if the term, "apartheid," was new—it appears never to have been used before 1943—the concept of "separation" or "segregation" for which it stood was a familiar one to all South Africans. Indeed, some historians would trace the practice of apartheid back to the days of the first Dutch governor of the Cape, Jan van Riebeck, when a hedge was planted to separate colonists from natives. Nationalist leaders then had some justification in speaking of apartheid as "the traditional policy of Afrikanerdom." Yet the coming to power of this generation of Afrikaner nationalists did represent a profound, even a revolutionary change in the tenor of South African politics. For the new men saw in the concept of apartheid not merely a useful legal convenience but a profound philosophical truth. They applied the conclusions to which this revolution led them with what one of their opponents has described as "a terrible consistency." [69] And they set about equipping themselves with the power needed to transform their ideas into reality.

"The party accepts," ran the National Party's manifesto, "the Christian trusteeship of the European race as the basic principle of its policy in regard to the non-European races. In accordance with this it desires to afford the non-European races the opportunity of developing themselves in their own fields, according to their natural ability and capacity, and it desires to assure them of fair and just treatment in the administration of the country, but it is emphatically opposed to any mixture of blood between the European and the non-European races." [70] To opponents of the system apartheid appeared as sterile and negative; to its supporters it was an essentially positive and progressive ideology. Accept the basic premise that "race" and "culture" are in some sense distinct entities, whose "purity" is to be preserved if their essence is not to be fatally impaired, and the ideology of apartheid acquires an immensely compelling logic. Deny this premise—and any historian, conscious of the process of change in history, has no alternative but to deny it—and the ideology becomes totally unacceptable. Nevertheless, the world has seen many ideologies which to the rational mind appear to possess a large element of absurdity exert a profound influence over human destinies for long periods of time. So it would seem to be with the ideology of apartheid. Moreover, behind the concept of apartheid, thinly concealed beneath the veneer of "trusteeship" and "development," lay another idea of equal antiquity and even greater emotional force, the concept of *baasskap,* of permanent white domination. Many societies in world history have provided examples of minority groups in dominant positions holding on to power with ferocious tenacity. But few such minorities have chosen to erect so clear and well-defined a set of notions to justify and confirm their position. To play down the force of this immensely powerful system of ideas is to fail to appreciate one of the basic realities of modern South Africa.

On achieving power in 1948 the Nationalists set to work to devise an elaborate series of laws designed to provide the necessary legal sanctions for the segregated society they aimed to produce. Hitherto the line between the white and the "Coloured" population had been imprecisely drawn. Between 1948 and 1950 a series of laws made both marriage and sexual intercourse between white and nonwhite illegal (an earlier Immorality Act, passed in 1927, prohibited sexual intercourse between European and African) and required every individual to have his "race" formally entered on a national register. The Group Areas Act of 1950 provided the government with the sanctions needed to unscramble the process which had occurred quite naturally over the generations in a number of South African towns whereby Europeans, Asians, "Coloureds," and sometimes even Africans came to live in the same street or district. Now each "group" was to have its own carefully designated area and amenities such as parks or cinemas which had been multiracial in character were to be confined to people of a particular pigmentation. In practical terms this act meant the removal of many nonwhite families from areas in which they and their forefathers had lived for generations; but it also involved the government in schemes for urban rebuilding on a massive scale.

To Hertzog the "Coloured" community had appeared as "an appendage of the white race," to Malan and his Nationalist followers they were clearly a distinct group. Therefore it was illogical that "Coloured" voters should still be allowed to vote on the same roll as Europeans, a feature of Cape politics that dated back to 1853. Accordingly, in 1951 a bill was introduced placing the "Coloured" voters on a separate roll and allowing them to elect four representatives. This bill when passed by simple majority provoked a long-drawn-out constitutional crisis. The new act represented a change in the constitution of a kind that could, according to the Act of Union, be sanctioned only by a two-thirds majority. Claiming the "ultimate sanction" of "the will of the people," the Nationalists set about altering the membership of the appeal court that had declared the act invalid and increased the size of the senate to their own advantage.

Nowhere was contact between the races so frequent as in the towns.

In their approach to the position of Africans in urban areas the Nationalist line was clear. "The native in our urban areas," declared a 1948 election document, "must be regarded as a 'visitor' who will never be entitled to any political rights or to equal social rights with the whites." [71] Accordingly the Pass Laws were tightened up and more strictly enforced, and many thousands of urban Africans who failed to comply with the stringent regulations governing residence in towns were "endorsed out" and sent back to their alleged "homelands."

The process of unscrambling convergent cultures was carried further in the Bantu Education Act of 1954. The act transferred the control of African education from provincial to the central government and put pressure on the missionary societies which were then responsible for running 90 percent of the schools to hand their educational institutions over to the government by withdrawing their subsidies. The new educational system laid greater stress on the importance of teaching in Bantu languages, although European languages were not neglected, and of helping the child to understand his own culture. The new system had much in common with the technocratic theory of education found in most authoritarian regimes, in which the state is assumed to know what type of education is suitable for each particular individual. A logical development of the new educational policy was the gradual removal of nonwhite students from the predominantly white universities and the establishment of separate university colleges for each distinct racial group. By 1969 there were 68,000 whites attending universities in South Africa, compared with 9,000 nonwhite students, of whom 4,000 were Africans.

Apartheid, supporters of the policy constantly pointed out, was not a purely negative policy. It involved the active encouragement of African initiative in those parts of the country, the reserves or "homelands" as they now came to be called, that could be regarded as exclusively African in character. From this there developed the idea of transforming the reserves into "Bantustans," quasi-autonomous "national states" within a great South African "commonwealth." By 1970 this policy had been carried furthest in the Transkei, by far the largest of the reserves, where a legislative assembly was set up in 1963 consisting of sixty-four chiefs and forty-five elected members. The new assembly possessed considerably greater powers than any other local government bodies, but the republican government provided more than 50 percent of the local budget, controlled the local security forces and so was well placed to exert pressure on the independent-minded chief minister, Kaizer Matanzima.

To provide itself with the necessary sanctions to deal with those who violently opposed its politics, the Nationalist government equipped itself with a formidable battery of legal weapons. The Suppression of Communism Act (1950) provided so broad a definition of "Communism" that action could be taken against "well-nigh anyone who thought radically." [72] The Unlawful Organizations Act (1960) led to the banning of the major nonwhite political organizations. The Criminal Law Amendment Act (1953) rendered it "an offence to advise, encourage or incite anyone to commit any offence by way of protest against a law" [73] with a maximum penalty of five years imprisonment. The General Law Amendment Act (1963) gave police officers the power to arrest without warrant and detain for ninety days persons suspected of committing certain types of political offenses. [74] To counter threats to its regime the government steadily increased the size of its security forces and developed a highly efficient system of internal intelligence based on a wide network of informers.

Opposition to the Nationalist government came from a very wide range of organizations and individuals drawn from every racial group, some operating openly in the parliamentary arena, others forming external lobbies, yet others engaging in subversive underground action. In parliament the United Party offered the greatest numerical opposition to the government, but the number of seats at the party's disposal fell from sixty-five in 1948 to thirty-nine in 1966. (In the same period the National Party increased its representation from 70 to 126, a development indicating that it was able to attract a considerable amount of English-speaking support.) The United Party accepted many of the racialist ideas of the Nationalists, but urged a more humane form of government and pressed for the creation of "a federation of races." At the same time, it stressed the need to protect "white leadership." The small Progressive Party, founded in 1959, represented by one vigorous member in parliament and attracting no more than 3 percent of the vote, denounced white domination as "morally indefensible" and urged the establishment of a qualified franchise based on educational standards, on income or property, and open to people of every race. The Liberal Party, founded in 1953, took a nonracial stand, pressed for a universal franchise, and spoke of the need for "strong measures to redress the imbalance of privilege which we have inherited." The party's spokesmen in parliament and the seven European representatives of African interests, were removed with the abolition of African representation in 1960. Eight years later, when the government declared racially mixed parties illegal, the Liberal Party decided to disband. Nevertheless, the views put forward by the party continued to be expressed by a number of European organizations, such as the Christian Institute or the South African Institute for Race Relations. Numerically, white South African Liberalism was weak, and many liberals, despairing of the possibility of change, chose to leave the country. Nevertheless, throughout the 1950's and 1960's the voice of liberal protest could be heard, from churchmen, from academics, from writers and artists, from businessmen, from journalists, from students, and from many ordinary white men and women shocked by some fresh example of government brutality. It was one of the paradoxes of the South African situation that these protests could be made openly in a state with many totalitarian characteristics —and some of the most courageous protesters were men of Afrikaner stock closely related to members of the ruling elite.

By far the most serious threat to the government came not from any white opponent but from the nonwhites. At the time the Nationalists came to power, the African National Congress, after a period of decline in the 1930's, had been stirred to vigorous action by the members of its newly founded Youth League, while in Natal the South African Indian Congress was engaged in a campaign of protest. Inevitably the steady stream of discriminatory legislation introduced by the Nationalists aroused increasingly bitter resentment, provoking nonwhite political movements to do all in their power to assert their views. In 1952, the two congresses, African and Indian, launched a campaign of defiance "against the unjust laws which keep in perpetual subjection and misery vast sections of the population." [75] More than 8,000 volunteers deliberately broke apartheid regulations, going into railway stations by "European only" entrances or parading the streets after curfew till they were rounded up and imprisoned. The campaign served as a splendid advertisement for the African National Congress whose membership rose from 7,000 to 100,000 within a few months. Yet in the face of ruthlessly deployed government power the campaign was doomed to failure, and when, toward its end, police brutality provoked savage outbursts of violence in three urban centers with both Europeans and Africans killed, the African National Congress found itself being accused of fomenting forms of violence its leaders had never condoned.

African nationalists in South Africa were confronted with two alternative lines of action: either they could stress the purely African and by implication anti-European character of their movement and aim at domination by the African majority, or they could work toward a truly integrated, nonracial, democratic state. Most Europeans believed that African nationalists were revolutionaries intent on shattering the whole structure of South African society. The events of the mid-1950's showed very clearly that most nationalists were in fact reformers, anxious to transform an unjust society gradually. The Freedom Charter of

1955, endorsed at a specially convened Congress of the People attended by 3,000 delegates including a number of Europeans, began by declaring that "South Africa belongs to all who live in it, black and white, and that no government can justly claim authority unless it is based on the will of all the people" and went on to sketch out a blueprint for a liberal, nonracial society.[76] To the government the charter was a highly subversive document: 156 leading members of the Congress of the People were arrested and put on trial on the charge of having been members of a conspiracy inspired by international Communism to overthrow the South African state by violence. The trial dragged on for four years, ending in the acquittal of the accused.

Meanwhile, between 1957 and 1962, the government found itself faced with a series of peasant revolts in some of the "Bantu homelands." In every case, government action—the imposition of unpopular chiefs, the introduction of oppressive laws—provoked the unrest. In every case force was promptly, even brutally deployed to restore order. But in some areas the situation bore an alarming resemblance to the last outbreak of rural violence, the Bambata rebellion of 1906 in Zululand. In Pondoland in the eastern Transkei, for example, peasant militants, with the help of ANC members, proved remarkably successful for a time in devising methods—boycotts, ostracism, and hut-burning—to intimidate collaborators and resist an all-powerful government. Even more alarming to the mass of South African whites were the series of demonstrations organized in 1960 by the Pan-African Congress, a new party founded in 1958 by a group of militant nationalists, more violent in their choice of methods, more exclusively African in their ideals than their elders in the ANC. Pan-Africanist agitation culminated in two spectacular incidents—the shooting at Sharpeville when the police opened fire on a crowd of Africans peacefully protesting against the Pass Laws, and the march on Cape Town when 30,000 Africans moved in orderly procession through the center of the city to present themselves at the parliament buildings. Government reactions were predictable: the proclamation of a state of emergency, the introduction of more stringent punitive legislation, including the outlawing of all African political organizations, and a further round of arrests.

In 1961, ANC leaders, driven underground by the ban on their party, decided to turn to more violent methods and founded a new organization, "The Spear of the Nation," to carry out acts of sabotage against selected installations. Sabotage, it was felt, could be carried on without causing any loss of life. The Pan-African Congress, on the other hand, favored more ruthless methods and established a terrorist organization, Poqo, to further its aims. Meanwhile, a large number of

African nationalists had found their way abroad and were able to count on increasing moral support from the United Nations, from the Afro-Asian states, and from liberals in North America and Western Europe. As the number of incidents of sabotage increased, the government introduced yet more repressive measures, holding suspects in solitary confinement for periods of ninety days without trial. By 1964 most of the leaders of the nationalist movement had been caught, tried and imprisoned, or forced to leave the country. The counterrevolution had won on every sector of the front. The government's security forces, increasingly ruthless, sophisticated and efficient in their methods, had succeeded in smothering every sign of open protest. In the late 1960's South Africa "enjoyed" a greater measure of internal "peace" than at any time for the last twenty years. But the supporters of the system might well have pondered on Burke's remark in his famous speech on conciliation with America: "The use of force alone is but *temporary*. It may subdue for a moment; but it does not remove the necessity of subduing again: and a nation is not governed which is perpetually conquered."

Nowhere on the African continent did the cause of African nationalism sustain so shattering a defeat as in South Africa. Some commentators ascribed the defeat to the tactics of the nationalists, to the "almost foolhardy decency" of the ANC and its concentration on nonviolent methods. But even if the ANC had chosen to follow the line of the FLN in Algeria and embark on a vigorous guerrilla war—a policy it began to follow in the late 1960's—it could hardly have been more successful. The Algerian rebels were exceptionally well-placed, it must be remembered, to receive material support from the outside; yet even then they were unable to achieve a clear-cut military victory. Only when French public opinion turned decisively against the war was it possible to organize a French withdrawal. In South Africa the government was in an entirely different situation. It had behind it the support of the vast majority of the white population, and it had so effectively intimidated the blacks, that few would dare to come out in support of a guerrilla movement organized from outside the country's borders. Given this resolute determination to maintain white supremacy at all costs, the doctrinal disputes among the Afrikaner elite that became so apparent in the late 1960's appeared of relatively trivial significance. *Verkrampte* and *verligte,* "reactionary" and "enlightened," might have argued bitterly over such trivial matters as the advisability of allowing African diplomats to reside in white suburbs or of permitting New Zealand rugby teams containing a few Maori players to tour the country, but on the essential need to maintain *baasskap* both groups were entirely in agreement.

▲▼ EXTERNAL RELATIONS

No independent polity in the modern history of Africa, with the possible exception of Egypt, has exerted so powerful an influence over such a wide area as the European-dominated state built up in South Africa. As early as the 1880's, the British colony at the Cape was serving as the base for expeditions reaching deep into Central Africa. Twenty years later a unified South Africa was exerting a magnetic influence on all its northern neighbors. Africans from many different countries came to work in the mines of the Witwatersrand. The country's famous mission schools attracted African students from far beyond South Africa's borders. And men of South African stock were to be found occupying a wide range of posts in all the British territories of East and Central Africa. World War I provided new evidence of South Africa's power, when troops from the Union overran the German colony of South West Africa and made a substantial contribution to the British victory in German East Africa. "It would be a great thing," wrote Smuts in 1922, "to round off the South African state with borders far flung into the heart of the continent." This was said at a time when there seemed some hope that the white Rhodesians would vote in favor of joining the Union. Should that happen, Smuts reckoned that South Africa would be able to "build economical and political bridges between all the territories of white settlement as far north as Kenya." [77] These grandiose hopes were not fulfilled in the 1920's and 1930's. Nevertheless, South African power was steadily consolidated, a process clearly demonstrated in World War II when the South African war effort was the greatest of any country in the continent, involving the enlistment of 210,000 Europeans and 123,000 non-Europeans, the latter being strictly confined to noncombatant duties.

Until the end of World War II South Africa had been immune to any threat of external assault. With the British navy guarding the country's sea lanes and the territories to the north firmly held by friendly colonial powers, the Union seemed to enjoy one of the most comfortable international positions in the world. The first sign of change occurred in 1946 when the Indian delegate to the United Nations launched an attack on the South African government for its treatment of its Indian population. "Colour," wrote Smuts sadly, "queers my poor pitch everywhere. But South Africans cannot understand. Colour-bars are to them part of the divine order of things. But I sometimes wonder what our position in years to come will be when the whole world will be against us." [78]

Smuts' foreboding was amply justified. Remorselessly South Africa's "policies of colour were in the way"—in Sir Keith Hancock's phrase —"to becoming the stuff and substance of her foreign policy." [79] As the movement of colonial emancipation spread from Asia to Africa, South Africans found themselves under increasingly bitter verbal attack. It was fortunate for the dominant white minority that their own power should have been steadily increasing in the same period. Expenditure on security and defense rose steadily throughout the 1960's. By 1970 South Africa was clearly the most effective military power in Africa. Moreover, the country was now strong enough to pursue a vigorous foreign policy designed to break down the barriers South Africa's enemies sought to erect against it and to reinforce its position of dominance over its traditional sphere of influence north of the Limpopo. Within the context of this broader pattern must be set the details of white South Africa's relations with its immediate neighbors on the African continent— South West Africa, the three former high commission territories, Rhodesia, and the Portuguese colonies, with the independent states to the north, and finally with the major countries of the outside world.

The German colony of South West Africa was conquered by South African troops in a swift and brilliant campaign in the first half of 1915. The South Africans hoped that they would be allowed to annex the conquered territory outright, but under the terms of the Treaty of Versailles South West Africa was given the status of a "C" class mandate. The terms of the mandate agreement allowed South Africa to govern South West Africa as an "integral part" of its own territory but required the Union government to "promote to the utmost the material and moral well being and the social progress of the inhabitants." Members of the Permanent Mandate Commission of the League of Nations soon had cause to criticize the manner in which South Africa maintained its "sacred trust." "Of all the native populations with which the Commission had to deal," Commissioner Rappard reported in 1936, "that of South West Africa seemed the most backward; its position was static and static on a deplorably low level." [80] The territory was, however, far from being totally immune to the process of change. White settlement steadily increased. As a German colony, South West Africa possessed a white population of 14,000. By 1926, even allowing for the repatriation of 6,000 Germans, the white population had doubled. In 1951 it numbered just under 50,000, by 1960 it had risen to 73,000. At the same time, there was a steady expansion of the economy. Between 1920 and 1962, with the development of mining, fisheries, and agriculture, South West Africa experienced an annual growth rate of just under 5 percent, slightly higher than that of South Africa itself. With its small population and with the promise of more mineral resources still to be discovered, South West Africa could be seen as potentially one of the richest areas of the entire continent.

The strategic importance of the territory, its growing wealth, and the close cultural ties between its white population—two-thirds of whom were of Afrikaner stock by 1960—and their neighbors across the Orange River made it inevitable that the South African government should do its utmost to absorb the territory fully within its own structure. In 1948, when all remaining mandates were transformed into "trust territories" under the supervision of the United Nations, South Africa refused to sign a trusteeship agreement. From then on the South African government found itself continually at loggerheads with the United Nations and was forced to play the defendant in two lengthy lawsuits at the International Court. At the same time, further steps were taken to integrate South West Africa into the republic as a fifth province. In the late 1960's the South African government began to extend its Bantustan policy to South West Africa, sharpening the distinction between "tribal areas" and the "Police Zone" in which European settlement was concentrated. In 1962 the tribal areas or reserves on which the Bantu homelands were to be based made up little more than one-quarter of the total area of the territory. It was planned to increase their size substantially, though the richest districts would still remain firmly in European hands. In 1959 two political parties were formed among the nonwhite population of the territory; a decade later political leaders in exile were organizing guerrilla activity in the extreme north of the country. Militarily, the South Africans might have had little difficulty mastering this threat, but the government's failure to secure international approval for its planned absorption of South West Africa left a serious chink in the republic's diplomatic armor. Legal experts might question the right of the outside world to intervene in the domestic affairs of the republic, but over South West Africa—or Namibia, as the territory was coming to be known in international circles—the United Nations clearly possessed sound legal grounds for taking further actions to assert its jurisdiction.

From 1910 on, every South African government was eager to persuade the British to renounce their protectorates over Basutoland, Bechuanaland, and Swaziland and to allow the three territories to be incorporated within South Africa. Distrust of South African racial policies, together with an awareness that any change in status would provoke immense local discontent induced the British to retain their hold over territories which offered no practical advantage to the metropolis. The British, indeed, did little to develop their three South African protectorates with the result that all three territories became increasingly closely integrated in the economic structure of the Union. In Swaziland half the agricultural land was owned by whites, some of them absentee landlords. White landownership was forbidden in Basutoland, but population pressure led large numbers of Basuto—as many as 42 percent of the adult male population in the early 1950's—to seek employment outside their country. There was also an extensive labor migration from Bechuanaland to the mines of the Rand, and in all three territories local trade was dominated by whites from South Africa. But for all its shortcomings British rule served to protect the African population of the three protectorates from the constraints imposed on their neighbors in the Republic. And when in the early 1960's the process of constitutional change so familiar from other British colonies in Africa was introduced to Bechuanaland, Basutoland, and Swaziland, the three territories were able to move relatively smoothly toward independence.

In each territory local politics could be broadly described as taking the form of a conflict between conservatives and modernists, with the conservatives represented and led in Botswana (Bechuanaland) by Seretse Khama, the Oxford-educated chief of the Bamagwato, in Lesotho by Chief Jonathan, leader of the Basutoland National Party, and in Swaziland by the Swazi Paramount—the title was changed to king after independence—Sobhuza. The development of the concept of Bantustans made it easier for the Nationalist government to accept the independence of these three independent African polities. At the same time, the leaders of the three new states, disregarding the policies advocated by their radical opponents, refused to allow their territories to become centers of subversive activity against the Republic, a refusal bred of a realistic appreciation of their own extreme vulnerability to South African pressure. Nevertheless, the mere existence of three such states whose leaders were prepared to condemn unreservedly their powerful neighbors' racial policies and to ensure that no color-bar was permitted within their own borders could hardly be regarded as anything less than deeply subversive to the ardent champions of apartheid. To the average South African tourist, shut out by passport restrictions from other parts of Black Africa, the opportunity to visit the casinos of Swaziland or the game reserves of Botswana might bring with it a few unexpected lessons in relaxed and harmonious race relations.

From its creation in 1890 the European polity known as Rhodesia possessed close links with South Africa, and there were men in both countries who could have liked Rhodesia to become a province of its powerful southern neighbor. In the 1923 referendum, 40 percent of the Rhodesian electorate voted in favor of union with South Africa. But cultural differences—the Britishness of Salisbury, the victorious Afrikanerdom of Pretoria—created a certain coolness between the two white-dominated governments. Thus, in 1955 Dr. Malan accused the Rhodesians of denying to their Afrikaner minority "the most elementary rights in the cultural and educational sphere." [81] In the case of the Portuguese territories of Angola and Mozambique, cultural differences were even greater. But in the 1960's the pressure of events—the emergence of formidable armed liberation movements in the two Portuguese colonies together with the consequences resulting from the unilateral declaration of independence in Rhodesia—forced the four white-dominated states to cooperate more closely than ever before. And the rapid development of the smaller countries' economies, a development to which South African capital made some contribution, created a situation in which the links between the four polities steadily ramified.

South Africa's interests were not confined to its immediate neighbors. In the 1890's Cecil Rhodes had dreamed of a British-dominated Cape to Cairo railroad. Thirty years later this vision had still not faded. In the 1920's Smuts was playing with the idea of "a great White Africa along the Eastern backbone" with railway and road communications connecting North and South," "a white State in time more important than Australia." [82] "Without large-scale permanent European settlement in this continent," Smuts declared in a famous series of lectures delivered at Oxford in 1929, "the African mass will not be moved, the sporadic attempts at civilization will pass, Africa may relapse to her barbaric and prehistoric slumbers." [83]

Seeing themselves as the agents of civilization, vividly aware of the contributions they could make through their own long experience of coping with African environments to the development of other parts of the continent, South Africans were shocked and pained by the rapid process of decolonization followed by the metropolitan powers in tropical Africa in the 1950's and 1960's. To many South Africans it seemed that "the Western colonial powers were much too eager to abandon their colonies by granting them *uhuru* before the road to independence had been thoroughly planned. In consequence," so the writers of a South African high school textbook, one of the most influential opinion-forming types of publication, pointed out, "inexperienced leaders and incapable officials who were not fit for the task had to assume the reins, with fatal results for the survival of their governments." [84]

Given the widespread acceptance of views such as these, it was impossible for the vast majority of South Africans to reach that sympathetic understanding of the dynamics of African nationalism achieved by many influential persons in the Western World. As the number of independent states increased, South Africa came under increasingly vigorous attack. South African representatives were forced to withdraw from numerous international bodies. South African aircraft were forbidden to use the air-space of independent African countries. And, in 1963, the Organization of African Unity set up a National Liberation Committee to assist freedom movements in Southern Africa with money and military training. Three years later, however, the position had changed sufficiently for the South African government to embark on an "outward-looking policy." At a time when many of the independent African states were beset by their own internal difficulties, South Africa seemed more powerful, more prosperous, more assured than ever. Extremely cordial relations were established with President Banda of Malawi and a harmonious *modus vivendi* with the three former high commission territories. No longer did it appear inconceivable that black diplomats would be treated with courtesy in South African establishments. There were shrewd reasons behind the new policy: it served to reassure a public opinion worried at the evidence of the republic's unpopularity, and it was the essential political counterpart to a move to find new African markets for the country's expanding manufactures. It was natural for the Republic to seek to assert itself as an African power. Yet even more important to the country's future was the maintenance of reasonably amicable relations with the major powers of the Western world.

In the course of the last sixty years South Africa's relations with the old metropolis, Britain, have been subject to many shifts and changes. In international diplomacy the personality of individual leaders must never be disregarded. There can be no doubt that the presence of J. C. Smuts, with his circle of intimate English friends, at the center of South African political life gave to Anglo-South African relations in the years before 1948 a cordiality they might not otherwise have achieved. For there were many potential sources of tension between the two countries. An influential section of British public opinion, the heirs of the nineteenth-century humanitarian tradition, viewed South Africa's racial policies with abhorrence. At the same time, all Afrikaner leaders, whether moderates like Smuts or extremists like Malan, were determined to achieve for their country the status of a truly independent power and resented the continuing manifestations of British paternalism and condescension. The advent to power of the Nationalists in 1948 coincided with the transformation of the Commonwealth from a comfortable "club for whites only" to a multi-racial association. In these circumstances increasing tensions became apparent. But the Nationalist government was not anxious to provoke an immediate break. Not until 1960 was the electorate asked to vote in a referendum on the issue, long discussed in

Nationalist circles, of a republic. Not until 1961 did South Africa formally withdraw from the Commonwealth, most of whose new Asian and African members were bitterly critical of the country's internal policies. Yet despite the severing of certain formal ties South Africa remained more closely bound to Britain than to any other country in the world. Britain was South Africa's major trading partner, taking in the mid-1960's about a third of South Africa's exports and providing about a quarter of its imports. The importance of South Africa as an export market to Britain declined dramatically in the late 1960's; in 1967 the Republic was Britain's second largest export market, but by 1969 it had fallen to ninth place. About 60 percent of all foreign investment in South Africa was British and British investment increased especially rapidly between 1961 and 1967. And there continued to be, of course, many strong ties based on culture and kinship between the two countries.

Ever since the end of the eighteenth century South Africa had occupied a position of vital importance in British imperial strategy. With the decline of British power in the East and the gradual abandonment of an "East of Suez" policy, South Africa's value to British strategists diminished. But the South African government was always eager to insist on its importance to the Western powers as an ally in the struggle against world Communism. There was no unanimity in the West in the 1960's about the reality of a Communist threat. Consequently the South African government found itself supported in its view of the world situation only by the more conservative elements in Britain and America. To British and American liberals too close an association with South Africa was seen as a serious liability, capable of gravely prejudicing relations with the countries of the Afro-Asian world. The real attractiveness of South Africa to the West lay in its position as a trading partner. During the 1960's Western European businessmen became increasingly aware of the opportunities offered by the South African market. Exports from EEC countries to South Africa increased by 50 percent in value between 1964 and 1969. Japan, too, developed a steadily mounting trade with the Republic, its imports to South Africa doubling in value in the same period. (For the sake of good trade relations the South African government found no difficulty in allowing Japanese businessmen to be classified as "honorary whites.") Trade was a powerful solvent to the tensions caused by differing political concepts. Thus the French government, with its notable record of cordial relations with the Third World countries, was perfectly prepared to disregard the U.N. ban on the sales of arms to South Africa and meet many of the South

African requirements in the field of planes and weapons. Here, indeed, in this nexus of cordial relations was one of white South Africa's strongest lines of defense.

As for relations with the Communist world, these were inevitably marked by bitter verbal hostility on both sides. But such modest evidence of Communist activity as the presence of a few Soviet warships in the Indian Ocean or of a number of Chinese engineers in Tanzania provided the South African government with valuable material which could be used to scare its own supporters into the belief that their country was under constant assault from vast and sinister external forces. But in fact it is reasonable to assume that to the rulers in Moscow and Peking South Africa was a country of purely marginal significance, a useful counter in a propaganda war but far too remote to be of any major concern in shaping a realistic foreign policy.

▲▼ SOUTH AFRICA: THE PROSPECT IN THE EARLY 1970'S

Every country in the modern world faces an uncertain future. But over few countries does there hang so dark and insistent a question mark as over the white-dominated Republic of South Africa. In the early 1970's, however, it would have been quite misleading to have suggested that the country faced a "revolutionary situation." Few governments in the modern world had so formidably equipped themselves to intervene in and control the lives of all their peoples as that of modern South Africa. There could be no analogy with the ramshackle *ancien régimes* of France in the 1780's, of Russia before 1917, or of China in the 1940's. Nor did it seem likely that South Africa would in the foreseeable future be seriously threatened by external pressures. The forces of militant African nationalism were far too weak, and even if—a highly speculative assumption—they were eventually to succeed in overthrowing white rule in Rhodesia and Mozambique, it seemed reasonable to assume that any black successor states in those two countries would face so many grave internal problems that they would find it impossible to develop into effective bases for action against South Africa; indeed, in all probability they would be irresistibly drawn into the South African sphere of influence, as the other black states in the area—Malawi, Botswana, Lesotho, and Swaziland—had already been. As for those powers which alone possessed the military and economic resources to put effective pressure on South Africa—the United States, the Soviet Union, Communist China, and the nations of Western Europe—to all of them South Africa represented an area of marginal importance. It seemed highly improbable that the governments of the United States, the Soviet Union, or the states of Western Europe, would desire to commit themselves in an already deeply troubled world to promote a revolutionary war of a kind likely to prove highly distasteful to large numbers of their own people. Nor did it seem probable that Communist China, with its own grave internal problems, would see an advantage in committing itself deeply to a struggle from which it could gain at most no more than a certain prestige in revolutionary circles but which would contribute little to the fundamental interests of the Chinese state. At the most, all that could be expected from the outside world was a certain amount of moral and financial support to the opponents of the South African government.

Yet clearly the situation was far from static. The steady expansion of industry, a process entirely dependent on interracial enterprise, made the practical difficulties of implementing the system of apartheid even more sharply apparent. Some commentators, indeed, were inclined to argue that the need to employ Africans in jobs previously reserved for whites would lead to the eventual collapse of enforced segregation. Other observers regarded this as a highly misleading prediction. Slave societies in the past—and in social structure South Africa presented certain obvious analogies with such societies—found it perfectly possible to employ the unfree in a variety of responsible posts without in any way affecting the basic legal and political inequality between freemen and slaves. Commentators also pointed to the likelihood of changes in the Bantustans, to which the government itself had made a promise of ultimate independence. Yet of the Bantustans only the Transkei appeared large enough to support a state structure as modest as that of Lesotho, itself one of the poorest countries in the world. No doubt political leaders in the Bantustans would press for a greater measure of autonomy, but their economic dependence on the government of Pretoria would always ensure that they retained the position of obedient satellites. Clearly the most powerful force making for change lay in the growth and pressure of population. By the year 2000 it was reckoned that South Africa would have a population of 40 million, only 8 million of whom would be white. Unless the white minority were prepared to make immense sacrifices and initiate a far more vigorous program for social and economic development in African areas than they had done in the past, the conditions in the homelands and in the urban locations, already apalling in many respects, were destined to grow steadily worse. African bitterness and frustration might well lead to renewed outbursts of violence. Even so, the white security forces were well-equipped to ensure that any such outbreaks would not spill over into white areas. As for effective African political activity, it must be accepted that in totalitarian regimes—and in its attitude toward nonwhites the South African government clearly behaved in a totalitarian manner—the experience of history appears to show that it is virtually impossible for a revolt from below to succeed.

But no regime is ever truly monolithic. Every regime contains cracks and fissures which may expand and lead to its collapse. The South African government of the early 1970's represented the domination of a minority group, the Afrikaners. Yet there existed a small but highly articulate group of Afrikaners—churchmen, academics, and writers among them—who rejected the exclusive nationalism of their kinsmen and saw the future of South Africa in terms of a nonracial or of a multi-racial society. To counterbalance the emergence of this relatively novel liberal Afrikaner group it should be recalled that many English-speaking South Africans, contemptuous though they might often appear in their everyday attitude toward their Afrikaner compatriots, were perfectly prepared to follow the lead of Afrikaner Nationalists if this would guarantee them the continuance of the materially satisfying life they had enjoyed for so long. Moreover, with many young liberals, stifled by the oppressive intellectual atmosphere of their country, choosing to make their homes overseas, the likelihood of a powerful liberal movement ever making an impact on the South African electorate seemed remote to the point of impossibility. Given all these considerations, it was hard for any liberal observer not to view the future of South Africa in any but the darkest terms. In the early 1970's the prospect facing South Africans seemed not to be of an era of violence, of revolutionary turmoil and upheaval, but of a steadily growing frustration—among the nonwhites the frustration that is bred of poverty and injustice, of the sense of wasted talents and stunted lives, among the whites the frustration bred of fear, guilt, or a soulless and entirely materialistic complacency.

Yet in a sense it was deeply unrealistic to think of South Africa, or indeed of any country, in these coldly analytical terms. Those who hurled abusive epithets at the South African regime—and there was hardly a country anywhere in the world, apart from Rhodesia and Portugal, whose leaders had not expressed their abhorrence of the system of apartheid—needed occasionally to remind themselves of Burke's famous dictum: "I do not know the method of drawing up an indictment against a whole people." The defenders of white supremacy in South Africa might well claim to be set in a unique or caught in a tragic situation. There was no country anywhere in the world where two such large groups, originally differing so greatly in culture, found themselves in such intimate juxtaposition. Moreover, it needed to be remembered that there existed in South Africa as in every country an enormous reservoir of human talent, of warmth, generosity, humor, vitality, compassion. It may well be that a historian three hundred years hence will see the greatness of South Africa in the twentieth century as lying not in the material achievements nor in the actions of its politicians but in the works produced by its men and women of letters, its novelists, poets, historians, and dramatists, many of whose works, it should be noted, were banned by official censors and so could never be read openly by their own compatriots. It was worth recalling, too, that it was from South Africa, from the pen of a young Afrikaner poet, Ingrid Jonker, that there came one of the great African poems of the mid-twentieth century, *The Child who was shot dead by soldiers at Nyanga.*

> *The child is not dead*
> *the child lifts his fists against his mother*
> *who shouts Afrika! shouts the breath*
> *of freedom and the veld*
> *in the locations of the cordoned heart . . .*
>
> *The child is present at all assemblies and law-givings*
> *the child peers through the windows of houses and into*
> *the hearts of mothers*
> *this child who wanted only to play in the sun at Nyanga*
> *is everywhere*
> *the child grown to a man treks on through all Africa*
> *the child grown into a giant journeys over the whole world*
>
> *Without a pass.*[85]

CHAPTER IX

The Islands

The Atlantic islands lying off the mainland of Africa—Madeira, the Canaries, the Cape Verde archipelago, Fernando Po, São Tomé and Principe, and St. Helena—fulfilled a historical role of some importance in the fifteenth, sixteenth, and seventeenth centuries. The Canaries became the scene of one of the first attempts made by Europeans since classical times to colonize land beyond the confines of their own continent, a process that involved the extermination of the Guanche, the native Berber population. Madeira and São Tomé, which European navigators found to be uninhabited, came to serve as the model for plantation colonies in other parts of the world, with African slaves providing the labor force and European settlers the capital and the management. São Tomé also provided an important base for Portuguese activities in Congo (Kongo) and Angola, while St. Helena was developed into a valuable port of call for English ships bound for the Indies.

In the course of the past century the islands' history has been less significant. Madeira and the Canaries have become so totally assimilated, both politically and culturally, with the rest of the Iberian peninsula that it is no longer appropriate to consider them in the context of African history. To travel today between Dakar or Freetown and the booming city of Las Palmas, the capital of the Canaries, is to be reminded in an exceptionally vivid manner of the extent of the cultural and technological divide between Europe and West Africa. The Cape Verde Islands, always poverty-stricken by virtue of their meager natural resources, are formally regarded as a province of Portugal. Sixty percent of their inhabitants are reckoned to be of mixed African and European descent. Lack of local opportunities forces the most enterprising to leave their homeland and seek employment in other parts of Portuguese Africa. The two other Portuguese islands, São Tomé and Principe, have always been dependent on imported labor to work their plantations. In the 1900's the Portuguese practice of recruiting contract labor in Angola to work on the islands' plantations was denounced as a modern form of slavery by English philanthropists. So vigorous was their campaign, so well-documented their evidence of abuses that the Portuguese authorities were forced to introduce reforms. But the islands still maintain their traditional character of plantation colonies with cocoa providing the main crop.

The recent history of Fernando Po has been more complex. The island, which lies within sight of the Nigerian-Cameroon mainland, came under Spanish sovereignty in 1778, but it was not until late in the nineteenth century that the Spaniards began to appreciate the value of their possession and set about building yet another plantation economy with labor supplied not by the indigenous Bubi but by Ibo and other workers from the mainland. The Spanish government also acquired a substantial enclave, known as Río Muni, on the Equatorial coast. The boundaries of the colony were laid down by international treaty in 1900, but it was not until the 1920's that the Spanish authorities were able to establish their hegemony over the independent Fang communities of the interior. In 1959 the Spanish government decided to make some concessions to the "wind of change" by hastily pushing through a policy of assimilation. As "the Equatorial Region of Spain" the two colonies were declared to have become an integral part of the metropolis, with the right to send their own deputies to the Cortes. These concessions failed to satisfy local nationalists, among whom those of Fang origin had been particularly active in forming new political parties. Anxious to avoid excessive criticism in the United Nations and to obtain Afro-Asian support in its dispute with Britain over Gibraltar, the Spanish government decided on an act of political withdrawal. In 1968 Fernando Po and Río Muni, which had already been granted a substantial measure of internal self-government, were transformed into an independent state, the Republic of Equatorial Guinea.

Few newly-independent African states faced such formidable political problems as the new republic. There were sharp ethnic divisions between the Bubi and the Nigerian immigrants of Fernando Po on the one side and the Fang of Río Muni on the other. But the Fang possessed a numerical superiority and so were able to gain control of the government. To maintain control was no easy task for the republic's capital was established at Santa Isabel on Fernando Po: there was talk of several thousand Fang being brought across to the island to help bolster up the position of their leaders. Equatorial Guinea's first year of independence was marked by two major crises. An outbreak of violent anti-European rioting led to the withdrawal of 90 percent of the

Spaniards—they numbered 7,000 in 1968—living in the republic. Shortly afterward the government narrowly escaped being overthrown by a coup in which some of its own most prominent ministers were implicated. There was evidence too of the growth of a secessionist movement in Fernando Po. Given the attractive power exerted on the republic by its richer and more powerful neighbors, Nigeria, Cameroon, and Gabon, Equatorial Guinea may well find it impossible to maintain its present status as an independent state.

▲▼ MADAGASCAR: THE KINGDOM OF IMERINA AND THE FRENCH CONQUEST

Two hundred miles of sea separate the great island of Madagascar from the mainland of Africa. Thus isolated, Madagascar has come to develop a highly distinctive character of its own with the culture of the Malagasy people presenting a remarkable blend of diverse elements, African, Asian, and European. In size Madagascar is as large as Kenya or Botswana or France and Belgium. In variety of climate and landscape it possesses a greater range than most of the countries of Africa. The *Hauts-Plateaux,* the bare, rolling hills of the country's highland spine, contrast sharply with the humid forests of the east coast or the savannah and dry scrub of the west and south. For all its size the island has a small population, about 2½ million in 1900 rising to 7 million by 1970. Even today, three-quarters of the island has a population density of less than three persons to the square mile.

The history of Madagascar may be presented, more clearly perhaps than that of most other countries, in terms of pioneering. Seemingly uninhabited at the beginning of the Christian era, the island began, in the course of the first millennium A.D., to receive small groups of colonists of Indonesian origin, adventurous seafarers who had made the arduous journey around the northern perimeter or across the empty equatorial wastes of the Indian Ocean. To these olive-skinned, straight-haired immigrants were added men and women of another physical stock, people of negroid type and Bantu culture, brought, probably as slaves, from the east coast of Africa. The extent to which this distinctively African element can be traced in the population varies from area to area, being most clearly marked among the communities of the island's west coast. But despite these differences of origin there came to develop among the people as a whole a remarkably uniform culture, with Malagasy, a language of Indonesian origin enriched by loan-words from other languages, emerging not merely as a *lingua franca* but as the only language of the entire island.

Until the end of the eighteenth century the population of Madagascar was divided up among a large number of ethnic groups, none of which possessed any overall measure of political unity. Out of this kaleidoscopic pattern of petty kingdoms and chiefdoms there emerged one state, Imerina, whose rulers succeeded in the course of the early nineteenth century in asserting their hegemony over two-thirds of the entire island. Imerina occupied an excellent strategic position, being sited in the very center of the island with its base astride the temperate highlands of the interior. Its economy was based on the production of rice in sufficient quantities so as to allow the maintenance of a comparatively wide range of specialists. But it required the leadership and insight of two remarkable monarchs, Andrianampoinimerina (1767–1810) and his son Radama I (1810–28), to translate these assets into political terms by embarking on a long series of campaigns which led to the formation of an empire as large as any to be found in contemporary Africa. Radama was anxious to modernize his country in much the same way as Muhammad Ali of Egypt. He made use of European military advisers to transform his feudal levies into an efficient fighting force, actively supported the schemes for evangelization and education put forward by a group of Christian missionaries, and welcomed the innovations introduced by European technicians. His death was followed by a period of reaction in which the missionaries were expelled and their converts persecuted. But the doors were not completely closed on all European influences and after the death of Radama's successor, Queen Ranavalona, in 1862, the missionaries were allowed to return.

By this time effective power in Imerina was in the hands not of the monarchs—the kingdom's last three rulers were all queens—but of a closely knit oligarchy headed by an extremely astute prime minister, Rainilaiarivony, who remained in office until the French occupation of 1895. In 1868, the prime minister, the queen, and many members of the Merina nobility accepted baptism at the hands of Protestant missionaries. Soon Imerina was proving itself to be a field more favorable for Christian evangelization than any part of mainland Africa. By 1895 Madagascar was reckoned to contain 455,000 Protestant converts and 136,000 Catholics. Inevitably, rivalry between Protestant and Catholic missionaries was intense, with both groups looking to their countries of origin, Britain for the Protestants, France for the Catholics, for diplomatic support. As a result of missionary labors Imerina acquired—in much the same was as some of the coastal settlements of West Africa —the nucleus of a Western-educated elite. Set in the remote interior of a still largely unexplored island and possessing a population which had given clear evidence of its capacity for adaptation, Imerina seemed particularly well set to resist excessive alien intervention.

But the kingdom was not as powerful as it appeared. It was true that Merina armies had fought in many parts of the island and that Merina governors, garrisons and colonists enforced Merina hegemony over the Betsileo, the Betsimisara, and other once independent people. But there were many other groups—such as the Bara of the south and some of the Sakalava chiefs of the west—who stoutly and effectively resisted Merina expansion, and the Merina army, though it might represent a formidable fighting force when set against local opponents, seemed notably ill-trained, ill-disciplined and ill-equipped when compared with contemporary European forces.

France and Britain were the two European powers most interested in Madagascar. A French stake in the island went back to the seventeenth century when an ambitious attempt had been made to establish French settlements on the southeastern coast. In 1875 the French controlled two off-shore islands, Nossi-Be in the northwest and Sainte Marie off the east coast. Far more important as a base for the penetration of Madagascar was the island of Réunion, many of whose European settlers looked with growing interest to the great island. Even before the French conquest of 1895 more than a thousand Réunionais were to be found in Madagascar. Together with the Catholic missionaries, the white settlers of Réunion came to represent a powerful lobby whose members constantly urged the government of the day to adopt a more vigorous policy in its dealings with Imerina and other Malagasy polities. The British also possessed a considerable stake in the island. British missionary enterprise in Imerina dated back to the 1820's and by the 1870's the London Missionary Society and other Protestant bodies could clearly claim a remarkable record of successful evangelization. At the same time, British subjects had acquired a preponderant position in the island's commerce, controlling 40 percent of its external trade, almost double the amount handled by the French. For the rulers of Imerina, Franco-British rivalry was clearly a factor that could be turned to their advantage. Indeed, so long as the two powers continued to oppose one another over Madagascar, Imerina could count on maintaining its independence.

In the early 1880's a number of relatively trivial incidents led to armed conflict between France and Imerina. Ever since the 1840's the French had laid claim to a vague protectorate over the Sakalava chiefdoms on the mainland opposite Nossi-Be. In 1881 certain Sakalava chiefs were persuaded by two British missionaries to accept Merina sovereignty. The French retaliated by sending naval parties ashore to cut down the flagstaffs flying the Merina flag. The Merina government then sent an embassy to London, Paris, and Washington to obtain international recognition for its claim to sovereignty over the entire island. Both the British and the American governments conceded the justness of the Merina case, but the British who had just become entangled in a major crisis with France over the occupation of Egypt were not prepared to heighten tension by becoming involved in a new dispute over an area of marginal strategic importance. The French, for their part, resorting to tougher forms of "gunboat diplomacy," blockaded Madagascar's main ports, bombarded Merina garrisons, and sent raiding parties on shore to burn Merina villages. Finally, in 1885, the two sides concluded a treaty which proved greatly to France's advantage. Under its terms the French government assumed responsibility for Imerina's external relations and obtained the right to station a resident, with a detachment of troops to protect him, at the Merina capital, Tananarive. At the same time, Diego Suarez, the island's best harbor, was ceded to France and the Merina government agreed to pay an indemnity of $1.2 million, an amount which could only be met by floating a loan in London. Thus the kingdom found itself deprived of one of its most important sources of revenue, for custom duties had to be set aside to meet the interest charges on the loan.

The years between 1885 and 1895 have been termed by some French historians the period of the "phantom protectorate." The Malagasy still possessed considerable freedom of action and in Imerina power remained concentrated in the hands of Rainilaiarivony, but the prime minister was now an old man with insufficient grasp of the complexities of the international situation to perceive the opportunities it might have offered. Moreover, he found himself faced with mounting opposition at home and with frequent revolts in the border areas nominally under Merina domination. Any prospect of British support was finally removed by the Anglo-French treaty of 1890 in which the British recognized the French protectorate over Madagascar in return for French acceptance of British claims over Zanzibar. Mounting tension between the French resident and the Merina government provided the pretext for forthright action. In October 1894, the French presented the Merina government with an ultimatum in the form of a draft treaty designed to establish a real protectorate. When the terms were rejected the resident was instructed to withdraw, and the French government set about preparing a grandiose military expedition.

Less than a year later (September, 1895), Tananarive, the Merina capital, was in French hands. The French paid a heavy price for their victory: more than a third of the French force of 15,000 men died of disease, while no more than 25 soldiers were killed in action. The old prime minister was removed from office and his successor ratified the treaty of 1894. The French were following the same line of policy that had worked so successfully in Tunis a decade earlier: preserving the structure of local institutions, establishing a system of indirect rule, gaining collaborators from among the members of the old ruling class. Their plans were foiled by popular resistance. Within a few weeks of the occupation of Tananarive revolt had broken out in a number of areas, directed not only against the French but also against the missionaries and against those members of the Merina aristocracy who could be represented as ruining the country by their acceptance of foreign ways. As rebellion spread, some of those who had formerly collaborated with the French began cautiously to throw in their hand with the rebels. Even the queen was implicated. "This is not a war of bandits, but a war made by the government," she is said to have written in a letter intended for widespread distribution. "All those who do not take part in it are guilty and shall be deprived of their possessions by the people and by me, for I consider them friends of the French." [1]

Faced with a rapidly deteriorating situation and under pressure from a strong lobby made up of Réunion settlers and of businessmen with an interest in Madagascar, the French government abandoned its plans for a protectorate and decided on outright annexation. In August 1896, Madagascar was formally declared a French colony. A month later a new resident-general, General J. S. Galliéni, was sent out to enforce the new policy; French aims were now, in Galliéni's own words, "to make Madagascar French, to undermine British influence and to bring down the Hova [Merina] pride and power." [2]

Galliéni was forty-six when he arrived in Madagascar. Behind him lay twenty years of varied and intensive experience of warfare and administration gained first in the Western Sudan and later in Indochina. Intellectual, rational, constructive, humane, he presented a splendid combination of qualities: few Europeans of his day were so well equipped to undertake the arduous task of administering peoples of alien culture. Animated by a dual loyalty—a passionate devotion to France and a deep concern for the Malagasy people—he left an enduring mark on the new dominion submitted to his charge. His first act was to shatter the structure of the Merina monarchy. In February, 1897, the queen was summarily forced into exile, the monarchy abolished, and, as a truly symbolic manifestation of the change in regime, the royal ceremony of the bath—a form of ritual purification by the rulers of Imerina —was replaced by the celebration of the fall of the Bastille. The execution of two Merina nobles accused of complicity in the rebellion provided a brutal warning to other members of the local aristocracy. At the same time, by enforcing measures for the emancipation of the slaves who made up about a third of the total population of Imerina, Galliéni gained the support of the lower classes of Merina society. The search for effective collaborators was carried further by the attention paid to non-Merina in areas that had once been independent but had come, in the last century, to be subjected to Merina hegemony.

In tackling the rebellion Galliéni applied those tactics—so vividly expressed in his metaphor of the "drop of oil"—that he had first worked out in the country between the Senegal and the Niger in the 1880's: the accumulation of exact information, the avoidance of flying columns and punitive expeditions, the establishment of one fortified post after another, the concentration of authority in the hands of a single local commandant, the introduction of practical schemes for social and economic development, with the soldiers of the garrison being encouraged to experiment with new crops on model farms or to build and equip local dispensaries. "Act in such a way," Galliéni told his officers —one of whom, Colonel Lyautey, was later to apply the same methods with equal success to the pacification of Morocco—"that the people whom you administer tremble only at the thought of your leaving." [3] By mid-1897 the French were firmly in control of all the territory that had once formed part of the ancient kingdom of Imerina. There remained the formidable task of asserting French hegemony over the many independent polities that had never been brought under Merina domination. "The sea," Andrianampoinimerina, the founder of Merina expansion, had told his son Radama, "marks the limits of my rice-fields," thus aphoristically expressing his ambition to bring the entire island under his sway. In accepting the same objective, Galliéni could regard himself as making a creative contribution to Malagasy development. His aim was not merely conquest, for he sought, in his own words, "to reverse and dilute the barriers that separate the various tribal groups of the island, to foster the fusion of tribes in an association of interests, to effect in sum an exchange of products and ideas that will in the end permit the realization of a political and administrative unity " [4] The process of nation-building, so frequently described by the nationalist leaders of the independent African states, could hardly be more effectively defined than in these words of one of the greatest imperial administrators of his generation. Galliéni left Madagascar in 1905, the island pacified and unified, his task completed.

▲▼ MADAGASCAR: FRENCH RULE AND
MALAGASY NATIONALISM

During more than half a century of French rule the people of Madagascar found themselves subjected to much the same pressures as their contemporaries in Morocco or the Ivory Coast. Strangers became increasingly common in their midst. In the early 1890's there were reckoned to be fewer than 2,000 Europeans in the entire island. By 1921, the European population had risen to 12,000, by 1958 to 55,000. In the early twentieth century many of the European immigrants were settlers from Réunion who acquired farms on the *Hauts-Plateaux* or plantations on the east coast. But European agricultural settlement in Madagascar never achieved the same measure of success as in Rhodesia or Kenya, and in time many of the farms came to be abandoned. Europeans were not the only newcomers. By 1958 there were 13,000 Indians in the island, together with a few thousand Chinese. Between them, the two Asian groups came to occupy a position of considerable importance, not unlike that of the Syrians and Lebanese in West Africa, in the commercial life of the island.

The arrival of these strangers affected the Malagasy in a number of ways. The Europeans represented a superior caste, not so rigidly separated from the mass of the population as in most parts of colonial Africa—there was a certain amount of intermarriage, and the French never established exclusive European residential areas in the towns—but enjoying many obvious privileges. Malagasy society had always been organized on a hierarchical basis. For members of the lower classes in Imerina and for non-Merina formerly subjected to Merina domination the French administrator replaced the Merina chief or governor without greatly upsetting the social structure. But for members of the Merina nobility it was peculiarly galling to find themselves deprived of their former privileges, forced to accept the status of *sujets*—the French term carried with it the concept of submission far more sharply than the English word "subject"—and exposed to the arbitrary punishments which French administrators could mete out under the terms of the native code, the *indigénat*. Many Merina notables sought to escape these frustrations by active collaboration, and the French were glad to make use of such able and experienced administrators in much the same way as the British in Uganda found it necessary to rely on the services of Ganda aristocrats. At the same time, a small number of Malagasy— less than 8,000 by 1939—succeeded in obtaining French citizenship. For the peasantry the most irksome aspect of French rule was probably represented by the demands made for labor service. In the late 1920's the French went so far as to organize a system of conscription for specially constituted labor battalions. The use of forced labor for public works was in accord with old Merina practice, but abuses crept into the French system when European planters began looking to local administrators to provide them with a regular supply of cheap labor.

In the field of economic development the French could claim to have laid the foundations of a modern infrastructure through the construction of roads, railroads, and harbor facilities and the encouragement of new cash crops, including coffee, vanilla, cloves, and sisal. There were also substantial advances in the field of public health, especially after World War II, with the launching of a large-scale campaign against malaria. Less impressive was the French achievement in the field of education. As a result of the work of Protestant and Catholic missionaries by the end of the nineteenth century, Madagascar had acquired an educational structure far in advance of almost every other part of Africa. In 1905, 230,000 children—about 10 percent of the entire population—were attending primary school. By 1939, given a substantial increase in the population, the proportion of children attending school had not greatly changed. Nevertheless, as a result of the educational progress made in the nineteenth century Madagascar came to possess a local intelligentsia comparable to but probably far more numerous than the class of *évolués,* the Western-educated Africans to be found in the coastal cities of West Africa.

Inevitably these Malagasy intellectuals—and especially those of Merina origin—came to take a leading part in the development of Malagasy nationalism. Before World War I, a Protestant minister from Imerina, Ravelojaona, formed the country's first proto-nationalist organization, the *Union Chrétienne de Jeunes Gens,* and created a considerable stir with a series of articles drawing the attention of Malagasy youth to the progress being made by Japan. The *Union* was quickly suppressed by the colonial authorities, but in 1915 a group of young men came together to form a secret society, *Vy Vako Sakelika*—a highly symbolic title meaning "the branches of stone and iron"—and talked of ejecting the French and recovering Imerina's lost independence. It was a not unfamiliar phenomenon, students playing at revolution, but it occurred in the middle of World War I, local officials were jittery, and local *colons* willing to swallow absurd rumors—the Malagasy were reported to be storing up barrels of poison to administer to their French overlords. Consequently the French reaction was unnecessarily harsh—more than 200 conspirators were arrested and some were given stiff prison sentences. During World War I more than 40,000 Malagasy saw overseas service in the French army, among them a young schoolteacher, Jean Ralaimongo, who stayed on in France after his demobilization, made contact with left-wing politicians and intellectuals and founded the *Ligue française pour l'accession des indigènes de Madagascar aux droits de citoyens français,* a body whose title bore witness to a fundamentally moderate and assimilationist form of nationalism. Returning to Madagascar, Ralaimongo joined forces with a number of Malagasy and European sympathizers. In 1929 the group staged a mass demonstration in Tananarive to which the authorites retorted with arrests, prison sentences, and banishments. The era of the Popular Front in the late 1930's brought a slightly more liberal climate, but no really serious attempt was made to devise an institutional structure for the expression of Malagasy hopes and grievances. The governors who succeeded Galliéni were for the most part able and energetic administrators but they lacked, as the French historian, Hubert Deschamps, himself a former administrator in Madagascar, has remarked, the great proconsul's capacity "to meditate on the evolution of the *Grande Ile* in a broad historical perspective," their policy was without political and sociological dimensions, and they showed themselves "singularly myopic" to the changes taking place around them.[5] The consequences of this myopia were brutally revealed in the rebellion of 1947.

A combination of circumstances served to create the conditions that made revolt possible. There was the blow to French prestige when the colony was attacked and overrun by British forces in 1942. (The British justified their invasion on the grounds that the pro-Vichy administration might provide bases for Japanese submarines.) There were the inevitable economic hardships associated with the war—inflation, black marketeering, and the levies imposed on local products. Then, immediately after the war, came the period of liberalization associated with the constitutional reforms that allowed Madagascar to send deputies to the French parliament. In 1946, the country's first national political party, the *Mouvement Démocratique de la Rénovation Malgache* (MDRM), was founded: based on Imerina, it gained a wide measure of support in other areas, though the French attempted to counter its influence by encouraging a rival non-Merina organization, the *Parti des Déshérités de Madagascar*. Thus the revolt which broke out in March 1947 must be put in the context of waning French prestige, considerable economic grievances, and mounting political excitement.

The organization of the revolt still remains something of a mystery. It is clear that there must have been a considerable amount of planning for attacks were launched on army barracks, administrative posts, and police stations simultaneously at a number of different places. It would seem that at least three distinct groups played an active part in the rebellion—ex-soldiers recently returned from France, members of the traditional priesthood—"witchdoctors and sorcerers" in European parlance—who resented the steady erosion of the old ways of life, and a small group of extremist nationalists; but the individual leaders of the revolt have never been satisfactorily identified. Violence was confined to a limited area, about one-sixth of the entire island, being concentrated in the districts around Tamatave on the east coast. Significantly, these were districts which contained a large number of European plantations. For the French the revolt presented a more serious threat to their authority than any they had had to meet in their colonial empire in Africa since the Algerian rising in Kabylia in 1871. The Malagasy rebels were miserably equipped, but they made up for their lack of modern arms by the fanaticism with which they charged French posts, their morale raised by their priests who assured them that the bullets of the enemy would be turned into drops of water. A year and a half of hard fighting was needed to suppress the rebellion. One hundred-forty Frenchmen and 16,000 Malagasy were killed by the rebels. Rebel losses have never been satisfactorily assessed, estimates ranging from 10,000 to 80,000 dead. As with the *Maji-Maji* rebellion in German East Africa forty years earlier, starvation and sheer misery appear to have been a far more frequent cause of death than the bullets of the colonial forces.

In suppressing the rebellion the French had also banned the MDRM, whose leaders were accused of complicity in the revolt. Consequently, throughout the early 1950's Malagasy nationalism remained without an effective voice. Indeed, the island might hardly have gained independence, had it not been caught up in the tide of decolonization that affected all the French colonies in Africa. When in the late 1950's Malagasy nationalists were free to express their views, a new political pattern emerged. As a result of the introduction of universal suffrage, it was no longer possible for the Merina to dominate local politics, and power passed to a largely non-Merina party, the *Parti Social Démocratique* whose leader, Philibert Tsiranana, came from Majunga on the west coast, and whose supporters were drawn from the rural masses. The main opposition party, the AKFM—the initials stand for the Malagasy words used to translate the party's original name, *Congres pour l'Indépendence de Madagascar,* was radical-Marxist in its ideology and could count on considerable support in the towns but was able to win only a handful of seats in the national assembly.

Along with most other French African territories, Madagascar slid smoothly into independence in 1960. The country's record in its first decade of independence proved exceptionally peaceful and uneventful. Tsiranana and the PSD remained firmly in power. Modest progress was made in the field of economic development, and the government pursued a cautious foreign policy, maintaining cordial relations with France, participating in the various interterritorial organizations of francophone Africa and going further than most African states in its willingness to establish links with South Africa. A new stage in Malagasy history opened unexpectedly in May, 1972 when Tananarive was the scene of violent riots in which both university students and urban workers participated. The president was forced to hand over executive powers to the senior army officer, General Gabriel Ramanantsoa. Five months later the general was elected president after a referendum.

▲▼ THE MASCARENES: MAURITIUS AND RÉUNION

In the middle of the nineteenth century the two major islands of the Mascarenes—British Mauritius and French Réunion—could be regarded as among the most valuable colonial possessions of their respected metropolitan powers. Both islands contained a substantial population of white settlers. (In 1875 there were far more Europeans in Mauritius alone than in the whole of tropical Africa.) Their contribution to European trade through the production of sugar was far greater than that of almost all the other economies of Africa. And they occupied a position of considerable strategic importance in the Indian Ocean. As the nineteenth century advanced, however, both islands were to find themselves deprived of much of their importance in the eyes of the outside world. Rapidly mounting European interest in the interior of Africa diverted attention from two such small, remote and peripheral possessions. Sugar, virtually their only product, was faced with growing competition, partly as a result of the development of a sugar-beet industry in Europe. And with the opening of the Suez Canal far fewer ships had cause to make use of the excellent facilities of Port Louis, the capital of Mauritius, or to call at the difficult landing places of harborless Réunion.

This decline in relative importance was accompanied by a process of increasing differentiation between the two islands. Their early history had been remarkably similar. Totally uninhabited at the time of their discovery by European navigators in the sixteenth century, both islands owed their later prosperity to French enterprise. The Dutch who occupied Mauritius in the seventeenth century failed completely to make a success of their settlement, but by introducing African slave labor the French were able to lay the foundations of a plantation economy and in so doing to create a social structure identical to that found in contemporary European settlements in the Caribbean.

During the Napoleonic wars Mauritius provided the French with an excellent base for attacks on British shipping in the Indian Ocean. The British retaliated by occupying the Mascarenes in 1810 and insisted on retaining Mauritius when peace was concluded five years later. But a modest British colonial presence in the island in no way affected the privileged social position of the French plantocracy, and French culture continued to play an important part in the intellectual development of the island. Far more important for the future of Mauritius was the decision made in 1834—the year in which slavery was finally abolished in all British possessions—to bring in indentured labor from India. Between 1834 and 1907, 450,000 Indian immigrants entered Mauritius, and a large number of them decided to make the island their home. Already by 1875 two-thirds of the island's population were of Indian descent, the remainder being either Europeans or "Creoles," descendents of the African slave population. Réunion, too, turned to India for assistance in meeting its labor requirements, but the period of Indian immigration was very much shorter, lasting only from 1861 to 1885, and the number of Indian immigrants did not exceed 100,000. To a remarkable extent Réunion's substantial Indian minority was gradually assimilated into the rest of the population. In part this process of assimilation has been ascribed to the work of Catholic missionaries, but it must also have been rendered possible by the fact that Réunion possessed a very substantial white population. Taking the last censuses in which whites were counted separately, Mauritius had 8,000 whites out of a total population of 91,000 in 1830, Réunion 44,000 out of 110,000 in 1848. In both islands the slave population was drawn from many different areas —Madagascar, East Africa, Ethiopia, even parts of West Africa—but, as in the West Indies, the slaves rapidly lost most aspects of their original culture and adopted the French *patois* known as Creole as their *lingua franca*. In Mauritius the Indian population was sufficiently numerous not only to maintain intact its own languages, religions, and customs but also to give a tone to the whole island. In Réunion, on the other hand, only two relatively small groups, the Chinese and the Indian Muslims from Gujerat—both also found in Mauritius—succeeded in resisting the tide of assimilation.

Politically, the two islands showed both similarities and differences. In both a great deal of political power lay for a long time in the hands of the old French landed families. Under the Third Republic Réunion was granted the right to send two deputies and a senator to the French parliament. Elections, conducted on the basis of a fairly wide franchise, were noted for their violence and corruption: in 1914, for example, as many as 12 people were killed and 150 wounded in election riots. Mauritius obtained its own legislative council in 1886 with eight officials, nine nominated and ten elected members, but property and income qualifications limited the vote to less than 2 percent of the total population. The first sign of change came in 1936 when a Creole doctor, Maurice Crué, founded the island's first political party, the Mauritius Labour Party, and began vigorously to express the many grievances felt by Creoles and Indians working on the sugar plantations. In 1948 the British government introduced a new constitution which provided for an enlarged legislative council with a majority of elected members and gave the vote to all who could pass a simple test of literacy. The new constitution inaugurated a peaceful revolution by transferring political power from the Franco-Mauritian oligarchy to the Hindu Indian community. The most prominent Indian politician, Dr. Seewoosagur Ramgoolam, had been an early member of the Labour Party, took over the leadership from Crué, and gave the party an increasingly Indian complexion. The path of constitutional advance was the conventional one for British colonial territories, though the pace was somewhat slower than in most British African territories, for Mauritius did not achieve final independence until 1968. In large part this delay was due to a bitter struggle which developed in the mid-1960's when the Franco-Mauritians with Creole support founded the *Parti Mauricien,* raised as their battle-cry the need to resist "Hindu domination," put forward the slogan, "Independence Means Starvation," and and spoke in favor of some form of continued association with Britain. Communal violence broke out on a number of occasions. In a bid to check communalism, the island's leading politicians came together a year after independence to form a nationl coalition under the leadership of the veteran Ramgoolam.

In the meantime, Réunion, in common with some of the islands of the French West Indies, had followed the opposite path of total assimilation with the metropolis, the island being given the status of a department of France under the constitution of 1946. Departmental status carried with it many tangible advantages: increasing French subsidies, a vast expansion of the local bureaucracy, with the expatriate Frenchmen who filled the top posts becoming a new and invigorating element in the local population, and easy access to France for those who wished to emigrate. The new arrangments gave to Réunion a prosperity such as it had never known before. Between 1880 and 1920, the island's population had actually declined from 210,000 to 173,000. Between the two world wars a rapid expansion in sugar production brought a measure of relief to the old landed families, but the lot of the mass of the population remained that of abject poverty. Much poverty still remains, but the 1950's brought in a visible improvement in the standard of living.

Nevertheless, for all the improvements that have taken place in their social services, both islands remained faced with a singularly daunting future. In few parts of the world does the problem of over-population present itself so starkly. Between 1880 and 1940 the population of Mauritius increased at the rate of no more than 0.5 percent per annum, while that of Réunion was a mere 10,000 more in 1940 than it had been in 1880. Only after World War II, largely as a result of an effective campaign to eradicate malaria, did population begin to leap forward, rising in Réunion from 220,000 in 1946 to 450,000 in 1970, by which year Mauritius had passed the 800,000 mark and possessed a population density of more than 1,000 people to the square mile. The social problems produced by population pressure were aggravated by the economic difficulties associated with monoculture and geographical isolation. In spite of strenuous efforts to diversify their economies, sugar still accounted for more than nine-tenths of their total exports, while the chances of promoting effective industrialization seemed to be ruled out by the islands' remoteness from world markets. Yet for all their problems, both islands have a lesson to teach the rest of the world. Within their narrow confines men and women of many different cultures, European, African, Malagasy, Indian, and Chinese, have learned to live and work harmoniously together. Here in these remote Indian Ocean islands is a microcosm of the world community.

CHAPTER X

The Process of Change in Modern African History

▲▼ THE ANALYSIS OF CHANGE

It is time to draw the threads together. To present the history of Africa in terms of a series of rigidly compartmentalized regional histories is to lay oneself open to the charge of ignoring the measure of unity implicit in the concept of a continent. Yet to what extent is it really possible to talk about African unity, when deeper study serves only to emphasize the continent's diversity? No doubt it may be said that all African peoples have shared a common experience in the course of the last century —the experience of conquest and alien rule followed, for most peoples, by liberation and regained independence. Yet the pattern of colonial conquest varied greatly from area to area and the experience of colonial rule was not the same for all the subject peoples. One might indeed assert as a rule of conquest situations that the larger the number of alien intruders, the more unpleasant life is likely to become for the subject population. In some parts of Africa—the Sudan, for example, or Northern Nigeria—the mesh of alien domination lay relatively lightly on local peoples. In others—such as Algeria or South Africa—the establishment of a large alien settler community was the cause of immense suffering for the defeated and the dispossessed. Again, liberation and the growth of local nationalism were processes that presented different patterns from one country to another. Moreover, to think of African history only in terms of colonialism and nationalism is to ignore many other aspects of the past in which purely political considerations are of minor or even negligible importance.

Only by thinking of history as a process of change can one find a unifying theme at once dynamic and comprehensive. And this is a theme which serves to link the history of Africa with that of other continents, with the history of mankind as a whole. Thus interpreted the history of Africa presents itself as basically no different from that of any other continent. Environments differ, the rate of change varies from society to society, some societies are clearly more complex, some cultures more elaborate than others. But the basic elements in any human situation— the relationship between man and his environment, and between man and man—always remain the same.

In *Africa to 1875,* the companion volume to the present study, an attempt was made to analyze the process of change. It seems worthwhile ending this lengthy essay on the history of a continent by returning to this analysis, for it was designed as a coherent and comprehensive framework in which could be set the varied phenomena of the past so as to reveal their interrelationship. Such an analysis may also serve to suggest reasoned lines of speculation about the future.

In the analysis of change one may begin by making a distinction between the *manifestations* of change and the *forces* making for change. Change manifests itself in many different fields—in natural objects, in manufactured objects, in techniques, in language and literature, in patterns of settlement, in communications, in institutions, and in modes of thought. Manifestation may take the form of innovation, of adaptation or of destruction. But simply to observe the manifestations of change tells one nothing of the way in which change occurs, of the forces making for innovation or destruction. The forces that serve to shape the development of social groups may be distinguished under six different headings: alterations in the natural environment; the pressures caused by the growth and movement of population; the stimulus of intercourse; the impact of ideas; the peaceful pursuit of well-being by individuals and social groups; and the violent pursuit of well-being. These manifestations and forces of change must now be illustrated with examples chosen from the last century of African history.

▲▼ THE MANIFESTATIONS OF CHANGE

Natural Objects

Measured in terms of geological time, one hundred years is but a moment. Yet there has probably never been a century in which the face of Africa has been so greatly changed as that covered by the present study. Many African landscapes have been transformed. In areas of high rainfall man has destroyed much of the original forest cover, while the widespread practice of bush-firing has served steadily to erode the forest fringes. In many parts of equatorial Africa the removal of the original vegetation has led to the destruction of the humus as a result of soil erosion. Elsewhere in the savanna belt, on the grassy steppes of East Africa, or on the South African veld, bush-firing and overgrazing have combined to produce a serious impoverishment of the soil in many areas. The large-scale exploitation of Africa's mineral resources is a very recent development, dating back in some parts of the continent no more than ten or twenty years. Clearly, Africa's total mineral resources have not yet been fully and adequately charted. Equally clearly, Africa cannot escape the problems that derive from the accelerating consumption of natural resources. But the most dramatic maifestation of man's destructive impact on the natural order is to be seen in the steady diminution of Africa's fauna. The continent still remains the world's greatest reservoir for the major wild animals. But African wildlife decreases rapidly from year to year, and in the course of the last century some species have become entirely extinct.

But if man has destroyed a great deal of the natural environment, he has also added greatly to it. The diffusion of useful crops from other continents—a process which probably began with the introduction of wheat and barley into Lower Egypt in the sixth millennium B.C.—has continued more vigorously than ever before. Many African landscapes have been transformed as a result of these innovations. New trees, such as the Indian mango or the Australian eucalyptus, new flowering shrubs such as hibiscus or bougainvillea, the latter of Oceanic origin, new cash crops, cocoa from South America, sisal from Mexico, tea from India, have been introduced. Older established innovations such as maize, manioc, or cotton have spread to new areas. And the work of the plant-breeder has led to the development of many improved strains. There have been changes too in the character of Africa's domestic animals, with white settlers playing a leading part in the introduction of new breeds of horses, cattle, or sheep.

Another manifestation of change which should be considered under the heading of "natural objects" is in the changing pattern of sickness and disease. Every disease has its own history, a history which must be largely concerned with the variations in its distribution from period to period. A wide range of diseases—malaria, sleeping sickness, yellow fever, smallpox and others—are endemic to the continent. But their distribution has changed in the course of the past century. The greater freedom of movement made possible by the establishment of the colonial peace and the construction of more efficient forms of communication played a considerable part in the rapid diffusion of sleeping sickness, a disease which caused great affliction to certain tropical African communities. In Uganda, for example, 10 percent of the entire population fell victim to the ravages of sleeping-sickness in the first decade of the twentieth century. Increasing contact with the outside world and greater internal mobility led to the introduction and diffusion of other diseases by which Africans appear to have been little afflicted in the past. Syphilis is in this category. New social conditions also led to the emergence of diseases previously little noted in Africa. Thus many newly created urban centers began to give evidence of an alarmingly high incidence of tuberculosis. Some outbreaks of diseases of alien origin reached epidemic proportions. Particularly serious was the great influenza epidemic of 1919–20 which caused deaths running into tens of thousands in many African countries. Hardly less serious in their impact on the lives of many communities were the diseases that affected domestic animals. The great rinderpest epidemic that swept through eastern and southern Africa in the 1890's caused terrible suffering to many pastoral peoples. Almost equally harmful were certain plant diseases. The ravages of "swollen shoot," a virus carried by the mealie bug which attacks and eventually kills cocoa trees had a far from insignificant bearing on the political and economic life of Ghana in the years immediately preceding independence. Man has countered the spread of disease partly by the introduction of artificially manufactured prophylactics, partly by direct attack on the vectors of disease. Thus certain diseases, like certain animals, have almost disappeared from areas in which they were once endemic.

Manufactured Objects

The expansion of trade and the development of industry have led to a massive increase in the number and variety of the manufactured objects available to the peoples of Africa. Household utensils made from wood, grass, leather, or clay have been superceded by manufactured objects of metal and plastic—tin basins, enamel pots, plastic containers, and so on. New forms of furniture based on European models—chairs, tables, wooden chests, iron bedsteads—have replaced or supplemented the sparse furnishing of the past. New materials have been utilized in the construction of houses: concrete blocks replace dried mud, thatch gives way to corrugated iron, window frames are built into previously blank walls. In clothing too there have been striking changes: European-style coats, shirts, trousers, and dresses, or, alternatively, as with the long gowns of Muslim Africans, clothes still cut in the traditional style but made from imported rather than from locally manufactured material. Modern African dress presents many fascinating sartorial variations: the meticulous formality of the Liberian elite, the elegant finery of the Northern Nigerian aristocracy, the Maoist rig of radical politicians, the jeans and flowery shirts of the emancipated young.

One may point to many other innovations in the field of manufactured objects. New tools: the saw, the plane, the screwdriver to supplement or replace the older tools of African craftsmen. New foodstuffs and beverages: bread made from imported flour, condensed milk, tea, beer, whisky, Coca-Cola. New forms of transportation: bicycles, cars, trucks, trains—all serving to eliminate the use of human porterage or of pack-animals. And many other useful innovations—pencils, cheap paper, patent medicines, paraffin lamps, electric flashlights—one has only to wander around any large African market to realize the extraordinary variety of objects available for those who can afford to purchase them. And in most of Africa the very objects used as the medium of exchange—the metal coin, the paper banknote—represent yet further examples of novelty.

But the traditional crafts have not yet disappeared. All over Africa pottery is still made by means of a technique that has changed little over the centuries. A variety of useful objects—bowls, platters, bottles, wall-plaques—are fashioned from the gourd or calabash. Cloth of great durability is woven on narrow looms. Grass is platted into mats or screens. Habitations, sometimes dark and squalid, sometimes clean and elegant, are erected using only locally available materials. Leather or animal skins are used for simple forms of covering, for girdles or for capes. For many communities the basic forms of diet have changed little in the course of the century, except to suffer some impoverishment from the disappearance of many once common species of game animals.

Techniques

Of the new techniques to be acquired by African societies in the course of the past century perhaps the most important—for those to whom it came as an innovation—was that of literacy. In 1875 literacy in the Arabic script was a technique fairly widely diffused throughout Muslim Africa. The expansion of Christian missionary activity led to a simpler technique of literacy based on Roman letters being introduced to many preliterate societies. Literacy immensely increased the opportunities of intercourse with the outside world and provided a far more effective means of storing information than reliance on human memory. Christian missionaries were responsible for introducing many other new techniques—carpentry, printing, accountancy, dressmaking, and improved forms of agriculture. With the expansion of European forms of education an ever increasing number of Africans were brought into contact with a range of techniques which steadily widened as the educational structure developed. In the last decades of the nineteenth century professional training in such fields as law or medicine was available only for those Africans whose particularly intimate contact with Europeans, often as a result of education at a mission school, provided the measure of support needed for obtaining entrance to centers of higher education overseas. The "been-tos" (the vivid term coined in West Africa in the 1950's to describe those who had "been to" an educational institution overseas) were drawn from a strictly limited range of countries, notably Egypt, South Africa, Sierra Leone, and the Gold Coast. By the 1960's, however, institutions of higher education had been founded in almost every country in the continent. (In 1945 there were no more than a dozen universities in Africa, only one of which was in tropical Africa; by 1972, the number of African universities or university colleges exceeded fifty.) At the same time, many thousands of Africans were provided with the opportunity of receiving some part of their education overseas. But formal schooling was not the only channel available for the transmission of new techniques. The conscript from Algeria who learned during his military service how to drive and maintain a truck, the Nigerian clerk who became familiar with commercial practices while in the employment of a European firm, the Kikuyu agricultural foreman who picked up modern farming techniques by working for an enterprising European settler—men such as these might well end up as independent transport contractors, successful businessmen in their own right, or prosperous yeoman farmers and at the same time serve as transmitters of their newly acquired techniques to a wide circle of associates.

Yet, at the same time, there was a measure of loss with old crafts and skills disappearing as a result of changing conditions: the hunter affected by the annihilation of the larger game animals, the woodcarver deprived of his chiefly patron, the metal-worker or weaver reduced to penury by competition from cheap manufactured imports. But there could also be adaptation—the carver, for example, turning from his work on objects of ritual significance to production of curios for the tourist trade. This process might well be regarded as one of degeneration and decline. But with the growing appreciation of African craftsmanship in the outside world, a new role, more akin to that of the independent European artist, began to open for the African carver or sculptor. And the introduction of novel materials—canvas, oil paint, ink, and so on—provided exciting new possibilities manifested in the emergence of new schools of painting, handicrafts, and sculpture.

Language and Literature

No language is ever static. Every language is exposed to a double process of change—change in its own structure as a result of modifications in grammar or syntax or accretions in vocabulary, change also in its distribution, whether in the form of expansion or contraction. It is reasonable to assume that all African languages have changed in this manner, though the degree of change clearly varies from language to language. The major indigenous languages—Arabic, Afrikaans, Hausa, Swahili, and others—have been shaped in the course of the past century into more effective media for the expression of novel concepts. Thus enlarged, these local *linguae francae* have demonstrated their superiority over their linguistic rivals. The number of distinct languages spoken in Africa is estimated to exceed 700. Many of these languages possess a very limited circulation, and some must be on the point of disappearing completely. But the most profound manifestation of change in the field of language is to be found not in African languages themselves but in the introduction of new *linguae francae* of alien origin, especially English and French. The wide distribution of these two languages throughout the continent has made it possible for many African peoples to communicate far more easily both with their own African neighbors and with the outside world. Of all the legacies of the colonial period this is clearly one of the most valuable.

Literature is not dependent on literacy. Preliterate societies possess their own verbal art forms—fables, riddles, praise poems, and so on—handed down from generation to generation. But the introduction of the technique of literacy and later of printing immensely increased the possibilities of literary expression. Many African writers made their first venture into print in the pages of a local newspaper. The history of an indigenous press dates back in some parts of Africa—Egypt, Sierra Leone, and South Africa—to the second half of the nineteenth century. In Egypt and South Africa the beginning of a modern literary tradition can be traced back to the work of nineteenth-century writers. In Black Africa, on the other hand, significant achievement in literary forms based on European models—the novel, poetry, and drama—has been a far more recent phenomenon. In the cultural development of francophone Africa two seminal events occurred in the late 1940's: the publication of L. S. Senghor's *Anthologie de la nouvelle poésie nègre et malgache* and the foundation of the literary journal, *Présence Africaine*. In Anglophone Africa the first work to receive international recognition came from a group of Nigerian writers—Ekwensi, Achebe, Soyinka, Okigbo, and others—whose first works, published in the late 1950's or early 1960's, helped to stimulate literary activity in other former British territories. The 1960's also saw the emergence of vigorous literary movements in North Africa, in Angola, and Mozambique, and in South Africa—French and Arabic serving as the media of expression in the first area, Portuguese in the second, and English and Afrikaans in the third.

Settlement Patterns

One of the most easily visible manifestations of change in many parts of the continent has been the emergence of great new urban settlements of a kind entirely unknown in earlier periods. In 1875 Africa contained a number of relatively ancient cities. Cairo, Tunis, Fez, and Kano could trace their history back to the first millennium A.D. Other cities—including Marrakesh, Algiers, Timbuktu, Benin, and Kilwa—had grown to prominence in the first half of the second millennium A.D. The seventeenth century saw the foundation of three important European settlements—St. Louis, Luanda, and Cape Town. And by the middle of the nineteenth century it was possible to point, especially in West Africa, to other important centers of African origin, some, such as Sokoto or Ibadan, of recent creation, others such as Segu, Kumasi, or Lagos with more than a century of growth behind them. But, at the same time, there were still vast areas of the continent which contained not a single settlement that could be described as truly urban. The expansion of European power and influence in the last quarter of the nineteenth century transformed this situation. The European conquerors founded a number of entirely new settlements as administrative, commercial, and industrial centers: Casablanca, Salisbury, Léopoldville, Dakar, and Johannesburg all fall into this category. Alternatively, Europeans took over existing urban settlements and transformed them by grafting on new suburbs or rebuilding and improving the older sections. Algiers, Alexandria, Khartoum, Accra, Lagos, Douala, and Dar es-Salaam are among the cities where this process of modernization could be observed. During the first half of the twentieth century these new or transformed urban centers began to attract an increasing number of people from neighboring areas. The rate of growth was relatively modest in the first four decades of the century, but a rapid acceleration in the pace of urbanization occurred after World War II and was maintained throughout the 1950's and 1960's.

In the past Africa provided a number of striking examples of great urban centers experiencing a total decline. Thebes (Luxor), Cyrene, Carthage, Kumbi Saleh (the capital of ancient Ghana), Meroe, and Zimbabwe are to be counted among the world's lost cities. The process of urban decline has been less noticeable in the past century, although the political changes consequent on the European conquest led some centers —such as Abomey or Sokoto—which had previously been the capitals of major African states to suffer a decline in importance.

Changes in settlement patterns were not confined to urban centers. With the establishment of the colonial *pax* the need to choose a place for settlement with a view to its defensive possibilities disappeared. In areas such as the Northern Nigerian plateau, the people of minor polities, long accustomed to suffer the raids of their more powerful neighbors, could now be encouraged to leave their inconvenient hilltop settlements and move down to the more fertile plains. The expansion of communications, of roads and railroads, also affected patterns of settlement, with villages springing up spontaneously at important crossroads or around railroad stations. And all the time, with the gradual increase in population and the emergence of new economic opportunities, that movement of pioneering which can be traced back to the earliest stages of human history was taking place, with groups of kinsmen hiving off from older communities to found new settlements in the virgin bush or forest. The cocoa farmers of Southern Ghana, the groundnut farmers of Senegal, the Cokwe elephant hunters and rubber tappers of the Angola-Congo borderlands provide vigorous examples of this process.

Another innovation in the pattern of settlement could be seen in the farms and plantations established by intrusive groups of Europeans. The vineyards of Algeria or the Cape, the palm-oil plantations of the Congo, the dairy farms of Kenya, the tea estates of Malawi, the cattle ranches of the Transvaal—alien domains such as these could be regarded as the manifestations of a profound change affecting both landscape and society. The plantation village, the farm-workers' quarters, the cluster of huts of a squatter community—these represented types of rural settlement whose novel features were easily apparent when set against the pattern of older hamlets or villages. Other groups of Europeans also had a profound influence on local settlement patterns. Mission stations sometimes acquired populations running into several hundreds: with their churches, schools, workshops, and farm lands they too presented entirely novel types of settlement. During the same period, European miners found it necessary to lay out camps for their workers. These rudimentary industrial sites sometimes emerged as the nuclei of substantial towns.

Other changes in rural settlement patterns were the product of government action. Resettlement schemes involving the removal of local populations from areas known to be particularly badly affected by diseases such as sleeping-sickness; "villagization," the transfer of people from scattered hamlets to centrally located villages, adopted as a counterinsurgency measure as in Kenya during the Mau Mau rebellion, but favored in more peaceful circumstances as the most practical means of making social services available to rural populations; agricultural projects associated with large-scale plans for irrigation, as in the Gezira of the Sudan—developments such as these profoundly affected the lives of those caught up in them.

Communications

In the middle of the nineteenth century, men undertaking journeys in Africa—traders, court-messengers, hunters, porters, pilgrims—moved along bush paths or bridle tracks, carrying their loads on their heads, driving pack-animals or, in the case of the European farmers of South Africa, using lumbering wagons drawn by teams of oxen. In 1875 the continent possessed no more than a few hundred miles of railroad and hardly any roads suitable for wheeled traffic. In those limited parts of the continent with access to navigable rivers or lakes, water transport was based on a wide variety of river-craft, but there was little coastal traffic. Port facilities were poor or nonexistent—on some stretches of coast, most notably in West Africa, ocean-going ships had to anchor off shore and transfer their cargoes to surf-boats to be landed on open beaches.

The communications system of Africa was revolutionized by technological innovations of alien origin, the steamship, the railroad engine, the motor car, the airplane, together with the various systems— submarine cable, telephone, radio—devised for transmitting the written or the spoken word over long distances. Steamship connections between European and African ports had already been established by 1875. With expanding trade the tonnage of ships visiting African ports steadily increased. This naturally led to a demand for improved port facilities, and all the colonial powers devoted a great deal of attention to the construction of modern wharves designed to facilitate the handling of cargo and passengers. In some territories it proved necessary to lay out entirely new ports, some of which developed into major urban centers: Dakar, Tema (Ghana), and Port Harcourt (Nigeria) fall into this category. Elsewhere, older ports, such as Algiers, Lagos, or Mombasa, were expanded and modernized. At an early stage in their penetration of the interior Europeans made use, both for military and for commercial purposes, of iron-clad ships propelled by steam on all the navigable rivers and lakes of the continent.

Railroads played a vital part in the first development plans prepared by the colonial powers for their newly conquered territories. In many parts of the continent the construction of railroads represented a truly heroic achievement, a cooperative venture between Europeans, Africans, and—in the case of the Uganda railroad—Asians, and one that sometimes involved a heavy loss of life. Some of Africa's great railroads were conceived with strategic objectives in mind, but all of them came to serve a commercial purpose, making possible the export of bulk products—copper, cotton, groundnuts—on a scale quite inconceivable in an earlier age when head porterage, cumbersome, slow and expensive, was the only form of transportation. Thus the building of such lines as those between Djibouti and Addis Ababa, Lagos and Kano, Benguela and Katanga, and Johannesburg and Lourenço Marques must be regarded as major events in the development of the areas concerned.

Not until the 1920's did motor transport begin to develop on a substantial scale. The motor car was a much more flexible instrument than the railroad engine, but it was greatly restricted by the absence of motorable roads. The elaborate system of wheeled traffic developed in Europe in the eighteenth and nineteenth centuries—the stage coaches, the farm wagons, and so on—made necessary the improvement of the bridle paths and farm tracks of an earlier age. In most parts of Africa wheeled traffic was entirely unknown during that period, and a network of roads had to be constructed from scratch. Not until after World War II could the governments of many African territories afford to devote much of their resources to road construction, but in the development plans of the 1950's and 1960's the improvement and expansion of the road system came very high on the list of priorities.

Again, it was not until after World War II that many parts of Africa came to be affected by the emergence of air transport and the improvement in systems of telecommunication. As late as the 1960's there must still have been millions of Africans who had never used a telephone, but there was one innovation which caught on with amazing rapidity in the 1960's—the transistor radio. Of all the forms of communication devised by man, the transistor, cheap, portable, easily maintained, may well be regarded as the most effective instrument for breaking down the intellectual isolation of remote communities.

Many of the new lines of communication—the roads and railroads —ran along older tracks or trade routes. But in one major area the new developments brought about a profound reorientation. For a thousand years the Sahara had been spanned by caravan routes that represented perhaps the most important commercial arteries in the entire continent. The development of West African ports and railroads created a situation in which most sections of the old caravan trade became uneconomical, and many of the old routes fell into disuse. But it would be wrong to talk of a complete abandonment of trans-Saharan communications. The introduction of the Land Rover made it easier for men to move in the desert than it had ever been before, and it is far from inconceivable that the Sahara may one day be spanned by broad arterial highways and trans-Saharan routes assume again something of the importance they enjoyed in earlier centuries.

Institutions

Every society is made up of a complex, interlocking mesh of institutions. Institutions vary in size: at one extreme the nuclear family embracing no more than a handful of individuals, at the other the nation-state with claims on the allegiance of populations to be numbered in millions. Institutions also vary in function: some exist primarily to serve political ends, others promote their members' well-being through spiritual, intellectual, social, or economic means. When institutions cease to fulfil a useful function, they break up or are destroyed. Others represent innovations introduced by peoples of other cultures. Yet others survive from generation to generation while experiencing profound inner transformations.

The family is the one universal institution. Yet patterns of family structure or kinship relationships vary subtly from society to society. This makes it hard to generalize about the changes that have taken place in African families in the course of the last century. But clearly older patterns—the polygamous household, the extended family in which many individuals are bound together by mutual obligations— have been profoundly modified by the transformation of subsistence economies, the greater opportunities for mobility, and the introduction of new concepts of family relationships based on alien models. In Algeria, Northern Rhodesia, and Nyasaland, together with parts of South Africa and the Belgian Congo, where the demands of the colonial regime produced for a time a high incidence of labor migration, a definite impoverishment of family life occurred. In the cities, too, family relationships often contracted when exposed to the pressure exerted by urban living—traditional forms of hospitality eroded by cramped accommodation, the need to purchase food, and the counterattraction of consumer goods. But it would be a mistake to assume that there is some sort of natural progression from the extended to the nuclear family. The currents are far more complex. While some individuals crave the wider freedom the nuclear family makes possible, others appreciate the warmth and security of the extended family.

It is a little easier to generalize about innovations in the sphere of political institutions. In 1875 Africa was divided into a very large number of independent polities. Some African communities lived in highly-organized states, with an elaborate system of authority extending over a considerable area. Many others were familiar only with stateless polities as represented by autonomous villages, by "clans" or "tribes" of nomads, or by bands of hunters. Over all these polities there was established, as a result of the European conquest, the novel structure of the bureaucratic state with its clearly defined frontiers, its more effective machinery for accumulating resources, and its multiplicity of distinct departments designed to enable it to intervene in many different aspects of the lives of its subjects. The extent to which the new type of state did, in fact, choose to intervene varied from territory to territory and from period to period. There were considerable variations too in the reactions of the rulers of the new states—the administrative officials of the colonial powers—to the older African polities within their area. Some African states—among them the Tukulor empire on the Upper Niger, the Zulu kingdom, and the Mahdist theocracy in the Sudan— were completely shattered or dismembered in the process of conquest. Others—among them the khedivate of Egypt, the sultanate of Morocco, and the kingdom of Buganda—were preserved by the alien rulers. In some territories, especially those where the colonial power pursued a policy of indirect rule, older polities became the basis for new systems of local government. In others, where greater emphasis was laid on direct administration, little attention was paid to the older structures, except at the lowest level. The change from colonial rule to independence brought about no really fundamental break in this pattern of development. Local men took over the offices vacated by the alien rulers, but their preoccupations were basically the same—to maintain the administrative structure needed to gird together a heterogeneous collection of communities possessing few natural bonds of unity.

After a decade of independence it became evident that a novel form of political institution—the political party—was hardly to be regarded as possessing an enduring significance. In most parts of Africa political parties served a double purpose: when organized on a mass scale they provided a highly effective instrument of protest; at the same time, they offered the only means by which the members of a group could stake out a claim for the spoils of office. In the period of decolonization political parties were formed either on the basis of ethnicity or of ideology. With the achievement of independence, parties tended to lose their rationale. Victorious parties merged themselves with the state machinery to create the one-party state; the defeated rapidly disintegrated. The late 1960's saw the eclipse of the professional politician in most parts of Africa. In Morocco and Ethiopia—significantly, the two African countries with the oldest unbroken indigenous tradition of monarchy— traditional rulers still maintained their prestige and exerted their power. In certain African countries outstanding leaders acquired the power and the prestige normally associated with monarchs and enjoyed reigns disturbed only by those conspiracies and protest movements from which no ruler can ever hope to be immune. Nasser of Egypt, Bourguiba of

Tunisia, Senghor of Senegal, Sékou Touré of Guinea, Houphouët-Boigny of the Ivory Coast, Kenyatta of Kenya, Nyerere of Tanzania, and Kaunda of Zambia, all achieved a position that may not unreasonably be described as monarchial. Elsewhere, notably in Ghana, Nigeria, and the Sudan, political leaders brought about their own downfall and were overthrown in coups led by army officers.

The creation of modern armies was a major institutional innovation brought about by the colonial powers. Some precolonial African states possessed substantial military forces: the Zulu, for example, built up a formidable war-machine, while the Ethiopians were well enough equipped to inflict a crushing defeat on the Italians in 1896. In general, however, precolonial African states lacked the resources needed to provide their armies with an adequate supply of modern weapons. The colonial powers made use of African troops from the start. Indeed, it would not be unreasonable to assert that most of Africa was in fact conquered by African armies stiffened and directed by a small cadre of white officers and N.C.O.'s. Though small in size—the armies of most independent African states numbered no more than a few thousand men —these tightly knit, efficiently organized institutions, usually possessing a near monopoly of the instruments of coercion, were well adapted to intervene in the political life of their respective countries, especially when the existing rulers, the politicians who had achieved power in the period of decolonization, showed signs of losing their grip. So it was hardly surprising to find in the decade after independence that a number of African countries saw the establishment of military regimes. But military regimes were far from monolithic: armies were riven by deep internal differences, army officers often assumed political power reluctantly and were glad to hand it over to civilian successors, and even military governments could not always hold out in the face of mass disapproval and protest.

The modern political institution created in every African country more important than the political party or the army was the central bureaucracy. Formed originally by the alien conquerors as an instrument for asserting their dominance over newly acquired territories, the bureaucracies, with their chain of command running in colonial days from the governor at the capital through the hierarchy of provincial commissioners or residents to the agents and district officers in the bush, came to exert an increasing influence on the mass of the population, an influence which usually tended to increase in the years after independence. For government offices were the places in which important decisions were taken, decisions about the amount and incidence of taxation, the provision of social services, the support to be given to projects for economic development, and so on. From a distance civil servants appeared as curiously anonymous individuals. Closer examination usually revealed that much could depend on the personality of a high official, the nature of his prejudices and enthusiasms. At first the new bureaucracies were extremely modest in size and scope, with officials often governing large districts single-handedly. But as African territories developed a cash economy, thus making it possible for governments to acquire more substantial revenue, so colonial bureaucracies began to ramify, establishing new departments with specialized functions. This process of growth and ramification also occurred at the level of local government, with the result that even quite modest local authorities came to have at their disposal a more abundant revenue and a larger staff of officials than many of the more substantial states of the precolonial period had ever had.

In the economic field a particularly striking innovation was the emergence of the large trading or mining company. This, too, was an innovation of alien origin, for local African entrepreneurs lacked the capital resources and the organizational experience needed to build up really large commercial undertakings. As in every other part of the world, a steady movement of absorption and amalgamation occurred, with smaller trading companies or mining concessions being taken over by larger and more dynamic businesses, a process well illustrated in the growth of the United Africa Company in West Africa or of the great gold mining combines of the Witwatersrand. From the start, many of the new alien governments were actively involved in economic undertakings; Léopold of the Belgians' Congo Free State provides the prime example of a state founded almost entirely for reasons of commercial profit. The systems of control devised by many colonial governments during World War II—particularly through the creation of various marketing boards—provided an effective machinery for intervention in major sectors of local economies. And, in the years after independence, many African governments pushed through measures of nationalization in their anxiety to ensure that the commanding heights of their economies should no longer be occupied by expatriate businessmen.

Those countries which experienced a rapid expansion in their economy also witnessed the creation of many other institutions whose functions were mainly economic in character—farmers' associations, cooperative societies, trade unions, and so on. Another important innovation in the field of economic institutions was the retail shop. In the past, buying and selling were activities confined to open markets, some permanent, the majority held at regular intervals. Markets still play a substantial role in the commercial life of most African countries, but retail shops and stores now serve to an increasing extent the same purpose. Throughout much of Africa the first shops were the creation of newcomers and aliens—Indians in East Africa, Syrians and Lebanese in West Africa, Greeks and Portuguese in parts of Equatorial Africa, supplemented in many areas by the agents of the great commercial companies. Urbanization naturally increased the opportunities for retail trading, and gradually—though in many areas not until the 1950's and 1960's—Africans began to take an active part in this sector of the economic life of their country.

In many African communities the new shops and the new government offices were often, in quite a literal sense, overshadowed by another type of institution, the church or the mosque. The spread of the two universalistic religions, Christianity and Islam, was a fruitful source of innovation in every part of the continent which felt their influence. Often, as in medieval Europe, the church was the largest building yet to be erected in a particular area. Both church and mosque became the focus for new sorts of communities, the congregations of the faithful. But there were obvious differences in the institutional structure of the two religions. Christianity was presented to Africa by the missionaries of many different denominations, often sharply divided one from another by fierce doctrinal disputes. This initial fragmentation was carried further with the establishment of indigenous churches, created by African Christians in reaction to the racist notions of certain European missionaries and to their ruthless denunciation of many revered traditional practices. Islam, too, had its divisions, which found institutional expression in the organization of *tariqas* or brotherhoods. But to the outside observer, Islam with its relatively simple ritual appeared almost monolithic in character. Moreover, being already well-established in many parts of Africa before the European intrusion of the latter half of the nineteenth century, it seemed a faith far less alien than Christianity and in many ways more tolerant of indigenous practices. But for the practitioners of the older religions of Africa, the local cults with their shrines and their multiplicity of gods and spirits, the steady expansion of Christianity and Islam meant, in the long run, the end of the old order. No doubt, as happened in Europe a thousand years earlier, something of the older religions would be incorporated in the ritual of the new faith; no doubt old cults would linger on for a time in many areas, but by the middle of the nineteenth century it seemed clear that the indigenous religions had been driven from their position of primacy in the lives of those whose fathers and grandfathers had been their devoted adherents.

With the new churches and mosques there came yet another new institution, the school. Both Christianity and Islam were religions based on a body of sacred literature. Fully to appreciate the meaning of the new faith, converts had to acquire the technique of literacy. Muslim education concentrated on passing on this technique often in a purely mechanical fashion, with students being required to memorize sections of the Koran in Arabic, a language with which they might otherwise be totally unfamiliar. But in its higher reaches a good Muslim education introduced the conscientious seeker after knowledge to a wide range of intellectual experiences in the fields of theology, law, literature, and history. The education provided by the Christian mission schools could offer at its best not only an introduction to many of the intellectual concepts of Western European culture but also an initiation in many practical skills. The educational work of the Christian missionaries was supplemented and in most territories eventually superceded by teachers in government service, with local educational structures steadily expanding as more revenue became available.

The new schools could be regarded as novel forms of organization, as formal education replaced the initiation ceremonies of older African communities. For those who found themselves uprooted from old-established patterns of life in rural communities, the first generation immigrants to the towns, other forms of social organization—tribal unions, *amicales* or friendly societies, literary societies, old boys' associations or sports clubs—came to provide an effective machinery for integration into a new pattern of life. Institutions such as these, though often based on alien models, were usually the product of indigenous initiative.

Modes of Thought

Every individual carries in his mind a set of concepts, generalizations, images, rules of conduct—a complex intermingling of mental processes or modes of thought. Clearly such modes are influenced partly by the character of the individual and by his hereditary endowments, partly by the environment and society in which he lives. Since environments and societies change, modes of thought change too. A modern generation will not view the world, using that term both in its narrow territorial sense and in the wider meaning of an extra-terrestial universe, in the same way as earlier generations have done. Rules of conduct designed to establish patterns of relationships between the old and the young, between subordinates and those in authority, differ from one society to another. Conventional notions of human destiny, the answers given to the great questions of life and death, vary from generation to generation and from culture to culture. It would be a useful exercise for the historian to construct a series of models of the characteristic modes of thought of the societies he studies and to note the changes that occur over a period of many generations. When dealing with a continent made up of many thousands of different societies such an approach is hardly practicable, but it is at least possible to point out in an impressionistic way some of the great changes in modes of thought experienced by most African societies in the course of the past century.

In 1875 most African communities lived an extremely isolated existence. In no case perhaps could one speak of total isolation: there must have been some form of intercourse with neighboring communities. But the appearance of strangers from farther afield must have been a rare event for communities lying far from the main arteries of trade. Isolation of such a nature was, of course, a common enough experience for peasant communities the world over. For preliterate communities caught in such a narrow territorial straitjacket, notions such as those of the terrestial globe, of oceans and continents, of the political divisions created by the European partition were entirely meaningless. Gradually the processes of education and of self-education began to erode the barriers. Geography lessons in village schools, encounters with strangers, journeys to towns, military service, courses of higher education overseas—by means such as these the concept of an infinitely wider and more complex world began to percolate down to communities whose earlier sense of terrestial space had covered a radius of no more than a few score miles.

Awareness of a wider world was accompanied by other concepts. Old accepted laws of causation came under attack: diseases which had previously been ascribed to some malignant spiritual or human agency were shown by modern science to be the product of natural causes. Yet old habits of thought die hard. The belief in witchcraft and magic is still rife in contemporary Africa, with many Western-educated Africans hovering uneasily between the two worlds of ancient magic and of modern science. In the same way, many recent converts to Christianity or Islam found it prudent to continue to render some form of offering to the ancient gods of their land.

Hardly less profound in their impact on older patterns of thought than the new religions and the new science were the new political concepts which developed in the period of colonial rule. In the past, most men were conscious of their obligations to their immediate kin and also in many areas of their allegiance to some local ruler or chief. The new political structures erected by the colonial powers also involved new sets of allegiances. Africans in official service were encouraged to develop a sense of loyalty and devotion to their distant metropolis, even at the expense of turning their backs on their own culture and society. Migrants to the new towns came to develop a certain sense of fraternity

with neighbors from different home-villages, people who would otherwise have been regarded as strangers but with whom they now shared
the bond of a common culture, a process that led to the emergence of a
spirit of ethnic solidarity or "tribalism" of a kind that few African peoples had known in the past. Above the concept of tribalism there
emerged the even more novel concept of nationalism, the idea that all
the peoples living within the confines of the most artificially defined African territory were bound together by certain almost spiritual ties.
Thus there developed a series of interlocking circles of allegiance, to
the kin group, to the local community, to the "tribe," and to the nation.
Often these allegiances appeared to conflict one with another, presenting
tough moral choices for the individual and hard political problems for
the leaders of larger groups. Much of what was described as nepotism
or corruption was the product of these conflicting loyalties, civil servants under pressure to observe the obligations of kinship making appointments that should have been more objectively considered or dis-
bursing to kinsmen money that legally belonged to that amorphous
entity "the general public."

New allegiances were accompanied by new patterns of relationship.
The term "class," as used in the Marxist sense, was one that could not
properly be applied to most African societies in the past. Stateless societies were usually egalitarian in character, and even in many demi-
states there was often little difference in wealth between a chief and his
most prominent followers. Only in the more elaborate states was it possible to note the emergence of a distinct aristocracy, and even here ties
of patronage and clientship served to cut across social barriers. The European conquest was followed in every part of Africa by the formal abolition of the status of slavery: gradually new opportunities of employment and greater mobility enabled many individuals to free themselves
from the disabilities of a servile position. At the same time, the development of European education led to the emergence of a new social
group, usually described as "the Western-educated elite" whose members were distinguished from their contemporaries initially not by
wealth or rank but by the prestige attached to the possession of the new
techniques introduced by the white man. With the advent of independence many members of this group were able to move into the posts vacated by the retiring colonial officials and so acquire salaries and other
emoluments that served to give them almost the status of plutocrats
when their income was compared with that of the mass of their countrymen. Yet even in modern African societies the familiar ties of patronage and clientship could still be noted, serving as they did to channel
some of the wealth acquired by a successful politician, businessman, or

civil servant into the hands of more needy kinsmen. Yet the cultural differences between the rich and the poor were now more sharply defined than they had been in the past, and the sense of division was made all the harsher in those countries of Southern Africa where all the most lucrative posts were kept as the monopoly of a single racial group.

In the past, most African societies, as indeed most societies in Asia and in Europe, were largely gerontocratical in character, decision-making posts being reserved for the elderly and the experienced. The spate of new techniques upset this pattern. Many of the alien conquerors —the proconsuls of the first generation of imperialism—were youngish men in their thirties and forties. And though the established colonial services came to lay great stress on seniority based on length of service, the successors to the colonial regimes, the successful politicians of the age of triumphant nationalism, were also youngish men—some only in their mid-twenties and few as old as fifty when they achieved power.

These new men, Western-educated for the most part, brought a new dynamism into their country's affairs. In the past, many African societies had been described as fatalistic, patiently accepting the blows dealt out by providence, whether in the form of famine, pestilence, or war. The triumphant nationalists, like their predecessors of half a century earlier, the great imperial proconsuls, refused to accept a passive and fatalistic view of their country's destinies. Society could progress toward more just sets of relationships. Man could control and exploit his environment for his own benefit. These were infectious ideas that could easily be transmitted to the members of a younger generation. "Life more abundant"—the slogan adopted by one of the major Nigerian parties in the 1950's—was a totally novel concept and one that no African society could have adopted two or three generations earlier. An awareness of future time, of a future that should somehow be better than the present, may well be regarded as one of the most striking manifestations of change in modern African history.

▲▼ THE FORCES OF CHANGE

Alterations in the Natural Environment

Alterations in the natural environment may occur either as the result of happenings—droughts, pestilences, floods, cyclones—over which man has little or no control, or they may be the product of human action. The history of most African communities has been punctuated, at least until very recent times, by natural disasters. In lands of irregular rainfall—a definition that might be stretched to include all but the equatorial regions of the continent—drought with its consequent famine was a constant hazard. Pestilences—epidemics of such diseases as cholera—caused a greater loss of life than any nineteenth-century African war. And most African environments bred a host of pests and disease-carrying parasites, creatures whose depredations served as a constant downdrag on human initiative, a continual drain on human energy. In most parts of Africa nature presents a harsher and more fickle face than in the temperate lands of Europe and North America.

Many of the alterations made by man to the natural environment have been harmful in their consequences: overgrazing and overcultivation leading to soil erosion; the total removal of forest cover affecting local rainfall; the destruction of certain species of animal upsetting a beneficial ecological balance. But man has also enriched his environment: producing through the transfer of useful plants a more varied and bountiful vegetation; creating artificial lakes and harnessing the power of rivers to produce electricity; cutting lines of communication through the wilderness and constantly extending the area of human settlement. Every plant introduced into Africa should be seen not only as a manifestation of change but also as a force contributing to the accelerating process of change. Cocoa, for example, made possible a great expansion of wealth on the Gold Coast, thus increasing the amount of revenue at the government's disposal and so serving to finance the construction of a wide range of public works. At the same time, cocoa laid the foundations of the private fortunes of successful farmers, thus contributing to the growth of an African bourgeoisie. In much the same way roads may be seen not only as evidence of new forms of human activity but also as revolutionary agents in themselves, vigorously demolishing the isolation of primitive communities.

The Pressure of Population Growth and Movement

Alterations in the size of the population of any locality are dependent on many variables: the incidence of disease, the production of food, the degree of internal security, the volume of immigration and emigration, the extent of industrialization, and so on. Population change is one of the more obscure aspects of the African past. Egypt, Algeria, South Africa, and the Mascarenes are the only African territories with population statistics reaching back to the nineteenth century. In many African countries reasonably thorough censuses were not held until as late as the 1950's, thus making it impossible to project back accurate figures of the rate of increase. It seems reasonable to assume that most African countries experienced a very slow increase in population in the centuries before the twentieth, but it is clear that certain areas witnessed, at least for limited periods, a significant decline in population. The population of Réunion is known to have fallen by about 15 percent between the

1870's and the 1910's; certain parts of tropical Africa—the eastern districts of the Central African Republic, for example, or the southern districts of Tanzania—were devastated by the activities of slave-raiders in the last quarter of the nineteenth century; and epidemics of smallpox or of cholera decimated the populations of the communities that lay in their paths.

Figures based on the years 1960–66, showing the annual percentage rate of growth, reveal considerable variations over the continent as a whole. Two countries—Somalia and Madagascar—reached the extraordinarily high rate of 4 percent. In Gabon and Portuguese Guinea, on the other hand, the rate of increase was less than 1 percent. The majority of African countries fell within the 2 and 3 percent brackets. Figures for population density revealed an even wider range of variations: at one extreme, Mauritius with almost 400 people to the square kilometer, followed by Réunion, Rwanda, and Burundi each with densities of more than 100; at the other, Botswana, Libya, and Mauritania, each with no more than 1 person to the square kilometer. Overall figures such as these convey too imprecise a picture. One needs an accurate impression of local variations. Many African countries combine limited areas of dense population with many thinly populated districts. The concepts of over- and underpopulation cannot adequately be measured in numerical terms. Some areas with a very low density may yet be overpopulated because the existing population presses too heavily on scarce resources. Other areas with very high population densities may still be able to absorb more growth because of the range of economic opportunities they are equipped to offer.

Population pressure is clearly one of the major forces making for change. It may lead to a growing shortage of land, the fragmentation of older properties, the emergence of a landless proletariat, widespread emigration, endemic unemployment, and so on. Yet out of such conditions there may well emerge a fierce desire to create a juster society, a willingness to experiment with new techniques in agriculture, a realization of the possibilities for industrial development, and a greater openness to the ideas of the outside world. All these points may be illustrated from the modern history of Egypt or of the Ibo areas of Nigeria, the Lower Nile Valley and Iboland being among the most densely populated areas in modern Africa.

Population growth and population movement do not necessarily go together. Men may move from one area to another for a variety of reasons, the greater opportunities offered by the new area or the more attractive life that it offers. Certain broad lines of migration may be noted. All over Africa the great urban centers exerted their magnetic pull over neighboring peoples, even though the opportunities they offered for employment were often far poorer than those held out a century earlier by the more highly industrialized towns of Western Europe and North America. Not all the migrants to the new towns of Africa became true townsmen; many were only transients, men who came to the towns for limited periods to earn a certain sum of money before returning to their homes in rural areas. Paradoxically it was the most highly industrialized country in Africa, the country best suited to acquire a settled urban population, which contained the greatest amount of transient labor. In South Africa the dominant white minority refused to allow the black majority freedom of tenure in urban areas and devised a highly elaborate system of regulations in order to restrict the number of Africans who became permanent residents in urban locations.

In the past, the vast majority of Africans lived out their lives in the same community or the same area. The greater mobility which became possible during the twentieth century meant that men moved more frequently and more freely than they had ever done before—and as they moved they were brought in touch with a wide range of new experiences and were exposed to the stimulus of intercourse with people whose cultures differed from their own.

The Stimulus of Intercourse

The more isolated a society, the less subject it is likely to be to the processes of change. Conversely, the more vigorous and extensive a society's intercourse with people of alien culture or of significantly different subcultures, the greater the incidence of innovation, whether adaptation or destruction. Intercourse may occur in a number of different forms—through commerce, conquest, migration, missionary activity, urbanization, or education. Each of these different forms of human activity can be amply illustrated from the recent history of Africa.

The expansion of commerce in late nineteenth-century and early twentieth-century Africa derived in large part from the need of the industrialized countries of Western Europe and North America for a steady flow of raw materials. Before 1875 African exports were confined to a limited number of commodities. The external trade in slaves, one of the major staples of African commerce only a generation earlier, had declined to a trickle as a result of vigorous European measures to abolish this cruel form of commerce. Gold, another of the great staples of the past, was of relatively minor importance, though the discovery of the fabulous deposits of the Transvaal was soon to make the precious metal once again one of the continent's major exports. Ivory, another ancient staple, had increased greatly in importance because of the demand created by the new tastes of the European bourgeoisie. Palm oil, used primarily as a component in soap manufacture, had developed within the last half-century into West Africa's major export. Wild rubber was just beginning to attract the interest of European buyers and was soon to experience a very rapid expansion. A vigorous trade in groundnuts had been established in the Senegambian areas. Egypt had become one of the great cotton-producing countries of the world. South Africa was largely dependent on the export of wool, though diamonds, recently discovered in the Kimberley area, had just begun to give a significant boost to the economy. Taking the continent as a whole it is clear that not only was the range of exports strictly limited but also that many areas seemed to have little or nothing to offer to the outside world.

The first half of the twentieth century brought a remarkable increase both in the production of cash crops and in the extraction of minerals. Old established crops were introduced to new areas. Cotton spread from Egypt to the Sudan, Uganda, Tanzania, and other tropical African countries. Groundnuts became a major export for all the countries lying in the Sudanic belt of West Africa. Coffee, a crop indigenous to Africa, was introduced to new areas and came to assume increasing importance in the economies of the Ivory Coast, Angola, Madagascar, and the countries of East Africa. With the development of effective methods of refrigeration, bananas from Somalia and from certain parts of West Africa found their way to the European market. Cocoa, a new crop of American origin, became well-established in certain parts of the forest area of West Africa. Sisal, another American plant, became an important source of wealth in Kenya and Tanzania. Tobacco became for a time the mainstay of the Rhodesian economy, while tea was introduced to favorable areas in Malawi and the countries of East Africa. Wine and citrus fruits acquired a place among the major exports of South Africa and Algeria. The island economies of the Mascarenes and of Zanzibar, however, remained almost as closely tied to a single crop, sugar in the Mascarenes, cloves in Zanzibar, as they had been during the nineteenth century.

One can trace three stages in the expansion of mineral production in modern Africa. The first, covering the last quarter of the nineteenth century, saw the significant activity almost entirely confined to South Africa where the new wealth derived from gold and diamonds provided the capital needed for later industrial development. The second stage covered the first four decades of the twentieth century and witnessed the exploitation of new mineral deposits, some of which had long been known to African miners, in other parts of the continent—tin in Nigeria, gold in Rhodesia and Ghana, copper in Zambia and the Congo. The third stage began after World War II and saw a rapid expansion both in the production of already established mines and in the exploitation of a wide range of new deposits, the existence of many of which had hardly been suspected a generation earlier. Particularly spectacular were the discoveries of oil, made first in the Sahara (Algeria and Libya) and later in Nigeria, Gabon, and Cabinda (Angola) and of exceptionally rich deposits of iron ore in Mauritania and Liberia. But there were also many other developments in the field of African mineral production: diamonds from South West Africa, Sierra Leone, and Tanzania, uranium from South Africa and the Congo, bauxite from Guinea, phosphates from Senegal, asbestos from Swaziland, and chrome from Rhodesia were among the new sources of wealth to be developed in the postwar years.

The expansion of trade and industry stimulated intercourse in many different ways. African peasant farmers and industrial workers, introduced for the first time to a cash economy, were able to acquire for themselves novel commodities of alien manufacture. Governments, their revenues steadily mounting as a result of the taxes imposed on expanding commerce, were able to spend more money on the improvement of communications and in so doing hit on the only practicable means for breaking down the isolation of remote communities. Along the new roads of Africa moved the traders, the produce buyers, the government officials, the missionaries and doctors and teachers, each of them serving as carriers of distrubing innovations.

European trade preceded European conquest. Conquest was followed by the establishment of a *pax* such as most parts of Africa had never known before. The new rulers were powerful enough to put a stop to local wars, feuds, and brigandage and in so doing created the conditions which made it possible for men to travel in safety far from their homes. If conquest stimulated intercourse in this manner, it could also in itself be regarded as a form of intercourse. For many African communities the first sight of a white man came when a European officer led a patrol of native troops into their village. In localities where the white man stayed on, established a military post or administrative headquarters, and began systematically to interfere in local life, African communities found themselves exposed to a particularly disturbing form of intercourse. Conquest stimulated the meeting of peoples of different cultures in another way. For the many thousands of Africans who served in the colonial armies were separated from their own communities, exposed to novel forms of training and discipline, and brought in the course of their service into contact with peoples of many different cultures. The role of the African soldier or ex-soldier as a transmitter of innovations is one that is often overlooked.

The significance of the missionary in this capacity is very much easier to understand. Indeed the whole function of the missionary, whether Christian or Muslim, was to serve as a transmitter, passing on to the unenlightened the essentials of his faith, the intellectual assumptions and the moral teaching together with the material objects and techniques that went with them. Thus if, as was almost invariably the case, the missionary, whether Christian or Muslim, regarded nakedness as a sin, then he was bound to introduce the novelty of dress and possibly also the technique of making clothes. Missionary enterprise was remarkable for embracing so wide a range of forms of human activity. Contact with the missionary was likely to be a far more disturbing experience for many Africans than contact with the alien administrator, soldier, or trader.

Missionary activity, both Muslim and Christian, was closely associated with education. Individuals were caught up in the process of education at a highly impressionable age. In the African context, education often brought students into contact with a teacher of an entirely different culture. In its higher reaches it also served to bring together students drawn from many different culture-areas in Africa. Literacy, the most important of all the new techniques imparted by the alien educators, was in itself an obvious means of promoting intercourse between different cultures. The diffusion of education based on literacy, even more than the expansion of missionary activity, served to familiarize African peoples with innovations of alien origin.

The literate, the adherents and converts of the two great universalistic religions, became members of the new elite, the dominant section of the community in all the newly independent states. But the literate were not the only ones to experience the powerful attraction of the new cultures brought in by the conquerors. In many parts of the continent long-distance migration provided a means of introducing individuals from remote and isolated communities to the ways of a larger world. In the first half of the twentieth century labor migration became an important feature in the lives of many African communities. From Algeria men in their thousands crossed the Mediterranean to seek work in France. Mossi from the Upper Volta traveled south to find employment on the cocoa farms of Ghana and the Ivory Coast. Population pressure and shortages of land brought about the diaspora of the Ibo of Eastern Nigeria, with dynamic Ibo communities springing up in most of the main towns of Nigeria's other regions. In South Africa the mines of the

Rand served as a magnet attracting many thousands of workers from as far north as Malawi and Zambia. The experience of the Algerian worker in the slums of Paris or of the miner from Malawi in the locations of Johannesburg might be harsh and cruel, but it served to emancipate him from the often constricting pattern of life of his own home-village and gave him some familiarity with many new things.

The growth of towns also involved a measure of migration, though the new townsmen might not have traveled as far as the labor-migrants nor found themselves so divorced from people of their own culture. But to move from the village to the town was to enter a new world, to be confronted with many previously unfamilair objects, to be subjected to novel strains and pressures. All cultures represent a synthesis, an interflowing of different currents. Most major African cities are to some extent cosmopolitan, though law or convention may attempt to maintain residential divisions between different sections of the population. Here in these great urban complexes, with their shops and their markets, their factories, banks and warehouses, their harbors and railway stations, their mosques and cathedrals, their schools, universities, newspaper offices, museums, cinemas, theaters, opera houses, their police stations, barracks, hospitals and government offices, innumerable different currents of life are brought together to interact ceaselessly one on another. Here in the great cities of Africa the stimulus of intercourse may be experienced in its most tangible form.

The Impact of Ideas

Of all the forces making for change perhaps ideas are capable of producing the most striking impact. Some ideas serve as simple and forceful guides to conduct. And there are some systems of ideas which equip those who hold them with a sort of moral armor, providing them with a set of satisfactory answers to the great questions of life and society. Ideas, whether in the form of rules of conduct or of statements based on simplifications of experience, play some part in the lives of most men. But the general historian can concern himself only with those well documented systems of ideas possessing, at least for a time, a certain infectious character which ensures their widespread acceptance. Two systems of ideas require special attention by any historian concerned with modern Africa: they may be identified by those two loose and capacious terms, "imperialism" and "nationalism."

"Imperialism" as a system of ideas may be defined as the concepts of ruling developed by any one group or people who aspire to dominate others. There have been many examples of imperialism in the course of the last two centuries of African history: Fulani imperialism as exemplified in the expansion of the caliphate of Sokoto, Turco-Egyptian as displayed in the policies of Muhammad Ali and his successors, Ethiopian as practiced by the Emperor Menelik, the imperialism of the Ganda, the Zulu, the Ashanti, and others. Each of these indigenous imperialisms had its own character. But the term "imperialism" tends to be limited in conventional usage to those concepts developed by certain European powers in the latter half of the nineteenth century, concepts which served at once to stimulate and to justify the expansion of European hegemony over many of the non-European peoples of the world. Concepts of imperialism varied from country to country: there were subtle ideological differences between the British, the French, the Germans, the Portuguese, and the Italians. Yet certain elements were common to all five powers and also to that group of isolated and independent Europeans, the Afrikaners of South Africa. There was first a profound sense of "racial" superiority. In the course of the nineteenth century, European nations had clearly achieved a massive technological superiority over peoples of other cultures. At the same time, Europeans had come to accept a highly simplified system of classification of the peoples of the world, a system which laid special stress on pigmentation. The term "race" was used to distinguish people of different skin color one from another, and "races" were arranged in order of superiority with the "white race" occupying the top rung of the ladder of human progress and the "black race," which covered most of the peoples of Africa, coming near the bottom. The importance of this profound sense of "racial" superiority can hardly be exaggerated. It equipped Europeans with an assurance, a total conviction of the rightness of their way of doing things, that contributed greatly to their success. Furthermore, if "races" were distinct one from another and some were superior to others, then it was in the interest of the "superior race" to preserve its "purity." People of "mixed race" were thought to be in some way degenerate; consequently physical intercourse between peoples of different skin color was discouraged. Put more colloquially, Europeans who "went native" were "letting down their side." These ideas of racial distinctiveness were carried furthest by the Afrikaners of South Africa and led to the development of the policy of apartheid, of rigid separation between the "races." But all the European colonial powers accepted the notion that white men were inherently superior to black men or brown men and that therefore only white men should be employed in posts of responsibility. These concepts had a profound influence on colonial systems of government until as late as the end of World War II.

The belief that Europeans were the agents of a "civilizing mission" in a "barbaric" land was another important strand in the European concept of imperialism. When Europeans talked of "civilizing" Africa, they tended to imply that African cultures should be so transformed as to develop into replicas of European models. Africans should be educated to accept the religion, the political institutions, the dress, the language, the technical skills of Europe. But if Africans could be transformed into replicas of Europeans, should they not then be regarded as the equals of Europeans? This was an extremely awkward question which threatened to undermine comfortable notions of "racial" superiority. To many colonial officials in the early decades of the twentieth century the "educated African" appeared as a distinctly unnatural figure: far better the "unspoiled" African out in the bush. For those who thought along these lines the concept of the "civilizing mission" needed modification. Certainly it was the task of the colonial power to maintain law and order, to prohibit "barbarous" practices, to promote a modest amount of economic development. But native institutions must be preserved whenever possible. This variation on the concept of the imperial mission received its most elaborate development in the writings of the theorists of indirect rule in British Africa.

A third strand in the imperialist system of ideas was concerned with the development of the continent's economy. Europe needed raw materials and markets to serve its expanding industries. Africa presented a great "undeveloped estate." Europeans were justified in applying their enormous technical skill to the exploitation of a continent whose inhabitants seemed, in European eyes, so lamentably incapable of developing its resources. At first this concept of exploitation was interpreted crudely in terms of the benefits that Europeans alone could hope to derive from the hitherto untapped wealth of the continent. But with the diffusion of liberal ideas after World War I, exploitation came to be seen in more balanced terms as a process that would benefit both Europeans and Africans. This was the concept of the "dual mandate," a concept widely accepted in colonial circles in the 1920's but gradually replaced by the idea that it was the duty of the colonial powers to do all they could to develop their territories primarily for the benefit of the colonial peoples themselves.

Imperialist ideas never gained universal acceptance. In every European power with a stake in Africa there were always to be found certain sections of opinion whose members regarded the acquisition of colonies with distaste. New colonial possessions were expensive to acquire and to maintain; they served to divert attention from other more important matters; and the establishment of colonial rule often involved actions deeply repugnant to the humane observer. But many English Liberals and French and German Socialists still continued to support the fundamental assumptions of European superiority and felt a glow of pride in their countries' "civilizing missions," even if they found some of the cruder actions of their compatriots intensely distasteful. A far more vigorous attack on the imperialist system came from Communist thinkers. The dynamic simplicity of Communist ideas—the equation of imperialism with the crudest form of exploitation—threw imperialist spokesmen on the defensive and forced them to seek means of justifying a system which an earlier generation had accepted as part of the natural order of things. Hardly less influential were the ideas popularized by the American president, Woodrow Wilson, toward the end of World War I, with their stress on the rights of small nations to determine their own futures. The decline of Britain and France, and the rise of the United States and Communist Russia to the status of superpowers profoundly affected the general climate of opinion. "Imperialist," a title proudly claimed by many European statesmen at the turn of the century, had become almost a term of abuse by the late 1940's.

The decline of imperialist sentiment in Europe was matched by the growth of nationalist sentiment in Africa. African nationalism had many roots. The ruling classes of the more substantial African polities had a deep and natural pride in their own traditions and culture. Some of these groups were able to reach a satisfactory bargain with the European intruder and so preserve many of their former privileges: such was the case in Morocco, Sokoto, and Buganda. Others witnessed the destruction of their ancestral institutions and were left with a profound sense of grievance. In many African communities embittered aristocrats were not the only group to resent the European presence. Peasants deprived of their land or exposed to oppressive forms of taxation; traders done out of business by competition from European commercial firms; civil servants, teachers, and clergymen in the new mission churches, and members of the newly-formed Western-educated elite who found their opportunities for promotion blocked by the color prejudice of their European superiors; devout Muslims alarmed by the spread of Christianity and shocked by the manifestations of European materialism— individuals in all these categories had cause to view the colonial regime with mixed feelings. Occasionally peculiar combinations of circumstances led to outright revolt, but taking the continent as a whole really violent disturbances were remarkably limited in number. In most parts of Africa the generation or two of undisputed European hegemony represented an astonishingly peaceful period.

Gradually increasing contacts with a wider world introduced small groups of African intellectuals to a highly stimulating range of new ideas. The young law student from British Africa came across the provocative slogan, "no taxation without representation"; the graduate from the French *lycée* was taught to honor the glorious principles of the revolution of 1789; the African who left his own country and came to live and work in Europe was likely sooner or later to come across the exhilaratingly abrasive attacks on the colonial system made by Communist writers and speakers; the African who crossed the Atlantic in the 1920's and 1930's was almost bound to hear something of the vigorous black nationalism of Marcus Garvey. The experience of conquest deflates and depresses those who suffer it. To learn that one is not alone, that there are others at different periods in the past who have fought for and won their freedom, that there are friends and well-wishers in other parts of the world, even in the heart of the colonial metropolis—experiences such as these are immensely stimulating for any individual who has been brought up in a state of subjection. At the core of every nationalist movement lies a new-born spirit of self-confidence and a conviction of the rightness and ultimate triumph of the nationalist cause.

The development of African nationalism can in part be presented as a double series of chain-reactions, with events in the outside world profoundly influencing the thoughts of responsive individuals throughout the continent, and with events in particular African countries having a particularly strong impact on neighboring territories. It is not difficult to list the external events that engraved themselves on many African minds: World War I, President Wilson's Fourteen Points, the Russian Revolution, World War II, the Atlantic Charter, the establishment of the United Nations, the British withdrawal from South Asia. The revolution in Egypt after World War I had a direct impact on the Sudan, and ideas emanating from Egypt and from other countries in the Middle East had wide circulation in the Maghrib in the 1920's and 1930's. Later, after World War II, all the countries of the Maghrib interacted one on another in their struggle for independence. In West Africa, Ghana emerged as the pace-setter in the movement for self-government. The Ghanaian example served to stimulate nationalist activities in other parts of British Africa. It also exerted a considerable influence on French policy in tropical Africa. The emancipation of the French territories proved a powerful incitement to African nationalists in the Belgian Congo. Meanwhile, in Southern Africa the electoral victory of the Afrikaner nationalists in 1948 aroused the fears of the British in Central Africa and so helped to expedite the creation of a Central African Federation. This in turn provoked the violent opposition of African politicians in the territories that were to become Zambia and Malawi.

The mounting tide of black nationalism was met by an even more formidable white nationalism in Rhodesia, South Africa, and the Portuguese territories. Thus Africa with its spreading nationalisms came to present a pattern of ideological development not altogether dissimilar from that of Europe in the late nineteenth and early twentieth centuries.

There are three other aspects of African nationalism that need to be noted. One of these aspects was the tendency of some nationalists to look back to the past for inspiration. Thus in Egypt and North Africa the famous deeds of the great centuries of Arab achievement were recalled with pride. In West Africa local historians recorded the customs and traditions of their people in a conscious attempt to arrest that movement to denigrate African culture from which even some Africans were not immune. And with the spread of nationalist sentiment there developed a growing awareness—encouraged in no small degree by the work of European scholars—of the richness of the African past. Another aspect was the emergence of what might be described as forms of subnationalism. In many African countries the most natural form of political combination was the party that directed its primary appeal to the people of a particular ethnic group. After independence the struggle for the spoils of office tended to strengthen this sense of ethnic identity. The third aspect of African nationalism ran counter to this trend, for it presented not the contraction of the spirit of group solidarity but its expansion beyond national frontiers. Pan-Africanism, a movement whose origins can be traced back to the first years of the twentieth century, drew its rationale from the experience of subjection to alien hegemony that was common to all the peoples of Africa. For a century and more, Africans had been dominated, exploited, and enslaved by outsiders; only by coming together and presenting an united front to the rest of the world could they guarantee their own freedom and integrity.

The complex of ideas associated with imperialism and nationalism were not the only intellectual forces that helped to shape the development of modern Africa. Possibly even more potent in their impact on many African societies were the novel concepts associated with the two great universalistic religions, Islam and Christianity, both of which experienced rapid expansion in these years. The ministers of the new religions derided and destroyed the old gods of Africa. They advocated new patterns of behavior and extolled new models of family life. For the first generation of converts the old life was still very close, but their sons and grandsons found themselves increasingly bound to accept the new cultural modes. No doubt an element of syncretism could often be detected, with older modes of behavior or belief persisting in a somewhat altered form. But between the devout Christian or Muslim and the adherent of one of the older religions there lay a very profound measure of difference.

Even more disturbing for the old Africa were the assumptions implicit in modern science and technology. The world of gods and spirits, of ghosts and witches, the world where men could be changed into animals or struck down by the malevolence of their neighbors—all these concepts were utterly repugnant and totally unacceptable to the rational mind trained in the discipline of modern science. The number of Africans with an opportunity to become familiar with these new modes of thought and above all to grow up in an environment where such modes were accepted as the norm was still very limited even as late as the 1960's. A larger number of Africans who had received some scientific training lived in a divided world, accepting some of the assumptions of the new learning but still retaining their belief in many of the older concepts.

The Peaceful Pursuit of Well-being

Every individual in full possession of his senses is moved by a certain inner dynamic—the desire to achieve and maintain a state of well-being. Well-being is a concept whose exact definition varies from society to society but which must always contain three distinct elements—material sufficiency, social harmony, and spiritual satisfaction. The degree of emphasis laid on each of these three elements is bound to differ from individual to individual, from social group to social group and, in periods of accelerating change, from generation to generation, but the three remain interdependent. A man who is constantly short of food, who comes from a violently dislocated society, who feels a sense of spiritual impoverishment finds himself falling far short of a true state of well-being.

The desire to achieve material sufficiency is clearly one of the most potent forces in human affairs. How else can one account for man's willingness to experiment with new techniques or to undertake the arduous work of pioneering in virgin lands? In the course of the past five centuries Europeans have become so conscious of their achievements in acquiring material wealth that they tend to assume that other societies —and particularly the peasant communities of Asia and Africa—have lacked the same thrusting power. Yet in fact the history of every peasant community is one of a slow battle to master a harsh environment. One has only to study the distribution of domesticated plants throughout Africa to realize that African peasant communities have always been ready to accept useful innovations. But innovations have to be fitted in to a pattern of well-being that embraces not only material suffi-ciency but also social harmony and spiritual satisfaction. In this connec-tion it is worth recalling a story told to the author several years ago by the European agent of a West African tobacco company. One of the agent's duties was to visit farmers living in the savanna belt to encour-age them to grow the new crop, tobacco. In one village the agent thought he had achieved a great success: the farmers took his seed, followed his instructions, and produced an excellent crop which earned them a con-siderable amount of money. But when the agent returned to the same village the next year with double the amount of seed, he was met to his astonishment by a stony refusal. "But surely," he asked the farmers, "you earned more money last year than you have ever done before?" "Certainly we did," the farmers replied, "but then we also worked a great deal harder. This year we want to celebrate, to use the money for feasts and dances. Besides we know that as soon as the district head has learned how much we have earned, he will come and ask us for more taxes." Material sufficiency should always be related to social harmony and spiritual satisfaction.

But clearly concepts of material sufficiency did begin to change throughout Africa in the course of the twentieth century. As African communities became aware of the marvelous objects—cloth, pots and pans, bicycles, sewing machines, transistor radios—the white man could offer those with the money to pay for them, they became infected by what has been vividly described as the "disease of the 'wants.'" Anx-ious to secure the goods they could see in the new shops and the ex-panded markets, many African communities turned eagerly to the pro-duction of the cash crops which would provide the money they needed. At the same time, the newly established colonial governments threw themselves into the tasks of economic development very much more vig-orously than most of the states they had supplanted had ever been able to do. Indeed, the whole concept of economic development, of the sys-tematic exploitation of the resources of a particular territory, gave a new edge to the urge for material sufficiency as a force making for change. And with the improvement in techniques and the rapid growth in the power and the resources of governments, economic development came to play an increasingly important part in the lives of many African peo-ples.

Political change can often be interpreted as an attempt to achieve a greater measure of social harmony, to eliminate the possibilities of vio-lence, to establish a proper sense of order, to relieve the frustrations of one group or another. The "civilizing mission" of the imperial powers could be regarded by its exponents as an attempt to establish a regime of social harmony among peoples who seemed to their conquerors to be living in a state of anarchy. African nationalism can be seen as an attempt to relieve the frustrations inherent in the colonial situation. And the various brands of African Socialism that made their appearance in the 1960's may be regarded as attempts to frame a new and more just social order.

Spiritual satisfaction was to be found for many African communities in the old indigenous religions, religions whose devotees seem to have been little affected by the missionary zeal that animated so many of the adherents of the two universalistic religions. Behind the zeal of the Christian or Muslim missionary lay a clear concept of the new order that needed to be established. The zeal of the missionary, the aspirations of the politician, the practical enthusiasm of the engineer, the shrewd calculation of profit made by the trader or the peasant farmer —mental processes such as these contributed, each in their own distinctive way, to the forces of change in African affairs.

The Violent Pursuit of Well-being

Often individuals or social groups seeking the same ends come into conflict one with another—nomadic herdsmen quarrel over grazing grounds or water-holes, peasant farmers rise up in protest against those attempting to dispossess them of their lands, precolonial states raid smaller neighboring polities for slaves and other forms of booty, colonial powers squabble over disputed territory, and so on. The larger, richer and more complex polities become, the more serious the consequences of conflict are likely to be. Thus it is hardly surprising that the most destructive wars to be fought in Africa in the course of the last hundred years have been those in which Europeans have been involved on both sides—the Anglo-Boer War of 1899–1902, the campaigns in the German colonies during World War I, the North African campaigns of World War II.

Conflict in precolonial Africa varied greatly in scale. Feuds between stateless polities might drag on for years yet cause only a handful of casualties. Larger African polities might place considerable armies in the field but were unable to maintain them for more than a short period. Perhaps the most destructive of precolonial conflicts were the raids for slaves carried on by most major African polities with the technical ability—acquired through the possession of firearms or horses— to dominate their smaller neighbors.

Another type of conflict was represented by the wars that accompanied the colonial conquest. A few African polities submitted peacefully to the European intrusion. The majority attempted to resist and were defeated by force of arms. Colonial campaigns varied greatly in character. Some were decided by a few set battles; others involved years of tough guerrilla warfare. In some areas a handful of troops proved sufficient to establish European claims to hegemony; in others—notably Morocco, Algeria, Libya, and Ethiopia—large armies, sometimes numbering more than 100,000 men, had to be brought in to break native resistance. In the first decades of colonial rule most African communities made no attempt to throw off the European yoke once it had been firmly established; but a few limited areas—parts of Algeria, South West Africa, Rhodesia, and Southern Tanzania among them—were the scene of violent revolts. Not until after the end of World War II was it possible for local nationalists to take up the struggle for independence with reasonable hopes of success. The decolonization of Africa was, on the whole, a remarkably peaceful process. With the exception of the Bamiléké revolt in Cameroon and the Mau Mau rebellion in Kenya, large-scale violence was confined to those territories—Algeria and the Portuguese colonies—where African nationalists found themselves confronted with a local European nationalism as strong as their own.

The most extreme cases of violent conflict in the postcolonial period occurred as a result of internal tensions in five of Africa's largest states —the Sudan, the Congo (Zaire), Ethiopia, Nigeria, and Chad—in each of which distinct ethnic or regional groups attempted to assert their rights to establish an independent or at least semiindependent state of their own. Interterritorial conflicts, on the other hand, were remarkable for their absence. Apart from a border dispute between Algeria and Morocco and the tension produced by Somali irredentism in the Horn of Africa, there were virtually no cases in the course of the 1960's involving violent incidents between the nationals of different African states.

One other type of violent conflict needs to be considered—that which may occur within a society as a result of mounting tension between different social groups. The colonial conquest was accompanied in many areas by revolutionary social changes as a result of the overthrow of many former ruling groups. Decolonization, on the other hand, appeared to involve a far less revolutionary process in many countries, as members of the Western-educated elite moved easily into the offices vacated by retiring European administrators. And many of the later political changes, though often brought about by violent means, did not produce any profound alterations in the structure of society. Only in Egypt with the overthrow of the Turco-Egyptian monarchy in 1952, in Zanzibar with the massacre of Arabs after the destruction of the sultanate in 1964, and in Rwanda with the total collapse of Tutsi hegemony could one speak of events that were truly revolutionary.

▲▼ FUTURE PROSPECTS

A historian who has carried his survey of a country or a continent over a long span of time and brought it up to the present can hardly resist engaging in some speculation about the future. Yet by the very nature of his profession the historian must be aware of the limitations of such speculations. The study of history provides a constant reminder of the complexity of events, of the wide range of variables that exist in any particular situation. Clearly it will never be possible to predict the exact course of human affairs. A shrewd political analyst may well be able to foresee that a particular country is on the verge of momentous changes. He may also be able to suggest in broad terms some of the forms these changes may take. But he will never be able to work out in advance the exact manner in which they will occur. Nevertheless, it should be possible for the historian who has acquired some grasp of the forces that have molded the past to project these same forces into the future and so indicate some of the possible developments that may reasonably be expected to occur.

The first of the six forces of change discussed in an earlier section of this chapter was described as alterations in the natural environment. With greater scientific knowledge and a more highly evolved technology at their disposal it is reasonable to assume that men in Africa will establish a more effective control over their environment than ever before. With every decade that passes Africa is likely to become progressively less wild—its natural fauna confined to game parks, its deserts traversed by broad arterial highways, its agriculture enriched by new and better-yielding crops, its mineral resources exploited with greater efficiency, its urban centers increasing in size and number. Many African landscapes will be tamed even as the landscapes of other continents have been tamed by centuries of human effort. Not all these developments are likely to be continuously beneficial. Just as the gold mines of ancient Nubia, once so lucrative a source of wealth to Kush and to Egypt, came in time to be worked out, so Liberia's sources of iron ore, Zambia's of copper, South Africa's of diamonds, Libya's of oil will one day be exhausted. Some countries may use their mineral wealth so productively that its gradual disappearance need not represent a really serious threat to their economy. In other countries, on the other hand, the bonanzas enjoyed for a few years or a few decades may well be followed by the revival of an older poverty. One has only to contemplate the ruined cities of Africa to be reminded that well-being is not an invariable constant.

There can be no doubt that the second force making for change—the pressure of population growth and movement—will make itself increasingly felt in the course of the next few decades. In the mid-1960's the population of the continent as a whole was put at 330 million. By the end of the century the population of Africa seems likely to exceed 750 million. The strains produced by a rapidly increasing population are bound to vary in intensity from country to country. Egypt, Mauritius, Rwanda, and the East-Central State of Nigeria, all of which already possess an exceptionally high population density, are likely to find themselves faced with the need to devise new political, social, and economic institutions to cope with the difficulties produced by population growth. In many other parts of the continent, on the other hand, a much larger population should be absorbed without undue difficulty. Indeed, by increasing the human resources in particular areas the growth of population is likely to serve as a powerful stimulant to further development.

One form of population movement seems bound to continue—the steady drift of people from rural areas to the major towns, some of which were expanding at the rate of 10 percent per annum in the late 1960's. The growth of population may well make the position of minority groups more uncertain and lead to their expulsion from certain areas. The position of most of the Asian communities in East Africa seems particularly vulnerable in this respect: they will survive only if they can contrive to find occupational niches not coveted by their African neighbors. In the long term, much the same may be said of the European communities of Southern Africa. At the same time it is difficult to imagine any great shifts of population taking place comparable to the major migrations of the African past. As minor cultural groups come to be absorbed by their neighbors, the population of many African countries seems likely to grow more homogeneous than it is at present, thus following a pattern of cultural development clearly evident in the history of most of the nations of Europe, Asia, and the Americas.

The emergence of a greater measure of cultural homogeneity can also be seen as one of the products of the third force making for change, the stimulus of intercourse. Immigrants to the expanding towns tend to adopt many of the cultural features of their new urban environments and even to abandon some of the distinctive features of their own ethnic group. But the movement of peoples is not the only cause of increased intercourse. Expanding commerce, the missionary activity of the followers of universalistic religions, and the establishment of new educational institutions serve equally forcefully to break down habits of mind associated with a high degree of isolation from other communities. All over the continent the tides of intercourse—between village and village, town and country, nation and nation, Africa and other parts of the world—are likely to grow more elaborate. New ties will lead to the emergence of new cultural syntheses and bring about the radical transformation of older modes of living.

Clearly Africa will also continue to be exposed to the fourth force making for change, the impact of ideas. Given the nature of modern methods of communication, ideas generated in other parts of the world —such as those associated with the concept of Black Power or the "Youth Revolution"—are likely to win substantial followings in African universities and urban centers within the space of a very few years. But the ideas which catch on rapidly in the great conurbations may well be expected to spread far less swiftly in the rural areas where the great mass of Africans have their homes. Here in these rural districts the expansion of one or other of the two great universalistic religions, Islam and Christianity, may indeed represent the most significant development in the field of ideology. As for the diffusion of the political ideas associated with one or other of the great power blocs of the world, the differing concepts of democracy accepted in Communist and non-Communist countries, these are certainly likely to remain subjects for passionate debate among the rapidly increasing number of Western-educated men and women. But it would be absurd to assume that any African country will ever find it either possible or desirable to reproduce political patterns derived from non-African models. Every African state will find itself absorbed in the unremitting task of working out its own solution to its own unique political problems.

No less significant than the introduction of novel political concepts will be the gradual acceptance of the gamut of ideas associated with modern technology—the belief in man's capacity consciously to increase his mastery of his own environment, the willingness constantly to accept productive innovations, the acceptance of the importance of exact observation, of the accumulation of data, of the need to formulate generalizations of universal application. Older modes of thought, reflected in mental attitudes which make possible a belief in the existence of ghosts or evil spirits, will linger on for a very long time, but it seems reasonable to assume that they will eventually disappear in Africa even as they have done in Europe.

What of the prospects for conflict in Africa, conflict which has been defined as the product of yet another force making for change, the violent pursuit of well-being? In answering this question, four different types of conflict need to be considered. The first involves outside powers, with African states finding themselves either being made the victims of external aggression or being drawn into some struggle between non-African states. The second is represented by conflict between individual African states. The third and the fourth both involve internal conflict, one between different ethnic groups, the other between different social classes. With the exception of Israel in its long struggle with Egypt, it is difficult to imagine any non-African power choosing to launch a direct assault on any African state, especially when such an action would provoke a highly critical reaction from the vast mass of world opinion. Some of the poorer African states, especially perhaps the ex-French colonies, may well retain a satellite status in their relationship with one of the Great Powers, but the opportunity of forming new commercial and diplomatic links with other states gives to every enterprising African government considerable room for manoeuver, and the opportunity to follow a more independent line is considerably enlarged by the greater number of outside powers, European, Asian, or American, with an interest in Africa. In these circumstances it is hard to imagine the revival of older forms of imperialism. Nor, with the exception of the Arab-Israeli conflict, does there seem much likelihood of any African state being drawn into any armed struggle between the major powers. Indeed should the future ever bring such a struggle in the form of a war fought with atomic weapons, Africa might well be one of those parts of the world that escapes relatively unscathed.

As for the possibility of conflict between African states, the area of greatest tension clearly lies along the line dividing the white-dominated states of Southern Africa from the black states to the north. Yet there seems little likelihood of a head-on confrontation. The white states cannot run the risk of incurring international odium through punitive action against their black neighbors. On the other hand, no black state is strong enough to contemplate an all-out war with Portugal, Rhodesia, or South Africa. Besides, the black states can resort to other tactics designed to weaken the position of their opponents: they can work to ensure their diplomatic isolation, and they can offer practical support to the African nationalist movements which are seeking to undermine white rule by means of guerrilla operations. The white regimes of the south are already under considerable external pressure—whether in the form of economic sanctions, as in Rhodesia, or of widespread moral disapproval, as is directed against South Africa. But Southern Africa seems likely to remain an area of peripheral strategic interest to the Great Powers of the world. In these circumstances it seems unreasonable to forecast a steady escalation in the volume of external pressure. If there is to be change in Southern Africa, it must come about largely as the result of internal forces. What impact are these forces likely to have on the structure of white supremacy?

In Rhodesia the position of the white minority seems least secure. Rhodesian whites find themselves faced with an African population which already outnumbers them by more than fifteen to one and which is increasing at a very rapid rate. In these circumstances the difficulties of maintaining a firm grip on the African-populated areas are bound to become increasingly formidable. Moreover, the majority of white Rhodesians are first generation immigrants. Such a population seems emotionally ill-equipped to sustain a long-drawn-out war against a nationalist guerrilla movement. In these circumstances the white minority may well find itself faced with only two options—either to place itself under South African protection, a protection the South African government may well not be willing to afford, or to seek the good offices of the British government in reaching a settlement with the African nationalists, a settlement that would be acceptable to the nationalists only if it allowed them to take over the seats of power within a short space of time.

The present rulers of Portugal obviously have it in their power to carry on their war with African nationalist forces in Angola and Mozambique for many years to come, but they are not likely to bring the war to what they would regard as a successful conclusion by military means. However ardent their sense of mission, they cannot ignore certain hard realities of the situation—the growing burden of military expenditure on the country's finances, the increasing resentment of the metropolitan population to the long periods of military service demanded of its young men, and the emergence of an attractive alternative to older ways of gaining wealth and prestige through the exploitation of colonial territories—the alternative presented by the prospect of more rapid economic development as a result of closer ties with the European Economic Community. In these circumstances there is the possibility of some sort of compromise settlement granting a greater measure of autonomy to the colonial territories. The experience of other African colonies suggests that autonomy is likely to be no more than a temporary stage on the road toward complete independence. It is impossible to predict what sort of adjustment is likely to occur between Portuguese settlers and African nationalists, but the absence of a legalized color-bar suggests that the Portuguese territories may eventually evolve the pattern of a multi-racial community similar to that found in some of the countries of Latin America.

In South Africa, on the other hand, there seems little likelihood in the immediate future of any substantial alteration in the present political balance. The Afrikaner Nationalist regime has a formidable array of resources at its disposal, and it can count on the support, tacit or vocal, of the vast majority of white South Africans. Yet the structure of South African society is not completely rigid. Certain significant changes could be observed in the early 1970's: the move toward autonomy of some of the Bantustans; the increase in the bargaining power of urban Africans as they acquire a wider range of industrial skills; the growth of "black consciousness"; the abandonment by many young white South Africans of the old notions of racial superiority. But none of these changes seem likely to lead to that dramatic solution, so often envisaged with relish or with foreboding, by people both inside and outside the country, a violent revolutionary upheaval. History affords many examples of minorities, ethnically distinct from the mass of the population, maintaining a privileged position for long periods of time: in the African record one may recall the experience of the Macedonian Greeks in Ptolemaic Egypt or of the Turks in many parts of North Africa in the sixteenth, seventeenth, and eighteenth centuries. In South Africa the processes of urbanization and industrialization seem likely to produce a more integrated population possessing a more homogeneous culture. In such a society wealth may come to seem more important than pigmentation as an index of social differentiation. In such circumstances the political situation in South Africa may well, in the course of the next few decades, come to resemble that of the Hapsburg Empire in the nineteenth century, a multi-national polity whose fissiparous tendencies were held in check by a conservative regime at the center.

In other African states conflict between different ethnic groups has been one of the most distinctive features of the first years of independence. On the other hand, there has been far less evidence of social conflict between different classes. Indeed, in their present stage of evolution, "class" is a term which seems inappropriate to apply to most African societies. But as economic development proceeds, differences in wealth between different sections of the community are likely to become more apparent. Already in many African countries one can point to the existence of an urban bourgeoisie and an urban proletariat. The wealth accumulated and displayed by small influential cliques is likely always to be a source of jealousy and resentment. Radical egalitarianism, whether expressed in Marxist or non-Marxist terms, seems bound to serve as the basis of the ideology of most opposition groups in late twentieth-century Africa. But every government, no matter how radical its ideology, inevitably acquires the character of an "in-group" and so incurs the resentment of those who envy its power and its privileges and the criticism of those who believe they could handle the direction of public affairs more effectively. To say this is to imply that tension must always be one of the basic elements of politics. Social systems change slowly and so convey the impression of great stability. Political regimes are far more fragile and contain within themselves the seeds of their own dissolution.

Finally, one must consider the peaceful pursuit of well-being as a force making for change in the Africa of the future. Everywhere in the world the vast majority of individuals live out their lives in a local or a private context. Yet the accumulation of private actions has a profound effect on the shaping of any society. Throughout Africa men and women have come in recent decades to acquire both new skills and new expectations. The man who builds himself a better house, the farmer who decides to make use of more modern tools or to sow improved strains of seed, the parents who are concerned to ensure for their children the best available education, the trader anxious to enlarge the scope of his business, the priest concerned about the spiritual welfare of his parishioners, the teacher enthusiastic to impart new tehniques or ideas to his students—individuals such as these act as a continual leaven within their own societies. To predict, in the manner of some contemporary prophets of doom, a dark future for mankind in general and Africa in particular, is to reveal a fundamental inability to appreciate the force of human vitality.

History is in large part the record of human achievement, of endeavor and creative action. The African past provides many splendid examples of such achievements. It is exhilirating to end a study of the history of Africa by reflecting on the many marvelous things the future is bound to bring forth—the new institutions, the new sources of wealth, the new art forms, the new ideas, but, above all, the new men and women who will make these achievements possible. Slowly, as the world shrinks, as modern communications bring countries and peoples ever closer together, a new culture is emerging, a culture based on tolerant and humane premises, a cosmopolitan culture that relishes the diversity of mankind, a culture that has been called "the civilization of the universal." To this culture, this civilization of the future the peoples of Africa will make many splendidly invigorating contributions.

Notes

▲▼ NOTES TO INTRODUCTION

1. In 1973 Africa, together with its neighboring islands, contained the following forty-one independent sovereign states: Algeria, Botswana, Burundi, Cameroon, Central African Republic, Chad, Congo-Brazzaville, Dahomey, Egypt, Equatorial Guinea, Ethiopia, Gabon, Gambia, Ghana, Guinea, Ivory Coast, Kenya, Lesotho, Liberia, Libya, Madagascar, Malawi, Mali, Mauritius, Morocco, Niger, Nigeria, Rwanda, Senegal, Sierra Leone, Somalia, South Africa, Sudan, Swaziland, Tanzania, Togo, Tunisia, Uganda, Upper Volta, Zaire (Congo), and Zambia. In addition the continent contained the following nonsovereign territories: under British control, St. Helena, and Seychelles; under French control, Afars and Issas Territory (French Somaliland), and Réunion; under Portuguese control, Angola, Cape Verde Islands, Mozambique, Portuguese Guinea, São Tomé, and Principe; under South African control, South West Africa; under Spanish control, Ceuta, Melilla, and Spanish Sahara. Rhodesia, *de jure* a British colony, was *de facto* independent.
2. B. Davidson, "The African Personality" in C. Legum (ed.), *Africa Handbook* (Harmondsworth, 1969), p. 535.
3. W. R. James, "A Crisis in Uduk History," *Sudan Notes and Records,* XLIX (1968), pp. 17–44. I am grateful to Miss W. James for other material on the Uduk contained in an unpublished seminar paper.
4. L. Tolstoy, *War and Peace,* tr. by L. and A. Maude (London, 1944), III, p. 390.

▲▼ NOTES TO CHAPTER II

1. Lady Duff Gordon, *Letters from Egypt, 1862–1869,* edited by G. Waterfield (London, 1969), p. 65.
2. Duff Gordon, *op. cit.,* p. 56.
3. Duff Gordon, *op. cit.,* pp. 301, 282.
4. P. J. Vatikiotis, *The Modern History of Egypt* (London, 1969), p. 112.
5. The Earl of Cromer, *Modern Egypt* (London, 1911), p. 46.
6. *Murray's Handbook for Travellers in Egypt* (London, 1873), p. 71.
7. Cromer, *op. cit.,* p. 795.

8. Quoted in Vatikiotis, *op. cit.*, p. 179.

9. D. S. Landes, *Bankers and Pashas* (London, 1958), p. 315.

10. A. Hourani, *Arabic Thought in the Liberal Age, 1798–1939* (London, 1962), p. 108.

11. N. R. Keddie, *An Islamic Response to Imperialism: Political and Religious Writings of Sayyid Jamal ad-Din al-Afghani* (Berkeley, 1968), p. 103.

12. Hourani, *op. cit.*, p. 109.

13. Cromer, *op. cit.*, p. 107.

14. Quoted in C. P. Harris, *Nationalism and Revolution in Egypt* (The Hague, 1964), p. 43.

15. Cromer, *op. cit.*, p. 194.

16. Cromer, *op. cit.*, p. 174.

17. W. S. Blunt, *Secret History of the English Occupation of Egypt* (London, 1922), p. 139.

18. Cromer, *op. cit.*, p. 164.

19. R. C. K. Ensor, *England, 1870–1914* (Oxford, 1936), p. 79.

20. Baring to Granville, 9.10.1883, quoted in R. E. Robinson, J. Gallagher, and A. Denny, *Africa and the Victorians* (London, 1961), p. 131.

21. Quoted in R. I. Tignor, *Modernization and British Colonial Rule in Egypt, 1882–1914* (Princeton, 1966), p. 83.

22. Baring to Salisbury, 15.12.1889, quoted in Robinson, Gallagher, and Denny, *op. cit.*, p. 285.

23. G. N. Sanderson, *England, Europe and the Upper Nile, 1882–1899* (Edinburgh, 1965), pp. 114, 116.

24. Salisbury to Cromer, 13.3.1896, quoted in Robinson, Gallagher, and Denny, *op. cit.*, p. 348.

25. Quoted in P. Magnus, *Kitchener* (London, 1958), p. 137.

26. Sanderson, *op. cit.*, p. 389.

27. Quoted in Sanderson, *op. cit.*, p. 360.

28. Cromer, *op. cit.*, p. 548.

29. A. W. Kinglake, *Eothen* (Everyman ed.; New York, 1928), p. 182.

30. Quoted in the Earl of Cromer, *Ancient and Modern Imperialisms* (London, 1910), p. 20n.

31. Quoted in the Marquess of Zetland, *Lord Cromer* (London, 1932), p. 89.

32. Cromer, *Modern Egypt*, p. 726.

33. Edgar Vincent, later Baron d'Abernon, quoted in A. Lutfi al-Sayyid, *Egypt under Cromer* (London, 1968), p. 64.

34. Quoted in Robinson, Gallagher, and Denny, *op. cit.*, p. 276.

35. Cromer, *op. cit.*, p. 908.

36. W. Wilcocks, *Sixty Years in the East* (London, 1935), p. 269.

37. Cromer, *op. cit.*, p. 882.

38. E. R. J. Owen, *Cotton and the Egyptian Economy, 1820–1914* (Oxford, 1969), p. 240.

39. Quoted by G. Baer, "Social Change in Egypt: 1800–1914" in P. M. Holt (ed.) *Political and Social Change in Modern Egypt* (London, 1968), p. 157.

40. Tignor, *op. cit.*, p. 251.

41. Lutfi al-Sayyid, *op. cit.*, p. 184.
42. The words used by the British chargé d'affaires quoted in Lutfi al-Sayyid, *op. cit.*, p. 172.
43. J. Ohrwalder, *Ten Years' Captivity in the Mahdi's Camp, 1882–1892*, 13th ed., revised and abridged (London, 1893), pp. 75–76.
44. Quoted in F. R. Wingate, *Mahdism and the Egyptian Sudan* (London, 1891), p. 45.
45. Quoted in Wingate, *op. cit.*, p. 111.
46. Quoted in B. M. Allen, *Gordon and the Sudan* (London, 1931), p. 140.
47. Ohrwalder, *op. cit.*, p. 393.
48. Quoted in Wingate, *op. cit.*, p. 309.
49. Ohrwalder, *op. cit.*, p. 458.
50. P. M. Holt, *A Modern History of the Sudan* (London, 1961), p. 106.
51. Quoted in J. S. R. Duncan, *The Sudan* (Edinburgh, 1952), p. 86.
52. *Report on the Finances, Administration and Conditions of Egypt and the Sudan* (London, 1902), p. 56.
53. Quoted in R. Wingate, *Wingate of the Sudan* (London, 1955), p. 160.
54. H. Macmichael, *The Anglo-Egyptian Sudan* (London, 1932), p. 108.
55. K. D. D. Henderson, *The Sudan Republic* (London, 1965), p. 50.
56. Henderson, *op. cit.*, p. 33.
57. E. J. Cox, "Munzinger's Observations on the Sudan," *Sudan Notes and Records* XXXIII (1952), quoted in K. M. Barbour, *The Republic of the Sudan* (London, 1961), p. 267.
58. Public Record Office (London) F.O./633/14. Cromer to Gorst, 12.11.1908, quoted in M. O. Beshir, *Educational Development in the Sudan, 1898 to 1956* (London, 1969), p. 27.
59. J. T. Bent, *The Sacred City of the Ethiopians* (London, 1893), pp. 11–12.
60. Quoted in J. L. Miège, *L'Impérialisme colonial Italien de 1870 à nos jours* (Paris, 1968), p. 54.
61. Quoted in Miège, *op. cit.*, p. 61.
62. Quoted in Miège, *op. cit.*, p. 62.
63. D. Mathew, *Ethiopia: the Study of a Polity, 1540–1935* (London, 1947), p. 226.
64. J. Rennell Rodd, *Social and Diplomatic Memoirs* (London, 1922), quoted in R. Pankhurst (ed.), *Travellers in Ethiopia* (London, 1965), p. 133.
65. L. Mosley, *Haile Selassie* (London, 1964), pp. 44, 46.
66. Quoted in R. Pankhurst (ed.), *The Ethiopian Royal Chronicles* (Addis Ababa, 1967), p. 194.
67. W. Thesiger, *Arabian Sands* (London, 1959), p. 4.
68. *Ibid.*, p. 5.
69. M. Perham, *The Government of Ethiopia*, 2d ed. (London, 1969), pp. 318–21.
70. D. Jardine, *The Mad Mullah of Somaliland* (London, 1923), p. 17.
71. I. M. Lewis, *The Modern History of Somaliland* (London, 1965), p. 43.
72. Quoted in V. Thompson and R. Adloff, *Djibouti and the Horn of Africa* (Stanford, Calif., 1966), p. 8.

73. Jardine, *op. cit.*, p. 313.
74. *Ibid.*, p. 308.
75. *Ibid.*, p. 305.
76. Lewis, *op. cit.*, p. 84.
77. G. Young, *Egypt* (London, 1927), p. 271.
78. P. G. Elgood, *The Transit of Egypt* (London, 1928), pp. 239–40.
79. Quoted in C. P. Harris, *Nationalism and Revolution in Egypt* (The Hague, 1964), p. 146.
80. J. Marlowe, *Anglo-Egyptian Relations, 1800–1956*, 2d ed. (London, 1965), p. 311.
81. P. Mansfield, *Nasser* (London, 1969), p. 35.
82. J. Gunther, *Inside Africa* (London, 1955), p. 202.
83. Quoted in N. Safran, *Egypt in Search of Political Community* (Cambridge, Mass., 1961), p. 201.
84. Mansfield, *op. cit.*, p. 74.
85. Quoted in M. Abd ar-Rahman, *Imperialism and Nationalism in the Sudan* (London, 1969), p. 99.
86. *Ibid.*, p. 100.
87. *Ibid.*, p. 109 n 1.
88. Sir D. Newbold, "Recent Political Developments in the Sudan," October, 1944, in K. D. D. Henderson, *The Making of the Modern Sudan* (London, 1952), p. 532.
89. Sir J. Maffey, minute of 1.1.1927, quoted in R. O. Collins and R. L. Tignor, *Egypt and the Sudan* (Englewood Cliffs, N.J., 1967), p. 128.
90. K. D. D. Henderson, *The Sudan Republic*, p. 163.
91. Civil Secretary's memorandum on "Southern Policy," 25.1.1930, in Abd ar-Rahman, *op. cit.*, pp. 244–49.
92. W. K. Hancock, *Argument of Empire* (London, 1943), p. 56, quoted by D. Newbold in a letter to J. W. Robertson, 23.6.1944, in Henderson, *The Making of the Modern Sudan*, p. 380.
93. Newbold's own phrase, *ibid.*, p. 380.
94. G. C. Scott, "Notes on Education in the Sudan" in Beshir, *op. cit.*, p. 221.
95. E. Atiyah, *An Arab Tells His Story* (London, 1946), p. 138.
96. The phrase used by Ismail al-Azhari in a letter to the Civil Secretary, quoted in Holt, *op. cit.*, p. 141.
97. Abd ar-Rahman, *op. cit.*, p. 126.
98. E. Atiyah, "Progress in the Sudan," *Spectator* (London), 31.3.1950.
99. Civil Secretary's memorandum on "Revision of Southern Policy," 19.12.1946, in Abd ar-Rahman, *op. cit.*, pp. 253–56.
100. The phrase used by "a senior district officer in the south in a private letter, 18.10.1944," quoted in Henderson, *The Sudan Republic*, p. 195.
101. Gunther, *op. cit.*, p. 237.
102. B. Davidson, "The Sudan: Arab or African?," *Manchester Guardian*, 19.2.1958.
103. Quoted in R. Greenfield, *Ethiopia: a New Political History* (London, 1965), p. 151.
104. Mosley, *op. cit.*, p. 148.
105. G. L. Steer, *Caesar in Abyssinia* (London, 1936), p. 38.

106. Quoted in Greenfield, *op. cit.*, p. 158.
107. Quoted in G. W. Baer, *The Coming of the Italian-Ethiopian War* (Cambridge, Mass., 1967), p. 17.
108. A. H. M. Jones and E. Monroe, *A History of Abyssinia* (Oxford, 1935), p. 182.
109. B. Mussolini, foreword to P. Badoglio, *The War in Abyssinia* (London, 1937), p. v.
110. Mosley, *op. cit.*, p. 203.
111. Quoted in Greenfield, *op. cit.*, p. 201.
112. Steer, *op. cit.*, p. 269.
113. Lord Hailey, foreword to F. Quaranta, *Ethiopia: an Empire in the Making* (London, 1939), p. vi.
114. Quoted in R. L. Hess, *Italian Colonialism in Somalia* (Chicago, 1966), p. 171.
115. I. M. Lewis in "The Somali Republic: A Special Report," *The Times* (London), 16.9.1969.
116. Lewis, *The Modern History of Somaliland*, p. 115.
117. Quoted in Lewis, *op. cit.*, p. 123.
118. *Annual Report for the Somaliland Protectorate for the Year 1948* (London, 1949), p. 15.
119. Quoted in Mansfield, *Nasser*, p. 21.
120. G. A. Nasser, *Egypt's Liberation: The Philosophy of the Revolution* (Washington, D.C., 1953), pp. 32–33.
121. Nasser, *op. cit.*, p. 103.
122. W. K., "Political Issues in the Fertile Crescent," *The World Today* (London) XXII (1956), pp. 219–20.
123. President Nasser's speech at the Arab Socialist Union meeting, 23.7.1964. Quoted in W. Lacquer, *The Struggle for the Middle East* (London, 1969), p. 239.
124. Quoted in Lacquer, *op. cit.*, p. 63.
125. Collins and Tignor, *op. cit.*, p. 146.
126. P. Mansfield, *Nasser's Egypt* (Harmondsworth, 1965), p. 122.
127. *Ibid.*, p. 168.
128. C. Issawi, *Egypt in Revolution* (London, 1963), p. 133.
129. Vatikiotis, *op. cit.*, p. 115.
130. Mansfield, *Nasser's Egypt*, p. 214.
131. B. Davidson, *Manchester Guardian*, 19.2.1958.
132. Gunther, *op. cit.*, p. 224.
133. Henderson, *The Sudan Republic*, p. 131.
134. Quoted in Henderson, *op. cit.*, p. 143.
135. *Ibid.*, p. 136.
136. J. Howell and M. B. Hamid, "Sudan and the Outside World," *African Affairs*, LXVIII/273 (October, 1969), p. 311.
137. *Ibid.*, p. 315.
138. M. Perham, *The Government of Ethiopia*, 2d ed. (London, 1969), p. lxxxii.
139. *The Guardian* (London), 8.11.1969.
140. Quoted in S. Touval, *Somali Nationalism* (Cambridge, Mass., 1963), p. 95.

▲▼   NOTES TO CHAPTER III

1.   S. H. Roberts, *History of French Colonial Policy* (London, 1929), vol. I, p. 208.

2.   Quoted in C. R. Ageron, *Les Algériens musulmans et la France (1871–1919)* (Paris, 1968), vol. I, p. 52.

3.   J. Berque, *French North Africa: The Maghrib between Two World Wars,* translated by J. Stewart (London, 1967), p. 345.

4.   Quoted in *The Annual Register, 1891* (London, 1892), p. 253.

5.   Quoted in Roberts, *op. cit.,* vol. I, p. 214.

6.   Berque, *op. cit.,* pp. 310–11.

7.   Quoted in D. L. Ling, *Tunisia: From Protectorate to Republic* (Bloomington, Ill., 1967), p. 27.

8.   Quoted in J. Ganiage, *Les Origines du protectorat français en Tunisie (1861–1881)* (Paris, 1959), p. 93.

9.   Quoted in Ganiage, *op. cit.,* p. 632.

10.   Quoted in Ganiage, *op. cit.,* p. 661.

11.   Quoted in Ling, *op. cit.,* p. 40.

12.   P. Leroy-Beaulieu, *L'Algérie et la Tunisie,* 2d ed. (Paris, 1897), p. 352.

13.   Quoted in N. Barbour, *Morocco* (London, 1965), p. 141.

14.   R. L. Playfair and R. Brown, *A Bibliography of Morocco* (London, 1892), p. x.

15.   E. Lévi-Provençal, quoted in R. Landau, *Moroccan Drama, 1900–1955* (London, 1956), p. 34.

16.   W. B. Harris, quoted in Landau, *op. cit.,* p. 54.

17.   Quoted in J. L. Miège, *Le Maroc et l'Europe (1830–1894)* (Paris, 1963), vol. IV, p. 136, n. 5.

18.   A. J. P. Taylor, *The Struggle for Mastery in Europe* (Oxford, 1954), p. 441.

19.   G. H. Selous, *Appointment to Fez* (London, 1956), p. 175.

20.   Quoted by P. Lyautey, "Marshal Lyautey" in *History of the Twentieth Century,* edited by A. J. P. Taylor and J. M. Roberts (London, 1968), p. 324.

21.   Quoted in R. Landau, *op. cit.,* p. 86.

22.   G. Maxwell, *Lords of the Atlas* (London, 1966), p. 145.

23.   General A. Guillaume, quoted in Landau, *op. cit.,* p. 90.

24.   Quoted in Landau, *op. cit.,* p. 92.

25.   Quoted in Landau, *op. cit.,* pp. 245–46. The text of the important report, dated 18.11.1920, in which this remark occurs, is given in P. Lyautey (ed.), *Lyautey l'Africain: Textes et lettres du Maréchal Lyautey* (Paris, 1953–57), vol. IV, pp. 25–36.

26.   Quoted in J. Brignon *et al., Histoire du Maroc* (Casablanca, 1967), p. 408.

27.   Quoted in D. S. Woodman, *Rebels in the Rif* (London, 1969), p. 116.

28.   J. I. Clarke, in R. M. Prothero (ed.), *A Geography of Africa* (London, 1969), p. 63.

29.   G. Tillion, *France and Algeria: Complementary Enemies,* translated by R. Howard (New York, 1961), p. 111.

30. Quoted in A. Bernard, *L'Algérie* (Paris, 1931), p. 211.
31. Berque, *op. cit.*, p. 93.
32. Consul Haggard, quoted in N. A. Ziadeh, *Origins of Nationalism in Tunisia* (Beirut, 1962), p. 44.
33. Berque, *op. cit.*, p. 57.
34. J. Gunther, *Inside Africa* (London, 1955), p. 151.
35. Berque, *op. cit.*, p. 143.
36. Napoleon Bonaparte in an address to the *Institut National* in 1797.
37. Berque, *op. cit.*, p. 44.
38. A. Memmi, *La Poésie algérienne de 1830 à nos jours* (Paris, 1963), pp. 34–36.
39. Quoted in Ageron, *op. cit.*, vol. II, p. 1054.
40. An English edition of this work translated by M. A. Shapor was published in Lahore in 1954.
41. C. F. Gallagher, *The United States and North Africa* (Cambridge, Mass., 1963), p. 87.
42. Quoted in Ziadeh, *op. cit.*, p. 92.
43. Quoted in R. Le Tourneau, *Evolution politique de l'Afrique du nord musulmane, 1920–1961* (Paris, 1962), p. 314.
44. *Ibid.*, p. 319.
45. Tillion, *op. cit.*, p. 115.
46. *Ibid.*, p. 8.
47. Quoted in C. R. Ageron, *Histoire de l'Algérie contemporaine, 1830–1969* (Paris, 1969), p. 116.
48. Quoted in E. E. Evans-Pritchard, *The Sanusi of Cyrenaica* (Oxford, 1949), p. 17.
49. B. Croce, *A History of Italy, 1871–1915*, translated by C. M. Ady, (London, 1929), p. 260.
50. Evans-Pritchard, *op. cit.*, p. 171.
51. *Ibid.*, p. 191.
52. R. Capot-Rey, *Le Sahara français* (Paris, 1953), p. 479.
53. R. Capot-Rey, "The Present State of Nomadism in the Sahara," *Arid Zone Research*, vol. XVIII (UNESCO, 1962).
54. *Ibid.*
55. J. Wright, *Libya* (London, 1969), p. 242.
56. *The Times* (London), 31.1.1968.
57. F. Fanon, *The Wretched of the Earth* (Harmondsworth, 1967), p. 30.

▲▼ NOTES TO CHAPTER IV

1. R. Jobson, *The Golden Trade,* new edition with introduction by W. Rodney (London, 1968), p. 78.
2. W. Winwood Reade, *Savage Africa* (London, 1863), p. 584.
3. *Ibid.*, p. 448.
4. F. Carrère and P. Holle, *De la Sénégambie française* (Paris, 1855), p. 127, quoted in M. A. Klein, "The Moslem Revolution in Nineteenth-Century Senegambia," in D. F. McCall, N. R. Bennett, and J. Butler (eds.), *Western African History,* Boston University Papers on Africa, vol. IV (New York, 1969), p. 74.

5. Quoted by C. A. Quinn, "Traditionalism, Islam and the European Expansion on the Gambia, 1850–1894," (Ph.D. thesis, University of California, Los Angeles, 1967), p. 235.

6. A. S. Kanya-Forstner, *The Conquest of the Western Sudan* (Cambridge, 1969), p. 40, summarizing an unpublished memorandum written by Faidherbe in 1858.

7. Le Général Faidherbe, *Le Sénégal* (Paris, 1889), p. 285.

8. *Ibid.*, p. 288.

9. J. D. Hargreaves, *Prelude to the Partition of West Africa* (London, 1963), p. 195.

10. J. S. Trimingham, *A History of Islam in West Africa* (London, 1962), p. 180.

11. Y. Person, "Samori et la Sierra Leone," *Cahiers d'études africaine,* 25 (1967), p. 25.

12. Quoted in C. W. Newbury and A. S. Kanya-Forstner, "French Policy and the Origins of the Scramble for West Africa," *Journal of African History,* X/2 (1969), p. 255.

13. *Ibid.*, p. 259.

14. *Ibid.*, p. 261.

15. J. Méniaud, *Les pionniers du Soudan . . . 1879–1894* (Paris, 1931), vol. I, p. 188.

16. Quoted in Kanya-Forstner, *op. cit.*, p. 89.

17. Quoted in P. Gourou, "Galliéni" in M. Baumann *et al., Les techniciens de la colonisation (XIXe–XXe siècles)* (Paris, 1946), pp. 95–97.

18. Quoted in Kanya-Forstner, *op. cit.*, p. 175.

19. Quoted in Gourou, *op. cit.*, p. 98.

20. Quoted in Kanya-Forstner, *op. cit.*, p. 187.

21. Colonel Baratier, *A travers l'Afrique* (Paris, 1912), quoted in M. Crowder, *West Africa under Colonial Rule* (London, 1968), p. 87.

22. A. Kouroubari, "Histoire de l'imam Samori," *Bulletin de l'Institut Français d'Afrique Noire,* series B. XXI (1959), p. 563.

23. Quoted in Kanya-Forstner, *op. cit.*, p. 167.

24. *Hansard,* 3rd series, CCCXLVIII, col. 459 (11.8.1890), quoted in R. Robinson, J. Gallagher and A. Denny, *Africa and the Victorians* (London, 1961), p. 303.

25. For a well-documented account of this extraordinary episode see Mme Klobb, *A la recherche de Voulet* (Paris, 1931).

26. W. Winwood Reade, *The African Sketch Book* (London, 1873), vol. II, p. 260.

27. A. Arcin, *La Guinée française* (Paris, 1907), pp. 582–83.

28. C.O. 806/325: Knutsford to officer administering the Government of Sierra Leone, 1.1.1890, quoted in C. Fyfe (ed.), *Sierra Leone Inheritance* (London, 1964), p. 203.

29. Quoted in C. Fyfe, *A History of Sierra Leone* (London, 1962), p. 556.

30. J. G. Liebenow, *Liberia* (Ithaca, 1969), p. 24.

31. C.O. 96/258: Governor Maxwell to Lord Ripon, 13.6.1895, in G. E. Metcalfe (ed.), *Great Britain and Ghana, Documents of Ghana History 1807–1957* (London, 1964), p. 478.

32. A. W. L. Hemming, "Memo. on relations with Ashanti," February,

1895, quoted in W. Tordoff, *Ashanti under the Prempehs, 1888–1936* (London, 1965), p. 55.

33. C.O. 96/378: Governor Nathan to Joseph Chamberlain, 19.3.1901, in Metcalfe (ed.), *op. cit.,* pp. 518–19.

34. J. B. Webster and A. A. Boahen with H. O. Idowu, *The Revolutionary Years: West Africa since 1800* (London, 1967), p. 117.

35. R. F. Burton, *A Mission to Gelele, King of Dahomey,* new edition with introduction by C. W. Newbury (London, 1966), p. 266.

36. J. D. Hargreaves, *Prelude to the Partition of West Africa* (London, 1963), p. 320.

37. The Togo Protectorate Treaty, quoted in C. W. Newbury, *The Western Slave Coast and Its Rulers* (London, 1961), p. 205.

38. C.O. 96/159: Governor Young to Lord Derby, 8.7.1884, in Metcalfe (ed.), *op. cit.,* p. 415.

39. C.O. 96/158: Minute by J. Anderson, *ibid.,* p. 417.

40. Confidential Prints, African 283: Derby to Young, 26.12.1884, *ibid.,* p. 419.

41. Robinson, Gallagher, and Denny, *op. cit.,* p. 408.

42. F.O. 84/1531: Simpson to Granville, 21.11.1871, quoted in C. W. Newbury, "Trade and Authority in West Africa" in L. H. Gann and P. Duignan (eds.), *Colonialism in Africa, 1870–1960.* Vol. I: *The History and Politics of Colonialism, 1870–1914* (Cambridge, 1969), p. 86.

43. F.O. 84/1750: Johnston to Anderson, 13.11.1885, quoted in K. O. Dike, *Trade and Politics in the Niger Delta, 1830–1885* (Oxford, 1956), p. 218.

44. Extracts from accounts written by British officers taking part in the Benin expedition, quoted in W. M. N. Geary, *Nigeria under British Rule* (London, 1927), pp. 116–17.

45. S. Johnson, *The History of the Yorubas* (Lagos, 1957), p. 607.

46. Chamberlain to Selbourne, 19.9.1897, quoted in Robinson, Gallagher, and Denny, *op. cit.,* p. 405.

47. M. Perham, *Lugard: The Years of Adventure, 1858–1898* (London, 1960), p. 59.

48. J. Guinness Rogers, "an old Gladstonian Liberal and Congregational Minister" in *The Nineteenth Century,* February, 1893, quoted in I. F. Nicholson, *The Administration of Nigeria* (Oxford, 1969), p. 128.

49. F. D. Lugard, *The Dual Mandate in British Tropical Africa,* 3d ed. (London, 1926), p. 615.

50. F. D. Lugard, "West African Administration" in *The Empire and the Century* (London, 1905), quoted in Nicholson, *op. cit.,* p. 170.

51. F.O. 84/1277: Livingstone to Stanley, 13.7.1867, quoted in Dike, *op. cit.,* p. 182.

52. F.O. 84/1852: Hewitt to Jaja, 11.7.1884, contained in Jaja to Salisbury, 5.7.1887, quoted in J. C. Anene, *Southern Nigeria in Transition, 1884–1906* (Cambridge, 1965), p. 66.

53. F.O. 84/1828: Johnston to Foreign Office, 28.7.1887, quoted in Anene, *op. cit.,* p. 83.

54. F. D. Lugard, Diary, 12.10.1894, quoted in Perham, *op. cit.,* p. 506.

55. Quoted in E. A. Ayandele, *The Missionary Impact on Modern Nigeria, 1842–1914* (London, 1966), p. 55.

56. Johnson, *op. cit.*, p. 619.

57. *Ibid.*, pp. 621–23.

58. J. D. Y. Peel, "Religious change in Yorubaland," *Africa* XXXVII/3 (1967).

59. Salisbury to Dufferin, 30.3.1892, quoted in Robinson, Gallagher, and Denny, *op. cit.*, p. 390.

60. D. Wellesley, *Sir George Goldie* (London, 1934), p. 91.

61. F.O. 2/83: Macdonald to Hill, 26.3.1895, quoted in Anene, *op. cit.*, p. 71.

62. Goldie to Iddesleigh, 31.12.1886, quoted in J. E. Flint, *Sir George Goldie and the Making of Nigeria* (London, 1960), p. 98.

63. *Parliamentary Papers*, 1896 LIX. Report by Sir John Kirk on the disturbances at Brass. Appendix B: The chiefs of Brass to Sir Claude Macdonald, 14.2.1895.

64. J. E. Flint, "Nigeria: The Colonial Experience" in L. H. Gann and P. Duignan (eds.), *Colonialism in Africa, 1870–1960*. Vol. I: *The History and Politics of Colonialism, 1870–1914* (Cambridge, 1969), p. 228.

65. Lugard to Chamberlain, 23.1.1903, quoted in D. J. M. Muffet, *Concerning Brave Captains: A History of Lord Lugard's Conquest of Hausaland* (London, 1964), pp. 59–60.

66. H. F. Backwell (ed.), *The Occupation of Hausaland, 1900–1904, being a Translation of Arabic Letters Found in the House of the Waziri of Sokoto, Bohari, in 1903* (Lagos, 1927), p. 73.

67. Acting High Commissioner Wallace to Colonial Secretary, 4.6.1903, quoted in Muffet, *op. cit.*, p. 161.

68. Quoted from a translation of the *Risalat* of the *Waziri* of Sokoto, Muhammad al-Bukhari b. Ahmad, in R. A. Adeleye, "The Dilemma of the Wazir," *Journal of the Historical Society of Nigeria*, IV/2 (1968), p. 309.

69. Alhaji Sir Ahmadu Bello, Sardauna of Sokoto, *My Life* (Cambridge, 1962), p. 19.

70. M. F. Smith, *Baba of Karo* (London, 1964), pp. 67–68.

71. W. R. Crocker, *Nigeria: A Critique of British Colonial Administration* (London, 1936), p. 200.

72. R. Delavignette, *Freedom and Authority in French West Africa* (London, 1950), p. 7.

73. R. Wraith, *Guggisberg* (London, 1967), p. 69.

74. Quoted in M. Crowder, *West Africa under Colonial Rule* (London, 1968), p. 382.

75. Wraith, *op. cit.*, p. 74.

76. *Ibid.*, p. 255.

77. W. R. Crocker, *On Governing Colonies* (London, 1947), p. 136.

78. Sir Frederick Lugard's "confidential" proposals on the amalgamation of Nigeria, May 1913, in A. H. M. Kirk-Greene (ed.), *Lugard and the Amalgamation of Nigeria* (London, 1968), p. 224.

79. *Ibid.*, pp. 224–25.

80. G. Gorer, *Africa Dances* (London, 1935), p. 131.

81. Naval Intelligence Division (British Admiralty), *French West Africa* (London, 1943), vol. I, p. 243.

82. R. Symonds, *The British and Their Successors* (London, 1966), p. 122.

83. Quoted in *ibid.*, p. 125.

84. Lord Hailey, *An African Survey* (London, 1938), p. 258.

85. Quoted in Symonds, *op. cit.*, p. 128.

86. W. M. Macmillan, *Africa Emergent* (Harmondsworth, 1949), p. 216.

87. M. Delafosse, quoted in R. L. Buell, *The Native Problem in Africa* (New York, 1928), vol. II, p. 21.

88. Delavignette, *Freedom and Authority in French West Africa*, p. 10.

89. Quoted in M. Perham, *Lugard: The Years of Authority, 1898–1945* (London, 1960), p. 148.

90. M. G. Smith, *Government in Zazzau* (London, 1960).

91. D. C. Dorward, "The Development of British Colonial Administration among the Tiv, 1900–1949," *African Affairs*, LXVIII/273 (1969).

92. J. Suret-Canale, "La fin de la chefferie en Guinée," *Journal of African History*, VII/3 (1966).

93. Smith, *op. cit.*, p. 231.

94. *Ibid.*, p. 291.

95. *Ibid.*, p. 293.

96. The text of van Vollenhoven's circular is given in J. D. Hargreaves (ed.), *France and West Africa* (London, 1969), pp. 210–14.

97. Suret-Canale, *op. cit.*, p. 471.

98. R. S. Rattray, "Recent Trends of African Colonial Government," *Journal of the Royal African Society*, XXXIII/130 (1934).

99. Hailey, *op. cit.*, p. 534.

100. L. P. Mair, *Native Policies in Africa* (London, 1936), p. 189.

101. J. Gunther, *Inside Africa* (London, 1955), p. 686.

102. G. Moore and U. Beier (eds.), *Modern Poetry from Africa* (Harmondsworth, 1963), p. 57.

103. T. J. Bowen, *Central Africa: Adventures and Missionary Labours . . . from 1849 to 1856* (London, 1857), p. 257, quoted in C. W. Newbury, "Trade and Authority in West Africa" in Gann and Duignan (eds.), *op. cit.,* vol. I, p. 68.

104. Newbury, in Gann and Duignan (eds.), *op. cit.*, vol. I, p. 77.

105. Quoted in Nicolson, *The Administration of Nigeria*, p. 70.

106. Hailey, *op. cit.*, p. 1561.

107. Northern Nigeria, Annual Reports, 1900–1911 (London), p. 711.

108. *Ibid.*, p. 413.

109. Macmillan, *op. cit.*, p. 246.

110. R. K. Udo, "British Policy and the Development of Export Crops in Nigeria," *The Nigerian Journal of Economic and Social Studies*, IX/3 (1967), p. 308.

111. C. Wilson, *The History of Unilever* (London, 1954), vol. II, p. 321.

112. *Ibid.*, p. 329.

113. Sir H. Clifford, *The Times* (London), 2.6.1925, quoted in Crowder, *West Africa under Colonial Rule*, p. 349.

114. V. Thompson and R. Adloff, *French West Africa* (London, 1958), p. 293.

115. A. Macmillan (ed.), *The Red Book of West Africa* (London, 1920), pp. 95–98.

116. P. T. Bauer, *West African Trade* (Cambridge, 1954), p. 358.

117. A. Macmillan (ed.), *op. cit.*, p. 184.

118. R. S. Morgenthau, *Political Parties in French-Speaking West Africa* (Oxford, 1961), p. xxi.

119. J. Richard-Molard, "Villes d'Afrique noire," *Présence Africaine*, 15 (1954), quoted in T. Hodgkin, *Nationalism in Colonial Africa* (London, 1956), p. 65.

120. T. Hodgkin, "The Islamic Literary Tradition in Ghana," in I. M. Lewis (ed.), *Islam in Tropical Africa* (London, 1966), p. 454.

121. E. P. Skinner, "Islam in Mossi Society," *ibid.*, p. 362.

122. J. C. Froelich, "Essai sur les causes et les méthodes de l'islamisation de l'Afrique de l'Ouest du XIe siècle au XXe siècle," *ibid.*, p. 170.

123. Sir H. Bell, *Journal of the African Society*, July, 1911, p. 391, quoted in Ayandele, *The Missionary Impact on Modern Nigeria*, p. 149.

124. Webster and Boahen, *op. cit.*, p. 252.

125. G. Parrinder, *Religion in an African City* (London, 1953).

126. C. Baëta, *Prophetism in Ghana* (London, (1962), p. 91.

127. Quoted in N. Smith, *The Presbyterian Church of Ghana, 1850–1960* (Accra, 1966), p. 90.

128. Ayandele, *op. cit.*, p. 332.

129. T. J. Alldridge, *A Transformed Colony* (London, 1910), p. 272.

130. Quoted in Smith, *The Presbyterian Church of Ghana*, p. 188.

131. J. C. Messenger, "Religious Acculturation among the Anang Ibibio," in W. R. Bascom and M. J. Herskovits (eds.), *Continuity and Change in African Cultures* (Chicago, 1959).

132. K. Little, *The Mende of Sierra Leone* (London, 1951), p. 121.

133. A. Moumouni, *Education in Africa* (London, 1968), p. 21.

134. Quoted in Hailey, *An African Survey*, p. 1265.

135. L. S. Senghor quoted in I. L. Markovitz, *Senghor and the Politics of Negritude* (London, 1969), p. 63.

136. Quoted in J. F. A. Ajayi, *Christian Missions in Nigeria, 1841–1891* (London, 1965), p. 133.

137. Hailey, *op. cit.*, p. 1183.

138. J. Foster, *Education and Social Change in Ghana* (London, 1965), p. 145.

139. Governor-General Brévié quoted in Moumouni, *op. cit.*, p. 42.

140. Moumouni, *op. cit.*, p. 55.

141. Morgenthau, *Political Parties in French-Speaking West Africa*, p. 15.

142. O. Awolowo, *Awo* (Cambridge, 1960), p. 27.

143. Moumouni, *op. cit.*, p. 49.

144. O. Awolowo, *Path to Nigerian Freedom* (London, 1947), p. 47.

145. Sir H. Clifford, Address to the Nigerian Council, 29.12.1920, quoted in J. S. Coleman, *Nigeria: Background to Nationalism* (Berkeley, 1963), p. 194.

146. E. J. Berg, "The Economic Dimension of Political Change in French West Africa," in W. J. Hanna (ed.), *Independent Black Africa* (Chicago, 1964), p. 615.

147. Quoted in R. W. July, *The Origins of Modern African Thought* (London, 1968), p. 344.

148. A. B. Ellis, *West African Sketches* (London, 1881), quoted in July, *op. cit.*, p. 299.

149. *Sierra Leone Weekly News*, 2.11.1912, quoted in Fyfe, *Sierra Leone Inheritance*, p. 303.

150. Coleman, *op. cit.*, p. 180.

151. Moore and Beier (eds.), *Modern Poetry from Africa*, p. 58.

152. O. Bassir (ed.), *An Anthology of West African Verse* (Ibadan, 1957), p. 39.

153. *Ibid.*

154. July, *op. cit.*, p. 277.

155. Quoted in D. Kimble, *A Political History of Ghana, 1850–1928* (Oxford, 1963), p. 150.

156. Morgenthau, *op. cit.*, p. 22.

157. E. W. Blyden, "The Negro in Ancient History," *Methodist Quarterly Review* (New York), LI (1869), quoted in H. R. Lynch, *Edward Wilmot Blyden* (London, 1967), p. 56.

158. Quoted in July, *op. cit.*, pp. 218–19.

159. *Sierra Leone Times*, 27.5.1893, quoted in Lynch, *op. cit.*, p. 61.

160. Quoted in July, *op. cit.*, p. 227.

161. Coleman, *op. cit.*, p. 189.

162. A. J. Garvey (compiler), *Philosophy and Opinions of Marcus Garvey* (New York, 1923), Part I, pp. 6, 4, 53.

163. *L'A.O.F.*, 11.4.1914, quoted in G. W. Johnson, "The Ascendency of Blaise Diagne and the Beginnings of African Politics in Senegal," *Africa*, XXXVI/3 (1966), p. 248.

164. Quoted in July, *op. cit.*, p. 407.

165. G. W. Johnson, *op. cit.*, p. 252.

166. July, *op. cit.*, p. 436.

167. J. C. Casely-Hayford, *Ethiopia Unbound* (London, 1911), pp. 69, 194.

168. Quoted in Coleman, *op. cit.*, p. 193.

169. July, *op. cit.*, p. 449.

170. Quoted in D. Austen, *Politics in Ghana, 1948–1960* (London, 1964), p. 10.

171. Quoted in Coleman, *op. cit.*, p. 198.

172. Hodgkin, *Nationalism in Colonial Africa*, p. 85.

173. Coleman, *op. cit.*, p. 214.

174. *Ibid.*, p. 220.

175. Gunther, *op. cit.*, p. 756–57.

176. "Report of the Commission of Enquiry into Disturbances in the Gold Coast" (1948), quoted in Metcalfe (ed.), *op. cit.*, p. 682.

177. "Minority Report of the Commission on Higher Education in West Africa," quoted in I. Wallenstein, *The Road to Independence: Ghana and the Ivory Coast* (Paris, 1964), p. 42.

178. Sir C. Arden-Clarke, "Eight years of Transition in Ghana," *African Affairs*, LVII/226 (January, 1958), p. 35.

179. H. Swanzy, "Quarterly Notes," *African Affairs*, XLV/181 (October, 1946), p. 168.

180. Sir J. Macpherson, Address to Legislative Council, 17.8.1948, quoted in Coleman, *op. cit.*, p. 311.

181. *Ibid.*, pp. 310–11.

182. Sir A. Burns, Address to Empire Parliamentary Association, 24.10.1946, quoted in Austin, *op. cit.*, p. 3.

183. W. E. F. Ward, *A History of Ghana* (London, 1959), p. 325.

184. K. Nkrumah, *Ghana: The Autobiography of Kwame Nkrumah* (Edinburgh, 1957), p. 45.

185. E. Huxley, *Four Guineas* (London, 1955), p. 93.

186. "Report . . . into Disturbances in the Gold Coast" (1948) in Metcalfe (ed.), *op. cit.*, pp. 682, 685.

187. Austin, *op. cit.*, p. 77, n. 5.

188. T. Hodgkin, *African Political Parties* (Harmondsworth, 1961), pp. 133–34.

189. Arden-Carke, *op. cit.*, p. 34.

190. Austin, *op. cit.*, p. 185.

191. G. Collier, *Sierra Leone* (New York, 1970), p. 18.

192. Quoted in W. A. Nielsen, *The Great Powers and Africa* (London, 1969), p. 84.

193. The texts of those sections of the French constitutions of 1946 and 1958 relevant to the African territories is given in Morgenthau, *Political Parties in French-Speaking West Africa*, pp. 379–92.

194. F. G. Snyder, "An Era Ends in Mali," *Africa Report*, XIV/3–4 (April, 1969), p. 14.

195. Morgenthau, *op. cit.*, p. 262.

196. Quoted in G. de Lusignan, *French-Speaking Africa since Independence* (London, 1969), p. 238.

197. Quoted in R. Segal, *African Profiles* (Harmondworth, 1962), p. 264.

198. Quoted in Morgenthau, *op. cit.*, p. 226.

199. *Ibid.*, p. 239.

200. An English translation of Sékou Touré's speech is given in O. R. Dathmore and W. Fenser (eds.), *Africa in Prose* (Harmondsworth, 1969), pp. 177–80.

201. Quoted in Morgenthau, *op. cit.*, p. 212.

202. A. R. Zollberg, "Ivory Coast" in J. S. Coleman and C. G. Rosberg (eds.), *Political Parties and National Integration in Tropical Africa* (Berkeley, 1964), pp. 86, 84.

203. *Ibid.*, p. 74.

204. *Ibid.*, p. 87.

205. Quoted in W. Schwarz, *Nigeria* (London, 1968), p. 152.

206. *Ibid.*, p. 167.

207. R. L. Sklar, "Nigerian Politics in Perspective," *Government and Opposition*, XII/4 (1967), p. 532.

208. Schwarz, *op. cit.*, p. 205.

209. Austin, *op. cit.*, p. 44.

210. Nkrumah, *op. cit.*, preface.

211. D. Apter, "Ghana" in Coleman and Rosberg (eds.), *op. cit.*, pp. 304–5.

212. Austin, *op. cit.*, p. 419.

213. Quoted in *West Africa*, 26.2.1966, p. 231.

214. Quoted from the later works of Sékou Touré in R. W. Johnson, "Sékou Touré and the Guinean revolution," *African Affairs*, LXIX/277 (October, 1970), pp. 361–62.

215. *Ibid.*, p. 352.

216. V. du Bois, "The Decline of the Guinean Revolution: Part 2. Economic Development and Political Expediency," *American Universities Field Staff Report Service*. West African Series, VIII/8 (1965), p. 18.

217. "A confidential party record" quoted in B. Davidson, *The Liberation of Guiné* (Harmondsworth, 1969), p. 32.

218. Party directive (1965) in A. Cabral, *Revolution in Guinea* (London, 1969), p. 70.

219. Davidson, *The Liberation of Guiné*, p. 119.

220. Buell, *Native Problem in Africa*, vol. II, p. 729.

221. J. G. Liebenow, *Liberia, The Evolution of Privilege* (Ithaca, 1969), pp. 74–75.

222. *Ibid.*, p. 175.

223. *Ibid.*, p. 182.

224. L. S. Senghor, "Rapport sur la doctrine et la programme du parti," *Nation et voie africaine du socialisme. Présence africaine* (Paris, 1961), quoted in K. Post, *The New States of West Africa* rev. ed. (Harmondsworth, 1968), p. 169.

225. De Lusignan, *op. cit.*, p. 133.

226. Charter for "The Union of African States," text in C. Legum, *Pan-Africanism* (New York, 1962), pp. 183–84.

227. The First Conference of Independent African States, Accra, April, 1958, text in Legum, *op. cit.*, pp. 139–48.

228. Austin, *op. cit.*, p. 130.

229. "The demographic situation in Western Africa," *Economic Bulletin for Africa*, VI/2 (1966), pp. 89–102.

▲▼ NOTES TO CHAPTER V

1. S. L. Hinde, *The Fall of the Congo Arabs* (London, 1897), pp. 184–85.

2. Quoted in A. Roberts, "Nyamwezi trade," in R. Gray and D. Birmingham (eds.), *Pre-Colonial African Trade* (London, 1970), p. 68.

3. D. Crawford, *Thinking Black* (London, 1912), p. 196, quoted in R. Slade, *King Leopold's Congo* (London, 1962), p. 121.

4. L. le Febvre de Vivy, *Documents d'histoire précoloniale belge* (Brussels, 1955), p. 23, quoted in N. Ascherson, *The King Incorporated* (London, 1963), p. 58.

5. *Ibid.*, p. 20, quoted in Ascherson, *op. cit.*, p. 55.

6. J. Stengers, *Textes inédites d'Emile Banning* (Brussels, 1955), p. 14, quoted in Slade, *op. cit.*, p. 36.

7. Ascherson, *op. cit.*, p. 101.

8. H. M. Stanley, *Through the Dark Continent* (London, 1880), p. 502.

9. H. M. Stanley, *Unpublished Letters* (London, 1957), p. 24, quoted in Ascherson, *op. cit.*, p. 112.

10. The text of the General Act of the Conference of Berlin, 26.2.1885, is given in A. B. Keith, *The Belgian Congo and the Berlin Act* (Oxford, 1919), pp. 302–16.

11. D. Crawford, *op. cit.*, pp. 324–25, quoted in R. Anstey, *King Leopold's Legacy* (London, 1966), p. 34.

12. J. Conrad, *Youth, Heart of Darkness, The End of the Tether* (London, 1946), p. 87. *Heart of Darkness* was first published in 1902.

13. H. M. Stanley in a letter dated 4.3.1885 in F. Bontinck, *Aux origines de l'Etat Indépendent du Congo* (Louvain, 1966), p. 300, quoted in J. Stengers, "The Congo Free State and the Belgian Congo before 1914" in L. H. Gann and P. Duignan (eds.), *Colonialism in Africa 1870–1960*. Vol. I: *The History and Politics of Colonialism, 1870–1914* (Cambridge, 1969), p. 274.

14. Stengers in Gann and Duignan (eds.), *op. cit.*, vol. I, p. 274.

15. A. Sharpe quoted in Slade, *op. cit.*, p. 128.

16. A. Berneart, *ministre d'Etat* and president of the *Société d'Etudes Coloniales*, in a speech of November, 1894, quoted in Slade, *op. cit.*, p. 118.

17. Report of a Congo Free State official obtained by British Consul Pulteney in 1899, quoted in Anstey, *op. cit.*, p. 6.

18. P. Balfour, *Lords of the Equator* (London, 1938), p. 219.

19. Quoted in J. Stengers, *Combien le Congo a-t-il couté à la Belgique?* (Brussels, 1957), p. 149.

20. *Daily News*, 16.4.1908, quoted in Anstey, *op. cit.*, p. 22.

21. A. A. Horn, *Trader Horn: The Ivory Coast in the Earlies* (London, 1933), p. 206.

22. Quoted in G. Hardy, "Origines et formation de l'Afrique Equatoriale Française" in *L'Encyclopédie coloniale et maritime. L'Afrique Equatoriale Française* (Paris, 1950), p. 55.

23. De Brazza in a speech of January, 1886, text in R. Delavignette and C. A. Julien (eds.), *Les Constructeurs de la France d'Outremer* (Paris, 1946), p. 324.

24. Quoted in Hardy, *op. cit.*, p. 59.

25. Quoted in A. S. Kanya-Forstner, *The Conquest of the Western Sudan* (London, 1967), p. 167.

26. R. L. Buell, *The Native Problem in Africa* (New York, 1928), vol. II, p. 221.

27. *Ibid.*, p. 222.

28. Quoted in H. F. Eydoux, *Savorgnan de Brazza* (Paris, 1932), p. 219.

29. Quoted in V. Thompson and R. Adloff, *The Emerging States of French Equatorial Africa* (London, 1960), p. 16.

30. G. M. Vassal, *Life in French Congo* (London, 1925), p. 127.

31. *Ibid.*, pp. 163–71.

32. Quoted in S. G. Ardener, *Eye-Witnesses to the Annexation of Cameroon, 1883–1887* (Buea, 1968), pp. 19–20.

33. *Protektoratsvertrag vom 12–13.7.1884,* original English text in H. Stoecker (ed.), *Kamerun unter Deutscher Kolonialherrschaft* (Berlin, 1968), vol. II, p. 259.

34. H. R. Rudin, *Germans in the Cameroons, 1884–1914* (London, 1938), p. 147.

35.   *Ibid.*, p. 152.

36.   Quoted in D. E. Gardner, "The British in the Cameroons, 1919–1939" in P. Gifford, W. R. Louis, and A. Smith (eds.), *Britain and Germany in Africa* (New Haven, 1967), p. 524.

37.   Balfour, *op. cit.*, pp. 102, 118.

38.   The words of a Belgian university teacher quoted in R. Anstey, *King Leopold's Legacy* (London, 1966), p. 40.

39.   T. Hodgkin, *Nationalism in Colonial Africa* (London, 1956), pp. 48–55.

40.   Quoted in Anstey, *op. cit.*, p. 51.

41.   *Ibid.*, p. 53.

42.   *Ibid.*, p. 77.

43.   *Ibid.*, p. 164.

44.   *Ibid.*, p. 155.

45.   *Ibid.*, p. 167.

46.   Hodgkin, *op. cit.*, p. 50.

47.   Quoted in Lord Hailey, *An African Survey* (London, 1938), p. 1271.

48.   T. Hodgkin, quoted in R. Lemarchand, *Political Awakening in the Belgian Congo* (Berkeley, 1964), p. 138.

49.   G. Hunter, *The New Societies of Tropical Africa* (London, 1962), p. 244.

50.   Quoted in B. Davidson, *The African Awakening* (London, 1955), p. 236.

51.   L. Mottoule quoted in *ibid.*, p. 166.

52.   J. Gunther, *Inside Africa* (London, 1955), p. 648.

53.   *Ibid.*, pp. 648–49.

54.   Quoted in R. L. Buell, *The Native Problem in Africa* (New York, 1928), vol. I, p. 769.

55.   Quoted in Anstey, *op. cit.*, p. 91.

56.   Hunter, *op. cit.*, p. 119.

57.   Quoted in C. Young, *Politics in the Congo* (Princeton, 1965), p. 71.

58.   Gunther, *op. cit.*, p. 656.

59.   C. M. Turnbull, *The Lonely African* (London, 1963), pp. 60–70; also quoted in Anstey, *op. cit.*, pp. 72–76.

60.   Quoted in G. Balandier, *The Sociology of Black Africa*, translated by D. Garman, (London, 1970), p. 75.

61.   *Ibid.*, p. 76.

62.   Quoted in B. Weinstein, *Gabon: Nation-Building on the Ogooué* (Cambridge, Mass., 1966), p. 36.

63.   *Ibid.*, p. 51.

64.   *Ibid.*, p. 68.

65.   Quoted in Anstey, *op. cit.*, p. 126.

66.   Quoted in Balandier, *op. cit.*, p. 418.

67.   Quoted in Anstey, *op. cit.*, p. 122.

68.   Balandier, *op. cit.*, p. 464.

69.   Young, *op. cit.*, pp. 440–41.

70.   Hodgkin, *op. cit.*, p. 72.

71.   J. A. Ballard, "Four Equatorial States" in G. M. Carter (ed.), *National Integration and Regionalism in Eight African States* (Ithaca, N.Y., 1966), p. 242.

72. V. Thompson and R. Adloff, *The Emerging States of French Equatorial Africa* (Stanford, Calif., 1960), p. 430.

73. Ballard in Carter (ed.), *op. cit.*, p. 288.

74. Thompson and Adloff, *op. cit.*, p. 489.

75. V. T. Le Vine, *The Cameroons from Mandate to Independence* (Berkeley, Calif., 1964), p. 148.

76. Mrs. Paul Robeson, quoted in C. Young, *Politics in the Congo* (Princeton, N.J., 1965), p. 275.

77. Davidson, *The African Awakening*, p. 162.

78. *Ibid.*, p. 162.

79. Quoted in R. Lemarchand, *Political Awakening in the Belgian Congo* (Berkeley, 1964), p. 155.

80. *Ibid.*, pp. 155–56.

81. *Ibid.*, p. 157.

82. *Ibid.*, p. 148.

83. *Ibid.*, p. 161.

84. *Ibid.*

85. Quoted in Anstey, *op. cit.*, p. 227.

86. *Ibid.*, p. 229.

87. *Ibid.*, p. 233.

88. Quoted in Lemarchand, *op. cit.*, p. 219.

89. *Ibid.*, p. 222.

90. The text of the two speeches is given in *Centre des Récherches et d'Information Socio-politiques* (C.R.I.S.P.), *Congo 1960*, (Brussels, 1961), vol. I, pp. 318–25.

91. Young, *Politics in the Congo*, p. 444.

92. N. Rudin, *Cameroun: An African Federation* (London, 1971), p. 91.

93. *Africa Contemporary Record, 1970–71* (London, 1971), p. B 305.

▲▼ NOTES FOR CHAPTER VI

1. J. Duffy, *Portugal in Africa* (Harmondsworth, 1962), p. 107.

2. H. A. C. Cairns, *The Clash of Cultures: Early Race Relations in Central Africa* (New York, 1965), pp. 129–31.

3. Quoted in Duffy, *op. cit.*, p. 117.

4. *Ibid.*, p. 118.

5. D. L. Wheeler and R. Pélissier, *Angola* (London, 1971), p. 81.

6. Duffy, *op. cit.*, p. 107.

7. Cairns, *op. cit.*, p. 8.

8. G. L. Caplan, *The Elites of Barotseland, 1878–1969* (London, 1970), p. 42.

9. Sir S. G. A. Shippard, Administrator of British Bechuanaland, quoted in L. H. Gann, *A History of Southern Rhodesia* (London, 1965), p. 68.

10. J. G. Lockhart and C. M. Wodehouse, *Rhodes* (London, 1963), p. 21.

11. *Ibid.*, p. 388.

12. M. Perham, *Lugard: The Years of Adventure* (London, 1956), pp. 158–59.

13. Quoted in R. Oliver, *Sir Harry Johnston and the Scramble for Africa* (London, 1959), p. 143.

14. *Ibid.*, p. 178.
15. Gann, *A History of Southern Rhodesia*, p. 137.
16. H. Rudin, *Les lois at l'administration de la Rhodésie* (Brussels, 1913), quoted in T. O. Ranger, *Revolt in Southern Rhodesia, 1896–97* (London, 1967), p. 337.
17. Oliver, *op. cit.*, p. 195.
18. *Ibid.*, pp. 235–36.
19. *Ibid.*, p. 254.
20. Quoted in L. H. Gann, *A History of Northern Rhodesia* (London, 1964), p. 95.
21. *Ibid.*, pp. 98–99.
22. Quoted in T. O. Ranger, "The Nineteenth Century in Southern Rhodesia" in T. O. Ranger (ed.), *Aspects of Central African History* (London, 1968), p. 126.
23. Quoted in P. Mason, *Birth of a Dilemma* (London, 1958), p. 105.
24. *Ibid.*, pp. 121–22.
25. Quoted in R. Brown, "Aspects of the Scramble for Matabeleland" in E. Stokes and R. Brown (eds.), *The Zambesian Past* (Manchester, 1966), p. 90.
26. Quoted in Mason, *op. cit.*, pp. 50–51.
27. Quoted in Caplan, *op. cit.*, p. 4.
28. *Ibid.*, p. 46.
29. *Ibid.*, p. 58.
30. *Ibid.*, p. 91.
31. Quoted in E. Stokes, "Barotseland: The Survival of an African State," in Stokes and Brown (eds.), *op. cit.*, p. 290.
32. Quoted in T. Ranger, "The Role of Ndebele and Shona Religious Authorities in the Rebellions of 1896 and 1897" in Stokes and Brown (eds.), *op. cit.*, p. 117.
33. Quoted in Ranger, *Revolt in Southern Rhodesia, 1896–97*, p. 79.
34. *Ibid.*, pp. 352–53.
35. Quoted in J. Duffy, *Portuguese Africa* (Cambridge, Mass., 1959), p. 271.
36. *Ibid.*, p. 277.
37. *Ibid.*, p. 270.
38. *Ibid.*, p. 292.
39. J. Gunther, *Inside Africa* (London, 1955), p. 584.
40. Duffy, *Portuguese Africa*, p. 266.
41. *Ibid.*, p. 288.
42. *Ibid.*, p. 282.
43. D. Livingstone, *Missionary Travels and Researches in South Africa* (London, 1857), pp. 371–72.
44. Gunther, *op. cit.*, p. 576.
45. Quoted in Wheeler and Pélissier, *op. cit.*, p. 112.
46. B. Davidson, *The African Awakening* (London, 1955), p. 197.
47. Quoted in Duffy, *Portuguese Africa*, p. 155.
48. Quoted in Davidson, *op. cit.*, p. 203.
49. *Ibid.*, p. 204.
50. Quoted in Mason, *op. cit.*, p. 214.
51. O. Ransford, *Livingstone's Lake* (London, 1966), p. 216.

52. Quoted in T. Ranger, "The Nineteenth Century in Southern Rhodesia" in Ranger (ed.), *Aspects of Central African History*, p. 113.
53. N. Sithole, *African Nationalism* (Cape Town, 1959), p. 146.
54. P. Mason, "Land Policy" in R. Gray, *The Two Nations* (London, 1960), p. 8.
55. Gray, *op. cit.*, p. 31.
56. Caplan, *op. cit.*, p. 87.
57. Quoted in R. I. Rotberg, *The Rise of Nationalism in Central Africa* (Cambridge, Mass., 1966), p. 27.
58. M. Read, "Native Standards of Living and African Cultural Change," supplement to *Africa* XI/3 (1938), pp. 42, 39.
59. Caplan, *op. cit.*, p. 144.
60. *Report of the Committee to Enquire into Emigrant Labour* (Zomba, 1936), quoted in R. Gray, *The Two Nations* (London, 1960), p. 120.
61. Quoted in Gray, *op. cit.*, p. 192.
62. Quoted in G. Shepperson and T. Price, *Independent African* (Edinburgh, 1958), p. 361.
63. *Ibid.*, p. 175.
64. Quoted in Rotberg, *op. cit.*, p. 79.
65. *Ibid.*, p. 82.
66. *Ibid.*, p. 86.
67. Quoted in Shepperson and Price, *op. cit.*, p. 156.
68. Gann, *History of Northern Rhodesia*, p. 170.
69. Gray, *op. cit.*, p. 117.
70. Quoted in T. Ranger, "African Politics in Twentieth-Century Southern Rhodesia" in Ranger (ed.), *Aspects of Central African History*, p. 229.
71. *Bulawayo Chronicle*, 14.4.1948, quoted in Gray, *op. cit.*, p. 289.
72. P. Gibbs, *Stranger than Armies*, quoted in Gray, *op. cit.*, p. 293.
73. Father Devlin, quoted in T. Ranger, "African Politics in Twentieth-Century Southern Rhodesia" in Ranger (ed.), *op. cit.*, p. 236.
74. Quoted in Rotberg, *op. cit.*, p. 189.
75. Quoted in Gray, *op. cit.*, p. 319.
76. Rotberg, *op. cit.*, p. 202.
77. *Ibid.*, p. 222.
78. Gray, *op. cit.*, p. 152.
79. *Ibid.*, p. 152.
80. *Ibid.*, p. 277.
81. Rotberg, *op. cit.*, p. 224.
82. Gann, *History of Northern Rhodesia*, p. 467.
83. Rotberg, *op. cit.*, p. 233.
84. *Ibid.*, p. 243.
85. Ranger, "African Politics in Twentieth-Century Southern Rhodesia" in Ranger (ed.), *op. cit.*, p. 238.
86. *Report of the Nyasaland Commission of Enquiry* (London, 1959), p. 13.
87. *Ibid.*, p. 35.
88. Rotberg, *op. cit.*, p. 293.
89. R. Hall, *Zambia* (London, 1965), p. 175.
90. Rotberg, *op. cit.*, p. 293.

91. Ranger, "African Politics in Twentieth-Century Southern Rhodesia" in Ranger (ed.), *op. cit.*, p. 239.
92. Rotberg, *op. cit.*, p. 304.
93. L. H. Gann and P. Duignan, *White Settlers in Tropical Africa* (Harmondsworth, 1962), p. 75.
94. *Ibid.*, p. 69.
95. C. Leys, *European Politics in Southern Rhodesia* (Oxford, 1959), p. 174.
96. J. Barber, *Rhodesia: The Road to Rebellion* (London, 1967), p. 148.
97. *Ibid.*, pp. 193–94.
98. J. Macrun, *The Angolan Revolution,* Volume I: *The Anatomy of an Explosion* (Cambridge, Mass., 1969), p. 6.
99. *Ibid.*, p. 48.
100. Wheeler and Pélissier, *op. cit.*, p. 237.
101. *Africa Digest,* XVI/3 (June 1969), p. 41.
102. J. G. Pine, *Malawi* (London, 1969), p. 171.

▲▼ NOTES FOR CHAPTER VII

1. Quoted from a letter of Lieutenant L. W. Mathews in R. Coupland, *The Exploitation of East Africa* (London, 1939), p. 242.
2. *Ibid.*, p. 266.
3. Quoted in R. Robertson, J. Gallagher and A. Denny, *Africa and the Victorians,* p. 49.
4. *Ibid.*, p. 190.
5. G. L. Steer, *The Judgment on German Africa* (London, 1939), p. 249.
6. The manifesto of the society is quoted by G. C. K. Gwassa, "The German Intervention and African Resistance in Tanzania" in I. N. Kimambo and A. J. Temu (eds.), *A History of Tanzania* (Nairobi, 1969), p. 98.
7. J. Flint, "The Wider Background to Partition and Colonial Occupation" in R. Oliver and G. Mathew (eds.), *History of East Africa* (Oxford, 1963), vol. I, p. 370.
8. Robinson, Gallagher, and Denny, *op. cit.*, p. 312.
9. D. A. Low, *Buganda in Modern History* (London, 1971), pp. 81, 78.
10. Quoted in Robinson, Gallagher, and Denny, *op. cit.*, p. 328.
11. C. Peters, *New Light on Darkest Africa* (London, 1891) quoted by G. S. P. Freeman-Grenville, "The German Sphere, 1884–1898" in Oliver and Mathew (eds.), *History of East Africa,* vol. I, p. 445.
12. *The Times* (London), 21.12.1901, quoted in M. F. H. Hill, *Permanent Way* (Nairobi, 1949), vol. I, pp. 272–73.
13. D. A. Low, "British East Africa: The Establishment of British Rule, 1895–1912" in V. Harlow, E. M. Chilver, and A. Smith (eds.), *History of East Africa,* (Oxford, 1965), vol. II, p. 32, n. 1.
14. *Ibid.*, p. 32.
15. Quoted in J. S. Mangat, *A History of the Asians in East Africa* (Oxford, 1969), p. 40.
16. *Ibid.*, p. 55.

17. M. P. K. Sorensen, *Origins of European Settlement in Kenya* (Nairobi, 1968), p. 42.

18. Quoted in E. Huxley, *White Man's Country* (London, 1938), vol. I, p. 82.

19. Low in Harlow, Chilver, and Smith (eds.), *History of East Africa,* vol. II, p. 1.

20. N. Leys, *Kenya* (London, 1924), p. 105.

21. F. H. Goldsmith, *John Ainsworth, Pioneer Kenya Administrator, 1864–1946* (London, 1955), p. 30.

22. Huxley, *op. cit.,* vol. I, p. 207.

23. Quoted in A. Redmayne, "Mkakwa and the Hehe Wars," *Journal of African History,* IX/3 (1968), p. 429.

24. *Ibid.,* p. 436.

25. J. Iliffe, "The Organization of the Maji-Maji Rebellion," *Journal of African History,* VII/3 (1967), p. 495.

26. *Ibid.,* p. 508.

27. D. A. Low, "The Northern Interior, 1840–1884," in Oliver and Mathew (eds.), *History of East Africa,* vol. I, p. 347.

28. Quoted in J. Flint, "Zanzibar, 1890–1950" in Harlow, Chilver, and Smith (eds.), *History of East Africa,* vol. II, p. 642.

29. M. Lofchie, *Zanzibar: Background to Revolution* (Princeton, 1965), p. 93.

30. *Ibid.,* p. 101.

31. R. Lemarchand, *Rwanda and Burundi* (London, 1970), p. 27.

32. Sir D. Cameron quoted in J. C. Taylor, *The Political Development of Tanganyika* (London, 1963), p. 47.

33. Lord Hailey quoted in R. C. Pratt, "Administration and Politics in Uganda, 1919–1945," in Harlow, Chilver, and Smith (eds.), *History of East Africa,* vol. II, p. 491.

34. *Ibid.,* p. 492.

35. J. Middleton, "Administration and Changes in African Life in Kenya, 1912–1945," in Harlow, Chilver, and Smith (eds.), *History of East Africa,* vol. II, p. 350.

36. B. A. Ogot and J. Kieran (eds.), *Zamani, a Survey of East African History* (Nairobi, 1968), p. 272.

37. C. Wrigley, "The Changing Economic Situation of Buganda" in L. A. Fallers (ed.), *The King's Men* (London, 1964), p. 18.

38. Quoted in Huxley, *op. cit.,* vol. I, p. 61.

39. C. Ehrlich, "The Uganda Economy, 1905–1945" in Harlow, Chilver, and Smith (eds.), *History of East Africa,* vol. II, p. 459.

40. C. C. Wrigley, "Kenya: Patterns of Economic Life, 1902–1945" in Harlow, Chilver, and Smith (eds.), *History of East Africa,* vol. II, p. 223.

41. *Ibid.,* p. 224.

42. *Ibid.,* p. 218.

43. J. Iliffe, "The Age of Improvement and Differentiation" in Kimambo and Temu (eds.), *A History of Tanzania,* p. 123.

44. C. G. Rosberg and J. Nottingham, *The Myth of Mau-Mau* (New York, 1966), p. 112.

45. Quoted in J. Middleton, "Kenya; Administration and Changes in Afri-

can Life, 1912–1945" in Harlow, Chilver, and Smith (eds.), *History of East Africa,* vol. II, p. 366.

46. Iliffe in Kimambo and Temu (eds.), *A History of Tanzania,* p. 136.
47. Middleton in Harlow, Chilver, and Smith (eds.), *op. cit.,* vol. II, p. 357.
48. Quoted in Iliffe, "The Age of Improvement and Differentiation" in Kimambo and Temu (eds.), *op. cit.,* p. 149.
49. *Ibid.,* pp. 159–60.
50. *Ibid.,* p. 156.
51. Quoted in J. Lonsdale, "Some Origins of Nationalism in East Africa," *Journal of African History,* IX/1 (1968), p. 144.
52. Quoted in A. J. Temu, "The Rise and Triumph of Nationalism" in Kimambo and Temu (eds.), *op. cit.,* p. 206.
53. Rosberg and Nottingham, *op. cit.,* p. 131.
54. P. Mitchell, *African Afterthoughts* (London, 1954), p. 219.
55. Quoted in Rosberg and Nottingham, *op. cit.,* p. 246.
56. *Ibid.,* p. 299.
57. Low, *Buganda in Modern History,* p. 97.
58. *Ibid.,* p. 105.
59. R. Lemarchand, "The Coup in Rwanda" in R. I. Rotberg and A. A. Mazrui, *Protest and Power in Black Africa* (New York, 1970), p. 920.
60. M. F. Lofchie, "The Zanzibar Revolution" in Rotberg and Mazrui (eds.), *op. cit.,* p. 965.
61. Quoted in Lemarchand, *op. cit.,* p. 286.

▲▼ NOTES TO CHAPTER VIII

1. Quoted by D. Hobart Houghton, "Economic Development, 1865–1965," in M. Wilson and L. Thompson (eds.), *The Oxford History of South Africa,* Vol. II: *South Africa, 1870–1966* (Oxford, 1971), p. 11.
2. *Ibid.,* p. 4.
3. L. Thompson, "The Subjugation of African Chiefdoms" in Wilson and Thompson (eds.), *op. cit.,* p. 265.
4. C. Webb, "Great Britain and the Zulu People, 1879–1887" in L. Thompson (ed.), *African Societies in Southern Africa* (London, 1969), p. 303.
5. Quoted in R. First, *South West Africa* (Harmondsworth, 1963), pp. 73–74.
6. H. Bley, *South West Africa under German Rule,* translated by G. H. Ridley (London, 1971), p. 127.
7. *Ibid.,* p. 151.
8. *Ibid.,* p. 68.
9. L. Thompson, "Great Britain and the Afrikaner Republics, 1870–1899," in Wilson and Thompson (eds.), *op. cit.,* p. 291.
10. Memorandum to the *Volksraad* at Ohrigsstadt, quoted in F. A. van Jaarsveld, *The Awakening of Afrikaner Nationalism,* translated by F. R. Metrowich (Cape Town, 1961), p. 30.
11. *Ibid.,* p. 54.
12. *Ibid.,* p. 122.

13. *Ibid.*, p. 109.
14. C. W. de Kiewiet, *The Imperial Factor in South Africa* (Cambridge, 1937), p. 145.
15. C. W. de Kiewiet, *A History of South Africa: Social and Economic* (London, 1941), p. 89.
16. D. Reitz, *Commando* (Harmondsworth, 1948), p. 19.
17. J. Buchan, *Memory-Hold-the-Door* (London, 1940), p. 470.
18. Quoted in R. Robinson, J. Gallagher, and A. Denny, *Africa and the Victorians* (London, 1961), p. 419.
19. Sir W. Butler, acting high commissioner in South Africa in 1899, quoted in G. H. Le May, *British Supremacy in South Africa, 1899–1907* (Oxford, 1965), p. 21.
20. *Ibid.*, p. 8.
21. O. Schreiner, *An English South African's View of the Situation* (London, 1899), quoted in *Dictionary of South African Biography* (Pretoria, 1968), vol. I, p. 698.
22. Le May, *op. cit.*, p. 86.
23. *Ibid.*, p. 151.
24. *Ibid.*, p. 149.
25. *Ibid.*, p. 186.
26. W. K. Hancock, *Smuts, Vol I: The Sanguine Years, 1870–1919* (Cambridge, 1962), p. 559.
27. Quoted by L. Thompson, "The Compromise of Union" in Wilson and Thompson (eds.), *op. cit.*, p. 356.
28. *Ibid.*, p. 364.
29. Sir J. Robinson, quoted in L. C. Knowles and C. M. Knowles, *The Economic Development of the British Overseas Empire, Vol. II: The Union of South Africa* (London, 1936), p. 28.
30. *Final Report of the Drought Investigation Committee* (Cape Town, 1923), quoted in F. Wilson, "Farming, 1866–1966" in Wilson and Thompson (eds.), *op. cit.*, p. 134.
31. *Ibid.*, p. 120.
32. De Kiewiet, *History of South Africa*, p. 193.
33. F. Wilson in Wilson and Thompson (eds.), *op. cit.*, p. 130.
34. S. T. Plaatje, *Native Life in South Africa* (London, n.d.), quoted in F. Wilson in Wilson and Thompson (eds.), *op. cit.*, p. 130.
35. *Ibid.*, p. 166.
36. M. Wilson, "The Growth of Peasant Communities" in Wilson and Thompson (eds.), *op. cit.*, p. 66.
37. D. H. Houghton, "Economic Development, 1865–1965" in Wilson and Thompson (eds.), *op. cit.*, p. 33.
38. Transvaal Chamber of Mines, *Mining Survey* (June, 1951), quoted in D. H. Houghton, *The South African Economy* (Cape Town, 1964), p. 85.
39. *Blue Book on Native Affairs* (1904), quoted in D. Welsh, "The Growth of the Towns," in Wilson and Thompson (eds.), *op. cit.*, p. 186.
40. *Ibid.*, p. 188.
41. Houghton, *The South African Economy*, p. 95.
42. M. Wilson in Wilson and Thompson (eds.), *op. cit.*, p. 67.

43. F. Wilson in *Ibid.*, p. 110.
44. M. Wilson, "Lovedale: Instrument of Peace," *South African Outlook,* March, 1971, p. 44.
45. De Kiewiet, *A History of South Africa,* p. 192.
46. S. Patterson, *The Last Trek* (London, 1957), p. 112.
47. *Ibid.*, p. 47.
48. L. Marquard, *The Peoples and Policies of South Africa* (London, 1969), p. 65.
49. R. de Villiers, "Afrikaner Nationalism" in Wilson and Thompson (eds.), *op. cit.*, p. 421.
50. L. Kuper, "African Nationalism in South Africa, 1910–1964," in Wilson and Thompson (eds.), *op. cit.*, p. 433.
51. M. Wilson in Wilson and Thompson (eds.), *op. cit.*, p. 91.
52. *Ibid.*, p. 77.
53. Marquard, *op. cit.*, p. 131.
54. M. Cobden, "The Bloodiest Place on Earth," *Rand Daily Mail,* 18.2.1967, quoted in Welsh, "The Growth of the Towns," in Wilson and Thompson (eds.), *op. cit.*, p. 220.
55. Marquard, *op. cit.*, p. 43.
56. Quoted in Welsh, *op. cit.*, p. 209.
57. E. Mphahlele, *The African Image* (London, 1962), p. 30.
58. M. S. Evans, *Black and White in South East Africa* (London, 1911), quoted in Welsh, *op. cit.*, p. 174.
59. De Kiewiet, *A History of South Africa,* p. 148.
60. Marquard, *op. cit.*, p. 28.
61. Hancock, *op. cit.*, p. 217.
62. W. K. Hancock, *Smuts, Vol. II: The Fields of Force, 1919–1950* (Cambridge, 1968), p. 46.
63. De Villiers, *op. cit.*, p. 370.
64. Hancock, *op. cit.*, p. 507.
65. *Ibid.*, p. 113.
66. J. Cope and U. Krige (eds.), *The Penguin Book of South African Verse* (Harmondsworth, 1968), p. 297.
67. *Ibid.*, p. 305.
68. Hancock, *op. cit.*, pp. 481, 488.
69. E. H. Brooks, *Apartheid* (London, 1968), p. xxviii.
70. *Ibid.*, p. 11.
71. Quoted in de Villiers, *op. cit.*, p. 407.
72. *Ibid.*, p. 412.
73. Brooks, *op. cit.*, p. 208.
74. *Ibid.*, p. 74.
75. Quoted in G. M. Carter, *The Politics of Inequality* (London, 1958), p. 370.
76. The text of the Freedom Charter is given in Carter, *op. cit.*, pp. 486–88.
77. Hancock, *op. cit.*, p. 152.
78. *Ibid.*, vol. II, p. 473.
79. *Ibid.*, vol. II, p. 473.
80. Quoted in J. Spence, "South Africa and the Modern World" in Wilson and Thompson, *op. cit.*, p. 506.

81. Patterson, *op. cit.*, p. 263.
82. Hancock, *op. cit.*, p. 223.
83. *Ibid.*, vol. II, p. 225.
84. J. J. Muller and G. H. P. de Bruin, *History for Standard Eight* (Cape Town, n.d.), p. 132.
85. Cope and Krige (eds.), pp. 235–36.

▲▼ NOTES FOR CHAPTER IX

1. Quoted in S. E. Howe, *The Drama of Madagascar* (London, 1938), p. 313.
2. Quoted in N. Heseltine, *Madagascar* (London, 1971), p. 142.
3. Quoted in H. Deschamps, *Histoire de Madagascar* (Paris, 1960), p. 229.
4. Quoted in R. K. Kent, *From Madagascar to the Malagasy Republic* (London, 1962), p. 71.
5. Deschamps, *op. cit.*, p. 255.

Suggested Readings

Anyone approaching the history of modern Africa for the first time is bound to feel himself overwhelmed by the sheer mass of information with which he is confronted. And even the professional Africanist is likely to react in much the same way as he notes the steadily mounting quantity of scholarly material produced every year by a rapidly expanding community of seekers after knowledge working in universities and research institutes, in government departments and newspaper offices in Africa itself and in that ever widening range of countries with an interest in Africa. The historian is by nature a jack-of-all-trades. Working in the African context he needs to be almost as familiar with studies made in related disciplines—geography, economics, social anthropology, and political science—as he is with the books and articles of his professional colleagues. For his task is to erect an adequate intellectual framework in which every aspect of human development may find its place.

How can this most effectively be done in the context of modern African history? It is essential in the first place to acquire some familiarity with the main themes, chronologically arranged, of the modern history of the continent as a whole: the precolonial background, the European conquest, the colonial interlude, the rise and triumph of nationalism, the progress of modernization. But in a continent of such immense variety, continental generalizations soon appear unsatisfactory. So one needs to follow up these themes on the smaller stages presented by individual African countries. Obviously it is not possible to study forty or more states in equal depth. In making a choice, there is something to be said for selecting one state from each of the regions into which Africa is conventionally divided. Yet the study of individual countries taken as single entities still fails to allow for that human variety every country contains. Hence the need to get down to more local studies, the history of a particular ethnic group or area, the development of some particular institution—a church, a mining company, a political party, a school, a bureaucracy. Only when one gets down to the local level does one really begin to get the "feel" of Africa, to catch in the mind's eye the faces of individuals, pick up their words, trace the tenor of their thoughts as they move purposefully about their distinct environments. Hence the prime importance of coming to grips with first-hand material—the speeches of politicians, the dispatches of officials, the narratives of travelers, the letters, journals, or reminiscences of observant individuals. In the African context, much of this material, at least in its more easily accessible forms, is the work of aliens. Yet is is vitally important for the historian to seek out the African voice with its distinctive note. From it he will learn how the process of conquest, the imposition of colonial rule, looks to a subject population, catch something of the animated debate between collaborators and resisters, and learn to recognize that there are large areas in the life of every individual which remain untouched by the local political situation, being taken up with the ordinary human processes, involved in intimate social relationships or in the struggle to gain a livelihood. For the non-African reader, the novels and poems and newspaper articles produced by African writers are of quite special value. This source can be supplemented by the oral record. Every man is a living historical document. For a really deep understanding of the African past, the historian needs to know much more than the easily accessible sources can, at present, offer him of the experiences of ordinary people. To be able to define the extent of one's own ignorance with reasonable precision may perhaps be regarded as the beginning of wisdom. The value of trying to construct a clear intellectual framework is that it allows one to perceive rather more clearly just how much one does not know. A keen sense of ignorance is one of the most stimulating of sensations. The pursuit of knowledge is a lifetime's occupation, an occupation that demands a certain flexibility of mind, a philosophical and enquiring spirit. To come deeply to grips with the history of any society involves one in hard and serious thought about the whole nature of the human condition.

The notes on suggested readings that follow have been divided into three parts. The first is concerned with works that cover Africa as a whole or at least a large part of the continent. Some of these works are wide-ranging studies, others are concerned with specific subjects; e.g., agriculture, education, urbanization. The second part is devoted to studies of particular regions or countries. The third considers the more easily available sources for the study of contemporary events in Africa. The section on suggested readings in *Africa to 1875,* the companion volume to the present work, lists the main bibliographies, historiographies, guides to libraries and archives, encyclopedias and other reference works, atlases and periodicals available for the student of African history. This information has not been repeated here and the reader is asked to refer to the earlier work for guidance on these particular aids to scholarship.

PART I

This part is intended as a guide to general works on Africa and to works on special subjects which draw their material from many different parts of the continent. It covers the following headings, alphabetically arranged: Administration; Agriculture; Economic History and Economic Development; Education; Ethnography; General History; Geography; Guides to Study; Health and Medicine; Ideologies; Imperialism and Colonialism; Intercontinental Affairs; Intracontinental Affairs; Journalism and Travel; Labor; Law; Literature; Nationalism and African Politics; Populations Studies; Reactions to Conquest; Readers; Religion; Social Change; Traditional Polities; Urbanization.

▲▼ ADMINISTRATION

During the high noon of the colonial era, administration and the practical problems involved in governing newly acquired territories took the place of politics as a subject for discussion among the alien rulers of Africa. L. P. Mair, *Native Policies in Africa* (1936) is a useful introductory work arranged on a comparative basis. R. L. Buell, *The Native Problem in Africa*, 2 vols. (1928) contains a mass of information on many aspects of administration in the 1920's. Lord Hailey, *An African Survey* (1938) also lays its main stress on administration: a revised and greatly extended edition of the *Survey* was published in 1957. See also the same author's *Native Administration in British African Territories*, 5 parts (1950–53). Of all the countries in Africa, Nigeria has produced the richest literature on administration. Much of the material contained in Lord Lugard's classic work, *The Dual Mandate in Tropical Africa* (1922) was derived from the author's Nigerian experience. Extensive extracts from Lugard's earlier writings are given in A. H. M. Kirk-Greene (ed.), *The Principles of Native Administration in Nigeria* (1965). See also M. Perham, *Native Administration in Nigeria* (1937) and the works by Crocker and Nicholson noted on p. 793. The africanization of colonial civil services is discussed in R. Symonds, *The British and Their Successors* (1966); see also A. L. Adu, *The Civil Service in Commonwealth Africa* (1969). On administration in the French colonies see W. B. Cohen, *Rulers of Empire: The French Colonial Service* (1971) and B. Weinstein's biography, *Éboué* (1972), together with the relevant works listed under Imperialism and Colonialism (p. 779).

▲▼ AGRICULTURE

The chapter by J. J. McKelvey. "Agricultural Research" in R. A. Lystad (ed.), *The African World* (1965) provides a useful introduction to the subject. See also W. Allan, *The African Husbandman* (1965); G. B. Masefield, *A Short History of Agriculture in the British Colonies* (1950); J. Phillips, *Agriculture and Ecology in Africa* (1959); and W. F. Thomas and G. W. Whittington (eds.), *Environment and Land Use in Africa* (1969). Notable agricultural studies confined to a particular country or project include A. Gaitskell, *Gezira, A Story of Development in the Sudan* (1959); E. Huxley, *A New Earth* (1960), on agricultural development in Kenya in the late 1950's; J. D. Tothill (ed.), *Agriculture in Uganda* (1940); J. B. Wills, (ed.), *Agriculture and Land Use in Ghana* (1962); and A. Wood, *The Groundnut Affair* (1950). See also G. B. Masefield, *A History of the Colonial Agricultural Service* (1972).

▲▼ ECONOMIC HISTORY AND ECONOMIC DEVELOPMENT

The economic history of precolonial Africa still presents a greatly underresearched field. Two recently published symposia—R. Gray and D. Birmingham (eds.), *Precolonial African Trade* (1970) and C. Meillassoux (ed.), *The Development of Indigenous Trade and Industry in West Africa* (1971)—break much new ground in this particular field. General works on the economic history of the colonial period include A. Pym, *The Financial and Economic History of the Tropical African Territories* (1940); S. H. Frankel, *Capital Investment in Africa* (1938) and W. A. Lewis (ed.), *Tropical Development, 1880–1913* (1970). There is a mass of material on the economic changes of the last twenty years. Useful general works include P. Robson and D. A. Lury, *The Economies of Africa* (1969); M. J. Herskovits and M. Harwitz (eds.), *Economic Transition in Africa* (1964); and G. Hunter, *Modernizing Peasant Societies* (1969). In 1968, the International Monetary Fund began publishing a series of *Surveys of African Economies;* Volume I (1968) covered the former French states of Equatorial Africa, Volume II (1969) East Africa, Volume III (1970) some of the states of West Africa. F. Arkhurst (ed.), *Africa in the Seventies and Eighties* (1970), surveys the "issues in development."

▲▼ EDUCATION

The Educated African, edited by H. Kitchen (1962) is a useful and comprehensive guide to the development of Western education in Africa to 1960, with separate chapters on individual countries. For British territories in Africa there are two wide-ranging surveys published during the colonial period: the first, financed by the Phelps Stokes Fund, produced two reports, *Education in East Africa* (n.d.) and *Education in Africa* (1922); the second, *African Education: A Study of Educational Policy and Practice in British Colonial Africa* (1953), was supported by the Nuffield Foundation. A. V. Murray, *The School in the Bush* (1928) gives an insight into educational thinking in the 1920's. The vastly changed atmosphere of postcolonial Africa is reflected in L. G. Cowan, J. O'Connel, and D. C. Scanlan, (eds.), *Ed-*

ucation and Nation-building in Africa (1965). Studies devoted to educational development in particular countries or regions include B. Rose (ed.), *Education in Southern Africa* (1970); J. Heyworth-Dunne, *An Introduction to the History of Modern Education in Egypt* (1939); and P. Foster, *Education and Social Change in Ghana* (1965). W. E. F. Ward, *Fraser of Trinity and Achimota* (1965) is one of the very few biographies devoted to educationalists who have left a profound mark on particular African territories.

▲▼ ETHNOGRAPHY

The monographs that form part of the *Ethnographic Survey of Africa* prepared by the International African Institute now cover a large part of the continent. Each monograph is devoted to a single people or to a closely related cluster of ethnic groups and provides a succinct summary of every aspect of the people's culture. More compact introductions to African ethnography are provided by J. L. Gibbs (ed.), *The Peoples of Africa* (1965) and F. P. Murdock, *Africa: Its Peoples and Their Culture History* (1959). See also J. Maquet, *Civilizations of Black Africa* (1972).

▲▼ GENERAL HISTORY

J. D. Fage (ed.), *Africa Discovers Its Past* (1970) contains a collection of brief but wide-ranging historiographies tracing the development of African historical studies on a regional basis. Fage is also the author of a useful brief survey of African historical studies in Lystad (ed.), *The African World*. General historical studies covering the whole or at least the greater part of the continent include H. H. Johnston, *History of the Colonization of Africa by Alien Races* (1899); G. Hardy, *Vue générale de l'histoire de l'Afrique* (1922); D. Westermann, *Geschichte Afrikas* (1952); R. Oliver and J. D. Fage, *A Short History of Africa* (1962); R. Cornevin, *Histoire de l'Afrique,* 2 vols. (1962, 1966); R. I. Rotberg, *A Political History of Tropical Africa* (1965); R. Oliver and A. Atmore, *Africa since 1800* (1967); B. Davidson, *Africa in History: Themes and Outlines* (1968); and R. W. July, *History of the African Peoples* (1970). Each of these works has its own particular virtues; each has inevitably been outdated by the rapid advance of contemporary historical research; each is now primarily of interest as showing how the history of Africa looked to an intelligent and well-informed observer at a particular period in the recent past. T. O. Ranger (ed.), *Emerging Themes of African History* (1968) is a particularly stimulating introduction to the present state of African historical studies.

▲▼ GEOGRAPHY

W. A. Hance, *The Geography of Modern Africa* (1964) is the most comprehensive single-volume geography of the continent. See also R. J. Harrison Church et al., *Africa and the Islands* (1964), A. T.

Grove, *Africa South of the Sahara* (1970), and the stimulating collection of geographical essays edited by B. W. Hodder and D. R. Harris, *Africa in Transition* (1967). P. Gourou, *The Tropical World* (third edition, 1962) is one of the classics of modern geography. In the course of the past twenty years, good single-volume geographies have been produced for most of the countries of Africa: some of these works are noted in Part II. Much of the current writing by geographers is of direct interest to historians of the recent past, and articles in geographical journals of the late nineteenth and early twentieth centuries now constitute valuable source material.

▲▼ GUIDES TO STUDY

R. A. Lystad (ed.), *The African World* (1965) offers a comprehensive survey of social research classified under the headings of "historical and socio-cultural," "physico-biological," and "psycho-cultural" studies. Serial publications relating to Africa have been listed by E. de Benko and P. L. Betts, *Research Sources for African Studies* (1969). See also Part I of "Selected Readings" in Hallett, *Africa to 1875*.

▲▼ HEALTH AND MEDICINE

The historian ought to possess some knowledge of the characteristics of the main diseases of Africa and their distribution. C. Wilcocks, *Health and Disease in the Tropics* (1955) provides a useful guide for the layman. On the development of medical research in Africa see M. Gelfand, *Medicine in Tropical Africa* (1961); H. H. Scott, *A History of Tropical Medicine*, 2 vols. (1939); and E. B. Worthington, *Science in the Development of Africa* (1938).

▲▼ IDEOLOGIES

R. W. July, *The Origins of Modern African Thought* (1967) provides a vivid introduction to the lives and thoughts of the more prominent members of the West African intelligentsia of the late nineteenth and early twentieth century. H. R. Lynch, *Edward Wilmot Blyden* (1967) is a biography of the outstanding Black African thinker of his day. One of Blyden's works, *Christianity, Islam and the Negro Race* (1887) has recently been republished with an introduction by C. Fyfe (1967). Works on contemporary Arab thought in Egypt and North Africa are noted on p. 787. J. R. Hooker's biography of George Padmore, *Black Revolutionary* (1967) is largely set in the late colonial period. Important statements of belief by nationalist leaders from South, Central, and East Africa have been collected under the title *Africa's Freedom* (1964). W. H. Friedland and C. G. Rosberg (eds.), *African Socialism* (1965) examines the ideologies of the more radical African states of the 1960's; see also, W. A. E. Skurnik (ed.), *African Political Thought* (1968), a study of the ideas of Patrice Lumumba, Kwame Nkrumah, and Sékou Touré. The writings of Frantz Fanon stand out as among the most influential works set in an African context to have appeared in the 1960's; among Fanon's works to have been translated into English are *The Wretched of the Earth* (1967), *Towards the African Revolution* (1967), and *Black Skin, White Mask* (1968).

▲▼ IMPERIALISM AND COLONIALSM

Important general studies of the concept of imperialism include R. Koebner and H. D. Schmidt, *Imperialism: The Story and Significance of a Political Word, 1840–1960* (1964), R. Owen and B. Sutcliffe (eds.), *Studies in the Theory of Imperialism* (1971), and A. P. Thornton, *Doctrines of Imperialism* (1965). R. F. Betts (ed.), *The "Scramble" for Africa* (1966) is a useful collection of readings, illustrating the different interpretations of the motives for the European conquest of Africa. Another imaginatively chosen collection of readings has been edited by R. W. Winks, *The Age of Imperialism* (1969). D. Fieldhouse, *The Colonial Empires* (1966) presents a succinct comparative survey. The most ambitious general survey by modern scholars is the multi-volume work, *Colonialism in Africa,* edited by L. H. Gann and P. Duignan, Vol. I, *The History and Politics of Colonialism, 1870–1914* (1969); Vol. II, *The History and Politics of Colonialism, 1914–1960* (1970); Vol. III, *Profiles of Change: African Society and Colonial Rule,* edited by V. Turner (1971). Gann and Duignan are also the authors of *Burden of Empire* (1967), one of the few apologias for imperialism to appear in the 1960's, and of *White Settlers in Tropical Africa* (1962). For an ironical impressionistic view of white settlers by an English journalist, see R. West, *The White Tribes of Africa* (1965). C. A. Julien (ed.), *Les Techniciens de la colonisation* (1946) is an interesting collection of biographical essays on many of the great proconsuls of the imperial age. See also the two massive symposia edited by P. Gifford and W. R. Louis, *Britain and Germany in Africa* (1967) and *France and Britain in Africa* (1971). Further studies of imperialism are devoted to the policies of individual colonial powers.

British imperialism: J. Hatch, *The History of Britain in Africa* (1969) and a well-illustrated volume by R. Lewis and Y. Fay, *The British In Africa* (1971) provide useful introductory surveys, while C. Cross, *The Fall of the British Empire* (1968) puts Britain's African possessions in a wider context. The third volume of *The Cambridge History of the British Empire, The Empire-Commonwealth, 1870–1919* (1959) presents imperial problems strictly from the viewpoint of the metropolis. R. E. Robinson, J. Gallagher, and A. Denny, *Africa and the Victorians* (1961), with its well-documented exploration of the "official mind of imperialism," has established itself as one of the seminal works in the modern historiography of imperialism. Equally stimulating is A. P. Thornton's "study of British power," *The Imperial Idea and Its Enemies* (1959). See also the collection of essays by D. A. Low, *Lion Rampant* (1973). The views and actions of the opponents of imperialism in the late nineteenth and early twentieth century are explored in more detail in B. Potter, *Critics of Empire* (1968). R. Heussler, *Yesterday's Rulers* (1963) is a well-documented study of the development of the British colonial service. J. Morris, *Pax Britannica* (1968), is a notably readable evocation of the British Empire at the height of its power. Works of a general nature by colonial civil servants include C. Jeffreys, *The Colonial Empire and Its Civil Service* (1938); A. Burns, *In Defence of Colonies* (1957); and A. Cohen, *British Policy in Changing Africa* (1958). M. Perham, *The Colonial Reckoning* (1963) reviews Britain's record as a colonial power. There is a valuable historiographical essay on British colonial rule in Africa by A. Smith and H. Pogge von Strandmann in P. Gifford, W. R. Louis, and A. Smith (eds.), *Britain and Germany in Africa* (1967).

French imperialism: The history of the growth of modern French imperialism is covered by J. Ganiage, *L'Expansion coloniale de la France sous la Troisième Republique, 1871–1914* (1968) and by H. Brunschwig, *Mythes et réalités de l'impérialisme colonial français, 1871–1914* (1960), available in English translation as, *French Colonization, 1871–1914* (1966). G. Hanotaux and A. Martineau, *Histoire des colonies françaises et de l'expansion française dans la monde,* 6 vols. (1930–34) reflects the characteristic attitudes of imperialist sentiment of the years in which it was produced. The intellectual history of French imperialism is briefly surveyed in H. J. Deschamps, *Les Méthodes et les doctrines coloniales de la France du XVIe siècle à nos jours* (1933). S. H. Roberts, *The History of French Colonial Policy, 1870–1925,* 2 vols. (1929) is the most comprehensive introduction to French colonialism in English. R. Delavignette and C. A. Julien (eds.), *Les Constructeurs de la France d'outre-mer* (1945) contains brief biographical sketches of the most prominent French imperialists, including Faidherbe, de Brazza, Galliéni and Lyautey, together with extracts from their writings. J. Suret-Canale, *French Colonialism in Tropical Africa 1900–45* (1971), the English translation of the second volume of *Afrique Noire: L'ère coloniale, 1900–45* (1961), is the work of a French Marxist and offers a stimulating antidote to the works of conventional imperialist historians. For other works on French colonialism see pp. 789 (North Africa), 793 (West Africa) and 796 (Equatorial Africa).

German imperialism: M. E. Townsend, *The Rise and Fall of the German Colonial Empire, 1884–1914* (1930) provides a sound general introduction. The contributions to the symposium edited by P. Gifford, W. E. Louis, and A. Smith, *Britain and Germany in Africa* (1967), indicate the reappraisal of German colonial policy now being made by European and American scholars. The historiographical essay in this volume by A. Smith and H. Pogge von Strandmann also covers German rule in Africa.

Italian imperialism: J. L. Miège, *L'Impérialisme colonial italien de 1870 à nos jours* (1968) is a compact introductory survey with a good bibliography.

Portuguese imperialism: See the works by Duffy, Hammond, and others listed on pp. 798 and 800.

Belgian imperialism: On the highly personal imperialism of King Leopold of the Belgians and on later Belgian rule in the Congo see the works listed on p. 796.

▲▼ INTERCONTINENTAL AFFAIRS

Two wide-ranging general studies, V. McKay, *Africa in World Affairs* (1963) and W. A. Nielsen, *The Great Powers and Africa* (1969), provide good introductions to the study of the place of Africa in a wider world. Studies of the relationship between individual powers and Africa include R. Emerson, *Africa and U.S. Policy* (1967); A. C. Hill and M. Kilson (eds.), *Apropos of Africa* (1969), a collection of statements by American Negro leaders on Africa from the 1800's to the 1950's; H. D. Cohen, *Soviet Policy Towards Black Africa* (1972); J. H. Rodrigues, *Brazil and Africa* (1968); and B. D. Larkin, *China and Africa, 1949–1970* (1971).

▲▼ INTRACONTINENTAL AFFAIRS: PAN AFRICANISM

C. Legum, *Pan-Africanism: a Short Political Guide* (1962) contains a historical commentary together with a valuable collection of documents. On the development of pan-Africanism see also I. Wallenstein, *Africa: The Politics of Unity* (1968) and V. B. Thompson, *African Unity: The Evolution of Pan-Africansim* (1968). The charter of the Organization of African Unity together with other important intercontinental agreements is given in I. Brownlie, *Basic Documents on African Affairs* (1971).

▲▼ JOURNALISM AND TRAVEL

Among the most readable books in the literature of African history are the impressionistic accounts left by journalists and other travelers. These must be read with caution, with due allowances for the prejudices of the hasty observer, but at their best they convey the "feel" of Africa with great sensitivity. Here one can give only a brief list, chronologically arranged, of some of the best of these works. Mary Kingsley, *Travels in West Africa* (1897) and *West African Studies* (1899); W. S. Churchill, *My African Journey* (1908); J. S. Huxley, *Africa View* (1931); Geoffrey Gorer, *Africa Dances* (1935); Patrick Blafuui (Lord Kinross), *Lords of the Equator* (1937); Negley Farson, *Behind God's Back* (1940) and *Last Chance in Africa* (1949); Elspeth Huxley, *The Sorcerer's Apprentice* (1948), *Four Guineas* (1954), and *Forks and Hope* (1964); Vernon Bartlett, *Struggle for Africa* (1953); John Gunther, *Inside Africa* (1955); Basil Davidson, *The African Awakening* (1955); James Cameron, *The African Revolution* (1961); Tom Hopkinson, *In the Fiery Continent* (1962); René Dumont, *False Start in Africa* (1966).

▲▼ LABOR

J. W. Davis, *Modern Industry and the African* (1933) and G. Orde-Browne, *The African Labourer* (1936) are among the earliest studies of labor in Africa. Recent general studies include W. H. Friedland,

Unions, Labor and Industrial Relations in Africa (1965) and J. Meynaud and A. Salah-Bey (eds.), *Trades Unionism in Africa* (1967). More detailed studies of African labor and trade unionism include W. Elkan, *Migrants and Proletarians: Urban Labour in the Economic Development of Uganda* (1960); S. T. van der Horst, *African Workers in Town: a Study of Labour in Cape Town* (1964); S. Fawzi, *The Labour Movement in the Sudan, 1946–1955* (1957); W. Ananaba, *The Trades Union Movement in Nigeria* (1969); and R. H. Bates, *Unions, Parties and Political Development* (1971), a study of mineworkers in Zambia. C. Kadalie, *My Life and the ICU* (1970) is the autobiography of the most prominent South African trade unionist of the 1920's.

▲▼ LAW

The chapter by A. A. Schiller on "Law" in R. A. Lystad (ed.), *The African World* provides a useful introduction to the study of law in Africa. Important works in this field include J. N. D. Anderson, *Islamic Law in Africa* (1954); A. N. Allott (ed.), *Judicial and Legal Systems in Africa* (1962); T. O. Elias, *The Nature of African Customary Law* (1956); J. N. D. Anderson (ed.), *Changing Law in Developing Countries* (1963); H. and L. Kuper, *African Law: Adaptation and Development* (1965).

▲▼ LITERATURE

R. Finnegan, *Oral Literature in Africa* (1970) provides a comprehensive introduction to the rich store of oral literature, some of which has been translated, edited, and published in an expanding series, *The Oxford Library of African Literature*. A. Tibble (ed.), *African-English Literature* (1965) contains a useful introductory survey of recent African writing in English. The most famous of all anthologies of African poetry is that edited by L. S. Senghor, *Anthologie de la nouvelle poésie nègre et malgache,* with an introduction by J. P. Sartre entitled *"Orphée noire"* (1948). Anthologies in English include G. Moore and U. Beier (eds.), *Modern Poetry from Africa* (1963) and O. R. Dathorne and W. Feuser (eds.), *Africa in Prose* (1969). The main literary journals concerned with Africa are *Présence Africaine* (Paris, from 1947, English edition from 1961); *Black Orpheus* (Ibadan, from 1957); *Transition* (Kampala, from 1963); *Africa South* (Cape Town, 1956–61).

Prominent European or American writers some of whose works are set in Africa include John Buchan, Albert Camus, Joseph Conrad, André Gide, Graham Greene, H. Rider Haggard, Ernest Hemingway, Edgar Wallace, Evelyn Waugh, and P. C. Wren. Works by writers such as these played a large part in helping to form the contemporary images of Africa held by outsiders.

▲▼ NATIONALISM AND AFRICAN POLITICS

Two good general surveys, R. Emerson, *From Empire to Nation* (1960) and H. Grimal, *La Décolonisation, 1919–1963* (1965), place the movement for African independence in a wider context. E. Kedourie, *Nationalism in Asia and Africa* (1970), combines a stimulating and critical essay on nationalist ideas with an anthology of relevant texts. Two short works by T. L. Hodgkin, *Nationalism in Colonial Africa* (1956) and *African Political Parties* (1961), stand out as among the most intelligent and sympathetic contemporary attempts to understand and explore the phenomenon of African nationalism. See also I. Wallenstein, *Africa: The Politics of Independence: An Interpretation of Modern African History* (1959). R. Segal (ed.), *Political Africa* (1961) and its abridgement, *African Profiles* (1963) provide useful guides to politicians and parties in the early 1960's. Political developments in the newly independent African states are described in a number of large composite volumes by American scholars: G. A. Almond and J. S. Coleman (eds.), *The Politics of the Developing Areas* (1960); G. M. Carter (ed.), *African One-Party States* (1962); G. M. Carter (ed.), *Five African States* (1963); J. S. Coleman and C. G. Rosberg (eds.), *Political Parties and National Integration in Tropical Africa* (1964). Toward the end of the 1960's political scientists found themselves forced by the turn of events to pay increasing attention to the role of the armed forces in newly independent states. Recent works in this field include W. Gutteridge, *The Military in African Politics* (1969); J. M. Lee, *African Armies and Civil Order* (1969); C. E. Welch (ed.), *Soldiers and Statesmen in Africa* (1970); and R. First, *The Barrel of a Gun* (1970).

▲▼ POPULATION STUDIES

Of African countries only Algeria, Egypt, South Africa, the Mascarenes, and some West African settlements have population records reaching back to the nineteenth century. Not until the 1950's were effective censuses held in many African countries. Two symposia, K. M. Barbour and R. M. Prothero (eds.), *Essays on African Population* (1961) and J. C. Caldwell and C. Okonjo (eds.), *The Populations of Tropical Africa* (1968), provide useful introductions to recent demographic studies in Africa. R. F. Stevenson, *Population and Political Systems in Tropical Africa* (1968) is a stimulating study examining the connection between population density and state formation. On migration, see the stimulating collection of essays edited by J. A. Jackson, *Migration* (1969).

▲▼ REACTIONS TO CONQUEST

In recent years historians have begun to pay increasing attention to African reactions to conquest in the first decades of rampant European imperialism. A massive symposium edited by R. I. Rotberg and A. Mazrui, *Protest and Power in Black Africa* (1971) brings together many of the most important recent studies in this field. See also M. Crowder (ed.), *West African Resistance* (1971) and the chapters on African resistance by J. D. Hargreaves and T. Ranger in Gann and Duignan, *Colonialism in Africa*, Vol. I.

▲▼ READERS

One of the most useful recent developments in African studies has been the production of "readers," collections of extracts drawn from primary or secondary sources, many of which are not otherwise easily available. For nineteenth-century Africa see the historical anthologies listed in *Africa to 1875,* p. 441. On European imperialism in Africa see the works edited by Betts and Winks noted on p. 779 above. For twentieth century Africa see P. J. M. McEwan, *Twentieth Century Africa* (1968); W. Cartey and M. Kilson (eds.), *The African Reader,* Vol. I, *Colonial Africa,* Vol. II, *Independent Africa* (1970); P. L. van der Berghe (ed.), *Social Problems of Change and Development* (1965) and P. J. M. McEwan and R. B. Sutcliffe (eds.), *The Study of Africa* (1965).

▲▼ RELIGION

G. Parrinder, *Religion in Africa* (1969) provides a brief, comprehensive introduction, covering traditional religion, Christianity, and Islam. The variety of traditional religious beliefs is well illustrated in two symposia, D. Forde (ed.), *African Worlds* (1954) and M. Fortes and G. Dieterlen (eds.), *African Systems of Thought* (1965). In recent years, social anthropologists have made a number of detailed studies of the traditional religious systems of a number of African peoples; see, for example, E. E. Evans-Pritchard, *Nuer Religion* (1956) and S. F. Nadel, *Nupe Religion* (1954). The contributors to *The Historical Study of African Religions,* edited by T. O. Ranger and I. N. Kimambo (1972), view traditional African religions in historical perspective, not in a "timeless ethnographic present."

On the expansion of Christianity in Africa the basic work is the richly detailed study by C. P. Groves, *The Planting of Christianity in Africa,* 4 vols. (1948–58). K. S. Latourette, *A History of the Expansion of Christianity,* 7 vols. (1937–45) deals with Africa more briefly. See also the more impressionistic account by G. Moorhouse, *The Missionaries* (1973). C. G. Baëta (ed.), *Christianity in Africa* (1968) is an important symposium indicating the lines of recent research in the field of mission history. See also T. O. Ranger and J. Weller (eds.), *Themes in the Christian History of Central Africa* (1973). Particular attention has been paid in recent years to the independent African churches, a line of research greatly stimulated by B. Sunndkler's seminal work, *Bantu Prophets in South Africa* (1948).

J. S. Trimingham, *The Influence of Islam upon Africa* (1968) provides a brief introduction to the role of Islam in Africa. Trimingham is also the author of detailed studies of *Islam in the Sudan* (1949), *Islam in Ethiopia* (1952), *Islam in West Africa* (1958), and *Islam in East Africa* (1964). I. M. Lewis (ed.), *Islam in Tropical Africa* (1966) is an important collection of studies, many of which are of particular interest to the general student of African history. See also, V. Monteil, *L'Islam noir* (1964).

▲▼ SOCIAL CHANGE

W. M. Macmillan, *Africa Emergent* (1938; revised and enlarged edition, 1948), "a study of social, political and economic trends in British Africa" and G. and M. Wilson, *The Analysis of Social Change* (1945), a brief study based on "observations in Central Africa," stand out as two of the first studies that attempted to generalize about the changes taking place in African society. See also, B. Malinowski, *Dynamics of Culture Change* (1945). Different aspects of social change are conveniently presented in a number of symposia or readers: W. R. Bascom and M. J. Herskovits (eds.), *Continuity and Change in African Cultures* (1959); S. and P. Ottenberg (eds.), *Cultures and Societies of Africa* (1960); A. Southall (ed.), *Social Change in Modern Africa* (1961); I. Wallenstein (ed.), *Social Change: The Colonial Situation* (1966). There are three stimulating general studies by individual authors: M. J. Herskovits, *The Human Factor in Changing Africa* (1963); G. Hunter, *The New Societies of Tropical Africa* (1962); and P. C. Lloyd, *Africa in Social Change* (1967). Two symposia discuss changes in the social structure of African countries: INCIDI, *The Development of a Middle Class in Tropical and Subtropical Countries* (1956) and P. C. Lloyd (ed.), *The New Elites of Tropical Africa* (1966).

▲▼ TRADITIONAL POLITIES

M. Fortes and E. E. Evans-Pritchard (eds.), *African Political Systems* (1940) and L. Mair, *Primitive Government* (1962) offer the best introductions to the variety of polities to be found in precolonial Africa. See also, I. Schapera, *Government and Politics in Tribal Societies* (1956) and J. Middleton and D. Tait (eds.), *Tribes without Rulers* (1958). Notable individual studies of African polities include E. E. Evans-Pritchard, *The Nuer* (1940); I. M. Lewis, *A Pastoral Democracy* (1961), a study of the Northern Somali; R. Montagne, *Les Berbères et le makhzen dans le sud du Maroc* (1930); M. G. Smith, *Government in Zazzau, 1800–1960* (1960), a study of a Northern Nigerian emirate; J. Maquet, *The Premise of Inequality in Rwanda* (1961); and J. H. M. Beattie, *Bunyoro, an African Kingdom* (1960). See also, the essays in D. Forde and P. M. Kaberry (eds.), *West African Kingdoms in the Nineteenth Century* (1967).

▲▼ URBANIZATION

Two symposia, H. Miner (ed.), *The City in Modern Africa* (1967) and INCIDI, *Urban Agglomerations in the States of the Third World* (1971), present a wide range of recent research on urbanization. R. W. Steel, "The towns of tropical Africa" in K. W. Barbour and R. M. Prothero, *Essays in African Population* (1961) is a useful introductory study. Particular attention has been paid to the development of urbanization in West Africa: see R. P. Simms, *Urbanization in West Africa:*

A Review of Current Literature (1965) and H. Kuper (ed.), *Urbanization and Migration in West Africa* (1965). Detailed studies of urban life in many of the major cities of Africa have now been made: see, for example, G. Balandier, *Sociologie des Brazzaville Noirs* (1955); R. Montagne, *Naissance du prolétariat marocain* (1952); and J. A. K. Leslie, *A Survey of Dar es-Salaam* (1963).

PART II

▲▼ NORTHEAST AFRICA

The differences between the various parts of Northeast Africa are so great that the region has never been considered to possess a measure of unity comparable to that of other regions of the continent. Consequently there is no single work to be recommended as providing an introduction to the region as a whole. General historians have concentrated on the individual countries—Egypt, the Sudan, Ethiopia, and Somalia—that make up the region.

EGYPT. P. J. Vatikiotis, *The Modern History of Egypt* (1969) provides a comprehensive and up-to-date introduction to Egyptian history. The collection of studies edited by P. M. Holt, *Political and Social Change in Modern Egypt* (1969), contains a number of important studies relating to nineteenth- and twentieth-century Egypt. J. Berque, *L'Egypte: impérialisme et révolution* (1967), the work of a distinguished French sociologist, is immensely stimulating and richly documented. J. Marlowe, *Anglo-Egyptian Relations, 1800–1956* (second edition, 1965) is a vivid introduction to the major theme of Egypt's external relations. A. E. Crouchley, *The Economic Development of Egypt* (1938) provides a succinct account of modern economic history; it should be supplemented by the more detailed study by E. R. J. Owen, *Cotton and the Egyptian Economy, 1820–1914* (1969).

J. McCoon, *Egypt As It Is* (1877) is a good contemporary account of Ismail's Egypt. The works of most European travelers in Egypt present a tourist's-eye view of the country, but Lady Duff Gordon, *Letters from Egypt*, edited by G. Waterfield (1969), conveys a marvelously sympathetic impression of the life of the *fellahin* in the 1860's. D. S. Landes, *Bankers and Pashas* (1958) contains a penetrating study of Ismail's financial transactions. The events that led to Ismail's downfall and later to the British occupation are narrated in the Earl of Cromer's magisterial work, *Modern Egypt* (1908). R. E. Robinson, J. Gallagher, and A. Denny, *Africa and the Victorians* (1961) contains a detailed study of the cross-currents of opinion in the British cabinet with regard to Egypt. W. S. Blunt, *Secret History of the British Occupation of Egypt* (1895) presents a highly critical view of British actions. The intellectual origins of Egyptian nationalism have been studied in a number of recent works: A. Hourani, *Arabic Thought in the Liberal Age* (1962); J. M. Ahmed, *The Intellectual Origins of Egyptian Nationalism* (1960); and N. Safran, *Egypt in Search of Political Community* (1961). M. Rowlatt, *Founders of Modern Egypt* (1962) provides a sympathetic account of the early nationalist movement.

Cromer's *Modern Egypt* provides a proconsular view of Egypt under the British; A. Milner, *England in Egypt* (1904) and Lord Lloyd, *Egypt since Cromer* (1933) are equally imperialist in tone. There are two useful studies of the British period by recent historians: R. L. Tignor, *Modernization and British Colonial Rule in Egypt, 1882–1914* (1865) and A. Lufti al-Sayyid, *Egypt under Cromer* (1968).

On the course of Egyptian politics from the ending of the British protectorate to the 1952 revolution, see the works by Vatikiotis and Marlowe already cited. The course of events that led to the ending of the British protectorate are clearly described in G. Young, *Modern Egypt* (1927) and P. G. Elgood, *The Transit of Egypt* (1928). C. P. Harris, *Nationalism and Revolution in Egypt* (1964) is a detailed study of the Muslim Brotherhood.

Two short books by P. Mansfield, *Nasser's Egypt* (1965) and *Nasser* (1969), provide a good introduction to the most recent period of Egyptian history. P. J. Vatikiotis, whose *Modern History* devotes much space to recent developments, has edited an important collection of scholarly studies, *Egypt since the Revolution* (1968). J. and S. Latourette, *Egypt in Transition* (1958) is a sympathetic account of the first years of the revolution by two French journalists. See also R. H. Dekmejian, *Egypt under Nasir* (1971), and R. Stephens, *Nasser* (1973). Recent developments in the economy are described in C. Issawi, *Egypt in Revolution* (1963) and P. K. O'Brien, *The Revolution in Egypt's Economic System* (1966). G. A. Nasser, *The Philosophy of the Revolution* (1955) is one of the seminal texts of modern African history A Ahdel Malek, *Egypte-société militaire* (1961) presents a critical view of Nasser's regime by an Egyptian Marxist. Among modern Egyptian novels to have been translated into English are A. R. Sharkawi, *Egyptian Earth* (1961) and F. Ghanen, *The Man Who Lost His Shadow* (1965).

THE SUDAN. There are two good introductory works: P. M. Holt, *A Modern History of the Sudan* (1961) and K. D. D. Henderson, *The Sudan Republic* (1965). These should be supplemented by the first-rate geographical study, K. M. Barbour, *The Republic of the Sudan* (1961).

R. Hill, *Egypt in the Sudan, 1820–1881* (1959) provides the best introduction to the period of Turco-Egyptian rule. Of the two most recent studies of the Mahdia the work by P. M. Holt, *The Mahdist State in the Sudan, 1881–1898* (1958) has the advantage of drawing much of its material from surviving Mahdist documents, while A. B. Theobald, *The Mahdiyya* (1951) is based largely on European sources. Gordon has been the subject of a very extensive literature: B. M.

Allen, *Gordon in the Sudan* (1931) is the most important secondary work. There is a particularly vivid account of the drama in which Gordon was involved in A. Moorehead, *The White Nile* (1960). Events in the Sudan in the 1880's and 1890's inspired a number of extremely exciting contemporary works: F. R. Wingate, *Mahdism in the Egyptian Sudan* (1891); J. Ohrwalder, *Ten Years Captivity in the Mahdist Camp* (1892); R. C. Slatin, *Fire and Sword in the Sudan* (1896); and W. S. Churchill, *The River War* (1899). The tangled European diplomacy of the struggle for the Upper Nile has been unraveled by G. N. Sanderson, *England, Europe and the Upper Nile, 1882–1899* (1965); the struggle is described more briefly from an exclusively British viewpoint in Cromer's *Modern Egypt* and in *Africa and the Victorians* by Robinson, Gallagher, and Denny. There are two detailed studies of events in the Southern Sudan in the last decades of the nineteenth century: R. Gray, *A History of the Southern Sudan 1839–1889* (1961) and R. O. Collins, *The Southern Sudan 1883–1898* (1962).

The two introductory works by Holt and Henderson contain useful surveys of the Anglo-Egyptian Condominium. The colonial period is now being studied in more detail by Sudanese historians: M. A. al-Rahim, *Imperialism and Nationalism in the Sudan* (1969); M. O. Beshir, *Educational Development in the Sudan, 1898 to 1956* (1969) and *The Southern Sudan: Development to Conflict* (1968). There are three biographical studies of European administrators who played a leading part in the development of the modern Sudan: R. Wingate, *Wingate of the Sudan* (1955); R. Hill, *Slatin Pasha* (1965); and K. D. D. Henderson, *The Making of the Modern Sudan* (1953), the life and letters of a far-sighted senior official, Sir Douglass Newbold. A different view of the condominium regime is provided by E. Atiyah, *An Arab Tells His Story* (1946). A vivid account of Sudanese life is contained in *The Memoirs of Babikir Bedri*, translated from the Arabic by Y. Bedri and G. Scott (1969).

There is at present no detailed study of the history of the Sudan in the years since 1956, but the works by Henderson and Holt provide brief accounts of the first years of the independent republic.

ETHIOPIA. Certain aspects of Ethiopia have been studied in great detail by European scholars, but the modern history of the country has only recently begun to be made the subject of scholarly research. Almost all the works presently available on Ethiopian history suffer from the thinness of their documentation. Introductory studies include A. H. M. Jones and E. Monroe, *A History of Abyssinia* (1935); D. Mathew, *Ethiopia: A Study of a Polity* (1946); E. Ullendorf, *The Ethiopians* (second edition, 1965); and R. Greenfield, *Ethiopia: A New Political History* (1965). Of these works Greenfield's provides the fullest account of the modern period. J. S. Trimingham, *Islam in Ethiopia* (1952) contains a good account of the history of the Muslim areas of the country.

There are a number of vivid accounts of Menelik's Ethiopia written by European travelers: Count Gleichen, *With the Mission to Menelik* (1898); A. B. Wylde, *Modern Abyssinia* (1901); J. Rennell Rodd, *So-*

cial and Diplomatic Memoirs (1922). Much interesting material is contained in two short anthologies edited by R. Pankhurst, *Travelers in Ethiopia* (1965) and *The Ethiopian Royal Chronicles* (1967).

L. Mosley, *Haile Selassie, the Conquering Lion* (1964) contains a good deal of information on Ethiopia in the 1910's and 1920's. The development of Italian ambitions represents the best documented theme of this period of Ethiopian history. J. L. Miège, *L'Impérialisme colonial italien de 1870 à nos jours* (1968) provides an excellent introduction to Italian activities. G. W. Baer, *The Coming of the Italian-Ethiopian War* (1967) is based on solid research in the Italian archives. P. Badoglio, *The War in Abyssinia* (1940) provides a contemporary account of the war from the Italian point of view, while G. L. Steer, *Caesar in Abyssinia* (1936) is the vivid narrative of an English journalist who accompanied the Ethiopian armies. G. K. N. Trevaskis, *Eritrea, a Colony in Transition* (1960) describes developments in the former Italian colony after its conquest and occupation by the British.

On the latest period of Ethiopian history there are three interesting studies all of which concentrate on the evolving structure of the imperial government: M. Perham, *The Government of Ethiopia* (second edition, 1969); C. Clapham, *Haile Selassie's Government* (1969); and R. L. Hess, *Ethiopia, the Modernization of Autocracy* (1970).

SOMALIA. I. M. Lewis, *The Modern History of Somaliland* (1965) is the most useful introductory work. The history of Italian Somalia is explored in more detail in R. L. Hess, *Italian Colonization in Somalia* (1966), while V. Thompson and R. Adloff, *Djibouti and the Horn of Africa* (1968) is a lengthy study of the French Somali coast. D. Jardine, *The Mad Mullah of Somaliland* (1923) is the best contemporary account, written by a senior colonial official, of the war against the Somali resistance leader, Muhammad Abdille Hassan. Another British official, J. J. Drysdale, has described recent Somali-Ethiopian relations in *The Somali Dispute* (1964).

▲▼ NORTHWEST AFRICA

There are a number of good introductory works on Northwest Africa. N. Barbour, *A Survey of North West Africa* (second edition, 1962) covers the entire region, including the Sahara. Other introductory works concentrate on the three principal countries of the region: R. M. Bruce, *Morocco, Algeria, Tunisia* (1964); C. F. Gallagher, *The United States and North Africa* (1963), a misleading title for an excellent general introduction; and S. Amin, *The Maghrib in the Modern World* (1970). These should be supplemented by two excellent geographical studies: J. Despois, *L'Afrique du Nord* (third edition, 1964) and R. Capot Rey, *Le Sahara français* (1953).

There is as yet no comprehensive general study of French rule in North Africa, but the French sociologist, J. Berque, presents a marvelously subtle portrait of the region at the height of the colonial era in *The Maghrib between Two World Wars,* translated by J. Stewart (1967). France's impact on the region is discussed in D. C. Gordon, *North Africa's French Legacy* (1962). The development of North African nationalism is described in considerable detail by C. A. Julien, *L'Afrique du Nord en marche* (1952) and by R. Le Tourneau, *Evolution politique de l'Afrique du Nord musulmane, 1920–1961* (1962). See also, L. Hahn, *North Africa: Nationalism to Nationhood* (1960) and A. al-Fasi, *The Independence Movements of North Africa* (1954), the latter the work of a leading Moroccan nationalist. For recent developments in North Africa the most useful source of material is the *Annuaire de l'Afrique du Nord*. See also E. Hermassi, *Leadership and National Development in North Africa* (1972).

ALGERIA. There is a good short history in the *Que sais-je?* series by C. R. Ageron, *Histoire de l'Algérie contemporaine (1830–1969)* (1969). Ageron is also the author of a massive and richly documented work, *Les Algériens musulmans et la France (1871–1919)* (1968). The same subject is dealt with much more briefly by V. Confer, *France and Algeria: The Problem of Civil and Political Reform, 1870–1920* (1966). The works by Julien and Le Tourneau—already cited— provide detailed narratives of the development of Algerian politics from 1920. The Algerian war of liberation has produced a copious literature. E. O'Balance, *The Algerian Insurrection, 1954–1962* (1967) offers a sober narrative by a military historian; E. Behr, *The Algerian Problem* (1961) is a vivid account by an English journalist; and G. Tillon, *Algeria: The Realities* (1957) and *France and Algeria, Complementary Enemies* (1961) are two moving studies by a French anthropologist deeply familiar with the Algerian scene. Franco-Algerian relations before 1962 are charted by D. C. Gordon, *The Passing of French Algeria* (1966), and W. G. Andrews, *French Politics and Algeria* (1962). The most recent period of Algerian history is described in D. and M. Ottaway, *Algeria: The Politics of a Socialist Revolution* (1970). See also W. B. Quandt, *Revolution and Political Leadership in Algeria* (1969).

MOROCCO. N. Barbour, *Morocco* (1965) is the most recent general history in English. J. L. Miège, *Le Maroc et l'Europe, 1830–1894*, 4 vols. (1961) stands out as the most detailed study yet made of the impact of Europe on a nineteenth-century African state. P. Guillen, *L'Allemagne et le Maroc de 1870 à 1905* (1967) is in the same richly documented tradition of scholarship as Miège's work. Two contemporary works, E. Aubin, *Morocco Today* (1904) and W. B. Harris, *Morocco That Was* (1921), provide vivid accounts of the sultanate in the last years of its independence. R. Montagne, *Les Berbères et le Makhzen dans le sud du Maroc* (1930) is a classic study of the dynamics of local politics. This should now be supplemented by E. Gellner, *Saints of the Atlas* (1969), and by the essays in the symposium edited by Gellner, *Arabs and Berbers* (1973). R. Landau, *Moroccan Drama* (1956) is a highly readable account of the development of Moroccan nationalism; it should be supplemented by the relevant sections of the general works by Julien, Le Tourneau, and al-Fasi and by J. P. Halsted, *Birth of a Nation: Origins and Rise of Moroccan Nationalism, 1912–1944* (1967). Franco-Moroccan relations are studied in S. Bernard, *The Franco-Moroccan Conflict* (1968). Political scientists have paid much attention to postindependence Morocco; works in this category include D. E. Ashford, *Political Change in Morocco* (1961); I. W. Zartmann, *Morocco: Problems of New Power* (1964); and J. Waterbury, *The Commander of the Faithful: the Moroccan Political Elite* (1970). F. E. Trout, *Morocco's Saharan Frontiers* (1970) is a detailed historical study of one of the most controversial borders in Africa. C. F. Stewart, *The Economy of Modern Morocco* (1967), should also be noted.

TUNISIA. W. Knapp, *Tunisia* (1970) and D. L. Ling, *Tunisia: From Protectorate to Republic* (1967) provide useful introductions to modern Tunisian history. J. Ganiage, *Les origines du protectorat français en Tunisie* (1959) is an outstanding study of the events leading up to the French occupation. The works by Julien and Le Tourneau describe the growth of Tunisian nationalism. Recent history is covered in C. H. Moore, *Tunisia since Independence* (1965).

LIBYA. J. Wright, *Libya* (1969) provides an excellent history of the country up to the 1960's. E. E. Evans-Pritchard, *The Sanusi of Cyrenaica* (1949) combines the techniques of the historian and the social anthropologist to produce one of the classic works of its kind.

MAURITANIA. A. G. Gerteiny, *Mauritania* (1967) is a competent historical introduction.

THE SAHARA. R. Capot Rey, *Le Sahara français* and L. Cabot Briggs, *Tribes of the Sahara* (1960) provide much useful information on recent changes in the Sahara.

For an introduction to recent North African writing see the anthology edited by L. Ortzen, *North African Writing* (1970).

▲▼ WEST AFRICA

There are two useful introductions to the region's history, both primarily designed as school textbooks: J. D. Fage, *A History of West Africa* (fourth edition, 1969) and J. F. A. Ajayi and I. Espie (eds.), *A Thousand Years of West African History* (1965). M. Crowder, *West Africa under Colonial Rule* (1968) contains a detailed account of the European conquest of West Africa and the establishment of European hegemony. J. D. Hargreaves, *Prelude to the Partition of West Africa* (1963) also considers the region in its entirety but concentrates on the period between the 1850's and the 1880's. The two-volume collection of documents edited by C. W. Newbury, *British Policy towards West Africa*, Vol. I, 1786–1874 (1965); Vol. II, 1875–1914 (1971) contains a mass of valuable material not easily accessible otherwise; so too does the somewhat similar collection edited by G. E. Metcalfe, *Great Britain and Ghana, 1807–1957* (1963). Documents relating to French policy are contained in the historical anthology edited by J. D. Hargreaves, *France and West Africa* (1969).

On the geography of West Africa the most comprehensive work is W. B. Morgan and J. C. Pugh, *West Africa* (1969). The variety of forms of government to be found in precolonial West Africa is well illustrated by the various contributions to *West African Kingdoms in the Nineteenth Century*, edited by D. Forde and P. M. Kaberry (1967). The impact of Islam is another theme which has been studied on a regional basis in a number of works: J. S. Trimingham, *A History of Islam in West Africa* (1962); I. M. Lewis (ed.), *Islam in Tropical Africa* (1966); and V. Monteil, *L'Islam noir* (1964). Detailed studies of particular aspects of Islam in West Africa include N. Levtzion, *Muslims and Chiefs in West Africa* (1968), a survey of the expansion of Islam in the Middle Volta basin in the precolonial period, and D. B. C. O'Brien, *The Mourids of Senegal* (1971).

Competent single-country histories are now available for all the anglophone states of West Africa and most of the francophone ones. Gambia: H. A. Gailey, *A History of the Gambia* (1964) and J. M. Gray, *A History of the Gambia* (1940). Sierra Leone: C. H. Fyfe, *A History of Sierra Leone* (1962), a massive work concentrating on the history of the colony and not going much farther than the end of the nineteenth century, and *A Short History of Sierra Leone* (1962), a much briefer but more comprehensive work by the same author. Ghana: W. E. F. Ward, *A History of Ghana* (1958) and J. D. Fage, *Ghana: A Historical Introduction* (1959). Nigeria: M. Crowder, *The Story of Nigeria* (1962). See also, J. E. Flint, *Ghana and Nigeria* (1967). French West Africa: J. D. Hargreaves, *West Africa: The Former French States* (1967) and V. Thompson and R. Adloff, *French West Africa* (1958). Senegal: M. Crowder, *Senegal: A Study in French Assimilation Policy* (1962). Ivory Coast: G. Rougerie, *Le Côte d'Ivoire* (1964). Togo: R. Cornevin, *Histoire du Togo* (1959). Dahomey: R. Cornevin, *Histoire du Dahomey* (1962). Niger: E. Série des Rivières, *Histoire du Niger* (1965). Liberia: E. J. Yancy, *The Republic of Liberia* (1959).

On Senegambia in the late nineteenth century the major contemporary work is General Faidherbe, *Le Sénégal* (1889). See also, J. D. Hargreaves, *Prelude to the Partition of West Africa* (1963); M. A. Klein, "The Moslem Revolution in Nineteenth-Century Senegambia" in D. F. MacColl, N. R. Bennett, and J. Butler (eds.), *Western African History*, Boston University Papers on Africa, Vol. IV (1969); and C. A. Quinn, *Mandingo Kingdoms of the Senegambia: Traditionalism, Islam and European Expansion* (1972).

On the French conquest of the Western Sudan there is an authoritative recent study by A. S. Kanya-Forstner, *The Conquest of the Western Sudan* (1969). Many French officers wrote accounts of their experiences; a representative work is J. Meniaud, *Les pionniers du Soudan,* 2 vols. (1931). On the Tukulor empire, the major Sudanic polity destroyed by the French, there is an excellent study by Y. Saint-Martin, *L'Empire toucouleur et la France* (1967). The state built up by Samory has been made the subject of a massive study by Y. Person, *Samori: une révolution dyula,* 2 vols. (Dakar, 1968 and 1970).

On the late nineteenth-century history of Upper Guinea, the area covered by the modern states of Guinea, Sierra Leone, Liberia, and the Ivory Coast, Hargreaves' *Prelude to Partition* provides the most comprehensive introduction. Of contemporary works A. Arcin, *La Guinée française* (1907) may be specially recommended.

The European conquest of the Gold Coast, Dahomey, and Togo is described in the general histories of these countries already cited. See also, W. Tordoff, *Ashanti under the Prempehs, 1886–1936* (1965), F. Agbodeka, *African Politics and British Rule in the Gold Coast, 1869–1900* (1972), and C. W. Newbury, *The Western Slave Coast and Its Rulers* (1961).

The late nineteenth-century history of Nigeria has been the subject of a great deal of research in recent years with a steadily mounting volume of publications being produced by Nigerian scholars. Important recent studies include K. O. Dike, *Trade and Politics in the Niger Delta, 1830–1885* (1956); J. C. Anene, *Southern Nigeria in Transition 1884–1906* (1965); E. A. Ayandele, *The Missionary Impact on Modern Nigeria, 1842–1914* (1966); R. A. Adeleye, *Power and Diplomacy in Northern Nigeria, 1804–1906* (1971); and S. A. Akintoye, *Revolution and Power Politics in Yorubaland, 1840–1893* (1971). There are good biographies of the two main architects of British rule: J. E. Flint, *Sir George Goldie and the Making of Nigeria* (1960) and M. Perham, *Lugard,* 2 vols. (1956, 1960). D. J. Muffett, *Concerning Brave Captains* (1964) presents a sympathetic view of the defeated side in the conquest of Northern Nigeria.

On the structure of European hegemony in West Africa there is a great deal of material in the two basic studies of colonial administration: Lord Hailey, *An African Survey* (1938; revised edition, 1957) and R. L. Buell, *The Native Problem in Africa,* 2 vols. (1928). On French rule see S. H. Roberts, *The History of French Colonial Policy 1870–1925* (1929) and R. Delavignette, *Freedom and Authority in French West Africa* (1950). See also M. Crowder and O. Ikime (eds.), *West African Chiefs* (1970). F. D. Lugard, *The Dual Mandate in Tropical Africa* (1922) was in its day the most influential work written by a colonial administrator in Africa. It should be read along with Perham's biography of Lugard and J. F. Nicholson, *The Administration of Nigeria* (1969), a study highly critical of Lugard but appreciative of the work of other British officials. W. R. Crocker, *Nigeria: A Critique of British Colonial Administration* (1936) is a vivid and lively study written by a young administrative officer. The African novels of Joyce Carey (*Aissa Saved, Mister Johnson,* and others) convey a memorable impression of Northern Nigeria in the first decades of colonial administration. For British administration on the Gold Coast see R. Wraith, *Guggisberg* (1967); D. Kimble, *A Political History of Ghana, 1850–1928* (1963) and W. Tordoff, *Ashanti under the Prempehs.*

For a survey of the economic history of West Africa see A. G. Hopkins, *An Economic History of West Africa* (1973). Other useful general works are C. W. Newbury, "Trade and Authority in West Africa" in L. H. Gann and P. Duignan (eds.), *Colonialism in Africa,* Vol. I (1969); W. K. Hancock, *A Survey of British Commonwealth Affairs,* Vol. I (1942); and P. T. Bauer, *West African Trade* (1954). The role of African producers is well illustrated in P. Hill, *The Gold Coast Cocoa Farmer* (1956), and of the big European firms in C. Wilson, *The History of Unilever,* 2 vols. (1954).

P. C. Lloyd, *Africa in Social Change* (1967), a work which, in spite of its title, draws its material entirely from West Africa, provides a good introduction to social and intellectual changes in the region. On urbanization see H. Kuper (ed.), *Urbanization and Migration in West Africa* (1965). There are also a number of good studies of individual West African cities: I. Acquah, *Accra Survey* (1958); M. Banton, *West African City* (1957), a study of Freetown; and P. C. Lloyd and others, *The City of Ibadan* (1967). On the impact of Islam and Christianity see, in addition to the more general works cited on p. 784, J. S. Trimingham, *Islam in West Africa* (1959); C. G. Baëta, *Prophetism in Ghana* (1962); N. Smith, *The Presbyterian Church of Ghana* (1966); and J. B. Webster, *The African Churches among the Yoruba* (1964). G. Parrinder, *Religion in an African City* (1953) provides a clear and detailed account of the variety of sects, Christian, Muslim, and traditional, to be found in the city of Ibadan. On education the general works cited on p. 776 should be supplemented by P. Foster, *Education and Social Change in Ghana* (1965), a stimulating and well-documented study. A. Moumoumi, *Education in Africa* (1968) contains a critical account of the system of education in French West Africa by an African teacher from Mali. Many of the studies in the symposium edited by P. C. Lloyd, *The New Elites of Tropical Africa* (1966) relate to West Africa. A. T. Porter, *Creoledom* (1963) is a sociological study of the descendants of the freed slaves of Sierra Leone, the first Western-educated elite group to emerge in West Africa. The largest European community in West Africa, the French in Senegal, are the subject of a study by R. C. O'Brien, *White Society in Black Africa* (1972). On the cultural impact of a European language, see the collection of essays edited by J. Spencer, *The English Language in West Africa* (1971).

The intellectual background to modern West African nationalism is vividly presented in R. W. July, *The Origins of Modern African Thought* (1968). J. S. Coleman, *Nigeria: Background to Nationalism* (1958) provides the most detailed account of political development in a West Africa country before World War II. On political developments in the period leading up to independence there are a number of richly documented studies: K. Ezera, *Constitutional Developments in Nigeria* (1960); R. L. Sklar, *Nigerian Political Parties* (1963); D. Austin, *Politics in Ghana, 1946–1960* (1964); M. Kilson, *Political Change in a West African State* (1966), a study of Sierra Leone; R. S. Morgenthau, *Political Parties in French-speaking West Africa* (1964) and A. R. Zolberg, *One-Party Government in the Ivory Coast* (1964). The highly complicated constitutional and political relations between France and her African colonies are clearly explained in E. Mortimer, *France and the Africans, 1944–1960* (1969); see also, W. J. Foltz, *From French West Africa to the Mali Federation* (1965). The literature on West African politics has been enriched by the writings of some of the most prominent West African politicians: K. Nkrumah, *Ghana* (1957) and other works; O. Awolowo, *Awo* (1960); N. Azikiwe, *Zik* (1960); Sir Ahmadu Bello, *My Life* (1962); L. Senghor, *On African Socialism* (1964); and M. Dia, *The African Nations and World Solidarity* (1962). See also K. W. J. Post and G. D. Jenkins,

The Price of Liberty: Personality and Politics in Colonial Nigeria (1972).

K. Post, *The New States of West Africa* (revised edition, 1968) provides a good introduction to the postindependence period. See also, G. Carter (ed.), *African One-Party States* (1962) and J. S. Coleman and C. G. Rosberg (eds.), *Political Parties and National Integration in Tropical Africa* (1964), both of which include contributions on several of the states of West Africa. On recent Ghanaian history see H. S. Bretton, *The Rise and Fall of Kwame Nkrumah* (1967); D. Austin, *Ghana Observed* (1972); and R. Pinkney, *Ghana under Military Rule, 1966–1969* (1972). W. Schwarz, *Nigeria* (1968) provides a clear account of the events leading up to the Nigerian Civil War. On the role of the army in Nigeria between 1960 and 1967, see R. Luckman, *The Nigerian Military* (1971). A mass of documentary material relating to the civil war has been edited by A. H. M. Kirk-Greene, *Crisis and Conflict in Nigeria,* two volumes (1971). For narrative histories of the war see J. de St. Jorre, *The Nigerian Civil War* (1972) and S. Cronje, *The World and Nigeria: A Diplomatic History of the Biafran War, 1967–70* (1972). For a briefer narrative see J. Hatch, *Nigeria* (1971). G. de Lusignan, *French-Speaking Africa since Independence* (1969) provides brief accounts of all the ex-French states of West Africa. See also V. Thompson, *West Africa's Council of the Entente* (1972). On Liberia there is a penetrating study by J. G. Liebenow, *Liberia; the Evolution of Privilege* (1969). B. Davidson, *The Liberation of Guinée* (1969) provides a vivid account of the development of the nationalist movement in the Portuguese colony.

In the course of the past twenty years West Africa has produced a remarkable variety of writers: Chinua Achebe (Nigeria: novelist); T. M. Aluko (Nigeria: novelist); Cyprian Ekwensi (Nigeria: novelist); Sembene Ousmane (Senegal: novelist); Lenrie Peters (Gambia: poet and novelist); L. S. Senghor (Senegal: poet); Wole Soyinka (Nigeria: dramatist, poet, and novelist); and others.

▲▼ EQUATORIAL AFRICA

There is no work which offers a satisfactory introduction to the entire region. A composite picture must be built up from a variety of works, most of which tend rather too strictly to observe the highly artificial boundaries laid down by the colonial powers. Single-country histories have now been written for most of the states in the region. Cameroon: E. Mweng, *Histoire du Cameroun* (1963) and N. Rudin, *Cameroun: An African Federation* (1971). Chad: P. Hugot, *Le Tchad* (1965). Central African Republic: P. Kalck, *Central African Republic* (1971). Zaire (Congo-Kinshasa): R. Cornevin, *Histoire du Congo-Léo* (1963) and R. Slade, *King Leopold's Congo* (1962). There is also a mass of useful material contained in the two colonial encyclopedias: the Belgian *Encyclopédie du Congo Belge,* 3 vols. (1950–52) and the French *Encyclopédie coloniale et maritime* of which volume 5 is devoted to French Equatorial Africa (1950) and volume 6 (1951) to Cameroon and Togo. The most comprehensive work on the ethnography of the region is J. Vansina, *Introduction à l'ethnographie du Congo* (1965).

Pre-European conquerors in Equatorial Africa. On the Adamawa Fulani there is a valuable article by P. F. Lacroix, "Matériaux pour servir à l'histoire des Peuls de l'Adamawa," *Etudes Camerounaises,* V/37–38 (1952). There is at present no comprehensive study of Rabih Zubair available, though a number of scholars have worked on the subject. Material about Rabih is derived from numerous contemporary sources of which the most useful is M. von Oppenheim, *Raḅeh und das Tschadseegebiet* (1902). On the Congo Arabs the most comprehensive recent study is P. Ceulemans, *La question arabe et le Congo* (1959). For Msiri and the Nyamwezi see A. Verbeken, *Msiri, roi du Garenganze* (1956). Cokwe expansion is vividly described by J. C. Miller, "Cokwe Trade and Expansion," in R. Gray and D. Birmingham (eds.), *Precolonial African Trade* (1970). On the Lunda kingdoms see J. Vansina, *Kingdoms of the Savanna* (1966).

The Congo Free State. The two most comprehensive studies in English are R. Slade, *King Leopold's Congo* and N. Ascherson, *The King Incorporated* (1963); see also, A. B. Keith, *The Belgian Congo and the Berlin Act* (1919). The dominant role taken by Leopold in the founding of the Congo Free State has been studied in great detail by Belgian scholars in a series of volumes published as *mémoires* of the *Institut Royal Colonial Belge* in the course of the 1950's. There is an excellent summary of this research by J. Stengers, the leading Belgian historian of the Congo, "The Congo Free State and the Belgian Congo before 1914" in L. H. Gann and P. Duignan (eds.), *Colonialism in Africa,* Vol. I (1969).

The Foundation of French Equatorial Africa. Detailed research on the early history of French Equatorial Africa has begun only recently, with the publication of a series of *Documents pour servir à l'histoire de l'Afrique Equatoriale Française,* edited by H. Brunschwig and others. There is at present no authoritative life of Savorgnan de Brazza, H. F. Eydoux's biography, *Savorgnan de Brazza* (1932) being no more than a modest but useful sketch. Brief accounts of the establishment of French rule are given in V. Thompson and R. Adloff, *The Emerging States of French Equatorial Africa* (1960) and R. L. Buell, *The Native Problem in Africa,* Vol. II. For a fuller account see C. Coquery-Vidrovitch, *Le Congo français au temps des grandes compagnies concessionaires, 1898–1930* (1972). There are a number of vivid contemporary accounts of French exploration and conquest including H. Alis, *Nos Africains* (1894) and H. Gentil, *La Chute de l'empire de Rabeh* (1902).

Cameroon: German Colony, British and French Mandate. H. E. Rudin, *Germans in the Cameroons, 1884–1914* (1938) stands out as one of the most detailed studies of the colonial period made before World War II. It should now be supplemented by the work of East German scholars edited by H. Stoecker, *Kamerun unter Deutscher Kolonialherrschaft,* 2 vols. (1968). For the British mandate see D. E. Gardner, "The British in the Cameroons, 1919–1939" in P. Gifford, W. R. Louis, and A. Smith (eds.), *Britain and Germany in Africa*

(1967); for the French mandate, V. T. Le Vine, *The Cameroons from Mandate to Independence* (1964).

Belgian rule in the Congo. R. Anstey, *King Leopold's Legacy* (1966) is the most comprehensive study of the period of Belgian rule by an English historian and uses a wide range of material published by Belgian scholars and administrators. See also, Buell, *The Native Problem in Africa* and Hailey, *An African Survey*.

African reactions to the colonial impact on Equatorial Africa. G. Balandier, *The Sociology of Black Africa*, English translation by D. Garman (1970), one of the classics of modern African studies, is based on anthropological research in Gabon and the French Congo. The work by Anstey already cited also devotes considerable attention to African reactions to colonial rule. C. M. Turnbull, *The Lonely African* (1963) is a remarkable study based on the recorded life-stories of a number of Africans from the Belgian Congo, each of whom was profoundly affected by the colonial impact.

The decolonization of French Equatorial Africa and Cameroun. For French Equatorial Africa see Thompson and Adloff, *The Emerging States of French Equatorial Africa* and J. A. Ballard, "Four Equatorial States" in G. M. Carter (ed.), *National Integration and Regionalism in Eight African States* (1966). On Cameroun see Le Vine, *The Cameroons from Mandate to Independence* (1964). The economic history of both Cameroon and French Equatorial Africa is described in outline in S. Amin and C. Coquery-Vidrovitch, *Histoire économique du Congo, 1880–1968* (1969).

The decolonization of the Belgian Congo. Anstey's account in *King Leopold's Legacy* should be supplemented by two more detailed studies of the last years of Belgian rule: C. Young, *Politics in the Congo* (1965) and R. Lemarchand, *Political Awakening in the Belgian Congo* (1964). There are interesting impressionistic accounts of the state of the Congo in the early 1950's in J. Gunther, *Inside Africa* (1955) and B. Davidson, *The African Awakening* (1955). For a Congolese view of Belgian rule in its last decade see P. Lumumba, *Congo My Country*, English translation by G. Heath (1962).

The independent states of Equatorial Africa. A series of year-books on the ex-Belgian Congo (*Congo 1959*, etc.) prepared by the *Centre des Récherches et d'Information Socio-politiques* (C.R.I.S.P.) in Brussels provides valuable collections of source material for recent Congolese history. For the history of the Congo in the first years of independence the two clearest surveys are C. Young, *Politics in the Congo* (1965) and C. Hoskyns, *The Congo since Independence* (1965). The Congolese crisis produced a considerable number of books written either by active participants, e.g., C. C. O'Brien, *To Katanga and Back* (1962), M. Hoare, *Congo Mercenary* (1967), or by journalists, e.g., C. Legum, *Congo Disaster* (1961), S. Hempstone, *Katanga Report* (1962). Studies on the former French territories which cover the post-independence period as well include B. Weinstein, *Gabon: Nation-building on the Ogowe* (1967); V. T. Le Vine, *The Cameroon Federal Republic* (1971); and P. Kalck, *Central African Republic* (1971).

Modern writers from Equatorial Africa include Mongo Beti (Cam-

eroon: novelist); Mbella Sonne Dipoko (Cameroon: novelist); Ferdinand
Oyono (Cameroon: novelist); and Tchicaya U Tam'si (Congo: poet).

▲▼ CENTRAL AFRICA

Two recent works provide the soundest introduction to Central African history: J. Vansina, *Kingdoms of the Savanna* (1966) and
T. Ranger (ed.), *Aspects of Central African History* (1968). Both these
studies are Afro-centric in their approach, in contrast to two earlier
works, A. J. Hanna, *The Story of the Rhodesias and Nyasaland* (1960)
and A. J. Wills, *An Introduction to the History of Central Africa*
(1964), both of which tend to concentrate their attention on European
activities. There are a number of good historical studies of the territories of former British Central Africa. Particularly richly documented
are the two works by L. H. Gann, *A History of Northern Rhodesia:
Early Days to 1953* (1964) and *A History of Southern Rhodesia:
Early Days to 1934* (1965). R. Hall, *Zambia* (1965), B. Pachai, *Malawi: The History of the Nation* (1973), and J. G. Pike, *Malawi* (1968)
take the history of these two countries up to the postindependence period. Malawi (Nyasaland) is also the subject of two attractive general
studies, F. Debenham, *Nyasaland* (1955) and O. Ransford, *Livingstone's Lake* (1966). An important collection of studies of Central African history has been edited by E. Stokes and R. Brown, *The Zam-
bezian Past* (1966).

The best introduction in English to the Portuguese territories is to
be found in two works by J. Duffy, *Portuguese Africa* (1959) and
Portugal in Africa (1962). *Portuguese Africa: A Handbook,* edited by
D. Abshire and M. A. Samuels (1969), is a useful work of reference.
D. L. Wheeler and R. Pélissier, *Angola* (1971) penetrates deeper into
the country's history than the earlier works by Duffy. There is as yet
no history of Mozambique in English. The bibliographical essay in
R. H. Chilcote, *Portuguese Africa* (1967) contains a brief guide to the
main Portuguese sources.

A great deal of anthropological research was carried out during the
colonial period on the peoples of British Central Africa. Two general
works, M. Tew, *The Peoples of the Lake Nyasa Region* (1950) and
E. Colson and M. Gluckman (eds.), *Seven Tribes of British Central Africa* (1954), convey an impression of the ethnic variety of a part of
the region.

Central Africa possesses a particularly rich literature of works by
nineteenth-century European travelers. Important works published between 1870 and 1910 include J. Waller, *Last Journals of David Livingstone* (1874); E. D. Young, *Nyasa* (1877); A. Serpa Pinto, *How I
Crossed Africa* (1881); F. C. Selous, *A Hunter's Wanderings in Africa* (1881); F. Coillard, *On the Threshold of Central Africa* (1897);
H. H. Johnston, *British Central Africa* (1897); W. A. Elmslie, *Among
the Wild Ngoni* (1899); and A. J. Swann, *Fighting the Slave-hunters*
(1910). There are two richly documented studies by modern scholars
of early European activities in Central Africa: E. C. Tabler, *The Far
Interior: Chronicles of Pioneering in the Matablele and Mashona*

Countries, 1847–1879 (1955) and H. A. C. Cairns, *The Clash of Cultures: Early Race Relations in Central Africa* (1965). (The English edition of Cairns' book has a different title, *Prelude to Imperialism: British Reactions to Central African Society, 1840–1890*.)

A series of four works issued under the auspices of the Institute of Race Relations in London provide a vivid, detailed and balanced account of the major theme of the modern history of Rhodesia: P. Mason, *Birth of a Dilemma: The Conquest and Settlement of Rhodesia* (1958); R. Gray, *The Two Nations: Aspects of the Development of Race Relations in the Rhodesias and Nyasaland* (1960); P. Mason, *Year of Decisions* (1960); and J. Barber, *Rhodesia: The Road to Rebellion* (1967). Three works by men closely connected with the work of the British South Africa Company convey the atmosphere of early European pioneering: F. C. Selous, *Sunrise and Storm in Rhodesia* (1896); H. M. Hole, *The Making of Rhodesia* (1926); and C. Harding, *Far Bugles* (1933). African reactions to the European intrusion are discussed in T. O. Ranger's splendidly detailed study, *Revolt in Southern Rhodesia, 1896–97* (1967). On white settler politics the works by Mason, Gray, and Barber should be supplemented by C. Leys, *European Politics in Southern Rhodesia* (1960) and by two biographies of leading Rhodesian politicians, J. P. R. Wallis, *The Story of Sir Charles Coghlan and the Liberation of Southern Rhodesia* (1950) and L. H. Gann and M. Gelfand, *Huggins of Rhodesia* (1964). The best introduction to the development of African political activity in Southern Rhodesia is given by Ranger in one of his contributions to *Aspects of Central African History* and *The African Voice in Southern Rhodesia* (1970). This should be supplemented by three works by Rhodesian Africans, L. Vambe, *An Ill-Fated People: Zimbabwe before and after Rhodes* (1972), N. Sithole, *African Nationalism* (1959), and N. Shamuyarira, *Crisis in Rhodesia* (1965), and by J. Day's study of the "Extra-Territorial Relations of Southern Rhodesian African Nationalists," in *International Nationalism*, ed. J. Day (1967).

On Zambia the general histories by Gann and by Hall should be supplemented by H. Langworthy, *Zambia before 1890* (1972) and G. Kay, *A Social Geography of Zambia* (1967). Two recent studies throw a great deal of light on the nature of the European impact on particular localities: G. L. Caplan, *The Elites of Barotseland, 1878–1969* (1970) and H. S. Meebelo, *Reactions to Colonialism and Prelude to the Politics of Development in Northern Zambia, 1895–1939* (1971). R. I. Rotberg, *The Rise of Nationalism in Central Africa* (1966) is based on a great deal of interesting material relating to African political movements in Zambia and Malawi.

The origins of British administration in Malawi have been studied by A. J. Hanna, *The Beginnings of Nyasaland and North-Eastern Rhodesia* (1956) and R. Oliver, *Sir Harry Johnston, and the Scramble for Africa* (1958). Missionaries played a particularly important part in the early years of European occupation; the atmosphere of early missionary work is vividly conveyed in W. P. Johnson, *My African Reminiscences* (n.d.) and in W. P. Livingstone, *Laws of Livingstonia* (1921). G. Jones, *Britain and Nyasaland* (1964) is a study of British administration by a former colonial official. African reactions to the European occupation are vividly illustrated in the splendid biography of John Chilembwe by G. Shepperson and T. Price, *Independent African* (1958). The growth of nationalist politics in Malawi is traced in R. Gray, *The Two Nations,* in Rotberg's study of nationalism in Central Africa, and in a chapter by J. MacCracken in *Aspects of Central African History.*

The controversial Central African Federation produced an extensive literature: narratives by prominent participants—R. Welensky, *Welensky's 1000 Days* (1964) and H. Franklin, *Unholy Wedlock* (1963); impressionistic accounts by journalists—C. Dunn, *Central African Witness* (1960), C. Sanger, *Central African Emergency* (1960); apologies for the Federation—C. E. Lucas Phillips, *The Vision Splendid* (1960); and critical analyses by outside observers—T. R. M. Creighton, *The Anatomy of Partnership* (1960) and E. Clegg, *Race and Politics* (1960). J. Barber, *Rhodesia: The Road to Rebellion* provides a clear narrative of the events leading up to Rhodesia's unilateral declaration of independence. The complexities of the Central African scene in the years after the declaration are unraveled by R. Hall, *The High Price of Principle: Kaunda and the White South* (1969).

On the Portuguese territories the general works by Duffy and Wheeler and Pélissier should be supplemented by R. H. Hammond, *Portugal and Africa, 1815–1910: A Study in Uneconomic Imperialism* (1966) and E. Axelson, *Portugal and the Scramble for Africa, 1875–1891* (1967). There are two detailed historical studies of the Portuguese in the Zambezi Valley: A. Isaacman, *Mozambique: The Africanization of a European Institution: The Zambezi Prazos, 1750–1902* (1972) and M. D. W. Newitt, *Portuguese Settlement on the Zambezi* (1972). B. Davidson, *The African Awakening* (1955) presents a critical impression of Portuguese rule in Angola in the 1950's; F. C. C. Egerton, *Angola in Perspective* (1957) is a pro-Portuguese view of the colony. The development of the Angolan nationalist movement is described in great detail by J. Macrun, *The Angolan Revolution.* Vol. I: *The Anatomy of an Explosion* (1969); see also B. Davidson, *In the Eye of the Storm: Angola's People* (1972). A year or two before his assassination, E. Mondlane, the leader of FRELIMO, wrote an account of the origins of African nationalism in Mozambique, *The Struggle for Mozambique* (1969). Documents relating to the nationalist movement in Mozambique have been edited by R. H. Chilcote, *Emerging Nationalism in Portuguese Africa* (1972). R. Gibson, *African Liberation Movements* (1972) covers the Portuguese territories, Rhodesia and South Africa.

▲▼ EAST AFRICA

The essential introduction to the history of the region is the *History of East Africa,* to be completed in three volumes. Volume I, edited by R. Oliver and G. Mathew (1963), traces the history of the region, defined to include Kenya, Uganda, and Tanzania, from the earliest times to the 1890's; Volume II, edited by V. Harlow, E. M. Chilver, and A. Smith (1965), covers the half-century between the mid-1890's and the end of World War II; and the third volume, devoted to the last years of the colonial era, is due to be published shortly. For a very much briefer survey of East African history based on recent research see *Zamani,* edited by B. A. Ogot and J. A. Kieran (1968). Other useful introductory works on East Africa include J. E. Goldthorpe, *Outlines of East African Society* (1958); A. M. O'Connor, *An Economic Geography of East Africa* (1966); and the *Report of the East African Royal Commission* (1953).

KENYA. The state of Kenya in the period immediately before the establishment of British rule is well described by D. A. Low, "The Northern Interior, 1840–84" in Volume I of *History of East Africa* (henceforth referred to as *H.E.A.*). For vivid contemporary accounts see J. Thompson, *Through Masai Land* (1885) and L. von Höhnel, *The Discovery of Lakes Rudolf and Stephanie,* 2 vols. (1894). J. S. Galbrath, *Mackinnon and East Africa, 1878–1895* (1972), traces the history of the Imperial British East Africa Company. On the origins of British administration see the chapters by M. de K. Hemphill, "The British Sphere, 1884–94" in *H.E.A.,* Vol. I and by D. A. Low, "British East Africa: The Establishment of British Rule, 1895–1912" in *H.E.A.,* Vol. II. The same period is covered in more detail in G. H. Mungean, *British Rule in Kenya, 1895–1912* (1966) and in M. P. K. Sorensen, *Origins of European Settlement in Kenya* (1968). E. Huxley, *White Man's Country: Lord Delamere and the Making of Kenya,* 2 vols. (1935), is a memorable biography of the most prominent of the Kenya settlers. M. F. Hill, *Permanent Way,* Vol. I, *The Story of the Kenya and Uganda Railway* (1950), stands out as the most richly detailed railroad history yet to have come out of Africa. Contemporary works of the early period of British rule include C. Eliot, *The East African Protectorate* (1905), F. J. Jackson, *Early Days in East Africa* (1930), and R. Meinertzagen, *Kenya Days, 1902–06* (1957).

The period between 1920 and 1945 is well covered in the chapters by C. C. Wrigley on the economy, by J. Middleton on social change, and by G. Bennett on politics in *H.E.A.,* Vol. II. See also, N. Leys, *Kenya* (1924) for a critical contemporary account of British rule. On the development of African responses to colonial rule in the inter-war years see J. M. Lonsdale, "Some Origins of Nationalism in East Africa," *Journal of African History,* IX: 1 (1968). G. Bennett, *Kenya: A Political History* (1963) provides a useful survey of the last decades of British rule. On the Mau Mau revolt see C. Rosberg and J. Nottingham, *The Myth of "Mau Mau"* (1967). Works by individuals who played a prominent part in postwar Kenya politics include P. Mitchell, *African Afterthoughts* (1954); M. Blundell, *So Rough a Wind* (1964); J. Kenyatta, *Facing Mount Kenya* (1938); T. Mboya, *Freedom and After* (1963); and O. Odinga, *Not Yet Uhuru* (1967); see also the biographical study by J. Murray-Brown, *Kenyatta* (1972). Postindependence politics are described in C. Gertzel, *The Politics of Independent Kenya, 1963–68* (1970).

UGANDA. The chapter by D. A. Low, "The Northern Interior,

1840–84" in *H.E.A.*, Vol. I covers Uganda as well as Kenya. On the history of Buganda, which is central to that of Uganda as a whole, see D. A. Low, *Buganda in Modern History* (1971) and *The Mind of Buganda* (1971), and C. C. Wrigley, "The Changing Economic Structure of Buganda" in L. A. Fallers (ed.), *The King's Men* (1964). For a contemporary account of Buganda before the European intrusion see H. M. Stanley, *Through the Dark Continent*, 2 vols. (1878). Recent studies of other interlacustrine kingdoms include J. Beattie, *The Nyoro State* (1971), and S. R. Karugire, *A History of the Kingdom of Nkore in Western Uganda to 1896* (1972). The establishment of British rule is described in the chapter by M. de K. Hemphill, in *H.E.A.*, Vol. I and by D. A. Low, "Uganda; The Establishment of the Protectorate, 1894–1919" in *H.E.A.*, Vol. II. The principal contemporary accounts are F. D. Lugard, *The Rise of Our East African Empire*, 2 vols. and H. H. Johnston, *The Uganda Protectorate*, 2 vols. (1900). See also the biographies of Lugard by M. Perham and of Johnston by R. Oliver.

The main period of British rule is covered by D. A. Low and R. C. Pratt, *Buganda and British Overrule, 1900–1955* (1960) and in the chapters by Pratt, "Administration and Politics in Uganda, 1919–1945" and by C. Ehrlich, "The Uganda Economy, 1903–1945" in *H.E.A.*, Vol. II. The impact of British rule on traditional polities is considered in A. I. Richards (ed.), *East African Chiefs* (1960). On the development of African politics in the 1950's see Low, *Buganda in Modern History* and D. E. Apter, *The Political Kingdom in Uganda* (1961).

TANGANYIKA (GERMAN EAST AFRICA). I. N. Kimambo and A. J. Temu (eds.), *A History of Tanzania* (1969) provides a good introduction based on recent research. The chapters by A. Roberts, "Political Changes in the Nineteenth Century" in *A History of Tanzania* and by A. Smith, "The Southern Section of the Interior, 1840–1884" in *H.E.A.*, Vol. I provide a comprehensive survey of the complex state of the interior before the establishment of alien rule. The German penetration and conquest is described by G. S. P. Freeman-Grenville, "The German Sphere, 1884–1898" in *H.E.A.*, Vol. I and by G. C. K. Gwassa whose chapter in *A History of Tanzania* lays special stress on African resistance. On the period of German rule the most recent accounts in English are contained in the chapters by W. O. Henderson and O. F. Raum in *H.E.A.*, Vol. II and in the study by J. Iliffe, *Tanganyika under German Rule 1905–1912* (1969).

The chapters by Iliffe and by T. O. Ranger in *A History of Tanzania* (1969) and by K. Ingham and M. L. Bates in *H.E.A.*, Vol. II describe the changes brought about during the period of British rule. D. Cameron, *My Tanganyika Service and Some Nigeria* (1939) describes the experiences of the best-known of the territory's interwar governors. J. Listowel, *The Making of Tanganyika* (1965) provides a narrative account of the growth of African nationalism; see also G. A. Macguire, *Towards Uhuru in Tanzania* (1969). For postindependence politics see L. Cliffe (ed.), *One-Party Democracy* (1967) and W. Tordoff, *Government and Politics in Tanzania* (1967). The speeches and writings of President Nyerere have been published in two collections, *Freedom and Unity* (1966) and *Freedom and Socialism* (1968); see also W. E. Smith, *Nyerere of Tanzania* (1973), and J. C. Hatch, *Tanzania: A Profile* (1972).

ZANZIBAR. R. Coupland, *The Exploitation of East Africa, 1856–1890* (1939) focuses its attention on the changes taking place in the sultanate of Zanzibar in this period. J. E. Flint's chapter, "Zanzibar, 1890–1950" in *H.E.A.*, Vol. II describes the impact of British rule on the sultanate. M. F. Lofchie, *Zanzibar, Background to Revolution* (1965) describes the political developments leading up to the 1964 revolution.

RWANDA AND BURUNDI. The two kingdoms formed part of German East Africa but were later handed over to Belgian control; consequently they tend to be neglected by anglophone historians. R. Lemarchand, *Rwanda and Burundi* (1970) is a detailed history with special emphasis on the events of the early 1960's.

Two themes of regional significance—the impact of Christian missionaries and development of the Asian minority—have received considerable attention from recent historians. R. Oliver, *The Missionary Factor in East Africa* (1952) offers a good introduction to the history of missionary activity. Other historical studies of East African Christianity include J. V. Taylor, *The Growth of the Church in Buganda* (1958); F. B. Welbourn, *East African Rebels* (1961); and M. Wright, *German Missions in Tanganyika* (1971). On the Asians in East Africa see J. S. Mangat, *A History of the Asians in East Africa* (1969) and D. P. Ghai (ed.), *Portrait of a Minority: Asians in East Africa* (1965).

Modern East African writers include Elspeth Huxley (Kenya: novelist and traveler); James Ngugi (Kenya: novelist); and Taban Lo Liyong (Uganda: poet).

▲▼ SOUTH AFRICA

The report of a symposium organized by the African Studies Association of the U.K. on Southern African Studies (1969) serves as a useful introduction to the present state of scholarship in the social sciences in South Africa. See also the review article by D. M. H. Schreuder, "History on the Veld: Towards a new dawn?", *African Affairs*, LXVIII/271 (April 1969). The article contains details of important work in progress much of which is likely to be published by the time the present work appears. The most recent and comprehensive survey of modern South African history is provided by the second volume of *The Oxford History of South Africa*, edited by M. Wilson and L. M. Thompson (1971), covering the period 1870–1966. There are a number of shorter introductory works to South Africa and its history; particularly recommended are C. W. de Kiewiet, *A History of South Africa, Social and Economic* (1941) and L. Marquard, *Peoples and Politics of South Africa* (1960). See also D. Denoon, *Southern Africa since 1800* (1972), and F. Troup, *South Africa: An Historical Introduction* (1972). An invaluable work of reference is the *Dictionary of*

South African Biography, the first volume of which, arranged so as to include names from every letter of the alphabet, was published in 1967. F. Wilson and D. Perrot (eds.), *Outlook on a Century* (1973) is an unusual historical anthology based on extracts from the liberal journal, *South African Outlook,* founded in 1870.

On the subjugation of the African polities the two best introductory works are J. D. Omer-Cooper's study, *The Zulu Aftermath* (1966) and the relevant chapter by L. Thompson in the *Oxford History.* Some of the studies in the collection edited by L. Thompson, *African Societies in Southern Africa* (1969) are also relevant to this period. For South West Africa there is an excellent study by H. Bley, *South West Africa under German Rule* (1971). Thompson's chapter on "Great Britain and the Afrikaner Republics, 1870–1899" in the *Oxford History* provides a succinct introduction to the relations between the two dominant white groups in the last quarter of the nineteenth century. Important studies of this period include C. W. de Kiewiet, *The Imperial Factor in South Africa* (1937); C. F. Goodfellow, *Great Britain and South African Confederation, 1870–1881* (1966); F. A. van Jaarsfeld, *The Awakening of Afrikaner Nationalism, 1868–1881* (1961); J. S. Marais, *The Fall of Kruger's Republic* (1961); and T. R. H. Davenport, *The Afrikaner Bond* (1966). There is as yet no really authoritative life of Cecil Rhodes. Of the large number of biographical studies the most recent, J. G. Lockhart and C. M. Wodehouse, *Rhodes* (1963), is the most useful. Two important recent works deal with the Anglo-Boer War and the period of unification: G. H. Le May, *British Supremacy in South Africa, 1899–1907* (1965) and L. M. Thompson, *The Unification of South Africa, 1902–1910* (1960). Thompson has also contributed the chapter on this period to the *Oxford History.* The first volume of W. K. Hancock's fine life of Smuts, *Smuts: The Sanguine Years, 1870–1919* (1962) should also be consulted for this period. D. Reitz, *Commando* (1931) provides a vivid personal account of the war from the Boer side. D. Denoon, *The Grand Illusion* (1973), studies British policy in the immediate postwar period.

On the transformation of the South African economy see the chapter by D. Hobart Houghton, "Economic Development, 1865–1965" in the *Oxford History* and the same author's *The South African Economy* (1967). Other relevant works include F. Wilson, "Farming, 1866–1966" in the *Oxford History,* and *Labour in the South African Gold Mines, 1911–1969* (1972); M. H. de Kock, *Selected Studies in the, Economic History of South Africa* (1924) and C. G. W. Schumann, *Structural Changes and Business Cycles in South Africa* (1938). See also the collection of readings from contemporary sources edited by D. H. Houghton and J. Dagut, *Source Book on the South African Economy, 1860–1970,* three volumes (1972–73). Two chapters in the *Oxford History,* "The Growth of Peasant Communities" by M. Wilson and "The Growth of Towns" by D. Welsh, cover many of the themes involved in the emergence of a plural society. For an introduction to Afrikaner society see S. Patterson, *The Last Trek* (1957). British emigrants to South Africa have been studied by J. Stone, *Colonist or Uitlander?* (1972). The changes in African society are illustrated and analyzed in the works of sociologists and social anthropologists: M. Hunter (M. Wilson), *Reactions to Conquest* (1936); L. Kuper, *An African Bourgeoisie* (1965); P. Mayer, *Tribesmen or Townsmen* (1961) and other works. A vivid impression of different aspects of African life is given in two books by African writers, S. T. Plaatje, *Native Life in South Africa* (n.d., c. 1913) and B. Modisane, *Blame Me on History* (1963). On the "Coloured" community the main work is still J. S. Marais, *The Cape Coloured People, 1652–1937* (1939). On the Indian community see M. Palmer, *The History of the Indians in Natal* (1957).

South African politics between 1910 and 1948 presents one of the least researched areas of recent South African history. W. K. Hancock's life of Smuts, Vol. I, *The Sanguine Years, 1870–1919* (1962) and Vol. II, *The Fields of Force* (1968) covers the period; so does A. Paton's biography, *Hofmeyr* (1964). R. de Villiers' chapter on "Afrikaner Nationalism" in the *Oxford History* is a useful survey of the period from 1910 to the present. A great deal has been written about white South African politics in the period since 1948. Two basic works are G. M. Carter, *The Politics of Inequality: South Africa since 1948* (1958) and L. M. Thompson, *Politics in the Republic of South Africa* (1966). E. H. Brookes (ed.), *Apartheid* (1968) is a useful collection of documents relating to this period. Much valuable factual material is contained in M. Horrell's annual *Survey of Race Relations in South Africa* (from 1956). For South Africa in the late 1960's and early 1970's see H. Adam, *Modernizing Racial Domination* (1971) and two symposia, one edited by H. Adam, *South Africa: Sociological Perspectives* (1971), the other by N. Rhoodie, *South African Dialogue* (1972). See also the series of reports produced between 1970 and 1973 by Spro-Cas (Study Project on Christianity in Apartheid Society).

The chapter by L. Kuper, "African Nationalism in South Africa, 1910–1964" in the *Oxford History* provides a compact introduction to the development of black South African politics. More detailed studies of this aspect of South African politics include M. Benson, *The African Patriots* (1963); H. Feit, *African Opposition in South Africa: The Failure of Passive Resistance* (1967), and *Urban Revolt in South Africa* (1971); E. Roux, *Time Longer than Rope* (1964); and P. Walshe, *The Rise of African Nationalism in South Africa: The African National Congress, 1912–1952* (1971). See also the "documentary history of African politics in South Africa" prepared under the general editorship of T. Karis and G. Carter, of which the first volume, *Protest and Hope* (1972), edited by S. Johns, covers the period up to 1934. Also relevant is the autobiography of the African trade union leader, C. Kadalie, *My Life and the I.C.U.*, edited by S. Trepido (1970).

For political developments in Botswana, Lesotho, and Swaziland during the colonial period see J. Halpern, *Basutoland, Bechuanaland and Swaziland, South Africa's Hostages* (1965). For postindependence politics see B. M. Khaketla, *Lesotho 1970: An African Coup under the Microscope* (1971), and C. P. Potholm, *Swaziland; the Dynamics of Political Modernization* (1972).

South Africa's external relations are discussed by J. Spence in "South Africa and the Modern World" in the *Oxford History;* for more detailed studies see R. Hyam, *The Failure of South African Expansion, 1908–1948* (1972), and J. Barber, *South Africa's Foreign Policy* (1973). R. First, *South West Africa* (1963) describes developments in the former German colony after it came under South African control; see also S. Slonim, *South West Africa and the United Nations* (1972).

No country in modern Africa has produced so rich a literature as South Africa. Any study of modern South Africa would be incomplete without reading a selection of South African autobiographies, novels, and poems. Prominent South African writers include Olive Schreiner, Roy Campbell, Alan Paton, Nadine Gordimer, Dan Jacobson, Peter Abrahams, Ezekiel Mphahlele, and Lewis Nkosi. See also, *The Penguin Book of South African Verse,* edited by J. Cope and U. Krige (1968).

▲▼ THE ISLANDS

THE ATLANTIC ISLANDS. There is a lack of detailed information in English on the Portuguese islands of São Tomé, Principe, and the Cape Verde Islands. For a brief account see D. M. Abshire and M. Samuels, *Portuguese Africa: A Handbook* (1969).

MADAGASCAR. H. Deschamps, *Histoire de Madagascar* (1960) and N. Heseltine, *Madagascar* (1971) provide good introductions to the history of the great island.

THE MASCARENES. The only available general history of Mauritius is a short school textbook by P. J. Barnwell and A. Toussaint, *A Short History of Mauritius* (1949). For an account of recent changes see B. Benedict, *Mauritius: The Problems of a Plural Society* (1965). For Réunion there is a good short history in the *Que sais-je?* series, A. Scherer, *Histoire de la Réunion* (1965).

PART III

▲▼ THE STUDY OF CONTEMPORARY AFRICA

The massive expansion of international interest in Africa has made it very much easier for the student of current affairs to keep abreast of contemporary developments in Africa. In the early 1950's the conscientious observer of the African scene had to make do with a limited press coverage, a handful of specialized periodicals, the reports published by colonial governments, and the impressionistic accounts produced by wandering journalists and other travelers. Almost all this material was written by Europeans: it was extremely difficult to come across an authentic African voice in print. During the late 1950's and early 1960's material relating to contemporary Africa became steadily more copious and more detailed. The main newspapers of the world paid more attention to African affairs. New universities and research institutes began producing their own publications. A greatly expanded market made feasible the establishment of new periodicals and works of reference. And a new generation of Africans began to turn to literary art forms for self-expression and in so doing laid the foundations of a modern African literature.

Newspapers obviously provide the most immediate source of detailed information about contemporary affairs. For the student who does not enjoy the advantage of access to a good press-cuttings service the *Africa Digest* (London, from 1954), published by the Africa Bureau, a liberal pressure group with a special interest in Southern Africa, is particularly valuable. The *Digest,* which is published six times a year, draws its material from the British, European, and Southern African press. Even more detailed is the *Africa Research Bulletin* (London, from 1964) which presents material derived from the press of most of the newly independent African states. Two leading British newspapers, *The Times* and the *Financial Times,* produce special supplements on individual African countries at irregular intervals, while much of the best contemporary reporting on Africa is to be found in the pages of the French newspaper, *Le Monde. Africa Confidential* (London, from 1960, originally published under the title *Africa 1960)* is particularly valuable for the range of its coverage and the quality of its comment; published every fortnight, each issue contains four or five articles concerned mainly with recent political developments. Some of the best contemporary comment on African affairs is to be found in *Africa Report* (New York, from 1956), published six times a year; this periodical includes science and the arts in its coverage of the African scene. The *Journal of Modern African Studies* (Cambridge, from 1963) and *African Affairs* (the journal of the Royal African Society, London, from 1901), both published quarterly, contain a number of articles concerned with recent events. The old-established weekly, *West Africa* (London, from 1917), is essential reading for any student of contemporary West Africa. Two monthly journals, *Africa* and *Afroscope,* were founded in 1971; both are devoted to a study of contemporary affairs. For a comprehensive guide to other serial publications see E. de Benko and P. L. Betts, *Research Sources for African Studies* (1969).

The most valuable of contemporary reference works on Africa is *Africa Contemporary Record,* edited by C. Legum and others and published annually from 1968. The *Record* contains lengthy articles on individual African countries and on the relations of the major powers with Africa together with an extensive collection of documents. Also useful, especially on account of its compactness, is *Africa Handbook,* edited by C. Legum (latest edition, 1969). The *Dictionary of African Biography,* compiled by E. Kay (1970), is the African equivalent of *Who's Who.*

158–62, in Libya, 57, 60,
233–38, in Somalia, 128–35,
163–67; relations, with Britain, 97, 568, with Congo Free
State, 435, with France, 46,
with Germany, 97
Itsekiri, Nigeria, and British, 289
Ivory, trade in, 15, 429, 727; in
Angola, 488; in Cameroon,
451; in East Africa, 560–61,
588; in Equatorial Africa, 427–
28; in Southern Sudan, 109, 119;
in Upper Congo, 425, 438
Ivory Coast, republic (since 1960),
former French colony, area,
304; economy, 327, 399–400,
418; education, 341, 416; foreign policy, 407, 408; French
conquest of, 53, 275–76;
French rule, 305, 310; nationalism and politics, 65, 379–81,
399–400; per capita income,
379; population, 379; "strangers" in, 380, 399, 414; trade,
413

Jaghbub, oasis, Libya, Sanusi
center, 234
Jaja of Opobo, and British, 289–
90, 294–96
Jallaba, Arab traders in Sudan,
109, 111, 423
Jallonka, ethnic group, Guinea,
259
Jameson, Dr. L. S., as British
South Africa Company's com-
missioner in Rhodesia, 498–
99; and raid on Transvaal, 631
Jameson's Raid, 25, 50, 499, 631
Jannsens, General, Belgian com-
mander of *Force Publique,*
Congo, 480
Japan, Japanese, and African
states, 72; influence of, on
Shakib Arslan, 222, on Malagasy
nationalists, 697; in South Af-
rica, 683; in World War II, 64
Jardine, D., quoted, 134

Jauréguibery, Admiral, French
minister for colonies, and
Senegal, 268
Jawara, Sir Daudu, nationalist
leader and president of The
Gambia, 368
Jebba, Nigeria, bridge over Ni-
ger at, 321
Jehovah's Witnesses, in Nyasa-
land, 529
Jenne, Mali, 263, 322, 331
Jews, in Morocco, 207; in North
Africa, 218–19, 251; in
South Africa, 648, 652
Jihads (Muslim "holy wars"), in
Adamawa, 422; in Central
Sudan, 286, 299; in Sudanic
belt, 12; in Western Sudan, 255,
257–60; and Mahdia, 114;
see also Abd al-Karim, Ma Ba,
Muhammad Abdille Hassan,
Sokoto caliphate, Umar Tall
Jijiga, Ethiopia, Dervishes attack
post at, 132
Jobson, R., quoted, 258
Johannesburg, Transvaal, South
Africa, crime in, 657; founda-
tion, 630, 711; population, 638
John (Yohannes), emperor of
Ethiopia, 114, 122–23
Johnson, Samuel, Yoruba histo-
rian 347; quoted, 296
Johnston, Sir Harry, British pro-
consul, character, 496; in Brit-
ish Central Africa, 496, 500–
501; and Jaja of Opobo, 295;
quoted, 515, 570
Jola, ethnic group, The Gambia,
257; in Dakar, 415
Jomart, C., quoted, 198
Jonker, Ingrid, South African
poet, quoted, 681
Jos plateau, Nigeria, 286, 292
Joubert, P. J., political leader,
Transvaal, 627
Journalists, Africans as, 57; *see
also* Press
Juba, River, Somalia, 131, 163
Jubaland, transferred from British